# Introduction

**Paul Ellerman**
Herbert Smith LLP

The use of employee share plans as a long-term reward remains an important part of the corporate landscape, both for listed and non-listed companies. Many companies choose to extend their employee share incentive plans internationally, either on a discretionary basis to senior executives or under "all-employee" arrangements.

These long-term incentive awards are generally delivered in one of two forms:

- *Market value options* where the executive receives a right to acquire shares at an exercise price which is set by reference to market value at the date of grant. The option can be exercised after a vesting period, provided that service and/or performance conditions have been met. Sometimes the market value option takes the form of an *equity-settled stock appreciation right* (often known as a SAR), which is simply the right to receive the "gain" on the option (ie the difference between the market value of the shares subject to the option at the date of exercise and the exercise price) in the form of shares.
- *Free shares* where the executive is given shares for no payment after a vesting period provided that service and/or performance conditions have been met. Free shares can be delivered under various mechanisms, the most common of which are:
  - *provisional allocations* where the executive receives an "unsecured promise" of free shares upon vesting, if service and/or performance conditions have been met;
  - *nil-cost options* where the executive can exercise a right to acquire shares for nil (or only nominal) consideration, if service and/or performance conditions have been met; and
  - *forfeitable securities* where the executive is awarded shares at the outset, but if the executive leaves employment within a specified period or if the company fails to meet performance conditions within a specified period, the executive must give up the shares without payment.

Whatever the arrangement, companies operating in the global marketplace need to consider various issues before extending their employee share plans in this way. These issues include: securities laws; tax and social security aspects (for both the employee and employer); the position of internationally mobile employees; reporting and withholding requirements; exchange controls; and employment and data protection laws. The chapters in this book highlight a number of these issues involved in different jurisdictions around the world.

The content of this book is, of course, for general information only. As laws and practice are constantly changing, it cannot, and does not, constitute legal advice and should not be relied upon as such. Specific advice should always be sought in any specific circumstances.

Finally, I would like to thank the contributors of each of the chapters in this book and, in addition, my colleagues Matthew Emms, Mark Ife and Melinda Rollinson who have assisted with the book's preparation.

*Paul Ellerman heads the employee incentives group at Herbert Smith LLP and has established a wide range of incentive plans (involving shares and/or cash) for a large number of quoted and unquoted companies, both UK and overseas. In addition, he has advised on the share plan aspects of many takeovers, IPOs, demergers and schemes of arrangement. He is a member of both the Tax Committee of the Share Plan Lawyers Organisation and of the Global Equity Organisation and is a regular conference speaker on employee share plan matters.*

*The employee incentives group advises on all advisory and transactional aspects of employee share plans and other types of share or cash-based long-term incentives in the United Kingdom and overseas, including the design of plans and current trends; tax-effective share allocations for participants and companies; how to deal with the cost of share plans; overseas regulatory and tax issues; financing of share plans; the impact of IPOs, demergers and other corporate actions on employee share plans; and corporate governance issues and remuneration committee support. The employee incentives group also advises on offerings to UK employees from companies in many overseas countries, particularly the United States and France.*

# Employee Share Plans

## International Legal and Tax Issues

Consulting Editor **Paul Ellerman**

**Consulting editor**
Paul Ellerman

**Publisher**
Sian O'Neill

**Marketing manager**
Alan Mowat

**Production**
John Meikle, Russell Anderson

**Publishing directors**
Guy Davis, Tony Harriss, Mark Lamb

*Employee Share Plans: International Legal and Tax Issues*
**is published by**
Globe Law and Business
Globe Business Publishing Ltd
New Hibernia House
Winchester Walk
London Bridge
London SE1 9AG
United Kingdom
Tel +44 20 7234 0606
Fax +44 20 7234 0808
Web www.gbplawbooks.com

Printed and bound in Great Britain by
Antony Rowe Ltd, Chippenham, Wiltshire

ISBN 978-1-905783-14-4

Employee Share Plans: International Legal and Tax Issues
© 2008 Globe Business Publishing Ltd

# Table of contents

# Australia

**John Cooper**
Freehills
**Jim Koutsokostas**
Greenwoods & Freehills
**Alexandra Moule**
Freehills
**Adrian O'Shannessy**
**Graham Warren**
Greenwoods & Freehills

---

> **Red flag issues**
> 1. Is ASIC class order relief available or will it be necessary to seek specific relief so that no prospectus is required?

## 1. Securities laws

**1.1 What prospectus and/or securities law requirements arise in connection with the grant, vesting or exercise of a long-term incentive award or on the eventual sale of the shares by the executive?**

*(a)* *Introduction*

The Corporations Act 2001 (Cth) (Act) regulates issues of securities and other financial products, including issues under employee and executive equity incentive schemes, in respect of disclosure, licensing and other considerations.

Securities are treated differently from other financial products from a disclosure perspective. While equity incentive schemes will usually involve a grant of securities, the term "financial product" is broadly defined in the Act, as set out below. Given this broad definition, it is possible that an equity incentive scheme might involve the issue of financial products.

In addition, listed entities (whether listed on the Australian Securities Exchange (ASX) or an "approved foreign exchange"[1]) are treated differently from unlisted entities.

---

*The authors would like to thank Sarah Shnider, Articled Clerk, Freehills, Melbourne, Australia for her kind assistance in the preparation of this chapter.

1    ASIC Class Order 03/184 lists those exchanges which are "approved foreign markets". As at October 1 2007, the approved foreign markets were: American Stock Exchange; Borsa Italiana; Bourse de Paris; Bursa Malaysia Main Board and Bursa Malaysia Second Board; Eurex Amsterdam; Frankfurt Stock Exchange; Hong Kong Stock Exchange; JSE Securities Exchange; London Stock Exchange; NASDAQ National Market; New York Stock Exchange; New Zealand Stock Exchange; Stock Exchange of Singapore; SWX Swiss Exchange; Tokyo Stock Exchange; Toronto Stock Exchange.

*(b)*    **Securities**
For the purposes of employee equity incentive schemes, a security is:[2]
- a share in a body (being a body corporate or an unincorporated body);
- a debenture of a body;
- a legal or equitable right or interest in a share or debenture of a body; or
- an option to acquire, by way of issue, a share or debenture of a body or a legal or equitable right or interest in a share or debenture of a body.

Market value options and free shares in the form of forfeitable securities (also known as "performance shares" or "deferred shares") clearly fall within the definition. General practice is to treat nil-priced options (or "performance rights") as options for these purposes, even where the performance right automatically vests on the occurrence of the applicable performance conditions.

Whether free shares in the form of provisional allocations are securities will depend on the circumstances and terms of the offer, and will need to be considered on a case-by-case basis.

*(c)*    **Financial products**
"Financial product" is broadly defined under the Act (and has specific inclusions and exclusions). Securities and derivatives are both listed as specific things that are financial products. In summary, a derivative arises where consideration or value is provided in the future and the amount of that consideration or value is determined having regard to the value of something else (such as an asset or an index). In Australia, equity settled stock appreciation rights are rare. However, traditional stock appreciation rights (SAR) (where the executive receives a cash payment linked to the growth in share price over the performance period) are becoming more common. A SAR, whatever its form, is likely to be classed as a derivative. Each case will need to be specifically considered at the time of offer.

As noted below, where a financial product is offered, the offeror will not be able to rely on the relevant class order relief[3] issued by the Australian Securities & Investment Commission (ASIC) and will instead need to apply to ASIC for specific relief.

*(d)*    **Requirement to prepare and lodge a prospectus: securities**
An offer of securities by a company to its employees requires the preparation and lodgement of a prospectus or other form of disclosure document,[4] unless a statutory exemption applies, or the conditions for relief under ASIC Class Order 03/184 (Equity Class Order) are satisfied.

While there are certain statutory exemptions which may apply to the company in respect of its obligation to provide a prospectus, the Equity Class Order is broader and will provide relief from the prospectus requirements, the on-sale restrictions and the financial services provisions in the Act, if the conditions set out within it are satisfied.

---

2    Section 761A of the Corporations Act 2001 (Cth).
3    ASIC Class Order 03/184. ASIC is the relevant regulatory body in Australia.
4    Sections 706 and 707 of the Corporations Act 2001 (Cth). Other forms of disclosure document provided under the Act include short-form prospectuses and offer information statements.

*(e)* **Statutory exceptions to the requirement to prepare and lodge a prospectus: securities**

There is no general statutory exception to the requirement to prepare a prospectus applicable for offers to employees. The statutory exceptions which may be available are quite specific, but do apply concurrently (so it is possible to rely on more than one exception). However, the exceptions only apply to the requirement to prepare a prospectus and, unlike the Equity Class Order, do not provide relief from the other applicable provisions of the Act.

There are two statutory exceptions which may apply to an offer to employees and executives:

- the "20/12 exception"; and
- the "senior manager exception".[5]

The "20/12 exception" applies where no more than 20 individuals are issued securities as a result of personal offers in any 12-month period, and no more than A$2 million is raised in any 12-month period. The exception will apply regardless of how many personal offers are made, provided no more than 20 people are issued with securities as a result of the offers. However, as it is not possible to control the number of people who accept an offer, it is recommended that the exception not be relied upon if more than 20 offers are made.

The "senior manager exception" applies to offers made to senior managers of the body or a related body, or to their spouse, parent, child or sibling. For these purposes, a "senior manager" is a person who is concerned, or takes part in, the management of the body (regardless of the person's designation and whether or not they are a director or secretary of the body).

Issues or sales for no consideration do not require a prospectus or other disclosure document to be prepared. While this exception might appear applicable to offers to employees, ASIC has, in the past, indicated that it views an employee's continued employment as constituting consideration for an offer.

*(f)* **Disclosure and licensing requirements: financial products and financial services**

The Act contains detailed provisions regulating financial services (including licensing requirements) and financial products.

A person who carries on a business of providing financial services in Australia must hold an Australian Financial Services Licence[6] (AFSL). In summary, "financial services" include:

- provision of a custodial or depository service;
- dealing in shares by an entity other than the issuer; and
- provision of financial product advice.

---

5   Sections 708(1)–(7) of the Corporations Act 2001 (Cth) apply to the 20/12 exception and Section 708(12) applies in respect of the senior manager exception. Previously Section 708(12) expressly applied to company directors, senior executives and company secretaries. An amendment to the Act to introduce the defined term "senior manager" changed its application, as directors and company secretaries are specifically excluded from the definition of senior manager. As a result, ASIC issued ASIC Class Order 04/899 to clarify the definition of "senior manager" for these purposes.

6   Chapter 7, Section 911A of the Corporations Act 2001 (Cth).

The breadth of these concepts means that "usual" activities related to an employee equity incentive scheme may be caught. External share plan administrators are likely to have an AFSL for their share plan roles. Otherwise, a statutory exception may apply,[7] or specific relief from ASIC may be available. The Equity Class Order will also provide relief from the licensing requirements if disclosure relief is available (see below).

The licensing requirements apply to all financial products, including securities. Separately from the disclosure requirements, the issue of financial products other than securities requires the preparation and distribution of a product disclosure statement.[8]

### (g)   ASIC Class Order relief: Class Order 03/184

The Equity Class Order provides relief from the disclosure requirements and financial services provisions (in so far as they apply to securities) of the Act in respect of employee share schemes.[9] If the conditions set out in the Class Order are satisfied, it can be relied upon without the need to apply formally to ASIC; however, copies of the relevant documents must be lodged.

The Equity Class Order provides for four exemptions:

- *first exemption:* disclosure relief for offers of shares, units of shares, options and stapled securities;
- *second exemption:* disclosure and other relief for offers involving a contribution plan;[10]
- *third exemption:* disclosure relief for offers of options by an unlisted body;[11] and
- *fourth exemption:* licensing and hawking relief.[12]

The conditions for relief under the first exemption of the Equity Class Order include:[13]

- the shares offered (or underlying the options offered) are fully paid and are in the same class as shares of the issuer which have been quoted on the ASX

---

7     See Section 911A(2) of the Corporations Act 2001 (Cth).
8     Section 1010A of the Corporations Act 2001 (Cth). The content requirements for a product disclosure statement is similar to a prospectus. The requirements for a product disclosure statement are set out in Chapter 7 of the Corporations Act 2001 (Cth).
9     ASIC Regulatory Guide 49 states that the Class Order also applies to the grant and issue of shares.
10    ASIC Class Order 03/184 defines "contribution plan" as a "plan under which a participating eligible employee may save money by regular deductions from wages or salary (including through salary sacrifice arrangements) towards paying for shares offered for issue or sale under an employee share scheme" where the terms and conditions of the contribution plan include the specific terms and conditions set out in the Equity Class Order. However, in our view, a "contribution plan" can only involve regular contributions from after-tax dollars.
11    ASIC Class Order 03/184 only provides relief for unlisted entities offering options, on specific conditions, which include that a prospectus for the underlying shares must be available when the options are able to be exercised. If these conditions cannot be satisfied, an unlisted entity would need to consider preparing a prospectus or offer information statement in relation to the grant of the securities.
12    Relief is available under the Fourth exemption if any of the First, Second or Third exemptions apply. This relief addresses the applicable financial services licensing requirements and exempts an issuer or associate of the issuer from the financial product advice, custodial/depository service and dealing licensing requirements if the conditions are met.
13    Refer to Class Order 03/184 conditions 1–4 of the Schedule, the definition of "eligible offer" and the definition of "offer document".

or an approved foreign market for at least 12 months (without suspension for more than two days);

- the offer is made under an employee share scheme extended only to eligible employees[14] of the issuer; and
- the person making the offer must:
  - include in the offer an "offer document" (which must contain certain information, such as the applicable terms and conditions and a copy or summary of the rules);
  - provide certain pricing details (including A$ equivalents) and an explanation of how the acquisition price will be determined at the time of the offer, and undertake to update the current share price during the period of the offer;
  - take reasonable steps to ensure that any employee to whom an offer is made is given a copy of the offer document; and
  - provide ASIC with a copy of the "offer document" and of each accompanying document within seven days of providing the material to employees.

If these conditions are not met, the company will need to apply to ASIC and obtain specific relief well in advance (approximately eight weeks) of making the offer to its employees.

## (h)   *Documentation*

If the Equity Class Order or specific relief is relied upon, eligible employees will be provided with an offer document which sets out the terms of the offer, summarises the rules (or includes a copy), discloses the risks of participating and contains the other specified information required by the relief.

Some companies use "opt out" arrangements for completely free grants of securities, but usually employees will be required to complete an application form to participate in the offer. The application form binds the employees to the terms of grant set out in the invitation, to the rules of the plan, and to the company's constitution.

If a statutory exception is relied upon it is worthwhile, though not required by law, to provide eligible employees with an offer document in a similar form to that described above. This will ensure that employees are clear as to the terms of participation and should minimise the risks of any disputes in the future.

Entities which cannot rely on the Equity Class Order specific relief or a statutory exception must prepare a disclosure document for an offer of securities. This could take the form of a prospectus or "offer information statement".[15] Entities offering to employees at the time of an initial public offering may be able to "wrap" their employee offer document with the general prospectus.[16] Entities offering financial products (other

---

14   For the purposes of the Equity Class Order, "eligible employee" means, in relation to an issuer, a person who is at the time of an offer under an employee share scheme, a full- or part-time employee or director of the issuer or of an associated body corporate of the issuer.

15   An offer information statement is a specific form of disclosure document which may be used where the body is raising (by the offer and all previous offers) not more than A$5million. Section 715 of the Corporations Act 2001 (Cth) sets out the content requirements.

16   ASIC Class Order 00/222.

than securities) which cannot rely on the Equity Class Order specific relief or a statutory exception must consider the requirements for product disclosure statements.

### (i) Misleading and deceptive conduct

A company cannot provide any misleading or deceptive information (including the omission of information) in respect of the issue of securities. This prohibition against deceptive and misleading conduct applies regardless of whether the Equity Class Order is relied upon.

### (j) Financial assistance

A company may give financial assistance to a person to acquire shares in the company or a holding company if giving the assistance does not materially prejudice the interests of the company or its shareholders, or the company's ability to pay its creditors.[17]

### (k) Restriction on on-sale: securities

Where securities are issued without a prospectus, the secondary trading provisions of the Act impose additional disclosure requirements where the securities are sold within 12 months.[18] These provisions prevent a company from intentionally avoiding its obligations to prepare a prospectus by making placement of securities to institutional investors, brokers or sophisticated investors who on-sell the securities. However, they may also apply to securities held as a result of employee offers.

Statutory exemptions may apply, or ASIC Class Order 04/671 may provide relief from these requirements.[19]

### 1.2 Is there an exemption from securities laws requirements either because the shares are being offered only to executives or because shares are being offered to a distinct group of named individuals?

While there is no general statutory exemption applying to offers to employees, there are statutory exemptions that provide relief from the requirement to lodge a prospectus where securities are issued to no more than 20 individuals in a 12-month period, or where offers are made only to "senior managers" of the company or a related body corporate.

Where the conditions for the Equity Class Order are met, the company will be exempt from both the prospectus and financial services provisions of the Act.

Where the conditions for the Equity Class Order are not met, the company may apply to ASIC for specific relief.

See discussion above at 1.1(e) and 1.1(g).

---

17    Section 260A(1) of the Corporations Act 2001 (Cth).
18    Sections 707(3) and (4) of the Corporations Act 2001 (Cth).
19    If one of the statutory exemptions to the need to prepare a prospectus is available at the time of and in respect of the on-sale, no prospectus is required. Separately, utilising the Equity Class Order may enable a company to rely upon ASIC Class Order 04/671.

**1.3** **If there is an exemption, will the exemption apply automatically or are there any applications/filings that need to be made?**

Statutory exemptions apply automatically. There will be automatic relief where the conditions for the Equity Class Order are met; however, copies of the relevant documents will need to be lodged with ASIC.

See discussion above at 1.1(e) and 1.1(g).

## 2. Employee tax and social security

**2.1** **When will the executive be liable to tax or social security (and at what rate) in respect of the long-term incentive award?[20]**

*(a)* *Up-front tax*

An executive will be taxed on the discount received on "non-qualifying" shares and rights acquired in respect of employment in the year acquired ("up-front"), at the executive's marginal rates (maximum 45% plus 1.5% Medicare Levy currently). Australia does not have a social security levy.

The discount will be equal to the market value of the shares or rights at the date of acquisition, less the consideration paid to acquire them (if any). The value of rights is determined by a statutory formula. Nil cost options, "provisional allocations" (being a promise of shares), equity settled stock appreciation rights and market value options would be considered "rights" for these purposes.

There will not be any further tax payable at the time when forfeiture conditions lapse, when restrictions on the sale of shares ends or upon the exercise of rights.

If the executive forfeits employee shares, the executive will not be eligible for a refund of the tax paid in the year of acquisition. Rather, the executive may be entitled to claim a capital loss in the year of forfeiture. Capital losses can be carried forward and can only be applied against capital gains. However, if the executive forfeits options, he will be eligible for a refund of the tax paid at the time of the acquisition.

*(b)* *Deferred tax*

Tax on "qualifying" shares and rights acquired in respect of employment is deferred unless the executive makes an election to be taxed up-front in the year of the acquisition. The election applies on a year-by-year basis and is only valid if made by the time of lodgement of the executive's tax return for the year in which the shares or rights are acquired.

A share or right is "qualifying" if all the following conditions are met:

- the share or right is acquired at a discount to market value;
- the employee is employed by the company or a subsidiary of the company issuing the shares or rights;
- all shares acquired must be ordinary shares and all rights must be in respect of ordinary shares;

---

20    The taxation of employee shares and rights is determined under Division 13A of Part III of the Income Tax Assessment Act 1936 (Cth).

- in the case of shares, at least 75% of the permanent employees of the employer company (broadly, employees of three years' standing) can, or have been entitled to, acquire shares or rights under the same or another plan; and
- the employee does not hold more than 5% of the company's shares (whether beneficially or legally) or more than 5% of the maximum number of votes that could be cast at a general meeting, immediately after acquiring the shares or rights.

"Ordinary shares" generally refer to shares other than preference shares. In this respect, the Australian Taxation Office has placed particular importance on features such as voting rights and rights to dividends from net profits. Any dividend restriction on the shares acquired may raise questions about whether the shares are "ordinary" shares.

The deferred taxing point will occur when the restrictions on sale of the shares or rights lift and forfeiture conditions lapse (or upon ceasing employment or 10 years from the acquisition, if earlier).

The executive will be taxed on the market value of the shares or rights at the taxing point, less any consideration paid by the executive for an acquisition of shares or rights, and in the case of exercised rights, the exercise price paid. If the shares or rights are sold within 30 days of the taxing point, the sale proceeds will be treated as the market value of the shares or rights at the taxing point.

*(c)*     *A$1,000 exemption*

If the employee elects to be taxed up-front on qualifying shares, up to the first A$1,000 discount on shares acquired in that year will be tax-free if the following conditions are met:

- the plan must not allow the shares to be disposed of until the earlier of three years after the acquisition of the shares, or cessation of employment;
- the plan must not contain any forfeiture conditions; and
- the offer must be made on a non-discriminatory basis (ie the essential features of each offer must be the same for at least 75% of permanent employees of three years' standing).

**2.2     How will the executive's tax and social security be collected? Will the executive be responsible for paying any liabilities himself or will the executive's employer be responsible for paying tax or social security liabilities on the executive's behalf?**

Tax payable on the acquisition of employee shares or rights is the responsibility of the executive. Tax is payable on assessment of the executive's tax return for the year in which the acquisition or deferred taxing point (as relevant) occurs.

The employer company need not withhold tax from the executive's salary.

**2.3     If the employer is responsible for the executive's liabilities, can the employer withhold the liabilities from the executive's salary? Are there any formalities in this respect?**

The employer is not responsible for the executive's tax liabilities on employee shares and rights.

2.4 **If the executive's salary in the month of exercise/release is not sufficient for the employer to withhold all of the liabilities, can the employer (or the parent company, if different) arrange for the executive to authorise to sell some of the executive's shares in the market and pass the money to the executive's employer?**
The employer is not responsible for the executive's tax liabilities on employee shares and rights.

2.5 **Will the executive pay tax on the eventual sale of his shares and if so at what rate?[21]**
On the eventual sale of shares or rights, the executive is essentially taxed at marginal rates on any gain made since the previous taxing point. The capital gain is the excess of the sale proceeds over the market value of the shares or rights at the date of the acquisition or deferred taxing point (as applicable), less any amount paid since then to exercise the rights (if relevant).

If the executive holds the shares for 12 months or more, the executive may be entitled to reduce the capital gain by 50%. The reduction is not available where rights are exercised, but the shares acquired are not held for a further 12 months.

The executive may also make a capital loss. The capital loss is the excess of the market value of the shares or rights at the date of acquisition or the deferred taxing point (as applicable), and any amount paid since then to exercise the rights (if relevant), over the sale proceeds. Capital losses can generally be applied against most capital gains. Capital losses remaining at the end of an income year can be carried forward.

If the executive defers tax on "qualifying" shares or rights and sells the shares or rights within 30 days from the taxing point, the executive is not liable for further tax on the sale.

## 3. Employer's social security

3.1 **Is the employer liable to pay (on its own account) any employer's social security in connection with the long-term incentive award?**
Australia does not have a social security levy. Employers are required to provide a minimum level of employee superannuation support, currently 9% of an employee's salary, but employee shares and rights are not salary for this purpose.[22]

The employer may be required to pay State or Territory payroll tax on the value of the shares or rights where services are performed in that State or Territory.[23] Payroll tax is payable only if the employer's total annual Australian wages exceed specified thresholds as follows:

- New South Wales: A$600,000;
- Victoria: A$550,000;
- Western Australia: A$750,000;

---

21  Taxation on the sale of shares or rights is generally determined under the capital gains tax provisions in Parts 3-1 and 3-3 of the Income Tax Assessment Act 1997 (Cth).
22  Superannuation Guarantee (Administration) Act 1992 (Cth); Superannuation Guarantee Charge Act 1992 (Cth).
23  Payroll Tax Act 2007 (NSW); Payroll Tax Act 2007 (Vic); Payroll Tax Assessment Act 2002 (WA); Payroll Tax Act (NT); Payroll Tax Act 1987 (ACT).

- Northern Territory: A$1,250,000; and
- Australian Capital Territory: A$1,250,000.

The rate at which payroll tax is payable (as at February 2008) is as follows:
- New South Wales: 6% (on the value of the shares or rights at the date of acquisition or vesting date);
- Victoria: 5.05% (on the value of the shares or rights at the date of acquisition or vesting date);
- Western Australia: 5.5% (on the value of the shares or rights at the date of acquisition);
- Northern Territory: 6.2% (on the value of the shares or rights at the date of acquisition); and
- Australian Capital Territory: 6.85% (on the value of the shares or rights at the date of acquisition or vesting date).

Payroll tax in Queensland, South Australia and Tasmania is not levied on the value of employee shares and rights issued.[24] However, the States and Territories have agreed to harmonise their payroll tax systems. Consequently, Queensland, South Australia and Tasmania are expected to levy payroll tax on the value of the shares or options issued commencing not later than July 1 2008.

**3.2 Can the liability of the employer be put onto the employee? What steps are required?**

Payroll tax is the employer's responsibility. The employment contract could require the employee to reimburse the employer for the tax or allow the employer to deduct an amount equal to the tax from cash payments to the employee. Such arrangements are common for independent contractors, but not for employees.

**4. Tax deduction for the employer**

**4.1 Is it possible for the employer to receive a tax deduction for the long-term incentive award? Would the employer need to be subject to recharge arrangements (eg if the employer is a subsidiary and provides funds to the parent company as part of a recharge arrangement in respect of the long-term incentive award)?**

Cash paid into a share plan trust or to a parent company under a recharge arrangement is deductible. The deduction is only available in the year the employee obtains a beneficial interest in the shares or rights.

A deduction for the issue directly to an employee of shares that qualify for the A$1,000 exemption is available up to the lesser of A$1,000 and the market value of the shares.[25]

---

24  Payroll Tax Act 1971 (Qld); Payroll Tax Act 1971 (SA); Payroll Tax Act 1971 (Tas). The Queensland Government has announced that it will harmonise key aspects of its payroll tax system with New South Wales and Victoria. Therefore, from July 1 2008, payroll tax will be payable on the value of employee shares or rights at the date of acquisition or vesting date. The exemption threshold for payroll tax in Queensland is A$1 million (total annual Australian wages) and the payroll tax rate is 4.75%.

25  A deduction is not otherwise available to the employer (eg upon exercise or vesting of shares or rights).

## 5. Tax beneficial arrangements

### 5.1 Are there any ways of making the long-term incentive award tax-efficient in Australia?

Concessions are available in the circumstances outlined above under which an executive can:

- defer tax on the discount for a maximum of 10 years; or
- elect to be taxed on the discount up-front in the year of acquisition and qualify for a tax exemption for the first A$1,000 of the discount.

## 6. Internationally mobile executives

### 6.1 What are the income tax consequences for an employee who is resident in Australia when the long-term incentive award is made, but who is no longer resident at the time of exercise/vesting?

#### (a) Tax on discount

Non-resident employees will not be subject to tax in Australia on the discount that relates to periods of foreign service after June 26 2005.

The rules do not prescribe how to calculate that part of the discount that relates to foreign service. Apportionment over any vesting or forfeiture period may be a means of pro-rating between foreign and domestic service. For example, assume that an employee is required to complete five years of service before obtaining an unrestricted right, and that the employee undertakes domestic service for four of the five years before commencing foreign service. Four-fifths of the discount, representing the four years of domestic service, would be included in the employee's Australian assessable income. However, apportionment on this basis is not readily reconcilable with tax up-front.

#### (b) Capital gains on eventual disposal

If an employee ceases being an Australian resident, a capital gain or a capital loss (if any) is calculated for each capital gains tax (CGT) asset owned by the employee just before the employee ceases being an Australian resident.[26] This includes employee shares and rights.

An employee can elect to ignore the capital gains and losses arising when he ceases to be an Australian resident and instead recognise any capital gain or loss on a later sale of the asset (which would mean that any gain accruing during the period of non-residence would also be subject to Australian tax).

An exception applies if an employee holds more than 10% of the shares, or rights to acquire more than 10% of the shares, in a company whose underlying value is principally derived from Australian real property. Ceasing to be an Australian resident does not give rise to a capital gain or loss, and the employee remains subject

---

26    The capital gain is the excess of the market value of the shares or rights at the date the employee ceases being an Australian resident over the market value of the shares or rights at the date of acquisition or the deferred taxing point (as applicable), less any amount paid since then to exercise the rights (if relevant).

to CGT on any later sale of the asset (regardless of election).

**6.2   What are the social security consequences for an employee who is resident in Australia when the long-term incentive award is made, but who is no longer resident at the time of exercise/vesting?**

Australia does not have a social security levy.

**6.3   What are the tax and social security withholding/reporting consequences for the employer for an employee who is resident in Australia when the long-term incentive award is made, but who is no longer resident at the time of exercise/vesting?**

Australia does not have a social security levy. There are no tax withholding or tax reporting obligations on an employer for employee shares or rights. This position does not change if the employee is, or becomes, non-resident.

## 7.   Reporting requirements

**7.1   Will the employer (or parent company, if different) have any reporting requirements as a result of the long-term incentive award?**

The financial reporting obligations of Australian companies extend to remuneration reporting. Every company listed on the ASX must publish a remuneration report[27] in its annual report. For these companies, the content requirements for the remuneration report are set by both the Act[28] and Accounting Standards.[29] For non-listed entities, the remuneration disclosures are governed by the Accounting Standards.

**7.2   Are there any tax rulings required in relation to the long-term incentive awards?**

Tax rulings (in the form of class rulings) are sometimes sought from the Australian Taxation Office to confirm that a share or right is "qualifying" and that any tax deferral is therefore available, or that the A$1,000 exemption is available. A ruling is not necessary for a straightforward plan.

Ruling applications generally take three months to process.

---

27   The remuneration report forms part of the directors' report, one of the statutory components of the annual report.

28   Section 300A of the Corporations Act 2001 (Cth). Disclosure requirements include details of specific remuneration components, a discussion on the company's remuneration policy for directors and senior managers (key management personnel) and the relationship with the company's performance, as well as details of performance conditions attaching to equity incentive arrangements.

29   AASB 124 Related Party Transactions, which requires entities (both listed and unlisted) to include in their financial report any share-based payment received by its key management personnel. Accounting Standard AASB 2 (Share-based payment) requires a company to reflect in its profit and loss and financial position the effects of share-based payment transaction, including expenses associated with transactions in which share-based options are granted. For financial years commencing on or after July 1 2007 disclosure need only be made in the remuneration report to meet the requirements of the Act, the Corporations Regulations and the Accounting Standards.

## 8. Exchange control issues

**8.1 Are there any exchange control issues that would prevent an employee from (a) remitting monies abroad to purchase shares or (b) repatriating monies from the sale of shares?**

Cash transactions of A$10,000 and above must be reported to the Reserve Bank of Australia for statistical purposes only.

Under Australian law there are no further exchange control regulations related to the offering in respect of the purchase or holding of foreign securities, the payment of the purchase price, the transfer of subscription payment abroad, or the receipt of dividends in foreign currency.

## 9. Employment law

**9.1 Are there any employment or local labour law issues which may arise as a result of the long-term incentive award? Are any consultations or authorisations required by law?**

While general employment laws will apply (eg anti-discrimination laws), inviting employees or executives to participate in a long-term incentive plan or granting securities under a plan does not give rise to any specific employment or local labour law issues. Other than as set out above, there are no additional consultations or authorisations required.

## 10. Translation

**10.1 Are there any language restrictions in Australia? Does any of the documentation provided to the employee in relation to the long-term incentive award need to be translated?**

There are no statutory requirements or regulations which specify that the offer document must be provided in English. However, the Act does require that any information contained in a disclosure document is worded and presented in a clear, concise and effective manner.[30] This requirement applies irrespective of whether the Equity Class Order is relied upon. It would be difficult to satisfy this obligation if an offer of securities was made to Australian employees in a language other than English.

Any document (eg rules of the plan under which a worldwide employee offer is made) which is lodged with ASIC that is not in English must be accompanied by a certified translation.

---

30    Section 715A(1) of the Corporations Act 2001 (Cth).

## 11.    Data protection

**11.1    Are there any data protection issues which may arise should the employer wish to outsource the administration of the long-term incentive award to a third party?**

The Privacy Act 1988 (Cth) and the National Privacy Principles regulate the handling of personal information.

A privacy "legend" (including specific consents) may need to be added to the material provided to employees to comply with the requirements of the privacy laws.

Where an overseas-based parent company issues securities pursuant to an employee equity incentive scheme, the restrictions on trans-border data flow contained in the National Privacy Principles must be adhered to by the Australian employing subsidiary.

## 12.    Source of shares

**12.1    Does it matter if shares are newly issued to an employee, provided out of treasury or delivered from an employee benefit trust?**

Shares for an employee incentive scheme may be sourced from new issues, or via on-market or off-market transactions. In Australia there is no treasury stock of shares. Shares may be allocated directly to employees (subject to appropriate trading restrictions if required), or to an employee trust.

### (a)    Insider trading

Where a company acquires shares on the market, it must be careful that the acquisition does not breach the insider trading provisions in the Act.

The Act prohibits a person from applying for, acquiring or disposing of securities or procuring another person to apply for, acquire, or dispose of securities, while in possession of information that is non-public, price sensitive and likely to have a material effect on the price of the entity's securities. It is also an offence to communicate (directly or indirectly) such information to another who is likely to deal with securities.[31]

Where the company issues shares pursuant to an equity incentive plan, the Corporations Regulations provide an exemption from the prohibition on insider trading.[32] However, there is no exemption in respect of on-market purchases of shares. Therefore, even where an independent broker has been engaged by the company to purchase shares on market, care must be taken that the shares are not purchased at a time when non-public information exists (even if that information came into existence after the broker was engaged).

### (b)    Shareholder approval for issues of securities

The ASX Listing Rules require listed entities to obtain shareholder approval for an

---

31    Section 1043A of the Corporations Act 2001 (Cth).
32    Regulation 9.12.01(b) Corporations Regulations 2001 (Cth).

issue of securities to directors.[33] The notice of meeting must include specified information so that shareholders can make an informed vote. Shareholder approval is not required for on-market acquisitions; however, companies may choose to seek approval (and, separately, must take care not to breach the insider trading provisions).

In certain circumstances, shareholder approval will also be required for financial benefits given to a related party (eg a director or employee).[34]

---

33    Australian Stock Exchange Listing Rule 10.14. Depending on the approval sought, ASX Listing Rules 10.15 and 10.15A will regulate the content requirements for the notice.

34    Approval is not required where the financial benefit constitutes "reasonable remuneration". See further Chapter 2E of the Corporations Act 2001 (Cth).

# Austria

Hans Georg Laimer
Gerold Zeiler
Schönherr

---

> **Red flag issues**
> 1. **Securities laws:** Since options are most likely considered to be "assessments" (*Veranlagungen*) and not securities, the Austrian Regulator (FMA), is of the opinion that the employee share scheme exemption under the Austrian Capital Market Act is not available for options.
> 2. **Securities laws:** From the position as set out above, options generally fall within the scope of the Austrian Capital Market Act. Accordingly, if no exceptions apply, a prospectus is considered necessary.

## 1.  Securities laws

**1.1  What prospectus and/or securities law requirements arise in connection with the grant, vesting or exercise of a long-term incentive award or on the eventual sale of the shares by the executive?**

Austria has implemented the EC Prospectus Directive through the Austrian Capital Market Act (KMG). Generally, under the KMG, an offer for transferable securities requires a prospectus unless the offer is excluded from the operation of the Act or exempt. Since options are most likely to be considered "assessments" (*Veranlagungen*) and not securities, the Austrian Regulator (Financial Market Authority – FMA) is of the opinion that the employee share scheme exemption provided within the Austrian KMG is not available for options.

Accordingly, for the following remarks on securities laws, please distinguish between the options and the shares provided as a long-term incentive award.

### (a)  Option plan

#### (i)  Securities laws on invitation

The law in Austria is uncertain on the issue of whether an offer of options is caught by the Prospectus Directive.

The FMA is of the opinion that the employee share-scheme exemption of the KMG is not available for stock option plans and that stock option plans fall within the scope of the KMG.

However, the requirement for a prospectus may be avoided by personal communication to the employees involved (private offer exemption). Otherwise, larger offers (roughly more than 100 employees; an individual assessment on a case-by-case basis may be necessary) may require a prospectus.

Generally, the Austrian securities rules do not apply if the offer does not qualify as a "public offer" (ie when the offer is made to a specified group of people). On this basis, it is likely that options can be offered to a number of employees (fewer than 100 is a rough rule, but the number has to be assessed on a case-by-case basis) without producing a prospectus or making any other filings under the KMG in Austria, provided that, before the offer is made, there is personal communication with each employee who is offered options. The company will need to write to employees twice; first, to say that it is intending to grant options; and then to confirm the grant (with applicable option documentation).

The grant of options to more than 100 employees will be deemed to be a "public offer", which means that a prospectus must be produced (even if it is made to a specified group of employees).

When a public offer is made, the following exemptions may be available:

- when options are not offered to more than 100 people (other than those registered as sophisticated investors) in each and every single member state of the EEA;
- to the extent that options are offered only to people who are registered as sophisticated investors in Austria – this may be suitable for very senior executives but is unlikely to be of help for a significant proportion of employees; or
- when the total value of the shares subject to options granted in Austria in any 12-month period is less than €100,000. (Austria did not implement the €2.5 million monetary limit exemption.) For offers of free shares the €100,000 limit is determined by the value of the underlying securities.

The requirements for an individual person to qualify as a sophisticated investor are, in accordance with Section 1(2) 1–3 KMG, as follows:

- the investor has carried out transactions of a significant size on securities markets at an average frequency of, at least, 10 per quarter over the previous four quarters;
- the size of the investor's securities portfolio exceeds €0.5 million;
- the investor works, or has worked, for at least one year in the financial sector in a professional position which requires knowledge of securities investment; and
- the investor is domiciled in Austria.

Individuals can apply to the FMA for the approval of the position as sophisticated investor. The application form has to contain all certificates to document the fulfilment of the requirements set out above. The FMA decides upon the application by official notice. Qualified investors are then listed in a register by the FMA. The requirements for the acceptance to the register have to be fulfilled on an ongoing basis.

If none of these exemptions is available and the offer qualifies as a public offer, a prospectus must be produced to operate the option plan. This must comply with detailed requirements set out in the legislation of the home member state of the company whose shares are being offered and may be prohibitively expensive and time consuming.

*(ii)*    *Securities laws on exercise/vesting*
No restrictions apply.

**(b)    Share (purchase) plan**

*(i)*    *Securities laws on invitation*
Generally, for employee share schemes, there are no restrictions for EU-listed companies (although special wording is required).

When the company whose shares are subject to the award are listed on a regulated market in the EU, no prospectus will be required. The Austrian authorities consider that the listing can be of any securities (eg debt or equity – not just those offered to the employees). Regulated markets include most major European stock exchanges. A full list on regulated markets within the EU is available on the EU website.

To take advantage of the employee share scheme exemption, certain fairly basic information about the share plan and the company must be published in accordance with the KMG (as detailed below). This can be provided to employees with explanatory material issued in connection with the share plan, but it could also be provided in other ways. We would not expect this to be unduly burdensome.

This information includes, but is not limited to:

- company name and principal place of business;
- details of where additional financial information on the issuer can be found (especially the most recent annual statement and financial publications of the issuer);
- explanation of the reasons for the offer (eg that the employees are offered shares under the plan to provide an additional incentive, or to encourage employee share ownership and to increase their interest in the company's success), or the admittance to a regulated market;
- details of the statutory provision that the document is based on (ie the reference to the section in the Austrian Capital Market Act on which the "basic information" is based);
- particulars of the offer, including:
  - addressees of the offer;
  - period of the offer;
  - the minimum and maximum amount of shares for each addressee and the applicable acquisition price;
  - information on the kind of securities and the rights and risks attaching to those securities; and
  - information on any additional requirements under the share plan; and
- the issuer having signed the document with the additional statement "as issuer". This additional statement constitutes the absolute presumption that the document was issued by the issuer and/or in his name respectively.

(ii)   *Making the information "available" to qualify for the share scheme exemption*
The basic information (outlined above) must be "published" under Section 10 of the KMG in the same way as a prospectus. This can be done in different ways, for example by publishing it on the internet, or by making a free paper version available to the public at the head office of the issuer and at the company in Austria. This must be done at least one working day before the offer starts or before the securities are admitted for trade (Section 10(2) of the KMG).

(iii)  *Gazette publication*
The company must also place a notice in the "Official Gazette attached to the Wiener Zeitung" (*Amtsblatt zur Wiener Zeitung*). The notice must contain information on how and where the prospectus directive information was published and where the document is available. This reference publication can be done either in German or in English.

In accordance with Section 10(4) of the KMG (Austrian Capital Market Act), the reference publication (*Hinweisbekanntmachung*) must contain the following information:
- the identification of the issuer;
- the type, class and amount of the securities to be offered, provided this is known at the time of the publication of the notice;
- the intended time schedule of the offer;
- a statement about where the information can be obtained;
- if the information has been published in a printed form, the addresses where and the period of time during which such printed forms are available to the public;
- if the information has been published in electronic form, the addresses to which investors should refer to ask for a paper copy; and
- the date of the notice.

For those companies that are not listed on a regulated market (eg those listed outside the EU or which are not listed at all) it may be necessary to take advantage of another exemption. An exemption may be available in the circumstances set out above.

(iv)  *Securities laws on exercise/vesting*
No restrictions apply.

## 2.   Employee tax and social security
### Tax regime
The start and end of the income tax year for individuals in Austria are January 1 and December 31 respectively.

Generally, individuals resident in Austria are subject to personal income tax. The income tax is a progressive tax with a current top rate of 50%. The personal income tax rates for 2008 are:
- 0% on first €10,000 of earnings;
- 23% on earnings between €10,001 and €25,000;

- 33.5% on earnings between €25,001 and €51,000; and
- 50% on earnings above €51,000.

### Social security regime

There will only be a social security liability for the employing company up to the monthly maximum, which is currently €3,930 (2008).

The monthly basis is the monthly total compensation per employee. Social security is only levied up to a monthly maximum base of €3,930. Once the monthly compensation is exceeded, no further social security becomes due. For separate payments a yearly maximum basis of €7,860 is given. Separate payments are special payments which are paid out regularly but not as often as the salary (eg Christmas pay, holiday pay etc.). These payments have a particular yearly maximum basis.

**2.1** **When will the executive be liable to tax or social security (and at what rate) in respect of the long-term incentive award?**

*(a)* *On grant*

No income tax or social security liability arises.

*(b)* *On vesting/exercise*

An income tax liability arises on the amount by which the fair market value of the shares acquired on exercise/vesting exceeds the acquisition price paid for the shares by the employees.

Social security contributions are also payable upon vesting of shares or exercise of the options and fall due on the last day of the month following the month in which the shares vested or the options were exercised.

*(c)* *Market price*

The market value is the same for both withholding purposes and employee tax purposes.

Generally, if the shares subject to the award are restricted because, for example, they have no voting rights, are granted no dividends or cannot be sold for a period of time, the employee is not considered to be the economic owner (*wirtschaftlicher Eigentümer*). A tax charge generally only arises when the employee becomes the economic owner of the shares. The employee is considered to be the economic owner once he/she can dispose of the shares without restrictions.

Accordingly, conditional awards which are transferred to the employee upon vesting are taxed on the date of transfer.

*(d)* *Forfeitable shares*

Forfeitable shares are generally transferred and taxed upon award if:

- the employees can freely dispose of the shares;
- there are no enduring restrictions on the selling or the transfer of the shares to third persons according to an agreement with the employer; and

- the employee cannot only dispose of the earnings resulting from the investment for a certain time (term of employment relationship) in an economic manner.

If the above conditions are not met, the tax charge will arise when the forfeiture conditions fall away.

If the shares are given at a reduced price or for free, one has to determine the money-equivalent advantage for the employee. According to Section 15(2) of the EStG (Austrian Income Tax Act) any payment in kind (*Sachbezug*) is to be calculated in accordance with the ordinary mid-market price of the place of use (*Verbrauchsort*). If the investments (shares or participations) are listed on a stock exchange, the mid-market value at the place of use is equivalent to the market price at the day of the transfer of the investment. If shares are acquired below their market value, the money-equivalent advantage is the difference to the market price.

**2.2 How will the executive's tax and social security be collected? Will the executive be responsible for paying any liabilities himself or will the executive's employer be responsible for paying tax or social security liabilities on the executive's behalf?**

The employee's tax and social security contributions will generally be withheld by the employer.

**2.3 If the employer is responsible for the executive's liabilities, can the employer withhold the liabilities from the executive's salary? Are there any formalities in this respect?**

Tax is payable on the fifteenth day following the month in which the shares vest or options are exercised. Tax payable upon vesting is generally withheld at the employees' marginal rates by the local company. Upon the vesting of the shares or exercise of the options there is a duty on the employer to provide an annual report to the tax and social securities authorities. Upon the sale or the transfer of shares by the participant, there is a duty on the employee to file a report for the annual tax return.

**2.4 If the executive's salary in the month of exercise/release is not sufficient for the employer to withhold all of the liabilities, can the employer (or the parent company, if different) authorise the executive to sell some of the executive's shares in the market and pass the money to the executive's employer?**

Yes. The employer (or the parent company, if different) can authorise the executive to sell some of the executive's shares in the market and pass the money to the executive's employer (if it is provided for in the participant's employment contract).

**2.5 Will the executive pay tax on the eventual sale of his shares and if so at what rate?**

If the employee sells or transfers shares within 12 months of acquisition, an income tax liability will arise unless the participant has held 1% or more of the shares in the company within the last five years. The amount of the gain subject to a tax liability is the amount by which the disposal proceeds exceed the acquisition cost of the shares and any amounts subject to taxation on vesting/exercise. Tax is payable once it is assessed by the tax authority.

*(a)*     *Income tax*

The current (2008) income tax rates and bands are set out above.

*(b)*     *Capital gains tax*

Capital gains tax is currently at a rate of 25%.

## 3.    Employer's social security

3.1    **Is the employer liable to pay (on its own account) any employee's social security in connection with the long-term incentive award?**
No. Please see above for the withholding obligation of the employer.

3.2    **Can the liability of the employer be put onto the employee?**
No.

## 4.    Tax deduction for the employer

4.1    **Is it possible for the employer to receive a tax deduction in respect of the long-term incentive award? Would the employer need to be subject to recharge arrangements (eg if the employer is a subsidiary and provides funds to the parent company as part of a recharge arrangement in respect of the long-term incentive award)?**
An Austrian entity may only claim a corporate tax reduction when it either bears the costs arising out of the offer to the employees or when such costs are recharged to it by the granting entity. To this end, the employing entity and the entity granting the offer may enter into a written agreement on the recharging of costs on arm's-length conditions prior to making the offer to the employees.

    Generally, the deduction may be claimed annually once the chargeback amount has been recognised in the subsidiary's accounts, not upon its payment. There is no difference in the participant's tax and social security position, whether a chargeback and/or corporate tax deduction is claimed.

## 5.    Tax beneficial arrangements

5.1    **Are there any ways of making the long-term incentive award tax-efficient in Austria?**

*(a)*     *Income tax*

Stock options granted after December 31 2000 enjoy favourable tax treatment if certain conditions are met (Section 3 para 1 litera 15c of the EstG):

- the options must be non-transferable (*nicht übertrager*) options for the acquisition of shares in the employing company or shares in affiliated companies;
- the employer must grant the options to all employees or to a group of employees which has been defined by objective criteria (eg all white/blue collar workers or occupational groups like technical or sales staff). All employees in a certain group do not have to accept the offer as long as the offer has been made to all of them, where:
  - a defined period must be stipulated for the exercising of the option; and
  - the value of the shares must not exceed €36,400 at the moment the option was granted.

Should the above conditions be met, the tax advantages available are as follows:
- if the option is exercised within one year of grant, 10% of the option gain (the amount by which the market value exceeds the acquisition price on the date of exercise/vesting) will be tax free; and
- if the option is exercised after one year but within two years of the date of grant, 20% will be tax-free and so forth, up until the maximum tax-free amount is achieved after five years from the date of grant.

There is no requirement that the option price has to be equal to or higher than the market value of the shares at the date of grant to receive the tax advantages noted above.

Income tax has to be withheld by the employer at the time of:
- exercise;
- the termination of the employment on the amount of the option gain (even if the option is not exercised); and
- at the latest on December 31 of the seventh year following the granting of the option on the amount of the option gain (even if the option is not exercised).

The acquisition of shares, pursuant to the exercise of an option or grant of free shares, can enjoy a tax exemption in relation to the first €1,460 per year. Acquisitions in excess of this amount are taxable at the ordinary progressive tax rates up to 50%. For the exemption to apply, the award/plan must satisfy the following conditions:
- the employer must award the shares to all employees;
- securities must be deposited by the employee at an Austrian credit institution after vesting, or must be transferred to the administration in trust of a legal entity determined by the employer and a representative of the employee; and
- the shares must not be transferred for five years after vesting (except in special circumstances, eg termination of employment).

## 6. Internationally mobile executives

Tax rules are complex and an individual's tax situation can be influenced by personal circumstances, laws and regulations. Individuals who move into or out of Austria between the grant of their options/shares and their vesting and/or exercise could be taxable in several locations. In general, however, and depending upon the country the employee affected goes to or comes from, foreign tax credits or exemptions usually apply to ensure that double taxation does not arise. Consequently, the taxation of options/shares could be affected by several factors including:

- the law of the country in which the employee is located when options/shares are granted, when they vest and when they are exercised;
- the law of the employee's country of citizenship at all relevant times; and/or
- any applicable tax treaties.

## 7. Reporting requirements

### 7.1 Will the employer (or parent company, if different) have any reporting requirements as a result of the long-term incentive award?

Yes. The employer (or parent company, if different) being obliged to withhold will have to fulfil reporting requirements as a result of the long-term incentive award. Accordingly, if the employer has to withhold, the employer is also obliged to file an annual report for the tax and social security authorities.

### 7.2 Are any tax rulings required in relation to the long-term incentive awards?

No.

## 8. Exchange control issues

### 8.1 Are there any exchange control issues that would prevent an employee from (a) remitting monies abroad to purchase shares, or (b) repatriating monies from the sale of shares?

Overall, there are no relevant exchange controls for remitting funds into or out of Austria. If a remittance is made, the bank transferring the funds will have to notify the National Bank of Austria for reporting purposes.

However, notification duties (for statistical purposes) under the Austrian Exchange Control Laws may apply. Primarily, it is the Austrian custodian who would be obliged to comply with these notification duties. If an Austrian custodian is not involved, it would be for the employee to notify, provided that the following thresholds are met or exceeded:

- on a yearly basis, when the value of the securities exceeds €5 million as at December 31 in any year; or
- on a quarterly basis, when the value of the securities exceeds €30 million as at the end of any quarter in any year.

## 9. Employment law

### 9.1 Are there any employment or local labour law issues which may arise as a result of the long-term incentive award? Are any consultations or authorisations required by law?

(a) *Incorporation into the employment contract*

If the rights deriving from the awards are incorporated into the individual's employment contract the benefits obtained may be pensionable.

(b) *Employee organisations*

There is no legal requirement to consult with employee organisations before granting.

(c) *Exclusion of liability*

A clause excluding the parent company and the local company from liability under the plans may not be effective. Even if the employer clearly states that a benefit or bonus is to be granted only once, there is no guarantee that the employer is completely excluded from any liability.

However, the employee should agree that any benefit granted does not create a right to any future benefit and can be unilaterally revoked at any time without the consent of the employee.

Generally, a severance payment includes base salary and all fringe benefits. However, any shares of the employer are not to be taken into consideration for calculating any claims with regard to the termination of employment pursuant to statutory law.

(d) *Forfeiture provisions*

According to recent case law, clauses stipulating the forfeiture of options during the vesting period are generally admissible. However, a vesting period of more than five years might not be enforceable to its whole extent as vesting periods of more than five years are considered to be improper employee retention by the Austrian Supreme Court. As a consequence, participants bound by a vesting period of more than five years may successfully claim for awards on a pro rata basis when their employment is terminated.

Moreover, the forfeiture of awards already vested seems problematic since vested awards are likely to be considered as remuneration already earned. Following the principle of Austrian Labour law that such claims must not be impaired, these clauses may not be enforceable. However, there is no case law dealing with the question of forfeiture of vested options.

(e) *Salary deductions*

The company may, with the (written) consent of the participant, deduct a regular contribution from the participant's salary. From an employment law point of view, the company does not need a permit or government consent to do this.

## 10. Translation

**10.1 Are there any language restrictions in Austria? Does any of the documentation provided to the employee in relation to the long-term incentive award need to be translated?**

Technically, as long as the employee is capable of understanding the text of the relevant contracts/plans/documentation, there is no need to provide the documentation in German. From a practical point of view, a rough guideline for the required capability of the employee would be whether the internal communication in the office is in English and whether the employee participates in that communication. However, the final assessment has to take into account every individual employee.

## 11. Data protection

### 11.1 Are there any data protection issues which may arise should the employer wish to outsource the administration of the long-term incentive award to a third party?

The employees will need to give explicit consent if the employing company wishes to pass information about them (eg names, addresses and payroll details) to another party (eg including a savings carrier or other plan administrator) by electronic means. Provided that data is transferred to a member state of the European Union or the employee explicitly agrees to the transfer, consent from the Data Protection Commission is not required. If data is transferred outside the EU, consent from the Data Protection Commission is required, unless certain exemptions apply (ie written consent of all affected employees, covering the required wording in accordance with the statutory laws).

Consent given by an employee for processing or transmitting of personal data can be withdrawn at any time. Under certain circumstances the employee may object to the use of personal data and the data processing manager must delete all data within eight weeks.

An agreement with the individual employee as to the possibility to transfer data should specifically mention: the exact kind of data, the clearly allocated and named recipient of the data, and the reason for the data transfer/collection/processing. Additionally, any such rule should explicitly mention that the employees can revoke their consent at any time.

An infringement of the provisions of the Data Protection Law may entitle the employee to claim for compliance and could lead to administrative penalty fees.

## 12. Source of shares

### 12.1 Does it matter if shares are newly issued to an employee, provided out of treasury or delivered from an employee-benefit trust?

There is no general employee exemption to the prohibition of financial assistance in connection with share plans in Austria; assistance by the company to its employees relating to the acquisition of existing shares in the company is prohibited. However, if newly issued shares are used, this does not, according to commentators, appear to be caught by the legislation. Thus, employee share plans in Austria are often run using newly issued shares.

# Belgium

Jérôme Aubertin
Herman Craeninckx
Stibbe

---

**Red flag issues**
1. The obligation in principle to issue a prospectus.
2. The absence of a favourable social security regime for long-term incentive awards other than stock options and shares with a rebate.
3. The obligation to pay the tax and social security contributions at the time of grant.

---

## 1. Securities laws

### 1.1 What prospectus and/or securities law requirements arise in connection with the grant, vesting or exercise of a long-term incentive award or on the eventual sale of the shares by the executive?

In Belgium, employee incentive plans typically take the form of either a stock option plan or a share purchase plan. Restricted Stock Awards (RSA) and Restricted Stock Units (RSU) can be implemented under Belgian law and would, in principle, take the form of contractual rights to acquire shares or the benefits resulting from shares. Depending on their nature and their terms and conditions, RSAs and RSUs may be considered as securities for the purposes of Belgian law. They would thus be subject to the securities law requirements discussed below.

For stock option plans, a distinction must be made between options on existing shares versus warrants over newly issued shares. An option is a mere contractual arrangement where the beneficiary is entitled to acquire at a certain point in time one or more existing shares at a certain price. A *warrant* is a type of security, subject to specific company law requirements, which entitles its holder to subscribe for newly issued shares from the issuer of the warrant. The grantor of options or the issuer of warrants can either be the employer itself or any other (related) party (eg the (ultimate) holding company of the employer). The beneficiaries of the options or warrants usually include the (top) management and sometimes also a larger group of (lower level) employees. It should be noted that in Belgium, managers here are often not engaged on the basis of an employment agreement but, rather, perform services independently on the basis of a management agreement. This may have important consequences from a corporate and financial law point of view.

From a securities law standpoint, the main concern is whether the scheme will be subject to the approval and distribution of a prospectus. The (public) offering of securities (such as shares or options on shares) is governed by the Belgian Act of June 16 2006 (the Prospectus Act). This implements the European Prospectus Directive 2003/71/EC, harmonising the public offering rules for the European Economic Area (EEA).[1] Pursuant to the Prospectus Act a company which intends to publicly offer securities in Belgium, must notify the competent authority of the contemplated transaction. Unless an exemption applies, the company must publish a prospectus on the transaction, which must be approved by the competent authority prior to its public release. However, these requirements only apply, when the issuance and/or distribution of the securities are considered as a public offering in Belgium. Private offerings are not subject to the requirement to publish an (approved) prospectus.

In light of the above, it is extremely important to determine:

- which authority will be the competent authority;
- whether the transaction envisaged is a public offering in Belgium; and
- whether the transaction can benefit from some kind of exemption from the prospectus requirements.

For companies that have their registered office within the European Economic Area (EEA), the competent authority will be the supervisory authority of such member state (home country control). For entities having their registered office outside the EEA and which have not publicly offered or listed securities within the EEA since December 31 2003, the competent authority will in principle be the supervisory authority of the EEA member state in which the shares are first offered. Entities which have publicly offered or listed securities within the EEA after December 31 2003 have been allocated a single competent authority, which is then authorised for all subsequent public offerings within the EEA regardless of whether the actual offering takes place in any other EEA member state than the home member state of the competent authority. In Belgium, this is the Belgian Banking Finance and Insurance Commission (BFIC).

The definition of a *public offering* is broad and encompasses any communication made to more than one person with information sufficient to make an investment decision. A transaction is, however, not considered a public offering in Belgium if any of the following conditions are met:

- the offering is of investment instruments (including securities) to qualified investors only;
- the offering is addressed to fewer than 100 persons (other than certain qualified investors) in each individual EEA member state;[2]
- the offering is of investment instruments representing an aggregate value of €50,000 per investor and per offering;
- the offering is of investment instruments having a nominal value of at least €50,000 each; or
- the offering is of investment instruments representing an aggregate value of less than €100,000 (to be calculated over a period of 12 months).

---

1    The EEA includes all EU Member States and Norway, Iceland and Liechtenstein.
2    This must be verified under the law of each member state.

Except for the exemptions under the second and fifth bullet points above, which may apply to smaller employee incentive plans, the other exemptions usually do not apply to employee incentive schemes. However, if the offering of shares or options is considered public (eg because it is offered to more than 100 individuals other than qualified investors) in any other EEA member state,[3] the offering would also be public in Belgium (regardless of the number of beneficiaries located in Belgium).

Furthermore, the Prospectus Act explicitly excludes the *grant of investment instruments for free* (including the grant of stock options for free, regardless of the price at which the shares can be acquired) from the definition of public offering. Accordingly, such grants fall outside the scope of the prospectus requirement. However, if within the Belgian territory a communication is made regarding the grant of investment instruments for free and such communication includes sufficient information regarding the instruments and their terms and conditions of allocation, the beneficiaries must receive a document including information on the number and nature of such investment instruments and the reasons and conditions of their allocation, except if:

- the investment instruments are allocated to qualified investors only;
- are allocated to less than 100 persons; or
- the investment instruments have a nominal value of at least €50,000 each.

If, as a result of the offering being considered a public offering in any other EEA member state, and a prospectus has been filed and approved by the competent authority, it can benefit from the EU passport regime. In practice, this means that the relevant competent authority will inform the competent authorities of the selected other EEA member states, as a result of which the same prospectus can also be used in relation to public offerings in those states. The only formality then required is a translation of the summary of the prospectus (typically about 2,500 words) in the language of those selected other EEA member states.

On the other hand, if notwithstanding the public nature of the offering, no prospectus would have to be registered with the competent authority pursuant to the rules of any other EEA member state (as a result of a potential exemption that would exist, eg for the offering of securities to employees), the issuer would in principle have to prepare a prospectus for the Belgian beneficiaries unless an exemption applies (see below).

**1.2    Is there an exemption from securities laws requirements either because the shares are being offered only to executives or because shares are being offered to a distinct group of named individuals?**

If, based on the criteria set out above, the offering is considered to be a public offering, a prospectus must be prepared unless the transaction would qualify for a specific exemption from the prospectus requirement. The exemptions which could be relevant to employee incentive schemes are discussed below. Accordingly, the following are exempt from the prospectus requirement:

---

3    This must be verified under the law of each member state.

- the (public) offering of securities (of the employer) by the employer itself or an affiliated entity, to current or former directors or employees, provided that such securities (of the employer) are already admitted to trading on a regulated stock exchange (eg offerings of Euronext listed securities to employees of such Euronext listed company);
- the (public) offering of securities (of the affiliate) by the affiliate of the employer to current or former directors or employees, provided that such securities (of the affiliate) belong to the same class of securities as the securities already admitted to trading on a regulated market (eg offerings of a Euronext-listed holding company to employees of its subsidiaries);
- the (public) offering of securities by the employer or an affiliated company to the current or former directors or employees, provided that:
  – the aggregate amount of the offering does not exceed €2.5 million; and
  – the securities offered belong to the same class of securities as those already admitted to trading of a properly operating and publicly accessible stock exchange outside the EEA, which impose information and disclosure requirements similar those applicable to regulated markets (eg offerings by a NYSE-listed US company to the employees of its (non-listed) Belgian subsidiary); and
- the (public) offering of securities to employees within the framework of a so-called participation plan within the meaning of the Act of May 22 2001, provided that the aggregate amount of the offering does not exceed €2.5 million.

Where the offering would benefit from the exemptions listed under bullet points one to three above, the offeror of the securities must make a document available to the beneficiaries which includes information on the number and nature of the securities offered and the reasons and the conditions for the offering.

Other than the general exemptions discussed above, no specific exemptions apply to executives or a distinct group of named individuals.

**1.3    If there is an exemption, will this apply automatically or do any applications/filings need to be made?**

The exemption applies automatically. However, the BFIC can verify at any time whether the conditions have actually been met.

## 2.    Employee tax and social security

**2.1    When will the executive be liable to tax or social security (and at what rate) in respect of the long-term incentive award?**

*(a)    Social security*

Here, a distinction must be made between the actual stock options and SARs. Under Belgian law, the stock option benefits granted by the employer to employees are exempt in principle from social security contributions. It should be stressed that both legitimate stock options (options over existing shares), and warrants (options over shares that must be issued) are not considered as remuneration subject to social security contributions.

However, there are two exceptions to this exemption in principle:

- *options in the money:* options whose exercise price is lower than the actual value of the underlying stock at the offer date. The difference between the exercise price and the value of the underlying share is considered as a benefit in kind subject to social security contributions; and
- *options granted pursuant to a scheme including clauses guaranteeing an ascertainable benefit:* this ascertainable benefit is regarded as remuneration subject to social security contributions.

In these two cases, the social security contributions are due at the time the options are granted, regardless of whether these options will subsequently be exercised.

Stock option benefits granted to self-employed agents are not subject to this favourable regime and are considered as remuneration subject to regular social contributions.

The grant of SARs is not subject to a specific regime under Belgian law. Therefore, in the author's view, social security contributions are payable when the "gain" is paid. The "gain" paid must be considered as remuneration subject to regular social security contributions (2008 rates quoted):

- employer social security contributions amounting to 35% of the gross amount when the beneficiary of the indemnity has the status of a white-collar employee and to approximately 45% of the gross amount when the beneficiary is a blue-collar employee; and
- employee social contributions of 13.07% of the gross amount withheld by the employer on the amount to be paid to employee and paid by the employer together with the employer social security contributions to the National Service for Social Security.

In Belgium, companies usually retain a payroll company to administer payments to their employees.

In principle, the grant of free shares is considered to be remuneration and is thus subject to regular social security contributions, the amount of which will be determined based on the fair market value of the shares at the time of grant.

The benefit granted to the employees when shares are offered at a price below the fair market value (discounted shares) can be exempt from social security contributions, provided the rebate does not exceed 20% and the following conditions are met:

- the shares must be granted within the framework of a capital increase;
- the company must have granted at least two dividends over the last three tax years;
- the capital increase and its modalities must be discussed with the works council, which will issue an opinion regarding the social aspects of the operation;
- the capital increase concerned as well as the increases made over the four

previous tax years cannot exceed 20% of the capital;
- the shares that will be issued must be on name and must be non-transferable during five years as from the subscription;
- the shares issued within the framework of the capital increase must be accessible to all personnel;
- the period of service required for employees to be eligible to acquire such shares cannot be lower than six months and cannot exceed three years;
- the timeframe within which employees must subscribe will be between 30 days and three months as from the opening of the subscription; and
- the period within which the employees must pay for their shares cannot exceed three years as from the subscription.

Apart from these strict conditions, the National Service for Social Security also accepts as exempt from social security contributions the grant of shares with a rebate, with the condition that the rebate does not exceed 16.66% of the fair market value and the shares are not transferable for at least two years.

*(b)* *Tax*

According to the general provisions of Belgian tax law, earned income includes "fringe benefits obtained by reason, or as a result, of the execution of an employment agreement". Fringe benefits are taxable for the year during which they are granted.

As to stock options, a distinction must be made between those that fall within the scope of the Law of March 26 1999 (the Law), and those that do not.

Under the provisions of the Law, benefits resulting from stock options are taxable income at the moment of grant. Options are deemed to be granted on the sixtieth day following the date of offer if the employee accepts the offer in writing at the latest on the sixtieth day following the date of the offer. If no written acceptance is given within the 60-day period, the options are not considered to be attributed and no taxable benefit arises (see below). Once the options are validly offered and accepted, the employee can be taxed on them, even if he cannot or does not effectively exercise the options. It is not relevant for Belgian tax purposes whether or not the options vest, whether the employee effectively exercises the options, or when he exercises such options. No tax is due on vesting or exercise of the options. Capital gains realised on the exercise of the options or on the sale of the shares received do not constitute taxable remuneration. Losses are not deductible.

If the shares are listed, the fair market value of the shares equals either the average closing price of the shares during a period of 30 days preceding the date of the offer, or the closing price of the shares on the last trading day preceding the date of the offer. If the shares are not listed, the board of directors of the grantor must determine the fair market value. This may not be less than:
- the book value of the shares as stated in the most recent annual accounts of the distributing company that was approved before the date of grant for securities representing share capital; or
- the value that results from the rights attributed by virtue of the articles of association for securities not representing the share capital.

For options which are not publicly traded, the benefit will, as a general rule, be valued on a lump-sum basis at the rate of 15% of the value of the underlying shares as determined at the moment of the offer. In addition, for options that are exercisable for more than five years after the date of offer, an additional 1% per year, or portion of a year, is added.

If the options meet a series of conditions, the valuation formula is reduced to 7.5% (plus 0.5% for each year exceeding five years) of the current value of the underlying shares. For the 7.5% formula to apply, the terms of the stock option plan must have all of the following features:

- the exercise price is definitively fixed at the moment of grant;
- the options may not be exercised after the tenth calendar year following the year of the offer;
- the options may not be exercised before the end of the third calendar year following the year of the offer;
- the options may not be transferred except upon death of the beneficiary;
- the risk inherent to the options cannot be covered either directly or indirectly by the company granting the options or by an affiliated company; and
- the options relate to shares of the employer company or a parent company of the employer company.

If the option plan does not contain the conditions mentioned under bullet points two, three and four above, the lower valuation will nevertheless apply if the beneficiary commits himself in writing to respect these restrictions. In the event of non-compliance, additional tax payments will be due.

If the option contains clauses attributing (at the moment of the offer or later, up to the end of the exercise period) a "certain benefit" to the beneficiary, the benefit constitutes additional taxable income for the year in which the benefit becomes certain, but only to the extent that this certain benefit is greater than the taxable amount as determined upon attribution of the option.

If an option is not granted free of charge, the value of the benefit is to be reduced by the amount paid for the options by the beneficiary.

The taxable advantage is also increased if the options are "in the money" (ie if the exercise price is lower than the fair market value of the underlying share at the moment of grant). The difference is added to the lump-sum taxable benefit. The late acceptance of the offer (ie after the 60-day period has lapsed) does not give rise to taxation of the benefit as an option (within the meaning of the Law), as it is considered not to be granted for Belgian tax purposes. If the "option" is exercised later, this benefit will be taxed as an advantageous stock plan. This means that, upon exercise, the beneficiary is taxable on the discount (ie on the balance between the fair market value of the shares upon exercise and the exercise price).

However, there is no actual choice for the beneficiaries as to the taxable moment (grant or exercise). Options falling within the scope of the Law are always taxable at grant; "options" falling outside the scope of the Law are not taxable at grant, but cannot benefit from the favourable tax and social security regime provided by the Law.

The benefit granted to the employees when (publicly traded) shares are offered at a price below the fair market value (*discounted shares*) can be tax exempt provided that:

- the discount equals 16.67% of the share's market value at the purchase date; and
- the employee committed himself not to trade the shares for a two-year period from the purchase date. A similar exemption applies if the number of share purchased by the employees could trigger a depreciation of the stock market price.

If shares are granted for free, the employee receives a taxable benefit-in-kind the value of which is equal to the fair market value of the shares at the date of grant.

**2.2 How will the executive's tax and social security be collected? Will the executive be responsible for paying any liabilities himself or will the executive's employer be responsible for paying tax or social security liabilities on the executive's behalf?**

The employer is liable for the payment of both the social security contributions of the employer and the employee.

The employer is also liable for the withholding and payment of wage withholding tax. In principle no wage withholding tax is due if a non-resident company without a base in Belgium grants benefits in kind.

**2.3 If the employer is responsible for the executive's liabilities, can the employer withhold the liabilities from the executive's salary? Are there any formalities in this respect?**

The employer withholds the employee's tax and social security contributions due on the amount to be paid. The employee receives a payslip with each payment made by the employer, stating the gross amounts and the different amounts that are withheld. Employers usually retain a payroll company to assist with this.

It is important to stress that the employer cannot force an employee to repay any social security payments overpaid to him in error by the employer.[4]

**2.4 If the executive's salary in the month of exercise/release is not sufficient for the employer to withhold all of the liabilities, can the employer (or the parent company, if different) arrange for the executive to authorise the sale of some of the executive's shares in the market and pass the money to the executive's employer?**

The employer and the employee can agree that the latter will sell the number of shares necessary to pay the social security contributions due on the benefits granted.

**2.5 Will the executive pay tax on the eventual sale of his shares and if so, at what rate?**

The shares are considered to be part of the executive's private fortune. In principle, any capital gains realised on sale of the shares are not subject to tax.

---

4    Article 26 of the Act of June 27 1969 revising the Decree-Act of December 28 1944 regarding the social security of employees.

## 3. Employer's social security

### 3.1 Is the employer liable to pay (on its own account) any employer's social security in connection with the long-term incentive award?

As mentioned above, the employer is liable for the payment of employer social security contributions. These can vary currently between 35% of the gross amount if the beneficiary is a white-collar employee and approximately 45% if the beneficiary is a blue-collar employee.

### 3.2 Can the liability of the employer be put onto the employee? What steps are required?

The employer cannot transfer its liability to the employee. In practice, the employer will fix the amount of the benefits taking into account its costs, including the employer social security contributions.

## 4. Tax deduction for the employer

### 4.1 Is it possible for the employer to receive a tax deduction in respect of the long-term incentive award? Would the employer need to be subject to recharge arrangements (eg if the employer is a subsidiary and provides funds to the parent company as part of a recharge arrangement in respect of the long-term incentive award)?

Any long-term incentive award is considered to be a professional expense and, therefore, tax deductible pursuant to the general tax law provisions. There are no recharge arrangements.

## 5. Tax beneficial arrangements

### 5.1 Are there any ways of making the long-term incentive award tax-efficient in Belgium?

The grant of options under the 1999 Stock Option Law provides for a rather low taxable benefit. The drawback of this regime is that the employee is taxed up-front.

## 6. Internationally mobile executives

### 6.1 What are the income tax consequences for an employee who is resident in Belgium when the long-term incentive award is made, but who is no longer resident at the time of exercise/vesting?

In this event, double taxation may arise if the employee's state of residence taxes the long-term incentive award at the time of exercise/vesting.

Double taxation may be avoided if a bilateral tax treaty applies. Generally, the Belgian tax authorities refrain from imposing tax if the long-term award incentive is made for employment exclusively executed in the partner state. In certain circumstances, differences in tax rules may lead to there being no taxation at all.

**6.2** **What are the social security consequences for an employee who is resident in Belgium when the long-term incentive award is made, but who is no longer resident at the time of exercise/vesting?**

It should be stressed that the applicable social security regime usually depends on the place where the employee carries out his/her work. A move to another country should therefore not impact on the applicable social security regime.

The rules explained above with respect to social security laws only apply if the employee concerned comes under the Belgian social security regime.

Social security contributions, if any, are due at the time the stock options benefits (including warrants as mentioned above) are awarded, regardless of whether or not these options will be exercised. The mobility of employees could mean they are doubly subject to social security contributions if they exercise their options in a country where stock options are subject to social security contributions at the time that they are exercised. This also applies to the award of free shares, as social contributions are due at the time of award.

As mentioned above, the author is of the opinion that social security contributions are due on SARs at the time the "gain" is paid. This could eventually mean that the "gain" is only paid once the employee concerned comes under a regime where the contributions on SARs are due at the time of award.

**6.3** **What are the tax and social security withholding/reporting consequences for the employer in respect of an employee who is resident in Belgium when the long-term incentive award is made, but who is no longer resident at the time of exercise/vesting?**

This situation should not arise as the withholding and reporting obligations under Belgian law exist at the time the social contributions have to be paid by the employer.

## 7. Reporting requirements

**7.1** **Will the employer (or parent company, if different) have any reporting requirements as a result of the long-term incentive award?**

The indemnity subject to social security contributions will be mentioned on the payslip of the employee concerned. This will indicate the gross amount, the social security contributions withheld, the taxable income as well as the advance tax payment withheld.

**7.2** **Are there any tax rulings required in relation to the long-term incentive awards?**

No, but the employer can always obtain a tax ruling confirming the tax regime of the long-term incentive awards.

## 8. Exchange control issues

8.1 **Are there any exchange control issues that would prevent an employee from (a) remitting monies abroad to purchase shares or (b) repatriating monies from the sale of shares?**

There are no foreign exchange requirements in Belgium.

## 9. Employment law

9.1 **Are there any employment or local labour law issues which may arise as a result of the long-term incentive award? Are any consultations or authorisations required by law?**

The validity of the clause requiring the employee still to be employed by the employer when exercising the option, or at the time the SARs are paid, is disputed in case law and in legal doctrine. Certain scholars are of the opinion that such benefits are remuneration, the payment of which cannot be made subject to any condition of presence. Others consider such clauses to be valid in principle. The Labour Tribunal of Brussels has already ruled in both directions, depending on the factual situation. It seems to consider the reason why the employee must still be employed, in order to assess whether or not this reason is acceptable and decide on whether the clause is valid.

Furthermore, in the event that the employee is dismissed, where he or she has been entitled to a long-term incentive over several years, this should be taken into consideration when determining the annual gross remuneration on the basis of which the indemnity in lieu of notice must be calculated.

The introduction of a long-term incentive plan does not necessarily have to be reviewed or approved by the works council or any other employee representatives, except when the incentive takes the form of shares with a rebate granted pursuant to Article 609 of the Company Code.

## 10. Translation

10.1 **Are there any language restrictions in Belgium? Does any of the documentation provided to the employee in relation to the long-term incentive award need to be translated?**

The use of language in employment relationships is strictly regulated in Belgium and consists of one national act (the Royal Decree of July 18 1966 on coordinated laws) and two regional legislative acts (the Flemish Decree of July 19 1973 and the Walloon Decree of June 30 1982). The contents of these three regulations and the sanctions they impose for infringement differ.

The documentation concerning incentive plans issued by the employer is usually regarded as a social document and is subject to strict regulations.

The location of the company's principal place of business (which need not necessarily be the same as its registered office) will determine the applicable legislation. Consequently, if the principal place of business is located in Flanders, all social documents used in employment relationships must be drafted in Dutch. If the documents are drafted in the wrong language, they will not have legal effect. In addition, the employee could invoke the provisions that are favourable to him and at the same time invoke the nullity of the document in order to prevent the application of the clauses that could be detrimental to him;

If the principal place of business is the Walloon Region, all social documents must be drafted in French. Failure to do so will result in the documents being devoid of legal effect (without any exception).

If the principal place of business is the Brussels-Capital Region (the city of Brussels, consisting of 19 communes), the German-speaking area or those municipalities with special language requirements, the social documents must be drafted in the language of the employee to whom they are addressed. This language can be Dutch, French or German. Any other foreign language is not acceptable. If the document is not written in one of these official languages it must be redrafted, and any violation can thereby be rectified.

The long-term incentive plan should be drafted in several languages if the employees carry out their work in different regions of Belgium.

## 11. Data protection

11.1 **Are there any data protection issues which may arise should the employer wish to outsource the administration of the long-term incentive award to a third party?**

The employer can outsource the administration of the long-term incentive award, provided the conditions of the Act of December 8 1992 with respect to the protection of private life are observed. The third party to whom the administration is outsourced must guarantee that the treatment of private information will comply with the measures of technical security and organisation as required by law. This guarantee will be dealt with contractually in the agreement between the employer and the third party. The contract will also provide for the respective liabilities of both parties with respect to the treatment of private information. Contractually, the third party must take over all commitments of the employer with respect to the way in which the private information can and must be treated.

The employer remains responsible for ensuring that the information is up-to-date and correct and that access to private information is strictly limited to the information that is necessary for the correct administration of the plan.

## 12. Source of shares

12.1 **Does it matter if shares are newly issued to an employee, provided out of treasury or delivered from an employee benefit trust?**

From a labour law perspective, this does not have any impact on the applicable rules.

# Brazil

Mihoko Sirley Kimura
Marcelo Rodrigues
Jorge Henrique Amaral Zaninetti
TozziniFreire Advogados

---

**Red flag issues**
- As a general rule, gratuitous benefits granted by an employer to its employees are considered remuneration and, therefore, awards of free shares are subject to labour and social security charges.
- As these benefits are granted without a payment in exchange for the shares, the value of the shares transferred to the executive will be treated as revenue received by him, subject to taxation under the Brazilian Individual Income Tax.

---

## 1. Securities laws

### 1.1 What prospectus and/or securities law requirements arise in connection with the grant, vesting or exercise of a long-term incentive award or on the eventual sale of the shares by the executive?

The grant of stock options and their exercise by executives must comply with regulations pertaining to public offerings of securities. As a general rule, a grant of stock options occurs by means of a private offer.

The offer of securities to the public in Brazil is regulated by the Brazilian Capital Markets Law (Law 6,385 76) and the Brazilian Securities Commission's (CVM) Ruling 400 03. By analysing the relevant law and regulations, one can determine whether an offer is private or public.

The main characteristic of a private offering is the fact that the offer is made on a person-to-person basis (ie the offeror makes the offer directly to a selected group of persons and not "the public in general").

### 1.2 Is there an exemption from securities laws requirements either because the shares are being offered only to executives or because shares are being offered to a distinct group of named individuals?

CVM Ruling 400 03 expressly excepts from the concept of "the pubic in general" any class, category or group of persons who have a regular and prior commercial, credit, corporate or labour relationship with the offeror. Therefore, to make sure that the offer may be charaterised as a private offer, the offeror has to be able to justify an existing relationship with the potential investor (ie management, employees and service suppliers of a company).

**1.3    If there is an exemption, will the exemption apply automatically or are there any applications/filings that need to be made?**
Unlike public offers, private offers may be implemented without any authorisation from, or registration with, a governmental agency.

## 2.    Employee tax and social security

**2.1    When will the executive be liable to tax or social security (and at what rate) in respect of the long-term incentive award?**
Concerning a market value option plan, the company usually grants an option to the executive and does not require a payment. As a result, the executive is not subject to taxation at the moment the option is granted.

When the executive exercises the option, the exercise price will comprise the acquisition cost for purposes of a future calculation of capital gains when the relevant shares are sold.

In a free shares award plan, since the executive will not make any payment in exchange for the shares, the tax authorities may consider the value of the shares transferred to the executive as revenue received. In this case, the executive's revenue will be subject to individual income tax (IRPF), which is calculated according to a monthly progressive table of income tax with rates ranging from 15 to 27.5%.

In terms of social security, according to Brazilian Labour Law, an executive's remuneration comprises not only the employee's fixed salary, but also any amount for commission, bonuses, fringe benefits, personal or family benefits and living expenses, among others.

The total remuneration is subject to labour and social security charges for the company, which correspond to approximately 60% of the remuneration, including FGTS – Severance Pay Fund (a fund constituted of deposits made by employers on behalf of each employee, which balance may be withdrawn in certain circumstances, including termination without cause), vacation, thirteenth salary (as provided by Brazilian law, all employees are entitled to receive one additional monthly salary per year), social security contributions of approximately 28% paid by the company, and social security for the executive at the rate of approximately 11% of salary (this is limited to R318.37).

As a general rule, gratuitous benefits granted by an employer to its employees are considered to be remuneration and, therefore, awards of free shares are subject to labour and social security charges.

There are no specific regulations or relevant court precedents indicating whether a stock option would constitute a gratuitous benefit. However, it is very likely that a stock option plan would be treated as a gratuitous benefit for the purposes of labour and social security charges if, for example, the employees can exercise the options for free or at a substantial discount to market value.

**2.2    How will the executive's tax and social security be collected? Will the executive be responsible for paying any liabilities himself or will the executive's employer be responsible for paying tax or social security liabilities on the executive's behalf?**

If the long-term incentive plan is operated by a Brazilian legal entity, it will be treated as income obtained from a Brazilian source. On payment to the executive, the company must withhold the amounts of IRPF.

If a foreign company operates the long-term incentive plan, it will be considered as income from a foreign source. Therefore, the applicable IRPF must be assessed and paid by the individual resident in Brazil by the last business day of the month following the month in which the income was received.

**2.3** **If the employer is responsible for the executive's liabilities, can the employer withhold the liabilities from the executive's salary? Are there any formalities in this respect?**
If the stock option is a gratuitous benefit and the company considers that the award is part of the executive's compensation, the employer must withhold the liabilities from the executive's salary. There are no specific formalities other than ordinary payroll procedures.

**2.4** **If the executive's salary in the month of exercise/release is not sufficient for the employer to withhold all of the liabilities, can the employer (or the parent company, if different) arrange for the executive to authorise the sale of some of the executive's shares in the market and pass the money to the executive's employer?**
If a stock option plan provides for this possibility, there are no labour law implications or prohibitions.

**2.5** **Will the executive pay tax on the eventual sale of his shares and if so at what rate?**
Any capital gains on a sale of shares for a price exceeding certain limits set by law will be subject to income tax of 15%. In the case of options, the capital gain is the difference between the market value of the shares as of the acquisition date and the sale price of the same shares.

The tax must be calculated and paid directly by the executive by the last business day of the month following the one in which the gain was earned.

**3.** **Employer's social security**

**3.1** **Is the employer liable to pay (on its own account) any employer's social security in connection with the long-term incentive award?**
If the benefit is gratuitous and the company considers that the award is part of the executive's compensation, the employer must pay social security contributions of approximately 28% of the award.

**3.2** **Can the liability of the employer be put onto the employee? What steps are required?**
The employer's liability cannot be put onto the executive.

## 4. Tax deduction for the employer

4.1 **Is it possible for the employer to receive a tax deduction in respect of the long-term incentive award? Would the employer be subject to recharge arrangements (eg if the employer is a subsidiary and provides funds to the parent company as part of a recharge arrangement in respect of the long-term incentive award)?**

In the event that a Brazilian subsidiary grants a benefit to its employee under a parent company's long-term incentive award, this expense would be considered a gift and would not be deductible for the purposes of calculating taxes on income, namely corporate income tax (IRPJ) and social contribution on profits (CSLL).

However, if the long-term incentive award is granted by a Brazilian company, expenses incurred by the Brazilian company will be considered to be deductible for IRPJ and CSLL tax purposes.

## 5. Tax beneficial arrangements

5.1 **Are there any ways of making the long-term incentive award tax-efficient in Brazil?**

The most tax efficient way to establish the long-term incentive award is by granting market value options, as these are not considered to be revenue paid by the employer to the executive.

## 6. Internationally mobile executives

6.1 **What are the income tax consequences for an employee who is resident in Brazil when the long-term incentive award is made, but who is no longer resident at the time of exercise/vesting?**

Brazilian tax law adopts a worldwide income system to impose taxation on Brazilian residents. Through this system, which is designed to avoid tax evasion, all income earned by the taxpayer, whether obtained from a Brazilian source or not, is subject to taxation.

For a Brazilian citizen, residence for tax purposes is determined when the individual resides in Brazil with a permanent status.

As far as overseas individuals are concerned, depending on the visa issued by the Brazilian authorities, the overseas individual may or may not be considered a resident for tax purposes immediately after his arrival in Brazil. Generally speaking, an overseas individual is considered resident in Brazil:

- as from the date of arrival in the country;
- when a permanent visa is obtained or when the individual obtains a temporary visa but comes to Brazil to work under an employment relationship with a Brazilian company;
- after a period of 183 days in the country, consecutively or not, within a period of 12 months, where the individual obtains any type of temporary visa; or
- when, before the period mentioned in the previous item, the individual obtains a permanent visa or a job under an employment relationship with a Brazilian company.

An individual is subject to taxation in Brazil on a worldwide basis, once he/she is considered to be tax resident in Brazil.

A Brazilian resident may become non-resident for tax purposes where:

- an individual leaves Brazil temporarily (ie without a permanent visa issued by the country of destination); that individual is considered to be non-resident after 12 months of absence, provided that a special income tax return is filed on the date that the 12-month period is completed; or
- an individual leaves the country permanently; such individual is considered non-resident as of the date of departure, provided an income tax return is filed at the date of leaving.

Non-Brazilian residents in general are taxed in Brazil when any income received derives from Brazilian sources or when the transaction giving rise to such earnings involves assets in Brazil. The income tax consequences for an employee who is resident in Brazil when the long-term incentive award is made, but who is no longer resident at the time of exercise/vesting are:

- where the award is granted by a Brazilian company under a free share structure, the value of shares transferred to the executive will be subject to withholding income tax at the rate of 15 or 25% if the non-Brazilian resident is located in a tax haven jurisdiction (ie those countries that do not impose any income tax, impose income tax at a maximum rate lower than 20% or permit restrictions on the disclosure of ownership in equity holdings); and
- where the plan involves the shares of a Brazilian company, the capital gains realised on the disposition of such shares, whether to other non-residents or Brazilian residents and whether made outside or within Brazil, is subject to taxation in Brazil at the rate of 15 or 25% if the non-Brazilian resident is located in a tax haven jurisdiction.

If the executive is not tax resident in Brazil and the options are granted by a foreign company, involving the shares of a foreign company, Brazilian tax rules will not apply.

6.2    **What are the social security consequences for an employee who is resident in Brazil when the long-term incentive award is made but who is no longer resident at the time of exercise/vesting?**

The answer depends on the plan's terms and conditions. Generally the plan rules set out that an executive is only able to exercise the options during employment, not following the termination of employment or resignation. Therefore, if the executive is living abroad, but is still rendering services to the company in Brazil, and if the options granted pertain to a Brazilian company, the social security rules will be the same as if the employee was residing in Brazil. If the employee is not resident in Brazil and the options are granted by a foreign company, Brazilian social security rules will not apply.

**6.3** **What are the tax and social security withholding/reporting consequences for the employer in respect of an employee who is resident in Brazil when the long-term incentive award is made, but who is no longer resident at the time of exercise/vesting?**

Please see 6.1 and 6.2 above.

## 7. Reporting requirements

**7.1** **Will the employer (or parent company, if different) have any reporting requirements as a result of the long-term incentive award?**

Any employee receiving benefits under a long-term incentive plan must inform the revenue authorities of any gains earned and any amounts received in connection with the plan in their annual income tax return. Where the employer is required to withhold the income tax due by the employee, the withheld amounts must be reported by the company to the tax authorities.

**7.2** **Are any tax rulings required in relation to the long-term incentive awards?**

No.

## 8. Exchange control issues

**8.1** **Are there any exchange control issues that would prevent an employee from (a) remitting monies abroad to purchase shares, or (b) repatriating monies from the sale of shares?**

As regards exchange control rulings, any individual or legal entity may purchase and sell foreign currency without limitation, provided that the transaction is legal and is evidenced by supporting documentation.

In view of the above, either a local employing subsidiary or employees of a given company located in Brazil may remit funds abroad for the acquisition of shares issued by a parent company under a share purchase or stock option plan.

## 9. Employment law

**9.1** **Are there any employment or local labour law issues which may arise as a result of the long-term incentive award? Are any consultations or authorisations required by law?**

No consultations or authorisations are required. If a company considers an award to be a non-gratuitous benefit, and thus does not pay and withhold social security contributions, and does not consider that the award gives rise to other labour charges, the relevant authorities and the executive may challenge the interpretation given by the company and claim the payment of labour and social security charges in court.

## 10. Translation

**10.1 Are there any language restrictions in Brazil? Does any of the documentation provided to the employee in relation to the long-term incentive award need to be translated into Portuguese?**

The documentation provided to an employee in relation to a long-term incentive award does not have to be in Portuguese. If the need arises to enforce rights in the courts of Brazil, however, the documents in which such right is set out, if written in a language other than Portuguese, would have to be translated into Portuguese by a sworn translator and registered with the appropriate Registry of Deeds and Documents in Brazil.

## 11. Data protection

**11.1 Are there any data protection issues which may arise should the employer wish to outsource the administration of the long-term incentive award to a third party?**

Protection of personal information pertaining to any Brazilian citizen is granted, in broad terms, by the Federal Constitution, which grants protection to a citizen's personal data.

Therefore, if the company intends to disclose any information pertaining to the executive, including any information related to a stock option plan, it should obtain prior written approval from the executive.

## 12. Source of shares

**12.1 Does it matter if shares are newly issued to an employee, provided out of treasury or delivered from an employee-benefit trust?**

The vast majority of stock option plans in Brazil are implemented through delivery of newly issued shares to employees. In a few specific circumstances, treasury shares are used. In any event, the legal consequences and relevant issues affecting the plan will remain the same, regardless of the source of shares.

# Bulgaria

Kalina S Tchakarova
Teodora Tsenova
Djingov, Gouginski, Kyutchukov & Velichkov

---

> **Red flag issues**
> 1. As at the time of writing, the authors are not aware of any relevant practice or instructions of the competent authorities on tax and social and health security liabilities relating specifically to the grant, exercise and/or vesting of long-term incentive awards.

## 1.     Securities laws

**1.1     What prospectus and/or securities law requirements arise in connection with the grant, vesting or exercise of a long-term incentive award or on the eventual sale of the shares by the executive?**

The Law on Public Offering of Securities (LPOS) defines the public offering of securities as any communication in Bulgaria to 100 or more people, or to an indefinite number of persons in any form and by any means, presenting sufficient information on the terms of the offer and the securities to be offered to enable an addressee to decide to purchase or subscribe to these securities. Provided that the offering of long-term incentive awards falls under the above definition, the rules of the LPOS apply. Additionally, to qualify as a security under the LPOS, the right offered must be transferable in nature. Therefore, if the long-term incentive award granted to the executive is not subject to provisions which allow for its transfer, its offering will not qualify as a public offering and consequently will not be subject to the rules of the LPOS.

**1.2     Is there an exemption from securities laws requirements either because the shares are being offered only to executives or because shares are being offered to a distinct group of named individuals?**

Provided that the shares are offered to a distinct group of individuals of fewer than 100 in number, then there will be no public offering, so the rules of the LPOS will not apply. Even if the information regarding the offering is communicated to more than 100 people in Bulgaria, there is no obligation to publish a prospectus in a number of cases, including where the offering and/or allocation of the shares is made to current or former members of management or supervisory bodies (jointly referred to as executives), or to employees by their employer or by an affiliated undertaking, provided that the shares are of the same class as shares already trading on a regulated market. In such a case a document should be provided to the concerned individuals containing information on:

- the number and nature of the shares;
- the rights thereunder and the rules on the exercise of such rights; and
- the rules and terms for acquisition of the shares as well as other information relevant to the offering.

Although exempt from the prospectus-related obligations, the remaining obligations for cases of public offering should be fulfilled.

**1.3 If there is an exemption, will the exemption apply automatically or are there any applications/filings that need to be made?**
Where an award qualifies as a public offering of securities but exemptions apply, these will apply automatically and no additional action is required.

**2. Employee tax and social security**

**2.1 When will the executive be liable to tax or social security (and at what rate) in respect of the long-term incentive award?**
As a general note it should be emphasised that the tax, social and health security liabilities of the executive, if any, will not be triggered at the moment of grant of the long-term incentive award, but at the moment of exercise of the option (ie the actual acquisition of shares under the award).

The tax, social and health security law consequences of the long-term incentive award will depend on whether the executive makes a payment to acquire the shares (ie whether it qualifies as a grant of an award with an exercise price (market-value options), or as a grant with no exercise price (free shares). Further, where the long-term incentive award has been granted with no exercise price, the consequences will differ depending on whether they were granted by or on the account of the direct employer, or by a third party.

If the executive is granted an option with an exercise price which tracks market value, then under Bulgarian law no tax, social or health security liability will arise.

However, if the long-term incentive award is granted either as free shares, or as an option with an exercise price which is lower than market value at exercise (eg options with an exercise price equal to market value at grant or nominal-cost options), then, provided that the award is granted by a person other than the direct employer (eg the group parent company or trustee), the difference will be treated as a gift and will be subject to gift tax at the moment of exercise. If the direct employer grants the option, gains are treated as income from employment and are subject to both social and health security and personal income tax.

Upon the acquisition of shares to which gift tax applies, the difference between the market value of the shares as of the date of exercise and the price paid (if any) will be subject to gift tax at a rate varying between 5% and 10%, subject to determination by the respective municipal council. Generally, the tax is payable by the executive within two months of the acquisition, unless the parties otherwise agree.

No social security or health security contributions are due for shares so acquired.

Upon acquisition of the shares, where the gain is treated as income from employment, the difference between the market value of the shares as of the date of exercise and the price paid (if any) will be subject to social and health security deductions (up to the maximum of the social security income) and to personal income tax. The liability for any payment of social and health security contributions due is split between the employer and the executive, while personal income tax must be paid by the executive. The employer must transfer these amounts to the state budget accounts.

The executive will also be liable for payment of personal income tax on any gain received from subsequent disposal of the shares (for further details see question 2.5 below). This gain will not be subject to health and social security charges.

Finally, any income accrued from the acquired shares in the interim period between exercise and disposal will be subject to taxation on dividends.

2.2    **How will the executive's tax and social security be collected? Will the executive be responsible for paying any liabilities himself or will the executive's employer be responsible for paying tax or social security liabilities on the executive's behalf?**

Where the acquisition of shares is subject only to gift tax, the executive is solely responsible for payment of the tax. If the long-term incentive award has been granted by the direct employer so that the benefit is taxed as income, the income tax and social and health contributions due on behalf of the executive will be subject to withholding tax by the employer. The employer must then make the respective transfer to the state budget accounts.

2.3    **If the employer is responsible for the executive's liabilities, can the employer withhold the liabilities from the executive's salary? Are there any formalities in this respect?**

As noted above, long-term incentive awards will not generally trigger any withholding liabilities for the employer, provided that the awards are granted by a third party to the employment relationship.

If income tax liabilities arise, then the employer must make the necessary withholdings from salary without any additional formalities.

2.4    **If the executive's salary in the month of exercise/release is not sufficient for the employer to withhold all of the liabilities, can the employer (or the parent company, if different) arrange for the executive to authorise the sale of some of the executive's shares in the market and pass the money to the executive's employer?**

Should income tax liabilities arise, it should be possible to deduct relevant amounts from future salary payments, or agree with the employee that sufficient shares are sold on the executive's behalf to reimburse the relevant amounts.

**2.5 Will the executive pay tax on the eventual sale of his shares and if so at what rate?**

Notwithstanding whether the shares were acquired for consideration or for free, the tax treatment of the income from the sale thereof will be identical in both cases. Where the executive transfers the title to the shares after the exercise of the award, he/she will be liable for payment of personal income tax on any profit realised by the transaction. Pursuant to the general rules of the Law on Taxation of Individuals, the basis for taxation will be the price received from the sale, less the documented acquisition price of the shares.

In the case of free shares, where the acquisition price is zero (where no cash is paid in consideration) the full sale price shall represent the taxable gain (notwithstanding the payment of any gift tax or income tax upon the acquisition, if applicable) and will be subject to income tax.

The tax due should be calculated and reported in the annual tax return of the executive selling the shares.

With respect to the applicable personal income tax rates, as of January 1 2008 a flat rate of 10% of taxable income applies.

## 3. Employer's social security

**3.1 Is the employer liable to pay (on its own account) any employer's social security in connection with the long-term incentive award?**

Where the long-term incentive award is granted by a third party to the employment relationship, this will not trigger any social or health security payments as it does not qualify as employment-related income. Therefore, neither the employer nor the grantor of the award will be liable to make any social and health security payments.

In cases where the award is granted by the employer directly, social and health security contributions are due. The employer must transfer the relevant amounts to the appropriate state budget accounts. However, the payment levy for the contributions is split between the employer and employee.

**3.2 Can the liability of the employer be put onto the employee? What steps are required?**

This is not applicable in most cases. If social and health security contributions are due, the employer's liability cannot be passed on to the employee.

## 4. Tax deduction for the employer

**4.1 Is it possible for the employer to receive a tax deduction in respect of the long-term incentive award? Would the employer need to be subject to recharge arrangements (eg if the employer is a subsidiary and provides funds to the parent company as part of a recharge arrangement in respect of the long-term incentive award)?**

No special statutory tax incentives are available in relation to the long-term incentive awards.

As noted above, if the awards qualify as a gift (as they are provided by a third party to the employment relationship), then under the rules of the Bulgarian Law on Corporate Income Taxation they should not be recognised as expenses of the employer for tax purposes and should not affect the employer's financial results (ie there is no reduction in the amount of corporate tax on business profits). Nevertheless, if the grantor of the award is a foreign entity, the accounting and tax rules of its jurisdiction would apply. In case of a grant where an incentive award qualifies as an employment-related income, the costs of the employer in relation to the award should be recognised as an expense of the employer for tax purposes and shown as a deduction in its accounts (the accounting profit/loss), which forms the basis of determining the corporate tax liability on business profits.

Recharge arrangements are possible, and would result in the incentive being deemed to have been granted on the account of the direct employer – a subsidiary of the grantor of the award. In this case, the incentive award would be treated as employment income, which would trigger social and health security liabilities for both the direct employer and the employee. Personal income tax rules would also apply.

## 5. Tax beneficial arrangements

### 5.1 Are there any ways of making the long-term incentive award tax-efficient in Bulgaria?

Provided that awards are structured so that they are not made by, or on behalf of, the direct employer, the grantor will not be liable to make any social and health security payments or tax deductions. Nor will the obligations arise for the direct employer. On exercise, the benefit to the employee is taxed at the more beneficial gift tax rate, rather than being subject to personal income tax and social and health security payments.

There are no tax-approved incentive arrangements in Bulgaria. Provided the grantor is a foreign entity, the tax rules of its jurisdiction will be taken into account.

## 6. Internationally mobile executives

### 6.1 What are the income tax consequences for an employee who is resident in Bulgaria when the long-term incentive award is made, but who is no longer resident at the time of exercise/vesting?

As the obligation to pay tax arises at the moment of exercising/vesting of the long-term incentive award, the issue of a change of residency prior to exercise/vesting of the award but after its grant is irrelevant. The executive will not qualify as a Bulgarian tax resident provided he/she spends less than 183 days in Bulgaria for every 12-month period and vice versa. If the executive qualifies as tax resident, then his/her worldwide income will be subject to taxation in Bulgaria. Where the executive is a tax resident of another country, the relevant local tax law will apply.

A gift of shares made by a foreign entity in favour of a foreign tax resident individual will have no Bulgarian gift tax implications. Similarly, a foreign tax resident will not be liable to any Bulgarian income tax on the gain from the sale of shares issued by a foreign company.

**6.2    What are the social security consequences for an employee who is resident in Bulgaria when the long-term incentive award is made, but who is no longer resident at the time of exercise/vesting?**

If the income realised is related to employment in Bulgaria, the fact that as of the date of exercise/vesting the employee is no longer resident is irrelevant.

**6.3    What are the tax and social security withholding/reporting consequences for the employer in respect of an employee who is resident in Bulgaria when the long-term incentive award is made, but who is no longer resident at the time of exercise/vesting?**

As long as the award is granted by a third party, the employer will not have to calculate tax and no withholding obligations arise, as the awards will not qualify as employment income. There are no social and health security obligations. In such cases, the responsibility for the payment of tax remains with the employee.

Provided the awards are granted by or on the account of the employer and qualify as income from employment, the employer's tax-related obligations will depend on the respective provisions of the country where the executive resides.

## 7.    Reporting requirements

**7.1    Will the employer (or parent company, if different) have any reporting requirements as a result of the long-term incentive award?**

Generally, the grant of awards to executives will not trigger any reporting obligations. However, pursuant to the Law on Currency and related ordinances, if a Bulgarian company acquires shares in a foreign entity for the purposes of granting them for whatever purpose, including to an employee, this acquisition may qualify as a direct foreign investment, provided that the acquired shares represent more than 10% of the voting rights in the foreign company. In such a case the employer will be obliged to report to the Bulgarian National Bank regarding the direct foreign investments. Sample statistical forms must be submitted to the bank on a quarterly basis, regarding the status of the investments.

**7.2    Are there any tax rulings required in relation to the long-term incentive awards?**

No such rulings are available. It should be noted, though, that notwithstanding the differences in the tax treatment, an obligation to declare the acquired shares occurs, irrespective of whether they are in a foreign or a local company, and stays solely with the employee if a local tax resident. The acquisition of shares should be declared in the annual tax return to be filed by the employee for personal income tax purposes not later than April 30 of the year following the reported year.

## 8.    Exchange control issues

8.1    **Are there any exchange control issues that would prevent an employee from (a) remitting monies abroad to purchase shares, or (b) repatriating monies from the sale of shares?**

As a general rule, there are no specific regimes applicable to remitting monies abroad for the purchase of shares or repatriating monies abroad from the sale of shares. However, there are general reporting requirements for the import/export of cash, as well as wire transfers of amounts exceeding the levels determined by statute.

In the event of an import of cash exceeding €10,000 (or its equivalent in another currency), the executive should report to customs the amount, type of currency, owner and recipient of the funds, the origin and purpose, as well as the transport vehicle's data and the itinerary. The same obligation applies in cases where an equivalent amount is exported in cash. Provided that the sum in cash subject to export exceeds Lev25,000 (approximately €12,821 at the time of writing), or its equivalent in foreign currency, the exporter should also present to customs a certificate issued by the respective revenue authorities stating that the person does not have overdue public liabilities in Bulgaria.

For the purposes of trans-border payment statistics, any local person receiving amounts equal to or exceeding Lev25,000 (approximately €12,821) (including the foreign currency equivalent thereof) should fill in and submit to the servicing bank a sample statistical form on the terms of the transaction performed. Wire transfers of sums from Lev5,000 (approximately €2,564) to Lev25,000 (approximately €12,821) require the filing of a sample statistical form with the servicing bank. Where the amount to be sent abroad via a wire transfer exceeds Lev25,000 (approximately €12,821) or the equivalent in foreign currency, a copy of the document certifying the grounds for the payment as well as the sample statistical form should be presented by the transferor to the servicing bank.

## 9.    Employment law

9.1    **Are there any employment or local labour law issues which may arise as a result of the long-term incentive award? Are any consultations or authorisations required by law?**

The long-term incentive awards would not trigger any implications from a labour law perspective, nor require the conduct of consultations and/or sending of notification to employees, work councils or trade unions. However, special consultation or other requirements might be provided for in a collective bargaining agreement, binding upon the particular employer.

## 10. Translation

10.1 **Are there any language restrictions in Bulgaria? Does any of the documentation provided to the employee in relation to the long-term incentive award need to be translated?**

Notwithstanding that under the Constitution of the Republic of Bulgaria the official language in the country is Bulgarian, local laws and regulations do not introduce any foreign language restrictions. Thus, all documents related to the long-term incentive award may be drafted and executed in a foreign language. However, all such documents might be subject to inspection by the authorities (eg the tax authorities) and in the event of an inspection should be presented, initially or upon request, with a Bulgarian translation, certified by a sworn translator. If the inspecting authority finds that the translation is not accurate, it may request another translation for the inspected entity or individual.

Thus, it is recommended that any and all documentation relating to the long-term incentive award is prepared in a bilingual format, in Bulgarian and in the respective foreign language, to avoid complications at a later stage. Further, it is recommended that bilingual documents are used where the respective employee is not fluent in English.

## 11. Data protection

11.1 **Are there any data protection issues which may arise should the employer wish to outsource the administration of the long-term incentive award to a third party?**

The relevant Law on Personal Data Protection applies for the processing of personal data by a data controller established on the territory of Bulgaria and such processing is carried out in the context of the activities of the controller. Further, Bulgarian law applies to data controllers who are not established in an EU member state or a member state of the European Economic Area (EEA), but who use data processors that are located in Bulgaria, unless these are only used for transitional purposes.

Provided that the Bulgarian law applies, different regimes will be relevant depending on whether the third party processes the personal data on its own behalf or on behalf of the employer. Thus, if a third party processes data on behalf of an employer under its direction, meaning that the employer will be the data controller, that third party will have the capacity of a data processor. By law the relations between the controller and the processor in relation to data processing should be in writing.

If a third party processes data on its own behalf (ie it has the capacity of a data controller), Bulgarian legislation would be applicable if that party is established (i) in Bulgaria or (ii) in a country other than an EU or EEA member state, if the means for processing are located in Bulgaria and are not used for transitional purposes only. If that is the case, the third party should observe all relevant data protection rules, such as the obligation to register as a data controller, to obtain the consent of the data subjects, etc. A third-party data controller may disclose data to the Bulgarian employer/assignor of the employees if prior to the first disclosure the employees are informed and are allowed to object to the intended disclosure.

If disclosure of the data will be made to a person outside the territory of Bulgaria (eg to a foreign employer or assignor of the executive), then no notifications, permissions or the like to or from any state authorities will be required. Provided that the data is transferred to a country outside the EU and EEA, the transfer should be permitted by the Commission on Personal Data Protection, provided that the said country gives an adequate level of protection of personal data. These requirements would not apply if any of the following are met:

- the European Commission has decided that the country of receipt offers adequate protection; or
- model clauses, approved by the European Commission as offering adequate level of protection, are used to regulate relations between parties with respect to the transfer.

The requirement for an adequate level of protection will not be applicable if the executives give their express, specific, informed and unequivocal consent to data transfer.

Finally, if the third party collects the data in its own name, and any of the above conditions for the applicability of Bulgarian legislation are not met, the collection shall not be subject to Bulgarian data protection legislation.

## 12.    Source of shares

**12.1    Does it matter if shares are newly issued to an employee, provided out of treasury or delivered from an employee-benefit trust?**

The origin of the shares does not have impact on the obligations of the grantor and the executive in relation to the grant of the awards.

# Canada

**Gary Nachshen**
Stikeman Elliott LLP

---

> **Red flag issues**
>
> 1. Criteria for half rate of tax on stock option benefits.
> 2. Personal and corporate tax implications of settling awards with new issue or treasury shares, with market purchase shares, or with cash.
> 3. Tax inefficiency of restricted stock grants.
> 4. Applicability of proposed non-resident trust taxation rules if shares sourced from offshore trust.
> 5. Risk of options or units vesting and/or remaining exercisable during reasonable notice period for employment termination.

## 1. Securities laws

**1.1 What prospectus and/or securities law requirements arise in connection with the grant, vesting or exercise of a long-term incentive award or on the eventual sale of the shares by the executive?**

Securities law in Canada is a matter of provincial and territorial jurisdiction. Each province and territory has its own securities laws, regulations, rules and policies, which can differ significantly from one another. Securities law in each province and territory of Canada is administered by its own regulator (a Securities Commission).

The various Securities Commissions in Canada have cooperated to develop rules known as multilateral instruments, which are adopted as law or at least as policy in the provinces and territories named in the particular multilateral instrument. There are also certain national policies and national instruments, which are generally applicable in all provinces and territories of Canada.

With respect to a stock-settled employee incentive plan (the Plan), the relevant governing instrument is National Instrument 45 – 106 – Prospectus and Registration Exemptions (NI 45–106), which came into force on September 14 2005. NI 45–106 serves to consolidate and harmonise most of the prospectus and dealer registration exemptions (such exemptions are discussed in more detail below) which had previously been contained in various provincial statutes and national, multilateral and local instruments.

As a general principle, securities[1] may not be "distributed" (within the meaning of applicable securities laws) in Canada except pursuant to a prospectus in the required form (the prospectus requirement). Further, no "trade" of securities (which includes distribution) may be undertaken without the involvement of a dealer registered in the particular jurisdiction for that purpose (the dealer registration requirement). An act in furtherance of a trade of securities, including any act, advertisement, solicitation, conduct or negotiation, is generally considered a trade under Canadian securities legislation.

Since it is often not practical for foreign issuers to prepare and file a prospectus in the required form or to obtain the necessary dealer registrations when completing an offering, such foreign issuers will look to rely on exemptions that are available from these requirements when distributing securities in Canada.

Interests in an incentive arrangement which can only be cash-settled, as opposed to stock-settled, are not considered "securities" under Canadian law and are therefore not subject to Canadian provincial or territorial securities legislation.

## 1.2 Is there an exemption from securities laws requirements either because the shares are being offered only to executives or because shares are being offered to a distinct group of named individuals?

Under NI 45–106, neither the prospectus requirement nor the dealer registration requirement applies to a trade by an issuer in a security of its own issue with a Canadian employee, executive officer, or director of the issuer or of a "related entity" of the issuer (each a Participant), so long as participation in the Plan by the Participant is "voluntary".[2]

Essentially, for participation to be voluntary, a Participant must not have been induced to acquire securities by expectation of employment or appointment or continued employment or appointment. A "related entity" means, for an issuer, a person that controls or is controlled by the issuer or that is controlled by the same person that controls the issuer. "Control" is generally evidenced by one entity having the power to direct the management and policies of another by virtue of ownership or direction over the voting securities of another or by other enumerated means.

Assuming, therefore, that the Participants are employed by the issuer or a related entity of the issuer and participation in the Plan by such Participants is voluntary, the issuance of shares under the Plan is exempt from the prospectus and dealer registration requirements and no filings[3] or fees are required.

Ideally, the Participants should confirm in writing that their participation in the Plan is voluntary (ie has not been induced by expectation of employment, appointment, continued employment or continued appointment, as applicable). It is therefore recommended that the issuer insert a passage along the lines of the following clause into the grant letter or enrolment form in respect of the Plan:

---

1   The securities, taxation, employment and other analysis in this chapter applies variously only to corporation shares or both to such shares and to other interests in legal entities, such as particular types of trust units. For ease of reference, the discussion in this chapter will refer expressly only to shares, but in certain cases the analysis would technically apply equally to other types of securities as well.

2   NI 45–106 also applies to consultants, but this chapter does not otherwise address the legal position as to consultants.

3   If the documents distributed to employees in the province of Quebec include marketing materials as opposed to just Plan rules and enrolment forms or agreements, then such documents must be filed with the Quebec Securities Commission pursuant to Section 37.2 of the Securities Regulation (Quebec).

*"By accepting this grant, you represent and warrant to the Company that your participation in the Company's [name of Plan] is voluntary and that you have not been induced to participate by expectation of engagement, appointment, employment, continued engagement, continued appointment or continued employment, as applicable."*

### (a) Options

#### (i) Grant of options

Under NI 45–106, a stock option grant is considered a right to purchase a share and, as such, would be treated as a security, and the analysis set out above would apply. Under NI 45–106, neither the prospectus requirement nor the dealer registration requirement applies to a trade by the issuer in a right to purchase a security of its own issue with a Participant, so long as such participation is voluntary.

#### (ii) Vesting of options

No dealer registration, consent or filing requirements will be triggered as a result of the vesting of a Participant's options, since the analysis set out above would equally apply.

#### (iii) Exercise of options

The issuance of shares upon the exercise of options under the Plan in accordance with the terms and conditions of the options is exempt from the dealer registration requirement and the prospectus requirement, and no registrations, consents or filings are required since the analysis set out above would equally apply.

#### (iv) Issuance of shares

There are no restrictions on the allotment or transfer of shares under the Plan and no registrations, consents or filings are required.

### (b) Sale of shares

Exemptions from the dealer registration requirement and prospectus requirement are also available for the first trade by the Participant of the shares acquired under the Plan. Sections 2.27 and 2.28 of NI 45–106 and Section 2.14 of Multilateral Instrument 45–102 – Resale of Securities set out the exemptions for the first trade of shares, which apply provided that the following conditions are satisfied:

- the issuer of the shares was not a reporting issuer in any Canadian jurisdiction at the distribution date or at the date of the trade;
- at the distribution date, after giving effect to the issue of the shares and any other shares of the same class or series that were issued at the same time or as part of the same distribution as the shares, residents of Canada:
  - did not own directly or indirectly more than 10% of the outstanding shares of the class or series, and
  - did not represent in number more than 10% of the total number of owners directly or indirectly of shares of the class or series; and
- the trade is made:

– through an exchange, or a market, outside of Canada; or

– to a person or company outside of Canada.

Provided that all of the aforementioned requirements are met, the first trade of shares by a Participant will be exempt from the dealer registration requirement and prospectus requirement.

*(c)*     ***Restricted stock***

*(i)*     *Grant of restricted stock*

An allocation of shares to a Participant would be considered a distribution and a trade, but the analysis set forth above would equally apply. Provided, therefore, that the Participants are employed by the issuer or a related entity to the issuer and participation in the trade is voluntary, the allocation of shares under the Plan would be exempt from the applicable prospectus and dealer registration requirements of Canadian securities legislation, and no filings or fees would be required.

*(ii)*     *Vesting of restricted stock*

This event is arguably not a "trade", and therefore would not attract the application of the prospectus or dealer registration requirements. To the extent that it did, however, the analysis set out above would equally apply.

If a forfeiture resulted in the issuer reacquiring previously issued shares from a Participant, then this could potentially raise an issue under Canadian "issuer bid" rules (discussed further below). There are potential exemptions available, but care would need to be taken to ensure that these exemptions are available. That being said, for the tax reasons examined below, restricted stock is rarely granted in Canada, so in practice this issue would rarely if ever arise.

*(iii)*     *Sale of shares*

The analysis with regard to the sale of optioned shares above would apply equally to the sale of restricted stock.

*(d)*     ***Stock-settled deferred share units, restricted share units and share appreciation rights***

*(i)*     *Grant of units or rights*

A grant of these types of awards to a Participant would be considered a distribution and a trade, but the analysis set out above would apply. Provided, therefore, that the Participants are employed by the issuer or a related entity to the issuer and participation in the Plan is voluntary, the allocation of shares under the Plan would be exempt from the applicable prospectus and dealer registration requirements of Canadian securities legislation, and no filings or fees would be required.

*(ii)*     *Vesting of units or rights*

This event is arguably not a "trade", and therefore would not attract the application of the prospectus or dealer registration requirements. To the extent that it did, however, the analysis set out above would apply equally.

*(iii)*   *Sale of shares*

The analysis with regard to the sale of optioned shares above would apply equally to the sale of shares acquired in this manner.

*(e)*   **Issuer bids**

There are rules in each province and territory of Canada dealing with "issuer bids" (ie the acquisition by an issuer of shares of its own issuance from shareholders in Canada, or shareholders with an address, as shown on the books of the issuer, in Canada). To the extent that the issuer acquires its own shares on the secondary market, care should be taken to ensure that this acquisition does not trigger the issuer bid requirements of Canadian law.

## 2.   Employee tax and social security

### 2.1   When will the executive be liable to tax or social security (and at what rate) in respect of the long-term incentive award?

Income taxation of Plan Participants is governed almost exclusively by the federal Income Tax Act (the ITA). The analogous rules at the provincial and territorial level are effectively identical, subject to a small number of relatively minor exceptions in Quebec. The following analysis addresses the taxation under the ITA primarily in respect of new issue or treasury shares granted to Participants under various types of Plan designs.[4] The taxation of Participants in a Plan involving the purchase of open market shares and/or cash settlement is addressed separately, where relevant.

The Canada Pension Plan (the CPP) is a contributory, earnings-related social insurance programme and operates throughout Canada, with the exception of Quebec which has its own virtually identical programme, the Quebec Pension Plan (the QPP). There are three kinds of CPP/QPP benefits: disability benefits, retirement pensions, and survivor benefits.

Employees pay one-half of the mandatory annual CPP/QPP contributions, at a rate of 4.95% of pensionable earnings. For CPP/QPP purposes, pensionable earnings include Plan benefits, up to the year's maximum pensionable earnings (the YMPE). The CPP/QPP YMPE for 2008 is C$44,900. Because the YMPE caps out at such a relatively low level, most Participants will reach the maximum C$2,049.30 annual employee contribution (for 2008) in respect of salary alone, making the CPP/QPP all but irrelevant for Plan purposes from a practical perspective.

*(a)*   **Options**

*(i)*   *Grant of options*

The grant of an option does not have any tax consequences.

---

4     There are a number of special rules applicable to shares of Canadian-controlled private corporations, as defined in the ITA, which rules are not addressed in this chapter.

*(ii)*    *Vesting of options*

The vesting of an option does not have any tax consequences.

*(iii)*   *Exercise of options*

Unless a Participant makes the election described below, he will be deemed to receive a taxable benefit from employment in the year that he exercises an option to acquire shares. The benefit is equal to the difference between the fair market value of the shares on the date they are acquired and the price paid to acquire the shares (and less any amount paid to acquire the options, where applicable).

The benefit is taxed in the same manner as all other employment income, at the Participant's combined federal and provincial/territorial marginal rate (which rate varies from jurisdiction to jurisdiction and from year to year), in the year of exercise. Importantly, the Participant may deduct 50% of the amount of the benefit from his taxable income in the year of exercise, providing that: (i) the exercise price is not less than the fair market value of the optioned shares at the time of the grant of the option; (ii) he is dealing at arm's length with the issuer (and with his employer, as applicable); and (iii) the optioned shares are "prescribed shares" within the meaning of the federal Income Tax Regulations (the ITR). In general terms, a "plain vanilla" ordinary or common share will constitute a prescribed share. More particularly, a minimum or maximum dividend or liquidation entitlement or certain types of conversion, put or call rights will disqualify optioned shares from prescribed share status.

Qualifying for this half rate of tax on stock option benefits, which is set out in Paragraph 110(1)(d) of the ITA, is a critical element in tax planning around employee compensation in Canada. With the exception of certain tax-qualified pension, retirement, and profit-sharing plans which are rarely encountered in the employee share plan context,[5] the "110(1)(d) deduction" is the only way for a Participant to pay tax on Plan benefits at less than his full marginal rate.[6]

*(b)*    **Sale of shares**

Subject to an annual limit, a Participant may elect to defer the taxation (but importantly, *not* the computation) of the stock option benefit realised on exercise of an option under the Plan from the year of exercise until the earliest of the year that the optioned shares are sold, the year the Participant ceases to be resident in Canada for ITA purposes, or the year the Participant dies. The Participant is eligible for the deferral if the following conditions are met:

- the shares are acquired after February 27 2000. Note that it does not matter when the option was granted, so long as the option is exercised after February 27 2000;
- the exercise price is not less than the fair market value of the optioned shares at the time the option was granted;

---

5    A discussion of the rules applicable to these tax-qualified, or tax-assisted, plans lies beyond the scope of this chapter.

6    Where the shares are publicly traded, the criteria for the 110(1)(d) deduction are met, and the Participant donates the shares to a registered charity within 30 days of exercising the option, he may deduct the *other* 50% of the amount of the stock option benefit from his taxable income as well.

- the Participant deals at arm's length with the employer, the issuer of the option and the corporation whose shares may be acquired under the option;
- the shares are prescribed shares;
- the Participant is not a "specified shareholder" of the employer, the issuer of the option, or the corporation whose shares may be acquired under the option, immediately after the option is granted. Generally, a "specified shareholder" is a shareholder who owns (directly or indirectly) 10% or more of the shares of any class of the relevant corporation, or of a corporation related to the relevant corporation; and
- the shares must be of a class listed on a prescribed Canadian or foreign stock exchange at the time the shares are acquired. The list of prescribed exchanges is contained in the ITR.

To obtain the deferral, the Participant must file an election before January 16 of the year following the year in which securities are acquired.

The annual limit of optioned shares vesting in a particular year for which the deferral may be elected is C$100,000. Generally, the "specified value" of a share for these purposes is the fair market value of the share at the time the option was granted. If the Participant has options vesting in a single year for shares with a value on the date of grant in excess of the C$100,000 annual limit, he may designate those options in respect of which the deferral will be claimed.

### (c)   *Market purchase shares*

The above discussion of stock options assumes that the optioned shares will be either newly issued, issued from treasury, or sold to the Participant by a corporation that does not deal at arm's length with the issuer.[7] If stock options can be settled using shares purchased on the open market, neither the half rate of tax nor the deferral described above would be available.

In addition, it is possible that a Plan using market purchase shares could be subject to the anti-avoidance "salary deferral arrangement" (SDA) rules in the ITA. An SDA is essentially a plan or arrangement under which a person has a right in one year to receive an amount after that year, where it is reasonable to consider that one of the main purposes for the creation or existence of the right is to postpone tax payable on amounts earned for the rendering of employment services, subject to certain enumerated exceptions.

The SDA rules would likely subject the Participant to tax in the year of grant and/or in any subsequent year prior to exercise during which the optioned shares increased in value, on a "mark-to-market" basis, unless all options would have to be exercised by the end of the third calendar year following the year of grant.[8] In such latter case, taxation would still be in the year of exercise, but at full marginal rates rather than the half rate. Where the SDA rules did subject the Participant to tax prior

---

7    That is, such discussion assumes the Plan is subject to Section 7 of the ITA.
8    This "three-year bonus rule" is one of the enumerated exceptions to SDA characterisation. In addition, a plan governed by Section 7 of the ITA or in which there is a substantial risk of forfeiture will not be subject to the SDA rules.

to the year of exercise, his tax position would be trued-up by way of a final income inclusion or a deduction, as applicable, in the year of exercise.

### (d) Cash settlement

If options over new issue or treasury shares can be cash-settled for their in-the-money value at the *Participant's* election, then the discussion in (a) (i), (ii) and (iii) above will apply, including most notably the potential availability of the half-rate of tax pursuant to the 110(1)(d) deduction. On the other hand, if options can be cash-settled at the *issuer's* or *employer's* election, then the same analysis with regard to market purchase shares in (c) above will apply.

### (e) Restricted stock

Where shares are issued at no charge to a Participant or to a trust for the absolute, conditional, or contingent benefit of a Participant, the Participant will be deemed to receive a benefit from employment equal to the fair market value of the shares on the date of issuance, taxable in the year of issuance. This is so even where the Participant has no discretion to deal in the shares for a period of time, or where the shares may subsequently be forfeited, although such factors may affect the shares' fair market value and thus the quantum of the above-mentioned benefit.

By contrast, where an award is structured such that the Participant receives only a right to receive shares at a future date provided certain events occur or time periods lapse, the Participant will be treated as receiving a taxable benefit only in the year of the actual issuance of the shares. If the shares are never issued (ie they do not vest), there are no tax consequences to the Participant. Certain variations on this alternative are addressed in detail in the section below.

Where shares are issued to the Participant but are subsequently forfeited, generally the Participant will only be entitled to claim a capital loss in the year of forfeiture.[9] As examined in more detail below, capital losses may only be set off against capital gains on other investments, not against taxable employment benefits.

For the above reasons, *restricted stock is rarely granted in Canada.*

### (f) Deferred share units

A deferred share unit (DSU) Plan, governed by Paragraph 6801(d) of the ITR, involves the grant of phantom stock, the value of which depends on the fair market value of a class of shares of the employer or a corporation related to the employer.[10] DSU Plans governed by Paragraph 6801(d) are expressly carved out from the SDA definition in the ITA, meaning the Participant will not be taxable in the year of grant or any subsequent year prior to settlement of the DSUs.

All amounts payable under a DSU Plan must be so paid *after* termination of

---

9   Where the shares are held in trust and certain specific criteria are met, the amount previously taxed as an employment benefit may be deducted from the Participant's income in the year of forfeiture.

10  Except as otherwise indicated, the discussion of DSUs, RSUs (as defined above) and SARs (as defined below) assumes that such units or rights would be settled in cash or market purchase shares rather than via issuance of new issue or treasury shares. Where DSUs, RSUs or SARs must be settled in new issue or treasury shares, there are no restrictions on timing of settlement because the SDA rules do not apply.

employment, either in the calendar year when employment terminates, or in the following calendar year. Payments are treated as employment income and taxed at the Participant's marginal rate in the year of settlement.

DSU Plans are virtually always unfunded. One tax risk associated with pre-funding a DSU Plan (eg by putting shares in trust with a third party) is that the funding could result in the Plan being treated as a "retirement compensation arrangement" under the ITA, meaning that a special 50% refundable tax would be payable on all contributions.

A DSU Plan may not provide any sort of backstop or guarantee to Participants to protect them against declining share prices. Recently, the CRA has begun to question DSU Plans which leave the amounts of individual grants to employer discretion, as opposed to prescribing some sort of standard grant formula or criteria, on the basis that such discretion could indirectly contravene the prohibition against share price backstops. This new administrative stance has made DSUs somewhat less attractive than in prior years.

*(g)*   *Restricted share units*

Besides DSUs, there is one other type of "full-value" phantom stock which is automatically exempt from the SDA rules, known as restricted share units (RSUs). RSUs are frequently granted in Canada in lieu of restricted stock and must be settled by the end of the *third* calendar year after the year of grant to qualify for the SDA exemption. Any other types of phantom stock which are "in the money" at the date of grant will ordinarily trigger taxation to the Participant in the year of grant. Payments in settlement of RSUs are treated as employment income and taxed at the Participant's marginal rate in the year of settlement.

RSU Plans are virtually always unfunded. Any pre-funding could trigger the application of the "employee benefit plan" rules in the ITA, one of the implications of which is that the funding would not generate a corporate tax deduction until the subsequent year in which the Participant was taxed.

*(h)*   *Share appreciation rights*

Share appreciation rights (SARs), or phantom stock options, involve the grant of units which have no value on the date of grant, but which track any increase in the value of the underlying class of shares. The Canada Revenue Agency (CRA) has stated that, generally, SARs are not treated as SDAs. Payments in settlement of such SARs are treated as employment income and taxed at the Participant's marginal rate in the year of settlement.

SAR plans are virtually always unfunded. Any pre-funding could trigger the application of the employee benefit plan rules in the ITA, one of the implications of which is that the funding would not generate a corporate tax deduction until the subsequent year in which the Participant was taxed.

One area of uncertainty is the timing of taxation for SARs which have vested (ie become exercisable at a time of the Participant's choosing). The CRA has stated that it is a question of fact whether such SARs should be treated as an SDA. To sidestep possible taxation of SARs before the year of settlement, it is preferable to provide that they must either:

- be settled by the end of the third calendar year after the year of grant; or
- stipulate only a single date for settlement as opposed to a window of exercisability.

It is not uncommon to add a cash-settled SAR feature to new issue or treasury share stock options, in which the choice of exercising the options for shares or surrendering the options for cash equal to their in-the-money value resides with the *Participant*. In such case, the taxable benefit associated with any cash payment may be reduced by one-half where the fair market value exercise price, arm's length status, and prescribed share conditions for the 110(1)(d) deduction are all met.

**2.2 How will the executive's tax and social security be collected? Will the executive be responsible for paying any liabilities himself or will the executive's employer be responsible for paying tax or social security liabilities on the executive's behalf?**

The ITA requires every employer paying salary or wages or making any various related payments (as enumerated in the ITA) to withhold tax and remit it to the Receiver General of Canada on account of each employee's income tax for the relevant pay period. The ITA authorises tax deductions to be made in "the amount determined in accordance with prescribed rules". The prescribed rules provide ranges of remuneration tied to the length of various pay periods. Having determined the range of remuneration which a payment to an employee falls into, the employer then calculates the tax to be withheld.

The CRA's administrative policy is that withholding on *non-cash* compensation such as stock option benefits need only be effected out of *cash* compensation (such as salary) paid by the same entity, and then only if the benefit is not so large or realised so late in the year as to cause undue hardship. One of the implications of this policy is that where the Participant is not employed by the issuer, and assuming the local Canadian employer does not reimburse the issuer for the issuance of the shares, then there would be nothing from which to withhold.

Whether tax is withheld and remitted by the employer or not, the Participant must report the associated income on his tax return, which must be filed by April 30 (or in some circumstances by June 30) of the next calendar year. In all cases, any tax owing must be paid by the Participant by April 30 of the next calendar year.

**2.3 If the employer is responsible for the executive's liabilities, can the employer withhold the liabilities from the executive's salary? Are there any formalities in this respect?**

Reference should be made to the immediately preceding response.

**2.4 If the executive's salary in the month of exercise/release is not sufficient for the employer to withhold all of the liabilities, can the employer (or the parent company, if different) arrange for the executive to authorise to sell some of the executive's shares in the market and pass the money to the executive's employer?**

There is no statutory or regulatory authority in Canada for requiring Participants to pay the amount of income tax withholding associated with Plan benefits by cheque or through the sale of a portion of their shares at the time they exercise their options or settle their units. Some employers do impose this requirement as a contractual matter. This is generally possible, subject to normal civil law and employment law principles governing employee authorisation to deduct at source.

## 2.5 Will the executive pay tax on the eventual sale of his shares and if so at what rate?

The sale of shares acquired under the Plan will result in the Participant realising a capital gain if the amount for which they are sold, net of any costs relating to the sale, is greater than the Participant's "adjusted cost base" (ACB) of the shares. 50% of the capital gain will be included in his income in the year of disposition and subject to tax at his marginal rate for that year.

The ACB of shares acquired under the Plan will be equal to their fair market value at the time they are acquired. If the Participant holds other shares of the issuer in the same share class, the ACB of each share will generally be determined by averaging the cost of all such shares. Averaging will not be required in respect of shares subject to the election to defer tax, noted above. Averaging will also not be required in respect of shares which are disposed of within 30 days of being acquired under the Plan, provided the Participant does not acquire any other shares of the issuer prior to the disposition and he identifies the disposed shares in his income tax return.

If the Participant sells shares for less than their ACB, he will sustain a capital loss and 50% of the capital loss may be deducted against taxable capital gains. To the extent that a capital loss cannot be deducted against taxable capital gains in the year the loss is incurred, this amount can be carried back three years and forward indefinitely and deducted against taxable capital gains in accordance with the detailed rules of the ITA.

There is no withholding or reporting obligation imposed on the issuer or employer in connection with the sale of the shares.

## 3. Employer's social security

## 3.1 Is the employer liable to pay (on its own account) any employer's social security in connection with the long term incentive award?

Employers pay one-half of the mandatory annual CPP/QPP contributions. The above analysis with respect to employee contributions is equally relevant in respect of employer contributions, including, in particular, the effect of the relatively low ceiling on CPP/QPP pensionable earnings.

Several provinces also levy a payroll tax to fund Canada's universal health insurance programme. This is paid by employers. Plan benefits are included in taxable payroll for these purposes. The payroll tax rate (expressed as a percentage of payroll in the relevant province) varies from province to province. There is no ceiling on taxable payroll for purposes of this tax.

**3.2 Can the liability of the employer be put onto the employee?**
No.

## 4. Tax deduction for the employer

**4.1 Is it possible for the employer to receive a tax deduction in respect of the long-term incentive award? Would the employer need to be subject to recharge arrangements (eg if the employer is a subsidiary and provides funds to the parent company as part of a recharge arrangement in respect of the long-term incentive award)?**

The ITA expressly prohibits a deduction for the sale or issue of shares to employees of the issuer or of the issuer's affiliate.[11] "Sale or issue" of shares has been interpreted for these purposes as an offer of new issue or treasury shares, or shares sold by a non-arm's-length corporation directly to an employee. This prohibition applies even to cash reimbursements by an employer to its foreign parent corporation of the cost of issuing shares under the Plan.

By contrast, a deduction for an award that is to be satisfied with market purchase shares would ordinarily be available in the year in which the employer incurred the expense of such shares (ie in the year the employer paid for the shares to be purchased on the open market by a third party or reimbursed its parent corporation for such purchase). A deduction in respect of cash paid to a Participant to settle Plan rights would ordinarily be available in the year in which the cash is paid by the employer to the Participant (or reimbursed to the parent, as applicable). This is the case whether the choice of cash or shares rests with the Participant or the company.

## 5. Tax beneficial arrangements

**5.1 Are there any ways of making the long-term incentive award tax-efficient in Canada?**

The most tax-efficient approach is to grant options which qualify for the 110(1)(d) deduction and can be stock-settled or cash-settled at the Participant's election. No matter what the form of settlement, the Participant will benefit from the half rate of tax. If the Participant chooses cash, the employer may claim a full deduction for the amount which it pays to the Participant or reimburses to its parent.[12]

---

11   That is, in any case where shares are sold or issued pursuant to Section 7 of the ITA.
12   Note that the cash settlement alternative can have accounting, as opposed to tax, consequences for the employer which are not always favourable. A discussion of such accounting treatment lies beyond the scope of this chapter.

## 6. Internationally mobile executives

6.1 **What are the income tax consequences for an employee who is resident in Canada when the long-term incentive award is made but who is no longer resident at the time of exercise/vesting?**

In principle, an award which is granted and which vests while the Participant is employed and resident in Canada will be subject to Canadian income tax. Depending on the particular factual circumstances and the terms of any applicable tax treaty, such Canadian tax liability can sometimes be reduced or eliminated.[13]

6.2 **What are the social security consequences for an employee who is resident in Canada when the long-term incentive award is made but who is no longer resident at the time of exercise/vesting?**

As noted above, social security is rarely relevant in the context of long-term incentive awards.

6.3 **What are the tax and social security withholding/reporting consequences for the employer in respect of an employee who is resident in Canada when the long-term incentive award is made but who is no longer resident at the time of exercise/vesting?**

The response to this question would depend on many of the same considerations as would affect the response to question 6.1 above.

## 7. Reporting requirements

7.1 **Will the employer (or parent company, if different) have any reporting requirements as a result of the long-term incentive award?**

The employer or other payor of benefits must file an annual information return with the CRA (and with Revenue Quebec in respect of recipients in Quebec) summarising all employment income paid or deemed to be paid in the prior calendar year, as well as send an individual tax slip to each recipient. Generally, the annual summary and slips must be submitted by the end of February of the year following the year of option exercise or other settlement of Plan benefits. In practice, the CRA will ordinarily accept the inclusion in the summary and slips prepared by the employer of amounts technically relating to share issuances by its foreign parent corporation.

7.2 **Are there any tax rulings required in relation to the long-term incentive awards?**

No. In certain cases, particularly for DSUs, Plan sponsors will sometimes wish to obtain an advance income tax ruling from the CRA to ensure that the anticipated tax treatment will, in fact, be available.

---

13    In late 2007, Canada and the US signed a protocol which may significantly revise the rules governing taxation of stock options in the hands of executives moving between those two countries. The protocol was not yet in effect at the time of writing.

## 8. Exchange control issues

### 8.1 Are there any exchange control issues that would prevent an employee from (a) remitting monies abroad to purchase shares or (b) repatriating monies from the sale of shares?

There are no such exchange control restrictions.

## 9. Employment law

### 9.1 Are there any employment or local labour law issues which may arise as a result of the long-term incentive award? Are any consultations or authorisations required by law?

There is no requirement to consult with non-unionised employee associations to which Participants belong. However, if Participants are represented by a labour union, the union must be consulted prior to implementing the Plan. If the Plan forms part of a collective bargaining agreement, the union must consent to any amendments to the Plan.

In Canada, unless otherwise contractually agreed, an employee is entitled to reasonable notice of termination of employment[14] or pay in lieu of that notice. Such pay in lieu of notice will include the value of Plan benefits that would have accrued during the Participant's reasonable notice period had he continued to work during that period, providing the Participant can establish (on a balance of probabilities) that he would indeed have received the particular Plan award had he not been terminated.

Where Plan documents explicitly exclude awards to employees who are terminated, lawfully or otherwise, the value of the award should not be payable to such employees. Therefore, it is advisable that specific wording be included in the Plan rules applicable to Canadian Participants to ensure that former employees cannot make successful claims for awards that would otherwise have vested or been exercisable during their respective reasonable notice periods.

## 10. Translation

### 10.1 Are there any language restrictions in Canada? Does any of the documentation provided to the employee in relation to the long-term incentive award need to be translated?

There are no statutory language requirements in Canada, except in Quebec. In Quebec, the law requires that all Plan documents be provided to a Participant in French, unless the Participant signs a written acknowledgement that he wishes to receive documentation in English. If the Plan sponsor does not wish to provide documents in French, and bearing in mind potential employee relations issues, a specific waiver to such effect (in both French and English) should be incorporated into the Plan enrolment form, option agreement, or other document signed by the Participant.

---

14 The reasonable notice period for a particular employee is determined on a case-by-case basis, having regard to a number of factors (eg age, length of service, position, and salary) established by common law.

## 11. Data protection

### 11.1 Are there any data protection issues which may arise should the employer wish to outsource the administration of the long-term incentive award to a third party?

The regulation of personal information in the private sector context is a fairly recent development in Canada. At the provincial level, three provinces – Quebec, British Columbia and Alberta – have adopted legislation dealing generally with the protection of personal information in the private sector. At the federal level, Parliament has enacted the Personal Information Protection and Electronic Documents Act (PIPEDA).

PIPEDA came into force on January 1 2001, in respect of the federally regulated private sector and information disclosed for consideration across national or provincial borders. Federally regulated sectors include industries such as banking, airlines, broadcasters, shippers and telecommunications companies. Effective January 1 2004, PIPEDA also became applicable to all personal information collected, used or disclosed in whole or in part within Canada in the course of "commercial activities", defined as "any particular transaction, act or conduct or any regular course of conduct that is of a commercial character, including the selling, bartering, or leasing of donor membership or fundraising lists".

PIPEDA applies in respect of personal information which is collected, used or disclosed in the course of commercial activities by federally regulated private-sector organisations, and personal information which is collected, used or disclosed by other private-sector organisations in the course of their commercial activities when it is transferred across Canadian or provincial borders or when it is collected, used or disclosed within a Canadian province that has not enacted legislation which is "substantially similar" to PIPEDA. To date, the federal government has recognised each of the Alberta Personal Information Protection Act (the APIPA), British Columbia Personal Information Protection Act (the BCPIPA) and Quebec's Act Respecting the Protection of Personal Information in the Private Sector (the Quebec Private Sector Act) to be "substantially similar" to PIPEDA. PIPEDA regulates the collection, disclosure and use of personal information in the private sector in all other provinces.

With respect to personal information of employees, PIPEDA only governs the collection, use, and disclosure of data relating to those persons employed by federal works or undertakings (ie employers in areas such as aviation, telecommunications, broadcasting and banking). Consequently, even if employee information is transferred across provincial borders, PIPEDA will not apply unless the business is federally regulated. APIPA, BCPIPA and the Quebec Private Sector Act regulate personal information of employees in the private sector in those provinces.

Under PIPEDA, individuals must be provided with the ability to exercise informed consent to the collection, use, or disclosure of their personal information. PIPEDA establishes rules governing the collection, use, and disclosure of personal information, and requires organisations to establish and enforce formal policies regarding the handling of personal data. Policies must strive to respect an individual's privacy rights, while permitting the valid gathering and use of personal information by organisations.

When comparing PIPEDA and the provincial privacy legislation, one matter that needs to be highlighted is the issue of consent. PIPEDA requires express ("opt-in") consent when the personal information collected, used or disclosed is sensitive (such as in the case of a person's health or financial information). Implied ("opt-out") consent is permissible under PIPEDA where the personal information is not sensitive (eg a person's mailing address in the case of a mainstream magazine subscription). Both the BCPIPA and APIPA, on the other hand, allow for implied consent for all types of personal information provided certain reasonableness criteria are met. In Quebec, consent must be manifest, free and enlightened, and must be given for a specific purpose.

## 12. Source of shares

### 12.1 Does it matter if shares are newly issued to an employee, provided out of treasury or delivered from an employee benefit trust?

Most of the above analysis does not depend on whether the shares governed by the Plan are newly issued shares, treasury shares or shares purchased on the open market. As described above, however, the source of shares is important for tax purposes.

The federal government has been attempting for some years to enact a series of amendments to the ITA designed to tax certain types of foreign passive investment income earned by Canadians in accordance with complex new deeming provisions. The most recent version of the proposed rules, released in November 2007 and intended to be effective retroactive to January 1 2007, was nearing passage as at the date of writing of the present chapter and would subject the worldwide income of a non-resident trust to Canadian income tax where the trust had certain specified connections with Canada. One such specified connection is where a non-resident trust had a Canadian resident contributor.

If the shares to be acquired by Canadian Participants were or could be sourced from a trust resident outside Canada, it is possible that the worldwide income earned by the trust could be subject to Canadian income tax under these proposed rules, should a Canadian-resident Participant or employer make contributions to it in connection with the Plan. To avoid this very negative potential consequence, it is advisable to ensure that no Canadian employer contributes to a non-resident trust (whether directly or indirectly) and that no shares for Canadian Participants be sourced from such a trust.

# China

Owen Cox
Gary Lock
Herbert Smith LLP

---

**Red flag issues**
1. Stock options should generally be limited to fewer than 200 people in China.
2. Stringent foreign exchange rules apply to Chinese nationals.
3. Stock options are generally taxed at the time of exercise.

---

## 1. Securities laws

### 1.1 What prospectus and/or securities law requirements arise in connection with the grant, vesting or exercise of a long-term incentive award or on the eventual sale of the shares by the executive?

The general rule is that any public offer of securities within China is subject to the approval of the China Securities Regulatory Commission (CSRC). Non-public offers by companies listed in China are also subject to CSRC approval.

Under China's Securities Law, an offer will be deemed public if: (i) shares are issued to unspecified persons, or (ii) securities are issued to an aggregate of 200 or more persons. While it will generally be straightforward to avoid application of the first of these tests – employees of a company will rarely, if ever, be unspecified persons – the second test means that employee stock options should generally be limited to 199 employees or fewer. This may require a change in policy for larger companies that elsewhere in the world extend share options to the full spectrum of their workforce.

A non-public offer of securities may not be advertised or circulated to the public in any manner. By way of practical guidance, an employer implementing an employee stock-option plan in China should take steps to ensure that information regarding the plan is not circulated beyond those employees immediately eligible to participate. Practical steps that may be taken include marking all plan documentation as "private and confidential" and addressing any associated correspondence to specific employees only. If information regarding the plan is available on the employer's intranet, then the information should be placed in a password-protected area with only those participating in the plan being given access.

In addition to securities law requirements, it should also be noted that only certain types of companies established in China can issue shares. In particular, most foreign-invested companies in China cannot issue shares. Only foreign-invested joint-stock companies can issue shares, although these have not proved historically popular with investors due to the relatively high registered capital amounts and higher-level approvals required.

**1.2    Is there an exemption from securities laws requirements either because the shares are being offered only to executives or because shares are being offered to a distinct group of named individuals?**

As discussed above, issuing shares to fewer than 200 specified people is not subject to CSRC approval.

A company wishing to offer stock options to 200 or more employees in China may choose to rely on the oral guidance of the CSRC that it does not require an employee stock-option plan to be approved if the stock-option plan is for stock listed on a foreign stock exchange. However, the extent to which a company can comfortably rely on such guidance depends largely on its risk appetite. National law clearly requires such an issuance to be approved by the CSRC, and oral confirmation from the CSRC that approval is not needed may be of little comfort in the face of future policy change. The prudent approach would simply be to limit an employee stock-option plan to fewer than 200 employees.

**1.3    If there is an exemption, will the exemption apply automatically or are there any applications/filings that need to be made?**

The exemption for the issuance of shares to fewer than 200 specified people is set out in the Securities Law, and it therefore applies automatically.

**2.    Employee tax and social security**

**2.1    When will the executive be liable to tax or social security (and at what rate) in respect of the long-term incentive award?**

Employees are not generally subject to tax in China on the receipt of options. Rather, they are subject to tax on the difference between the exercise price and the closing price of stocks (for listed companies) on the day of exercise. The taxable amount for unlisted companies is calculated on the basis of net assets. Once the taxable amount is calculated, the taxable income may be spread over the number of months to which the options relate (up to a maximum of 12 months). This method of calculation, which is similar to the taxation of bonuses, means an employee does not have to pay tax at his or her highest marginal rate.

If options are transferred at any time prior to exercise, then the employee will be subject to tax on consideration for the transfer, and there are no applicable apportionment provisions.

**2.2    How will the executive's tax and social security be collected? Will the executive be responsible for paying any liabilities himself or will the executive's employer be responsible for paying tax or social security liabilities on the executive's behalf?**

Employers in China must withhold individual income tax and pay withheld amounts to the government. Individuals who have more than one source of income, and those with an annual income of over Rmb120,000, are required to declare their income and pay income tax by themselves.

**2.3** **If the employer is responsible for the executive's liabilities, can the employer withhold the liabilities from the executive's salary? Are there any formalities in this respect?**
Withholding tax may be withheld from an employee's salary.

The employee stock-option plan, together with other required documentation, must be submitted to the tax bureau for their records before the plan is implemented. An employer must also notify the relevant local tax bureau prior to an employee exercising any stock option. In practice, the stock-option documentation would require the employee to give notice to the employer of an intention to exercise an option.

**2.4** **If the executive's salary in the month of exercise/release is not sufficient for the employer to withhold all of the liabilities, can the employer (or the parent company, if different) arrange for the executive to authorise to sell some of the executive's shares in the market and pass the money to the executive's employer?**
PRC law does not specifically give such a right. A company that finds itself in such a position should – either directly or though a tax advisor – consult with its local tax bureau.

**2.5** **Will the executive pay tax on the eventual sale of his shares and if so at what rate?**
As noted above, an employee will generally be subject to tax at the time of exercising share options.

China's individual income tax rates are progressive. The rates are currently:

| Monthly taxable income | Tax rate |
| --- | --- |
| Up to Rmb500 | 5% |
| More than Rmb500 and up to Rmb2,000 | 10% |
| More than Rmb2,000 and up to Rmb5,000 | 15% |
| More than Rmb5,000 and up to Rmb20,000 | 20% |
| More than Rmb20,000 and up to Rmb40,000 | 25% |
| More than Rmb40,000 and up to Rmb60,000 | 30% |
| More than Rmb60,000 and up to Rmb80,000 | 35% |
| More than Rmb60,000 and up to Rmb80,000 | 40% |
| More than Rmb100,000 | 45% |

An amount of Rmb2,000 is deducted from the salary or wages of a Chinese national to arrive at the monthly taxable income. The deduction for foreign nationals is Rmb5,200. Certain benefits received by a foreign national are also non-taxable.

## 3. Employer's social security

### 3.1 Is the employer liable to pay (on its own account) any employer's social security in connection with the long-term incentive award?

No. Stock options are not included in the salary of an employee for the purpose of calculating the amount of social security payments (such as pension, medical insurance, unemployment insurance and housing) that must be made on behalf of an employee.

### 3.2 Can the liability of the employer be put onto the employee? What steps are required?

As noted for the previous question, the employer has no liability to social security in respect of stock options.

## 4. Tax deduction for the employer

### 4.1 Is it possible for the employer to receive a tax deduction in respect of the long-term incentive award? Would the employer need to be subject to recharge arrangements (eg if the employer is a subsidiary and provides funds to the parent company as part of a recharge arrangement in respect of the long-term incentive award)?

The general rule is that expenses incurred for reasonable salary and wages are deductible. The definition of "salary and wages" includes monetary and non-monetary remuneration as well as bonuses and any other expenses relating to the work or employment of employees.

To claim deductions for overseas expenses relating to the issuance of stock options by, or the exercise of, stock options relating to an overseas affiliate, those expenses must first be charged back to the employer in China.

## 5. Tax beneficial arrangements

### 5.1 Are there any ways of making the long-term incentive award tax-efficient in the People's Republic of China?

Taxable stock-option income will generally be apportioned over 12 months as outlined above. No other tax-efficient structuring is allowed under Chinese law.

## 6. Internationally mobile executives

### 6.1 What are the income tax consequences for an employee who is resident in the People's Republic of China when the long-term incentive award is made but who is no longer resident at the time of exercise/vesting?

China-sourced income for foreign nationals, and the global income of Chinese nationals, is subject to individual income tax in China. (Foreign nationals may also be subject to tax on their global income if they have been resident in China for more than five years.) Accordingly, tax would be payable in China at the time of exercise if the grant of options relates to time spent working in China. If the grant relates to time in China and time out of China, then tax in China will only be payable for the amount attributable to work in China.

**6.2 What are the social security consequences for an employee who is resident in the People's Republic of China when the long-term incentive award is made, but who is no longer resident at the time of exercise/vesting?**
None. See above.

**6.3 What are the tax and social security withholding/reporting consequences for the employer for an employee who is resident in the People's Republic China when the long-term incentive award is made, but who is no longer resident at the time of exercise/vesting?**
Theoretically, the employer will have a withholding obligation. In practice – particularly if the individual is no longer an employee – the employee will be responsible for declaring his/her own income.

## 7. Reporting requirements

**7.1 Will the employer (or parent company, if different) have any reporting requirements as a result of the long-term incentive award?**
An employer will be required to file an employee stock-option plan with the relevant local tax bureau (see above), may be required to seek CSRC approval (see above), and may be required to file documentation for the employee stock-option plan with the State Administration for Foreign Exchange (SAFE) (see below). An employer also has a filing obligation prior to an employee exercising his/her options.

**7.2 Are there any tax rulings required in relation to the long-term incentive awards?**
Many tax rulings relating to stock options have been issued, although tax rulings are not required in every case.

## 8. Exchange control issues

**8.1 Are there any exchange control issues that would prevent an employee from (a) remitting monies abroad to purchase shares or (b) repatriating monies from the sale of shares?**
Chinese nationals have an annual quota of US$50,000 for buying and selling foreign currency. However, rules applicable the purchase of foreign stock require Chinese nationals to purchase foreign stock via qualified domestic institutional investors (QDII), which are permitted to buy foreign "financial products" in the capacity of an agent. In part, this reflects the limited convertibility of Chinese currency. A trial scheme in Tianjin for Chinese nationals to invest directly in the Hong Kong stock market was announced in 2007. However, the government has been slow to implement the scheme.

 With effect from early 2007, Chinese nationals are also specifically allowed to purchase stock under an employee stock-option plan, provided that the stock-option plan is approved by SAFE prior to implementation. SAFE's requirements set out the manner in which stock-option plans over foreign stock are permitted to operate in China.

According to an "internal" SAFE guideline that has not been publicly issued, a domestic agent is required to handle foreign exchange in connection with employee stock options. The domestic agent may be a Chinese subsidiary of the offshore listed company, or may be a financial institution in China qualified as an asset custodian. The domestic agent is required to authorise a foreign asset manager (or securities company) to sell and purchase the offshore shares. An offshore custodian bank is also required under the internal SAFE guidelines. The domestic agent needs to apply to local foreign exchange authority for an annual quota of foreign exchange conversion and payment. The proceeds will be paid to the bank accounts opened by the domestic agent, who will then settle the foreign exchange or transfer the proceeds to the employees' saving accounts directly. Chinese nationals are not permitted to fund the exercise of stock options with funds from outside China. Rather, they must purchase foreign exchange from within China. Moreover, all proceeds from the sale of options or shares must be repatriated back into China.

The internal SAFE guideline also required Chinese nationals who participated in any stock-option plan for foreign-listed stock to register their participation in the stock-option plan with SAFE prior to July 5 2007.

The internal SAFE guideline, however, has not been officially promulgated or publicly disclosed and this leads to questions about whether it may be validly implemented. Under the terms of China's accession to the WTO, laws and regulations regarding foreign exchange are required to be publicly disclosed prior to implementation. While it arguably follows from China's WTO obligations that the internal SAFE guideline should not be enforced, it appears that various SAFE bureaux have begun to enforce its provisions on the basis that the internal SAFE guidelines assist them in exercising their approval powers under other foreign exchange regulations.

Prior to early 2007, foreign investment approvals and foreign exchange restrictions for Chinese nationals meant that multinationals wishing to benefit their Chinese national employees with stock options had to resort to alternatives. Two alternatives that have been used in China are phantom stock and the cashless exercise of stock options. Both alternatives allow Chinese nationals to enjoy economic benefits associated with an increased share price. However, neither alternative allows Chinese nationals to become shareholders, which is an important purpose of employee stock options elsewhere in the world. Both alternatives are subject to the above-mentioned internal SAFE guideline (to the extent that it creates valid obligations).

Under a cashless exercise of stock options, the underlying stock is sold at the same time as the option is exercised and the employee is given the difference between the selling price and the option price. Foreign investment approvals are not needed because the employee does not take title to any stock and no foreign exchange is needed to purchase the stock. In effect, however, the stock option becomes a bonus plan under which entitlements are indexed to the performance of the stock.

Phantom stock options are similar, although there is no sale of stock involved. Rather, employee entitlement to payments under a phantom stock-option plan is based on how much an employee would get if a share were to be sold. The incentive payment needs to be funded out of a company's profits, which can make phantom stock options less attractive.

Non-Chinese nationals who fund the exercise of stock options with income that is not sourced in China are not subject to SAFE rules. A non-Chinese national who wishes to buy foreign currency within China must provide various documents to show that the funds were legitimately earned in China.

## 9. Employment law

**9.1 Are there any employment or local labour law issues which may arise as a result of the long-term incentive award? Are any consultations or authorisations required by law?**

China's recent Labour Contract Law requires various matters, including labour remuneration and any other matters that may have a material impact on the interest of employees, to be discussed at an employee representative meeting or by all employees. Trade unions also have a right to negotiate with the employer prior to a decision being made. It is unclear whether employee representatives or labour unions would have a right of veto over a stock-option plan.

If an employee stock-option plan is included in any collective contract, then the rules applicable to collective contracts will give the local labour bureau an opportunity to object to the stock-option plan (as with anything else in the collective contract) within 15 days of filing.

## 10. Translation

**10.1 Are there any language restrictions in the People's Republic of China? Does any of the documentation provided to the employee in relation to the long-term incentive award need to be translated into Chinese?**

Chinese governmental authorities typically require Chinese-language translations of any English-language materials required to be submitted for approval or filing. In some instances, a translation of the key points may also be accepted.

## 11. Data protection

**11.1 Are there any data protection issues which may arise should the employer wish to outsource the administration of the long-term incentive award to a third party?**

An employer must maintain the confidentiality of personal data relating to its employees. In particular, an employer must obtain the consent of an employee before disclosing his/her personal data to a third party.

In addition to the above employment-related regulation, China is planning to pass a more general law on the protection of personal data. The scope of this law, and the timing of its introduction, is presently unclear. In the meantime, some commentators argue that the general prohibition against damaging an individual's "honour" under the General Principles of Civil Law can be extended to offer a measure of additional legal protection to personal data.

## 12. Source of shares

### 12.1 Does it matter if shares are newly issued to an employee, provided out of treasury or delivered from an employee-benefit trust?

Companies in China may repurchase their own shares for the purpose of implementing an employee stock-option plan. New shares may also be issued. Moreover, trust companies are permitted to hold shares for the benefit of employees. However, the source of the shares does not affect an employer's or an employee's income tax obligations.

# Czech Republic

**Veronika Odrobinová**
Gleiss Lutz
**Lenka Pazderová**
Vorlíčková & Leitner

---

> **Red flag issues**
> 1. Restrictions on providing long-term incentive awards to members of a statutory body.
> 2. Taxation in case of sale of the shares.
> 3. Social security provisions applying to recharge arrangements.

## 1.  General introduction

The tax and legal implications of receiving long-term incentive awards in the Czech Republic differ depending on whether the recipient is a member of a statutory body (ie an executive of a limited liability company, or a member of the board of directors of a joint stock company), or is an employee. In this chapter, the term "executive" refers to both employees and members of a statutory body.

Statutory bodies comprise the management of a company, who can generally act on behalf of the company in all matters. The relationship between the company and its statutory body is governed by Act No 513/1991 Coll., the Commercial Code, as amended (the Commercial Code), and not by Act No 262/2006 Coll., the Labour Code, as amended (the Labour Code). Statutory bodies are subject to stricter rules, for example, with regard to their liabilities, remuneration, transactions with the company etc. If the recipient of the long-term incentive award is a member of a statutory body, additional provisions apply from a legal perspective.

The tax regime for employees (including managing employees) is comparable with the tax regime for the members of a statutory body of a limited liability company. However, the tax regime for the members of the statutory body of a joint stock company differs in certain aspects from the tax regime for the statutory body of a limited liability company. Where necessary, the differences are explicitly cited.

Significant changes were implemented in the Czech tax legislation from January 1 2008, and this chapter does not refer to the previous tax regime.

## 2.  Securities laws

### 2.1  What prospectus and/or securities law requirements arise in connection with the grant, vesting or exercise of a long-term incentive award or on the eventual sale of the shares by the executive?

*(a)*     ***Grant of a long-term incentive award***

The grant of a long-term incentive award generally qualifies as a public offer of shares. A public offer of securities arises where the offeror provides a broad group of people with sufficient information in relation to the offered securities and the conditions for their acquisition to enable an investor to make a decision in relation to the purchase or subscription of those securities.

In accordance with Act No 256/2004 Coll., on Business Activities on the Capital Market, as amended (the Capital Markets Act), a public offer of securities requires the issue of a prospectus unless, or to the extent that, an appropriate exemption is available.

Long-term incentive awards implemented in the Czech Republic will usually fall within the exceptions from the obligation to publish the prospectus (see question 2.2 below) and, thus, no prospectus would be required.

*(b)*     ***Vesting and exercise of long-term incentive award***

Generally, the vesting and exercise of long-term incentive awards do not trigger a public offer of the underlying securities, because no public offer is made at that time.

*(c)*     ***Sale of shares***

As for the prospective sale of the shares by an executive, whether issues arise that relate to securities laws will depend entirely on whether and under what circumstances such an offer is made and whether the statutory exceptions from the obligation to publish the prospectus apply (see below).

**2.2     Is there an exemption from securities laws requirements either because the shares are being offered only to executives or because shares are being offered to a distinct group of named individuals?**

The Capital Markets Act provides that it is not necessary to publish a prospectus if the offer is addressed to current or former employees of a Czech company, or members of the statutory body of a Czech company provided that:

- the securities are issued by a Czech company, or by a controlled or controlling company, or by a company controlled by the same person;
- the securities offered are of the same type as securities listed on a regulated market (as defined by the Capital Markets Act); and
- the Czech National Bank receives a notification stating the number and type of securities offered and the reasons for, and details of, the offer.

Furthermore, the provisions of the Capital Markets Act in relation to public offers and the need to publish a prospectus do not apply if the total sale or issue price of the securities does not exceed €200,000. This amount is calculated for all securities offered during a 12-month period.

A prospectus is not required if the offer is addressed to a limited group of persons not exceeding 100 participants in any EU member state (qualified investors, such as banks, securities traders or financial institutions, are not included in this limit).

A number of additional exceptions are set out in the Capital Markets Act. However, these are not generally relevant for long-term incentive awards.

**2.3** **If there is an exemption, will the exemption apply automatically or are there any applications/filings that need to be made?**

Generally, the exceptions apply automatically, unless the law specifically provides otherwise. For example, there is an obligation to notify the Czech National Bank where the exception applies to offers addressed to current or former employees of a Czech company or members of the statutory body of a Czech company (see above).

**3.** **Employee tax and social security**

**3.1** **When will the executive be liable to tax or social security (and at what rate) in respect of the long-term incentive award?**

*(a)* *Income tax*

In accordance with Act No 586/2004 Coll. on income taxes, as amended (the Income Taxes Act), any income resulting from "dependent activities", regardless of whether they are in a monetary or a non-monetary form, is subject to income tax. Examples of income from a dependent activity include wages, salaries, director's fees, bonuses, and remuneration of statutory bodies.

In addition, a long-term incentive award qualifies as income from a dependent activity. An income tax liability arises on the amount by which the market value of the shares acquired exceeds the acquisition price paid (if any) when an option is exercised, or free shares are acquired.

The same regime applies to income received in connection with current, previous or future employment (ie the "dependent activity"). It does not matter if the income is received on a regular basis or in the form of a lump sum, or whether there is a legal entitlement to such income or not. For tax purposes, the person providing the income or benefits is referred to as the "employer" (whether or not there is an employment contract between the parties).

Taxpayers having their tax domicile in the Czech Republic are liable to tax on income generated from sources within both the Czech Republic and abroad, even if the income is based on a contractual relationship with a person or company with a registered seat or residence abroad.

Taxpayers who do not have their tax domicile in the territory of the Czech Republic are liable to tax only on income derived from sources in the territory of the Czech Republic (ie for the activities carried out in the Czech Republic), again irrespective of whether the income is paid by a Czech or a foreign person or company.

Income is taxed at a rate of 15% (and this will be reduced to 12.5% from 2009). The basis for the calculation of income tax from dependent activities is the executive's gross salary/remuneration, together with any health and social insurance contributions payable by the employer. The total tax liability is then reduced by the personal and other allowances.

*(b)* *Social security and health insurance*

Provided that (i) the executive is subject to the Czech social security system; and (ii) the costs related to the long-term incentive plan can be attributed to the executive by the employer, the income (non-monetary benefit) derived from the exercise or vesting of the long-term incentive award will be subject to Czech social security and health insurance.

The remuneration of members of statutory bodies is subject to mandatory health insurance contributions, but not social security contributions.

The basis for calculating contributions to social security and health insurance is the amount of the difference between the market value of the shares acquired and the price paid by the executive. Where free shares are acquired, this is equal to the full market value of the shares.

Contributions to social security and health insurance are capped on an annual basis at 48 times the average monthly wage. The cap currently amounts to approximately Kr1.035 million (approximately €40,800).

The total contributions amount to 47.5% and consist of the following:

|  | Employee (%) | Employer (%) | Total (%) |
|---|---|---|---|
| Social security | 8.0 | 26.0 | 34.0 |
| Unemployment insurance | 0.4 | 1.2 | 1.6 |
| Pension insurance | 6.5 | 21.5 | 28.0 |
| Sickness insurance | 1.1 | 3.3 | 4.4 |
| Health insurance | 4.5 | 9.0 | 13.5 |
| Total | 12.5 | 35.0 | 47.5 |

**3.2 How will the executive's tax and social security be collected? Will the executive be responsible for paying any liabilities himself or will the executive's employer be responsible for paying tax or social security liabilities on the executive's behalf?**

*(a)* *Income tax*

If the long-term incentive award is granted by a Czech company, or by a foreign group company but in circumstances where the local employer accounts for the transaction in its books, the employer is obliged to withhold wage tax (in the form of a tax advance) from the remuneration and to transfer it to the Czech tax administrator.

Tax advances must be withheld on the day the remuneration is received (ie on the day the option is exercised or the free shares are acquired), regardless of the period to which it relates. They must then be transferred to the tax authority's bank account before the twentieth day of the calendar month following the receipt of the remuneration.

At the end of the year, the executive either asks the employer for an annual account in respect of his tax advances or files his own personal income tax return.

If the long-term incentive award is granted by a foreign group company and the local employer does not account for the transaction at all, the executive must file his own personal income tax return and declare this income therein. The tax return has to be filed, and the respective income tax paid, before the end of March of the following calendar year (or before the end of June if a tax advisor is appointed to prepare and file the tax return).

*(b)*     *Social security and health insurance*
A similar procedure applies for the collection of social security and health insurance contributions.

The employee's contributions must be deducted by the employer from the executive's remuneration and transferred, together with the employer's contributions, to the bank account of the competent authorities (the local social security office and the executive's health insurance company) on the day the company has determined as its "payday". Should this day not be determined, then the transfer must be made at the latest by the eighth calendar day of the following month.

The above procedure also applies to foreign employers provided that the executive is liable to Czech social security (eg this is the case for expatriates seconded to a Czech subsidiary of their employer where the executive and his employer do not possess Form E101 to certify that the executive is to remain in the social security system of his home state).

**3.3     If the employer is responsible for the executive's liabilities, can the employer withhold the liabilities from the executive's salary? Are there any formalities in this respect?**
The employer is able to withhold income tax and social security liabilities from the executive's salary without any special formalities. The benefit must be entered into the employer's salary administration system and processed the same way as a salary.

**3.4     If the executive's salary in the month of exercise/release is not sufficient for the employer to withhold all of the liabilities, can the employer (or the parent company, if different) arrange for the executive to authorise to sell some of the executive's shares in the market and pass the money to the executive's employer?**
Generally, withholdings from an employee's salary can be performed only if this is stipulated by legal regulations (eg tax, social security, health insurance), or if agreed in writing with the employee. The withholdings (on both a statutory and a contractual basis) cannot exceed the statutory minimum which must always be paid to the employee. Therefore, an agreement on a subsequent settlement of the amounts the employer transferred to the authorities but could not deduct from the employee's salary should be concluded.

The situation is different in the case of members of a statutory body; for these individuals, the above statutory limitations do not apply. For members of a statutory body, such liabilities are not collected on the basis of a withholding agreement, but as a set-off against other receipts by the individual.

The company can arrange for the sale of a proportion of the shares acquired and use the proceeds to settle the executive's liabilities, but only with the executive's consent. In addition, such agreement should not be made before the shares are acquired. The tax consequences of such a sale are set out below.

**3.5 Will the executive pay tax on the eventual sale of his shares and if so at what rate?**

On a sale of an executive's shares, any gain realised (ie the sale proceeds less the amount paid for the shares) is added to the employee's income and taxed as set out above However, it is currently not clear whether the tax paid at the moment of exercising the option may be credited against the tax liability resulting from the sale of the executive's shares if the tax exemptions mentioned below are not available.

In order to achieve a tax exemption in relation to the sale of publicly tradable shares acquired after January 1 2008, those shares must have been held for six months from the date of acquisition. In addition, the executive must not have had a direct or indirect holding of more than 5% of the registered capital or voting rights of the issuer during a 24-month period preceding the sale of the shares. If this condition is not met, the tax exemption on the sale of shares will only apply if the shares have been held for at least five years prior to sale. In relation to the sale of shares in a non-publicly traded joint-stock company, the holding period for the purposes of the tax exemption is also five years.

The income from the sale of shares is not subject to social security and health insurance contributions.

**4. Employer's social security**

**4.1 Is the employer liable to pay (on its own account) any employer's social security in connection with the long-term incentive award?**

If the long-term incentive award is subject to Czech social security and/or health insurance (see above), the employer is obliged to pay employer's contributions. For the rates, terms and procedures, see above.

**4.2 Can the liability of the employer be put onto the employee? What steps are required?**

The employer's contributions cannot be put onto the employee. The employer can authorise the executive (or a third person) to pay the employee's social security and health insurance contributions directly to the relevant authorities. This authorisation is made on a contractual basis (a mandate or instruction contract) and is not regulated by any tax or social security legislation. Even in the case of such an appointment, however, the employer remains responsible for the correct payment of all the employer's statutory liabilities.

## 5. Tax deduction for the employer

**5.1** **Is it possible for the employer to receive a tax deduction in respect of the long-term incentive award? Would the employer need to be subject to recharge arrangements (eg if the employer is a subsidiary and provides funds to the parent company as part of a recharge arrangement in respect of the long-term incentive award)?**

If any costs relating to the long-term incentive award are invoiced by the foreign group company to the Czech employer, these recharge costs will represent a tax deductible item of the employer if:

- the costs are actually borne by the employer; and
- the granting of the long-term incentive award to the executive had been agreed in a collective bargaining agreement, internal directive, employment contract or another contract (eg a mandate contract or a contract on the performance of the position).

However, amounts received by the members of a statutory body (except for the statutory body of a limited liability company) are not tax deductible for the company and so any recharged costs related to the long-term incentive award are not tax deductible either.

From a social security and health insurance point of view, it may be advisable for the costs related to the long-term incentive award not to be recharged by the foreign group company (not being the executive's legal employer) to the Czech employer. If the employer accounts for those costs as being for the executive's benefit, social security and health insurance contributions must be deducted.

## 6. Tax beneficial arrangements

**6.1** **Are there any ways of making the long-term incentive award tax-efficient in the Czech Republic?**

Unfortunately, it is not possible to avoid or reduce the tax which arises on benefits-in-kind (ie the income arising from the acquisition of shares subject to the long-term incentive award). This is always taxed as the executive's income from dependent activities.

As noted above, there will be no further tax on the sale of the shares if the executive has held those shares for at least six months. This exemption applies, without any restrictions, to all shares acquired before January 1 2008. Publicly tradable shares acquired on or after January 1 2008 are subject to a six-month test, if the executive does not possess, directly or indirectly, a share in voting rights and capital of the issuing company of more than 5% in the 24 months immediately preceding the sale of the shares. Otherwise, capital gains from the sale of shares are subject to a five-year test before the tax exemption applies.

As noted above, where costs relating to the long-term incentive award are recharged to the Czech employer, these are accounted for as a benefit to the executive and are subject to social security and health insurance contributions. In order to avoid such a charge, it is advisable that where the company granting the long-term incentive award is not the executive's legal employer, such costs are not recharged.

## 7. Internationally mobile executives

### 7.1 What are the income tax consequences for an employee who is resident in the Czech Republic when the long-term incentive award is made, but who is no longer resident at the time of exercise/vesting?

According to the Income Taxes Act, the income derived in connection with previous employment is also subject to taxation as income from dependent activities.

If the executive no longer has his tax domicile in the Czech Republic at the moment of exercising the stock option, or acquiring the free shares, he is liable to tax only in relation to any income derived from Czech sources. The term "from Czech sources" is generally understood to be income for any dependent activities carried out in the Czech Republic.

As mentioned above, the benefit from the long-term incentive award is to be taxed at the moment it is exercised (or the free shares are acquired). However, Czech tax law does not contain any provisions for the treatment of this income if the recipient is no longer a Czech resident. Therefore, the principles set out in the OECD Commentary on Article 15 of the Model Convention with Respect to Taxes on Income and on Capital apply.

In practice, this means that it has to be determined to which activity and to which period the long-term incentive award relates. If the award was granted for the executive's past performance (eg financial results in a certain year), it must be attributed to the employment in that year. An award granted to the executive on the condition that he provides the services to the same employer (or to another group company) for a certain period in the future must be attributed to employment carried out during this future period.

Where an award is considered to be derived from activities carried out in more than one country, the benefit attributable to the award should be considered to be derived from the Czech Republic as a proportion of the number of days the executive provided services there, as compared to the total number of days for which the award is provided.

The Czech Republic has concluded double taxation treaties with more than 60 countries. Therefore, double taxation of the income taxable in the Czech Republic based on the above principle should be able to be avoided in the country of the executive's current residence in many cases.

### 7.2 What are the social security consequences for an employee who is resident in the Czech Republic when the long-term incentive award is made, but who is no longer resident at the time of exercise/vesting?

According to Czech legislation, the withholding of social security and health insurance contributions is based on benefits provided in each calendar month. Therefore, these contributions are to be withheld in the month in which the conditions mentioned above are fulfilled. The Czech Republic, as a member of the European Union, must also comply with Council Regulation No 1408/71 of June 14 1971. In accordance with this Regulation, if the executive is no longer subject to the Czech social security system at the relevant time, no social security or health insurance contributions may be deducted.

7.3 **What are the tax and social security withholding/reporting consequences for the employer for an employee who is resident in the Czech Republic when the long-term incentive award is made, but who is no longer resident at the time of exercise/vesting?**

The consequences are the same as the employer's liabilities where the award is exercised, or shares are acquired, by an executive who still is resident in the Czech Republic (see above). In short, the related duties can be summarised as follows:

- deduction of the wage tax advance by the employer and its transfer to the competent local tax authority (this applies if the employer is/was a registered wage tax payer);
- preparation of the annual account in respect of wage tax advances by the employer, if the executive so requests;
- filing of a personal income tax return by the executive and declaring the income therein (this is obligatory if the executive was, at the time of his or her activity in the Czech Republic, responsible for fulfilling his or her tax duties and is voluntary if a wage tax advance is withheld by the employer and no preparation of respective annual accounts has been requested);
- deduction of the employee's social security and health insurance contributions by the employer and their transfer, together with the employer's part, to the competent authority (this is only the case where such contributions are legally to be withheld – see above); and
- keeping proper salary administration in line with the legislation in force.

## 8. Reporting requirements

8.1 **Will the employer (or parent company, if different) have any reporting requirements as a result of the long-term incentive award?**

There are no particular notification requirements or general restrictions on Czech or foreign companies offering shares or awards to employees in the Czech Republic.

Some reporting requirements may apply under the relevant foreign exchange, securities law and data protection legislation (see above).

Additional requirements apply if listed securities of a foreign company in the same group are offered to the employees or members of a statutory body of the Czech company. If these securities are offered to members of a statutory body or other employees qualifying as "leading" employees (and to certain additional persons connected with them), these transactions must be notified to the Czech National Bank within five days of the execution of the transaction. However, this is a duty incumbent on the respective individuals and not on the Czech company.

In order to meet the conditions for the application of the exception from the duty to publish the prospectus, there is an additional duty to notify the Czech National Bank (see above).

8.2 **Are there any tax rulings required in relation to the long-term incentive awards?**

No.

## 9. Exchange control issues

### 9.1 Are there any exchange control issues that would prevent an employee from (a) remitting monies abroad to purchase shares, or (b) repatriating monies from the sale of shares?

There are generally no foreign exchange issues which would prevent an employee from (a) remitting monies abroad to purchase shares; or (b) repatriating monies from the sale of shares, if the relevant payment is made by wire transfer. Payments exceeding €15,000 must always be made by wire transfer.

Legal entities having their seat in the Czech Republic must fulfil the notification duties within the periods of time stipulated in a decree implementing Act No 219/1995 Coll., the Foreign Exchange Act, as amended (the Foreign Exchange Act), if the relevant payment exceeds Kr1 million. The notification duty applies to natural persons only if requested by the Czech National Bank.

The Czech National Bank must be notified, inter alia, in connection with:

- direct investments (ie if the participation in a company exceeds stipulated thresholds);
- financial credits; and
- acquisition of foreign securities.

These notifications can be made electronically, and no costs are involved.

The Czech government reserves the right to amend the current foreign exchange laws in case of "emergency" (as defined by legal regulations). In such a case, additional restrictions could be implemented.

Strict rules apply if the Czech company helps the employees and statutory bodies in the currency conversion in respect of making the payments for the long-term incentive award. The Czech Foreign Exchange Act states that only certain individuals can carry out the exchange of foreign currency and such individuals must have the permission of the Czech National Bank. Such activities are also subject to a trade license requirement.

## 10. Employment and corporate law issues

### 10.1 Are there any employment or local labour law issues which may arise as a result of the long-term incentive award? Are any consultations or authorisations required by law?

### (a) Employees

### (i) Consultation

The employer is obliged to inform its employees regarding remuneration for their work. These details should be included in the salary assessment, employment contract, collective bargaining agreement or internal directive.

The employer is obliged to consult with the respective trade union (if established) about the system of evaluation and remuneration of employees, regardless of the number of employees affected. The granting of long-term incentive awards could be considered as a part of this system.

The consultation should take place in advance, so that trade unions can express their views. These should be taken into account before the long-term incentive award is implemented. In this respect, consultation means negotiations between the parties and the exchange of views and explanations so as to achieve agreement. Within consultation, trade union representatives have the right to be provided with a substantiated reply to any views they have expressed. The employer is only obliged to inform the trade unions and to discuss the matter with them; the trade unions do not have to give their consent/approval (unless this has been otherwise agreed, eg in a collective bargaining agreement).

If no trade union exists, the employees can appoint a works council. In this case, consultation is not required.

The Labour Code also provides for the general obligation of an employer to inform employees (or trade unions/work councils if established) about any important changes related to working conditions. A long-term incentive award could be considered to be such a change in working conditions (depending on how many employees are affected by the long-term incentive award etc).

(ii)    *Non-discrimination*
When implementing the long-term incentive award, the general prohibition against discrimination must also be respected. According to the Labour Code, the employer is obliged to ensure equal treatment for all employees. This means that the employer is only entitled to treat an employee differently based on objective criteria such as a higher level of responsibility, workload, or experience.

Additional restrictions or requirements may result from collective bargaining agreements, internal directives, employment documentation of the company, employment contracts and so on.

At the time of writing, the new anti-discrimination legislation is still being discussed in the Czech Parliament and has not been approved. However, the proposed implementation date (January 1 2008) has not yet been changed in the discussed draft Act.

(b)    **Statutory bodies**
If the persons eligible for the long-term incentive award include members of a statutory body, there are additional issues to be taken into account (eg no consultation with employee representatives is required).

On the other hand, even in a foreign company, shares or awards granted to members of a statutory body must be approved by a specified body of the Czech company, usually the general meeting or supervisory board.

Additional restrictions or requirements may result from the corporate documentation of the company, contracts with the statutory bodies, etc.

## 11. Translation

### 11.1 Are there any language restrictions in the Czech Republic? Does any of the documentation provided to the employee in relation to the long-term incentive award need to be translated?

Yes. To be binding on all parties, the participants must understand the language in which the document implementing the long-term incentive award is executed. Otherwise, these documents must be translated into Czech. If the participant does not understand the documents, the grant of the long-term incentive award may be rendered invalid.

If the grant of the long-term incentive award documentation is only in a foreign language, an official translation (by a certified translator) of the documents into Czech may be required by the local authorities (ie the Labour Office, Work Inspectorate, Financial Authority and Social Insurance Authority) on an ad hoc basis.

## 12. Data protection

### 12.1 Are there any data protection issues which may arise should the employer wish to outsource the administration of the long-term incentive award to a third party?

Yes. Generally, a Czech company must not disclose any data concerning its employees or statutory bodies to any third party without prior consent according to Act No 101/2000 Coll. on Personal Data Protection, as amended, the Labour Code and Act No 64/1964 Coll. (the Civil Code), as amended.

A number of obligations for a person dealing with personal data of individuals have been imposed in the Czech Republic (certain exemptions apply):

- the consent of the employee must be obtained where the Czech company processes the personal data for purposes other than those required by the applicable legal regulations (Although this is not required by the relevant legal regulations, it is strongly recommended that consent in writing should be obtained as the data controller must be able to prove that it has the consent of the data subject to personal data processing during the whole period of processing.);
- the Office for the Protection of Personal Data must be notified prior to the commencement of any collection and/or processing of personal data regarding the intention to administer the personal data of employees or statutory bodies in connection with the implementation of the long-term incentive award;
- numerous rules relating to the contents of the database must be followed; and
- the consent of the Office for the Protection of Personal Data must be obtained prior to the transfer of any personal data abroad unless it is transferred to an EU member state, or if an international treaty in respect of non-EU countries states otherwise. In other cases, the application should be submitted to the Office for the Protection of Personal Data for approval, with

evidence of the written consent to such a transfer from the employee or statutory body. The consents should ideally be signed by the employee or statutory body after they have been provided with a written explanation of the reason for the data transfer.

If the long-term incentive award is administered by a third party, an agreement must be executed in writing which will specify to what extent, purpose and time the agreement is concluded. It should further include the representations and warranties of the third party as regards the technical and organisational security of the personal data.

## 13. Source of shares

**13.1 Does it matter if shares are newly issued to an employee, provided out of treasury or delivered from an employee-benefit trust?**
No.

## 14. Prohibited financial assistance

A Czech joint stock company may not grant any advance payment, loans or credit for the purpose of the acquisition of its shares or shares in a company which controls it. It may not secure credit or loans provided for such purposes or other obligations relating to such an acquisition.

# Denmark

Claus Juel Hansen
Kromann Reumert

---

**Red flag issues**
1. Provisions purporting to reduce employees' rights to retain equity awards upon termination of employment may not be fully enforceable.
2. The granting of equity awards will normally trigger a requirement to distribute a so-called employer statement to the employees no later than 30 days after implementation of equity incentive awards.
3. SARs may be taxable at grant.

---

## 1. Securities laws

### 1.1 What prospectus and/or securities law requirements arise in connection with the grant, vesting or exercise of a long-term incentive award or on the eventual sale of the shares by the executive?

*(a)* *General*

Denmark has implemented the EU Prospectus Directive. Under the Danish Prospectus regime, the main rule is that any offer of transferable securities to the public in Denmark with an aggregate value above €100,000 entails an obligation to publish a prospectus on the offering.

*(b)* *Offer of securities*

In accordance with Section 2b of the Danish Securities Trading Act, an offer of securities to the public is a communication to natural or legal persons in any form and by any means, presenting sufficient information on the terms of the offer and the securities to be offered so as to enable an investor to decide to purchase or subscribe to these securities.

*(c)* *Transferable securities*

The Danish prospectus regulation only applies to "transferable securities". Hence, non-transferable securities granted to employees are not encompassed by the Danish Prospectus regime. Further, it should be noted that, at the time of exercise of the non-transferable securities, there is no public offer within the meaning of Article 2.1(d) of the EU Prospectus Directive as interpreted by the Danish Financial Supervisory Authority (FSA).

*(d)* *Free securities (shares)*

If the offering entails an offer of securities free of charge with no element of *choice* on the part of the employee, there is no obligation to publish a prospectus.

If there is an element of choice (ie the employee decides whether to accept the offer), the offer is regarded as an offer for zero consideration and will as such be subject to the exemption for offers of less than €100,000. However, this analysis does not prevent the Danish FSA from assessing whether an offer presented as an offer of free securities in fact disguises a "hidden" consideration. If so, the offer may be caught by the prospectus requirement if the offer has an aggregate value above €100,000 and none of the other exemptions are applicable.

1.2   **Is there an exemption from securities laws requirements either because the shares are being offered only to executives or because shares are being offered to a distinct group of named individuals?**

Notwithstanding the generality of the main rule to publish a prospectus, a number of exemptions may apply to an offering. The exemptions can be divided into two main categories, namely:

- securities which are not listed or admitted for trading on a regulated market (ie stock exchanges and similar) operating from within the EU/EEA (unlisted securities); and
- securities which are listed or admitted for trading on a regulated market (ie stock exchanges and similar) operating from within the EU/EEA (listed securities).

Securities which are listed or admitted for trading outside, but not inside, the EU/EEA belong in the category of unlisted securities for the purposes of the rules.

The following exemptions are of general relevance. The list is not exhaustive, and other exemptions may be applicable for reasons specific to a particular offering. Thus:

- Unlisted securities:
  - *100-offeree exemption:* Offerings of unlisted securities addressed to fewer than 100 natural or legal persons in Denmark; and
  - *Employee exemption:* Unlisted securities which are offered, allotted or to be allotted to existing or former directors or employees by their employer, which has securities already admitted for trading on a regulated market within the EU/EEA (but outside Denmark), or by an affiliated company. Note the obligation for the employer to have securities already admitted for trading on a regulated market within the EU/EEA; and
- Listed securities:
  - *100-offeree exemption:* If the listed securities will not be listed or admitted for trading on a regulated market in Denmark, the 100-offeree exemption is available;
  - *Employee exemption:* Securities offered, allotted or to be allotted to existing or former directors or employees by their employer or an affiliated company, provided that the said securities are of the same class as the securities already admitted to trading on the same regulated market; and

– *10% exemption:* Shares representing, over a period of 12 months, less than 10% of the number of shares of the same class already admitted to trading on the same regulated market.

Under "the employee exemptions", the employer must provide employees with a document "containing information on the number and nature of the securities and the reasons for and details of the offer".

CESR (The Committee of European Securities Regulators) has published "CESR's recommendations for the consistent implementation of the European Commission's Regulation on Prospectuses No 809/2004" (CESR/05-054b) in which paragraphs 173–76 specify that the document should normally include:

- information on the employer, and where additional information on the employer can be found if required;
- the reasons for making the offer, and the exemption due to which no prospectus is required;
- standard details of the offer (terms and conditions); and
- the rights attaching to the securities offered.

The employee exemptions and the CESR-recommendation do not contain any language requirements. Hence, the document may be made available to Danish employees in a Danish or English version.

**1.3    If there is an exemption, will the exemption apply automatically or are there any applications/filings that need to be made?**
The exemptions will apply automatically if the offering may avail itself of an exemption from the prospectus requirement.

## 2.    Employee tax and social security

**2.1    When will the executive be liable to tax or social security (and at what rate) in respect of the long-term incentive award?**

*(a)    Stock options*
The executive will be subject to income tax on the spread at exercise of each option. Any payments made by the executive for the options will reduce the taxable amount. The taxable amount will be subject to personal income tax rates of up to approximately 63%, including 8% social security, currently.

*(b)    SARs*
Danish law does not contain any express provision regarding taxation of SARs, which are not defined instruments or structures and have no immediate equivalent under Danish tax law. As a starting point, it is likely that SARs will be subject to taxation – including social security charges – upon grant (ie taxation will not be deferred until the SARs vest or are exercised). However, if the SARs are subject to performance conditions as in the current instance – or other conditions, the

fulfilment of which is not certain – it is likely that the taxation will be postponed until the point in time when such conditions are met.

The market value of the shares representing the "gain" will currently be subject to personal income tax rates of up to approximately 63%, including 8% social security.

### (c)   *Provisional allocation of free shares*

Provided the vesting of the shares is subject to performance conditions, as in the current instance – or other conditions, the fulfilment of which is not certain – the shares will probably be subject to taxation when such conditions are met. The market value of the shares will be subject to personal income tax rates of up to approximately 63%, including 8% social security, currently.

### (d)   *Nil-cost options*

With regard to nil-cost options, where the executive can exercise a right to acquire shares for no cost, the taxable event is identical with the description above regarding the provisional allocation of free shares.

If, however, the nil-cost options give the executive a right to acquire shares for a price above nil (eg to the nominal value of the shares or to 1% of the market value of the shares at grant), the executive will be subject to income tax on the spread at exercise. Any payments made by the executive for the options will reduce the taxable amount (ie the taxation is postponed until exercise, regardless of whether or not the nil-cost options are subject to any conditions). According to a Danish ruling, any option that has an exercise price above nil may potentially become out of the money and therefore will only be taxed at exercise.

The taxable amount will be subject to personal income tax rates of up to approximately 63%, including 8% social security, currently.

### (e)   *Forfeitable securities*

Danish law does not contain any express provision regarding taxation of forfeitable securities, which are not defined instruments or structures and have no immediate equivalent under Danish tax law. As a starting point, it is likely that forfeitable securities will be subject to taxation – including social security charges – upon grant. However, if the forfeitable securities are subject to performance conditions as in the current instance – or other conditions, the fulfilment of which is not certain – it is likely that the taxation will be postponed until the point in time when such conditions are met.

The market value of the shares representing the "gain" will be subject to personal income tax rates of up to approximately 63%, including 8% social security.

**2.2**   **How will the executive's tax and social security be collected? Will the executive be responsible for paying any liabilities himself or will the executive's employer be responsible for paying tax or social security liabilities on the executive's behalf?**

With regard to the employer, there is no withholding requirement in Denmark. The executive is required to pay all taxes (including social security charges) and to report the taxable amount on his or her tax return.

2.3     If the employer is responsible for the executive's liabilities, can the employer withhold the liabilities from the executive's salary? Are there any formalities in this respect?

See 2.2 above.

2.4     If the executive's salary in the month of exercise/release is not sufficient for the employer to withhold all of the liabilities, can the employer (or the parent company, if different) arrange for the executive to authorise to sell some of the executive's shares in the market and pass the money to the executive's employer?

See 2.2 above.

2.5     Will the executive pay tax on the eventual sale of his shares and if so at what rate?

When the executive sells the shares any potential gain will be taxable. Accordingly, capital gains on the shares are taxed as share income (ie at a rate of 28% up to an aggregate amount of share income of Dkr46,700 (Dkr93,400 for a married couple), 43% of an aggregate amount of share income between Dkr46,700 (Dkr93,400 for married couples) and Dkr102,600 (Dkr205,200 for married couples) and 45% of any share income in excess of the above threshold (2008 figures).

Losses on unlisted shares held by the executive are fully deductible, while losses on listed shares can only be set against gains on listed shares.

The executive has to pay the potential tax in connection with the income tax return relating to the year during which the executive sold the shares.

## 3.     Employer's social security

3.1     Is the employer liable to pay (on its own account) any employer's social security in connection with the long-term incentive award?

No.

3.2     Can the liability of the employer be put onto the employee? What steps are required?

See 3.1 above.

## 4.     Tax deduction for the employer

4.1     Is it possible for the employer to receive a tax deduction for the long-term incentive award? Would the employer need to be subject to recharge arrangements (eg if the employer is a subsidiary and provides funds to the parent company as part of a recharge arrangement in respect of the long-term incentive award)?

The employer will receive a tax deduction in respect of the long-term incentive award. If no recharge agreement is entered into, from a Danish tax perspective the parent company has awarded a contribution to the employer.

As a general rule contributions are included in the taxable income for the Danish subsidiary. However, with effect from income year 2007, a contribution from a parent company to a Danish subsidiary is tax exempt provided the parent company cannot deduct the contribution awarded. Consequently, with effect from the income year 2007, the Danish subsidiary is not subject to tax on the long-term incentive award costs as an intra-group contribution by the parent company to the Danish subsidiary, provided that the parent company cannot deduct the long-term incentive award costs.

Consequently, if no contribution is awarded – because a recharge agreement is entered into – the Danish employer will in total receive a tax deduction. In addition, the Danish employer will in total receive a tax deduction if no recharge agreement is entered into and the contribution is tax exempt: see above. If, however, the contribution is not tax exempt – the parent company can deduct the expenses – the Danish employer will receive a tax deduction and in addition the Danish employer will be taxed on the contribution. This means that, overall, the taxable event will be neutral for the Danish employer (ie the Danish employer will not, under those circumstances, in total receive a tax deduction).

## 5. Tax beneficial arrangements

### 5.1 Are there any ways of making the long-term incentive award tax-efficient in Denmark?

Where certain conditions are met, executives may receive shares pursuant to a qualified plan under Section 7A of the Danish Tax Assessment Act which defers all taxation until the underlying shares are sold (ie no taxation will apply at grant, vesting or exercise). At the subsequent sale of shares, the gain is calculated as the difference between the purchase price for the shares and the sale price. The gain is taxed at ordinary rates (see above regarding tax on sale of shares). It is a requirement that the following conditions are met:

- the long-term incentive award must, in principle, be open to all employees;
- the value of the options offered must not amount to more than 10% of an employee's annual income, or exceed Dkr22,000 (2008) per year per employee;
- the long-term incentive award can use newly issued shares or shares already on the market, including treasury shares;
- the shares must have the same rights as other shares in the same class;
- the shares must be held for the year the option is exercised, plus five years for all Danish employees and the they must be deposited with a bank;
- the employer's auditor/lawyer must give an auditor's/lawyer's certificate concerning the truth of the information submitted to the tax authorities (latest January 20); and
- the employer must prepare and maintain records of the number of shares held by each employee and is obligated to report to the Danish tax administration.

Alternatively, the executives may receive shares pursuant to another qualified plan under Section 7H of the Danish Tax Assessment Act that similarly defers all taxation until the underlying shares are sold (ie no taxation will apply at grant, vesting or exercise). At the subsequent sale of shares, the gain is calculated as the difference between the purchase price for the shares and the sale price. The gain is taxed at ordinary rates (see above regarding tax on sale of shares). It is a requirement that the following conditions are met:

- the employee and the employer agree to opt for the regime;
- the value of the shares, options, and warrants does not exceed 10% of the employee's annual salary; or the exercise price for the options and warrants is at least 85% of the market value of the underlying shares, and the value of any shares received does not exceed 10% of the employee's annual salary;
- the employee's employer or a group company offers the shares, options, or warrants;
- the offered options or the underlying shares to be acquired upon exercise of the options or warrants are shares in the employer or a group company;
- no special share classes are created for the shares;
- the employee or the employer has a right to receive or issue shares, respectively, that is, instruments that can only be settled in cash do not qualify for the scheme;
- the employer's external legal counsel or accountant must certify that the above conditions are met; and a copy of this attestation and of the agreement regarding the application must be filed with the tax authorities; and
- the options (including rights to purchase shares), and warrants may not be transferred.

## 6. Internationally mobile executives

### 6.1 What are the income tax consequences for an employee who is resident in Denmark when the long-term incentive award is made, but who is no longer resident at the time of exercise/vesting?

*(a)* *Stock options*

If the employee moves away from Denmark and is no longer taxable there, the option will be taxable at personal income rates of up to approximately 63%, including 8% social security (current rates) for the year in which the employee moves from Denmark.

When calculating the taxation, the value of the stock options on the date when the employee moves is decisive. The value of the stock options can be determined as the difference between the market value of the shares at the time when the employee moved from Denmark, and the exercise price.

The employee can choose to pay the tax or ask for an extension. There will therefore be an exit charge when the employee leaves Denmark, even if the option is not exercised.

When the stock options are actually exercised, the employee can choose to calculate the taxation in the light of the value of the stock options at the time of actual exercise (a new calculation), instead of the value when the employee moved. Of course, it is better to choose a new calculation if the value decreased after the employee left Denmark.

*(b)*     *SARs, provisional allocation of free shares, nil-cost options, forfeitable securities*
As a rule, employees will be taxed in Denmark as if the shares were sold at the time the employee become non-resident. However, if the incentive award is not vested at the time of transfer, the tax treatment is uncertain. Certainty can only be achieved by means of a binding ruling – see 7.2 below.

6.2     **What are the social security consequences for an employee who is resident in Denmark when the long-term incentive award is made but who is no longer resident at the time of exercise/vesting?**
See 6.1 above.

6.3     **What are the tax and social security withholding/reporting consequences for the employer in respect of an employee who is resident in Denmark when the long-term incentive award is made but who is no longer resident at the time of exercise/vesting?**
See 2 above and 7 below.

7.     **Reporting requirements**

7.1     **Will the employer (or parent company, if different) have any reporting requirements as a result of the long-term incentive award?**
The employer is liable to report stock options that have been exercised and the value at the time of exercise, on a monthly basis to the Danish tax authorities.

The employer is liable to report SARs, provisional allocation of free shares, nil-cost options and forfeitable securities that have been granted and the value at grant on a monthly basis to the Danish tax authorities.

7.2     **Are there any tax rulings required in relation to the long-term incentive awards?**
A tax ruling is not required under Danish tax law. It is, however, possible to obtain a binding ruling; and it may, based on a case-by-case assessment, be expedient to obtain a binding tax ruling. It will take three to eight months to obtain such a tax ruling.

8.     **Exchange control issues**

8.1     **Are there any exchange control issues that would prevent an employee from (a) remitting monies abroad to purchase shares or (b) repatriating monies from the sale of shares?**
No. However, employees who are liable to tax in Denmark are required to report foreign bank accounts to the tax authorities.

## 9. Employment law

### 9.1 Are there any employment or local labour law issues which may arise as a result of the long-term incentive award? Are any consultations or authorisations required by law?

#### (a) Managing directors

The managing director of a company and, in certain cases, other directors who work independently (primarily referring to the board of directors), who cannot be said to be salaried employees, are not subject to any mandatory protective rules regarding long-term equity incentive awards. The legal treatment of long-term equity incentive awards for such directors in the event of termination of employment will be as stipulated in the long-term equity incentive award agreements and plans, unless the provisions of such agreements and plans can be said to be unreasonable within the meaning of the Danish Act on Contracts. (Ordinary forfeiture provisions will generally not be considered unreasonable.)

No consultations or authorisations are required by law.

#### (b) Other employees

All grants of rights to acquire or subscribe for shares at a later point in time (ie stock options, provisional allocation of free shares and nil-cost options) made after July 1 2004 will be subject to the termination provisions in the Danish Stock Option Act (see below).

#### (c) Termination by the employee

If an employee himself resigns his position by giving notice of termination to his employer, the Danish Stock Option Act says that all his rights to retain equity awards will be forfeited unless otherwise agreed. This will also apply to any future grants of equity awards that the employee could have expected to receive had he continued his employment.

#### (d) Termination by the employer and termination by the employee due to special reasons

If an employee is given notice of termination by his employer for any reason other than misconduct, or if an employee retires because he has attained the retirement age of that particular industry or that particular company or because the employee is entitled to receive a retirement or old-age pension from the employer, then the Danish Stock Option Act says that he will retain all rights to retain and exercise equity awards that have already been granted. In addition, the employee will be entitled to receive a share, proportionate to the length of his employment in the accounting year, of the grants to which he would have been entitled according to agreement or custom, had he still been employed at the end of the accounting year, or at the date of grant.

The Danish Stock Option Act cannot be deviated from to the detriment of the employee, but the above are minimum rules, and all entitlements providing more rights for the employees than the minimum rules will be enforceable.

No consultations or authorisations are required by law.

The employer is obliged to provide all employees with a so-called employer statement (see 10 below).

### (e) SARs

The use of SARs in employment relationships has not been expressly regulated under Danish law, but grants of SARs will generally be considered to constitute part of the employees' remuneration and consequently dealt with under Section 17a of the Danish Salaried Employees Act.

It has not yet been decided in case law, and the legal treatment is thus uncertain, but in the author's view there is a significant risk that SARs will be considered to be fully acquired on the date of grant even if they vest at a later date and over a certain period, and whether they are based on past or future performance (similar to the legal treatment of stock options granted before July 1 2004 as established in case law).

Consequently, by analogy with Section 17a of the Salaried Employees Act, it follows that SARS granted to an employee cannot be forfeited due to termination of the employee's employment, regardless of whether termination is voluntary or involuntary and the employee will be entitled to retain and exercise all granted SARs as if he had still been employed. This applies irrespective of contrary agreements or provisions in the SARs plan/agreement.

No consultations or authorisations are required by law.

### (f) Forfeitable securities

The use of forfeitable securities in employment relationships has not been expressly regulated under Danish law, but grants of forfeitable securities will generally be considered to constitute part of the employees' remuneration and consequently dealt with under Section 17a of the Danish Salaried Employees Act.

It has not yet been decided in case law, and the legal treatment is thus uncertain, but the authors believe that there is a significant risk that forfeitable securities will be considered to be fully acquired on the date of grant even if forfeiture provisions exist relating to termination of employment, and whether they are based on past or future performance (similar to the legal treatment of stock options granted before July 1 2004 as established in case law).

Consequently, by analogy with Section 17a of the Salaried Employees Act, it follows that forfeitable securities granted to an employee cannot be forfeited due to termination of the employee's employment, regardless of whether termination is voluntary or involuntary and the employee will be entitled to retain all granted forfeitable securities as if he had still been employed. This applies irrespective of contrary agreements or provisions in the forfeitable securities plan/agreement.

However, there are good arguments to suggest that the employees should only be entitled to retain a pro rata share of the forfeitable securities on termination of employment; but it is to be expected that the lower courts will be reluctant to reach a judgment differing from the case law regarding stock options granted before July 1

2004. Accordingly, if a pro rata right is applied, the employer should – if challenged by the employees – be ready to pursue cases to the Supreme Court to obtain approval of this legal treatment of forfeitable securities in connection with termination of employment, and even the outcome of a Supreme Court case regarding forfeitable securities will be highly uncertain.

Provisions providing for forfeiture on the basis of the company's or the employees' performance are generally enforceable unless they can be said to be unreasonable within the meaning of the Danish Act on Contracts.

No consultations or authorisations are required by law.

(g)   *Stock options, SARs, provisional allocation of free shares, nil-cost options, forfeitable securities*
Pursuant to general employment law principles, an employee who has repeatedly been granted equity awards may in some situations be entitled legally to claim that such equity awards continue on roughly similar terms.

It is not possible to say for exactly how long the equity awards should be granted before a customary right to awards on a continuing basis arises. However, repeating the same type of grant annually for two years will in many cases be enough, and repeating the grant annually for three years will almost always establish a customary right for the employees to receive awards on a continuing basis.

Such customary right can be established regardless of explicit contrary agreements.

## 10.   Translation

10.1   **Are there any language restrictions in Denmark? Does any of the documentation provided to the employee in relation to the long-term incentive award needed to be translated?**

(a)   *Stock options, provisional allocation of free shares, nil-cost options*
The employer shall give to the employees a so-called employer statement which is a separate written statement containing the following particulars about the equity incentive award:
- the date of granting;
- criteria or conditions for granting the equity incentive awards;
- the exercise date or period, or the rules for determining such date or period;
- the price at which the exercise can take place;
- the legal position of the employee upon termination of his employment; and
- the financial aspects of participating in the equity incentive award.

The employer statement shall be drafted in Danish, and must be distributed to the participating employees no later than 30 days after implementation of the equity incentive award. The employer statement is merely a formal document, and will normally not be longer than two to three pages. No other documents are required to be translated.

*(b)* *SARs, forfeitable securities*
There are no restrictions.

## 11. Data protection

11.1 **Are there any data protection issues which may arise should the employer wish to outsource the administration of the long-term incentive award to a third party?**
The Danish Act on Processing of Personal Data imposes a number of restrictions on the processing of data, including data relating to employee equity incentive awards. In most cases, the processing of data relating to such equity incentive awards will be considered a necessary and unavoidable consequence of the employment agreement with the employee. On this basis, the data processing can take place within the EU/EEA without the specific consent of the employee (including outsourcing of the administration of the equity incentive awards). However, the scope of the Act is not completely clear and it would therefore be advisable to obtain prior written consent from the employees for the processing of the data; and the employees' explicit consent is required for the transfer of that data to a group company or a third party (eg an equity incentive award administrator) located in a non-EU/EEA country. Note that a Danish company can only process personal data that reveals the employee's racial or ethnic origin, political opinions, religious or philosophical beliefs, trade-union membership, or information about the employees' health or sex life, if the employees give their explicit written consent and the processing of data is registered with the Danish Data Protection Agency. Again, if a Danish company wishes to transfer sensitive personal data to another group company, the data can only be transferred with the employees' explicit written consent.

## 12. Source of shares

12.1 **Does it matter if shares are newly issued to an employee, provided out of treasury or delivered from an employee benefit trust?**
No.

# Estonia

Maret Hallikma
Gerli Kilusk
Liina Linsi
Lepik and Luhaäär LAWIN

---

> **Red flag issues**
>
> **1.** Grant, vesting or exercise of a long-term incentive award by an executive is subject to a prospectus requirement if it could be considered a public offer of securities under the Estonian Securities Market Act.
>
> **2.** A long-term incentive award is a fringe benefit under the Estonian Income Tax Act.
>
> **3.** An employer shall pay income tax and social tax on fringe benefits granted to employees, ie it is the obligation of an employer, not the employee, and the respective sums may not be withheld from the employee's remuneration.

## 1. Securities laws

### 1.1 What prospectus and/or securities law requirements arise in connection with the grant, vesting or exercise of a long-term incentive award or on the eventual sale of the shares by the executive?

The grant, vesting or exercise of a long-term incentive award or on the eventual sale of the shares by the executive is subject to a prospectus requirement if it could be considered a public offer of securities in the essence of the Estonian Securities Market Act.

According to the Estonian Securities Market Act, an offer of securities is deemed to be public, unless:

- it is addressed solely to qualified investors;[1] or
- it is addressed to fewer than 99 people per contracting state,[2] other than qualified investors; or
- it is addressed to investors who acquire securities for a total consideration of at least €50,000 per investor for each separate offer; or
- the denomination per unit amounts to at least €50,000; or

---

1   Qualified investors are credit institutions, investment firms, management companies, investment funds, insurance undertakings or other people subject to financial supervision in Estonia or a foreign state, the Republic of Estonia or a foreign state, or a local or regional government or the central bank of Estonia or a foreign state, international organisations, including the International Monetary Fund, the European Central Bank, the European Investment Bank, the financial institutions of Estonia or a foreign state whose only business activity is investment in securities, or other persons who meet the requirements of a qualified investor as set forth in the Securities Market Act.
2   Parties to the European Economic Area Agreement.

- it is an issue or offer of securities with a total consideration of less than €100,000 in a period of 12 months.

If a grant, vesting or exercise of a long-term incentive award or on the eventual sale of the shares by the executive involves more than 99 people per contracting state, it is likely to be considered a public offer.

As a general rule, any person arranging a public offer is required to compile a prospectus containing all data as required by the provisions of the Prospectus Regulation[3] and register it with the Estonian Financial Supervision Authority prior to announcing the offer. A prospectus must be made publicly available when the offer is announced.

**1.2** **Is there an exemption from securities laws requirements either because the shares are being offered only to executives or because shares are being offered to a distinct group of named individuals?**

There is an exemption from the requirement to make the prospectus public and file it with the Estonian Financial Supervision Authority if the securities are issued by (a) an issuer whose securities are traded on a regulated market; or (b) a company belonging to the consolidated group of such an issuer is offered to existing or former members of the management board or employees of the issuer, provided that a document is made available which, in the opinion of the Estonian Financial Supervision Authority, contains information on the number and nature of the securities and the reasons for, and details of, the offer. In other words, the information package on the offer to be provided to existing or former members of the management board or employees must first be filed with the Estonian Financial Supervision Authority for a formal opinion regarding the sufficiency of the information.

The Estonian Financial Supervision Authority is currently drafting guidelines on seeking the opinion of the Estonian Financial Supervision Authority regarding employee share-purchase plans and similar issues. As yet, these guidelines have not been adopted.

**1.3** **If there is an exemption, will the exemption apply automatically or are there any applications/filings that need to be made?**

There is no need to submit any applications or filings of a public nature to rely on the exemption described above – it applies automatically.

**2.** **Employee tax and social security**

**2.1** **When will the executive be liable to tax or social security (and at what rate) in respect of the long-term incentive award?**

---

3    Commission Regulation (CE) 809/2004 of April 29 2004 implementing Directive 2003/71/EC of the European Parliament and of the Council as regards information contained in prospectuses as well as the format, incorporation by reference and publication of such prospectuses and dissemination of advertisements.

The long-term incentive award is a fringe benefit under the Estonian Income Tax Act. The moment of taxation depends on whether or not the long-term incentive awards have a monetary value for the receiving employee at the moment of grant. Whether a long-term incentive award has a monetary value depends on the terms and conditions of the award. (For example, where an award is conditional and is related to the fulfilment of special conditions or criteria in the future, it would only have a monetary value after these criteria had been fulfilled.)

Long-term incentive awards (transferable employee stock options or free share awards) that have a monetary value to the receiving employee at the moment of grant are taxable at the moment of grant. In such a case, the employer is under an obligation to pay fringe-benefit taxes (income tax and social tax) on the difference between the amount paid by the employee for the award (if any) and the fair market value of the option premium.

The rate of income tax applicable in 2008 is 21%. The law provides for a reduction of this rate by 1% per annum until 2011 and so, from January 1 2011, the rate will be 18%. The rate of social tax payable is currently 33%.

Long-term incentive awards (non-transferable employee stock options) with no monetary value at the moment of grant trigger tax implications upon exercise of the stock option by the employee. Fringe-benefit taxes (income tax and social tax) are imposed on the difference between the exercise price of the underlying shares and the market value of the shares at that moment.

2.2 **How will the executive's tax and social security be collected? Will the executive be responsible for paying any liabilities himself, or will the executive's employer be responsible for paying tax or social security liabilities on the executive's behalf?**

The taxable income of a natural person does not include fringe benefits. Employers pay income tax and social tax on fringe benefits granted to employees (ie it is the obligation of the employer, not the employee), so the respective sums may not be withheld from the employee's remuneration. The rate of income tax applicable in 2008 is 21%. The law provides for a reduction of this rate by 1% per annum until 2011 and so, from 1 January 2011, the rate will be 18%. The rate of social tax payable is currently 33%.

The period of taxation is the calendar month. An employer granting its employee a fringe benefit is required to submit a tax return to the regional division of the Tax and Customs Board by the tenth day of the calendar month following the period of taxation in which the fringe benefit was granted. The employer is required to transfer the tax payable to the bank account of the Tax and Customs Board not later than by the tenth day of the calendar month following the period of taxation.

2.3 **If the employer is responsible for the executive's liabilities, can the employer withhold the liabilities from the executive's salary? Are there any formalities in this respect?**

As an employee has no tax liability in respect of the long-term incentive awards and as the tax liability lies solely on an employer, the employer may not withhold any taxes arising in connection with a fringe benefit from the employee's salary.

Taxes paid on the long-term incentive award are not individually registered, so there are no additional formalities except as described above.

**2.4 If the executive's salary in the month of exercise/release is not sufficient for the employer to withhold all of the liabilities, can the employer (or the parent company, if different) arrange for the executive to authorise the sale of the executive's shares in the market and pass the money to the executive's employer?**

Estonian law does not recognise tax-related arrangements under which an employer and employee agree upon the division of tax obligations other than as set out in applicable law. Thus, as all the relevant tax liability of the long-term incentive award is borne solely by the employer, it would be against Estonian law for the employer to arrange for the employee to authorise the sale of shares in the market and then to pass the money on to the employer.

**2.5 Will the executive pay tax on the eventual sale of his shares and if so, at what rate?**

According to Estonian law an employee must pay income tax on the eventual sale of his shares. Income tax is levied on the amount received on the eventual sale of the shares less the acquisition cost. The acquisition cost refers to all certified expenses made by the taxpayer to acquire the securities, including any commission and fees paid. If the shares acquired at exercise/vesting were deemed to be a taxable fringe benefit, the employee will be taxed on the difference between the sale price and the amount already subject to tax as a fringe benefit. The tax rate is 21% in 2008 and is decreasing by 1% per annum until 2011.

## 3. Employer's social security

**3.1 Is the employer liable to pay (on its own account) any social security in connection with the long-term incentive award?**

An employer is liable to pay social tax at the rate of 33% on the value of fringe benefits, as well as on income tax payable on fringe benefits (see above).

**3.2 Can the liability of the employer be passed on to the employee? What steps are required?**

The obligation to pay social tax is on an employer and this obligation cannot be split between the employer and the employee (see above).

## 4. Tax deduction for the employer

**4.1 Is it possible for the employer to receive a tax deduction for the long-term incentive award? Would the employer need to be subject to recharge arrangements (eg if the employer is a subsidiary and provides funds to the parent company as part of a recharge arrangement for the long-term incentive award)?**

It is important to note that Estonia has a unique corporate income tax system. According to this system, there is no income tax liability on earned profits. This means that the profits of a company are not taxed as they are generated, rather as they are distributed (ie direct distribution (dividends), as well as fringe benefits or payments not related to the business). Therefore, there is no scope for tax deductions related to corporate income tax.

## 5. Tax beneficial arrangements

**5.1 Are there any ways of making the long-term incentive award tax-efficient in Estonia?**

There are no tax schemes or arrangements which could be implemented according to Estonian law that would make the long-term incentive award tax-efficient in Estonia.

## 6. Internationally mobile executives

**6.1 What are the income tax consequences for an employee who is resident in Estonia when the long-term incentive award is made, but who is no longer resident at the time of exercise/vesting?**

All fringe benefits granted by an employer to its employees or members of the management board or other management or supervision bodies are subject to income tax irrespective of whether the recipient of fringe benefits is a resident or non-resident.

**6.2 What are the social security consequences for an employee who is resident in Estonia when the long-term incentive award is made, but who is no longer resident at the time of exercise/vesting?**

All fringe benefits granted by an employer to its employees or members of the management board or other management or supervision bodies are subject to social tax irrespective of whether the recipient of fringe benefits is resident or non-resident.

**6.3 What are the tax and social security withholding/reporting consequences for the employer in respect of an employee who is resident in Estonia when the long-term incentive award is made, but who is no longer resident at the time of exercise/vesting?**

All fringe benefits granted by an employer to its employees or members of the management board or other management or supervision bodies are subject to income tax and social tax irrespective of whether the recipient of fringe benefits is resident or non-resident. (See above for withholding/reporting consequences.)

## 7. Reporting requirements

**7.1 Will the employer (or parent company, if different) have any reporting requirements as a result of the long-term incentive award?**

A company listed on the Tallinn Stock Exchange is required to indicate in its annual report the number of its shares that are held by the members of its management board or other management or supervision bodies, as well as by the latter's affiliated persons, as of the end at the financial year. Any shares to be acquired by these individuals by share options in future periods must be indicated separately. Information must also be presented on any unexpired share options granted during the financial year to members of the issuer's management and supervisory boards, along with information on the management and supervisory board members who are entitled to exercise their options.

The employer must submit a tax return to the regional division of the Tax and Customs Board by the tenth day of the calendar month following the period of taxation regarding the fringe benefits granted during the calendar month. The employer is required to transfer the tax payable to the bank account of the Tax and Customs Board no later than the tenth day of the calendar month following the period of taxation.

**7.2** **Are there any tax rulings required in relation to the long-term incentive awards?**
There are no tax rulings required.

## 8. Exchange control issues

**8.1** **Are there any exchange control issues that would prevent an employee from (a) remitting monies abroad to purchase shares or (b) repatriating monies from the sale of shares?**
There are no exchange control issues that would prevent an employee from (a) remitting monies abroad to purchase shares, or (b) repatriating monies from the sale of shares applicable in Estonia.

## 9. Employment law

**9.1** **Are there any employment or local labour law issues which may arise as a result of the long-term incentive award? Are any consultations or authorisations required by law?**
If the long-term incentive award is granted by an Estonian employer to its employees,[4] it is likely that the award will be considered to be granted within the context of an employment relationship. This may give rise to certain labour law implications. The employer would be required to ensure equal treatment of all its comparable employees and avoid discriminating against any of its employees on a prohibited ground (eg gender, nationality, race, social position, religious or political beliefs, attitude towards military service, etc). In light of these requirements, it is possible, for example, that employees on certain types of leave would be required to be eligible to participate in, or obtain grants under, the long-term incentive award. No consultations or authorisations are required by law.

---

4        Members of a management board or any other management or supervisory bodies are not considered to be employees under Estonian labour law.

## 10. Translation

10.1 **Are there any language restrictions in Estonia? Does any of the documentation provided to the employee in relation to the long-term incentive award need to be translated?**

According to the Estonian Language Act, all information provided to employees in connection with their employment relationship must be made available in the Estonian language and there is a view that all long-term incentive award-related documents must be translated into Estonian. Due to lack of relevant jurisprudence, there is no definitive opinion regarding the language issue.

## 11. Data protection

11.1 **Are there any data protection issues which may arise should the employer wish to outsource the administration of the long-term incentive award to a third party?**

As a general rule, the consent of a data subject is required to process any personal data. The processing of personal data is only permitted if it is used under the terms of a contract entered into with the data subject. Processing personal data in connection with the long-term incentive awards granted to employees and members of a management board or other management and supervisory bodies could be considered to take place in the course of the contract executed between an employer and an employee.

Despite the above, an employer cannot transmit personal data or give a third person access to it without the consent of the data subject. If the employer wishes to outsource the administration of the long-term incentive award to a third party, it must have the unambiguous and freely given consent of the employer or the executive.

## 12. Source of shares

12.1 **Does it matter if shares are newly issued to an employee, provided out of treasury or delivered from an employee benefit trust?**

There are no differences whether or not the shares are newly issued or transferred from an employee benefit trust.

# Finland

Tiina Hakri
Eva Nordman-Rajaharju
Vesa Rasinaho
Roschier, Attorneys Ltd

---

**Red flag issues**

1. Employer's deduction right of costs resulting from an incentive plan is often uncertain or not available at all.

2. Forfeitable securities are generally taxed already upon grant.

3. Due to recent case law, rights obtained under incentive plans may in the future be regarded as part of an employee's salary for employment law purposes.

---

## 1. Securities laws

### 1.1 What prospectus and/or securities law requirements arise in connection with the grant, vesting or exercise of a long-term incentive award or on the eventual sale of the shares by the executive?

According to a general provision of the Finnish Securities Market Act (495/1989) (the SMA), anyone offering securities to the public in Finland must prepare and publish a prospectus approved by the Finnish Financial Supervision Authority (the FFSA) before the launch of the offering, absent available exemption. Please see 1.2 below for a description of the possible exemptions.

Long-term incentive awards (as defined) qualify as "securities" for the purposes of the SMA, provided that such awards (options, shares etc) are transferable.

Regardless of whether an exemption to publish a prospectus is available, the issuer of the securities is required to make available to the employees sufficient information on factors which may have a material effect on the value of the securities offered. There is no clearly established interpretation as to what would qualify as information of material significance. Generally, all the relevant details of the issuing company together with recent historical financial statements should be provided. The issuer is further required to ensure that no untrue or misleading information is given and that the procedures or methods used are not contrary to good practice or unfair to the employees. In addition, the employees must be treated equally, meaning that employees in Finland must receive the same information as employees in any other country and in a language they can understand. The above information may be given on the issuer's intranet site.

No securities law requirements arise in connection with the eventual sale of the shares by the employees and/or executives.

**1.2** **Is there an exemption from securities laws requirements either because the shares are being offered only to executives or because shares are being offered to a distinct group of named individuals?**

*(a)* *Exemption based on limited number of offerees*

According to guidelines issued by the FFSA, an offering of securities will not be considered a public offering but rather a private placement if:

- the addressees of the offer consist of a group of pre-selected potential investors (regardless of their sophistication as investors);
- the number of such investors in Finland does not exceed 99; and
- no persons other than the named, pre-selected potential investors can participate in the offer in Finland. In this case, the offeror must prepare a list of the potential investors in Finland that must be approached before any promotion is made. The list must be submitted to the FFSA upon request. An offering of securities considered a private placement is not subject to the prospectus requirements of the SMA.

*(b)* *Exemption based on total consideration of the offering*

There is an automatic exemption available under the Finnish regulations (Decree 538/2005 on national prospectuses issued by the Finnish Ministry of Finance) in the case of an offer of securities with a total consideration of less than €100,000 for a period of 12 months as well as in the case of an offer of securities to (current or former) employees and/or executives with a total consideration of less than €2.5 million in the European Economic Area (EEA) for a period of 12 months. The consideration given by the employees and not the value of the shares subject to award is counted when calculating the above exemptions. Under the exemptions, there is no registration or prospectus requirement.

However, should the total consideration of the offer be €2.5 million or more in the EEA for a period of 12 months, the provisions of the EU Prospectus Directive (2003/71/EC), as implemented in Finland, would be applied, meaning that no automatic exemption would be available for such employee offerings. In such a situation, an exemption would need to be applied for from the FFSA. This would only be available to listed companies in the EEA.

*(c)* *Other exemptions*

There is no prospectus requirement (i) if the shares are granted free of charge or against no consideration by the employee/executive; or (ii) in connection with the grant of non-transferable awards/options as they do not qualify as "securities". Furthermore, there is no prospectus requirement in connection with the exercise of non-transferable options, as it is considered as the exercise of pre-existing contractual rights based on the exercise of a previous offer. However, the disclosure requirement discussed in 1.1 above is nevertheless applicable for free shares/securities.

1.3 **If there is an exemption, will the exemption apply automatically or are there any applications/filings that need to be made?**
The following exemptions are available automatically by operation of law:
- an exemption based on a limited number of offerees: maximum of 99 investors;
- an exemption based on the total consideration of the offering: €100,000 for a period of 12 months; and
- an exemption based on total consideration of less than €2.5 million in the EEA for a period of 12 months if securities are offered to employees and/or executives.

An application needs to be made to the FFSA in connection with an exemption based on total consideration of €2.5 million or more in the EEA for a period of 12 months, if securities are offered to employees and/or executives.

## 2. Employee tax and social security

2.1 **When will the executive be liable to tax or social security (and at what rate) in respect of the long-term incentive award?**
The benefit accruing from employment option rights, defined in Finnish tax law as any rights based on an employment relationship to receive or acquire shares in a corporate entity for a price below fair market value on the basis of a convertible bond, bond loan with warrants, option rights or other comparable agreement or commitment, is taxable income in the year when the employment option right is exercised. The sale of employment option rights is generally treated as an exercise of such rights. The donation or sale of an employment option right to a party related to the executive is not treated as an exercise. In such situations, the taxation of the executive will be deferred until the year during which the donee or related party exercises the options.

Free share grants or other awards or benefits that do not constitute employment option rights are taxed in the calendar year during which the benefits are received as money or other benefit having monetary value. This generally means that provisional shares are taxed only when they vest (when the right of ownership to the shares is actually transferred to the executive). Forfeitable securities are also taxed at the time when the ownership of shares is transferred to the executive, irrespective of possible transfer restrictions and return obligations. If the award is carried out in the form of share issue to the majority of the employees of the Finnish employer, the benefit is taxable income only for the part that the discount of the subscription price exceeds 10 per cent of the fair value of the share.

Benefits accruing from incentive awards are subject to earned income tax at progressive rates up to approximately 54%.

Employee social security charges become payable in connection with the withholding of advance tax on the basis of an exercise of an incentive award (see below). With the exception of an employee's medical care premium, social security charges only become payable for that proportion that the payment or benefit constitutes as a part of the employee's salary for the purposes of pension benefits or social security. Those benefits related to employment share issues are generally not considered to constitute part of salary for the purposes of pension benefits or social security. These are:

- issues of shares to the majority of employees of the issuing company on the basis of employment relationship;
- employment option rights; and
- payments made on the basis of an employment relationship, with an amount depending on the development of the employer company's share price.

If the incentive award qualifies as salary for social security charge purposes, the following become payable by the employee:

- a medical care premium at 1.24%;
- a daily allowance premium at 0.67%;
- an employee's pension insurance contribution at 4.1 to 5.2%; and
- an unemployment insurance contribution at 0.34%.

If the incentive award does not qualify as salary (most incentive awards fall under this category), only the medical care premium becomes payable, but at an increased rate of 1.41%.

All the above rates are for the year 2008.

**2.2 How will the executive's tax and social security be collected? Will the executive be responsible for paying any liabilities himself or will the executive's employer be responsible for paying tax or social security liabilities on the executive's behalf?**

As a rule, the executive's employer is liable to withhold advance tax and social security charges from cash payments made to the executive. The executive is liable to pay any deficit and is entitled to receive any surplus between his final income tax and the amount of advance tax after his final taxation for the relevant year has been completed, generally in December of the year following the relevant tax year and in February of the second following year. If the executive wishes to avoid interest on the deficit, he/she has to pay the deficit to the tax authorities by the end of January of the year following the relevant tax year.

**2.3 If the employer is responsible for the executive's liabilities, can the employer withhold the liabilities from the executive's salary? Are there any formalities in this respect?**

Yes, as described above. The withholding of liabilities relating to long-term incentive awards is, however, restricted only to cash payments made in the same calendar year during which the benefit has become taxable. Thus, especially for benefits accruing at the end of the year, it is possible that cash payments made to the executive are not sufficient to cover such withholding. In such cases, the executive is liable to pay on his/her own initiative any social security charges not withheld in addition to the payment of final tax as described above.

The employer must submit the withheld taxes and social security charges by the tenth day of the month following the payment of salaries to the Finnish tax authorities. Furthermore, the employer is obliged to report the amounts of salaries, taxable benefits, income tax withheld and social security contributions in a monthly and in an annual report to the Finnish tax authorities. The monthly tax report must be submitted by the fifteenth of the month following the payment of salaries. The annual report must be filed with the tax office by the end of January of the following year.

**2.4** **If the executive's salary in the month of exercise/release is not sufficient for the employer to withhold all of the liabilities, can the employer (or the parent company, if different) arrange for the executive to authorise to sell some of the executive's shares in the market and pass the money to the executive's employer?**
This is generally possible, subject to normal civil and labour law provisions governing authorisation. Any sale of shares owned by the employee triggers normal income tax and transfer tax liabilities for the executive.

**2.5** **Will the executive pay tax on the eventual sale of his shares and if so, at what rate?**
The eventual sale of shares by the executive triggers capital gains taxation for the executive at a tax rate of 28% (in 2008). The capital gain is calculated as the difference between the sale price and the aggregate amount of the price paid for the shares, if any, the amount of benefit taxed as employment-related benefit, and any costs related to the sale of shares. Alternatively, the executive can deduct from the sales price the so-called presumptive acquisition cost of shares, which is 20% of the sales price, or if the shares have been held for a period of at least 10 years, 40%. If the presumptive acquisition cost is used, the executive cannot deduct any other expenses from the sales price.

Capital gains are exempt from tax if the aggregate transfer prices of all otherwise taxable transferred assets of the executive within the same tax year do not exceed €1,000.

If the shares in question have been issued by a Finnish entity, the sale is in general subject to Finnish transfer tax at 1.6%, unless the shares are listed in a stock exchange, sold against a fixed cash consideration and the sale is carried out using an authorised securities broker.

## 3. Employer's social security

**3.1** **Is the employer liable to pay (on its own account) any employer's social security in connection with the long-term incentive award?**
Generally, employers' social security payments rarely fall payable in connection with long-term incentive awards.

The employer's social security charges only become payable for any part of the payment or benefit which constitutes part of the employee's salary for the purposes of pension benefits or social security. Benefits related to employment share issues (issues of shares to the majority of employees of the issuing company on the basis of the employment relationship), employment option rights and payments made on the basis of the employment relationship with an amount depending on the development of the employer company's share price are generally not considered to constitute a part of salary for the purposes of pension benefits or social security.

If the incentive award constitutes a payment subject to social security payments, the following are payable by the employer: employer's social security contribution; pension insurance premium; unemployment insurance premium; accident insurance premium; and group life insurance premium. The employer's social security contribution varies between 2.771% and 5.871%. In aggregate, the insurance premiums vary between approximately 21.3% and 26.6%.

All above rates are for the year 2008.

3.2  **Can the liability of the employer be put onto the employee?**
No.

## 4.  Tax deduction for the employer

4.1  **Is it possible for the employer to receive a tax deduction for the long-term incentive award? Would the employer need to be subject to recharge arrangements (eg if the employer is a subsidiary and provides funds to the parent company as part of a recharge arrangement in respect of the long-term incentive award)?**
Generally, computed costs incurred in relation to share-based incentive plans, such as the cost of share-based remunerations under IFRS 2 are not deductible, unless the costs are deemed to correspond to the "factual" expenses of the employer. Cash bonuses, including cash payments made on the basis of the development of the value of the employer's shares, are generally deductible. In a recent ruling by the Finnish Supreme Administrative Court, the court approved the deduction of compensation paid by a Finnish subsidiary to its US parent (company) on the basis of the US parent's computational expenses incurred in granting its own shares to the employees of the Finnish subsidiary. An initiative is currently pending explicitly to forbid the deduction of the amount of benefit received on the basis of share-based incentive plans. This includes the acquisition cost of own shares of the company (if these are granted as an employment benefit) as well as payments made to other companies in relation to such plans. (This overturns the Supreme Administrative Court ruling.) So far, no government bill has been published concerning this initiative.

## 5.  Tax beneficial arrangements

5.1  **Are there any ways of making the long-term incentive award tax-efficient in Finland?**
Generally, it is difficult to achieve arrangements aiming at transferring part of the increase in the value of a share accrued before the executive has acquired ownership of the share to be taxed as capital gains, instead of progressive earned income. Tax optimisation in listed companies often aims at ensuring that the employer can make deductions in connection with the plan (eg by using cash payments instead of direct

share grants or options). Tax optimisation may also aim to eliminate any liability to pay transfer tax in connection with the plan.

An employment share issue offered for the majority of the employees of a Finnish employer has the benefit that only the part of the discount in subscription price in excess of 10% of the fair value of the shares is taxable income. As this discount is not included in the acquisition cost of the shares, the discount generally increases the taxable capital gain if the shares are subsequently sold.

The scope of the application of capital gains taxation instead of earned income taxation may be increased through transferring ownership of the shares to the executive at an earlier date/point in time, eg through the use of forfeitable securities or other transfer restrictions or through the use of highly leveraged holding companies as vehicles for holding the executive's shares. Such mechanisms are usually complicated and have the drawback that if earned income taxation is accelerated through such a plan, the executive does not have the cash to pay the initial earned income tax, as the shares received are subject to restrictions and cannot be sold.

## 6. Internationally mobile executives

### 6.1 What are the income tax consequences for an employee who is resident in Finland when the long-term incentive award is made, but who is no longer resident at the time of exercise/vesting?

If the executive exercises his incentive award when working abroad for a period of at least six months, it is possible that such part of the increase in value of the award that has accrued during the work abroad is not taxable in Finland, if:

- there is a tax treaty in place between Finland and the country where the work is carried out;
- the award income is taxed in the same way as salary in that country; and
- the executive has duly reported the award income to the tax authorities of that country.

If the executive has moved abroad due to retirement or transfer to the employment of another, unrelated, employer and exercised his award abroad, the incentive award has been treated as fully taxable income for the time that the executive has been abroad. The tax treaties possibly applicable to the income received by the executive may additionally limit Finland's right to tax the incentive award.

For non-residents receiving income taxed as salary in Finland, a fixed tax rate of 35% is applied as a final withholding tax. If the executive does not receive any cash payments from which to withhold tax, or only receives payments exempt from Finnish tax on the basis of Finnish tax laws, the Finnish tax authorities impose the tax on the executive directly. An executive resident within the EEA but not in Finland may, under certain qualifications, elect to choose the same progressive income taxation as Finnish residents instead of the fixed withholding tax rate.

**6.2** **What are the social security consequences for an employee who is resident in Finland when the long-term incentive award is made, but who is no longer resident at the time of exercise/vesting?**

As a general rule, liability to pay social security charges is connected with the executive's entitlement to Finnish social security. If the executive does not fall under (the scope of application of) Finnish social security, social security charges are generally not payable. As most share-based incentive awards are only subject to the employee's medical care premium, the question of the applicability of most social security charges on incentive awards very seldom arises. As the basis for the calculation of the employee's medical care premium is connected with the amount taxable as earned income in Finland, the medical care premium generally becomes payable to the extent that the incentive award benefit is taxable (see above).

**6.3** **What are the tax and social security withholding/reporting consequences for the employer for an employee who is resident in Finland when the long-term incentive award is made, but who is no longer resident at the time of exercise/vesting?**

If the incentive award is deemed to relate wholly or partly to the executive's work carried out in Finland for the employer, the employer is liable to withhold tax, pay social security charges and report the payments to the tax authorities irrespective of whether the employee is still resident or otherwise working in Finland at the time of payment. However, if the employee is working for the same employer abroad during the time of exercise, and the employee's salary for the work carried out abroad has been exempt from Finnish tax on the basis of Finnish domestic legislation, the employer is not liable to withhold tax payable on the incentive award taxable in Finland from such salary that is not taxable in Finland. The employer reports the salaries paid to non-residents and taxes withheld in the annual report. In addition, the employer must give the non-resident employee a receipt for the payments made and the taxes withheld.

## 7. Reporting requirements

**7.1** **Will the employer (or parent company, if different) have any reporting requirements as a result of the long-term incentive award?**

The employer or other payer, which has paid withheld taxes or social security contributions to the Finnish tax authorities, must report such payments in a monthly report by the fifteenth day of the month following the payments.

The employer or other payer of benefits is liable to make an annual report on salaries and other benefits paid and the amounts withheld during a calendar year. Generally the annual report has to be filed by the end of January of the year following the payments. As an example, in the report the employer has to specify the payments that are not subject to the employee's daily allowance premium (ie most long-term incentive awards).

**7.2** **Are there any tax rulings required in relation to the long-term incentive awards?**

There is no mandatory obligation to apply for tax rulings in connection with long-term incentive awards. If the plan involves any uncertainties relating to Finnish taxation, it is possible to ensure the tax treatment in advance by applying for an advance ruling. The need for such rulings should be decided on a case-by-case basis.

## 8. Exchange control issues

**8.1 Are there any exchange control issues that would prevent an employee from (a) remitting monies abroad to purchase shares or (b) repatriating monies from the sale of shares?**

There are no such exchange control restrictions.

## 9. Employment law

**9.1 Are there any employment or local labour law issues which may arise as a result of the long-term incentive award? Are any consultations or authorisations required by law?**

The Finnish Employment Contracts Act (55/2001) does not include any provisions regarding employee stock options, bonuses and other comparable incentives (ie discretionary benefits granted to an employee under a separate scheme, though based on the employment relationship). Therefore, unless otherwise agreed in an individual employment contract, long-term incentive awards granted to an employee are generally not regarded as part of an employee's salary under Finnish law, but rather as an additional "benefit". Furthermore, as long-term incentive awards based on a separate scheme are generally not regarded as part of the employee's salary, it is unlikely that the rights obtained under such a scheme would become incorporated into a participating employee's employment contract (as an implied term), especially if such rights are expressly excluded and the wording of the employment contract and the scheme clearly reflect this exclusion. Note, however, that the practices adopted by the employer must also support such exclusion (ie in the event that, according to an incentive plan, provisional awards are payable only if certain financial targets have been met, the employer must not pay the award if the targets have not been met).

However, it should be noted that the Finnish Supreme Court gave a ruling in 2006 concerning the income from employment-related stock options as part of salary. The Supreme Court ruled that employee stock options should be taken into account as part of the employee's salary when defining the amount of compensation for unlawful termination (KKO:2006:42). The ruling deviates from previous practice, where income arising from employee stock options has not been regarded as the employee's salary when determining the compensation for unlawful termination. The ruling raises more questions than it answers.

In general, there is no legal requirement to consult (or obtain any authorisations from) any employee organisations about the implementation of an employee share scheme unless otherwise agreed (eg in the terms of the scheme concerned or in the works council rules of the employer company). It is emphasised, however, that in one specific case the employer may have an obligation to negotiate with employees (or their representatives) about the implementation of a scheme. This negotiation obligation exists if the award is given in the form of the employer company's (or a company belonging to the same group) listed shares or a comparable benefit or even cash, provided that the value of such award depends on the possible increase in the value of such shares no less than one year after the promise to allocate the award.

## 10. Translation

**10.1 Are there any language restrictions in Finland? Does any of the documentation provided to the employee in relation to the long-term incentive award need to be translated?**

There are no statutory language requirements in Finland. Therefore, it is up to the employer to assess whether the potential participating employees have the necessary language skills to receive the information in English, or whether the information should be given in Finnish. If the employer is of the opinion that the eligible employees have sufficient language skills (eg if the corporate language is English), then the necessary information could be given in English only.

## 11. Data protection

**11.1 Are there any data protection issues which may arise should the employer wish to outsource the administration of the long-term incentive award to a third party?**

The Finnish Personal Data Act (523/1999) includes an obligation to notify the Finnish Data Protection Ombudsman of any outsourced processing of personal data (ie when the data controller acquires data-processing services from an external party). When outsourcing personal data processing, an employer shall obtain sufficient undertakings from the third-party processor to ensure that the processing will be conducted in accordance with Finnish law and good processing practices. In the event that the third-party processor processes employees' personal data on behalf of a Finnish employer, a specific notification regarding the outsourcing of data processing must be submitted to the Data Protection Ombudsman.

In the event that the processing of personal data is outsourced outside the EU/EEA, stricter rules will be applied. As a general rule, personal data collected under the Personal Data Act may only be transferred to and/or processed in a country in which the level of protection for such data is considered to be adequate. This is evaluated in the light of the nature of the data, the purpose and duration of the intended processing, the country of origin and the country of final destination, as well as the general and sector-specific legal provisions, codes of conduct and security measures applied in the country of destination. The transfer of personal data to countries outside the EU/EEA is allowed if:

- the data subject has unambiguously consented to the transfer;
- the transfer is necessary to protect the vital interests of the data subject;
- the data receiving entity has subscribed to the safe-harbour regime (which applies to the US only); or

- the model clauses issued by the EU Commission are used.

If the personal data file is transferred from an entity within the EU/EEA to an entity of the same corporate group outside of the EU/EEA, the rules regarding transfer outside of the EU/EEA apply.

## 12. Source of shares

### 12.1 Does it matter if shares are newly issued to an employee, provided out of treasury or delivered from an employee benefit trust?

For the purposes of tax law, an issue of new shares has been treated as a capital investment. As such, it is not a taxable event for the issuing company; nor is it subject to transfer tax. However, the transfer of existing shares has been treated as a taxable event both for corporate tax and transfer tax purposes (with the possibility of incurring a deductible loss if the shares are transferred for a price less than the acquisition cost). Finnish tax laws are expected to be amended so as to make the transfer of own shares a non-taxable (but also non-deductible) event for the Finnish company for corporate tax (but not for transfer tax) purposes.

In case law, the rule exempting 10% discounts on employment share issues from tax has been deemed to apply only to issues of new shares. However, the validity of such interpretation is no longer clear due to the amendment of the Finnish Companies Act (624/2006) in 2006, whereupon the transfer of own shares was, for virtually all corporate law purposes, equated with an issue of new shares. Whether this means that transfers of own shares should be treated as share issues for all relevant tax purposes remains to be seen.

# France

Sophie Brézin
Jean-Luc Calisti
Jérôme Le Berre
Emma Röhsler
Herbert Smith LLP

---

> **Red flag issues**
>
> **1.** Possible favourable tax and social security regime if a sub-plan is implemented, tailored to the French legal and tax requirements.
>
> **2.** A tax deduction may be available for the issuing company or the local employer with respect to the costs incurred in relation to the long-term incentive plan.
>
> **3.** Particular attention should be paid to information given to executives with regard to the impact of a termination of their employment on their vested and/or non-vested awards.
>
> **4.** In practice, the documentation should be drafted in French where the number of employees involved is significant.

## 1. Securities laws

**1.1** **What prospectus and/or securities law requirements arise in connection with the grant, vesting or exercise of a long-term incentive award or on the eventual sale of the shares by the executive?**

With regard to the need for establishing a prospectus in relation to the grant, vesting or exercise of such award, the French Market Authority (Autorité des Marchés Financiers – AMF) recently summarised its position as follows (*Revue mensuelle de l'Autorité des Marchés Financiers* Nr. 39, September 2007).

*(a)* *Free shares*

The AMF considers that to the extent that free shares are granted for no consideration (ie the employees are not required to pay consideration for the award made to them), such awards do not constitute a public offering within the meaning of Article L 411-1 of the French Monetary and Financial Code (*Code monétaire et financier* – CMF). Accordingly, the implementation of free share plans does not require that a prospectus be established and filed with the AMF.

*(b)* *Stock options*

The AMF considers that stock options (ie options to subscribe for newly issued shares, or to purchase existing shares within the meaning of Articles L 225-177 to L 225-186 of the French *Code de commerce* (French Commercial Code)) cannot be regarded as financial instruments within the meaning of Article L 211-1 of the CMF because they are not transferable by book entry or manual transfer. Option plans do not therefore constitute a public offering and the granting of options does not require that a prospectus be established and filed with the AMF.

The AMF confirmed that this also applies to options granted over shares in a foreign issuer, provided that the granted options have the same characteristics as options granted under French law.

With regard to the exercise of options by employees, the AMF also considers that the latter does not constitute a public offering, since the exercise is a mere execution of the original grant. The exercise does not require that a prospectus be established and filed with the AMF.

Notwithstanding this, it should be noted that the listing on a regulated market of the shares resulting from the exercise of the options constitutes a public offering within the meaning of Article L 411–1 of the CMF. However, such a listing may be exempt from the obligation to establish a prospectus either (i) under Article 212–5 1° of the AMF General Regulations (*Réglement général* – AMF) if less than 10% of the total number of the issuer's shares have been admitted on the same regulated market over a 12-month period, or (ii) under Article 212–5 6° of the AMF General Regulations.

**1.2**  **Is there an exemption from securities law requirements either because the shares are being offered only to executives or because shares are being offered to a distinct group of named individuals?**

As stated above, the position of the AMF is based on the legal nature of the options (ie they are not considered to be financial instruments) and on the fact that free shares are offered for no consideration, so that such an offering may not be regarded as a public offering within the meaning of the AMF General Regulations.

**1.3**  **If there is an exemption, will the exemption apply automatically or are there any applications/filings that need to be made?**

Based on the above-mentioned position of the AMF, the exemption applies automatically.

**2.**  **Employee tax and social security**

**2.1**  **When will the executive be liable to tax or social security (and at what rate) in respect of the long-term incentive award?**

For French tax (and social security) purposes, a distinction must, in principle, be made between long-term incentive awards that qualify for a favourable tax and social security regime (so-called qualifying plans) and those which do not benefit from such a favourable regime (non-qualifying plans).

Awards made under non-qualifying plans will generally trigger a tax liability upon exercise (options) or vesting (free shares).

Conversely, under qualifying plans, the tax liability will only arise upon the disposal (sale) of the underlying shares, save in certain limited circumstances (ie under stock option plans, where a discount of more than 5% is granted over the exercise price of the shares – see below).

Any acquisition gain (ie the difference between the market value of the underlying shares upon vesting or exercise and their exercise price (if any)), is treated as additional salary income and subject to income tax (up to 40%) and social security contributions at the rates of around 20% (employee's part) and 50% (employer's part).

The position is different in relation to qualifying plans (see below).

**2.2  How will the executive's tax and social security be collected? Will the executive be responsible for paying any liabilities himself or will the executive's employer be responsible for paying tax or social security liabilities on the executive's behalf?**

Regardless of whether the award is made under a "qualifying plan" or not, the employee will be solely responsible for the payment of income tax for the long-term incentive award.

As regards social security, the employer will generally be responsible for deducting at source the employee's contribution, preparing to pay the employer's contribution and then paying both to the relevant authorities.

If the award is made under a "qualifying plan", the acquisition gain (as defined above) is not treated as salary income but taxed as a capital gain and the social contributions that become due are payable by the executive.

**2.3  If the employer is responsible for the executive's liabilities, can the employer withhold the liabilities from the executive's salary? Are there any formalities in this respect?**

The employer may deduct the employee social contribution from the executive's salary, but not income tax or employer's social security contributions.

There are no specific formalities in this respect. However, the deduction should be expressly mentioned in the relevant plan rules. Moreover, the deduction should be mentioned on the relevant payslip.

**2.4  If the executive's salary in the month of exercise/release is not sufficient for the employer to withhold all of the liabilities, can the employer (or the parent company, if different) arrange for the executive to authorise to sell some of the executive's shares in the market and pass the money to the executive's employer?**

In theory, nothing prevents the employer or the parent company from doing so. However, this possibility should be expressly provided for in the rules of the plan to avoid any dispute with the executive.

**2.5  Will the executive pay tax on the eventual sale of his shares and if so at what rate?**

Any capital gain realised on the sale of the underlying shares will be subject to:

- income tax at the proportional rate of 18% (rate applicable as from January 1 2008); and
- social contributions at the global rate of 11% (*cotisation sociale généralisée* (CSG) at the rate of 8.2%, *contribution au remboursement de la dette sociale* (CRDS) at the rate of 0.5% and a special levy of 2.3%).

Please note, however, that capital gains are exempt from income tax (and social contributions) when the total amount of the proceeds received by the executive's household as a result of the sale of shares during the relevant calendar year does not exceed €25,000 (threshold applicable as from January 1 2008).

In addition, a further tax benefit may be available, as from January 1 2006, if the shares are owned for at least six years. As from the sixth year of ownership, the capital gain realised upon the sale of the shares is reduced by one-third, so that a full exemption is available after eight years of ownership. This exemption only applies with respect to income tax (ie social contributions remain due).

Where a capital loss is incurred upon the sale of the underlying shares, it may be deducted from the acquisition gain realised by the executive in relation to his options or free shares.

## 3. Employer's social security

**3.1 Is the employer liable to pay (on its own account) any employer's social security in connection with the long-term incentive award?**
As stated above, the employer will be liable to social security contributions (employer's part) at the rate of around 50% on any acquisition gain realised by the executive, unless the long-term incentive award is made under a "qualifying plan".

**3.2 Can the liability of the employer be transferred to the employee? What steps are required?**
As a matter of law, it is not possible for an employer to transfer the liability for employer's social security contributions to the employee. It may, however, be possible to provide in the plan for damages to be paid by the employee if the employee triggers a liability for the employer as a result of a breach of the rules of the relevant plan. Such provision will, however, be difficult to implement in practice.

## 4. Tax deduction for the employer

**4.1 Is it possible for the employer to receive a tax deduction for the long-term incentive award? Would the employer need to be subject to recharge arrangements (eg if the employer is a subsidiary and provides funds to the parent company as part of a recharge arrangement for the long-term incentive award)?**
French tax law expressly provides for a tax deduction for the employer for costs and expenses incurred in connection with long-term incentive awards under a qualifying plan (ie stock option plans and free share award plans).

By virtue of Section 217 *quinquies* of the French Tax Code, the costs incurred by the employer (and charged back to the local entity) in relation to the exercise of options by their employees which fall within the favourable tax regime are deductible for corporation tax purposes. In particular, deductibility covers the costs incurred by the issuing company in connection with:

- the buy-back of its shares;
- the costs of increasing its capital;

- the costs relating to the administration of the shares bought back or issued until the exercise of the options by the employees; and
- the costs directly relating to the exercise of the options.

Any capital losses suffered by the issuing company with respect to the difference between the price paid by the employees exercising their options and the market value of the shares in question for the issuing company are also tax deductible. In this respect, note that the French tax authorities consider such capital losses are only deductible with respect to options over existing shares which are bought by the issuing company.

The law relating to employees' savings (*loi pour le développement de la participation et de l'actionnariat salarié*) dated December 30 2006 has expressly confirmed the tax deductibility of certain costs incurred by a company in offering free shares under a tax-qualified plan.

Thus, where a company operates a free share plan, the company can claim a tax deduction for an amount equal to the difference between the exercise price/offer price, and the market value of the shares at the time of the offer.

The aforementioned law has extended this tax deductibility to capital loss incurred by companies under free share plans in relation to newly issued shares. To be eligible for the deduction the company must offer the plan to all employees, and the shares must be offered equally to employees according to their remuneration and/or position.

When the employer is not the issuing company, it is admitted that the costs and expenses incurred by the issuing company may be recharged to the employer (eg the French subsidiary of a foreign issuing company). The recharge arrangement should be entered into at arm's length and should provide for the principles retained for the allocation of the costs (ie costs charged back to the local entity on a pro-rata basis), to avoid the risks of challenge by the French tax authorities.

## 5. Tax beneficial arrangements

### 5.1 Are there any ways of making the long-term incentive award tax-efficient in France?

French tax law provides for a favourable tax and social security regime in connection with both stock option grants and free share awards, subject to certain conditions being fulfilled. Foreign plans may be eligible for the favourable regime, provided that they meet the principal French legal and tax requirements.

### (a) Stock options

In order to be eligible for the favourable tax regime, options granted to French tax-resident employees over shares in a foreign legal entity must fulfil the following conditions (listed in a Statement of Practice of the French tax authorities issued on May 16 1998):

- the company issuing the options must hold, directly or indirectly, at least 10% of the shares of the French company which employs the persons subscribing to the options;
- the options must be granted by the body which is competent to take such decisions within the issuing company; and

- the terms of the options must comply with the provisions of Articles L 225–177 to L225–186 of the French Commercial Code, and in particular:
  - the option price must be definitely fixed on the date of grant;
  - the option holder must be an employee of the employing company; options may also be granted to corporate officers and directors of the employing company provided that shares in the foreign parent company over which the options are granted are listed on a regulated market;
  - the option holder must not hold more than 10% of the share capital of the issuing company;
  - where the shares to be purchased on exercise of the options are listed shares, the price at which the options are granted must be no less than 80% of the arithmetical average of the middle market quotation of the shares on the 20 business days preceding the date of grant;[1] and
  - no option may be granted to any employee less than 20 trading days after payment of a dividend or an attribution of extra shares.

In addition, the regime requires that the shares resulting from the exercise of the option:

- remain registered in the name of the French employee for a period of four years from the date the options were granted; and
- *are not disposed of during that four-year period* (early disposal of the shares is, however, allowed in the event of disability, death, dismissal, redundancy or retirement.)

If all the above conditions are fulfilled, the notional capital gain realised on the exercise of the option (the "acquisition gain"), which corresponds to the difference between the exercise price of the option and the market value of the shares in question on the date of the exercise of the option by the employee, is taxed as follows:

- with respect to that fraction of the acquisition gain which does not exceed €152,500 during any one calendar year, at a fixed rate of 41%, including social contributions (ie CSG (8.2%), CRDS (0.5%) and the social contribution of 2.3%); and
- above that threshold,[2] at a rate of 51% (including CSG, CRDS and the social contribution of 2.3%).

However, if the employee holds the shares received in exchange for exercising the option for a further two-year period after the first four-year holding period has expired, these rates of tax are reduced as follows:

- to 29% with respect to that fraction of the acquisition gain which does not exceed €152,500; and
- to 41% above that threshold.

---

1     The shares over which the options are granted may be newly issued or existing shares. However, specific rules apply for existing shares.

2     The employees can also opt for the acquisition gain to be taxed as supplementary salary (ie to pay subject to income tax at his/her top marginal rate).

Please note that there is a further liability to tax and social security contributions if the difference between the market value of the shares on the date on which the option is granted and the option price exceeds 5%. That part of the discount which exceeds 5% is taxed if and when the option is exercised, as if it were supplementary salary. Thus, it is subject to income tax in the hands of the employee at his or her top marginal rate (the top marginal rate is currently 40%), and generates employee and employer social security contributions. That part of the discount which does not exceed the 5% limit is included in the acquisition gain and taxed accordingly as described above.

The acquisition gain is exempt from employee and employer social security contributions.

However, it should be noted that the law relating to the financing of French social security for 2008, which was adopted on November 23 2007, introduced two additional social contributions in connection with stock options which may be paid by both employer and employee.

For options granted on or after October 26 2007, the employee will be liable for a 2.5% social security contribution assessed on the acquisition gain realised and the employer will be liable for a 10% social security contribution assessed on either (a) the fair value of the options, as determined for the drawing up of consolidated accounts in accordance with International Accounting Standards, or (b) 25% of the value of the underlying shares at grant.

When the employee sells his or her shares after having exercised his or her option, any increase in the value of the shares between the market value on the date of exercise of the options and the sale price is taxed as a capital gain at a rate of 29% (including CSG, CRDS and the social contribution of 2.3%).

Finally, where the employee does not comply with the minimum holding requirement, the favourable tax and social security regime does not apply and the acquisition gain is considered as supplementary salary. It is subject to income tax in the hands of the employee at his or her top marginal rate.

## (b) *Free shares*

To qualify, a free share plan (whether French or foreign) must comply with the provisions of Articles L 225–197–1 to L 225–197–5 of the French Commercial Code.

The company awarding the free shares must hold, directly or indirectly, at least 10% of the share capital or voting rights of the company employing the French resident participants. However, where that company is listed, it may also grant free shares to employees and officers of both its parent and sister companies.

In addition to the above, the benefit of the favourable tax and social security regime is subject to compliance with minimum vesting and holding requirements, namely:

- a minimum vesting period of at least two years, during which time the employee is not the owner of the shares; and
- a minimum holding period of at least two years between the date of vesting and the date of sale of the shares, during which time the employee is the shareholder. Accordingly, even if a company provides for the award to vest after three years, the holding period would still need to be at least two years long.

These requirements are regarded as "substantial" by the French tax authorities. This means that the preferential tax and social security regime does not apply to awards of free shares which do not meet these requirements.

Other requirements of the French Commercial Code, while not being defined as substantial requirements by the French tax authorities, should also be complied with by foreign companies making awards to French resident employees of their group to secure the benefit of the regime. These are as follows:

- the total number of free shares awarded cannot exceed 10% of the company's share capital;
- no participant may hold more than 10% of the shares in the awarding company both before and after the award;
- the heirs of a deceased participant must be able to require the transfer of the shares during the six months following the participant's death; and
- once the holding period has elapsed, shares in the company cannot be sold:
  - within the ten dealing days both preceding and following the date on which the accounts of the company are made public; and
  - during the period beginning on the date on which the subsidiaries of the awarding company are made aware of information which, if made public, could have significant impact on the market price of the shares, and ending on the date ten dealing days after the date on which such information is made public.

The shareholders of the company are responsible for establishing the criteria for the conditions of granting the award and the portion of share capital to satisfy the award.

When there is a sale of the shares, provided all the provisions of Articles L 225–197–1 to L225–197–5 of the French Commercial Code are fulfilled, qualified employee free-share plans will currently be taxed as follows:

- the benefit realised at vesting will be taxed at a flat income tax rate of 41% (including social contributions at the global rate of 11%), or, as an option, at an ordinary income tax rate on salaries;
- this flat income tax charge on the benefit realised at vesting is deferred until the date the shares are sold; and
- the capital gain (the difference between the fair market value at vesting and the sale price) realised at sale is subject to tax at a flat rate of 29% (including social contributions at the global rate of 11%).

Moreover, the acquisition gain will be exempt from French social security contributions for both employees and employers. However, it should be noted that for awards made on or after October 26 2007, social contributions at the rate of 2.5% and 10% will be payable by the employee and the employer,[3] respectively, pursuant to the law relating to the financing of French social security for 2008 (see above).

---

3    With regard to free shares, the 10% social contribution due by the employer is assessed on either (a) the fair value of the shares, as determined for the drawing up of consolidated accounts in accordance with International Accounting Standards, or (b) the value of the shares at grant.

### 6. Internationally mobile executives

6.1 **What are the income tax consequences for an employee who is resident in France when the long-term incentive award is made, but who is no longer resident at the time of exercise/vesting?**

As a general statement, it should be noted that in cross-border situations the sourcing of the acquisition gain (relating to stock options or free shares) remains a grey area, since French tax law does not provide for specific rules in connection with the impact of a change of tax residency on long-term incentive awards.

Since the acquisition gain is treated as salary income, the French tax authorities generally consider that the latter should be taxable in the country where the corresponding salaried activity is/has been carried out.

On the basis of the above, the method of allocation of the taxable income between the two (or more) relevant countries will depend on which of the following two interpretations is retained:

- the options or free shares were granted in consideration for an activity performed prior to their date of grant. According to this interpretation, if the grant of the options occurred when the employee was resident and carried out his activity in France, the gain realised upon the subsequent exercise of his options or the vesting of his shares would be taxable in France, irrespective of the country in which the employee will be tax resident on the date of the subsequent exercise of his options or vesting of his free shares; or
- the gain relates to the activity performed by the employee concerned between the date of grant and the date of exercise of the options. According to this interpretation, the taxable gain is sourced in the place or places where the salaried activity was performed throughout the life of the options or free shares.

Practitioners in France have generally supported this second interpretation in the past. The latter also appears to be in line with the general principles proposed by the OECD in its 2004 report entitled *Cross-border Income Tax Issues Arising from Employee Stock Option Plans*.

The French tax authorities have recently confirmed that they were keen to implement the recommendations of the OECD report. However, they have not issued any statement of practice in this respect so far, so that the exact methodology that will be retained remains unclear and that these principles remain difficult to implement in practice.

6.2 **What are the social security consequences for an employee who is resident in France when the long-term incentive award is made but who is no longer resident at the time of exercise/vesting?**

There are no specific rules applicable for social security purposes with regard to the impact of a change in tax residency on the assessment of the acquisition gain.

As a general rule, French social security authorities tend to follow the position of the French tax authorities.

6.3     **What are the tax and social security withholding/reporting consequences for the employer in respect of an employee who is resident in France when the long-term incentive award is made, but who is no longer resident at the time of exercise/vesting?**
There are no specific withholding or reporting requirements for the employer upon a change of tax residency of the executive.

The employer may, however, remain liable for any social security contributions that may become due as a result of the executive exercising/selling his shares, where the plan under which the options or free shares were granted does not comply with French legal and tax requirements or, for instance, where the executive does not comply with the minimum holding requirements provided for by French tax law once he has transferred his tax residency.

## 7.     Reporting requirements

7.1     **Will the employer (or parent company, if different) have any reporting requirements as a result of the long-term incentive award?**
With regard to stock options, the employing company is required to issue a certificate to its employees who have exercised their options, by February 15 of the year following the date of exercise, and it is required to send a copy to the French tax authorities.

Furthermore, the employing company is required to provide the employees with a further certificate (and to send a copy to the French tax authorities) by February 15 of the year following that during which they dispose of their shares, if such disposal takes place less than four years from the date the options were granted to them.

A similar reporting requirement applies for free shares awards, whereby the employer is required to inform the French social security authorities of the vesting of the free shares that have been granted.

7.2     **Are there any tax rulings required in relation to the long-term incentive awards?**
No tax rulings are required in connection with long-term incentive awards.

A tax ruling may be sought on a case-by-case basis, in particular in connection with certain corporate operations that may have an impact on options or free shares that have already been granted (eg mergers or takeover bids), or with regard to particular features of an incentive plan (eg use of a trust to retain the shares granted to the employees).

## 8.     Exchange control issues

8.1     **Are there any exchange control issues that would prevent an employee from (a) remitting monies abroad to purchase shares or (b) repatriating monies from the sale of shares?**
Long-term incentive awards do not raise exchange control issues in France.

French residents are not required to obtain any specific authorisation to purchase foreign stock. French residents may hold stock outside France provided they make a declaration to the French tax authorities on an annual basis regarding any foreign bank or stock account opened abroad.

In addition, Article 1649 *quater* A of the French Tax Code (*Code général des impôts*) provides that French resident or non-resident individuals must declare to the Customs authorities the cash and securities they import or export without the use of a financial institution when the value of such cash and securities exceeds €7,600.

## 9. Employment law

### 9.1 Are there any employment or local labour law issues which may arise as a result of the long-term incentive award? Are any consultations or authorisations required by law?

The main issue that may arise from an employment law perspective in connection with a long-term incentive award relates to the termination of the employment and its impact on the executive's rights to existing and non-vested options or free shares.

First and foremost, the rules of the plan should clearly stipulate the consequences of a termination of the executive's employment on his entitlement to existing and non-vested options and free shares. The employer should also, from the outset, seek confirmation from the employee that he has been adequately informed of such consequences. This requires, in particular, that the executive be provided with a copy of the rules of the plan.

Failing to do so may mean that the executive may try to bring a claim before French courts for the loss of his existing or non-vested options or shares in the event of termination.

A similar issue may arise upon unfair dismissal of the executive, whereby French courts have already ruled in the past that an employee should be indemnified for the loss of his options or free shares if such loss was the result of a termination without cause.

As a general principle of French law provided by Article L 432–1 of the Employment Code, it is compulsory to inform and consult the works council on questions relating to the organisation, management and operation of the business, and, in particular, on measures which may affect jobs and working conditions. In the event of share plans, the works council is informed and consulted when these plans concern a significant number of employees, are of a collective nature or concern a significant part of the share capital.

When the share plans are granted by a parent company, it seems that the works council of the company which employs the beneficiaries need not be consulted. Nevertheless, it should be noted that, given the generality of the obligation to inform and consult with the works council, it remains a grey area. Should a special sub-plan be set up for the French employees, it is advisable to ensure that the works council is informed and consulted prior to the finalisation of such sub-plan.

Non-compliance with the provisions relating to the powers of the works council constitutes a criminal offence (*"délit d'entrave"*) punishable by up to one year's imprisonment and/or a maximum fine of €3,750.

## 10. Translation

### 10.1 Are there any language restrictions in France? Does any of the documentation provided to the employee in relation to the long-term incentive award need to be translated?

French law does not specifically require that the documentation relating to long-term incentive awards is drafted in French. French courts have indeed ruled that a long-term incentive award is not part of the employment contract of the executive and therefore need not be drafted in French.

However, it is generally advisable in practice, in particular where the award is made to a significant number of employees (as opposed to a limited number of senior executives), to provide the employees with a French translation of the relevant documentation, to ensure that they have a clear understanding of the rules.

## 11. Data protection

### 11.1 Are there any data protection issues which may arise should the employer wish to outsource the administration of the long-term incentive award to a third party?

In general terms and pursuant to the Data Protection Act of January 6 1978, as amended by the laws of August 6 2004 and January 23 2006, the collection, processing and retention of personal data[4] must respect the following principles:[5]

- *Good faith:* all data must be collected in good faith and in a lawful manner.
- *The principle of the aim:* the data of a personal nature must only be collected and processed for a specific and legitimate use and must not be processed subsequently in a manner incompatible with such aims.
- *Proportionality:* the data must be adequate, relevant and not excessive given the aims for which it was collected. The treatment of the data must not unduly restrict the rights and freedoms of the persons in a manner disproportionate to the stated aims for collection of the data.
- *Keeping the information for a limited time:* the data must not be retained indefinitely; a fixed duration for retention of the data must be established depending on the aim of each file. By way of example, data may be retained for the length of an employee's employment if this relates to management of careers, five years for payroll purposes etc.

---

4     The expression "personal data" includes all information relating to an identified physical person or who could be identified, directly or indirectly, by reference to an identification number or other specific elements specific (eg name, registration number, telephone number, photograph etc).
The "processing of personal data" is defined as an operation or series of operations which relate to such data, whatever procedure is used and, in particular, the collection, recording, organisation, retention, adaptation or modification, extraction, consultation, use or communication by transmission, diffusion or any other form of means of access, approach or connection, as well as the passwording, deletion or destruction of such data.

5     These principles shall apply to the processing of personal data if the data controller is established on French territory, or if the data controller, although not established on French territory or in any other member state of the European Union, uses means of processing located on French territory (with the exception of processing used only for the purposes of transit through this territory).

- *Protection of data:* the employer is responsible for the processing of the data and, in this regard, has an obligation to protect such data: he must establish measures necessary to guarantee the confidentiality of the data.
- *Transparency:*
  - The relevant employees must be clearly informed of the identity of the person responsible for processing data (the person who determines the aims and means of the processing), the relevant objectives, whether the provision of data is mandatory or voluntary, the possible consequences of failing to respond to requests to provide data, the persons to whom data may be sent, whether the data may be transferred outside the EU and the means by which data subjects may have access to the data, and may amend and correct this.
  - The employee representative bodies must be consulted.
  - A prior declaration must be filed with the *Commission Nationale de l'Informatique et des Libertés* (CNIL) before personal data is processed. Processing personal data without respecting such prior formality is punishable by up to five years' imprisonment and a fine of €300,000. This can be increased to €1.5 million for corporate entities.
- *The transfer of data:* personal data may not be transferred to outside the EU other than to countries where the European Commission has recognised that a minimum level of protection for the private life, freedoms and fundamental rights of the data subjects is assured. As at today's date, the Commission has recognised Switzerland, Canada, Argentina, Guernsey, the Isle of Man and the US Safe Harbor programme as providing adequate protection. Nonetheless, the transfer of data to other countries may also be authorised by the CNIL under certain conditions.[6]

Failure to comply with the above-mentioned requirements is usually sanctioned by five years' imprisonment and a fine of €300,000. Civil sanctions may also be imposed, where relevant.

## 12. Source of shares

### 12.1 Does it matter if shares are newly issued to an employee, provided out of treasury or delivered from an employee benefit trust?

From a legal and tax perspective, the shares offered under a long-term incentive award may be either existing or newly issued shares.

As a general rule, the French tax authorities tend to be suspicious of foreign trusts (especially where they are located in low-tax jurisdictions) within the context of employee share plans. Where there are foreign legal requirements which justify the use of a trust (eg prohibition on a foreign company holding its own shares), they have admitted in the past, although not officially, that a trust may be used for the purpose of holding the shares offered under a foreign plan on behalf of the employees.

---

6    Subject to the company having put in place Internal Rules (Binding Corporate Rules) which each member of the Group must respect, which are approved by the CNIL, or by the relevant French companies and any other entity to which data may be transferred entering into a contract including model clauses approved by the European Commission for the transfer of data to another country.

# Germany

Thomas Müller-Bonanni
Michael Müntefering
Freshfields Bruckhaus Deringer

---

**Red flag issues**
1. No special tax advantages for long-term incentive awards.
2. Works councils may need to be involved in the implementation of the plan.

## 1. Securities laws

**1.1 What prospectus and/or securities law requirements arise in connection with the grant, vesting or exercise of a long-term incentive award or on the eventual sale of the shares by the executive?**

According to Section 3, para 1 of the German Prospectus Act (*Wertpapierprospektgesetz*) a prospectus must be made available on every public offer of securities unless an exemption is available.

Non-transferable instruments do not qualify as securities within this meaning (cf Section 2, item 1 of the Prospectus Act). Therefore, the granting of non-transferable share options does not trigger the prospectus requirement. However, the German regulator BaFin (*Bundesanstalt für Finanzdienstleistungsaufsicht*) holds the view that, upon the exercise of non-transferable share options, a public offer of the underlying shares may occur. Employers must ensure that an exemption is available on the exercise of the share options.

As the award of shares will normally qualify as a public offer of securities, a prospectus must be published unless an exemption is available. The mere fact that shares are solely granted to employees does not make the offer non-public. There is no official guidance on whether the award of shares on a provisional or forfeitable basis qualifies as a public offer of securities. Given that the award of shares on a provisional or forfeitable basis comes close to the granting of an option, however, it should be possible to argue that this is not the case. Under this approach there will normally be a public offer of securities when the shares vest.

The granting of equity-settled stock appreciation rights does not involve an offer of securities. Accordingly, a prospectus need not be made available.

**1.2 Is there an exemption from securities laws requirements either because the shares are being offered only to executives, or because shares are being offered to a distinct group of named individuals?**

There are a number of exemptions available that employers may rely on when operating share schemes in Germany. The most important exemptions are:

- the limited circle of investors exemption;
- the small-scale offer exemption; and
- the employee-offer exemption.

Under the limited circle of investors exemption (Section 3, para 2, item 2 of the Prospectus Act) a prospectus does not have to be made available if the public offer of securities is addressed to fewer than 100 non-qualified investors in every member state of the European Economic Area (EEA). Experience shows that administering share schemes under this exemption can be difficult in practice as it requires regular reviews of the number of scheme participants in all member states. Exceeding the limit of 99 non-qualified investors in any one member state means the exemption does not apply.

Under the small-scale offer exemption (Section 3, para 2, item 5 of the Prospectus Act), a prospectus is not needed where the purchase price for all securities offered is less than €100,000. Where the issuer's shares are already listed on a regulated market the threshold is €2.5 million (Section 1, para 2, item 4 of the Prospectus Act). These figures will be calculated over a 12-month period. From a practical point of view, these exemptions are rarely available for market-value options. However, they are normally available for free shares as the Prospectus Act looks at the purchase price for the shares, not their value.

Under the employee-offer exemption (Section 4, para 1, item 5 of the Prospectus Act) a prospectus should not be published if the shares are offered solely to active or former employees (including board members) of the issuer or a related company, provided that the issuer has securities registered on a regulated market. There is no official guidance on whether the employee exemption requires that the issuer has equity shares listed on a regulated market, or whether a listing of debt instruments is sufficient.

Under the employee exemption, an information document must be made available containing information on the number and type of securities which are offered and setting out the reasons and the details of the offer. This information document does not have to be (and cannot be) filed with the German regulator for approval. Careful drafting of the information document is crucial.

1.3 **If there is an exemption, will the exemption apply automatically or are there any applications/filings that need to be made?**

The aforementioned exemptions apply by operation of law. It is not necessary (or possible) to apply for an official ruling. However, the German regulator is normally open to a discussion of legal issues.

## 2. Employee tax and social security

2.1 **When will the executive be liable to tax or social security (and at what rate) in respect of the long-term incentive award?**

Taxes arise on the transfer of the economic ownership of the shares. The granting or vesting of market value options or nil-cost options is, therefore, not a taxable event. Similarly, a provisional or forfeitable allocation of shares is normally not a taxable event. Rather, taxes arise when the options are exercised or the provisional/forfeitable shares vest, more precisely when the shares are booked out of the company's share account.

With regard to market-value options, taxes will be calculated on the difference between the exercise price and the market value of the shares on the date of exercise. When the executive is given free shares, taxes will be calculated on the market value of the shares on the day of the share transfer. In both cases, a benefit of up to €135 may be tax-exempt.

Income tax is charged at progressive rates, currently ranging from 15% to 45%. In addition, a so-called solidarity surcharge amounting to 5.5% of the income taxes due (not of the taxable benefit) and, where applicable, church taxes (8 or 9% of the income taxes due) will be charged. Under certain circumstances (eg termination scenarios), the applicable income-tax rate may be reduced according to an income averaging rule for extraordinary income (*Fünftelungsregelung*).

In principle, the taxable benefit is also subject to social security contributions (old-age pension, unemployment, health and long-term care insurance). However, no social security contributions are due on income that exceeds certain threshold figures (so called *Beitragsbemessungsgrenze* – social security ceiling). The threshold figures for 2008 are €63,600 per year (in the former East Germany: €54,000 per year) for old-age pension and unemployment insurance, and €43,200 per year for health and long-term care insurance. No social security contributions are charged on income which is greater than this, so if the executive's employment income exceeds the threshold figures, the gain from the long-term incentive awards is not liable to social security contributions.

Social security contributions, if any, are split equally between the employer and the employee. The rates for 2008 (based on the taxable benefit and only up to the threshold figures) are:

- old age pension     19.9 %
- unemployment     3.3 %
- health     14.0 % (average)
- long -term care     1.7 %

Social security contributions, if any, are due at the same time as taxes (ie in the case of market-value options, when the shares are booked out of the company's share account).

2.2   **How will the executive's tax and social security be collected? Will the executive be responsible for paying any liabilities himself or will the executive's employer be responsible for paying tax or social security liabilities on the executive's behalf?**
The employer is obliged to withhold wage taxes from the cash remuneration paid to the executive and to transfer them to the tax authorities. Employers who do not (fully) comply with this obligation will be liable for the unpaid amount (secondary liability). In any event, the executive remains liable for any unpaid income tax and

must report any income in an annual tax return. Withheld wage taxes are then credited against the income tax due.

The employer is also obliged to withhold any social security contributions from the cash remuneration paid to the executive and to transfer them to the relevant authorities (Beitragseinzugsstelle).

### 2.3 If the employer is responsible for the executive's liabilities, can the employer withhold the liabilities from the executive's salary? Are there any formalities in this respect?

The employer is obliged to withhold wage taxes and social security contributions from the executive's salary (see above). There are no specific formalities with regard to share schemes. In general, the employer must report the wage taxes withheld to the tax authorities. The employer must also operate a payroll account for each employee, in which all data which is relevant for tax must be recorded. Similar obligations are in place with regard to social security contributions via the competent authority (the *Beitragseinzugsstelle*). In addition, the employer must record the social security contributions withheld and the underlying calculation for each employee, and keep the documents for inspection by the relevant authorities.

### 2.4 If the executive's salary in the month of exercise/release is not sufficient for the employer to withhold all of the liabilities, can the employer (or the parent company, if different) arrange for the executive to authorise to sell some of the executive's shares in the market and pass the money to the executive's employer?

Yes, it is common practice to authorise the employer to arrange for a partial sale of the executive's shares to satisfy the executive's tax and social security obligations. Most employee share plans also address the situation in which the executive does not have enough cash to pay for all of the shares at the time of exercise. In this case, most plans authorise the employer to sell that part of the shares which is sufficient to finance the exercise price.

Where the share plan does not provide for the possibility of selling part of the executive's shares to finance tax and social security liabilities, the executive must pay the outstanding amount to the employer. If the executive is unable to do this, the employer can avoid secondary liability for the outstanding amount by notifying the tax authorities that he was unable to withhold the relevant amounts.

### 2.5 Will the executive pay tax on the eventual sale of his shares and if so at what rate?

If the shares are acquired before January 1 2009, the capital gain derived from the sale of shares will only be taxable if (i) the executive sells the shares within one year after he received them; or (ii) he holds, or has held within the last five years prior to the sale, 1% or more of the issuer's capital. With regard to market value options, the capital gain is defined as the difference between the sale proceeds and the acquisition cost. The acquisition cost will be determined by reference to the exercise price and the amount which was taxed upon the exercise of the options.

Where capital gain taxation applies, only 50% of the capital gain will be subject to taxes. The tax rate for the taxable 50% of the capital gain is equal to the executive's individual income tax rate (plus solidarity surcharge and, where applicable, church tax). Thus, the maximum effective rate will be 22.5% (= 50% taxable × maximum income tax rate 45%) plus solidarity surcharge and, where applicable, church tax. However, capital gains are entirely exempt from taxation if all capital gains realised in one calendar year do not exceed €511.

If the shares are acquired in 2009 or later, the capital gain derived from the sale of shares will always be taxable. In principle, a flat tax rate of 25% (plus solidarity surcharge and, where applicable, church tax) applies, irrespective of how long the executive has held the shares. If the executive holds, or has held within the last five years prior to the sale, 1% or more of the issuer's capital, the applicable tax rate will be equal to the executive's individual income-tax rate (plus solidarity surcharge and, where applicable, church tax), although 40% of the capital gain is tax-exempt.

No social security contributions are due on the sale of shares.

## 3. Employer's social security

### 3.1 Is the employer liable to pay (on its own account) any employer's social security in connection with the long-term incentive award?

Technically, the employer is liable for all social security contributions. However, the employer has the right to take recourse against the employee for 50% of the social security contributions so that, ultimately, both the employer and the employee bear a 50% share.

### 3.2 Can the liability of the employer be put onto the employee? What steps are required?

It is not possible to shift the liability of the employer onto the employee.

## 4. Tax deduction for the employer

### 4.1 Is it possible for the employer to receive a tax deduction for the long-term incentive award? Would the employer need to be subject to recharge arrangements (eg if the employer is a subsidiary and provides funds to the parent company as part of a recharge arrangement for the long-term incentive award)?

It depends on the details of each case, (for instance on the source and the issuer of the shares) whether it is possible for the employer to receive a tax deduction for the long-term incentive award. The following statements can only provide a quick overview over the most common arrangements.

Where the employer grants long-term incentive awards to its own employees by issuing new shares, the prevailing view is that there is no tax deduction as the employer bears no costs (the costs of the grant are borne by the shareholders via the dilution effect). Where the employer grants treasury shares (ie shares acquired in a buy back) there will often be costs to the employer, especially if the purchase price is higher than the share option exercise price. However, it is unclear whether such costs are tax deductible or not as, in general, corporations cannot claim tax deductions for capital losses incurred from a sale of shares and there is no authority on whether or not this general rule also applies to long-term incentive awards.

Where long-term incentive awards are granted by the employer's parent company, the prevailing view is that, in the absence of a recharge agreement between the employing subsidiary and the parent company, there will be no tax deduction as the employer bears no costs. A recharge arrangement often improves the chances of the employer receiving a tax deduction. It should be noted, however, that the German tax authorities have established a complex set of rules that must be observed when drafting recharge agreements. Payments under inter-company agreements must be at arm's length, the recharge agreements must be in writing and they must normally be signed before the share scheme is implemented.

## 5. Tax beneficial arrangements

### 5.1 Are there any ways of making the long-term incentive award tax-efficient in Germany?

There is currently no favourable tax regime for share schemes in Germany. Depending on the circumstances, a tax-free amount of €135 may be available.

## 6. Internationally mobile executives

### 6.1 What are the income tax consequences for an employee who is resident in Germany when the long-term incentive award is made, but who is no longer resident at the time of exercise/vesting?

If an executive is no longer resident in Germany on the date of vesting and/or exercise, he will be liable to German income tax when exercising the options on a pro rata basis (ie for that proportion of the benefit that is attributable to the period of time the executive lived and worked in Germany). The reference period for this calculation is currently unclear. According to a ruling of the Federal Fiscal Court (*Bundesfinanzhof*) from 2001, the time between the grant and the exercise of the options shall serve as the reference period. However, the Federal Ministry of Finance (*Bundesfinanzministerium*) recently issued a paper which states that the time between the grant and the vesting of the options serves as the reference period. It remains to be seen whether the Federal Fiscal Court will follow this opinion.

Tax is due on the difference between the market value of the shares on the date of the exercise and the exercise price. Tax relief may be available if the employee exercises the option in a jurisdiction which has signed a double taxation agreement with Germany.

### 6.2 What are the social security consequences for an employee who is resident in Germany when the long-term incentive award is made, but who is no longer resident at the time of exercise/vesting?

If an executive is no longer resident in Germany on the date of vesting and/or exercise, he will only be liable to social security contributions when exercising the options if he is still subject to the German social security system. As a general rule, this is only the case if the executive is temporarily posted to another country and will return to Germany within a foreseeable period of time. If posted to another EU member state, the executive will normally remain in the German social security system if the anticipated duration of his posting does not exceed 12 months..

### 6.3 What are the tax and social security/withholding/reporting consequences for the employer in respect of an employee who is resident in Germany when the long-term incentive award is made, but who is no longer resident at the time of exercise/vesting?

When the executive exercises the options, the employer is obliged to withhold income tax with regard to the benefit that relates to the executive's work in Germany (see above). The employer must report the amount withheld and transfer it to the tax authorities.

Social security contributions are only payable if the executive is still subject to the German social security system at the time of exercise (see above). Where this is the case, the normal withholding process must be complied with.

## 7. Reporting requirements

### 7.1 Will the employer (or parent company, if different) have any reporting requirements as a result of the long-term incentive award?

The employer must report all wage taxes withheld to the tax authorities. Moreover, the employer must operate a payroll account for each employee in which all data which is of relevance for tax is to be recorded.

With regard to social security contributions, the employer must inform the competent authorities (*Beitragseinzugsstelle*) about the number of employees it has. In addition, the employer must keep records on the social security contributions withheld and the underlying calculation for each employee, and keep those records available for review by the relevant authorities..

### 7.2 Are there any tax rulings required in relation to the long-term incentive awards?

There is no obligation to apply for tax rulings in connection with long-term incentive awards. If the share scheme creates uncertainties with regard to German taxation, it is possible to apply for an advance tax ruling. Such rulings are subject to charges. Whether there is a need for an advance tax ruling should be decided on a case-by-case basis.

## 8. Exchange control issues

### 8.1 Are there any exchange control issues that would prevent an employee from (a) remitting monies abroad to purchase shares or (b) repatriating monies from the sale of shares?

There are no exchange control restrictions in Germany. However, if an executive who is resident in Germany remits abroad a sum of more than €12,500, the German

Central Bank (*Bundesbank*) must be informed. The same obligation arises where such an amount is transferred to the executive by a natural or legal person not resident in Germany. The relevant forms are normally available from the bank.

## 9.    Employment law

**9.1**    **Are there any employment or local labour law issues which may arise as a result of the long-term incentive award? Are any consultations or authorisations required by law?**

*(a)*    *Involvement of employee representative bodies*
If a company has a works council and the employees entitled to receive share options under the plan are not executives (*leitende Angestellte*) within the meaning of Section 5, para 3 of the Works Constitution Act (*Betriebsverfassungsgesetz*), the works council has a codetermination right. This means that, while a company is free to decide whether it wants to introduce a share plan, the works council must consent to the distribution criteria and other details of the plan. The company cannot implement the plan without the consent of the works council.

The works council has no codetermination right with regard to share plans/share plan rules relating to members of the board (*Vorstände/Geschäftsführer*) or executives (*leitende Angestellte*). If an executives' representative body (*Sprecherausschuss*) exists, the company must inform and consult with it, but does not need its consent to implement the plan.

If the share scheme is set up by a foreign (parent) company, the legal situation is unclear. The majority view is that there is no obligation to involve German employee representative bodies (unless the German subsidiary is involved in the administration of the plan). The works council has a right to information to ascertain the (non)-existence of its codetermination right.

*(b)*    *Business transfers*
In case of a business transfer, the employee's rights under the share option scheme do not transfer across to the buyer if the options are granted by a foreign parent company. The Federal Labour Court (*Bundesarbeitsgericht*) has held that such options granted by the foreign parent normally do not constitute remuneration and therefore are not part of the employment contract which transfers across. However, the employee will normally remain entitled to exercise vested options after the business transfer.

Where share options are not exercisable following a business sale or the sale of the subsidiary, the new employer is not obliged to set up an equivalent or comparable scheme. However, he may be required to pay cash compensation for the loss of options if they form a substantial part of the employee's remuneration. Court decisions in this area concern the loss of bonus payments rather than share options but indicate that if options form more than 15% to 20% of the employee's income, an obligation to compensate may arise.

## 10. Translation

### 10.1 Are there any language restrictions in Germany? Does any of the documentation provided to the employee in relation to the long-term incentive award need to be translated?

There is no legal obligation to provide documents in German. The information can therefore be given in English. However, translations should be made available where the addressees do not have an adequate command of the English language.

## 11. Data protection

### 11.1 Are there any data protection issues which may arise should the employer wish to outsource the administration of the long-term incentive award to a third party?

When the employer wishes to outsource the administration of the long-term incentive award he must ensure that the third party complies with data protection laws when processing the employees' personal data. This means that the contract between the employer and third party must be in writing and it should outline the purpose and scope of the data transfer.

If the plan administration is outsourced within Germany or to another country of the EU/EEA, the prevailing view among legal commentators is that the employee does not need to consent to the data transfer. If the plan administration is outsourced to a country outside the EU/EEA, stricter rules apply. In principle, a transfer of personal data to such a country is only permitted if that country has an adequate level of data protection. This will be assessed in light of the nature of the data, the purpose and duration of the proposed processing operation, the country of origin and country of final destination, as well as the rules of law, professional rules and security measures existing in that country.

Some countries are generally recognised as having an adequate level of protection (eg Switzerland and Hungary). However, this does not apply to the United States and data transfer to there is only permitted if:

- the third party subjects itself to the so-called Safe Harbor principles, which are recognised by both the EU Commission and the Federal Trade Commission as ensuring an adequate level of data protection;
- the third party enters into an agreement with the employer based on the EU's standard contractual clauses; or
- (in case of a data transfer within the company group) if there is a code of conduct which ensures an adequate level of data protection and is binding for all companies of the group.

The transfer of personal data to a country that has no adequate level of data protection is only permitted in certain cases (eg if the executive consents to the transfer).

## 12.    Source of shares

12.1    **Does it matter if shares are newly issued to an employee, provided out of treasury or delivered from an employee-benefit trust?**

In principle, the source of shares does not matter for the executive's taxation. Depending on the terms and conditions of an employee-benefit trust, the executive may be considered to be the economic owner of the shares held in trust, although the shares were not yet transferred to the executive.

From the employer's perspective, the source of shares may influence whether the employer can claim deductible expenses (see 4 above).

# India

**Aakash Choubey**
Khaitan & Co

---

**Red flag issues**
- Fringe benefit tax as a cost to the employer unless recharged to the employee.
- Uncertainty on employer tax deductions.
- Proportionate taxation in India of employees for the time spent in India during the life of the award.

---

## 1. Securities laws

### 1.1 What prospectus and/or securities law requirements arise in connection with the grant, vesting or exercise of a long-term incentive award or on the eventual sale of the shares by the executive?

There are no prospectus or securities law requirements in India where a foreign company grants long-term incentive awards to Indian employees (although there are restrictions on certain Indian companies making grants to their own employees).

The grant of long-term incentive awards to Indian executives is regulated by Indian foreign exchange laws. An Indian-resident employee or director of a foreign company, or of the Indian offices (branch or liaison or otherwise) of a foreign company, including an Indian subsidiary of a foreign company having a foreign holding of at least 51%, is permitted to acquire foreign securities in the foreign company pursuant to an employee stock option plan both under a "cashless" employee stock option scheme and by way of remittance from India for exercise of such options.

The concept of "foreign securities" under Indian law includes American Depository Receipts (ADRs) and Global Depository Receipts (GDRs) issued by an Indian company, including a subsidiary of a foreign company. Resident employees of Indian companies engaged in the "knowledge-based sectors" such as information technology, entertainment software, pharmaceuticals and biotechnology are permitted to acquire foreign securities issued under ADR/GDR-linked stock option schemes issued by Indian listed and unlisted companies under applicable Indian law, up to a prescribed purchase consideration threshold.

Foreign exchange laws permit the sale of securities acquired pursuant to long-term incentive awards provided that the sale proceeds are repatriated to India within 90 days.

Foreign employers can repurchase securities issued to Indian-resident executives in compliance with Indian foreign exchange laws, as long as the terms were documented to the Indian executives at the time of the grant of the long-term incentive awards.

**1.2    Is there an exemption from securities laws requirements either because the shares are being offered only to executives or because shares are being offered to a distinct group of named individuals?**

There are no prospectus or securities laws which would apply to the grant of long-term incentive awards. In relation to the foreign exchange laws noted above, there are no exemptions available.

## 2.    Employee tax and social security

**2.1    When will the executive be liable to tax or social security (and at what rate) in respect of the long-term incentive award?**

Fringe benefit tax (as detailed below) arises in respect of the long-term incentive award when shares are allotted or transferred to an employee. However, fringe benefit tax will be payable only on the difference between the exercise price (if any) and the fair market value of such shares on the date on which the long-term incentive award vests. Further, the concept of social security in relation to long-term incentives does not exist in India. It is pertinent to note that several recommendations have been made proposing amendments to the tax regime governing long-term employee incentives in India.

Issues relating to the taxation of long-term incentive awards have stimulated significant debate and interest. Since options are granted to employees in respect of shares at a predetermined price, there is an element of benefit accruing to employees at the time of exercise of options.

The (Indian) Finance Act 2005 introduced the concept of Fringe Benefit Tax (FBT), which was further amended in 2007 to be levied in respect of any specified security allotted or transferred free of cost or at a concessional rate to employees. These included options and free shares ("share incentives").

As regards the question of whether a foreign company is liable for FBT on share incentives allotted/transferred to employees of their subsidiaries in India, the Central Board of Direct Taxes (CBDT) has clarified that since share incentives are allotted or transferred to employees of an Indian subsidiary by virtue of their employment with the subsidiary company, the liability to pay FBT on such share incentives rests with the Indian subsidiary, not on the foreign company. Further, an Indian subsidiary is liable to FBT irrespective of whether or not there is a charge back of cost by its foreign holding company. However, CBDT circulars are not binding on taxpayers, so some ambiguity on the applicability of the clarification still exists.

*(a)    Tax rates*

FBT is payable at the rate of 30% (plus applicable surcharge and education levy) on the fringe benefit value. This is the fair market value of the share incentives on the date on which the option vests, but reduced by the amount actually paid by, or recovered from, an employee in respect of such share incentives. FBT is non-deductible for the employer for the purposes of taxation.

2.2 **How will the executive's tax and social security be collected? Will the executive be responsible for paying any liabilities himself or will the executive's employer be responsible for paying tax or social security liabilities on the executive's behalf?**

The primary responsibility for paying FBT rests with the employer. However, where share incentives are transferred or allotted to employee(s) on or after April 1 2007, the employer can recover such FBT from its employee(s). The employer can vary the agreement or scheme under which such share incentives have been allotted or transferred to recover FBT from an employee to the extent to which the employer is liable to pay FBT.

2.3 **If the employer is responsible for the executive's liabilities, can the employer withhold the liabilities from the executive's salary? Are there any formalities in this respect?**

Where payment of FBT is not the employee's liability, the question of withholding the liability from an employee's salary does not arise. However, if the employer opts to recover this amount from its employee and an employee does not pay, then the employer can resort to withholding such tax liability from that employee's salary, depending on company policy.

2.4 **If the executive's salary in the month of exercise/release is not sufficient for the employer to withhold all of the liabilities, can the employer (or the parent company, if different) arrange for the executive to authorise the sale of some of the executive's shares in the market and pass the money to the executive's employer?**

Where the employer is responsible for paying FBT, it cannot arrange for an employee to authorise the sale of his shares in the market and pass the money to the employer. However, if the employer chooses to recover the FBT from an employee, then the employer can use these methods, depending on company policy.

2.5 **Will the executive pay tax on the eventual sale of his shares and if so at what rate?**

Under the Tax Act, any gain arising from transfer of a capital asset, such as shares, is subject to capital gains tax. The gain will generally be based on the sale proceeds. However, where shares are transferred under a gift or irrevocable trust by an employee, the market value of the shares at the date of such gift or irrevocable trust will be treated as the full consideration received or accruing as a result of the transfer. The rate of capital gains tax will depend on the period for which such shares have been held by the employee prior to transfer (the "holding period"). If this is less than 12 months and an employee realises a capital gain on such a transfer, there will be a short-term capital gains tax at the rate of 15% for listed companies (increased by applicable surcharge and educational levy), where it arises from the sale of shares of a company listed on a stock exchange and is subject to a securities transaction tax of 0.125% on the value of the transaction, and at normal slab rates for unlisted companies. If the holding period is more than 12 months and an employee realises a capital gain on the transfer, there will be no long-term capital gains tax. A securities transaction tax will be paid by listed companies (if the sale is made on the floor of the stock exchange), while unlisted companies will pay a 20% long-term gains tax.

As the employer and employee are treated as separate taxpayers in India, and the liability for FBT remains with the employer (although it may be recovered from the employee), the employee will not receive any credit under Indian tax law for the FBT when he sells the shares. Further, the Indian tax authorities do not allow credit for tax paid by an employee in any international jurisdiction. In view of the Finance Bill 2008 (which comes into effect on April 1 2008), the Government of India has proposed that FBT recovered from employees in the case of stock options will be deemed as tax paid by the employee. This could enable an expatriate to claim credit for the FBT paid on stock options against his tax liability in his home country, although it remains unclear whether an Indian employee will be able to offset these amounts against capital gains taxable in India.

## 3.    Employer's social security

Indian laws do not provide for any employer's social security.

## 4.    Tax deduction for the employer

### 4.1    Is it possible for the employer to receive a tax deduction in respect of the long-term incentive award? Would the employer need to be subject to recharge arrangements (eg if the employer is a subsidiary and provides funds to the parent company as part of a recharge arrangement in respect of the long-term incentive award)?

There are two views on the question of whether an employer can claim a tax deduction in respect of long-term incentive awards. One view is that since the expense of a long-term incentive award is charged to the income statement of the employer on a notional basis based on either intrinsic value or fair value (both of which are without actual cash outflow), such expense is not tax deductible. Another view, which has been taken by the Indian income tax tribunals, is that, as the grant of options is an ascertained expenditure, not being contingent on various factors, it is tax deductible. Considering that there is no binding ruling in this regard, this issue needs a definitive clarification from the Ministry of Finance, India.

## 5.    Tax beneficial arrangements

### 5.1    Are there any ways of making the long-term incentive award tax-efficient in India?

Considering that tax laws relating to long-term incentive awards are in their nascent stage, there are no definitive ways of making such awards tax efficient.

## 6. Internationally mobile executives

**6.1 What are the income tax consequences for an employee who is resident in India when the long-term incentive award is made, but who is no longer resident at the time of exercise/vesting?**

Where an employee has been based in India at any time during the period beginning with the grant of the long-term incentive award and ending with the date of vesting ("grant period"), irrespective of the location of an employee at the time of grant or vesting, a proportionate amount of the value of the fringe benefit is liable to FBT. The proportionate amount is determined by applying to the value of the fringe benefit the proportion which the length of the period of stay in India by an employee during the grant period bears to the length of the grant period.

**6.2 What are the social security consequences for an employee who is resident in India when the long-term incentive award is made, but who is no longer resident at the time of exercise/vesting?**

Social security does not exist in relation to long-term incentives in India.

**6.3 What are the tax and social security withholding/reporting consequences for the employer in respect of an employee who is resident in India when the long-term incentive award is made, but who is no longer resident at the time of exercise/vesting?**

Under the Tax Act, an employee is not liable to pay FBT. However, the employer can recover any tax it has paid from its employee.

## 7. Reporting requirements

**7.1 Will the employer (or parent company, if different) have any reporting requirements as a result of the long-term incentive award?**

Indian companies that are subsidiaries of a foreign company which is making awards to Indian employees must make an annual statement to the Reserve Bank of India (RBI) about: (a) the number of securities allotted; (b) the number of employees or directors who accepted securities; and (c) the amount which is remitted from India for the acquisition of such securities. The Indian subsidiary must also inform the RBI about the level of the foreign company's shareholdings and must make an annual statement concerning the repurchase of securities by their foreign parent companies from their Indian employees or directors.

Where long-term incentives are granted by a foreign parent company to employees of its Indian subsidiary, the Indian subsidiary is required to disclose the costs incurred in the "Notes to the Accounts" of its financial statements. In the event that the subsidiary reimburses the costs incurred by its parent in relation to the grant of the long-term incentive award, the Indian company must disclose those payments, as applicable, in the "Notes to the Accounts" of its respective financial statements.

**7.2   Are any tax rulings required in relation to the long-term incentive awards?**
No tax rulings are required under Indian law.

## 8.   Exchange control issues

**8.1   Are there any exchange control issues that would prevent an employee from (a) remitting monies abroad to purchase shares, or (b) repatriating monies from the sale of shares?**
Previously, persons resident in India were permitted to acquire foreign securities issued by a company incorporated outside India using either a cashless exercise facility, where the acquisition does not involve any remittance from India, or by limiting the amount which could be remitted from India. However, over the years the Reserve Bank of India has liberalised the rules relating to the acquisition of foreign securities by resident individuals who are either employees or directors of an Indian office or branch of a foreign company in which foreign holding is not less than 51%. It is now possible for such individuals to acquire foreign securities under a share option scheme without any monetary limit.

Where a cashless exercise facility is made available, the foreign company may itself fund, or permit an empanelled stock broker(s) to fund, the payment of the exercise price, which is adjusted against the sale proceeds of some or all of the shares.

Indian law further permits Indian-resident individuals who are either employees or directors of an Indian office or branch of a foreign company in which the foreign holding is not less than 51% to sell foreign securities acquired under a long-term incentive scheme without any monetary limit, provided the proceeds from the sale of such foreign securities are repatriated to India.

## 9.   Employment law

**9.1   Are there any employment or local labour law issues which may arise as a result of the long-term incentive award? Are any consultations or authorisations required by law?**
There is no such requirement under Indian law.

## 10.   Translation

**10.1   Are there any language restrictions in India? Does any of the documentation provided to the employee in relation to the long-term incentive award need to be translated into English?**
There is no such requirement under Indian law.

## 11.    Data protection

11.1    **Are there any data protection issues which may arise should the employer wish to outsource the administration of the long-term incentive award to a third party?**

There is no statutory data protection legislation in India and, therefore, no such issues may arise under Indian laws.

## 12.    Source of shares

12.1    **Does it matter if shares are newly issued to an employee, provided out of treasury, or delivered from an employee-benefit trust?**

Where shares of a foreign parent company are acquired by employees in India, there are no restrictions on how these shares are delivered. If a trust structure is used, the accounts of the employer are required to be prepared on the same basis as if the trust was not being used.

*Aakash acknowledges the valuable guidance and contributions of his colleagues, Daksha Bakshi, Rabindra Jhunjhunwala and Tarunya Krishnan, for his chapter.*

# Ireland

Emily Ennis
Marie Griffin
Stephen Hegarty
Arthur Cox

---

> **Red flag issues**
> 1. When an offer of shares is made to executives, consideration should be given to whether the offer of shares will benefit from an exemption from the obligations to publish a prospectus relating to the offer of shares.
> 2. Executives may be liable to pay tax and file a tax return within 30 days of the exercise of a right to acquire shares.

## 1.    Securities laws

1.1    **What prospectus and/or securities law requirements arise in connection with the grant, vesting or exercise of a long-term incentive award or on the eventual sale of shares by the executive?**

*(a)*    *Prospectus requirements*

The Prospectus (Directive 2003/71/EC) Regulations 2005 (SI 324 of 2005) (the "Prospectus Regulations") implemented Directive 2003/71/EC (the "Prospectus Directive") which requires a prospectus to be published and the Financial Regulator to be notified when securities are to be offered to the public or admitted to trading. The Prospectus Regulations regulate offers of securities to the public and are enforced by the Irish Financial Services Regulatory Authority. An offer of securities to the public is defined as a communication to persons in any form and by any means that presents enough information on the securities and the offer terms to enable an investor to decide whether to purchase or to subscribe for these securities. When shares are offered to employees under employee share schemes, the Prospectus Regulations must be considered.

*(b)*    *Market-value options*

Options granted to executives which are non-transferable are not subject to the Prospectus Directive requirements as these only apply to transferable securities. The Committee of European Securities Regulators have agreed that non-transferable options granted to employees do not constitute an offer of securities to the public and are thus outside the requirements of the Prospectus Regulations.

### (c) Free shares

Where securities are offered free of charge, a prospectus is not required provided that there is no element of choice (including no right to repudiate the allocation) on the part of the recipient. Where an offer of free shares is made and the recipient decides whether to accept the offer, then the offer is for zero consideration and will fall within the excluded offers. These are also subject to the exemption for offers of less than €100,000 (see further below) and no prospectus would be required. However, if shares are expressly offered in the place of quantifiable financial benefits in another form then this may disguise a "hidden" consideration, which might restrict the availability of the exemption.

### (d) Securities requirements

A director of an Irish company will be required to notify his award to the company within five business days of the date of grant in accordance with the requirements of Part IV of the Companies Act 1990. He will also be required to notify any assignment or termination of the interest or right in shares within five business days of such an event. The notifications must then be maintained by the company in a register which is open to inspection by the public. The details will also need to be disclosed in the Irish company's accounts. If the company's shares are listed on a regulated market, this notification must be made within four days by the directors and any senior executives who are designated by the company as persons who discharge a managerial responsibility.

If the value of the shares to be acquired by any director of an Irish company or subsidiary could exceed €63,490 (or 10% of the relevant net assets of the local company), and the Irish company is to discharge the cost of providing shares in respect of the grant, it is recommended that the grant of the options should be approved in advance by an ordinary resolution of the shareholders of the local Irish subsidiary for the purposes of Section 29 of the Companies Act 1990. Ideally, the approval should occur prior to the date of grant, although any time up to a reasonable period after the date of exercise is also sufficient.

**1.2    Is there an exemption from securities laws requirements either because the shares are being offered only to executives or because shares are being offered to a distinct group of named individuals?**

An employer is exempt from requirements of the Prospectus Regulations for the public offer of securities if it offers shares in a company that already has securities admitted to trading on an EEA-regulated market. In such cases, the company need only make available a document containing information on the number and nature of the shares and the reasons for, and details of, the offer. Alternatively, the employer may rely on any of the following exceptions from the obligation to publish a prospectus:

- the offer is made to fewer than 100 people; or
- the total price of the offer of securities, together with the price of any other shares offered in the 12 months preceding the offer, is equal to at least €100,000, but does not exceed €2.5 million, and is accompanied by a local

offer document. The figure of €2.5 million is for the offer of shares by the relevant entity Europe-wide. In most cases companies with operations in several European countries who put equity-based compensation arrangements in place in Ireland ensure that the shares are offered by the local Irish subsidiary or trustee, rather than by a European/US parent company, as this kind of offer is more likely to exceed the threshold. Two or more separate companies (such as a US parent and a local subsidiary) could make separate offers so that a €2.5 million limit applied to each; or

- the total consideration paid for shares offered under the scheme in any 12-month period is less than €100,000; or
- the offer of securities is addressed to investors and the minimum consideration payable is at least €50,000 per investor for each separate offer; or
- the securities being offered have a denomination per unit of at least €50,000.

## 1.3 If there is an exemption, will the exemption apply automatically or are there any applications/filings that need to be made?

The exemptions apply automatically however, where the offer expressly limits the total consideration paid for shares (when aggregated with the consideration for all previous offers of securities of the same type made in the 12 months preceding the offer) to less than €2.5 million, then Irish law requires that a "local offer document" is made available and that it is registered in the Companies Registration Office prior to, or simultaneous with, it being "made available". The local offer document is a short-form document setting out particulars in relation the offer together with certain other informational requirements and health warning and restrictions set out in Regulation 8(1)(h) and Section 49 of the Investment Companies (Miscellaneous Provisions) Act 2005.

## 2. Employee tax and social security

## 2.1 When will the executive be liable to tax or social security (and at what rate) in respect of the long-term incentive award?

*(a)* *Approved share option schemes*

Irish legislation currently provides favourable tax treatment for Revenue-approved employee share schemes. However, these schemes must apply to all employees in the company in order to benefit from favourable tax treatment. Every participant must participate in the scheme on similar terms and the award of shares or share options under the scheme must be based on objective criteria. Under a Revenue-approved profit-sharing scheme or share-option scheme, there is no charge to income tax or social security on receipt of the shares or the exercise of the option provided the shares are held for a period of not less than three years between the date of the grant and the date of the disposal of the shares. The relevant conditions imposed by Revenue must be complied with. Capital gains tax (CGT) will be payable on the amount of any gain realised on the disposal of the shares.

**(b)** *Market value options – unapproved share option schemes*

Where a share option scheme is not approved by the Irish Revenue Commissioners, income tax will be due on the exercise of the options based on the difference between the option price and the market value of the shares at the date of exercise. Any income tax due must be paid by the individual within 30 days of the date of exercise of the option at the higher rate of income tax (currently 41%) (unless permission is granted by the Irish Revenue Commissioners to apply the standard rate of tax (currently 20%)). The employee must also file a special return (Form RTS01), reporting details of the exercise within 30 days of the exercise of the share options.

Where a share option is capable of being exercised more than seven years after grant, the Revenue Commissioners reserve the right to tax the individual on the grant of the option. The individual is taxed on the difference between the market value of the shares at the date of grant and the price payable on exercise of the option. The individual will be entitled to offset the income tax paid on the grant of the right against any income tax payable when the option is exercised.

The grant and exercise of share options by employees does not give rise to any other tax charge, nor is it subject to PRSI/Health Levy. However, when the employee sells the shares, he may be liable to CGT on any gain he makes.

**(c)** *Free shares*

An executive may be liable to tax under the self-assessment system for free shares. This means that an individual must file an income tax return containing details of the benefit, and must also pay income tax (at the individual's marginal rate (currently 20%/41%)) in respect of the market value of the benefit.

If executives receive free shares under a scheme which prevents the immediate disposal of the shares, then an abatement of the income tax charge may be available in the year in which the shares are acquired. The abatement ranges from 10% discount for one-year clog (ie the number of years prohibiting disposal) to a maximum 55% discount for a clog in excess of five years. For this treatment to apply, the prohibition on disposal must be absolute and imposed for genuine commercial reasons (such as securities law considerations). It will only apply to a grant of shares made in the employer company or the parent company.

The company also has an obligation to provide details of the benefits to the Revenue.

**2.2 How will the executive tax and social security be collected? Will the executive be responsible for paying any liabilities himself or will the executive's employer be responsible for paying tax or social security liabilities on the executive's behalf?**

The employer is not required to withhold any tax or social security contributions in relation to benefits in the form of shares, provided the shares are received by the executive in the company in which the executive holds his employment or a company which has control of the employer company.

Employees are obliged to account for income tax due on the exercise of options under the self-assessment system and are obliged to file an income tax return and to pay any income tax due by a specified date.

If shares are issued to the executive partly paid, the amount left outstanding is treated as a preferential loan from the employer and will be subject to tax. The company will be obliged to deduct income tax (under the PAYE system) and social security contributions (PRSI/Health Levy).

The Irish employer is required to provide information to the Irish Inspector of Taxes regarding the grant, assignment and release of rights or allotment of shares or options. This reporting is done on a special disclosure form (Form S02) which must be submitted on or before March 31 following the end of the tax year. If requested by the Revenue Commissioners, share awards must be reported through the submission of Form P11D.

**2.3** **If the employer is responsible for the executive's liabilities, can the employer withhold the liabilities from the executive's salary? Are there any formalities in this respect?**

The employer is not responsible for any income tax payable by the executive as a result of the executive exercising his share options.

**2.4** **If the executive's salary in the month of exercise/release is not sufficient for the employer to withhold all the liabilities, can the employer (or the parent company, if different) arrange for the executive to authorise to sell some of the executives shares in the market and pass the money to the executive's employer.**

See the answer to 2.3 above.

The employee's shares could only be sold if the executive gave his consent, or it was expressly provided for in the rules of the Scheme.

**2.5** **Will the executive pay tax on the eventual sale of his shares and if so, at what rate?**

If the employee is resident and domiciled in Ireland, CGT is charged currently at 20% on any gain made from selling the shares. CGT is also payable regardless of where the executive is resident if the shares derive the greater part of their value from land or minerals located in Ireland. The amount of the gain chargeable is the excess of the market value of the shares at the time of disposal over the cost of acquisition of the shares. The acquisition cost is the total amount paid by the employee or executive for the shares, including any income tax paid on the grant. An individual is entitled to receive a gain of €1,270 free from CGT each year.

**3.** **Employer's social security**

**3.1** **Is the employer liable to pay (on its own account) any employer's social security in connection with the long-term incentive award?**

Neither exercise of an option nor the vesting of an award will trigger any liability on the part of the employer to pay employer's pay-related social insurance (PRSI). The matching share award is regarded as a benefit-in-kind for tax purposes, but no social security charge (PRSI) arises for the employer in connection with free shares or matching shares under a long-term incentive award. However, the employer must report the award of shares and exercise and grant of share options to the Revenue Commissioners on the relevant annual return form.

**3.2    Can the liability of the employer be put onto the employee? What steps are required?**

Not applicable.

## 4.    Tax deduction for the employer

**4.1    Is it possible for the employer to receive a tax deduction for the long-term incentive award? Would the employer need to be subject to recharge arrangements (eg if the employer is a subsidiary and provides funds to the parent company as part of a recharge arrangement in respect of the long-term incentive award)?**

A corporation tax deduction is available for expenditure incurred by the company on the acquisition of shares at an arm's length price and also for arm's length payments to connected companies for the issue of shares. A corporation tax deduction is also available for expenditure incurred or payments made to a connected company by the company in connection with the right to receive shares, provided such expenditure is incurred for bona fide commercial purposes.

An employer will not be entitled to claim a corporation tax deduction for contributions made to employee-benefit schemes until such contributions become liable to tax in the hands of its employees/directors. Exceptions are made for certain approved employee share schemes or pension plans, as well as accident benefit schemes.

## 5.    Tax beneficial arrangements

**5.1    Are there any ways of making the long-term incentive award tax-efficient in Ireland?**

As noted above, favourable tax treatment is available for certain employee-share schemes which have received the approval of the Revenue Commissioners in Ireland. These schemes apply to all employees of the company. Every employee must participate in the scheme on similar terms and the award of shares or share options under the scheme must be based on objective criteria (eg shares or rights attaching to share options must be allocated on the basis of objective conditions such as length of service or level of remuneration). In limited instances, an approved share option scheme may contain an element providing benefits or incentives for key employees with terms which are dissimilar to those applicable to other employees. However, this element of a share option scheme must only be an adjunct to a main share option scheme which is applicable to all employees.

## 6.    Internationally mobile executives

6.1    **What are the income tax consequences for an employee who is resident in Ireland when the long-term incentive award is made, but who is no longer resident at the time of exercise or vesting?**

If an employee receives a grant of a share option while resident in Ireland, and subsequently moves to a country with which Ireland has a double taxation treaty prior to exercise of that option, that employee will remain within the charge to Irish tax for the proportion of the gain made which relates to the discharge of the duties of the employment in Ireland. The Revenue Commissioners will examine the period of employment during which the employee held the right and the period of time will depend on the individual facts and circumstances of each case and the terms and conditions under which the executive received the right. They would then generally apportion the total number of working days during the relevant period of employment between those spent working in Ireland and those spent working abroad, and the relevant proportion of the gain relating to the time spent working in Ireland will be regarded as subject to Irish tax.

If the resident executive exercises the right in a country that does not have a double taxation treaty with Ireland, the Irish Revenue Commissioners have indicated that they would assert taxing rights on the entire benefit derived from exercise of the option. The executive can deduct any foreign tax paid from the benefit.

6.2    **What are the social security consequences for an employee who is resident in Ireland when the long-term incentive award is made, but is no longer resident at the time of exercise/vesting?**

Social security (PRSI/Health Levy) is not payable on share options/share awards. See the answer to 6.1 above.

6.3    **What are tax and social security/withholding/reporting consequences for the employer in respect of an employee who is resident in Ireland when the long-term incentive award is made but is no longer resident at the time of exercise/vesting?**

See the answer to 6.1 above.

## 7.    Reporting requirements

7.1    **Will the employer (or parent company, if different) have any reporting requirements as a result of the long-term incentive award?**

The employer must report both the grant and the exercise of share options or share awards to the Revenue Commissioners by March 31 in the year of assessment following the year of grant and/or exercise. The relevant reporting form contains details of the names of the employees as well as Revenue and social insurance numbers of employees to whom options or share awards are granted and those employees who have exercised options/awards during the year. Certain details on the terms and conditions relating to the award of shares are also required.

**7.2   Are there any tax rulings required in relation to the long-term incentive awards?**

A tax ruling is not required in relation to unapproved long-term incentive awards. If the share scheme is to be approved by the Revenue Commissioners for favourable tax treatment, then formal approval will be required.

## 8.   Exchange control issues

**8.1   Are there any exchange control issues that would prevent an employee from (a) remitting monies abroad to purchase shares, or (b) repatriating monies from the sale of shares?**

There are no general currency restrictions in force. However, dealing with certain countries (such as those subject to EU or UN embargoes) is restricted. Therefore, in these cases it is prudent to check that no prohibition applies.

## 9.   Employment law

**9.1   Are there any employment or local labour law issues which may arise as a result of the long-term incentive award? Are any consultations or authorisations required by law?**

Where a share scheme is operated on a consistent basis over a number of years it may be regarded as part of the employment environment of the company, so if a business or undertaking of the employer is ever transferred to a new company in circumstances which are subject to the transfer of undertaking regulations, then it may be necessary to replicate the scheme.

If there is a collective agreement with the trade union which requires consultation before any change can be made to remuneration arrangements, then the employer must consult with the employee representatives. Otherwise the employer has no consultation obligations.

## 10.   Translation

**10.1   Are there any language restrictions in Ireland? Does any of the documentation provided to the employee in relation to the long-term incentive award need to be translated?**

If participation in the scheme is part of the executive's terms and conditions of employment, the executive will have a right to have the scheme documentation made available to him in English. Where it is not part of his terms and conditions of employment, an English translation is recommended to avoid any uncertainty/disputes.

## 11.   Data protection

**11.1   Are there any data protection issues which may arise should the employer wish to outsource the administration of the long-term incentive award to a third party?**

Under Ireland's Data Protection Acts 1988 and 2003, the employer and/or the administrator will come within the category of a "data controller" (ie a person who, either alone or with others, controls the contents and use of personal data). A data controller is subject to the data protection responsibilities set out in the legislation and is required to register with the Data Protection Commissioner in Ireland.

The Acts provide that personal data may only be collected for specified, explicit and legitimate purposes and the personal data must be accurate, relevant and not excessive. The transfer of personal data to a third party (including another group company or share plan administrator) for commercial purposes (including for the purpose of administering a share plan) is a legitimate cause. However, those persons whose data is transferred are entitled to object to the transfer. For this reason written consent should be obtained from the employee prior to the transfer of data and preferably sought and obtained at the time of collection of the data.

The legislation also restricts the transfer of data outside the European Economic Area. Under these restrictions, the transfer of personal data to outside the European Union is allowed only if the country ensures an adequate level of protection or if other requirements are fulfilled. These restrictions do not apply where the data subject has given consent to the transfer of personal data. In seeking such consent, the employee should be asked unambiguously to give his or her consent to the transfer of personal data to all relevant parties and specify to what extent the file supervisor has access to such data.

## 12. Source of shares

### 12.1 Does it matter if shares are newly issued to an employee, provided out of treasury or delivered from an employee-benefit trust?

Unlike the general allotment of shares in the company, shareholder approval is not required to allot shares in pursuance of an employee share scheme provided the company has sufficient authorised share capital. Furthermore, shares which will be issued in pursuance of an employee share scheme are not subject to the usual statutory pre-emption requirements.

If a company reissues treasury shares, the Companies Act 1990 requires the shareholders to approve maximum and minimum price ranges before the shares can be reissued. Companies listed on the Official List of the Irish Stock Exchange or on the Irish Enterprise Exchange of the Irish Stock Exchanges may also be subject to additional rules and notification requirements. For example, the Listing Rules of the Irish Stock Exchange restrict the sale or transfer of treasury shares during specified periods and require the company to send an official notification to the Exchange of certain transactions, such as sales or transfers for an employee share scheme.

There may also be accounting advantages if shares in respect of an employee share scheme are sourced from purchased shares.

# Malaysia

Phua Pao Yii
Skrine

---

> **Red flag issues**
> 1. There are no major hindrances or obstacles in respect of the implementation of an employee share scheme in Malaysia.

## 1. Securities laws

**1.1 What prospectus and/or securities law requirements arise in connection with the grant, vesting or exercise of a long-term incentive award or on the eventual sale of the shares by the executive?**

The main legislation pertaining to employee share schemes is the new Capital Markets and Services Act 2007 (CMSA) which came into force on September 28 2007.

Under Section 212 of the CMSA, the prior approval of the Securities Commission must be obtained before any person may "make available, offer for subscription or purchase, or issue an invitation to subscribe for or purchase *securities* in Malaysia".

The term "securities" has been defined to include shares of overseas companies and therefore the requirement for Securities Commission approval under the CMSA would extend to the shares of an overseas company.

However, the CMSA provides that:
- the making available of, offering for subscription or purchase of, or making an invitation to subscribe for or purchase, securities of a company pursuant to an employee share or employee share option scheme is exempt from the requirement to obtain the approval of the Securities Commission;
- an offer or invitation made to employees or directors of a company or its related company pursuant to an employee share or employee share option scheme would be an "excluded offer" or an "excluded invitation", which is exempt from various provisions pertaining to prospectus requirements under the CMSA; and
- the issue of securities which are acquired by employees or directors of a company or its related company pursuant to an employee share or employee share option scheme would be an "excluded issue", which is exempt from various provisions pertaining to prospectus requirements under the CMSA.

**1.2 Is there an exemption from securities laws requirements either because the shares are being offered only to executives or because shares are being offered to a distinct group of named individuals?**

The exemption from securities law requirements (specifically the requirement to obtain the approval of the Securities Commission and the requirement to comply with prospectus requirements) applies to "an issue of securities which are acquired by employees or directors of a company or its related company pursuant to an employee share or employee share option scheme".

It is to be noted, however, that there is no definition of the term "employee share or employee share option scheme" in the CMSA.

Interestingly, the term "directors" includes non-executive directors who, by definition, are not employees.

**1.3    If there is an exemption, will the exemption apply automatically or are there any applications/filings that need to be made?**

The exemption applies automatically. There is no need for an overseas company or its Malaysian subsidiary to make any application/filings.

Public limited companies in Malaysia operating employee share schemes and employee share option schemes are no longer required to obtain the approval of the Securities Commission. However, in the case of public limited companies in Malaysia which are listed on Bursa Malaysia, regulatory parameters governing proposals on employee share schemes and employee share option schemes are administered by Bursa Malaysia.

*(a)    Information memorandum*

If an overseas company issues an information memorandum in relation to the grant of its shares or its options, it must deposit a copy of the information memorandum with the Securities Commission within seven days after it is first issued. There is, however, no requirement to prepare an information memorandum.

The term "information memorandum" is not defined in the CMSA. The form of the information memorandum is also not prescribed by the CMSA and its regulations. The only guidance, under Sections 229 and 230 of the CMSA, as to what constitutes an "information memorandum" is that it is a document issued by a person that describes the business and affairs of the person and is in respect of an "excluded offer" or an "excluded invitation" or an "excluded issue". A document providing information to employees in relation to the grant of shares or options *per se* would not constitute an information memorandum unless the document issued by the person also describes the business and affairs of the person.

**2.    Employee tax and social security**

**2.1    When will the executive be liable to tax or social security (and at what rate) in respect of the long-term incentive award?**

*(a)    Tax*

The grant of an award/option to acquire shares pursuant to an employee share scheme would be deemed by the Inland Revenue Board (IRB) as a "perquisite", which would be taxable in the hands of the employee at progressive rates of income tax (currently from nil to 28%). The term "perquisite" refers to benefits that are convertible into money and which are received by an employee from the employer or third party in respect of the employment.

From the year of assessment 2006, for the purposes of income tax where an employee acquires any right to acquire shares in a company, the value of the benefit to be included in the employee's gross income is based on the difference between the market price on the date the share option is exercisable or exercised, whichever is lower, and the discounted price offered by the employer. This is as follows:

- in a case where the right must be exercised, assigned, released or acquired *on a specified date*, the market value of the shares on that specified date; or
- in a case where the right can be exercised, assigned, released or acquired *within a specified period*, the market value of the shares on the first day of that period; or
- the market value of the shares on the date of the exercise, assignment, release or acquisition of the right, whichever is lower, less the amount paid for the shares.

For purposes of the above, "market value" means:

- in the case of a company listed on the Malaysian Stock Exchange (ie Bursa Malaysia), the average of the highest and lowest price of the shares for that day; or
- in any other case, the net asset value of the shares for the day.

*(b)*     *Social security*

Under the Employees' Provident Fund Act 1991 (EPF Act), the employees' provident fund (EPF) contribution is a form of compulsory pension contribution (for the benefit of the employee) by both the employer and the employee. The amount of monthly contribution which every employer and employee is liable to pay is set out in the Third Schedule to the EPF Act, and is based on the amount of wages or salary paid to the employee. However, perquisites are not normally brought into the calculation of wages or salary for the purposes of calculating EPF contributions by either the employer or employee.

The EPF Board has indicated that benefits arising from an employee share scheme or an employee share option scheme do not fall within its scope and are not subject to EPF contributions.

Under the Employees' Social Security Act 1969 (SOCSO Act), the employees' social security (SOCSO) contribution is a form of compulsory contribution (for the benefit of the employee) by both the employer and the employee and is paid to the Social Security Organisation. The monthly contributions are paid at the rate specified in the Third Schedule to the SOCSO Act, which are determined in accordance with the wages of the employee.

"Perquisites" are not normally brought into the calculation of "wages" for the purposes of calculating SOCSO contributions by either the employer or employee so that in practice a liability to SOCSO contributions (in respect of the perquisites) will not arise.

**2.2    How will the executive's tax and social security be collected? Will the executive be responsible for paying any liabilities himself or will the executive's employer be responsible for paying tax or social security liabilities on the executive's behalf?**

The value of taxable benefits received by an employee must be reported by his employer on Form EA. This is issued by the employer at the end of each year. The employee should declare this amount as part of his employment income in his income tax return, which currently must be filed by April 30 of a calendar year for income received in the previous calendar year.

*(a)    Employee's responsibilities*

The employee is required to:

- report in his tax return the amount in respect of benefits from the award/option that have been exercised;
- make an assessment by including the benefit as stated above as income from employment for the basis period in which that benefit is offered; and
- ensure that income tax on the benefit is paid:
  - by deductions from remuneration under the Schedular Tax Deductions scheme ("STD scheme") in the month the option is exercised or that total tax is paid by instalments based on the STD scheme; or
  - on furnishing the tax return. Nevertheless, the employee can arrange with the IRB to pay the amount of tax owing by way of instalments, in which case the employer is required to comply with the directive issued by the IRB.

*(b)    Employer's responsibilities*

Where an employee who has been granted an award/option and has exercised his right under the award/option, the employer must ensure that the tax to be charged on the benefit which arises from the award/option is deducted from the employee's salary based on the STD scheme (in the month in which the option is exercised).

Where the employee chooses to pay the tax by instalments through the STD scheme, the employer must make the tax deductions from the remuneration of the employee each month (for a maximum of 12 months) commencing from the month in which the option is exercised.

Where an employee elects to pay the income tax arising on the perquisite at the end of the year, the employer must ensure that the election is made in writing.

The employer is also required to report this benefit on the employee's Form EA for the year the option is exercised. At the same time, the employer is also required to submit a copy of the names of employees who have exercised their rights under an option to the Director, Technical Department, IRB.

**2.3    If the employer is responsible for the executive's liabilities, can the employer withhold the liabilities from the executive's salary? Are there any formalities in this respect?**

As described in the response to question 2.2, an employer must ensure that the tax to be charged on the benefit that arises from the award/option is deducted from the employee's salary based on the STD scheme. The amount of tax which an employer is liable to pay under the STD scheme will be a debt due from the employer to the Government and shall be recoverable by civil proceedings as if the employer were the person charged therewith.

**2.4** **If the executive's salary in the month of exercise/release is not sufficient for the employer to withhold all of the liabilities, can the employer (or the parent company, if different) arrange for the executive to authorise to sell some of the executive's shares in the market and pass the money to the executive's employer?**

Not applicable.

**2.5** **Will the executive pay tax on the eventual sale of his shares and if so at what rate?**

Any profits or gains made on the sale of shares will be of a capital gains nature and would not attract any liability to tax in Malaysia.

**3.** **Employer's social security**

**3.1** **Is the employer liable to pay (on its own account) any employer's social security in connection with the long-term incentive award?**

As set out above, social security liabilities do not arise in connection with employee share schemes.

**3.2** **Can the liability of the employer be put onto the employee? What steps are required?**

Not applicable, by virtue of the response to 3.1 above.

**4.** **Tax deduction for the employer**

**4.1** **Is it possible for the employer to receive a tax deduction in respect of the long-term incentive award? Would the employer need to be subject to recharge arrangements (eg if the employer is a subsidiary and provides funds to the parent company as part of a recharge arrangement in respect of the long-term incentive award)?**

In order for an employer to qualify for any tax deduction in respect of operating an employee share scheme, the expenses associated with operating the scheme have to be "wholly and exclusively incurred in the production of gross income of the employer". The employer will have to prove that:

- it incurred the expenses concerned; and
- the expenses were wholly and exclusively incurred in the production of its gross income.

It is not possible to get a tax deduction for the difference between the value of the shares acquired by the employees and the amount paid for them (ie on the so-called "spread" on exercise).

## 5. Tax beneficial arrangements

### 5.1 Are there any ways of making the long-term incentive award tax-efficient in Malaysia?

Whether or not any arrangements can be made to achieve tax benefits for an employee would depend on the particular employee's individual circumstances (eg whether or not the employee is a citizen/expatriate) and whether any double taxation agreement/treaty is applicable to the employee.

Specific tax advice on arrangements that can be implemented to enhance the tax position of particular employees would have to be obtained by the relevant employee.

## 6. Internationally mobile executives

### 6.1 What are the income tax consequences for an employee who is resident in Malaysia when the long-term incentive award is made, but who is no longer resident at the time of exercise/vesting?

If an employee is resident in Malaysia when the award or option (under an employee share scheme) is granted, but is no longer resident at the time of exercise, then, for purposes of income tax, the employee would be non-resident for the year of assessment in which he exercises his award/option and would be taxed at the current flat rate of 28%.

### 6.2 What are the social security consequences for an employee who is resident in Malaysia when the long-term incentive award is made, but who is no longer resident at the time of exercise/vesting?

As set out above, social security liabilities do not arise in connection with employee share schemes.

### 6.3 What are the tax and social security withholding/reporting consequences for the employer in respect of an employee who is resident in Malaysia when the long-term incentive award is made, but who is no longer resident at the time of exercise/vesting?

If the employee is still employed by the employer, then the employer must still ensure that the tax to be charged on the benefit that arises from the award/option is deducted from the employee's salary based on the STD scheme, regardless of whether the employee is a resident or non-resident for tax purposes.

## 7. Reporting requirements

### 7.1 Will the employer (or parent company, if different) have any reporting requirements as a result of the long-term incentive award?

The Malaysian employer/Malaysian subsidiary is required to file a notification with the IRB pertaining to the launch of an employee share scheme. Notification to the IRB is made by completing Form BT/ESOS/2005, along with supporting documents such as the rules of the employee share scheme, the resolution of the directors or members approving the scheme and any documents which are to be supplied to the eligible employees. The notification must be filed within 30 days after expiry of the period of acceptance of the offer as specified in the scheme's rules.

The IRB will determine the taxable benefit in kind and confirm any other taxation issues. The determination by the IRB may take between three and six months. However, receiving a determination from the IRB is not a pre-condition to implementing a share option scheme.

The IRB has, in this regard, issued Public Ruling No 4/2004 for employee share option schemes. A Public Ruling is issued for the purpose of providing guidance for the public and officers of the IRB. The Public Ruling sets out the interpretation of the Director General of IRB in respect of particular tax laws and the policy and procedures that are to be applied.

7.2     **Are there any tax rulings required in relation to the long-term incentive awards?**
See above.

## 8.     Exchange control issues

8.1     **Are there any exchange control issues that would prevent an employee from (a) remitting monies abroad to purchase shares, or (b) repatriating monies from the sale of shares?**
Malaysia's currency, the ringgit (M$) is not valid tender outside Malaysia.

At present, individuals are permitted to remit or invest any amount in foreign currency for foreign shares offered by the overseas parent or related company under an employee share option scheme. Payment for such shares can be made in foreign currency other than the currency of Israel.

If the funds are financed through a deduction from the employees' salary, they must be deposited with an approved local financial institution prior to remitting the funds as payment for the shares in the employee share scheme.

There are no restrictions on the repatriation of the proceeds of the sale of shares back to Malaysia. The previous requirement by Bank Negara Malaysia (BNM) that all dividends, profits and proceeds from the sale of shares (under an employee share scheme) should be repatriated back to Malaysia as soon as they are received and that the prior approval of BNM is required for the retention or reinvestment of these proceeds overseas no longer applies. As such, if an employee share scheme provides for dividend distributions to be automatically reinvested to purchase more shares in the scheme, this is now permitted.

## 9.     Employment law

9.1     **Are there any employment or local labour law issues which may arise as a result of the long-term incentive award? Are any consultations or authorisations required by law?**

*(a)* *Labour issues*

If the implementation of an employee share scheme changes the remuneration of employees, their express consent should be obtained. For employees who are members of trade unions, although there is no statutory or regulatory requirement in this respect, approval from the union must generally be obtained.

*(b)* *Legality of payroll deductions*

The amounts deducted from payroll for participation in the employee share scheme are subject to payroll taxes as regular wages. It is also preferable for the employee to sign a written agreement authorising the payroll deductions.

If employees are subject to the Malaysian Employment Act (ie where the employee earns below M$1,500 per month or where the employees are engaged in manual labour), approval for any payroll deduction is required from the Department of Labour if the deduction is towards repayment of a loan made to the employee to enable him or her to purchase shares. Otherwise, approval is not required.

The total salary deduction (for employees subject to the Malaysian Employment Act), including statutory deductions (such as EPF and monthly tax withholding), should not exceed 50%.

## 10. Translation

10.1 **Are there any language restrictions in Malaysia? Does any of the documentation provided to the employee in relation to the long-term incentive award need to be translated?**

In so far as offer documents are concerned, there are no language restrictions in Malaysia. The forms/documents provided to the employees in relation to an employee share scheme or employee share option scheme need not be translated.

## 11. Data protection

11.1 **Are there any data protection issues which may arise should the employer wish to outsource the administration of the long-term incentive award to a third party?**

At present, Malaysia does not have any legislation dealing with data protection or the protection of privacy. In 2001, Malaysian legislators prepared a draft Personal Data Protection Bill. However, due to various unresolved issues, the PDP Bill has not been tabled in Parliament and the proposed Personal Data Protection Act has not been passed and there has been no development on the legislative front since 2003.

Notwithstanding the lack of laws/regulations pertaining to data protection or data privacy, it is advisable (but not imperative) that participants consent to the use and transfer of personal data.

In particular, the employee's consent/authorisation should be obtained to transfer and disclose personal data to any relevant parties (ie brokers, agents, etc) or to third parties (to whom the employer wishes to outsource the administration of an employee share scheme).

## 12. Source of shares

12.1 **Does it matter if shares are newly issued to an employee, provided out of treasury or delivered from an employee-benefit trust?**

It is immaterial whether the shares of the company are newly issued to an employee or provided out of treasury or delivered from an employee-benefit trust.

# Mexico

**Raúl Moreyra**
Goodrich, Riquelme y Asociados

---

> **No red flag issues**

## 1. Securities laws

**1.1** **What prospectus and/or securities law requirements arise in connection with the grant, vesting or exercise of a long-term incentive award or on the eventual sale of the shares by the executive?**

Under Mexican Law there is no legal requirement to provide executives with a prospectus or any written communication in connection with the grant, vesting or exercise of a long-term incentive award, or on the eventual sale of the shares. Nevertheless, it is advisable to have the executives sign a copy of the plan.

**1.2** **Is there an exemption from securities laws requirements either because the shares are being offered only to executives or because shares are being offered to a distinct group of named individuals?**

See 1.1 above.

**1.3** **If there is an exemption, will the exemption apply automatically or are there any applications/filings that need to be made?**

See 1.1 above.

## 2. Employee tax and social security

**2.1** **When will the executive be liable to tax or social security (and at what rate) in respect of the long-term incentive award?**

The executive will be liable to tax when exercising the incentive award. The income tax rate is progressive, with the maximum rate currently being 28%.

Social security charges are applicable only when the subsidiary absorbs the cost of the incentive award by reimbursing the parent company or otherwise.

The social security charges are as follows:

- paid by employee – 3% to 5% of salary (capped at Ps39,442.50 per month);
- paid by employer – 25% to 28% of salary (capped at Ps39,442.50 per month).

The base salaries for computing are capped at the equivalent of 25 times the minimum daily salary in force in Mexico City. At the time of writing, this daily minimum salary is Ps52.59. The minimum daily salary is updated every year in January. Therefore, at the time of writing, the cap equals approximately the monthly amount of Ps39,442.50 (Ps 52.59 × 25 × 30). The exchange rate of the peso to the US$ is around 11 pesos to a dollar. The exchange rate fluctuates freely. In the case of share options, income tax and social security charges will be calculated on the difference between the amounts paid by the employee when the options are granted, if any, and the market value of the shares at the time of exercising the options.

Where free shares are granted, the consequences will be the same, but the taxable amount (including social security charges) will be the market value of the shares when delivered.

2.2　**How will the executive's tax and social security be collected? Will the executive be responsible for paying any liabilities himself or will the executive's employer be responsible for paying tax or social security liabilities on the executive's behalf?**

The company employing the executive is liable for withholding income tax on the executive's behalf when the incentive award is exercised by the executive or the free shares are delivered; and social security charges must be paid in the same fashion when costs of the incentive award are absorbed by the employer.

2.3　**If the employer is responsible for the executive's liabilities, can the employer withhold the liabilities from the executive's salary? Are there any formalities in this respect?**

The employer is jointly liable with the executive for the payment of the tax and social security charges. Mexican labour law forbids any other withholding of liabilities by the employer from the employee's salary.

The only withholding from the employee's salary authorised by the Mexican labour law is for savings purposes, and requires prior written consent from the employee; but it can never exceed 30% of the surplus over the applicable minimum wage in Mexico City in one month (the daily minimum wage currently being Ps 52.59).

2.4　**If the executive's salary in the month of exercise/release is not sufficient for the employer to withhold all of the liabilities, can the employer (or the parent company, if different) arrange for the executive to authorise to sell some of the executive's shares in the market and pass the money to the executive's employer?**

The executive can authorise the sale of shares of his property and instruct as how to use the proceeds.

2.5　**Will the executive pay tax on the eventual sale of his shares and if so at what rate?**

The executive must make an advance payment of 20% of the price received from the sale within 15 days of the sale and make payment of the balance, or apply for the credit for the difference in his favour, if that is the case, in the annual tax return to be filed by the employee in April of the following year.

### 3. Employer's social security

**3.1** Is the employer liable to pay (on its own account) any employer's social security in connection with the long-term incentive award?

Yes, the employer is liable to pay its social security quota and also that of the employee through withholding the social security in the case mentioned above.

**3.2** Can the liability of the employer be put onto the employee? What steps are required?

It is forbidden under Mexican Law to put the liability of the employer onto the employee.

### 4. Tax deduction for the employer

**4.1** Is it possible for the employer to receive a tax deduction in respect of the long-term incentive award? Would the employer need to be subject to recharge arrangements (eg if the employer is a subsidiary and provides funds to the parent company as part of a recharge arrangement in respect of the long-term incentive award)?

The employer can receive a tax deduction for any reimbursement to the parent company of the cost incurred by the latter on the long-term incentive award; but in such a case the employer is liable for social security charges as described above.

### 5. Tax beneficial arrangements

**5.1** Are there any ways of making the long-term incentive award tax-efficient in Mexico?

This benefit is considered as an income from wages for the executive, so the way to make it tax efficient would be to apply the tax treaty between Mexico and the country of residence of the executive to avoid double taxation (see also below).

### 6. Internationally mobile executives

**6.1** What are the income tax consequences for an employee who is resident in Mexico when the long-term incentive award is made, but who is no longer resident at the time of exercise/vesting?

The social security consequences for an employee are the same as for tax, namely that if the employee is no longer resident in Mexico at the time that the option is exercised by the executive or the shares are delivered, there are no social charges or tax is to be paid in Mexico by the employee.

**6.2** What are the social security consequences for an employee who is resident in Mexico when the long-term incentive award is made, but who is no longer resident at the time of exercise/vesting?

See 6.1 above.

**6.3** **What are the tax and social security withholding/reporting consequences for the employer in respect of an employee who is resident in Mexico when the long-term incentive award is made, but who is no longer resident at the time of exercise/vesting?**

If the employer reimburses the parent company for the cost of the long-term incentive award, then the employer is liable to withhold the tax and social security charges.

## 7. Reporting requirements

**7.1** **Will the employer (or parent company, if different) have any reporting requirements as a result of the long-term incentive award?**

Neither the employer nor the parent company has any reporting requirements as a result of the long-term incentive award.

**7.2** **Are there any tax rulings required in relation to the long-term incentive awards?**

No tax rulings are required.

## 8. Exchange control issues

**8.1** **Are there any exchange control issues that would prevent an employee from (a) remitting monies abroad to purchase shares, or (b) repatriating monies from the sale of shares?**

There are no exchange controls or restrictions that would prevent an employee from remitting monies abroad, purchasing shares, or repatriating monies from the sale of shares.

## 9. Employment law

**9.1** **Are there any employment or local labour law issues which may arise as a result of the long-term incentive award? Are any consultations or authorisations required by law?**

In order to avoid the benefits being incorporated to the executive's employment contract, the benefits should be expressly excluded in the plan offered to the executive.

If the plan is offered by the parent company, it is unlikely to be considered a labour benefit granted by an employer to its employees. If there is a chargeback to the employer by the parent company, Mexican courts could hold that the plan is an employment benefit granted by the employer to the employees.

If the plan is considered to be a labour benefit, employees may include this benefit in any claim against the employer.

## 10. Translation

10.1 **Are there any language restrictions in Mexico? Does any of the documentation provided to the employee in relation to the long-term incentive award need to be translated?**

There is no requirement to translate any documentation that is provided to the employees and there are no language restrictions.

## 11. Data protection

11.1 **Are there any data protection issues which may arise should the employer wish to outsource the administration of the long-term incentive award to a third party?**

It is not necessary to obtain the employee's consent, but it would be prudent to do so.

## 12. Source of shares

12.1 **Does it matter if shares are newly issued to an employee, provided out of treasury or delivered from an employee-benefit trust?**

It does not matter if the shares come from any of the three sources mentioned above, but it is important to determine whether the income received by the employee is from a low-tax jurisdiction. A low-tax jurisdiction is one where the income tax paid is less than 75% of the level of tax that would be paid in Mexico.

Income obtained by Mexican residents from these jurisdictions is that obtained directly or indirectly from legal entities or legal structures created or constituted pursuant to foreign law.

Taxpayers must account for any income, dividends and profits originating from low-tax jurisdictions and inform the tax authorities in February of every year. Income derived from low-tax jurisdictions is deemed to be received at the time it is generated. The income may not be commingled with other income; the profit is taxed separately and any tax is paid annually.

Where the taxpayer does not directly participate in the investment (ie he does not, either directly or through a third party, decide on the timing of the distribution of yields, profits or dividends), income is not deemed to be obtained from the low-tax jurisdiction.

# Netherlands

Arjan Hovenkamp
Stibbe

---

**Red flag issues**

1. Costs related to stock options plans are, as of January 1 2007, no longer tax deductible for corporate income tax purposes. Expenses related to SARs settled in cash are still tax deductible for corporate income tax purposes.

2. Internationally mobile employees are taxed on the proportion of the option gain that arises during such part of the vesting period that they are resident in the Netherlands.

3. Options are now taxed at the date of exercise and not on the vesting date.

---

## 1. Securities laws

### 1.1 What prospectus and/or securities law requirements arise in connection with the grant, vesting or exercise of a long-term incentive award or on the eventual sale of the shares by the executive?

In the Netherlands the EU prospectus Directive (2003/71/EC) has been implemented in the Financial Supervision Act (*Wet op het Financieel Toezicht*). Based upon this legislation, in principle a prospectus must be published when transferable securities are offered to the public. The Dutch Authority for Financial Markets (AFM – *Autoriteit Financiële Markten*) must approve such a prospectus before securities can actually be offered. Exemptions usually apply to this prospectus obligation (see below).

When a company with no listing in any of the European Economic Area (EEA) countries wants to implement a long-term incentive plan for its employees working in the Netherlands, in principle the plan will be subject to the obligation to publish a prospectus with the AFM to obtain approval. In case a prospectus has already been made for the introduction of the plan in another EEA country, this prospectus can be used for the Netherlands as well. To be able to use this prospectus for the Netherlands, the financial authorities in that other EEA country will have to file the prospectus with the Dutch AFM.

### 1.2 Is there an exemption from securities laws requirements either because the shares are being offered only to executives or because shares are being offered to a distinct group of named individuals?

The Committee of European Securities Regulators (CESR) is of the opinion that no prospectus obligation arises when long-term incentive plans are introduced that relate to non-transferable securities. In general, options and free share awards granted to employees are non-transferable, which means that no prospectus obligation arises. A prospectus obligation would only arise if the options or free share awards are transferable.

When options are actually exercised, a Dutch issuing company can refer to an exception as included in the Dutch Financial Supervision Act. According to this exception, no prospectus is needed when the issuing company offers shares which represent less than 10% of the total number of those shares that are already available to the market.

When a long-term incentive plan is issued by a company which does not have a listing in an EEA country, the company generally has the obligation to publish a prospectus. The company should investigate whether it qualifies for an exemption, as a result of which it would not need to publish a prospectus.

One of these exceptions is made in the event that the long-term incentive plan is offered to fewer than 100 employees per year, in which case no prospectus obligation arises. A company could therefore grant the long-term incentives to different employees each year, as long as the total number of eligible employees for that particular calendar year remains below 100.

Another exception would exist where employees are invited to participate in a long-term incentive plan for free.

**1.3** **If there is an exemption, will the exemption apply automatically or are there any applications/filings that need to be made?**

When an exemption applies and no prospectus has to be published, the exemption applies automatically. There is no need to apply for the exemption to the Dutch Authority for Financial Markets.

**2.** **Employee tax and social security**

**2.1** **When will the executive be liable to tax or social security (and at what rate) in respect of the long-term incentive award?**

*(a)* *Stock options*

At the moment of grant, no tax charge arises. Stock options are taxed at the moment of exercise rather than on vesting. It is irrelevant whether or not the options are made conditional or unconditional. The taxable benefit is calculated by taking the market value of the share at the moment of exercise, less the exercise price of the option. This difference is taxed against the applicable (progressive) tax rate (top rate for 2008: 52%, which applies to a taxable income from employment and principal residence (box 1[1])). If the executive does not exercise his options, no taxable moment

---

[1] The Dutch income tax is levied through three "boxes". Each of the boxes levies taxes on certain types of income. Box 1 collects the taxable income from employment and principal residence. This income is taxed against progressive income tax rates, which vary from 2.45% for the first €17,579 of income to 52% for taxable income higher than €53,860 (rates for 2008). Box 2 collects the taxable income from substantial share ownership. The applicable tax rate is 25%. Box 3 collects the taxable income from savings and investments. In this box, the taxable income is determined not based on actual income from savings and investments, but the annual average net value of the assets of the taxpayer are deemed to have brought in a 4% yield. This fictitious income is taxed against a flat income tax rate of 30%.

occurs. For the purpose of taxation, it is irrelevant whether or not the options are granted to the executive at an exercise price below the actual market price at the moment of grant. Taxation still only occurs at the moment of exercise. Note that, based on Dutch corporate governance guidelines, options may not be granted to executives against an exercise price below market value of the underlying shares at the moment of grant.

The term *exercise* has a broader meaning for tax purposes. Also the disposal of option rights to a third party is considered as "exercise", thus leading to a taxable moment.

Options granted to an executive prior to January 1 2005 (when a different tax regime applied) but that vested after January 1 2005 will follow the new tax regime applicable as of January 1 2005, outlined above.

*(b)*     ***Free share award***
If the employee receives a grant of free shares, where the actual acquisition by the employee depends on certain conditions that must be met, the taxable moment will not occur before the conditions are indeed met and the employee actually has the unconditional right to acquire the shares. In fact such a grant must be regarded as a conditional grant. At the moment the grant becomes unconditional, the taxable benefit is the actual value of the shares that can be obtained.

If the employee receives a grant of free shares which is subject to forfeiture provisions, such a grant will be subject to taxation at the moment of grant. The taxable benefit is again the market value of the shares. If the shares are granted to and acquired by the employee, but restrictions apply to the shares during a certain period of time, these restrictions can be regarded as an element which lowers the taxable benefit. In general it can be stated that, due to such restrictions, the taxable benefit from such restricted shares can be determined at 2.5% of the taxable benefit per year of restriction.

2.2     **How will the executive's tax and social security be collected? Will the executive be responsible for paying any liabilities himself or will the executive's employer be responsible for paying tax or social security liabilities on the executive's behalf?**
When a taxable moment occurs, in principle the employer of the executive needs to withhold wage tax and (if applicable) social security premiums on the taxable benefit on behalf of the executive. The taxable benefit must be processed through the payroll in the month in which the taxable moment occurred. The benefit is regarded as a benefit-in-kind. To withhold Dutch wage tax and social security premiums, the Dutch employer must be regarded as a withholding agent for the Dutch Wage Tax Act (*Wet op de Loonbelasting* 1964).

In international situations it often occurs that the foreign parent company grants options to its executives working in other countries, without the local company where the executive is employed at that time being aware of this. The executive might also have been granted options prior to his assignment to the Netherlands. In general it can be stated that, also in these situations, the Dutch employer/wage tax agent is obliged to withhold wage tax and (possible) social security premiums on the taxable income from the executive if the Dutch entity where the executive is working at that moment. This applies even if the Dutch entity has no knowledge of the long-term incentive plan and the participation of any employee working in the Netherlands (this would only apply in affiliated company situations).

The executive will also have to report his income from equity incentives in his Dutch personal income tax return. As the taxes and premiums on this benefit have already been paid through wage tax withholding, in principle no additional payment takes place through the executive's income tax assessment as far as this is related to income from equity incentives.

**2.3     If the employer is responsible for the executive's liabilities, can the employer withhold the liabilities from the executive's salary? Are there any formalities in this respect?**

Yes. The employer as a wage tax withholding agent must pay taxes on the taxable benefit from the long-term incentives on behalf of the executive to the Dutch tax authorities. This obligation arises based upon the Dutch Wage Tax Act. As mentioned above, the executive would also have to report the income in his personal income tax return.

**2.4     If the executive's salary in the month of exercise/release is not sufficient for the employer to withhold all of the liabilities, can the employer (or the parent company, if different) arrange for the executive to authorise the company to sell some of the executive's shares in the market and pass the money to the executive's employer?**

If it turns out that the regular salary payment in that particular month is not sufficient to withhold the taxes due, the employer has the right to recover the additional taxes from the executive. This is based upon a specific clause in the Dutch Wage Tax Act. In general, equity incentive plans will contain a specific clause that refers to the taxation of benefits obtained through the incentives. Based on this specific clause in the plan, the executive remains fully liable for any tax and or social security implications. This is also advisable to avoid any discussions about possible net benefits from the incentives. Employees granted the incentives might otherwise take the view that any tax implications should be accounted for by the company.

An obligatory sale of (some of the) securities on behalf of the executive to be able to pay the wage tax due on the taxable benefit is not a tool that the employer can use to obtain the necessary funds for payment of the taxes due. Only the executive can decide to do this. In some cases, the employer can also provide the executive with a loan to cover the taxes due on the taxable benefit from equity incentives. Granting such a loan does have wage tax implications if the company does not charge interest on the loan.

**2.5     Will the executive pay tax on the eventual sale of his shares and if so at what rate?**

As soon as the executive exercises his options and the taxable moment has occurred for wage tax purposes, the shares are, in principle, no longer considered as a wage element. The shares are from that moment considered to be a personal investment of the executive. This means that the market value of the shares will be taken into consideration annually when the taxable income from savings and investments (box 3) are determined.[2] When the shares are sold, no additional taxable moment will occur, as the Netherlands do not have a capital gains tax. An exception can be found if the shares are sold back to the company against a value which is higher than the actual market value of the shares at that moment in time. In that situation, the additional value that is received by the executive for his shares must be considered as taxable income from employment, which is taxable against the applicable progressive income tax rate (box 1).

## 3. Employer's social security

**3.1 Is the employer liable to pay (on its own account) any employer's social security in connection with the long-term incentive award?**

In principle every executive will be covered for Dutch employee insurances. Most of the premiums due for these insurances (disability and unemployment), are (partly) for the account of the employer. Payment for these premiums is limited to a certain level of taxable income. Employee social security premiums are only calculated on a maximum annual premium income of €46,205 (2008 figures). If the total income of the executive is higher, no additional premiums are due on the income from the incentive plan.

**3.2 Can the liability of the employer be put onto the employee?**

No.

## 4. Tax deduction for the employer

**4.1 Is it possible for the employer to receive a tax deduction in respect of the long-term incentive award? Would the employer need to be subject to recharge arrangements (eg if the employer is a subsidiary and provides funds to the parent company as part of a recharge arrangement in respect of the long-term incentive award)?**

As of 2007, the Dutch government changed corporate income tax in such way that expenses regarding the provision of stock options or other share-related incentives are no longer tax deductible. The Dutch government made this change so that stock-option and share plans must be considered as capital transactions which do not actually cost the company anything. The only effect of the options will be that the company's capital will be divided over more shares by the time the options are exercised.

Until December 31 2006, expenses related to long-term incentive plans could be

---

2    This means that the average annual value of the shares will be annually taxed against effectively 1.2% income tax (4% deemed income from the annual average net value of assets, taxed against 30% income tax).

deducted from taxable income for corporate income tax purposes. Only the company where the employees are employed could deduct the expenses related to the long-term incentive plan on the date the options vested.

Together with the implementation of this new legislation, transitional legislation was introduced for already existing incentive plans. This allows deduction of expenses for corporate tax purposes in relation to options and share plans granted prior to May 24 2006 (the date on which the new corporate income tax plans for options were announced). This transitory legislation will remain in place until December 31 2009.

### (a) Stock Appreciation Rights (SARs)

With respect to SARs, these expenses could and can still be deducted by the company. SARs granted as of 2007 are therefore not affected by the abolition of the deduction of expenses related to share incentive plans. This distinction is caused by the fact that SARs are only related to shares, but the actual benefit the executive receives is an amount in cash. The abolition of the deduction of expenses related to stock options caused a movement from option plans to SARs.

When the company is dealing with an equity-settled SAR, the expenses can no longer be deducted by the company. This is in line with the general treatment of option plans as of January 1 2007.

If an option plan is structured so that the employee is obliged to transfer any shares obtained on exercise to the company to receive the cash equivalent of his shares, the option plan should in fact not be regarded as an option plan but merely as an SAR, a payment in cash. This also implies that the expenses of such a plan remain tax deductible for the company.

For SARs, the amount that can be deducted is similar to the value at the moment of grant. If 500 SARs are granted against an exercise price of €5.50, then the deduction at the moment of grant amounts to €2,750.

## 5. Tax beneficial arrangements

### 5.1 Are there any ways of making the long-term incentive award tax-efficient in the Netherlands?

In principle long-term incentive awards are considered as employment income, which is taxed against the progressive income tax rates that apply at the taxable moment. No special tax rates apply to income from long-term incentives.

In case an executive is recruited from abroad and the executive is benefiting from the so-called 30% ruling,[3] the 30% ruling also applies to the taxable income from equity incentives. In that case, the progressive income tax rate is in fact lowered from 52% to 36.4% (70% of 52%).

---

[3]     This ruling allows the employer of the executive to pay 30% of the agreed salary free of tax to cover expenses related to the fact that the executive is recruited from abroad regardless of the actual expenses.

## 6. Internationally mobile executives

6.1 **What are the income tax consequences for an employee who is resident in the Netherlands when the long-term incentive award is made, but who is no longer resident at the time of exercise/vesting?**

In a special decree in 2002, the Dutch State Secretary of Finance announced how stock options should be taxed in an international situation. Until that moment, options could only be taxed in the Netherlands if the executive was actually present when, for Dutch tax purposes, the taxable moment occurred. In other words, if the executive was not actually present in the Netherlands, the benefit from options would not be taxable.

The 2002 decree seeks ways of concurring with the general rules of the international taxation of employment income. The allocation of the taxable benefit is the key element of the decree. Assuming that options granted to executives are almost always conditional options, the period between the moment of grant and the moment that the options become exercisable should be regarded as the relevant period to determine the allocation of the taxable benefit. When the executive actually exercises his option, the taxable benefit should be divided between the countries where the executive was employed during the period between grant and vesting of the options. This can be best shown by an example.

*Example*
On January 1 2007, a Dutch executive living and working in the Netherlands is granted an option to acquire 500 shares in the company at an exercise price of €15 per share. The options vest after two years, on January 1 2009. On July 1 2008, the executive is asked to go to the US for a period of three years. The executive exercises his options on March 31 2008, when the market value of the share is €22.50.

The taxable benefit amounts to 500 * (22.50 – 15) = €3,750

The period between the grant and vesting of the options is 24 months. During this period, the executive worked and lived in the Netherlands for 18 months. In the last six months of the vesting period, the executive became a resident of the US, while working there. The taxable benefit received by the executive needs to be allocated for Dutch tax purposes.

The option gain needs to be apportioned between the period the employee was resident in the Netherlands and in the United States. The employee was resident of the Netherlands for 18/24ths (or 75%) of the vesting period and therefore 75% of the option gain, that of €2,812.50, will be taxed in the Netherlands (ie 75% × €3,750). This is the taxable benefit to be reported in the Netherlands even though the executive is no longer living there. Note that the period between vesting and actual exercise is irrelevant.

One point to note in respect of this allocation is a possible conflict with respect to the taxation of the taxable benefit from stock options in the country of residence at the moment of exercise. In the example given above, the United States will most likely initially include the full taxable benefit of the stock options in the executive's taxable income. As three-quarters of the total benefit is taxed in the Netherlands, the United States would have to provide relief under the Netherlands/US double-taxation treaty to avoid double taxation. Whether or not this will always occur in an international situation is questionable.

Although the decree only speaks about options, it is generally considered that it should also apply to other long-term incentive plans.

**6.2** **What are the social security consequences for an employee who is resident in the Netherlands when the long-term incentive award is made, but who is no longer resident at the time of exercise/vesting?**

The income from options in this particular situation should be regarded as after-acquired benefit. In general this income will be subject to employee social security premiums, but there are some exceptions. As well as employee insurances such as unemployment and disability insurance, other national social security premiums (eg old-age pension premiums) should also be considered. In general, a non-resident of the Netherlands who receives income subject to Dutch wage withholding tax (as in this particular situation) will also be subject to national social security premiums. Exceptions may exist due to the international allocation of the right to levy social security premiums.

**6.3** **What are the tax and social security/withholding/reporting consequences for the employer in respect of an employee who is resident in the Netherlands when the long-term incentive award is made, but who is no longer resident at the time of exercise/vesting?**

If the executive no longer lives in the Netherlands at the moment of exercise, the Dutch company must still withhold wage tax on the taxable benefit from equity incentives. This means that the company will have to continue to monitor the employee. If a taxable moment occurs while the employee no longer works in the Netherlands, the employer is faced with additional administrative obligations due to the fact that wage tax must be withheld on the taxable benefit. As the company will not pay any regular salary and only the benefit-in-kind from stock options is processed through the payroll, the company will have to ensure that the employee pays back the taxes due. Employer and employee could make a separate arrangement when the employee is about to leave the Netherlands to ensure that it can collect the taxes due from the employee by the time the taxable moment occurs.

**7.** **Reporting requirements**

**7.1** **Will the employer (or parent company, if different) have any reporting requirements as a result of the long-term incentive award?**

In general there are no reporting requirements in the Netherlands for the grant of long-term incentives.

**7.2    Are any tax rulings required in relation to the long-term incentive awards?**

A company can introduce a long-term incentive plan without the need to obtain prior approval from the tax authorities regarding the plan concerned. If certain fiscal aspects of the plan are not clear upfront, it is possible to contact the tax authorities to obtain their opinion regarding the tax consequences for the participants. Thus, companies can assure certainty upfront on all relevant aspects that might influence the tax implications of the long-term incentives. However, in general, such plans are introduced without first contacting the tax authorities.

**8.    Exchange control issues**

**8.1    Are there any exchange control issues that would prevent an employee from (a) remitting monies abroad to purchase shares, or (b) repatriating monies from the sale of shares?**

No.

**9.    Employment law**

**9.1    Are there any employment or local labour law issues which may arise as a result of the long-term incentive award? Are any consultations or authorisations required by law?**

Yes. When implementing a long-term incentive plan, the company must be aware of certain employment law-related aspects. When such a plan is introduced, the company usually selects only particular group(s) of employee(s) who are eligible for incentives. However, the company cannot make any distinction between genders when granting the incentives. When deciding who will be granted incentives, the company must not consider if an employee is full- or part-time. However, the company can take an employee's hours into consideration when determining the size of the awards.

Exceptions to the above-mentioned issues can only be made in cases where there is an objective and legitimate reason to make the distinction.

Incentive plans often contain a clause stipulating that the employee will lose his or her rights if employment is terminated. From an employment law perspective it is questionable to what extent such a stipulation is enforceable. Although the Dutch Supreme Court has never given an actual decision in such a case, it is generally assumed that this kind of clause is acceptable. Only if it would be unreasonable of the employer to rely on this clause should it be regarded as invalid (eg if termination of the employment agreement is caused merely by the employer).

Implementation of a long-term incentive plan could also be subject to prior consent of the works council. Whether or not a company will need to install a works council depends on the workforce that is employed by the company and whether it qualifies under the Works Council Act. Every company with a regular workforce of at least 50 employees (full- or part-time) must have a works council. Furthermore, only if the long-term incentive plan can be regarded as a "reward system", the works council must give its prior consent. Although it is not always clear when a long-term incentive plan must be regarded as a reward system, in a lot of cases its implementation must be considered as such, making it a topic that must be approved by the works council before it can be introduced. If approval has not been obtained, the works council can invoke the nullity of the introduction of the plan. However, this does not affect the rights of employees who have already been granted options under the plan. These employees will remain entitled to the benefits of this grant.

## 10. Translation

### 10.1 Are there any language restrictions in the Netherlands? Does any of the documentation provided to the employee in relation to the long-term incentive award need to be translated?

No. The long-term incentive plan will probably be written in Dutch or English. The company does not have to provide a translation of the plan to be able to present a copy of the plan in the employees' language. The employer must be aware, though, that long-term incentive plans written in languages other than the employees' language might cause interpretation problems. If these problems are brought to court, they are usually decided in favour of the employee.

## 11. Data protection

### 11.1 Are there any data protection issues which may arise should the employer wish to outsource the administration of the long-term incentive award to a third party?

When the company has implemented a long-term incentive plan, it needs to act in line with the regulations of the Personal Data Protection Act (PDPA) which deal with the personal data of employees. The general rule is that the company must process data from its employees in a fair and lawful way. In practice, this means that the processing of any personal data is only allowed after consent has been obtained from the employee, or when the processing of the data is necessary for the execution of an agreement. This could be the employment agreement of the option agreement that has been signed by the employee. The participating employee should be informed about the fact that the administration regarding the option plan will be performed by a third party and that the employer will have to provide information to this third party so it can carry out its duties. The personal data the company has obtained from the employee may only be processed as necessary to carry out the option plan.

If the company decides to outsource the services regarding the administration of the option plan, the company remains responsible for proper processing of the data provided to the third party, as well as for the security of the information. The DPA requires that the employees involved must consent to the transfer of the data.

The company outsourcing the administration will need to inform the authorities (among other issues) about the purpose of the administration, the way the information will be processed and the way the personal information will be safeguarded. There are certain exceptions where this is not necessary. The outsourcing of the administration of the options plans might be a decision that needs the prior consent of the works council, if the outsourcing is regarded as a "general regulation regarding processing personal data".

## 12. Source of shares

**12.1 Does it matter if shares are newly issued to an employee, provided out of treasury or delivered from an employee-benefit trust?**

No. When an employee decides to exercise its options, the company can choose three ways of providing the shares to the employee. The company can issue new shares, obtain the shares at the stock exchange, or it can use shares it has repurchased at an earlier stage.

# New Zealand

Mark Todd
Bell Gully

---

**Red flag issues**

1. Unless an exemption applies, an overseas company offering a long-term incentive award scheme to its New Zealand employees may need to produce a New Zealand Prospectus and Investment Statement under New Zealand securities laws. Doing this is likely to involve prohibitive cost in many cases. Therefore, it will be important to fall within a relevant securities law exemption.

2. An overseas company offering a long-term incentive share award scheme to New Zealand employees may need to file financial statements with the New Zealand Companies Office. Where this requirement applies, the overseas company should check that it is able to meet the relevant specific New Zealand requirements.

3. Executives receiving long-term incentive awards will be subject to New Zealand income tax on the difference between the price paid for the shares (if any) and the market value of the shares on the date that the shares are received or the relevant option is exercised.

---

## 1. Securities laws

### 1.1 What prospectus and/or securities law requirements arise in connection with the grant, vesting or exercise of a long-term incentive award or on the eventual sale of the shares by the executive?

*(a)* *Overview of New Zealand securities legislation*
The principal legislation governing New Zealand securities offerings is the Securities Act 1978 (the Act). Broadly speaking, the Act regulates "offers of securities to the public for subscription".

The principal requirements of the Act in relation to an offer of securities to which it applies are as follows:

- a requirement to produce and register a prospectus which meets the prescribed content requirements of the Act. The prospectus will generally need to contain detailed information about the issuer (including financial information) and the offer of securities. The prospectus must be registered with the New Zealand Companies Office and a copy must be provided to prospective subscribers on request;

- a requirement to distribute an investment statement to all investors before they subscribe for the relevant security. An investment statement is a form of key features document which meets the prescribed content requirements of the Act. Under the Act, the purpose of the investment statement is to: *"... provide certain key information that is likely to assist a prudent but non-expert person to decide whether or not to subscribe for securities"*. The investment statement does not need to be registered with any government agency; and

- various other requirements, such as a requirement to operate a securities register.

Significant criminal and civil liabilities can potentially arise for breaches of the Act for an issuer and its directors. An offer may also be void or voidable where a breach occurs.

As a starting point for any offer of a long-term incentive award scheme in New Zealand, it is necessary to consider whether the offer falls within the scope of the Act. If so, then the next question is whether an exemption applies to relieve the issuer of some or all of the substantive requirements of the Act.

Note that producing a New Zealand registered Prospectus and Investment Statement involves a significant amount of work and cost. Therefore, for most offers it is important to fall within an applicable exemption.

The following sections outline the key elements of any analysis of how the Act applies to an offer of a long-term incentive award scheme.

## (b) Do employees constitute "the public" for the purposes of the Act?

### (i) Introduction
The Act applies only in relation to an offer of securities to "the public" in New Zealand. Accordingly, if the offer is not being made to the public then the Act will not apply.

### (ii) Employees not excluded
The Act does not contain a definition of "the public" as such. However, it does state that: *A person shall not be precluded from being regarded as a member of the public in regard to any offer of securities by reason only that he or she is ... an employee ... of ... the issuer or any promoter of the securities."*

Accordingly, the fact that the offer of a long-term incentive award scheme is limited to employees does not preclude the Act from applying to the offer.

### (iii) Offer to senior executives only
In some cases, the class of offerees of the long-term incentive award scheme in New Zealand may be sufficiently narrow in that it does not amount to the public for the purposes of the Act. Factors of relevance here include:
- the number of employees to whom the offer is made in New Zealand;
- the seniority of those employees; and
- the manner in which those employees are selected.

Generally speaking, only a very limited offer will be likely to be excluded from the Act on this basis.

### (c) *Other relevant factors*

### (i) *Introduction*

In addition to the question of whether the offerees constitute the public for the purposes of the Act, several other factors need to be considered when analysing the application of the Act to the offer of a long-term incentive award scheme in New Zealand. These are outlined in this section.

### (ii) *Does the offer involve new securities or existing securities?*

In certain limited circumstances, the prospectus and investment statement requirements of the Act do not apply where the offer involves the offer of securities that have previously been allotted. This may be relevant where existing securities (including treasury stock) are used for the purposes of the long-term incentive award scheme, rather than newly issued securities.

However, the prospectus and investment statement requirements do generally apply to an offer involving existing securities where: *"... the holder or offeror, not being the original allotter, offers the security for sale to the public and the original allotter advises, encourages, or knowingly assists the holder or offeror in connection with the offer or sale of the security."*

Accordingly, careful analysis is required before concluding that it is not necessary to produce a prospectus or investment statement on the basis that existing securities are being used.

Further, where an offer is made without a prospectus or investment statement on the basis that existing securities are being used, the Act prescribes that it is an implied term of the offer that: *"... except to the extent disclosed for the purposes of the offer of the security, the offeror has no information in relation to the original allotter that is not publicly available and that would, or would be likely to, affect materially the price of the security if it were so disclosed."*

### (iii) *Is there a subscription?*

As mentioned, the Act only applies where there is an offer of securities to the public for subscription. Accordingly, in each case, it is necessary to consider whether the offer involves a subscription by the employee. For this purpose, subscription is broadly defined to include: *"... purchase and contribute to, whether by way of cash or otherwise"*.

Some long-term incentive award offers may involve the grant of securities to an employee without the need for any payment of money by the employee. By way of example, this could occur where options are granted to an employee at no cost (whether or not an exercise price is subsequently payable to exercise the options). It could also occur where the employee is given shares for no payment after a vesting period in circumstances where service and/or performance conditions have been met.

In these circumstances, consideration can be given to whether the Act does not apply on the basis that there is no subscription for the securities. However, given the broad definition of "subscription", some caution is required in relation to any such analysis.

*(d)* *At what point(s) in time does the Act apply?*

The Act is most likely to apply at the points in time at which participation in the long-term incentive award scheme is offered to employees in New Zealand. It is at these points in time that the criteria of the Act are most likely to be met.

However, it is possible that the Act can apply at more than one point in time in relation to a particular offer of participation in a long-term incentive award scheme. For example, in relation to a scheme based on options, the Act can potentially apply both at the point in time when the options are granted and then when the options are exercised. Where this occurs the requirements of the Act must be complied with at each relevant point in time.

The Act is unlikely to apply to the eventual sale of securities by an employee. Such a sale is unlikely to constitute an offer of securities to the public for subscription of a type that falls within the Act.

**1.2** **Is there an exemption from securities laws requirements either because the shares are being offered only to executives or because shares are being offered to a distinct group of named individuals?**

*(a)* **Introduction**

It is necessary to consider four exemptions that may potentially be relevant to the offer of a long-term incentive award scheme in New Zealand. These are as follows:

- The "exemption" that may potentially apply where the offer is made to such a narrow class of executives as to not involve an offer to the public. This is dealt with above.
- The exemption that may potentially apply where existing securities (including treasury stock) are used for the purposes of the scheme. Again, this is dealt with above.
- The exemption that applies to offers that are only made to persons who are wealthy or who are experienced in investing money or in the industry or business to which the security relates. This is considered below.
- The class exemption applicable to overseas employee share-purchase schemes that meet certain specified criteria. Again, this is considered below.

*(b)* *Exemption for wealthy persons and persons who are experienced in investing money or in the industry or business to which the security relates*

*(i)* *Introduction*

The Act contains a broad exemption for offers that are only made to "wealthy" or "experienced" persons (as defined in the Act). Such offers are exempt from the requirement to produce a New Zealand prospectus and investment statement.

(ii) *Definition of "wealthy"*

A person is "wealthy" if an independent chartered accountant certifies, no more than six months before the offer is made, that the chartered accountant is satisfied on reasonable grounds that that person:

- has net assets of at least NZ$2 million; or
- had an annual gross income of at least NZ$200,000 for each of the last two financial years.

(iii) *Definition of "experienced"*

A person is "experienced in investing money or in the industry or business to which the security relates" if an independent "financial service provider" is satisfied on reasonable grounds that that person, as a result of having experience of that kind, is able to assess:

- the merits of the offer;
- the value of the security;
- the risks involved in accepting the offer;
- that person's own information needs; and
- the adequacy of the information given by the person making the offer.

For this purpose, "financial service provider" is defined to mean a person whose principal business consists of giving investment advice, receiving investment money or receiving investment property.

(c) **Class exemption notice applicable to overseas employee share-purchase schemes**

(i) *Introduction*

The Act is administered by the New Zealand Securities Commission. The Securities Commission is given the power to grant exemptions from the requirements of the Act to certain issuers. The exemptions may be granted on a class basis, or in relation to specific individual issuers.

The Securities Commission has recognised that the cost and time involved in producing a New Zealand prospectus and investment statement is likely to be prohibitive for many companies wishing to offer their international employee share participation schemes in New Zealand. Accordingly, the Commission has granted a relevant class exemption called the Securities Act (Overseas Employee Share Purchase Schemes) Exemption Notice 2002 (the Exemption Notice).

(ii) *Exemptions provided under the Exemption Notice*

Where the Exemption Notice applies, the issuer will not be required to produce a New Zealand prospectus or investment statement in relation to the offer of its employee share purchase scheme to employees in New Zealand. This means that, broadly speaking, the issuer will be able to make that offer based on its general offer documentation. This is a significant exemption.

The Exemption Notice does not absolve the issuer from the liability provisions of the Act. It also does not absolve the issuer from the general requirement to ensure that any advertisement relating to the offer does not contain any information that is likely to deceive, mislead or confuse with regard to any particular that is material to the offer.

(iii)   *Period of the exemption*
The Exemption Notice has recently been renewed for a further five-year period, expiring on September 30 2012. While there is no guarantee, it is likely to be renewed for further periods after that.

(iv)    *Scope of the Exemption Notice*
In broad terms, the Exemption Notice applies to the offer of participation in an employee share purchase scheme made by a qualifying overseas issuer to employees in New Zealand. In summary, the key points about the Exemption Notice are as follows:

- the offer can only be made to employees (including directors) of the issuer or any of its subsidiaries;
- the offer must be made under an employee share purchase scheme that is established under the laws of the jurisdiction in which the issuer is incorporated or listed (or a regional variation of such a scheme);
- the scheme may involve the offer of a share or common stock in the relevant issuer or a right or option to acquire such a share or common stock. Certain other related security interests (such as interests in certain trust arrangements associated with the employee share purchase scheme) can also be offered under the Exemption Notice; and
- The issuer must:
  - be incorporated in a qualifying overseas jurisdiction;
  - be listed on a securities exchange in that jurisdiction; and
  - have shares or common stock which are quoted or approved for quoting by a securities exchange in that jurisdiction.

The Exemption Notice can also extend to issuers that have made an application to have their shares or common stock quoted on a securities exchange in a qualifying overseas jurisdiction and to issuers who are specifically approved by the Securities Commission to be covered by the Exemption Notice.

For the purposes of the Exemption Notice, qualifying overseas jurisdictions are:

- Australia
- Canada
- Denmark
- Finland
- France
- Germany
- The Netherlands
- Norway
- Singapore
- South Africa

- Sweden
- Switzerland
- the United Kingdom
- the United States.

The Exemption Notice also extends to apply to certain savings schemes securities offered in connection with employee share purchase schemes. This is unlikely to be relevant to long-term incentive award schemes.

*(v)*    *Conditions in the Exemption Notice*
As well as meeting the basic eligibility criteria outlined above, the issuer must comply with the following conditions under the Exemption Notice:
- The offer in New Zealand must be made after or at the same time as the offer under the same employee share purchase scheme is being made/was made in the jurisdiction in which the scheme is established.
- Every person to whom the offer is made must have received, before subscribing for the security (ie agreeing to participate in the scheme), an English version or English translation of the following:
  – the most recent annual report of the issuer of the securities;
  – the most recent published financial statements of the issuer of the securities;
  – the current rules of the scheme or a summary of those rules; and
  – the terms of the offer in New Zealand, where "published financial statements" means financial statements that are published, issued, or prepared in accordance with the laws of the jurisdiction in which the issuer is incorporated or listed.
- As an alternative to the above, employees may be given a notice stating:
  – that the information described above is available on an Internet or Intranet site operated by or on behalf of the issuer;
  – the address of that Internet or Intranet site; and
  – that the information will be sent, without fee, to the person to whom the offer is made on request, and how and to whom that request may be made.
- The issuer will need to file a copy of the information set out above with the New Zealand Companies Office prior to allotment.

**1.3    If there is an exemption, will the exemption apply automatically or are there any applications/filings that need to be made?**
See 1.2 above.

## 2.    Employee tax and social security

**2.1    When will the executive be liable to tax or social security (and at what rate) in respect of the long-term incentive award?**
Different tax rules apply depending on whether the long-term incentive award scheme involves the grant of options or the award of shares. Some of the material differences between the taxation of option-based schemes and share awards are outlined below.

## *(a)* **Taxation of options**

### *(i)* *Taxation on grant*
The grant of an option is not taxed.

### *(ii)* *Taxation on exercise*
Income tax will be payable in the tax year (beginning April 1 and ending March 31) in which the option is exercised, on the difference between the price paid for the shares and their value on the date of exercise.

The marginal income tax rates and income bands for individuals are currently set at:
- income up to NZ$38,000 – 19.5%;
- income exceeding NZ$38,000 and up to NZ$60,000 – 33%; and
- income exceeding NZ$60,000 – 39%.

## *(b)* **Taxation of share grants**
Income tax will be payable by the employee in the tax year in which the shares are received on the difference between the price paid for the shares and their value on the date of receipt.

Restrictions on the disposal of shares are only taken into account in determining the taxable benefit received by an employee if the restriction applies:
- for at least eight years from the end of the tax year in which the employee acquires the shares (or until the employee's death if earlier); or
- for at least eight years from the end of the tax year in which the employee acquires the shares (or until the employee's death if earlier) and also provides that an employee who ends employment before this time must transfer his or her shares to the employer (or the entity from whom the employee acquired the shares, ie a trustee), either for no consideration or for consideration that does not exceed the amount paid by the employee to acquire the shares.

If the long-term incentive award involves shares being held by a trustee on behalf of the employee before vesting (in the case of a provisional vesting, for example) those shares will be treated as having been acquired by the employee at the time that the trustee holds allocated shares beneficially for the employee.

## *(c)* **Holding and disposing of foreign shares**
The rules for the taxation of shares held by New Zealand residents in foreign entities (the FIF rules) have recently been amended. The FIF rules tax the value of foreign shares on an unrealised basis. Taxation of dividends only was viewed as inappropriate in many cases by the New Zealand Government because foreign companies often have a policy of paying low or no dividends. However, an investor can still make an economic gain through an increase in the share price which, in most cases, would not be taxable to the investor when realised.

The FIF rules will apply to an employee and his or her foreign shareholding if the total cost of his or her investments in foreign companies and unit trusts exceeds NZ$50,000. The cost threshold must be calculated for each tax year after April 1

2007. Not all foreign shares and units are taken into account in determining whether the NZ$50,000 cost threshold is exceeded in a particular tax year. For example, the cost of shares in Australian resident companies listed on an approved index of the Australian Stock Exchange and units in certain Australian unit trusts are not taken into account.

If foreign shares or units have been acquired before January 1 2000, an employee may elect that the cost of those investments be treated as one-half of the market value of the investment on April 1 2007 (the commencement date of the revised rules).

Note: The FIF rules can only apply if an employee acquires shares in a non-New Zealand resident company.

(i)    *If the FIF rules apply*

If the FIF rules apply, an employee must use an authorised calculation method to determine his or her taxable income and gains from the shares in a particular tax year.

The fair dividend rate (FDR) method is the calculation method which is most commonly applied. Under this method an investor is taxed each year on a total of 5% of the market value of his or her total offshore portfolio at April 1 each year. Dividends received on shares and gains on the sale of shares (that are not "quick sale" investments – see below) are not taxed separately.

An employee would be entitled to select the comparative value method (the CV method) instead of the FDR method in a particular tax year if this would result in less taxable income than under the FDR method. Taxable income under the CV method is the amount that is the total realised and unrealised gain (ie the net gain in the market value over the year, dividends received and net sale proceeds) in the tax year. Generally, if an investor applies the CV method in a given tax year he or she cannot apply the FDR method to his or her other foreign investments which are subject to the FIF rules.

Where an investor acquires and disposes of an offshore investment in the same income year (referred to as "quick sale" investments), the investor will be taxed on the lesser of:

- 5% of the cost attributable to the quick sale investments (the cost per unit of any quick sale investment is the average per-unit cost of all investments acquired or increased during the year); and
- The investor's actual return on the quick sale investments (ie all distributions received and proceeds received on the sale of the investment, less all costs incurred in acquiring the investment).

If an employee who is subject to the FIF rules sells shares to meet the purchase price or the exercise price of an option, these quick sale rules may apply. If shares are "withheld" by the employee to satisfy the share price, these rules may also apply depending on whether or not the employee could be said to have acquired and disposed of the "withheld" shares under the terms of the particular scheme.

Where it is not practical to apply the FDR method because the "market value" of an investment cannot be determined except by independent valuation, an investor may choose to pay tax on 5% of the cost (initially determined by obtaining an independent valuation) of the investment each year under the "cost method". The "cost" of the investment is increased by 5% each year for the purposes of applying this method. "Cost" can be reset once every five years through an independent valuation.

In no case is an investor entitled to claim a deduction for a net reduction in the value of his or her overall portfolio during an income year. The FDR method, the CV method and the cost method apply to the circumstances of each tax year irrespective of any fluctuation in value of investments from year to year.

Foreign withholding tax deducted from dividends can be applied to reduce the amount of New Zealand tax payable in respect of the shares under the FIF rules.

*(ii)*    *If the FIF rules do not apply*
Any dividends received in respect of any shares acquired will be taxable in the hands of the employee at the employee's marginal tax rate. The employee will be required to include the full amount of the dividend plus any foreign withholding tax deducted from the dividend (converted to New Zealand dollars at the time of the dividend is declared) in an income tax return or statement. A credit should be available against the employee's New Zealand income tax liability for any tax withheld overseas (although the credit may not exceed the investor's New Zealand tax liability on the dividend).

New Zealand does not have a capital gains tax, but does have tax gains on the sale of property which is: acquired as part of a business of dealing in that property; or acquired with a purpose of re-sale; or acquired or sold in the course of carrying on or carrying out a profit-making undertaking or scheme. Whether or not the gain on the sale of shares is taxable depends on the facts and circumstances relevant to a particular employee. However, generally:

- if the employee acquires the options, intending to exercise the options and dispose of the shares shortly afterwards, any gain on the sale of the shares is likely to be taxed. The taxable gain is the difference between the price paid for the shares and the sale proceeds; and
- if the shares are retained with a view to long-term investment, then unless the employee is a frequent trader in shares, any gain in the value of shares from the date of exercise until sale is unlikely to be taxable.

In calculating the amount of any taxable gain, the amount paid by the employee to acquire the shares must be converted to New Zealand dollars at the time the shares are acquired and the sale proceeds must be converted to New Zealand dollars at the time of the sale (ie exchange gain or losses are also taken into account in calculating the taxable gain).

**2.2    How will the executive's tax and social security be collected? Will the executive be responsible for paying any liabilities himself or will the executive's employer be responsible for paying tax or social security liabilities on the executive's behalf?**
The taxable benefit must be included as income in the employee's tax return or statement in the income year in which the employee exercises his or her options or receives his or her shares. Tax on this income will not be paid by the employer and the employee will need to meet the tax liability.

There is no PAYE or other withholding tax obligation on the local employer, as the employee is responsible for paying the tax.

2.3 **If the employer is responsible for the executive's liabilities, can the employer withhold the liabilities from the executive's salary? Are there any formalities in this respect?**

Not applicable.

2.4 **If the executive's salary in the month of exercise/release is not sufficient for the employer to withhold all of the liabilities, can the employer (or the parent company, if different) arrange for the executive to authorise to sell some of the executive's shares in the market and pass the money to the executive's employer?**

Not applicable.

2.5 **Will the executive pay tax on the eventual sale of his shares and if so at what rate?**

See above.

3. **Employer's social security**

3.1 **Is the employer liable to pay (on its own account) any employer's social security in connection with the long-term incentive award?**

No.

3.2 **Can the liability of the employer be put onto the employee? What steps are required?**

Not applicable.

4. **Tax deduction for the employer**

4.1 **Is it possible for the employer to receive a tax deduction in respect of the long-term incentive award? Would the employer need to be subject to recharge arrangements (eg if the employer is a subsidiary and provides funds to the parent company as part of a recharge arrangement in respect of the long-term incentive award)?**

There are no special deductions available for a share option scheme. However, the costs of establishing and operating a scheme should be deductible for tax purposes under general deductibility principles if those costs are incurred by the local employer. Recharge payments made by a subsidiary employer to a parent company in connection with the operation of a scheme should also be deductible.

The deductions available to the subsidiary can be claimed in the year in which they are incurred.

The dilution effect of issuing shares at less than their market value is not deductible as it does not result in any expenditure by the issuer or the employer.

Employees will be taxed on the difference between the price paid for, and the market value of, the shares but the employer cannot deduct an equivalent amount.

Transfer pricing issues can arise in situations such as this where a non-resident parent company is issuing shares to employees of a New Zealand subsidiary, depending on the arrangements between the parent company and the New Zealand subsidiary.

## 5.     Tax beneficial arrangements

### 5.1   Are there ways of making the long-term incentive award tax-efficient in New Zealand?

Some long-term incentive share award schemes do not give rise to income tax being payable on share price gains during the period after the initial grant of the share right. Examples of employee share purchase schemes that operate in this manner include certain schemes:

- under which the employee receives the shares at the outset (rather than options or rights in respect of the shares);
- involving the use of convertible notes; and
- involving the use of partly paid shares.

Specific advice would be required in relation to the establishment of schemes of this nature.

## 6.     Internationally mobile executives

### 6.1   What are the income tax consequences for an employee who is resident in New Zealand when the long-term incentive award is made but who is no longer resident at the time of exercise/vesting?

Generally, the benefit derived by an employee under a long-term incentive award who is no longer resident in New Zealand at the time of exercise/vesting will be subject to tax in New Zealand if the benefit is treated as being derived from a source in New Zealand. Income which is "earned in New Zealand in the service of an employer" resident in New Zealand or elsewhere is treated as being derived from New Zealand.

In the context of long-term incentive awards, the best approach may be to determine the portion of the benefit received under the award which vests in the employee for services performed in New Zealand and the benefit attributable to services performed overseas. Only the portion of the benefit attributable to the services performed in New Zealand should be subject to New Zealand tax. Note that the benefit under a long-term incentive award would not generally be regarded as relating to any services rendered after the vesting period.

This approach is broadly consistent with the approach advocated by the OECD in its 2004 report *Cross-border Income Tax Issues Arising from Employee Stock Option Plans* and is likely to represent the approach adopted by New Zealand in its tax treaty negotiations.

**6.2** **What are the social security consequences for an employee who is resident in New Zealand when the long-term incentive award is made but who is no longer resident at the time of exercise/vesting?**

No New Zealand social security implications arise for long-term incentive share awards.

**6.3** **What are the tax and social security withholding/reporting consequences for the employer in respect of an employee who is resident in New Zealand when the long-term incentive award is made but who is no longer resident at the time of exercise/vesting?**

None.

## 7. Reporting requirements

**7.1** **Will the employer (or parent company, if different) have any reporting requirements as a result of the long-term incentive award?**

Under the Financial Reporting Act 1993, offering securities to New Zealand employees may mean that the issuer must comply with certain reporting obligations in relation to the preparation, content and registration of financial statements. This will be the case where the issuer falls within the Securities Act 1978 or relies on certain exemptions granted by the Securities Commission under that Act.

Where these requirements apply, financial statements for the issuer and the issuer's group (ie consolidated accounts alone will not suffice) must be filed with the New Zealand Companies Office within five months plus 20 working days from the issuer's year-end.

The financial statements should generally include an audit report, statement of cash flows, statement of financial performance, statement of financial position, notes to the accounts and a statement of accounting policies. They must be signed by two directors.

The Companies Office is entitled to insist on financial statements that comply with New Zealand accounting requirements.

It is possible to apply to the Companies Office or the Securities Commission for an exemption from some or all of the requirements of the Financial Reporting Act 1993. The ability to apply for such exemptions resulted from a recent law change and it is currently uncertain what criteria will need to be met in order to obtain an exemption. A class exemption has been issued in respect of certain issuers incorporated in the United States (subject to conditions).

**7.2** **Are there any tax rulings required in relation to the long-term incentive awards?**

No.

**8. Exchange control issues**

8.1 Are there any exchange control issues that would prevent an employee from (a) remitting monies abroad to purchase shares, or (b) repatriating monies from the sale of shares?

No.

**9. Employment law**

9.1 Are there any employment or local labour law issues which may arise as a result of the long-term incentive award? Are any consultations or authorisations required by law?

It is unlawful for an employer to discriminate against employees engaged in the same or substantially similar work on any prohibited grounds of discrimination such as gender, age and family status under the New Zealand Human Rights Act 1993 (HRA).

Under the terms of some overseas employee share purchase schemes, employees who are retiring (ie leaving service having reached a certain age) are treated more favourably than those who decide to leave service in other circumstances. This is generally differentiating on the basis of age, which is discriminatory and hence unlawful under the HRA.

The HRA prohibits not only direct discrimination but also indirect discrimination (ie discrimination which does not discriminate against one of the prohibited grounds but may have the effect of doing so).

In general, share purchase schemes are not subject to works council/union/employee representative body approval, notification, or consultation. However, review of agreements with such bodies or applicable collective bargaining agreements, if any, is recommended. The Employment Relations Act 2000 provides that employers must act in good faith, which, among other things, requires employers to be "active and constructive" in maintaining an employment relationship in which the parties are "responsive and communicative".

**10. Translation**

10.1 Are there any language restrictions in New Zealand? Does any of the documentation provided to the employee in relation to the long-term incentive award need to be translated into English?

An English version of certain documents may need to be provided to employees under securities laws (see above).

## 11. Data protection

11.1 **Are there any data protection issues which may arise should the employer wish to outsource the administration of the long-term incentive award to a third party?**

The Privacy Act 1993 sets out certain principles which place obligations on agencies (including employers) in relation to the collection, storage and use of personal data. In particular, individuals must be informed thus:

- the fact that the data is being collected;
- why the data is being collected;
- the intended recipients of the information;
- the name and address of the agency collecting and holding the data;
- the consequences (if any) for the individual if all or any part of the requested data is not provided; and
- the rights of access to, and correction of, any personal data provided.

Where personal data about an employee is proposed to be passed on to a third-party administrator, the provisions of the Privacy Act 1993 will need to be considered. It is likely to be prudent to obtain the express written consent of the employee as to the proposed treatment of the relevant data. This consent can generally be sought at the time the employee applies for the long-term incentive award.

## 12. Source of shares

12.1 **Does it matter if shares are newly issued to an employee, provided out of treasury or delivered from an employee-benefit trust?**

This can make a difference to the treatment of the offer under the Securities Act 1978 in that, if certain conditions are met, it may be possible to make an offer without requiring a prospectus or an investment statement (see above). It can also impact on the requirements under the Financial Reporting Act 1993 in that, if a prospectus and investment statement are not required under the Securities Act 1978 and certain other conditions are met, it may not be necessary to comply with New Zealand financial reporting requirements (see above).

# Poland

Przemysław Pietrzak
Gleiss Lutz

---

> **Red flag issues**
> 1. Ambiguity relating to tax deduction for the employer.
> 2. Polish language requirements for documents relating to employment relationships.

## 1. Securities laws

**1.1** What prospectus and/or securities law requirements arise in connection with the grant, vesting or exercise of a long-term incentive award or on the eventual sale of the shares by the executive?

### (a) Public offering

Provided that long-term incentive awards (as defined) are non-transferable, they will not qualify as "securities" for the purposes of the Polish Act on a Public Offering, Conditions Governing the Introduction of Financial Instruments to Organised Trading, and Public Companies, dated June 29 2005 (the POA). Therefore, the grant or exercise will not be a public offering which requires a prospectus. Options which, from the point of view of corporate law, take the form of subscription warrants or convertible bonds or bonds with the priority right will usually also be non-transferable.

### (b) Prospectus requirements; information memorandum

If the long-term incentive awards are transferable, the company will be deemed to have made a public offer of securities in Poland which will require the publication of a prospectus approved by the Polish Financial Supervision Commission (the PFSC) before the offer is made. The relevant exemptions are described below.

The prospectus must contain information specified in detail in the POA and in Commission Regulations (EC) No 809/2004 of April 29 2004, implementing Directive 2003/71/EC of the European Parliament and of the Council. This information relates to the content and format of prospectuses, incorporation by reference, publication of prospectuses and dissemination of advertisements. In particular, the prospectus must include the identification data of the issuer, information on the form of the securities, persons responsible for information, shareholders with a significant number of shares, risk factors, issuer's assessment and forecast prospects and financial statement.

If, under the POA, a public offer takes place within a member state of the European Union or European Union Area (EEA) other than Poland, the prospectus may be prepared in Polish or in English, according to the choice of the issuer.

If there is an exemption from the requirement to prepare a prospectus before offering securities to the public (see below), according to the POA, it is necessary to prepare an information memorandum. In such cases, the public offer of securities requires the information memorandum to be submitted to the PFSC. In general, the information contained in the information memorandum is less detailed than that which is included in the prospectus. Securities may be offered to the public, if the PFSC does not raise any objection to the public offer, within 20 working days from the submission of the information memorandum.

The approved prospectus or the information memorandum, to which no objection has been raised, must be announced publicly (in a national newspaper, at the registered office of the company, on the issuer's website, or on the website of the company responsible for the relevant regulated market).

The issuer is under a duty to provide the PFSC within 24 hours with any information, in the form of an attachment to the prospectus or information memorandum, which could have a significant impact on the value of the securities until the public offer is conducted or cancelled.

1.2 **Is there an exemption from the requirement of the law on securities either because the shares are being offered only to executives or because shares are being offered to a distinct group of named individuals?**
There are exemptions from the general rules relating to the public offering and prospectus requirements which are described above. These are set out next.

*(a)* *No public offering*
In the light of the POA, an offering of securities is not a public offering and is to be treated as a private placement if:
- the addressees of the offer consist of a group of specified pre-selected potential investors (eg employees of the issuer);
- the number of investors in Poland is less than 100; or
- the addressees of the offer are exclusively qualified investors (who may also be natural persons), if they have a registered office in Poland (are Polish residents) and are registered in the register of qualified investors, or have a registered office in (are residents of) one of the member states of the European Union or EEA and have the status of qualified investor in one of these states.

In order to be entered in the register of qualified investors, it is necessary to fulfil two of the three conditions below:
- the addressee of the offer who is a qualified investor must currently work, or have at least one year's work experience, in the field in which the knowledge concerning the investment in securities is required; or
- he/she must have concluded in the last 12 months, prior to registration as a

qualified investor, at least 10 transactions in the amount of €50,000 per transaction; or

- the total value of the investment in securities concluded by him/her must amount to at least €500,000.

### (b) Prospectus requirements

#### (i) Exemptions based on total consideration of the offering

The POA provides for exemptions from the prospectus requirements as described above, particularly in the case of:

- an offer of securities the total value of which, calculated on the basis of the issue price or selling price, does not exceed – over a period of 12 consecutive months – €100,000;
- an offer of securities addressed only to investors, each of which purchases securities of a value, calculated in accordance with their issue price or sale price, of at least €50,000;
- an application to admit to the regulated market shares which, within the next 12 months, constitute less than 10 per cent of all the issuer's shares of the same type admitted to trade on the same regulated market;
- an offer of securities where the total value of their issue over the period of 12 consecutive months, calculated on the basis of the issue price, is less than €2.5 million;
- an offer relating to securities of which the unit nominal value is at least €50,000.

#### (ii) Other exemptions

Under the POA there is no prospectus requirement in certain other circumstances, in particular in the case of:

- an application to admit to the regulated market securities of the same type as other securities of the issuer admitted to trade on the same regulated market which were the subject of the purchase offer, or were issued by the issuer or by a connected entity to (current or former) employees and/or executives;
- an offer where the shares are granted free of any consideration to shareholders (from company funds) or as a payment of dividend on the shares, and the shares issued are of the same type as the shares on which a dividend is paid; and
- an application to admit to the regulated market shares of a company whose other shares of the same type are admitted to trade on the same regulated market, if the purchase offer or issue of these has been made for holders of other securities of this company to exercise their rights.

### 1.3 If there is an exemption, will the exemption apply automatically or are there any applications/documents which must be submitted?

The law expressly sets out when a placement of securities is a public offering or a private placement, and also when prospectus requirements apply. Thus, there is no need to request authority for the application of a statutory exemption.

## 2. Employee tax and social security

### 2.1 When will the executive be liable to tax or social security (and at what rate) in respect of the long-term incentive award?

#### (a) On grant

The grant of a non-transferable option does not have any tax consequences.

Free shares will be subject to Polish personal income tax (PIT) at the date of grant on their fair market value, irrespective of whether the shares are subject to forfeiture should the beneficiary leave the company or the performance conditions not be achieved.

#### (b) On exercise

An income tax charge will arise on the exercise of a non-transferable option on the amount by which the market value of the underlying shares at the date of exercise exceeds the exercise price (plus any amount paid for the option) (option gain).

Social security obligations arise at the same time as the tax obligations. The principles of taxation and those relating to social security, described below, apply to executives engaged both under an employment agreement or managerial agreement (commission agreement).

However, if specific conditions are satisfied, the Polish tax provisions allow exemption from the above taxation.

The option gain is added to other income during that year (which is not taxable separately). The taxation takes place according to a progressive tax scale, which is currently at 19% on annual taxable amounts up to around PLN43,500, 30% on amounts from around PLN43,500 up to around PLN85,500, and 40% above the threshold of around PLN85,500.

#### (c) Tax exemption

Under the provisions in force relating to PIT, the income of an employee on the exercise of an option, or on the grant of shares, will not be subject to taxation if the shares are taken up by employees/executives authorised under a resolution of the general meeting of the company issuing the shares.

The above exemption is also applied in cases where shares are awarded by the company of an intermediary which has taken up the shares solely for the purpose of transferring them to employees/executives authorised under a resolution of the general meeting. Under the PIT Act, it is not clear whether the authorised employees/executives must be indicated by name, or whether a general description of the category of the beneficiaries is sufficient.

#### (d) Social security

The social security contributions are calculated on the basis of the income which is calculated in the same manner as for tax purposes and amount to:

- pension contribution – 19.52% of income (half of which the employer contributes);

- retirement pension – 6% of income (three-quarters of which the employer contributes);
- sickness insurance – 2.45% of the income (paid by employee only);
- health insurance – 9% of income excluding pension, disability allowance and sickness benefit (paid by the employee only);
- accident insurance – of between 0.67% and 3.6% of income (paid by the employer only);
- benefits fund for employees guaranteed under employment law – 0.1% of income (paid by employer only); and
- employment fund contribution – 2.45% of income (paid by the employer only).

*(e)* *Sale of transferable option rights and shares*

Income subject to taxation is also generated in each case where the employee/executive sells the shares to a third party, irrespective of whether or not they were awarded to him/her free of any consideration. The income subject to taxation will be the sale price minus the exercise price, if any, and any amount paid for the option. This income is not added to other income subject to taxation according to the progressive scale, and the applicable rate in this case is 19%. Such income is considered as a capital gain and the tax is to be paid by the employee/executive. Additionally, the sale is subject to transfer tax of 1% to be paid by the purchaser.

Social security obligations do not arise in the case of the sale of shares because the income received at this stage is not treated as remuneration resulting from employment or a managerial agreement (commission agreement).

**2.2 How will the executive's tax and social security be collected? Will the executive be responsible for paying any liabilities himself or will the executive's employer be responsible for paying tax or social security liabilities on the executive's behalf?**

Advance PIT and social security contributions are deducted each month by the employer for the employee. This applies to executives engaged on the basis of an employment contract or managerial agreement (commission agreement).

**2.3 If the employer is responsible for the executive's liabilities, can the employer withhold the liabilities from the executive's salary? Are there any formalities in this respect?**

Yes. The employer is able to make deductions from the executive's monthly remuneration (which includes benefits in the form of shares) for the entire advance income tax contribution and pays it into the relevant tax office, together with the monthly declaration by the twentieth day of the month following the payment of salaries.

An annual declaration must be submitted by the end of January of the following year. The employer deducts an amount (see above) for the social security contribution from the executive's monthly remuneration and makes payment, together with its own liability, to the relevant social insurance office by the fifteenth day of the month following the payment of salaries. It must also make the appropriate monthly declarations.

2.4 **If the executive's salary in the month of exercise/release is not sufficient for the employer to withhold all of the liabilities, can the employer (or the parent company, if different) arrange for the executive to authorise to sell some of the executive's shares in the market and pass the money to the executive's employer?**
Yes. The authorisation has to be in writing.

2.5 **Will the executive pay tax on the eventual sale of his shares and if so at what rate?**
Yes. Each sale of shares by the executive is subject to taxation at a flat tax rate of 19% PIT after deduction of the costs of purchasing the shares. The Polish provisions on PIT do not provide any additional exemptions. Income on the sale of shares as capital gains is not added to other income. Moreover, the sale of shares is subject to transfer tax of 1% of the price. The tax is to be paid by the purchaser.

3. **Employer's social security**

3.1 **Is the employer liable to pay (on its own account) any employer's social security in connection with the long-term incentive award?**
Yes, in respect of a liability which may arise in connection with the grant of free shares and the exercise of an option.

3.2 **Can the liability of the employer be put onto the employee?**
No.

4. **Tax deduction for the employer**

4.1 **Is it possible for the employer to receive a tax deduction for the long-term incentive award? Would the employer need to be subject to recharge arrangements (eg if the employer is a subsidiary and provides funds to the parent company as part of a recharge arrangement for the long-term incentive award)?**
Yes. The costs involved in satisfying a long-term incentive award can be deducted from the employer's profits subject to taxation, if the employer can demonstrate the connection between these costs and income (eg incentive payments to employees which increase their output and therefore the employer's income). These costs are in particular the administration costs of a long-term incentive award.

However, opinion is divided as to the settlement of recharged costs of long-term incentive awards by a subsidiary, which is financed by the parent company, on the basis of which the employees of the subsidiary obtain shares of the parent company. As a rule, the tax authorities do not acknowledge such costs connected with income of the subsidiary as tax-deductible. The tax authorities are beginning to change their stance on this, but to date there is still a risk that they will question any amounts that are re-charged to the subsidiary.

## 5. Tax beneficial arrangements

### 5.1 Are there any ways of making the long-term incentive award tax-efficient in Poland?

Yes, if the free shares granted or shares acquired on exercise of a non-transferable option are taken up by employees/executives authorised by a resolution of the general meeting. This will avoid a tax charge on the grant (of free shares) and exercise (of an option). (See 2.1(c) above.)

## 6. Internationally mobile executives

### 6.1 What are the income tax consequences for an employee who is resident in Poland when the long-term incentive award is made, but who is no longer resident at the time of exercise/vesting?

If, at the time of exercise, an employee/executive who has been granted a long-term incentive award is no longer a Polish resident within the meaning of the Polish tax law, his/her income will not be taxed in Poland, provided he/she is no longer employed and does not conduct any economic activity in Poland and does not achieve any other income which is taxable in Poland.

On the sale of shares acquired pursuant to the exercise of a non-transferable option, or the grant of free shares, income subject to taxation in Poland may arise if the company's property comprises mainly, either directly or indirectly, real estate assets situated in Poland or rights forming part of these assets. Most agreements on the avoidance of double taxation provide for taxation of this nature.

### 6.2 What are the social security consequences for an employee who is resident in Poland when the long-term incentive award is made, but who is no longer resident at the time of exercise/vesting?

There are no social security obligations in Poland if, at the time of exercise, an employee who has been granted a long-term incentive award is no longer a Polish resident within the meaning of the Polish social security law. His/her income will not be taxed in Poland, provided that he/she is not employed or does not conduct economic activity in Poland and does not achieve any other income subject to taxation in Poland.

### 6.3 What are the tax and social security withholding/reporting consequences for the employer in respect of an employee who is resident in Poland when the long-term incentive award is made but who is no longer resident at the time of exercise/vesting?

If the exercise is not subject to taxation or an obligation to pay social security contributions in Poland as a result of the circumstances described above, the employer will not have any additional obligations.

## 7. Reporting requirements

### 7.1. Will the employer (or parent company, if different) have any reporting requirements as a result of the long-term incentive award?

Companies whose securities have been admitted to public trading on a regulated market must provide the PFSC with information relating to the companies or their shares, if such information might influence the price of shares in a significant manner. The above duty applies, in practice, to the duty to submit to the PFSC a report containing information on the options scheme.

### 7.2. Are there any tax rulings required in relation to the long-term incentive awards?

Polish law does not stipulate any obligatory application for tax rulings in reference to long-term incentive awards. If there is any uncertainty with regard to tax treatment of the intended long-term incentive awards, then legal certainty can be achieved by applying for an advance ruling. Such a tax ruling may be granted by the competent tax authority if there is no pending tax or control procedure relating to the relevant case. If the interpretation given by the tax authority is followed by the taxpayer, conduct which is in accordance with such interpretation may not be questioned any further by any tax authority, even though such interpretation may be inconsistent with the applicable law.

## 8. Exchange control issues

### 8.1 Are there any exchange control issues that would prevent an employee from (a) remitting monies abroad to purchase shares or (b) repatriating monies from the sale of shares?

According to the Polish Exchange Law of July 27 2002, the purchase of shares in companies with registered offices in a member state of the European Union, EEA or OECD does not require a permit. The general permit issued by the Polish Minister of Finance of September 4 2007 also allows the purchase of shares of companies with a registered office in countries with whom Poland has concluded an agreement on the promotion and protection of investments. In all other cases, a permit issued by the President of the National Bank of Poland is required.

## 9. Employment law

### 9.1 Are there any employment or local labour law issues which may arise as a result of the long-term incentive award? Are any consultations or authorisations required by law?

The Polish Labour Code of June 26 1974 does not contain any explicit provisions relating to long-term incentive awards.

Long-term incentives in Poland are based, in principle, not on individual employment agreements but rather on the general schemes applying to specific groups of employees, defined according to objective criteria. However, it is possible, though not obligatory, also to regulate them in the remuneration rules issued by the employer. If there is a trade union in the company, such remuneration rules must be agreed with the trade union.

## 10. Translation

10.1 **Are there any language restrictions in Poland? Does any of the documentation provided to the employee in relation to the long-term incentive award need to be translated?**
Yes. According to Clauses 7 and 8 of the Polish Language Act of October 7 1999, all documentation addressed to employees must be in Polish, especially with regard to employment agreements, provided the relevant agreement is exercised within Poland and Polish labour regulations apply.

## 11. Data protection

11.1 **Are there any data protection issues which may arise should the employer wish to outsource the administration of the long-term incentive award to a third party?**
Processing, collecting or forwarding the personal data of beneficiaries of long-term incentives to other entities generally requires the consent of the relevant individuals. Moreover, when databases containing such data are created, they must be registered with the General Supervisor for Data Protection.

The administrator of the personal data of beneficiaries of long-term incentive awards may, in a written agreement, under Article 31 of the Personal Data Protection Act (the PDPA), entrust the processing of personal data to another entity. The entity to which the administration of data has been entrusted has sole authorisation according to the scope and purpose defined in the agreement. This also relates to the time which is necessary to process the data in order to realise the purpose of data processing and to give effect to the long-term incentive award. Moreover, before it commences the data processing, this entity must safeguard the database against access by unauthorised persons, by taking technical and organisational measures to safeguard it. It should also keep documents relating to the data's protection, as it could at a future point be liable as if it were the administrator.

Entrusting the data processing to another entity does not release the administrator from liability for administration. Liability for failure to observe the provisions of the PDPA lies both with the administrator of the data, and the entity with which it concluded an agreement.

Entrusting the administration of data to an entity with its registered office in another country is permitted on condition that standards are, at the very least equivalent in that country to those in Poland, unless the person whose data is processed consents in writing or the data being processed is necessary to perform an agreement between the administrator of the data and the person to whom the data relates.

Where an entity which processes data has its registered office in a foreign country, it must appoint a representative in Poland.

## 12. Source of shares

### 12.1 Does it matter if shares are newly issued to an employee, provided out of treasury or delivered from an employee-benefit trust?

No. It is of little significance whether employees exercising their rights under the incentive award purchased shares from the company which were bought on the market by the company, or whether they took up newly issued shares by the company for this purpose.

# Portugal

Ana Paula Basílio
Ana Sofia Silva
Sandra Lima da Silveira
Gonçalves Pereira, Castelo Branco & Associados, RL

---

**Red flag issues**
1. No withholding tax for residents.
2. Social security liability.
3. Exemption of prospectus in specific situations.

## 1. Securities laws

### 1.1 What prospectus and/or securities law requirements arise in connection with the grant, vesting or exercise of a long-term incentive award or on the eventual sale of the shares by the executive?

The following rules apply to the grant, vesting or exercise of a long-term incentive award.

According to the Portuguese Securities Code (Decree-Law No. 486/99, dated November 13 1999, as subsequently amended), offers specifically addressed to Portuguese residents are governed by Portuguese law and are subject to the supervision of the Portuguese Securities Commission (*Comissão do Mercado de Valores Imobiliários* – CMVM).

The main distinction to be made is that between public and private offers. Under the terms of the Portuguese Securities Code, any offer of securities specifically addressed to Portuguese residents shall be considered as public where it is:

- addressed to an undetermined number of addressees;
- addressed to all the shareholders of a company which is open to public investment, irrespective of the shares being in nominative form;
- wholly or partially preceded or accompanied by a prospectus or an invitation to invest from unidentified addressees or in the form of promotional material; or
- addressed to more than 100 persons, who are not qualified investors resident or established in Portugal.

The offer to employees of non-transferable options and free share awards is also subject to the above rules.

The concept of a private offer is residual, as an offer is considered to be private where it does not qualify as a "public offer". Portuguese law also provides some situations that should be regarded as private offers, irrespective of the fact that they fall under the legal criteria referred above (eg offers addressed to qualified investors only, which is not the case under analysis).

Accordingly, whether a stock options plan qualifies as a public or private offer will depend on the number of eligible executives/employees. Private offers do not need a prospectus or an information document to be produced.

Public offers:

- must take place through a duly authorised financial intermediary (registered with CMVM), who will provide assistance and placement services;
- shall be subject to prior registration with the CMVM;
- require a Public Offer Announcement;
- require a prospectus; and
- require that all publicity material related to the public offer is subject to prior approval by the CMVM.

However, (i) public offers for distribution of securities with a denomination per unit equal to or greater than €50,000 or whose subscription or sale price, per addressee, is equal to or greater than that amount; and (ii) public offers for distribution of securities where the total consideration of the offer is less than €2.5 million (which shall be calculated over a 12-month period) are not subject to the rules mentioned above.

The eventual sale of the shares by the executive is not subject to any specific rules, pursuant to Portuguese law.

**1.2    Is there an exemption from securities laws requirements either because the shares are being offered only to executives, or because shares are being offered to a distinct group of named individuals?**

There is an exemption from securities laws requirements if the offer qualifies as private.

Offers for the distribution of securities to 100 or more existing or former members of the board of directors or to employees by their employer or an affiliated company which already has securities trading on a regulated market are exempt from the prospectus, provided that a document is made available which contains information on the number and nature of the securities and the reasons for, and details of, the offer.

**1.3    If there is an exemption, will the exemption apply automatically or are there any applications/filings that need to be made?**

For private offers, the exemption applies automatically. If the offer is made by a public company (a company whose share capital is open to public investment) or by a company whose share capital is listed on a regulated market, the CMVM must be informed for statistical purposes. In the above case, the prospectus exemption applies automatically.

## 2. Employee tax and social security

### 2.1 When will the executive be liable to tax or social security (and at what rate) in respect of the long-term incentive award?

*(a)* *Tax*

The long-term incentive awards are treated as income from employment. For individual income tax purposes, where the employee:

- is *resident* in Portugal, for tax purposes, the award is taxed at the general progressive rates from 10.5% to 42%. The resident employee submits an annual tax return where all income received during the previous year, including this specific type of employment income, is disclosed and the tax authorities then make the income tax assessment. This assessment is then notified to the resident employee, who must pay the tax due within 30 days; or
- is *non-resident* in Portugal, there is a 20% rate, through withholding tax.

The date where such income is considered to be obtained and the point the tax liability arises will depend on the particular type of incentive award granted to the employees, as described below.

*(b)* *Award of shares*

Where the incentive award corresponds to the effective granting of shares and to the extent that there is a minimum vesting period – during which the employee is bound to keep those shares and cannot assign, charge or otherwise dispose of them, or during which the employee, to comply with his contractual obligation and entitlement to the incentive award, must not terminate his employment relationship – the shares will be taxable when the restrictions fall away and the shares fully vest.

The income tax liability will arise on the amount by which the fair market value of the shares exceeds the acquisition price paid by the employee to acquire them on the date they fully vest. If the shares have been granted free of charge, the employee will be subject to a tax charge equal to the fair market value of the shares on the date they vest.

However, if the incentive award is not subject to the vesting period restrictions described above, any income will be taxable immediately at the date the shares are granted to the employee.

Should the shares granted to the employee be repurchased by the employer for an amount in excess of the shares' fair market value, the excess will be treated as employment income and will be subject to an income tax charge.

*(c)* *Options on grant*

No income tax charge will arise on the grant of an option to acquire shares in the company, regardless of whether the exercise price is equal to, or less than, the fair market value of the shares at the date of grant.

*(d)* *On exercise*

An income tax charge will arise on the exercise of the option on the amount by which the fair market value of the shares exceeds the exercise price.

If the option is a transferable option and the employee sells it, an income tax charge will arise on the amount by which the sale proceeds exceed the price paid by the employee to acquire the option (if any).

### (e) Social security

According to technical internal guidance issued by the Social Security General Direction (*Direcção Geral da Solidariedade e Segurança Social*) in February 2004, benefits under share schemes are equivalent to bonuses and should be treated as such. As per the applicable legislation, a bonus will only be subject to social security obligations if its grant qualifies as regular and periodical. The fact that the plan allows the granting of options over the years and does not constitute a one-off benefit may lead to its qualification as a regular and periodical benefit and make it subject to social security obligations.

Notwithstanding the above, this administrative information is internal guidance for social security officers, and as such does not constitute a legal obligation for employers. This means that although social security officers may wish to enforce this interpretation of what is considered to be income subject to social security contributions, it is possible for employers to oppose any decision based on this administrative information.

In the absence of any express rules about share schemes, general rules will apply and the benefit (the amount by which the fair market value of the shares exceeds the exercise price) will be liable to social security when the options are exercised.

**2.2** **How will the executive's tax and social security be collected? Will the executive be responsible for paying any liabilities himself or will the executive's employer be responsible for paying tax or social security liabilities on the executive's behalf?**

### (a) Tax

#### (i) Portugal-resident employees

In the context of long-term incentive award plans, income arising from the award of shares or grant of options is not subject to withholding tax where the employee/beneficiary of the income is resident in Portugal for tax purposes.

Therefore, this income will only be taxed in final terms – along with the other income of the employee received in the same year. It must be disclosed by the employee, in his annual tax return corresponding to the year the income is considered to be obtained, with the employee being solely responsible for paying the tax due for the incentives awarded.

#### (ii) Non-Portugal-resident

If the employee is not resident in Portugal for tax purposes, any income earned will be subject to withholding tax at a 20% flat rate by virtue of the award of shares or the exercising of options.

Here the employer must withhold this tax and pay it to the Portuguese tax authorities. If it is not withheld (or, being withheld, is not paid to the tax authorities), the employer is responsible for payment and will be charged interest at 4% per year for any late payment. A penalty, ranging from 20% to 100% of the amount corresponding to the tax not withheld (or that, having been withheld, was not paid to the tax authorities), up to a limit of €30,000, may also be levied.

*(b)*    *Social security*

The employer must make a monthly declaration to the social security services about payments made to employees. This is due by the fifteenth day of the month following the month in which the payments were made. The employer must pay any due amounts on the same day.

Contributions rates for the declared payments are currently:
- 23.75% (liability of the employer);
- 11% (liability of the employee).

**2.3**    **If the employer is responsible for the executive's liabilities, can the employer withhold the liabilities from the executive's salary? Are there any formalities in this respect?**

*(a)*    *Tax*

As previously mentioned, the employer is only responsible for the employee's tax liabilities if the employee is not resident in Portugal for tax purposes. Here, the employer will be responsible for withholding the corresponding tax from the employee's salary, at a 20% flat rate.

Furthermore, the employer must comply with some registry and "compliance" obligations relating to the employment income paid to its employees and, in particular, to the employment income granted under stock option plans or similar plans. The employer must:
- by the end of July of each year, submit a statement/form to the tax authorities stating the employment income paid to any employees who are not resident in Portugal during the previous year, and any corresponding tax withheld;
- by the end of February of each year, submit a statement/form to the tax authorities stating the income paid to employees resident in Portugal during the previous year and any corresponding tax withheld. (This applies to other sorts of employment income, as this type of income arising from the granting of shares or stock options is not subject to withholding tax, when received by Portugal-resident employees);
- by the end of June of each year, submit a statement/form to the tax authorities whereby the employer informs the tax authorities that a stock option plan, a subscription plan or other long-term incentive award plan was implemented in the previous year;
- hold and update a registry of the employees which are entitled to this kind of income, containing their name, taxpayer number and code, and the date and value of each income payment, even if no tax has been withheld; and
- by January 20 of each year, deliver to the employees a document stating the

amounts/income due in the previous year and, where applicable, the corresponding tax withheld.

*(b)* *Social security*
The amount for which the employee is liable (currently 11%) should be withheld by the employer from the payment made (or benefit granted) to the employee.

**2.4** **If the executive's salary in the month of exercise/release is not sufficient for the employer to withhold all of the liabilities, can the employer (or the parent company, if different) arrange for the executive to authorise to sell some of the executive's shares in the market and pass the money to the executive's employer?**

*(a)* *Tax*
As previously mentioned, this issue could only arise if the employee is a non-resident of Portugal, as no withholding tax is due over this kind of employment income where the beneficiary is resident in Portugal.

*(i)* *Non-resident employees*
No. The employer has no right to sell the shares of a non-resident employee. The non-resident employee could agree to sell sufficient number of shares to satisfy the liability and pass the proceeds to the employer; but the employer cannot enforce this.

*(b)* *Social security*
Please see the tax section above.

**2.5** **Will the executive pay tax on the eventual sale of his shares and if so at what rate?**

*(a)* *Sale of the shares to third parties*
The employee will be taxed on the capital gains arising from the sale of the shares, at a special 10% rate, except where those shares have been held (by the employee) for more than 12 months, prior to their disposal and the assets of the company whose shares are being disposed of are not made up of more than 50% of real estate located in Portugal. If these two requirements are met, there will be no capital gains liability on the disposal of the shares.

If the employees are non-residents of Portugal, capital gains on the sale of the shares will be exempt, even if the above requirement concerning the 12-month retention period is not met, as long as the assets of the company whose share are being disposed of are not composed, by more than 50%, of real estate located in Portugal. If this last condition is not met (and, thus, the exemption does not apply), the capital gain obtained by the employee, as a result of the sale of the shares, will be taxed, at the 10% rate (except where the employee is tax-resident in a country which has signed a double taxation treaty with Portugal and that treaty grants exclusive rights to tax this kind of capital gains to the state of residence of its beneficiary/employee).

If a capital gains tax liability arises, the taxable capital gain shall correspond to the amount by which the disposal proceeds exceed the adjusted basis which was considered in the computation of the income from the employment previously taxed (ie the fair market value of those shares (i) at the date the vesting period terminates, (ii) at the date the option is exercised, or (iii) at the date the shares were purchased at a discount, depending on the type of right granted to the employee and, therefore, on the regime previously applied to the employment income element).

Capital gains tax liability is not subject to withholding; it is instead paid when the liability is disclosed by the employee in his annual tax return corresponding to the year where the shares have been sold. This applies whether or not the employee is resident in Portugal.

*(b)*     *Sale of the shares to the employer*
It should be noted that if the shares are repurchased by the employer, the amount by which the disposal proceeds exceed the fair market value of the shares (if any) will qualify and be taxed as employment income (as mentioned above) and the balance will be treated as a capital gain.

It should further be noted that the base cost of the shares, for the purposes of the computation of the capital gain, will not correspond to the price effectively paid by the employee on the date the shares were acquired, but to its fair market value (i) at the date the vesting period had terminated, (ii) at the date the option was exercised, or (iii) at the date the shares were purchased at a discount (depending on the type of right granted to the employee and, consequently, on the computation of the employment income element that was previously taxed), to avoid part of the gain from being taxed twice (as an employment income by the date the shares were acquired and as a portion of the capital gain, by the date the same are disposed of).

## 3.     Employer's social security

3.1     **Is the employer liable to pay (on its own account) any social security in connection with the long-term incentive award?**
The employer will be liable to pay 23.75% (of the amount by which the fair market value exceeds the option price) as a result of the exercise of the option.

3.2     **Can the liability of the employer be put onto the employee?**
No.

## 4.     Tax deduction for the employer

4.1     **Is it possible for the employer to receive a tax deduction in respect of the long-term incentive award? Would the employer need to be subject to recharge arrangements (eg if the employer is a subsidiary and provides funds to the** parent company as part of a recharge arrangement in respect of the long-term incentive award)?

Yes. For the computation of its taxable results, the employer may deduct the costs incurred by the long-term incentive awards granted to its employees, as being costs with salaries. As they are related to its corporate activities, these costs will be deductible for corporate income tax purposes. Where the incentive is an option, the costs arising to the employee, which would be tax deductible, would correspond to the amount by which the fair market value of the shares paid by the employer in the acquisition of the shares exceeds the exercise price. In awards of shares, the total acquisition price of the shares, paid by the employer, would be deductible.

If recharge arrangements are entered into between the local employer and its foreign parent company, costs arising from these arrangements would be fully tax deductible as long as those costs comply with the Portuguese transfer pricing rules (ie are determined on an arm's-length basis).

## 5. Tax beneficial arrangements

### 5.1 Are there any ways of making the long-term incentive award tax-efficient in Portugal?

The point of taxation will depend on the type of awards that are granted. Shares awarded without vesting conditions will be taxed at grant, whereas should share awards be subject to a specified vesting period during which they may be forfeited, the employee will not be subject to a tax charge until the end of the vesting period when the shares are no longer subject to a risk of forfeiture.

Shares that are held for a minimum period of 12 months will be exempt from a capital gains tax charge on their disposal.

## 6. Internationally mobile executives

### 6.1 What are the income tax consequences for an employee who is resident in Portugal when the long-term incentive award is made, but who is no longer resident at the time of exercise/vesting?

As previously mentioned, the income arising from a long-term incentive award plan will be deemed to be obtained when the vesting period ends or the options are exercised.

Therefore, if the employee is resident in Portugal when the long-term incentive award is granted and is no longer resident in Portugal on the date the employment income is deemed to be obtained, then the employee will be taxed, for the relevant employment income, as a non-resident and, through withholding tax, at a 20% flat rate.

For the purposes of non-Portuguese individuals, it should be noted that employment income is deemed to be obtained in Portugal when the work performed by the employee is carried out in Portuguese territory and (even if the work is not performed in Portuguese territory) when the employment income is due by a Portuguese resident entity (ie when the employer is a company resident in Portugal). If the employee is resident in a country that has signed a double taxation treaty with

Portugal, the regime foreseen in that treaty concerning employment income should also be analysed, to ascertain if any employment income would be taxable in Portugal.

**6.2** **What are the social security consequences for an employee who is resident in Portugal when the long-term incentive award is made, but who is no longer resident at the time of exercise/vesting?**

There are no express rules or procedures established by the social security authorities for this type of benefit or for this specific situation. As a result of the applicable general rules and principles, the above obligations will apply if the employee is still subject to the Portuguese social security regime

**6.3** **What are the tax and social security withholding/reporting consequences for the employer in respect of an employee who is resident in Portugal when the long-term incentive award is made, but who is no longer resident at the time of exercise/vesting?**

*(a)* *Tax*

This employment income would be taxed in Portugal under the rules applicable to non-residents of Portugal and, through withholding tax, at a 20% flat rate.

Therefore, in these cases, the employer will be under an obligation to withhold such tax and deliver it to the Portuguese tax authorities (by the twentieth day of the month following the date that the tax liability arose) and to comply with the corresponding reporting requirements as stated in 7 below.

*(b)* *Social security*

The employer should declare the payment to the employee by the fifteenth day of the month following the social security liability arising. On the same date the employer must pay the amount that is due under the applicable rates.

If the employee is no longer subject to the Portuguese social security system, express reference should be made to the fact that the payment relates to a benefit granted when the employee was resident in Portugal and was therefore subject to the Portuguese social security system.

**7.** **Reporting requirements**

**7.1** **Will the employer (or parent company, if different) have any reporting requirements as a result of the long-term incentive award?**

*(a)* *Tax*

The employer must comply with some compliance obligations relating to the employment income paid to its employees as a result of the long-term incentive award plan, as follows:

- by the end of July of each year, submit to the tax authorities a statement/form regarding the employment income paid to employees that are not resident in Portugal, during the previous year and corresponding tax withheld (this includes income arising from the award of shares, or exercise of stock options);

- by the end of February of each year, submit to the tax authorities a statement/form regarding the income paid to employees resident in Portugal during the previous year and the corresponding tax withheld (this includes income arising from the award of shares, or exercise of stock options);
- by the end of June of each year, submit to the tax authorities a statement/form where the employer informs the tax authorities that a stock option plan or other long-term incentive award plan was implemented in the previous year;
- maintain and update a registry of the employees that are entitled to this kind of income, containing their names, taxpayer number and code, date and value of each income payment, even if no tax has been withheld; and
- by January 20 of each year deliver to the employees a document stating the amounts/income due in the previous year and, where applicable, the corresponding tax withheld.

*(b)    Social security*

Long-term incentive awards will imply the same reporting requirements for the employer as mentioned above (namely a declaration to the social security services of the benefits received by employees).

**7.2    Are any tax rulings required in relation to the long-term incentive awards?**
No.

**8.    Exchange control issues**

**8.1    Are there any exchange control issues that would prevent an employee from (a) remitting monies abroad to purchase shares, or (b) repatriating monies from the sale of shares?**
No such exchange control rules are applicable, pursuant to Portuguese law.

**9.    Employment law**

**9.1    Are there any employment or local labour law issues which may arise as a result of the long-term incentive award? Are any consultations or authorisations required by law?**
There are no express employment law provisions that impact on employee share schemes. The analysis of such plans is therefore based in the general principles of labour law. Considering these general principles, the following issues are often raised:

*(a)    Criteria used for the selection of the employees*

Only the objective criteria of exclusion or admission may be used, otherwise general principles of non-discrimination could be deemed to have been violated. Implementation of the scheme raises no issues on this matter.

*(b)* *Protection of employees' acquired rights*

The fact that the employees participate in the scheme over a number of years means that the right to participate in the scheme and receive its related benefits is a right of the employee that cannot be withdrawn, altered or suspended without his consent.

## 10. Translation

**10.1 Are there any language restrictions in Portugal? Does any of the documentation provided to the employee in relation to the long-term incentive award need to be translated?**

From an employment law perspective, no specific provision of the Labour Code requires the documentation to be in the local language. Therefore, considering the general rules of civil law applicable to contractual declarations, provided that the employee has skills in the language used in the document and is able fully to understand its contents, the fact that the documentation is not in Portuguese would not raise any issues.

However, pursuant to the Portuguese Securities Code, information disclosed in Portugal that is able to influence the decision of the investors (in this case the executives) in relation to public offers, securities markets, financial intermediation activities and issuers should be written in Portuguese or accompanied by a duly sworn Portuguese translation.

Should the CMVM consider that the interests of the investors are duly protected, it may waive the requirement of a translation.

## 11. Data protection

**11.1 Are there any data protection issues which may arise should the employer wish to outsource the administration of the long-term incentive award to a third party?**

Yes. According to the Portuguese data protection legislation, the processing of employees' personal data by employers has to be notified before the Portuguese data protection authority (*Comissão Nacional de Protecção de Dados*, CNPD), unless in cases of exemption of notification as provided by some Authorisations of Exemption issued by the CNPD (namely, Authorisation No 1/99 related to salary payments, and Authorisation No 4/99 related to the general management of employees). Nevertheless, employees must always be informed of the terms under which their data is processed by employers.

Apart from those general obligations established by the PDPL, employees must be always informed if their personal data is given to any third parties (including clients). This communication must be unequivocally authorised by employees, unless it is considered necessary for the performance of an agreement of which the employees are a part.

Furthermore, the employee must also be informed should their data be transferred outside Portugal to a country within the European Union (EU).

If the destination of the data is a country outside the EU, the transfer must comply with the provisions of the PDPL:

- the unequivocal consent of the employees; or
- a safe harbour with the company located in the country of destination; or
- the transfer was subject to an agreement containing the standard clauses issued by the European Commission for this matter; or
- other circumstances are met that allow the transfer, as authorised by the CNPD.

The CNPD must be informed of international transfers to the EU. In the case of international transfer outside the EU, CNPD authorisation will be required unless any of the requirements above are met, in which case the CNPD must be notified of the operation to verify the compliance with the PDPL.

## 12. Source of shares

12.1 **Does it matter if shares are newly issued to an employee, provided out of treasury or delivered from an employee-benefit trust?**
No. There are no specific rules regarding the type of shares subject to the stock option plan.

# Russia

Irina Bakaeva
Oleg Konnov
Herbert Smith CIS LLP

---

**Red flag issues**
1. The Russian market has not yet developed standard employee share schemes.
2. Exchange control restrictions have recently been lifted, thereby expanding opportunities.
3. Options are normally taxed on exercise and not on grant.

## 1.    Securities laws

### 1.1    What prospectus and/or securities law requirements arise in connection with the grant, vesting or exercise of a long-term incentive award or on the eventual sale of the shares by the executive?

The grant of an option by a foreign company is not subject to securities law requirements in Russia. As discussed below, the award of free shares, or vesting/exercise of a long-term incentive award may be subject to Russian securities law, depending on whether the award is satisfied by newly issued or existing shares.

### (a)    Newly issued shares

If new shares are issued by a foreign company in Russia to an employee of its Russian subsidiary by way of a free share award, or in satisfaction of the exercise of an option, the issue of the shares must be in accordance with the rules established by a relevant international treaty between the Russian Federation (Russian securities authorities) and a country of the issuer's residency (its securities authorities) as well as the rules applicable to Russian issuers to the extent that such rules do not contradict the respective treaty. Russia has not yet concluded a single international treaty governing the issuance of shares.

The share issuance should be registered with the Russian securities authorities, irrespective of the number of potential subscribers, even if the shares are issued to a distinct group of people. No shares issued in Russia may be transferred prior to the registration of share issuance with Russian securities authorities. There is an exhaustive list of grounds on which registration may be denied or invalidated.

If the shares are issued by a foreign company to more than 500 Russian employees (even if the issuance is made to a distinct group of people), the company must prepare and register a prospectus and disclose information in accordance with the requirements of the Russian federal securities authorities. Where a prospectus must be prepared, stricter disclosure rules apply. The prospectus must include detailed information about the issuer, its financial position, management bodies, interested-party transactions and other essential information. All information included in the prospectus is open to the public.

The issuance of shares, the registration of a prospectus and certain other actions are subject to stamp duty. The amount of stamp duty is capped and is relatively insignificant. Independent registrars normally charge fees in connection with the movement of shares, as well as other fees.

*(b)* *Existing shares*

If existing shares are transferred by a foreign company (or its employee-benefit trust) to an employee of its Russian subsidiary by way of a free share award, or in satisfaction of the exercise of an option, it is not subject to Russian securities regulations, irrespective of the number of potential subscribers and regardless of whether or not the shares are transferred to a distinct group of people.

*(c)* *Disposal of shares*

Russian securities legislation does not regulate the subsequent disposition of shares by employees in detail.

There are no capital, share issuance or share transfer taxes in Russia.

**1.2** **Is there an exemption from securities laws requirements either because the shares are being offered only to executives or because shares are being offered to a distinct group of named individuals?**

The exercise of an option over existing shares is not subject to specific securities law requirements.

If the foreign company uses new issue shares, it will be subject to securities law requirements at the time when the shares are issued. However, prospectus and certain other requirements are not applicable if:

- the shares are offered to a distinct group of individuals by way of a closed subscription; and
- the number of subscribers or potential subscribers is less than 500.

**1.3** **If there is an exemption, will this apply automatically or are there any applications/filings that need to be made?**

An exemption from the prospectus requirement applies automatically.

**2.** **Employee tax and social security**

**2.1** **When will an executive be liable to tax or social security (and at what rate) in respect of the long-term incentive award?**

*(a)* *On grant*

There are no income tax or social security obligations on grant.

*(b)* **On exercise**

A personal income tax liability will arise on the date an employee exercises his option, or on the date his free share award vests, on the amount by which the market value of the shares at the date of exercise/vesting exceeds the acquisition price. The amount is deemed to be taxable income.

*(c)* **Income tax rates**

Income is subject to tax at a fixed rate.

Russian residents (as a general rule, any individuals regardless of their citizenship or domicile who are physically present in Russia for at least 183 days in any consecutive 12 months) are subject to tax at the rate of 13%.

All other individuals (non-residents) are subject to tax at the rate of 30%, unless an applicable tax treaty provides for an exemption or a lower rate.

*(d)* **Social security liability**

Employees are not subject to social charges on the exercise of an option/the vesting of free shares.

Social charges only apply to the employer if the option/free shares are structured as part of the employee's contractual compensation package. Here, the employer becomes liable to social charges as described below at the time when the option is exercised/the free shares vest.

2.2 **How will the executive's tax and social security be collected? Will the executive be responsible for paying any liabilities himself or will the executive's employer be responsible for paying tax or social security liabilities on the executive's behalf?**

Employers that are either Russian or foreign companies operating through a permanent establishment in Russia are liable for withholding and remittance to the authorities of the personal income tax from any cash payments due to the employee, if they are the source of the employee's taxable income. If for any reason the tax is not withheld and/or paid to the authorities or, in the cases where shares are granted by a foreign company not having a permanent establishment in Russia, the employee is personally liable for the tax.

Social charges are levied on employers, not on employees. Accordingly, the employer is liable for social charges. In fact, there is no mechanism for an employee to pay social charges unless he or she is registered as a private entrepreneur.

2.3 **If the employer is responsible for the employee's liabilities, can the employer withhold the liabilities from the employee's salary? Are there any formalities in this respect?**

Employers (other than non-Russian companies not having a permanent establishment in Russia) that are the source of taxable income for an employee are liable to withhold tax from any cash payments due to the employee, including salary, bonuses and other similar payments. Withholding may not reduce cash available to the employee by more than 50%. Penalties may be imposed on the employer for the failure to withhold personal income tax. Employers are also responsible for personalised accounting of income paid to their employees, and for tax amounts withheld from such income and transferred to the authorities.

Russian law explicitly prohibits employers from using their own funds to satisfy employees' personal income tax liability. In particular, this means that if no cash payment is due to the employee, or if the cash due to the employee is insufficient, the employer may not satisfy its withholding obligation. If the tax cannot be withheld for any reason, the employer must report this to the Russian tax authorities and the employee is then personally liable for the income tax. In particular, employees are personally liable for payment of the tax if the shares or income are received from a foreign company which is not permanently established in Russia and does not qualify as a tax agent and cannot withhold tax. In this case, the employee must file a tax return by April 30 of the year following the year when the taxable income was received, and then transfer the tax due to the authorities.

2.4 **If the executive's salary in the month of exercise/release is not sufficient for the employer to withhold all of the liabilities, can the employer (or the parent company, if different) arrange for the executive to authorise the sale of some of the executive's shares in the market and pass the money to the executive's employer?**

The employer may not sell any of the employee's shares without the employee's authorisation.

If the employee's salary is not sufficient for the employer to withhold all of the liabilities and the employer expects that it will be unable to withhold the tax within the 12-month period, the employer must notify the Russian tax authorities to this effect and state the amount of outstanding tax. In this case, the employee will be personally responsible for any outstanding tax liabilities.

2.5 **Will the executive pay tax on the eventual sale of his shares and if so at what rate?**

Capital gains from the sale of shares is subject to Russian personal income tax, but not to social security charges. The tax rate is currently 13% for Russian residents and 30% for non-residents (subject to provisions of applicable tax treaties).

Employees are personally liable for payment of this tax and are required to file an annual tax return and report taxable income from the sale of shares not later than April 30 of the year following the year when the capital gain was received. As a general rule, the tax must be paid by July 15.

Russian tax legislation has special rules for calculating personal income tax for any income arising from the sale of shares. In accordance with these rules, tax should be paid on the net income (income less expenses) of an individual. Expenses must be properly documented and can relate to both the acquisition and disposal of shares. The expenses can include the purchase price, legal fees, brokerage fees, etc. Furthermore, if shares were received by the employee free of charge or with a discount, the amount of income which was subject to tax is considered as a deductible expense. For instance, if the employee receives shares free of charge and thus has no acquisition cost, at the time of exercise of the option he or she will be liable to tax on the market value of the shares. After tax, the market value of the shares will be allowed as a deductible tax cost on the subsequent sale of the shares. The costs are deductible in full in the year the income from the sale of shares is received by the employee. Any losses from the sale of shares cannot be carried forward.

## 3. Employer's social security

**3.1 Is the employer liable to pay (on its own account) any employer's social security in connection with the long-term incentive award?**

Payroll expenses are generally subject to social security charges as long as they are deductible for profits tax purposes. These expenses are deductible for profits tax purposes by Russian companies or foreign companies operating through a permanent establishment in Russia if they are incurred in accordance with the obligations imposed on the employer pursuant to employment and/or collective bargaining agreements.

Therefore, if the option providing for the shares free of charge is deemed to be part of the compensation package contemplated by the employment or collective bargaining agreement (which is not always the case), the employer is liable for social security on the exercise of the option.

Social charges are assessed in accordance with the regressive rate. Annual wages up to Rb280,000 (per employee) are subject to a 26% rate; annual wages up to Rb600,000 (per employee) are subject to a 10% rate plus a fixed amount of Rb72,800; annual wages in excess of Rb600,000 (per employee) are subject to a 2% rate plus a fixed amount of Rb104,800. Compulsory contributions for insurance against injuries at work are excluded and assessed at various rates ranging from 0.2% to 8.5% depending on the level of professional risk.

If the long-term incentive award is not contemplated by the labour agreement and/or collective bargaining agreement, it will not be deemed a payroll expense. In such a case, it will not be deductible for profits tax purposes but will be exempt from social security charges.

If, as a result of a market value option structured as a part of the compensation package, the employee acquires shares at an exercise price, the employer will not be liable for social charges.

**3.2 Can the liability of the employer be put onto the employee? What steps are required?**

Under no circumstances may the liability for social security be put onto the employee. The individual may be held liable for social security only if he/she is deemed to be a private entrepreneur and not an employee.

## 4. Tax deduction for the employer

**4.1 Is it possible for the employer to receive a tax deduction in respect of the long-term incentive award? Would the employer need to be subject to recharge**

arrangements (eg if the employer is a subsidiary and provides funds to the parent company as part of a recharge arrangement in respect of the long-term incentive award)?

The cost of the long-term incentive award is deductible for the employer (a Russian company or a permanently established foreign company acting via a permanent establishment within Russia) as long as it is contemplated by the employment and/or collective bargaining agreement.

In accordance with the general principles set out in Russian tax law, only economically justified expenses may be deducted for tax purposes. Accordingly, the employer should be prepared to justify the business need for granting the long-term incentive award. Economically justified expenses should be proper and consistent with market practice incentives.

If the option is included in the employment package contemplated by the employment contract or a collective bargaining agreement the tax costs of the shares and expenses related to the acquisition and disposal of the shares can generally be deducted for profits tax purposes provided that no option reserve is created by the employer.

If a Russian employer provides funds to the parent company as part of a recharge arrangement in respect of the long-term incentive award, it is theoretically possible to deduct these costs. However, there is a practical risk that the tax authorities will challenge such an arrangement.

Capital gains realised by a Russian company or a permanent establishment of a foreign company on the sale of shares/options to employees is subject to profits tax in Russia at the current rate of 24%. The gain is calculated on the difference between the market value of the disposed shares/options and the tax costs of the shares and expenses related to acquisition and disposal of the shares/options. Special rules apply to capital gains from the sale of shares/options.

## 5. Tax beneficial arrangements

**5.1 Are there any ways of making the long-term incentive award tax-efficient in Russia?**

In practice, Russian companies use different ways of structuring their option programmes to achieve tax efficiency. These include granting employees non-listed shares or interests in limited liability companies, or using intermediate companies which are exempt from the unified social tax, etc.

However, it is important to structure such arrangements carefully. Artificial or tax-driven arrangements may be challenged by the tax authorities based upon the "business substance" doctrine or other similar grounds.

## 6. Internationally mobile executives

**6.1 What are the income tax consequences for an employee who is resident in Russia when the long-term incentive award is made, but who is no longer resident at the time of exercise/vesting?**

Russian tax legislation has no special tax rules for internationally mobile employees. Income is subject to tax when received. Accordingly, if employees or former employees are no longer residents of Russia at the time when the incentive award is exercised, they will be taxed as non-residents. This should be the case even if the option was granted at the time when the employees were Russian residents, but was exercised later.

Non-residents are generally subject to tax on Russian-source income unless this income is exempt because of an applicable tax treaty. Income from the exercise of an option on the shares of a non-Russian company may qualify as Russian-source income if it relates to employment in Russia. Income realised by non-residents from the exercise of an option related to their employment in Russia could arguably be deemed as Russian-source income. It may be exempt under an applicable tax treaty.

6.2   **What are the social security consequences for an employee who is resident in Russia when the long-term incentive award is made, but who is no longer resident at the time of exercise/vesting?**
As mentioned above, the employee has no social security liability in connection with the long-term incentive award.

6.3   **What are the tax and social security withholding/reporting consequences for the employer in respect of an employee who is resident in Russia when the long-term incentive award is made, but who is no longer resident at the time of exercise/vesting?**
No special rules apply to cases where the employees are internationally mobile and, therefore, general withholding/reporting tax legislation applies. In particular, Russian companies or a permanently established foreign company from which an individual receives a taxable income are responsible for the calculation and payment of personal income tax on the individual's behalf.

If the employee's salary is not sufficient for the employer to withhold all of the liabilities, the employer must inform the Russian tax authorities of this fact and the amount of tax outstanding.

The employer's social security obligations do not depend on whether the employee is a Russian tax resident or not.

## 7.   Reporting requirements

7.1   **Will the employer (or parent company, if different) have any reporting requirements as a result of the long-term incentive award?**
Apart from securities law requirements, the grant of an option/award of free shares is not subject to any reporting requirements. If an employer is unable to withhold tax when due, it must report this to the tax authorities. In addition, employers are subject to general periodic reporting obligations for all income paid to employees (including, but not limited to, income under the share schemes, if any).

7.2   **Are there any tax rulings required in relation to the long-term incentive awards?**
No rulings are required.

## 8. Exchange control issues

### 8.1 Are there any exchange control issues that would prevent an employee from (a) remitting monies abroad to purchase shares, or (b) repatriating monies from the sale of shares?

Following recent changes to Russian exchange control regulations, Russian resident and non-resident individuals may freely transfer funds to and from foreign jurisdictions in connection with the acquisition and disposal of shares. All transfers should be made through bank accounts. If a Russian national wishes to use a bank account with a non-Russian bank, special reporting requirements apply with respect to opening and the maintenance of a foreign bank account. All settlements between Russian residents must be made in Russian currency (roubles).

## 9. Employment law

### 9.1 Are there any employment or local labour law issues which may arise as a result of the long-term incentive award? Are any consultations or authorisations required by law?

Russian labour law does not specifically regulate stock option plans or similar incentive programmes.

The long-term incentive award may be contemplated by the employment agreement, collective bargaining agreement or an internal resolution of the employer.

If the purchase of shares under a stock option plan is structured as a partial payment of an eligible employee's salary via shares (which is not very common), any relevant Russian labour law requirements should be complied with. In particular, limitations apply to shares granted as part of a salary. In such cases, granting shares to employees under such a stock option plan should be treated as the part-payment of salary in a non-monetary form (ie in the form of shares). Salary paid in a non-monetary form should not exceed 20% of the full amount of the employee's salary. This means that under such a stock option plan, formally, an eligible employee could receive shares monthly in amount equal to 20% of his monthly salary.

A stock option plan which is linked to an eligible employee's salary could require salary deductions. These employees would not automatically receive shares as the part of their salary (as in previous case), but would obtain a right to purchase shares in the future.

Since such a stock option plan would involve deductions from the salaries of the eligible employees, the following restrictions should be observed. First, deductions from an employee's salary may only be made automatically in the limited cases specified by law, such as the withholding of personal income tax or the deduction of unearned advance salary payments or alimony. In other cases, such as the deduction of the payment under the stock option plan, the deduction can only be made pursuant to a written request of the employee. Therefore, to implement such a stock option plan, the eligible employees would need to submit such requests. Alternatively, the deductions may be formalised in a bilateral instrument signed by both employee and the employer.

The aggregated amount of deductions from an employee's salary cannot exceed 20% (50%/70% in specific cases where a higher cap is permitted by law). However, there are good arguments that this limitation is established for the protection of employees, so it should not extend to cases where a deduction in excess of the 20% cap is not stipulated by law but is made as a part of the incentive programme at the request of the employee. This request would be formalised in either a unilateral application of the employee, or in a bilateral document signed by both the employee and the employer.

## 10.  Translation

10.1  **Are there any language restrictions in Russia? Does any of the documentation provided to the employee in relation to the long-term incentive award need to be translated?**
Yes. All Russian entities are obligated under the law to maintain documentation in Russian. If necessary, this can be translated into a foreign language.

## 11.  Data protection

11.1  **Are there any data protection issues which may arise should the employer wish to outsource the administration of the long-term incentive award to a third party?**
Yes. The transfer of personal data is restricted and may be carried out only with the consent of the employee. No exemptions are provided for employee share schemes. Accordingly, consent of the employees is required for the transfer of personal data. In addition, restrictions apply to the transfer of information to outside Russia.

## 12.  Source of shares

12.1  **Does it matter if shares are newly issued to an employee, provided out of treasury or delivered from an employee-benefit trust?**
Russian law does not recognise the notion of trusts, including employee-benefit trusts.

As described above, issuance of new shares is connected with rather complicated corporate and securities law procedure. Share issuance, however, should not result in profits tax consequences for the issuer.

Disposition of treasury shares may subject the employer to profits tax. In addition, the acquisition by the company of its own shares is subject to a number of restrictions. For this and other reasons, options are often granted through special purpose vehicles.

# Spain

**Juan Bonilla**
Cuatrecasas Abogados, SRL

---

> **Red flag issues**
>
> 1. The profit arising out of the vesting/exercise of long-term incentive awards may increase severance or redundancy payments upon termination of employment.
>
> 2. An employee terminated without cause may claim continuation of long-term incentive awards even after the termination of employment.
>
> 3. The first €12,000 of profit arising out of the vesting/exercise of long-term incentive awards may be exempt from income tax.

## 1. Securities laws

**1.1 What prospectus and/or securities law requirements arise in connection with the grant, vesting or exercise of a long-term incentive award or on the eventual sale of the shares by the executive?**

Long-term incentive awards, in the form of either market value options or free shares, are usually neither transferable nor marketable for the employees prior to the effective conversion into shares.

Spanish securities regulations state that if a financial instrument is not transferable or marketable, it does not constitute a public offering and, therefore, the implementation of the long-term incentive award will not require any registration, communication or notification procedure before the Spanish Securities and Exchange Commission (*Comisión Nacional del Mercado de Valores*).

In addition, the vesting or exercise of the long-term incentive awards will not be considered a public offering, because it will merely be an execution of a previous offer which was not deemed to be a public offering in Spain. Therefore, no registration, communication or notification procedure will be required at the vesting or exercise of the long-term incentive awards.

If long-term incentive awards are only transferable to a limited and restricted number of potential investors (ie investors selected by the company offering the awards), but are not transferable generally to any third party, the offering of a long-term incentive award would not constitute a public offering for Spanish law purposes. The offer of such restricted transferable awards would not require registration, communication or notification before the Spanish Securities and Exchange Commission (*Comisión Nacional del Mercado de Valores*).

**1.2** **Is there an exemption from securities laws requirements either because the shares are being offered only to executives or because shares are being offered to a distinct group of named individuals?**

As explained above, since long-term incentive awards are usually granted as non-transferable (or only as partly transferable in the sense that they would only be transferable to selected investors), the offering would not constitute a public offering of securities from a Spanish law standpoint. Consequently, there is no need to seek or apply for an exemption from securities law requirements.

**1.3** **If there is an exemption, will the exemption apply automatically or are there any applications/filings that need to be made?**

On the assumption that the long-term incentive awards are not transferable, the exemption would apply automatically and there would be no applications/filings to be made.

**2.** **Employee tax and social security**

**2.1** **When will the executive be liable to tax or social security (and at what rate) in respect of the long-term incentive award?**

Assuming the long-term incentive awards are not transferable, the grant of the award will not constitute a taxable event for Spanish income tax purposes. Long-term incentive awards will become subject to tax either at the vesting date or at the exercise date.

Market value options will generally be taxable upon the exercise of the options and conversion into shares. Taxation for income tax purposes would arise on the difference between the market value of the shares subject to the option at the date of exercise, and the exercise price.

If the market value option takes the form of equity-settled stock appreciation rights, they will be subject to tax upon the exercise of the right, which is the moment when the executive receives the gain on the option in the form of shares. In this case, taxation would be for the gain on the option, equal to the market value of the shares received.

The same would apply for nil-cost options, as they will also be subject to taxation on the exercise of the options. In this case, taxation for income tax purposes would be equal to the market value of the shares subject to the option.

Free shares, either in the form of provisional allocations or forfeitable securities, will be subject to tax on vesting once the service and/or performance conditions have been met and the executive is then the owner of the shares. The market value of the shares will be then subject to income tax upon vesting.

For income tax purposes, the profit arising from the long-term incentive awards is considered as employment income. Applicable income tax rates range up to 43% currently, and vary according to a progressive scale depending on the amount of the taxable base for the executive, which includes not only the profit from the long-term incentive awards, but also any other salary-related or bonus income received by the executive. For an explanation of the ways of making the long-term incentive award tax-efficient in Spain, please see 5 below.

In terms of social security, long-term incentive awards are also subject to social security contributions upon vesting or exercise, in exactly the same way as described above for income tax purposes. However, it is important to note that there is a maximum cap for social security contributions in Spain. If the taxable base exceeds the cap (for 2008, the cap for the taxable base is €3,074.10), the excess is not subject to social security contributions.

Employer social security contributions are generally at a rate of 30.15%, while rates for employee social security contributions are 6.35%.

2.2    **How will the executive's tax and social security be collected? Will the executive be responsible for paying any liabilities himself or will the executive's employer be responsible for paying tax or social security liabilities on the executive's behalf?**

The executive's income tax and social security obligations will be collected in the form of withholdings from the executive's payroll. Based on the foregoing, the local employer is responsible for withholding the amounts due for income tax and also for social security contributions on the side of the executive. Social security contributions on the side of the employer will not be withheld from the payroll but will be paid directly by the employer to the social security bodies.

If the long-term incentive awards are made by a holding company which is not located in Spain, the local employer – the Spanish subsidiary of the issuer of the awards as the Spanish tax resident of the group – will be obliged to make the withholdings from the executive's payroll, on account of the executive.

2.3    **If the employer is responsible for the executive's liabilities, can the employer withhold the liabilities from the executive's salary? Are there any formalities in this respect?**

Since the employer is responsible for the executive's liabilities, both in terms of income tax and social security obligations, the employer can withhold the liabilities from the executive's salary. For the avoidance of doubt, it is advisable to incorporate, within the terms of the long-term incentive award, a specific provision that tax payments will be withheld from the executive's monthly salary.

The long-term incentive award can also provide that income tax obligations will be satisfied through an arrangement whereby the executive authorises the sale of some shares in the market and the money is passed on to the executive's employer.

However, careful consideration should also be given to the situation where the executive receives the full profit from the long-term incentive award, and then undertakes to give his employer the money required to satisfy his income tax payments. If the executive has not reimbursed the employer by the time the payments to the Spanish tax authorities are due, the employer must make the payments. In addition, the employer may have difficulties in reclaiming this money, as it is not clear if the tax or employment courts would be competent to deal with such a claim. This is particularly relevant if the executive has received the profit from the long-term incentive award in the days before or after his employment is terminated, as the company could not make any deductions from the payroll.

**2.4** **If the executive's salary in the month of exercise/release is not sufficient for the employer to withhold all of the liabilities, can the employer (or the parent company, if different) arrange for the executive to authorise to sell some of the executive's shares in the market and pass the money to the executive's employer?**

The long-term incentive award can provide that the executive's income tax and social security obligations will be satisfied through an arrangement where the executive authorises the sale of some of his/her shares and the money is then given to the executive's employer to satisfy such obligations. This provision can apply whether or not the executive's salary in the month of exercise/release is sufficient for the employer to withhold all of the liabilities.

**2.5** **Will the executive pay tax on the eventual sale of his shares and if so at what rate?**

The eventual sale of the shares to a third party will give rise to a taxable event for income tax purposes. The difference between the market value of the shares at the date of sale to a third party and the market value of the shares at the exercise of the options or vesting of the free shares will be subject to income tax as a capital gain. The applicable tax rate for the profit arising out of the sale of his shares is currently 18%.

Social security contributions are not due on the eventual sale of the shares.

## 3. Employer's social security

**3.1** **Is the employer liable to pay (on its own account) any employer's social security in connection with the long-term incentive award?**

The employer is liable to pay, on its own account, the employer's social security in connection with the long-term incentive award. Such contributions are to be made upon the exercise of the options or the vesting of the free shares. Currently, the employer's social security rate is 30.15%.

As explained below, there is a maximum cap for social security payments. If the taxable base, including not only the profit arising out of the long-term incentive awards but also of the base salary, or any bonus, commissions or remuneration-in-kind earned by the executive, exceeds the maximum cap (for 2008, this is €3,074.10), then any excess does not trigger any social security contributions on the side of the employer.

**3.2** **Can the liability of the employer be put onto the employee? What steps are required?**

Liability for the employer's social security contributions cannot be put onto the employee. Each party, the employer and the employee, is obliged to satisfy its respective social security obligations.

## 4.    Tax deduction for the employer

4.1    **Is it possible for the employer to receive a tax deduction in respect of the long-term incentive award? Would the employer need to be subject to recharge arrangements (eg if the employer is a subsidiary and provides funds to the parent company as part of a recharge arrangement in respect of the long-term incentive award)?**
The employer can consider as a tax-deductible expense the amount of employment income obtained by the employees upon the exercise of the options or the vesting of the free shares.

If the long-term incentive awards are granted by a foreign company, the Spanish subsidiary can consider as a tax-deductible expense the amount of employment income obtained by the employees only if there is a recharge agreement between the foreign company and the Spanish subsidiary. This agreement can be made in respect of the long-term incentive award, or more generally for a variety of purposes, but it must specify the nature of the services to be provided and must establish the methods for the distribution of the expenses in accordance with the criteria of continuity and rationality.

## 5.    Tax beneficial arrangements

5.1    **Are there any ways of making the long-term incentive award tax-efficient in Spain?**
Spanish tax legislation provides for a tax-efficient system to certain grants of long-term incentive awards if the following requirements are met:

- no employee may have on his or her own, or with his or her family or close relatives, a direct or indirect participation in more than 5% in the company where he/she renders his/her services or in any group company;
- the employee must hold the shares for at least three years from the date the employee actually owns the shares;
- the shares must be offered as part of a general remuneration policy of the company or group of companies and should enhance the participation of the employees in the equity of the company.

If all these requirements are met, there is an exemption of €12,000 per year which will apply on the employment income obtained by the executive on the exercise of the options or the vesting of the free shares. If the profit of the executive exceeds €12,000 per year, then such excess will be subject to taxation.

It should be noted that the employee must hold the shares for at least three years from the date he actually obtained ownership of the shares. In this connection, if the employee sells the shares to a third party before the end of the three-year period, the amount initially considered to be exempt from income tax will then be taxed at the regular rate. The employee will have to file an additional tax return corresponding to the tax period in which the profit was due and declare the corresponding taxes previously considered to be exempt. In principle, there are no reporting obligations from the employer if the employee sells the shares once the tax year has finished.

A different way to benefit from a favourable tax regime is to apply a partial reduction of 40% of the taxable base. To do this, the income obtained from the long-term incentive awards must be considered as non-regular income, in the sense that it is generated over more than two years. In this regard, the Spanish tax authorities have clarified that income obtained from long-term incentive awards can only be considered as non-regular income when (i) there is a period of more than two years from the grant of the award to the exercise of the options or the vesting of the free shares, and (ii) when the awards are not granted on a periodical or regular basis. Long-term incentive awards granted on an annual basis would not qualify for this partial deduction of the taxable base, but long-term incentive awards granted only once may qualify. This partial reduction is subject to a maximum cap. For the purposes of applying the reduction, the maximum taxable base to which the partial deduction can be made is limited to an amount resulting from multiplying the annual standard wage (€22,100 for 2008) by the number of years lapsed from the grant date of the award to the exercise of the options or the vesting of the free shares. This limit can be doubled under certain circumstances, particularly if the shares are held by the executive for a period of three years.

## 6.    Internationally mobile executives

6.1    **What are the income tax consequences for an employee who is resident in Spain when the long-term incentive award is made, but who is no longer resident at the time of exercise/vesting?**

In principle, an employee who is resident in Spain when the long-term award is made, but who is no longer resident at the time of exercise of the options or vesting of the shares will not be subject to taxation in Spain. However, rules for the taxation of non-resident individuals in Spain as well as international conventions addressed to avoid double taxation may require payment of taxes in Spain, as a non-resident, at a flat rate of 24%.

Due to the complexity of this area of the law, and fast-changing rules and the existence of international conventions with different provisions depending on the destination country, the analysis of taxation of internationally mobile employees requires assessment on a case-by-case basis.

6.2    **What are the social security consequences for an employee who is resident in Spain when the long-term incentive award is made, but who is no longer resident at the time of exercise/vesting?**

In terms of social security, an employee who is resident in Spain when the long-term incentive award is made, but who is no longer resident at the time of exercise of the options or vesting of the free shares, can be under one of the following scenarios:

- The employee can be posted to a third country but still remain registered within the Spanish social security system. This may be the case if the destination country is a member of the European Union or a country with which Spain has signed a totalisation agreement for social security. If the employee remains within the Spanish social security system, the exercise of the options or vesting of the free shares will give rise to social security contributions, on the basis of the rules explained above.

- The employee can be registered on the social security system of the country of destination, having previously been registered in Spain. From the Spanish social security standpoint, there are, in principle, no social security consequences arising out of the exercise of the options or the vesting of the free shares.

It is important to note that registration for social security purposes does not necessarily need to coincide with tax residency. As explained in this section, deviations frequently arise because employees may still be registered on the Spanish social security system even if they are working for another company of the group in a country that has signed a totalisation agreement with Spain (eg any member state of the European Union).

**6.3    What are the tax and social security withholding/reporting consequences for the employer in respect of an employee who is resident in Spain when the long-term incentive award is made, but who is no longer resident at the time of exercise/vesting?**

As explained in 6.1 above, in principle the profit from the long-term incentive award would not be subject to taxation in Spain based on the fact that the employee would no longer be resident in Spain at the time of exercise of the options or vesting of the free shares. Consequently, in terms of income tax reporting requirements, the local employer would not be subject to any withholding or reporting requirements. However, for the avoidance of doubt, it may be advisable to request a certificate of residency from the destination country of the employee.

In terms of social security obligations, a withholding obligation will arise if the employee is still registered with the Spanish social security authorities, even though he or she is working in another country. See above.

**7.    Reporting requirements**

**7.1    Will the employer (or parent company, if different) have any reporting requirements as a result of the long-term incentive award?**

The employer generally has no reporting requirements as a result of the long-term incentive award.

**7.2    Are any tax rulings required in relation to the long-term incentive awards?**

No tax rulings are required to implement long-term incentive awards. However, the company can file a consultation request before the Spanish tax authorities (ie on the potential application of the tax exemption). The outcome of a consultation is binding on the tax authorities.

**8.    Exchange control issues**

**8.1    Are there any exchange control issues that would prevent an employee from (a) remitting monies abroad to purchase shares, or (b) repatriating monies from the sale of shares?**

Following Spanish exchange control regulations, an employee acquiring shares in a foreign company through the exercise or vesting of long-term incentive awards, or the financial institution or investment company where the shares of the employee are registered, will have to declare the acquisition to the Spanish Directorate of Commerce and Investments (*Dirección General de Comercio e Inversiones*). This is done for statistical purposes only.

## 9. Employment law

### 9.1 Are there any employment or local labour law issues which may arise as a result of the long-term incentive award? Are any consultations or authorisations required by law?

In terms of worker participation and consultation, if the long-term incentive award is designed as a new benefit and is not replacing any other benefit previously in place, there is no need for the approval of the works council or body for employee representation. Consultation would only be required if the long-term incentive awards are replacing another benefit still in force, or if the long-term incentive awards are to be substantially altered within the term of enforceability of the award.

In connection with employment law, there are two issues worthy of special mention. Both regard the potential implications of termination of employment, particularly when the termination is unfair.

The first implication relates to the calculation of the severance or redundancy payments due under a termination without cause or in a redundancy situation. Spanish employment law does not recognise the concept of employment at will and requires payment of severance or redundancy payments as damages for an unfair dismissal or for redundancy. These payments are generally calculated based on the employee's salary and length of service.

Spanish case law has held that the profit obtained by the vesting/exercise of the long-term incentive awards is to form part of the salary used to calculate statutory severance or redundancy payments. The inclusion of such profit within the calculation base for termination payments is considered as a "public order" rule and consequently cannot be contracted out under the terms of the long-term incentive award.

Based on the above, the profit arising out of the long-term incentive award will increase the amount of severance or redundancy payments due upon a termination of employment. In practical terms, case law tends to suggest that only the profit generated in the 12 months prior to the termination date is to be considered for the calculation of the termination payments. To calculate the impact of the long-term incentive awards over the termination payments, the following alternatives have been upheld by the Spanish courts:

- Market value options can be calculated thus:
  - the profit obtained from the exercise of the options within the last 12 months prior to the termination of employment, divided by the number of years from the grant date to the exercise date of the options; or
  - the profit obtained from the exercise, within the last 12 months of

employment, of options which have vested in the last 12 months of employment;
- Free shares can be calculated thus:
  - if the free shares are granted annually: the profit obtained from the vesting of the free shares within the last 12 months prior to the termination of employment; or
  - if the free shares are only granted once: the profit obtained from the vesting of the free shares within the last 12 months prior to the termination of employment, divided by the number of years from the grant date to the vesting date of the free shares.

There is still some uncertainty from the Spanish courts on how to calculate the value of the long-term incentive awards. More case law on this specific issue is expected in due course.

The second employment law implication of the vesting/exercise of the long-term incentive awards relates to a potential request to continue the benefits even after the termination of employment. Such a request has been reviewed in several cases when the termination was unfair, and where the terminated employees claimed that the terms of the long-term award requiring continuity of employment for the vesting or exercise of the awards were void. Case law has been contradictory and unclear on these issues, and consequently there has been a high degree of uncertainty in this area of the law.

The majority of the case law held that, irrespective of the terms of the long-term incentive award, an employee who has been unfairly dismissed or has been made redundant does not lose his rights to the award, which remains in full force and effect as if the employee was subject to a non-voluntary termination (ie retirement, death and disability).

Most of the cases deal with long-term incentive awards where continuity of employment or service is required for vesting and exercise, but there are no performance criteria attached. It remains to be seen if long-term incentive awards which must comply with certain performance goals will be subject to the same rules of continuation as described above.

## 10. Translation

### 10.1 Are there any language restrictions in Spain? Does any of the documentation provided to the employee in relation to the long-term incentive award need to be translated?

There are no rules that require the terms of the long-term incentive awards to be drafted or translated into Spanish, as long as the employees that are being offered the awards understand the language in which it is drafted.

However, it is advisable to translate certain documents into Spanish, particularly the grant of the long-term incentive award. If there is no Spanish translation, in the event of litigation, a sworn translation of the documents will be required to accept the terms of the long-term incentive award as evidence for the case.

## 11. Data protection

### 11.1 Are there any data protection issues which may arise should the employer wish to outsource the administration of the long-term incentive award to a third party?

If an employee's personal data is to be transferred to a third party (ie if the employer wishes to outsource the administration of the long-term incentive award to a third party), the consent of the employee would be required. The consent form must contain the purpose of the transfer (ie administration of the long-term incentive award) and identify the parties that may have access to such personal data.

If such a transfer to a third party is deemed to be a cross-border transfer, it would require not only the employee's consent, but also prior written authorisation by the Spanish Data Protection Agency if the country of destination of the personal data is a country which has a lower level of protection than the level provided under Spanish law. If the country of destination has a level of protection comparable to that under Spanish law (eg in member states of the European Union), then there is no need to seek prior authorisation from the Spanish Data Protection Agency and a notification to the Agency of the cross-border transfer will suffice.

## 12. Source of shares

### 12.1 Does it matter if shares are newly issued to an employee, provided out of treasury or delivered from an employee-benefit trust?

The same legal implications would arise if the shares satisfying the long-term incentive awards are newly issued, provided out of treasury, or delivered from an employee-benefit trust. However, since the institution of trusts is not recognised in Spain, the use of an employee-benefit trust would pose additional difficulties for Spanish employers wishing to grant long-term incentive awards using this method. In particular, the issuer of the long-term incentive awards would have to reach an agreement with a third party – usually a third company – whereby such a third party will be the legal owner of the shares required to satisfy the long-term incentive awards, but will be subject to certain obligations to sell the shares to the beneficiaries of the awards when the conditions for the exercise of the options or vesting of the free shares are fulfilled. A complex set of rules to set up the rights and obligations of the third party, including the potential charge of a fee for the deposit of the shares and the limitations of the sale of such shares except in favour of the beneficiaries of the awards, will have to be agreed.

# Sweden

Annika Andersson
Karin Gustafsson
Helena Rempler
Mannheimer Swartling

---

**Red flag issues**

1. For Swedish tax purposes it is not entirely clear when the taxable event of a long-term incentive award arises; it will depend on the complete terms and conditions for the award.

2. The Swedish employer is responsible for the social security contributions (in 2008 at 32.42%) and not subject to any earnings cap.

---

## 1. Securities laws

### 1.1 What prospectus and/or securities law requirements arise in connection with the grant, vesting or exercise of a long-term incentive award or on the eventual sale of the shares by the executive?

Sweden has implemented the EU Prospectus Directive (2003/71/EC). The Swedish prospectus rules are provided for in the Swedish Financial Instruments Trading Act. Accordingly, Swedish prospectus requirements are triggered when securities intended for public trading are offered to the public or are admitted to trading in a regulated market, unless an exemption from the prospectus requirements applies. If no exemption from the Swedish prospectus requirements is available, a prospectus must be published and approved by the competent authority of, in general, the issuer's home member state. Once a prospectus has been approved, it may be used for offerings or admissions to regulated markets in all states within the EEA without the need for further approval of the document in those member states. For a description of relevant exemptions from the prospectus requirements in connection with an offer of incentive awards to employees, see below.

Under Swedish law, an offer of securities intended for public trading directed towards present or former employees or board members in the company would be considered as a public offer. It should be noted that incentive awards consisting of shares or options in private limited liability companies are not considered as securities intended for public trading under Swedish law. Hence, the grant of incentive awards in the form of shares or options in private limited liability companies are not subject to Swedish prospectus requirements.[1] If the incentive

---

1      See the preparatory work to the new Securities Markets Act, prop 2006/07:115, p. 283, which entered into force on November 1 2007, by which legislation Markets in Financial Instruments Directive 2004/39/EC (MiFID) was implemented in Sweden.

awards consist of shares or options in a public limited liability company, these would be considered as securities intended for public trading under Swedish law, even if the company is an unlisted company. Also, non-transferable employee options (*personaloptioner*), see definition below, may be considered as securities intended for public trading under Swedish law.

An offer will not trigger any prospectus requirements under Swedish law as there is no element of choice on the part of the recipient, including the right to repudiate the allocation of the security, since, in such a case, there is no offer for the purpose of the prospectus rules. If incentive awards are allocated to employees without an element of choice on the part of the employee, no prospectus requirements would be triggered in Sweden.

Further, the Committee of European Securities Regulators (the CESR), which includes the Swedish Financial Supervisory Authority (FSA), has agreed that non-transferable options granted to employees do not trigger prospectus requirements, either at the time of the grant or at the time of the exercise, because at the time of the exercise there is no public offer but merely the execution of a previous offer. The Swedish Financial Supervisory Authority has made an equivalent statement with respect to non-transferable employee options (*personaloptioner*), see the definition below. Hence, no prospectus is required in Sweden at the time of the grant of non-transferable options or employee options to employees, nor at the time of the exercise of such non-transferable options or employee options.

A subsequent sale of the shares by the employee would not trigger any prospectus requirements in Sweden, unless of course such sale of shares is made through a public offer and no exemptions for such an offer would be available.

If the company is a public company listed on a regulated market, it should be noted that additional corporate and securities rules are applicable under Swedish laws and regulations. For example, there are binding guidelines on how public companies listed on a regulated market are to act and give information to their shareholders when offering incentive awards to their employees. Moreover, an incentive award to employees in a public company (including unlisted public companies) where the shareholders will not have pre-emption rights is to be decided by the general meeting in some cases. In such cases, the decision must be supported by nine-tenths of both the shares voted and the shares represented at the general meeting. Also, insider rules and notification rules may need to be taken into account in connection with the grant and exercise of long-term incentive awards.

**1.2 Is there an exemption from securities laws requirements either because the shares are being offered only to executives or because shares are being offered to a distinct group of named individuals?**

In Sweden, securities offered to present or former employees or board members are exempt from prospectus requirements if the securities are the same as those already listed on a regulated market or related to such listed securities. Further, if the securities in question are newly issued securities, no prospectus would be required in connection with the admission to trading of such securities on the same regulated market. However, in order to benefit from this exemption, an information memorandum should be made available for the participants of the incentive plan, which describes the securities and the motives and terms of the plan. It is not necessary to file this information memorandum with the Swedish Financial Supervisory Authority.

Further, no prospectus (or an information memorandum referred to above) is required in Sweden if:

- the total number of eligible employees is less than 100 persons (other than qualified investors) in Sweden;[2]
- the minimum investment amount for each employee is at least €50,000;
- the nominal value of the securities is at least €50,000; or
- the total consideration of the offer is less than €1 million within the EEA, which limit is to be calculated over a period of 12 months.[3]

Offers of free securities, where the recipient decides whether to accept the offer, are regarded as an offer for zero consideration. Hence, such an offer is exempt from prospectus requirements in Sweden. It should be noted that if the securities are offered in place of quantifiable financial benefits in another form, the offer may not be considered as a free offer.

### 1.3 If there is an exemption, will the exemption apply automatically or are there any applications/filings that need to be made?

Yes, the exemption will automatically apply so no applications/filings need to be made. It should be noted that, according to Swedish market practice, eligible employees usually receive an information brochure regarding the incentive plan, even if no prospectus requirements apply.

## 2. Employee tax and social security

### 2.1 When will the executive be liable to tax or social security (and at what rate) for the long-term incentive award?

Options granted to employees are generally characterised either as employee stock options (*personaloptioner*) or as securities (*värdepapper*).

Employee stock options are not taxed at grant, but when the options are exercised. The option gain (ie the fair market value of shares acquired minus the strike price, minus any amount paid for the grant of the option) is then taxed as employment income.

Options characterised as securities are taxed as employment income at grant to the extent the option premium paid is less than the fair market value of the options. Thus, if such options are acquired at fair market value there will be no recognition

---

2    In October 2007, the Swedish FSA resolved to change its previous praxis to the effect that if the total number of eligible persons in the offer is less than 100, no prospectus requirements are triggered, even if the offer would be directed to more than 100 persons in another state within the EEA.

3    It should be noted that public offers directed to qualified investors, as defined in the Financial Instruments Trading Act, are also exempt from prospectus requirements in Sweden. However, the definition of qualified investors only includes certain legal entities, not individuals. This exemption is not relevant in Sweden in connection with the offer of incentive awards to employees.

of employment income. The fair market value is generally determined by applying the Black & Scholes option pricing model. What then determines whether options are characterised as employee stock options or as securities? Options that are non-transferable and subject to vesting are normally treated as employee stock options. To be characterised as securities, options must be freely transferable and not subject to vesting so that the option holder, as a rule of thumb, is able to realise the fair market value of the award at all times.

Hence, market value options will generally be taxed at exercise. The same applies to options that do not entitle the option holder to acquire shares. Hence, an equity-settled stock appreciation right which only entitles the option holder to receive a cash consideration calculated on the difference between the market value of the shares subject to the option at the date of exercise and the exercise price, which is tied to the employment and subject to a vesting requirement, will generally be taxable at exercise. However, if the employer has a unilateral right under the terms of the option to decide whether cash should be delivered in lieu of all or a portion of the shares deliverable, it follows from a Supreme Administrative Court case that the taxable event arises on the first day when the employee is able to exercise his or her option (that is, at vesting).

Provisional allocations and nil-cost options will also generally be taxed as employee stock options (that is, taxed at exercise), provided that the employer not at his own discretion can decide to settle the options in cash in lieu of shares. If, the employer at his own discretion can decide to settle such options in cash, the taxable event will occur at vesting. Should these options be freely transferable and not tied to the employment, they will be treated as securities and the taxable event will be at grant.

To determine the taxation of restricted shares (forfeitable securities), it has to be determined whether the employee is the owner of the restricted shares or has merely acquired a promise to receive shares at a future date (ie after the restriction period). If the employee (for all legal and practical purposes) is already treated as the owner of the shares during the period when the restrictions apply, he or she will be taxed for any benefit when the restricted shares are acquired. If the employee cannot be viewed as the owner of the restricted shares (by virtue of the restrictions being too far-reaching), then – for as long as the restrictions apply – the employee will be taxed when the restrictions lapse and as a consequence not taxed at all if the shares are instead forfeited without any payment to the employee. In certain cases, the Swedish Tax Agency has taken the position that the transfer restrictions and leaver provisions agreed in shareholders' agreements shall have the effect that no acquisition of securities has taken place. (Cases are currently pending in the lower courts on appeal by the taxpayers.)

A taxable benefit received due to the long-term incentive award will be added to the employee's other employment income and taxed accordingly. (The marginal tax rate in Sweden currently varies from approximately 32% to 57%, including an employee's social security liabilities.)

**2.2** **How will the executive's tax and social security be collected? Will the executive be responsible for paying any liabilities himself, or will the executive's employer be responsible for paying tax or social security liabilities on the executive's behalf?**

The employer is responsible for deducting the executive's income tax. However, the responsibility is limited to deducting income tax from the cash salary for the month when the employee's tax liability arises. Any remaining tax is payable by the employee.

**2.3** **If the employer is responsible for the executive's liabilities, can the employer withhold the liabilities from the executive's salary? Are there any formalities in this respect?**

See 2.2 above.

**2.4** **If the executive's salary in the month of exercise/release is not sufficient for the employer to withhold all of the liabilities, can the employer (or the parent company, if different) arrange for the executive to authorise to sell some of the executive's shares in the market and pass the money to the executive's employer?**

It would be possible for the employee to give authorisation to sell some of the shares to cover the tax liability. The employee could also ask the employer to withhold additional tax from his salary for the remaining months of the year.

**2.5** **Will the executive pay tax on the eventual sale of his shares and if so, at what rate?**

Any gain realised on a sale of shares is taxed as investment income at a current rate of 30%. However, only five-sixths of a capital gain on certain unlisted shares[4] is taxable (ie the effective tax rate for capital gains on such shares will be 25%). The taxable gain is the difference between the sale price and the acquisition cost of the shares. The acquisition cost is the total of the price paid by the employee and the value of the taxable benefit.

## 3. Employer's social security

**3.1** **Is the employer liable to pay (on its own account) any employer's social security in connection with the long-term incentive award?**

An employer's social security contributions will be payable on the value of taxable benefits received by the employees at a rate of 32.42% for the 2007/08 income year. Employer social security contributions are not subject to any earnings caps.

Generally, the person paying the benefit will be liable for social security contributions. However, when the benefit is paid by a foreign legal entity for work

---

4   This rule is applicable on unlisted shares in a Swedish or foreign company that are not closely held. For the rule to apply to shares in non-Swedish companies, the foreign company must generally be subject to at least 15% tax on its net income.

performed under the employment of a Swedish company, the Swedish company will be liable for the social security contributions.

**3.2 Can the liability of the employer be put onto the employee? What steps are required?**

Generally, no. However, should a Swedish individual be employed by a foreign employer which does not have a permanent establishment in Sweden, it is possible to enter into an agreement that the employee should pay the social security contributions. The employee must give information about the agreement in his income tax return.

## 4. Tax deduction for the employer

**4.1 Is it possible for the employer to receive a tax deduction in respect of the long-term incentive award? Would the employer need to be subject to recharge arrangements (eg if the employer is a subsidiary and provides funds to the parent company as part of a recharge arrangement in respect of the long-term incentive award)?**

Generally, costs incurred in connection with a new issue of shares have not been regarded as costs for the company but for the shareholders (due to equity dilution) and, as a consequence, they have not been considered deductible for tax purposes. Nevertheless, in a June 2002 tax ruling, a branch with a permanent establishment in Sweden was granted a deduction for the acquisition cost of new shares issued by the foreign parent company, as salary costs.[5]

Two other rulings deal with the same kind of question. A Swedish corporate group implemented a worldwide incentive scheme, under which the employees were granted employee stock options. The group also implemented a share savings plan. Each company within the group granted stock options to its employees, giving the employees the right to acquire shares in the parent company. The parent company planned to deliver shares free of charge to its subsidiary so that the subsidiary could fulfil its obligations under the incentive scheme. The Council for Advance Tax Rulings held that both the parent and the subsidiary would be entitled to a tax deduction for wages in an amount corresponding to the market value of the shares delivered to the employees (less any price paid by the employee).[6]

A Swedish employer may be entitled to deduct any costs charged by the parent company. However, the legal situation in this regard is uncertain (although there are strong arguments to suggest that such expenses should be tax-deductible for the Swedish subsidiary).

---

5     Note that the Supreme Administrative Court has not addressed the issue, because the ruling was not appealed to the higher court.

6     These rulings were appealed to the Supreme Administrative Court, which confirmed the view established by the Council for Advance Tax Rulings.

## 5. Tax beneficial arrangements

### 5.1 Are there any ways of making the long-term incentive award tax-efficient in Sweden?

No. Swedish tax legislation does not contain any regulations providing for a favourable tax treatment of long-term incentive awards in Sweden. It should be noted that, from a Swedish tax perspective, securities could be more favourable, as any increase in value between grant and exercise will be taxed as investment income not subject to social security contributions. However, the tax treatment of securities requires that the incentive award is freely transferable and not subject to vesting. This is often an impossible solution for commercial reasons.

## 6. Internationally mobile executives

### 6.1 What are the income tax consequences for an employee who is resident in Sweden when the long-term incentive award is made, but who is no longer resident at the time of exercise/vesting?

If the employee holds an employee stock option that has vested (become exercisable) but has not been exercised, he is deemed to have received a taxable benefit from the day he no longer lives in Sweden or does not stay there on a regular basis. The value of the benefit is the difference between the market value of the shares and the exercise price. If the option has not vested, he is not deemed to have received a benefit when he moves from Sweden. The Swedish Tax Agency does not apply this rule to individuals who move from Sweden to another country within the European Union. Those individuals will be taxed on exercise, assuming that they then still have unlimited tax liability in Sweden.

It should be noted that these rules are currently under review and that new rules most likely will enter into force as from July 1 2008.

### 6.2 What are the social security consequences for an employee who is resident in Sweden when the long-term incentive award is made, but who is no longer resident at the time of exercise/vesting?

The social security liability for the employee is tied to the tax liability of the employee; see 2 above.

### 6.3 What are the tax and social security withholding/reporting consequences for the employer in respect of an employee who is resident in Sweden when the long-term incentive award is made but who is no longer resident at the time of exercise/vesting?

Employers' social security contributions are levied on the same base as income tax. In addition, the social security contributions of Swedish employers will also be due for work performed abroad by employees who, according to EC law or a social security convention, are covered by Swedish social security. Sweden has concluded social security conventions, which contain provisions for employees working abroad, with approximately 20 countries.

Should a taxable event arise when the employee moves from Sweden, the employer will be liable to withhold tax. The employer will also be obliged to report this to the Tax Agency.

These rules are also currently under review.

## 7. Reporting requirements

**7.1 Will the employer (or parent company, if different) have any reporting requirements as a result of the long-term incentive award?**

The employer must report to the Tax Agency any remuneration that is treated as income from employment. Should the issuer of the benefit be a foreign company, the Swedish employer has this obligation if (i) there is no employment relationship between the foreign company and the employees, and (ii) the benefit is deemed to emanate from the employment in Sweden.

**7.2 Are there any tax rulings required in relation to the long-term incentive awards?**

No.

## 8. Exchange control issues

**8.1 Are there any exchange control issues that would prevent an employee from (a) remitting monies abroad to purchase shares or (b) repatriating monies from the sale of shares?**

There are no relevant exchange control restrictions although there are some reporting requirements, such that any person (generally, a remitting bank) who carries out a payment exceeding Skr150,000, where the payment is made (i) from Sweden to a foreign jurisdiction by an individual or a legal entity fiscally resident in Sweden, or (ii) from abroad to an individual or a legal entity fiscally resident in Sweden, must report such payment to the Swedish Tax Agency.

## 9. Employment law

**9.1 Are there any employment or local labour law issues which may arise as a result of the long-term incentive award? Are any consultations or authorisations required by law?**

Under Swedish law, an employer may implement a long-term incentive award at its own discretion, provided that the benefits under such a plan are granted in addition to the employees' normal employment benefits (which in turn should be in line with the market standard). It is essential that employees fully understand the conditions for obtaining benefits under the award (eg that the benefits will be contingent upon continued employment).

In addition, the following employment law issues should also be taken into account before introducing a long-term incentive award.

Under Swedish law, employment benefits can either be granted as a contractual benefit or as a unilaterally given benefit. Whereas unilaterally given benefits, as a rule, may be withdrawn at the employer's discretion, a variation of contractually agreed terms enforced by the employer is not permitted and may be deemed a termination of employment which is subject to the relevant restrictions and limitations.

Under Swedish law, an employer may not discriminate against employees on grounds of, for example, gender, ethnic origin or disability. In addition, unfair treatment of employees with part-time employment and fixed-term employment is prohibited. If the long-term incentive award is only offered to employees with permanent and full-time employment, there is a risk that this would constitute discrimination under the Act on the Prohibition on Discrimination of Part-time Employees and Employees with Fixed-term Employment. However, the prohibition under this Act does not apply if the application of certain terms could be justified on reasonable grounds. For example, nothing prevents the amount of the benefit paid to be commensurate with the degree of employment. Violation of the Act could lead to a liability to pay damages and to rectify the unlawful decision, if challenged in court.

It should be noted that the implementation of the long-term incentive award could give rise to an obligation to consult with the trade unions to which the employer is bound by collective agreement or, if the employer is not bound by any collective agreement, with the trade unions having members at the workplace. It should be noted that such consultations should be initiated and concluded before the decision to implement the award is made. A failure to negotiate with the trade unions does not affect the validity of the employer's decision to implement the award, but could lead to a liability to pay damages to the relevant unions.

## 10. Translation

10.1 **Are there any language restrictions in Sweden? Does any of the documentation provided to the employee in relation to the long-term incentive award need to be translated?**

There are no legal requirements that the documentation must be translated into Swedish, unless prospectus requirements are triggered in Sweden. In such cases, the prospectus must normally be prepared in Swedish, unless it concerns a prospectus which has been approved by a Financial Supervisory Authority in another state within the EEA, in which case only the summary of the prospectus can be required to be translated into Swedish. Even if no prospectus requirements are triggered in Sweden, the information should be given in a language that the employees understand, preferably in Swedish to Swedish employees.

## 11. Data protection

11.1 **Are there any data protection issues which may arise should the employer wish to outsource the administration of the long-term incentive award to a third party?**

The main principle pursuant to the Swedish Personal Data Act is that personal data may only be processed if the person registered gives his consent. The employee should be informed of the processing of his/her personal data and it is appropriate to ask for the employee's consent in connection with this. Therefore, the employee should also give his consent to the processing of his personal data, when he or she agrees to participate in the long-term incentive award.

## 12. Source of shares

**12.1 Does it matter if shares are newly issued to an employee, provided out of treasury or delivered from an employee-benefit trust?**
No.

# Switzerland

Balz Gross
Peter Müller
Thomas Pietruszak
Homburger AG

---

> **Red flag issues**
>
> 1. Vesting/forfeiture conditions and other restrictions may not be enforceable if the long-term incentive award is qualified as part of the salary, and not as a discretionary payment.
>
> 2. The date of taxation of stock options or employee shares, and the date of charging of social security contributions, depend on whether any forfeiture/vesting restrictions apply to the stock options or the employee shares, respectively.
>
> 3. For cantonal/communal income tax rates, there can be substantial differences between cantons and, within a canton, between the communities.

## 1. Securities laws

**1.1 What prospectus and/or securities laws requirements arise in connection with the grant, vesting or exercise of a long-term incentive award or on the eventual sale of the shares by the executive?**

*(a) Reporting requirements*

Reporting duties may exist under stock exchange and securities trading rules. If the company is foreign listed, foreign law will determine the reporting duties. The Swiss Stock Exchange and Securities Trading Act applies to companies listed on a Swiss stock exchange. Its reporting provisions were amended on December 1 2007. The reporting duties also cover option rights and could also be triggered if a Swiss listed company issues shares or options in connection with long-term incentive plans. Under the general rules, the issuance of shares or option rights representing more than 3, 5, 10, 15, 20, 25, 33, 50 or 66⅔ of the voting rights must be reported.

*(b) Issues triggered if new shares are issued in connection with the long-term incentive award*

Prospectus issues arise if new shares are issued in connection with a long-term incentive award. Swiss company law may apply if a Swiss or foreign company issues new shares to Swiss employees in connection with the long-term incentive award. The issuance of new shares in connection with long-term incentive awards triggers the requirement to draw up a listing prospectus within the meaning of Article 652a

273

of the Swiss Code of Obligations (CO) if the issuance is considered a "public offer". It remains unclear under which circumstances the issuance of shares to employees could be considered a public offer. It is generally assumed that there could not be a public offer if fewer than 20 employees receive an offer, but there may be a public offer if more than 500 employees are involved. Despite these accepted rules of thumb, the issue of whether there is a public offering not only depends on the number of offerees, but also on the manner in which the offer is made (individual identification of offerees, method of communication (individual letter or public announcement), number of offerees). If a prospectus were indeed required, Article 652a, para 1 of the CO requires a prospectus with rather basic information on the legal structure of the issuer and on the issuer's current financial situation. In addition, there is no requirement to distribute the prospectus unless specifically requested.

Additional Swiss rules may apply if the newly issued shares are listed on the SWX Swiss Exchange. In particular, there is a requirement to draw up a listing prospectus unless the shares are allotted to employees only and are of the same class as already listed shares.

If the shares that are listed on the SWX Swiss Exchange are traded on virt-x, certain EU laws, such as the EU Prospectus Directive, and implementing national laws apply, because virt-x is considered a regulated market under EU law.

**1.2    Is there an exemption from securities laws requirements either because the shares are being offered only to executives or because shares are being offered to a distinct group of named individuals?**

Yes, if the issue of shares is considered to be a private placement, where no offering prospectus is required. See above.

**1.3    If there is an exemption, will the exemption apply automatically or are there any applications/filings that need to be made?**

Neither applications nor filings are required if the above-stated exemptions (see above) of a private placement apply (Article 652a of the CO). There is no application or filing requirement if securities of the same class are already listed on a Swiss stock exchange and the newly issued equity securities are solely allotted to employees (Article 38, para. 1, no. 4 SWX Listing Rules).

**2.    Employee tax and social security**

**2.1    When is the executive liable to tax or social security (and at what rate) in respect of the long-term incentive award?**

*(a)    Employee's tax liability*

The system of taxation of long-term incentive awards is not explicitly regulated in the Swiss federal or cantonal tax laws. Instead, it is rather based on case law and the administrative practice of the Swiss federal tax administration and the cantonal tax administrations. The practice may, to a certain extent, differ from canton to canton.

(i)   *Taxation of stock option awards*

As a general rule, the date of taxation of stock option awards depends on whether the stock options are granted subject to vesting/forfeiture conditions. If no vesting/forfeiture conditions apply, the amount of taxable income depends on whether transfer restrictions apply to the stock option. The date of income taxation is also relevant for wealth taxation. The following concepts apply:

- *No restrictions:* unrestricted stock option awards (ie stock options not subject to any vesting/forfeiture conditions and/or transfer conditions) whose value can be properly appraised at grant, are taxable at grant.
- *Transfer restrictions:* stock option awards subject to transfer restrictions (but not subject to vesting/forfeiture conditions) and whose value is properly determinable at grant are taxed at grant. A discount of 5.66% is given on the underlying shares for each full year the transfer restrictions apply. The discount is currently capped at 25.274% for a five-year maximum transfer restriction.
- *Vesting/forfeiture conditions:* stock option awards subject to vesting/forfeiture conditions are taxed at exercise on the fair market value of the shares at exercise, less the strike price, if any.

(ii)   *Taxation of share awards*

The date of taxation of share awards depends on whether any forfeiture/vesting conditions apply. Thus:

- *Provisional allocations of shares,* where the executive receives an "unsecured promise" of free shares on vesting if certain service and/or performance conditions are met, are taxed at vesting on the fair market value of the shares.
- *Forfeitable shares,* where the executive is awarded shares at the outset but will lose them without indemnification if he leaves employment within a specified period or if the company fails to meet performance conditions within a specified period, are taxed at grant on the fair market value of the shares. Any shares forfeited/lost after the time of grant usually lead to negative taxable income at the time of forfeiture, which can usually be set off against the income earned in the year of forfeiture. If the shares are subject to transfer restrictions, a discount of 5.66% on the fair market value of the shares for each full year the transfer restrictions apply is granted. The discount is currently capped at 44.161% for a 10-year maximum transfer restriction.
- *Progressive income tax rates:* any income derived from employee stock options, employee shares and other long-term incentive awards is aggregated with the global income of the employee and is taxed at progressive income tax rates. Federal income tax is 0% to 11.5% of the net taxable income (gross income less certain expenses and allowances) provided for in the tax laws, whereas cantonal/municipal income tax is between 0% and 28.5% of the net taxable income, depending on the canton and municipality of residence, the income, the marital status and the number of children of the employee. The cantonal/communal income tax rates differ substantially between cantons and, within a canton, between the municipalities.

*(b)*     ***Social security contributions***

Any remuneration the executive receives for performing his work, including benefits from a long-term incentive award, is subject to social security contributions. Exactly when the social security contributions have to be made for long-term incentive awards is not explicitly set out in law. The Swiss Federal Social Insurance Office has published guidelines which essentially provide that the social security liabilities, as set out below, will arise at the same time as the income tax liabilities (see above).

The following social security rates apply in 2008:

- AHV (1st pillar coverage of old age and survivorship): 8.4%;
- IV (1st pillar coverage of disability): 1.4%;
- EO (coverage of salary payment in case of military service and motherhood): 0.3%.

The total rate of 10.1% is to be shared equally by the employer and the executive (5.05% each). Contributions to the 2nd pillar mandatory and non-mandatory coverage of old age, survivorship and disability (BVG) may be due depending on the relevant insurance contract. Wages of up to Sfr126,000 are also subject to contributions for ALV (coverage of unemployment: 2.0%) and mandatory accident insurance.

**2.2     How is the executive's tax and social security to be collected? Is the executive responsible for paying any liabilities himself or is the executive's employer responsible for paying tax or social security liabilities on the executive's behalf?**

*(a)*     ***Responsibility for tax payments***

Different concepts apply concerning the collection of tax depending on the executive's nationality and place of residence.

*(i)*     *Collection of income tax from the executive*

Except where an executive is exclusively subject to wage tax withholding (see below), he or she must file an annual tax return for any worldwide income in the tax year and worldwide wealth at the end of the tax year (normally December 31), based on which any income tax and wealth tax due are determined. Certain income derived from foreign sources and wealth that can be allocated to foreign jurisdictions (real property abroad, business conducted through a permanent establishment or a fixed place of business situated abroad) will be tax exempt under a progression proviso pursuant to domestic law. If wage tax withholding was deducted from any of the executive's income, such wage tax withholding is credited against the tax assessed by the tax inspector, considering the tax declaration made in the annual tax return.

Employment income from foreign sources may be exempt under the progression proviso based on a double taxation treaty. Net income attributable to Switzerland (ie gross income less attributable expenses and allowances) is taxable at the progressive rates set out above. The tax authorities collect income and wealth tax directly from the executive, who is solely responsible for paying any tax liabilities.

*(ii)*   *Wage tax withholding*
Wage tax withholding exclusively applies to:

- non-Swiss nationals who have not been granted a long-term residence permit, and who are not married to a Swiss national;
- holders of a long-term residence permit, whose taxable income for the respective tax year does not exceed Sfr120,000;
- income earned by non-Swiss resident executives or executives who have ceased to be resident in Switzerland and who have derived taxable income from long-term incentive awards (as regards the latter case, see Internationally mobile executives below).

Employers must register their employees subject to wage tax withholding with the tax authorities of the canton in which the employer resides. The employer must deduct the wage tax withholding at the applicable tax rates from the executive's remuneration and must remit the respective amounts on behalf of the employee to the competent tax administration.

*(b)*   ***Responsibility for social security contributions***
Employers must register all their employees with the competent social security authorities and are responsible for payment of their own and their executive's social security contributions.

**2.3**   **If the employer is responsible for the executive's liabilities, can the employer withhold the liabilities from the executive's salary? Are there any formalities in this respect?**
Where wage tax withholding applies and with regard to social security contributions, the employer must withhold tax and social security contributions from the executive's salary or, respectively, from the executive's long-term incentive award.

The employer must annually (usually in January of the following year) provide the executive with a written salary statement. If the executive has been granted a long-term incentive award, the employer must complete a sheet additional to the salary statement stating all details of the award, in particular the number and the market value of the options or shares subject to the award, the restriction period and the amount of the tax discount, if any. In certain cantons, the employer is obliged to file a copy of the salary statement directly with the cantonal tax authorities. Where wage tax withholding applies, the employer must monthly or quarterly (as applicable) report the wages and wage tax deductions to the tax authorities. In addition, the wages and social security deductions must be reported annually to the social security authorities.

**2.4**   **If the executive's salary in the month of exercise/release is not sufficient for the employer to withhold all of the liabilities, can the employer (or the parent company, if different) arrange for the executive to authorise to sell some of the executive's shares in the market and pass the money to the executive's employer?**
Whether or not the company needs the executive's consent to sell shares in the market depends on the structure of the plan, in particular the parties to the plan and

the nature of the awards. In any event, it is advisable that the applicable plan rules explicitly provide that the initial award is subject to any applicable wage tax withholding and social security deductions.

**2.5    Will the executive have to pay tax on the eventual sale of his shares and if so at what rate?**

As a general rule, capital gains realised on the sale of privately held movable assets are not taxable as income in Switzerland. Executives who hold the shares as private assets realise a tax-free capital gain on the eventual sale of their shares. Conversely, capital losses are not tax-deductible. However, income taxes may become due if the executive is exceptionally considered a professional securities trader for income tax purposes. In that case, the capital gains realised are treated as income from an independent business activity.

**3.    Employer's social security**

**3.1    Is the employer liable to pay (on its own account) any employer's social security in connection with the long-term incentive award?**

Yes, any benefit the executive receives under a long-term incentive award qualifies as salary, which is subject to social security contributions from both the employee and the employer. The employer must, at the relevant date (see above), remit both the employer's and the executive's portion on such contributions to the competent authorities. While the executive's portion is deducted from the payments to the executive, the employer must pay his own portion on top.

**3.2    Can the liability of the employer be put onto the employee? What steps are required?**

No, under Swiss law the employer cannot put his social security liability onto the executive.

**4.    Tax deduction for the employer**

**4.1    Is it possible for the employer to receive a tax deduction in respect to the long-term incentive award? Would the employer need to be subject to recharge arrangements (eg if the employer is a subsidiary and provides funds to the parent company as part of a recharge arrangement in respect to the long-term incentive award)?**

Yes, the expenses/provisions booked by a Swiss employer for long-term incentive awards are tax-deductible. Such costs are genuine business expenses for the Swiss employing entity whether they are actually paid for in cash or just provisioned for in the accounts. Exemptions may apply where stock options are exercised against contingent share capital and no proper structure has been put in place.

Generally under Swiss tax law, a taxpayer is obliged to provide evidence that the expenses deducted from the taxable income are commercially justified. There are no specific rules on how such evidence must be given. However, for transactions between affiliated parties and also for accounting purposes, it is recommended that a written agreement (a recharge agreement) is put in place to support the commercial legitimacy and tax-deductibility of expenses incurred in connection with employee participation together with the usual invoices and accounting records and to facilitate the recharge process (invoices and records can refer to the agreement). A written agreement as part of proper documentation is particularly relevant for the purposes of Swiss VAT (ie as proof that the recharged plan costs are not subject to Swiss VAT).

## 5. Tax beneficial arrangements

### 5.1 Are there any ways of making the long-term incentive award tax-efficient in Switzerland?

As a rule, capital gains realised on privately held movable assets are not taxable as income in Switzerland (as long as the employee is not considered a professional securities trader for income tax purposes – see above). Accordingly, taxation of long-term incentive awards at grant can be more beneficial to Swiss tax-resident employees than if the award is taxed at vesting/exercise. This holds particularly true in bullish markets.

Taxation at grant bears, however, the risk that the long-term incentive awards decrease in value over time and that income tax and social security charges are paid on a basis that is higher than the actual benefit earned from the award upon sale, exercise or vesting, respectively.

Furthermore, by submitting the long-term incentive award to transfer restrictions a tax discount is available (see 2.1 above) of up to 25.274% (for a five-year maximum transfer restriction period on the underlying shares) in case of the award of option, respectively up to 44.161% (for a 10-year maximum transfer restriction period) of the shares in case of an award of shares.

## 6. Internationally mobile executives

### 6.1 What are the consequences on income tax for an employee who is resident in Switzerland when the long-term incentive award is made, but who is no longer resident at the time of exercise/vesting?

There are no specific regulations in Swiss tax law, nor is there a standard tax treatment of long-term incentive awards, for an employee who is resident in Switzerland when the long-term incentive award is made, but who is no longer resident at the time of exercise/vesting. In practice, the following concepts apply.

### (a) Past performance

Long-term incentive awards have been granted for the past performance of the executive for work performed in Switzerland. Long-term incentive awards granted while the employee is resident in Switzerland will be taxable in Switzerland at exercise/vesting, irrespective of where the employee is resident at the time of exercise/vesting (in an emigration situation).

*(b)*   *Future performance*

Long-term incentive awards have also been granted for the future performance of the employee. Such awards remain subject to income tax in Switzerland even if the employee is, at the time of exercise/vesting, no longer residing in Switzerland. However, income tax is usually levied on a pro rata basis considering the time the employee was resident in Switzerland and the time when the award is exercised/vested. Here, the income tax rate is calculated considering the entire income earned from the long-term incentive award, but such income is taxed on a pro rata basis only.

Any capital gain derived upon disposal of the vested shares/unrestricted options is out of the scope of Swiss income tax of the respective fiscal year, as the employee is not subject to income tax at the time of disposal of the long-term incentive award.

6.2   **What are the consequences on social security for an employee who is resident in Switzerland when the long-term incentive award is made, but who is no longer resident at the time of exercise/vesting?**

There are no consequences on social security contributions if such contributions were charged at grant of the long-term incentive award and the employee leaves Switzerland later on.

The legal situation is unclear, however, if the social security contributions should be due upon exercise or vesting, but the employee falls at that time out of the scope of Swiss social security legislation. It is possible that the social security authorities would also apply either the tax-related concept of past performance or the concept of future performance, as set out above.

6.3   **What are the tax and social security withholding/reporting consequences for the employer in respect of an employee who is resident in Switzerland when the long-term incentive award is made, but who is no longer resident at the time of exercise/vesting?**

The employer by whom the employee was employed at the time of grant of a long-term incentive award is under the obligation to report wages and wage tax deductions (by means of wage tax withholding) and wages and social security deductions to the tax authority and the social security authority, respectively, and to remit the tax and social security to the respective authorities.

## 7.   Reporting requirements

7.1   **Does the employer (or parent company, if different) have any reporting requirements as a result of the long-term incentive award?**

A listed Swiss company is required to disclose in the annex of its balance sheet (i) the remuneration of its members of the board of directors, its members of the management and its members of the advisory council (Beirat), and (ii) the shares and options/warrants held by each individual member of the board of directors, the management and the advisory council (in each case including persons closely related to them). If the company is foreign listed, foreign law will determine the reporting duties, and there are no reporting requirements under Swiss law in relation to the grant of long-term incentive awards to Swiss employees of a company which is not listed in Switzerland. (For reporting to the tax authorities, see above.)

In addition, a listed Swiss company may have reporting duties under the Swiss Stock Exchange and Securities Trading Act if shares or option rights representing more than 3, 5, 10, 15, 20, 25, 33, 50 or 66⅔ of the voting rights are issued.

**7.2    Are there any tax rulings required in relation to the long-term incentive awards?**
No, there are no tax rulings required in relation to the long-term incentive awards.

It is, however, a customary practice in Switzerland to seek an advance tax ruling with the Swiss tax authorities covering the tax treatment of the granting of long-term incentive awards, in particular if a substantial number of Swiss tax-resident employees are invited to participate in the plan and/or if the amount of awards granted under the plan is substantial.

## 8.    Exchange control issues

**8.1    Are there any exchange control issues that would prevent an employee from (a) remitting monies abroad to purchase shares or (b) repatriating monies from the sale of shares?**
In general, there are no exchange control issues in Switzerland.

Pursuant to the Swiss Law on the Enforcement of Sanctions, certain transactions with certain countries or persons can be banned. There is a regularly updated list of banned transactions with specific countries or specific persons on the website of the State Secretariat for Economic Affairs (SECO). The website address is: www.seco.admin.ch.

## 9.    Employment law

**9.1    Are there any employment or local labour law issues which may arise as a result of the long-term incentive award? Are any consultations or authorisations required by law?**

*(a)    Enforceability of the plan rules*
Swiss employment law does not have specific regulations on long-term incentive awards. However, such awards are considered to be employment-related and, therefore, must be in accordance with mandatory provisions of Swiss employment law and general principles of Swiss contract law.

As regards the employee's compensation, Swiss employment law subdivides the employee's overall remuneration (also including long-term incentive awards) into salary and gratification:

- *Salary* is the actual remuneration the employee receives for performing his work. The amount of the salary can be fix or variable depending on the employee's performance (commissions, achieving specific targets, etc). However, the employer has no discretion with respect to the salary. Once the amount of the salary or, respectively, the factors according to which the salary is calculated, have been agreed between the parties, they form part of the employment contract which can only be amended by mutual consent.

- *Gratification* is, if compared to the salary, a remuneration of secondary importance. To qualify as gratification and not as salary, the employer must have discretion either to determine the amount of the award or to grant an award at all. If the employer lacks such discretion (eg because it has been agreed that the employee shall receive a particular amount if certain accountable targets are achieved), the respective award qualifies as salary and not as gratification.

The distinction between salary and gratification is crucial. Pursuant to mandatory Swiss law, salary must be paid at certain time intervals (usually monthly) and be free of any conditions or restrictions. Any agreement preventing the employee from disposing freely of his salary (eg if salary includes shares or stock options, vesting/forfeiture conditions or transfer restrictions) is null and void. This protection applies to all employees regardless of their position within the company; so it also applies to executives. However, in Swiss doctrine and jurisprudence there is a tendency to argue that employees with very high salaries as well as employees who act as investors do not deserve such protection in relation to long-term incentive awards. Swiss courts have confirmed this view in relation to employees acting as investors, but the very high salary argument has not yet been tested in court. In the case of gratification, however, these principles do not apply. Gratification can therefore be granted under conditions and/or restrictions.

Swiss courts use several criteria in order to qualify a long-term incentive award as part of the employee's salary or as a gratification. The respective decisions are often made on a case-by-case basis taking into consideration all relevant circumstances. As a general rule, the value of the long-term incentive award must be of secondary importance if compared with the compensation the employee can immediately and freely dispose of (cash salary, cash bonus, non-deferred shares, etc). In addition, if awards have been made for three or more consecutive years, it is important that the employer has actually made use of his discretion; otherwise the employer would be deemed to have waived it and the award would be considered as salary.

If the long-term incentive award is qualified as gratification, the rules of the long-term incentive plan, including vesting/forfeiture conditions and transfer restrictions, are, in principle, enforceable. However, any deferral (including vesting periods and transfer restrictions) exceeding 10 years is not accepted by the Swiss courts and will be accelerated accordingly. Moreover, the Swiss Federal Supreme Court held that a provision contained in a stock option plan, according to which an unvested option award is forfeited if the employee ceases to be in employment, is not enforceable if the employer terminates the employment relationship unfairly. The stock options concerned were therefore deemed to have been vested, and the employer had to reimburse the employee the value of these options.

*(b)*   *Information/Consultation obligations*

Swiss law requires the employer to conduct a formal information and/or consultation procedure with the employee's representative body or, if there is none, with each employee only in very limited cases (see Article 10 of the Swiss Act on Information and Co-Determination of Employees in Enterprises). There is no such statutory requirement in connection with long-term incentive awards, either when the plan is being implemented or carried out. However, the employer must clarify whether it is under an obligation pursuant to an applicable collective employment agreement, or the company's internal work rules, as these may provide for additional information/consultation obligations.

*(c)*   *Applicable law; jurisdiction*

Due to their close connection to the employment relationship, long-term incentive awards are usually subject to the rules on conflict of laws in employment matters. It is unclear, however, whether this is also the case if the award is not granted by the employer but by a different legal entity (eg the parent company abroad). Swiss courts usually consider the specific circumstances of the individual case. They tend to apply the conflict rules in employment matters if the main purpose of having the award made by a different legal entity abroad is to make it more difficult for the employee to enforce his claims.

As a general rule, employment contracts are governed by the laws of the state where the employee usually performs his work. Instead, the parties may subject the employment contract to the laws of either the state in which the employee usually resides, or the state in which the employer has its branch, domicile or usual residence (Article 121, paras 1 and 3 of the Swiss Act on Private International Law). The choice of any other law would not be recognised by the Swiss courts.

## 10.    Translation

**10.1    Are there any language restrictions in Switzerland? Does any of the documentation provided to the employee in relation to the long-term incentive award need to be translated?**

There are no specific language requirements under Swiss law. However, according to general principles of Swiss contract law, the executive is only deemed to have agreed to the terms and conditions of the long-term incentive plan if they were provided in a language the executive is capable of reading and understanding. Many companies in Switzerland have their plan rules and other employment-related documents in English, with the option of having them in German or French, which is usually considered sufficient. Depending on the persons involved, however, full German, French or Italian translations of the relevant plan rules may be recommended.

## 11. Data protection

**11.1 Are there any data protection issues which may arise should the employer wish to outsource the administration of the long-term incentive award to a third party?**

Swiss data protection laws apply to the employer, any incentive award plan administrator and any other party processing data that is related to an identified or identifiable employee. The main data protection restrictions are thus:

- The sole purpose of the data processing (which includes collecting, storing, archiving and all other operations related to the data) must be to serve the purposes of the plan as agreed with the employee.

- The data processing must be limited to what is necessary for the above-mentioned purpose.

- The employee must be informed in advance about the processing of data, including the fact that processing may take place abroad and may be carried out by third parties. The employee should expressly consent to this (it is advisable to document this for evidence). The employee also has the right to request access to or correction or deletion of personal data.

- All data must be secured against unauthorised access and processing for other purposes.

- No data shall be shared with any third parties (including affiliates and authorities) except where consent has been given by the employee or is allowed under (Swiss) law.

- Any country outside Switzerland which is about to receive data is contractually obligated fully to comply with Swiss data protection laws, unless that country has a similar level of data protection (as is the case in many countries of the European Union, but not the United States). There is no data protection restriction for anonymous data, provided the data subject cannot be identified indirectly (through information on salary, position, age etc). The supply of information about employees to foreign authorities (eg tax authorities) may also be subject to separate criminal law provisions in Switzerland. It might be considered to constitute a prohibited act for a foreign state or economic intelligence service (Articles 271 and 273 of the Swiss Penal Code). Banking secrecy provision may also apply to accounts opened for employees in the context of incentive awards.

A revised Swiss Federal Act on Data Protection (DPA) and its implementing ordinance came into effect on January 1 2008. The revision will redefine the limitations on the transfer of data abroad. There is no material impact of the new law. For data transfer abroad, the revised law requires generally appropriate data protection. Even if appropriate data protection abroad is not safeguarded, the revised law explicitly foresees certain exceptions, of which the consent by the person whose personal data is transferred may be the most important.

## 12. Source of shares

**12.1 Does it matter if shares are newly issued to an employee, provided out of treasury or delivered from an employee-benefit trust?**

The company is free to decide whether it uses newly issued shares or already existing treasury shares or shares delivered from an employee-benefit trust.

However, if newly issued shares are used, Swiss and foreign companies will have to comply with the prospectus requirements of Article 652a of the CO if the offer to the employees is considered a public offer. Companies listed on a Swiss exchange will also have to prepare a listing prospectus unless the shares are allotted to employees only and are of the same class as shares that are already listed.

# United Kingdom

**Mark A Ife**
Herbert Smith LLP

---

> **Red flag issues**
> 1. Prospectus requirements for non-EU issuers.

## 1. Securities laws

### 1.1 What prospectus and/or securities law requirements arise in connection with the grant, vesting or exercise of a long-term incentive award or on the eventual sale of the shares by the executive?

The United Kingdom is subject to the provisions of EU Prospectus Directive (2003/71/EC), which provides rules for the publication of a prospectus when securities are offered to the public. The UK provisions implementing the Prospectus Directive are contained in the Prospectus Rules issued by the UK Listing Authority of the Financial Services Authority (FSA), and also in Part VI of the Financial Services and Markets Act 2000 (as amended).

The Financial Services and Markets Act 2000 provides that a prospectus must be issued whenever transferable securities are offered to the public, or a request for the admission of securities to a regulated public market is made.

In relation to employee share plans, the FSA has provided guidance on what constitutes a "transferable security" for the purpose of the Prospectus Rules. The FSA does not consider that options granted to employees, provided that those options are non-transferable, fall within the provisions of the Prospectus Rules, either at the time of the option grant or when that option is exercised and the underlying securities are acquired. This is because the option is not a transferable security itself and, on exercise, there is no offer to the public but, rather, the fulfilment of a contractual entitlement. The Prospectus Rules will not, therefore, apply to share option grants.

The definition of an "offer to the public" is set out within the legislation as being any communication giving sufficient information to enable an investor to decide to "buy or subscribe" for securities. The FSA has confirmed that it does not consider offers of shares to employees for nil consideration (ie free shares) to fall within this definition, as there will be no purchase or subscription for those shares. The Prospectus Rules will not, therefore, apply to free share awards.

Offers to employees to subscribe to or purchase shares will, however, fall within the Prospectus Rules and will require a prospectus to be published, unless one of the relevant exemptions applies.

Where a prospectus has been produced and approved in another EU jurisdiction in respect of the offer, an application can be made to the FSA to use that prospectus in the United Kingdom for the offer being made, without the need to produce and file a separate prospectus. This procedure is referred to as "passporting".

1.2 **Is there an exemption from securities laws requirements either because the shares are being offered only to executives or because shares are being offered to a distinct group of named individuals?**

There are a number of exemptions which may apply where an offer does not fall outside of the requirement to produce a prospectus. The exemptions which are most likely to be used in connection with employee share plans are:

- offers to fewer than 100 persons in each EU jurisdiction;
- offers where the total consideration for the securities offered is less than the equivalent of €100,000 (when taken together with similar offers in the same 12-month period);
- securities included in an offer where the total consideration of the offer is less than the equivalent of €2.5 million; and
- offers to existing or former directors and employees of transferable securities which are already admitted to trading on a recognised EU market, provided that a document is made available containing information on the number and nature of the securities offered, and the reasons for, and details of, the offer.

It is important to note, in relation to the exemption for offers to directors and employees, that this will not be available to unlisted companies or to companies which do not have a listing (whether primary or secondary) on an EU market. It is therefore important for non-EU issuers to consider whether the Prospectus Rules will apply to them and whether there are other exemptions available on which they may rely.

1.3 **If there is an exemption, will the exemption apply automatically or are there any applications/filings that need to be made?**

Where an exemption from the need to produce a prospectus applies, there will be no requirement to make any application or filing to the FSA. Generally, exemptions will apply automatically without the need for the issuer to produce any documentation.

The exception to this rule is in relation to the exemption for offers to directors and employees. For this exemption to apply, the issuer must produce a document which sets out specific information in relation to the offer. The details for the content of the document are set out both in the Prospectus Rules and also in guidance issued by the Committee of European Securities Regulators (CESR). The Prospectus Rules provide that the document must contain details of the number and nature of the securities available and the reasons for, and details of, the offer. In addition, the CESR guidance provides that the document should also set out the identification of the issuer and details of where further information can be found (generally this will be a reference to the company's website).

Where a company produces an employee guide in connection with the offer, it is likely that this guide will suffice as a "document" for the purposes of the Prospectus Rules.

## 2. Employee tax and social security

### 2.1 When will the executive be liable to tax or social security (and at what rate) in respect of the long-term incentive award?

*(a)* *Share options*

In relation to share options (including market value, discounted and nil-cost options), there is no charge to tax at the time that the option is granted provided that the employee is resident and ordinarily resident in the United Kingdom at the time of the grant (for options granted from April 6 2008, this tax treatment is also extended to employees who are resident but not ordinarily resident at grant). Neither is there a tax charge when the option becomes exercisable (ie at vesting). At the time that the option is actually exercised and the employee acquires the shares, the value of the shares acquired, less the amount of the price paid (if any), will be a taxable benefit and will be subject to income tax and national insurance (NI, ie social security) contributions.

For options granted prior to April 6 2008, if the employee was resident but not ordinarily resident in the United Kingdom at the time of grant, then there would have been no tax at grant, provided that the option was granted with an exercise price at least equal to the market value of the shares at that time. Any discount to market value would, however, have been treated as a benefit and subject to income tax and NI contributions. On the exercise of such an option, the employee will be treated as acquiring shares at an undervalue and any difference between the market value of the shares and the price paid (plus any amount which has already been subject to income tax at grant) will be treated as a notional loan until the shares are sold. Each year, or part year, that the shares are held, deemed interest on this notional loan (currently, 6.25%) is treated as a benefit and is subject to income tax for the employee, but not NI contributions (although employer NI is due – see 3.1 below). When the shares are sold, this is treated as a write-off of the notional loan, and this benefit is subject to income tax and NI contributions.

*(b)* *Free shares – conditional allocations*

There is no charge to tax at the time that the conditional allocation is granted to the employee, as the employee has only an unsecured promise to the shares. When the shares are transferred to the employee, the value of the shares received will be a taxable benefit and will be subject to income tax and NI contributions.

*(c)* *Free shares – restricted securities*

Where an employee acquires shares which are subject to a forfeiture provision which lasts for no longer than five years from the date on which the shares were acquired, the default position for an employee who is resident and ordinarily resident in the United Kingdom is that there is no charge to tax at this time (for restricted securities acquired from April 6 2008, this tax treatment is also extended to employees who are resident but not ordinarily resident at acquisition). At the stage that the forfeiture provision is lifted (or falls away), the value of the shares received will be a taxable benefit and will be subject to income tax and NI contributions. Shares will be subject to forfeiture provisions if the terms on which they are acquired provide that they must be cancelled or transferred for less than market value if certain conditions have not been met within a specified period.

For restricted shares acquired prior to April 6 2008, if the employee was resident, but not ordinarily resident, in the United Kingdom at the time that the shares were acquired, then the value of the shares at that time would have been treated as a benefit and subject to income tax and NI contributions. There will, however, be no additional income tax or NI at the time that the forfeiture provision is lifted (or falls away).

### (d)   Tax rates

Where income tax arises, this will be due at the employee's marginal rate of income tax (for the tax year April 6 2008 to April 5 2009, the income tax rates are 20% for a basic rate taxpayer and 40% for a higher rate taxpayer).

NI contributions are due at 11% on annual earnings of up to £40,040 (for the tax year April 6 2008 to April 5 2009) and at 1% thereafter.

NI contributions will not apply in the above circumstances if the shares which are acquired are not "readily convertible assets", ie essentially where there are no trading arrangements (eg a listing on a stock market, or an employee-benefit trust willing to purchase the shares) in place which would allow the employee to realise the value of the shares at that time. Shares will, however, be deemed to be "readily convertible assets" where they do not meet the qualifying conditions for a statutory corporation tax deduction (see below).

### 2.2   How will the executive's tax and social security be collected? Will the executive be responsible for paying any liabilities himself or will the executive's employer be responsible for paying tax or social security liabilities on the executive's behalf?

Where both income tax and NI arise, these amounts must be accounted for to HM Revenue & Customs by the employing company under the Pay-As-You-Earn (PAYE) system within 14 days following the end of the tax month in which the liability arises. This amount will then need to be reimbursed by the employee to his employer within 90 days of the tax liability arising. If the employee has not made this reimbursement, the outstanding amount will be treated as a benefit and will be subject to an additional charge to income tax.

Where PAYE is due, the employer is liable for this amount to HM Revenue & Customs, who may only seek direct payment from the employee in certain specified circumstances (eg where the employee is aware that PAYE has been operated incorrectly).

Where income tax arises, but NI does not (eg in respect of the notional loan charge referred to above for options exercised by employees who are not ordinarily resident in the United Kingdom or where the shares acquired are not "readily convertible assets") the income tax is accounted for by the individual completing a self-assessment return. Where income tax is to be accounted for under self-assessment, the return (along with the payment of the tax) must be submitted by January 31 in the year following the end of the tax year in which the liability arises.

**2.3    If the employer is responsible for the executive's liabilities, can the employer withhold the liabilities from the executive's salary? Are there any formalities in this respect?**

The statutory rights to deduct PAYE amounts from an employee's salary are strictly limited. Generally, it is only possible to recover PAYE amounts from payments made to an employee in the same tax month. However, by agreement, the employee can allow deductions to be made either from salary in future months (but note the penal tax charge where reimbursement is not received within 90 days), or can make alternative arrangements for the recovery of the PAYE. Where an employer makes a payment in respect of PAYE on behalf of an employee, the employer has a legal right in restitution to such reimbursement and may bring a claim for such recovery (although in most cases this will not be necessary as the employee will have agreed to make arrangements for reimbursement).

**2.4    If the executive's salary in the month of exercise/release is not sufficient for the employer to withhold all of the liabilities, can the employer (or the parent company, if different) arrange for the executive to authorise to sell some of the executive's shares in the market and pass the money to the executive's employer?**

Although not a statutory right, plan rules should provide that on the exercise of an option, or on the transfer of shares, the employer or parent company of the employer can arrange for sufficient shares to be withheld and sold on behalf of the employee in order to reimburse the employer for the PAYE amount. Alternatively, the employee can agree with the employer that this withholding is made. Generally, the employer will instruct a broker to sell sufficient shares to cover the PAYE and will retain the proceeds of such sale.

**2.5    Will the executive pay tax on the eventual sale of his shares and if so at what rate?**

On a sale of the shares acquired by the employee, capital gains tax may be due on the difference between the sale price and the purchase price paid for the shares (plus any amount on which income tax has already been paid). Any gains made may be reduced by the employee's annual exemption. Individuals are allowed to make £9,600 of capital gains per year (for the tax year April 6 2008 to April 5 2009) before becoming subject to capital gains tax. Any gain above this amount will be subject to capital gains tax at 18%.

No NI contributions are payable on capital gains.

For shares sold up to April 5 2008, if an employee shareholder had remained employed by the company whose shares were acquired, to the date of sale, "business asset taper relief" would have been available which would have resulted in only 50% of any gain remaining chargeable to capital gains tax if the shares had been held for one whole year from the date of acquisition. This reduction was increased to 75% where the shares had been held for two whole years or more from the date of acquisition. For former employee shareholders who had left the company whose shares had been acquired, the sale of shares qualified only for less favourable rates of "non-business asset taper relief" (where reductions of only up to 40% were available over a 10-year period).

As a result of the UK Government's reform of capital gains tax to simplify the tax system, taper relief was abolished for disposals from April 6 2008. However, employees or directors who hold at least 5% of the shares in their employer will be able to take advantage of a relief in respect of their first £1 million of lifetime chargeable gains on such shares, which will result in their paying capital gains tax at an effective rate of 10%. This relief is known as "entrepreneur's relief".

## 3. Employer's social security

### 3.1 Is the employer liable to pay (on its own account) any employer's social security in connection with the long-term incentive award?

The rate of employer's NI is currently 12.8% and applies generally whenever income tax and NI is collected via PAYE.

In relation to the notional loan which arises on the exercise of an option, by employees who were not ordinarily resident in the United Kingdom at the time of the option grant, although NI is not payable by the employee, employer's NI is due on this amount.

### 3.2 Can the liability of the employer be put onto the employee? What steps are required?

In certain circumstances a transfer of employer's NI to the employee is possible. In the context of options and free shares, these circumstances are limited to the exercise of a share option and the award of restricted (forfeitable) securities. Where the liability is passed to the employee, the employee will receive a deduction against income tax for the amount of the liability for employer's NI.

The Social Security Contributions and Benefits Act 1992 provides for two methods of passing the liability for employer's NI to the employee. The first method is for the employee to agree with his employer that the liability is to be transferred. In this case, the liability to HM Revenue & Customs for the employer's NI remains with the employer, although the employer has a contractual right to recover this amount from the employee. The second method is a more formal approach and requires the employee and employer to enter into an "election" in a form which has been approved by HM Revenue & Customs. By entering into the election, the liability to HM Revenue & Customs for the employer's NI is formally transferred from the employer to the employee. The benefit of this is that the employer is no longer required to accrue for this liability in its accounts and the employer's NI is treated in the same manner as the employee's.

## 4. Tax deduction for the employer

4.1 Is it possible for the employer to receive a tax deduction in respect of the long-term incentive award? Would the employer need to be subject to recharge arrangements (eg if the employer is a subsidiary and provides funds to the parent company as part of a recharge arrangement in respect of the long-term incentive award)?

Where employees exercise share options or acquire shares in their employer (or in the parent company of their employer) a corporation tax deduction for the UK employer will be available at the time that the shares are acquired, provided that certain statutory conditions are met. First, the shares must either be listed on a recognised stock exchange or must be shares in a company which is either not controlled by another company, or is controlled by a company with shares listed on a recognised stock exchange. Secondly, the business for which the employee's work must be carried on by the employing company and must be within a charge to UK corporation tax. Finally, the option exercise or share award must constitute earnings from employment.

Where the statutory conditions are met, the employing company will be able to claim a deduction against the profits of the business for which the employee works equal to the amount of the gain made by the employee. The deduction will, therefore, be equal to the value of the shares acquired, less the amount of the price paid (if any).

This statutory corporation tax deduction is available irrespective of whether recharge arrangements are in place. If recharge arrangements are in place, there will be no corporation tax deduction for such arrangements where the statutory deduction is available, as the legislation provides for the statutory deduction to take precedence.

The rate of UK corporation tax, effective from April 6 2008, is 28%.

## 5. Tax beneficial arrangements

5.1 Are there any ways of making the long-term incentive award tax-efficient in the United Kingdom?

There are four types of share-based incentive arrangement available in the United Kingdom which may receive tax-beneficial treatment following approval by HM Revenue & Customs. Two of these – the Sharesave Scheme and the Share Incentive Plan – are all-employee arrangements (ie they must be offered on similar terms to all UK employees). The remaining two, however, may be offered on a discretionary basis.

Both of the discretionary tax-approved share plans are option schemes. It is not, therefore, possible to provide for discretionary free share allocations or restricted shares on a tax-approved basis.

The first of the approved share option plans is the Company Share Option Plan. Under this plan, an employer may grant up to £30,000 worth of market value options to each participating employee and, provided that the option is exercised more than three years after grant (but not more than 10 years after grant), the gain on exercise will not be subject to income tax. In addition, where the option is exercised in certain specified circumstances (death, injury, disability, retirement or redundancy), exercise may be effected without an income tax charge even if exercise is within the first three years of grant. Where shares are later sold, the full difference between the sale price and the exercise price paid will be subject to the more beneficial rates of capital gains tax (see above), and also allows the employee to use the capital gains tax annual exemption. To qualify for this beneficial tax treatment, the shares acquired must satisfy the statutory conditions (ie the shares must be fully paid up and not redeemable, and they must either be listed on a recognised stock exchange or be shares in a company which is either not controlled by another company, or is controlled by a company with shares listed on a recognised stock exchange), there must be no restrictions on the shares which do not apply generally to all shareholders, and the employee must not already hold 25% or more of the company's shares.

The second approved share option plan is the Enterprise Management Incentive (EMI) Plan. This plan is more flexible in that options do not need to be market value options, but may be discounted or nil-cost options (ie free shares). However, there are additional restrictions as to which companies are eligible to operate an EMI plan. Essentially, the company whose shares are acquired pursuant to the option must be an independent trading company that has gross assets of no more than £30 million and has fewer than 250 employees. In addition, certain businesses are excluded from participating, such as banking, shipbuilding, coal and steel production, insurance, certain property businesses, farming and legal or accountancy businesses. The limit for individuals is that no employee may hold unexercised qualifying EMI options over shares with a market value at grant of more than £120,000 (from April 6 2008; the previous limit being £100,000). Any number of employees may hold EMI options in a company or group, subject to a maximum of £3 million as the total value of shares under EMI options. As with the Company Share Option Plan, the gain over the market value at grant on the exercise of an EMI option will not be subject to income tax (although any upfront discount will be subject to income tax and National Insurance at exercise). Where shares are later sold, the full difference between the sale price and the exercise price paid (taking into account any amounts on which income tax has already been paid) will be subject to the more beneficial rates of capital gains tax (see above), and also allows the employee to use the capital gains tax annual exemption.

## 6. Internationally mobile executives

**6.1 What are the income tax consequences for an employee who is resident in the United Kingdom when the long-term incentive award is made but who is no longer resident at the time of exercise/vesting?**

*(a) Share options*

In relation to share options, for an employee who was resident and ordinarily resident at the date of grant of the option, but who is no longer resident in the

United Kingdom at exercise, the UK legislation continues to apply to tax the full gain on exercise (and, from April 6 2008, this tax treatment is also extended to employees who are resident but not ordinarily resident at grant). However, as a result of double taxation treaties (or, in certain cases, unilateral relief from UK tax allowed by HM Revenue & Customs), the gain on exercise is generally apportioned for tax purposes between the United Kingdom and the country of residence at exercise based on the residence of the employee during the vesting period (ie up to the time that the option became exercisable). Under the UK–US double taxation treaty, however, the apportionment is based on the time that the option has been held to the date of exercise. This will only be the case, however, where the employee would suffer double taxation without the relief from the UK tax.

For options granted prior to April 6 2008, in respect of employees who were not ordinarily resident at the date of grant of the option and who are not resident at the time of exercise, provided that the employee has no taxable UK earnings at that time, there will be no tax when the option is exercised.

*(b)* *Free shares – conditional allocations*
As a conditional allocation of free shares is taxed only as a benefit when the shares are received, there will only be a charge to UK tax if the employee is resident in the United Kingdom when he receives the shares. If the employee is no longer resident in the United Kingdom at this time, the acquisition of the shares will only be taxable in the employee's country of residence at that time.

*(c)* *Free shares – restricted securities*
The same provisions as apply to share options will apply to an employee who was resident and ordinarily resident at the date on which restricted securities were acquired if, as a result of the forfeiture provisions lasting for less than five years, he was not subject to income tax on acquisition and is no longer resident in the United Kingdom when the forfeiture provision falls away (although, for apportionment purposes, the view of HM Revenue & Customs is that the earnings period in relation to restricted securities will generally fall prior to the award rather than being based on the forfeiture period). For restricted securities acquired from April 6 2008, this tax treatment is also extended to employees who are resident but not ordinarily resident at acquisition.

*(d)* *Capital gains tax*
If an individual makes capital gains from selling shares during a period of temporary residence (ie five or fewer years) outside the United Kingdom, he may still be subject to UK capital gains tax under the temporary non-residence rules.

6.2 **What are the social security consequences for an employee who is resident in the United Kingdom when the long-term incentive award is made but who is no longer resident at the time of exercise/vesting?**
An employee's social security position will depend on the terms of applicable EC Regulations and also any bilateral social security agreement between the United Kingdom and the jurisdictions in which the employee is then resident.

*(a)*     **Share options**

In relation to share options, for an employee who was resident and ordinarily resident at the date of grant of the option (and for options granted from April 6 2008, where the employee is resident but not ordinarily resident at grant), but who is no longer resident in the United Kingdom at exercise, HM Revenue & Customs considers that, as the option was granted for UK employment, the whole of any gain should be subject to UK NI. Where, however, a bilateral social security agreement exists, this will set out the provisions which will apply to NI charges.

In respect of options granted prior to April 6 2008, for employees who were not ordinarily resident at the date of grant of the option and who are not resident at the time of exercise, HM Revenue & Customs will not seek to apply UK NI contributions provided that exercise takes place in a new tax year following departure from the United Kingdom.

*(b)*     **Free shares – conditional allocations**

A conditional allocation of free shares is treated as a benefit when the shares are received. The general position is that employees will remain liable for UK National Insurance for 52 weeks following leaving the United Kingdom. This, however, is subject to EC Regulations, which require social security to be paid in the member state in which the individual is then working, and the terms of any bilateral social security agreement.

*(c)*     **Free shares – restricted securities**

The same provisions as apply to share options will apply to an employee who was resident and ordinarily resident at the date on which restricted securities were acquired if, as a result of the forfeiture provisions lasting for less than five years, he was not subject to NI on acquisition and is no longer resident in the United Kingdom when the forfeiture provision falls away. For restricted securities acquired from April 6 2008, this treatment is also extended to employees who are resident but not ordinarily resident at acquisition.

6.3     **What are the tax and social security/withholding/reporting consequences for the employer in respect of an employee who is resident in the United Kingdom when the long-term incentive award is made, but who is no longer resident at the time of exercise/vesting?**

Where income tax and NI contributions arise for share awards made to individuals who are no longer UK tax resident, the employer continues to be liable to account to HM Revenue & Customs under the PAYE system in respect of these amounts. In the case of non-resident employees, however, PAYE is operated at the basic rate of tax (20% for the tax year April 6 2008 to April 5 2009) and NI is operated based on weekly rates (11% on an amount between £105 and £770, and 1% thereafter). Employer's NI remains at 12.8% on the full amount which is subject to UK income tax. Any additional amount of income tax due (ie for higher rate tax payers) must be accounted for to HM Revenue & Customs by the individual under self-assessment.

## 7. Reporting requirements

**7.1 Will the employer (or parent company, if different) have any reporting requirements as a result of the long-term incentive award?**

No formal approval is required from HM Revenue & Customs or from the FSA for employee share plans. Should the employer wish to adopt an approved Company Share Option Plan, this must have received prior approval from HM Revenue & Customs before options may be granted. Although not requiring formal approval before grant, EMI options must be notified to HM Revenue & Customs within 92 days of grant.

HM Revenue & Customs requires employers to comply with detailed reporting requirements where employees acquire shares or an interest in shares. Annual returns must be submitted to HM Revenue & Customs (using prescribed forms) by July 7 in each year and penalties may apply if this deadline is not adhered to. In addition, HM Revenue & Customs requires disclosure of any unapproved share plan which provides significant tax advantages to participants.

**7.2 Are there any tax rulings required in relation to the long-term incentive awards?**

No tax ruling will be required for shares that are listed on the London or New York stock exchanges. For unlisted shares or shares listed on other markets, Shares and Assets Valuation at HM Revenue & Customs will generally need to be consulted to agree the value of the relevant shares for tax purposes.

## 8. Exchange control issues

**8.1 Are there any exchange control issues that would prevent an employee from (a) remitting monies abroad to purchase shares or (b) repatriating monies from the sale of shares?**

There are no exchange control laws in the United Kingdom.

## 9. Employment law

**9.1 Are there any employment or local labour law issues which may arise as a result of the long-term incentive award? Are any consultations or authorisations required by law?**

There are generally no requirements to consult with employee representatives before share awards are made to employees. Consultation may, however, be required if the employer has entered into a collective agreement with a union which requires such consultation (eg in respect of changes to remuneration arrangements).

The Information and Consultation of Employees Regulations 2004 include an obligation for certain employers (currently, those employing more than 100 individuals) to inform and/or consult employees in relation to the economic situation of the business, their employment prospects and decisions likely to lead to substantial changes in work organisation or contractual relations, including redundancies and transfers. Whilst these obligations will not generally extend to the making of share awards, they may be relevant in certain situations.

## 10. Translation

**10.1 Are there any language restrictions in the United Kingdom? Does any of the documentation provided to the employee in relation to the long-term incentive award need to be translated into English?**

There are generally no requirements for documents sent to individuals to be translated into English.

Where a prospectus is submitted to the FSA for approval it must be in English. If a prospectus has been "passported" into the United Kingdom in a language other than English, the FSA requires that the summary is translated into English in cases where the prospectus is solely being used for public offers (rather than admission to trading). Similarly, if the company is relying on the exemption from producing a prospectus for offers to directors and employees and a document setting out specific information in relation to the offer is being produced, this document should be translated into English.

## 11. Data protection

**11.1 Are there any data protection issues which may arise should the employer wish to outsource the administration of the long-term incentive award to a third party?**

The Data Protection Act 1998 governs the processing of personal data in the United Kingdom. The most relevant obligations imposed in respect of the transfer of the personal data of individuals are the obligation to maintain a notification (ie registration) with the UK Office of the Information Commissioner and to ensure that the transfer is "fair and lawful".

Fairness and lawfulness require at least one of the conditions contained in the legislation to be met. These include the individual having given his consent to the processing, or the processing being necessary for the performance of a contract to which the individual is a party or for the taking of steps at the request of the individual with a view to entering into a contract. It will also be lawful to transfer personal data if the processing is necessary for the purposes of "legitimate interests" pursued by the data controller or by a third party or parties to whom the data is disclosed. The controller of the data must ensure that the rights and freedoms or legitimate interests of the individual are protected.

There are also additional requirements to be met if sensitive personal data is being transferred (eg information as to a person's health, sexual life, political opinions, racial or ethnic origin, trade union membership or criminal record).

In order to carry out any processing of personal data, organisations are required to file a suitable notification with the UK Information Commissioner's Office and to keep this up-to-date. The notification requires a generic description of the kinds of personal data processed by an organisation and the purposes for which they are processed. There are only very narrow exemptions from the requirement to notify. Failure to maintain an up-to-date data protection notification (unless exempt) is a criminal offence punishable by way of potentially unlimited fine.

Employees affected by the proposed processing will need to be made aware of the identity of the entity processing their personal data, the purposes for which the data is being processed and any further information which is necessary, having regard to the specific circumstances, to enable processing in respect of the employees to be "fair".

## 12. Source of shares

### 12.1 Does it matter if shares are newly issued to an employee, provided out of treasury or delivered from an employee-benefit trust?

It is possible for options and share awards to be satisfied by an issue of shares or transfer of shares from treasury or from an employee-benefit trust without affecting the tax position for the individual, save that stamp duty tax is payable where shares are transferred from an employee-benefit trust for consideration. This stamp duty will usually be paid by the employing company.

Where the issuing company has a listing in the United Kingdom on the main market of the London Stock Exchange, shareholder approval is required for share awards which may make use of new issue shares or treasury shares. In addition, where share awards are made to directors of a company which has a main market UK listing, shareholder approval will generally be required.

# United States

**Susan P Serota**
Pillsbury Winthrop Shaw Pittman, LLP

---

**Red flag issues**

1. Compliance with the registration and reporting requirements of the securities laws for initial issuances and re-sales of plan securities or exemptions from such requirements.

2. Compliance with new Internal Revenue Code §409A imposing tax penalties on deferred compensation.

3. Compliance with state securities laws by equity plans of companies whose shares are not traded on a US national exchange.

---

## 1. Types of equity-based compensation

The types of long-term equity compensation awards commonly offered by US corporations are stock option plans, employee stock purchase plans (ESPPs), stock appreciation rights (SARs), restricted stock (also known as forfeitable securities), and performance shares or restricted stock units (RSUs). The tax, securities law, and other reporting requirements related to equity compensation may vary depending on the nature of the plan and the type of awards offered.

The two basic types of option plans – distinguished by their respective tax consequences – are incentive stock options (ISOs) and non-qualified stock options (NQSOs).[1] While for both types the executive receives a right to acquire company shares, ISOs qualify for favourable tax treatment from the executive's perspective whereas NQSOs do not. Also a type of option plan, SARs allow the recipient to receive (either in shares or cash) the spread between the value of a share on the date the SAR is granted and the date the SAR is exercised. Performance shares function like SARs, but derive their value from a measurement external to the price of company stock (ie cost reduction, cash flow, earnings per share or book value multiples). By comparison, RSUs are provisional allocations for which neither stock nor options are actually issued at the date of grant, but which represent the company's promise to distribute shares, or the cash equivalent of such shares, when the recipient satisfies

---

[1]     To qualify for ISO status, which allows the employee to defer award income until the stock purchased with the option is sold, the option must be granted with an exercise price that at least equals the fair market value of the stock at the time of grant, and must meet other requirements, including shareholder approval and limits on the term of the option, exercisability, and grant value; and upon exercise, the acquired shares are subject to a post-exercise holding period. See section 422 of the Internal Revenue Code of 1986, as amended, (the Code), 26 USC1 *et seq* (2000).

certain service and/or performance vesting requirements.

With respect to pure stock awards, an ESPP allows a broad-based group of employees to purchase employer stock at a discount, typically through payroll deductions. As with ISOs, ESPP recipients enjoy favourable tax treatment under the plan.[2] Restricted stock is stock that is granted to the employee either without consideration or for a nominal purchase price that is subject to transferability, vesting, forfeiture, and/or repurchase restrictions for a certain service period.[3]

## 2.      Securities laws

### 2.1      What prospectus and/or securities law requirements arise in connection with the grant, vesting or exercise of a long-term incentive award or on the eventual sale of the shares by the executive?

Equity awards to employees will generally implicate a variety of federal and state securities laws.[4] In the absence of an exemption, these awards are subject to the registration requirements of the Securities Act 1933 (the Securities Act) and, if not traded on US exchanges, most state securities laws. Furthermore, reporting companies under the Securities Exchange Act 1934 (the Exchange Act) must make ongoing equity compensation disclosures; companies whose securities trade on a US exchange must also comply with the rules adopted by that exchange. In addition, the securities laws often impose restrictions on the recipient's ability to resell stock, including strict reporting obligations and trading limitations imposed on certain key employees.

### (a)      Securities Act of 1933 – Registration

In the absence of an exemption, equity awards are generally subject to the registration and prospectus requirements of the securities laws at the time of sale or offer to sell such securities to employees, with the exception that, under the "no-sale" theory, registration is not required if the employee provides nothing of value in exchange for the award.[5] Because stock options require the payment of value (ie the exercise price) to receive the shares, the securities underlying the options generally are subject to registration when the options first become exercisable, which is deemed the point at which such securities are offered by the employer.[6] Similarly, while stock awards bargained for individually by employees, such as performance-based awards, are generally subject to registration, awards broadly available to

---

2       To qualify for ESPP status, which allows the employee to defer the recognition of income until the stock is sold, the discount price at which the stock is offered to employees cannot exceed 15% below the fair market value of the stock (determined either at grant or at exercise); the ESPP must be approved by stockholders, and the acquired shares are subject to a post-acquisition holding period. See Code §423 (2000).

3       During the restricted period, the recipient may receive dividends declared and vote the shares.

4       State laws are pre-empted and do not apply where the issuer's securities are listed on any of the national exchange markets regulated by the Securities and Exchange Commission (SEC). See Sections 18(a) and 18(b)(1) of the Securities Act,.

5       See SEC No Action Letters to Verint Systems Inc. (May 24 2007), Goldman Sachs Group, Inc. (August 24 1998), MCA Inc. (May 26 1992) and Farmers Group, Inc. (December 1 1995).

6       See Securities Act Release No. 33–6188, at Pt II.A.5.d (February 1 1980).

employees (where employees do not individually bargain to contribute value to the plan) are not subject to registration because there is no offer or sale under the Securities Act. Likewise, if ESPP stock is acquired directly from the employer, registration is required unless an exemption is available; but if ESPP stock is acquired on the open market, registration is necessary only if the employer has solicited employees to participate in the plan.[7]

Rule 701 of the Securities Act exempts from registration certain written compensation plans to employees, directors, general partners, trustees, officers, or certain consultants of companies who are not subject to the reporting requirements of §13 or §15(b) of the Exchange Act (otherwise known as private companies) and are not investment companies. Rule 701 is subject to disclosure[8] and volume[9] limitations and does not exempt resales by plan recipients. Other exemptions that may be relied upon by the issuer of plan benefits include Regulation S, which applies to certain offshore transactions, Section 4(2), which applies in the context of a private offering, and Regulation D, which provides specific safe harbours for limited offerings. While some of these exemptions may require the issuer to follow certain formalities, a full-blown registration process is avoided.

For sales by plan recipients, any plan securities issued by the employer in reliance on an exemption are restricted securities which must be registered upon resale or resold in reliance on an exemption. Conversely, plan securities that have been registered under the Securities Act are generally freely tradable by recipients without any resale restrictions at all. However, affiliates of the issuer (generally directors, key executive officers and controlling stockholders), as well as recipients who are non-affiliates holding restricted securities (ie unregistered securities issued in reliance on an exemption), cannot offer or sell their securities unless either the securities are separately registered for resale purposes or an exemption from such registration is available. The primary exemption normally relied upon in this context is Rule 144, which provides a specific safe harbour for resales that comply with certain holding period and manner of sale requirements.

The SEC has recently approved amendments to Rule 144 that will dramatically ease the resale limitations on holders of unregistered securities.[10] The amendments shorten the required resale holding periods for both affiliates and non-affiliates holding restricted securities. They permit non-affiliates of a reporting company that has been subject to Exchange Act reporting requirements for at least 90 days prior to the sale of the securities to freely sell restricted securities without a resale registration after holding them for six months (instead of the previous one-year holding period), subject only to the requirement that the company be current in its Exchange Act

---

7     Solicitation implies an offer or sale under the Securities Act and whether a solicitation has occurred depends primarily on the degree of the employer's involvement in the plan.

8     Prior to any sales of plan securities, the employer must provide each recipient with a copy of the plan. If the aggregate sales price of securities issued during any consecutive 12-month period exceeds $5 million, the employer must also provide detailed financial statements, risk factor disclosures, and a summary description of the plan.

9     The amount of securities sold over a 12-month period is limited to the greater of $1 million; 15% of the issuer's total assets; or 15% of the outstanding securities of that class.

10    Revisions to Rules 144 and 145, Securities Act Release No. 33-8869 (December 6 2007) (effective February 15 2008).

reporting. After one year (instead of the previous two-year holding period), non-affiliates of both reporting and non-reporting companies can sell their restricted securities without registration and without complying with any other Rule 144 condition (ie volume limits and current public information). The other resale exemptions available to plan recipients are judicially crafted Section 4(1½), which applies to certain private resales, and Regulation S, which applies in the context of offshore resales and is very useful to non-US public companies.

In the absence of a valid exemption from registration for sales pursuant to plans, interests in the plan, and resales of plan shares, a Form S-8 is typically used by a US publicly traded company to register equity compensation awards. The Form S-8 prospectus materials must contain, among other things, material information regarding the plan and its operation that will enable recipients to make informed investment decisions.[11] The prospectus should describe the tax effects of plan participation and any restrictions on resale of the underlying securities. It must also be regularly updated to reflect any material changes during any period in which offers or sales of securities are made. Furthermore, registering with Form S-8 generally requires the employer to deliver or properly incorporate by reference many of the same documents routinely delivered to stockholders, including a Form 10-K containing the employer's audited financial statements.

Significantly, regardless of whether an exemption from registration is available, securities transactions are subject to anti-fraud and other liability under the securities laws. Indeed, the general anti-fraud provisions of SEC Rule 10(b)(5)[12] – which cover all security transactions – require the disclosure of honest and complete information regarding the plan securities. Liability for material misrepresentations in a registration statement is also triggered under Sections 11[13] and 12(a)(2)[14] of the Securities Act, which are considerably more generous to plaintiffs than Rule 10(b)(5).

#### (b)   Securities Exchange Act of 1934 – Registration

The Exchange Act provides that an issuer must register with the SEC any security, including plan securities, if it is listed on a national securities exchange, or if the issuer has a class of 500 or more persons holding such security and total assets exceeding $10 million.[15] Upon such registration, the issuer becomes a reporting company and is subject to ongoing reporting obligations (eg Forms 10-Q, 10-K, and 20-F), including the specific disclosure rules of Regulations S-K[16] (qualitative disclosures) and S-X[17] (quantitative disclosures).[18] While SEC Rule 12g3-2(a) traditionally provided the primary exemption from such registration for certain foreign issuers, the SEC recently approved specific exemptions for issuers of

---

| 11 | See generally, Form S-8 and the related instructions. |
| 12 | 17 CFR §240.10b-5 (2007). |
| 13 | 15 USC §77k (civil liabilities on account of false registration statement). |
| 14 | 15 USC §77l (civil liabilities in connection with prospectuses and other communications). |
| 15 | Exchange Act §§ 12(a), 12(g)(1). |
| 16 | 17 CFR §229.10 et seq (2007). |
| 17 | 17 CFR §210.1-01 et seq (2007). |
| 18 | Regulations S-K and S-X are the focal point of the SEC's integrated disclosure system, and carry a common link both across the initial offering and in later periodic reporting. |

employee stock options that conform to certain eligibility requirements; such issuers are no longer subject to Exchange Act registration even if they have more than 500 option holders and more than $10 million in assets.[19]

The Exchange Act also requires each US securities exchange to adopt rules that regulate issuers whose securities are listed on its exchange; such rules must be considered whenever an equity plan is introduced. The rules of the major exchanges, for example, typically require stockholder approval and certain notification procedures for new plans and any revisions to plans.

(c)   *Securities Exchange Act of 1934 – Section 16, short-swing profit rules*
The "short-swing profit" rules of Section 16 of the Exchange Act impose strict liability on certain trades by key executives for all trading "profits" realised within a period of less than six months. For Section 16 purposes, the term "profits" captures all differences in transaction prices within the six-month time span, regardless of whether the purchase or the sale occurs first, or whether the shares initially purchased or sold are the same shares subsequently sold or purchased. Accordingly, plan recipients who also happen to be key executives must pay close attention to their trading activity to avoid liability under the mechanical application of the short-swing profit rules.

Rule 16b-3, however, exempts transactions between an issuer and its officers or directors that satisfy any one of four possible alternative exempt categories set out in the Rule. Notably, tax-conditioned plans (eg 401(k) plans), and grants and dispositions pursuant to board or shareholder approval, are generally exempt from Section 16 liability under the Rule.

(d)   *Securities Exchange Act of 1934 – executive compensation disclosures*
While the SEC has a variety of disclosure rules in place that require reporting companies, among other things, to disclose material qualitative and quantitative information regarding their equity plans, in 2006 it adopted a comprehensive set of disclosure rules governing executive compensation (including equity compensation).[20] The new rules require companies to provide detailed disclosure as to amounts payable under equity plans. Furthermore, where uncertainties exist (ie the possibility of payments upon a change in control), companies are required to make reasonable estimates and to disclose material assumptions underlying such estimates.

2.2   **Is there an exemption from securities laws requirements either because the shares are being offered only to executives or because shares are being offered to a distinct group of named individuals?**
When plan securities are offered or sold to a group of sophisticated executives in a private transaction, as opposed to a general offering made to a broad-based group of

---

19    Exemption of Compensatory Employee Stock Options From Registration Under Section 12(g) of the Securities Exchange Act of 1934, Exchange Act Release No. 34-56887 (December 3 2007).
20    See generally Executive Compensation and Related Person Disclosure, Securities Act Release Nos. 33–8732A, Exchange Act 34–54302A, 71 Fed. Reg. 53,158 (September 8 2006).

employees, the issuing employer may be exempt from registration pursuant to either Section 4(2) or the specific safe harbours of Regulation D. Rule 505 of Regulation D, for example, provides an exemption from registration for offerings of up to $5 million to an unlimited number of accredited investors (ie executives who meet the wealth requirements set out in the Rule), as long as, among other requirements, no more than 35 non-accredited investors also participate in the offering. Alternatively, Rule 506 of Regulation D provides a similar exemption, yet without limiting the offering amount as long as the non-accredited investors, if any, have the requisite knowledge and experience in financial and business matters to enable them to fend for themselves. Further, as noted above, SEC Rule 701 is specifically designed as an exemption from registration under the Securities Act for plans of issuers which are reporting companies under the Exchange Act.

**2.3    If there is an exemption, will the exemption apply automatically or are there any applications/filings that need to be made?**

Under federal law, valid reliance on an exemption from registration generally requires no special filings or applications but rather applies automatically if the substantive provisions of the exemption are met. A notable exception is the requirement to file Form D[21] when relying on any of the Regulation D safe harbours. Furthermore, compliance with certain formalities is often required to perfect an exemption. For example, prior to the sale of more than $5 million in plan securities during a 12-month period, issuers relying on Rule 701 must provide recipients with the plan documentation, a summary description of the plan, detailed financial statements and other disclosures.[22] Likewise, Rule 144 is generally conditioned on the availability of current public information, which in turn is often satisfied by the filing of other forms such as Form 10-K or Form 10 under the Exchange Act.

Generally speaking, when an exemption is valid under the federal laws, the company need not meet additional requirements under state Blue Sky laws. In fact, most states offer an automatic exemption from registration for employee-benefit plans, without any filings or applications. Certain states offer such exemption provided merely that procedures for notification and disclosure are followed. In some states, such as New York, a formal application for exemption must be filed. Yet compliance with some other states' securities laws may be even more complicated. Under California law, for example, employers offering equity awards in reliance on Rule 701 must make a notice filing within 30 days after the initial issuance of any security under the plan, pay a filing fee, and seek shareholder approval if more than 35 plan recipients are California residents. The other California exemptions often require analysis of grantees on a continuing basis, or, alternatively, the filing of an application, including copies of organisational documents and audited financial statements.

---

21    Form D, which must be filed with the SEC within 15 days of the first sale of securities, requires that the issuer sets out the following information: (i) the identity of the issuer, its promoters, chief executive officer, and the names of all persons who receive compensation for solicitation of the purchasers; (ii) a description of the securities offered and of potential investors; (iii) the offering expenses and the use of proceeds; and (iv) an undertaking to furnish the SEC upon request with additional information.

22    See Rule 701(g); 17 CFR §230.701(g) (2007).

## 3. Employee tax and social security

### 3.1 When will the executive be liable to tax or social security (and at what rate) in respect of the long-term incentive award?

Section 83 of the Code, which governs the taxation of property (including plan securities) transferred to an employee in connection with the performance of services, provides that such property is taxable to the employee as ordinary income in the year in which the property is transferable or is no longer subject to a substantial risk of forfeiture. Because plan securities are issued as remuneration for services, the amount of such ordinary income recognised by the employee is characterised as wages[23] and is subject to withholding of income tax and Federal Insurance Contributions Act (FICA) tax,[24] which consists of social security and Medicare. Currently, the ordinary income tax rates in the United States range from a minimum of 10% up to a maximum of 35% depending on the taxpayer's income and tax-filing classification. The FICA tax is 12.4% for social security and 2.9% for Medicare, but only one-half of those respective percentages are paid by the employee. The other half is paid by the employer.

ISOs and ESPPs, on the other hand, are eligible for more favourable taxation from the employee's perspective, since award income is generally characterised as a capital gain and is taxed at the capital gain rate. This taxation is deferred until the time the securities are sold. While short-term capital gains are taxed at the ordinary income tax rates, the long-term capital gain tax for plan investments held over one year is currently capped at 15%, which is generally the applicable rate given an executive's taxable income. This favourable tax treatment is conditioned on numerous restrictions affecting both the plan's design and transferability of shares.[25]

If such restrictions are met, since no taxable income is recognised at the time of exercise, there similarly can be no income characterised as wages for income tax and FICA withholding purposes at that time. Likewise, the sale of stock received under an award will generally not trigger the withholding of income tax to the extent that the income recognised is characterised as capital gain. The ESPP recipient, for example, recognises taxable income only upon sale, at which time the recipient includes in ordinary income characterised as wages only the discount by which the fair market value of the stock at the time of grant exceeds the exercise price. The recipient then recognises a capital gain equal to the excess of the proceeds of the sale over the exercise price, plus the amount of any such discount recognised as ordinary income.

Similarly, in the case of ISOs, provided the shares received upon exercise are held for the minimum holding period, the employee will defer the recognition of income until the ultimate sale, at which point the employee is taxed at the capital gain rates. However, the spread between the exercise price and the fair market value of the stock upon exercise of the option, though not taxable as compensation, must be included

---

23   In the current context, the term "wages", with certain exceptions, means all remuneration for services performed by an employee for an employer, generally including equity compensation.

24   See Code § 3101.

25   The tax qualifications for ISOs and ESPPs (see fns 1 and 2) are set out in Code §§422 and 423 respectively.

by the ISO recipient as an adjustment in computing the alternative minimum taxable income in the year of exercise.[26]

In the case of NQSOs, there are generally no tax consequences at the time option awards are granted because no property is yet considered to be transferred within the meaning of Code §83. But the recipient will recognise wage income subject to income tax and FICA withholding at the time of exercise (unless the shares obtained are restricted) equal to the difference between the fair market value of the stock received and the exercise price. When the shares acquired upon exercise of an NQSO are sold, the difference between the fair market value of the stock on the date of exercise and the sale price should be treated as short or long-term capital gain, depending on whether the shares were held for more than one year following the date of exercise.

Significantly, if the exercise of otherwise exercisable options is deferred by the recipient, unless the NQSO plan satisfies Code §409A,[27] income taxation of the deferred compensation element, including a 20% penalty tax plus a premium interest tax, is imposed at the time the option first becomes exercisable. These adverse tax consequences also result from the issuance of NQSOs where the exercise price is less than the fair market value of the stock on the date of grant.

For restricted stock, unless a Section 83(b) election is made within 30 days after the grant, the inherent value in the stock at the time of grant is generally not taxed to the employee. However, when the transferability and forfeiture restrictions lapse and the shares become vested in the employee, the awards are taxed as ordinary income characterised as wages measured by the value of the stock at vesting, less the consideration, if any, contributed by the recipient for the award. Due to the substantial restrictions during the vesting period, restricted stock is generally not considered deferred compensation subject to the penalties and interest provisions of Code §409A.

Where a voluntary Section 83(b) election is made by the employee, the excess of fair market value of the shares at the grant date over the amount, if any, contributed for the stock is taxed to the employee as ordinary income and is subject to payroll tax withholding at the time of grant. When the shares are ultimately sold, the excess, if any, of the sale price over the fair market value of the shares at the date of grant is recognised as a short- or long-term capital gain depending on the holding period of the stock. A Section 83(b) election is typically made where the net benefit of being taxed on stock increases during the vesting period at the lower capital gain rates rather than the ordinary income rates exceeds the detriment of paying income and FICA taxes on the excess of fair market value over the purchase price, if any, upfront

---

26     The alternative minimum tax sets a minimum tax rate of either 26% or 28% (depending on the amount of the taxpayer's "alternative minimum taxable income") on some taxpayers so that they cannot use certain types of deductions to lower their tax. See Code. §55.

27     Section 409A regulates non-qualified deferred compensation plans, and requires that the election to defer compensation as well as the time and form of distribution of the deferred compensation is made before the beginning of the calendar year in which the employee performs the services, or within 30 days after the employee first becomes eligible to participate in the plan. See Code §409A (2007). IRS Notice 2007–86 extends to December 31 2008 the transitional relief period for amending non-qualified deferred compensation plans to comply with Section 409A.

at the time of grant. Further, the forfeiture of restricted stock after a Section 83(b) election has been made will result in a capital loss and not an ordinary loss for federal tax purposes.

With respect to SARs, the award recipient will recognise ordinary income characterised as wages and subject to withholding only when the SAR is exercised in an amount equal to the cash and/or the fair market value of property received, unless the property received is otherwise restricted. SAR awards also generally pose deferral issues under the principles of Code §409A.[28]

## 3.2 How will the executive's tax and social security be collected? Will the executive be responsible for paying any liabilities himself or will the executive's employer be responsible for paying tax or social security liabilities on the executive's behalf?

Employers must deduct and withhold income and FICA tax from the employee's wages.[29] Further, FICA tax and Federal Unemployment Tax Act (FUTA) tax are imposed on the employer[30] in an amount equal to a percentage of the wages paid by that employer, who must pay these taxes independent of the employee's separate tax obligations. For example, the employer must withhold as a payroll deduction federal income tax on equity awards characterised as wages, plus half of the FICA taxes, and is responsible for paying the other half. The amount of federal income tax withheld from the recipient's wages is ultimately credited towards the overall annual income tax liability computed on the recipient's income tax return.

## 3.3 If the employer is responsible for the executive's liabilities, can the employer withhold the liabilities from the executive's salary? Are there any formalities in this respect?

The employer is ultimately responsible for withholding the executive's tax liabilities, and is liable for the executive's tax obligations if it fails to withhold. There are no formalities or special elections to enable the employer to withhold tax liabilities from the executive's salary; rather, the employer is automatically required to do so by law.

The employer must also comply with the applicable Form W-2 or Form 1099 reporting requirements under Code §§6041 and 6041A for the amount of compensation income required to be recorded by, and taxed to, the employee. Copies of these withholding reports are submitted to employees, the Internal Revenue Service (IRS), and the Social Security Administration.[31] The employer must formally deposit federal income tax withheld and both the employer and employee FICA obligations, and must file Form 941 or 944 with the IRS to record all wages paid and withholdings made.

---

28    SARs with the amount payable that is or could be greater than the spread between the fair market value on the date of exercise over the fair market value on the date the SAR was granted are treated as deferring compensation.

29    See Code §§3402(a), 3101.

30    See Code §§3111, 3301.

31    See IRS Publication 15 (2007), *Employer's Tax Guide*, available at www.irs.gov/publications/p15/index.html.

**3.4** **If the executive's salary in the month of exercise/release is not sufficient for the employer to withhold all of the liabilities, can the employer (or the parent company, if different) arrange for the executive to authorise to sell some of the executive's shares in the market and pass the money to the executive's employer?**

The employee's tax obligations may be satisfied with sale proceeds of plan securities in a cashless exercise, which involves the simultaneous exercise of an option and sale of the shares through a broker (commonly referred to as "broker-assisted exercise"). Under this method, the employee authorises the exercise of an option and the immediate sale of the option shares. On the same day, the company notifies the broker of the sale order and the broker executes the sale. On the settlement day, the broker makes a cash payment to the company for the exercise price and the statutory withholding taxes and remits the balance of the net sales proceeds to the employee.

Depending on the terms of the employee share plan, employees may provide payment of taxes by cheque, wire transfer or indirectly through a broker-assisted exercise to satisfy their withholding obligations. In addition, such plans may permit an employee to satisfy their tax withholding obligations by using either plan or personally owned shares.

**3.5** **Will the executive pay tax on the eventual sale of his shares and if so at what rate?**

The executive will pay tax on the ultimate sale of securities received in connection with a ISO or ESPP, a non-qualified stock option plan, or a restricted stock award plan at the short- or long-term capital gain rates (depending on the holding period).[32] Such tax will be applied to the excess of the fair market value of the stock at the date of sale over the employee's basis in the stock, which is typically the exercise price or other contribution made plus the amount, if any, of ordinary income previously recognised in relation to the award.

## 4. Employer's social security

**4.1** **Is the employer liable to pay (on its own account) any employer's social security in connection with the long-term incentive award?**

The employer must pay one-half of the employee's FICA taxes on the value of incentive awards characterised as wages and subject to payroll tax withholdings, and is ultimately liable for the withholding and payment of the employee's income tax and FICA obligations.

**4.2** **Can the liability of the employer be put onto the employee? What steps are required?**

The obligation of the employer to comply with the payroll tax withholding procedures and to pay employment taxes is imposed by federal law and is not

---

32  As previously mentioned, the long-term capital gains rate in the context of plan securities is currently capped at 15%; if the shares are held for one year or less, then the ordinary income tax rates apply.

assignable to the employee. However, the employer's obligation runs only with respect to employees and does not apply to independent contractors. Employee status is defined under both common and statutory law, and generally refers to a relationship where a worker provides services under the control of his master.

## 5. Tax deduction for the employer

5.1 **Is it possible for the employer to receive a tax deduction in respect of the long-term incentive award? Would the employer need to be subject to recharge arrangements (eg if the employer is a subsidiary and provides funds to the parent company as part of a recharge arrangement in respect of the long-term incentive award)?**

Under Code §83, the employer is entitled to an income tax deduction (subject to Code §162(m) as discussed below) equal to the amount of compensation income characterised as wages by and taxed to the employee, and may take this deduction at the same time that such compensation income is required to be recognised by the employee. Accordingly, in the case of NQSOs, the employer is generally entitled to a deduction at the time of exercise for the spread between the exercise price and the fair market value of the stock upon exercise of the option. By contrast, in the case of ISOs, the employer receives no deduction either at the time of exercise or sale because no corresponding wage income is taxable to the employee. As with ISOs, no employer deductions are permitted for ESPPs where the tax qualifications for employee-favourable tax treatment are met.

With respect to restricted stock, the employer is entitled to a deduction for the compensation element recognised as ordinary income by the employee either upon the lapse of the restrictions or at the time a Code §83(b) election is made. Likewise, with respect to SARs, the employer is entitled to a deduction only at the time the SAR is exercised, for an amount equal to the corresponding ordinary income recognised by the employee. And with respect to all plan securities, under US tax law it is not necessary to have a recharge arrangement between a parent and its subsidiary for the subsidiary to obtain a deduction for the compensation element of incentive awards granted to employees, even if the awards are actually funded by the parent.

Code Section 162(m), however, limits a public corporation's income tax deduction to $1 million for compensation paid to a covered employee who is either the chief executive officer of the corporation or among the four highest paid officers whose total compensation must be reported under the Exchange Act. Performance-based awards that meet certain conditions (ie stockholder disclosure and approval) are exempt from the limitations of Code §162(m).[33] Accordingly, stock options and SARs generally satisfy the performance-based exemption as long as the exercise price is at least equal to the fair market value of the stock on the date of grant, and certain other procedural requirements are met. Restricted stock, however, would rarely qualify for an exemption from §162(m) unless the vesting conditions are performance based.

---

33    Code. §162(m)(4)(C)(i).

## 6. Tax beneficial arrangements

**6.1 Are there any ways of making the long-term incentive award tax-efficient in the US?**
Tax efficiency from the employee's perspective may be achieved through the implementation of incentive awards such as ISOs and ESPPs. These awards are favourable to employees because taxes are not paid until the ultimate sale, and even then gains are generally taxed at the relatively lower long-term capital gain rates. In the case of ISOs, however, the spread between the exercise price and the fair market value of the stock upon exercise of the option, though not taxable as wages, must be included by the ISO recipient as an adjustment in computing alternative minimum taxable income in the year of exercise. Moreover, from the employer's perspective, tax awards are not necessarily favourable because the employer is not entitled to a tax deduction for the value of the award as compensation paid to the employee.

## 7. Internationally mobile executives

**7.1 What are the income tax consequences for an employee who is resident in the United States when the long-term incentive award is made, but who is no longer resident at the time of exercise/vesting?**
The US taxes its citizens and non-citizens residing in the United States on all of their worldwide income, regardless of the geographic origin of that income. Accordingly, an employee who is a US citizen or a permanent resident (a "green card holder") will ultimately pay income tax related to incentive awards no matter the origin of that income or where the employee resides. A non-citizen employee who was US-resident[34] for only a portion of a taxable year is generally taxed on his or her worldwide income on a pro-rata basis for only that portion of the year.[35] If a foreign person who is a non-resident alien[36] has US-based award income that is not effectively connected with a US business (either because the person has no such business or because the income is not related to the business), the income may generally be taxed at a flat rate of 30%. In addition to US taxes, the recipient of plan securities is also subject to taxation in the relevant foreign jurisdiction. However, bilateral income tax treaties with many countries as well as foreign income tax credits against US tax often mitigate, or even eliminate, the effects of international double taxation.

**7.2 What are the social security consequences for an employee who is resident in the United States when the long-term incentive award is made, but who is no longer resident at the time of exercise/vesting?**
In general, FICA taxes apply to payments of wages for services performed as an employee in the United States, unless the person performing the services is considered a non-resident

---

34   A resident for tax purposes is someone who, for the majority of the tax year, had the right of legal permanent residence in the United States (ie had a "green card," or who was "substantially present" in the US). "Substantial presence" is based on the number of days the individual is in the United States over a period of several years.
35   Treas. Reg. §1.871-13(a)(1).
36   A non-resident alien is an individual who is not a citizen and is not considered a resident of the US.

alien. Accordingly, the recipient must pay FICA taxes on the portion of the award representing services performed in the United States. In certain instances, treaty provisions may provide eligible taxpayers with some relief from international double taxation.

**7.3** **What are the tax and social security withholding/reporting consequences for the employer in respect of an employee who is resident in the United States when the long-term incentive award is made, but who is no longer resident at the time of exercise/vesting?**

The employer's tax withholding obligations are identical for citizen and resident employees. Where a non-citizen resides in the United States for only a portion of the taxable year, award income is pro-rated for that portion of the year. The employer must then withhold income and FICA taxes on the pro-rata amount reflecting that portion of the year.

## 8. Reporting requirements

**8.1** **Will the employer (or parent company, if different) have any reporting requirements as a result of the long-term incentive award?**

The employer must comply with the applicable Form W-2 or Form 1099 reporting requirements under Code Sections 6041 and 6041A with respect to the amount of compensation income required to be recorded by, and taxed to, the employee. These reporting requirements ensure that the correct amount of taxable compensation income is taxed to and included by the employee. The employer must also furnish a statement to each employee who exercises an ISO, which must contain identifying information of both the issuing corporation and the person to whom the shares are transferred, the date the option was granted, the number of shares transferred to the recipient, and the fair market value of the stock at the time of exercise.[37] The employer also has reporting obligations under the new requirements of Code §409A, including an obligation to report the total amount of deferrals for the relevant tax year.

Lastly, the employer may also have a series of securities law reporting obligations, including proxy disclosures, 8-K filings to disclose material events, disclosures to comply with Exchange Act Regulations S-K and S-X, and registration requirements under the Securities Act.

**8.2** **Are there any tax rulings required in relation to the long-term incentive awards?**

No tax rulings are required.

## 9. Exchange control issues

**9.1** **Are there any exchange control issues that would prevent an employee from (a) remitting monies abroad to purchase shares, or (b) repatriating monies from the sale of shares?**

There are no exchange control issues unless cash (as opposed to a cheque) exceeding

---

37    Treas. Reg. §1.6039-1, Statements to persons with respect to whom information is furnished.

$10,000 is used to remit monies abroad for the purchase of shares or to repatriate monies from the sale of shares, in which case IRS Form 8300 must be filed to report the transaction. Cash is generally considered currency and coins of the United States and any other country. Because cash transactions are very unlikely in the context of a stock option exercise payment or even a sale of shares, generally speaking there are no exchange control issues to consider.

## 10. Employment law

### 10.1 Are there any employment or local labour law issues which may arise as a result of the long-term incentive award? Are any consultations or authorisations required by law?

Employment law issues may implicate the issuance of incentive awards in the context of collective bargaining agreements. For example, labour-union agreements often include provisions that limit the company's ability to issue incentive awards as a form of compensation. In addition, issues may arise in the context of wrongful termination claims under standard common law. If the termination cuts off the option vesting, for example, employment-based claims for damages may arise. Also, stock options have become an issue in employment discrimination cases under federal law as well as in cases involving attempted enforcement of non-compete provisions.

## 11. Translation

### 11.1 Are there any language restrictions in the United States? Does any of the documentation provided to the employee in relation to the long-term incentive award need to be translated?

Plan documentation need not be translated unless the plan is governed by the Employee Retirement Income Security Act of 1974 (ERISA). Because executive compensation plans generally are not created for the express purpose of providing retirement income, such plans are normally not governed by ERISA. Where ERISA regulations apply, however, an employer must provide a notice in another language that offers speakers of that language assistance in learning about their benefits. Many employers go beyond such notice and translate plan written materials into a foreign language as needed, or at least allow translators to participate in benefits meetings.

## 12. Data protection

### 12.1 Are there any data protection issues which may arise should the employer wish to outsource the administration of the long-term incentive award to a third party?

The federal laws tend to focus on the regulation of financial institutions and other organisations maintaining consumer information, but do not generally govern employee information maintained by employers in connection with equity plans. State laws, however, often regulate keepers of personal data more broadly. Many states have adopted data breach notification procedures that require those who keep personal data to notify individuals whose information is believed to have been misappropriated in an unauthorised fashion. In New York, for example, companies that own or license computerised data that includes "private information" must notify its residents, the state attorney general, the consumer protection board, and the state office of cyber security of any breach of the database storing their data. Many states have also adopted provisions relating to data destruction and procedures for maintaining reasonable security measures.

## 13.    Source of shares

13.1    **Does it matter if shares are newly issued to an employee, provided out of treasury or delivered from an employee-benefit trust?**

It generally does not matter whether the plan shares are newly issued, provided out of treasury, or placed in an employee-benefit trust. However, if a trust is used to defer compensation in the context of non-qualified plans, the requirements of a "rabbi trust" must be met or the plan may be subject to adverse tax consequences.[38] The IRS will find a valid rabbi trust exists if all three conditions are met: (1) the trust's assets must be available to all the general creditors of the employer if the employer files for bankruptcy, (2) there are no insolvency triggers that hasten payments to employees when the employer's net worth falls below a certain point, thereby bypassing creditors before insolvency is declared, and (3) there is a procedure to provide notice to the trustee of the bankruptcy of the employer or financial hardship of the employer.

---

38    See Rev. Proc. 92-64, 1992-2 C.B. 422.

# Vietnam

**Konrad Hull**
**Nguyen Thi Xuan Trinh**
LWA Vietnam Ltd

---

> **Red flag issues**
> 1. Consent of State Bank of Vietnam required.
> 2. Awaiting Circular to implement Decree 160.
> 3. Distinction between shares offered in foreign companies and shares offered in Vietnamese companies.

## 1. Securities laws

**1.1 What prospectus and/or securities law requirements arise in connection with the grant, vesting or exercise of a long-term incentive award or on the eventual sale of the shares by the executive?**

There are no prospectus or securities law requirements in respect of the granting, vesting or exercise of the long-term incentive award or the eventual sale of the shares by the executive in a foreign company. However, if the long-term incentive award is granted in a Vietnamese company, certain securities law requirements apply.

*(a) Long-term incentive awards or shares granted in foreign companies*

Until recently, and pursuant to Vietnamese law, approval from the State Bank of Vietnam (SBV) has been required for Vietnamese nationals to "invest" in the shares of foreign companies, whether or not monies are transferred abroad. This approval was required for the Vietnamese individual, although it would more readily be given if the relevant incentive award had been previously approved by the SBV. If the shares were issued in a Vietnamese company, or in a foreign company but to foreign individuals, SBV approval was unnecessary.

In relation to the above, it had been unofficially indicated by the SBV that its policy was not to approve any monetary share/option purchase schemes. The reason given for this policy was to encourage the Vietnamese people to purchase shares in Vietnamese companies listed on the recently formed Vietnamese stock exchange. However, the SBV had indicated that it did not object to what it referred to as "non-cash" share/option schemes. That is, it did not object to schemes that did not involve the employee "paying" for shares/options in cash or in kind. Whilst the SBV has in the past approved several non-cash schemes, all previously approved schemes have been option schemes where the employee never actually held any shares in the offshore company (ie at the option exercise date, the shares would be sold on the

317

employee's behalf and the employee would receive the cash from such sale).

However, whilst the previous position was relatively clear, the current position is somewhat unclear. The law governing the investment by Vietnamese nationals in foreign shares has recently been amended by the issuance of the Ordinance on Foreign Exchange, which took effect from June 1 2006, and Decree 160 implementing the Ordinance, which took effect in January 2007. As yet, SBV has not issued a Circular to implement Decree 160, so the position in relation to Vietnamese nationals investing in foreign shares remains unclear. However, it appears from the Decree that Vietnamese nationals will be permitted to invest in foreign shares provided that they satisfy all the conditions set out by the SBV in the (yet to be issued) Circular. From informal discussions with the SBV, it has confirmed that under the terms of the new Circular, Vietnamese nationals will be permitted to use their own foreign currency to purchase foreign shares or be permitted to receive foreign shares without payment (ie by virtue of a non-cash employee-share scheme). Therefore, it appears that both "monetary" share schemes and "non-cash" shares schemes will be allowed provided the investor (ie the employee) first obtains an approval from the SBV to do so. However, given that the Circular is still being drafted, it is not clear what conditions and procedures will need to be complied with to obtain SBV approval. Further, it is unclear whether or not incentive plans will also need to be registered with the SBV, or whether it will only be for the Vietnamese investor to obtain all necessary approvals.

### (b) Long-term incentive awards or shares granted in companies established in Vietnam

Pursuant to the Law on Securities of Vietnam, a "share purchase right" is defined as "a type of security issued by a shareholding company as part of an additional share-issuing tranche, aimed at ensuring existing shareholders have the right to purchase new shares in accordance with stipulated conditions". Therefore, Vietnamese companies can grant "share purchase rights", which can then be granted to employees. However, it appears from the law that a "share purchase right" can only be granted to existing shareholders. If the executives/employees to whom such rights are intended to be granted are not existing shareholders, they will not be entitled to "share purchase rights".

In addition to the granting of a "share purchase right", pursuant to relevant securities laws Vietnamese public companies can grant "bonus" shares to their employees (including executives) or they can issue shares under "option programmes" to employees. It is unclear from the law what constitutes an "option programme" but, in order to issue shares to employees, the company must satisfy the following conditions:

- it must have an option programme and a share issuance plan approved by the shareholders in general meeting;
- the total volume of shares issued under the programme must not be more than 5% of the shareholdings of the company; and
- the board of management must specifically publish the standards and the list of employees entitled to the programme, the principle for determination of the selling price and the time for implementation.

Further, the company is required to submit certain documents to the State Securities Committee of Vietnam (SSC) and/or the Stock Exchange and publish certain specified information in mass communication media not later than 10 days before the above issuance. Within 10 days after completion of the issuance, the company must report the results thereof to the SSC and/or the Stock Exchange.

In respect of shareholdings in Vietnamese listed companies, it should be noted that foreigners cannot currently own more than 49% of total shares of any such company. Therefore, any long-term incentive awards must comply with this rule.

1.2    **Is there an exemption from securities laws requirements either because the shares are being offered only to executives or because shares are being offered to a distinct group of named individuals?**
No. There is no exemption from securities law requirements because the shares are being offered only to executives or because the shares are being offered to a distinct group of names individuals.

1.3    **If there is an exemption, will the exemption apply automatically or are there any applications/filings that need to be made?**
As noted above, there is no exemption because the shares are only being offered to executives or because the shares are being offered to a distinct group of named individuals.

2.    **Employee tax and social security**

2.1    **When will the executive be liable to tax or social security (and at what rate) in respect of the long-term incentive award?**
Pursuant to Official Letter No. 4252 TCT/DTNN, issued by the Ministry of Finance General Department of Taxation and dated December 22 2004 ("Official Letter 4252"), for a "share purchasing right" granted in foreign companies, income arising from the exercise of a share purchasing right is to be included in any income subject to the personal income tax (PIT) of employees.[1] The income arising from the exercise of the share purchasing right will be the net difference between the share value calculated at the market price at the selling time and the share value calculated at the price set in the option, after having subtracted costs in connection with the transaction. The income is held to be of a regular nature and should be included in income subject to PIT in the month when the income arises.

Whilst Official Letter 4252 is based on the assumption that the employee never actually holds any shares and the SBV is currently unlikely to approve any scheme whereby the employee holds shares (at least until such time as the Circular to implement Decree 160 is issued), in the event that such a scheme were to be approved and dividends were to be paid to the employee on shares held by him, PIT

---

[1]    Please note that Official Letter 4252 is written on the assumption that on exercise of an option, employees receive the value of the shares, but never actually hold them. This appears to be consistent with the views of the SBV referred to above.

*should not* be payable on those dividends.

In respect of "bonus" shares granted to employees, if the company issues shares and grants them as a bonus to its employees, the employees are required to pay PIT on the total par value of the bonus shares.

Both Vietnamese citizens and foreign residents are liable for PIT at rates ranging from 0% to 40%. These tax rates are incremental, and each portion of income is taxed at the rate applicable to the band in which it falls. However, for foreign residents the bands are higher than for Vietnamese citizens, with the top tax rate of 40% applying to income over D40 million for Vietnamese citizens and to income over D80 million for foreign residents.

2.2 **How will the executive's tax and social security be collected? Will the executive be responsible for paying any liabilities himself or will the executive's employer be responsible for paying tax or social security liabilities on the executive's behalf?**

Social and health insurance will not be payable on income generated from the grant of the shares, the sale of the shares or on the exercise of the rights to purchase the shares.

Pursuant to Vietnamese law, the employer is responsible for declaring and withholding an employee's PIT liabilities on income arising from employment with the employer and paying such amounts directly to the tax authorities.

On the assumption that any monies generated from the sale of shares will be paid through the employing entity in Vietnam, then the obligation will be on the employing entity to declare and withhold the employee's PIT liability and pay such liability directly to the tax authorities. However, where monies generated from the sale of shares will be paid directly from an offshore entity to the employee, the obligation will be on the employee to declare such income and make payment of PIT liabilities to the tax authorities.

If employees obtain bonus shares in a Vietnamese public company, the company must deduct the employee's PIT liability and pay it to the tax authorities.

2.3 **If the employer is responsible for the executive's liabilities, can the employer withhold the liabilities from the executive's salary? Are there any formalities in this respect?**

The employer's liability to withhold PIT liabilities arises when:

- the employee receives money from the sale of the shares and therefore there would be no need to withhold any amount from an employee's salary (ie it should be withheld from the income generated from the sale of shares). In any event, pursuant to Vietnamese law, an employer could not deduct PIT liabilities arising from the sale of shares from an employee's salary unless the employee requests the employer to do so; and
- the employee receives bonus shares, in which case the employee can provide the employer with his/her PIT liability amount or request the employer to deduct the liability for his/her salary so that the employer can pay such PIT to the tax authorities.

**2.4** **If the executive's salary in the month of exercise/release is not sufficient for the employer to withhold all of the liabilities, can the employer (or the parent company, if different) arrange for the executive to authorise to sell some of the executive's shares in the market and pass the money to the executive's employer?**

Yes, the employer (or parent company, if different) can arrange for the executive to authorise it to sell some of the executive's shares in the market and pass the money to the executive's employer.

**2.5** **Will the executive pay tax on the eventual sale of his shares and if so at what rate?**

Please see above.

**3.** **Employer's social security**

**3.1** **Is the employer liable to pay (on its own account) any employer's social security in connection with the long-term incentive award?**

Social and health insurance will not be payable on income generated from the sale of the shares or on the exercise of the rights to purchase the shares or from the grant of free shares.

**3.2** **Can the liability of the employer be put onto the employee? What steps are required?**

As noted above, social and health insurance will not be payable on income generated from the sale of the shares or on the exercise of the rights to purchase the shares or from the grant of free shares.

**4.** **Tax deduction for the employer**

**4.1** **Is it possible for the employer to receive a tax deduction in respect of the long-term incentive award? Would the employer need to be subject to recharge arrangements (eg if the employer is a subsidiary and provides funds to the parent company as part of a recharge arrangement in respect of the long-term incentive award)?**

If the benefits being granted are in an offshore entity, then there would generally be no cost to the employing entity in Vietnam, so the employing entity in Vietnam could not claim any tax deduction. Further, the associated costs for operating the scheme would also generally be the offshore entity's, so no tax deduction could be obtained for these costs. However, in the event that there are costs to the employing entity in Vietnam through a recharge arrangement, then such costs may be able to be deducted for Corporate Income Tax (CIT) purposes, although this would be scrutinised on a case-by-case basis by the tax authorities.

If the benefits being granted are in a Vietnamese entity, it is legally unclear whether or not the cost of the shares themselves and the costs for operating the scheme can be claimed by the employer as a tax deduction, although it appears unlikely. Vietnamese law is silent on this issue and in unofficial discussions with relevant authorities it has been indicated that without a specific provision in the law allowing for such costs to be deductible, they will not be treated by the authorities as deductible.

## 5. Tax beneficial arrangements

### 5.1 Are there any ways of making the long-term incentive award tax-efficient in Vietnam?

From a the executive's perspective there are unlikely to be any ways to make the long-term incentive award tax efficient as the awards would count in the executive's personal income tax liabilities in accordance with the above. From the company's perspective, the long-term incentive awards would only be tax efficient if there were costs in Vietnam which were considered to be deductible for corporate income tax purposes. It would be necessary to work with the tax authorities to determine which costs and in what circumstances they would be deductible, as this is a relatively new area under Vietnamese law.

## 6. Internationally mobile executives

### 6.1 What are the income tax consequences for an employee who is resident in Vietnam when the long-term incentive award is made, but who is no longer resident at the time of exercise/vesting?

Pursuant to Official Letter 4252, PIT liability only arises when the employee exercises the long-term incentive award. Therefore, if the employee is no longer resident in Vietnam at the time of exercise/vesting, he is not liable to Vietnamese PIT for income from exercise/vesting of the long-term incentive award.

### 6.2 What are the social security consequences for an employee who is resident in Vietnam when the long-term incentive award is made, but who is no longer resident at the time of exercise/vesting?

As noted above, social and health insurance will not be payable on income generated from the exercise of a long-term incentive award.

### 6.3 What are the tax and social security withholding/reporting consequences for the employer in respect of an employee who is resident in Vietnam when the long-term incentive award is made, but who is no longer resident at the time of exercise/vesting?

As noted above, pursuant to Official Letter 4252, PIT liability only arises when the employee exercises the long-term incentive award. Therefore, if the employee is no longer resident in Vietnam at the time of exercise/vesting, he is not liable to Vietnamese PIT for income from exercise/vesting of the long-term incentive award and, as a result, there are no tax and social security withholding/reporting consequences for the employer.

## 7. Reporting requirements

**7.1 Will the employer (or parent company, if different) have any reporting requirements as a result of the long-term incentive award?**

Apart from SBV approval and reporting to SSC and/or the Stock Exchange referred to under the heading "Securities laws", there are no other reporting requirements.

**7.2 Are there any tax rulings required in relation to the long-term incentive awards?**

Please see above under the heading "Employee tax and social security".

## 8. Exchange control issues

**8.1 Are there any exchange control issues that would prevent an employee from (a) remitting monies abroad to purchase shares, or (b) repatriating monies from the sale of shares?**

Without SBV approval Vietnamese individuals cannot transfer foreign currency abroad to pay for shares. Pursuant to Vietnamese law, Vietnamese nationals can only convert Vietnamese dong to US dollars for transfer abroad, or, if they have US dollars available, transfer US dollars abroad, without relevant authority approvals, for specified purposes. The exercise of a share option/right does not fall into the specified purposes.

Vietnamese individuals are required to repatriate the profit and other income from their investment in overseas shares to Vietnam no later than 60 days from the date of ending of the fiscal year of the country where the shares are issued.

Whilst technically a foreign resident of Vietnam is also under foreign exchange control restrictions, provided the foreigner can show that any monies to be remitted were lawfully obtained in Vietnam (ie through employment etc) and tax has been paid on such amounts, a foreigner can repatriate money abroad for the purchase of shares. There are no requirements on a foreigner to repatriate money from the sale of shares into Vietnam, although a foreign resident is liable to taxation on worldwide income as noted above.

## 9. Employment law

**9.1 Are there any employment or local labour law issues which may arise as a result of the long-term incentive award? Are any consultations or authorisations required by law?**

There are no employment or labour law issues that arise as a result of the long-term incentive award. However, if the long-term incentive award is being offered by way of an "annual bonus", this is regulated by Vietnamese law. Specifically, effective as of January 1 2003 there is no longer an obligation under Vietnamese law for employers to pay employees a bonus. Current Vietnamese law provides that:

- payment of bonuses shall be based on the annual results of production and business and the degree of completion of work by employees;[2]

---

2    The payment of a bonus should be based on the annual results of the employer company and not any "group" results.

- bonuses shall be payable in accordance with labour contracts and the collective labour agreement signed by both parties;
- enterprises are responsible for issuing regulations on bonuses after consultation with the executive committee of the relevant trade union;[3] and
- the regulations on bonuses must be publicised within the enterprise.

Whilst the employer has an obligation to consult with the executive committee of the trade union of the enterprise (if any) and to publicise the regulations on bonuses within the enterprise, there is no obligation to pay a specific bonus. Therefore, it is possible for an enterprise to formulate an entirely discretionary bonus plan[4] provided this has been discussed (and, presumably, agreed) with the trade union (if any), publicised within the enterprise and is not contrary to any employment contract or collective labour agreement.

## 10. Translation

### 10.1 Are there any language restrictions in Vietnam? Does any of the documentation provided to the employee in relation to the long-term incentive award need to be translated?

There is no legal requirement for the documentation to be in Vietnamese. However, in the event of a dispute before a Vietnamese court (or arbitration not involving a foreign party), if the documents were not in Vietnamese it would be necessary to have the documents officially translated into Vietnamese (using the relevant government translators) and the quality of such translation cannot be controlled. Therefore, it is often preferable to provide the documentation in Vietnamese as well, ensuring the quality of the translation, to avoid this issue.

## 11. Data protection

### 11.1 Are there any data protection issues which may arise should the employer wish to outsource the administration of the long-term incentive award to a third party?

From a privacy perspective, whilst Vietnam does not have a consolidated privacy law, the Civil Code of Vietnam specifies that the collection or publication of information and materials regarding the "private life" of an individual must have the individual's consent, except if the collection or publication is carried out under the decision of a competent State authority. Further, Article 8 of Decree 55–2001–ND–CP dated August 23 2001 on management, provision and use of internet services (Decree 55) specifies that the confidentiality of private information of organisations and individuals on the internet shall be ensured in accordance with provisions of the Vietnamese constitution and law. Article 11 of Decree 55 prohibits stealing and illegally using

---

3   Whilst the law only imposes and obligation to "consult" with the trade union, by implication it probably means that the regulations must be agreed with the trade union.

4   However, it is still standard practice in Vietnam (although not compulsory) to pay a thirteenth month salary by way of bonus shortly prior to the Vietnamese New Year.

private information of organisations and institutions on the internet. Pursuant to the Law on Electronic Transactions, an organisation or individual is not permitted to use, provide or disclose any information on privacy or information about another organisation or individual that the former has accessed or controlled in an electronic transaction without the consent of the latter, unless otherwise stipulated by law.

Whilst no clarification is provided as to the meaning of what constitutes the "private life" or "private information" of an individual, it seems clear that if information regarding employees was provided to an outsource company administrating the long-term incentive award, the consent of the employee would be required before a copy of any such information could be forwarded to the third party.

## 12. Source of shares

### 12.1 Does it matter if shares are newly issued to an employee, provided out of treasury or delivered from an employee-benefit trust?

No. It does not matter from a Vietnamese law perspective if shares are newly issued, provided out of treasury or delivered from an employee-benefit trust.

# About the authors

**Annika Andersson,**
Senior Associate, Mannheimer Swartling
aik@msa.se

Annika Andersson is a senior associate in the securities group at the Stockholm office of Mannheimer Swartling. Annika specialises in domestic and international public transactions on the Swedish market involving mergers and acquisitions, takeovers, listings and other corporate transactions. Annika is a member of the Swedish Bar Association.

**Jérôme Aubertin**
Associate, Stibbe
Jerome.aubertin@stibbe.com

Jérôme handles all aspects of collective and individual employment law. He focuses on technical aspects related to salaries and incentives and frequently advises on employee benefits.

**Irina Bakaeva**
Associate, Herbert Smith CIS LLP
irina.bakaeva@herbertsmith.com

Irina Bakaeva is a tax associate at Herbert Smith. Prior to joining Herbert Smith, Irina spent five years with major international audit firms. Irina has wide experience in dealing with foreign investors and Russian taxpayers on complex tax and tax-planning issues, and with pre-trial and court resolution of tax disputes.

**Ana Paula Basílio**
Associate, Gonçalves Pereira, Castelo Branco & Associados, RL
abasilio@gpcb.pt

Ana Paula Basílio is an associate of the law firm Gonçalves Pereira, Castelo Branco & Associados, RL. Her main areas of practice include tax law. She focuses essentially on legal/tax issues related to banking and financing business, including corporate reorganisation, structuring of financing and real-estate transactions. She is a member of the Portuguese Bar and member of *Associação Fiscal Portuguesa* (Portuguese Tax Association).

**Juan Bonilla**
Partner, Cuatrecasas Abogados, SRL
juan.bonilla@cuatrecasas.com

Juan works for the Barcelona Office of the leading law firm of Cuatrecasas in Spain. He specialises in international labour and employment law, pensions and incentives, and has broad experience in employee equity participation and business-transfer laws, both in contentious and non-contentious matters. He has a strong background in international practice, advising international clients on major transactions on a worldwide basis, particularly in the European Union and Latin America.

About the authors

**Sophie Brézin**
Partner, Herbert Smith LLP
sophie.brezin@herbertsmith.com

Sophie Brézin is head of the labour law group of Herbert Smith's Paris office. She handles all aspects of French employment law, including advising major corporations on the reduction and reorganisation of staffing capacities (redundancies, outsourcing); the employment law aspects of large corporate transactions (consultations with works council, transfers of employees and consequences); collective issues (personnel representatives, unions, negotiation of collective agreements); expatriate and international secondment issues; retirement schemes, employee savings schemes and share options; the implementation of new employment regulations; and employment litigation.

**Jean-Luc Calisti**
Partner, Herbert Smith LLP
jean-luc.calisti@herbertsmith.com

Jean-Luc Calisti heads the tax group of Herbert Smith's Paris office. He specialises in domestic, cross-border and international acquisitions, and has solid experience assisting clients based in the United Kingdom, France and other jurisdictions on tax issues arising from management incentives and employee benefits schemes. He has notably advised on tax aspects of management ownership of shares, on incentive schemes for selected French employees of French subsidiaries of international groups, on the relocation of foreign employees in France, on the optimisation of tax packages for the hiring of senior executives, as well as personal income tax issues of management in connection with public takeovers.

**Aakash Choubey**
Associate, Khaitan & Co
aakash@khaitanco.com

Aakash is based in the Mumbai office of Khaitan & Co, where he is part of the corporate and commercial laws practice. He focuses on mergers and acquisitions. Aakash is a member of the Bar Council of Maharashtra & Goa. He is the author of numerous articles in Indian legal journals. Mr Choubey has co-authored the India chapter in *Mergers & Acquisitions: A Practical Global Guide* (Globe Law and Business, 2007), *International Encyclopaedia of Agency and Distribution Agreements* (Kluwer Law International, 2006) and *Company Formation: A Practical Global Guide* (Globe Law and Business, 2006).

**John Cooper**
Partner, Freehills
John.Cooper@freehills.com

John advises clients on recruitment, remuneration and benefits, employment of executives and terminations. He has more than 30 years' experience in all aspects of industrial relations and employment law across many industries, acting for Australian and international companies.

He has acted for companies in many industry sectors including retailing, transport, building and construction, finance, logistics, manufacturing and professional service firms in a variety of employment and industrial-relations matters throughout his career.

He contributes to various international publications, including the American Bar Association's *International Labour and Employment Laws*.

**Owen Cox**
Practice Support Lawyer, Herbert Smith LLP
owen.cox@herbertsmith.com

Owen Cox is the Practice Support Lawyer for Herbert Smith's Shanghai and Beijing offices. In this role, he focuses on knowledge management and provides a range of assistance to lawyers within Herbert Smith's China practice. Prior to joining Herbert Smith in late 2005, Owen was a corporate lawyer with another international law firm in Shanghai where he advised multinationals on the establishment of green-field operations, on mergers and acquisitions, and on corporate reorganisations and various employment-related matters. Owen is qualified in Australia and has worked in China since 2001.

**Herman Craeninckx**

Partner, Stibbe

herman.craeninckx@stibbe.com

Herman focuses on all aspects of collective and individual dismissals, including their financial aspects, and frequently takes an active part in the negotiation of severance packages. He also advises company boards on highly technical issues related to management salaries and incentives and deals with pension and employee benefits, such as bonus schemes, stock options or warrant plans. He is a frequent speaker at seminars, both in Belgium and abroad, concerning corporate restructuring, transfers of undertakings, the financial aspects of dismissals, social elections and various issues with respect to remuneration and incentives.

**Paul Ellerman**

Partner, Herbert Smith LLP

paul.ellerman@herbertsmith.com

Paul Ellerman heads the employee incentives group at Herbert Smith LLP and has established a wide range of incentive plans (involving shares and/or cash) for a large number of quoted and unquoted companies, both UK and overseas. In addition, he has advised on the share plan aspects of many takeovers, IPOs, demergers and schemes of arrangement. He is a member of both the Tax Committee of the Share Plan Lawyers Organisation and of the Global Equity Organisation and is a regular conference speaker on employee share plan matters.

**Emily Ennis**

Associate, Arthur Cox

emily.ennis@arthurcox.com

Emily Ennis is an associate in the corporate department of Arthur Cox. Emily advises a range of public companies, private companies and state-related entities on their corporate governance obligations and business issues. She was called to the Bar in Ireland in 2001 and was admitted as an attorney to the New York Bar in 2003.

**Marie Griffin**

Associate, Arthur Cox

marie.griffin@arthurcox.com

Marie Griffin is an associate in the Tax Department of Arthur Cox. Marie advises on the tax aspects of share acquisitions and disposals. She also advises on tax planning for domestic and international companies, including tax aspects of acquisitions, disposals, reorganisations and securitisations. Marie has lectured in Revenue Law in the School of Law, University College Dublin, and has lectured for the Law Society of Ireland.

**Balz Gross**

Partner, Homburger AG

balz.gross@homburger.ch

Balz Gross is a partner in Homburger, one of Switzerland's premier business law firms. He is a member of Homburger's dispute resolution team and of the interdisciplinary employment law group. His practice focuses on international arbitration proceedings and complex domestic and international litigation, including employment-related disputes.

He frequently represents Swiss and international clients in high-profile employment disputes before the Swiss courts. He also regularly advises clients on the setting up and drafting of employee equity ownership plans and on employment-related issues in connection with transactions.

**Karin Gustafsson**
Partner, Mannheimer Swartling
kgn@msa.se

Karin Gustafsson is a partner in Mannheimer Swartling's corporate tax group. Focusing on corporate tax law, she advises on a broad range of tax matters including domestic and international restructuring, mergers and acquisitions as well as reorganisations and transfers of companies. Her experience and practice also include employee benefits, including incentive plans, double tax analyses and tax issues relating to potential conflicts with EC law. She frequently represents clients in court procedures, tax audits and advance ruling proceedings. Karin is a member of the Swedish Bar Association and the International Fiscal Association.

**Tiina Hakri**
Senior Associate, Roschier, Attorneys Ltd
tiina.hakri@roschier.com

Tiina Hakri specialises in employment law, social security law (including pensions) and tax law. Before joining Roschier, Attorneys Ltd., Tiina worked with a leading international US tax consultancy firm in Finland, where she specialised in the international taxation of individuals, particularly in relation to the expatriation of employees as well as employee incentive and share plans. She also has experience in payroll-related issues.

**Maret Hallikma**
Tax Counsel, Lepik & Luhaäär LAWIN
maret.hallikma@lawin.ee

Maret Hallikma has advised several multinational companies on taxation issues related to their activities in Estonia. Before joining Lepik & Luhaäär LAWIN, Maret was the head of the Legal Department of the National Tax and Customs Board. She has also participated in the elaboration of Estonia's Taxation Act.

**Claus Juel Hansen**
Partner, Kromann Reumert
cjh@kromannreumert.com

Claus Juel Hansen is a partner in the employment law department of Kromann Reumert, a leading law firm in Denmark. He has particular expertise in bonus and incentive schemes, including stock-based remuneration and the remuneration and employment conditions of directors and managers. In 2005, Mr Hansen published a commentary on the Danish Stock Option Act and regularly lectures on this subject.

**Stephen Hegarty**
Partner, Arthur Cox
Stephen.Hegarty@arthurcox.com

Stephen Hegarty is a partner in the Commercial Department of Arthur Cox. He has considerable experience in acting for large public companies in stock exchange work. He also advises state-owned companies, particularly in regard to ESOP and corporate governance.

Stephen is the author of the Irish section of the *Guide to European Company Laws* (Sweet & Maxwell) and he has contributed to several journals on the subject of corporate governance.

**Arjan Hovenkamp**
Senior Associate, Stibbe
Arjan.Hovenkamp@Stibbe.com

Arjan Hovenkamp is a senior associate at Stibbe. He works for the employment tax and benefits department of Stibbe and is part of their equity incentive expert group. Mr Hovenkamp has more than 11 years of work experience as a tax advisor. In the last six years he has worked for one of the "big four" tax firms in Amsterdam, where he specialised in the taxation of employment income in an international environment, Dutch withholding obligations, and the tax implications of equity incentives.

**Konrad Hull**

Partner and Head of Branch, LWA Vietnam Ltd

Email: info@lwavietnam.com

Konrad Hull is an Australian-qualified barrister and solicitor, partner and Head of Branch of LWA Vietnam Ltd. Konrad has a broad corporate/commercial background, advising clients on mergers and acquisitions, listings, due diligence, corporate governance, FDI and general commercial matters. He has also been recognised by *Asia Pacific Legal 500* as a leading individual in Vietnam for employment-related dispute resolution and he regularly advises clients on employment-related matters.

**Mark A Ife**

Partner, Herbert Smith LLP

mark.ife@herbertsmith.com

Mark Ife is a partner in the employee incentives group at Herbert Smith LLP and is involved in advising on the establishment and operation of share plans and cash bonus arrangements for both quoted and unquoted companies. Mark also advises on the share plan aspects (including taxation) of corporate transactions.

**Gerli Kilusk**

Associate Partner, Lepik & Luhaäär LAWIN

gerli.kilusk@lawin.ee

Gerli Kilusk advises Estonian and international clients on general corporate and commercial law, mergers and acquisitions, banking and finance issues. Ms Kilusk is also a regular contributor to annual finance and securities-related publications, legal magazines and various studies. Her working languages are Estonian, English and Russian.

**Mihoko Sirley Kimura**

Partner, TozziniFreire Advogados

mkimura@tozzinifreire.com.br

Mihoko Sirley Kimura is a partner in the Labour and Social Security Law practice groups of TozziniFreire Advogados. Mihoko is co-author of "Direct Investment: Setting up", a chapter in the book *Doing Business in Brazil*, (Britcham Brazil Publications, 2001 and 2005 editions), and of the Brazil chapter in *International Employee Equity Plans – Participation Beyond Borders*, published by Kluwer Law International.

**Oleg Konnov**

Partner, Herbert Smith CIS LLP

oleg.konnov@herbertsmith.com

Oleg Konnov is a partner at Herbert Smith. He has 14 years of experience covering a wide range of tax advisory and litigation services. Oleg has represented clients at all stages of disputes with Russian tax authorities, including tax audits, and administrative and court appeals. He has advised clients on both inbound and outbound transactions and complex tax structures.

Oleg is fluent in Russian and English and is a frequent writer on international and domestic taxation matters for various journals and other publications.

**Jim Koutsokostas**

Tax Consultant, Greenwoods & Freehills

Jim.koutsokostas@gf.com.au

Jim Koutsokostas advises on a broad range of corporate tax matters including corporate restructures, tax consolidation, international structuring and cross-border transactions, capital gains tax and employee share plans. Jim has advised a broad range of clients from multinational public corporations to privately owned companies and high net-worth individuals. He acts on behalf of clients in the retail, financial services, transport and telecommunications industries.

Jim is a member of the Law Institute of Victoria and an associate of the Taxation Institute of Australia.

**Hans Georg Laimer**
Associate, Schönherr
h.laimer@schoenherr.at

Hans Laimer is an associate in the employment law practice group of Schönherr. He has practised employment law for more than five years. He drafts contracts and policies, and he advises employers on issues such as handling disciplinary and grievance procedures, long-term incentive plans, incentive option schemes and share schemes, restructuring and redundancies, termination of employment and conducting employment tribunal claims.

**Jérôme Le Berre**
Tax Associate, Herbert Smith LLP
jerome.leberre@herbertsmith.com

Jérôme Le Berre is a senior associate in the tax group of Herbert Smith's Paris office. His practice covers the tax aspects of domestic, cross-border and international mergers and acquisitions. He also advises on tax issues related to the implementation in France of management incentives and employee benefit schemes.

**Liina Linsi**
Partner, Lepik & Luhaäär LAWIN
liina.linsi@lawin.ee

Liina specialises in real property law, civil and administrative litigation, employment law, construction and planning law and general business and contract law.

Ms Linsi is also a member of the International Bar Association and acts as a member of the Court of Honour of the Estonian Bar Association. Her working languages are Estonian, English and Russian.

**Gary Lock**
Managing Partner, Herbert Smith LLP
gary.lock@herbertsmith.com

Gary is the managing partner of the Shanghai office of Herbert Smith. He has extensive experience in advising on mergers and acquisitions, corporate reorganisations, privatisations and joint ventures. He is also widely recognised as a leading capital markets lawyer in connection with Hong Kong and China-related matters. He has advised on many major transactions in mainland China and Hong Kong for leading corporates and banks, both foreign and Chinese.

Gary has lived in Shanghai for more than 10 years and, prior to that, he worked in London and Hong Kong. He speaks fluent Cantonese, Putonghua and English.

**Raúl Moreyra**
Partner, Goodrich, Riquelme y Asociados
rmoreyra@goodrichriquelme.com

Raúl Moreyra is a partner in the tax department at Goodrich Riquelme and Associates, a leading international law firm in Mexico. Mr Moreyra has been the head of the tax practice in Goodrich for more than 10 years. He has particular experience in mergers and acquisitions, tax planning, tax litigation and tax advice in general. He has been invited by the Mexican government and private organisations to deliver lectures in Mexico and abroad on tax and other legal aspects of investing in Mexico. He is the author of several works and articles published in books and magazines specialising in taxation.

**Alexandra Moule**
Senior Associate, Freehills
alexandra.moule@freehills.com

Alexandra Moule, Senior Associate, advises clients on equity incentive plans for executives and employees, share plans for non-executive directors, corporate governance, shareholder and Australian Securities Exchange (ASX) communications, shareholder meetings and trends in incentive arrangements. Her practice is focused on head office and internal company management issues.

## Peter Müller
Tax Director, Homburger AG
peter.mueller@homburger.ch

Peter Müller is a tax director at Homburger. He is a member of Homburger's tax team and of the interdisciplinary employment law group. His practice focuses on national and international tax law, particularly corporate tax and reorganisations. Other areas of work include administrative law, social security law and corporate law.

## Thomas Müller-Bonanni
Partner, Freshfields Bruckhaus Deringer
thomas.mueller-bonanni@freshfields.com

Thomas Müller-Bonanni is a partner in the labour and employment law department of Freshfields Bruckhaus Deringer, a leading international law firm. He specialises in labour and employment law with a special focus on share-based remuneration systems. He is the author of numerous legal publications and is a regular lecturer at specialist seminars.

## Michael Müntefering
Associate, Freshfields Bruckhaus Deringer
michael.muentefering@freshfields.com

Michael is an associate in the labour and employment law department of Freshfields Bruckhaus Deringer, a leading international law firm. He specialises in labour and employment law with a special focus on remuneration systems, restructurings and senior executive matters. He is a dually qualified German Rechtsanwalt and English solicitor.

## Gary Nachshen
Partner, Stikeman Elliott LLP
gnachshen@stikeman.com

Gary Nachshen is the director of Stikeman Elliott's national pension and benefits practice group. His practice focuses on the areas of executive compensation, employee benefit programmes, pension plan governance, pension fund investments, and pension plan surpluses, deficits and restructurings. He is the editor of the monthly law report *Canadian Cases on Pensions and Benefits* and has published and spoken widely on pension and benefits matters in both English and French.

## Nguyen Thi Xuan Trinh
Partner, LWA Vietnam Ltd
Email: info@lwavietnam.com

Trinh has worked for Lucy Wayne & Associates (now LWA Vietnam Ltd) since 1998. Trinh advises on a broad range of direct and indirect foreign investment in Vietnam, as well as corporate, oil and gas, maritime, construction, employment, litigation, IP, commercial, taxation, banking, project financing and securities. She has worked closely with various Vietnamese state authorities.

## Eva Nordman-Rajaharju
Partner, Roschier, Attorneys Ltd
eva.nordman@roschier.com

Eva Nordman-Rajaharju is a partner in Roschier, Attorneys Ltd in Helsinki. She has particular experience in employment and labour law issues as well as patent law, biosciences and dispute resolution. Ms Nordman-Rajaharju is the author of a number of articles on various aspects of human resources law, as well as patent law and litigation.

**Veronika Odrobinová**
Senior Associate, Gleiss Lutz
Veronika.Odrobinova@gleisslutz.com

Veronika Odrobinová is a senior associate at the Prague office of Gleiss Lutz. She has worked in the area of employment law for almost nine years. She has particular experience in compensation and benefits, including the implementation of stock option plans. She regularly contributes to professional publications, including her recent templates for employment contracts prepared for the C H Beck publication entitled *Large Book of Contract Templates* (in Czech: *Velká kniha smluvních vzorů*), 5th edition. She is a native Czech speaker and is fluent in English and French.

**Adrian O'Shannessy**
Director, Greenwoods & Freehills
adrian.o'shannessy@gf.com.au

Adrian O'Shannessy advises public and multinational companies on all aspects of domestic and international tax planning, with a focus on corporate head office issues such as employee share and dividend reinvestment plans, mergers and acquisitions and structured finance. He speaks regularly at various conferences. He lectures in taxation at the University of Melbourne and contributes to various tax journals. He has a monthly tax column in *The Australian* newspaper.

**Lenka Pazderová**
Manager, Vorlíčková & Leitner
lenka.pazderova@vorlickova.com

Lenka Pazderová is a manager in the tax department of Vorlíčková & Leitner, a member of the Leitner + Leitner Group. She specialises in value added tax, international taxation and international secondment of employees as well as related social security issues.

She is a member of the Chamber of Tax Advisors of the Czech Republic and of the International Fiscal Association. She is fluent in Czech, English and German.

**Phua Pao Yii**
Partner, Skrine
ppy@skrine.com

Phua Pao Yii is a partner in the corporate division at Skrine in Malaysia and has more than 14 years' experience as a corporate lawyer. His main areas of practice include mergers and acquisitions, corporate restructuring, joint ventures, employee share schemes and advising clients on foreign investments in Malaysia. He also regularly advises clients on general corporate and commercial legal issues. Pao Yii was also admitted as an Advocate and Solicitor of the Supreme Court of Singapore and prior to joining Skrine practised in Singapore.

**Thomas Pietruszak**
Associate, Homburger AG
thomas.pietruszak@homburger.ch

Thomas Pietruszak is an associate at Homburger. He is a member in Homburger's dispute resolution team and of the interdisciplinary employment law group.

Thomas frequently represents Swiss and international clients in high-profile employment disputes before the Swiss courts. He also regularly advises clients on the setting up and drafting of employee equity ownership plans, on employment-related issues in connection with transactions and on all other employment matters. He teaches employment law at a Swiss business school and contract law at the University of Zurich. He is the author of several publications, among them a commentary on the legal provisions of the employment contract.

**Przemysław Pietrzak**
Partner, Gleiss Lutz
przemyslaw.pietrzak@gleisslutz.com

Przemysław Pietrzak is a partner at the Warsaw office of Gleiss Lutz. He has worked in Polish corporate law, M&A and real-estate transactions for almost 15 years, advising major international investors from all over Europe, North America and Asia in several languages.

**Vesa Rasinaho**

Specialist Counsel, Roschier, Attorneys Ltd

vesa.rasinaho@roschier.com

Vesa Rasinaho has extensive experience of transactions involving private and public companies with a particular focus on corporate and tax law. He was the secretary of the Finnish Company Law Working Group responsible for drafting the new Companies Act in Finland in 2001 to 2003 and has been expert counsel to the Ministry of Justice since then. In addition to the leading commentary on the Companies Act in Finland, Mr Rasinaho has published several books and articles on company and tax law.

**Helena Rempler**

Partner, Mannheimer Swartling

hr@msa.se

Helena Rempler is a partner of Mannheimer Swartling. She divides her practice between the banking and insurance group and the tax group and works mainly for banks, insurance companies and other Swedish and international groups of companies in the financial services sector. She regularly advises on international structured financings, derivative products and related tax planning and assists clients in discussions with the tax authorities and in applications for advance tax rulings. Helena Rempler is a member of the Swedish Bar Association, the International Bar Association and the International Fiscal Association and is the author of several articles published in Swedish and international tax publications.

**Marcelo Rodrigues**

Partner, TozziniFreire Advogados

mrodrigues@tozzinifreire.com.br

Marcelo Rodrigues is a partner in the Mergers and Acquisitions and Corporate Law practice groups of TozziniFreire Advogados and has been closely involved with some of the most relevant M&A transactions handled by the firm, with a particular focus on deals with publicly held corporations.

**Emma Röhsler**

Associate, Herbert Smith LLP

emma.rohsler@herbertsmith.com

Emma is a dual English- and French-qualified associate in the labour law group of Herbert Smith's Paris office. She advises and assists clients on a wide range of French employment law matters including cross-border labour issues arising from the establishment of operations in France, redundancies, reorganisation, outsourcing, the employment law aspects of corporate transactions, the transfer of employees, contracts of employment, terminations and international secondment issues.

**Susan P Serota**

Partner, Pillsbury Winthrop Shaw Pittman LLP

susan.serota@pillsburylaw.com

Susan Serota is a partner and National Chair of Pillsbury's executive compensation and employee benefits practice. A significant part of her practice concerns executive compensation and global share plans for multinational companies. Ms Serota is the immediate-past Chair of the American Bar Association Section on Taxation, a former Chair of the employee benefits committee of the section on taxation and a former Chair of the ABA Joint committee on employee benefits. She is a frequent speaker on Executive Compensation and ERISA fiduciary issues. She is the editor of *ERISA Fiduciary Law* (BNA Books, 2nd edn, 2006).

**Ana Sofia Silva**

Associate, Gonçalves Pereira, Castelo Branco & Associados, RL

asofiasilva@gpcb.pt

Ana Sofia Silva has been an associate of the law firm Gonçalves Pereira, Castelo Branco & Associados, RL since 2002. Her main areas of practice include banking and finance law, structured finance (namely cross-border leasings), corporate finance, capital markets, debt issues, financial derivatives and insurance law. Ms Silva obtained a law degree from the Law School of the University of Lisbon in 2000 and a post-graduate qualification in banking, securities and insurance law from the Law School of the University of Coimbra. She has been a member of the Portuguese Bar since 2000.

**Sandra Lima da Silveira**

Associate, Gonçalves Pereira, Castelo Branco & Associados, RL

slimasilveira@gpcb.pt

Sandra Lima da Silveira is an associate of the law firm Gonçalves Pereira, Castelo Branco & Associados. Her main areas of practice include labour and social security law. She is a member of the Portuguese Bar.

**Kalina S Tchakarova**

Partner, Djingov, Gouginski, Kyutchukov & Velichkov

kalina.tchakarova@dgkv.com

Kalina is a partner at Djingov, Gouginski, Kyutchukov & Velichkov. She is the leading lawyer of the labour and social security law practice of DGKV. She has extensive expertise on advising the prime international and domestic corporate clients of DGKV on all aspects of labour law and social security.

Kalina has contributed to publications on various aspects of labour and social security law.

**Mark Todd**

Partner, Bell Gully

mark.todd@bellgully.com

Mark Todd is a partner in the corporate department at Bell Gully. Mark has advised on employee share purchase schemes for almost 15 years, initially becoming involved in this area with one of London's "magic circle" law firms. He has advised clients from many jurisdictions about offering their schemes to New Zealand employees.

**Teodora Tsenova**

Associate, Djingov, Gouginski, Kyutchukov & Velichkov

teodora.tsenova@dgkv.com

Teodora is a member of the labour and social security law practice at Djingov, Gouginski, Kyutchukov & Velichkov. She has been actively involved in advising a large number of national and international clients of the firm on all aspects of labour and social security law issues. She has contributed to various publications on labour and social security matters.

**Graham Warren**

Senior Associate, Greenwoods & Freehills

graham.warren@gf.com.au

Graham Warren, Senior Associate, advises on a broad range of corporate tax matters including debt and equity financing arrangements, corporate restructures, taxation of superannuation funds and employment taxes, tax consolidation, public – private partnerships, international tax, capital gains tax and taxation of trusts. Graham also advises clients in the mining, financial services, property and transport industries.

Graham is a Fellow of the Taxation Institute of Australia and has written regularly for the tax industry journal *Taxation in Australia*.

**Jorge Henrique Amaral Zaninetti**
Partner, TozziniFreire Advogados
jzaninetti@tozzinifreire.com.br

Jorge Henrique Amaral Zaninetti is a partner in the tax practice group of TozziniFreire Advogados. He is co-author of the book *Planejamento Fiscal*, published by Quartier Latin, and of the book *Os Negócios e o Direito – Sobrevivência Legal no Brasil* (winner of the Jabuti Literature Award – Business, Administration and Law category), published by Maltese.

**Gerold Zeiler**
Partner, Schönherr
g.zeiler@schoenherr.at

Gerold Zeiler is a partner of Schönherr. He heads the employment law department and also specialises in international arbitration. He has practised employment law since being admitted to the Vienna bar in 1993. He drafts contracts and policies, advises employers on issues such as employee incentive plans, bonus arrangements, restructuring and redundancies, and negotiating settlements. He also provides advice on post-termination restrictive covenants and directors' duties.

encontra, como resulta do exame da mesma feito pelos illustrados historiographos pernambucanos commendador Antonio Joaquim de Mello e dr. Francisco Augusto Pereira da Costa. E' pena que esteja ainda inedita tão importante obra, cuja manuscripto se guarda no convento de S. Bento em Olinda, ao qual pertence.

*Nobiliarchia Paulistana* pelo sargento-mór Pedro Taques de Almeida Paes Leme, integralmente publicada nos tomos XXXII a XXXV da nossa *Revista*, verdadeira obra de benedictino, que no conceito dàs pessoas competentes collocou já o seu auctor no numero dos nossos melhores historiadores.

Na obra do dr. Augusto de Siqueira Cardoso segue-se a genealogia deste estimado historiador até ao seu ascendente *Martim Lem*, cavalheiro flamengo, senhor de muitos feudos no condado de Flandres e que emigrou para Portugal no reinado de El-Rei D. Affonso V ; e dahi segue a linha genealogica até aos actuaes representantes daquelle remoto tronco.

Em trabalhos deste genero, como se dá nas supracitadas obras de Pedro Taques e de Borges da Fonseca, a genealogia é apenas a teia em que se entrelaça a narrativa dos acontecimentos correlatos e nisto está o seu valor historico.

E' honroso para o dr. Augusto de Siqueira Cardoso poder dizer-se, depois do exame de sua obra, que ella constitue uma util continuação e legitimo complemento da estimada obra de Pedro Taques.

E assim a Commissão a reputa obra digna do apreço deste Instituto.

Sala das Sessões do Instituto Historico Brazileiro, 22 de Maio de 1903.

(Assignados) *Barão Homem de Mello.*
*Miguel A. Galvão.*

Foi approvado em sessão de 22 de Maio de 1903.
E' enviado á Commissão de Admissão de Socios para emittir parecer, sendo relator o sr. Conselheiro Manoel Francisco Correia.

O escripturario,
*Francisco Martins Guimarães.*

---

## PARECER

« Tendo em consideração as ponderações feitas pela illustrada Commissão de Historia, em seu elaborado trabalho de 22 do mez findo, acerca da obra escripta pelo sr. dr. Augusto de Siqueira Cardoso, sob o titulo *Notas Genealogicas* sobre os ascendentes e descendentes de Pedro Taques de Almeida Paes Leme, auctor da *Nobiliarchia das Principaes Familias da Capitania de S Paulo e S. Vicente*, obra que serviu de titulo á sua admissão e que aquella illustrada commissão julga digna de apreço deste Instituto, a Commissão de Admissão de Socios, é de parecer que seja approvada a proposta do dr. Augusto de Siqueira Cardoso, para socio correspondente do Instituto Historico e Gegraphico Brasileiro, em 8 de Junho de 1903.

(Assignados) *Manoel Francisco Correia.*
*Antonio de Paula Freitas.*

O escripturario,
*Francisco Martins Guimarães.*

# Ascendente em linha recta de Pedro Taques de Almeida Paes Leme, auctor da nobiliarchia Paulistana

## CAPITULO PRIMEIRO

### LINHA — *A*

A linha A desta genealogia tem por progenitor Martim Leme, cavalleiro nobre e rico, senhor de muitos feudos na cidade de Burges, uma das principaes do condado de Flandres, na Belgica. Passando esta familia a Portugal por causa do commercio e se estabelecendo Martim Leme em Lisbôa, El-rei D. Affonso V o tomou por fidalgo de sua casa e alli corrompendo-se com a pronunciação portugueza a verdadeira voz do seu appellido se chamou Leme—o que era Lem

Pedro Taques—Nobiliarchia Paulistana – na Revista do Instituto Hist·rico, Geographico e Ethnographico do Brazil XXXV —1.º trimestre de 1872 em titulo —Lemes—.

Nobiliaires des Gayos Bas par de Vegians em 7 volumes.

Desta linha procede a nobre familia dos Lemes da capitania de S. Paulo que teve por progenitor Antão Leme, (1) fidalgo que veiu para o Brazil com Martim Affonso de Souza, ou logo depois, quando este donatario da capitania de S. Vicente mandou buscar canna de assucar á ilha da Madeira.

Foi Antão Leme um dos nobres povoadores da villa de São Vicente, a qual fundou pelos annos de 1531 o seu donatario Martim Affonso de Souza, que trouxe muitos e nobres povoadores por mercê d'El-rei D. João III e por este principe feito capitão-mór governador das terras do Brazil, para o dito Martim Affonso as poder repartir de sesmaria com as pessoas que comsigo trazia para as povoarem, como se vê da sua carta patente datada da villa de Crato a 20 de Novembro de 1530, registrada no cartorio da Provedoria da Fazenda Real da capitania de S. Paulo Liv. de sesmaria tit. 1554.

---

(1) Frei Gaspar da Madre de Deus, Memorias para á historia da capitania de S. Vicente Liv. I 77.

Antão Lemes natural da Madeira e senhor dos morgados da sua casa era irmão de Aleixo Leme e Pedro Leme, fidalgos da casa real e de D. Antonia Leme, mulher de Pedro Affonso de Aguiar e de d. Leonor Leme, mulher de André de Aguiar da Camara, e primos do capitão donatario da capitania do Funchal —os quaes Lemes são fidalgos nos livros de Sua Magestade e Reino de Portugal.

Antão Leme—a quem El-rei D. Affonso V constituiu chefe dos Lemes, com as armas desta familia (1); e a quem competia essa illustre qualidade herdada, da cidade de Burges em Flandres, aonde a sua casa, que floresceu por espaço de 500 annos produzindo varões illustrissimos, era uma das maiores daquelle condado, como referem os auctores genealogicos.

Foi juiz ordinario em S. Vicente em 1544—casado no Funchal com Catharina de Barros e teve entre outros filhos Pedro Leme (2) (tronco e origem dos Lemes em S. Paulo) que foi casado com Luiza Fernandes, e desse casamento houve uma filha com o nome de Leonor, que é a do texto genealogico seguinte.

1

#### LEONOR LEME—A QUAL CASOU-SE COM BRAZ ESTEVES, AMBOS PORTUGUEZES

Leonor Leme veio para o Brazil em companhia de seu pae Pedro Leme que embarcou na ilha da Madeira, e pelos annos de 1550 já estava em S. Vicente com sua mulher Luzia Fernandes e veio fazer assento na villa capital de S. Vicente, onde desembarcou com varios criados de seu serviço, e alli foi estimado, e reconhecido com o caracter de fidalgo. Foi pessoa de maior autoridade na dita villa, e com a mesma se conservaram seus netos. Pedro Leme, natural do Funchal e filho de Antão Leme, justificou em S. Vicente a sua filiação e fidalguia em 2 de Outubro de 1564 perante o dr. Desembargador Braz Fragoso, provedor-mór da fazenda e ouvidor geral de toda a costa do Brazil, e foi escrivão dos autos Antonio Rodrigues de Almeida, cavalleiro fidalgo da casa real, e obteve sentença extrahida do processo e passada em nome d'El-rei D. Sebastião.

---

(1) São as suas armas em campo de ouro, cinco meiros de preto, postos em aspas, sem pés nem bicos; e por timbre um dos meiros entre uma aspa de ouro. Assim se acham illuminadas na torre do Tombo em Lisboa no Livro de Armeria, e assim o refere o dr. Antonio de Villas-Boas e Sampaio na sua nobiliarchia Portugueza—edição de 1727, cap. 37 fls. 295.

(2) Frei Gaspar da Madre de Deus, Memorias para a historia da capitania de S. Vicente I, 78.

Estabelecido na villa de S. Vicente—foi o primeiro povoador da fazenda de Sant'Anna — foi casado a primeira vez no Funchal com Luzia Fernades, fallecida em S. Vicente em 1560 e tantos, e foi sepultada na capella mór da igreja dos padres Jesuitas, o que tudo consta do testamento de Pedro Leme — e deste matrimonio teve uma filha *que é o objecto deste texto primeiro.*

Casou-se segunda vez em S. Vicente com Garcia Rodrigues de Moura, filha de Gaspar Rodrigues de Moura e não teve descendencia. (1)

Falleceu Pedro Leme em S. Paulo no mez de Março de 1601 em casa de seu genro Braz Esteves—e marido de sua filha Leonor que já era casada quando veio da ilha da Madeira—em 1550.

Leonor Leme e seu marido viveram muitos annos na villa de S. Vicente, abastados com lucros do engenho de assucar chamado S. Jorge dos Erasmos (2).

Depois se passou com sous filhos para a villa de S. Paulo onde fez o seu estabelecimento e foi uma das primeiras pessoas da governança da republica. Falleceu Leonor Leme com testamento a 13 de Janeiro de 1633 e teve cinco filhos, nascidos na villa São Vicente :

1) Pedro Leme, casado com Elena do Prado, filha de João do Prado, natural da Olivença em Alemtejo (3)

Domingos Leme da Silva, que occupou em Sorocaba posição saliente, casou em primeiras nupcias, com d. Francisca Cardoso, filha de Antonio Lourenço e d. Izabel Cardoso e tem sete filhos; e em segundas nupcias com d. Maria da Abreu, de quem tem um unico filho, Domingos Leme da Silva, mestre de campo, fallecido em Cuyabá — Confira-se Azevedo Marques. Apontamentos historicos, geographicos, biographicos, ettatisticos e noticiosos da provincia de S. Paulo, no nome Domingos Leme da Silva.

---

(1) Confira-se Frei Gaspar da Madre de Deus, Memorias para a Historia da capitania de S. Vicente—Liv. I pags. 79-80 e 81 e uma carta de Pedro Taques de Almeida Paes Leme, escripta ao mesmo. Frei Gaspar é publicada no vol. IV p 21 da publicação official do Archivo do Estado de S. Paulo.

(2) Assim chamou-se o primeiro engenho de canna de assucar que houve na ilha de S. Vicente, mandado construir por Martim Affonso.

(Frei Gaspar da Madre-Deus, *Memorias para a Historia da Capitania de S. Vicente.*

(3) João do Prado é tronco de numerosa desoendencia de seu appellido na Capitania de S. Vicente e nas visinhas, e que veio para o Brazil com Martim Affonso de Sousa, estabelecendo-se na ilha de S. Vicente, onde servio os cargos da republica — e casou se com D. Philippa Vicente, filha de Pedro Vicente e d. Maria de Faria, portuguesas Pedro Taques—citado XXXIII. Tit. Prados—p. 80. Nos tres seculos coloniaes, as palavras —republica e republicanos não tinham a significação hostil ao Rei : ao contrario, a republica e os republicanos eram d. El-Rei. Os paulist s antigos apreciavam muito a denominação de cidadãos republicanos, i é, leaes vassallos d'El-Rei.

Deixou do seu primeiro matrimonio entre outros filhos (sete) a mais velha Izabel Cardoso casada com Bartholomeu Bueno—chamado o *Anhanguera* (1) sobrlnho de Amador Bueno— o aclamado.

Pedro Leme— chamado pela alcunha o *Torto* e coxo. Pedro Taques—citado XXXV titulo Leme a pag. 34—falleceu em Ytú. Paulista que soube desempenhar os nobres espiritos do sangue que lhe adornavam as veias como revelou na acção do valor e fidelidade que praticara na campanha e sertão da Vaccaria. Entre os cinco filhos que deixou, do seu casamento com d. Domingas Gonçalves tem menção especial João Leme da Silva e Lourenço Leme da Silva que tiveram tão triste fim (2).

2) Matheus Leme, casado em primeiras nupcias com d. Antonia Chaves, deixando d'ste matrimonio sete filhos ; em segundas com d. Antonia Gago, de quem não teve filhos.

3) Aleixo Leme, foi casado com d. Ignez Dias (irmã inteira. de d. Antonia Chaves, Mulher de Matheus Leme (com dez filhos.

4) Braz Esteves Leme — (Pedro Taques, citado XXXV em titulo Lemes — Cap. IV a pag. 84) falleceu solteiro (3).

5) D. Lucrecia Leme, da qual se tratará no texto seguinte

## II

LUCRECIA LEME, A QUAL CASOU-SE COM FERNANDO DIAS PAES

Fernando Dias Paes, natural da villa de Abrantes, em Portugal, foi casado em S. Vicente a primeira vez com Hélena

---

(1) Azevedo Marques no nome Bartholomeu Bueno da Silva, vol. 1 pag. 48 que tornou-se um sertanejo notavel e foi chamado Anhanguera—diabo velho—pelos indios. Fez invasões pelos sertões além do Rio Grande e descobriu minas de ouro em territorio occupado pelos indios *Goyá* e voltou do sertão trazendo tantos indios que, dizem os chronistas, davam para fazer um' boa villa. Voltando a Parnahyba, lá fallecen em fius do século XVII deixando nove filhos, dos quaes o mais velho chama-se Bartholomeu Bueno da Silva, tambem denominado *Anhanguera*, como seu pai.

(2) Os incidentes da vida e morte tragica dos irmãos Leme narram Pedro Taques citado XXXV em titulo Leme a pag. 39 e seguintes e Azevedo Marques citado, no nome Lemes a pag. 45 do Tomo II, e a morte desses dois irmãos não foi devida aos crimes por elles praticados, porquanto esses crimes eram comparativamente antigos: e recentemente o Capitão General que não podia ignoral-os, os tinha enchido de favores e honras e usado para com elles da linguagem mais lisong ira. expressando a confiança que depositava no caracter e nas qualidades pessoaes de ambos. O premio offerecido pelas cabeças dos Lemes e o consequente assassinato de ambos foram devidos a intriga, ao enredo, a avareza, de um gatuno portuguez, Sebastiam Fernandes do Rego, que residia em S Baulo, aqui era provedor da Fazenda Real conselheiro intimo do Capitão General Rodrigo Cezar de Menezes.

(3) Não foi casado. mas teve 14 filhos de diversas mulheres da raça indigena do paiz Possuiu grande fortuna. em consequencia do muito ouro que extrahiu das riquissimas minas da serra do Jaraguá, descobertas por Affonso Sardinha em 1597, e falleceu no sertão do Jaraguá. O juiz de orphãos procedeu o inventario de todos seus bens para serem partilhados pelos referidos 14 filhos; mas não o permittindo as leis em razão da nobreza e qualidades de seu pai, foram excluidos da herança por sentença proferida a favor dos dois irmãos de Pedro Leme e D. Lucrecia Leme que lhe sobreviveram.

Teixeira, cujos 3 filhos Francisco Vicente e Antonio foram para a Bahia em companhia de um parente, e a segunda com d. Lucrecia Leme.

Foi uma das pessoas de maior respeito e occupou os lugares da republica nas villas de S. Vicente e Santo André (1) e S. Paulo do Piratininga (2) como se vê dos livros da Camara da cidade de S. Paulo, e no anno de 1570. era juiz ordinario.

Fez depois seu estabelecimento no sitio dos Pinheiros onde teve uma grande fazenda de cultura, cujas terras de matos e campos chegaram até a ribeira do Yporanga (3) comprehendendo a distancia de uma legoa. Falleceu Fernando Dias em S. Paulo, a 5 de Outubro de 1605 e d. Lucrecia Leme falleceu com testamento em S. Paulo em 1.º de Julho de 1641 deixando deste 2.º matrimonio os seguintes filhos:

1) Leonor Leme, casada com Simão Borges de Cerqueira, moço da camara d'El-rei D. Henrique e natural de Mezamfrio, em Portugal; passou-se a esta capitania no serviço do mesmo senhor, com o foro de moço fidalgo de sua real camara, que se acha no archivo desta com geração.

2) Fernando Dias Paes Leme, casado com d. Catharina Camacho, filha de João Maciel e d. Paula Camacho, teve um unico filho, o padre jesuita Francisco de Moraes por alcunha—malagueta—e por isso fizeram em 24 de Janeiro de 1624 doação de todos os seus bens, entre os quaes as terras do MBoy ao collegio dos jesuitas de S. Paulo, com a pensão de uma festa annual á Imagem de N S. do Desterro, em um altar fundado por elles. Foi administrador das aldêas do real padroado

3) Maria Leme, casou com Manoel João Branco, natural de Setubal, que adquiriu grande cabedal extrahido das minas de ouro de S Paulo —e teve 3 filhos.

4) Izabel Paes, casada em primeiras nupcias com Marcos Mendes de Oliveira e em segundas nupcias com José Serrão— sem descendencia.

5) Pedro Dias Paes Leme, o qual é o do texto seguinte.

6) Luiza Leme casada com o capitão-mór Pedro Vaz de Barros, natural de Lisboa, Portugal, donde veio para S. Vicente com seu irmão Antonio Pedroso de Barros, pelos annos de 1600,

---

(1) Antiga e extincta povoação fundada em aprasivel situação, á margem direita do Ribeirão *Guapituba*, por João Ramalho e sua familia com os indios que se lhe agregaram na paragem chamada *Borda do Campo*, territorio hoje da freguesia de S. Bernardo Vide linha B titulo II p. 24 v.

(2) Começou por uma casa de educação e catechese creada pelos padres Manoel de Paiva e José Anchieta, na aldea de Piratininga e depois passou a chamar-sse S. Paulo de Piratininga, mais tarde villa de S. Paulo e por carta regia de D. João V. de 11 de Julho de 1711 a categoria de cidade e hoje capital do Estado.

(3) E' a ribeira do Ypiranga.

ou pouco antes. Serviram de capitães-móres locos-tenentes de Lopo de Souza, neto de Martim Affonso, então Senhor de duas capitanias em 1602 e em 1607.

Tratando, Pedro Taques cit. XXXV no titulo Pedrosos, Barros, Vazes a pag. 44—desses dous irmãos diz que eram « pessoas de qualificada nobresa, e vieram providos Antonio Pe- « droso em capitão-mór governador da capitania de S. Vicente « e S. Paulo, e o irmão Pedro Vaz de Barros em ouvidor da « mesma capitania, com clausula que, fallecendo Antonio Pe- « droso fosse capitão-mór governador e tambem ouvidor o irmão « Pedro Vaz, e fallecendo este, fosse Antonio Pedroso o capitão- « mór governador e tambem ouvidor. » Ahi Pedro Taques expõe com abundancia o que foi Pedro Vaz de Barros, capitão-mór e governador.

Pedro Vaz falleceu em S. Paulo a 28 de Março de 1644 deixando 8 filhos (1).

7) Luiz Dias Leme, foi paulista de tanta autoridade e respeito, que nem antes, nem depois delle se conheceu outro que o excedesse. Casado com d. Catharina Pelaes, filha de Alonso Pelaes cavalheiro castelhano e d Luzia de Siqueira Mendonça: do matrimonio de Luiz Dias Leme deixaram seis filhos.

## III

### PEDRO DIAS PAES LEME CASOU-SE COM MARIA LEITE

Pedro Dias Paes Leme, occupou os cargos da republica muitas vezes : foi paulista de uma grande estimação e respeito. Falle- ceu a 16 de Julho de 1633, sepultado na capella-mór da igreja do Carmo em jazigo proprio.

---

(1) a) Jeronymo Pedroso de Barros que falleceu sem descendencia. b) Valentim Pedroso de Barros,--casado com d. Catharina de Góes Siqueira que enviuvando passou a segundas nupcias com d. João Matheus Rendon tambem viuvo. c) Antonio Pedroso de Barros, casado com d. Maria Pires de Medeiros filha do capitão Salvador Pires e de d. Ignes Monteiro, Azevedo Marques, citado - mesmes nomes ; deixando Antonio Pedroso de Barros 4 filhos entre elles Pedro Vaz de Barros casado com d. Maria Leite Mesquita que foi senhor do engenho de catauna com mais de 600 indios administrados. d) Pedro Vaz de Barros foi fundador da actual cidade de S. Roque e falleceu solteiro. e) Sebastião Paes de Barros casado com d. Anna Tavares—com descendencia. f) D. Lucrecia Pedroso de Barros casada com Antonio de Almeida Pimentel, portuguez. g) Fernando Paes de Barros, grande sertanejo e cidadão muitissimo illustre, e dos seus dois consorcios, sendo um com d. Maria de Mendonça, não deixou filhos. h) Luiz Pedroso de Barros um dos mais audazes exploradores dos sertões e conquistadores de indios do seu tempo, pelo que grangeu grande fortuna. Foi capitão de infantaria. e como tal marchou em 1629 a soccor- rer Pernambuco, possuidos dos inimigos hollandezes, não contente com os annos que con- sumio nessa guerra, ainda depois passou ao Perú, colonia hespanhola, onde falleceu em 1662 Tendo estado na Bahia, alli casaram-se elle, e seu irmão Valentim de Barros com duas irmãs germanas do desembargador João de Góes Araujo.

Foi casado com D. Maria Leite, natural de São Paulo, filha de Paschoal Leite Furtado (1) da ilha de Santa Maria (Açores) e de sua mulher D. Izabel do Prado, (2) irmã do padre jesuita Domingos do Prado. D. Maria Leite falleceu a 13 de Maio de 1667 e se sepultou no seu jazigo da capella-mór da igreja dos carmelitas.

Deste matrimonio nasceram em S. Paulo nove filhos (1.ª cart. de orph. de S. Paulo).

1) Fernandes Dias Paes, sogro de Manoel de Borba Gato, o encarregado da descoberta das minas de prata e de famosas esmeraldas (3); era casado com D. Maria Garcia Rodrigues Betim. Os historiadores e muitos documentos officiaes o tratam sómente por *Fernão Dias Paes*, confundindo-o com o avô, que apenas assim era chamado. Seu filho Garcia Rodrigues Paes, o acompanhou nessa expedição a s sertões do *Sabarabossú* (4) e dos inlios *Maxapós* em 1672; e continuou, após sua morte 168C, as explorações; tendo sido nomeado, por provisão de 23 de Outubro de 1683, capitão mór das entralas e descobrimento das esmeraldas. Em 1702, por carta regia de 27 de Março, foi no-

---

Elle casou-se com D. Leonor de Siqueira, filha de Jorge de Araujo de Góes, e de sua mulher D. Angela de Siqueira, ambos naturaes da Bahia, neta por parte paterna, de Gaspar de Araujo, natural da Villa de Ponte de Lima, e de sua mulher D. Catharina de Góes, natural de Lisboa. E, pela materna, de Seba stião Pedroso Barbosa, natural da villa de Vianna do Minho, e de sua mulher D. Leonor de Siqueira, natural da cidade da Bahia. Tudo isto escreveu Pedro Taques de Almeida Paes Leme que consta do autos de *puritate et nobilitate probanda* do desembargador João de Góes Araujo, para lêr no Paço em Lisboa.

Jorge de Araujo Goes foi irmão gemeo de Simão de Araujo de Góes, muito conhecido na guerra da Bahia contra os hollandezes. E ainda teve ao serviço real, na mesma guerra, seus filhos Ignacio de Araujo de Góes, Antonio de Araujo de Góes e Francisco de Araujo de Góes. O desembargador João Góes de Araujo prestou muitos serviços; e. entre estes, o das negociações para a fabrica de fragatas de alto bordo no *Estado do Brasil*.

Luiz Pedroso de Barros deixou do seu consorcio duas filhas:
— D. Maria de Araujo, casada com Lourenço Castanho Taques —o moço; 2) D. Angela de Siqueira, casada em segundas nupcias com Pedro Taques de Almeida como se verá nos textos IV e V da linha *B*

(1) Este Paschoal Leite Furtado, filho de Gonçalo Martins Leite, era neto de Jorge Furtado de Sousa, que teve o foro de fidalgo da casa real. Pedro Taques de Almeida Paes Leme, *Nobiliarchia Paulistana*, na *Revista do Instituto Historico. Geographico e Ethnographico do Brasil*, XXX parte 2·, titulo «Prados», pag. 84; e XXXV parte ·', titulo *Lemes* a pag. 96 faz referencia ao *Nobiliario* do reverendo Dr Gaspar Fructuoso, III. 3 IV, 16 para demonstrar a nobilissima e muito antiga linhagem de Paschoal Leite Furtado. e dá integralmente o brazão de armas, do qual se ve que esta D. Maria Leite descendente de D. Maria Alvares Cabral, irmã de Pedro Alvares Cabral o descobridor do Brasil;

(2) Filha de João do Prado, descripto no texto 1 desta linha.

(3) Acerca desta descoberta veja-se Azevedo Marques citado, na chronologia e acontecimentos de 26 de Julho, 1.º de Setembro e 11 de Desembro de '681.

(4) Antigos sertões da provincia de Minas-Geraes onde esses prestimosos e incomparaveis pauli tas fizeram á descoberta do ouro esmeralda em 1681.

O mestre de campo Mattias Cardoso de Almeida vid. J. Mendes pag. 259.

Machado de Oliveira Quadro historico de s. Paulo pag. 106.

J. Mendes—Notas genealogicas pag. 445 notas pag. 318 e Pedro Taques XXXV pag. 129 e 130.

Azevedo Marques—chronologia p 238, 239, 242 e 243.

meado fidalgo cavalleiro da casa real. Abrindo a sua custa, no espaço de cinco annos, a estrada para as minas-geraes, El-rei escreveu-lhe uma carta para louvar-lhe esse acto. Teve o titulo o o privilegio de guarda-mór de minas por tres vidas, que findaram na pessoa de seu neto Fernando Dias Paes Leme. Garcia Rodrigues Paes falleceu em 7 de Março de 1738.

Os serviços destes Fernãos Dias Paes e Garcia Roiz Paes constam da Historia Patria, da legislação de Portugal e de todos os archivos e cartorios publicos em S. Paulo e no Rio de Janeiro.

Fernando Dias Paes foi casado com D. Maria Garcia Rodrigues Betimk, filha de Garcia Roiz Velho, natural e cidadão de S. Paulo, e de sua mulher D. Maria Betimk. D'ahi o appelido Betim entre os Paes Leme. Deixou oito filhos seguintes:

*a)* Garcia Roiz Paes, capitão-mór, casado com D. Maria Antonia Pinheiro da Fonseca, filha do capitão João Rodrigues da Fonseca e de D. Antonia Pinheiro Rapozo Tavares. Este distincto continuador do genio inccansavel e do espirito emprehendedor de seu pae, acompanhou-o sempre durante os 7 annos que andou pelos sertões do interior do Brazil na descoberta de ouro e pedras preciosas. Falleceu em 1738 deixando 2 filhas e 3 filhos, dos quaes dois, Fernando Dias Paes e Pedro Dias Paes, foram homens de muito merito e occuparam cargos publicos. *b)* Pedro Dias Paes Leme casado com D. Maria de Lima de Moraes, filha do capitão-mór Guilherme Pompéo de Almeida, des·ripto no texto III da linha B. *c)* D. Marianna Paes Leme casada em primeiras nupcias com Francisco Paes de Oliveira Horta e em segundas nupcias com Fernando de Moraes Madureira e com descendencia. *d)* D. Custodia Paes Lema casada com Gaspar Gonsalves Moreira. *e)* D. Izabel Paes casada com o coronel Jorge Moreira de Godoy. *f)* D. Catharina Paes, casada com Luiz Soares Ferreira. *g)* D. Anna Maria Leme, casada com João Henrique de Siqueira Baruel—*h)* e D. Maria Leite, casada com o mestre de campo Manoel de Borba Gato.

2) Paschoal Leite Paes, foi casado duas vezes, a primeira em Santos, com D. Maria da Silva e com uma filha unica, Margarida da Silva que foi casada com Salvador Jorge Velho e a segunda com D. Agostinha Rodrigues, sem geração.

3) Pedro Dias Leite casado com D. Anna de Proença veja-se o texto IV da Linha B, filha de Lourenço Castanho Taques, o Velho, com descendencia.

4) Dr. João Leite da Silva, clerigo do habito de São Pedro.

5) Maria Dias Leite, casou-se duas vezes, sendo a primeira com Diniz Cardoso, natural de Portugal, sem geração, a segunda com Domingues Rodrigues de Mesquita, natural de Portugal, com uma unica filha, Maria Leite de Mesquita.

6) Izabel Paes da Silva, que é a do texto seguinte.

7) Potencia Leite, casada em primeiras nupcias com Pedro Taques veja-se o texto III da linha B, que por desavença em 1640 com Fernando de Camargo, foi assassinado por este á falsa fé; sem descendencia. Casou se, depois oom, Manoel de Carvalho Aguiar cuja nobreza e brazam de armas prendem-a aos *Moraes do Antas*; e desse consorcio nasceram em S. Paulo 4 filhos (1).

8) Veronica Dias Leite, casou-se com Manoel Ferraz de Araujo, natural do Porto, com tres filhos.

9) Sebastiana Leite da Silva, foi casada com Bento Pires Ribeiro capitão de tropa, filho de Salvador Pires de Medeiros e D. Ignez Monteiro de Alvarenga, chamada — Matrona — por suas virtudes e animo varonil (2). Deixaram sete filhos.

IV

IZABEL PAES DA SILVA A QUAL CASOU-SE COM BARTHOLOMEU
SIMÕES DE ABREU

Izabel Paes da Siva casou-se duas vezes : sendo a primeira na matriz de S. Paulo, a 29 de Janeiro de 1636 com Bartholomeu Simões de Abreu, natural da villa de Santos, filho de João de Abreu, nobre cidadão da villa de Santos, almoxarife que foi da fazenda real, em 1591 e de sua mulher Izabel de Proença Varella, natural da villa de Santos, filha de Paulo Proença,

---

(1) João Carvalho Aguiar, caasado com D. Marianna Bueno, neta do Amador Bueno o aclamado Manoel Carvalho de Aguiar, casado com Francisca da Silva Teixeira, neta de Amador Bueno o aclamado D. Maria Leite casada com o capitão mór Manoel Bueno da Fonseca, neto de Amador Bueno o aclamado. D. Izabel Barbara de Aguiar e Silva, casada com *Domingos da Silva Bueno* neta de Amador Bueno o aclamado, que foi por seu merito o primeiro mestre de campo do terço de auxiliares de S. Paulo, que em 1697 levantou o governador Arthur de Sá Em 1710 tendo o governador Antoio de Albuquerque Coelho de Carvalho de ausentar-se de P. Paulo para Minas, deixou o governo interino ao mestre de campo Domingos da Silva Bueno. Anteriormente por occasião da descoberta das linhas de *Sabarabossu* passou a ellas em 1700 servindo de governador e guarda-mór onde se houve de tal modo que foi elogiado pela carta Regia de 9 de Dezembro do mesmo anno; voltou logo depois a S Paulo e tornou ás Minas onde grangeou boa fortuna. Na 2.ª invasão dos francezes no Rio de Janeiro, em 1711 soccorreu com tropa e mantimentos áquella praça, tudo pago a sua custa. Confira-se Azevedo Marques citado vol. I p. 129.

(2) Confira-se João Mendes de Almeida em suas Notas Genealogicas Cap. IV Linha A tit. 3 p. 363.

natural da villa de Alemquer e de sua mãe Izabel Cubas, filha de Braz Cubas (1).

Sendo a 2.ª — com Simão Ferreira Delgado (segundo Pedró Taques de Almeida Paes Leme) era natural da cidade da Bahia e professo da ordem de Christo, de cuja praça era capitão de infanteria da companhia de seu pae Sebastião Fernandes Tourinho de quem era filho e de sua mulner D. Maria Braz Reis, que foram senhores do engenho e de grandes cabedaes na Bahia. Fallecendo o dito mestre de campo Sebastião Fernandes Tourinho, passou para a Bahia seu filho e unico herdeiro desta grande casa — o Capitão Simão Ferreira Delgado e dalli embarcou para o reino a tratar dos seus serviços com o concurso dos que ficaram por morte de seu pae. Teve a infelicidade de ficar o navio de seu transporte captivo dos mouros e para o poder destes barbaros foi tambem captivo o capitão Simão Ferreira Delgado, e encontrando o seu destino rigores e crueldades, não lhe durou muito tempo o tormento, porque aos effeitos delle perdeu a vida.

D. ızabel Paes da Silva, falleceu na villa de S. Sebastião a 8 de Abril dé 1666 teve do seu

### 1.º Matrimonio

1) Francisco Paes da Silva que casou-se em primeiras nupcias com Ignez Monteiro filha de Antonio Pires de Medeiros e Anna Luiza Grou sem geração ; e em 2.ªª nupcias com d. Maria Bueno do Amaral neta de Amador Bueno o—acclamado.

2) Potencia Leite da Silva casada com o Cap.ᵐ Diogo de Escobar Ortiz natural de S. Sebastião irmão de Estevam Raposo Boaarro e teve 2 filhas.

3) Maria de Abrou Pedroso Leme que é a do texto seguinte :

### 2.º Matrimonio

4) Lucrecia Leme casada com José de Godoy Moreira que depois de viuvo, ordenou-se de presbytero de S. Pedro na cidade da Bahia—era filho de Gaspar de Godoy Moreira e Anna Lopes

(1) Braz Cubas, cavalheiro fidalgo da casa real — era natural do Porto, filho de João Pires Cubas e Izabel Nunes e neto de Nuno Rodrigues, e passou-se para o Brasil com Martin Affonso de Sousa no estado de viuvo: foi '.º alcaide-mór da villa de Santos — seu fundador e provedor — e depois provedor da fazenda real, capitão-mór, governador e ouvidor da Capitania de S Vicente Seu filho Pedro Cubas, moço fidalgo da Camara d'Elrei, foi tambem provedor da fazenda — capitão-mór, governador e ouvidor da dita Capitania, vieram juntamente com Braz Cubas seus irmãos: Antonio Cubas — Gonçalo Nunes Cubas — Francisco Nunes Cubas e D. Catharina Cubas que casou-se com Francisco Ferreira. Confira-se Frei Gaspar da Madre de Deos, Memorias para a Capitania de S. Vicente, 1, 93,

Moreira e teve uma filha Maria Leme das Neves casada co Timotheo Corrêa de Goes. (1)

5) Sebastiana Paes Leme casada com Antonio do Rego Sá, natural da ilha de S. Miguel, sem filhos.

6) Anna Ferreira Tourinho falleceu solteira.

## V

### D. MARIA DE ABREU PEDROSO LEME—A QUAL CASOU-SE COM ESTEVÃO RAPOSO BOCARRO

Estevão Raposo Bocarro — da governança da republica da villa de S. Sebastião e natural della, onde foi pessoa de tratamento e grandes cabedaes de numerosa escravatura e senhor do engenho chamado da Praia de Barro que tinha sido de seus avós, primeiros fundadores e povoadores da ilha de S. Sebastião (2)— foi guarda-mór da marinha desta ilha dos Porcos até a barra da

---

(1) Timotheo Correa Goes, natural de Santos filho de Sebastião Fernandes Correa e de D. Angela de Siqueira Araujo (vide o texto V da linha B) foi o 2.º provedor o contador da Real Fazenda e juiz da Alfandega por sobrevivencia no officio de seu pai. Ainda mui jovem succedeo a seu pae no emprego sobredito e a este respeito refére miudamente o genealogista Pedro Taques de Almeida Paes Leme a seguinte historia : Sendo sua mãe D. Angela Siqueira mulher de animo varonil e tendo ella o previlegio, concedido por El-rei D. Affonso VI. de nomear para o cargo de provedor e contador da real fazenda e juiz da Alfandega em Santos, nomeara durante a menoridade de seu filho Timotheo Correa de Goes, o segundo marido capitão-mór Pedro Taques : chegado porém, o tempo de exercer dito cargo, como herdeiro empossou-se Timotheo Corres de Goes no cargo e retirou-se para S. Paulo, deixando commissão ao escrivão para os despachos dos cargos.
Nao quiz pagar este imposto um individuo, compadre e protegido do ex-capitão-mór governador da capitania Diogo Pinto do Rego, pessoa de distincta qualidade e nobresa, e muito abastado de fortuna : e resultando disso a prisão do referido individuo. Diogo Pinto do Rego o mandara soltar em desprestigio de Timotheo Correa de Goes. Este facto foi considerado uma injuria : depois, os parentes de Timotheo Correa de Goes determinaram que passada a festa de Paschoa, baixasse o provedor a Santos, acompanhado do padrasto e de outros parentes de authoridade e respeito, que lh'o sustentariam a jurisdicção e o prestigio, castigando os réos conforme o direito.
Com a noticia preparou-se, em Santos, Diogo Pinto do Rego para a lucta, fortificando e municiando suas casas, e passada a Paschoa, descendo Timotheo Correa Goes em companhia de sua mãe, de seu padrasto e de numerosos parentes, entre os quaes Fernão Paes de Barros, Pe'ro Vaz de Barros, Antonio Pedroso de Barros, Pedro Taques Pires, Lourenço Castanho Taques, formara sobre esse pessoal um corpo de mais de mil pessoas.
Felizmente chegados a Santos, após preparativos de ambos os lados para a lucta armada, durante dias, intervindo religiosos dos conventos do Carmo e de Santo Antonio e muitos moradores do lugar, os quaes todos ponderaram as desgraças para os contendores, Diogo Pinto do Rego resolveu entregar o infractor, o qual voltou á cadeia com ferros aos pés, ainda que para ser solto apos duas horas, como justa satisfacção ao provedor.
E' inutil relatar que as pazes foram feitas com geral applauso. Falleceu Timotheo Correa de Goes em Santos a 21 de Outubro de 1732 e deste seu consorcio teve 11 filhos : dos quaes, D. Izabel Caetana de Araujo casou-se com Diogo Pinto do Rego, cavalheiro fidalgo da casa real e neto do acima mencionado Diogo Pinto de Rego.
Vide Azevedo Marques em Sedição Militar em Santos—vol II p. 164.
(2) Elevada a villa por provisão do conde de Monte Santo, em 16 de Março de 1638.

Fortaleza da Bertioga (1) no tempo que o inimigo e pirata francez andava roubando as embarcações, que navegavam para aquella costa. Foi filho do capitão Gaspar Picam, natural da villa de Santos, morador na ilha de S. Sebastião e senhor do sobredito engenho da Praia de Barro, e da governança da republica, onde occupou os cargos della repetidas vezes e de sua mulher Catharina de Oliveira como consta do cartorio de orphãos, nos maços de inventarios da dita villa de S. Sebastião. Catharina de Oliveira foi irmã inteira de Antonia de Escobar, mulher de Manoel Pinto, chamado o Passarilho, de cujo matrimonio nasceu Domingos Thomaz da Silva, que foi pae do padre mestre frei Bernardino de Jesus, natural do Rio de Janeiro, religioso franciscano e commissionario do Santo Officio, um dos grandes talentos em letras e virtudes de sua provincia.

Foi Estevão Raposo Bocarro neto por parte paterna de Gaspar Fernandes Palha, natural da cidade de Funchal da ilha da Madeira, descendente de Ruy Vaz de Almeida, a quem El-rei D. João I deu o appellido de Palha com as armas, (2) como consta de muitos nobiliarios. Foi da governança da villa de Santos. Foi provedor de orphãos, dos defuntos e ausentes, capellas e residuos da capitania da S. Vicente de S. Paulo e casou-se na dita villa de Santos com d. Antonia Acqueixa de Peralta, filha de Antonio Raposo, natural da cidade de Beja, e de sua mulher d. Antonia Acqueixa de Peralta natural de Hespanha, de onde veiu com seu marido Antonio Raposo, para a capitania de São Vicente na armada real, de que foi general d. Diogo de Flores Boldez, como tudo melhor consta do alvará, que se passou ao dito Antonio Raposo quando em S. Paulo foi armado cavalheiro no anno de 1601 por d. Francisco de Souza, governador geral do Estado do Brazil, que para o fazer tinha decreto d'El-rei D. Felippe, em premio de serviços feitos á corôa, o qual alvará se acha registrado no archivo da camara de S. Paulo em caderno de registros, titulo 1600, de fls. 31 a 38.

E pela materna foi o guarda-mór Estevão Raposo Bocarro neto de Francisco de Escobar Ortiz que foi o primeiro povoador da ilha de São Sebastião, a qual lhe concedeu para si e seus descendentes o donatario da capitania de cem leguas Pedro Lopes de Souza para elle com a sua nobre geração a povoar, como fez sahindo da capitania do Espirito Santo com sua mulher Ignez

---

(1) A fundação deste forte data da chegada de Martim Affonso de Souza na distancia de 5 legoas a sueste da cidade de Santos. Bertioga—corrupção de *Buriquioca*, nome dado a esse lugar pelos indigenas ; e significa—casa de *buriquis* casa de macacos.

(2) Procedem de Ruy Vaz de Almeida, a quem El-rei D. João I chamara o Palha, porque e ordinario trazia uma palha na boca, usam das mesmas armas dos Almeidas.

de Oliveira Cotrim e com filhas já casadas. Dentro das sete leguas da dita ilha que lhe foi concedida se estabeleceu Francisco de Escobar Ortiz e seu cunhado Nuno Cavalleiro. Foi senhor de dois engenhos de assucar, os primeiros que houve naquella ilha, onde foi pessoa de grandes cabedaes com um navio de duas cobertas, que navegava para Angola.

Na capitania do Espirito Santo teve uma irmã chamada Antonia Escobar, casada com o fidalgo Vasco Fernandes Coutinho, que era filho natural do fidalgo do mesmo nome, capitão e senhor donatario da dita capitania por mercê d'El-rei D. João III

Antonia de Escobar fez procuração na dita capitania no anno de 1633 para se receber em S. Paulo a herança que lhe tocou por morte de seu filho o capirão Frederico de Mello Coutinho; que falleceu sem geração em S. Paulo a 28 de Janeiro de 1633 estando casado com D. Maria a qual depois foi mulher de João Barreto, como tudo se vê do testamento do capitão Fréderico de Mello nos autos de inventario de seus bens, no 1.º cartorio do judicial e notas de S. Paulo. Este Frederico de Mello foi conhecido e estimado em S. Paulo por homem fidalgo, como consta assim no archivo da camara no caderno de registros titulo 1623 a fls. 22.

Francisco Escobar, falleceu na ilha de S. Sebastião com testamento no anno de 1652, e sua mulher Ignez de Oliveira a 3 de Agosto de 1675 tambem com testamento, onde se mostra que de seu matrimonio fôra filha Catharina de Oliveira, mulher do capitão Gaspar Picam, senhor do ongenho da Praia do Barro.

Do matrimonio do guarda-mpr Estevão Raposo Bocarro e de D. Maria de Abreu Pedroso Leme, nasceram na ilha de S. Sehastião doze filhos que foram :

*1)* Pedro Dias Raposo — casou-se duas vezes : a 1.ª com Isabel Ribeiro da Silva Bueno (Pedro Taques nobil. Paul. XXXII 2.º trimestre pag. 218 Buenos da Ribeira) sem geração, e a 2.ª com Rosa da Apresentação, com descendencia.

*2)* Estevão Raposo Boccarro—deixou do seu matrimonio duas filhas e um filho.

*3)* João Leite da Silva Ortiz—um dos descobridores das minas de Goyaz em 1725, em companhia do seu sogro Bartholomeu Bueno da Silva (1) do seu casamento com D. Isabel Bueno da Silva deixou quatro filhos.

*4)* Diogo de Escobar Ortiz—foi casado com Catharina Nunes de Freitas e teve cinco filhos.

---

(1) Bartholomeu Bueno da Silva filho de outro de igual nome (nota * ao texto I desta linba) tambem conhecido couo seu pai por Anhanguera e sobre este paulista leia-se Azevedo Marques, *Apoutamentos Historicos, geographicos, biographicos, estatisticos e noticiosos da Provincia de S. Paulo* vol. I p. 49 e na sua *Chronologia* a p. 255ª

5) Bartholomeu Paes de Abreu—que casando-se com Leonor de Siqueira Paes—fundiu em uma linha A e B desta genealogia—como adiante será explicado.

6) Bento Paes da Silva—casado com uma filha de Urbano de Castro Pereira deivou dois filhos.

7) Ignez de Oliveira Cotrim—casada com Antonio de Faria Sodré, com descendencia. Destes descendem a familia Silva Prado.

8) Veronica Dias Raposo— casou-se cem Miguel Gonçalves Martins e teve tres filhos.

9) Isabel Paes da Silva—casada com Manoel André Vianna e teve dous filhos.

10) Catharina de Oliveira Cotrim—casada com o cap.ᵐ Marcos Soares de Faria e teve sete filhos.

11 Antonia Recqueixa de Peralta—foi casada com Salvador Nunes—sem geração

12) Leonor Corrêa de Abreu — cassada com José Dias da Silva—deixaram no ve filhos.

# CAPITULO SEGUNDO

## LINHA—B

Esta linha tem por progenitores Antonio Rodriguez de Almeida e D. Maria Castanho, ambos portuguezes.

E' esta a linha dos Almeidas-Custanhos-Proenças-Taques-Laras-Toledos-Godoys-Anhaias-Moraes e Pompeos.

E' a linha nobilitada á moda européa desde sua origem; porque Antonio Rodriguez de Almeida era cavalleiro fidalgo da casa d'El-rei D. João III.

Por D. Magdalena Fernandes de Moraes Feijó, mulher de D. Diogo de Lara, cuja filha D. Maria de Lara casou-se com Lourenço Castanho Taques— o velho, esta linha prende-se á dos Antas Moraes. De facto, D. Magdalena Fernandes de Moraes Eeijó era filha de Pedro de Moraes de Antas e de sua mulher D. Leonor Pedroso, esta filha de Fstevão Ribeiro Bayão e de sua mulher D. Magdalena Fernandes Feijó, todos portuguezes. Aquelle Pedro de Moraes de Antas era descendente, em decimoquinto gráo, de D. Mendo Alam, senhor da então villa be Bragança; o qual vivia em tempo de El-Rei D. Affonso VI de Leão avô de D. Affonso Henriques, primeiro rei de Portugal, e casarase com uma princeza de Armenia, qne com seu pae viera á romaria em Compostella a visitar o corpo do apostolo S. Thiago. Deste casal procedeu D. Fernando Mendes —o velho, rico homem, o qual suecedeu a seu pae no senhorio de Bragança, e mais ter-

— 56 —

ras, na provincia de Traz-os-Montes; este rico homem foi casado com uma unica filha d'El-rei D. Affonso Henriques, ou segundo outros, com a infanta D. Sancha Henriques (1).

O ultimo desta Linha, em relação às estas notas genealogicas, foi o capitão mór governudor Pedro Tagues de Almeida asado com D. Angela de Siqueira. Sua filha D. Leonor de Siueira Paes casando-se com Barthelomeu Paes de Abreu, reunio final as duas linhas A e B.

I

ANTONIO RODRIGDES DE ALMEI A, CASADO COM D. MARIA CASTANHO AMBOS PORTUGUEZES.

Antonio Rodrigues de Almeida, natural de Monte-môr o Novo em Portugal, veio para a capitania de S. Vicente em 1547, pouco mais ou menos (2), e tinha o fôro de cavallaria fidalgo da da casa d'El rei D. João III. (1).

(1) Pedro Taques de Almeida Paes Leme *Nobiliarchia Paulistana na Revista do Instituto Historico XXXIII*, parte segunda, paginas 27 e seguintes, 1870. Faz referencias ao chronista Brandão e ao genealogista conde D. Pedro ; e por outro lado, á *Genealogia da Casa Real de Portugal*.

(2) A seguinte carta de sesmaria pode esclarecer esse ponto, que as chronicas não determinam: chegando alguns chronistas a dizer que Antonio Rodrigues de Almei'a viera com Matrim Affonso de Souza em 1831 ! Eis a carta de sesmaria :

« Pedro Ferraz Barreto, capitão e ouvidor com alçada na capitania de S Vicente por Martim Affonso de Souza, senhor da dita capitania. do conselheiro d'El-rei nosso Senhor, e senhor das villas de Alcoenta. Tagarro e Rio Maior, etc. Faço saber que por Antonio Rodrigues de Almeida, cavalleiro fidalgo da casa d'El-rei nosso Senhor, almoxarife, chanceller, escrivão da ouvidoria e das datas a petição em que diz . Que elle ha 16 annos que em ella vive, e tem sua mulher e filhas. e uma casada, e me pedia terras no Rio de Janeiro a entestar com uma aldêia, que por nome dos indios se chama *Ita-oca* meia legua de terra, etc. E se lhe concedeu a 6 de Janeiro de 1565.»

Parece que o requerimento foi feito em 1562 ou 1565. Assim pois, sua vida foi em 1646 ou 1547.

Confira-se João Mendes em seu livro *Algumas notas genealogicas* á pag. 97 usque 99 e notas Frei Gaspar da Madre de Deos, memorias para a victoria da Capitania de S. Vicente I, 92.

(1) A lei de 25 de Maio de 1776, embora promulgada para diminuir os privilegios dos nobres, conforme os intuitos de El-Rei D. José I, incluio não obstante na primeira nobreza do Reino nos tempos antigos «os escudeiros, os cavalleiros armados pelos Reis, ou pelos capitães-móres nas guerras da Africa e da Asia, os que conseguiam o honrado titulo de *Vasallos*, e outros da mesma gerarchia.»

El-Rei D Manuel havia feito definir em suas Ordenações quaes os fidalgos, e e a e:sa a legislação no tempo d'El-rei D. João III : «em cujo reinado (segundo escreveu Pedro Taques citado-*Nobiliarchia Paulistana)* foi o foro de cavalleiro fidalgo o *mais superior* que constituia gráo de fidalguia, até que alterou a ordem dos filhamentos o Snr. Pei D. Sebastião, de cujo tempo até o presente ficou este foro de cavalleiro fidalgo sendo *infimo*». E accrescentou o mesmo Pedro Taques: «Esta materia tratou Moraes, *de cecutiombus* : e muito melhor o revm padre-mestre D. Antonio Caetano de Souza no seu livro *Grandes de Portugal*, impresso em 1755».

O citado Moraes, IV, 8, 70, explicando os gráos de nobreza, com o apoio de *Brandão* e outros, relata:

«Cavalleiro da casa d'El-rei, nos tempos antigos em que não havia distincção, que hoje ha, de fidalgos cavalleiros e de cavalleiros fidalgos, se acha tomado em um e outro sentido, de maneira que muitas vezes se entendia por aquelles que hoje chamamos *Fidalgos-cavalleiros, ut notat Cabedo II, dec. 106, n. 1.*

Tendo deixado a mulher e duas filhas em Portugal, permaneceu em S. Vicenie até 1556. Durante esse tempo tomou parte em todas as guerras contra os *Tamuyas* que, ligados aos selvagens de *Ubatyba* e mais aldêas da costa, atacavam incessantemente as povoações dos portuguezes, e até penetravam a ilha de Guaibe onde apossaram-se do forte construido por ordem do donatario Martim Affonso de Souza.

Voltando a Portugal em 1556 d'alli regressou em 1557, constituido em capitão-mór governador e ouvidor da Capitania de Santo Amaro de *Guaibe*. (1)

Alem da sesmaria de meia legua de terra, proxima á aldêa de *Itaóca*, no Rio de Janeiro, (2) cujo titulo já foi transcripto, obteve elle mais duas na capitania de S. Vicente.

· Em 1560 «um pedaço de terta que, partindo por um regato que está a par do mosteiro de *Piratiiinga* (3) e que irá cortando pelo dito regato até entestar com roças de Fernão Alves, onde foi o primeiro *tugipar*, e d'alli irá cortando ao longo do campo até partir com terras de Antonio Piuto, e irá partindo com elle até findar no rio da *Tapera do Cacique*, e d'alli irá por elle abaixo até chegar ao dito regato, onde começou primeiro a partir que será onde se vê o dito regato metter-se no rio *Anhangavahy»* (4).

Em 1567, para confirmação de concessão anterior em 1556; uma legua de terra com todas as aguar interiores, para fazer engenhos no *Cubatão*, demarcada da maneira reguinte; «Indo desta villa de Santos pelo rio Cubatão arriba, da borda do dito rio da banda do norte, direito ao cume da serra mais alta, partindo com terras de Francisco Pinto, ou de quem foram, lhe

---

(1) Outros escrevem *Guaymbe*. 8ó depois de 1645 é que esta capitania tomou a denominação de *Santo Amaro*, por haverem algnns devotos edificado na villa de *Guaibe* uma capella com essa vocação, como bem o demonstrou frei Gaspar da Madre de Deus, *Memorias para a Historia da capitania de S. Vicente*, II §§ 20 a 31. O titulo da capella passou á ilha, e desta a capitania inteira das cincoenta leguas ; sem comprehender portanto as trinta de *Itamaraca*, em Pernambuco, as quaes continuaram com este nome. - J. Mendes cap. 3 pag. 38 nota esplica a significação dessa palavra.

(2) Balthazar da Silva Lisboa, *Annaes do Rio de Janeiro*, menciona Antonio Rodrigues de Almeida como um dos que acompanharam Mem de Sá, na expedição de S. Vicente contra os Franceses. E pertencendo aquelle territorio do Rio de Janeiro á capitania de S. Vicente, a qual começava 13 leguas ao norte do Cabo-Frio até o rio Curupace (55 leguas), e desde o rio S. Vicente até 12 leguas ao sul da ilha de Cananéa (45 leguas), Antonio Rodrigues de Almeida teve a exercitar alli duas funcções de escrivão da ouvidoria e outras, ainda que simultaneamente fosse capitão-mor loco-tenente na capitania de Santo Amaro de *Guaibe*

(3) Collegio dos padres da Companhia de Jesus, em S. Paulo. *Piratininga* peixe secco, srguet elica J. Mendes cit a p 91 nota .

(4) Confr ntando com os titulos de sesmaria de supra-citado Antonio Pinto, transcripto por Asevedo Marques *Apontamentos historicos, geographicos, estatisticos e noticiosos da provincia de S. Paulo*, no nome *Piratininga*, parece que esra seamaria de Anto Rodrigues de Almeida comprehendia o territorio hoje urbano das duas actuaes freguesias de Santa Ephigenia e de Nossa Senhora da Consolação. O *Anhangavahy* é que é affluente do rio *Tamandaathey*, mencionando no titulo de sesmaria supra como nm regato.

— 58 —

irá correndo pelo cume da serra mais alta, uma legua em comprido para a banda do sudoeste, e dalli, donde se acaba a dita legua, descerá por ahi abaixo ao rio do Cubatão, que vem ao longo da serra, em chãos della correndo para a banda do nordeste, e dalli virá correndo pelo dito rio abaixo até onde primeiro começou a partir com o dito Francisco Pinto; e assim lhe dava mais agua grande, que chamam o Cubatão (1), que apparece desta villa de Santos, com todas as mais que dentro de suas confrontações houver».

Ainda que exercendo o cargo de capitão-mór governador da capitania de Santo Amaro de *Guaibe*, em virtude da procuração de D. Izabel de Gambôa lhe entregou em Lisboa, lavrada aos 22 de setembro de 1557 (2), servia tambem os de

(1) Escreveu Azevedo Marques que *Cubatão* significa entre os indigenas «porto de mar morto nas fraldas das serras e montes.»
(2) Eis o inteiro theor desta procuração:
« Saibam quantos este poder virem que no anno do nascimento de N. S. J. C. do 1557 annos, aos 22 dias do mez de Setembro, na cidade de Lisboa, na rua do Outeiro junto da porta de Santa Catharina, nas casas em que vive a Sra. D. Izabel da Gambôa, mulher de Pedro Lopes de Souza, que Deos haja em gloria, estando ella dita sra. D. Izabel ahi presente, disse que ella, em nome e como tutora e administradora do Snr. seu filho Martim Affonso de Souza, capitão governador de 50 legoas de terra na costa do Brasil, que lhe succedeu e herdou por fallecimento do dito Pedro Lopes, seu pai, e por virtude de uma provisão que tem de El-Rei, que na santa gloria haja, e por nisso sentir fazer 'erviço a Deos, em bem e prol da capitania que tem em Santo Amaro de Guaibe, que está na dita sua capitania; e por se augmentar e povoar faz, como effeito fez, seu procurador bastante e Antonio Rois de Almeida, cavalheiro fidalgo da casa d'El-Rei nosso senhor, que ora volta para S. Vicente, o amostrador deste instrumento, e lhe deu seu poder comprido e mandado especial, para que, por ella, e em seu nome e do dito filho, a todas as pessoas que se vão povoar, beneficiar, aproveitar e reedificar conforme as ordens, elle Antonio Rodrigues de Almeida possa dar as taes terras, aguas e cousas sobredictas de sesmaria a quem lhe aprouver isso mesmo; e lhe dá poder para que possa dar quaesquer outras terras do dito seu filho em a dita capitania de Santo Amaro de Guaibe, conforme as ordens das sesmarias, e das terras que lhe aprouver comedidamente lhe fará cartas de sesmarias, e possa pôr na dita capitania capitão ouvidor, taes quaes devão ser, e querendo elle dito Antonio Rodrigues de Almeida ser capitão e ouvidor, lhe dá poder de capitão e ouvidor, para que em nome do dito seu filho *seja todo tempo que lhe aprouver*, e a ella senhora lhe bem parecer, e manda que lhe obedeção no alto e no baixo; e assim ao capitão ouvidor que elle Antonio Rodrigues de Almeida ordenar, tirar a um e por a outro quando justo e razão lhe parecer, e que possa receber ella Antonio Rodrigues de Almeida todas as redizimas e rendas que pertencerem ao dito seu filho por seu foral e doação; e assim para tomar conta e razão a Jorge Ferreira, que esteve por capitão na dita capitania e teve poder disso, e o deporá do dito poder e lhe tomará conta da que em si recebido tem; e assim a quaesquer outras pessoas ou pessoa que lhe devão suas rendas e ao diante deverem, e que obrigados lhe sejão, e de tudo e quo lhe deverem possa receber, e do que receber dará conhecimento e quitações, e haverá suas contas por acabadas, e procurará por toda fazenda do dito seu filho e suas rendas, e possa citar e demandar a quem lhe aprouver, em juizo e fóra delle allegar, defender, e etc. e de toda a fazenda de escravos do cathecismo e dos Carijós que o dito Jorge Ferreira tiver recebido para o dito seu filho. E assim de outras quaesquer cousas, artilharias e munições, e de tudo tomará conta e razão, e dará conhecimento e quitações do que receber; e dá poder ao dito Antonio Rodrigues de Almeida, que como capitão possa fazer e faça tabelliães do publico e do judicial e dos orphãos e da camara e do ouvidor, e lhes dará os seus assignados, com declaração de se virem confirmar por ella senhora em certo tempo que lhes será limitado para ella senhora lhes mandar passar carta ou cartas em forma sellado com o sello do dito seu filho assim outorgou: testemunhas as sobreditas. E eu Antonio do Amaral, Tabellião publico de el-rei nosso senhor nesta cidade de Lisboa e seus termos, que este instrumento de poder no livro de minhas notas escrevi, etc.

almoxarife, escrivão da onvidoria, promotor da justiça, escrivão
das datas de terras de sesmarias e chanceller, na capitania de
São Vicente, como proprietario de taes officios, por mercê do
donatario Martin Affonso de Souza, casado com d. Maria Cas-
tango, natural tambem de Monte-mór o Novo, a qual veio em
1560, mais ou menos, fundou na capitania de São Vicente a
familia dos *Almeidas, Laras, Toledos, Toques, Moraes, Casta-
nhos, e outros* (1).

Deste consorcio nasceram duas filhas, em Portugal; e um
filho, na então villa de Santos, da capitania de S. Vicente, em
1573, o qual foi o padre André de Almeida, citado pelo padre
Simão de Vasconcellos, na obra *A vida do padre João de Almeida*,
II, 4 (2), nos termos o mais significativos para um sacerdote.
Tomou a roupeta de jesuita em 1589, com 16 annos de idade,
e serviu sessenta pois que falleceu no collegio do Rio de Janeiro,
onde ficaram seus ossos, em 22 de outubro de de 1649 — na
idade de 76 annos. Naquelle collegio e no anniversario de sua
morte, era costume lêr no refeitorio a vida deste padre (3).

Das duas filhas, uma, d. Catharina de Almeida, falleceu
solteira (não sendo, portanto, exacta a asseveração de frei Gaspar
da Madre de Deus—que ambas casaram-se em Santos); a outra
d Maria Castanho, tambem natural de Monte-mór o Novo,
casou-se na villa de Santos em 1564-1565 com Antonio de
Proença, egualmente fidalgo (4).

---

(1) Frei Gaspar da Madre de Deus, *Memorias para a historia da capitania de S Vicente*, I, 92 o qual accrescentou. «Ainda hoje conhecido por gente principal na cidade de S. Paulo, e em algumas villas de serra acima.»

(2) Escreveu o padre Simão de Vasconcellos, na citada obra impressa em Lisboa—1658 «Outro varão insigne foi o padre veneravel André de Almeida de mui sandosa memoria em toda esta provincia, de cujas exemplares virtudes fizera de boa vontade uma larga relação:. direi sómente por ora que foi em tal gráu a santidade deste padre, que o comparam ordinariamente ao mesmo João de Almeida, e não é pequeno abono da sua virtude Foi extremado em todas as virtudes . Era notavelmente austero para comsigo mesmo, e sobremaneira affavel com os outros: delle se contam muitos sentimentos de Deus e casos propheticos... Faz, porém, muito naquelle varão o conceito que delle fazia o referido padre João de Almeida nas notaveis palavras seguintes: *O padre André de Almeida, unica pedra preciosa e de muita estima de Deus, pelo qual o Senhor tem feito, fas e ha de fazer muitos bens de muita gloria sua, e honra desta provincia e de toda a campanhia, como Deus Nosso Senhor irá descobrindo algum tempo.* Asev. Marques, 1.º vol, pag. 13.

(3) Pedro Taques de Almeida Paes Leme *Nobiliarchia Paulistana na Revista do Instituto Historico Geographico e Eta. do Brazil* XXXIII parte 1ª a pags. 240 a 242; 1870.

(4) Acerca da fidalguia de Antonio Rodrigues de Almeida e de Antonio Proença, é util transcrever o que escreveu Frei Gaspar da Madre de Deus, obra ditada 1, 98: «De proposito apontei as éras, em que os sobreditos se encontram com o tratamento de Cavalleiros fidalgos, para mostrar que todos chegaram a esta graduação antes do anno de 1572, em que D. Sebastião deu o regimento novo dos filhamentos Ora, nenhum delles conseguiu o fôro no dia em que se lavraram os documentos por mim citados; antes disso já o tinham, e por consequencia precederam seus filhamentos ao anno de 1557, em que morreu D. João III.»

II

D. Maria Castanho, casou-se com Antonio de Proença,
ambos portuguezes

Antonio de Proença, natural da villa de Belmonte, em
Portugal, era moço da camara do infante D. Luiz.
Estabeleceu-se em S. Paulo (Pirotininga), já então villa;
onde fez muitos serviços ao rei e ao paiz, e por provisão de
15 de outubro de 1599, do governador geral do Estado do
Brasil, D. Francisco de Sousa attendendo este aos auxilios de
armas e de escravos, sob a direcção de seu filho Francisco de
Proença, para a descoberta de minas de ouro, foi nomeado capitão da gente de cavallo. Antes dessa epocha; havia servido
os cargos de ouvidor, auditor e capitão-mór da capitania de
São Vicente, 1580-1582; além de varios outros cargos da villa
de São Paulo, inclusive no de capitão della no impedimento de
Diogo Arias de Aguirre, 1602, por nomeação do mesmo governador geral D. Francisco de Souza em 15 de maio daquelle
anno: — e tambem em 1582 o de juiz ordinario e de orphams (1).
Possuiu uma fazenda de terras de cultura e campos na
ribeira Itiporanga (2).
Em 1694, o capitão-mór Pedro Taques de Almeida, de
quem adeante se tratará, seu bisneto, provou no juizo ecclesiastico de São Paulo, a nobreza, qualidade e pureza de sangue de
seu ter-avô Antonio Rodrigues de Almeida, que é o mesmo do
texto I desta linha, cavalleiro fidalgo, natural de Monte-mór o
Novo, casado com d. Maria Castanho, do mesmo logar; e a
qualidade, nobreza e pureza de sangue da seu bis-avô Antonio
de Proença, moço da camara do infante D. Luiz, e natural de
Belmonte. Quanto a Antonio de Proença, foi expedida uma carta
requisitoria ao bispo da guarda, em Portugal; e, nessa mesma

---

(1) Pedro Taques de Almeida Paes Leme *Nobiliarchia Paulistana*, na *Revista do
Instituto Historico, Geographico e Etnographico do Brasil*, XXXIII, parte primeira. 1.º
trimestre de 1870 a paga 206 a 211.
(2) E' o actual *Ypiranga* tambem chamado em titulos de sesmaria, dos seculos XVI
e XVII, *Guarapirauga*. Esta fásenda pertenceu posteriormente a Pedro Taques, como
cabeça de sua mulher; e destes a herdou seu filho Lourenço Castanho Taques, como
adiante se dirá. O sitio de Francisco de Proença, cunhado de Pedro Taques, era visinho, para os lados de Santo Amaro. Balthazar da Silva Lisbôa, *Annaes do Rio de Janeiro*, escreveu que um fidalgo de nome Antonio Mariz, em 1561 pedio terras a Pedro
Collaço, capitão-mór de S. Vicente por Martim Affonso de Sousa, dizendo ser morador
naquella capitania, casado. e que na Borda do Campo, onde se chama *Ypiranga*, termo
da villa Piratininga, pedia em uma matta virgem um pedaço de des tiros de bésta comprido, de largura outro tanto ; que lhe fôra concedido por carta dada em S. Vicente aos
1º de Junho de 1561.» E o mesmo Antonio Mariz passou-se por o Rio de Janeiro em
1567, com a familia. Parece, pois que, de Antonio Mariz, por qualquer modo legal,
passaram estas terras no Ypiranga talvez a Antonio Proença.

occasião, foram outras cartas requisitorias para Portugal e Hespanha, quanto á qualidade, nobreza e pureza do sangue de Pedro Taques, de D. Diogo de Lara e de Balthazar de Moraes Antas. Tudo isto foi julgado por sentença (1).

Antonio de Proença deixou um filho e quatro filhas:

1°.) Francisco de Proença, já referido. De seu primeiro casamento, com D. Isabel Ribeiro, teve um unico filho, João Ribeiro de Proença, casado com D. Paula Moreira; com descendencia. Do segundo casamento, com D. Mécia Bicudo, teve uma unica filha, D. Anna Proença a qual, casou com Salvador Pires de Medeiros, filho de outro de egual nome, e neto de Salvador Pires e de D. Mécia Fernandes: os quatro unicos filhos de D. Anna Proença fallereram ainda pequenos.

Este Francisco de Proença teve o fôro de cavalleiro fidalgo por seu avô Antonio Roiz de Almeida, que, como já ficou referido, tinha o mesmo fôro. Seu estabelecimento agricola era no logar denominado *Borda do Campo*, no caminho de Santos, indo até o rio Jaraigbatiba, além de Santo Amaro, e confinando com o de seu pae, segundo já foi dito.

2.°) D. Anna de Proença, que é a do texto genealogico seguinte.

3.°) D. Catharina de Almeida, a qual se casou com Antonio Castanho da Silva, natural da villa de Thomar, em Portugal, onde era morgado (vide Pedro Taques XXXIII a pag. 213 e 214 e 215—Azevedo Marques Tom. I fl. 21) deixou os seguintes filhos:

Antonio Castanho da Silva, casado com Filippa Gago, filha de Paschoal Delgado Lobo e de D. Anna da Costa. Luiz Castanho de Almeida, fallecido em 1671, casado com D. Izabel de Lara, filha de Diogo de Lara e de D. Magdalena Fernandes Feijó de Moraes.

4.°) D. Isabel de Almeida e Proença, a qual se casou com Francisco Vaz Coelho, portuguez: com descendencia.

Deste casal descende a familia Anhaia, pelo casamento de sua primeira filha D. Maria Coelho com Paulo de Anhaia, natural da cidade do Porto, mas de origem hespanhola.

5.°) D. Maria de Almeida, a qual tendo-se casado em S. Paulo com João Lopes de Ledesma, portuguez, o acompanhou para o Rio de Janeiro, onde fixaram residencia e tiverem descendencia.

_____

(1) Esta noticia a dá Pedro Taques citado XXXIII, 1 parte de 1870, pag. 210 a 211.

## III

D ANNA DE PROENÇA CASOU SE COM PEDRO TAQUES, PORTUQUEZ

Pedro Taques era filho de Francisco Taques Pompeu e de sua mulher D. Ignez Rodrigues.

Francisco Taques Pompeu, natural de Brabante, dos Estados de Flandes, de nobilli-sima familia do seu appellido, passára a Portugal por causa do commercio e estacelecera-se na villa de Setubal, onde casou-se com D. Ignez Rodrigues -tendo deste ma· trimonio nasci lo dois filhos —*Francisca Taques* que foi casada em Setub il com Rei·aldo João e *Pedro Taques* e com este principiou em s. Paulo esta familia Taques.

A pureza e nobreza de sangue dos Taques Pompeus constam de uma justificação *de genere*, cujo instrumento, passado em 30 de Dezembro de 1697, foi remettido á camara episcopal do Rio de Jane.ro ; por onde se tinha expedido a requisitoria para as diligencias a favor de Pedro Taques de Almeida, natural da villa de S. Paulo, e neto do sobredito Pedro Taques. A justificação supra-referida fôra completa ; e, por isso, foi dado aquelle instrumento, com todas as precisas declarações.

Pedro Taques passou ao Brazil em 1591, na qualidade de secretario do setimo governador geral do mesmo Estado, D. Francisco de Sousa. Este governardor, depois de residir na cidade da Bahia até 1699, dirigiu-se, por ordem régia, á capitania de S Vicente e á villa de S. Paulo, por amor das minas de ouro descobertas em 1590, na serra *Jaguamimhaba* (Mantiqueira), e com elle o secretario Pedro Taques. Recolhendo-se, em 1602, a Portugal, o referido governador geral, Pedro Taques deixou de exercer o cargo ; preferindo ficar em S. Paulo, por ter-se casado com D. Anna de Proença.

Tornando-se cidadão da villa de S. Paulo, Pedro Taques serviu os cargos mais honrosos. E, quando em 1609 voltou D. Francisco de Souza, revestido dos mais amplos poderes, entre os quaes o de dar a serventia vitalicia de officios de justiça, mandou-lhe passar, em 6 de Junho do mesmo anno, provisão para o officio de juiz de orphams da villa de S. Paulo.

Pedro Taques falleceu em S. Paulo, aos 26 de Outubro de 164 l. (1)

Do seu consorcio com D. Anna de Proença teve oito filhos ; mas cresceram apenas seis.

---

(1) Confira-se Pedro Taques de Almeida Paes Leme—*Nobiliarchia Paulistana*, na *Rev. do Inst. Hist.* XXXII, parte 1.ª 1869 pags. 241 a 261.

1) Pedro Taques, casado com D. Potencia Leite, irmãn germana do governador Fernão Dias Paes.

Por desavenças, em 164⁰, com Fernando de Camargo, foi assassinado por este, á falsa fé. Não deixou descendencia.

2) Guilherme Pompeu de Almeida, foi muito rico de bens e de consideração publica. Residindo no territorio da villa de Parnahyba, alli serviu o cargo de capitão-mór, por El-rei D. Pedro II, sendo ainda regente

Mereceu a honra de receber cartas dos Reis D. João IV, D. Affonso VI e D. Pedro II. Fundou no territorio daquella villa, em Vuturuna, a capella de Nossa Senhora da Conceição; dotando-a além de grande patrimonio, com ornamentos ricos e as precisas alfaias: — essa capella já não offerece quasi vestigios do que foi.

Deixou á sua descendencia o encargo da administração da capella; e instituiu duas missas por sua alma em cada mez. Seria primeiro administrador seu filho mais velho, o reverendo Guilherme Pompeu de Almeida; e por morte deste, seu genro Antonio de Godoy Moreira.

Fernando de Camargo era neto de Francisco Camargo e de sua mulher D. Beatriz de la Peña, naturaes da Hespanha, vindos para S. Paulo em meado do seculo XVI. E filho de José Ortiz Camargo e de sua mulher D. Leonor Domingues.

Este José Ortiz Camargo foi o tronco da familia de *Camargos*, rival e inimiga da dos *Pires*.

Foi o seu filho, do mesmo nome, o promotor da guerra entre aquellas familias.

Nega-se Azevedo Marques, *Apontamentos Historicos de S. Paulo* nos nomes *José Ortiz de Camargo e Salvador Pires*, pae e filho.

De seu casamento com D. Maria de Lima Pedroso, filha de João Pedroso de Moraes e de sua mulher D. Maria de Lima, teve apenas 3 filhos; o dito reverendo Guilherme Pompeu de Almeida (1), D. Maria de Lima e Moraes, e D. Anna de Lima e Moraes. Esta ultima, casada com Antonio de Godoy Moreira,

___

(1) O Padre Guilherme Pompeu de Almeida herdou uma grande fortuna, e a despendia em sumptuoso tratamento. E, contrastes da vida! era homem illustrado e lido em philosophia e em theologia : pelo que merecêra o gráu de doutor por bulla pontificia.

Residia em Araçariguama, onde fundara a capella de Nossa Senhora da Conceição, de cuja imagem era muito devoto, fazendo sua festa annualmente. no dia 8 de Dezembro com um oitavario de missas cantadas, sacramento exposto. e sermões a varios santos de sua especial devoção. Foram-lhe concedidas as honras de Bispo missionario; e logo falleceu, 1713.

A sumptuosidade no cerimonial de seu enterro correspondeu á grandeza do seu tratamento em vida. Jaz sepultado ao pé do altar de S. Francisco Xavier, que elle fundára na egreja do collegio dos padres Jesuitas.

natural de Parnahyba, filho de João de Godoy Moreira e de D. Eufemia da Costa. Foi cidadão prestante e muito considerado em seu tempo. Falleceu a 15 de Julho de 1721, foi a que deixou descendencia. (1)

3) Lourenço Castanho Taques — *o velho*, que é o do texto genealogico seguinte.

4) D. Sebastiana Taques, sem geração.

5) D. Maria Pompeu Taques, casada com Manoel de Góes Raposo, filho de Antonio Raposo e de Isabel de Góes. Com descendencia.

6) Antonio Pompeo de Almeida. Depois de ter viajado até Lisboa e Angola, voltou a S. Paulo.

Tendo de prestar contas de administração das rendas geraes, na capitania de S. Paulo e S. Vicente, recolhia-se da cidade da Bahia aonde fôra, aquelle fim, quando se enamorou, no Rio de Janeiro, de uma viuva D. Maria de Sousa Coutinho e com ella se casou. Passado algum tempo, foram ambos assassinados no leito em que dormiam, por um bando de individuos que invadiram-lhes a casa. Sem geração.

## IV

LOURENÇO CASTANHO TAQUES, DENOMINADO — O VELHO; CASOU-SE COM D. MARIA DE LARA

Lourenço Castanho Taques—*o velho*—foi notabilissimo e nobre cidadão de S. Paulo. Como homem opulento que era em bens, e tambem em virtudes privadas e civicas, prestou muitos serviços ao governo de metropole, e á administração da Capitania de S. Vicente. (2)

Exerceu como seu pae, o cargo de juiz de orphams ; adquirindo, por sua justiça, o respeito dos jurisdiccionados.

Quando em 1.º de Abril de 1641, Amador Bueno da Ribeira, foi acclamado *Rei* em S. Paulo, Lourenço Castanho Taques, a

(1) Este casal produziu cinco filhos ; destes, falleceram solteiros José Godoy e Guilherme de Godoy de Almeida: João de Godoy de Almeida, casado com D. Anna da Silva, tavo uma unica filha, D. Rita de Godoy de Almeida e Silva a qual, casada em Parnahyba com João de Mattos Raposo, natural da ilha de S. Miguel, deixou numerosa prole : D. Escholastica de Godoy foi casada em primeiras nupcias com Bento do Amaral da Silva tronco de numerosa familia de seu appellido e, em segundas nupcias, com José Pinto Coelho da Mesquita (sem dec ), natural do Rio de Janeiro, deu origem aos Amaral Gurgel, de Ytú—e, finalmente Francisco de Godoy Moreira, que, capitão-mór em Minas Geraes, de lá voltou e fixou residencia em Mogy das Cruzes, onde se casou com D Maria Jorge, teve um unico filho Antonio Jorge de Godoy, que residu em Jundiahy, exercendo alli o posto de sargento-mór das ordenanças
(2) Só por provisão de 22 de Março de 1681, a cabeça da capitania passou a villa de S. Paulo: elevada a cidade por carta régia de 11 de Junho de 1711.

convite do mesmo Amador Bueno e dos frades do mosterio de S. Bento, accudiu immediatamente com sua influencia para que o povo não insistisse no seu revoluncionario proposito. Então, gosava de prestigio quasi egual (1) ao do Amador Bueno; existindo até uma certa rivalidade entre as respectivas famílias. De então em deante, tornou-se elle o cidadão preponderante na villa, e mesmo na capitania. Entendendo que os padres da Companhia de Jesus eram necessarios ás missões e á cathechese, não cessou de sustental-os com os meios moraes e politicos, de que dispunha.

Por isso andou sempre identificado com o governador Salvador Corrêa de Sá e Benevides, accusado de favorecer os jesuitas.

Auxiliou com pessoal e dinheiro as despesas das descobertas de minas, quando em 1659 o referido Salvador Corrêa de Sá e Benevides, nomeado administrador geral das minas de ouro e prata, reunidamente com o governo das tres capitanias — Espirito Santo, Rio de Janeiro e S. Vicente, chegou á villa de S. Paulo, trazendo-lhe uma carta d'el-rei D. João IV (2) para que lhe desse ajuda e favor

São conhecidos os conflictos, que se deram no Rio de Janeiro, revoltando-se alli a população contra o governador de praça Thomé Corrêa de Alvarenga, o sargento-mór Martim Corrêa Vasques, e o provedor da fazenda real Pedro de Souza Pereira, em fins de 1660. Quando a S. Paulo chegou a noticia do insulto, resolvendo o governador geral Salvador de Sá e Benevides «pôr-se a caminho e ir para o Rio de Janeiro socegar o tumulto e dar o merecido castigo aos cabeças e auctores da sedição», apressou-se Lourenço Castanho Taques a demovel-o de tão imprudente proposito, supplicando com instancias de leal vassallo não quizesse sua senhoria pôr em tão evidente risco a vida e a auctoridade».

Resistindo o governador geral a tão sinceras ponderações, Lourenço Castanho Taques assentou accompanhal-o com armas; mas nem este auxilio admittio. «Com este total desengano, fomentou Lourenço Castanho que a nob·eza se juntasse em corpo de união com o senado da camara, para, por carta e por parte de sua Magestade, se lhe ponderar a materia com esperanças de acceitar as ponderações que se lhe fizessem.»

---

(1) Nesse mesmo anno de 1641, Lourenço Castanho Taques havia entendido que não devia retriar-se de S. Paulo, após o assassinato de seu irmão Pedro Taques, como o fizeram aos outros irmãos, "porque e seu grande respeito e força d'armas o promptificara para pôr em cerco aos inimigos". Adduzimos este facto só para mostrar seu poderio naquella epocha referida no texto supra.

(2) Sendo a ordem d'Elrei D. João IV, de 7 de Junho de 1641, para descoberta de taes minas, é provavel que a carta supra fosse tambem desse anno. Elrei D. João IV fallecera em 1656.

Afinal, feito, assim, accedeu ; limitando seu regresso até a
ilha Grande, sem embargo da resposta já dada a aquella carta,
em 2 de Março de 1661. (1)

Annos depois, desenvolvendo-se ainda mais no governo em
Lisbôa a mania da descoberta de minas, Lourenço Castanho Taques, «achando se com disciplina militar na guerra contra os
indios, e tendo pratico conhecimento dos sertões que havia pe-
netrado na conquista de varias nações dos mesmos indios, recebeu uma carta do Princive Regente o infante D. Pedro (2),
datada de 23 de Fevereiro de 1674 (3), sobre o descobrimento

---

(1) Pedro Taques de Almeida Paes Leme, *Nobiliarchia Paulistana na Revista do Instituto Historico, Geogr. Eth. do Brasil* XXXIII parte primeira pags. 11 e 12, transcreveu
o inteiro theor da « resposta do governador. geral, Salvador Corrêa de Sá e Benevides,
á carta que lhe escreveu a nobreza de S. Paulo, com os prelados das religiões o reverendo D. Abbade de S Bento frei Hyeronimo do Rosario, o prior do Carmo frei André
de Santa Maria, o guardião de S. Francisco frei Gaspar de Santo Innocencio. o vigario
da egreja Domingos Gomes Albanes; os camaristas Estevão Bayão Parente, Constantino
de Saavedra, Francisco Dias Leme, Manoel Cardoso e Paulo Gonçalves, os da primeira
nobreza Lourenço Castanho Taques e seu filho Lourenço Castanho Taques, o moço.—o
capitão-mór Antonio Pibeiro de Moraes. D. Francisco de Lemos, João de Godoy Moreira,
João Ortis de Camargo Hyeronimo de Camargo, Antonio Pires: D. Simão de Toledo Piza, Paulo da Fonseca Bueno, Antonio Lopes de Medeiros, Manoel Dias da Silva, Antonio
do Canto de Mesquito, Antonio de Godoy Moreira, Estevão Fernandes Porto, Gabriel
Barbosa de Lima, Estevão Gomes Cabral, Gaspar Maciel Aranha, Manoel Alves de Souza e outros muitos paulistas de veneração e respeito, que constam do mesmo accordão
a fis. 117 do Liv. do registro n. 4 tit. 1658, do archivo da Camara de S. Paulo, onde
se encontram 58 pessoas assignadas ». Eis o theor da resposta: » Conheço o zelo com
que Vmes e mais ministros, camara, cidadãos e povo tratam do serviço de sua Magestade, com tão leaes vassallos seus : eu lhe representarei em todas as occasiões que se
offerecerem do augmento destas capitanias e moradores d'ellas e da parte fico com o
devido agradecimento da mercê que me fazem em abandonar as minhas acções; suppos-
hão sido cim o desejo de acertar, ás vezes não são agradecidos.

A Vmes. lhes é presente o que tenho obrado, e que me não fica que fazer por
esta banda do Sul; e não é justo que, estando no derradeiro quartel da vida, eu fique
nesta villa tratando de conveniencias proprias, quando posso occupar o tempo nas do
serviço de sua magestade, indo-me chegando á cidade do Rio oe Janeiro a dar calor á
obra dos galeões que ali está começada, porque considero que os moradores, á vista do
banJo que já mandei lanJoa e lhes pava modo ne bom governo, *accomodondo-me as suas
desconfianças*, espero que obrem como leaes vassallos, conhecendo que a minha tenção não
é mais que conservar a jurisdicção real; que supposto com ajud de Vmes e desta capitania, e zelo dos moradores della no serviço real, podia eu tratar do castigo, me con-
formo antes em obrar, *em materias do povo*, com toda a prudencia, até a resolução de
sua magestade, para com ella obrar o que me mandar.

Espero que nesta occasião e em todas as mais que se offerecerem do serviço de
sua Magestade, e por me fazerem mercê, os ache com a mesma vontade que em esta
occasião experimento—S. Paulo, 2 de Março de 1661—Salvador Corrêa de Sá Benevides »

E' um documento de grande valor politico, pela maderação que revelou o seu as-
signatario.

Algum tempo depois: El-rei dignou-se agradecer a Lourenço Castanho Taques a
intervenção de sua influencia em favor do governador geral, o referido Salvador Corrêa de Sá e Benevides.

(2) Depois de El-rei D. Pedro II. denominado o *Pacifico* que falleceu em Portugal
em 9 de Dezembro de 1706 com 59 annos de idade sendo substituido do throno por seu
filho d. João V.

(3) A dada desta carta regia é de 23 de Março de 1664, segundo Azevedo Marques,
*apontamentos historicos, geographicos, biographicos, estatisticos e noticiosos da provincia de
S. Paulo*, no nome Lourenço Castanho Taques—o pae.

Mas foi engano seu; porque a carta é do Infante D. Pedro que em 1664 ainda não
era regente.

de minas de ouro e de prata, para cuja diligencia tinha já partido Fernão Dias Paes (1), com patente de governador de sua leva ou tropa : e pois, Lourenço Castanho tomou a si, pelos seus cabedaes e força do corpo de armas, penetrar o sertão de barbarbaros indios *Cataguazes*, e entrou para esta conquista com patente de governador, com jurisdicção e poder correspondente ao caracter de sua patente, largando a serventia do officio de juiz de orphãos, que occupava por provisão, de mercê vitalicia, como tinha tido seu pae Pedro Taques.

E conseguiu o primeiro conhecimento, que depois veiu a produzir a fertilidade das minas de ouro chamadas no principio do seu descobrimento *Cataguazes*, e, depois, estendendo-se em muitas leguas de distancia, mas no mesmo sertão, os novos descobrimentos, vieram estas Minas a ficar concluidas com a nomenclatura de *Geraes*, em que se conservam. »

Sua propriedade rural era a mesma fazenda da ribeira do Ypiranga, herdada de seus paes ( 2 ).

Parece que esta propriedade abrangia, em seus limites, tudo o que mostra actualmente naquelle lugar vestigios de cultura antiga e de bemfeitorias e edificações. As sesmarias eram sempre muito extensas: e homens ricos, como Antonio de Proença, Pedro Taques e Lourenço Castanho Taques, não deixaram de as possuir nas proporções de seus cabedaes e de suas grandes forças.

---

D. Maria de Lara, tambem paulista, era filha de D. Diogo de Lara e de sua mulher D. Magdalena Fernandes Ferreira Feijá. Casou-se com Lourenço Castanho Taques, na matriz de S. Paulo—em 24 Novembro de 1631.

---

A data do texto, tirada da *Nobiliarchia Paulistana*, de Pedro Taques de Almeida Paes Leme, é a exacta; mesmo porque copiada do livro respectivo, tit. 1673, como elle declara na nota a mesma data.

Ainda mais que a carta regia, citada por Azevedo Marques, o elogiou por ter sido um dos descobridoures das Minas de *Cataguazes* e dos sertões de *Casthé*; e pois, não podia ser senão *posterior* a de 23 de Fevereiro de 1674, que recommendara-lhe essa descoberta.

(1) Veja-se a linha *A* no texto III.

(2) E' a mesma fazenda que pertencera a Antonio de Proença: Ribeira de *Ypiranga* é a mesma de *Ypiranga* tambem mencionadr por Pedro Taques de Almeida Paes Leme, *Nobiliarchia Paulistana, na Revista do Inst. Historico Brasil*, XXXIII, parte I 2.º trimestre de 1870, pag. 211.

A parte, que ficara pertencendo a Francisco de Proença. é assim descripta por Pedro Taques citado, pag. 212: « teve estabelecimento de fazenda da mesma natureza de seu pae, á qual estava contigua, cujos dilatados campos e ferteis terras se estendem em grande distancia pelas faces da ribeira de Ytiporanga, de uma parte pelo caminho de Santos até o sitio chamado *Borda do Campo*, e de outra do caminho dos carros até o Rio de Jaraigbatiba, além da freguezia de Santo Amaro.

D. Diogo de Lara, seu pae, era filho legitimo de D. Diogo Ordonhez de Lara, natural da cidade de Zamora, Hespanha, de sangue muito illustre, como consta dos autos *de genere* e outros, na camara municipal de S. Paulo. Sua mãe era D. Antonia de Oliveira.

Foi o progenitor da familia Lara, na capitania de S. Vicente e S. Paulo Era geralmente respeitado e venerado por suas virtudes. Vivia mais na egreja de Nossa Senhora do Carmo, junto ao alta-mór, onde estava o Santissimo Sacramento no sacrario, do que em sua casa. Residindo em uma quinta, que legou ao convento do Carmo, d'alli sahia vestido diariamente no habito de irmão terceiro, trazendo flores para ornar o altar de Nossa Senhora do Carmo, na capella-mór.

Fallecendo em 22 de Outubro de 1665, seu corpo foi sepultado na capella dos irmãos terceiros, com a veneração de Santo. por sua exemplar e penitente vida.

Deixou 8 filhos : Joaquim de Lara e Moraes, casado na Ilha-Grande ; Mariano do Lara, carmelita com o nome de frei Alberto do Nascimento ; Pedro de Lara e Moraes, clèrigo, tambem mudado para a Ilha-Grande ; João de Lara e Moraes, casado com D. Maria de Góes e Medeiros : D. Maria de Lara casada com Lourenço Castanho Taques : D. Anna de Lara, casada com Francisco Martins Bonilha : D. Maria Pedrosa, casada com Tristão de Oliveira Lobo ; e D. Izabel de Lara, casada com Luiz Castanho de Almeida.

D. Madaglena Fernandes Feijó, sua mãe era filha legitima de Pedro de Moraes de Antas e de D. Leonor Pedrosa. Falleceu em 18 de Julho de 1661.

Este Pedro de Moraes Antas (1) era filho legitimo de Balthazar de Moraes de Antas, com Brites Rodrigues Annes, e por sua nobreza, prende-se ao titulo dos *Braganções* (2), como bem

---

(1) Pedro de Moraes de Antas foi o fundador e primeiro padroeiro da Capella de Nossa Senhora *del Populo*, situada no bairro do Rio Grande no Caminho de S. Paulo a Santos. Pedro de Moraes de Antas falleceu, segundo Pedro Taques de Almeida Paes Leme, em 14 de Julho de 1636; mas segundo Azevedo Marques citado em Desembro de 1649. E isto elle o affirma, em formal con testação a Pedro Taques, dizendo ter lido seu testamento, e o inventario, dos quaes era guarda como primeiro escrivão de orphams de S. Paulo.

(2) D. Antonio Caetano de Souza, *Genealogia da casa real Portugueza*, e outros genealogistas fazem descender de D. Mendo Alam, senhor da villa de Bragança, casado com uma princeza armenia, os denominados *Braganções*, de Portugal. Succedeu a seu pae, no senhorio de Bragança, seu filho D. Fernando Mendes, rico homem, chamado o —velho; cujo neto D. Fernando Mendes também rico homem, denominado-o *Bragançção*, casou-se, segundo uns com D Theresa Affonso, filha illegitima de El-rei D. Affonso Henriques, segundo outros com D. Sancha Henriques, irmã do mesmo rei D. Affonso Henriques, -, segungo alguns, com D. Theresa Soares, filha de D. Soeiro Mendes—o Bom da Maia.

O citado Pedro Taques de Almeida Paes Leme, no logar supra indicado, discute todas essas historias de casamentos.

demonstrou Pedro Taques de Almeida Paes Leme, *Nobiliarchia Paulistana*, na *Revista do Instituto Historico*, *Geographico e Ethnographico do Brasil*, XXXIII, parte segunda desde pag. 27 a pag. 35.

De seu lado. D. Leonor Pedrosa era filha legitima de Estevão Ribeiro Bayão, natural da cidade de Beja (parente de Estevão Liz, morgado em Villa Real) e de sua mulher, D Magdalena Fernandes Feijó de Madureira, natural do Porto, donde veio para S. Paulo, já casada (1)

A este tronco pertencem todos os religiosos da Companhia de Jesus, de appellidos *Moraes, Pedroso e Ribeiro*: e delle tambem sahiram varios familiares e commissarios do Santo Officio, cavalheiros da Ordem de Christo, fidalgos da casa real, governadores e um donatario— o conhecido e já referido Bento Maciel Parente (2), que, em 1638, foi governador do Estado do Maranhão.

Outrosim delles procede o famoso sertanista João Amaro Maciel Parente, que, em fins do seculo XVII, penetrou os sertões a Bahia (3).

Lourenço Castanho Taques, de seu casamento com D. Maria de Lara, teve 7 filhos e 3 filhas.

1.º) Lourenço Castanho Taques — o moço. Serviu os mais honrosos cargos na villa de S. Paulo. Imitando a seu pae em todas as virtudes privadas e civicas, foi como elle muito estimado e respeitado de seus concidadãos.

Tornára-se pacificador infallivel das desavenças entre os desvairados para a inimizade. Tambem tratava-se a lei da nobreza; não esquecendo nunca os preceitos christãos. Mereceu a honra de uma carta de El rei D. Pedro II. de 20 de Outubro de 1698, agradecendo-lhe os serviços e auxilios que prestára ao governador e capitão-general do Rio de Janeiro, Arthur de Sá Menezes. Depois de ter casado os filhos e dotado as filhas, «apurou o resto de sua grandeza na fundação e construcção do Recolhimento de Santa Theresa», com auxilio de dinheiro que seu irmão, o capitão-mór e alcaide-mór Pedro Taques de Almeida, prestou-lhe. Era casado com D. Maria de Araujo, natural de S. Paulo, filha legitima de Luiz Pedroso de Barros (4) capitão

---

(1) Alguns chronistas não trazem o sobrenome de *Madureira*.
(2) Este Bento Manoel Parente foi o que ficou feito prisioneiro dos hollandezes, na cidade de S. Luiz do Maranhão, vide o cap. VIII pag .. de J Mendes.
(3) Sebastião da Rocha Pitta, *America Portugueza*, a tribúe a este capitão-mór João Amaro Maciel Parente a conquista dos gentios que offendiam as villas de Cairá, Camamú e Boypeba, na Bahia, mas, Pedro Taques dit. *Nobiliarchia Paulistana*, faz restituir ao governador Estevão Ribeiro Bayão, pae do dito João de Amaro, essa proeza sem que as do de nome João Amaro, de egual natureza, sofiam prejuizo.
(4) Veja-se o texto II da linha A.

de infanteria na restauração de Pernambuco, e de D. Leonor de Siqueira Góes e Araujo, da cidade da Bahia, irman germana do desembargador João de Góes Araujo. Segundo affirma *Pedro Taques*, falleceu elle com evidentes signaes de *predestinado*, em Dezembro de 1708. Deixou descendencia; 5 filhos e 6 filhas.

1 Lourenço Castanho Taques casado com D. Anna de Araujo.

2 Maximiano Góes de Araujo casado com D. Maria de Arruda.

3 Luiz Pedroso de Barros casado com D. Agostinha Rodrigues. Tomou parte na guerra contra *Emboabas*, foi quem pelos annos de 1723 a 1725 abriu o caminho de S. Paulo até o rio *Paraná*, pelo que lhe foi conferida a mercê do habito de Christo com tença de 50$000.

4 José Pompeu Castanho casado com D. Izabel Sampaio.

5 D. Leonor de Siqueira casada com Domingos Dias da Silva que tambem tomou parte em 1709 na guerra entre os paulistas e emboabos, sendo immediato ao capitão-mór Amador Bueno da Veiga no commando dos paulistas.

D. Angela de Siqueira—casada com o Cap.ᵐ M.ᵉˡ do Rego Cabral, filhos de Francisco de Arruda Sá.

D. Maria de Araujo—casada com José de Sá e Arruda.

D. Ignacia de Góes—casada com José do Barros.

D. Theresa de Góes—casada com José Barbosa Pires.

Antonio Taques Pompeu.

D. Maria de Lara—casada com o C.ᵐ João Conçalves Fiqueira.

2.°) Francisco de Almeida Lara. Tomou ordens em Lisboa; e foi doutor e protonatario apostolico por bulla pontificia, com uso do habito prelaticio e varão de grandes virtudes.

3.°) Pedro Taques de Almeida, que é o do texto genealogico seguinte.

4.°) Thomé de Lara e Almeida. Residiu na Villa de Sorocaba. Foi casado duas vezes: a primeira, com D. Maria Pimentel, filha unica do capitão Antonio de Almeida Pimentel e sua mulher D. Lucrecia Pedroso de Barros. Deixou o capitão-mór Thomé de Lara e Almeida deste 1.° matrimonio entre outros filhos (onze) D. Lucrecia Pedrosa de Barros que foi casada com Fernando Dias Falcão, D. Luiza casada com João Antunes Maciel. (1) a segunda com D Maria de Campos deixou 5 filhos e destes só deixou geração Thomé de Lara Campos.

5.°) Diogo de Lara e Moraes. Casado com D. Izabel de Godoy filha de João Godoy Moreira e de sua mulher D. Eufe-

---

(1) Entre os descobridores das minas de Cuyabá se encontravam pessoas de grande valor, riqueza o merito como os irmãos Maciel—Lemes--Fernando Dias Falcão e outros. Confira se Azevedo Marques—citado - em os nomes *Bernando Dias Falcão* e *João Antunes Maciel* e a Publicação official do Archivo do Estado de S. Paulo vol. XIII annexos *a* pag. 171 e *E* p. 220.

mia da Costa Motta «Passou a viver na cidade do Rio de Janeiro, occupando o emprego de commissario da junta de fragatas d'El-rei».

6.°) Antonio de Almeida. Residio em seu sitio de Araçariguama districto da villa de Parnahyba, onde servio de juiz ordinario e de orphams. Era casado com D. Potencia Leite do Prado ; e apenas deixou duas filhas, as quaes casaram-se e tiveram geração. (1)

7.°) José Pompeu de Almeida. Tomou ordens em Lisboa, tambem como seu irmão Francisco de Almeida Lara. Rebellando-se contra a disciplina ecclesiastica, ausentou-se para os sertões de Paraguay, onde falleceu miseravelmente, senão de fome, devorado por alguma fera. (2)

8.°) D. Anna de Proença. Casou-se duas vezes ; a primeira com Pedro Dias Leite, (3) irmão germano do governador Fernando Dias Paes ; a segunda com Manoel de Brito Nogueira. De ambos os casamentos deixou descendencia.

9.°) D. Branca de Almeida. Casou-se com João Pires Rodrigues, «paulista de muita veneração, chamado por autonomasia *Pai da Patria*, pelo grande zelo que mostrou sempre pelos interesses do bem publico della». Entre os doze filhos, tem menção especial Pedro Taques Pires, sustentou longa e custosa pendencia contra o ouvidor e corregedor da comarca, pela infração ao alvará que garantia as duas familias Pires e Camargo seus logares de vereadores. (4) Azevedo Marques chronologia-p. 236.

10.) D. Maria de Lara. Casou-se com João de Toledo Castelhanos (5): o qual, enviuvando, contrahio segundas nupcias com D. Maria do Canto de Mesquita. D. Maria de Lara deixou numerosa descendencia.

Lourenço Castanho Taques falleceu no dia 5 de Março de 1677 ; e foi inhumado, em sepultura rasa, na egreja dos Carmelitas, no jazigo proprio que ahi dexara seu pae Pedro Taques. D. Maria de Lara tinha fallecido no dia 8 de Dezembro de 1670

---

(1) D. Maria de Lara que foi casada com João Raposo da Fonseca Leme que na ausencia de Ro rigo Cesar de Menezes para o Cuyabá em 1727 ficou governador interino ; com 2 filhos ; Anna de Ribeiro Leite que foi casada com seu tio José de Góes e Moraes — e Antonio Almeida Lara.

(2) D. Anna Ribeiro Leite que foi casada com Antonio Pedro de Barros.

(3) O Padre Manoel da Fonseca. *vida do padre Belchior de Pontes*, narra que o padre Pontes, mesmo de S. Paulo transportara-se em espirito até o lugar em que estava a morrer o padre José Pompeu de Almeida, e confessara-o.

(4) Veja-se a Linha A no texto III.

(5) Confira-se J. Mendes em suas notas genealogicas a pag. 116 e nota por sua filha . . . . . . . . . casada com . . . . . . . . . deste casal descendem os Toledos Lara. Deste casal por sua filha D. Francisca de Almeida Taques casada com Simão de Toledo Piza da Cunha e D. Anna Ribeiro descendem os actuaes *Toledo Pizas*.

(6) Confira-se J. Mendes em suas notas genealogicas a pag. 427 a 429.

## V

PEDRO TAQUES DE ALMEIDA, CASOU-SE COM D. ANGELA DE SIQUEIRA

Pedro Taques de Almeida, nobre cidadão da villa de S. Paulo, occupou ahi os principaes cargos.

Foi tambem commandante da fortaleza de Vera Cruz, de Itapema, em Santos; capitão-mór governador da capitania de S. Paulo e S. Vicente, por patente régia, 1684-1687, com jurisdicção para prover postos militares e outros cargos. Em 1704, por carta régia de 13 de Setembro, foi nomeado alcaide-mór e administrador das aldeias no real padroado.

Era muito considerado pelo governo real em Lisbôa: e, só com informação sua (1), o goverao resolvia as pendencias, demittindo e nomeando funccionarios da capitania.

Por seus conselhos foi que, não podendo continuar a visitar as aldeias, El-rei determinou que fossem governadas, cada uma dellas, por um missionario, com jurisdicção parochial para os sacramentos; havendo tambem, para administração politica e economica, um capitão-mór, um sargento-mór, e alguns capitães escolhidos entre os mesmos indigenas.

Pelos grandes serviços prestados á corôa, sempre á custa de sua fazenda e com maior zelo, El-rei D. Pedro II o tomou para fidalgo de sua ca-a, com o fôro e moradia de cavalleiro fidalgo, que era o que tinha seu ter-avô Antonio Rodrigues de Almeida. Nem disso precisava elle, porquanto, afim de provar a pureza de seu nobre sangue, requereu no juizo ecclesiastico as deligencias de genere, pelos costados de seus quatro avós, e foram expedidas as seguintes cartas requisitorias:

1.º Ao Bispo da guarda, em Portugal, para inquisições sobre a pureza de sangue de Antonio Proença, de Belmonte, moço da camara que tinha sido do infante D. Luiz.

2.ª Ao Arcebispo de Lisbôa, tambem em Portugal, quanto á pureza de sangue de Pedro Taques, de Setubal.

---

(1) Exemplo disso é a carta régia de 3 de Abril de 1709, escripta aos officiaes da camara de S Paulo
« Officiaes da camara na villa de S. Paulo — Eu el-rei vos envio muito saudar. Havendo visto a conta que me deu Pedro Taques de Almeida, sobre a incapacidade de Bento do Amaral da Silva a quem o ouvidor geral João Saraiva de Carvalho deixou em seu lugar. ausentando-se para o Rio de Janeiro por ser um homem criminoso; me pareceu ordenar-vos, como por esta faço, lhe não obedeçais, nem ao mesmo ouvidor-geral proprietario, se tornar a entrar na correição. E porque o mesmo Pedro Taques me representou a grande perturbação que causou nesse povo as *moedas falsas* que se acharam nessa capitania, vos ordeno que neste particular, procedais com aquella diligencia e cuidado que pede materia tão importante.
Escripta em Lisboa a 3 de Abril de 1709 com a rubrica de sua Magestade».

3.ª Ao bispo de Zamora, em Hespanha, quanto á pureza de sangue de D. Diogo Ordonhez de Lara.

Além destas foi expedida outra requisitoria acerca de Balthazar de Moraes de Antas, fidalgo da casa real, natural da villa de Mogadouro, tambem de Portugal.

E as sentenças proferidas pelos vigarios geraes e juizes das justificações *de genere*, do bispado do Rio de Janeiro (ainda então não havia sido creado o bispado de S. Paulo, que só o foi em 1745), existiam na respectiva camara episcopal, donde foram transferidas depois para a do bispado de S. Paulo. Tambem em juizo civel, por sentença do ouvidor geral e corregedor da camara de S. Paulo, em 16 de Maio de 1702, foi julgada a fidalguia hereditaria de seus ascendentes. E, porque a estes autos de *puritate et nobilitate probanda* juntou os instrumentos de Balthazar de Moraes de Antas, seu bisavô, processados na villa de Mogadouro em 1567 foi julgado por este costado de Moraes de Antas, tambem legitimo setimo neto de Mendes Affonso de Antas senhor donatario e alcaide-mór da villa de Vimioso, como consta dos ditos instrumentos. E dos livros genealogicos, entre os quaes tem toda a primazia a obra do conde D. Pedro consta o mesmo que foi escripto nos mencionados instrumentos de Balthazar de Moraes de Antas, «que veio casar-se em S. Paulo em 1580.» Balthazar de Moraes de Antas, com effeito casou-se em S. Paulo com D. Brites Rodrigues Annes, filha de Joanne Annes Sobrinho, e irman de outras duas que egualmente casaram se com pessoas de conhecida nobreza; e tiveram sómente dous filhos e duas filhas, entre os quaes Pedro de Moraes de Antas, já referido no texto genealogico antecedente.

Fundou e fez construir, á sua custa, na egreja da Ordem Terceira do Carmo, o altar do Carmo o altar do Senhor Bom Jesus da Bôa Morte, em talha; e um jazigo para si e sua familia. E, bem assim, fundou na egreja do mosteiro de S. Bento outro altar, de talha dourada, para a imagem de Nossa Senhora da Conceição (1). Em quanto vivo fazia celebrar nos dias 3 de Maio e 8 de Dezembro, nas egrejas do Carmo (ordem terceira) e de S. Bento, respectivamente as solennidades da Santa Cruz da Conceição.

E, para depois da sua morte, providenciou no testamento, instituindo um vinculo com a renda precisa para serem continuadas aquellas festividades; cuja administração ficou a cargo

_____

(1) Segundo Pedro Taques de Almeida Paes Leme—*Nobiliarchia Paulistana* «o pavimento todo desse altar, que é collateral ao pé do arco da capella-mór da parte da epistola, ficou pertencendo, por escriptura de transacção, ao seu fundador, para seu jazigo e o dos seus legitimos descendentes, *in perpetuum*.»

de seus descendentes por varonia, dos quaes o ultimo foi o brigadeiro Bernardo José Pinto Gavião Peixoto (1).

Concorreu com o dinheiro preciso, segundo já ficou escripto, para que seu irmão Lourenço Castanho Taques—*o moço* concluisse o Recolhimento de Santa Theresa, «com os dormitorios cêrca, egreja, côro e tudo o mais em sua ultima perfeição.»

Falleceu em S. Paulo, a 4 de Agosto de 1724; e seu corpo foi sepultado no jazigo de sua propriedade, junto ao altar do Senhor Bom Jesus da Bôa Morte (2);—em cujo campa estão abertas as armas dos *Taques, Proenças, Laras e Moraes*; em quatro quarteis dentro de um escudo, na fórma que lhe foram illuminadas no brazão, tirado em Lisbôa aos 5 de Julho de 1707, e que se não acha no livro de registro e ordens reaes da Camara municipal de S. Paulo—anno de 1721, fl 51—e archivo da Camara do Rio de Janeiro, Portugal, Rey de armas nestes Reinos e senhorios de Portugal do muito alto e poderoso Rey e senhor nosso D. João V, por graça de Deus, Rey de Portugal e dos Algarves, d'aquem e d'alem mar em Africa senhor de Guinés da conquista, navegação e commercio da Ethiopia, Arabias, Persia e da India etc.

Faço saber aos que esta minha carta de certidam do Brazam de Armas, Fidalguia e nobreza, digna de fé e crença virem que por parte do capitam-mór Pedro Taques de Almeida morador na villa de S. Paulo Capitania do Rio de Janeiro me foi feito petiçam por escripto, dizendo que pela sentença junta, que offerecia passada em nome sua Magestade e pela chancellaria da côrte e promulgada pelo Dr. Gonçalo da Cunha Villas Boas, do desembargo do dito senhor Desembargador da casa da suplicação e corregedor com alçada dos feitos e causas civeis em sua corte; consta ser elle supp.° das nobres e illustres famílias dos Taques—Proenças—Laras—Moraes, que neste Reyno são fidalgos antigos de cota de armas, por ser elle filho legitimo do capitam Lourenço costanho Taques e sua m.er Maria de Lara, naturaes e moradores na dita villa de S. Paulo: netto pela parte paterna de Pedro Taques natural de Setubal e

(1) Por effeito da lei de 6 de Outubro de 1835: comquanto o art. 3 não proteja a extincção do vinculo no caso do instituido no testamento referido no texto supra.

Tambem ha o decreto de 29 de Maio de 1837; segundo o qual «todas as disposições testamentarias, ou doações para instituições de morgados e vinculos, que se não verificaram, são havidos como não escriptos, e os bens que dellas fizeram objecto, pertencem aos herdeiros instituidores »

(2) Emquanto viveu, «fazia celebrar neste altar, todas as sextas-feiras de cada semana, uma missa, antes da qual se corria o veu que encobria a Sagrada Imagem. Havendo nesse acto doctos de incenso e na missa o mesmo», segundo o que escreveu Pedro Taques de Almeida Paes Leme, *Nobiliarchia Paulistana*.

Segundo este mesmo genealogista, «antes de dispor o seu testamento, havia o capitão-mór governador Pedro Taques, de commum accordo com sua mulher, mandado estabelecer no reino de Portugal uma missa quotidiana».

Baptisado na freguezia de Sam Juliam e de sua mulher Anna de Proenças natural da dita de S. Paulo, e pela parte materna da de Lara e da sua m.er Madalena Fernandes, naturaes da dita villa de S. Paulo epor sinão perder a memoria dos obitos des eus progenitores, e de sua antiga fidalguia e nobreza, queria elle supp.° para conservação della um brazam das armas das ditas 4 gerações; pelo que me pedia lhes mandasse passar na forma assim como elle supp.° devia mandar usar e Receberia Mercê. E visto por mim a dita sua dita petição e sentença que fica no cartorio da nobreza em poder do Escrivão que esta subscreveo, e como por ella consta estar o supp.° julgado por legitimo descendente das 4 ditas gerações do Taques — Proenças Laras e Moraes em virtude delle procurei os livros da Fidalguia e nobreza deste Reyno que em meo poder tenho, e nelles achei registradas as armas que as ditas familias pertencem, que sam as que nesta lhe dou divizadas com os metaes e cores a ellas pertencentes, a saber um escudo esquartelado posto ao Belém:

No primeiro quartel as armas dos Taques que são: escudo partido em faxa, na primeira em Campo de ouro, uma aguia Imperial de duas cabeças e sobre ella uma corôa real — o segundo em campo de prata e partido outra vez em palla; — na primeira sobre um campo verde um javali (porco montez) azul, e na segunda um penhasco azul. No segundo quartel as armas dos Proenças, que são: escudo partido em palla a primeira de campo verde com uma aguia parda de duas cabeças armado de ouro e segunda em campo azul cinco flores de liz de ouro em santor.

No terceiro quartel as armas dos Laras, que são: em campo de prata duas caldeiras pretas guarnecidas de ouro nas bocas e azas e postas em palla. No quarto as armas dos Moraes que são : escudo partido em palla, na primeira em campo sanguineo uma torre de prata picada e lavrada de preto assentada junto de um rio, com telhado de ouro e sobre ella uma bandeira de prata, na segundo em campo de prata uma amereira verde com raizes. Elmo de prata aberto e bem guarnecido de ouro. Paquife dos metaes e cores das armas. Timbre a aguia das armas dos Taques e por differença um trifoléo de sua côr·

E porque estas são as armas que ás ditas familias pertencem e eu Antonio de Aguiar Rei de armas de Portugal e principal com o poder do meu muito nobre real officio lhes dou e assim como vão no dito escudo ; das quaes armas poderá usar, como acto e prerogativo de sua nobreza e fidalguia, e com ellas gosar de todas as graças, liberdade e honras e mercês que pelos senhores Reis deste Reino foram concedidas

aos fidalgos e nobres delles. especialmente aos das ditas gerações, e com ellas poderá entrar em batalhas e em todos e qualquer actos militares assim de paz, como de guerra tanto nas
cousas graves e de necessidade, como nas volumtarias e do
passa-tempo : assim como justos torneios e em tudo o mais, que
licito e honesto for, e os poderá fazei pintar e bordar em seus
reposteiros, bandeiras, estandartes e abrir e esculpir nas bai-
xellas de sua casa e em seus asseios, sinetes e em todas as
peças de ouro e de prata pedraria e grimpas e nos portões de
suas casas e quintas; finalmente as poderá esculpir e deixar sobre sua propria sepultura. servindo-se, honrando-se e aproveitando se dellas como a sua nobreza e fidalguia convém, e como o
fazem os mais fidalgos e nobres deste Reino. Felo que requeiro
aos Dezembargadores, Corregedores, Ouridoses, Juizes e mais
justiça de sua magestade da parte do dito senhor e da minha
por bem do officicio que pertenço, e em especial mando aos
officiaes da nobreza, como juiz que sou della, Rei de armas,
arautos e passavantes, a cumpram e façam inteiramente cumprir
como por mim é determinado e julgado ; e por firmeza de tudo
vai por mim assignado com o signal publico do nome do meu
officio Lisbóa 5 de Julho de 1707 *Daniel Monteiro* o fez por
*José Duarte Salgado*, cavalheiro da casa real e escrivão de nobreza nestes Reinos e senhorias de Portugal e eu *José Duarte
Salgado* o fiz escrever—Rei de armas—proximo passado fica registrado a fls. 28 do livro grande do registro dos brazões de
nobreza.

Lisbôa 5 de Julho de 1707—*José Duarte Salggado·*
Cumpra-se e registre-se S. Paulo 12 de Julho de 1714
*Rasquinho.*
Cumpra-se *Manço.*
Cumpra-se e registre-se S. Paulo 10 de Outubro de 1714
*Abreo Castellanos, Pires, Torres.*

D. Angela de Siqueira, nascida em S. Paulo em 1648, era
filha de Luiz Pedro de Barros e de sua mulher D. Leonor de
Siqueira de Góes Araujo; elle, capitão da infanteria na restauração de Pernambuco, ella irmã germana do desembargador João
de Góes de Araujo, da cidade da Bahia.

Tambem, D. Angela de Siqueira e sua irmã D. Maria de
Araujo, ambas casaram se igualmente com dous irmãos o alcaide-mór Pedro Taques de Almeida e Lourenço Castanho Taques—*o moço.*

D. Angela de Siqueira, quando casou-se com o alcaide-mór
Pedro Taques de Almeida, já era viuva de Sebastião Fernandes Corrêa, segundo provedor e contador da fazenda real da ca-

pitania de S. Vicente e S. Paulo; de cujo matrimonio tivera um unico filho, Thimoteo Corrêa de Góes.

D. Angela de Siqueira ainda enviuvou do seu segundo marido· A ella refere-se o padre Manoel da Fonseca, na obra *Vida do Padre Belchior de Pontes XXXV.*

A' sua custa, fizera ella reconstruir a egreja do collegio dos padres da Companhia de Jesus, em S.Paulo. Falleceu em 1728.

O capitão-mór governador e alcaide-mór Pedro Taques de Almeida; de seu consorcio com D. Angela de Siqueira, teve sete filhos e um unico filho (primogenito):

1.°) José de Góes e Moraes, casado com sua sobrinha, 1834 D. Anna de Ribeiro Leite, foi sargento-mór de S. Paulo, onde tambem exerceu os maiores cargos, inclusive o de juiz ordinario, e posteriormente o de capitão-mór governador da capitania de S. Paulo e S. Vicente com patente. Foi este José de Góes e Moraes que, conforme escreveu frei Gaspar da Madre de Deus, *Memorias para a historia da capitania de S. Vicente,* II, 89, «entrou no projecto de comprar as cincoenta leguas (1) de Pedro Lopes de Souza»; mas foi atalhado em seu proposito por El-rei D. João V, como consta do alvará de 22 de Outubro de 1709 e da escriptura publica de compra de 19 de Setembro de 1711, para serem adjudicados a coroa real pelo preço de 40.000 cruzados, e mais 4.000 de luvas (2).

O vendedor foi o Marquez de Cascáes, então na posse da successão do donatario. Este acto do governo causou a José Góes de Moraes um enorme prejuizo, porque foi perdido o grande cabedal remettido a Lisboa para esta arrojada negociação. Com effeito, empregado o dinheiro em mercadorias para o commercio no Rio de Janeiro e outros lugares do Brasil, o navio que as trazia foi assaltado e tomado por piratas francezes. Não arruinou, porém, a José de Góes e Moraes este infeliz successo: porque, fundando fazendas de gado nos campos geraes, denominados de Curytiba, refez em pouco tempo aquelle prejuizo. Deixou 5 filhos.

1 Escolastica Jacintha da Ribeira Góes e Moraes, casada com o coronel Francisco Pinto do Rego, deste casal descendeu os *Pintos Gaviões.*

---

(1) Era a mesma capitania de Santo Amaro de *Guaibe*, da qual fôra capitão-mór Antonio Rodrigues de Almeida, primeiro antepassado do mesmo José de Góes e Moraes, nesta linha B.

(2) Este alvará e a escriptura publica, frei Gaspar da Madre de Deus transcreveu no fim de sua supradita obra. São dous documentos historicos de grande importancia para S. Paulo, Pernambuco e Parnahyba: porquanto o alvará explica detalhadamente a capitania de Pedro Lopes de Sousa, e dá outra explicações de valor. O capitão mór José de Góes e Moraes offereceu 40 000 cruzados e mais 4 000 de luvas Os 40 000 seriam pagos immediatamente e posto a juros para serem empregados em bens de raiz, quando se offerecesse a occasião.

2   Capitão-mór João Raposo da Fonseca Góes.
3   Anna Maria da Ribeira Góes e Moraes falleceu solteira.
4   Leonor Thereza da Ribeira Góes e Moraes casada com o coronel Manoel Antunes Bethlem de Andrade.
5   D. Maria de Lara Leite, casada com José de Góes Siqueira.

Deste casal por sua filha D. Angela de Siqueira Rendou de Quevedo casada com Diogo de Toledo Lara filha de João de Toledo Castelhano e D. Maria de Lara descendem os filhos do Dr. J. Mendes.

2) D. Appollonia de Araujo casada com Martinho de Oliveira Leitão, falleceu sem geração.

3) D. Branca de Almeida Taques; a qual casando-se com Antonio Pinto Guedes, deixou uma unica filha, D. Izabel Ribeira de Alvarenga, que apezar de casar-se duas vezes, a 1.ª com Sebastião Pinheiro, e a 2.ª com seu primo João Barbosa de Lara, não deixou descendencia.

4) D. Maria de Araujo casou-se com D. Francisco Matheus de Rendon. Do seu consorcio nasceram 2 filhos e 4 filhas.

5) D. Leonor de Siqueira Paes casada com Bartholomeu Paes de Abreu—fundindo em uma unica as linhas A e B desta genealogia, como adiante no texto será explicado.

6) D. Thereza de Araujo falleceu solteira.
7) D. Catharina de Siqueira Taques falleceu solteira.
8) D. Angela de Siqueira     »     »     »

## CAPITULO TERCEIRO

### Linha — A e B

Esta linha é a união das linhas precedentes A e B; e tem por progenitores Bartholomeu Paes de Abreu, da linha A — e D. Leonor de Siqueira Paes da linha B — filha do governador e alcaide-mór Pedro Taques de Almeida.
Esta linha A e B começou no seculo XVIII.

### I

LEONOR DE SIQUEIRA PAES CASOU-SE COM BARTHOLOMEU
PAES DE ABREU

Bartholomeu Paes de Abreu, natural da villa de S. Sebastião, filho de Estevão Raposo Bocarro e D. Maria de Abreu Pedroso Leme, todos de S. Paulo.

Foi juiz ordinario, pelos annos de 1705 e seguintes.

Naquelle anno, tendo havido um assassinato nas immedia-ções do largo do Carmo da então villa de S. Paulo no exercicio deste cargo, fez prender o assassino que era um *mameluco* (1), indo pessoalmente no logar do delicto, e sendo o criminoso con-duzido á cadeia, ao passar pelo Recolhimento de Santa Thereza, pôde agarrar-se ao ferrolho da porta principal da egreja, cla-mando pela immunidade della.

Observou Bartholomeu Paes de Abreu, e com elle a gente que havia concorrido á diligencia, que a corrente com que fôra seguro o preso não sahira das mãos dos officiaes de justiça, e portanto mandou que o conduzissem á cadêa. O vigario da vara, padre André Baruel, entendendo que o juiz ordinario menospre-sara a immunidade eclesiastica, o declarou logo por escommun-gado. Mas, Bartholomeu Paes de Abreu não quiz tambem at-tender á excomunhão, e continuou a proceder como se ella não lhe tivesse sido lançada. Então o vigario André Baruel repre-sentou, ao Bispo diocesano, carregando as côres do facto, e o bispo, que era o D. frei Francisco de S. Jeronymo, preoccupa-do com as repetidas reprosentações do vigario, aggravou ainda mais as censuras ao ponto de pretender que o juiz largasse a vara, ao que este não se submetteu, e apoiado por numeroso sequito de parentes e amigos, continuou no exercicio de seu cargo. Houve processo, que foi á Relação metropolitana da Bahia, e esta absolveu o accusado juiz, não obstante, o vigario André Baruel, apoiado pelo Bispo, não quiz cumprir o accordo do tribunal, porque chegado a epocha quaresmal, Bartholomeu Paes de Abreu fôra ao collegio dos padres jesuitas com os quaes estava de harmonia e lá se desobrigara—e apresentando ao pa-rocho a certidão de sua absolvição, este não admittio e repre-sentou ao prelado, que decidiu que a absolvição não era legiti-ma, e chegou a escrever ao juiz ordinario, que emquanto não cedesse com humildade de filho obediente da Santa Igreja pe-dindo absolvição ao vigario, ficasse certo que não lhes valeriam os recursos em que fundava as suas esperanças. Tomava já esta luta sérias proporções; os partidistas de um e de outro lado agi-tavam-se, e nestas circumstancias, o alcaide-mór Pedro Taques de Almeida sogro do juiz ordinario; o qual pelo conceito que muito merecia a El Rei, tomou o expediente de representar ao governo em Lisboa, expondo o caso e suas circumstancias, e pedíndo justiça. Não a demorou El-Rei; e pois mandou conse-lho Ultramarino expedir ordens ao Bispo para fazer levantar a

---

(1) Os europeus assim denominavam o mistiço nascido do ajuntamento da mulher india com o branco.

excommunhão, remettendo-se duas vias desta ordem, além da primeira dirigida ao Bispo ; e assim terminou esta pentencia, que alvorotou tanto a capitania naquelles tempos.

Passados alguns annos depois deste acontecimento, concebeu Bartholomeu Paes de Abreu. o projecto de abertura duma entrada que communicasse a villa da Laguna, e em requerimento datado de 23 de Março de 1720, propondo a El-rei dizia: «Acho-me com talento e cabedaes para com forças de um avultado corpo de armas, fazer entrada no Rio Grande sem a menor despeza da fazenda real, talar aquelle vasto sertão e abrir caminho pelo centro delle, demandando o rumo da comarca de S. Paulo, tendo por premio deste particular serviço, a custa de minha fazenda e risco de vida, as mercês seguintes. Ser donatario de quarenta leguas de terra, abeirando o *Rio Grande* (1) vinte para a parte do norte e vinte para a do Sul, medidos por costa, com todo o sertão que se achar pertencer a Vossa Magestade, de juro e herdade para sempre. com um padrão de 200$000, estabelecido na passagem do Rio Grande, sendo capitão-mór daquellas capitanias. Os primeiros nove annos livres de direitos os animaes que extrahir por mim ou socios meus; ser guarda-mór de quaesquer minas que se descobrirem nas vertentes do Rio Grande e serras annexas, com os mesmos ordenados que se conferio ao guarda-mór das Minas Geraes em S. Paulo».

Pareceram ao governo excessivas estas exigencias e por isso não foram acceitas; mas chegando a S. Paulo, o governador Rodrigo Cesar de Menezes procurou a Bartholomeu Paes de Abreu para entrar com elle em ajuste sobre estas proposta o que não conseguio, porque a esse tempo já se achava Bartholomeu Paes em Cuyabá, donde voltou a associar-se com seu irmão João Leite da Silva Ortiz, e Bartholomeu Bueno da Silva (2) nos lucros das descobertas das minas de Goyaz entrando com dinheiros para as despezas da expedição. Realizada porém, a descoberta das minas, não auferio Bartholomeu Paes lucro algum porque falleceu em S. Paulo de variola a 1.° de Janeiro de 1738.

Foi casado em 1.as nupcias com D. Maria Gomes Moraes filha de Gaspar de Godoy Moraes—o *Tavaymana* e D. Custodia Moreira—seg. Pedro Taquis cit XXXV 2.° trim. de 1872 em titulo —*Godoys*— pag. 362 n. 3—4.

---

(1) Este Rio Grande é o canal que communica a lagôa dos Patos com o mar, de duas leguas de extensão sobre uma de largura. A mesma lagôa, porém, foi denominada *Rio Grande* pelos primeiros navegantes; e mesmo depois tem conservado este nome.
(2) Veja linha A no texto V.
Confira-se Pedro Taques de Almeida Paes Leme Nobiliarchia Paulistana na Revista do Instituto Historico, Geographico, Ethnographico do Brasil XXXIII segundo trimestre de 1870 pag. 73.

Do seu casamento em 17 de Setembro de 1701 com D. Leonor de Siqueira Paes deixou os seguintes filhos; 1) Maria Paes Leme falleceu solteira em 1750; 2) Angela Maria Paes falleceu solteira; 3) Theresa Paes da Silva casada com o mestre de campo Manoel Dias da Silva natural de S. Paulo filho do notavel Paulista Domingos Dias da Silva e de D. Leonor da Siqueira.— Manoel Dias da Silva serviu de juiz ordinario e de orphams em S. Paulo por algum tempo, deixando de seu casamento dois filhos, que foram o Dezembargador do paço Alexandre da Silva Corrêa, e D. Anna Leonor da Silva ambos fallecidos no estado de solteiros.

4). Escholastica Paes da Silva, regente do Recolhimento de Santa Theresa, muitas vezes, sob o nome de irmã Escholastica de Santa Theresa.

5). Bento Paes da Silva formado em Coimbra e fallecide de desastre na barra de Lisboa.

6). Pedro Taques de Almeida Paes Leme que é do texto genealogico seguinte:

7). Leonor Caetana de Escobar e Silva.

8). Antonio Paes da Silva Lara e Abreu.

# Origens da civilisação sul-americana, antes da conquista [1]

ENSAIO DE PHILOLOGIA AMERICANISTA, APRESENTADO AO INSTITUTO HISTORICO GEOGRAPHICO, DE SÃO PAULO

Não é nosso intuito, aqui, estudarmos a origem dos povos americanos, isto é, a sua autochtonia ou a sua procedencia primitiva da Asia ou da Europa, questão ardua, que, ha muitos seculos, absorve a attenção dos sabios e tem dado logar a tantas hypotheses e fantasias arrojadas, mas sem base scientifica, em sua maioria.

Entretanto, sempre diremos que a tendencia actual do nosso espirito é para adoptar a theoria das migrações originarias, quer da Asia, (elemento mongolico e budhista) quer da Europa, (elemento aria, representados pelos islandezes e normandos, sobretudo).

O nosso escopo verdadeiro aqui, é, porem, averiguar somente as origens das civilisações pre-incasica, no Perú, e chibcha ou muysca, no Equador e Columbia, ista é, se ellas constituem centros de cultura originaes e independentes de outras, ou se, pelo contrario, procedem de uma fonte commum, em época remotissima, ramificando-se e differenciando-se profundamente no decurso de seculos, pelas migrações e fusões de povos differentes.

E' hoje, como se sabe, opinião acceita pela grande maioria dos americanistas, que se deve procurar, no planalto bolivio-peruano, o *habitat* dos povos e tribus que se disseminaram, antes da conquista hespanhola, pelo continente sul-americano, incluidos nelles, não só os quechuas e aymaras, como os araucanos, os caraibas, os tupis-guaranys e tribus connexas.

Aquelle planalto representa, na proto-historia americana, o mesmo papel singular que o Pamir e os contrafortes do Hymalaia representaram, na proto-historia dos indo-europeus, segundo muitos autores.

As affinidades linguisticas verificadas entre o quechua-kallu e o aymará, por um lado, e o abaneenga, seus dialectos e linguas correlatas, por outro (2); as migrações dos symbolos religiosos e

---

(1) Enssaio elaborado para o Congresso scientifico latino-americano e que não alcançou em funccionamento.

(2) Baptista Caetano. *Apontamentos sobre o Abaneenga*. Rio de Janeiro, 1876, pag. 17.

amuletos de jadeite, os emblemas cruciformes, etc. *(1)*: o encontro,
em diversos pontos do Brasil, de petroglyphos e de artefactos de
cobre, de evidente origem peruana *(2)*: a identidade de certos
costumes e tradições entre as diversas tribus, separadas por grandes
distancias *(3)*; a reproducção de certas denominações geographicas
*(4)*; a analogia do *Folk-lore*: o origem commum naquelle planalto
de muitos rios caudalosos e extensos de continente—vias de communicação naturaes para as regiões cisandinas, tudo isso força a
convicção de que o referido planalto, foi, em tempos remotos, o
fóço de irradiação daquelles povos·

Donde, porem, procederam elles primitivamente, ou melhor
qual a origem das civilisações preincasica e chibcha ou muysca;
especialmente, qual a origem do povo constructor dos monumentos
de Tiahuanaco?

Sobre esse ponto, parece que tambem se vae firmando o parecer dos competentes, após muitas controversias e debates.

O estudo comparativo das linguas, da architectura, dos symbolos religiosos, das tradições e dos costumes, concernentes aos
antigos toltecas, aztecas, zapotecas e mayas, em confronto com
os monumentos e tradições de Tiáhuanaco e com os elementos
de cultura dos aymarás, quechuas e chibchas, já tem encami-
nhado muitos americanistas para a identificação das civilisações tolteca e peruana antiga.

E' fóra de duvida que, em tempos remotos, deram-se, no
Mexico e na America Central, grandes invasões e migrações,
a exemplo de que se passou, na ultima phase do imperio romano, como as incursões dos godos e hunos, e, na edade media
com as dos arabes, na Hespanha e em Byzancio·

Attestam n'o de modo evidente, as ruinas das grandiosa
cidades do Yucatan, do Honduras e as ruinas dos monumentos
de Tiahuanaco, no alto Perú, ruinas já existentes, na época das
expedições de F. CORTEZ e de PIZARRO.

Quaesquer que fossem as causas da tremenda avalanche de
nações ou de tribus, que, desde as regiões do Texas e da
California, se despenharam para o Sul, quer fóssem cataclysmas

(1) Barbosa Rodrigues. *O muirakytan e os idolos symbolicos*. 1899, 1.º vol. pag.
7 e seguintes Quiroga. *La Cruz en America*. Buenos Aires, 1901, pags. 242 e 243.
(2) Dr H Hiering *Rev. do Museu Paulista* vols. 1 ∘ pags. 125 e 151 e 6.º pags.
570    C. von Koseritz. *Bosquejos ethnologicos*. Porto Alegre, 1884, pags 63 e seguintes
(3) Dr. P Ehrenreich. *Divisão e distribuição das tribus no Brasil*, na •Rev. Petermann», de Gotha, em Abril e Maio de 1891, e *Ethnographia da America do Sul*, nos
•Archivos de Anthropologia•, 1904, ambas as memorias publicadas, em traducção, pelo
*Jornal do Commercio*, do Rio.
(4) V. F. Lopez. Geographia historica del territorio argentino, em sua *Historia
argentina*, e Lafone Quevedo. *Prologo a traducção do livro* de M. Schmidel pag. 80 e
seguintes. Vide mais: Nadaillac. *L'Amerique Préhistorique*, pags. 469 e 469.

naturaes, dissenções religiosas, invasões mongolicas, simples transbordamento de população sedenta de conquista e de saque, a verdade é que o facto se deu, chegando alguns escriptores, como D. Charnay e Moke, a traçar—o primeiro, a rota da migração tolteca, desde o golpho de California até a cidade de Copan, no Honduras, e—o segundo a descrever a migração azteca, baseado em Clavigero e em um quadro antigo in'erpretado por tradições que assignalam para essa migração o periodo que decorre de 1991 a 1245, data em que os aztecas attingiram a Chapoltepec (1).

As ruinas de Tiabunaco, sobretudo, só podem ser estudadas e classificadas pelas migrações.

Larrabure Unanue, o illustrado americanista de Lima, o mesmo qne acaba de ser nomeado ministro do Perú, perante o nosso governo, diz em seu importante livro —*Monografias historico-americanas* o seguinte :

« Me parece indudable que el territorio peruano servió de centro, entempos muy remotos, á una serie de invasiones de hombres civilisados : que los invasores debieron aliar-se unos, chocar-se otros, en sus fronteras, y instalar-se al cabo, en determinadas provincias ; pero que contribuyron todos a formar essa civilisacion original cuya marcha se ignora.»

Accrescenta elle adeante :—« Apesar de que se ha pretendido estabelecer diferencias profundas entre los monumentos peruanos y los de aquellas regiones (America Central, Yucatan e Mexico), la verdad, a mi juicio, és más bien que existen analogias que prueban haber estado dichos pueblos en contacto.» (2)

Topinard, baseado em Morton, reconhece entre os indigenas do México, Perú e Nova Granada, caracteres anthropologicos quasi identicos. (3) Opina elle pela ascendencia tolteca e nahua dos indigenas de Ancon, do Perú.

Sob o ponto de vista linguistico, basta saber se que todas as linguas americanas se baseiam no principio do *polysynthetismo* e da *incorporação*, para presumir que têm ellas uma origem commum. (4)

As differenças, entre as mesmas notadas, explicam-se, como diz o marquez de Nadaillac, pela rapidez com que se alteram e se transformam os dialectos oriundos de uma fonte commum, (5)

L. Angrand, o illustre americanista francez, de quem disse C. Wiener ser o *mais competente em tal assumpto* e cujas con-

(1) Nadaillac. Obr. cit , pags 261, 273, 274 e 590; Quiroga, obr. cit. pag. 244:
Moke — *Histoire des peuples Américains.* Bruxellas, 1847, pag. 167.
(2) *Monogr. historico-americanas.* Lima, 1893, pags. 119 e 120, 271 e 272.
(3) *L'Antropologie.* Paris, 1876, pags. 201 e 508.
(4) Hovelaque. *La Linguistique.* Paris, 1881, pags. 173 e 177.
(5) Obr. cit., pag. 264.

elusões foram adoptadas por Nadaillac, reproduzindo e desenvolvendo a hypothese genial de A. de Humboldt, depois de um estudo profundo dos monumentos de Tiahuanaco, declara o seguinte

« Le peuple qui a élevé les monuments de Tiaguanaco était une branche de la grande famille Tolteque Occidentale, d'origine Nahuatt ou Californienne á tête droite descendue veis le sud á l'epoque des grandes migrations ». (1)

Quanto aos quechuas, dá-lhes elle a origem maya, attentos os caracteres ethnologiccs e religiosos communs.

Recentemente o dr. P Ehrenreich, o sabio collaborador do expedicionario allemão C von den Steinen, em publicação nos *Archivos de anthropologia*, de Brunschweg, já citados declarou o seguinte :

« Do mesmo modo que podemos considerar uma a raça americana, independente de misturas ulteriores, ao Noroéste, procedentes da Asia, *devemos considerar a America do Norte sua patria primitiva, isto é, o theatro de sua differenciação* ». (2)

As recentes explorações do archeologo e geologo americano Edwin Walters demonstraram a existencia, ao N. O. do paiz dos choctaws, de um immenso deposito de ossos humanos, restos, segundo elle, de uma multidão de guerreiros, 60 a 100 mil talvez, mortos em combate, o que se evidencia pelo facto de estarem quasi todos os craneos fracturados ou atravessados por flexas de silex. (3)

Isso attesta as lutas dos diversos povos que se dirigiam para o Mexico e Yucatan, e depois, comprimidos pela estreiteza do Isthmo, se derramaram pelas regiões andinas.

Entre os vestigios demonstrativos dessas grandes deslocações de povos, nenhum, para nós, tem tão convincente alcance, como o da reproducção de nomes geographicos, que se apresentam indecifraveis e extranhos, em meio das linguas dos povos que habitam as localidades respectivas.

O vocabulo—*Copacabana* p. ex., é um delles, pois até hoje não pôde ser interpretado ou traduzido devidamente. Como se sabe, é esse nome dado, desde tempos immemoriaes, a uma peninsula, no lago de Titicaca, no Alto Perú, não longe das ruinas de Tiahuanaco.

O mesmo nome de *Copacabana* é dado tambem a uma povoação da Republica Argentina, junto a Tinogasta, a uma antiga

(1) *Antiquités américaines. Lettre sur les antiquités de Tiaguanaco*. Paris, 1880 pag. 44. Wiener. *Perou et Bolivie*. Paris, 1880, pag. 427 e Nadaillac cit. pag. 390.
(2) *Jornal do Commercio*. de 3 de Maio de 1905.
(3) Transcripção do *Jornal do Commercio*, Janeiro de 1898.

reducção jesuita, no territorio das Missões, e a uma praia e egreja, na cidade do Rio de Janeiro.

Por outro lado, vemos um affluente do rio Madeira (que, como se sabe, nasce no planalto bolivio-peruano), com o nome de *Capana*. De modo que, de Sul a Norte, vemos reproduzido o vacabulo, por uma transmissão regular, coincidindo com as migrações dos povos sul-americanos. (1)

Assim, o dr. P. Ehrenreich, o sabio collaborador de C. von den Steinen, em recentes publicações tem demonstrado que « a distribuição muito espalhada dos povos sul-americanos explica-se da maneira mais simples, pela *irradiação de um centro*... Tudo indica que devemos procurar o ponto do exodo dos tupis, onde ainda hoje vemos junta a massa mais compacta dessas tribus, isto é, no Paraguay e suas visinhanças, *como tambem nos pontos orientaes da Bolivia* ». (2)

Traça elle então tres linhas, como roteiro das migrações, entre aquellas, uma que segue o Madeira e o Ucayale, dirigindo-se para o Norte.

Qual póde ser, porém, a origem ou significação da palavra *Copacabana*?

Eis um problema de difficil solução.

Larrabure Unanue, o eminente americanista de Lima, já citado, em carta dirigida ao abaixo assignado, expende a opinião de que « essa palavra, assim como as de *Viracocha* e *Huaca*, são hoje indecifraveis, pois, a seu vêr, pertencem a uma lingua primitiva, cujo vocabulario e theoria grammatical se perderam ha muitos seculos ».

Nós, embóra incompetente, suggerimos, outróra, a hypothese de que esse vocabulo era *aymará*, e não, *quechua*, como o quizeram o padre Affonso Ramos e o dr. V. F. Lopes, e deveria ser decomposto, como substantivo verbal, em dois: — *Capac* e *Apana*.

Traduzimol-os então, do seguinte modo:

(*Logar onde*) *o rei* (ou *o Senhor*) *se levantou*.

Assim ligavamos a etymologia dessa palavra á lenda de *Manco Capac*, surgindo inopinadamente do lago de Titicaca, junto á peninsula de Copacabana, para fundar o imperio incasico. Démos essa interpretação, como méra tentativa philologica, em assumpto, até então completamente inexplorado, e assim foi publicado em traducção o nosso modesto trabalho, na *Revista Nacional*, de Buenos Aires (Anno 16.º vol. 1.º pag. 519 e seguintes).

---

(1) Como diz o dr. T. Sampaio, o tupi, em contacto com outras linguas americanas, não poucos vocabulos extranhos adquiriu. (Rev. do Instituto Historico Paulista vol. VI pag. 552).
(2) Rev. Petermann cit.

Acatando, porém, como devemos, a auctorizada opinião de Unanue, de que só mais tarde tivemos conhecimento, reiteramos o estudo sobre o assumpto, e hoje estamos inclinado a adoptar aquella opinião de Unanue.

Occorre, porém, um facto singular, que é digno de preoccupar a attenção dos competentes. Existem, no Honduras, ruinas de duas cidades muito importantes e antiquissimas, que, além de muito proximas uma da outra, têm nomes que, ligados, entre si, formam, com pouca alteração, o vocabulo—*Copacabana* e são—as velhas cidades de *Copan* e *Coban*.

Será essa circumstancia mera casualidade?

Não parece.

A cidade de *Coban* é referida por Stephens e por D. Charnay, como tendo sido muito antiga e importante.

Quanto a *Copan*, refere o licenciado D. Diogo Garcia de Palacio, em seu relatorio ao rei de Hespanha, sobre as provincias central-americanas, escripto em 1576, que «essa antiquissima cidade, já então, continha ruinas tão imponentes e artisticamente ornamentadas que contrastavam com o estado selvagem dos habitantes do Honduras, na occasião da conquista.

Já nessa época, estes haviam perdido toda e qualquer tradição sobre a origem e causa da decadencia daquelles edificios, pelo que se presume que são elles mais antigos do que a civilização azteca». (1)

Os monumentos de Copan, em ruinas hoje, mas attestando estas sua importancia, foram em 1891 explorados *s*eriamente por uma commissão de sabios enviada pela Universidade de Harvard, e tambem pelo inglez Madsley. (2)

A referida commissão assignalou alli ruinas que se estendem por uma superficie de sete a oito milhas de comprimento por duas de largura, e contem ruas, praças, pateos calçados, monumentos, palacios, templos, columnas e até um systema de exgottos, tudo isso demonstrando a existencia alli de uma civilização antiquissima, que a commissão presumiu até ser anterior á dos mayas.

Ora, considerando que essa cidade é assignalada por D. Charnay, fundado em tradições e chronicas fidedignas, como ultimo ponto de escala ao sul, da grande migração tolteca e nahua, é claro que essa cidade offerece grande interesse para o estudo do assumpto que nos occupa.

Brasseur de Bourbourg, fundado em Herrera, dá os *Carios*, que elle identifica aos *Nahuas*, como fundadores de Copan. (3)

(1) C. Koserits—*Bosquejos ethnologicos* pags. 47 e 48.
(2) *Rev. das Revues*, 1 de Fevereiro de 1898, *Rev. Encyclopedique*, 1892, pag. 843.
(3) *Sources da l'histoire primitive du Mexique*, pg. 13,nota 1, pg. 67 nota 1 epg. 73.

*Pan*, segundo B. de Bourbourg, significa *bandeira*, *estandarte*, e applicava-se á capital ou cidade principal ; e *Co* parece derivar do nome do Hercules dos povos daquella região—*Con* ou *Cum*, pelo que se poderia traduzir—*Copan*, por *capital do deus Con* (1)

Assim damos as razões da nossa convicção, que só cederá a prova mais convincente em contrario.

Não ignoramos que alguns ethnologos, que se têm occupado da civilização peruana, como Stubel e Uhle, Kean e G. Rialle, contestam a theoria da procedencia *tolteca* ou maya dessa civilização ; mas os seus argumentos não nos convencem, deante das demonstrações de Angrand, de C. Markham de Middendorf e outros que citámos. (2)

Sobretudo a filiação de vocabulos nos parece justificar plenamente aquella theoria, pois, como diz o sabio Frei C. de Monserrate :

« *Não é extraordinario encontrar-se na denominação geographica de algumas localidades da America, indicios que revelem o ponto de partida das populações que outróra aqui se estabeleceram*». (3)

Em conclusão, a civilização antiga sul-americana é de origem *tolteca* ou *nahua*, isto é, procede do Norte do continente e não antochtone, como querem alguns escriptores, aliás de peso.

S. Paulo, 1 de Outubro de 1905.

J. C. GOMES RIBEIRO.

———•◦●◦•———

---

(1)  Ob. cit. pag. 42.
(2)  Keane, *Ethnology*, pag. 189.
(3)  Frei C. Monserrate, *Biographia pelo Sr. Ramiz Galvão*, Appendice 28,.

# Sete de Setembro

( A' MOCIDADE DAS ESCOLAS BRASILEIRAS )

O Brasil rememora hoje a data magnificente da sua entrada para o convivio das nações livres.

Ha oitenta e tres annos, n'um dos arredores da actual e opulenta cidade de S. Paulo, nas campinas do Ypiranga, ás margens do riacho deste nome, e ao lado dessa mesma estrada de rodagem, outr'ora a unica via de communicação entre as villas de *Piratininga, Santo André da Borda da Matta* e o littoral do *Engaguassú*, desferia o principe regente, em seguida Pedro I, do Brasil e mais tarde Pedro IV, de Portugal, o brado significativo de *Independencia ou morte!* — accre-cido destas memoraveis palavras: *E' tempo... Estamos separados de Portugal.*

Antes, porém, desse brado, sello que valorisou o pacto solennissimo promanado dos desejos irreprimiveis dos nossos compatriotas daquellas éras, já tinha sido lançada em nossa Patria, cento e tantos annos atráz, a primeira pedra para a construcção do edificio magestoso da sua independencia.

A acclamação de Amador Bueno para rei de S Paulo, embora abafada pela prudencia daquelle, ou pela propria fidelidade dos paulistas. que quizeram ver nesse acto uma cavilosa machinação dos hespanhóes, como vindicta á Restauração de Portugal em 1640, segundo a versão de varios historiadores, — foi em todo o caso o echo que accordou de novo o sentimento da emancipação entre nós, embora tantos annos depois...

Villa Rica, capital de Minas Geraes, então a mais intellectual e a mais prospera capitania entre as suas irmãs, foi o quartel general desses bravos guerrilheiros das liberdades patrias e delineadores do audacioso plano da mallograda conspiração de 1789, conchavada entre José Joaquim da Maia, o sympathico e infortunado emulo de Guilherme Tell no Brasil. Alvares Maciel, Claudio Manoel da Costa, Thomaz Gonzaga, Silva Xavier, o *Tiradentes*, e outros desventurados patriotas, que sonhavam a grandeza moral de nossa terra, todos victimados pela delação ignobil de Silverio dos Reis, o judas dessa primeira e heroica tentativa de liberdade.

Em seguida ao mallogro da Inconfidencia estacionaram, mas nao morreram, os ideaes em pról da independencia, os quaes foram de novo aviventados em 1808 pelo proprio D. João VI, que assim se pronunciára em manifesto, quando a côrte portugueza se transferira para o Rio de Janeiro, por motivo da invasão napoleonica: — *ergo a vóz no seio do novo imperio que venho fundar...*

Estava dado por essa fórma o passo decisivo, revelando-se D. João VI tão açorado pela libertação da terra de Santa Cruz, quanto os rebellados de Villa Rica.

Em 7 de Setembro de 1822 o cavalheirismo, a coragem, a franqueza e a actividade de D. Pedro 1, no dizer judicioso de notavel historiador nacional, incumbiram-se de fazer o resto, isto é: — separar o Brasil de Portugal

O desejo de desmembrar o Brasil da Metropole vinha já de mui longa data como dissemos; era uma aspiração natural a que serviram de pretexto varios factos, alguns occorridos entre nós, outros passados em terras extranhas, todos constituindo fortes aculeus e precipitando os acontecimentos...

A Metropole revelava-se simplesmente imprevidente despachando para aqui certos representantes, que mantinham em continua irritação o animo dos brasileiros, os quaes não lhes podiam tolerar o espirito de auctoritarismo e de corrupção, alliado á mais completa ignorancia, degenerando tudo isso na mais ferrenha e revoltante das tyrannias.

O plano habillissimo de reconciliação, posto em pratica pelo espirito atilado de Sebastião José de Carvalho e Mello, esse extraordinario estadista, que foi conde de Oeiras e falleceu marquez de Pombal, adoptando a politica de aqui prover os brasileiros nos cargos publicos, fôra desastradamente abandonado pelos seus successores...

Não possuiam elles a invejavel subtileza de espirito de Pombal e ignoravam que o favoritismo aos interesses metropolitanos em detrimento das posses sões—traria a perda desses dominios, segundo lhes aconteceu comnosco, conforme pondera com tanto acerto W. Pessôa Allen, no seu recentissimo e valioso estudo, referente ás possessões portuguezas em Africa e intitulado — «O Imperio Portuguez», ou «A Alliança Anglo-Luza».

Não possuiam tambem, esses ridiculos reformadores dos soberbos projectos do grande Pombal, o criterio dos directores da Companhia das Indias, que dirigiam, ainda em Dezembro de 1854, ao governo britannico, as seguintes e frisantes palavras, transcriptas no citado estudo de Pessôa Allen:

«Não é favorecendo a ambição official, mas reprimindo os crimes, garantindo a propriedade, incutindo a confiança, assegurando á industria o fructo do seu trabalho, protegendo todos os individuos no pleno uso dos seus direitos, e no livre exercicio das suas faculdades, que o governo melhor ministra ao publico riqueza e felicidade.

Effectivamente o livre accesso aos cargos officiaes é principalmente valioso, quando elle é apenas *uma parte* da liberdade geral».

Realmente... o segredo do poderio da Inglaterra é oriundo precisamente desse facto: ouvir e praticar tão sensatos quão liberaes conselhos dos seus representantes.

Entre nós, entretanto, fazia-se tudo ao contrario, ao ponto do grande Antonio Vieira dirigir-se ao rei Pedro II, pedindo-lhe que nomeasse para os empregos do Brazil as pessoas da terra e não de Elvas, nem de Flandres...

«Porque este estado, tendo tantas leguas de costa e de ilhas e de rios abertos, não se ha de defender, nem póde, com fortalezas, nem com exercitos, senão com assaltos, com canôas, e principalmente com indios: e esta guerra só o sabem fazer os moradores que conquistaram isto e não os que vem de Portugal. E bem se viu por experiencia que um governador, que veio de Portugal, perdeu o Maranhão, e um capitão-mór, Antonio Teixeira, que cá se elegeu, o restaurou e isso sem soccôrro do reino. Aqui ha homens de boa qualidade que podem governar com mais justiça e tambem com mais temor; e ainda que tratem do seu interesse, sempre será com muito maior moderação, e tudo o que grangearam ficará na terra com que ella se irá augmentando: e se desfructarem as herdades, será como donos e não como rendeiros, que é o que fazem os que vem de Portugal».

Accirrando ainda mais a tendencia de emancipação dos brasileiros, surgiu o brado insurrecional de Boston, que deu em resultado a independencia da America do Norte, facto este amplamente divulgado e enthusiasticamente commentado no Brazil por varios dos seus filhos que regressavam então da Europa, onde tinham ido lapidar a intelligencia nessas grandes officinas do saber humano: as Universidades e as Academias, que aqui ainda não existiam.

A ideia sublime e santa, não obstante, dos conjurados; fôra abafada pela oppressão dos encarceramentos e por ultimo ensopada no sangue generoso do *Tiradentes!*...

Mas, doutrina Ancillon, o famoso historiographo e publicista prussiano: «Succede com o pensamento o mesmo que com a terra; a guerra póde destruir as seáras, e paralisar por algum tempo os trabalhos da cultura; mas a natureza e a alma conservam a fecundidade, e sempre tornam a reproduzir». .

Em 7 de Setembro de 1822 transformou D. Pedro I em realidade o sonho dourado dos patriotas de 1789, bem assim o açoramento de D. João VI, que afinal consubstanciavam a aspiração continua dos filhos deste paiz maravilhoso.

Entretanto, releva notar, para orgulho do velho e heroico Portugal, que este paiz nenhuma opposição odiosa fez contra a indepenpencia do Brasil, reconhecendo antes a legitimidade dos seus direitos.

A independencia fez-se devido a uma lei fatal a que não poude se furtar Portugal, como não poderam se furtar a Hesem relação ás suas colonias da America e a Inglaterra em relação aos Estados Unidos.

Cabe á sempre sublimada Luzitania a gloria de ter sido a Metropole a mais conscienciosa e liberal em face das suas colonias, apesar dos desvios de alguns dos seus representantes, verdade essa reconhecida pelo Brasil, que sempre e muito venerou a sua Mãe Patria, á qual, além do mais se sente gostosamente preso pelos laços indestructiveis da bella linguagem em que fallou Camões e do mesmo sangue que correu nas veias dos Viriato, dos Albuquerque, dos Castro Forte, dos Nun'Alvares' dos Gama, dos Pedr'Alvares Cabral e tantissimos outros, *a quem Neptuno e Marte obedeceram e em quem poder não teve a morte!*

Luciano Esteves Junior.

Limeira, 7 de Setembro de 1905.

# Viagem do Capitão General Franca e Horta a Sorocaba, Ytú e Porto-Feliz, em 1804

Ill mo e Ex mo Snr.: Acabo de chegar de uma jornada que fiz ás villas de Parnahyba, Ytú, Sorocaba, e Porto Feliz, afim de as visitar e conhecer se aquelles vassallos de Sua Alteza Real viviam satisfeitos ou opprimidos com o commando dos seus respectivos chefes, qual fosse o merecimento e conducta das pessoas em auctoridades publicas e, finalmente, para providenciar sobre os mesmos logares tudo aquillo do que o Estado e bem publico pudessem tirar algumas vantagens.

A factura de um novo caminho da villa de Ytú para esta cidade, caminho ha muitos annos projectado, mas sobre o qual eram quasi tantas as opiniões como as cabeças, foi um dos objectos que me levaram a fazer esta jornada. Ha d'aqui a villa de Ytú 18 leguas de caminho a que chamarei *velho* e se me propunha com instancia a abertura de um novo que encurtava mais de quatro (1).

Todas os informes a que mandei proceder me vinham cheio de contradicções e duvidas e a circumstancia de ser elle o canal por onde passa quasi toda a riqueza dos effeitos da Capitania obrigou a tratar este objecto com a seriedade que pedia, sustando na decisão até que occularmente o pudesse examinar.

Achei com effeito ser o caminho novo muito superior ao antigo, assim pela qualidade do seu terreno como por encurtar as ditas quatro leguas, que se me dizia, e com este desengano se está já trabalhando nelle a custa de varias pessoas interessadas na sua factura o que é de um beneficio geral para o publico e com especialidade para os conductores de assucar, por atalharem quasi um dia de jornada.

Com tudo o motivo mais forte foi a criação de duas novas irmandades de Misericordia, uma na villa de Ytú, e outra na de Sorocaba, ambas villas notaveis pela sua população, agricultura e commercio, e portanto da maior ponderação tão util estabelecimento. O zelo com que as pessoas principaes daquelles districtos me estão vendo promover a desta Capitania lhes serviu

---

1) A distancia de S. Paulo á Ytú pela estrada de rodagem era de 18 leguas; se a nova estrada encurtou 4 leguas é porque a antiga tinha 22.—(*N. da R.*)

de estimulo para imitacão e daqui se vê bem quanto é efficaz o exemplo para tudo (1).

Na villa de Ytú se lançou pedra para a fundação de dois hospitaes, um destinado aos lazaros e outro para todo o mais genero de molestias, funcção que se executou com o maior concurso e applauso do povo, trabalhando-se após disto com tanto fervor que nos poucos dias que alli estive de demora deixei quasi cheios os alicerces dos hospitaes e capellas.

O dos Lazaros foi feito quasi que a custa de um clerigo que alli ha de boa vida (2), o qual voluntariamente se me offereceu para uma tão pia obra; o outro é fundado em um edificio immediato a uma egreja que obtive para a Misericordia e Hospital pelo consentimento que deu o capitão-mór da mesma villa, administrador que era da referida capella (3).

Com igual alegria popular se lançou tambem a pedra para o hospital da villa de Sorocaba e tenho todo o fundamento de esperar que estas fundações prosigam sem intervallo e sirvam muito brevemente de asylo aos desgraçados pelo zelo e capacidade das pessoas a quem as deixei encarregadas. São ellas, na na villa de Ytú, o capitão-mór Vicente Taques e o sargento-mór Joaquim Duarte do Rego, homens que pelas suas bôas qualidades devo fazer chegarem ao conhecimenio de V. E⁴. Ambos elles são grandes servidores do Estado; ambos forcejaram quanto delles cabia para que avultasse o donativo voluntario pedido por Sua Alteza; ambos se distinguiram muito no estabelecimento que acabo de referir e ambos, de mãos dadas no exercicio do seu commando, conservam em tão perfeito socego aquella villa, que affirmo a V. Ex.⁴ ser a que menos cuidado me dá.

E' em Sorocaba o capitão-mór Francisco José de Souza, homem de estimaveis qualidades, igualmente benemerito e zeloso do real serviço, o qual além da despesa que tem feito não só offertou uma attendivel quantia a edificação daquelle hospital, mas tem promovido o haver esmola e deixar taes que posso contar haver já com que elle se complete.

O desejo de fazer conhecer quanto estes estabelecimentos são do agrado de Sua Alteza Real e de mostrar ao mesmo tempo o muito que me interesso por aquelles homens que servem com zelo e honra os postos em que se acham conservados, me

---

1) A ninguem mais do que ao auctor deste officio se póde applicar o proverbio «louvor em bocca propria é vitupério», porque o seu exemplo não aproveitava por ser um tyrano e máu administrador.
2) Padre Antonio Pacheco da Silva, sacerdote dos mais illustres do tempo.
3) Trata-so de Vicente da Costa Taques Góes e Aranha, capitão mór do Ytú de 1779 a 1825, bom poéta e latinista, de uma das mais illustres familias da capitania. (N. da R.)

obriga a supplicar a V. Ex·ᵃ haja de implorar ao mesmo Senhor a graça do habito de Christo para estes tres vassallos, que tanto se distinguem pelas suas qualidades estabelecimentos e serviços, desejando de mais a mais que, annuindo Sua Alteza a esta supplica, se especificassem na confirmação da graça os motivos que originaram, isto é, tanto pelo zelo e honra com que se portam nos deveres dos seus postos como pela parte que tiveram no instituição de um tão util e pio estabelecimento.

Faço a V. Ex.ᵃ esta rogativa olhando para o bem que dahi pode resultar a este Estado. Vejo occupados muitos destes postos, que são de consequencia nesta America, por homens indignos e sem nenhum merecimento. O premio dos bons fará entrarem em si os mais e todos acabarão de conhecer que no meu tempo só o obrar bem os pode fazer attendidos. Deste modo conseguirão delles não só a probidade precisa no desempenho dos seus deveres, mas que de boamente concorram e me ajudem e em todas aquellas disposições que exigem o augmento e o bem geral da Capitania.

Finalmente, Exm.° Senhor. visto tratar aqui de homens benemeritos e bons servidores do Estado, devo de justiça lembrar tambem a V. Exm.ᵃ Manoel Lopes da Resurreição, capitão-mór da villa de S. Sebastião, que é um vassallo raro no serviço de Sua Alteza, porque todo elle, o seu socego, os seus interesses e até a propria vida despresa para cumprir exactamente com as suas obrigações, e como é um homem de 80 annos parece justo ver em seus dias recompensados seus longos serviços. premiando-os o mesmo Senhor com o habito de uma das suas ordens, o que não sendo de dispesa para o Estado é muito conveniente para animar os homens a emprehenderem acções, de honra e magnificencia por que se distigam.·—Deus guarde a V. Ex.ᵃ S. Paulo, 30 de Outubro de 1804.— Illm·° e Exm ° Sr. Visconde de Anadia.—*Antonio José da Franca e Horta*.

## RUINAS DO GUAYRÁ

Ill.ᵐᵒ e Ex.ᵐᵒ Senhor :—Este anno passado sahiram desta praça alguns povoadores a pescar no Rio Grande (1), de onde se recolheram com perto de 300 arrobas de peixe, entre os quaes foi Salvador Leme, filho de Francisco Leme de Freitas, natural

---

(1) O Rio Grande, aqui mencionado, é o Paraná, pouco acima do salto das Sete Quedas, e a praça donde partiram os pescadores Yguatemy, em territorio de Matto Grosso, mas fundada pelos paulistas em 1766 e destruida pelos hespanhóes do Paraguay em 1777.

de Araraytaguaba, o qual, passando pela barra do rio Piquiry (1), viu enterrado da parte do sul da barra um limoeiro gallego e algumas laranjeiras doces, e para colher algumas laranjas e limões entrou dentro da barra do rio, saltou em terra e, encaminhando-se para as laranjeiras, encontrou ve~tigios de uma casa de taipas, grande, onde acharam algumas telhas inteiras e outras quebradas, e andando mais para deante encontrou uma pedra furada e parte della lavrada como para mó de moinho, e a pouca distancia vestigios de outras casas que pareciam ser de parede de mão.

Deu-me parte do que havia visto e logo preparei uma cousa e mandei ao alferes Joaquim Xavier de Moraes Sarmento e ao sargento Fabiano Alves Ferreira que navegassem desta praça em direitura ao salto do Guayrá ou Sete Quedas, que observassem o sol, porque desejava saber a altura daquelle logar, e que penetrassem o matto a rumo de nordeste para vêr se encontravam campos; mas nem uma nem outra cousa teve effeito por impedimento das chuvas, e lhe ordenei mais que, não encontrando campo subissem o rio Piquiry para vêr se por aquella parte se podiam descobrir; assim o intentaram, porém o não conseguiram tambem pela muita chuva e depois por falta de mantimentos.

No logar que acharam a pedra furada e os vestigios da casa continuaram por deante e acharam vestigios de uma larga povoação, e me affirmou o sargento Fabiano que elle andára em uma rua que lhe pareceu ter mais de meia legua, que o arruamento era regular e que a povoação estava entre o rio Piquiry e outro ribeirão que lhe passa pela parte do sul, e que occupa tambem a margem do Rio Grande e se deixa vêr distinctamente que fora cercada pela parte da campanha, porque ainda o fosso estava em todas as partes conhecido, e que fôra deste fosso tinha um arrabalde grande, encostado á parte do Piquiry, que tambem fôra cercado sobre si por ter tambem fosso semelhante ao primeiro.

Dizem os velhos desta terra que alli fôra a cidade do Guayrá, que tomára o nome de um cacique que vivia naquelle logar (2).

Com a parte que me deram o alferes e o sargento, mandei ao ajudante Manuel José Alberto (3), com 20 soldados, que se

---

(1) Riacho do Estado do Paraná, que desagua no rio Paraná acima do salto e em cuja embocadura estava *Ciudad Real*, povoação hespanhola destruida pelos paulistas nos annos de 1630—32.

(2 Os velhos da terra eram todos idos das povoações paulistas e pouco sabiam sobre as origens do Guayrá.

(3) Manuel José Alberto Pessoa, ajudante de ordens do capitão-general Dr. Luiz Antonio de Sousa; morreu de peste em Yguatemy.

arranchasse na barra do Piquiry e ao sargento Fabiano que subisse novamente o rio Piquiry até á cachoeira e dalli abrisse uma picada a rumo de leste a vêr se descobria campamha. Andou alguns dias nesta diligencia e por causa de enfermidades se recolheu á barra do Piquiry, onde delineou uma estacada, em que se está trabalhando, para cobrir aquelle destacamento de alguma invasão de indios, e nesta diligencia se descobriram mais duas mós de moinho, cada uma em differente logar da povoação. O matto é tão grande que dentro da povoação excede as mattas virgens.

Tambem me diz o ajudante Manuel José que se encontrou uma bella fonte de agua e mostrou ser tão bôa que logo a tropa della bebeu, preservou aos sãos e sararam os enfermos.

Agora proximamente mandei outra vez ao sargento Fabiano subir o rio Piquiry até á cachoeira e della, a caminho de lesnordeste, abrisse picada até encontrar campo apezar de todo o trabalho, porque sei que se ha de encontrar. Caso se encontre intento mandar romper deste campo para o porto de São Bento; si se conseguir, como desejo, brevemente mandarei amostra dos cavallos de Curityba á cidade de S. Paulo.

Denominei esta fundação com a invocação de *S. José da Pedra Furada do Piquiry*. Tenho reparado que me dizem desta povoação, primeiramente, que é divertida, alegre, amena e deliciosa; isto é quando voltam, porém quando vão é com má vontade, Praça dos Prazeres de Yguatemy, 23 de Março de 1773. Ill.ᵐᵒ e Ex.ᵐᵒ Sr. D. Luiz Antonio de Sousa.—*João Alves Ferreira.*

———

Este officio foi-nos enviado de Lisboa pelo engenheiro Alves Lima, acompanhado das seguintes notas do brigadeiro José Custodio de Sá e Faria:

« Na barra do rio Piquiry foi fundada pelos castelhanos *Ciudad Real*, no anno de 1557, que se havia mudado do outro lado logo acima do Salto grande, onde havia sido erigida no anno de 1538, com a denominação de *Cidade de Guayrá*, descobrindo-se no anno de 1773 vestigios della........

« Dentro do rio Ivahy tiveram os castelhanos *Villa Rica*, fundada no anno de 1588, e para o interior do sertão quinze aldeias dos jesuitas, que todas foram arruinadas pelos paulistas, sem ficar nem jesuita nem castelhano do Salto Grande para norte, desde o anno de 1631........

« Para segurar a fronteira do rio Paraná da parte de leste seria preciso fazer povoações nos rios Piquiry, Ivahy, Paranapanema e Tieté, retiradas para o interior do sertão, em paragens onde não chegassem as epidemias do rio Paraná, e dando ellas reciprocamente as mãos para a defesa de qualquer irrupção que tentassem os castelhanos.........»

———

Acompanhou tambem o officio o seguinte roteiro, que é interessante e convem ser vulgarizado:

«Em o dia 9 de Julho de 1773 principiamos a nossa derrota da praça de Yguatemy, pela Guarda da Boccaina, seguindo o rumo de norte por campanha descoberta até ao ribeirão dos Bugres, onde só encontrámos alguns pantanos e ribeiras que ficaram com pontes feitas e aquelles onde não se achavam desvios ficaram com aterrados, e deste ribeirão seguimos a procura do Amambahy, cortando ou seguindo o rumo de leste por nos desviar muito o do norte. Deste passo fomos encontrando mattas e entre ellas campinas e accommodados pastos para os que seguirem este caminho com animaes.

« A este rumo caminhámos sempre, fazendo pontes e aterrados e abrindo as mattas de modo que sempre ficasse o caminho já feito e desembaraçado, por cujo motivo nos foi preciso mandar buscar o primeiro soccorro, pois a dilação do serviço nos faz dilatado o tempo, e chegado que foi o soccorro caminhámos para deante e chegando ao dito rio Amambahy explorou-se a navegação delle e achou-se sem o minimo inpedimento até ao Rio Grande.

« Deste passo continuamos a mesma derrota do caminho, fazendo-o com toda a perfeição até chegarmos ao rio Avenhauma ou Tres Barras, achando sempre mattas e campinas accommodadas para os pousos. e chegámos a esse rio com nove mezes de dilação pelo grande trabalho da factura do caminho a assentos dos desvios dos pantanos, em cuja diligencia se gastou muitos dias.

« Deste rio Avenhauma sahiu uma bandeira solta, guiada por Francisco Xavier Bezerra, a procurar a barra do Rio Pardo e gastando nesta diligencia vinte dias chegou dizendo que descobrira aquelle ponto que o capitão-mór regente (1), quando veiu para esta praça, mandára assignalar em um campo cerrado que fica meia legua apartado da barra do Rio Pardo, por onde o dito regente queria que sahisse o caminho, e que mais se

———

1 João Martins de Barros, ituano distincto. fundador da colonia de Yguatemy e lá fallecido de febres palustres. O caminho de que aqui se fala corria em terreno de Matto Grosso e o Rio Grande é o Paraná, em cuja margem direita corria o caminho.
(N da R.)

certificava que não se enganára no ponto porque viu a ilha
que fica no Rio Grande, defronte da barra; e com esta certeza,
por nos acharmos falta de polvora e chumbo, unico refugio para
os que em tal diligencia andamos, me resolvi embarcado em
uma canoa que fizemos rodar pelo rio Avenheuma, e com mar-
chas violentas gastei trez dias para sahir no Rio Grande, em
um braço do Tres Barras, e seguir até á praça onde me acho.

« Este rio Avenheuma ou Tres Barras tem mais largura no
tempo presente do que o Tieté na sua maior largura; é todo
navegavel, sem cachoeira nem embaraços..........

« Por este modo supponho vencida a diligencia do caminho,
em que se julga gastar desta praça ao Rio Pardo, depois de
concluido, quinze dias de viagem pouco mais ou menos. Não
encontramos vestigios dos gentios, senão tão sómente rodar pelo
Avenheuma um remo quebrado e pedaços de cuias e da outra
parte do mesmo rio algumas abelheiras furadas, já antigas.
Persuado-me que no fim de Maio ou principio de Junho po-
deremos estar nesta praça com a diligencia finda. Praça de
Yguatemy, 26 de Março de 1774.—*Joaquim Rodrigues de Oliveira.*

# Cartas de Alexandre de Gusmão

Pelo socio desembargador Bernardo Gavião Peixoto foi offerecido ao Instituto um folheto manuscripto contendo algumas cartas de Alexandre de Gusmão, que vão publicadas em seguida. Com ainda o folheto cópias de outros documentos que vão tambem publicados por serem da penna de pessoas proeminentes e versarem sobre materia historica de interesse para os leitores.

A lettra do folheto manuscripto parece ser do marechal Arouche Rendon E' de crêr que Arouche, quando estudante de Direito na universidade de Coimbra tivesse occasião de ver em Lisbôa, as cartas de Alexandre de Gusmão e dellas tivesse extrahido as cópias que temos á vista, juntando-lhes as dos outros documentos que vão annexos.

Voltando a S. Paulo o bacharel Arouche se fez militar, subindo ás mais altas patentes, e se tornou amigo do brigadeiro Bernardo José Pinto Gavião Peixoto, que ficou senhor do manuscripto e o transmittiu ao seu filho desembargador Bernardo Gavião Peixoto, que gentilmente o offereceu ao nosso Instituto.

E' a explicação mais plausivel do facto de ser o manuscripto da lettra do marechal Arouche e de ser propriedade da familia Gavião Peixoto.

*A Redacção.*

# CORRESPONDENCIA DE ALEXANDRE DE GUSMÃO

CARTA DE D. LUIZ DA CUNHA PARA O SECRETARIO DE ESTADO DIOGO DE MENDONÇA CORTE REAL

O atteptado que commetteu a familia de Pedro Alvares Cabral, nosso Ministro na Côrte de Madrid, nos obriga a tomar as armas a tempo que gosavamos da mais deliciosa paz. As irregulares acções deste cavalheiro estão sabidas nas Côrtes da Europa por avisos de seus ministros residentes na Côrte de Madrid: nenhum delles dá razão ao de Portugal, que para todos ficou sem credito e sómente poderá encontral-o do caso como são muitos do nosso reino.

O Secretario da Enviatura e os criados que se seguiram e executaram o seu empenho merecem exemplar castigo por causarem todas estas desordens, com que perderam o Ministro, que era fidalgo bem intencionado; e chegaram os dois reinos a emprehendêr uma guerra de que se poderão seguir muitas despesas, trabalhos e perdas  Tanto se pode esperar de uma familia mal educada, sem policia e viciosa, como era a do nosso ministro segundo sentem geralmente as pessoas que o conheceram criminoro em Direito o procedimento da Côrte de Madrid com esta familia do Cabral; mas o que praticou em Lisbôa com a familia do Marquez de Capicio Castro é bem facil de arguir e me admiro querer V. S.ª persuadir-me o contrario, pois sendo a Côrte de Madrid a que foi offendida pelo insulto que os ditos criados do Cabral fizeram á sua Justiça no sitio do Pardo, espancando-a e tirando-lhe violentamente um preso, que conduziram á casa de seu amo, escandalosamente armados, e com cujo preso, réu de grave delicto, conversava publicamente á janella e á porta da rua do secretario de Cabral, e não fazendo mais que prender a este Ministro dois criados graves e lacaios, com um moço da cosinha, mandou El-Rei, nosso Amo, como V S.ª confessa, prender todos os criados graves, os lacaios e os cosinheiros de Capicio Castro, deixando a este ministro sem criados para servir-se, e diz-me V. S.ª que, como a Côrte de Madrid foi a primeira neste procedimento, devia dar uma satisfação.

Extranha politica!

Eu não me atreveria a fazer similhante proposição se fosse Ministro na Côrte de Madrid; mas para que nos cansarmos? Aqui não ha mais caminho que tornarmos á ignorancia de Cabral e aos erros de sua familia, expondo que não é justo mover-se uma guerra por causa de procedimentós errados, que foram depois dos acontecimentos de Madrid os que se seguiram em Lisbôa, e isto é não tenho instado, pois o contrario não tinha logar.

Não é o intento de Castella querer conquistar Portugal, como erradamente entendem todos os nossos ministros; mas é por este modo querer satisfazer-se da injuria com que se considera gravada. Da mesma sorte não é empenhada França nesta supposta conquista; porém deseja desmanchar nossa alliança com Inglaterra e como se lhe offerece esta occasião procura ajustar-se nella a beneficio dos seus interesses.

E como no caso de fazer a guerra ignoramos todos o seu fim, por serem incertos os acontecimentos della, devemos sempre fugir de chegarmos a esse extremo, que é muito arriscado.

Eu bem me tenho cançado e não desconfio das minhas diligencias; mas para coadjuval-as necessito com muita brevidade de cem mil cruzados e das tres joias que já mencionei na minha carta precedente, as quaes bastará que sejam de valor de 30 até 40 mil cruzados, e com esta despesa de cento e trinta até cento e quarenta mil cruzados me parece venceremos a negociação, sem serem necessarios os dois milhões que nosso Amo se offerecia a despender.

Por ora não se me offerece mais que lombrar a V. S.ª que rogo a El-Rei, nosso Amo, não desattenda os dictames do Conde D Luiz e do auctor da *Instrucção* (1) que veiu para Marco Antonio, que é um chefe d'obra. Eu lh'a remmetti logo, acompanhada com os meus sentimentos. Fico á obediencia de V. S.ª, que Deus guarde como desejo.—Paris, 4 de Janeiro de 1735.

CARTA DE ALEXANDRE DE GUSMÃO PARA DIOGO BARBOSA MACHADO

Mᵗᵒ R. Sr. Diogo Barbosa Machado :— Sinto que Vm.ᶜᵉ tomasse o incommodo de procurar-me, e que o não achasse em casa e me roubasse o gosto da sua es·imavel conversação, da qual procurei aproveitar-me sem molestia sua.

Muito tenho que agradecer a Vm.ᶜᵉ occorrer-lhe o meu nome ao formar um *Catalogo dos Portuguezes Eruditos*, sendo maior o agradecimento quanto menos razão havia para que eu devesse lembrar-lhe; e supposto não desconheça ou deixe de apreciar a henra que Vm.ᶜᵉ me faz, é justo tambem que me não induza o amor proprio a abusar della.

Alguns amigos me fazem a mercê de espalhar no publico um conceito vantajoso dos meus estudos; porem como estes,

---

1) O auctor desta Instrucção tinha sido Alexandre de Gusmão.

emquanto se não dão a conhecer pelas obras, dependem de mui
pia fé para se acreditarem, não devo attribuir o estabelecimento
daquella fama senão á benevolencia dos que me a favorecem,
pois até ao presente não tenho.... posição por onde pudesse adqui-
ril-as; e fazendo contas do meu talento tenho por mui provavel
que apprenderia de todo se sabisse á luz com algum volume.

Supposta esta verdade, que sou obrigado a confessar, ainda
que me cause confusão, discorro que tambem Vm.<sup>ce</sup> se tem deixado enganar com aquella não merecida opinião, o que seria
extranhado á execução e boa critica de Vm.<sup>ce</sup> contar na Bibliotheca Luzitana, entre os auctores, um individuo que o não é.
Assim que, como não tenho que responder ao interrogatorio
principal das obras que compuz, julgo superfluo dar satisfacção
aos mais quesitos que contém a carta de Vmce.

No seu livro terei que invejar aos varões que, pelos seus
trabalhos, se fizeram merecedores dos elogios de tão discreto e
intelligente juiz e sempre conservarei uma viva lembrança do
logar que a bondade de Vmce me queria dar nelle, que será um
motivo para desejar repetidas occasiões em que possa, servindo
a Vm.<sup>ce</sup>, mostrar o meu reconhecimento. – Deus guarde a Vm.<sup>ce</sup>
muitos annos. Casa, 2 de Maio de 1740.–De Vm.<sup>ce</sup> mnito Am,°
Ven.<sup>or</sup> e Cr., *Alexandre de Gusmão.*

---

PARA O CONDE DE UNHÃO, GOVERNADOR DO REINO DO ALGARVE

Ill<sup>mo</sup>. e Ex<sup>m</sup>°. Sr.—Nesta cidade se acham presos Antonio
Fernades Pereira e Luiz José da Rosa á ordem do Corregedor
do bairro de S. Paulo pelo contrabando que lhes foi achado no
hiate por invocação *Santo Antonio,* vindo do porto dessa cidade, que é destes negociantes, a quem pertence a sua carga.

Nas perguntas que lhe fez o Corregedor confessou Antonio
Fernandes que um caixotinho de relogios inglezes pertencia a
João de Azevedo, criado particular de V. Ex.ª e provou a sua
confissão com algumas cartas do mesmo Azevedo e com duas
ordens, como portarias, assignadas por V. Ex.ª e passadas pelo
secretario do governo.

Este vergonhoso facto pedia exemplarissimo castigo se delle
se tomasse conhecimento e fosse com effeito sentenciado como
mandam as leis, pois que em todas as circumstancias é igual
inteiramente ao despotismo que praticaram os senhores acastellados e os regulos da ignorancia e barbaridade, com escandalo
e horror da humanidade, com injuria ao poder dos Reis e, o que
é mais, sem temor de Deus.

que os chamados povo e tropa da cidade de S. Paulo, instigados por alguns DESORGANIZADORES E REBELDES QUE POR DESGRAÇA DA PROVINCIA, SE ACHAM ENTRE OS MEMBROS DO SEU ACTUAL GOVERNO, se têm ultimamente, comportado : Querendo, pois, dar um prompto remedio a taes desordens e attentados, que diariamente vão crescendo, HEI POR BEM CASSAR O PRESENTE GOVERNO e orden r que os eleitores de parochias, convocados nas cabeças dos districtos, segundo o meu decreto de 3 do corrente e instrucções á elle annexas, depois de procederem á nomeação de deputados para a Assembléa Geral Constituinte e Legislativa deste reino do Brasil, passem immediatamente a nomear um governo provisorio legitimo, composto de um presidente, um secretario e cinco membros, cuja apuração se fará pelo mesmo methodo com que deve se apurar a nomeação dos deputados para a assembléa geral, na camara da capital, a qual passará logo a dar-lhe posse. A este governo provisorio, assim nomeado e installado, fica competindo toda a auctoridade e jurisdicção, que exercerá segundo as leis existentes na parte civil, economica, administrativa e policial, como uma delegação do meu poder executivo. As auctoridades a quem competir a execução deste decreto o tenham assim entendido e façam cumprir debaixo da sua maior responsabilidade. Paço, em 25 de Junho de 1822.—COM A RUBRICA DE SUA ALTEZA REAL O PRINCIPE REGENTE.—*José Bonifacio de Andrada e Silva*».

Não satisfeito com a expedição de um tal decreto, severo pelo espirito e aspero pela sua linguagem, o Principe Regente remetteu-o ao governo de S. Paulo acompanhado da seguinte portaria :

«Sendo-me presentes os vossos officios de 24 de Maio e 11 do corrente, em que me participastes que as duvidas occorreram e se vos offereceram para não cumprir as portarias de 10 e 21 de Maio, em que se vos ordenava fizesseis partir immediatamente para esta côrte ao presidente do governo e ao ouvidor nomeado para essa comarca de S. Paulo, debaixo do *falso pretexto* de que assim vos requereram o povo e tropa dessa cidade e porque assim o exigia o socego publico dessa provincia ; rogando-me por isso que houvesse de approvar similhantes medidas. Informado eu, porêm, dos verdadeiros motivos que deram causa ao motim de 23 do dito mez, em que a tropa miliciana e *um punhado de miseraveis e facciosos dentre o povo* INSTIGADOS E SEDUZIDOS POR ALGUNS DE VÓS E OUTROS VOSSOS APANIGUADOS, com manifesta desobediencia e rebeldia á minha real auctoridade, como Principe Regente deste reino do Brasil e seu Perpetuo Defensor, e contra o juramento que me prestastes no dia da installação desse governo : Portanto, desejando eu que fique para sempre illibada a honra dessa briosa e leal provincia de S. Paulo, a que eu e este reino tanto devemos pela fidelidade e energia dos seus sentimentos e nobres acções, vos ordeno que logo, logo deis fiel e prompta execução ás ditas portarias, acima mencionadas, debaixo da mais rigorosa responsabilidade para commigo e para com a Assembléa Geral Constituinte e Legislativa que mandei convocar. O que me pareeeu participar-vos para vossa cabal intelligencia e fiel execução. Escripta no Palacio do Rio de Janeiro em 25 de Junho de 1822.—PRINCIPE REGENTE.—*José Bonifacio de Andrada e Silva.*

Estavam cassados os poderes do governo sedicioso de São Paulo, nos termos os mais aviltantes, e em toda a legislação brasileira talvez não se encontre um acto de tão formal reprovação por parte de uma auctoridade superior para com um seu subordinado. Tanto o decreto como a portaria deviam ter sido recebidos pelo governo entre os dias 5 e 10 de Julho, gastando no maximo quinze dias na viagem ; porém o governo, que se achava em sessão permanente desde 29 de Maio, occultou esses documentos por varios dias e só o apresentou em sessão a 16 de Julho, mandando-lhes pôr o «cumpra-se e registe-se» accrescentando lhe João Carlos de Oeynhau-sen o seguinte com a sua assignatura :

«Recebi a intimação que muito fielmente cumprirei, e dou-me por demittido da auctoridade que só conservei até saber a real vontade do serenissimo senhor Principe Regente, que desta carta régia consta», como se tal vontade não estivesse claramente expressa na portaria de 10 de Maio, que o chamou ao Rio pela primeira vez.

Esta declaração do ultimo capitão general de S. Paulo e ex-presidente do governo provisorio não é verdadeira no seu fundo, mas é habilmente sophistica na fórma. Deixando-a escripta servia perante a posteridade de uma attenuante para o seu procedimento faccioso e de uma desculpa deante dos contempora, neos. Elle não obedeceu ao primeiro chamado do Principe Regente porque não lhe convinha, nem aos seus amigos e partidarios, deixar o governo de S. Paulo entregue a Martim e Jordão e tinha esperança de que a quéda destes paulistas e sua expulsão desta capital repercutissem no Rio em detrimento do ministro José Bonifacio e que este tambem fosse derribado do poder, não por D. Pedro, mas pelo partido retrogrado fluminense, interessado na restauração da perdida influencia portugueza.

Era corrente em S. Paulo, espalhada pelos sediciosos, a

noticia de que o elomento portuguez no Rio estava em actividade, que contava com o apoio do marechal Joaquim de Oliveira Álvares, ministro da Guerra, que se incumbiria de expulsar
do ministerio o seu collega José Bonifacio, e que Lazaro Gonçalves, commandante dos *Leaes Paulistanos*, em guarnição no
Rio, não se opporia a esta violenta medida. O proprio coronel
Francisco Ignacio e os seus officiaes fingiam estar de tal fórma
convencidos da victoria final da causa sediciosa que defendiam,
que Francisco Ignacio chegou a declarar, em logar publico e
perante pessoas gradas da cidade, que passaria o chicote em D.
Pedro, se este principe se obstinasse em conservar José Bonifacio no ministerio e o capitão Pedro Taques se propunha a ir ao
Rio realizar na pessoa do Principe Regente a ameaça de leval-o
pelas ruas da cidade amarrado á cauda do seu cavallo

Entretanto, nem a esperada esquadra portugueza vinha a
Santos se aproveitar da artilharia encravada pelo capitão Silva
Valente, nem Jose Bonifacio era apeado do poder no Rio; pelo
contrario, o general Candido Xavier vinha tomar o commando
da praça de Santos e recebia ordem de marchar sobre S. Paulo,
e Martim Francisco entrava para o ministerio, na pasta da Fazenda, fortificando a causa nacional e desalentando o espirito
dos retrogados mais prudentes e cautelosos.

Tendo-lhe falhado totalmente os calculos, entendeu João
Carlos de Oeynhausen que era tempo de abandonar os seus companheiros da sedição em S. Paulo e de tirar partido das suas
habilidades diplomaticas para evitar as más consequencias que
lhe poderia resultar de se ter feito solidario com os facciosos
desta capital. Não esperou mais tempo, deixou o governo e
partiu para o Rio de Janeiro em 21 de Julho.

No mesmo dia 16 de Julho, em que o governo de S. Paulo,
acceitou a renuncia de João Carlos da presidencia da junta go-
vernativa provincial, estando a cidade em armas e as forças de
promptidão, sob as ordens do coronel Francisco Ignacio, realisa-
va-se o casamento do ouvidor Costa Carvalho com a sogra daquelle coronel, viuva do brigadeiro Luiz Antonio. Chamado ao
Rio de Janeiro pela portaria de 21 de Maio, desobedeceu e dei-
xou-se ficar em S. Paulo, seguindo o exemplo de João Carlos
de Oeynhausen e levado pelas mesmas esperanças, porém estas
se não realizavam e a prudencia o aconselhava a que obedecesse áquelle chamado, deixando o seu procedimento futuro, no Rio,
dependente da habilidade com que, ao lado de João Carlos,
sonber-se explicar satisfactoriamente a sua franca participação nos
motins da capital paulista. Entretanto partir para um destino
desconhecido e deixar a noiva exposta no meio agitado da pro-

vincia de S. Paulo, onde ficavam o cunhado Paulo Souza e os seus irmãos capitães Bento de Barros e Francicco de Barros, capazes de influencial-a, importavam em tornar problematico o projectado casamento; realizou-o, portanto, nesse mesmo dia, 16 de Julho, e cinco dias depois partiu tranquillo para o Rio de Janeiro em companhia de João Carlos, deixando a esposa nesta cidade, para ella seguil-o mais tarde escoltada pelo seu genro, o coronel Francisco Ignacio.

Não constam dos papeis que tenho á vista, nem dos autos da devassa a que se procedeu, nem do archivo da Camara Municipal, quando os viajantes chegaram ao Rio e como foram recebidos por D. Pedro e seus ministros; porém, constam outros factos de gravidade occorridos nesta cidade e que não devem permanecer desconhecidos.

## IX

Tratando o coronel Francisco Ignacio dos preparativos da sua viagem para o Rio, em companhia de sua sogra, que lá ia se juntar ao seu joven esposo, alarmaram-se os sediciosos paulistas com a perspectiva de ficarem privados do seu chefe e representaram aos restantes membros do governo — Oliveira Pinto, Müller e Quartim, todos extraugeiros para que não consentissem nessa viagem, visto que a situação não permittia que se dispensassem os serviços daquelle coronel, que se deixou ficar na cidade e continuou no seu cargo de mantenedor da ordem e do socego publico, sem abandonar a chefia dos sediciosos.

No quartel estava em armas o batalhão de infanteria de milicia, augmentada por mulatos e negros, livres e captivos, recrutados nas ruas da cidade, todos espiritualmente dirigidos pelo padre Bernardo Conrado e pelo frade Antonio do Menino Jesus, armados de espada e trabuco e mais cheios de espirito militar do que de sentimentos evangelicos; estavam alli como excitadores de rebellião e não como capellães da força armada, nem pertenciam ao cleio paulista, parecendo terem ambos sido importados para as funcções que estavam desempenhando.

Estava a força armada servida por banquete permanente, com abundancia de vinhos generosos e mais bebidas alcoolicas suppridas pelo armazem de Gabriel Henrique Pessoa, a custa do coronel Francisco Ignacio. Os soldados sentavam-se ás mesas e eram servidos por officiaes, que se prestavam ao papel de creados e obedeciam a direcção do tenente-coronel Jeronymo Chrispim, e todos saudavam o chefe Francisco Ignacio e o mais turbulento dos sediciosos, na pessoa do capitão Pedro Taques.

Este ultimo explicava ao povo e aos soldados que os depostos Martim e Jordão não eram membros do governo, como erradamente se dissera no olficio dirigido a D. Pedro pelos sediciosos, mas dois *ladrões desavergonhados*, e a todos se procurava intimidar e irritar com a affirmação de que a tropa que vinha de Santos, sob o commando do marechal Candido Xavier, trazia ordem de levar a cidade a saque. Era necessario estimular os animos e para alcançar este fim o expediente de collocar clerigos armados e bellicosos à frente da tropa sediciosa, de encharcar esta de vinho e cachaça e de espalhar pela arraia miuda a noção de ser o marechal Candido Xavier o commandante de salteadores que vinham saquear a cidade, não podia deixar de produzir os resultados desejados, como se vê das actas continuas da sessão permanente do governo sedicioso, já por mim publicadas no vol. I dos *Documentos interessantes* do Archivo do Estado de S. Paulo.

No dia 19 de Julho á noite, foi o governo avisado pelo coronel Francisco Ignacio de estar gente do povo se reunindo no quartel em consequencia da noticia da approximação da força do general Candido Xavier, com quatro peças de artilharia, pela estrada de Santos. Esta noticia, corroborada por um aviso do commandante da povoação de S. Bernardo, dizendo que o transito da estrada estava embaraçado pela vanguarda das forças daquelle general, foi plenamente confirmada por um officio do proprio Candido Xavier, datado de Santos do dia 17 e trazido pelo coronel Joaquim Arranha Barreto, que se apresentou em palacio acompanhado pelo brigadeiro Nogueira da Gama.

Nesse officio o marechal Candido Xavier participava ao governo que marchava sobre esta capital para fazer cumprir as ordens do Principe Regente. Os membros do governo—Oliveira Pinto, Müller e Quartim,—em vez de se submetterem ao representante de um poder legal superior correram ao quartel da força armada e recommendaram ao coronel Francisco Ignacio toda a vigilancia e energia na boa ordem do quartel e em seguida resolveram que Müller, acompanhado pelo brigadeiro Nogueira da Gama, partisse pela estrada de Santos a se encontrar com o marechal Candido Xavier, a quem entregaria um officio do governo relatando os inconvenientes da sua projectada entrada nesta capital e a necessidade daquelle general fazer alto, longe da cidade, e ao mesmo tempo se fez uma proclamação no quartel aconselhando ordem aos que alli se achavam.

As tropas de Candido Xavier não podiam estar muito distantes desta cepital; entretanto, tendo-se passado muitas horas, sem que Müller e Nogueira da Gama voltassem a dar conta da sua missão, espalhou-se na cidade a idéa de que elles podiam estar presos e aventou-se no quartel a opinião de que se deveria ir libertal-os. O governo se oppoz a isso e despachou um outro emissario a Candido Xavier com *ordem* a este general para que fizesse alto e viesse elle mesmo a esta capital conferenciar com o governo, o que Candido Xavier executou na noite de 21 de Julho.

O general se apresentou em palacio, munido de uma ordem do marechal Joaquim de Oliveira Alvares, ministro da Guerra do Principe Regente, e declarou que vinha encarregado de uma commissão que devia ser desempenhada de accordo com o marechal José Arouche de Toledo Rendon e que a presença deste general se fazia necessaria. Veio Arouche ao palacio e expostas ao governo as ordens que os dois marechaes traziam de fazer cumprir as portarias de 10 de maio, que chamava João Carlos para o Rio, a de 20 de Maio, que nomeava Arouche commandante das armas da provincia, e a de 21 de Maio que ordenava a partida de Costa Carvalho para o Rio, obrigou se o governo a dar cumprimento immediato a essas portarias e o marechal Candido, por seu lado, se obrigou a voltar a Santos com as suas forças. E' o que se lê naz actas das sessões do governo.

Continuava o governo em sessão permanente desde o dia 29 de Maio e as actas das suas sessões, mal redigidas por Souza Chichorro, contém phrases arrogantes, como se os extrangeiros detentores do governo de S. Paulo estivessem tratando de egual para egual com o marechal Candido Xavier, delegado e representante immediato do Principe Regente. Assim, diz a acta, no § 30, que no officio levado por Müller o governo *exigia* que Candido Xavier fizesse alto, quando este general, que já tinha mais de cincoenta annos de serviços á sua patria, desde o descobrimento dos campos de Guarapuava em 1771 e explorações das Sete Quédas em 1786, não era homem para obecer a uma tal intimação e as tropas que trazia de Santos, sendo militares de profissão, estavam em condições de levar de vencida as forças do coronel Francisco Ignacio, composta como era de milicianos, negros e mulatos, libertos e captivos, e até de clerigos armados de espadas e de trabucos, em parte animados pelo vinho e cachaça de Gabriel Henrique Pessoa.

O brigadeiro Francisco Antonio de Paula Nogueira da Gama, que acompanhou Müller na missão perante Candido Xavier, era brasileiro de nascença e de sentimentos, muito opposto á *Bernarda* de 23 de Maio, como se vê pelo seu longo e importante depoimento na devassa que depois se tirou sobre

aquella sedição, e sua ida em companhia da Múller naquella
missão só se explica como a de um intermediario insuspeito de
que o governo sedicioso lançou mão para obter do marechal
Candido algumas concessões. Estas concessões precisavam ser
discutidas e combinadas e isto occasionou a demora da volta
de ambos, que tanto impressionou aos sediciosos, ao ponto de
se lembrarem de ir libertal-os.

No § 31 da mesma acta ainda fez o governo escrever que
mandou uma segunda embaixada ao general, com *recommendação* para fazer alto e vir pessoalmenta se apresentar em palacio
como se estivesse agora tratando com um subordinado. Convinha ao governo deixar aos posteros estas informações, todas
suas, que o apresentam sobranceiro e dominando os acontecimentos, quando a sua situação era das mais precarias, cortado
de communicações com todo o interior e com o valle do Parahyba, privado do apoio de Santos com forças inimigas e artilharia nas vizinhanças e ainda tendo abertamente contra si os melhores elementos da população civil da capital, em que se in-
cluiam a propria Camara Municipal, com o seu presidente, capitão Bento José Leite Penteado, e todo o corpo das ordenanças ou segunda reserva, tendo á sua frente o capitão- mór Eleu-
tero da Silva Prado.

Ora, um governo assim cercado de inimigos externos, ameaçado por forças militares sob as ordens de um experimentade
general, contando, com fortes antipathias na capital, tendo do
luctar com homens da ordem de Paula Souza no interior, do
general Arouche nas villas do norte, do marechal Candido em
Santos, de José Bonifacio e Martim Francisco no Rio de Janeiro e
dispondo sómente de um batalhão de milicianos inconscientemente
arrastado a figurar de sedicioso e auxiliado por alguns plebeus
recrutados nas ruas da capital e estimulados sómente pelo vinho
e cachaça e pelo temor de um saque problematico e inventado
*ad hoc* e *ad rem* era evidentemente um governo condemnado a
uma ruina certa e a uma morte ingloria.

O marechal Candido Xavier, paulista e patriota, tinha e
direito de ser generoso e de fazer aos extrangeiros facciosos do
governo a concessão de não derramar sangue dos paulistas tomando a cidade de assalto, uma vez que esses extrangeiros se
obrigavam a dar cumprimento as portarias regias, remettendo
para o Rio de Janeiro a João Carlos de Oeynthaussn e Costa
Carvalho, e dando ao merechal Arouche a posse do commando
das armas. O ex-presidente e o ouvidor, que já contavam com
esse resultado final, estavam promptos para a viagem e partiram
immediatamente para o Rio, abandonando á sua sorte os seus
companheiros de sedição.

Entretanto, retirada a força de Candido Xavier para Santos, voltaram os sediciosos a se oppor á posse do marechal Arouche, e este julgou prudente assignar um termo de desistencia de tomar aquella posse e se retirar da cidade, que continuou entregue aos revoltosos. Apesar de terem estes perdido as suas cabeças pensantes nas pessoas de João Carlos e Costa Carvalho, recobraram parte do animo perdido e tentaram chamar a si as povoações do interior e as forças armadas de que elles dispunham, mandando clandestinamente Paulo Macedo a Ytú e Porto Feliz, Pedro Taques ao valle do Parahyba e um outro emissario a Sorocaba, na esperança de ainda poder apresentar ao governo do Principe Regente uma apparencia de força que lhes trouxesse a probabilidade de uma capitulação menos desastrada.

Estas missões todas se mallograram, não tendo havido uma só povoação do interior, um só commandante de milicias e um só capitão-mór de ordenanças que se prestassem a trahir os interesses da causa brazileira no conflicto travado com os extrangeiros do governo e os retrogrados desta capital. Este facto é muito caracteristico; da clara noção da intensidade do patriotismo e sentimentos liberaes das populações paulistas e de alguma fórma explica, sinão justifica, as violencias que em Ytú, soffreu o emissario Paula Macedo considerado pela gente da confederação ytúana como delegado do odioso governo dos extrangeiros que eram em S. Paulo a personificação da ideia recolonizadora do Brasil.

O governo, esphacelado como se achava, mettido em um becco sem sahida, procurava lançar nas actas continuas das suas sessões permanentes as desculpas do seu procedimento, respeitando pouco a verdade para dar aos factos uma apparencia menos condemnavel, como se vê dos §§ 34 e 35, que convem trancrever aqui:

«34.—Chegando a noticia a este governo, no dia 26 (de Julho), que a camara de Ytú, espalhando noticias vagas e *mal fundomentadas* de que reinava a anarchia nesta cidade, ordenava aos commandantes de milicias que retivessem as praças de milicias que deveriam destacar para esta cidade no mez proximo futuro, o governo expediu logo sobre este objecto officios que providenciassem medida tão arbitraria e incompetente, enviando para este fim áquella villa o sargento-mór do regimento de *Sertanejos* Francisco de Paula Macedo.

«35.—Voltando este e participando ao governo, por officio de 5 do corrente mez de Agosto, que o seu tenente-coronel, commandante do regimento, Pedro José de Brito não quizera attender, nem dar execução ás ordens do mesmo governo, o qual asseverava estar deposto por Sua Alteza Real e que assim obrava em observancia de ordens de que se dizia munido, mas que nem mostrava, nem dizia de quem; tomou o governo a deliberação de participar aquelle successo a Sua Alteza Real por officio de 6 do predicto mez (Agosto), rogando ao mesmo Augusto Senhor viesse com promptidão á provincia para, com sua desejada presença, socegar estes tumultos—rogativa que reiterou em officio de 12 do mesmo mez por haver recebido o do tenente-coronel-commandante do regimento de milicias de Sorocaba, João Floriano da Costa, datado a 5 do mesmo e o da camara da dita villa de 6, que egualmente repugnaram cumprir as ordens do governo; e tambem por ser presente ao mesmo governo o officio original que a camara de Ytú dirigiu á desta cidade, em data de 6, com a cópia do decreto de Sua Alteza Real, em 25 de Junho proximo passado, convidando a a desobedecer ao governo e participando-lhe que ia formar um governo temporario naquella villa, até á installação do novo governo provisorio que o predicto decreto manda eleger, na falsa idéia que o actual governo estava deposto por Sua Alteza Real ainda antes da sobredita installação».

A cidade de S. Paulo estava, de facto, em completa anarchia; os facciosos e a arraia miuda, congregados no quartel e alimentados a carne, arroz, farinha *vinho* e *cachaça*, estavam sendo ensinados que a cidade ia ser levada a saque; os vereadores eram violentados, alguns a fazerem sessão e outros a fugirem da cidade, bem como a população pacifica, que tinha de se ausentar para evitar attritos com os sediciosos; o proprio coronel Francisco Ignacio, encarregado da ordem e socego da cidade, apregoava em logares publicos que passaria o chicote em D. Pedro se não despedisse José Bonifacio do ministerio; Pedro Taques ameaçava de amarrar o Principe Regente á cauda da seu cavallo, e assim passear com elle nas ruas do Rio de Janeiro, e em presença destes factos o governo dos extrangeiros em S. Paulo fazia escrever nas actas de suas sessões que a camara de Ytú espalhava noticias *vagas e mal fundamentadas* de que reinava a anarchia nesta capital!

No longo e mal redigido § 35, acima transcripto, diz o governo que appellou para a vinda do Principe Regente a S. Paulo afim de apaziguar os tumultos, que elle mesmo provocára a 23 de Maio e que vinham desgraçando a cidade até ao mez de Agosto, tendo o primeiro appello a D. Pedro sido feito a 6 de Agosto e o segundo a 12 do mesmo mez, quando a vinda do Principe era coisa já combinada desde Julho entre os confederados de Ytú e José Bonifacio. A vinda de D. Pedro se de-

morou por motivos fornecidos pela politica fluminense e essa
demora deu logar a que Paula Souza mandasse ao Rio o seu
amigo Candido Motta para expor a Martim Francisco a necessidade de apressar quanto possivel aquella vinda, como se vê
de documento datado do 23 de Julho e já publicado.

Resolvida a viagem de D. Pedro para o mez de Agosto,
partiu elle do Rio de Janeiro no dia 14, pelo caminho de terra,
e chegou a esta capital no dia 25. O governo sedicioso de S.
Paulo, que teve a noticia antecipada da vinda do Principe Regente e se conservou em sessão permanente até 17 de Agosto,
se apressou em mandar lavrar na acta de suas sessões as seguintes interessantes declarações:

« 36.º — Havendo noticias, por cartas do Rio de Janeiro, de
que Sua Alteza Real vinha com toda a brevidade a esta provincia, se deram de novo as precisas ordens para se apromptarem,
tanto pela estrada como nesta cidade, todo o necessario para o
*mais pomposo recebimento* do mesmo Augusto Senhor, e que para
isso se ajuntassem os millicianos dos cinco regimentos da cidade
e as Camaras e capitães-móres das villas mais vizinhas mandas-
sem suas deputações para cumprimentarem ao predito serenissimo
Princepe Regente.

« 37.º — Comparecendo na sessão do dia 17 do corrente o
reverendo padre João de Santa Candida, guardião do convento
da villa de Santos, da ordem de S. Francisco, que nesse dia
chegou da Côrte do Rio de Janeiro, e vertificando a proxima e
desejada vinda de Sua Alteza Real a esta cidade, onde lhe af-
firmara havia de chegar no dia 22 (pois que encarregára de
fazer apromptar os poisos), o governo, recebendo com *particular
satisfacção e agrado tão plausivel noticia*, passou a completar as
ultimas providencias para o recebimemto, nomeando uma deputação de dois de seus membros para ir ao encontro do mesmo
Augusto Senhor prestar-lhe os *mais ardentes votos do seu respeito, obediencia e homenagem* ».

Estas declarações são de 17 de Agosto de 1822 e estão assignadas por Oliveira Pinto, presidente interino, Müller, secretario, Quartim e Francisco Ignacio, unicos que restavam em
exercicio dos quinze primitivos membros do governo provisorio
de S Paulo; ellas servem para bem caracterizar a coherencia
politica destes tres extrangeiros e do seu alliado Francisco Ignacio.

Solidarios com os sedicisoos de 23 de Maio e mesmo seus
chefes pela posição que occupavam, revoltaram-se contra a ordem
de coisas estabelecida pela revolução liberal de 23 de Junho de
1821 e approvada pelo Princepe Regente pelo decreto de 30 de

Julho daquelle anno; coherentes comsigo mesmos como sediciosos, não se deram por offendidos, nem melindrados, com o decreto
e officio de 25 de Junho de 1822, que lhes cassavam os poderes,
es qualificavam *rebeldes* e de *instigadores* de *miseraveis facciosos;*
continuando a usufruir os proveitos do poder e a tirar delle todo
o partido para o apoio da causa que defendiam resistiram com
as armas nas mãos ao marechal Candido Xavier, portador das
ordens de D. Pedro; um delles, exactamente o unico brasileiro
de nascença, o coronel Francisco Ignacio, chegou mesmo a levar
o seu desembaraço revoltoso ao ponto de ameaçar D. Pedro com
o seu chicote, de longe bem entendido, mas em logar publico e
em presença de pessoas gradas, se o Princepe Regente não despedisse José Bonifacio do ministerio, emquanto o seu precioso
auxiliar Pedro Taques promettia fazel-o palmilhar as ruas do
Rio de Janeiro atado á cauda do seu ginete; e depois de tudo
isto, quando D. Pedro se resolve a vir a S. Paulo, a pedido da
confederação de Ytú, para por um termo á anarchia que vinha
assolando a provincia e desgraçando esta capital desde 23 de
Maio, são estes mesmos homens, Oliveira Pinto, Müller, Quartim
e Francisco Ignacio, que decidem festejar a sua vinda, mandar
uma commissão ao seu encontro e prestar-lhe os mais ardentes
votos de respeito, obediencia e homenagem!

O coronel Francisco Ignacio, mesmo por ser o mais compro-
mettido de todos na sedição, não sómente pelos actos que praticou, mas tambem pela linguagem violenta que empregava, foi
quem mais procurou se salientar nos festejos que se preparavam
para a recepção do Principe Regente; era militar e rico e nessa
qualidade tratou de montar a sua custa um luzido corpo de
trinta e duas praças, sob o seu commando, com que pretendia abrilhantar aquellas festas, dando-lhes especial realce.

A D. Pedro, cuja viagem era motivada pela necessidade de
restabelecer a ordem nesta provincia e syndicar dos factos deli-
tuosos aqui praticados durante mais de dois mezes, não convinha
de modo algum acceitar cumprimentos e obsequios dos deliquen-
tes e se collocar em obrigação para com elles.

Informado a tempo da natureza dos festejos com que ia ser
recebido nesta capital, mandou do caminho aviso adeantado ao
governo sedicioso de que não receberia os seus emissarios e ao
coronel Francisco Ignacio de que dispensava os seus cumpr-
mentos militares, e aos vereadores sediciosos, que assignaram as
actas de 23 e de 29 de maio, ordenou positivamente que não
figurassem nos festejos e que entregassem as suas cadeiras na
municipalidade aos camaristas transactos para estes repeesentarem
officialmente o povo paulista nas solemnidades da sua recepção.

Assim se cumpriu, e Francisco Ignacio, Siqueira Morres, Caetano Pinto e Cunha Bastos se recolheram ás suas casas, donde *assistiram* as festas pela chegada do Principe Regente .e onde naturalmente aguardavam, com aperto de coração, as consequencias pouco lisonjeiras da situação em que se achavam, que nada tinha de agradavel.

## X

D Pedro, chegando á freguezia da Penha na tarde de 24 de agosto, alli pernoitou e só na manhã do dia 25 foi que fez a sua entrada solemne nesta cidadade, onde foi recebido com grandes festas, por muito povo, tanto da capital e suas visinhanças como de Jundiahy, Campinas, Ytú Sorocaba e outros logares, com as respectivas auctoridades, todos anciosos por tributar-lhe as suas homenagens e agradecer lhe de antemão a paz e o socego que vinha restituir a esta cidade e a toda a provincia.

Para guardar a pessoa do Principe Regente contra os possiveis perigos que offerecesse uma cidade anarchisada durante longos mezes ,no meio de gente que ainda trinta dias antes ameaçava de chicote e de arrastal-o atado á cauda de um cavallo, trouxeram ytuanos um corpo de tropa, formado de gente bôa e de confiança e para a manutenção da ordem na cidade foi organizado um corpo especial denominado *guarda civica* e composto da melhor gente que havia na cidade, inclusive muitos clerigos. Eram guardas civicos, e fazim timbre de o ser, o desembargador Velloso de Oliveira, o coronel Anastacio Trancoso, depois membro do governo. Antonio da Silva Prado, depois barão de Iguape, o dr. Justiniano de Mello Franco, medico notavel naquelle tempo o cirurgião Joquim Theobaldo Machado de Vasconcellos, pae do celebre medico e grande politico Alvares Machado, o conego Ildefonso Xavier Ferreira e muitos outros clerigos liberaes e um bom numero de cidadãos mais ou menos conhecidos nesta capital, cujos nomes constam de um documento que reproduzirei depois.

Com a chegada de D. Pedro a esta cidade desappareceu o residuo do antigo governo provisorio de S. Paulo, que havia sido acclamado com tantas festas no dia 23 de Junho de 1821, que tantas illusorias esperanças havia gerado nos corações paulistas e que tantos males trouxe, immediatamente para a provincia e remotamente para todo o paiz.

Assumiu o Principe Regente o governo, restabeleceu a ordem e a união em toda a provincia e, depois de um rapido passeio a Santos, na sua volta proclamou a independencia nos campos do Ypiranga, na tarde de 7 de Setembro de 1822.

Tratando de regressar depressa para o Rio de Janeiro, onde o chamavam importantes negocios, partiu D. Pedro de S. Paulo a 10 de Setembro, deixando de aqui installado um governo provisorio, composto do bispo D. Matheus de Abreu Pereira, do marechal Candido Xavier de Almeida e Souza e do dr José Corrêa Pacheco e Silva, ouvidor da comarca da capital e ytúano de familia illustre.

Este triumvirato, por ordem superior, mandou proceder a uma devassa sobre os factos sediciosos occorridos nesta capital nos mezes de Maio a Julho daquelle anno. O magistrado que devia presidir a esse inquerito era o ouvidor Pacheco e Silva, que fazendo parte do governo, se achava impedido e foi substituido pelo dr· Antonio de Almeida Silva Freire, juiz de fóra de Santos, servindo de escrivão da devassa o dr. Manuel Joaquim de Ornellas, que depois representou importante papel na politica da provincia.

Enquanto se procedia á devassa julgou o governo que era prudente remover os indiciados desta capital para varias partes. Para o Rio de Janeiro, onde já se achavam João Carlos de Oeynhausen e Costa Carvalho, seguiram o coronel Francisco Ignacio, Oliveira Pinto, o capitão Santos Cruz, e o bellicoso frade Antonio do Menino Jesus ;—para Jundiahy foi Antonio Maria Quartim, ex-membro do Governo, e para a Cutia Amaro José Vieira, o escrivão da Ouvidoria que se fizera redactor das actas encommendadas por Costa Carvalho ;—para os lados de Faxina foi o capitão Antonio Cardoso Nogueira, o mesmo que pretendeu uma reforma prematura e o monopolio das carnes verdes nesta capital, e para Nazareth foi mandado Antonio de Siqueira Moraes, o vereador intruso que figura na acta dn 23 de Maio. O ardoroso padre Bernado Conrado, que tanto se notabilisou nas scenas do quartel, esteve algum tempo em Araçariguama, Daniel Muller em Atibaia, Paula Macedo em Campinas e Silva Telles em Piracicaba ;—Gabriel Henrique Pessoa, o fornecedor de vinho e cachaça aos sediciosos, foi a Santos, o brigadeiro Moraes Leme a Parnahyba, Oliveira Netto a Porto-Feliz e Pedro Taques a Paranaguá. Os tenentes Mamede e Pinto *Patarata* e outros facciosos de menor valia foram para varias partes, emquanto o turbulento alferes *Fadiga* conseguiu fugir para Portugal, que julgo ter sido a sua patria.

Depois dos factos de 23 de Maio André Gomes e os padres Oliveira Bueno e Paula Oliveira tiveram a imprudencia de continuar por algum tempo a figurar nas sessões do governo, dando a entender com a sua presença que sanccionavam aquella sedição ; foram por isso mandados sahir de S. Paulo, indo André Gomes passar algum tempo na Cutia, Paula Oliveira em Juquery e Oliveira Bueno na aldêa de indios do Baruery; porém a devassa que se tirou foi toda em seu favor e provou cabalmente que elles foram inteiramente extranhos á sedição e constituiam a minoria no governo.

Os autos desta devassa, que deveriam estar no cartorio da extincta ouvidoria desta capital, desappareceram durante muitos annos, assim como desappareceram tambem dos respectivos cartorios as autos relativos ao assassinato de Badaró e os referentes aos revolucionarios de 1842, que ultimamente foram encontrados em poder de particulares nesta capital e estão agora sendo aproveitados para estudos dos factos com que se relacionam. Azevedo Marques teve em suas mãos a devassa sobre a *Bernarda de Francisco Ignacio*; elle assim o declara nos seus « Apontamentos Historicos » e até copiou della mal e publicou, todo trucado, o depoimento de uma das testemunhas, o capitão Bento José Leite Penteado, que podia ser uma das melhores, por ter sido uma das victimas da sedição, e que entretanto disse pouco em relação ao muito que podia dizer.

Essa devassa, que tornou a desapparecer durante trinta annos, está hoje em meu poder e vai ser recolhida ao archivo do Instituto; faltam-lhe peças no começo, que não prejudicam o seu valor historico; mas contém os depoimentos completos de todas as testemunhas que juraram no processo—em numero de 23,—todas enumeradas desde a primeira até á ultima, com os respectivos termos de assentada. Depuzeram um brigadeiro, um tenente-coronel, dois majores, sete capitães, dois cirurgiões, quatro clerigos seculares e mais seis pessoas menos graduadas, porém bem conhecedoras dos factos e seus depoimentos serão opportunamente publicados.

Havia na devassa provas bastantes para um ministro *arbitrario*, como se dizia que era José Bonifacio, ordenar a formação de conselbos militares e fazer condemnar os sediciosos de 23 de Maio a penas quasi tão severas como as que os seus *humanos* successores applicaram a Ratcliff, Frei Caneca e outros rebeldes de Pernambuco. Os delictos eram pouco menos graves; a confederação do Equador tentára desmembrar o paiz e criar no norte uma nova nação para fugir ao dominio já conhecidamente oppressivo e immoral de Pedro I, e os sediciosos de S. Paulo pretenderam retirar a provincia do dominio ainda esperançoso do Principe Regente para recollocal-a sob o asperrimo, odiado e apodrecido regimen colonial portuguez.

Entretanto esta commettedora devassa não produziu effeito algum criminal porque, proclamada a independencia a 7 de setembro e voltado D. Pedro ao Rio de Janeiro, tratou-se imediatamente de completar a independencia do paiz proclamando-o « Imperador do Brazil », importante solemnidade que se realisou dentro de menos de um mez, a 12 de Outubro de 1822. O 7 de Setembro e o 12 de Outubro, seu complemento necessario, formam o facto mais importante e faustoso da nossa historia e mereciam bem que fossem, como effectivamente foram, o primeiro de perto acompanhado e o segundo de perto precedido por uma amnistia para os accusados de delictos politicos.

Aproveitaram-se os sediciosos de S. Paulo desse acto de generosidade do governo regencial e voltaram todos para as suas casas, com alguma experiencia a mais e curados de manias recolonizadoras, mas cheios de odios contra os confederados de Ytú, que se tinham mostrado fieis á causa nacional, e contra os ministros José Bonifacio e Martim Francisco, que os tinha feito soffrer os rigores de um curto exilio.

Durante os poucos dias de sua estada nesta capital, D. Pedro, sempre leviano e devasso, teve a infelicidade de travar conhecimento com a celebre Domitila, iniciando aqui aquellas relações illicitas que se prolongaram durante sete annos, até 1829, que o fizeram esquecer os seus deveres de chefe de familia e de primeiro magistrado da nação e que foram a causa immediata ou remota de todos os males que affligiram o seu curto reinado. Feito este fatal conhecimento, não demorou a famosa cortezã em seguir o jovem monarcha ao Rio de Janeiro, onde conseguiu assenhorear-se de tal fórma do seu irreflectido espirito que se tornou, de facto, a imperatriz do Brazil e a suprema dispensadora das graças e favores officiaes, representando na côrte fluminense papel identico ao que junto do rei Luiz XV, da França, desempenharam a marqueza de Pompadour e a condessa Du Barry.

José Bonifacio, procurando moralisar a casa imperial e excluir da direcção dos negocios publicos a influencia deleteria daquella perniciosa mulher, cahiu logo no seu desagrado e foi a primeira e a mais illustre das suas victimas.

Costa Carvalho, já então deputado constituinte e intimamente ligado aos elementos hostis ao ministerio que fez 7 de Setembro e restaurou a unidade nacional, serviu-se della para a sua meditada vingança pessoal e para a realisação dos seus planos politicos, e, segundo nos conta o chronista Vasconcellos Drumond, pagou-lhe doze contos de reis para que ella obtivesse do seu imperial amante a dissolução da Assembléa Constituinte e a deportação dos Andradas e de outros patriotas para fóra do paiz,—acto este de inaudita violencia, producto directo da *Bernada de Francisco Ignacio*, que atirou D. Pedro na senda tortuosa que devia leval-o ao 7 de Abril de 1831.

Naquelle grave momento, tendo nomeado o calumniado e perseguido José Bonifacio tutor das imperiaes creanças, que aqui ficavam entregues á revolução victoriosa, e retirado a bordo de um navio extrangeiro, que devia leval-o para sempre deste paiz, que tanto o amou e que elle tão mal serviu, só tinha D. Pedro a seu lado João Carlos de Oeynhausen, que coherente comsigo mesmo, o acompanhou a Portugal, abandonando a sua cadeira de senador do Imperio, emquanto os outros que tinham igualmente lisonjeado na prosperidade, apredrejando o sol no occaso para adorar o sol nascente, se apressavam em ir se alistar sob a bandeira vencedora de Evaristo da Veiga.

E singrando os mares a bordo da *Volage*, que o tranportou com a sua pequena comitiva para o velho mundo, o ex-imperador, ainda joven e apparentemente cheio de vida, sequestrado á roda viciada que o cercava no Rio de Janeiro e entregue á propria consciencia, teria muitas accasiões de concentrar o seu espirito, de passar em revista os tormentosos acontecimentos do seu ephemero reinado e de fazer algumas amargas considerações sobre o caracter e os methodos dos politicos de profissão e sobre as vicissitudes das coisas humanas

S. Paulo 20 de Maio de 1905.

A. DE TOLEDO PIZA.

# Episodios da Independencia

---

### JOSÉ BONIFACIO E O «FICO»

Deposto João Carlos de Oeynhausen do seu cargo de capitão-general de S. Paulo, que vinha exercendo desde 25 de
Abril de 1819, e substituido por um governo provisorio que fôra
acclamado pelos paulistas em 23 de Junho de 1821, estava a
provincia de S. Paulo em condições apparentemente boas para
caminhar na senda do progresso e alcançar aquelle gráu de
prosperidade a que lhe davam incontestavel direito a riqueza
do seu sólo, a salubridade de seu clima e a intrepida energia
dos seus filhos, tantas vezes manifestada nos lances os mais he-
roicos, que illustram a nossa historia desde o primeiro seculo
do descobrimento.

Estavam juradas as «Bases» da Constituição que as Côrtes
Constituintes de Lisboa haviam decretado para o Reino Unido
de Portugal, Brasil e Algarves; o paiz gosava de relativa tranquillidade, desde a sanguinaria suppressão da rebellião pernan-
bucana, e recebia alguns importantes melhoramentos introduzi-
dos por D. João VI, bem aconselhado pelo governo inglez e
por alguns estadistas de merito que delle se acercaram durante
os treze annos de sua permanencia no Rio de Janeiro.

Entretanto, essas mesmas Côrtes Portuguezas, que pareciam
querer romper com um longo passado de absolutismo incontrastado e do direito divino dos réis, para entrar em um regimen
novo e constitucional, estabelecido sobre principio da soberania
popular, se propuzeram a usar para com o Brasil de uma politica repressiva e retrogada, com tendencias recolonizadoras, que

não podia deixar de produzir no espirito dos brasileiros profundos desgostos e irritações, que só serviam para por em perigo a unidade da mornachia portugueza, enchendo os brasileiros de odios contra os seus irmãos de além mar e fazendo brotar os germens latentes da separação da sua colonia americana

Aquellas Côrtes forçaram D. João VI a voltar a Lisboa em Abril, de 1821, ficando no Rio de Janeiro o principe D. Pedro como regente do Brazil; dividiram as antigas capitanias do norte em circumscripções politico-administrativas, com governos autonomicos entre si e independentes do Principe Regente, mas directa e immediatamente sujeitos ao governo de Lisboa, destruindo assim a integridade territorial da colonia e applicando a ella o principio machiavelico de dividir para mais facilmente subjugar e opprimir; aboliram algumas instituições uteis fundadas no Brasil por D. João VI, e acabaram ordenando que tambem o Principe Regente voltasse para Portugal, sob o pretexto de que precisava ver algumas côrtes européas e se instruir no manejo dos negocios publicos.

A partida de D. João VI deu causa a movimentos populares e armados, que derribaram dos respectivos governos os antigos capitães-generaes, de pouca saudosa memoria, e os substituiram por juntas provinciaes ou governos provisorios acclamados pelos revolucionarios. Em S. Paulo o movimento revolucionario teve logar a 23 de Junho de 1821, e na formação do novo governo pedia o povo que nelle não entrassem «aquelles que até aqui têm sido os nossos oppressores».

Entretanto, para o novo governo entraram muitos dos «nossos antigos oppressores», por condescendencia de José Bonifacio, que fôra chamado á ultima hora para auxiliar o movimento liberal e tomar parte na selecção do pessoal que para o mesmo governo se ia escolher, e que entendia ser aquelle momento o mais proprio para se lançar um veu sobre o passado e iniciar uma éra de reconciliações, de esquecimento de odios antigos e de congraçamento geral.

Ficou este governo provisorio composto de quinze membros, sendo sómente sete brasileiros e oito extrangeiros, dos quaes seis eram militares de profissão. Os extrangeiros, militares de carreira, eram João Carlos de Ceynhausen, Oliveira Pinto, Daniel Muller, Antonio Quartim, Lazaro Conçalves e Gama Lobo, e civis eram Vergueiro e André Gomes; os membros brasileiros eram José Bonifacio, Martim Francisco, brigadeiro Rodrigues Jordão, padres Oliveira Bueno, Paula Oliveira e Felisberto Jardim, e o coronel Francisco Ignacio de Souza Queiroz.

A vida «arrastada» que levava este heterogeneo governo,

desde o seu inicio, se tornava dia a dia mais penosa pelas más noticias que vinham chegando de Lisboa, relativas ao incorrecto e inepto procedimento das Côrtes Portuguezas, para com os brasileiros, procedimento que irritava o espirito publico e augmentava os odios contra os portuguezes, em contrario aos desejos de José Bonifacio, que recommendará aos seus patricios calma e tolerancia.

A chamada do principe regente veio fazer transbordar o calix das amarguras brasileiras e de diversas partes se dirigiam petições a D. Pedro para que não abandonasse o Brasil e ficasse no Rio de Janeiro, porque a sua partida para Lisboa daria logar á separação do Brasil.

Sendo o Rio de Janeiro escala obrigada das noticias vindas de Portugal a S. Paulo, está claro que os actos acintosos e irritantes das Côrtes de Lisboa deviam ser conhecidos e produzir os seus naturaes effeitos naquella capital antes de serem conhecidos nesta cidade, tanto mais que as communicações eram difficeis e morosas, tanto por terra como por mar.

Conhecidas no Rio as ordens das Côrtes para que D. Pedro voltasse a Lisboa, moveram-se alguns cidadãos patriotas e trataram dos meios de excitar uma reacção contra aquellas exigencias, começando por se obterem das juntas governativas provinciaes, das camaras municipaes e até dos bispos convenientes representações ao principe regente para que não obdecesse áquellas ordens e se deixasse ficar no Rio, onde a sua presença era necessaria para a tranquilidade da colonia e conservação da integridade da monarchia. Para Minas Geraes foi mandado como agente Paulo Barbosa da Silva, que partiu a 20 de dezembro de 1821, e para S. Paulo veio Pedro Dias Paes Leme, depois marquez de Quixeramobim, que deixou o Rio de Janeiro a 22 de dezembro e só podia chegar a S. Paulo no fim do mez ou nos primeiros dias do mez seguinte, porque a viagem não se fazia em menos de oito dias.

Estava Pedro Dias Paes Leme apenas com dois dias de viagem e, portanto, ainda muito longe de S. Paulo, quando José Bonifacio já estava aqui em acção e a 24 daquelle mesmo mez redigia uma vigorosa e eloquente representação que, ás 11 horas da noite daquelle mesmo dia 24 de Dezembro, fez approvar pelos seus collegas do governo e remetteu ao Principe Regente, com a maxima brevidade, por um estafeta, que chegou ao Rio a 1 de Janeiro e fez a D. Pedro a entrega de mão propria do notavel manifesto ás 8 horas da noite daquelle mesmo dia.

Recebendo a representação paulista, impressionou-se D. Pedro por tal fórma com a sua leitura que, estando a partir no dia 4 de Janeiro para Lisboa o navio-correio «Infante Dom Sebastião», remetteu por elle a seu pae uma cópia daquelle importante documento, acompanhada de uma carta que começa pelas seguintes palavras:

« Meu pae e meu Senhor: — Hontem pelas 8 horas da noite, recebi de S. Paulo um proprio com ordem de me entregar em mão propria o officio que ora remetto incluso, para que Vossa Magestade conheça e faça conhecer ao soberano Congresso quaes as firmes tenções dos paulistas e por ellas conhecer quaes as geraes do Brazil».

Dava D. Pedro a entender a seu pae que a opinião dos paulistas era a synthese da opinião dos brazileiros em geral e que o sentimento de S. Paulo era a fiel expressão do sentimento geral do Brazil; estava lançado o germen do Fico, que só precisava de um momento opportuno para brotar e produzir os seus fecundos effeitos, e fôra José Bonifacio quem o semeára, dando assim o primeiro passo na senda que nos devia levar á independencia, que ainda por sua decisiva intervenção se realizou dahi a nove mezes.

Chegando o emissario fluminense Pedro Dias a S. Paulo quando a representação paulista já estava a chegar ás mãos do Principe Regente, no Rio, só restava obter as representações da Camara Municipal e do bispo para completar o pedido dos paulistas para que D. Pedro se deixasse ficar no Brazil. Estas representações da municipalidade e do bispo foram feitas no ultimo dia do anno de 1821 e só chegaram ao Rio de Janeiro depois do Fico, que teve logar a 9 de Janeiro de 1822, quando o povo carioca foi ao paço real, capitaneado por José Clemente Pereira, e a elle declarou D. Pedro que, sendo para bem de todos, ficava no Brazil.

Pretendeu José Clemente Pereira que a elle e aos seus amigos fluminenses pertence a prioridade do Fico quando elle só em principio de Janeiro de 1822 foi que obteve de D. Pedro audiencia para o dia 9 e não fez mais do que colher fructos de terreno semeado por José Bonifacio. Si a primeira idéa de resistir ás ordens das Côrtes de Lisboa brotara do cerebro de alguns fluminenses — José Mariano, José Joaquim da Rocha, Pedro Dias, Paulo Barbosa e alguns outros, o proprio José Clemente confessa que José Mariano foi á sua casa tratar disso e que elle respondera que só se moveria, como presidente que era da Camara Municipal do Rio, de accôrdo com as corporações governistas e municipaes das provincias, o que elle fez, começando a mover-se no dia 26 de Dezembro de 1822, quando José Bonifacio já estava em movimento desde 24 de Dezembro e isto sem inspiração de ninguem porque o emissario Pedro Dias só aqui chegou muito depois de feita, assignada e remettida a representação paulista.

Além desta representação, resolvera o governo collectivo de S. Prulo enviar ao Rio os seus membros Martim Francisco e Gama Lobo, em missão especial perante o Principe Regente para reforçarem com os seus argumentos pessoaes as razões dadas na representação para que D. Pedro não, partisse para Lisboa. Esta resolução fôra tomada no dia 21 de Dezembro, isto é, antes que José Clemente e os seus amigos se movessem para dirigir ao Principe Regente egual pedido.

A camara municipal de S. Paulo no dia seguinte, 22 de Dezembro, se reuniu e resolveu nomear o marechal Arouche para ir, da sua parte, apresentar ao Principe as mesmas idéias defendidas pelo governo provisorio e dirigiu-lhe o seguinte officio, que está registrado em livro da mesma Camara e que é desconhecido dos leitores:

« Illustrissimo e Excellentissimo Senhor:—Sendo de abso-
« luta necessidade que vá á côrte do Rio de Janeiro um depu-
« tado pela camara desta cidade a representar a Sua Alteza Real
« a dignidade e interesses desta provincia, que se identificam
« com os de todo o Brasil, e sendo incontestavel que em Vossa
« Excellencia, além dos sentimentos de patriota «benemerito, se
« acham como epilogadas todas as qualidades e virtudes que
« constituem o homem honrado, em sessão de hoje o nomeam
« e de bom grado o elegem para tão alto e ponderosa commis-
« são, como verá do accordam constante da copia inclusa: lou-
« vando-se, além disto, nos illustrissimos senhores deputados do
« Governo Provisorio, coroneis Martim Francisco Ribeiro de An-
« drada e Antonio Leite Pereira da Gama Lobo, a mesma ca-
« mara se lisonjeará assás de que Vossa Excellencia se queira
« della encarregar, assim como lhe assegura sua sincera e cor-
« dial gratidão. A pessoa de Vossa Excellencia guarde Deos
« muitos annos. S. Paulo, em vereação de 22 de Dezembro de
« 1821. Illustrissimo e Excellentissimo Senhor Marechal José
« Arouche de Toledo Rendon.—José de Almeida Ramos.—An-
« tonio de Siqueira Moraes.—Antonio da Silva Prado.—Antonio
« Cardoso Nogueira·—Amaro José de Moraes».

Neste mesmo dia 22 de Dezembro, por motivos que não podem ser investigados neste artigo, reuniu-se cedo o governo de S. Paulo e resolveu substituir Martim Francisco por José Bonifacio na missão que ia enviar a D. Pedro. A camara municipal que ainda se achava reunida, foi avisada immediatamente da troca e modificou de conformidade o seu officio ao mare-

chal Arouche, dirigindo lhe um outro, datado do mesmo dia e
egualmente constante do livro de registos, em que lhe participava que os seus companheiros na jornada para o Rio seriam
José Bonifacio e Gama Lobo.

A camara se limitava então a mandar a D. Pedro o seu
emissario, sem instrucção alguma particular, devendo elle proceder de accôrdo com os enviados do governo.

Por motivos diversos demoraram elles a sua partida, que
teve logar no começo do mez de Janeiro. Entretanto chegára
Pedro Dias a S. Paulo e só então foi que a camara, em 31 de
Dezembro, se resolveu a escrever uma representação a D. Pedro,
que foi redigida no mesmo sentido da representação do governo
e que devia ser levada pelo marechal Arouche. Não transcrevo
os dizeres dessa representação porque ella é longa demais para
caber aqui, mas será opportunamente publicada para elucidação
dos factos daquelles tempos.

Assegura Machado de Oliveira, no seu «Quadro Historico
da Provincia de S. Paulo», que no dia 9 de Janeiro de 1822
as commissões reunidas do Rio, Minas e S. Paulo foram ao palacio do Principe Regente e delle obtiveram a declaração de
que ficava no Brasil. Affirma José Clemente Pereira que a
commissão paulista foi esperada no Rio e que até se fizeram
preparativos de festas pera recebel a, mas que ella só lá chegou
depois do dia 9 de Janeiro. Quem está com a verdade neste
ponto é José Clemente Pereira, estando Machado de Oliveira,
aliás contemporaneo dos factos, enganado, porque os emissarios
paulistas só chegaram ao Rio nove dias depois da declaração
feita por D. Pedro ficar no paiz.

O engano de Machado de Oliveira será talvez devido ás
lacunas existentes no Archivo do Estado de S. Paulo, onde faltam
documentos importantes, livros inteiros, relativos aos factos do
tempo da independencia. Os responsaveis por estas lacunas
seriam talvez os proprios interessados que tinham ingresso franco
no mencionado archivo ou seriam os caçadores de documentos
curiosos que não respeitaram a propriedade da provincia, em
tempo em que o archivo não era um repartição organizada, como
hoje, mas um simples deposito de papeis velhos, confiado á guarda
de um famulo do palacio presidencial e accessivel a toda a gente
que nelle quizesse entrar.

O archivo da camara municipal tem os seus papeis em melhor estado e mais completos e offerece um recurso subsidiario
importante a quem se propõe a fazer investigações sobre a nossa
historia. Lá se encontra um importante documento, que Manoel
da Cunha de Azeredo Coutinho Sousa Chichorro, secretario do

governo de S Paulo em 1821-22, truncou por ordem superior, tornando-o incompleto e defeituoso, mas ainda assim de valor para a historia do tempo. E' o resumo de uma carta que José Bonifacio, Gama Lobo, e Arouche dirigiram do Rio de Janeiro ao governo de S. Paulo, narrando a sua viagem e chegada áquella capital e pedindo que o seu conteúdo seja communicado á camara municipal, de quem Arouche era delegado ; mas Sousa Chichorro, em vez de remetter á camara cópia fiel e integral da carta, cujo original não está no Archivo do Estado, como devia ou resumo bem feito, truncou-a desastradamente, remettendo aos vereadores as seguintes notas :

. . . . . . . . . . . . . . . . . .

. . . . . . Chegaram felizmente a Sepetiba, levando em sua companhia o desembargador João Evangelista, que na villa de S. Sebastião desamparou a barca de vapor, em que ia, para separar-se alguns mal intencionados que nella viajavam.

« Na côrte se desejava a chegada dos senhores deputados como um bem geral. A Princeza Real estava em Santa Cruz com seus filhos, em consequencia dos acontecimentos dos dias 11 e 12 com bastante cuidado do seu esposo. Ella tinha mandado pôr em Sepetiba tres cavallos seus para serviços dos senhores deputados, com um piquete de dois soldados e um cabo para os acompanhar ao Rio de Janeiro, com ordem de se lhe dar aviso logo que os senhores deputados chegassem, e não bastante isso já tinha ido de passeio a Sepetiba no dia 16.

« Chegou a Sepetiba a deputação em o dia 17 e como achasse ahi um carro de posta, em que tinha ido um particular nelle partiu para Santa Cruz a deputação do governo ; logo chegou mas em meio do caminho topou com Sua Alteza a Princeza, que a ella se dirigia. Conversou com os senhores deputados com summo contentamento e ainda depois de se retirar para Santa Cruz tornou a voltar a trote e a galope e conversou muito em francez com o excellentissimo senhor José Bonifacio, sendo, porém, mui notaveis as expressões : que estimaria muito que os senhores deputados vissem os seus brasileirinhos (eram seus augustos filhos e nossos adoraveis patricios) além dos quaes tinha um terceiro no ventre e que os entregaria ao cuidado dos honrados paulistas.

« Esta estimavel Princeza mandou ordem a Sepetiba para que toda a despeza que alli fizessem os senhores deputados fosse a custa da mesma senhora, favor que não foi acceito.

« Tendo já chegado a Sepetiba ás 10 horas da noite, o terceiro deputado da Camara, o sr. marechal Arouche, á 1 hora da manhã do dia 18, partiram para a cidade e pelas 9 horas da noite, com os mesmos vestidos de viagem e por uma porta particular, foram falar em S. Christovam a Sua Alteza Real, o serenissimo senhor Principe Regente por expressa ordem sua.

« Sabendo então o excellentissimo senhor José Bonifacio de Andrada da sua nomeação para secretario de Estado dos Negocios do Interior e Extrangeiros, resistiu quanto pode ao amavel Princepe, que assim e distinguia, e só aceitou na certeza de poder promover a felicidade deste reino.

« No mesmo dia 13 chegou ao Rio de Janeiro o desembargador José Teixeira da Fonseca Vasconcellos, vice-presidente do governo provisorio de Minas e doutado pela mesma provincia, está de accôrdo com os sentimentos desta provincia, que são os mesmos de Sua Alteza Real, isto é, de salvar a existencia do Reino Unido, que alguns pretendem destruir com a capa de zelo e de constituição.

« Estava a entrar uma fragata, que se dizia ser da Bahia e trazer deputados daquella provincia a Sua Alteza Real.

« A provincia do Rio de Janeiro esta no maior enthusiamo pela boa causa. Nos acontecimentos do dia 11 pegaram em armas, a mais de seis mil pessoas de todas as classes.

« Quanto a noticias da Europa, dizem que está a chegar a tropa destinada para o Rio de Janeiro e que só pcderia estar no Rio a 15 do mez de Fevereiro e que o tenente general Palmeirim a vem commandando como futuro general das armas da provincia do Rio de Janeiro·

Este extracto traz sómente a assignatura de Souza Chichorro, secretario do governo e não tem data; a carta de que, se fez este resumo tem a data de 21 de Janeiro e devia ter sido recebida nos primeiros dias de Feveriro, o resumo foi enviado á Camara no dia 4, acompanhado de · um officio que convém transcrever aqui ;

« Illmos. srs·—O Governo Provisorio, havendo recebido de seus deputados na côrte do Rio de Janeiro, o Illustrissimo senhor couselheiro José Bonifacio de Andrada e Silva, ministro e secretario de Estado dos Negccios deste Reino e Extrangeiros e o senhor coronel Antonio Leite Pereira da Gama Lobo, um officio datado de 21 de Janeiro proximo passado, escripto e assignado tambem pelo deputado dessa Camara, o sr. marechal José Arouche de Toledo Rendon, em que participam sua chegado áquella côrte e o muito bem que foram recebidos por Suas Altezas Beaes, o serenissimo senhor Principe Regente e sua augusta consorte, pedindo que esta participação seja communicada a essa Camara, o Governo remette a vossas mercês um extracto do dito cfficio para sua intelligencia e lhes dá o parabem do alto conceito em que Sua Alteza Real tem os honrados e fieis paulistas e da consideração que lhe mereceram os seus deputados·

« O governo manda agora publicar por bando que Sua Alteza Real, o serenissimo senhor Principe Regente, por portaria de 17 do mez de Janeiro, expedida pela secretaria de Estado dos Negocios deste Reino, lhe mandou participar que resolveu no dia 9 do precitado mez suspender a sua sahida de Portugal por entender, á vista das differentes representações que se dirigiram á sua real presença que assim convém ao bem geral dos povos e ao importante fim da união dos dois reinos ; e que egualmente o Governo manda participar a vossas mercês, remettendo-lhes por cópia, a citada portaria. Deus guarde a vossas mercês : Palacio do Governo de Paulo, 4 de Fevereiro de 1822 —Jão Carlos Augusto de Oeyhausen, presidente—Martim Francisco Ribeiro de Andrada, secretario—Miguel José de Oliveira Pintc, secretario.

Estes documentos são decisivos, dando positivameute a data em que os representantes do governo e municipalidade de S. Paulo chegaram ao Rio e alguns promenores da viagem e da recepção que elles tiveram por parte da familia real.

José Bonifacio não esteve presente ao Fico, assim como tambem não estiveram o marechal Arouche, delegado da Camara de S. Paulo, e o desembargador José Teixeira da Fonseca Vasconcellos, vice-presidente e representante da provincia, de Minas. Só José Clemente Pereira, com a sua gente, é que assitiu áquella famosa declaração do Principe Regente, e como foi elle o orador official da occasião por ser então o presidente da Oamara do Rio, a elle incumbiu D. Pedro de dizer ao povo que ficava no Brazil.

Entretanto, no proprio officio acima transcripto e na portataria nelle mencionada se lê que o Principe Regente se resolveu no dia 9 de janeiro, a ficar no Brasil «em virtude das differentes representações» que se dirigiam á sua real presença», Foram estas representações que decidiram D. Pedro a não partir, e de todas estas representações a que fôra escripta por José Bonifacio foi a primeira que o Principe recebeu e a mais eloquente, pelo fundo e pela forma, tanto que foi immediatamente remettida a D. João VI, em Lisboa, como a synthese dos sentimentos brasileiros.

Foi José Bonifacio quem sacudiu a consciencia adormecida de D. Pedro e lhe fez conhecer os perigos da situação politica em que se achava a monarchia portugueza e a elle cabe a prioridade official do Fico, restando a José Clemente uma parte secundaria e o prazer de ter colhido sazonados fructos de terrenos semeados por outrem,

## II

Na sessão da Camara dos Deputados de 14 de junho de 1841 José Clemente Pereira, portuguez de nascimento e membro do ministerio liberticida de 23 de março, em que occupava a pasta da Guerra e se fez responsavel pelas leis reaccionarias que trouxeram as desastradas rebelliões de S. Paulo e Minas Geraes, em 1842, pronunciou nm curioso discurso em que, recordando factos do tempo da independencia, pretendeu chamar a si as glorias resultante do famoso Fico, que foi o primeiro passo no caminho da nossa emancipação politica.

Para bem se apreciar a força dos argumentos do pretencioso ministro e comparar as datas fornecidas por elle em contrario a documentos officiaes ainda existentes, em beneficio da verdade historica, transcrevo abaixo um longo trecho daquelle seu discurso, referente aos factos do dia 9 de janeiro de 1822 :

« O nobre deputado (Antonio Carlos), por occasião de uma declaração que eu fiz, de ter tido a principal parte na representação para a convocação de uma assembléa no Brasil, disse que entendia que eu me referia ao dia 9 de janeiro, conhecido pelo dia do Fico, e que a ser assim queria reclamar porque a gloria da preferencia neste caso pertencia a S. Paulo e não ao Rio de Janeiro.

« O nobre deputado, com muita razão, desempenha o seu officio de bom procurador dos paulistas, mas ha de permittir-me que, como procurador dos fluminenses, chame a sua attenção sobre alguns factos dos, quae se deduz que «a prioridade, si prioridade houve, pertence aos fluminenses», A mim me parece que, na cooperação para a independencia, a gloria é egual para todas as provincias ; mas si é necessario que alguem tenha a prioridade, ha de permittir-me que o conteste e que diga que ella pertence aos fluminenses.

« O nobre deputado conhece, e não ha duvida, que a representação por parte da providcia do Rio de Janeiro «teve logar em 9 de janeiro e que a representação por parte de S. Paulo teve logar dias depois.

(Ha um aparte de Antonio Carlos que não foi tomado).

« Perdoe-me; a representação teve logar dias depois de 9 de janeiro; é verdade que já nós esperavamos a deputação de S. Paulo e alguns preparativos se fizeram para recebel-a, mas o facto é que ella não poude aqui chegar senão depois do dia 9.

Mas o nobre deputado quer que a representação seja datada do dia da deliberação do governo de S. Paulo e não do dia em bue foi apresentada; pois bem, acceito a declaração do nobre deputado e desejo que se escreva nos annaes da historia que o quer que se conte a prioridade do dia em que se tomou a deliberação em cada uma das provincias: a de S. Paulo é marcada pelo nobre deputado no dia 3 de janeiro, que foi quando o governo da Provincia se dirigiu ás municipalidades participandolhes a deliberação do governo ou convidando-as para cooperarem. (Ha outro aparte de Antonio Carlos, que não foi tomado.

«Pois bem ainda mesmo como quer que seja, o nobre deputado ha de ter lembrar-se de que em 22 de dezembro de 1821 sahiu um commissario mandado do Rio de Janeiro ao governo de S. Paulo, convidando-o para cooperar para a ficada do Principe Regente; foi o snr. Pedro Dias, hoje marquez de Quixeramobim. E no dia 20 sahiu daqui para Minas outro commissario, tambem por parte do Rio de Janeiro, encarregado de egual commissão; foi o snr. Paulo Barboza da Silva.

UM SENHOR DEPUTADO.—Foi o sr. conego Januario.

O ORADOR.—Não, senhor; esse foi para a acclamação; estou bem certo nos factos: foi o senhor Paulo Barbosa da Silva. Em virtude destas enviaturas aconteceu que alguns povos de Minas mandaram as suas representações com data de dezembro; eu quero dar aos mineiros a parte da gloria que lhes pertence. A villa de Barbacena enviou a sua representação com data de 27 de dezembro; a camara de Marianna enviou tambem a sua, em data de 2 de janeiro; mas no Rio de Janeiro foi este negocio tratado com muita antecipação, e convém que se dê o seu a seu dono. Devo declarar que os primeiros que se lembraram desta medida foram o sr. José Marianno e o sr. José Joaquim da Rocha.

O SR. ANDRADA MACHADO.—E' verdade.

O ORADOR.—E isto antes do dia 15 de dezembro. Isto creio que anda impresso, e tanto que se me fez crime porque não fui dos primeiros a concordar com a medida como se me apresentava. O sr. José Marianno foi á minha casa, por ser eu então presidente do Senado da Camara, communicar-me a resolução em que se achavam de pedir ao Principe Regente do Brazil que quizesse ficar no Brazil porque assim convinha aos interesses do paiz. Nessa occasião eu disse que julgava de necessidade a ficada do Principe, mas que não julgava prudente que o Rio de Janeiro fizesse a representação só por si, porque não havia a força necessaria, muito mais existindo no Rio de Janeiro uma força portugueza assás forte que, como o nobre deputado sabe por informações, até nos ameaçou com as armas.

Tratava-se de nomear então um governo, esse governo de tres cabeças, que o Brazil não queria e contra o qual eu me tinha pronunciado, e por isso foi-me objectado: — Si o governo tem de nomear-se, que ha de fazer o Principe? A isto respondi: — m uanto se pede a cooperação das provincias immediatas, Minas e S. Paulo, póde o Principe ir para Santa Cruz; logo que cheguem as representações pede-se ao Principe que se deixe ficar no Brazil. — Estas minhas palavras serviram até depois para uma devassa por crime de republicano, na qual houvera quem forse jurar que eu era tão republicano que tinha feito as observações que acabo de referir.

Mas o caso é que o sr. José Mariano e o sr. José Joaquim da Rocha acharam boas as minhas observações e concordaram em que se deviam dirigir aos governos de S. Paulo e de Minas, e em consequencia deste accôrdo partiram, para S. Paulo como já disse, o sr. marquez de Quixeramobim e para Minas o sr. Paulo Barbosa da Silva.

Ora, ogora accresce mais que, tendo eu, como me convinha. tratado de saber do Principe Regente qual era a sua opinião a este respeito, porque corria a noticia de que elle queria ir para Portugal (o que depois reconheceu-se que era politica sua, porque sempre teve vontade de ficar), dirigi-me, logo depois da communicação do sr. José Mariano, a S. Christovam, e Sua Alteza; com effeito ainda «reservou de mim a sua verdadeira opinião», mas, tomando consistencia a opinião do povo fluminense e estando eu decidido a cooperar para ella em todo o caso, procurei novamente o Principe (lembro-me bem) na vespera do dia de Natal e falei-lhe na tribuna da Capella Imperial, dizendo a Sua Alteza Real que o povo do Rio de Janeiro tratava de dirigir-lhe uma supplica no sentido de que lhe havia participado dia antes e que devia esperar egual representação de Minas e S. Paulo, porque era impossivel que estas duas provincias não annuissem as communicações que lhe foram feitas pelo Rio de Janeiro. e Sua Alteza teve a bondade de responder-me que ficaria.

No dia 26 de dezembro fui á casa do sr. José Mariano, onde se achavam o senhor Rocha e O SENHOR PADRE FREI FRANCISCO DE SAMPAIO, QUE FOI QUEM REDIGIU A REPRESENTAÇÃO... Creio que estas observações não são indifferentes para a historia, e fui dizer-lhes que o representação devia fazer-se, que estava disposto a cooperar para ella e que deveria ter logar no dia 9 de janeiro».

A presente exposição não obedeceu á ordem chronologica e tem alguns pontos mal esclarecidos; entretanto a linguagem simples e clara de José Clemente Pereira permitte ao leitor apanhar bem o seu pensamento e apreciar a força dos seus raciocinios. Do discurso se conclue o seguinte:

*a*) Que, chegando ao Rio as más noticias de Lisboa, sendo de todas a peor a da ordem ao Principe Regente para voltar a Portugal, alarmaram-se alguns patriotas — José Mariano, Paulo Barbosa, Rocha e Pedro Dias — e trataram dos meios de impedir que D. Pedro obedecesse áquella ordem, e isto sem determinação do dia, mas, antes de 15 de Dezembro de 1821;

*b*) Que José Mariano foi á casa de José Clemente Pereira tratar disso e que José Clemente, presidente da Camara do Rio, não julgou prudente que o Rio se movesse sòsinho nesse sentido, devendo agir de accôrdo e simultaneamente com os governos das provincias;

*c*) Que, concordando José Mariano e Rocha com esta declaração, seguiram, para Minas Geraes, Paulo Barboza, a 20 de Dezembro, e, para S. Paulo, Pedro Dias, a 22 daquelle mesmo mez;

*d*) Que, espalhando-se nestes dias a noticia de que D. Pedro partiria para Lisboa, foi José Clemente ao paço e perguntou ao Principe Regente qual era o seu pensamento e que D. Pedro «se negou a dizer-lhe o que pensava»;

*e*) Que, no dia 24 de Dezembro, vespera do Natal, foi José Clemente á capella real e em uma das tribunas falou a D. Pedro que o Rio de Janeiro tratava de dirigir-lhe uma supplica, que seria reforçada por eguaes supplicas que deveriam vir de S. Paulo e Minas, e que então o Principe Regente lhe respondera que ficaria no Brazil;

*f*) Que no dia 26 foi o mesmo José Clemente á casa de José Mariano, onde encontrou Rocha e frei Francisco de Sampaio, «que escreveu a representação», e lhes disse que a representação devia fazer-se no dia 9 de Janeiro, como realmente se fez.

Toda a acção do Rio de Janeiro, segundo esta narrativa, desde 15 até 24 de Dezembro, não passou de simples conferencias entre José Mariano, Rocha e José Clemente, em que o agente principal foi José Mariano e não José Clemente, ficando inteiramente malograda a geitosa tentativa deste ultimo de obeter de D Pedro alguma informação sobre as suas intenções.

No dia 24, na capella real, José Clemente contou ao Principe Regente que o Rio de Janeiro, S. Paulo e Minas iam dirigir-lhe um pedido para que ficasse no Brazil e D. Pedro lhe respondeu que ficaria. Houve, portanto, duas scenas do Fico, uma presenciada só por José Clemente, na capella real, a 24 de Dezembro, e outra assistida por elle e pelo povo fluminense no dia 9 de Janeiro. Mas José Clemente não nos diz quaes os argumentos de que lançou mão para convencer D. Pedro de que devia ficar no Brazil, nem mesmo diz que argumentasse nesse sentido; apenas nos conta que na quinta de S Christovam sómente perguntou ao Principe a sua opinião, que aliás lhe foi negada, e que na capella real se limitou a dizer a D. Pedro que o Rio, S. Paulo e Minas iam lhe fazer representações para que não partisse, e que então o principe lhe respondera que ficaria.

Depois disto elle só foi, no dia 26 de Dezembro, á casa de José Mariano contar que a representação seria apresentada no dia 9 de Janeiro e em seguida confessa que elle nem mesmo escreveu essa representação, que foi redigida pelo illustre frade Francisco de Sampaio, de modo que no dia 9 de Janeiro elle não foi mais do que méro portador de uma representação popular, da qual nem ao menos elle teve o merito da redacção e de cujo conteudo D. Pedro não teve conhecimento a não ser no acto da entrega.

No trecho do discurso acima transcripto diz José Clemente que D. Pedro, por conveniencia politica, «fingia» que desejava voltar a Lisboa, mas que de facto elle queria ficar no Brazil. Esta declaração, si fosse verdadeira, podia ser encarada por duas faces diametralmente oppostas; entretanto ella não foi tomada em consideração, nem mesmo pelos deputados presentes á sessão.

Si D. Pedro, de coração, desejava ficar no Brazil e sómente pelas necessidades da politica é que partia para Portugal, era necessaria uma exposição clara, firme, logica e incisiva, como a representação redigida por José Bonifacio, para convencel-o de que exactamente pelas necessidades da politica é que elle devia ficar no Brazil, desobedecendo ás ordens das Côrtes de Lisboa e rompendo de uma vez com a subordinação ao governo portuguez. Ahi é que estão o merito da obra dos patriotas e a grandeza e magestade do Fico.

Porém, si as palavras de José Clemente exprimem que D. Pedro não deixaria o Brazil, porque não queria nos deixar, que desobedeceria de «motu proprio» ás Côrtes Portuguezas e que só por hypocrisia é que fingia querer voltar á Europa, então desapparece por completo a importancia do Fico, que se reduz a um acto politico menos do que trivial, inteiramente nullo e producto de refinada hypocrisia, que não encontra explicação e menos justificativa naquelle importante momento historico.

A nossa historia nos apresenta D. Pedro I como um personagem dotado de algumas qualidades intellectuaes, mas de crassa ignorancia, até dos mais rudimentares elementos da lingua vernacula, de caracter violento, de incuravel leviandade e de infrene devassidão, e agora vemos que, para José Clemente Pereira, era elle ainda um refalsado que juntava a todos os seus vicios e deffeitos o mais horrivel dos vicios, que é a hypocrisia, no dizer do grande moralista Fenelon.

E' possivel que esta opinião de José Clemente Pereira, manifestada no parlamento nacional de um modo indirecto e um tanto velado sobre o caracter fingido e refalsado de D. Pedro, encontre apoio nos pamphletos politicos de Torres Homem e do velho Mello Moraes; mas parece que sendo o dominio de si mesmo e o imperio sobre as proprias paixões os requisitos essenciaes da hypocrisia, não podia ser hypocrita o Principe impulsivo e violento que, durante todo o seu reinado, não teve um só momento de importancia e de gravidade em que mostrasse poder refrear o seu genio irascivel ou dominar as suas condemnaveis paixões, como bem o attestam as suas intimas e immoralissimas relações com pessôas da ordem do Chalaça e da Domitila e os desnecessarios rigores exercidos contra a Assembléa Constituinte e os revolucionarios de diversas provincias, de 1823 a 1829.

Luiz Francisco da Veiga, no seu livro « O Primeiro Reinado», paginas 166-67, disse:

« Dois dos mais tremendos instrumentos do despotismo de D. Pedro, dois dos seus ministros mais liberticidas e, portanto, menos clementes, chamavam-se «Clemente» e foram CLEMENTE FERREIRA FRANÇA e JOSÉ CLEMENTE PEREIRA. O primeiro foi o referendario dos famosos decretos de 1824 e 1825 (sobre a lei marcial), entre os quaes figura o que manda executar promptamente as sentenças de morte, em vez de commutal-as, como próva de paternal clemencia. O segundo foi o ferrenho satrapa que mandára comprar dez mil armas na Europa para firmar em bases solidas, neste imperio, o minotauro do despotismo, e tão odiento, odioso e odiado que, em 1830, eleito deputado á Assembléa Geral, quizeram muitos deputados já reconhecidos expellil-o do parlamento ou não admittil-o nelle por indigno (textual).

« Temos em nosso poder uma longa carta, toda pela propria letra de Bernardo Pereira de Vasconcellos, datada de 8 de Abril de 1830 e dirigida a Evaristo Ferreira da Veiga, onde se lêm as seguintes vehementes palavras: « José Clemente, reconhecido e condemnado pela opinião publica como trahidor ao throno constitucional, deverá sentar-se na Camara?». Deixemos os dois «mentirosos» Clementes e reatemos a nossa interrompida apreciação».

*
* *

Nas «Actas das Sessões» do governo provisorio de S. Paulo, pags. 99 e 100 da primeira edição, lê-se o seguinte:

«Com a chegada da «Gazeta» extraordinaria do Rio de Janeiro e nella o decreto das Côrtes de 1 de outubro deste anno (1821), que manda retirar a Sua Alteza Real, o serenissimo senhor Principe Regente, daquella côrte para fazel-o viajar incognito por determinadas côrtes da Europa, e outrosim o decreto da mesma data relativo á nova fórma dos governos provisorios para as provincias do Brazil, o governo accordou unanimente que se escreva a Sua Alteza Real e se lhe rogue que suspenda a execução de taes decretos emquanto não forem chegados a côrte do Rio de Janeiro seus deputados, que sobre estes dois objectos lhe vão representar por parte delle, governo. E sendo consultada a camara desta cidade e ouvida sobre este mesmo objecto respondeu que em sessão de 19 ella tinha já tomado o mesmo accôrdo que agora toma o governo e que ella nomeava para levarem suas representações a Sua Alteza Real os dois senhores deputados nomeados pelo governo, além de um terceiro que ajunta a estes.

Accordou mais que se officie ao governo de Minas Geraes para que, de mãos dadas com esse governo, represente a Sua Alteza Real sobre esta materia, que é de tanto interesse para a felicidade e prosperidade deste reino de Portugal, e que o mesmo se pratique com todos os demais governos deste reino».

Estas resoluções foram tomadas em sessão extraordinaria de 21 de dezembro de 1821, em virtude de noticias trazidas pela «Gazeta» do Rio de Janeiro, que devia ter chegado a S. Paulo tres dias antes. A camara municipal já se tinha reunido no dia 19 e acceitava para seus representantes os mesmos do governo, aos quaes ajuntaria um terceiro. O pessoal do governo era muito numeroso e difficil de se reunir para uma sessão extraordinaria, em que se ia tratar de materia importante e para qual convinha que concorressem todos os membros, si fosse possivel; estiveram presentes treze, que assignaram a acta, faltando Vergueiro e Felisberto Jardim. Esta seria a causa da demora da acção do governo, que deu tempo a que a camara lhe tomasse a deanteira, reunindo-se e providenciando no dia 19, emquanto o governo só poude funccionar a 21.

Estes actos são todos officiaes, e ao tempo em que elles se passavam aqui na capital paulista, no Rio de Janeiro só se tratava de simples conferencias entre José Mariano, Rocha e, depois, José Clemente, sem nenhum caracter official. A camara aqui agiu a 19 e só a 20 é que Paulo Barbosa partia do Rio para Minas; o governo aqui providenciava no dia 21 e se communicava com o de Minas Geraes, e só a 22 foi que o emissario Pedro Dias partiu do Rio para S. Paulo. A 24 José Bonifacio redigia a representação paulista, energica e solemne, qualificada por Homem de Mello como uma fulminação poderosa atirada ás faces das Côrtes de Lisboa, approvada alia noite e remettida immediatamente a D. Pedro, e só a 26 fci que José Clemente obteve de um illuttre frade, frei Francisco de Sampaio, que escrevesse a representação fluminense, de que elle se fez o portador para o Principe Regente quinze dias depois.

Antonio Carlos, deputado presente á sessão, não podia contestar com vantagem as affirmações de José Clemente, porque ao tempo do Fico se achava em Lisboa, defendendo com calor e coragem os interesses brazileiros desrespeitados pelas Côrtes, e não estava ao corrente dos pormenores da politica fluminense e paulista em fins de 1821 e começo de 1822; seu irmão Martim Francisco, que conhecia bem os factos porque nelles tomará parte das mais activas, é quem poderia apresentar ao parlamento o lado paulista da questão, mas não esteve presente áquella sessão e assim as affirmações de José Clemente passaram á posteridade como a fiel exposição dos factos, que têm duas faces, e naturalmente elle considerou aquella que mais lhe convinha.

Chegadas ao Rio as más noticias de Lisboa, relativas à politica e á administração do Brazil, sómente alguns poucos espiritos patrioticos se moveram no sentido de uma energica reacção; mas eram elles – José Mariano, Rocha, Barbosa e Pedro Dias—simples cidadãos que não tinham autoridade para falar e agir em nome da collectividade politica e social. Entretanto, foi um delles que procurou José Clemente, então presidente da camara do Rio, para que este providenciasse em nome do povo fluminense, e José Clemente não tomou a iniciativa, allegando que não seria prudente agir sinão de accôrdo com os governos e municipalidades das provincias vizinhas.

Ficava elle satisfeito com um logar na rectaguarda dos patriotas; a vanguarda estava ameaçada pelas tropas portuguezas aquarteladas no Rio e a cautela aconselhava que se repartissem com os vizinhos as glorias, assim como os perigos do Fico. Tinha razão o historiador Abreu e Lima quando disse:

«Entretanto D. Pedro se preparava para obedecer á ordem da sua retirada no meio de sustos e clamores de todos os partidos. A reprovação da partida do Principe Regente se tornava geral. Na cidade de S. Paulo, onde os patriotas eram em maior numero do que na capital (Rio), as coisas levaram caminho mais prompto e seguro. José Bonifacio, vice-presidente da junta provincial, informado da proxima retirada do Principe, convocou os seus collegas ás 11 da noite de 24 de dezembro e conseguiu que assignassem uma representação em que se fazia ver a Sua Alteza Real que a sua partida seria o signal da separação do Brazil.

Tenho motivos para estar convencido de que realmente assim foi; porém, José Clemente de proposito confundiu os factos, não distinguindo entre representação paulista e deputação paulista, e procurou dahi tirar partido para a causa que defendia. A deputação paulista, de facto, chegou ao Rio muitos dias depois de 9 de janeiro, mas a representação paulista, escripta e approvada no dia 24 de dezembro e urgentemente remettida a D. Pedro, foi a primeira que o Principe recebeu e a que mais impressionou o seu espirito voluvel e indeciso. A José Bonifacio e não a José Clemente pertence a prioridade official do Fico, que continúo a considerar como a manifestação de uma ephemera, mas honesta convicção politica e não como o producto de refinada hypocrisia principesca.

## III

### A DEPOSIÇÃO DE MARTIM FRANCISCO E SUA DEPORTAÇÃO PARA O RIO DE JANEIRO

Em dias diversos do primeiro trimestre de 1821 foram juradas em varias partes do Brazil as «Bases» da Constituição que as Côrtes de Lisboa haviam decretado para o Reino Unido de Portugal, Brasil e Algarves. D. João VI, que ainda se achava no Rio de Janeiro, acceitára aquellas «Bases», mas em Abril daquelle mesmo anno regressára a Lisboa, depois de uma ausencia de treze annos, e nos deixára seu filho mais velho, o principe D. Pedro, como regente do Brasil.

As colonias hespanholas da America, desde Buenos Aires até ao Mexico, estavam todas em plena revolução para se libertarem do pesado jugo da mãe patria e para o estabelecimento do regimen constitucional republicano.

O Brasil se mantinha em relativa tranquillidade sob o governo de D. João VI e os echos das revoluções hispano-americanas só encontraram repercussão na ephemera e desastrada rebellião de Pernambuco, de 1817, que custou a vida a diversos patriotas, como Abreu e Lima, Barros Lima, Domingos Theotonio, Domingos Martins, padres Miguel de Almeida e Antonio Pereira, Amaro Coutinho, Albuquerque Maranhão e outros, que pretenderam estabelecer um regimen republicano independente naquella parte do paiz.

Com a retirada de D. João VI agitou-se a opinião publica·
no Brasil, e em quasi todas as provincias se tratou de· substituir o capitão-general, representante directo do velho regimen,.
por um governo eleito pelos povos e mais capaz de se accommodar cem as idéias liberaes em voga. Já não bastavam as
«Bases» da Constituição que havia pouco tinham sido juradas
e já não satisfazia as exigencias do espirito publico a pequena
representação que ao Brasil foi permittido mandar ás Côrtes.
Constituintes de Lisboa ; a alma popular aspirava por uma
Constituinte Brasileira, por uma constituição brasileira e por·
um regimen autonomico que permittisse um pouco de vida propria ao paiz, embora politicamente continuasse o Brasil a fazer·
parte do Reino Unido de Portugal, Brasil e Algarves.

A agitação politica em S. Paulo culminou no dia 23 de·
Junho de 1821, quando a massa popular e a força armada se·
reuniram no largo de S. Gonçalo, hoje praça Dr. João Mendes,
declararam o conselheiro João Carlos de Oeynhausen deposto·
do seu cargo de capitão-general e trataram de formar um governo nacional em que não entrassem aquelles que até aqui
têm sido os nossos oppressores».

José Bonifacio, que dois annos antes havia voltado da Europa, onde residira trinta e nove annos, achava-se na cidade a
passeio ou a negocio, e os revolucionarios julgaram de bom·
conselho convidal-o para que viesse á camara municipal aju-
dal-os na escolha do pessoal que devia compor o governo que·
se ia eleger.

Acceitou o patriarcha o convite que lhe era feito ; mas,
conhecendo pouco os homens e as coisas paulistas, não só não
tomou em consideração o pedido que se lhe fez de que não entrassem para o governo os nossos antigos oppressores», como·
recommendou o esquecimento do passado e uma reconciliação·
geral entre os opprimidos e seus oppressores, entre brasileiros·
e portuguezes, entre liberaes e reaccionarios, e conseguiu que
o povo e tropas acceitassem um governo composto do seguinte·
pessoal :

1—João Carlos Augusto de Oeynhausen—presidente.
2—José Bonifacio de Andrada e Silva—vice-presidente.
3—Martim Francisco Ribeiro de Andrada— secretario da Fazenda.
4—Coronel Lazaro José Gonçalves—secretario da Guerra.
5—Miguel José de Oliveira Pinto—secretario da Marinha..
6 e 7—Coroneis Antonio Leite Pereira da Gama Lobo e·
   Daniel Pedro Müller—representantes da força armada.

8 e 9—Brigadeiro Manoel Rodrigues Jordão e coronel Francisco Ignacio de Souza Queiroz —representantes do commercio.

10 e 11—Dr. Nicolau Pereira de Campos Vergueiro e tenente-coronel Antonio Maria Quartim—representantes da agricultura,

12 e 13—Padre Francisco de Paula Oliveira e professor André da Silva Gomes—representantes da instrucção e letras.

14 e 15—Padres João Ferreira de Oliveira Bueno e Felisberto Gomes Jardim—representantes do clero.

Este pessoal era excessivamente numeroso para ser activo e expedito nos despachos dos negocios publicos e muito mesclado e heterogeneo para ser harmonico como convinha aos interesses politicos da provincia na quadra agitada que ella estava atravessando.

João Carlos de Oeynhausen e Müller eram militares portuguezes, de origem allemã, em commissão no Brasil; Lazaro Gonçalves, Gama Lobo e Oliveira Pinto eram portuguezes e militares; Vergueiro e André Gomes eram nascidos, criados e educados em Portugal e Antonio Quartim era miJlitar hespanhol. Os outros todos eram paulistas, menos Felisberto Jardim, que era rio grandense de nascimento e morador em S. Paulo. Estavam, portanto, fazendo parte de um governo de origem revolucionaria e que devia ser a personificação do espirito nacionalista, liberal, oito extrangeiros, dos quaes quatro eram militares de carreira, e sómente sete eram brasileiros.

Quando ás idéias, gostos e inclinações, dividia-se o pessoal do governo em dois grupos muito diversos dos primeiros, acima considerados; representavam o elemento estatico, conservador, retrogado, João Carlos, Müller, Oliveira Pinto, Quartim e Francisco Ignacio, sendo este ultimo paulista de nascimento, mas muito ligado aos seus collegas extrangeiros e militares do governo, emquanto os restantes membros adheriram mais ou menos francamente ás idéias novas e se puzeram sem reservas ao serviço do Brasil.

Aos cinco reaccionarios que formavam o grupo estatico se applica com cabimento a designação de «bernardistas», pela parte activa que tomaram na sedição de 23 de Maio de 1822, conhecida na nossa historia pelo nome de «Bernarda de Francisco Ignacio».

Installado este governo no mesmo dia em que foi eleito, em 23 de Junho de 1821, tratou elle logo de mandar dois dos seus membros, o brigadeiro Jordão e o coronel Gama Lobo, ao

Rio de Janeiro para communicar a D. Pedro a sua eleição e posse e pedir ao principe a sua approvação, que lhe foi dada por decreto de 30 de Julho do mesmo anno Estava sanccionada a revolução popular e os paulistas se mostravam cheios de esperanças de um futuro lisonjeiro.

Apparentemente caminhava o governo sem maiores attritos e difficuldades; os mezes se foram passando e com o correr do tempo noticias más vinham chegando ao Brazil, relativas ao espirito reaccionario e ás tendencias recolonizadoras manifestados pelas côrtes de Lisbôa, que annullavam os beneficios que D. João VI nos havia feito, fraccionavam o nosso paiz, estabelecendo nas partes fraccionadas governos só dependentes de Lisbôa, e chamavam para Portugal o principe D. Pedro para nos tirar os ultimos restos da autonomia politica e administrativa que ainda tinhamos.

Alarmou-se o espirito publico e de toda a parte se faziam representações a D. Pedro para que não abandonasse o Brazil, José Bonifacio foi o auctor da mais eloquente dessas representações, que elle dirigiu a 24 de Dezembro de 1821, fez os seus collegas do governo approvarem alta noite daquelle mesmo dia e remetteu com toda a urgencia ao Principe Regente, que a recebeu no ultimo dia daquelle mez ou a 1 de Janeiro de 1822. Oito dias depois tambem seguiu elle proprio para o Rio, afim de reforçar com a sua presença e com a sua auctorizada palavra as razões dadas na representação para que D. Pedro não partisse para Lisbôa.

Com a partida de José Bonifacio, que era o mais habil membro do governo collectivo de S. Paulo e seu vice-presidente, ficou um tanto enfraquecida a influencia paulista na administração da provincia e, como disse Americo Brasiliense, sentiu-se João Carlos com mais liberdade de acção, faltando-lhe sómente para completar a restauração da influencia portugueza eliminar do governo Martim Francisco, que ficara occupando a vice-presidencia e se tornára, na ausencia de seu irmão, o homem mais habil e energico daquella corporação; e porque o brigadeiro Jordão era seu amigo e partidario politico de grande prestigio, convinha eliminal-o tambem para que a reacção contra o elemento brasileiro e paulista fosse completa.

Não consta das «Actas das Sessões» do governo que houvesse um motivo de queixa contra a presença de Martim Francisco e do brigadeiro Jordão naquella corporação, internamente corroida de ciumes e de intrigas; nellas não se encontram uma questão que dividisse os membros do governo em grupos hostis, nem a menor referencia ou critica a qualquer acto menos digno praticado por estes dois paulistas ; entretanto cá fóra se tramava á surdina a expulsão de ambos do governo, sendo o presidente João Carlos de Oeynhausen e o ouvidor Costa Carvalho as cabeças pensantes da secreta conspiração, que devia ter por seus braços fortes os coroneis Francisco Ignacio de Sousa Queiroz e Francisco Alves Ferreira do Amaral e o brigadeiro Joaquim José Pinto de Moraes Leme, commandantes das forças armadas que se achavam aquarteladas na cidade de S. Paulo.

Faltava um pretexto para a conspiração sahir á rua e executar os seus fins e este não tardou muito em apparecer na portaria do Principe Regente de 10 de Maio de 1822, ordenando que João Carlos de Oeynhausem e Costa Carvalho seguissem sem demora para o Rio de Janeiro, por necessidade do serviço publico. Entenderam os conspiradores, e parece que entenderam bem, que Martim Francisco ficou ao corrente da conspiração e que, para fazel-a abortar, se entendera reservadamente com José Bonifacio, que então era ministro de D. Pedro, para que o Principe chamasse para o Rio aquellas duas cabeças directoras da projectada sedição, e aproveitaram-se daquella portaria para sahirem á rua, no dia 23 de Maio, á frente da força armada, deporem do governo Martim e Jordão e impedirem que João Carlos de Oeynhausen e Costa Carvalho sahissem de S. Paulo, tudo em completa desobediencia ás ordens do Principe Regente.

João Carlos, general em commissão do governo de S. Paulo, e Costa Carvalho, ouvidor da comarca, eram funccionarios publicos immediatamente dependentes do Principe Regente, que por motivo de serviço publico podia legalmente chamal-os para o Rio e mesmo remettel-os para qualquer outra parte em que os seus prestimos fossem necessarios para o bem do paiz ; porém os sediciosos dos quarteis, aconselhados por estes mesmos funccionarios, vieram á rua, debaixo de armas, protestar que aquella portaria estava errada e que as necessidades do serviço exigiam exactamente o contrario, isto é, que João Carlos e Costa Carvalho fizessem nos seus cargos e que Martim e Jordão deixassem os seus logares, mesmo pela força si fosse preciso, por assim ser conveniente ao socego e á tranquillidade dos paulistas.

A theoria era das mais extranhas, mas propria dos quarteis, onde a acção sobrepuja o raciocinio e a força vence o direito: D. Pedro, chamando a serviço aquelles seus subordinados, estava errado, mas os homens dos quarteis, depondo violentamente dois membros de um governo legal, estavam certos ; entretanto, como a sedição se fazia em nome do socego e da tranquillidade dos paulistas, ameaçados por aquella portaria, que daqui retirava dois individuos extranhos á provincia e funccionarios publicos, con-

vinha que a todo o custo se procurasse dar ao movimento uma
apparencia de popularidade e para isso os capitães Pedro Taques
e Oliveira Netto e alguns outros foram mandados á rua, de trabuco em punho, a « convidar » o povo para se ajuntar aos sediciosos e fortalecer com a sua presença a causa que elles defendiam.
E, como o « convite » era feito á bocca de uma pistola, a recusa
era difficil e os vereadores e alguns populares se julgaram ao
dever de acceder a elle e de comparecer no edificio da camara
municipal para assignar uma representação que os mesmos sediciosos fizeram a D. Pedro, explicando as causas da rebellião e
pedindo para os seus actos a approvação do Principe Regente.

Esta representação, que esta registrada em um dos livros
da Camara Municipal de S. Paulo, contém 192 assignaturas,
das quaes 107 são de militares, desde um brigadeiro até soldados, musicos do batalhão, meirinhos e carcereiros; 3 são de
clerigos obscuros e o resto pertence a individuos desconhecidos,
recrutados nas ruas por Pedro Taques, Oliveira Netto e seus
comparsas, e levados ao paço municipal para fazerem o papel
do povo ausente, sendo a lista encabeçada por Costa Carvalho,
que assignou em primeiro logar, depois dos vereadores.

Depostos do poder, Jordão retirou-se para Santos, onde
havia ordem e segurança, porém, Martim Francisco se deixou
ficar na cidade, dominada pelo militarismo turbulento Irrita-
ram-se com isso os sediciosos, que se reuniram de novo, a 29
de Maio, sempre debaixo dos auspicios de João Carlos e Costa
Carvalho, e representaram ao governo para que fizesse Martim
Francisco sahir da cidade em 24 horas e da provincia em 8 dias,
e o governo, então nas mãos de tres militares extrangeiros—
João Carlos, Oliveira Pinto e Daniel Muller — se apressou em
expedir a portaria de 30 de Maio, dirigida ao capitão portuguez
José Fernandes da Silva, para que este militar, com o cabo
Felisberto Dias de Camargo e os soldados Antonio Joaquim da
Silva e Francisco Pereira Bueno, escoltasse Martim Francisco
até ás fronteiras da provincia do Rio de Janeiro e para que
dalli em diante o acompanhasse até ao logar onde o mesmo
Martim o despedisse.

Si os extrangeiros detentores do governo de S. Paulo queriam, como pretendem alguns, honrar a pessoa de Martim Francisco, dando-lhe uma guarda de honra que o acompanhasse até
aos limites da provincia ou até ao logar onde bem conviesse ao
deportado ir na companhia dessa guarda, era justo que lhe dessem uma escolta commandada por um official brasileiro e amigo,
que lhe amenizasse as agruras da situação em que se achava;
mas deram-lhe por companheiro um official portuguez que, natu-

ralmente, era da confiança dos sediciosos e dos seus chefes no governo e que, lnoge de ser um agradavel companheiro em longa jornada para o exilio, seria antes um espião que lhe vigiasse os actos e observasse as conversas durante o trajecto de S. Paulo ao Rio

Partiu Martim Francisco nesta má companhia, pelo caminho de terra, para o Rio de Janeiro e no fim de alguns dias chegou a Bananal, onde pernoitou. Alli encontrou Martim um corpo de milicia de S Paulo, que voltava da cidade do Rio, onde fôra a serviço de D. Pedro, e pedio ao commandante desse corpo que lhe désse um official para o acompanhar até ao Rio· Foi-lhe dado o capitão Joaquim José de Almeida, e a este pediu Martim Francisco que intimasse, em nome de D. Pedro, ao capitão José Fernandes da Silva, commandante da sua escolta, para que tambem seguisse até ao Rio.

Partiram todos e, chegados ao Rio, puzeram Martim em segurança, naturalmente na casa do seu irmão José Bonifacio, ministro do Interior e de Extrangeiros do Principe Regente. Apresentando-se ao ministro da Guerra o capitão Joaquim José Almeida, recebeu elle do ministro, segundo affirma, ordem para de novo intimar ao capitão Jose Fernandes da Silva que não se retirasse do Rio de Janeiro sem expressa ordem do Principe Regente, intimação que aquelle official jura que fez e que o capitão Jose Fernandes da Silva desobedeceu, partindo para S. Paulo sem mais ceremonias e trazendo, como passaporte, a mesma portaria de 30 de maio que o incumbia de escoltar o deportado até ás fronteira au até ao logar onde fosse despedido.

Ficou o capitão José Fernandes garantido na sua liberdade e impune da sua desobediencia emquanto se mantiveram no governo de S. Paulo os audaciosos extrangeiros qde delle estavam senhores e que se propunham a tratar D. Pedro, seus ministros e seus delegados Candido Xavier e Arouche de egual para egual. Porém, em agosto, D Pedro chegou a S. Paulo qeu cabo dos restos do governo sedicioso e, ao voltar para o Rio em 10 de setembro de 1822, aqui deixou installado um novo governo composto do bispo D, Matheus, do ouvidor José Corrêa e do marechal Candido Xavier, que era tambem commandante das armas da provincia.

Cessaram então as immunidades do capitão José Fernandes da Silva, que foi preso e mettido na fortaleza da barra de Santos. Instaurou-se-lhe o competente processo perante um Conselho de Guerra, que tinha por presidente o coronel Joaquim José de Moraes Abreu, por auditor o dr. José Corréa Pacheco e Silva e por vogaes os majores João Pereira Simões e Antonio José Bordini, os capitães Matheus Fernandes Cantinho e Francisco da Silva Prado, os tenentes João Ribeiro de Camargo o Segismundo de Lima e os alferes Joaquim José da Silva e Salvador Pires da Silva.

Correu o processo com rapidez, tendo começado logo que .o novo governo tomou posse e ficando julgado e terminado em 14 de novembro do mesmo anno. Depuzeram seis testemunhas, das quaes só uma, o capitão Joaquim José de Almeida, falou com conhecimento pessoal da materia por ter feito parte da comitiva de Martim Francisco do Bananal até ao Rio de Janeiro, referindo as outras cinco sómente aquillo que tinham ouvido dizer e que allegavam ser corrente na cidade de S. Paulo

O accusado apresentou defesa escripta em onze artigos e alguns documentos que favoreciam a sua causa. Allegou que éra surdo e provou que, por esse defeito physico, se achava retirado do serviço militar activo, comquanto não fosse reformado, e fora dispensado de seguir para o Rio de Janeiro na brigada dos «Leaes Paulistanos» em, principio de 1822, a defender o Principe Regente contra as aggressões do rebelde general portuguez Avillez.

Allegou mais que no Bananal ouvira a intimação para acompanhar Martim Francisco até ao Rio, mas que, lá chegado, não teve ou não, ouviu nenhuma intimação, por parte do ministro da Guerra para que não voltasse a S Paulo sem ordem expressa de D. Pedro; que antes de voltar fôra jantar com Martim Frncisco e lhe perguntára se queria alguma coisa para S Paulo tendo em resposta que este nada desejava de cá ou para cá, e finalmente declarou que a mesma portaria, que lhe serviu de passaporte para a ida, devia servir-lhe para a volta; que tinha 50 annos de edade, era casado e negociante e que occupava nesta cidade o cargo de juiz almotacel por nomeação da Camara Municipal.

A accusação de ter o reu voltado do rio sem licença expressa de D. Pedro ficou, portanto, limitada a uma questão de veracidade entre elle e o capitão José Joaquim de Almeida, que affirmava ter-lhe intimado essa ordem por parte do ministro da Guerra, e o Conselho de Guerra votou unanimemente pela sua absolvição, que foi confirmada, tambem unanimemente, pelo Supremo Conselho Militar do Rio de Janeiro.

O Conselho de Guerra era composto de officiaes paulistas, sendo o presidente Moraes Abreu, filho do coronel Corrêa de Moraes, capitão-mór que foi de Porto Feliz durante um quarto de seculo, e o auditor José Corrêa, filho de uma illustre familia ytúama e ainda membro do governo de S. Paulo e amigo dos Andradas, e todos esses officiaes foram nomeados para esse conselho peló marechal Candido Xavier, tambem membro do governo e egualmente amigo e partidario dos Andradas.

Entretanto, ninguem votou pela condemnação do official portuguez e até no Conselho Supremo do Rio, de que faziam parte o barão de Bagé e mais cinco militares, que se achavam debaixo das vistas immediatas de José Bonifacio e Martin Francisco, ministros do Principe Regente, não teve o accusado nenhum voto desfavoravel.

Esta sentença é importante pelas deducções que della se podem tirar: Absolveu-se o acusado em uma época de profundas agitações politicas e de odios irreconciliaveis, pelo facto de não haver provas que justificassem a accusação; fez-se justiça ao reu.

Mas essa justiça feita até a reus militares sujeitos ao severo regulamento do conde de Lippe, vem demonstrar que o governo de S. Paulo. composto de amigos dos Andradas e por elles influenciado, sabia elevar-se acima de mesquinhas vinganças e fazer justiça aos seus inimigos, reduzindo a menores proporções a pecha de arbitrarios e violentos que os seus desaffectos se comprazem em lhes atirar.

Quando já elles estavam longe do seu paiz natal, deportados em França, D. Pedro e seus ministros encontraram meios de obter de um outro conselho de guerra a condemnação traiçoeira de Ralcliff, cujo sangue, no dizer de Torres-Homem, negrejou na fronte imperial e ainda mancha a memoria de Pedro I.

IV

### A ELEIÇÃO DA ASSEMBLÉA CONSTITUINTE

A « Bernarda de Francisco Ignacio de 23 de Maio de 1822, que tantos males trouxe a S. Paulo e ao Brazil todo, esphacelara o Governo Provisorio e deixara as redeas da administração entregues aos portuguezes João Carlos de Oeynhausen e Oliveira Pinto, ao allemão Daniel Müller e no hespanhol Antonio Quartim, de mãos dadas com o coronel Francisco Ignacio de Souza Queiroz, que era filho de portuguez, fora educado em Portutal e lá sevira como alferes de tropa de linha, tendo idéas, habit's e gostos portuguezes.

Fôra elle o braço forte, emquanto Costa Carvalho, depois marquez de Monte-Alegre, era a cabeça pensante, daquella audaciosa sedição, que tomou o seu nome e deu origem á confederação dos municipios do interior, com séde em Ytú, para a defesa dos interesses brasileiros contra os extrangeiros acastellados no governo de S. Paulo.

José Bonifacio já era ministro do principe D. Pedro, desde meado de Janeiro daquelle anno de 1822, e Martim Francisco, derribado do poder pela « Bernarda de Francisco Ignacio» e remettido preso para o Rio, era lá elevado a ministro da Fazenda, em quanto o seu irmão e sogro regia as pastas do Interior e Extrangeiros.

Não podia D. Pedro se conformar com os factos occorridos em S. Paulo a 23 de Maio de 1822, que alterara profundamena ordem e a paz nesta provincia, e expediu o decreto de 25 de Junho, redigido em phrases energicas até á offensa, cassando os poderes dos extrangeiros sediciosos e ordenando a eleição de um outro governo paia esta provincia e de deputados que deveriam formar a nossa primeira Assemblèa Constituinte.

Os extrangeiros do governo não deram por cassado os seus poderes e continuaram como uma ameaça aos interesses brazileiros, confiados á guarda da confederação de Ytú, sob a chefia de Paulo Souza, Candido Motta, major José Custodio de Oliveira, capitão Salvador Martins, Domingos Soares de Barros, padre Miguel Archanjo Ribeiro e outros ardentes nacionalistas, delegados de varios municipios.

Viera D. Pedro a S. Paulo, onde chegou a 25 de Agosto do mesmo anno de 1822, dissolveu o governo sedicioso, de que só restavam quatro membros, e passou a nomear um outro composto de tres membros, que foram o bispo D. Matheus de Abreu Pereira, o general Candido Xavier de Almeida e Souza e o ouvidor Jose Correia Pacheco e Silva.

A 5 de Setembro, tendo apaziguado as discordias na provincia e recebido as homenagens dos municipios do interior, entre festas que fizeram os bons paulistas para celebrar a visita principesca, desceu D. Pedro a Santos, onde falhou o dia 6 em visita ás fortalezas e aos membros da familia Andrada, que lá residiam, e voltou a esta capital no dia 7, encontrando á tardinha nos campos do Ypiranga o correio que do Rio lhe mandava José Bonifacio, com importantes despachos de Lisboa, officio dos ministros e carta da princeza Leopoldina, que alli mesmo, naquelles campos, proximo ao ribeiro do Ypiranga, o decidiram a dar o famoso grito « Independencia ou morte.»

Acceitaram os paulistas, com prazer e alegria, as consequencias que dahi podiam resultar e no meio de extraordinarios festeja os sanccionaram a declaração da independencia com outro grito «Viva o rei do Brazil.»

No dia 10 de Setembro regressára D. Pedro ao Rio de Janeiro, onde o chamavam graves responsabilidades oriundas da declaração da independencia, e deixava empossado das redeas do governo desta provincia o triumvirato acima mencionado, que administrou os negocios publicos até 9 de Janeiro de 1823.

Procedendo se ás eleições ordenadas pelo decreto de 25 de Junho de 1822, foram eleitos membros do governo collectivo de S. Paulo o marechal Candido Xavier de Almeida e Souza, presidente; o dr. José Corrêa Pacheco e Silva, secretario.; o dr. Manoel Joaquim de Ornellas, o padre João Gonçalves L'ma e os coroneis Anastacio de Freitas Trancoso, João Baptista da Silva Passos e Francisco Corrêa de Morces.

Este ultimo, que foi capitão-mòr de Porto Feliz durante um quarto de seculo, de 1797 a 1822, não acceitou o cargo, allegando velhice e doença, e deixou vago o seu logar, que não foi preenchido. Silva Passos era capitã-mór de Santos, e Gonçalves Lima vigario de Parnahyba; Anastacio Trancoso era um militar já edoso e muito distincto, que, no governo de Martim Lopes, montára a sua custa um bom corpo de tropas e com elle marchára para o Rio Grande do Sul, em 1776, lá prestando bons serviços e voltado coberto de louro á sua provincia, onde continuou a prestar importantes serviços até á sua morte, occorrida em 1839. O dr. José Corrêa pertencia a uma illustre familia ituana; occupára os cargos de juiz de fóra de Santos e de ouvidor de S. Paulo e fez figura na politica do seu tempo. Do marechal Candido Xavier bastará dizer que falleceu em 1831 com 62 annos de activos serviços ao seu paiz, desde o descabrimento dos campos de Guarapuava, em 1771, e explorações no famoso salto de Sete-Quedas, em 1786, até no governo de São Paulo, de que fez parte importante durante os annos de 1822— 23—24.

Para deputados á Assembléa Constituinte foram eleitos os cidadãos abaixo mencionados, com o numero de votos que obetiveram, que não costa da nossa historia publicada:

1 — Dr. Nicolau Pereira de Campos Vergueiro 275 votos
2 — Dr. Antonio Carlos Ribeiro de Andrada
    Machado e Silva. . . . . . . . . 254 »
3 — Desembargador Antonio Rodrigues Velloso
    de Oliveira . . . . . . . . . . 234 »
4 — Dr. José Ricardo da Costa Aguiar Andrada 193 »
5 — Marechal José Arouche de Toledo Rendon. 176 »
6 — Francisco de Paula Sousa e Mello . . . 150 »
7 — Dr. Diogo de Toledo Lara e Ordonhes. . 143 »
8 — Dr. José Bonifacio de Andrada e Silva. . 125 »
9 — Dr. José Feliciano Fernandes Pinheiro . . 122 »

De 9 foi o numero dos deputados que a provincia ne São Paulo elegia para a Assembléa Legislativa Geral desde a independencia até á quéda da monarchia, em 1889. Havia supplentes dos deputados proprietarios das cadeiras, e esses supplentes foram :

1 — Coronel Martim Francisco Ribeiro de Andrada 121 votos
2 — Dr. Manoel Joaquim de Ornellas . . . 114 »
3 — Dr. José Corrêa Pacheco e Silva . . . 108 »
4 — General Manoel Martins do Couto Reis. . 90 »
5 — Dr. João de Medeiros Gomes. . . . . 90 »
6 — Padre Diogo Antonio Feijó . . . . . 84 »
7 — Coronel Ignacio José Vicente da Fonseca . 55 »
8 — Padre João Chrysosthomo de Oliveira Salgado . . . . . . . . . . . . . 50 »
9 — Coronel Antonio José Vaz . . . . . 48 »

Além destes, ainda obtiveram votos os seguintes individuos Joaquim Roberto de Carvalho Macedo, 46; Antonio José Vicente da Fonseca, 44; conego Januario da Cunha Barbosa, 43; Antonio Manoel de Oliveira Bueno, 43; commendador Manoel da Cunha de Azeredo Coutinho Souza Chichorro, 40 padre Francisco de Paula e Oliveira, 35; padre José Ignacio Rodrigues de Carvalho, 26 ; coronel José Vicente de Oliveira, 18; desembargador Estevam Ribeiro de Resende, 16; padre José Gonçalves da Silva, 16 ; desembargador D. Nuno Eugenio de Lossio Seibz, 16; padre João Gonçalves Lima, 15; capitão-mór João Baptista da Silva Passos, 15, e professor Francisco de Paula Simões, 14·

Vergueiro era portuguez e formado em leis na universidade de Coimbra; veiu para S. Paulo em 1802, quando ainda era muito moço pois nascera em 1779 ; aqui se casou e criou familia, dedicando se algum tanto á advocacia e muito à agricultura que lhe deve importantes serviços. Era homem moderado e bemquisto, como se vê pela grande votação que teve e em politica subiu ás mais altas posições que um cidadão podia alcançar no antigo regimen, inclusivé a do regente do imperio durante a menoridade de D. Pedro II.

Antonio Carlos foi o grande tribuno da Assembléa Constituinte e o maior orador politico que o Brazil tem tido Nascido em 1773 e formado em leis, em Coimbra, foi juiz de fóra de Santos e depois ouvidor em Pernambuco, onde se envolveu na rebellião de 1817 e soffreu alguns annos de prisão. Como deputado ás Côrtes de Lisboa, cm 1821-22 fez saliente figura e se tornou tão odiado pelos portuguezes, quanto admirado pelos seus patricios, que o elegeram para a Constituinte Brazileira com uma bonita votação, só inferior a de Vergueiro. Preso e deportado, com seus irmãos, em 1823, ficou no exilio até 1838,

quando voltou ao Brazil, e, não achando logar na representação
paulista, que lhe ficou fechada pela influencia de Feijó, seu
mortal inimigo, fez politica por fóra e chegou a ir a Portugal
na esperança de fazer Pedro I a occupar de novo o trono do
Brazil. Rompendo finalmente a barreira que lhe oppunham os
seus inimigos, entrou na camara em 1838, foi o chefe real da
revolução da maioridade, em 1840, e falleceu em 1845, occupando uma cadeira de senador por Pernambuco.

Velloso de Oliveira é menos conhecido dos paulistas do que
merece. Nascido em S. Paulo, formou-se em direito em Coimbra e de volta á sua patria, subiu na magistratura até ao Desembargo do Paço. Em politica foi moderado, e nas horas vagas dava-se a escriptor, deixando alguns trabalhos que estão
publicados e são pouco lidos hoje. O facto de occupar elle o
terceiro logar na votação indica a popularidade de que gosava
entre os seus patricios.

José Ricardo não era um simples portador de um nome
illustre. Sobrinho carnal dos Andradas, elle não rivalizava com
os seus tios em capacidade int-llectual, mas era um homem de
real merecimento. Formado tambem em lei:, em Coimbra foi
deputado ás Cortes de Lisboa e á Constituinte Brazileira, e na
magistura subiu até ao Supremo Tribunal de Justiça, de que
foi um dos membros mais illustres. Era muito viajado em paizes
extrangeiros.

O marechal Arouche, que póde charmar-se « o ultimo fidalgo paulista», era irmão mais moço de Diogo Ordonhes e, como
este, formado em direito, em Coimbra; preferiu seguir a carreira das armas, em que attingiu a um alto posto, e foi o primeiro director que teve a Academia de S. Paulo.

São muitos os serviços que fez á sua provincia, e o seu
nome é justamente respeitado pelos seus patricios.

Paula Souza, por sua constituição fraca e doentia, não poude
seguir para Coimbra, como era costume, e formou-se nas « arêas
de Ytú » ; entretanto, por seu extraordinario talento e variada
instrucção, não desmerecia ao lado dos seus companheiros da
deputação paulista ; era intensamente brasileiro e foi o chefe da
reacção effectuada no interior contra o dominio dos extrangeiros
« bernardistas », acastellados no governo da capital. Em politica,
sempre liberal, subiu até aos postos de senador do imperio e
;residente do Conselho.

Diogo Ordonhes não tomou posse da sua cadeira de deputado
constituinte ; estava velho, cansado e, parece, não se dava bem
com a politica para seguil-a como carreira, para o que estava,
além disso, muito avançado em annos. Foi magistrado dos mais

distinctos e percorreu todos os cargos, desde os de juiz de fóra
e ouvidor de Cuyabá até ao de membro do Dezembargo do Paço;
foi socio da Academia Real das Sciencias de Lisbôa e, fallecendo
em 1826 sem familia propria, legou seus beus á Santa Casa de
Misericordia desta capital.

De José Bonifacio basta dizer que, como homem de sciencia,
honrou o Brasil na Europa, que percorreu quasi toda; como poeta
é dos mais illustres e como politico está justamente sagrado « O
PATRIARCHA DA INDEPENDENCIA ».

Fernandes Pinheiro foi um dos mais illustres brasileiros do
seu tempo, aliás fecundo em grandes homens; é mais conhecido
pelo seu titulo de visconde de S Leopoldo. Como politico
occupou com brilho todos os cargos mais importantes, até o de
senador do imperio; como ministro de Estado fundou as academias de Direito de S. Paulo e Pernambuco, e como escriptor
deixou obras de merecimento, entre as quaes estão os importantes
« Annaes do Rio Grande do Sul ».

Dos nove deputados constituintes, quatro eram nascidos em
Santos—José Bonifacio, Antonio Carlos, José Ricardo e Fernandes
Pinheiro; tres eram naturaes de S. Paulo—Diogo Ordonhes, marechal Arouche e Velloso de Olivera; Paula Sousa era filho de
Ytú e Vergueiro, de Lisbôa. Diogo Ordonhes, que era o mais
velho de todos, tinha 70 annos de edade e Paula Sousa, o Benjamim da representação paulista, tinha apenas 32 annos. Velloso
de Oliveira devia ter uns 60 annos de edade, visto que seu pae
fallecera em 1770, e José Ricardo não andaria longe dos 35. O
marechal Arouche tinha 66 annos, José Bonifacio, 59, Antonio
Carlos, 49, Fernandes Pinheiro, 48 e Vergueiro, 43.

Era realmente de superior qualidade a representação paulista
na Assembléa Constituinte e poderia figurar com honra no parlamento de qualquer nação européa. José Bonifacio e Paula
Sousa eram a encarnação do espirito liberal do tempo e da resistencia contra o dominio portuguez; Antonio Carlos era a
personificação da eloquencia tribunicia; José Ricardo e Velloso
de Oliveira eram jurisconsultos e Arouche e Vergueiro symbo-
lizavam o bom senso, a circumspecção e a prudencia.

Fernandes Pinheiro, tendo sido eleito deputado constituinte
pelo Rio Grande do Sul, optára por lá e deixou vaga a sua
cadeira por S. Paulo; devia ser substituido poo Martim Francisco, que era o supplente mais votado, porém, tendo Martim
sido eleito supplente pelo Rio de Janeiro, por lá tomou assento

na vaga do deputado Agostinho Corrêa da Silva Goulão, e isto deu logar a que fosse Ornellas chamado a occupar a cadeira que devia ser de Fernandes Pinheiro, uma vez que era elle o segundo votado dos supplentes.

Diogo Ordonhes, como já foi dito, não tomou posse da sua cadeira, que foi occupada pelo dr. José Corrêa Pacheco e Silva, o terceiro votado na lista dos supplentes.

Vergueiro, sempre muito occupado com as suas lavouras e outros muito negocios particulares, demorou muito para ir tomar posse da sua cadeira e para que ella não ficasse assim vaga com prejuizo da representação paulista, foi occupada pelo tenente general Manoel Martins do Couto Reis, santista muito distincto e grande servidor da patria, que era o quarto votado dos supplentes e mais velho do que o ouvidor João de Medeiros Gomes, que tivera egual numero de votos.

A Camara Municipal da cidade de S. Paulo, fazendo a apuração dos votos e expedindo diplomas aos eleitos e aos seus supplentes, julgou-se com o direito de tomar conhecimento das incompatibilidades resultantes dos cargos que occupavam alguns dos votados. Os drs. Ornellas e Pacheco e Silva eram membros do Governo Provisorio de S. Paulo, e o dr. João de Medeiros Gomes era ouvidor da comarca da capital, e por estes motivos a Camara negou-lhes os respectivos diplomas e passou a dal-os aos immediatos em votos—Diogo Feijó, coronel Ignacio Fonseca e padre Oliveira Salgado

José Bonifacio, ministro do Interior, a quem talvez não conviesse a presença de Feijó na Assembléa Constituinte, pela animosidade que já havia entre elles e que durou até a morte do patriarcha, contestou á Camara Municipal o direito de intervir na materia, ordenando-lhe que expedisse os diplomas aos mais votados e que deixasse á Assembléa Constituinte, como unico poder competente, a tarefa de julgar do merito da questão. A Camara obedeceu e, realmente, a Assembléa Constituinte não julgou incompativeis os logares de membros do Governo Provisorio de S. Paulo e de deputados áquella Assembléa e deu assento a Ornellas e Pacheco e Silva, nas vagas de Fernandes Pinheiro e Diogo Ordonhes, com exclusão de Feijó, que Azevedo Marques, nos seus « Apontamentos Historicos », pagina 118, erradamente dá como membro da Assembléa Constituinte.

*
* *

E' para notar a desegualdade da votação obtida pelos deputados constituintes e seus supplentes. A eleição não era por districtos, mas por provincia, e de dois graus, como sempre foi durante o imperio, até 1881, e parece que um pouco de trabalho eleitoral teria trazido mais uniformidade na votação. O partido « bernadista » composto dos sediciosos de 23 de Maio, estava esmagado e seus chefes—João Carlos de Oeynhausen e Costa Carvalho—estavam no Rio sob as vistas do governo imperial, e os seus braços fortes—coroneis Francisco Ignacio e Ferreira do Amaral, majores Oliveira Netto e Araujo Macedo, capitão Pedro Taques, Silva Telles e outros de menos valia, estavam deportados para varias partes da provincia, e os dominadores da occasião, senhores absolutos da situação, poderiam, si quizessem, obter uma votação cerrada nos seus candidatos; entretanto foi enorme a dispesção de votos e os membros do ministerio do joven D. Pedro foram os que tiveram menos votação. Vemos José Bonifacio apparecer no penultimo logar entre os votados e Mártim Francisco apenas alcançar o primeiro logar entre os supplentes.

Como se explica similhante facto?

Não se poderá dizer que a victoria que elle e Martim alcançaram sobre os « bernardistas » e a deportação dos sediciosos por trez mezes os tivessem tornado odiosos à provincia, porque a provincia esteve quasi toda a seu lado na lucta contra os extrangeiros acastellados no governo e a deportação dos sediciosos para varias partes da provincia, por trez mezes, não foi pena tão severa que revoltasse a consciencia popular e viesse influir de modo sensivel na eleição para deputados constituintes. Além disso, Antonio Carlos, irmão de ambos aquelles ministros e solidario com elles em todas as suas idéas e actos politicos, teve grande votação e occupa o segundo logar, tendo sómente Vergueiro acima de si na lista dos votados.

Tambem não se poderá explicar a grande votação de Antonio Carlos pelos serviços por elle prestados ao Brazil como deputado ás Côrtes de Lisboa, porque em tal caso tambem Feijó devia ter boa votação, visto lá ter estado ao lado de Antonio Carlos, ter feito egualmente bons serviços ao Brazil, ter corrido eguaes riscos de vida e ter com elle fugido para a Inglaterra, onde juntos publicaram o «Manife-to de Falmouth». Entretanto Feijó não conseguiu siquer occupar um logar entre os supplentes que tomaram assento na Constituinte, porque foi o sexto votado na lista e os supplentes empossados dos cargos foram sómente os quatro mais votados.

Tambem não se poderá allegar que José Bonifacio, ministro e inimigo de Feijó, tivesse efficazmente influido para a pequena votação que teve o futuro ministro da Justiça e regente do

imperio, porque, si José Bonifacio tivesse poder e força bastantes
para isso, deveria tel-os egualmente para impedir o córte que
soffreu e que o atirou ao penultimo logar e, mais ainda, para
salvar a candidatura de Martim Francisco, seu irmão, genro e
collega no ministerio, e impedir que elle viesse figurar apenas
como o mais votado dos supplentes e ficar dependendo da inva-
lidez de Diogo Ordonhes ou da opção de Fernandes Pinheiro
para ter assento na Assembléa Constituinte.

As vagas deixadas por Agostinho Goulão, deputado fluminense, e por Fernandes Pinheiro, que optára pelo Rio Grande
do Sul, eram imprevistas ao tempo da eleição e José Bonifacio
não poderia se satisfazer com factos possiveis, porém não provaveis, e deixar a candidatura do seu irmão e melhor companheiro
dependente de acontecimentos furtuitos.

Martim Francisco, senhor de duas supplencias, uma por S.
Paulo e outro pelo Rio de Janeiro, optou por esta ultima e deu
logar a que o dr Ornellas, seu amigo, entrasse na Constituinte
por S. Paulo; mas seria de melhor effeito moral que elle tivesse
obtido votação sufficiente para tomar assento como proprietario
de uma cadeira do que como supplente de Fernandes Pinheiro
ou de Agostinho Goulão.

O facto em si mesmo não tem grande relevancia, mas assume
uma certa importancia por se ter dado com José Bonifacio e
Martim Francisco, ex-membros do primeiro Governo Provisorio
de S. Paulo e membros do ministerio de D. Pedro e por ser a
primeira manifestação official da sympathia popular pelos politicos
da terra depois dos graves acontecimentos de 23 de Maio de
1822, em que os Andradas foram violentamente hostilizados pelos
elementos extrangeiro e retrogrado, senhores do governo de S.
Paulo e da força armada desta capital, mas em que tambem
foram fortemente apoiados pelo elemento nacional representado
pela confederação dos municipios do interior, sob a chefia de
Paula Sousa, o mais extremado liberal daquelles agitados tempos.

Si a votação, relativamente pequena, que tiveram os dois
ministros paulistas, não foi o resultado de alguma combinação
amigavel, cujos segredos não pódem constar dos livros officiaes que
tenho á vista, mas consequencia obrigada do desprestigio politico
resultante da reacção que ambos fizeram contra os sediciosos de
23 de Maio, seria caso dos eleitores parochiaes completarem
a sua vindicta dando alguns votos a João Carlos de Oeynhausen
e, principalmente, a Costa Carvalho, como demonstração de sympathia senão pelas suas pessôas, ao menos pelos principios retrogrados que representavam. Entretanto isto não aconteceu e
os nomes dos «bernardistas» todos primaram pela ausencia nos
comicios eleitoraes.

João Carlos, Francisco Ignacio, Moraes Leme e Ferreira do Amaral não tiveram voto algum, sendo todos militares proeminentes em S. Paulo e dados á politica; mas o militar Manoel Martins do Couto Reis, que aliás não se envolvia em politica activa, obteve votos bastantes para funccionar por alguns mezes como supplente de Vergueiro. O ex-ouvidor Cósta Carvalho tambem não teve um voto siquer, mas o ex-ouvidor José Corrêa Pacheco e Silva recebeu votação sufficiente para lhe garantir um assento permanente na Constituinte como supplente de Diogo Ordonhes e, si o ouvidor Medeiros Gomes não tomou assento por falta de mais cadeiras vagas, teve comtudo mais votos do que Feijó, inimigo acerrimo dos Andradas e, portanto sympatico aos «bernardistas» e seus adherentes.

A dispersão de votos, grande como foi, podia ter, politica e moralmente, prejudicado a José Bonifacio e Martim Francisco e coincidio com a ephemera despedida de ambos do ministerio pelo joven imperador, já influenciado pela celebre cortezã Domitilla, que tanto envergonhou e desgraçou o seu reinado, mas não aproveitou directamente a nenhum dos que figuram na «bernada de Francisco Ignacio», nem os que abertamente hostilizarm a politica andradina, a que elles se compraziam em chamar arbitraria» e capazde trazer a supressão da liberdade e a ruina do Brazil.

Feijó, conego Januario, Lossio Seilbz e Estevam de Rezende trez «vitimas das arbitrariedades» dos Andradas e tres estranhos, a provincia, receberam alguma votação, mas tão pequena que não foi julgada digna de menção na historia publicada da provincia de S. Paulo e só agora sai á luz pela primeira vez.

## V

### A ELEIÇÃO DO GOVERNO PROVISORIO

Em 1822 a cidade de S. Paulo, politicamente, continha apenas duas freguezias: a da Sé, que abrangia o Braz, Norte e Sul da Sé e Villa Mariana, e a de Santa Ephigenia, em que ficavam incluidas a Consolação, Santa Cecilia e Sant'Anna.

O municipio da capital abrangia as povoações da Penha, Nossa Senhora do O', Santo Amaro, Cutia, Juquery, Conceição dos Guarulhos e S. Bernardo, não passando Itapecerica de um méro aldeamento de indios, que vinha durando desde o seculo XVII e qu só foi elevado a freguezia, definitivamente, em 1841.

A comarca abrangia todas as povoações acima mencionadas e mais as de Parnahyba e Araçariguama, S. Roque, Jundiahy,

Atibaia e Nazareth, Bragança, Mogy das Cruzes e Santa Izabel
e Parahybuna.

Tinha o municipio da capital 47 eleitores parochiaes ou do
2.º gráu assim distribuidos pelas suas freguezias:

| | |
|---|---:|
| Sé . . . . . . . . . . | 12 |
| Santa Ephigenia . . . . | 5 |
| Penha . . . . . . . . | 2 |
| N. Senhora do O' . . . . | 2 |
| Cutia . . . . . . . . | 6 |
| Santo Amaro . . . . . | 9 |
| S. Bernardo . . . . . . | 2 |
| Guarulhos . . . . . . | 6 |
| Juquery . . . . . . . | 3 |
| | — |
| Somma . . . . | 47 |

O eleitorado da comarca abrangia mais os seguintes eleitores:

| | |
|---|---:|
| De Parnahyba . . . . . . | 4 |
| » Araçáriguama . . . . . | 1 |
| » S. Roque . . . . . . | 5 |
| » Jundiahy . . . . . . | 6 |
| » Atibaia . . . . . . . | 7 |
| » Nazareth . . . . . . | 7 |
| » Bragança . . . . . . | 8 |
| » Mogy das Cruzes . . . . | 16 |
| » Santa Isabel . . . . . | 6 |
| » Parahybuna . . . . . | 3 |
| | — |
| Somma . . . . . | 67 |

Todo o eleitorado da comarca da capital se compunha,
portanto de 114 pessoas, das mais graduadas, porque a funcção
do eleitor era então de muita responsabilidade e o cargo era
considerado como muito honroso.

José Vaz Leite de Carvalho, eleitor por duas parochias,
optou pela da Cutia e deixou vago o seu logar na representação de Parnahyba, e, porque não houvesse supplentes, o numero
dos eleitores da comarca ficou desfalcado de um e reduzido a
113, cujos nomes estão conservados no livro das actas das
eleições.

A sedição de 23 de Maio de 1822 appellidada «A Bernarda de Francisco Ignacio», tinha entregado a cidade de S.
Paulo aos reaccionarios e as eleições primarias, feitas sob o seu

dominio, lhes tinham dado ganho de causa, dando logar a que a maioria dos eleitores do 2.° grau, da cidade pertencesse ao partido « bernardista » ; alguns chefes deste partido eram eleitores, como o brigadeiro Joaquim José Pinto de Moraes Leme, o coronel Francisco Ignacio de Souza Queiroz e o capitão Antonio de Siqueira Moraes.

Quando, em cumprimento do decreto de 25 de Junho de 1822, se tratou de eleger um novo governo provisorio para a provincia de S Paulo, reuniu-se o gollegio eleitoral da comarca da capital a 29 de Agosto de 1822, quando o principe D Pedro aqui se achava, tendo chegado a esta cidade quatro dias antes, no dia 25. Os bernardistas », expulsos do poder pelo principe, que aqui viera syndicar do seu procedimento, não se intimidaram e concorreram todos ao collegio eleitoral e deram os seus votos sem serem molestados. Reunido o collegio no paço do Camara Municipal, sob a presidencia do dr. Manuel Joaquim de Ornellas, secretariado pelo coronel Luiz Antonio Neves de Carvalho, e escolhidos para escrutinadores o brigadeiro Moraes Leme e o tenente João Baptista Vaz, eleitores da parachia da Sé, passou-se a fazer a eleição do governo provisorio, com o seguinte resultado :

### FARA PRESIDENTE DO GOVERNO PROVISORIO

|  | votos |
|---|---|
| Dom Luiz de Saldanha da Gama . . . . . | 42 |
| Conselheiro João Carlos Augusto Oeynhausen. . | 23 |
| Dr. Manoel Joaquim de Ornellas. . . . . | 7 |
| Desembargador João de Medeiros Gomes . . . | 7 |
| Marechal Candido Xavier de Almeida e Souza . | 5 |
| Intendente Miguel José de Oliveira. . . . . | 5 |
| Brigadeiro Joaquim José Pinto de Moraes Leme . | 4 |
| Dr. José Corrêa Pacheco Silva . . . . . . | 4 |

O marechal José Arouche de Toledo Rendon, o coronel Daniel Pedro Müller, o coronel Luiz Antonio Neves de Carvalho e o padre Frencisco das Chagas Lima tiveram um voto cada um.

### PARA SECRETARIO DO GOVERNO

|  | votos |
|---|---|
| Coronel Luiz Antonio Neves de Carvalho . . . | 62 |
| Coronel Daniel Pedro Müller. . . . . . . | 12 |
| Dr. José Corrêa Pacheco e Silva . . . . . | 9 |
| Intendente Miguel José de Oliveira Pinto. . . | 7 |
| Dr. Manoel Joaquim de Ornellas . . . . . . | 5 |
| Capitão Elesbão Francisco Vaz . . . . . . . | 2 |

O brigadeiro Francisco Antonio de Paula Nogueira da Gama, o coronel Bernardo José Pinto Gavião, e o tenente-coronel Ignacio José Vicente da Fonseca, tiveram um voto cada um.

Para os cargos de presidente e secretario do governo o voto era uninominal e o seu numero indica os eleitores presentes— 101. Para presidente teve maioria de votos Dom Luiz de Saldanha da Gama, ministro itinirante de d. Pedro e com elle presente na cidade ao tempo da eleição; não era paulista, nem tinha relações em S. Paulo que justificassem a grande votação que recebeu.

Esta demonstração de apreço não representa, portanto, mais do que uma certa adulação ao ministro, a quem parece que se queria propiciar para a syndicancia a que se ia proceder pelos factos sediciosos de 23 de maio. Que essa votação foi quasi toda de « bernadistas » se deduz dos factos de estarem elles em grande maioria no collegio eleitorar, do seu ex-chefe João Carlos de Oeynhausen, ausente de S. Paulo, desde 21 de Julho precedente, occupar o segundo logar na lista e de ainda sobrarem alguns dos seus votos para serem dados aos « bernadistas » intendente Oliveira Pinto, brigadeiro Moraes Leme e coronel Daniel Müller, emquanto que os legalistas Medeiros Gomes e Ornellas apenas tiveram 7 votos cada um e os marechaes Candido Xavier 5, e Arouche 1.

Para secretario votaram 103 eleitores e teve maioria absoluta de votos o coronel Luiz Antonio Neves de Carvalho, homem reconcentrado, insociavel, quasi neurasthenico, que nunca se declarára pró ou contra as liberdades reclamadas pelos brasileiros e nem siquer se apresentou nas festas paulistas pela chegada de D. Pedro a S. Paulo. A votação que recebeu foi de« bernadistas », que ainda tiveram votos para Müller e Oliveira Pinto, emquan- os legalistas drs. José Corrêa e Ornellas figuraram com votações minimas.

O governo, que ia ser eleito, devia ser composto de sete membros, sendo um presidente, um secretario e cinco vogaes ou deputados. O presidente e secretario estavam já votados e só faltava se proceder ao escrutinio para os deputados do governo, devendo cada eleitor votar em cinco pessoas.

O numero de votos subiu a 530, indicando a presença de 106 eleitores entretanto a acta está assignada por 105, parecendo que um eleitor se retirou antes de se apurar o resultado e de se lavrar o respectivo termo. Houve uma tal dispersão de votos que na acta se encontram 71 nomes votados, quando os lugares eram apenas 5, e como estas votações deitam alguma luz sobre o estado da opinião publica na cidade e indicam a intensidade do predominio « bernadista » no collegio eleitorar, convem transcrever o resultado da votação em beneficio da historia paulista daquelle tempo ; esse resultado foi o seguinte :

.PARA DEPUTADOS DO GOVERNO PROVISORIO

| | | VOTOS |
|---|---|---|
| 1 | Intendente Miguel de Oliveira Pinto. . . | 43 |
| 2 | Coronel Daniel Pedro Müller . . . . | 42 |
| 3 | Coronel Francisco Ignacio de Sousa Queiroz | 33 |
| 4 | Brigadeiro Joaquim J. Pinto de Moraes Leme | 31 |
| 5 | Padre João Gonçalves Lima . . . . . | 31 |
| | Capitão-mór João Baptista da Silva Passos. . | 26 |
| | Coronel Luiz Antonio Neves de Carvalho . . | 22 |
| | Dr. Manuel Joaquim de Ornellas. . . . . | 20 |
| | Coronel Anastacio de Freitas Trancoso . . . | 18 |
| | Capitão-mòr Eleuterio da Silva Prado . . . | 18 |
| | Capitão Elesbão Francisco Vaz . . . . . | 17 |
| | Coronel Antonio José Vaz . . . . . . | 16 |
| | Coronel Joaquim José Cesar de Cerqueira . . | 13 |
| | Coronel 'Bernardo José Pinto Gavião. . . . | 12 |
| | Padre Francisco das Chagas Lima . . . . | 12 |
| | Padre João Ferreira de Oliveira Bueno. . . . | 12 |
| | Padre José Rodrigues de Carvalho. . . . . | 11 |
| | Padre Manuel J Gonçalves de Andrade . . . | 11 |
| | Padre Manuel Caetano de Oliveira. . . . . | 11 |
| | Padre Francisco Moreira da Costa. . . . . | 10 |
| | André da Silva Gomes . . . . . . . . | 8 |
| | Brigadeiro Manuel Rodrigues Jordão. . . . . | 5 |
| | Tenente-coronel Bento Alberto da Gama e Sá. . | 5 |
| | Tenente-coronel José da Cunha Abreu. . . . | 5 |
| | Coronel Joaquim Antonio de Guimarães. . . . | 5 |
| | Padre Francisco José Lobo. . . . . . . | 4 |
| | Capitão José dos Santos. . . . . . . . | 4 |
| | Capitão Francisco Mariano da Cunha. . . . | 4 |
| | Capitão Francisco de Paula Simões . . . . | 4 |
| | Tenente-coronel José de Almeida Leme. . . . | 4 |
| | Dr. José Corrêa Pacheco e Silva. . . . . | 4 |
| | Desembargador João de Sousa Oliveira Bueno. . | 4 |
| | Capitão-mór Vicente da Costa Taques Góes Aranha. | 4 |
| | Brigadeiro Francisco A. de Paula Nogueira da Gama | 3 |
| | Tenente-coronel José A. da Silva Valente. . . | 3 |
| | Tenente-coronel José Fernandes Nunes. . . . | 3 |
| | Tenente João Baptista Vaz. . . . . . . | 3 |
| | Coronel Joaquim José dos Santos. . . . . | 3 |

Coronel Antonio Fernandes da Silva. . . . . 2
Padre Francisco de Paula Oliveira. . . . . 2
Desembargador João de Medeiros Gomes. . . 2
Joaquim Roberto de Carvalho Macedo. . . . 2
Capitão José Lopes França. . . . . . . 2
Padre Joaquim Ribeiro de Araujo. . . . . 2
Tenente-coronel Ricardo Carneiro. . . . . 2

Receberam um voto cada um os seguintes individuos: co-
ronel Antonio L. P. da Gama Lobo, padre Antonio Joaquim da
Silva, major Angelo Leite de Siqueira, major Bento Dias Pacheco, capitão Bento J. Leite Penteado, coronel Francisco Pinto
Ferraz, coronel Francisco Alves Ferreira de Amaral, FRANCISCO
DE PAULA SOUSA E MELLO, brigadeiro José Vaz de Carvalho,
coronel Jacintho José de Castro, coronel João Xavier da Costa
Aguiar, brigadeiro Joaquim Mariano Galvão, coronel Jeronymo
Pereira Chrispim, padre José Gonçalves da Silva, padre Joaquim A. Fernandes de Saldanha, padre José Ignacio Rodrigues,
padre José Francisco Aranha, dr. José da Costa Carvalho, capitão José de Almeida Ramos, Dom Luiz de Saldanha da Gama,
coronel Matheus da Silva Bueno, Manuel Lopes Guimarães, capitão Manuel J. da Silva Castro, DR. NICOLAO PEREIRA DE CAM-
POS VERGUEIRO e major Thomaz Gonçalves Gomide.
Os tres mais votados desta longa lista foram chefes dos
mais activos da celebre «Bernarda de Francisco Ignacio» e receberam as melhores votações sem interferencia de D. Pedro,
que estava em S. Paulo, nem de José Bonifacio, seu ministro,
que havia ficado no Rio. O quarto votado, brigadeiro Moraes
Leme, era um militar muito distincto, fidalgo de alta linhagem
e rico, que montou á sua custa um corpo de tropas e a sua
frente marchou para o Rio Grande do Sul, em 1776, fazendo o
mesmo que fizera o coronel Anastacio Trancoso e prestando importantes serviços ao seu paiz; depois fez-se um dos heróes da
«Bernarda» e apparece aqui em politica como candidato dos
«bernardistas» ao governo da provincia.
O quinto da lista, padre João Gonçalves de Lima, era um
velho de 70 annos, vigario de Parnahyba e muito boa pessoa:
porém, tinha para os «bernardistas» o defeito, de que o accu-
saram, de ser amigo dos Andradas e por isso imprestavel para
membro do governo de S. Paulo, em cujo cargo não se prestaria
a servir aos reaccionarios. A votação que teve foi, naturalmente, do eleitorado de fóra da cidade, que tambem honrou os
nomes do capitão-mór Silva Passos, do dr. Ornellas e do coronel Anastacio Trancoso, todos amigos e partidarios dos Andra-

das; porém, estas votações foram tão pequenas que não lhe darriam entrada no governo si na eleição dependesse só da comarca da capital

Examinando-se a lista vê-se que, nellas figuram mais militares clerigos, muitos dos quaes são homens obscuros de quem a historia paulista não guardou os nomes, emquanto que alguns homens de merito, como Paulo Souza, Costa Carvalho, e Vergueiro, apparecem apenas com um voto cada um e o marechal Candido Xavier e o coronel Francisco Corrêa de Moraes tiveram os seus nomes totalmente deslumbrados pelos eleitores da capital.

Si não houvesse outros collegios eleitoraes das comarcas de Ytú, de Curityba e do valle de Parnahyba, o governo ficaria constituido do seguinte modo :

Presidente, d. Luiz Saldanha da Gama e na sua falta o conselheiro João Carlos de Oeynhausen, que era o segundo votado.

Secretario, coronel Luiz Antonio Neves de Carvalho, homem pouco estimado pelos nacionalistas, e na sua falta pelo coronel Muller, um dos chefe da «Bernarda».

Deputados do governo, intendente Miguel José de Oliveira Pinto, coroneis Daniel Pedro Müller e Francisco Ignacio de Souza Queiroz, brigadeiro Joaqnim José Pinto de Moraes Leme —todos chefes activos da «Bernarda» —e padre João Gonçalves Lima, velho quasi decrepito e incapaz de enfrentar com os seus collegas do governo quando se tratasse dos interesses brasileiros em conflicto com os interesses portuguezes na crise politica de que resultou a nossa independencia.

Pelos resultados desta eleição se vê que os «bernadistas» de S. Paulo pretenderam, com os seus votos, aunullar os effeitos do decreto de 25 de Junho de 1822, que lhes cassou os poderes governamentaes, e reeleger os mesmos individues demittridos por d. Pedro do governo provisorio por causa da parte activa que haviam tomado na sedição de 23 de Maio de 1822.

Continuariam assim no poder e a sancção dos seus actos voto popular importaria condemnação da politica cntão adoptada por José Bonifacio e Martim Francisco, membros do ministerio do principe regente contra os sediciosos da «Bernarda»,

Seria uma victoria moral e politica do mais alto alcance.

Felizmente, porém, para os nacionalistas e para os interesses brasileiros por elles defendidos, só na cidade de S. Paulo é que estava influenciada pelos reaccionarios ; todo o interior estava congregado na confederação de Ytú, sob a chefia de Paula Souza, Santos estava bem guardada pelo marechal Candido Xavier e o vale do Parahyba ficava firme nas idéas novas, sob a influencia do general Arouche, inspector geral das milicias, —todos paulistas genuinos e chefes proeminentes do nacionalismo.

Nestes termos, as eleições occorridas em toda a provicia deram tão estrondosa victoria aos candidatos nacionalistas que o seu resultado geral annullou completamente as votações desta capital e garantiram a eleição de um governo composto sómente de paulistas liberaes, que foram os seguintes:

1.º Marechal Candido Xavier de Almeida e Souza, presidente.
2.º Dr José Corrêa Pacheco e Silva, secretario.
3.º Dr. Manoel Joaquim de Ornellas, deputado.
4.º Padre João Goncalves Lima, deputado.
5.º Coronel Anastacio de Freitas Trancoso, deputado.
6.º Capitão-mór João Baptista da Silva Passos, deputado.
7.º Coronel Francisco Corrèa de Moraes, deputado.

Tomaram elles posse a 6 de janeiro de 1823 e governaram a provincia até 1 de abril de 1824, quando foram substituidos por Lucas Antonio Monteiro de Barros, depois visconde de Congonhas do Campo, que foi o primeiro presidente que S. Paulo teve depois da promulgação da constituição outorgada em 25 de março de 1824.

A. DE TOLEDO PIZA.

# Recordaçoes historicas

## I

D. João VI. tendo residido no Rio de Janeiro durante treze annos, de 1808 a 1821, e gosando mesmo de alguma estima popular pelos importantes melhoramentos que, sob o seu governo, se introduziram no paiz, se affeiçoara muito ao Brazil e aos brasileiros e desejaria viver e morrer entre nós.

Foi com grande desgosto que elle recebeu o chamado das Côrtes Constituintes de Lisboa para voltar com a familia real ao velho Reino. A principio vacillou elle em acudir áquelle chamado, entendendo que as necessidades da politica em Portugal ficariam satisfeitas mandando elle para Lisboa o seu filho primogen to D. Pedro mas os cortezãos, chefiados pela rainha Carlota Joaquina, decidiram de modo contrario e assim o pae é que foi e o filho é que ficou.

Resolvida a partida do rei, embarcou-se D. João VI no dia 25 de Abril, mas elle só deixou a bahia do Rio de Janeiro na manhã do dia 26, chorand lagrimas amargas e já curtindo saudades do paiz que tanto amava, emquanto a sua perversa esposa exultava por voltar ao velho mundo e limpava dos sapatos a terra do sólo brasileio. A esquadra que levou e rei era composta de doze navios e chegou a Lisboa em Julho, nella seguindo a familia real, que não era pequena e muita gente da côrte.

A 22 daquelle mesmo mez de Abril o rei nomeou regente do Brazil o principe D. Pedro, que entrou officialmente a exercer as funcções magestaticas; porém, como desde dias antes os preparativos da partida occupavam a attenção da côrte; D. Pedro já vinha de facto governando o Brazil e fazendo-se moralmente responsavel pela paz e socego publico.

No dia 21 de Abril, vespera da sua investidura do cargo de regente, estavam reunidos na Praça do Commercio os eleitores parochiaes que tinham de eleger os representantes do Rio de Janeiro nas córtes Constituintes de Lisboa, quando o edificio foi assaltado pela força armada, que fez fogo sobre os eleitores e mais gente alli presentes, produzindo muitas mortes e ferimentos E' a este facto que Evaristo Veiga se referiu, quando disse que « D. Pedro começou a sua vida publica por um acto de ferocidade, que foi a trahição da Praça do Commercio, e a terminou por um acto de demencia, que foi a nomeação do ministerio das 24 horas», compostos dos fidalgos e retrogrados marquezes de Paranáguá, de Aracaty, de Baependy e de Inhambupe, do conde de Lages e do visconde de Alcantara e que o levou ao abysmo do 7 de Abril de 1831.

D. João VI durante os treze annos que residiu no Brazil, teve sómento um gabinete e oito ministros, que foram D. Pedro de Souza Holstein, depois duque de Palmella; D. Fernando José de Portugal, depois marquez de Aguiar; Antonio de Araujo Azevedo, depois conde da Barca; D. João de Almeida Mello Castro, depois conde das Galveas; D. Marcos de Noronha, depois conde dos Arcos; D Rodrigo de Sousa Coutinho, mais tarde conde de Linhares; João Rodrigues de Sá e Mello, que foi visconde de Anadia, e Thomaz Antonio de Villa Nova Portugal. Estes foram ministros effectivos e João Paulo Bezerra exerceu interinamento as funcções de ministro por alguns mezes pertencendo todos ao periodo do regimen absoluto.

Juradas as bases da Constituição das Córtes de Lisboa, foram mantidas as mesmas pastas ministeriaes, do Reino, da Marinha e Ultramar, da Guerra e Extrangeiros e das Finanças que se chamava *Real Erario*, mas a 26 de Fevereiro de 1821 entrou pessoal novo, composto dos almirantes Costa Quintella e Monteiro Torres, do jurisconsulto Sylvestre Pinheiro Ferreira e do fidalgo conde de Louzã.

Estava este novo gabinete no caso de governar o paiz durante annos, como acontecia com os ministros de D. João VI, entretanto, durou menos de dois mezes e foi despedido a 22 de Abril, no mesmo dia em que D. Pedro assumiu o cargo de regente. Foi então que começou a contradança ministerial, especie de fogo da gangorra, com que o primeiro imperador se devertiu durante os dez annos do seu reinado.

Se D. João VI, nos treze annos da sua permauença no Rio de Janeiro, teve sómente um ministerio, de que fizeram parte oito pessoas, algumas das quaes da ordem de duque de Palmella, do conde de Barca e de Sylvestre Ferreira, a volubilidade e inconstancia de Pedro I levaram-no a ter, em muito menos tempo, desaseis ministerios, em que entraram cincoenta politicos diversos, sem contar os dois ministros itinerantes.

Estevam Ribeiro de Rezende e Lujz Saldanha da Gama. que o acompanharam nas viagens que fez a Minas e S. Paulo, em 1822. As pastas ministeriaes no começo eram quatro, depois passaram a cinco e subiram a seis antes do fim do primeiro reinado. Muitos dos ministerio de D. Pedro exerceram o cargo diversas vezes,, de modo que o numero dos ministros subiu a cento e trinta e nove. A duração dos ministerios merece uma especial menção, porque nos dá uma idéa mais ou menos exacta das phantasias politicas de D. Pedro e da sua caprichosa interferencia na direcção dos negocios publicos.

O gabinete que teve vida mais longa foi o sexto, que durou 24 mezes e 7 dias, de 14 de Novembro de 1822 e 21 de Novembro de 1825; o segundo na duração foi o decimo segundo que viveu anno e meio, de meado de Junho de 1828 a meado de dezembro de 1829; um durou 11 mezes e 24 dias; um 10 mezes e 5 dias; um 9 mezes e 20 dias; tres viveram 8 mezes e alguns dias; dois 5 mezes e dias; dois 3 mezes e dias; um durou 16 dias; outro 4 dias; outro 2 dias e finalmente, o ultimo viveu sómente um dia.

No primeiro gabinete organizado por D. Pedro entraram dois politicos que tinham servido com D. João VI e cinco homens novos; estes serviram oito mezes e dias e foram despedidos a 16 de janeiro de 1822, quando se orgauisou outro gabinete composto de pessoal quasi todo novo.

Do segundo ministerio fez parte José Bonifacio desde o seu começo, e a 3 de julho para elle entrou Martim Francisco, pouco antes expulso do governo provisorio de S. Paulo pela sedição da *Bernarda de Francisco Ignacio*; os outros membros foram Caetano Pinto de Miranda Montenegro, o marechal Oliveira Alves, Luiz Pereira Nobrega de Souza Coutinho e Manuel Antonio Farinha, depois conde de Souzel.

Foi este o ministerio que fez a independencia a 7 de Setembro de 1822 e a acclamação do imperador a 12 de outubro do mesmo anno; porém, D. Pedro, ingrato e já dirigido por influencias extranhas que dominavam o seu espirito leviano, o despediu a 28 de outubro, cincoenta e um dias depois da proclamação da independencia e dezeseis dias depois da sua acclamação, e formou um outro gabinete de gente quasi desconhecida, como eram os desembargadores Sebastião Luiz Tinoco da Silva e João Ignacio Cunha, o barão de Santo Amaro, o capitão de mar e guerra Luiz da Cunha Moreira e o tenente-coronel João Vieira de Carvalho, sendo este ultimo um dos aulicos mais protegidos por D. Pedro.

A substituição do ministerio dos Andradas por um outro composto de homens relativamente desconhecidos, produziu grande indignação entre os brazileiros e as manifestações de desgosto não se fizeram esperar. D. Pedro, reconsiderando em parte o seu acto imprudente, recompoz o ministerio, fazendo voltar a elle José Bonifacio, Martim Francisco e Miranda Montenegro, mas conservando dois dos seus protegidos, Vieira de Carvalho e Cunha Moreira, de modo que o gabinete impopular que foi assim modificado veiu a durar sómente dois dias, de 28 a 30 de outubro de 1822. Em S. Paulo a opinião publica se alarmára com a noticia da quéda inesperada e desnecessaria do ministerio dos Andradas e o povo logo se reunio no Paço Municipal e de accôrdo com os vereadores, dirigiu ao imperador uma importante representação, que diz assim:

« No meio de publicos festejos, signaes não equivocos do regosijo que transporta nossos corações, pela gloriosa acclamação do senhor D. Pedro de Alcantara, imperador sem par, idolo des brazileiros ouvimos e lemos com espanto que um partido de vis carbonarios, de monstros da especie humana, solapava a estabilidade do throno brasileiro e, servindo-se de tramas e cabalas, pretendeu murchar em flor nossas esperanças, offuscar a gloria do immortal Pedro, privando-o de um ministerio sabio, justo e forte.

« Oh! Só meros automatos não se sentiriam arrebatados de rancor e de desesperação pela avidez de morder esses corações perfidos que manejavam a intriga e a desordem, que pretendiam levar de rojo o recem-nascido e florescente imperio, estabelecendo a anarchia, a destruição e a guerra civil!!!

«Como veriamos sem horror malogrados nossos trabalhos, menoscabado nosso nome, e nossos inimigos exultando em alegria, vendo o Brazil, descer do seu throno magestoso e abafando nos labios o grito da independencia que levantou com denodo e jurou com coragem?

«Como não seria insultado de novo nesse denominado *Soberano Congresso Lisbonense* o nosso anjo tutelar, o magnanimo Pedro? Como não zombariam de suas acertadas e maduras resoluções e de seus justos decretos, attribuindo-os ás vascillações de um menino que, de sua opinião, devia ainda aprender os primeiros elementos de litteratura nas côrtes extrangeiras?

«Que série de males, que abysmo de horrores!... Mas, oh ventura! os bons brazileiros, habitantes do Rio de Janeiro, idolatras da patria, do imperador e das virtudes, souberam apagar o incendio, que começava a atear-se, e anniquillar o partido que ousadamente queria dominar. Elles viram bambalear o magestoso edificio da nossa bem entendida liberdade e ir a cahir por terra os mais firmes esteios do throno e, calculando as consequencias, dando desafogo ás suas virtudes innatas, deram o passo

que só podia salvar-nos de novo: representaram ao imperador
que a patria exigia que elle fizesse o sacrificio maior a seu
coração, restituindo ao ministerio os benemeritos brazileiros, os
nossos dignos patricios, (com que gloria o dizemos!) os grandes,
os sabios, os justos Andradas.

«Os infra-escriptos, pois, querendo dar um publico teste
munho de seus sentimenios patrioticos, completamente identicos
aos do bom povo do Rio de Janeiro, exigem que com toda a
camara desta cidade, como orgam do povo agradeça a Sua Magestade Imperial o restabelecimento dos seus bons ministros e
roguem a sua conservação, pois nelles confiam a segurança da
patria, a conservação e o progresso do imperio brasileiro, porquanto é incontestavel que o ministerio é a mola real dos
imperios e desde que esta se entorpece, retarda-se e até se des-
tróe o movimento regular destas grandes machinas.

«Não é necessario procurar demonstrações desta verdade;
ella é de evidencia politica, e os ministerios do sr. rei D. João
VI e mesmo de Sua Magestade Imperial, até aos começos deste
anno, são bem eloquentes testemunhos ; e se renovem os protestos
da ma·s firme adhesão á sua sagrada pessôa e á santa causa do
Brazil, que os paulistas juram defender até ao ultimo alento, e
rogue outrosim a Sua Magestade Imperial o mais exemplar
castigo desses infames que procuram denegrir a nossa gloria.

«Agradeça-se á camara e ao honrado povo do Rio de Janeiro
o passo heroico que deram pedindo a Sua Magestade a conservação dos sabios ministros que nada têm a invejar aos Colberts,
aos Sullys e aos Pitts e que rivalizam a gloria dos Franklins,
assegurando-lhes que os valentes e briosos paulistas, desejando
imitar suas virtudes patrioticas, hão de sempre collaborar com
denodo na conservação do imperio do Brazil e do seu immortal
imperador e nos progressos da sua felicidade, quaesquer que
sejam os sacrificios que devam fazer e quaesquer que sejam os
perigos que devam affrontar.—S. Paulo, 11 de novembro de 1822.—
*Anastacio de Freitas Trancoso*, coronel reformado e commandante
interino da guarda civica—*Miguel Angelo da Silveira*, tenente-coronel reformado e segundo commandante interino da guarda civica.—
*Antonio Joaquim de Abreu Pereira*, chantre.—*Francisco Nunes Ramalho*, capitão reformado e major da guarda civica.—Conego *Joaquim
José Carlos de Carvalho*, guarda civica.—Conego *Francisco José
Lobo*.— Conego *José Gomes de Almeida*.—Padre *Fernando Lopes
de Camargo* —Commendador *Manuel da Cunha Azeredo Coutinho Souza Chichorro* —*Antonio da Silva Prado*, guarda civica.—
Padre *Manuel Joaquim do Amaral Gurgel*, guarda civica.—Padre
—*Ildelfonso Xavier Ferreira*, guarda civica —*Francisco de*

*Assis Lorena*.— Conego *Lourenço Justiniano Ferreira*.—Conego *Antonio P. de Camargo* —*Francisco de Paula Tavares*, guarda civica.—*Manoel José Chaves*, guarda civica.—*José Rodrigues Velloso de Oliveira*, guarda civica.— *Ignacio José Cesar*, guarda civica. —*João Manoel de Almeida Bueno*, guarda civica. --*Francisco Pinto do Rego*, guarda civica. *Joaquim Rodrigues Goulart*, guarda civica.—*Francisco Jorge de Paula Pibeiro*, guarda civica. *José Maria Rodrigues Goulart*, guarda civica.—*João Nepomuceno Freire Souto*, guarda civica·—*José Porfirio*, guarda civica.—*Joaquim José Terxeira Baptista*, guarda civica.—*Thomaz Gonçalves Gomide*, guarda civica.—*Joaquim Gonçalves Gomide*, guarda civica. —*José Gonçalves Gomide*, guarda civica.—*Thomaz M. das Dores Tibeiro*, guarda civica.—*Thomaz de Aquino e Castro*, tenente de caçadores.—*José de Freitas Saldanha*, mestre de cerimonias — *Antonio Mariano de Azevedo Marques*, guarda civica.—*Manuel Emygdio Bernardes*, sub-chantre da Sé.—Padre *Leão José de Senna*.—*Joaquim Manuel de Azevedo Marques*, guarda civica.—*João Olyntho de Carvalho e Silva*, guarda civica.—*João Rodrigues de Camargo Pires*, tenente —*Manuel Franrisco da Matta*—Dr. *Manuel Joaquim de Ornellas*.—Fr. *João do Espirito Santo*, guardião de S. Francisco.—*Januario Antonio de Araujo*, guarda-civica.—*Joaquim M da Costa Ferreira*, capitão ás ordens do governo.—*João José Moreira*, guarda-civica.—*Joaquim Antonio Alves Alvim*, alferes.—*José Gomes Segurado*, guarda-civica —*José Maria da Silveira*, guarda-civica.—*Joaquim Cardoso*, cirurgião-mór do hospital e guarda-civica.—*Innocencio José Rodrigues de Vasconcellos*, guarda-civica.—*Thomaz Gonçalves Gomide*, official da Contadoria e guarda-civica.—*Manuel Gomes de Gouvêa*, guarda-civica.— *Antonio Xavier Ferreira*, guarda-civica —*José Clemente de Mesquita*, guarda-civica.—*Joaquim Antonio Rodrigues de Vasconcellos*, guarda-civica.--*Miguel Antonio de Godoy*, guarda-civica. —*José Antonio de Camargo*, guarda-civica.—*Caetano Felix Theodoro Xavier*, guarda-civica.—*João Nepomuceno de Almeida*, guarda-civica.—*José Francisco Xavier dos Santos*, guarda-civica.—*Joaquim Borges de Sampaio*, guarda-civica.—*Antonio José Pessoa*, guarda-civica.—*Candido Gonçalves Gomide*, guarda-civica. — *Martim Gonçalves Gomide*, guarda-civica·—*João Gonçalves Gomide*, guarda-civica.—*José Mathias Ferreira de Abreu*, major da guarda-civica.—*Jeronymo Maximo Rodrigues Cardim*, guarda-civica.—*Francisco Martins Bonilho*, guarda-civica —*Manuel Francisco da Costa Silveira*.—*Joaquim Theodoro de Araujo*, guarda-civica.—Fr *Antonio de Santo Gertrudes*, prior do Carmo.—*José Xavier de Azevedo Marques*,

guarda-civica.—*Francisco Antonio Pinto Bastos,—Candido Igna
cio da Silva*, guarda-civica.—*Joaquim José Machado de Oliveira*, guarda-civica.—*Antonio Marques Henriques*, conego cura
da Sé.—*Antonio Monuel de Abreu*, coadjuctor da Sé —*Antonio
Mariano da Silva*, sacristão da Sé.—*Antonio de Padua de Gusmão*, tenenre-coronel.—*Francisco Antonio Romano*, alferes.—
*José Joaquim de Carvalho.*—Padre *Francisco de Faula Oliveira*,
guarda-civica.—*José Joaquim Cesar de Cerqueira Leme*, coronel.—*Joaquim José de Moraes Abreu*, tenente-coronel· —Dr.
*Justiniano de Mello Franco*, physico-mór interino e guarda
civica.—*Manuel Innocencio de Vasconcellos*, sargento-mór -
guarda-civica.—*José Joaquim de Vasconcellos Alambary* sargento-
mór e ajudante de ordens.—*Manuel de Campos Penteado*, sargento-mór.—*Francisco Pinto Ferraz* capitão de cavallaria.—*Francisco
da Silva Prado*, capitão.—*Joaquim José dos Santos Silva*, alferes.—*Antonio de Almeida da Silva Freire*, juiz de fóra de
Taubaté e soldado da guarda-civica.—*Manuel Joaquim Leite
Penteado*, guarda-civica.—*Mario de Faria Doria*, guarda-civica.
—O vigario *Antonio Joaquim da Silva.—Pedro Antonio Ferreira*, alferes.—*Antonio Nunes Ramalho*, guarda-civica.—Padre
*José Joaquim de Oliveira Brazeiro*, guarda-civica.—*Joaquim
José de Almeida*, capitão.—Padre *Antonio Joaquim de Araujo
Leite*, guarda civica.—*Joaquim José Freire da Silva*, guarda-
civica.—*Joaquim José Freire Filho*, guarda-civica. - *Manuel J.
da Silva Castro*, guarda-civica.—*Joaquim Floriano de Toledo*,
tenente.—*José Rodrigues da Silva*, ajudante.—*Ignacio Antonio
de Toledo*, guarda-civica.—*José Teixeira dos Santos*, guarda-
civica.—*Francisco de Assis Cruz*, tenente.—*José Francisco Serpa*,
*Bento Francisco de Moraes.*—Padre *José Manuel de Sousa*,
guarda-civica.—*Manuel Delfino da Fonseca*, official da Contadoria e guarda civica.—*Francisco de Paula Xavier de Toledo.—
José Antonio Fernandes*, alferes.—*Bento Dias Vieira.—Thomaz
Antonio Duarte*, guarda-civica. — Padre *João Ferreira de Oliveira Bueno*, thesoureiro da Sé e guarda-civica.— Padre *Marcellino Ferreira Bueno*, guarda civica.—Padre *Vicente Pires da
Motta*, guarda-civica.—*Bento Corrêa Leme*, capitão de cavallaria.—*Manuel J. Rodrigues da Silva*, guarda-civica.—*Roberto
Watkins*, guarda-civica.—*Manuel Nunes Ramalho*, guarda-civica.
—*Francisco de Assis Pinheiro Prado*, guarda-civica.—Dr. *José
Corrêa Pacheco e Silva*, ouvidor da comarca.—*Segismundo Honorio de Lima*, tenente.—*Antonio Joaquim da Costa Ribeiro*,
capitão.—*Luiz Antonio de Sá Brazeiros*, capitão.—*Manuel Francisco da Cruz Almeida*, capitão.—*João Baptista de Oliveira*,
tenente.—*Francisco Bernardes Corrêa*, tenente.—*Manu l Gon-*

çalves da Luz Paralhão, tenente.—*Manuel Ribeiro de Araujo*, guarda-civica.—*José Ferreira Leite*, guarda-civica.—*José F. Leite Filho*, guarda-civica.—*José da Silva Carvalho*, sargento-mór. — Padre *Joaquim A Fernandes de Saldanha*, lente regio de Theologia e guarda-civica.—*Manuel dos Santos Lima*.—*Luiz José Carneiro*, sargento-mór,—*José Manuel da Silva*, capitão.—*Marcellino J. de Vasconcellos Nardy*, capitão e guarda-civica.—*Antonio Rodrigues Moreira*.—*Luiz Pedroso da Silva*.—*Julião de Moura Negrão*, coronel de milicias.—*Antonio José Bordini*, sargento-mór.—*José Manuel da Luz*, sargento-mór.—*João Pereira Simões*, tenente-coronel.—*Floriano da Costa e Silva*, guarda-civica.—*Ignacio José de Macedo*, tenente.—*Severino Pinto da Silva*, capitão.—*Manuel P. de Toledo*, guarda-civica.—*Diogo Corrêa Marzagão*.—*Francisco Pereira de Araujo*.—*Joaquim José do Rosario*, alferes.—*Antonio José de Faria*.—*Joaquim P. de Castro*, guarda-civica.—*José da Silva Marceana*, advogado e guarda-mór da Junta de Justiça. — Padre *Sebastião A. de Oliveira Cruz*.—*José Joaquim Monteiro*.—*Aleixo Corrêa Vieira*.—*Salvador Pedroso de Barros*, guarda-civica.—*João Homem Guedes Portilho*, alferes.—*Antonio R. Freire de Vasconcellos*.—*João C. Marzagão*.—*André da Silva Gomes*, guarda civica.—Padre *Manuel Dias de Abreu*.—*Bento José de Moraes*, capitão.—*Antonio Pedro do Silva Gomes*.—*Bento José da Silva Rego*. guarda-civica.—O vigario *José Basilio Rodrigues Cardim*, guarda-civica.—*Francisco S dos Santos Cardim*, tenente.—*Antonio Bernardo Bueno da Veiga*, capitão de milicias e guarda-civica, —*Gregorio Ignacio Ferreira Nobre*, capitão.—*José Lopes França*, capitão.—*José Antonio Pimenta*, guarda-civica.—*Manuel Ferreira Duarte*.—*Diogo José Machado de Castro*, sargento-mór.—*Francisco José Barbosa*.—*José Joaquim de Jesus e Silva*.—*José Rodrigues de Almeida*.—*João de Almeida Bueno*, guarda-çivica. —*Joaquim Firmino Gonçalves*, guarda-civica.—*Luiz Manuel Feliciano Kelli*.—*Francisco de Assis Ludgero*, alferes.—*José Feliciano de Lara Moraes*.—*Manuel Neves de Jesus*.—*Luiz Antonio do Valle Quaresma*.—Padre *Florentino Antonio Maria* guarda-civica.—Alferes *José Mendes da Silva*.

Cerca de 200 pessoas assignaram esta representação e entre ellas se encontram homens de todas as classes sociaes e das mais proeminentes familias paulistas. O numero de clerigos é grande, e todos pareciam ter gosto em declarar que pertenciam á guarda civica, que aqui fôra creada em seguida á proclamação da independencia, para a defesa dos interesses brazileiros em lucta com os interesses portuguezes e retrogrados.

A geração actual encontrará na lista das assignaturas muitos nomes de antepassados seus e terá satisfacção de saber como elles: pensavam sobre a politica nacional e que idéa faziam dos aulicos, que ao tempo da independencia e da acclamação já estavam dominando o espirito de D. Pedro e levando-o á pratica de actos, revoltantes para os corações patrioticos e dedicados á causa do Brazil.

Hão de ainda notar os leitores que assignaram este importante documento, em que os Andradas são chamados *sabios*, *grandes e justos*, diversos individuos, como Padua Gusmão, Severino Silva, coronel Cesar, Pinto Bastos, Thomaz Gomide e outros, que fizeram figura nos motins da *Bernarda de Francisco Ignacio* e seguintes ou que subscreveram as accusações dos sediciosos contra os paulistas Martim Francisco e Brigadeiro Jordão, confirmando assim o que alguns disseram na devassa, que então se fez, que foram arrastados pela violencia a tomar parte naquelles degradantes acontecimentos.

Pede-se na representação que sejam «exemplarmente punidos os infames que procuraram denegrir a nossa gloria, que pretenderam levar de rojo o recem-nascido e já florescente imperio brazileiro e estabelecer no paiz a anarchia, a destruição e a guerra civil», denotando estas affirmações que em S. Paulo se sabia que o espirito leviano e vacillante de D. Pedro, como de um menino, já estava sendo trabalhado e dirigido por influencias extranhas e contrarias aos sentimentos brazileiros e aos interesses nacionaes.

João Carlos de Oeynhausen, Costa Carvalho, Francisco Ignacio e Domitila estavam no Rio de Janeiro e a sua presença na capital do imperio, coincidindo com a quéda precipitada e justificada do ministerio dos Andradas, parece estar indicando que a mudança inesperada do gabinete obedecia á influencia dos retrogrados, nacionaes e extrangeiros, alliada aos odios ainda recentes e não amortecidos da *Bernarda* de 23 de Maio de 1822.

Deante das manifestações populares no Rio de Janeiro, o joven imperador se apressou em restituir as pastas a José Bonifacio e Martim Francisco, sem esperar pelas representações dos paulistas e de outros povos mais distantes; porém o ministerio já não era o mesmo e tinha em seu seio elementos extranhos e hostis ao espirito liberal, e desses máos elementos João Vieira de Carvalho, valido do Paço e depois conde de Lages, era o mais genuino representante e Cunha Moreira era um dos fieis adeptos.

Caetano Pinto era um residuo dos tempos coloniaes, que vinha se accommodando as novas condições do paiz ou se ageitando ás caprichosas feições da politica imperial; fôra capitão general de baraço e cutello, puro representante do despo—

'tismo portuguez, como fôra membro do ministerio libertador de 16 de Janeiro de 1822 e do gabinete reaccionario de 17 de Julho de 1823, que substituiu o ministerio dos Andradas, definitivamente derribado nessa data; servia á pessôa de D. Pedro e não ao paiz adoptivo

Assim reorganizado, com um elemento quasi neutro na pessoa de Caetano Pinto e com dois elementos hostis representados por Vieira de Carvalho e Cunha Moreira, o novo ministerio dos Andradas arrastava comsigo a má vontade do imperador e da sua roda immediata e não podia estar em condições de servir ao paiz com a mesma energia e vantagens da sua primeira phase.

Luctando com a leviendade e inconstancia de D. Pedro e com a aversão dos aulicos, viveria o ministerio sómente o tempo necessario para se preparar um novo plano de despedil-o; tinha os seus dias contados, mas ainda nessa precaria situação proseguiram os Andradas no trabalho de completar a grande obra da independencia, que haviam iniciado, e tanto a adeantaram que a sua quéda definitiva a 17 de julho de 1823, a violenta e criminosa dissolução da Assembléa Constituinte, as consequentes deportações e a rebellião conhecida por *Confederação do Equador* não pouderam impedil-a de ser completada tres annos depois.

A 17 de Julho de 1823 foram José Bonifacio e Martim Francisco definitivamente despedidos do terceiro ministerio organizado por D. Pedro e formou-se nesse mesmo dia um quinto gabinete, em que entraram tres membros do ministerio anterior —o velho Caetano Pinto de Miranda Montenegro, que servia a todos os governos, o palaciano João Vieira de Carvalho, protegido do imperador, e o official de marinha Cunha Moreira.

Para as pastas vagas pela retirada de José Bonifacio e Martim entraram Carneiro de Campos, então deputado constituinte e depois marquez de Caravellas, e Manoel Jacintho Nogueira da da Gama, mineiro absolutista e depois marquez de Baependy, cujo nome Evaristo Veiga dizia ironicamente ser do «melhor agouro» para a liberdade.

A presença de Carneiro de Campos em um tal ministerio, composto de um conhecido absolutista, como era Nogueira da Gama, de um residuo do governo colonial, como Caetano Pinto, e de dois militares subalternos, creaturas do Paço, como Vieira de Carvalho e Cunha Moreira, faz suppor que o futuro marquz de Caravellas estava de accôrdo com as idéas dos seus companheiros de gabinete e que o governo deste modo organizado estaria nas graças do imperador e da roda aulica que o cercava, tendo assim e principal dos elementos necessarios para uma longa e prospera vida.

Entretanto, ou pelos caprichos e volubilidade de D. Pedro ou pelas exigencias palacianas, foi este ministerio despedido a 10 de Novembro ddquelle mesmo anno de 1823, tendo durado sómente 3 mezes e 23 dias. A Assembléa Constituinte estava funccionando ; o projecto de constituição sujeito á apreciação dos dos deputados não era do agrado dos aulicos e dos retrogados, que o julgavam por demais liberal e offensivo ás imperiaes regalias ; na propria assemléa havia discordia e as relações entre brasileiros e portuguezes eram tensas e mesmo azedas, de modo que a situação politica da capital do imperio era então das mais precarias.

D. Pedro e os aulicos, que pareciam estar á espera de um pretexto para medidas violentas, precisavam de um gabinete de acção e capaz de vencer as difficuldades daquelle grave momento politico. Foi então organizado o ministerio de 10 de Novembro de 1823, o sexto do primeiro do reinado e composto de Francisco Villela Barbosa, despota e futuro marquez do Paranaguá ; de Clemente Ferreira França, homem sanguinario, que mais tarde encheu as provincias de commissões militares e de cadafalsos e que julgava ser acto de misericordia enforcar depressa os condemnados politicos ; de Cunha Moreira; o mesmo que vinha servindo em varios ministerios anteriores ; de Sebastião Tinoco, já mencionado como membro do ministerio de 28 do Outubro de 1823, que durou dois dias, até 30 daquelle mesmo mez, e de José de Oliveira Barbosa, homem inteiramente desconhecido.

Foi este o ministerio que se responsabilizou pela dissolução da Assembléa Constituinte e prisão de varios deputados — o maior crime politico do primeiro imperio e origem de todas as desordens que levaram D. Pedro ao abysmo de 7 de Abril de 1831. Dissolvida a Assembléa á mão armada e presos os deputados mais temidos e odiados pelos aulicos e pelas cortezãas, a 12 de Novembro de 1823, já D. Pedro despediu do ministerio, do dia seguinte, Sebastião Tinoco, e José de Oliveira Barbosa, que serviram sómente tres dias, tempo que bastou para a pratica daquelle grande crime.

A pasta de Oliveira Barbosa, que era a da Guerra, passou interinamente para Villela Barbosa, e para a vaga de Sebastião Tinoco, na Fazenda, entrou Mariano José Pereira Fonseca, futuro marquez de Maricá, bom literato e auctor das famosas *Maximas e Pensamentos*. Esta modificação ministerial durou apenas 24 horas, porque no dia seguinte, 14 de Novembro, D. Pedro poz abaixo todo o gabinete e organizou um outro, de seis pastas, que durou dois annos e sete dias até 21 de Novembro de 1825.

Desde que assumiu o cargo de Regente do Brasil. a 22 de Abril de 1821, até a dissolução da Assembléa Constituinte, teve D. Pedro seis ministerios, dos quaes um durará dois dias e outro, não obstante as recomposições. viveu sómente quatro dias, dando logar a que um dos ministros, o marquez de Maricá, carregasse com a sua pasta sómente um dia!

O ministerio *mathusalem*, que se formou a 14 de Novembro de 1893 e durou um pouco mais de dois annos, foi muitas vezes recomposto, de maneira que teve quinze membros. Delle fizeram parte o tenente-coronel Costa Barros e Pedro de Araujo Lima, futuro marquez de Olinda, que foram despedidos tres dias depois ; Clemente Ferreira França, que foi posto na rua dentro de sete dias, Estevam de Rezende, visconde de Barbacena, marquez de Queluz, Carvalho e Mello, Sebastião Tinoco, Silveira Mendonça, o valido do Paço, Vieira de Carvalho, já barão do Lages, Villela Barbosa: que servia effectivamente na pasta dos Extrangeiros e interinaments occupou varias outras, e finalmente Mariano José Pereira Fonseca, o famoso moralista, que entrou já no fim do biennio ministerial e carregou a pasta da Fazenda durante 38 dias até 21 de Novembro de 1825, dia em que todo o ministerio foi depedido e se organizou um outro. cuja composição darei depois.

Este ministerio se incubiu da deportação dos Andradas e de outros patriotas presos em consequencia da dissolução da Assembléa Constituinte ; decretou a constituição de 25 de Março de 1824, mas não convocou os corpos legislativos creados pelo codigo fundamental ; tramou a proclamação do governo absoluto e chegou mesmo a proclamal-o em varias partes por intermedio de seus agentes, Chichorro em Taubaté, Itaparica na Bahia, Niemayer no Ceará, o cabildo em Montevidéo, que então era a capital da nossa provincia da Cisplatina ; não poude impedir a revolta de algumas provincias do norte, que se uniram para formar a mallograda *Confederação do Equador* e da Cisplatina, ao sul, que acabou por se fazer independente com o nome de Republica Oriental do Uruguy ; mas multiplicou as commissões militares em Pernambuco e adjacencias e depressa fuzilou e enforcou frei Caneca, Ratcliff, e mais uma duzia de liberaes nortistas.

Não faltavam homens notaveis nesse ministerio, mas tal era o caracter do imperador e as condições sociaes e politicas do paiz que o gabinete não era mais do que um espelho que sómente reflectia a leviandade e inepcia admininistactiva de D. Pedro e a perversidade da roda aulica e feminina que o cercava. Até mesmo o reconhecimento da independencia do Brazil, imposta ao governo portuguez pela Inglaterra, foi obtido a peso de dinheiro e á custa de varias concessões feitas a Portugal. A concessão de titulos honorificos aos politicos palacianos tambem foi um dos careteristicos deste macrobio ministerio.

Despedido o gabinete em 21 de Novembro de 1825, organisou D. Pedro um outro cuja composição e recomposições vieram ainda uma vez por em evidencia a leviandade e os caprichos do imperador na direcção dos negocios nacionaes.

Formou-se ministerio com o visconde de Barbacena na pasta da Fazenda e interinamente na do Imperio, Sebastião Tinoco na da Justiça, visconde de S. Amaro na dos Extrangeiros, o valido barão Lages na da Guerra e o despota visconde de Paranaguá na da Marinha. Dois mezes depois Lages passou a reger interinamente a pasta do Imperio: saltando Barbacena fóra e entrando para a da Fazenda o visconde de Inhambupe, que já occupava a dos Extrangeiros, em logar de Santo Amaro, despedido a 18 de Janeiro. Assim as contradanças ministeriaes fizeram com que as seis pastas tivessem nove occupantes em 59 dias comquanto, fosse este um gabinete de titulares palacianos foi todo elle despedido á 21 de Janeiro de 1826 quando completava apenas dois mezes de precaria existencia.

O novo gabinete que nesse dia se formou era composto dos titulares viscondes de Baependy, de Paranaguá, de Inhambupe e de Caravellas, do barão de Lages e de Fernandes Pinheiro, que então recebeu o titulo de visconde de S. Leopoldo, emquanto o que era barão subiu a visconde e os que eram viscondes passaram a marquezes, saltando por cima da graduação de conde. Os ministros pareciam mais interessados na concessão de titulos honorificos a si proprios, a cortezãs e á creadagem do Paço do que na direcção da guerra da Cisplatina, que ia mal e ameaçava arrebatar de nós aquella bellissima provincia.

Barbacena fôra nomeado commandante das forças brasileiras no Sul e o imperador, para animar a campanha, para lá partiu a 24 de novembro, deixando no Rio gravemente enferma a imperatriz, que falleceu desoito dias depois, a 11 de Dezembro de 1826. Voltou D. Pedro depressa para o Rio de Janeiro, de onde não devera ter sahido em vista do mau estado da saúde de sua esposa, e apenas desembarcado despediu o ministerio, a 15 de janeiro de 1827, não por motivos de serviço publico, mas por causa de desavenças occorridas entre o ministro Paranáguá e a cortezã predilecta do imperador.

Foi durante este ministerio que se reuniu pela primeira vez, a 3 de Maio de 1826, os corpos legislatsvo creados pela constituição outorgada em 25 de Março de 1824. Mais de dois annos levaram o imperador e os seus aulicos governando o paiz com uma constituição em suspenso, sem leis ordinarias e com commissões militares, deportando, enforcando e fuzilando desembaraçadamente aquelles que se insurgiam contra as violencias do incontrastado poder imperial. Reunido o parlamento nacional, parece que o espirito publico se desafogou algum tanto; reinou calma relativa nas provincias e cessaram por algum tempo as execuções summari s de delinquentes politicos; mas na Cisplatina continuava a rebellião, que se approximava do seu desastrado termo, com o auxilio das armas argentinas.

Triumphante a celebre cortezã e demittido o ministerio, que ousára desattender aos seus caprichos durante a ausencia imperial no Sul, formou-se novo gabinete a 15 de Janeiro de 1827, composto só de gente afidalgada pelas graças imperiaes— marquezes de Queluz, de Maceió e de Nazareth, o valido conde de Lages, membro obrigado de todos os ministerios, o conde de Valença e o visconde de S. Leopoldo.

Foi o ministerio que creou as academias de Direito do Recife e S. Paulo, que representam o mais sério e o mais duradouro melhoramento introduzido no paiz pelo primeiro reinado. Até então os estudantes de direito tinham de ir a Coimbra para se diplomarem na materia e os que não aproveitavam a opportunidade para uma visita ás grandes nações de Europa vinham em regra imbuidos de idéas portuguezas ou cheios de odios contra o Portugal.

A batalha de Ytuzaingo, occorrido pouco depois da posse deste ministerio, e a ruina completa de nossas esperanças de reconquistar á provincia rebellada da Cisplatina, devem ser levadas á conta do gabinete anterior e do proprio imperador, que não providenciaram em tempo sobre as medidas necessarias para evitar tamanho desastre

Despedindo este ministerio de marquezes, condes e viscondes, a 20 de Novembro de 1827 formou-se no mesmo dia um outro em que não entrou titular algum, a não ser João Carlos de Oeynhausen, o ex-capitão general de S. Paulo e ex-presidente do nosso governo provisorio nos annos de 1819-21 e de 1821-22, mas já então elevado a marquez de Aracaty e a senador do Imperio, continuando entretanto a ser bom portuguez e melhor amigo de D. Pedro do que dos brasileiros, se por *melhor amigo* se entender dedicação pessoal ao imperante.

Durou apenas cinco mezes e 25 dias este gabinete e foi, 15 de Junho de 1828, substituído por um outro que merece especial menção pelo numero do seu pessoal e pela sua relativamente longa vida, pois que, sendo o decimo segundo dos ministerio do primeiro reinado, foi o segundo pela sua longividade, de dezoito mezes.

Nelle apparecem Clemente Pereira e o militar Mello Alvim occupando as pastas do Imperio e da Marinha durante todo o periodo ministerial, e Clemente Pereira, portuguez nacionalizado e pau para toda a obra, apparece ainda interinamente nas pastas da Justiça, Extrangeiros, Guerra e Fazenda. O magistrado Teixeira de Gouvêa figura duas vezes na pasta da Justiça; *o bom senhor* Aracaty tambem apparece duas vezes na do Extrangeiros e Miguel Calmon egualmente duas vezes na da Fazenda. José Bernardino Baptista Pereira regeu as pastas da Justiça e da Fazenda, emquanto a da Guerra foi ainda occupada por Cordeiro Torres e Oliveira Alvares. As seis pastas, durante a vida do gabinete, foram occupadas por 16 funccionarios representados por 8 pessoas distinctas

Foi debaixo deste ministerio que se tratou de reformar a constituição de 25 de março de 1824, para tornal-a *verdadeiramente monarchica*, e para alcançar este objecto, tão do agrado da roda aulica que cercava o imperador, se trataria de conciliar os soberanos da França e Austria para obter delles força armada que auxiliasse esta perigosa empresa politica. Foi tambem este ministerio que restabeleceu o systema das commissões militares e das execuções summarias, praticado em larga escala pelo ministerio de 14 de novembro de 1823 e que victimou tantos liberaes illustres.

O estado de sitio foi novamente estabelecido em Pernambuco por decreto de 27 de fevereiro de 1827, firmado pelo ministro e magistrado Lucio Soares Teixeira de Gouvêa, emquanto no mesmo dia se decretava a creação de commissão militar e as execuções summarias sob a responsabilidade de Oliveira Alvares, ministo de guerra, que ainda subscreveu o seguinte «DECRETO— de 27 de fevereiro de 1829.

« Não se fazendo dignos da minha Imperial Clemencia réos que forem convencidos do horrendo crime de rebelião contra o systema de Governo Monarchico Constitucional estabellecido e jurado neste imperio : Hei por bem, tendo ouvido o meu conselho de Estado, que as sentenças proferidas na Commissão Militar que eu mandei crear, por decreto de hoje, para a provincia de Pernambuco, *sejam immediatamente executadas, sem que primeiramente subam a minha Imperial presença*, não obstante o art. 1.ª da lei de 14 de setembro de 1826. As auctoridades, a quem o conhecimento deste pertencer, o tenham assim entendido e assim façam executar. Paço em 27 de fevereiro de 1829, oitavo da Independencia e do Imperio. COM A RUBRICA DE SUA MAJESTADE IMPERIAL.—*Joaquim de Oliveira Alvares.*

A séde de sangue e o odio ao liberalismo exaltado levavam

o imperador a apressar as execuções de pena capital imposta a réos politicos e, para facilitar essas rapidas execuções, D. Pedro delegava á commissão militar a parte mais preciosa do seu Poder Moderador, que era a faculdade de commutar e de perdoar as penas impostas pelos tribunaes do paiz. Entendia o imperador que, uma vez condemnados á morte os delinquentes politicos, era obra de caridade mandal-os enforcar ou fuzilar sem demora, afim de acabar com os seus soffrimentos moraes, e isto fôra antes officialmente declarado pelo sanguinario ministro Ferreira França, que por uma ironia da sorte, tinha o nome christão de *Clemente*.

Ainda a 31 de outubro de 1829, já nos ultimos dias da vida deste ministerio, mandou o governo extender o estado de sitio ao Ceará, porque lá se agitava a opinião publica no sentido de se destruir o regimen constitucional *para se estabelecer o governo absoluto*. Em 1825 os cearences não acudiram ao convite do general Niemeyer para se destruir a constituição e estabelecer o regimem absoluto, mas quatro annos depois agitam-se nesse sentido, sendo necessario que o imperador e seus ministros os obriguem, pela applicação do estado de sitio, a permanecerem dentro do regimen constitucional então vigente!

Foi ainda este ministerio que mandou metter Antonio Carlos e Martim Francisco em processo por terem voltado á sua patria, depois de cinco longos annos de exilio, sem prévia licença do governo imperial. Consideravam-se ainda em vigor, em 1828, em regimem que devia ser plenamente constitucional e com o parlamento funccionando,—as ordens de deportação decretadas em 1823, quando não havia constituição e muito menos leis ordinarias que garantissem a liberdade e os direitos dos cidadãos. Os grandes paulistas foram, entretanto, absolvidos pelo tribunal encarregado de julgal-os.

Foi ainda este desastrado ministerio que, incapaz de conter as leviandades e caprichos do imperador e bastante subserviente para se responsabilizar por todos os seus erros, iniciou as desavenças entre D. Pedro e o parlamento, as quaes continuaram durante todo o periodo legislativo de 1829, e consentiu que o imperador encerrasse as Camaras com o seguinte discurso:

*« Augustos e Dignissimos Senhores Representantes da Nação.*

ESTÁ FECHADA A SESSÃO

IMPERADOR
CONSTITUCIONAL E DEFENSOR PERPETUO DO BRAZIL».

Este discurso grosseiramente laconico e provocador parece um desafio atirado aos brazileiros por D Pedro e seus aulicos e marca o começo da ladeira que foi dar ao abysmo do 7 de Abril, no qual se precipitaram o imperador e a influencia portugueza, que o vinha dirigindo desde alguns mezes antes da dissolução da Assembléa Constituinte.

Pelos decretos de suspensão das garantias constitucionaes, da creação dos tribunaes militares e da immediata execução das penas de morte por delictos politicos, foi dada denuncia á Camara contra os ministros Lucio Soares Teixeira de Gouvêa e Joaquim de Oliveira Alvares, que tinham referendado aquelles sanguinarios decretos.

Joaquim Gonçalves Ledo, deputado, e liberal exaltado de 1822-23, que tanto se incommodava com os processos arbitrarios de José Bonifacio, quando ministro, em um tempo em que ainda não havia constituição e em que não se enforcou, nem fuzilou ninguem, esquecido do seu intransigente liberalismo anterior, se fez no parlamento o defensor daquelles sanguinarios ministros e dos seus actos violentos. A respeito deste rasgo de duplicidade daquelle notavel politico diz um chronista o seguinte, com relação ao ministro Oliveira Alvares:

«O imperador se empenhava para que a accusação não proseguisse. A discussão na Camara foi calorosa e o imperador ia todos os dias se collocar em uma das janellas do Paço, que ficava em frente á Camara, para dahi expedir os seus agentes afim de saber o que se passava; e dizendo-se-lhe que LEDO estava fazendo um brilhante discurso em favor do ministro accusado, o imperador, virando-se para os que o cercavam, disse: «E' a terceira vez que o compro e de todas tem-me servido bem».

«Este facto foi referido pelo marquez de Quixeramobim, Pedro Dias Paes Leme, que se achava presente como camarista do imperador. O imperador, para salvar o ministro accusado, nada poupou, nem mesmo a propria dignidade; prometteu, solicitou e corrompeu, chegando a ir em pessôa procurar os deputados em suas casas para esse fim».

Ledo conseguiu o seu fim e salvou os ministros da accusação que se lhes fez; mas parece que esta empreitada de alguma fórma o malquistou com os liberaes daquelles agitados tempos e principalmente com Evaristo da Veiga, porque na *Aurora Fluminense*, de 19 de Fevereiro de 1830, fez Evaristo a seguinte pergunta, que é maliciosa e traz agua no bico:

*«Porque não se fala ha tanto tempo no sr. Ledo? Perderia elle o volume que occupava no mundo politico?»*

A má impressão que no espirito dos liberaes produziu o facto

de Ledo se incumbir da defesa de actos violentos de ministros
liberticidas durou annos e parece que o liberal oxaltado de outrora se tinha mesmo bandeado para os reaccionarios porque,
quando Feijó foi tambem denunciado em 1832, por actos que
praticou como ministro da Justiça do periodo regencial, o mesmo
Ledo, que defendera os ministros em 1829, votou contra elle,
quando Feijó era então o braço forte dos liberaes moderados,
chefiados por Evaristo Veiga.

Esta nova manifestação de Ledo contra Evaristo deu logar
a mais recriminações contra o ex-liberal de 1822-23, como se
vê em um dos numeros do *Observador Constitucional*, de Setembro de 1832, que diz o seguinte:

«Os 15 deputados que votaram para que se procedesse á
accusação do sr. Feijó são os seguintes: LEDO, Almeida Torres.
Perdigão Ernesto, M. do Amaral, F. França, Rebouças, Montezuma, L. Cavalcanti, Castro Moraes, Francisco Rego. H.
Cavalcanti, Vallasques, Paula e Albuquerque e Lobo. Todos
os mais em numero de 56, votaram contra.

« O *Tempo* nota, e como muita razão, que na accusação
do sr. Oliveira Alvares, militares votassem por ella, que na do
sr. Lucio Soares magistrados votassem por ella e que na do sr.
Feijó não votasse por ella um padre!!!

A *Aurora* diz que O *Tempo* podia ainda fazer outra reflexão e era que os srs. LEDO e Almeida Torres, defensores dos primeiros ministros, não temeram votar agora contra o terceiro.
Quid inde?.. Não se acham no numero dos 56, outros LEDOS e
Almeida Torres!... Os que em outro tempo votaram contra
Oliveira Alvares e Lucio não votaram tambem agora a favor
do sr. Geijò?. Na verdade somos obrigados a confessar que
o *tempo tem tudo mudado*!!! »

A 14 de Dezembro de 1829, depois de anno e meio de
vida penosa, foi, despedido este gabinete e organizado um outro
composto de fidalgos, reaes e adventicios—marquezes de Barbacena, de Paranáguá e de Caravellas, conde do Rio Pardo e
visconde de Alcantara, com Miguel Calmon e José Antonio Barbosa para democratizar a organização. Durou este ministerio
sómente nove mezes e dias, mas nesse curto periodo soffreu
recomposições, que fizeram quatro pastas serem occupadas por
sete ministros e vieram ainda uma vez demonstrar a volubilidade
e caprichos de D. Pedro na direcção dos negocios nacionaes.

A 4 de Outubro de 1830 desmanchou-se esta organização
ministerial por questões suscitadas entre o imperador o seu
principal ministro, o marquez de Barbacena, sobre materia de
dinheiro. Depois de terminada a guerra com a Cisplatina, em

que Barbacena foi general infeliz das forças brazileiras, foi elle mandado á Europa em busca de uma noiva para o imperador, com carta branca sobre as despesas a fazer e com recommendação de arranjar princeza de alto nascimento, bonita, boa de genio e bem educada.

Em Vienna da Austria o emissario de D. Pedro não foi feliz, porque a proposta que trazia foi rejeitada por seis princezas da familia imperial dos *Habsbourg*, e Barbacena foi *convidado* a sahir depressa daquella capital por Metternich, o celebre ministro de Francisco II. Retirado precipitadamente para Munich, a capital da Baviera, conseguiu Barbacena lá obter para o imperador a mão da princeza Amelia, duqueza de Leuchtenberg, que elle trouxe ao Brazil, entrando elle para o governo, na primeira organização ministerial que se seguiu.

Se a missão á Europa, de que Barbacena fóra incumbido, tivesse o caracter nacional, ao thesouro publico cumpria occorrer ás despezas della resultantes: mas foi elle em missão particular do imperador e as despesas tiveram de ser satisfeitas á custa de imperial bolsinho. D. Pedro encantado com a noiva, chamou o seu « S. Gonçalo » para o ministerio e demorou a tomada de contas das despesas e presente do noivado; mas o dia para isso chegou, a prestação das contas não agradou ao imperial committente e elle e seu mandatario desceram a expresões dignas da « praia do peixe », e o ministerio se esphacelou.

Em jornaes daquelles tempos fez Barbacena em sua defesa, neste escandaloso ajuste de contas, algumas curiosas publicações, que não transcrevo aqui, mas que bem evidenciam quanto era impulsivo e irrefletido o caracter do primeiro imperador. Estes incidentes da vida palaciana, os decretos da suspensão das garantias constitucionaes, as commissões militares, as ordens para execuções summarias dos criminosos politicos e outros actos imprudentes ou violentos só serviram para apressar a marcha do imperador pela ladeira abaixo e dar com elle e seus aulicos no pego do 7 de Abril, que estava mais perto do que elles suppunham.

A reorganização ministerial de 14 de Outubro de 1830 importou em um novo gabinete, em queentraram quatro ex-membros do ministerio demissionario—Paranaguá, Rio Pardo, Alcantara e Lisboa, ficando com duas pastas o marquez de Paranaguá o *irresistivel, o nosso Polygnac-mirim*, como o qualificava Evaristo Veiga, e entrando Silva Maia para completar o gabinete

Durou sómente cinco mezes e meio este ministerio, que nesse curto periodo foi modificado varias vezes, entrando Francisco Carneiro de Campos em 9 de Outubro para a pasta interinamente regida por Paranaguá, saltando Lisboa fóra, em 3 de

Novembro, para dar logar a Hollanda Cavalcanti e sendo o visconde de Alcantara substituido em 18 de Março, pelo visconde de Goyanna, que carregou a pasta uma só noite, porque no dia seguinte ao da sua nomeação, a 19 de Março foi todo o ministerio despedido.

D. Pedro se tornava de dia para dia mais impopular, o parlamento mais independente e a imprensa mais aggressiva. Desanimado com o regimen constitucional, existente no papel e não praticado, os liberaes brasileiros começavam a volver as vistas para o federalismo e mesmo para a Republica, e em Minas Geraes essas manifestações eram mais formaes e perigosas para a Monarchia. Entendeu D. Pedro que devia ir visital-a e resuscitar entre os mineiros os enthusiasmos que a sua pessoa lá provocara na primeira viagem que fizera áquella provincia em 1822

Entretanto os tempos estavam mudados e o adorado principe regente, do tempo da independencia, era agora o odiado imperador das violações constitucionaes, das suspensões de garantias, das commissões militares, das execuções summarias do do desenfreado validismo, de Rocha Pinto, Chalaça e João Maria. A viagem a Minas foi uma temerosa decepção para D. Pedro, que era por toda a parte recebido com estudada frieza e até com dobres de sinos a finados. De Ouro Preto atirou elle aos povos uma proclamação aggressiva, que só podia aggravar sua situação e contribuir para tornal-a irremediavel.

Partira D. Pedro para Minas a 30 de Dezembro e voltára ao Rio em 11 de Março de 1831, ficando uma semana inteira recolhido em seu palacio de S. Christovam e curtindo as amarguras da situação que elle mesmo se havia creado. Querendo os amigos pessoaes do imperador e, principalmente, os portuguezes fazer-lhe algumas festas que o consolassem do mau resultado da sua viagem, deram-se os gravissimos factos da noite de 13 para 14 de Março, conhecidos na nossa historia pela denominação de *Noite das garrafadas*, em que tomaram parte portuguezes, brasileiros exaltados e até officiaes militares.

Desde esse dia D. Pedro era um homem condemnado e a sua quéda era questão de mais ou menos tempo, uma vez que elle não tinha força para corrigir os defeitos do seu caracter leviano e provocador, nem energia para conter os aulicos, os retrogrados e os portuguezes, que o empurravam para a perdição.

A 17 de Março voltou o imperador á actividade e veiu á cidade e a 19 deitou abaixo o ministerio, organizando um outro em que entraram Hollanda Calvacanti, Goyanna e Carneiro de Campos, vindos do gabinete anterior, e mais tres homens novos e inteiramente desconhecidos no mundo politico—Manoel José de Souza França, José Manoel de Moraes e José Manoel de Almeida.

Esta organização de um gabinete de homens menos conhecidos e sem grande responsabilidade pelos erros da politica imperial, que vinham se accumulando desde 1823, podia servir de ponte entre o passado e o futuro e facilitar a D. Pedro o inicio de uma nova politica mais conforme aos interesses nacionaes e aos sentimentos liberaes dos brasileiros ; mas sempre incorrigivel, o imperador mudava os seus ministerios sem mudar de politica e, imprudente como de costume, sem ser convidado, foi assistir ao *Te-Deum*, que, em acção de graças, se rezava a 25 de Março na egreja de S. Francisco de Paula, sendo lá mal recebido e provocando com a sua não desejada presença manifestações hostis á sua pessoa.

Tão penosa situação não podia prolongar-se indefinidamente, e o imperador, desatinado, foi quem primeiro procurou dar-lhe uma sahida qualquer. A 5 de Abril deitou elle abaixo o ministerio, que teve sómente 16 dias de vida, e organizou um outro em que entraram seis titulares marquezes de Aracaty, de Paranaguá, de Baependy e de Inhambupe, conde de Lages e visconde de Alcantara, alguns dos quaes eram portuguezes e outros brasileiros retrogrados e todos representantes de tudo quanto havia de mais antipathico aos sentimentos liberaes do paiz.

As reclamações populares, que exigiam a despedida deste antipathico ministerio, deste mostrengo politico, respondia D. Pedro que tudo faria *para o povo, mas nada pelo povo*, não consentindo em se desfazer daquelle monstruoso producto do aulicismo palaciano. O golpe do Estado e a revolução eram as unicas sahidas possiveis para a situação. A corda, esticada de mais em 1823 e em 1824-1825, rebentára na ponta mais fraca, que era segurada pelos Andradas e por Manoel de Carvalho, Ratcliff e Frei Caneca; porém, em 1831, os tempos e os homens estavam mudados, a começar pelo proprio imperador, que, de adorado que era pelos brasileiros, se fizera o fóco attrahente dos odios nacionaes contra as cortezãs, aulicos, retrogrados e portuguezes, que influiam sobre o espirito de D. Pedro e davam á sua politica a feição anti-nacional que a caracterizou.

Ao povo rebellado se juntou a força armada e a corda desta vez rebentou pelo lado do imperador, que no dia seguinte abdicou a corôa na pessoa de seu filho, deu-lhe como tutor José Bonifacio, o homem que tanto elle havia odiado e perseguido, e a 7 de abril deixou para sempre o sólo brasileiro para se recolher a bordo de um navio extrangeiro, que o transportou para o velho mundo, onde elle tinha uma missão a cumprir, que era a restauração das liberdades portuguezas destruidas pelo seu irmão, o feroz D. Miguel de Bragança.

A libertação do velho reino do despotismo miguelista e a restauração do regimen constitucional sob o governo de D. Maria II rehabilitam a sua memoria perante a Historia, mas não augmentam os seus direitos á nossa gratidão

Não sou daquelles que acreditam que o bello monumento em fórma de uma estatua equestre, que se ergueu em uma das praças da capital do Brasil á memoria de Pedro I, represente a gratidão dos brasileiros pelos serviços por elle prestados á nossa independencia e á formação da nossa nacionalidade. A independencia se faria com elle ou sem elle; o espirito publico estava maduro para isso e já não mais podia supportar o pesado jugo colonial. O Brasil estava crescido demais para continuar em tutela e Portugal estava pequeno demais para o sem papel de metropole.

D. Pedro sabia disso e mesmo seu pae lhe tinha dado, a respeito, conselhos de se fazer rei da colonia emancipada, que podia se tornar a presa de qualquer aventureiro; mas o seu interesse, como herdeiro presumptivo da corôa, era manter a unidade da monarchia e não favorecer a separação da sua mais futurosa parte. O grito do campo do Ypiranga não foi mais do que o producto suggestionado ao seu espirito impressivo pelos actos imprudentemente provocadores das Côrtes de Lisboa e pela influencia decisiva de José Bonifacio.

Pessoalmente D. Pedro não tinha nenhuma das grandes qualidades necessarias ao fundador de uma nação; estudos, planos, constancia, methodo, sisudez, circumspecção, estima-propria, consciencia da missão a desempenhar — tudo lhe faltava, de quanto caracteriza o verdadeiro estadista. Nada nelle se encontra que recorde algum traço de caracter de Victor Manoel e de Guilherme I, fundadores do reino da Italia e do Imperio Allemão. D. João VI, «refalsado e suspeitoso, irresoluto e poltrão», como dizia Torres Homem, soube rodear-se de homens capazes, que deram algum brilho ao seu reinado; mas nem do exemplo paterno soube D. Pedro se aproveitar para escolher os seus conselheiros e dar ao seu governo uma apparencia siquer de bons desejos e de honestas intenções. O pessoal de que se rodeou, os politicos com que formou os ephemeros ministerios e os altos e baixos do seu governo retratam fielmente a sua personalidade moral e politica.

Proclamada a independencia e acclamado o imperio em 1822 sob a immediata direcção dos Andradas, que emprestavam alguma coherencia e logica ao caracter multiforme de D. Pedro, depedidos estes do governo em 1823, começou a serie de erros e de crimes, que se extendeu desde a violenta dissolução da Assembléa Constituinte, atravez das deportações, das rebelliões, das leis marciaes, das commissões militares, das execuções summarias, do desmembramento territorial! pela perda da Cisplatina, das tentativas de restabelecimento do governo absoluto, do mais desenfreado e baixo validismo, até á nomeação do «ministerio das 24 horas» e ao 7 de Abril de 1831, que marca o termo da sinuosa evolução da politica imperial.

Tendo D. Pedro continuado a governar o paiz discrecionariamente durante dois longos annos depois de jurada a Constituição de 1824, póde a outorga do codigo fundamental ser considerada como um acto politico de intenção reservada, e a creação das academias de Direito em 1827, melhoramento reclamado desde 1823 e devido aos esforços de Fernandes Pinheiro, não resgata os erros do primeiro reinado ; entretanto, são estes os seus unicos actos de caracter duradouro e que influiram favoravelmente sobre a formação e desenvolvimento do caracter nacional.

## II

### UM DOCUMENTO APOCRYPHO—JAPYASSÚ—RAPHAEL TOBIAS

Corre impressa pelo Brasil inteiro uma importante affirmação historica, que diz assim :

« A primeira vez que o sr. José Bonifacio foi denominado *Heróe* da independencia foi a 7 de Setembro de 1832, em uma reunião popular, amalgama monstruoso de alguns festeiros das *garrafadas* de Março, de heróes das ceias de camarão em 1822, e de varios curiosos » (*Aurora Fluminense*, de 14 de Setembro de 1832).

A *Aurora Fluminense* foi o orgam de Evaristo Veiga, o grande politico de 7 de Abril de 1831, e quem lér esta sentença condemnatoria é levado a crer que ella partiu do cerebro daquelle notavel cidadão e que foi escripta pela sua adestrada penna, mas ficará enganado como eu o fui quando, pela primeira vez, se me deparou tão peremptoria declaração.

Os jornaes daquelles agitados tempos não tinham *secção livre*, nem *publicações a pedido*, para regalo dos *romões* da imprensa. Os artigos que não eram da redacção, mas que offereciam algum interesse aos leitores sahiam publicados em uma secção especial, chamada *Variedade* ; podiam ser anonymos, podiam trazer a assignatura do auctor ou podiam ser firmados por pseudonymos, mas não tinham o cunho, a responsabilidade moral da redacção.

Examinando uns velhos numeros da *Aurora Fluminense*, existentes no Archivo do Estado e já muito estragados pelas traças e em parte totalmente rotos, encontrei esse trecho no numero 675, da mencionada data, em uma correspondencia particular, sob a costumada epigraphe *Variedade*; diz assim:

« Sr. Redactor :—Nada tem vm. dito das festas com que no dia 7 de Setembro foi obsequiado o *heróe da independencia*, alcunha que recentemente se deu ao sr. José Bonifacio de Andrada e Silva? Porque?

« Foram tão pouco notaveis os gritos e vozerias com que esses representantes da opinião publica correram as ruas da cidade, dando vivas e morras, aonde os srs. Andradas eram sempre os heróes e malvados aquelles que se suspeita de lhe serem menos affeiçoados!

« Se não quer dar os detalhes relativos a este nobre assumpto, indique ao menos quem eram os directores do festejo, que começou e foi traçado no *Palais Royal dos novelleiros caramurús*, aonde, por principio de justa, investiram contra um moço que tinha a desventura de não ser bemquisto do sr. Girão. Dalli se levou ao *patriarcha* a coroa de flôres na bandeja, que por um resto do pudor, o emissario escondia debaixo da casaca; alli se formou o primeiro grupo a que se reuniram depois todos os da comitiva, amalgama monstruoso de alguns festeiros das garrafadas de Março, de heróes das ceias de camarão em 1822, e de varios curiosos . . . . . . . . . . . . . . .
. . . . . . . . . . . . . . . . . . . . . . . . . .

O *Gi...te*

O final do artigo está roto e illegivel, mas o começo bem indica que o escripto não è de Evaristo Veiga e até critica o facto da *Aurora* nem sequer fazer menção dos acontecimentos. Na assignatura, que é um pseudonymo, falta a syllaba do meio, indicando as syllabas existentes que o nome é *Gigante*, *Gingante* ou *Ginete* unicas palavras que encontro em *Aulete*, que começa por *Gi* e acabam em *te*. (1)

Aquella opinião, portanto, não é de Evaristo Veiga, mas de um annonymo qualquer, e o facto de vir ella publicada no jornal do grande liberal mineiro não lhe empresta importancia, alguma nem serve de arma contra a reputação daquelle que a historia nacional elevou á dignidade unica de patriarcha da nossa in-

---

(1) Segundo Mello Moraes - que transcrevo esse artigo da *Aurora* de 14 de Setembro,—a assignatura era—*O Girante*
Vide—A INDEPENDENCIA E O IMPERIO DO BRAZIL, pelo Dr. M. Moraes—1897 Pg. 137 a 139 no Cap: —*Quando começou a idéa do Patriarchado da Independencia do Brasil, atribuido a J. Bonifacio de Andrada e Silva.* (N. da Redacção da Revista.

dependencia. E' um documento apocrypho, sem valor, encartado nas nossas chronicas.

*Caveant historiographi!*

* * *

Durante o primeiro reinado dois homens havia em S. Paulo que se tornaram notaveis pelo odio popular que sobre si elles souberam attrahir

O primeiro delles foi Sousa Chichorro, ex-secretario do governo, ex-juiz de fóra de Taubaté e ouvidor desta capital, cujo retracto moral foi feito por Badaró no *Observador Constitucional* e reproduzido ha pouco no *Correio Paulistano*; era um partidario acerrimo do regimem absolutista e tentou proclamal-o nas villas do valle do Parahyba.

Gorado esse plano, foi Chichorro mettido em processo, que não teve resultado algum, e recebeu de D. Pedro a recompensa da sua ousadia na promoção que teve para ouvidor de S. Paulo.

O outro individuo foi Candido Ladislau Japyassú, que em 1830 era ouvidor de S. Paulo e muito combatido por Badaró por suas idéas absolutistas e seus sentimentos retrogrados. Assassinado Badaró na noite de 20 de Novembro de 1830, a opinião publica apontava Japyassú como envolvido naquelle crime, realizado, segundo se disse, pelos allemães Stockler, e a sua vida correu grandes riscos no meio da indignação dos estudantes e do exaltamento popular, occasionados por aquelle assassinato. O governo teve de subtrahil-o á furia popular e de o remetter para o Rio de Janeiro, em canóa de voga e remo pela costa maritima, viagem perigosissima que só mesmo podia ser feita por quem fugia para salvar a vida.

No processo que se instaurou contra os assassinos nada se apurou que legalmente compromette-se Japyassú e elle ficou livre de culpa e pena e tambem desembaraçado dos ataques do grande jornalista, proprietario e redactor do *Observador Constitucional*: porém a sua vida em S. Paulo se tornou impossivel por algum tempo, pelo menos emquanto duravam as paixões populares e a indignação produzida pelo assassinato do medico italiano, que se fizera verdadeiro idolo dos estudantes e do povo paulista.

No Rio, onde elle ficou por algum tempo, pretendeu obter o cargo de vereador, em 1832, e apresentou-se candidato a uma cadeira na Camara Municipal naturalmente como absolutista e não como representante de idéas brasileiras.

Evaristo Veiga, chefe do liberalismo moderado de então, que não podia apreciar as qualidades politicas de Japyassú, nem concordar com semelhante candidatura, escreveu e fez publicar na *Aurora Fluminense*, a 21 de Setembro daquelle anno, um artigo politico com algumas vagas insinuações, que Japyassú tomou como offensa a si e ataque á sua candidatura. Então o offendido dirigiu a Evaristo o seguinte desafio, que vem publicada na *Aurora* de 13 de Outubro do mesmo anno.

« Sr. Redactor:—Lendo na *Aurora* n. 678 um ataque aos meus direitos de cidadão brasileiro, quando diz que a minha *candidatura para a Camara Municipal marca de côr vergonhosa as influencias do ministerio passado*, muito desejoso de responder-lhe em regra, exijo que Vm., para que não fique marcado com a côr vergonhosa do crime de calumniador, haja de publicar os motivos que o obrigam a julgar-me indigno da eleição dos meus concidadãos e que na vossa mesma *Aurora* haja de publicar estas linhas.—*Candido Ladisláo Japiassú*».

Não tem data esta exigencia, nem traz o nome do logar onde foi escripta; porém, sendo de mais de vinte dias o tempo que decorreu da publicação das insinuações de Evaristo á do desafio, é de suppor que Japyassú estivesse ausente do Rio e só com a demora de tres semanas é que poude fazer esta impertinente reclamação. Publicando-a no seu jornal, como era exigido pelo reclamante, Evaristo fel-a acompanhar da seguinte interessante resposta:

« Responderemos em poucas palavras ao sr. Candido Ladisláo Japiassú. Primeiro que tudo, não é exacto que houvesse atacado os sous direitos de cidadão brasileiro na *Aurora* que elle menciona; pode-se ser cidadão do Brasil e todavia não merecer o voto dos amigos das liberdades publicas. E' o caso em que julgamos estar o sr. Japiassú.

« Conhecido em Coimbra por seu phrenesi politico, opiniões exaggeradas e anti-monarchicas, veiu elle exercer no Rio Grande do Sul as funcções de um cargo judiciario, onde é arguido pela voz publica de haver praticado vexames contra alguns habitantes de Porto Alegre, ora por espirito de rancor e vingança, ora pelo desejo de fazer a côrte a D. Pedro I quando este principe para alli se dirigiu.

« Magistrado na cidade de S. Paulo nós não trataremos de fazer reviver suspeitas que sobre elle recahiram em consequencia de um horrivel attentado; ha uma sentença formal que o absolveu e devemos nesta parte considera-lo innocente. Porém que explicação satisfactoria dará o sr. Japiassú da sua conducta no caso das facas, no negocio do jury, no crime de assuada que ainda não existia e de outros factos com que se tornou odioso á população de S. Paulo e adquiriu no Brasil um nome tão abominado?

« Apenas solto, as suas relações intimas com os antigos servos de D. Pedro, com os circulo dos homens do partido *Caramurú*, contrastam tristemente com as opiniões que dantes professara e o fizeram apparecer como candidato para a nossa Camara Municipal, recommendado pelos agentes e directores desse mesmo partido.

« Eis, em resumo, as razões que temos para crer que a sua candidatura marca de cor vergonhosa as influencias da quarentena que decorreu de 3 de Agosto a 13 de Setembro. E' esta a nossa convicção, que não damos como dogma. Estamos persuadidos que o dr. Japiassú não será do nosso parecer a semelhante respeito mas permitta-nos que lhe digamos : « elle é na materia juiz incompetente ». Concluindo faremos notar ainda que na *Aurora* n. 678, a que o nosso correspondente se refere, não haviamos falado nas *influencias do ministerio passado* expressão que nos é attribuida pelo ser Japiassú, sem duvida por inadvertencia ».

Temos nesta resposta um exemplo de severas censuras expressas em linguagem moderada e digna de um homem como Evaristo Veiga, em completo contraste com aquillo que acima se leu relativo a José Bonifacio e escripto ahi por um *Gi...te* qualquer.

Refere-se Evaristo á « quarentena que decorreu de 3 de Agosto a 13 de Setembro de 1832 », que deu origem á antipathica candidatura de Japyassú a uma cadeira da Camara Municipal do Rio e que aqui apparece de modo obscuro : convém dizer sobre essa phrase algumas palavras.

Naquelles tempos, as mutações ministeriaes eram frequentes e rapidas, mais pelos caprichos do Executivo do que pela influencia do Poder Legislativo. D. Pedro I, nos dez annos que governou o Brazil, de Abril de 1821 a Abril de 1831, teve nada menos de dezeseis ministerios, alguns dos quaes foram verdadeiros meteoros, que mal brilhavam e já morriam. O gabinete de 28 de Outubro de 1822, composto de um barão, dois desembargadores, um tenente-coronel e um capitão de mar e guerra, durou apenas dois dias e o ministerio de 5 de Abril de 1831, o ultimo do primeiro reinado e composto de um visconde, um conde e quatro marquezes, incluindo o de Aracaty, João Carlos de Oeynhausen, que tanto se celebrizou em S. Paulo, tambem durou sómente dois dias.

Derribado D. Pedro a 7 de Abril, organizou-se no mesmo dia uma regencia trina *provisoria*, que durou setenta dias e foi substituida por uma regencia trina *permanente*, que durou menos de quatro annos e funccionou grande parte desse tempo com um membro sómente. Esta regencia permanente teve tres ministerios: o primeiro, de 16 de Julho de 1831 a 3 de Agosto de 1832 : o segundo, de 3 de Agosto a 13 de Setembro de 1832 ; é o da «quarentena», mencionada por Evaristo Veiga e composto só de tres membros, Hollanda Cavalcanti, Araujo Lima e Barroso

Pereira, cada um delles occupando duas pastas. Não era esse ministerio do agrado de Evaristo Veiga, alma e espirito virificador da politica regencial, e não poude viver mais tempo por falta do sopro inspirador; protegia a candidatura de Japyassú ao cargo de vereador e isto bastava para se aquilatarem os sentimentos liberaes do ministerio da «quarenteua».

O juizo que Evaristo fazia de Japyassú não era mais lisonjeiro do que a opinião, já por mim publicada, que Badaró tinha das qualidades de Sousa Chicorro, ambos juizes de S. Paulo por algum tempo, ambos protegidos por Pedro I e ambos notaveis por suas idéas contrarias ás liberdades publicas. Odiados pelo povo, que os considerava como espectros vivos do morto despotismo colonial, é de crêr que ambos fossem victimas de muitas accusações injustas e que carregassem até á sepultura a responsabilidade de muitas culpas que não commetteram.

#### *⁎*

O brigadeiro Raphael Tobias de Aguiar foi, por certo, um dos mais notaveis paulistas do seu tempo: como Paula Souza, elle não foi a Coimbra e apenas frequentou as escolas poucas e defeituosas que havia em S. Paulo nos tempos coloniaes. Não era um talento como Paula Souza, nem um caracter positivo como Feijó; mas guardava um justo meio termo que o habilitou a fazer notavel figura na politica paulista durante muitos annos, em um tempo abundante em homens proeminentes.

Depois de ter occupado os cargos de conselheiro do governo e conselheiro geral, foi nomeado presidente da provincia de São Paulo em Novembro de 1831, quando tinha 38 annos de edade. Feijó, seu intimo amigo e correligionario politico, era então, ministro da regencia trina permanente e naturalmente influiu para essa nomeação, que lhe garantia a conservação de sua influencia sobre esta provincia e a continuação da da exclusão dos Andradas da politica paulista.

Evaristo Veiga, que era o mais valente sustentaculo da regencia trina e de seu ministro Feijó, naturalmente esteve de accôdo com a nomeação de Raphael Tobias para presidente de S. Paulo, e com a exclusão dos Andradas da politica da provincia. Um obscuro jornal, O Cometa, que não era orgão do partido moderado, de que Evaristo era o chefe, mais que seria a expressão de qualquer das muitas facções politicas daquelle tempo, publicou o seguinte, com relação ao presidente de S. Paulo:

«O sr. Raphael Tobias não tem merecimento algum, nem aptidão para governar povos; elle apenas saberá ler e assignar o seu nome».

A injustiça deste deprimente conceito era ainda agravada por estar publicada em gryphos e ser seguido de um elogio ás boas qualidades do *honrado* Pedro Taques de Almeida Alvim, capitão de milicias, absolutista, profundamente beato e mentalmente tão desenquilibrado que perdeu totalmente o juizo pelo resto da vida. Evaristo Veiga, indignado responden chamando *O Cometa* «vesgo e torvo» e defendendo o presidente de São Paulo nos seguintes termos:

«O sr. Raphael Tobias, conhecido desde muito tempo pela firmeza e honradez do seu caracter e uns dos mais abastados capitalistas da provincia de S. Paulo, recebeu na sua mocidade educação cultivada, frequentando com louvor os chamados estudos preparatorios, unicos que então se podiam obter no paiz. Verdade é que não foi a Coimbra e que, faltando-lhe o diploma de bacharel em leis, aos olhos dos idiotas não póde ser homem instruido, titulo que só compete aos *formados*. Sem duvida neste sentido é que o *O Cometa* o dá como pessoa que *apenas saberá ler e assignar o seu nome.*

«A sua provincia, reconhecendo nelle as bôas qualidades e patriotismo de que é dotado, o elegeu seu representante á Assemb'éa Geral e elle é o mais votado dos conselheiros presidiaes (presidenciaes, é que se deve ler). Tal foi o cidadão de quem a regencia lançou mão para o logar de presidente de S. Paulo, cargo que o sr. Raphael Tobias acceitou a instancias dos seus amigos e em cujo desempenho ha satisfeito geralmente aos paulistas.

«O atilamento e prudencia, de quem tem dado provas no exercicio das funcções delicadas que lhe foram incumbidas, o socego de que a provincia tem gosado, a reconciliação dos partidos, quasi de todo operada, tudo justificou a optima escolha da regencia e faz morder de raiva aquelles que desejariam ver na presidencia de S. Paulo um *Japiassú* ou um *Almeida Torres*. Eis a razão do seu odio contra o sr. Raphael Thobias.

«Quanto ao sr. Pedro Taques, tem elle a honra de ser *caramurú* e em todos os tempos, reputado como acerrimo absulutista; merece, portanto, os panegyricos do *Cometa*. E quem não rirá da importancia que o partido retrogado está hoje dando ao sr. Pedro Taques?

Fraca alavanca tem o partido para mover os animos e fazer seita em S. Paulo. O sr. Taques, ou devida ou indevidamente, não gosa alli de nenhuma consideração e a facção *caramuruuna* é conhecida em poucos logares da provincia.»

Japyassú toma aqui mais uma pedrada; é justo o conceito que Evaristo faz de Pedro Taques, que tinha por norma apregoar que diante do rei se devia pôr um joelho em terra e deante de Deus os dois joelhos. Entretanto, se ser *caramurú* qver aqui dizer partidario dos Andradas, o conceito é menos verdadeiro, porque Pedro Taques era inimigo figadal dos Andradas e foi um dos peores sediciosos da *Bernarda*, que derribou Martim Francisco do governo e o deportou de S. Paulo para o Rio.

Tambem Almeida Torres não era tão mau como aqui se dá a entender; não foi bom juiz nos tempos coloniaes, mas se portou regularmente bem como presidente que foi de S. Paulo por duas vezes, em 1829—30 e em 1842—43, e depois da rebellião de 1842 fez cessar muitas perseguições injustas iniciadas por Costa Carvalho. Na correspondencia de Paula Sousa em meu poder, e nos livros de registros do Archivo do Estado se encontram traços evidentes da sua moderação comparada com as exigencias do Costa Carvalho, então barão de Monte Alegre.

## III

### A HISTORIA E SEUS BASTIDORES

Os dois maiores historiadores que escreveram sobre o Brazil foram Southey e Varnhagem, tendo ambos deixado monumentos dignos de serem apreciados pelos amantes dos estudos historicos.

O primeiro, que era inglez, dedicou tolo o seu trabalho em narrar com minuciosidade e relativa exacticão os factos da nossa historia nos tempos puramente coloniaes e parou em 1808, com a chegada de D. João VI ao Rio de Janeiro, occupando a sua *History of Brazil* seis bons volumes, que foram traduzidos para o portuguez pelo literato Luiz de Castro, redactor que foi do *Jornal do Commercio*.

Pereira da Silva continúou este trabalho, trazendo-o até os nosos dias, mas dividindo os seus escriptos em partes distinctas. Começa a sua narrativa em 1808, época em que Southey parou, e a primeira parte, que se intitula a *Historia da Fundação do Imperio*, termina com a independencia completa do Brasil; seguem-se a esta as historias do primeiro reinado e da regencia e as *Memorias do meu tempo*.

Apesar de alguns lapsos e lacunas são as obras de Pereira da Silva a melhor fonte de informações sobre a historia constitucional do Brasil; para tel-as completas é necessario possuir tambem a obra de Southey e todas reunidas custam tanto dinheiro que a grande maioria dos estudantes da historia patria não póde compral-as.

Varnhagem escreveu dois grossos volumes, pesados e difficeis de serem manuseados, e parou em 1820, sem motivo algum que justifique tal acto, porquanto aquelle anno não apresenta nada de importante na nossa historia e com mais um pequeno esforço elle poderia ter ido até 1822 ou 1825, annos que se fizeram notaveis pela proclamação da independencia e pelo seu reconhecimento pelo governo de Lisboa. A obra é excellente, mas não encontrou um continuador que a trouxesse aos nossos tempos; serve para o periodo colonial sómente, rivalizando com a de Southey nas minudencias da narrativa.

De todos os outros historiadores nacionaes talvez o padre Galanti seja o mais completo; não passando os outros de auctores de compendios para uso de collegios e academias. *A America Portugueza* de Rocha Pitta, é resumida e pára em 1724, com a posse do vice-rei Vasco Fernandes Cesar de Menezes.

Algumas das divisões politicas do Brasil tiveram bons chronistas.

O Rio de Janeiro é de todas as partes a melhor servida, com as *Memorias* de Pizarro e os *Annaes* de Balthazar Lisbôa; vem em seguida a Bahia com as *Memorias Historias* de Accioli, Pernambuco com as *Memorias* de Gama, o Maranhão com os *Annaes* de Berredo, Goyaz com os *Annaes* de Alencastro e o Rio Grande do Sul com os *Annaes* do visconde de S. Leopoldo. Todas estas obras se referem aos tempos coloniaes e offerecem boas informações sobre o inicio das conquistas e povoamento das respectivas regiões.

S. Paulo foi menos feliz; foi a primeira donataria estabelecida no Brasil e formou depois a mais vasta capitania que jámais tivemos; os seus habitantes, cedo transformados em caçadores de indios e exploradores das minas dos sertões, se fizeram famosos como *bandeirantes* e contribuiram mais que outros brasileiros para a formação da actual geographia nacional.

Foram elles que, com Raposo, expelliram do Guayrá os invasores castelhanos; que, com o mesmo Raposo, foram luctar contra os hollandezes em Pernambuco; que, com Estevam Bayão, varreram do Reconcavo da Bahia as tribus *tupynambás*, que tantos estragos faziam aos moradores da região; que, com Maciel Parente, devassaram e povoaram os sertões do Piauhy e Maranhão; que com Pedroso Xavier e Campos Bicudo, invadiram o Paraguay e se mediram com os hespanhoes de Assumpção e Villa Rica; que, com Pedroso de Barros, cortaram o Brasil de leste ao oeste e visitaram as minas de prata da Bolivia e Perú; que, com Domingos Jorge, se incumbiram de dar cabo da lendaria colonias africana dos Palmares; que, com Dias Velho, iniciaram o povoamento de Santa Catharina; qus, comBrito Peixoto, exploraram, os pampas do Rio Grande Sul; que, com Fernando Dias Paes descobriram o sertão aurifero de Minas Geraes; que, com Bartholomeu Bueno, fizeram conhecidas as riquezas mineraes de Goyaz e que, com os Lemes, Macieis, Cabraes e Sutis, abriram á civilização os sertões de Matto Grosso.

Entretanto, a esta gente, a mais audaciosa e destimida que o Brasil jámais produziu, ainda não encontrou um chronista que, narrando os seus grandes feitos, lhe fizesse a devida justiça. As *Memorias* de Frei Gaspar, como elle mesmo as qualificou, servem para a historia da capitania de S. Vicente, mas não contém essa historia. Encontra-se nellas mais a discussão de factos do que a narrativa dos acontecimentos. Machado de Oliveira, no seu *Quadro Historico*, é resumido demais; atropela os acontecimentos, acceita informações menos verdadeiras sobre alguns factos aliás bem conhecidos, como a morte dos irmãos Lemes, e emprega no seu livrinho uma linguagem pesada e ás vezes obscura, que torna sua narrativa pouco agradavel.

Alimentamos a esperança de que o dr. Washington Luiz Pereira e Souza, moço de brilhantes talentos, de gosto para os estudos historicos de amor ao trabalho, de sisudo criterio e já vantajosamente conhecido no nosso meio historico, se queira incumbir de supprir tamanha lacuna, dando-nos opportunamente senão uma historia completa de S. Paulo, desde os primeiros descobrimentos da costa brasileira até hoje, ao menos um trabalho que faça justiça aos *bandeirantes* e nol-os apresente taes quaes elles foram — de uma intrepidez á toda próva, de uma ealdade nunca desmentida e de uma liberalidade proverbial.

\*  
\*  \*

Ha na historia geral do nosso paiz muitos factos que são de interesse especial para S. Paulo e que, entretanto, são geralmente desconhecidos pelo publico paulista porque os escriptores que trataram desta provincia, como Machado de Oliveira, foram muito resumidos e não tiveram occasião de referil-os ou apenas delles fizeram ligeira menção.

O imperador Pedro I, sempre leviano e impulsivo, parecia um desatinado que corria ao encontro de um fatal destino. Desde logo assediado pela roda desmorulizadora dos Gomes *Chalaça*, Rocha Pinto e Domitila a explorada pelos retrogrados e portuguezes, chefiados pelos Paranágua, Lages, Clemente Pereira e outros politicos, começou o jovem monarcha a sua carreira de pesatino com a dissolução da Assembléa Constituinte e deportação de alguns patriotas e a terminou com a sua abdicação a 7 de abiil.

Na côrte imperial o mais temido e odiado de todos os nossos grandes homens era exactamente José Bonifacio, por ter tentado moralizal-a e tornar seria e decente a direcção dos negocios publicos. Seis annos de exilio custou a elle, e a seus dois irmãos, essa tentativa de reforma nos habitos e processos palacianos, emquanto os seus successores, nos ministerios que se seguiram, trouxeram a confederação do Equador, afogada em precioso sangue, a não convocação dos corpos legislativos por dois annos, a perda da nossa provincia da Cisplatina depois do desastre de Ytuzaingo, os insultos do almirante francez Roussin e, finalmente, o 7 de Abril, que veiu coroar a obra iniciada a 12 de novembro de 1823. Voltados á patria em 1828, sem licença da roda que cercava Pedro I, foram Martim Francisco e Antonio Carlos mettidos em processo pelo governo imperial: mas, como o excesso do despotismo ou da violencia provoca sempre uma justa reacção, foram ambos absolvidos e Jose Bonifacio, ao voltar tambem ao Brasil no anno seguinte, nada soffreu da parte do imperante e dos seus aulicos.

Não frequentavam elles o palacio, nem assistiam as festas imperiaes, mas diz-nos um chronista que Jose Bomifacio fizera uma visita ao imperador e que este o apresentara a imperatriz, que ja não era mais a martyr princeza Leopoldina, mas a energica e imperiosa D. Amelia de Leuchtenberg, e accrescenta que «em uma curta allocução dirigida em francez a imperatriz, Jose Boniacio expoz o estado do Brasil com cores vivas e concluiu pedindo-lhe que fosse ella o anjo que conciliasse o imperador com a nação e a nação com imperador; durante a conversa o imperador interrompia a Jose Bonifacio, mas este, que o conhecia de perto, voltando-se para elle, lhe disse : —*não me interrompa, deixe-me dizer a verdade porque ella interessa a Vossa Magestade e a vossos filhos»*.

Era verdade, exposta em linguagem clara e talvez dura, que offendia os ouvidos do joven monarcha e escandalizava a roda aulica que o bajulava e o separava da nação ; mas Dom Pedro, incorrigivel por indole e viciado pelo habito da sua roda, que era nelle uma segunda natureza, não se corrigiu e o 7 de Abril foi a consequencia. Na vespera da sua abdicação, com certeza sem consultar os aulicos que não o largavam, lavrou elle o seguinte decreto que é o acto mais solemne de reparação que a nossa historia regista :

« Tendo maduramente reflectido sobre a posição politica deste imperio, conhecendo quanto se faz necessaria a minha abdicação e não desejando mais nada neste mundo senão gloria para mim e felicidade para a minha patria, hei por bem, usando direito que a Contituição me concede, no capitulo V. artigo 130, nomear como por este meu imperial decreto nomeio, tutor dos meus muito amados filhos ao MUITO PROBO, HONRADO E PATRIOTICO CIDADÃO José BONIFACIO DE ANDRADE E SILVA MEU VERDADEIRO AMIGO. Paço da Boa Vista, aos 6 de Abril de 1831, decimo da Independencia e do Imperio.— *Imperador Constitucional e Defensor Perpetuo do* BRAZIL.»

Mas onde estavam os cortezãos do tempo da prosperidade os aduladores de 1823 a 1830 e os conselheiros da dissolução da Assembléa Constituinte, das deportações, dos tribunaes maiciaes e dos fuzilamentos, que não foram lembrados, pelo infeliz monarcha para a delicada e honrosa funcção de tutor das imperiaes creanças? Tinham-se cautelosamente posto á sombra, para logo depois apparecerem filiados ao partido victorioso de Evaristo Veiga, em que não tardaram alguns em galgar as mais elevadas posições.

O ex-imperador, arrependido e penitenciado, explicou o seu acto ao parlamento nacional em um officio que tambem merece ter melhor conhecimento pelos paulistas e que diz assim;

«AUGUSTOS E DIGNISSIMCS SENHORES REPRESENTANTES DA NAÇÃO :—Participo-vos, senhores, que no dia 6 do corrente mez de Abril usando do direito que a Constituição me concede no capitulo V, artigo 130, nomeei tutor dos meus amados filhos ao MUITO PROBO, HONRADO E PATRIOTICO CIDADÃO, O MEU VERDADEIRO AMIGO, José BONIFACIO DE ANDRADA E SILVA.

«Não vos hei, senhores, feito esta participação logo que a augusta Assembléa Geral principiou seus importantes trabalhos, porque era mister que o MEU AMIGO fosse primeiramente consultado e que me respondesse favoravelmente, como acaba de fazer, dando deste modo mais uma prova da sua amizade. Resta-me agora, como pae, como amigo da minha patria adoptiva e de todos os brasileiros, por cujo amor abdiquei duas coroas para sempre, uma offerecida e outra herdada, pedir á augusta. Assembléa Geral que digne confirmar esta minha nomeação.

« Eu assim o espero confiado nos serviços que de todo o meu coração fiz ao Brazil e que a augusta Assembléa não deixará de querer alliviar-me desta maneira um pouco as saudades que me atormentam, motivadas pela separação dos meus amados filhos e da patria, que adoro. Bordo da nau ingleza *Warspite*, surta neste porto, aos 8 de Abril de 1831, decimo da Independencia do Imperio.—PEDRO.»

A reparação não podia ser mais cabal e estrondosa da

parte do offensor, mas ella só ficou completa quando a opinião nacinal elevou o offendido á categoria de *Patriarcha da Independencia* e levantou-lhe uma estatua em uma das praça da capital do Imperio.

\*\*\*

Se a gloria da independencia está indefectivelmente ligada ao nome de José Bonifacio, o heróe civil do 7 de Abril foi sem duvida Evaristo da Veiga. Não póde ser elle juiz dos seus proprios feitos, mas justificando e glorificando a revolução triumphante, diz Evaristo o seguinte, na *Aurora Fluminense* de 11 de Abril de 1831 :

«As intenções do ex-imperador, quando mudou o Ministerio, foram as mais *puras*. Os nomes de um *Paranaguá*, de um *Lages*, de um *Baependy*, ETC., eram do *melhor agouro para a liberdade*. Tudo havia a esperar de tão *bons* senhores e o Ministerio da confiança imperial *mostrara claramente* quanto o imperial animo *estava de accôrdo* com a opinião publica. Porém, não contente com isso, sua ex-magestade foi nomear para o commando do corpo da policia aquelle mesmo homem que, em 1824, fôra mandado a S. Paulo para ahi proclamar o absolutismo (o sr. Gavião)!

«Quem não acreditará nos *bons* desejos com que Dom Pedro I escolheu o aristocratico ministerio das 24 horas? O nosso *Polignac* burlesco, o irresistivel Paranaguá nutria... *(roto)*... esperanças que... *(roto)* ... tinha na .. *(roto)* .. Contam mesmo que até á ultima hora elle aconselhara ao ex-imperador que se puzesse á frente da tropa e cahisse sobre os rebeldes...»

Os ministerios do imperador obdeciam aos seus caprichos na duração; alguns viveram mezes, outros prolongaram-se por semanas e houve gabinete que, como a rosa de Malherbe, durou sómente um dia; este foi o ministerio composto dos marquezes de Paranaguá. de Baependy, de Aracaty e de Inhambupe, do conde de Lages e do visconde de Alcantara—seis fidalgos que Evaristo chama «*bons* senhores» e cujos nomes eram do *melhor agouro para a liberdade*. Sómente os nomes de tres vem mencionados, por serem estes os mais antipathicos aos sentimentos liberaes dos brazileiros; porém os outros tres estão claramente incluidos naquelle suggestivo ETC., que interrompe a lista.

O marquez de Aracaty, um dos seis, era talvez o mais afidalgado delles e se fez muito conhecido em S. Paulo em 1819-22 como capitão general e como presidente do governo collectivo acclamado a 23 de Junho de 1821 : foi aqui um dos chefes da famosa *Bernarda* de 23 de Maio, trabalhou contra a independencia e contribuiu para a impopularidade e quéda de Pedro I, mas não virou as costas ao imperador decahido e o acompanhou a Portugal, abandonando a sua cadeira de senador do imperio, dando assim a próva de que amava mais Dom Pedro e o velho reino do que o Brazil e os brazileiros.

Tem havido um trabalho constante de rehabilitação da sua memoria, procurando-se definir a sua individualidade moral e politica e apresental-o ao nosso publico como um grande amigo do Brazil; mas, politicamente morto a 7 de Abril de 1831, Evaristo Veiga se incumbiu de lançar a ultima pá de terra sobre a sua sepultura e de repetir o costumado *requiescat in pace.*

*\*
\* \**

Dissolvendo a Assembléa Constituinte a 12 de Novembro de 1823, prendendo e deportando alguns homens dos mais proeminentes e obrigando outros a fugirem do paiz, apressou-se Dom Pedro a outorgar ao Brazil uma constituição politica toda sua, redigida sob a sua presidencia por um conselho de homens da sua absoluta confiança. Essa constituição foi jurada na capital do imperio, a 25 de Março de 1824, mas o imperador não tinha firme intenção de executal-a, considerando-a sómente como uma valvula de segurança contra os perigos de uma explosão nacional; a opinião publica ficaria na expectativa e elle ganharia tempo para traçar os planos convenientes para burlar o codigo fundamental, sophismal-o ou executal-o de accôrdo com as circumstancias.

Começou-se por não convocar os corpos legislativos durante dois annos e depois distribuiram se emissarios para varias partes do paiz. Gavião em S. Paulo, Souza Chichorro em Taubaté. Itapagipe na Bahia, etc.—para proclamarem as vantagens do governo absoluto sobre o regimen constitucional.

Todo o plano se mallogrou porque a revolta da nossa provincia da Cisplatina absorveu toda a attenção dos poderes publicos, occupou todas as forças armadas do governo imperial e acabou assegurando a independencia daquella região, em virtude de desastre soffrido pelas forças imperiaes no combate de Ytuzaingo; mas a proclamação platonica do absolutismo chegou a realizar-se em Taubaté e na Bahia, acompanhada de perto de uma branda censura e de boas recompensas aos seus auctores.

Terminada a guerra Cisplatina com a independencia daquella provincia em 1828, voltou o governo imperial aos seus planos de absolutismo e no anno seguinte já os aulicos, por si ou por ordem de D. Pedro I, iniciavam os estudos dos meios de abolir a constituição ou, pelo menos, de tornal-a *verdadeiramen te monarchica*, como se vê da seguinte declaração feita por Evaristo da Veiga na *Aurora Fluminense* em 13 Abril de 1831:

Sempre negaram os aulicos que houvesse, em 1829, de parte do Poder o designio de alterar a constituição brasileira. Agora houvemos á mão os quesitos que naquella época foram feitos sobre este assumpto a differentes personagens. Só as circumstancias e o desenvolvimento muito rapido da opinião publica impediram a verificação dos planos tenebrosos que então se traçavam. Vejam-se os quesitos: comparem-se com a linguagem hypocrita e absurda da proclamação de Ouro Preto e diga-se que especie de confiança podiamos nós ter na ex-monarchia e em seus conselheiros:

1.º Em que estado de fermentação se deve considerar o Brazil?

2º. Que remedios se lhe pódem applicar?

3.º Se será melhor, DEPOIS QUE SUA MAGESTADE SE CONCILIAR E INTELLIGENCIAR COM OS DIFFERENTES SOBERANOS INFLUENTES, QUE ESTÃO INDISPOSTOS CONTRA SUA MAGEST.DE, VER SE MANDAM UMA FORÇA PARA APOIAR A NOSSA EM CASO DE NECESSIDADE, e Sua Magestade então dar nova constituição, *verdadeiramente monarchica*.

4.º Quaes serão os meios de fazer a concilliação e intelligencia com os differentes soberanos.

5.º Em que época se deverá por em pratica este plano?

« Estes quesitos eram feitos pelos homens que moveram ceus e terra, que clamaram contra o perjurio quando, em 1830, se falou em alterar, pelos tramites que a Constituição marcou, alguns artigos da lei fundamental. E elles queriam nado menos do que mudar a sua substancia, tornal-a monarchia, isto com o apoio de forças extrangeiras!... »

Referem-se o terceiro e o quarto quesitos a differentes soberanos européus, influentes e indispostos contra o imperador do Brasil, e sobre a necessidade de os conciliar para se obter delles o auxilio de força armada que facilitasse a desejada reforma constitucional no sentido de tornar o nosso codigo fundamental *verdadeiramente monarchico*. Estes soberanos só podiam ser Carlos X, rei de França, parente não muito distante de D. Pedro, visto que ambos eram da familia *Bourbon* e descendentes do grande Henrique IV, e Francisco II, imperador da Austria o ex-sogro do monarcha brasileiro.

Com a guerra da Cisplatina, que durou de 1825 a 1828 e na qual interveiu a Republica Argentina, os interesses francezes no Rio da Prata soffreram consideravelmente e alguns navios mercantes da França foram mesmo aprisionados pela esquadra

brasileira. Carlos X fez as costumadas reclamações, mas Dom
Pedro, leviano e irreflectido por natureza e sempre rodeado pelos
Rocha Pinto, *Chalaça* e Domitila e mal dirigido por politicos
incapazes de incutir a necessaria seriedade nos seus actos, não
soube levar as negociações diplomaticas a bom termo e o rei da
França, indisposto contra o primo do Brasil mandou para cá o
almirante Roussin, que, a 6 de Julho de 1828, surgiu com uma
esquadrilha de tres navios no porto do Rio de Janeiro e exigiu
do governo a entrega immediata dos navios francezes aprisionados e uma indemnização por perdas e damnos. Os navios foram
logo entregues, mas a indemnização só foi paga no anno seguinte
de 1829, exactamente quando se tratou de *conciliar* e *intilli-
genciar* os soberanos europeus para os fins politicos do imperador
e dos seus aulicos.

Com o imperador da Austria a indisposição era de natureza
mais grave, porque provinha de questões pessoaes e de negocios
da familia.

A imperatriz Leopoldina, sempre maltratada por Dom Pedro,
estava frequentemente a escrever ao imperador da Austria, seu
pae, narrando os soffrimentos que Dom Pedro e suas messalinas
lhe inflingiam no Rio de Janeiro e que acabaram por matal-a
na flôr da edade, deixando-nos cinco creanças—D. Maria da
Gloria com 7 annos de edade, D. Januaria com 4, D. Paula
com 3, D. Francisca com 2, e Dom Pedro II apenas com um anno.

Era natural que o imperador da Austria vivesse indisposto
com o genro, que tanto lhe maltratava a filha, e falou-se mesmo
que elle mandaria ao Brazil a outra filha, D. Maria Luiza, viuva
de Napoleão I, para levar daqui a infeliz irmã e talvez isto se
realizasse se a imperatriz Leopoldina não fosse tão cedo arreba-
tada deste mundo.

Fallecendo a imperatriz em Dezembro de 1826, ficou Dom
Pedro qnasi tres annos viuvo e todo entregue á perniciosa roda
aulica e feminina que o vinha desde muito sequestrando da
nação ; mas, afinal cançou da vida desregrada e tratou de casar
segunda vez, devendo a noiva possuir qualidades de nascimento,
virtude, instrucção e formosura, que viessem fazer a felicidade
do noivo e do paiz. O marquez de Barbacena, Felisberto Caldeira Brant, encarregado da espinhosa missão de escolher nas
côrtes européas uma noiva com taes requisitos, bateu seis vezes
nas portas de diversos membros da familia imperial da Austria
donde foi repellido outras tantas vezes, porque aquellas princezas
austriacas tinham noticias certas da vida atormentada que no Fio
de Janeiro havia levado a fallecida imperatriz Leopoldina·

Desanimado, o marquez de Barbacena deixou Vienna d'Austria e foi a Munich, onde conseguiu obter para o seu imperial committente a mão da princeza Amelia de Leuchtenberg, neta do rei da Baviera. Não teria ella, talvez, todos os requisitos exigidos pelo imperador, mas tinha formosura, e Dom Pedro, por esse lado, ficou bem servido com uma bella noiva, mas continuou a ser o objecto de indisposição da parte dos poderosos monarchas da França e da Austria, que eram membros proeminentes da Santa Alliança e acerrimos adversarios das liberdades publicas.

O tenebroso plano de *monarchizar* a constituição brasileira não se realisou, como bem disse Evaristo Veiga, porque o rapido desenvolvimento da opinião publica e ás circumstancias o impediram e não por falta de *bons* desejos da parte de Dom Pedro e dos seus aulicos. As idéas liberaes tinham se expandido de tal forma na mesma Europa que o reaccionario Carlos X foi derribado do throno no anno seguinte, de 1830, e o proprio imperador da Austria se viu incommodado por movimento revolucionarios na Italia, onde possuia algumas importantes provincias e varias dependencias.

A Inglaterra, monarchia livre e bem governada, era então um freio que continha as tendencias invasoras do absolutismo continental europeu e a *Doutrina de Monroe*, que já annos antes tinha feito recuarem os soberanos representados no Congresso de Verona, seria mais um impedimento a qualquer tentativa de desembarque de forças européas nas costas do Brasil, para a violenta transformação do regimen constitucional, estabelecido e já acceito pelo paiz, em um imperio *monarchizado*, que só beneficiaria a Dom Pedro e aos seus conselheiros, entre os quaes se contavam João Carlos de Oeynhausen, Villela Barbosa, Clemente Pereira e outros absolutistas portuguezes e alguns aberrados brazileiros, do grupo de Nogueira da Gama, marquez de Baependy.

Estes factos, ligeiramente mencionados pelos jornaes do tempo não constam todos da nossa historia *compendiada*, exectamente porque os nossos chronistas, por demais resumidos, se limitam a condensada narrativa dos acontecimentos principaes e deixam na sombra as suas causas e os factos de menor importancia intrinseca ou de resultados negativos; e se um ou outro jámais fez alguma breve referencia á tentativa de estabelecimento de um governo absoluto no Brasil depois de outorgada a constituição politica de 1824, foi sómente porque este plano chegou a se manisfestar por actos e a ter um começo de execução em Taubaté e na Bahia.

Mallogrado o tenebroso plano, Dom Pedro I se viu na necessidade de desauctorar publicamente aos seus adeptos, mas teve o cuidado de recompensar com honras e altos cargos aos

mais compromettidos, entre os quaes se achava o commendador
Souza Chichorro, que de juiz de fóra da villa de Taubaté foi
elevado a ouvidor da cidade de S. Paulo, emquanto um outro,
no norte do imperio, foi nomeado barão de qualquer coisa. São
factos da vida nacional do Brazil e não devem ficar em perpetuo esquecimento.

*⁎*

A literatura historica é dividida em duas partes: a *Historia*
propriamente dita e os *Bastidores da Historia*; aquella nos apresenta os acontecimentos da vida dos povos e as razões publicas
que os explicam ou justificam e estes se incumbem do registo
dos factos reservados e das razões occultas que, a bem dos governos e ás vezes da moral social, não convém que passem ao
dominio do publico, pelo menos emquanto vivem os protogonis-
tas dos acontecimentos.

Entretanto é tão estreita a ligação entre a *Historia* e seus
*Bastidores* nos governos de monarchas sensuaes, como Carlos II
da Inglaterra, Luiz XV da França e Pedro I do Brazil, que
não se póde traçar entre elles um limite claro e positivo que
determine os seus dominios. O famoso Luiz XIV pensionava as
cortezãs da côrte ingleza e por ellas obtinha que Carlos II não
se envolvesse na politica expansiva do rei francez; a imperatriz
da Austria, Maria Thereza, não se julgava rebaixada em manter
correspondencia secreta com a marqueza de Pompadour e com o
concurso desta celebre cortezã obter o auxilio de Luiz XV na
guerra dos *Sete Annos* contra o grande Frederico, rei da Prus-
sia, e D. Pedro não fazia mysterio da influencia sobre elle exer-
cida pelas cortezãs que desgraçaram o seu curto reinado.

Na côrte de Pedro I quem menos influia e menos acção tinha era exactamente a sua esposa, a infeliz D. Leopoldina da
Austria; desde a dissolução da Assembléa Constituinte, em 1823,
até á volta de D. Pedro de sua viagem ao Sul, em 1827, e
consequente perda da nossa provincia da Cisplatina, tudo era
movido pelas cortezãs, marquezas, baronezas e outras, que atra-
vessavam o palacio imperial e decidiam des mais altos e importantes interesses nacionaes. Os sobejos é que tocavam aos aulicos de profissão e á fidalguia adventicia criada pelo imperador,
que o sequestravam do amor dos seus subditos.

Entre os creados do Paço havia dois que se tornavam notaveis pela estima e protecção que lhes concedia o imperador:
eram João da Rocha Pinto e Francisco Gomes da Silva—o *Chalaça*—, ambos portuguezes de baixa estirpe, corruptos e ignoran-
tes. Gosando e abusando da absoluta confiança de D. Pedro,

eram ambos no palacio o prolongamento de José Clemente Pereira e de outros chefes do partido portuguez do Rio de Janeiro e, como taes, eram naturalmedte os objectos de especial aversão e odio dos brazileiros em geral e dos fluminenses em particular.

Com a chegada ao Rio de Janeiro da energica e imperiosa imperatriz Amelia de Leuchtenberg, as cortezãs mais perniciosas evacuaram o palacio imperial, mas Rocha Pinto e Chalaça, não pertencendo á roda immediata da nova imperatriz e sendo protegidos pelo imperador, deixaram-se ficar e pretenderam continuar no seu papel de validos do Paço. Foi preciso que o marquez de Barbacena, homem habil e confidente da imperatriz, cujo casamento elle havia arranjado, entrasse para o ministerio, em fim de 1829, para impôr a D. Pedro a exclusão desses indignos portuguezes do palacio imperial.

Quiz D. Pedro reluctar ainda, não podendo se resignar a perder a companhia destes seus amigos ursos; mas a intervenção da imperatriz poz termo á questão e ambos os validos foram forçados a sahir do palacio. D. Pedro, para consolar a ambos e a si proprio, nomeou Rocha Pinto encarregado de negocios do Brasil em Napoles e deu ao Chalaça egual cargo na Suecia, sendo os decretos destas nomeações firmados por Miguel Calmon, futuro marquez de Abrantes. Um chronista, muito familiar com os Bastidores da historia palaciana, nos conta o seguinte sobre a partida e a historia destes dois personagens:

«Os dois validos partiram por ordem do imperador, a bordo de um paquete inglez para a Inglaterra. O imperador concedeu do seu imperial bolsinho uma pensão annual a Chalaça de vinte e cinco mil francos e a Rocha Pinto, de vinte mil, por todo o tempo que ficassem ausentes do Rio de Janeiro.

«Ao imperador custou muito a separação destes dois validos encarregando-se elle proprio de todo o necessario da bagagem, para que nada lhes faltasse. Lembrava-se das coisas as mais miúdas para commodo dos seus dois amigos.

«Tudo o que fazia, o imperador communicava aos ministros, entretendo-os antes do despacho com essas ridicularias: «Estive toda esta manhã a fazer arranjar tal ou tal mala; um estojo para aqui, um copo para alli, um talher e outras coisas para Francisco Gomes levar». Isto mortificava o ministerio

«Como o Chalaça bebia muito, o imperador teve muito cuidado em arranjar-lhe os frasquinhos para a viagem. No dia do embarque o imperador abraçou, beijou e chorou pela separação dos dois intimos amigos. Nunca se gastou tão boa cera com tão ruins defuntos.

«Em Londres ligaram-se com os emigrados portuguezes e fizeram por persuadir o imperador que, se fosse para a Europa, seria imperador da Peninsula. *Chalaça* foi commandante de um esquadrão da guarda de honra, official do gabinete do imperador, conselheiro, official do Cruzeiro e possuia as commendas da Torre e Espada e da Rosa. Rocha Pinto foi guardaroupa, gentilhomem, estribeiro-mór e superintendente das quintas e da fazenda de Santa Cruz. Depois da morte do imperador a ex-imperatriz Amelia nomeou o *Chalaça* seu secretario e mordomo da sua casa e o levou para Munich. Rocha Pinto suicidou-se em Lisboa».

Termina o chronista citado dizendo que, em 1831, estando *Chalaça* em Londres no meio de emigrados portuguezes: foragidos da tyrannia de D. Miguel, lá publicou umas *Memorias offerecidas á Nação Brazileira*, que elle não podia ter escripto por ser muito ignorante e que estão todas recheiadas de falsidades e mentiras. Sahindo do Brazil contra a vontade, levando comsigo a aversão e o odio dos brasileiros e, logo depois, vendo-se sem esperança de voltar ao Brazil pela queda do seu amigo e protector Pedro I, era natural que *Chalaça* só mandasse escrever falsidades e mentiras sobre o nosso paiz e seus habitantes.

Parece que D. Pedro, na cegueira da sua dedicação por estes validos, se limitou a melhorar a sua condição de *deportados*, dando-lhes cargos que eram verdadeiras sinecuras, e que, não tendo verbas no orçamento do ministerio de Extrangeiros para custeio do nenhum serviço de que ambos foram encarregados, pagou-lhes pensões annuaes, de 25.000 francos a um e de 20.000 francos ao outro, tirados do seu imperial bolsinho. Entretanto não foi sómente isto e *Chalaça*, apesar de ser um tanto borracho, teve de D. Pedro a incumbencia de desempenhar na França uma commissão de summa importancia. que só a leviandade e irreflexão do imperador podiam confiar a um tal representante, quando lá tinha o Brasil um bom embaixador na pessoa do politico baiano Domingos Borges de Barros, visconde da Pedra Branca.

Não podendo D. Pedro ser simultaneamente imperador do Brasil e rei de Portugal, cujo throno herdára por morte de seu pae D. João VI, em 1826, abdicára elle a corôa portugueza na pessoa de sua filha primogenita, D. Maria da Gloria, princeza que então tinha sete annos de edade e que devia ser casada ao seu tio D. Miguel, regente do reino de Portugal durante a menoridade da noiva. D. Miguel, principe perverso e de má fé, apossou-se do throno e descartou-se da noiva, que foi obrigada a voltar ao Rio de Janeiro e aqui esperar o desdobramento dos factos e das relações entre seu pae, no Rio, e seu tio, em Lisboa.

O imperador, que vivia absorvido pela roda de cortezãs e de aulicos, levou annos em contemporisações com o irmão, que se fez rei do velho reino e algoz das liberdades publicas da sua patria. Em 1829 ainda estava elle protelando a reivindicação da corôa de Portugal, pertencente á sua filha, e cuidava antes no plano de *monarchisar* a constituição brazileira, tanto do agrado da sua gente, com o auxilio de forças extrangeiras, que só poderiam lhe ser fornecidas pelos soberanos da França e da Austria, Carlos X e Francisco II, indispostos contra elle e necessitados de conciliação. Com o auxilio destes dois monarchas poderia elle não sómente *monarchisar* o governo brasileiro, a seu gosto, como tambem derribar do throno portuguez o usurpador D. Miguel e restabelecer nelle a sua filha Maria da Gloria, parente de Carlos X e neta de Francisco II.

Estariam as negociações em andamento para a realização deste projecto, quando, em fins de Julho de 1830, foi Carlos X derribado do throno francez e Francisco II se viu atarefado com revoluções na Italia, que tanto affectavam interesses seus como de diversos principes, seus parentes, alli reinantes. Luiz Felippe foi logo acclamado rei dos francezes e D. Pedro, que já não tinha mais esperanças no auxilio do monarcha decahido e do seu ex-sogro, se apressou em travar relações, as mais estreitas, com os Orleans, pedindo a Luiz Felippe para fazer um dos seus filhos casar com D. Maria da Gloria. O visconde da Pedra Branca iniciara a necessaria negociação para isso e o *Chalaça* foi por D. Pedro encarregado de a concluir.

E' simplesmente pasmoso que o Imperador do Brazil levasse a sua dedicação por este indigno valido ao ponto de confiar-lhe uma tarefa tão delicada e que tanto interessava á felicidade de sua filha e ao bem do povo portuguez, do qual ella era a rainha legal. Eis o que a respeito publicou Evaristo Veiga em editorial da *Aurora Fluminense*, de 20 de Abril de 1831, convindo notar que *Chalaça* tinha ainda a alcunha de *Bem conhecido* e que ás vezes denominado *Conselheiro Gomes*,

« Os nossos leitores terão tido grande curiosidade de saber como vae e o que tem feito na Europa o *Bem Conhecido, o fidus Achates*, o homem da privança, o *Sully do nosso Henrique IV*, em uma palavra, o *Conselheiro Gomes* da Silva. Dir-lhes-emos alguma cousa sobre tão importante personagem:

« O *Conselheiro Gomes* veiu a Pariz e pediu uma audiencia ao ministro dos Negocios Extrangeiros, general Sebastiani; tendo-a alcançado, apresenta-se o nosso homem carregado de commendas, principiando deste modo a alvoraçar todo o Ministerio dos Negocios Extrangeiros, e roga ao ministro que lhe obtenha dia e hora para falar á Sua Magestade El-Rei dos Francezes a quem tinha de communicar negocios da mais grave importancia.

« Diz-lhe o ministro que desejava saber o objecto da audiencia para prevenir Sua Majestade. Respondeu o sr. Gomes que trazia uma carta do imperador, *seu amo*, para Luiz Felippe, com recommendação de entregal-a em mão propria. Pergunta-lhe o ministro se trazia copia da carta, como era de estylo· O nosso diplomata improvisado tornou-lhe que copia naquella occasião não tinha, mas que lh'a traria, o que era escusado, porque tudo o que ella comprehendia era relativo ao casamento da rainha de Portugal, D. Maria com um filho do rei dos francezes.

« Despediu-se o ministro dizendo que pediria as ordens do rei a respeito das audiencias e lhe daria a resposta. Não a recebendo, começou o nosso diplomata a affligir-se e valeu-se do seu amigo Rezende, que o apresentou ao rei. Então o *Bem conhecido*, triumphante, da-lhe a carta que continha mais ou menos o seguinte :

« *Mr. Le Lieutenant General du Royaume* (e aqui, quando a carta foi escripta, já se sabia da acclamação do rei Luiz Felippe).—*Apprenant que vous avez temoigné le desir de marier un de vos fils à ma fille bien aimée la reine de Portugal, et mon intention étant de recevoir avec le plus grand interét toutes propositions que vous aurez a me faire sur cet object si important à nos maisons royales, jai chargé mon marechal de palais, etc».*

« O rei não deu resposta e como se lembrasse que, havia largo tempo, o visconde da Pedra Branca lhe falara sobre a possibilidade de um tal casamento, a que o duque de Orleans não dera decisão alguma, mandando-o chamar e lhe disse : «Que fizestes? Que mandastes dizer para o Brazil sobre casamento da filha do imperador com meu filho? Estou admirado de receber agora uma carta por via de certo homem que se diz *marechal de palais* e das primeiras familias da vossa côrte, contando-se nella que eu havia manifestado desejos de casar meu filho etc.»

« O visconde da Pedra Branca escapou-se como poude e o negocio ficou em nada. Agora accusam o conselheiro privado de ter accumulado disparate sobre disparate nesta nogociação e de haver sabido fóra das formulas usadas em casos semelhantes. O certo é que elle deu todo o logar ao ridiculo na côrte de França, onde pelo enviado se ficou formando idéa bem pouco vantajosa do amo. Mas disto não tem culpa o sr. Gomes, que não foi educado para estas cousas e que passou por semelhantes vergonhas só para servir a quem o mandou. S. exa, achava-se ultimamente na Inglaterra e de boa saude».

O duque de Orleans, de que acima se faz menção, era o filho mais velho do rei Luiz Felippe e o herdeiro presumptivo da corôa da França; não poderia casar com a princeza D. Maria da Gloria, futura rainha de Portugal, pela inconveniencia da união das duas corôas, que viria influir sobre o equilibrio da politica européa; mas Luiz Felippe tinha mais quatro filhos— os duques de Nemours, de Montpensier e de Aumale e o principe de Joinville, e qualquer destes estava no caso de ser um bom consorte para a rainha de Portugal.

Não havia preconceito ou opposição contra a alliança das suas familias, como se viu logo depois: o duque de Montpensier veio casar na Hespanha com uma princeza, irmã da rainha Isabel e prima de Pedro I, e o principe de Joinville veio se alliar no Rio de Janeiro a D. Francisca, filha do mesmo Pedro I e irmã da rainha de Portugal. Um quarto de seculo depois ainda vinham o conde d'Eu e o duque de Saxe, netos de Luiz Felippe, receber-se em matrimonio com princezas brasileiras, netas de Pedro I, e ainda ultimamente a princeza Amelia de Orleans, bisneta do rei dos francezes, foi tomada por esposa pelo rei D. Carlos de Portugal, bisneto do primeiro imperador do Brasil.

Talvez não haja na Europa outras familias reaes tão entrelaçadas como se acham as de *Orleans*, *Bourbon* e *Bragança*; entretanto D. Pedro, por sua pessima politica e por seu ainda peor emissario, não poude conseguir entre os principes de Orleans um noivo para D. Maria da Gloria; casou-se ella depois com o duque de Leuchtenberg, irmã da imperatriz Amelia e cunhado do imperador, seu pae, e ficando viuva dois mezes depois, foi procurar um segundo esposo entre os *Saxe-Cobourg*, das pequenas dynastias ducaes da Allemanha, emquanto o desastrado *Chalaça* passava de Portugal para a Baviera e ia servir de secretario da ex-imperatriz Amelia, a mesma que, com Barbacena, o havia deportado do Rio de Janeiro, com a ficha de consolação de uma sinecura diplomatica na capital de Suecia e 25.000 francos de subsidio annual do imperial bolsinho de Pedro I.

Não reconhecendo D. Pedro a seu irmão D. Miguel como rei de Portugal, cuja corôa pertencia de direito á D. Maria da Gloria, filha e pupilla de Pedro I, precisava o imperador manter dupla representação diplomatica nas côrtes européas, uma por sua conta, por parte do Brasil e outra por conta de D. Maria da Gloria, por parte de Portugal e ambas dirigidas pelo nosso monarcha.

Nos negocios internacionaes referentes ao Brazil, naturalmente D. Pedro havia de ouvir os membros do gabinete; porém, estes ministros não tinham competencia alguma para se envolverem na politica externa de Portugal, quando os interesses brazileiros não estivessem em jogo. Nas relações do velho Reino com outros paizes, D. Pedro intervinha *pessoalmente,* elle só, como pae e tutor de D. Maria da Gloria; mas sempre incapaz de agir com seriedade e circumspecção, fazia elle do *Chalaça* o seu confidente e secretario particular e chegava mesmo a confiar ao seu valido a redacção, até a responsabilidade de importantes documentos, apesar da sua ignorancia e falta de idoneidade moral, como se vê do seguinte officio :

« *Imperial gabinete* :—As cartas de 24 e de 26 Maio, que dirigiu a S. M. o Imperador meu amo, ordena-me o mesmo Augusto Senhor responda que louva a maneira por que V. Exa. se houve na occasião que recebeu o decreto de 3 de Maio demittindo-se do emprego de suas funcções, como embaixador de Portugal em Londres, e escrevendo ao Ministerio dos negocios extrangeiros, Visconde de Santarem, o seu officio reservado de 24 de Maio, expondo-lhe os motivos de as fazer cessar, o que certamente é uma prova do patriotismo e fidelidade de V. Exa.

« S. M. tendo abdicado a corôa de Portugal em sua Augusta Filha, a Sra. D. Maria da Gloria, hoje Rainha de Portugal D. Maria II, não deixou por isso de ser seu tutor, e nesta qualidade S. M. tem tomado e continuará a tomar as medidas que julgar convenientes, para que sejam mantidos illesos os inauferiveis direitos de sua filha, e para que a leal Nação Portugueza se conserve firme no juramento que prestou á Carta Constitucional.

« Aproveito esta occasião para significar a V. Exa. que sou com toda a consideração—Illm.° e Exm.ª Sr. Marquez de Palmela—De V. Exa. attencioso venerador *Francisco Gomes da Silva*—Rio de Janeiro, 22 de Julho de 1828».

O duque de Palmella, a quem este officio foi dirigido, era D. Pedro de Souza Holstein, um dos mais habeis politicos que Portugal jamais teve, homem de brilhante talento, de fina educação, muito viajado e amigo de Humboldt, de Gay-Lussac, de Barante, de Benjamim Constant, de Madame de Stael e de outros luzeiros do pensamento, e para corresponder com um tal homem D. Pedro não encontrava no Rio de Janeiro um amigo decente e lançava mão do *Chalaça*, que em nome do imperador, *seu amo,* tratava o estadista de além mar de egual para egual, como se fosse ahi um qualquer Rocha Pinto.

Já depois de ter sido deportado em 1829 e estando na

Europa, teve o *Chalaça* occasião de lêr ou de saber de certo
aspero artigo que Evaristo Veiga escreveu a seu respeito. D.
Pedro ainda era imperador e o valido ausente chamou á responsabilidade a *Aurora Fluminense* pelas duras verdades que disse sobre a sua pessoa. A causa foi julgada a 22 de Março de
1830, por um conselho de jurados presidido pelo literato conego Januario da Cunha Barbosa, e por unanimidade se decidiu
que não havia criminalidade nos conceitos que o grande jornalista enunciara sobre o famoso valido do primeiro imperador.

Commentando a decisão do jury, pergunta Evaristo qual
seria a sua sorte si o processo fosse julgado pela antiga Casa
da Supplicação da Côrte, que não encontraria penas bastante
severas para punil-o pelo horroroso crime de ter dito sobre o
*Chalaça* algumas verdades sem rebuço.

## IV

### DOIS CAPITÃES-GENERAES E UM OUVIDOR

Revendo a papelada velha do Archivo do Estado, encontro
algumas coisas curiosas sobre os nossos antepassados.

Alguns desses factos foram publicados pelos primeiros jornaes
que appareceram logo depois da independencia, mas estão inteiramente esquecidos hoje, emquanto outros não tiveram a honra de
vir á luz do dia e jazem sepultados na mais profunda ignorancia
por parte da geração actual. Convem recordal-as a beneficio dos
leitores e da vulgarização da nossa historia colonial.

D. Bernardo José de Lorena, que foi capitão-general de
S. Paulo, de 1789 a 1797, passava por ser filho adulterino do rei
D. José I. Moço espiloteado, devasso e leviano, era um tram-
bolho na côrte da sua irman, a rainha D. Maria I, que o remetteu
para o Brazil como capitão-general de S. Paulo, dando-lhe como
mentor José Romão Jeunot, personagem de certa capacidade
administrativa, cauteloso e circumspecto, que deu algum lustre
ao governo de D. Bernardo nos nove annos que permaneceu
nesta capital.

m uanto o mentor se entregava ao serviço publico e
realizava alguns melhoramentos de que S. Paulo muito precisava,
o amo se entregava aos seus gostos devassos e epicuristicos,
saltando alta noite os muros dos quintaes das casas de familia,
vencendo pelo exilio e pelo assassinato as resistencias aos seus

condemnaveis desejos e praticando outras tropelias que, não trazendo a desgraça das suas victimas, serviam para caracterizar o genio, o caracter e os costumes daquelle pimpolho da realeza luzitana.

Autonio Augusto da Fonseca, ytúano muito distincto e dado a estudos historicos, deixou-nos a narrativa dos assassinatos de um capitão e de um alferes paulistas, praticados por ordem de D. Bernardo, e Benedicto Octavio, poeta campineiro, poz em drama, escripto em excellentes versos, a sóva de chicote que tomára o capitão-general em consequencia de umas experiencias libidinosas que tentára e que conseguira levar avante nesta capital.

Na *Aurora Fluminense*, celebre jornal do notavel politico Evaristo Veiga, numero de 26 de Fevereiro de 1830, encontra-se a seguinte historia, que aquelle jornal diz ser extrahida *do Observador Constitucional*, periodico egualmente celebre por ter sido o orgam das ideias liberaes e da propaganda politica de Libero Badaró, assassinado em S. Paulo a 30 de Novembro daquelle anno:

« Era dia de jejum e o exmo. sr. capitão-general Bernardo José de Lorena era acostumado jejuar; mandou o seu criado comprar peixe fresco, mas como fosse tarde já não o havia. Encontrou, porem, um preto do conego Patricio, que levava umas tabaranas para seu senhor, e pediu o criado de s. exa. ao preto que lhe houvesse de vender as tabaranas; recusou este e levou para a casa o peixe, que se poz logo a cozinhar. Voltou para o palacio o servo do capitão-general, com as mãos vazias, e contou a s. exa. todo o acontecido.

« *Bem*, disse o sr. Bernardo de Lorena, *já dois soldados á casa do conego e tragam-me o peixe tal qual está*».

A expedição partiu: trouxeram conquistado o peixe já meio cozido. Sua exa. teve o gosto de comer tabaranas naquelle dia, e não consta que mandasse restituir a panella ».

O conego Patricio deve ser Patricio de Andrada, irmão de José Bonifacio, Antonio Carlos e Martim Francisco; perdeu o jejum que pretendia fazer de tabaranas, perdeu o dinheiro que ellas lhe custaram e até a panella em que estavam sendo cozidas, emquanto o capitão general se regalava a custa alheia, desrespeitando a propriedade particular, assim como desrespeitava a honra das familias paulistas.

Ao cabo de nove longos annos ficamos livre deste capitão-general, despotico, lascivo e agatunado, que nos deixou para ir por algum tempo infelicitar os povos de Minas Geraes, donde passou para Angola, e lá ainda teria occasião de empregar as suas habilidades no contacto com algum dos infelizes companheiros de Tiradentes, deportados para a costa da Africa.

\* \*

Deixando-nos para sempre, foi Bernardo de Lorena substituido no governo de S. Paulo por Antonio Manoel de Mello Castro e Mendonça, homem de melhores entranhas e de melhores intenções do que o seu antecessor, porém de uma incuravel fatuidade e amigo de certa pompa, que não estava de modo algum de accôrdo com a pobreza e atrazo da capitania, sempre mal governada, desde que subiu ao throno o devasso e beato rei João V até a independencia, sem exceptuar mesmo a administração vigorosa e regeneradora do marquez de Pombal.

O capitão-general Mello Castro, sem deixar de cuidar nos serviços publicos, que delle receberam alguns melhoramentos, atormentava os povos das villas paulistas com frequentas e prolongadas paradas, manejos e festas militares nesta capital, em que eram obrigados a tomar parte os batalhões de milicias do interior.

Estes batalhões vinham do interior equipados e sustentados nas viagens á custa dos respectivos commandantes e, como nesta capital não houvesse quartel capaz de os accommodar, ficavam por ahi alojados em barracas, em parte sustentados pela caridade publica, porque o Thesouro nunca tinha recursos para os pagamentos pontuaes das forças de linha e muito menos para satisfazer ás despesas das féstas militares e caprichosas do capitão-general, que não tinha lei, nem autorização alguma em que se apegasse para fazer esses gastos inuteis.

Tinha o capitão-general Mello Castro o appellido de *Pilatos*, que agarrou-se a elle de modo a nunca mais o largar ; donde lhe veiu essa alcunha, não encontro explicação em nenhum dos nossos chronistas.

Si já não o trouxe de Portugal, então é provavel que lhe fosse dado aqui pelos paulistas, qualificando os seus gostos por fofa pompa e apparatosa exhibição da sua pessoa em publico, nas festas que fazia sem recursos pecuniarios e sem leis que as permittissem, não se importando com as más consequencias que dellas resultavam para o povo da capital, que tinha de sustentar tanta gente chamada do interior, nem tendo a menor consideração para com o vexame que impunha aos milicianos, obrigados a vir de grandes distancias tomar parte nos divertimentos officiaes, deixando em abandono as suas familias, lavoura, negocios e todas as fórmas de interesses que os ligavam ás respectivas terras nataes.

Não demoraram as representações dos povos paulistas dirigidas ao governo de Lisboa contra os desmandos do capitão-

general; porém, este, cioso do seu socego e da boa administração
que elle dizia ao mesmo governo de Lisboa estar fazendo em
S. Paulo, sequestrava aquellas representações na sua passagem
por esta capital. Deste modo as queixas dos paulistas não chegavam ao ouvido da rainha Maria I e o capitão-general ficava
sabendo a natureza das accusações que lhe faziam e conhecendo
os queixosos para delles tirar a vingança que estivesse ao seu
alcance.

Governou elle sómente cinco annos, de 1797 a 1802, pouco,
em relação a Bernardo de Lorena, mas muito para soffrimento
dos paulistas, e deixou o governo entregue a Antonio José da
Franca e Horta, vindo de Portugal expressamente para o substituir, homem friamente perverso, tyranno, hypocrita, enredeiro
e intrigante, que desgraçou a capitania durante nove annos, de
1802 a 1811, e fez os paulistas repetirem por muitas vezes
aquelle celebre dito da velha de Syracusa: «Mal com elle, peior
sem elle».

Realmente, a substituição de Mello Castro por Franca e Horta
foi uma calamidade para a capitania de S. Paulo, que viu a espionagem e a delação estabelecidas nas repartições publicas,
nos quarteis e nas casas particulares como meios regulares de
governo e o recrutamento na mais alta escala promovido em
toda a parte e até dentro das egrejas, em dias de festas religiosas, além das violencias ordinarias e proprias do regimen colonial portuguez.

O modo, um tanto brusco e mysterioso, pelo qual se fez a
substituição de Mello Castro por Franca e Horta, era assim nar-
rado pelo dr. Ricardo Gunbleton, illustre medico inglez, domi-
ciliado em Campinas e muito entendido em materias relativas á
antiguidade paulista:

«A Camara de Ytú, no tempo do capitão-general Antonio
de Mello Castro e Mendonça, conhecido pelo nome de *Pilatos*,
fez uma accusação contra este governador e a remetteu directamente ao governo de Lisboa, mas não obteve resposta; repetiu
a accusação duas ou tres vezes e sempre o mesmo silencio.

«Então alguem, em Ytú, se lembrou de que essas representações podiam ter sido subtrahidas em viagem e não terem chegado ao seu destino. Residia então em Lisboa D. Isabel de
Campos, ytúana de familia illustre, intelligente e casada com
um portuguez que residira algum tempo nesta capitania e voltára a Portugal, levando comsigo a esposa. Esta senhora tinha
sido apresentada no palacio real e tinha adquirido certa intimi-
dade com a rainha, convindo portanto que se remettesse nova
representação a D. Isabel de Campos, em fórma de carta par-

ticular, pedindo-se a ella que fosse a sua portadora para as mãos de D. Maria I.

«A rainha já se achava louca nesse tempo, pois perdêra o uso da razão em 1800; porém, ou porque este facto não fosse ainda conhecido em Ytú, ou porque o regente do reino, que era o seu filho, mais tarde rei com o titulo de João VI, agisse sempre em nome da rainha, era a esta que o povo ytúano se dirigia, pedindo providencias contra os excessos de Mello Castro na administração da capitania de S. Paulo.

«Passados alguns mezes, os sufficientes para se ter uma resposta de qualquer communicação feita a Lisboa, apresentou-se em S. Paulo o general Franca e Horta e foi a palacio como um simples viajante que desejava cumprimentar o capitão-general em exercicio, mas levando comsigo dois companheiros que com elle tinham vindo de Portugal e cujos nomes a tradição não conservou.

«Depois de uma pequena palestra Franca e Horta tomou as mãos do Pilatos e disse-lhe: «Esteja preso á ordem da rainha»; entregou-lhe então o decreto da sua nomeação para capitão-general de S. Paulo e confiou o preso á guarda dos seus dois companheiros, que se incumbiram de escoltal-o até Portugal, passando em seguida o novo governador a fazer a apprehensão de todos os papeis do Pilatos, publicos e particulares, na esperança de descobrir nelles alguns valiosos segredos que satisfizessem o seu genio novidadeiro e intrigante e ao mesmo tempo justificassem a severidade empregada contra o governador demittido».

Não encontrei no Archivo do Estado documento algum que confirme esta tradição; porém, creio na verdade da narrativa, porque os factos estão de accôrdo com o caracter de Franca e Horta e com a natureza do regimen colonial portuguez e hespanhol e porque a honestidade e a sizudez que distinguiam o dr. Ricardo Gunbleton nos auctorizam a crer que elle não teria inventado esta historia para alta recreação sua e de seus ouvintes. Demais, o sr. Antonio Augusto da Fonseca, ytúano illustre, ha pouco fallecido e amigo do dr. Ricardo, foi quem me transmittiu esta tradição, accrescentando que acreditava na sua veracidade, sem comtudo conhecer com precisão a natureza das accusações que os ytúanos, seus antepassados, faziam contra Mello Castro, que aliás não praticou acto algum que justificasse a violencia de que foi victima por parte de Franca e Horta, estando as suas arbitrariedades muito áquem das violencias e crueldades commettidas pelos seus antecessores Rodrigo Cesar, Caldeira Pimentel, Martim Lopes, Bernardo de Lorena e mesmo D. Luiz Antonio de Sousa, morgado de Matheus, que aliás foi o mais habil e capaz dos capitães generaes que o governo portuguez mandou a S. Paulo.

Rodrigo Cesar assassinára judicialmente os irmãos João e Lourenço Leme, para satisfazer a violencia do seu genio e a cupidez do seu valido Sebastião Fernandes do Rego; Caldeira Pimentel roubara os quintos reaes, de parceria com este mesmo Sebastião Fernandes, que era o provedor daquelles quintos, atirando ambos a culpa sobre o paulista Jacintho Barbosa Lopes, que muito soffreu por isso, e não contente com os roubos praticados e falsidades levantadas contra um innocente, ainda Caldeira Pimentel fez assassinar João Lopes da Silva Ortiz, que estava em viagem para Lisboa, receando que este paulista distincto e sertanejo destemido denunciasse ao rei as suas falcatruas; Martim Lopes tão incapaz como tyrannico, tambem assassinou judicialmente o infeliz Caetaninho, companheiro das orgias do seu filho Antonio Lopes; Bernardo de Lorena assassinava o alferes José Corrêa e roubava as tabaranas e panellas do conego Patricio, por simples caprichos de lascivia e de glutoneria, e D. Luiz Antonio remettia gente algemada para as longinquas e pestiferas regiões de Yguatemy, que aliás não eram da sua capitania e nem da sua obrigação povoar, conservando nas prisões a mãe, a esposa e muitas vezes a familia inteira de alguem que se escondia para evitar taes violencias, até que o refugiado apparecesse. Entretanto, nenhum destes tyrannetes foi tratado por seu successor com tanto rigor como Mello Castro foi tratado por França e Horta, em uma época em que o sentimento de humanidade devera estar mais desenvolvido pela influencia dos principios moraes propagados pela Revolução Franceza e já expurgados das excrescencias nelles introduzidas pelo regimen do Terror.

*⁎*

No primeiro quarto do seculo passado residia na cidade de São Paulo, á rua da Tabatinguera n. 20, o coronel Manuel da Cunha Azeredo Coutinho Souza Chichorro, que no tempo da independencia tinha 50 annos de edade. Era casado com uma D. Catharina, tinha um filho de nome João Maria, que aos 15 annos era já cadete, e possuia onze escravos de serviços domesticos, todos menores de 30 annos.

Organizado em 1821 o governo provisorio de quinze membros, em virtude da revolução de 23 de Junho, que depoz o capitão-general João Carlos de Oeynhausen, passou Souza Chichorro a exercer o cargo de secretario do novo governo, cargo que elle já vinha exercendo desde longa data, sob a administração do triumvirato composto do bispo d. Matheus, do ouvidor Lossio Seilbz e do intendente Oliveira Pinto e sob o governo do capitão-general Oeynhausen.

Vivia elle da renda dos seus escravos e do ordenado do seu emprego, que podia desempenhar melhor do que o fazia. Era homem de alguma instrucção e mesmo publicou alguns trabalhos de real interesse para S. Paulo, mais por compilação do que por esforço do proprio talento. As actas das sessões do governo, escriptas por elle, são laconicas, cheias de falhas e mal redigidas, como se poderá verificar no vol. II do *Archivo do Estado de S Paulo* E' imperdoavel a falta que elle commetteu não registando nos livros da secretaria do governo a narrativa que José Bonifacio, Gama Lobo e marechal Arouche, delegados do governo e da municipalidade de S. Paulo junto a D. Pedro, fizeram da sua viagem desta cidade ao Rio de Janeiro, e truncando a cópia que mandou á Camara e que lá se acha registrada, sem notar outras faltas que praticou.

Profundamente absolutista em politica, adheriu por necessidade á independencia e pouco depois foi nomeado juiz de fóra de Taubaté. D. Pedro, que já havia decretado a constituição de 25 de Março de 1824, permanecia influenciado por individuos da ordem do Chalaça e Rocha Pinto, estava dominado pela celebre cortezan Domitila, era mal aconselhado por despotas e retrogrados, demorava a convocação dos corpos legislativos e preparava os meios de abolir a constituição outorgada e se fazer imperador de baraço e cutello, do mesmo paiz que com delirio o acclamára e que ainda não tinha perdido as doces esperanças nelle depositadas.

Rebentara em 1825 a revolta da nossa provincia da Cisplatina, que se fez independente em 1828 com o auxilio dos argentinos, e as tropas de que D. Pedro precisava para garantir o bom resultado dos planos absolutistas, seus ou da sua côrte tiveram de marchar para o sul e o plano dos reaccionarios se mallogrou inteiramente por falta de elementos para fazel-o effectivo. Entretanto o grito «*Viva o absolutismo, abaixo a constituição*», foi ouvido em mais de um logar, sendo Sousa Chichorro, coronel, commendador e juiz de fóra, quem o proferiu em Taubaté e villas vizinhas, dependentes da sua auctoridade.

A tentativa teve resultados inteiramente negativos : o Brazil, como nação, nada perdeu com ella, porém serviu para desmascarar os cortezãos e a cortezan, que sequestravam D. Pedro do seu povo, e para tornar o commendador Souza Chichorro intensamente odiado pelos brazileiros em geral e pelos liberaes patriotas em particular. Este odio popular o acompanhcu até á sua morte, occorrida muitos annos depois e fez delle um *outcast* politico e social.

O marechal Arouche, paulista liberal e patriota, foi dos primeiros a protestar contra o procedimento indigno de Chichorro e escreveu contra elle um violento artigo, que vem publicado nas paginas 117—118—119 do vol. V, da *Revista* do Instituto Historico de S: Paulo, e, ainda annos depois, Libero Badaró publicava contra elle o seguinte artigo, que tirei do *Observador Constitucional*, de 8 de Março de 1830, com todos os seus griphos :

« Não pretendiamos falar mais no *celebre Chichorro* e sim eutregal-o ao bem merecido desprezo de que se faz credor; porém, como O *Telegrapho* diz que este *heróe tem em seu favor a opinião dos homens sensatos* da provincia de S. Paulo e do Imperio, bom é que digamos duas palavras ácerca delle, para que se persuada o vil *Telegrapho (Analysta* de Minas) qual a *opinião* de que gosa nesta provincia o *incomparavel* Chichorro.

« Na qualidade de secretario do governo (logar que occupou ha annos) respondam as raspadelas dos livros e o aviso pelo qual foi reprehendido, infructiferamente, pois vergonha, queremo-nos persuadir que é qualidade que sua senhoria não tem.

« No tempo que exerceu o cargo de juiz de fóra de Taubaté quiz nos mimosear proclamando o absolutismo, para o que convocou a Camara, e foi tão feliz este heróe, que sahiu absolvido e, o mais é, *logo* despachado ouvidor para esta cidade

«Quando é preciso indicar em S. Paulo o pessimo dos magistrados, é o Chichorro; quando se quer indicar o homem sem vergonha, é o Chichorro; quando se quer indicar o homem desmoralizado, é o Chichorro: um sevandija é o Chichorro; si se deseja um homem sem nenhuma sombra de virtudes, é o Chichorro. Em uma palavra, podemos afiançar ao servil *Telegrapho*, sustentado, protegido e redigido pelo J. J. Lopes, que si alguma opinião tem o Chichorro nesta provincia é para com os moleques e não podia deixar de assim ser, pois que *similis similem querit.*

«Prova-se tanto a opinião deste Chichorrão, que nas ultimas nomeações populares, que a pouco acabámos, sua senhoria contou apenas um magro voto, sem duvida por mangação. Será isto força de opinião? Responda sr. servil *Telegrupho.* Quem gosa da opinião dos homens sensatos não póde obter nem o logar de bliguim? Venha, sr. *Telegrapho,* feche os olhos, agarre no primeiro que encontrar na rua e pergunte-lhe: «Quem é o Chichorro?» Certamente ha de ouvir uma bellissima ladainha do tal freguez. Sr. *Thelegrapho*, si quer fazer alguma fortuna, si quer grangear alguma opinião para o seu confrade, tome o nosso conselho: vá para a Turquia, que de certo será alli muito estimado de todos; porém no Brazil, meu rico senhor absolutista, não faz colheita, pois é bem conhecidinho.

«Que parelha bella de tres podia sahir da provincia de Minas os—CHICHORRO, TELEGRAPHO & ASSIS LORENA!!!!!!».

A linguagem usada por Libero Badaró, aspera como se vê acima, não éra mais violenta do que ,a dos outros jornaes do tempo. A causa do seu assassinato, occorrido alguns mezes depois, não foi a fórma dos seus ataques aos adversarios, mas o espirito da propaganda liberal que fazia contra a politica reaccionaria de D. Pedro e seus auxiliares, que os levou ao 7 de Abril e entregou o Brazil ao dominio de si mesmo.

*O Observador Constitucional* era publicado na typographia do *Pharol Paulistano* e tinha apenas 30 centimetros do alto á base e 20 centimetros de largura, incluindo nestas dimensões as margens, quatro paginas de duas columnas, e nenhum annuncio; sahia duas vezes por semana, sendo a assignatura de 1$440 por trimestre e 80 réis o numero avulso. Era intensa a animosidade da redacção contra o absolutismo e este nobre sentimento, levado ás vezes á exaggeração, se manifestava em artigos de fundo, em maximas e pensamentos, em anecdotas, quasi sempre em prosa, mas as vezes em verso. Em todos os numeros vem no alto da primeira pagina o seguinte *moto*, tirado de Felinto Elysio;

« E leis mais brandas regerão o mundo
Quando homens mais humanos,
Com o raio da verdade, a luz espalhem».

No jornal de 5 de Março de 1830 se diz que os brazileiros devem observar os dez mandamentos seguintes:

1.—Amar de coração a Sua Magestade Imperial e Constitucional.

2.—Não jurar outra fórma de governo, sinão a actual constitucional, pinte-se como se pintar.

3.—Guardar e observar exactamente tudo quanto emanar do governo, emquanto fôr constitucional.

4.—Honrar ao nosso ministerio por ser constitucional e respeital-o como a nosso pae, emquanto for constitucional.

5.—Não matar aos absolutistas, nem mesmo aos do club Wandeque, isto é, á pessoa alguma.

6.—Não observar outra coisa que não seja mandado por Deus no sexto mandamento.

7.—Não furtar cousa alguma, ainda sendo dos absolutistas, por ser isso só proprio delles.

8.—Não levantar falso testemunho aos despoticos, nem ainda sendo do partido *chalacino*.

9.—Não desejar a mulher de ninguem, por isso ser manha despotica e indigna da sociedade.

10.—Não cobiçar honras, nem pensões, e deixar isso aos mandões absolutistas, como sanguesugas do Estado, e ao partido *chalacino*.

Termina o jornal dizendo que estes dez mandamentos podem ser condensados em dois : UNIÃO E OLHO VIVO.

O partido *chalacino* era naturalmente composto daquelles que resavam pela cartilha do *Chalaça*, o mais vil dos cortezãos que rebaixavam a côrte de Pedro I, de que o *Analysta* era o orgam para apregoar ao mundo as virtudes de Pedro I e dos partidarios do regimen absolutista. Dahi veio Badaró dizer que *O Telegrapho*, jornal mineiro e apreciador das qualidades de Chichorro, era o *Analysta* de Minas Geraes.

Na collecção d'*O Observador Constitucional*, que tenho á vista, faltam os numeros todos de meiado de Julho ao fim de Dezembro de 1830 e, portanto, não contém informação alguma sobre o assassinato do seu redactor. O jornal continuou a ser publicado ainda por mais de um anno e sustentava os mesmos principios liberaes, mas já não offerecia a mesma feição interessante que lhe sabia dar o grande liberal italiano.

## V

### DESAPROPRIAÇÕES EM 1820

Para a reconstituição da nossa historia colonial, geralmente mal estudada e pouco conhecida, servem muitos documentos que apparentemente não têm importancia, mas que entretanto deitam muita luz sobre um ou outro ponto da vida da nossa antiga sociedade, dos costumes dos nossos avós e da lenta expansão das nossas cidades e populações.

Em 1820 a cidade de S. Paulo, a grande e bella capital de nossos dias, não tinha mais de 15.000 habitantes, e estava toda situada no espaço contido pelos ribeirões do Tamanduatehy e Anhangabahú e pela rua Tabatinguera, prolongando-se a certa distancia as ruas da Liberdade e de Santo Amaro, em direcção ás povoações de Santo Amaro e M'Boi a da Consolação ao longo da estrada geral para Sorocaba, Ytú e Jundiahy, a da Gloria no caminho para Santos, e a actual avenida Tiradentes em segui-mento da estrada de rodagem que, através da serra da Cantareira, se dirigia para Juquery, Atibaia e Bragança.

Neste resumido terreno estava a cidade colonial, de ruas estreitas, tortas mal calçadas e guarnecidas de casarias baixas, mal construidas, sem gosto artistico, sem luz, sem hygiene, de rotulas abrindo para fóra e de telhados projectando sobre as ruas, sem encanamento para guiar as aguas pluviaes, que dos tectos despejavam sobre os transeuntes.

Não havia illuminação regular, porque o kerozene não estava ainda descoberto e ninguem pensava na possibilidade da illuminação a gaz e a electricidade. Os exgottos eram em fossas nos quintaes e algum lixo era deitado no Tamandutehy á noite ou nos terrenos baldios das vizinhanças da cidade. A agua era boa, mas pouca, tirada de cisternas ou comprada na porta, a tanto por barril, de vendedores ambulantes que andavam com carrocinhas pelas ruas e viellas da povoação. Os quintaes eram viveiros de corvos, que faziam gratuitamente o papel de agentes da limpeza publica.

Não havia mercado e as ruas eram inundadas de quitandeiras de verduras, que faziam da rua do Commercio, a mais central da cidade, estreita e torta, o seu centro de reunião e logar de despejo dos residuos e dos generos deteriorados. Era rua commercial e importante e os mercadores nella estabelecidos viviam desgostosos com as más consequencias que para ellas resultavam daquella pouco aggradavel agglomeração na sua visinhança; reclamaram providencias da camara municipal, que expediu a seguinte curiosa.

### PORTARIA

« Sendo repetidas as representações que os negociantes de fazenda secca e outros mercadores da rua do Commercio, desta cidade, têm feito subir a esta camara, sobre o damno que experimentam em suas fazendas, proveniente do enxame de moscas que tem grassado naquella rua, a que dão causa as quitandeiras que se postam nas portas dos mesmos; Ordenamos a vossa mercê que, para evitar similhantes clamores e prejuizos, passe immediatamente a ordenar ás mesmas quitandeiras, impondo-lhes a pena de condemnação, que só do canto do alferes José Antonio Fernandes por deante, travessa que vae sahir á rua de S. Bento, é que devem fazer ponto com as suas quitandas, bem como do lado opposto, principiando na esquina das casas de Luiz Gonzaga, parallelo ás outras, e nunca em outra qualquer parte. Deus guarde á vossa mercê. S. Paulo, em vereação de 20 de

Março de 1822 —*Bento José Leite Penteado, José Mariano Bueno, Luiz Manoel da Cunha Bastos.*—Senhor alferes *Francisco Manoel de Andrade Figueiredo e Albuquerque*, juiz almotacel.

Com esta energica medida ficaram os negociantes de fazendas seccas e mais mercadores da rua do Commercio alliviados da importunação das moscas attrahidas pelas quitandeiras, flagello que passou naturalmente a affligir o alferes José Antonio Fernandes e os inquilinos das casas de Luiz Gonzaga, cujas visinhanças passaram a ser o ponto de reunião das verdureiras e das moscas que formavam o seu infallivel sequito.

Havia, entretanto, na cidade um estabelecimento publico a que se dava o nome de «As Casinhas», onde se vendiam toucinhos e outros generos vindos das villas vizinhas. Estava na rua Quinze de Novembro, na esquina onde hoje está o paço da Camara Municipal; pertencia a uma viuva o predio que alli existia ha cerca de 120 annos, quando se tratou de desaprorial-o para serviço publico. Dava frente para a rua Quinze de Novembro e tinha quintal que corria, pela rua do Thesouro, até à rua do Commercio, com mais de uma porta para armazem ou venda, que não era da dona do predio

Quando se tratou da desapropriação foi avaliado por 800$000, mas a proprietaria protestou contra a avaliação e recorreu ao capitão-general, allegando que o predio lhe dava o aluguer de 8$000 mensaes ou 96$000 por anno, quantia esta que representava o juro legal de 6 por cento sobre 1:600$000, e que seria uma violencia sem nome obrigal-a a ceder por 800$000 um predio que lhe dava juros do dobro dessa somma.

Parece que o capitão-general deu provimento ao recurso, porque a viuva se calou e o predio foi desappropriado e transformado em «As Casinhas» para servidão publica.

\*\*\*

Na mesma rua Quinze de Novembro, esquina da travessa do Collegio, hoje rua do Palacio, havia uma casa fóra do alinhamento e saliente para a rua Quinze de Novembro, de modo a embaraçar o transito publico, diminuindo ainda mais a largura da rua, que nesse logar já é muito estreita. Pertencia essa casa ás «Mocinhas da Casa Verde», que não são desconhecidas dos paulistas e que, não obstante, merecem uma especial menção nesta palestra com os leitores.

Agostinho Delgado Arouche foi um fidalgo paulista, que exerceu nesta capital os cargos de thesoureiro dos bens dos defunctos e ausentes e de escrivão da ouvidoria geral, não porque precisasse dos rendimentos desses empregos para viver, mas porque era cidadão republicano e pertencia á governança da terra, como era costume se dizer dos fidalgos paulistas naquelles tempos. Possuia terras de sesmaria no interior e muitas propriedades nesta capital. Fallecendo a cerca de cento e trinta annos, deixou 11 filhos, sendo 4 homens e 7 mulheres.

Os homens foram o marechal José Arouche de Toledo Rendon, os drs. Francisco Leandro de Toledo Rendon e Diogo de Toledo Lara Ordonhes e o padre Francisco Joaquim de Toledo Arouche. Os primeiros tres foram educados em Portugal, formaram-se em direito na universidade de Coimbra e fizeram boa figura em S. Paulo, antes e depois da independencia.

As moças eram D. Caetana, D. Pulcheria, D. Maria Rosa, D. Gertrudes, D. Joaquina, D. Reduzinda e D. Anna Thereza. Nenhuma dellas se casou ; moravam todas juntas em um sobrado da rua do Palacio e se tornaram conhecidas na cidade pelo appellido de «Mocinhas da Casa Verde», nome de uma propriedade agricola que ellas possuiam no bairro de Sant'Anna. O sobrado em que residiam tinha em 1820, o numero 11, com dependencias que se extendiam desde a esquina da rua Quinze de Novembro, pela rua do Palacio até ao predio do telegrapho nacional e cartorio do tabellião Victorino Carmillo. Possuiam, além destas, outras propriedades urbanas e quarenta escravos de serviço domestico e de aluguer, segundo se vê nos recenseamentos do tempo.

Para alargar a rua Quinze de Novembro, que então se chamava rua do Rosario, e rectificar o seu alinhamento resolveu a Camara Municipal desapropriar a casa das moçinhas da Casa Verde, commettendo aliás os vereadores a leviandade de fazerem de um escravo das moças o intermediario para a compra amigavel do predio. A' proposta responderam algumas das moças com a seguinte carta, existente no Archivo do Estado :

« Illmos. Srs. do Nobre Senado:—Respondendo ao recado que Vossas Senhorias nos mandaram pelo nosso escravo Suterio Caio, somos a dizer que nos causa mui grande incommodo vender a casa que possuimos no canto da rua do Rosario para a travessa do Collegio : mas, attendendo ao bem publico, venderemos sómente a parte que fôr preciza para o alinhamento da rua, por 1:400$000, livres de siza, aliás não. E' o que podemos responder a Vossas Senhorias, a quem Deus guarde muitos annos. São Paulo, 18 de abril de 1822.—*D. Caetana Antonia de Toledo Lara e Moraes—D. Pulcheria Leocadia Domitila Ordonhes—D. Maria Rosa de Toledo Rendon—D. Gertrudes Genebra de Toledo Rendon Freire—D. Joaquina Luiza Delgado de Toledo e Luna»*.

Não concordou a Camara com o preço pedido por uma parte do predio, sómente a necessaria para o alinhamento da rua, e mandou os avaliadores officiaes, Manuel José Antunes da Silva e José Joaquim de Carvalho para procederem ao exame da casa e a avaliarem de accôrdo com o seu estado de conservação; estes deram-lhe o valor de 472$000; com isto não se conformaram as moças, que enviaram ao governo o seguinte interessante

## RECURSO

« Illmos. e Exmos. Senhores:—A Vossas Excellencias representam D. D. Caetana Antonia de Toledo Lara e Moraes e suas irmãs que a Camara desta cidade ha dias mandou chamar, por um official de justiça, um escravo das supplicantes e por este lhes mandou dizer que esse excellentissimo governo quería saber quanto queriam ellas supplicantes, pela casa terrea que possuem na esquina da travessa do Collegio, para a rua do Rosario, afim de se deital-a abaixo em parte para melhor se arruar a dita rua do Rosario.

« As supplicantes, por escripto, responderam á Camara que só pela parte preciza para o arruamento queriam 1:400$000, quantia esta proporcional ao rendimento que por vezes se tem offerecido ás supplicantes pelo aluguer da dita casa e que as supplicantes não têm acceitado por quererem conservar o actual inquilino; porém a Camara a mandou avaliar e consta as mesmas supplicantes que só lhes pretende dar 600$000 por todo o predio.

« As supplicantes, fiando muito da rectidão desse governo, passam a expôr que ellas têm rejeitado um conto de réis por aquelle predio, que lhes offereceu o negociante D. Thomaz; rejeitaram do coronel Antonio Leite Pereira da Gama Lobo o aluguer de 8$000 mensaes, juros de um grandioso principal; logo aquella avaliação é muito diminuta ao verdadeiro valor da casa, principalmente pela sua posição local.

« Além disto, as supplicantes têm grande precisão da parte que fica fóra do alinhamento da rua do Rosario, não só para fazerem a segurança do oitão da casa do sobrado em que moram mas para melhor accommodarem a grande familia que têm, e nunca jamais convém na venda da dita parte restante, nem tam pouco no diminuto preço porque a Camara as quer forçar a venderem-na.

« O direito de propriedade foi sempre mui sagrado e agora muito mais, e as supplicantes esperam que esse Excellentissimo Governo lhes o mantenha, até porque se fazem credoras disso pelos sacrificios que ellas têm feito pelo Estado, porquanto as supplicantes têm cedido gratuitamente para obras publicas o terreno que hoje é a praça do Ouvidor, na cidade nova, parte do terreno em que se acha o Jardim Botanico, uma parte do actual Hopital Militar e, não ha muito tempo, uma parte do quintal das casas que venderam ao reverendo Joaquim Manuel.

« A' vista do exposto parece que não devem ser as supplicantes compellidas a novos sacrificios, com tanto prejuizo por seus bens, e assim o esperam da rectidão de Vossas Excellencias

E. E. R. M »

Mandou o governo que a Camara informasse sobre a materia deste requerimento e ella confessou que as ponderações das supplicantes eram dignas de toda a consideração, mas que a dita avaliação, feita com todas as formalidades legaes, abrangia sómente a parte necessaria para o alimento, não julgando ter feito ás supplicantes violencia alguma, e accrescentou:

« Quanto aos sacrificios que referem as supplicantes terem feito ao Estado, não duvidamos que assim tenha acontecido, pois da probidade das supplicantes não se deve presumir o contrario; mas só sabemos da parte do quintal das casas que hoje são do reverendo Joaquim Manuel, bem como a respeito da praça denominada do « Ouvidor », na cidade nova, porque estas duas coisas eram da competencia desta Camara, e de facto cederam gratuitamente. E quanto aos outros terrenos para o Jardim Botanico e Hospital Militar, ignoramos, por não ter a Camara tido intendencia alguma nessas obras ».

A casa em questão estava na esquina onde hoje se levanta o sobrado cujos baixos são occupados pela loja da firma Lebre, Filho & Companhia. Mais acima estavam duas casas tambem salientes para a rua do Rosario, hoje Quinze de Novembro, que precisavam ser recuadas para o alargamento da rua; uma, de dois lances, no meio do quarteirão, pertencia a Dionysio Ereopagito da Motta e foi avaliada por 900$000 na parte destinada á desapropriação, e a outra ficava na esquina onde está o « Café Girondino » com dois lances, duas portas para negocio fronteando a rua Direita e uma janella para o largo da Sé, onde fazia canto, avaliada por 500$000, com a declaração de ser muito velha. Era esta ultima de propriedade do alferes Joaquim Ribeiro dos Santos, pae do grande orador paulista e eximio jurisconsulto dr. Gabriel José Rodrigues dos Santos.

O negociante D. Thomaz, que offerecera um conto de réis pelas das moças Arouche era D. Thomaz de Molina, que se tornou sogro de Bernardo Quartim, director do Jardim Publico, progenitor de boa descendencia nesta cidade, e filho do hespanhol Antonio Maria Quartim, que foi membro do governo de S. Paulo em 1821—22 e tomou parte na sedição da « Bernarda » contra Martim Francisco e o brigadeiro Jordão.

O coronel Gama Lobo, de quem as moças tambemfazem menresidiu algum tempo na travessa do Collegio, perto das mesmas ção, moças, em casa que mais tarde serviu de residencia do conselheiro Carrão Foi homem notavel por mais de um titulo; portuguez e militar, veiu residir em S. Paulo e aqui, alliado aos Andradas e adherente ás idéas liberaes, fez figura importante nos acontecimentos que precederam à independencia. Casou-se nesta capital com uma filha do dr. Francisco Le ndro de Toledo Rendon, sobrinha do marechal Arouche, e delle são bisnetos os drs. Mendes de Almeida, advogados conhecidos no fôro de S. Paulo.

Dionizio Europagito da Motta era homem de 57 annos, paulista, solteiro e de cor parda; vivia do rendimento de sua pharmacia e ainda tinha onze escravos de serviço domestico e de aluguer. Com elle moravam duas irmans solteiras, sexagenarias, uma sobrinha já idosa, dois aggregados e o padre Vicente Pires da Motta, que foi criado e educado por elle do melhor modo que o tempo permettia. O engeitado cresceu e ordenou-se ainda no tempo colonial e depois formou-se em Direito, foi lente e director da Academia, presidente de provincias importantes e um dos politicos mais proeminentes que tivemos.

Geralmente se pensa que o terreno do largo do Arouche, antigo largo do Ouvidor, foi dado á Camara para servidão publica, pelo marechal José Arouche de Toledo Rendon, que foi o proprietario da grande chacara que alli existia e que está hoje transformada na Villa Buarque, um dos mais lindos bairros da cidade. Entretanto, pela petição das « Mocinhas da Casa Verde » e pela informação dos vereadores, se verifica que foram ellas que doaram á Camara aquelle grande terreno, em que hoje está um dos mais bellos e espaçosos largos da cidade.

Não está bem applicado o nome de « largo do Arouche », dado a este pateo, pelo erro a que induz o publico, fazendo-o suppor que a doação foi feita pelo marechal e não pelas suas irmans; entretanto, não ha outro nome applicavel áquelle logradouro publico, porque não tinham as moças um sobrenome commum que pudesse ser approveitado para o caso e o seu appellido de « Mocinhas da Casa Verde » era absolutamente inaceitavel para designar aquelle largo. Nestes termos o nome que lhe deram é ainda assim o mais approximado por ser o appellido geral da familia.

O terreno que ellas deram para o Jardim Pnblico foi aproveitado em 1825 para esse importante fim pelo presidente Lucas Antonio Monteiro de Barros, sendo o marechal Arouche o seu primeiro director, e o chão destinado ao Hospital Militar, tambem doado por ellas, estava na rua que se chama do «Seminario», porque o prédio nelle costruido, perto do mercadinho da rua de S. João, passou depois a servir de «Seminario das Educandas», e está hoje arrendado a uma firma particular. Estas duas doações não foram feitas á Camara, mas ao governo colonial, como se vê pela informação da propria Camara, acima transcripta.

Para a Camara do tempo, que era muito pobre. fazer simultaneamente a desapropriação de partes de 3 predios na importancia de 1:872$000, quando as suas rendas talvez não excedessem a esta quantia, era necessario que os predios em questão estivessem realmente muito avançados para a rua Quinze de Novembro, reduzindo a um estreito becco a sabida dessa rua no largo da Sé; mas a opposição dos proprietarios venceu a boa disposição da Camara, os prédios ficaram como estavam, e só muito mais tarde é que foram recuados para a posição em que hoje se acham.

Da esquina da casa Lebre á esquina do «Café Girondino» a distancia é cerca de 40 metros, toda occupada pelos tres predios, que tinham nove frestas e espaços lateraes que os separavam. Suppondo que elles deviam ser recuados dois metros, teriamos 80 metros quadrados para serem desapropriados pela quantia de 1:872$000, relação esta que nos dá 23$400 por metro quadrado de chão. Isto nos habilita a bem appreciar a alta dos preços do terreno na rua Quinze de Novembro entre os annos de 1822 e 1904, tendo em vista varias desappropriações e compras que a actual Camara tem feito ultimamente e que não lhe custaram menos de 650$000 por metro quadrado.

m uanto a população da cidade crescia quasi vinte vezes nestes oitenta annos, de 15.000 a 260.0 0, o valor dos terrenos na sua principal rua subia cerca de vinte e oito vezes, de 23$000 a 650$000 por metro quadrado, ao mesmo tempo que a sombria e melancholica povoação daquelles tempos se transformava na bella, asseada, prospera e alegre capital que hoje vemos.

## IV

### A FEIRA DE PILATOS

Não pensem os leitores que eu vou tratar do famoso delegado romano na Judéa que, por condemnavel fraqueza e indisculpavel timidez, ou com revoltante hypocrisia, lavára as mãos e friamente consentira no supplicio do martyr do Golgotha, e de alguma feira estabelecida por elle em qualquer das historicas povoações do lendario valle do rio Jordão. Não.

Vou tratar de um acontecimento que só tem importancia para nós, que nos toca mais de perto e nos apresenta uma das muitas feições da vida colonial de nossos avós; vou dar uma noticia documentada de uma feira ou mercado annual que se estabeleceu no largo da Luz, desta capital, em frente ao Jardim Publico, no anno de 1800, pelos esforços de Antonio Manuel de Mello de Castro e Mendonça, que foi governador e capitão-general de S. Paulo, de 1797 a 1802, e ficou conhecido na nossa historia pela alcunha de « Pilatos », que por algum justo motivo lhe deram os seus contemporaneos.

\*\*\*

As feiras annuaes, domingueiras ou diárias, de então para cá, nunca deixaram de existir nesta muito desmembrada e ainda extensa circumscripção politico administrativa que hoje se chama « Estado de S. Paulo ».

Era afamada a feira annual de Sorocaba, estabelecida ha muitos annos, para a qual concorriam negociantes de toda a parte, desde do Rio Grande do Sul até a Bahia, para compra e venda de centenas de milhares de animaes e tambem mercadores de todas as qualidades, principalmente de arreios e outras obras de couro, de freios, « chilenas » e varios artefactos de ferro, de joias, de metaes preciosos; jogadores de todas as cathegorias, desde os refinados batoteiros do esquecido « lasquenet », até os modestos atiradores de buzio na praça publica; vivandeiras de todas as classes, de todas as raças, de todas as feições, que lá iam, não em busca da Gloria que só acompanha os soldados, mas á cata do dinheiro, alli espalhado ás mancheias pelos generosos e liberaes peregrinos dessa curiosa Méca, e milhares de visitantes que lá iam por simples divertimento.

A feira de Sorocaba, que mereceu ser posta em drama levado á scena, muito decahida e quasi extincta hoje, é uma tradição viva e representa um passado saudoso para muitos paulistas, ainda mocetões e robustos, que se lembram com pesar desses bons tempos que não voltarão mais.

Os mercados domingueiros de algumas cidades do valle do Parahyba são interessantes e dignos de obervação, principalmente o de Taubaté, que era admiravel pela multidão de expositores e visitantes e pela profusão e diversidade dos objectos expostos á venda.

A primeira vez que o vi, em 1871, fiquei em verdade maravilhado pela novidade do curioso espectaculo, pela ordem e harmonia que presidiam ao conjuncto, pelo relativo asseio do local, em pateo aberto, e pela infinita variedade das mercadorias, que abrangiam todas as classes imaginaveis, desde o « pito de barro», ornado com o serio focinho do cão amigo ou com o sorridente rosto do macaco brejeiro, pela escala ascendente das fazendas molhadas e seccas, dos vertebrados, dos quadrupedos e bipedes, até o odioso comboio de luzidos negros, importados do norte pelos ainda mais odiosos traficantes de carne humana.

Si a mercadoria humana desappareceu para sempre com a redemptora lei de 13 de Maio, os mercados semanaes de Taubaté e das villas do Parahyba só ganharam com isso, porque, com ella, desappareceu tambem a unica variedade que desgostava á vista dos visitantes desinteressados no trafico de escravos.

Em todas as cidades paulistas do oeste, de certa importancia, ha mercados diarios, que supprem os habitantes com generos de que necessitam dia a dia, mas não ha feiras periodicas a não ser em Araras, cujo bom exemplo não tem encontrado imitadores, como era para desejar e como tanto convem aos interesses das populações.

**\***

Na cidade de S. Paulo, até o anno de 1800, não havia mercado diario nem feiras periodicas, que merecessem esses nomes. O estabelecimento de «As casinhas», na antiga rua do Rosario, hoje Quinze de Novembro, e esquina da rua do Thesouro, no logar onde hoje está o grande predio em que funcciona a Camara Municipal, para servirem de mercado permanente, não satisfez de modo algum as necessidades publicas e as quitandeiras de verduras e fructas iam fazer o seu ponto de parada na rua do Commercio, com grave damno para o asseio daquella via publica e grandes prejuizos para os negociantes nella estabelecidos.

Não havia, pois, em S. Paulo nem mercado diario que prestasse, nem feira periodica que animasse o intercambio de mercadorias e estimulasse a agricultura e a industria, offerecendo-lhes um recurso prompto para a disposição dos seus productos.

D. Bernardo de Lorena, o espurio pimpolho do rei D. José e capitão general de S. Paulo de 1789 a 1797, cuidava pouco em coisas serias e muito em saltar os muros dos quintaes, emquanto o seu mentor, José Romão Jeunot, se incumbia de dar uma pouca fama á sua adminsstração, cuidando seriamente em alguns trabalhos de interesse geral, que não vem ao caso mencionar aqui e a cidade continuava sem mercado regular e sem feiras animadoras do commercio e ind▪stria

Em 1797 foi o «Lovelace» D. Bernardo transferido para Minas Geraes, sendo substituido no governo de S. Paulo por Antonio Manuel de Mello Castro, militar energico, de bom fundo moral, bem intencionado e desejoso de acertar. Apesar de ser um tanto fatuo e apparatoro, ao ponto de fazer grandes revistas militares nesta capital, de tropas chamadas de todo o interior, só para ter o prazer de se apresentar fardado e se fazer admirar pelos seus governados, metteu hombros aos negocios publicos e realizou alguns consideraveis melhoramentos, tanto no interior como nesta capital.

Augmentou o fornecimento de agua da cidade, iniciou a fundação de um jardim publico por meio de uma subscripção publica, que lhe rendeu uma dezena de contos de réis, e organizou uma feira annual, que elle mesmo descreve no seguinte interessante officio, dirigido a um dos ministros em Lisboa, com um longo preambulo :

«Illm.º e exm.º sr.—Tendo sempre em vista as reaes ordens de sua alteza, cuja pontual execução faz todo o objecto dos meus cuidados e do meu desvelo, por effeito necessario da minha obrigação, devia eu dar cumprimento á ordem de 24 de Julho de 1797, em que v. exc. tão efficazmente me recommenda que anime o commercio interior e exterior desta capitania.

«Em meu officio de 23 de Novembro do mesmo anno tive a honra de participar a v. exc. o que já, em observancia da mesma ordem, tinha feito ; e na continuação dos meus officios verá v. exc. que a nada me tenho poupado para realizar as sábias e penetrantes vistas que abrangem as reaes determinações expressadas naquella ordem. E, si me é licito produzir algumas provas indirectas para abono desta verdade, eu não quero lançar mão sinão do conhecido augmento da agricultura, que bem se manifesta pelo accrescimo do rendimento dos dizimos e pelos mappas de exportação que vou dirigir a v. exc. Mas, como pela mesma ordem sou obrigado a participar todos os annos os esforços que se fizer sobre este objecto e os bons resultados que ob-

tiveram as minhas diligencias, devo pôr na presença de v. exc.
o que este anno pratiquei e qual foi o fructo do meu trabalho.

«Para animar, pois, o commercio interior e, por consequencia, o exterior da capitania julguei que devia estabelecer um mercado publico ou feira, na qual se vendessem e permutassem todos os generos do paiz e os de fóra. Escolhi, para esse effeito, a melhor occasião do anno, que é desde a dominga da Santissima Trindade até a que se segue, tudo inclusivamente, e isto por ser nesta conjunctura o estio neste clima, por estar então parada a agricultura, cujos trabalhos começam de Julho por deante, e por ser a unica vez que concorrem á cidade todos os povos circumvisinhos, a assistirem á festa de «Corpus Christi», vindo egualmente os soldados milicianos fazer a sua mostra annual, os seus exercicios, e por fim cobrir as ruas na procissão com que termina aquella solemnidade.

«Fiz antecipadamente aos capitães-móres desta cidade e villas visinhas o aviso constante da ordem n. 886, que envio por cópia, e, tendo desta sorte feito os povos scientes da minha deliberação, principiaram a concorrer no tempo aprazado ao logar que lhes determinei, que foi no Passeio Publico, defronte do Jardim Botanico e da praça da Luz, onde se fazem os exercicios militares.

«Todos os negociantes da cidade, a quem particularmente fiz demover para alli irem armar as suas lojas, da mesma sorte concorreram, e para esse fim, na falta de barracas proprias, fiz armar em toda a extensão do terreno as de Sua Alteza Real, que se achavam nos armazens, e com esta providencia consegui irem todos, muitos dos quaes o não fariam por não estarem preparados para isso.

«A novidade deste estabelecimento attrahiu á cidade muito mais gente fóra do costume e excitou a curiosidade dos seus habitantes, de maneira que todo o tempo que durou se achou aquelle campo coberto de gente, ainda de pessoas que rarissimas vezes eram vistas em concursos, e isso tanto de dia como de noite.

«Todos os generos vindos das villas visinhas, algumas das quaes mandaram 100 cavallos carregados, logo se venderam. Os mesmos indios, que são os que fazem a louça ordinaria, repetiram tres e quatro vezes as suas conducções, e os mercadores deram extracção á immensa fazenda e entre ella alguma em que já têm reputado o seu dinheiro. Em uma palavra, no ultimo dia da feira não se achava um traste delicado, porque o que era de gosto ou de luxo se tinha vendido.

« Eu tive a satisfação de assistir todos os dias no campo da

feira, onde tinha a minha barraca, e pude conseguir acharem-se
alli tambem todas as familias da cidade, o que concorreu para
a extraordinaria venda que se fez, e foram tão ajustadas as providencias que tomei que não houve um só furto ou desordem.

« Todos os habitantes da cidade e os que concorreram de
fóra, tanto a vender como a comprar, ficaram tão gostosos que
uns pediam que se prorogasse mais o tempo da feira e outros
que se a repetisse duas vezes no anno; mas nem a uma nem a
outra supplica deferi, por me parecer que ella não deve ser re-
petida sinão no tempo que arbitrei, pelas razões já ponderadas,
e nesta certeza desde já se estão preparando os negociantes para,
na compra que fizerem no Rio de Janeiro, se fornecerem das
coisas de melhor e mais propria extracção, a que deu logar o
ajuntamento das senhoras da cidade que, não costumando ir ás
lojas comprar coisa alguma, nesta occasião toda a fazenda era
pouca para saciar o seu desejo.

« Posso certificar a v. exa., sem exaggeração, que ainda não
vi uma feira onde mais se ligasse a modestia com a alegria do
povo e que entretivesse com egual prazer todas as classes de
pessoas, de fórma que por gosto se podia andar passeiando por
ella, principalmente de noite, vendo a illuminação que de seu
«motu proprio» fizeram os negociantes e os vivandeiros, e ouvindo a musica do regimento que para alli eu tinha mandado para
mais attrahir, com esta variedade. a attenção dos espectadores.

« Todo o meu desejo é que sua alteza real approve esta
minha deliberação como deduzida das suas sábias e previdentes
determinações e que, attendendo ao bom exito que teve este
anno, e a vantajosa extracção que promette para o futuro, tanto
dos generos do paiz como dos de fóra delle, além de ser um dos
meios, talvez o mais efficaz, para policiar e fazer trataveis os
povos desta capitania, se digne confirmal-a para sempre e mandar
que, assim como, por virtude daquella referida ordem de 24 de
de Julho de 1797, os generaes que me succederem devem dar
conta do que praticarem para a sua execução, da mesma sorte
fiquem ligados a conservar um estabelecimento que é, sem con-
tradicta, o mais apropriado e que mais corresponde ás instrucções
de Sua Alteza, em cuja sempre augusta e real presença espero
que v. exa. se digne, por especial mercê, fazer constar os puros
sentimentos de humilde vassalagem e de patriotismo com que me
empenhei, com toda a extensão das minhas forças, para assim o
cumprir na fórma recommendada. — Deus guarde a v. exc.—S.
Junho de 1900.—Antonio Manoel de Mello Castro e Mendonça ».
Paulo, 16 de

*\*\*

A bôavontade do capitão general Mello Castro e os bons conselhos que deu para que os seus successores continuassem a feira não tiveram bom resultado e a feira cessou logo por motivos muito poderosos e independentes da vontade popular.

Em 1802 deixou Mello Castro o governo de S Paulo e foi substituido por Antonio José de França e Horta, que foi um dos peiores delegados que o governo de Lisboa mandou a S. Paulo e aqui permaneceu durante nove longos annos, até 1811.

Homem de vistas curtas e retrogrado, não era violento como Martim Lopes; mas, friamente perverso, mesquinho, intrigante e enredeiro, encheu a capitania de espiões e delatores arvorados em agente do seu governo. Cada official ou soldado era espião e secreto delator do que se passava nos quarteis e cada escravo ou famulo era egualmente de tudo quanto occorria na casa de seu senhor ou patrão, de modo que, arvoradas a espionagem e a delação em meios regulares do governo, ninguem mais se julgava seguro em sua casa ou nos quarteis e todos se retrahiram de maneira a serem vistos ou lembrados o menos que fosse possivel.

E, como si isto não bastasse para dar um golpe mortal na actividade e expansão popular, renovou-se o recrutamento e com dobrado vigor, não sómente caçando a gente valida por toda a parte para o serviço militar, mas até cercando de surpreza e traiçoeiramente as egrejas em dias de festas religiosas, agarrando a todos quanto nellas se achavam, capazes de carregar um mosquete em tempo de guerra, e remettendo-os para as campanhas do sul, onde muitos se deixaram ficar para sempre, para não mais voltarem a esta odienta tyrannia.

Fugindo o povo do contacto das vistas do refalsado e perverso capitão general, a quem foi dado o muito acertado appellido de «Mexeriqueiro», ninguem mais se animou a concorrer com os seus productos e mercadorias para a renovação annual da feira estabelecida nesta capital por Mello Castro, e assim desappareceu para sempre a FEIRA DE PILATOS, que se inaugurára com tantas festas e que tantas illusorias esperanças despertára nos ingenuos corações paulistas.

## VIII

### VITALICIEDADE DOS ENADO—OBSERVADOR CONSTITUCIONAL—PRIMEIRA MENÇÃO NO BRAZIL DA DOUTRINA DE MONROE

Com a queda de Pedro I, a 7 de Abril de 1831, as idéas liberaes tomaram grande desenvolvimento; porém, o povo brasileiro, ainda mal educado para o verdadeiro *self-government*, não distinguia entre a liberdade e a anarchia, e atirou-se a revoluções que duraram até 1848 e se extenderam por quasi todas as provincias do Imperio, desde o Pará até ao Rio Grande do Sul.

Entretanto, os *moderados*, senhores do governo, tinham noção mais ou menos exacta das necessidades politicas do paiz e tentaram algumas reformas uteis, que conseguiram realizar, e outras que se mallograram pelo concurso de muitos interesses particulares, ligados ao espirito conservador do tempo.

Em 1832, tratou-se no parlamento de abolir a vitaliciedade do Senado, que foi considerada como um dos males do regimen imperial, e que nunca poude ser removida. A ideia cahiu por uma votação de 58 contra 57, e talvez tivesse sido victoriosa, si houvesse um pouco mais diligencia da parte de alguns deputados, que não compareceram no momento preciso.

Em um velho e estragadissimo numero do *Correio Paulistano*, publicado a 12 de Outubro 1832, lê-se o seguinte sobre esta materia :

« Foram pela vitaliciedade do senado os senhores senadores Evangelista, Saturnino, *Paranaguá*, Santos, Gomide, *Palma*, Lourenço de Andrade, Costa Barros, Patricio, *Lages*, Furtado de Mendonça, Manoel Caetano, *Maricá*, *Cayrú*, Carneiro de Campos, Carvalho, *Barbacena*, *Barpendy*, *Caravellas*, *Itapoan*, *Inhambupe*, *Valença*, *Queluz*, Oliveira, Duque Estrada, Bacellar, *Jacarépaguá*, *Alcantara*, Tinoco, Rodrigues de Carvalho, *Congonhas do Campo*, padre Marcos, Aguiar e d. Nunes Eugenio. Deputados Almeida Torres, Perdigão, Lopes Gama, Rebello, Miranda Ribeiro, Manoel Cavalcanti, Mendes Ribeiro, Rebouças, Paim, Calmon, Veiga, Getulio, Soares da Rocha, Maciel, Mello Mattos, Montezuma, Martim, Vallasques, Cavalcanti Lacerda, Pedro Cavalcanti e Netto.—Ao todo 58.

« Votaram contra a vitaliciedade os senadores Vergueiro, Alencar e Borges e os deputados Limpo, Lemos, Belisario, Pinto Peixoto, Pinto da Gama, Carneiro da Cunha, Brito Guerra, Bello, Fortuna, Andrade Lima, Rezende, Deus e Silva, G. Mendes, Souto, Amaral, Paca de Barros, Moura, Evaristo, padre Ignacio da Costa, Junqueira, Gervasio, Gomes da Fonseca, Ferreira, França, Ernesto, Lobo de Souza, Lessa, Custodio Dias, Fernandes da Silveira, Baptista de Oliveira, Nascimento, Sebastião do Rego, Ferreira de Castro, Ferreira de Mello, padre Valerio, Pereira Ribeiro, Ledo, Muniz Barreto, Vasconcellos, Lino, Jacobina, May, Costa Ferreira, Francisco do Rego, Toledo, Sá Ribas, padre Simões, Jardim, Corrêa Pacheco, Aureliano, Odorico Mendes, Duarte Silva, Paula Araujo, Moura e Costa Miranda.—Ao todo 57.

«Faltaram os deputados Clemente Pereira, Monteiro de Barros, Castro Alvares, Sá Palacio, Alves Branco, Araujo, Franco e Baptista Ferreira.—Senadores, nem um só!!! Os srs. Inhambupe e Aguiar, que não tinham ido ás primeiras sessões por enfermos, compareceram logo que se agitou a questão da vitaliciedade e o sr. marquez de Queluz, apesar do estado de paralysia em que se acha, fez-se transportar á casa da reunião, para dar o seu voto».

Esta resenha, aliás interessante por nos dar uma idéia dos sentimentos reformadores e conservadores dos parlamentares de 1832, não está completa. Os senadores paulistas daquelle tempo eram quatro—o marquez de Palma, o visconde de Congonhas do Campo, o visconde de S. Leopoldo e o bispo José Caetano ; os primeiros figuram na lista como votando pela permanencia da vitaliciedade, porém os ultimos dois não apparecem na votação, o que indica que a lista é sómente dos que estavam então no Rio e que compareceram ou deixaram de comparecer na sessão.

Os deputados paulistas então eram Paula Souza, Feijó, Raphael Tobias, Corrêa Pacheco, Ornellas, Sá Ribas, barão de Piracicaba e Monteiro de Barros e na qualidade de supplentes tomaram tambem assento na camara o coronel Joaquim Floriano de Toledo, e os padres Simões e Valerio. Destes figuram na lista como votando contra a vitaliciedade do Senado os padres Valerio e Simões, Corrêa Pacheco, Joaquim Floriano de Toledo e Sá Ribas. Deixou de comparecer o deputado Monteiro de Barros, estando no Rio, e dos outros não se faz menção, nem de um lado, nem do outro.

Os que têm seus nomes em italicos eram os titulares do Senado, da fidalguia creada por Pedro I.

Feijó tinha deixado, havia pouco, o Ministerio da Justiça e provavelmente estava fóra da capital do Imperio, descançando das temerosas luctas que teve de sustentar contra violenta opposição no parlamento e contra rebeldes nas ruas do Rio de Janeiro. Vergueiro era senador e Martim Francisco deputado por Minas Geraes ; aquelle votou contra e este a favor da vitaliciedade. Vergueiro era então ministro da Justiça, não em substituição de Feijó, mas de Pedro de Araujo Lima, um dos ministros do gabinete que Evaristo Veiga chamava da «quarentena».

O marquez de Queluz, que mesmo paralytico se fez transportar á casa da sessão para votar a seu favor, em causa propria, se chamava João Severiano Maciel da Costa e foi um dos mais importantes politicos do primeiro reinado e um espirito muito conservador.

Os jornaes liberaes do tempo não o poupavam e um delles, *O Universal*, disse que o fim de uma viagem que este fidalgo fizera a Minas, pelos annos de 1829-30, fôra comprar alguns predios ruraes para constituir um morgado ou vinculo da ANTIGA E NOBRE CASA DOS QUELUZES e tambem tratar de alguns negocios politicos de alta monta ; mas a *Aurora Fluminense*, de Evaristo Veiga, disse que a viagem do titular a Minas fôra com o fim de fazer imprimir em uma das typographias daquella provincia um catecismo politico em que o conhecido titular mostrava, com razões muito attendiveis, que a outorga da Constituição de 25 de Março de 1824 foi um erro e que o governo constitucional não convém aos paizes mal povoados, como o Brazil.

No Brazil nunca houve morgados e muito menos uma *antiga e nobre casa dos Queluzes* ; havia nobresa de sangue, devidamente certificada por competentes autos *de genere*, mas não a nobreza advencia, creada por decretos, algumas vezes em favor dos servidores da patria e outras vezes a beneficio do validismo imperial. O marquez devia o seu titulo aos serviços que fez ao governo de Dom Pedro e não era dos adventicios ; mas era de um conservatorismo theorico, mais intenso do que convinha á sua condição de brazileiro nato e filho de Minas, e a imprensa liberal da provincia o recebeu com pouca sympathia e recommendou aos seus leitores que tivessem com elle o cuidado que se deve ter com homens perigosos, porque « cautela e caldo de gallinha não fazem mal a ninguem ».

*\*

O *Observador Constitucional* de Badaró era publicado na typographia do *Pharol Paulistano* e fazia violenta opposição a Pedro I e aos seus methodos de governar o Brasil. Depois do assassinato do seu redactor-chefe, a 20 de Novembro de 1830, passou o *Observador* a outra direcção, a ser impresso em outra typographia e diminuiu muito o seu formato, que já era pequeno.

E' difficil conhecer a nova orientação do jornal, quaes as idéas politicas e sociaes que defendia, porque a sua redacção já não estava entregue a um homem feito e de reputação firmada como o assassinado Badaró, mas fazia violenta opposição ao governo estabelecido depois do 7 de Abril.

Este facto parece indicar que o jornal mudou inteiramente de rumo. Badaró fazia opposição á politica de D. Pedro I e logicamente estava de accôrdo com Evaristo Veiga, que desempenhava egual missão nas columnas da *Aurora Fluminense* ; porém, cahindo o imperador e passando o governo a uma regencia

inspirada por Evaristo, era natural que o *Observador*, se mantivesse a mesma politica, continuasse solidario com a ordem de
cousas creada pelo 7 de Abril.

O jornal, entretanto, combatia a situação e contra o Poder
Legislativo atirava as suas mais fortes envectivas, dizendo que
era o « patronato mais atrevido que se podia encontrar em uma
assembléa que tornou se um conselho do governo, que perdeu
de vista o rumo que devera trilhar, que armou em guerra auctoridades que a constituição queria que só apparecessem ao povo
com o espirito de paz e de concordia, que manchou a legislação
com leis revolucionarias, e que nada fez que preenchesse a sua
espectação ».

Ainda pouco acostumadas com o uso e com o abuso da liberdade da imprensa, as auctoridades chamaram o *Observador
Constitucional* á responsabilidade pelos ataques, acima transcri-
ptos, ao Poder Legislativo da nação. Havia naquelle tempo dois
jurys—um de accusação e outro de sentença; formou-se o jury
de accusação para decidir se havia materia para criminalidade
do jornal, ficando o conselho composto por Francisco da Silva
Prado, Antonio Bernardo Bueno da Veiga, Antonio José Bordini, José Manuel da Luz, João Olyntho de Carvalho, padre Manuel Joaquim do Amaral Gurgel, José Gonçalves Gomide, José
Manuel da Silva. Manuel Joaquim de Vasconcellos, Domingos
Francisco de Andrade e um senhor Segurado e um senhor Reis,
cujos nomes estão dilacerados e rotos no original.

Este conselho se compunha de gente bôa e conhecida nesta
capital ; Francisco Prado era de familia rica e proeminente ; José
Manuel da Silva foi o futuro barão de Tieté, Bueno da Veiga
vinha da linha dos Amador Bueno; o padre Amaral Gurgel foi
um dos mais illustres filhos de S. Paulo; Gomide pertencia a
uma raça de cirurgiões ; Olyntho de Carvalho contava na sua
familia generaes e sertanejos; Bordini era um official que fez
certa figura em S. Paulo ; José Manuel da Luz, chamado *Tralhão*,
foi um dos *bernardistas* de 1822 e os Segurados e os Andrades
ainda hoje têm representantes nesta capital, não se devendo
confundir Andrade com Andrada, nome este só pertencente á
familia do PATRIARCHA DA INDEPENDENCIA.

Este conselho, composto como era de gente solida, julgou
unanimemente que não havia criminalidade nos ataques do *Observador Constitucional*, contra os representantes da nação, nas publicações trazidas á sua consideração, ficando o redactor livre de
culpa, pena e custas. O *Correio Paulistano* de 1832, orgam da
situação, noticiando o resultado deste julgamento, derramou lagrimas de sentimento, ao vêr que homens de tanta responsabili-

dade sanccionassem com o seu voto as censuras e calumnias que o *Observador* atirava contra os legisladores da patria, que podiam ser esclarecidos, mas não lançados ao ridiculo e á odiosidade por uma imprensa pouco interessada pela causa publica.

No mesmo dia foram ainda julgados mais dois processos de abuso da liberdade de imprensa por queixa do dr. Aymberé, juiz de Taubaté, um por publicação feita no mesmo *Observador Constitucional* e o outro por artigos sahidos no *Pharol Paulistano*. Em ambos os casos ficou egualmente decidido que não havia materia para accusação, sendo o conselho de jurados composto dos srs. Manuel Dias de Toledo, ainda estudante de direito, Francisco da Silva Prado, João Olyntho de Carvalho, Lucio Manuel Felix dos Santos Capello, Antonio Rodrigues de Almeida Jordão, Francisco Garcia Ferreira, Anselmo José da Silva, João Manuel de Almeida Bueno, Manuel Joaquim de Vasconcellos, Antonio Joaquim Xavier da Costa e Manuel Alves Alvim. E o *Correio Paulistano* de 1832, continuando a chorar lagrimas amargas sobre o descalabro social representado por estes julgamentos, termina assim:

« Mas, que importa a certa gente que de nada sirva a lei da liberdade da imprensa e que só prevaleçam os caprichos particulares? Estes homens não querem as instituições para o interesse commum, querem-na, sim para seu proveito. Oh! E a quantos não pesa bastante que não fosse adoptado o artigo da acta de S. Felix em que se ordenava que se queimasse a lei da liberdade da imprensa!! Pois bem, homens que vos intitulaes conscienciosos e amigos da Liberdade, continuae a dar-nos estas exuberantes provas da vossa *boa fé*, do vosso prestimo e do vosso patriotismo. Nós bem vos conhecemos e no nosso juizo daremos o justo preço que merecem as acções que praticaes».

Quando em fins de 1823, James Monröe presidente dos Estados Unidos, tomou na devida consideração a ameaça que das nações da Santa Alliaça, reunidas no Congresso de Verona, partiram contra a independencia das antigas colonias hespanholas da America, já a Inglaterra se tinha mostrado algum tanto contraria a qualquer acção daquellas nações no sentido de auxiliar a Hespanha na reconquista das suas colonias revoltadas, de modo que o presidente Monröe agia de alguma fórma estimulado pelo apoio moral da Gran-Bretanha no desafio que ia atirar ás faces da Santa Alliança e que se tornou famoso com o nome de *Doutrina de Monöe*.

Esta doutrina fora formulada em mensagem que Monröe dirigiu ao congresso americano em Dezembro de 1823 e só poderia ter tomado uma fórma positiva depois de estar o seu auctor bem certo, pelas informações diplomaticas, das intenções dos paizes representados no congresso de Verona. Estas informações estavam ainda sendo colhidas pelo governo de Washington, quando um jornal de New York publicou a seguinte carta, que lhe foi dirigida pelo seu correspondente na capital americana:

« A resposta do Poder Executivo ao pedido do Congresso de informações relativas ás intenções e designios da Santa Alliança para com as colonias emancipadas da America do Sul ha de ser em substancia que a segurança publica o bem do Estado não permittem a administração communicar as informações que tem a este respeito.

« Ora, não póde haver a menor duvida que tenha o Congresso sobre esta importante materia informações positivas e muito importantes e tambem não é duvidoso que seja verdade o que se disse—ter a Inglaterra dado a segurança de se oppor e de resistir aos santos alliados, sendo essa segurança e os motivos que a determinaram o que provavelmente o Poder Executivo julga nocivo publicar presentemente.»

Ao chegar ao Rio de Janeiro o jornal de New-York, que continha esta carta em começo de março de 1824, ainda não era aqui conhecida a *Doutrina de Monröe* publicada em Dezembro de 1823. Traduzindo a carta supra e publicando·a, *A Extrella Brazileira* fez os seguintes commentarios :

« Tudo, pois, confirma de mais a mais o fundamento do boato espalhado, tanto na União Americana, como no Reino Unido Britanico, de ter o ministro inglez feito certas proposições ao governo dos Estados-Unidos para se oppor, até com a força das armas, a qualquer ataque *directo ou indirecto* dirigido pela Santa Allinça contra a independencia dos novos Estados Unidos da America do Sul (?).

«Bastante impaciencia temos, na verdade, de vêr qual será emfim a ultima determinação dos santos alliados, quando se lhes antolhar, em perspectiva das suas tentativas a favor da Hespanha, uma guerra inevitavel com a Inglaterra e os Estados Unidos. Isto dá materia sufficiente para reflectir.»

A materia era, realmente, digna de serias reflexões, porque imminentes eram os perigos que então corriam ás revoltadas colonias hespanholas de uma invasão das legiões da Santa Alliança. O Brazil não estava, por esse lado, exposto a perigo algum, porque Dom Pedro aqui estava já como imperador e como um seguro prolongamento do imperialismo europeu.

Entretanto, como os hispano-americanos de 1823 estavam ainda na primeira infancia da vida constitucional e não tinham ainda o habito, nem a capacidade precisa para serias reflexões politicas, que muitos delles ainda hoje não têm, James Monröe se incumbiu de reflectir e de agir por elles e o fez tão bem que obrigou os santos alliados a reflectirem egualmente e a comprehenderem que era enviavel o projecto que alimentavam de recolonizar a America Hespanhola e estas ficariam independentes; mas a *Doutrina* ahi ficou lançada até hoje e aquelles mesmos que mais se aproveitaram da sua efficacia, parecem ser os que mais duvidam da utilidade da sua existencia.

A. DE TOLEDO PIZA.

# Auto de eleição do Governo Provisorio de S. Paulo em 23 de Junho de 1821

TERMO DE VEREANÇA GERAL E EXTRAORDINARIA DA CAMARA, FEITO A REQUERIMENTO DO POVO E TROPAS DESTA CIDADE DE SÃO PAULO (1).

Aos 23 dias do mez de Junho de 1821, nesta cidade de São Paulo e casas da camara e paços do conselho della, onde foram vindos o dr. juiz de fóra, presidente Nicoláo de Siqueira Queiroz, vereadores actuaes e o actual procurador (2), assistindo o povo e as tropas, pelos quaes foram convocados os ditos extraordinariamente para se proceder á formação de um governo provisorio, jurar as bases da constituição, decretada pelas Côrtes de Lisbôa, e observar religiosamente as leis que garantem a segurança individual, a propriedade e os direitos dos cidadãos; jurar, outrosim, obediencia ao muito alto e poderoso senhor D. João VI, nosso rei constitucional do Reino Unido de Portugal, Brasil e Algarves e a Sua Alteza Real, o principe hereditario regente do reino do Brasil e á real dynastia da serenissima casa de Bragança, tudo na conformidade do que Sua Alteza Real praticou de proximo na Côrte do Rio de Janeiro e mandou praticar em todo o reino do Brasil. E neste ajuntamento e vereação foram nomeados por unanime acclamação do povo e tropas, que se achavam reunidos e postados no largo destes paços do Conselho: — Para presidente o Illmo. e Exmo. Sr. João Carlos Augusto de Oyenhausen; para vice-presidente o conselheiro José Bonifacio de Andrada e Silva; para secretarios do governo, do Interior e Fazenda o coronel Martim Francisco Ribeiro de Andrada, dos Negocios da Guerra o coronel Lazaro José Gonçalves e da Marinha o chefe de esquadra Miguel José

---

(1) Estrahido do livro 50 de vereanças da Camara Municipal da cidade de São Paulo, dos annos de 1821-22 e inédito

(2) Os vereadores eram Antonio Pereira dos Santos, João Francisco da Rocha e José de Almeida Ramos e servia de procurador Amaro José de Moraes.

(*N. da R.*)

de Oliveira Pinto; para deputados e vogaes da junta, pelo
Ecclesiastico o Revdmo. Arcipreste Felisberto Gomes Jardim e
o Revdmo. Thesoureiro-mór João Ferreira de Oliveira Bueno;
pelas Armas o coronel Antonio Leite Pereira da Gama Lobo e
o coronel Daniel Pedro Muller, pelo Commercio o coronel Francisco
Ignacio de Sousa Queiroz e o brigadeiro Manoel Rodrigues Jordão,
pela Sciencia e Educação o Revdmo. Padre Francisco de Paula
e Oliveira e o professor André da Silva Gomes, pela Agricultura o dr. Nicoláu Pereira de Campos Vergueiro e o coronel
Antonio Maria Quartim; dos quaes aos presentes se deu logo
posse e o juramento seguinte: «Juro as Bases da Constituição
decretadas pelas Côrtes Geraes, Extraordinarias e Constituintes
de Lisboa; juro obediencia a Sua Magestade o Sr. D. João VI,
rei constitucional do Reino Unido de Portugal, Brasil e Algarves;
juro, outrosim de vigiar pela exacta e prompta execução das
leis existentes e promover todo o bem desta provincia em particular e da nação em geral; assim Deus me salve».—E depois
de findo este acto de vereação, para constar, mandaram lavrar
este termo em que esta camara, todas as auctoridades, povo e
tropas presentes assignaram, e eu João Nepomuceno de Almeida
escrivão da camara, que o escrevi e assignei. — *João Carlos
Augusto de Oyenhausen —José Bonifacio de Andrada e Silva.
—Lazaro José Gonçalves.*—O arcipreste da Cathedral, *Felisberto
Gomes Jardim.*—O thesoureiro-mór, *João Ferreira de Oliveira
Bueno.—Antonio Leite Pereira da Gama Lobo —Francisco
Ignacio de Souza Queiroz.—Manoel Rodrigues Jordão.— Francisco
de Paula e Oliveira* (1).—*André da Silva Gomes.—Antonio Maria
Quartim.—Nicoláu de Siqueira Queiroz —Antonio Pereira dos
Santos —João Franco da Rocha.—José de Almeida Ramos.—
Amaro José de Moraes.—João Nepomuceno e Almeida.—D.
Matheus,* bispo de S. Paulo.—*D. Nuno Eugenio de Locio e
Seilbiz.—Manoel da Cunha de Azeredo Coutinho Souza Chichorro.
Francisco Antonio de Paula Nogueira da Gama —José Antonio
da Silva Valente.—Bernardo José Pinto Gavião.— Gregorio Ignacio
Ferreira Nobre.—Joaquim Maria da Costa Ferreira —Nabor
Delphim Pereira.—Francisco de Paula Xavier de Toledo.—Mo-
desto Antonio Coelho Netto.—João da Costa Ferreira.—Ildefonso
Xavier Ferreira.—José Gonçalves Gomide.—Manoel Joaquim do
Amaral Gurgel.—José Mathias Ferreira de Abreu —Francisco
Pinto Ferraz Filho.—José Antonio Teixeira Cabral.—Fortunato
Corrêa de Mello.—Antonio Manoel de Jesus e Azevedo.—Fran-*

---

(1) Era padre e representante das Sciencias e Educação no governo; ensinava latim
e passava por bom orador sagrado; era paulista e tinha o appellido de *Mimí.*

cisco Jorge de Paula Ribeiro.—Joaquim Olintho de Carvalho.—
José Clemente de Mexquita —Januario Antonio de Araujo.—
José Gomes Segurado.—Manoel de Campos Penteado —Antonio
José Vieira Barbosa.—Rodrigues Goulart.—Alves Alvim (1).—
Thomé Manoel Jesus Varella.—Antonio Rodrigues Moreira.—
Antonio Xavier Ferreira.—Joaquim José Rodrigues.—Antonio
José Pereira dos Santos.—P.ᵉ Antonio Morato da Costa.—Fran-
cisco de Azevedo.—João Anastacio da Silva Portilho, tenente-
coronel.—Rufino José Felizardo e Costa, tenente engenheiro.—
P.ᵉ Vicente Pires da Motta.—José Innocencio Alves Alvim.—
Jeronimo José de Andrade, ajudante.—Francisco Garcia Ferreira.
—Candido Gonçalves Gomide.—Antonio José Barbosa.—João
Lopes da Silva.—José Felippe de Macedo, sargento.—P.ᵉ Mar-
celino Ferreira.—José da Cunha Paes Leme.—Francisco de Paula
Lustoza. — P.ᵉ Jeronymo Maximo Rodrigues Cardim — Manoel
José Rodrigues da Silva—João Manoel de Almeida — Joaquim
José Machado—Joaquim Antonio Alves Alvim—Antonio Ezequiel
Pereira — Candido Joaquim Justiniano de Sousa — Francisco
Gomes da Silva — Fortunato P. do Rego — Francisco de Assis
Pinto—Manoel Rodrigues de Almeida Bueno—Candido Ignacio
da Silva—José Antonio Pimenta — P.ᵉ Manoel Dias de Abreu—
Manoel José de Campos Bueno—Francisco das Chagas de Abreu
Piteco—José Maria de Oliveira Cezar—José Martins de Sousa—
Vicente Diniz Caldeira — Joaquim José da Silveira Baptista —
Joaquim Dias Vieira—Francisco Antonio de Moraes—José An-
tonio do Nascimento—Francisco Luiz Penna—Joaquim Domin-
gues da Silva—João Jacomo de Baumann—José de Sousa Lima
— Agostinho Lourenço da Silva — Joaquim José de Almeida —
Antonio Joaquim de Oliveira—Floriano da Costa e Silva—Francisco
Alvares Ferreira do Amaral — Jeronymo Pereira Chrispim de
Vasconcellos — José Manoel de Sousa—Caetano Pinto Homem—
João Francisco Bellegarde, sargento-mór—Carlos Maria de Oli-
va, capitão — José Osorio da Fonseca Pina Leitão, capitão—
Domingos Anacleto da Silva — Bernardo Bueno de Sousa Lobo,
tenente — Manoel Correia de Oliveira Doria, ajudante — João
Carlos de Baumann, alferes—José Joaquim dos Santos, capitão
—José Marcellino do Amaral, alferes—Bento Thomaz Gonçalves,
alferes—João Vicente Pereira Rangel, tenente—Joaquim Lopes
Guimarães, alferes—José Ramos de Oliveira, picador—José Joa-
quim de Abreu, capitão dos reaes engenheiros — Joaquim José

*dos Santos*, coronel — *Pedro Fernandes de Andrade*, tenente — *Francisco Antonio Pinto Bastos*, alferes — *Manoel Francisco de Salles*, capitão — *José de Freitas Saldanha*, mestre das cerimonias — *Joaquim Alves Moreira*, capitão — *Gaspar Ribeiro da Rosa*, sargento-mór — *Francisco M. Pereira da Motta*, tenente — *Antonio José do Valle*, alferes — *Antonio de Padua Gusmão*, tenente-coronel — *D. Antonio de Locio e Seilbz*, alferes — *Carlos Lourentzo Dannwardo*, capitão — *Joaquim da Silva Lima*, capitão — *Pedro Antonio Ferreira*, alfere s — *Francisco de Assis Ludgero*, alferes — *João Feliciano da Costa Ferreira*, secretario do regimento — *Francisco Jacintho Pereira*, alferes — *Antonio Joaquim da Silva*, vigario — *Custodio José Gomes de Lima Guimarães*, sargento — *José de Freitas Saldanha*, capitão de milicias — *José Marcellino Fernandes*, cirurgião-mór dos caçadores — *P.e Ignacio Eduardo da Silva.* — *João Gonçalves Bastos*, tenente-coronel graduado. — Tenente-coronel *Joaquim José de Moraes Abreu.* — Quartel-mestre *José Pereira Jorge.* — Ajudante *Manoel Pereira Jorge.* — *Manoel Joaquim Gonçalves de Andrade*, arcediago, provisor e vigario geral do bispado. — Chantre *Antonio Joaquim de Abreu Pereira.* — Conego *Manoel Caetano de Oliveira.* — Conego *Antonio Paes de Camargo.* — Conego cura *Antonio Marques Henriques.* — Padre *Manoel Teixeira de Almeida.* — *José Branco de Barros*, sargento do 2.º regimento. — *Lourenço Justiniano*, furriel. — *Ponciano Joaquim de Góes*, furriel. — *José da Cunha Abreu*, tenente-coronel *José Rodrigues Pereira de Oliveira Netto*, sargento-mór. — *Manoel Innocencio de Vasconcellos*, sargento-mór. — *Joaquim Ignacio Ribeiro*, capitão. — *Antonio Cardoso Nogueira*, capitão. — *Francisco Candido Sagalerva*, capitão. — *Luiz Antonio Quaresma*, tenente. — *Luiz Rodrigues da Cunha*, tenente. — *Joaquim Floriano de Godoy*, tenente. — *Antonio Gonçalves Mamede*, tenente. — *Jaime da Silva Telles*, alferes. — *Francisco Manoel de Andrade Figueiredo e Albuquerque*, alferes. — *Flaminio Antonio de Vasconcellos*, tenente. — *Francisco de Assis Cruz*, tenente. — *Antonio Sergio da Silva*, sargento-mór do regimento de caçadores. — *Francisco Bernardes Correia*, sargento. — *Ezequiel de Moraes*, cabo de esquadra. — *Antonio da Cunha Lobo*, capitão. *Manoel Francisco da Costa Silveira.* — *José Corrêa de Miranda*, sargento-mór. — *Amaro José Vieira.* — *Bento Corrêa Leme*, capitão. — *Francisco Alves Ribeiro*, cabo de esquadra. — *Joaquim José do Nascimento*, sargento de milicias. — *Manoel Floriano Vitorio*, sargento. — *Joaquim José de Lima*, sargento de milicias. — *Manoel José dos Santos*, cabo de milicias. — *Joaquim José Soares*, cabo de milicias. — *Francisco de Borja*, cabo de ordenança. — *José Elias da Silva*, tenente. — *Francisco Xavier Pinheiro*, sargento reformado de caçadores.—*José Joaquim dos Santos Prado*, sargento-mór de milicias.—*Luiz Antonio Pinto do Rego*, ajudante reformado da legião de tropas ligeiras.—*Antonio José Brandão*, ajudante de cavallaria.—*João Baptista de Oliveira*, alferes do 1.° regimento de cavallaria.—Conego *Francisco Joaquim de Toledo Arouche.*—Conego *Melchior Fernandes Nunes de Camargo.*—*José Antonio Abranches*, porta-estandarte de milicias.—*Domingos Antonio Fernandes*, furriel de milicias.—Conego *José Gonçalves de Almeida.*—*Manoel Delphino da Fonseca.*—*João José Moreira.*—*Innocencio José Rodrigues de Vasconcellos.*—*Joaquim Theodoro de Araujo.*—*Manoel Leite de Oliveira*—*Diogo José da Silva.*—*Francisco de Paula Leite Prestes*, capitão de milicias.—*José Floriano Lara de Moraes*, sargento-mór.—*Pedro Taques de Almeida Alvim*, capitão.—*Segismundo de Lima*, tenente.—P.ᵉ *Lourenço Justiniano Ferreira.*—*Joaquim de Abreu Rangel*, administrador dos correios. —*José Teixeira dos Santos.*—*João da Silva Brito.*—*Carlos José Cardoso*—*Feliciano Telles Gonçalves da Trindade.*—*Francisco Gonçalves dos Santos Cruz.* capitão.—*Joaquim José da Silva.* *Leonardo Luciano de Campos*, alferes do 2.° batalhão de caçadores.—*João Olintho de Carvalho.*—*Francisco da Silva Prado*, capitão. —*Matheus Fernandes Coutinho.* capitão — *Bernardo Guedes Cardoso de Vasconcellos*, capitão.—*Luiz Manoel da Cunha Bastos*, capitão.—*Manoel Gonçalves Lessa*, sargento.—*José Joaquim da Rocha Penteado.*—*João Pires de Camargo*, porta-estandarte.—*Luiz Antonio de Sá Brazeiro*, ajudante —*Francisco de Paula Macedo*, major.—Conego *Joaquim José Carlos de Carvalho.*—*João Maria de Souza Chichorro*, alferes de caçadores.— *José Rodrigues Pereira*, capitão.—*Antonio Rodrigues Salgado.*— *Bento Simão Vieira.*—*Manoel Domingues Martins e Souza.*— *Gaspar Antonio de Souza*, capitão de caçadores.—*Francisco de Paula Barbosa.*—*Francisco de Paula Oliveira*, tenente.—*Antonio Joaquim de Almeida.*—*João Pereira Simões*, tenente-coronel graduado.—*Manoel José da Costa*, sargento-mór —*João Lopes França*, capitão.—*Theodoro José de Cerqueira Cesar*, sargento de cavallaria.—*Joaquim José da Fonseca*, sargento de cavallaria.—Cirurgião-mór *Joaquim Theobaldo Machado de Oliveira e Vasconcellos.*—P.ᵉ *Leão José de Senna.*—*José Arouche de Toledo Rendon.* marechal de campo graduado e inspector geral de miliciaas.—*Francisco Xavier dos Santos*, brigadeiro.—*Anastacio de Freitas Trancoso*, coronel reformado das tropas ligeiras.— *José Joaquim de Vasconcellos Alambary*, sargento-mór e ajudante do marechal inspector geral do milicias.—P.ᵉ *Joaquim Ribeiro de Oliveira.*—P.ᵉ *Bruno Ferreira da Costa.*—*Manoel Coe-*

*lho Netto*, tenente-quartel-mestre do 1.° regimento.—*Antonio José de Almeida.*— *Manoel Peixoto de Azevedo*, furriel.—*Manoel Neves de Jesus*, alferes.—*Manoel Francicco Borja.*—*João Pedro Thomaz*, sargento.—*José Mariano de Assumpção Bailão*, tenente de milicias.—*Francisco Pereira de Araujo.*—*Eleuterio da Silva Prado*, capitão-mór *Antonio da Silva Prado*, capitão de ordenanças.—*Manoel Joaquim Coelho*, capitão de ordenanças.— *Joaquim da Silva Prado*, ajudante.—*José Manoel da Silva*, capitão.—*João Baptista Tavares*, alferes.—*Joaquim da Silva Abreu Vianna*, alferes.—*José Antonio Fernandes.*—*Manoel José da Silva*, alferes.—*P.° Bartholomeu Pereira Mendes.*—*Manoel Eugenio Barbosa*, alferes.—*Joaquim Pereira Vianna de Lima*, capitão pagador.—*Francisco José Barbosa.*—*José Joaquim de Jesus e Silva.*— *Bento José da Silva Rego.*—*Antonio Joaquim Furquim Justino* —*Demetrio de Jesus.*—*Ignacio Bueno de Oliveira.* —*José Dias de Quadros Aranha.*—*José Manoel Soares da Silva Araujo*, tenente.— *João Evangelista*, cabo de milicias.- -*Luiz Pedroso da Silva*, ajudante.—*Francisco Nunes Ramalho*, capitão reformado —*Francisco José de Assis* —*José Rodrigues Coelho.* *José Pedro Galvão de Moura Lacerda*, brigadeiro. *João Hilario Grellet.*—*José Maria de Mello e Souza*, sargento mór.—*Francisco Barbosa Ortiz*, tenente.—*Manoel Benedicto de Toledo.*—*José Telles Peixoto.*- *Jacintho José de Sant'Anna*, tenente.—*José Antonio de Camargo.*—*Luiz Gonzaga de Araujo*, alferes de milicias.—*José Ponciano de Godoy.*—*José da Silva Carvalho.*— sargento-mór.—*Manoel de Jesus Costa Cintra.*—*Francisco de Salles Borralho*, ajudante de milicias.—*Gabriel Henriques Pessoa.*—*Joaquim José dos Santos.*—O vigario *André Joaquim da Silva Macaré.*—*Francisco Manoel de Borja*, sargento.—*Antonio Victorino de Moraes*, capitão.—*Francisco Vieira da Silva*, porta-bandeira.—*José Francisco Serpa.*—*Manoel Ribeiro de Araujo*, furriel reformado.—*José Ferreira Leite*, alferes de milicias.— *Manoel da Silva Moraes*, sargento.—O vigario *Antonio José de Carvalho.*—*José Moreira de Souza.*—*José Domingues Damaceno.*—*Martinho da Silva Santos*, meirinho geral *Antonio Manoel Pereira.*—*Francisco Lourenço.*—*Fernando Antonio da Silva Macaré.*—*Manoel Pereira da Silva.*- *Joaquim de Souza Guirães*, cadete de caçadores.—*José Delphino de Camargo*, cadete de caçadores.—*Luiz Gonzaga*, furriel. —*Joaquim Pereira Braga*, sargento.—*Ignacio José de Vasconcellos*, cabo.—*Ignacio José de Macedo*, tenente.—*Antonio Floriano Alves Alvim* —*P.° Antonio José Corrêa.*—O vigario *Francisco de Paula Teixeira.*—*José Galvão da Fonseca e Camara*, capitão,—*Manoel Barbosa da Silva.*— *Matheus Corrêa de Vasconcellos.*—*Antonio Freire de*

Menezes, capitão.—*Salvador de Oliveira Paes.—Ignacio Ribeiro do Espirito Santo.—Benedicto dos Santos.—Manoel Joaquim de Oliveira*, sargento.—P.ᵉ *João Joaquim de Carvalho Porto.—P.ᵉ Francisco Emigdio de Toledo.—P.ᵉ José Manoel de Souza.* P.ᵉ *Joaquim Manoel de Azevedo Marques.—Antonio José Bordini*, sargento-mòr.—*José de Oliveira Prado.—Francisco Pinto Ferraz*, coronel reformado do 2.° regimento de cavallaria.—*Vicente da Silva Carvalho*, furriel.—*Severino Pinto da Silva*, capitão.—*José Joaquim dos Santos.* — P.ᵉ *Antonio Pedro Garcia da Silva Gomes.—Fr. Antonio de Santa Gertrudes*, prior do convento do Carmo.—P.ᵉ *Joaquim Manoel de Oliveira e Castro.—P.ᵉ Ignacio Pedroso de Aveiros.—P.ᵉ Manoel Emigdio Bernardes.—Fr. Hygino de Santa Narcisa.—Fr. José de Santa Delphina.—Fr. Lucas José da Purificação —Fr. Joaquim de S. José.—P.ᵉ Joaquim José de Almeida.—P.ᵉ Manoel José Rodrigues. —João Rodrigues de Camargo Pires.—Antonio de Siqueira Moraes*, capitão.—*O Guardião de S. Francisco.—Francisco Mariano da Cunha*, capitão.—*Joaquim José Pinto de Moraes Leme*, brigadeiro de cavavallaria.—*Manoel Joaquim de Ornellas.—Joaquim Floriano de Toledo*, tenente de milicias e official da Secretaria do governo.—P.ᵉ *Manoel Gomes de Gauvê.a—P.ᵉ Antonio José de Souza Lima.—P.ᵉ Mariano Pinto Tavares.—P.ᵉ Bento Pedroso de Camargo.—P.ᵉ Felippe José Pereira·—P.ᵉ Amaro José Martins.—Fr. Manoel da Natividade Marques*, presidente do S. Bento.—*Fr. Joaquim dos Prazeres.—Fr. Francisco de S. Miguel.— Pᵉ Antonio Maximo.—Pᵉ Raphael Antonio de Barros.—P.ᵉ Antonio Manoel de Abreu.—Manoel Gomes de Gouvea.—Fr. José da Purificação*, carmelita.—*Fr. Francisco Bernardes da. Virgem Maria*, carmelita.—*José Vaz de Carvalho.—Eleuterio José Pinto. —P.ᵉ Joaquim Montairo da Silva Buris, O vigario collado.— Bento Manuel dos Passos.—José Rodrigues Velloso de Oliveira. —O vigario collado, Joaquim José Rodrigues.—P.ᵉ João Nepumuceno.—P.ᵉ Bernardo Conrado da Cunha e Faria.—O professor, Antonio Mariano de Azevedo Marques.—o vigario collado, José Rodrigues de Moraes.—Pᵉ José Antonio dos Reis. -P.ᵉ Joaquim José de Oliveira.—O vigario collado, José Basilio Rodrigues Cardim.—Francisco Severiano dos Santos Cardim*, tenente de milicias.—*Joaquim Antonio de Carvalho.—O vigario collado, Francisco José de Abreu.—P.ᵉ Joaquim José da Silva Lisboa.— O vigario collado, Feliciano Cavalheiro Leite.—José Antonio Pereira*, alferes de ordenanças.—*Manoel Felizardo de Carvalho e Almeida*, ajudantes de ordenanças.—P.ᵉ *João José Vieira Ramalho. —Antonio José Fernandes.—P.ᵉ Francisco Emigdio de Toledo. —José Rodrigues de Almeida.—Antonio José Vaz.—Elesbão Fran-*

cisco Vaz Manoel José da Silva Castro.—João Baptista Vaz.—
O vigario, José Alves Dantas.—P.ᵉ Fernandes Lopes de Camar-
go.—P.ᵉ Manoel Joaquim de Oliveira.—Francisco Figueira de
Assumpção, clerigo, in minoribus.— José Manoel Ferraz.—João
Garcia da Fonseca.—O conego, Fidelis José de Moraes.—P.ᵉ Fran-
cisco Antonio de Araujo Souto.—Francisco Josè de Jesus.—
Joaquim José Colaço.—P.ᵉ Francisco Metello Homem.—Floriano
José Luiz Antonio Neves de Carvalho, coronel.—Luiz Antonio da
Silva Freire.—José Mendes da Silva.—Cosntantino José dos San-
tos, alferes.=José Felippe de Santiago, alferes.—Joaquim José
Pedro Maia.—P.ᵉ Francisco Coelho Aires.—Bento José Leite
Penteado. capitão.—P.ᵉ Manoel José Pereira de Andrade.—O vi-
gario, José Branco de Oliveira.—João Antonio Rosa.—Sylvestre
Ferreira da Silva, sargento mór Januario Antonio de Lima, co-
ronel.—José Mariano Bueno, capitão.—Antonio Bernardo Bue-
no da Veiga, capitão de milicias.—Balthazar de Godoy Cardoso,
capitão de milicias.—Dr) Justiniano de Mello Franco.—Antonio
José Ribeiro da Silva.—Manoel Ferreira Duarte.—José Antonio
de Assumpção.—Manoel José Villaça.—Manoel Guilherme da
Silva Cruz.—Ignacio Antonio de Toledo.—O coadjutor da Cutia,
Ignacio Francisco do Amaral.—Thomaz Gançalves Gomide.—
Francisco José de Carvalho Faro —P.ᵉ José Joaquim de Toledo.—
Joaquim José Correia.—Theodosio Pinto da Silva.—Pedro Antonio
da Encarnação.—João José Rodrigues, capitão.—Matheus Jorge
da Silva.—Francisco Bernardes da Silva, sargento-mór.—Manoel de Barros.—Joaquim Josè de Oliveira.—Manoel Joaquim de
Vasconcellos, alferes. —Manoel José Chaves.—P.ᵉ Antonio Joaqim
de Araujo Leite. — Manoel José de Castro, — Salvador Paes
da Costa. — Joaquim José de Andrade e Aquino. — Alexandre Gonçalves Barroso de Souza e Silva sargento de caçadores.

REPRESENTAÇÃO DA CAMARA DE S. PAULO AO PRINCIPE REGENTE,
PARA QUE FIQUE NO BRAZIL, LEVADA PELO MARECHAL JOSÉ
AROUCHE DE TOELDO RENDON.

Senhor: Si é indubitvael que a nação portugueza, por
seus feitos immortaes, tem sido em todas as épocas considerada
como uma nação de heróes; si é certo que nenhum povo da
terra lhe póde disputar virtudes sublimes, que tanto a ennobre-
cem, taes como a adhesão e fidelidade aos seus reis, enthusiasmo pela gloria e patriotismo exaltado; tambem é incontestavel
que ella é sempre a mesma, que os mesmos sentimentos a animam, quer habite um ou outro hemispherio.

A historia do Brasil attesta esta verdade. As heroicas proezas dos pernambucanos por espaço de sete annos contra seus tyrannos invasores, os hollandezes ; os gloriosos e felizes esforços dos bahianos, fluminenses e outros povos, repellindo por vezes aggressões extrangeiras, são exemplos que assaz evidenciam quanto os portuguezes nascidos no Brazil prezaram sempre a sua independencia, ainda quando agrilhoados pelo barbaro despotismo.

Era impossivel, pois, Real Senhor, que os brasileiros de hoje, herdeiros dos nobres sentimentos e valor dos seus antepassados e illustrado pelas luzes do seculo, não vivessem possuidos do amor da gloria e cada vez mais inflamados no desejo de ver livre e independente o seu paiz natal, era impossivel que, depois de tão lisongeiras esperanças de uma melhor sorte, elles não tremessem agora de horror e indignação prevendo desde já o medonho futuro que os ameaça, si se realizarem os planos de escravidão que lhes preparam os portuguezes da Europa.

Com effeito, o generoso Brasil, que tão francamente se prestou a fazer causa commum com Portugal, vendo illudida a sua boa fé e ultrajado o seu decoro nacional, reconhece hoje o seu erro e, á vista de procedimentos nunca esperados, parece jazer amadornado, podendo apenas acreditar tão absurdas disposições a seu respeito. Os paulistas, porém, não podendo por mais tempo disfarçar seu justissimo resentimento, são os primeiros que ousam levantar sua voz e protestar contra actos inconstitucionaes, com que se pretende illudir e escravizar um povo livre, cujo crime é haver dado demasiado credito a vans promessas e doces palavras :

Desnecessario seria narrar aqui por extenso todas as causas de nosso descontentamento; Vossa Alteza Real bem as conhece. Sim, Real Senhor, parece que um destino fatal pugna para arrastar ás bordas do precipicio a esses mesmos portuguezes que na sua regeneração politica attrahiram sobre si a admiração do mundo. Depois de haverem conseguido o principal objecto do seu plano, o arrancar do Brasil o precioso deposito que o Céu lhe confiára em 1808, depois de haverem recebido dos brasileiros as mais decisivas provas de uma confraternidade sem egual, mudaram inteiramente de tom a respeito destes mesmos sinceros brasileiros, a cuja indiscreta cooperação devem em grande parte o feliz resultado de sua perigosissima empresa.

Os representantes de Portugal, sem esperarem pelos do Brasil, começaram a discutir um projecto de constituição que devia ser commum a ambos os reinos, projecto em que a cada pagina se descobre o machiavelismo com que, com douradas ca-

dêas, se intenta escravizar este riquissimo paiz e reduzil-o a mera
colonia. Os represenrantes de Portugal, depois de haverem,
pelo artigo 21 das Bases, reconhecido o direito, que só competia aos representantes do Brasil, de fazer a lei para o seu paiz,
repentinamente se arrogaram esse mesmo direito e começaram a
legislar sobre os mais sagrados interesses de tod·· o Brasil; elles lhes prescreveram governos provinciaes organizados de tal
maneira que só parecem destinados de proposito para enfraque-
cer-nos, dividir-nos em partidos e desligar as provincias, afim de
melhor imperarem sobre cada uma.

Elles nos tem enviado tropas sob pretextos especiosos, sem
que houvesse inimigos externos a combater ou dissensões internas a suffocar. Mas que homem é tão estupido que não pe-
netre o verdadeiro fim de taes expedições?

Os brasileiros, Real Senhor, estão persuadidos de que é por
meio de baionetas que se pretende dar a lei a este reino;
muito se enganam de certo os seus inimigos que intentam pôr
em pratica. O Brasil conhece perfeitamente toda a extensão
dos seus recursos.

A noticia da extincção dos tribunaes do Rio de Janeiro,
a da retirada dos vasos de guerra e os decretos de 29 de Setembro (1) vieram pôr o cumulo á nossa desesperação. Orde-
nam que Vossa Alteza Real vá quanto antes para Portugal,
deixando o reino do Brasil sem centro commum de governo e
união e tornando-o dependente de Lisboa em todas as suas relações e negocios, qual vil colonia sem contemplação.

Esta medida, a mais impolitica que o espirito humano
podia dictar, tomada sem se consultarem os representantes do
Brasil, é o maior insulto que se podia fazer aos seus habitantes e a sua execução, nós o ousamos dizer, será o primeiro signal da desunião e da discordia, será o principio das desgraças
incalculaveis que tem de arruinar a ambos os Reinos.

A ameaçadora perspectiva de tantos males convenceu aos
habitantes desta capital da necessidade de se reunirem para
obrarem de commum accôrdo e tratarem das medidas que as
circumstancias exigem a bem da patria. A Camara e os cidadãos abaixo assignados, persuadidos de que da resolução de
Vossa Alteza Real dependem os destinos deste reino, resolveram enviar á Augusta Presença de Vossa Alteza Real uma
deputação composta de tres cidadãos, o conselheiro José Bonifacio de Andrada e Silva (2), o coronel Antonio Leite Pereira
da Gama Lobo e o marechal José Arouche de Toledo Rendon,

---

(1) Decreto chamado o Principe Regente para Portugal.
2) Foi tambem como delegado do governo da provincia.

cujo objecto é representar a V ossa Alteza Real as terriveis consequencias que necessariamente se devem seguir da sua ausencia e rogar-lhe haja de differir o seu embarque até nova resolução do Congresso Nacional (1), pois é de esperar que elle, ρ melhor illustrado sobre os reciprocos e verdadeiros interesses dos dous reinos, decrete outro systema de união, fundado sobre bases mais justas e razoaveis, a principal das quaes será certamente a conservação de Vossa Alteza Real neste reino, sem a qual jámais os brasileiros consentirão em uma união ephemera.

A deputação terá a honra de expressar a Vossa Alteza Real os puros sentimentos dos paulistas e a firme resolução em que se acham de preferirem a morte á escravidão e de não pouparem sacrificios até exgottarem a ultima pinga de seu sangue para sustentarem seus direitos. Praza aos Céos que Vossa Alteza Real, cheio de prudencia e de sabedoria, annúa aos nossos votos, pois de outra sorte rios de sangue têm de inundar este bello paiz, que de certo não merece a sorte que lhe pretendem destinar. A Augusta Pessoa de Vossa Alteza Real guarde Deos muitos annos, como havemos mister. S. Paulo, em vereação de 31 de Dezembro de 1821.--O ouvidor interino, *José da Costa Carvalho.*—O juiz de fora pela lei, presidente, *José de Almeida Ramos.*—O vereador *Antonio de Siqueira Moraes.*—O vereador *Antonio da Silva Prado.*—O vereador, *Antonio Cardoso Nogueira.*—O procurador *Amaro José de Moraes.*—O escrivão *João Nepomuceno de Almeida.*—*Matheus,* Bispo de S. Paulo.—*Manoel Joaquim Gonçalves de Andrade,* arcediago e vigario geral deste bispado de S. Paulo.—*Antonio Joaquim Pereira de Abreu,* chantre da Sé.—O conego *Manoel Caetano de Oliveira*—O conego *Francisco José de Toledo Arcuche Rendon*—O conego *Lourenço Justiniano Ferreira*—O conego *Joaquim José Carlos Aires de Carvalho*—O conego *Melchior Fernandes Nunes*—O conego *Fsanetsca José Lobo*—O conego *José Gomes de Almeida*—O conego *Fidelis José de Moraes*—O conego cura *Antouio Marques Henriques*—O sub-chantre *Antonio Marianno de Azevedo Marques*—O mestre de cerimonias *José de Freitas Saldanha*—O capellão *Leão José de Senua*—O capellão *José Joaquim de Toledo*—O capellão *Manoel Joaquim de Oliveira*—O capellão *Joaquim José de Oliveira*—O capellão *José Manoel de Sousa*—O capellão *Bernardo Conrado e Cunha*

---

(1) D. Pedro annuiu aos pedidos que de diversas partes lhe foram feitos neste sentido, mas a representação que mais influiu sobre o seu espirito foi a que o governo de S. Paulo lhe mandou em 24 de Dezembro de 1821 e que elle remetteu a D. João VI, em Lisboa, como a real expressão dos sentimentos dos brasileiros.

—O capellão *Joaquim Aatonio Rodrigues*—O capellão *Joaquim Manoel de Azevedo*—O capellão *Manoel Emygdio Bernardes*— O capellão *Antonio Pedro Garcia*—*Lazaro José Gonçalves*, coronel de caçadores—*Carlos Maria de Oliva*, capitão — *Antonio Mariano de Bittencourt*, tenente—*D. Antonio de Locio e Seilbz*, alferes— *João Carlos Baumann*, alferes — *José Marcellino do Amaral*, alferes— *João Maria de Sousa*, alferes— *Antonio Correia Pinto*, alferes—*Domingos Anacleto da Silva*, capitão—*José Pereira Jorge*, quartel-mestre—*Antonio João Fernandes Gabizo*, alferes — *Francisco de Paula Gomes*, tenente—*Bernardo José Pinto Gavião*, tenente-coronel —*Carlos Lorentezo Damkvard*, capitão—*João Vicente Rangel*, tenente— *Joaquim José Lopes*, alferes— *Antonio Manoel de Mello*, alferes—*Nabor Delfim Pereira*, ajudante —*João Feliciano da Costa*, secretario —*José Ramos*, quartel-mestre—*Manoel da Cunha de Azeredo Coutinho e Sousa Chichorro*, secretario do expediente geral—*José Mathias Ferreira de Abreu*, official maior—*Joaquim Flariano de Toledo*, 2.° official— *Francisco Xavier dos Santos*, brigadeiro — *João Vicente da Fonseca*, coronel — *Luiz Manoel Feliciano Queles* — *Joaquim José Rodrigues*, almotacel —*Francisco Xavier de Toledo*, juiz almotacel — *José Francisco Serpa* — *Bento Alberto da Gama e Sá*, governador da villa de Santos— *Manoel Joaquim de Ornellas*—*Antonio Safino da Fonseca*—*Joaquim José dos Santos*—*Candido Gonçalves Gomide* — *Antonio de Almeida e Silva Freire* — juiz de fóra de Taubaté — O vigario *Modesto Antonio Coelho Netto* — *Francisco de Paula Macedo*, major—*José Innscencio Alves Alvim*—*Manoel Innocencio de Vasconcellos*, contador geral—*João José Moreira* — *José Clemente de Mesquita* — *Manoel Delfino da Fonseca* — *Francisco de Assis Cruz*—*Luiz Antonio da Silva Freire*—*João Baptista Vaz*—O padre *João Neponucemo*—*José Ferreira Leite*, alferes—*Manoel Ribeiro de Araujo*— *Antonio José Brandão*, ajudante — *Francisco Alves Ferreira do Amaral*, coronel — *Thomé Manoel de Jesus Varella*, alferes — *Thomaz Gonçalves Gomide Juntor* — *Joaquim Theodoro de Araujo*—*Manoel Gomes de Gouvêa*—*Joaquim José Pinto de Moraes Leme*, brigadeiro—*Francisco Pinto Ferraz*, capitão — *Francisco Mariano da Costa*, capitão— *José Ferraz da Silva*, capitão—*Joaquim Theobaldo Machado de Oliveira Vasconcellos*, cirurgião-mór—*João Rodrigues de Camargo Pires*, tenente—*Joaquim José de Moraes Abreu*, tenente-coronel— *Matheus Fernandes Cantinho*, capitão—*Pedro Taqúes de Almeida Alves Alvim*, capitão— *Luiz Antonio de Sá Brazeiro*, ajudante — *Francisco da Silva Prado*, capitão—*Sigismando de Lima*, tenente — *Bernado José Guedes Cardoso*, tenente—*Domingos de Araujo Roso*, alferes—*Joaquim José da Silva*, alferes—*José Ro-*

*drigues Pereira de Oliveira Netto*, major — *Francisco Candido
Sagalerva*, capitão — *Luiz Antonio do Valle*, capitão — *Joaquim
Ignacio Ribeiro*, capitão—*Manoel Pereira Jorge*, ajudante—*Antonio Gonçalves Mamede*, tenente — *Luiz Gonzaga de Araujo*,
tenente — *Joaquim dos Santos Silva*,alferes—*Jayme da Silva
Telles*, tenente— *Antonio Fernandes da Motta*, alferes—*Jeronymo
Pereira Chrispim de Vasconcellos*, tenente-coronel—*José Manoel
da Luz*, major— *Francisco Jorge de Paula Ribeiro*, major—*Caetano Pinto Homem*, capitão — *Joaquim José de Almcida*, capitão
—*Flaminio Antonio de Vasconcellos*, tenente—*Fracisco Antonio
Pinto Bastos*, tenente— *Manoel Guilherme da Silva Cruz--José
Joaquim Alves Rodrigues.—P.ᵉ Francisco Rodrigues Coelho.—
Floriano Antonio Rodrigues.—Joaquim Cardoso.—Antonio Telles Barreto.—Manoel Gonçalves dos Santos.* (1)

---

(1) Contém este documento 450 assignaturas, sendo 280 de pessoas que assistiram
á deposição de João Carlos e á eleição do governo provisorio e nellas tomaram parte
directa, immediata ; as restantes 170 são de pessoas que vieram depois sanccionar o
feito de 23 de Junho de 1821 e prestar juramento de obediencia ás bases da constituição. Ha entre os signatarios um marechal, brigadeiros, coroneis, capitães, muita gente
da governança da terra—capitão-mór, vereadores, juizes, etc.; e até o bispo da diocese
acompanhado de muitos clerigos, tanto regulares como seculares; mas o ouvidor Costa
Carvalho não appareceu naquelle dia e nem achou occasião depois para vir prestar homenagem ao codigo constitucional !

Em sessão de 22 de Dezembro de 1821 a Camara escolheu para seus delegados José Bo.
nifacio, o marechal Arouche e o coronel Gama Lobo junto ao Principe afim de pedir em-
lhe que não deixe o Brasil. Em sessão de 31 do mesmo fez a camara a representação
a D. Pedró, que foi assignada por mais gente além dos vereadores e foi dada a
Arouche para leval-a ao Rio.

A. PIZA.

## Processo do Capitão José Fernandes da Silva, que acompanhou Martim Francisco, de S. Paulo ao Rio de Janeiro em Maio de 1822

Ao 1.º do mez de Outubro de 1822, nesta cidade de S. Paulo e quartel das tropas da guarnição da mesma, tendo sido presente ao Ex.ᵐᵒ Governador das Armas desta Provincia, o Marechal de Campo Candido Xavier de Almeida e Souza, que o capitão do 2.º regimento de cavallaria miliciana José Fernandes do Silva fora mandado pelo ex-Governo Provisorio desta mesma provincia acompanhar ao Ex.ᵐᵒ Martim Francisco Ribeiro de Andrada, quando o mesmo ex-Governo o obrigou a uma rapida sahida desta cidade para o Rio de Janeiro, até aonde o mesmo quizesse, e fora ao depois intimado á ordem de Sua Alteza Real para o acompanhar até á corte, o que assim cumpriu, e que chegando á corte recebêra ahi ordem do Ex.ᵐᵒ Ministro da Guerra para se não retirar a esta cidade sem expressa ordem de Sua Alteza Real, o qual assim não cumpriu, porquanto retirou-se para esta cidade sem que tivesse ordem de Sua Alteza Real para isso, como tudo consta da parte do capitão mandante do sobredito regimento, ao deante junta, vindo a faltar, com semelhante procedimento á devida obediencia ás ordens de Sua Alteza Real; portanto, mandou o dito Governador das Armas proceder a Conselho de Guerra para nelle se averiguar o crime de que é arguido o dito capitão, sendo presidente e vogaes os nomeados na relação ao deante junta; do que tudo mandou o presidente do Conselho fazer este auto, escripto por mim Auditor, para por elle se proceder á inquirição de testemunhas, interrogatorios e sentença contra o réo; do que fiz este termo eu, José Correa Pacheco e Silva, Auditor, que o escrevi por ordem do mesmo.—O Auditor, *José Correa Pacheco e Silva.*

Candido Xavier de Almeida e Souza, Commendador da Ordem Militar de S. Bento de Aviz, Marechal de Campo dos Reaes Exercitos e Governador das Armas desta Provincia de S. Paulo, por Sua Alteza Real, que Deus guarde, etc., etc., etc.

Para o Conselho de Guerra que mando fazer, em conformidade das ordens do mesmo Augusto Senhor, ao capitão do 2.º regimento de cavallaria de 2.ª linha desta provincia, José Fernandes da Silva, pela culpa de que é arguido pela parte accusatoria junta, de desobediencia contra o artigo 1.º de Guerra, descripto á folhas 166 do Regulamento de Cavallaria, de 25 de Agosto de 1764, em observancia do § 2.º do Capitulo 11. descripto á folhas 179 do mesmo Regulamento.

O senhor tenente coronel Joaquim José de Moraes Abreu, com o presidente, fará convocarem observancia das Reaes Ordens.

Para Auditor — o senhor doutor Juiz de Fora do termo desta cidade, José Corrêa Pacheco e Silva.

Para Vogaes — os senhores majores João Pereira Simões, interrogante, e Antonio José Bordini; capitães Matheus Fernandes Cantinho, interrogante, e Francisco da Silva Prado; tenentes João Ribeiro de Camargo e Sigismundo de Lima; alferes Joaquim José da Silva e Salvador Pires da Silva.

Serão convocadas tres testemunhas da culpa ou mais, até que esta seja provada.

Quartel General de S. Paulo, 25 de Setembro de 1822. — *Candido Xavier de Almeida e Souza.*

———

Ill.mo e Ex.mo Senhor: — Em observancia do que V. Ex.ª me ordena participo a V. Ex.ª que o capitão José Fernandes da Silva foi em diligencia para a corte do Rio de Janeiro, acompanhar ao Ex.mo Sr. Martim Francisco Ribeiro de Andrada até aonde o mesmo Senhor o determinasse, por portaria do ex-Governo de 30 de Maio do corrente anno.

Na freguezia do Bananal, segundo me informa o capitão Joaquim José de Almeida, lhe mandou o Ex.mo Sr. Andrada intimar, á ordem de Sua Alteza Real, ao capitão Fernandes de o acompanhar até á côrte do Rio de Janeiro, o que cumpriu: e depois de alli chegado o mesmo capitão Almeida teve ordem do Ex.mo Ministro da Guerra para se não retirar daquella côrte e o capitão José Fernandes da Silva sem expressa ordem de Sua Alteza Real, o que o capitão Almeida communicou ao capitão Fernandes, que regressou para esta cidade com a mesma portaria do ex-Governo e sem outro nenhum passaporte.

E' o que informo a V. Ex.ª, repertando-me a documentos que tenho em meu poder.

Deus guarde a V. Ex.ª muitos annos. Qualtel em S: Paulo, 19 de Setembro de 1822. Ill.ᵐᵒ e Ex.ᵐᵒ Sr. Marechal Commandante das Armas da Provincia.—*Francisco Pinto Ferraz*, capitão Mandante.

———

Francisco Pinto Ferraz, Cavalleiro da Ordem de Christo, capitão da 3.ª Companhia de Cavallaria de Milicias e Commandante interinamente do 2.° Regimento de Cavallaria, etc.

Attesto e faço certo que, revendo o Livro Mestre do Regimento do meu commando, nelle, á folhas 32 verso, se acha o assento do teôr seguinte:

José Fernandes da Silva, de idade de trinta e quatro annos, filho do Porto, assentou praça de furriel no regimento dos sertanejos a 28 de Maio de 1807. Fez passagem para este regimento a 21 de Outubro de 1812. Passou ao posto de tenente quartel-mestre a 20 de Agosto de 1813. Confirmado a 9 de Outubro do dito anno. Passou a capitão por despacho do Governo de 22 de Dezembro de 1818.

E nada mais se continha no Livro Mestre e assento da 2.ª companhia. E por me ser mandado passar a presente fé de officio, o certifico debaixo da minha palavra de honra.

Quartel de São Paulo, 17 de Setembrro de 1822.—*Francisco Pinto Ferraz*, Capitão-Mandante.

———

Ao 1.° dia do mez de Outubro de 1822, primeira sessão deste, Conselho, ahi presente elle, foram perguntadas as testemunhas seguintes pelos officiaes interrogantes, o major João Ribeiro Simões e o capitão Matheos Fernandes Cantinho, sobre o crime arguido ao réo; de que fiz este termo eu, *José Correa Pacheco e Silva*, Auditor, que o escrevi.

### TESTEMUNHA 1.ª

Joaquim José de Almeida, capitão de Milicias; casado, natural desta cidade e nella morador, e onde vive de seu negocio, de idade que disse ter trinta e quatro annos; testemunha jurada aos Santos Evangelhos para dizer a verdade do que souber e lhe for perguntado. E sendo perguntado pelo conteúdo no auto retro, que todo lhe foi lido e declarado, disse elle, testemunha, que sabe que o réo acompanhou ao Exmo. Martim Francisco Ribeiro de Andrade quando daqui partiu para o Rio de Janeiro, até ao Bananal, por ordem do ex-Governo Provisorio; o que sabe elle, testemunha, por ver a portaria do mesmo ex-Governo que commetteu ao réo esta diligencia, e que do dito logar elle, testemunha, intimou ao réo, por mandado do dito Exmo. Martim Francisco, que á ordem de Sua Alteza Real o acompanhasse até ao Rio de Janeiro, e que chegando elle, testemunha, ao Rio, lhe determinou o Exmo. Ministro da Guerra que se não retirasse para esta cidade sem ordem de Sua Altezo Real e que a mesma intimasse ao réo, o que elle, testemunha, assim fez, intimando .a dita ordem; e que elle, réo viera para esta cidade sem ordem de Sua Alteza Real, o que elle, testemunha, sabe por ouvir dizer ao padre João de Carvalho e mais a outro sujeito cujo nome ignora; e nada mais disse; e nos costumes disse que tinha alguma amizade ao réo, e se assignou com os officiaes interrogantes, sendo-lhe primeiro lido o seu depoimento, e o achar conforme ao que havia exposto, e eu. José Correa Pacheco e Silva, Auditor, que o escrevi.—*Simões.*—*Cantinho.*—*Joaquim José de Almeida.*

## TESTEMUNHA 2.ª

Ignacio José de Macedo, tenente de Milicias, casado, natural desta cidade, onde mora e vive de seu negocio, de idade que disse ter trinta e oito annos; testemunha jurada aos Santos Évangelhos para dizer a verdade do que souber e lhe for perguntado, e aos costumes disse nada. E seudo perguntado pelo conteúdo do auto retro, que todo lhe foi lido e declarado, disse elle, testemunha, que sabe, por lhe contar o réo e por ver a portaria do ex-Governo Provisorio, que o réo acompanhou ao Exmo. Martim Francisco Ribeiro de Andrade, com ordem do dito ex-Governo para voltar de onde elle quizesse e o despedisse, porem que o acompanhou até ao Rio de Janeiro por isso que o dito Exmo. Martim Francisco o levou do districto da capitania e mandou que o acompanhasse até ao Rio de Janeiro.

Disse mais elle, testemunha, que sabe por ouvir contar o mesmo réo que no Rio de Janeiro, indo jantar em casa do dito Exmo. Martim Francisco, lhe perguntou se queria alguma cousa mais delle e respondeu o mesmo que não, e por isso, pensando que a mesma portaria, que o levou, o podia trazer, voltou para esta cidade; e que tambem o réo lhe dissera não teve ordem alguma para que se não retirasse daquella côrte, e nada mais disse e se assignou com os officiaes interrogantes, sendo-lhe primeiro lido o seu depoimento e o achar conforme ao que havia deposto, e eu, José Correa Pacheco e Silva, Auditor, que o escrevi.—*Simões.*—*Cantinho.*—*Ignacio José de Macedo.*

## TESTEMUNHA 3.ª

Raymundo Pinto Homem, alferes de milicias, casado, natural de Lamego e morador nesta cidade, onde vive de suas agencias, de idade que disse ter 32 annos, testemunha jurada aos Santos Evangelhos, para debaixo delle dizer a verdade do que souber e lhe for perguntado, e aos costumes disse nada. E sendo perguntado pelo conteúdo no auto retro, que todo lhe foi lido e declarado, disse elle testemunha que sabe, por ver, que o réo acompanhou ao Exmo. Martim Francisco Ribeiro de Andrade quando daqui foi para o Rio de Janeiro por isso que se encontrou com elle em caminho, no pouso de Itaguassava, e que elle testemunha, voltando desta cidade para aquella côrte, ahi o governador das Armas, Joaquim Xavier Curado, determinou a elle testemunha que procurasse ao rêo, o que assim fazendo não o achou mais naquella corte, do que deu parte ao dito governador das Armas, e nada mais disse e se assigna com os officiaes interrogantes, sendo lhe primeiro lido o seu depoimento e o achar conforme ao que havia deposto, e eu, José Correa Pacheco e Silva, Auditor, que o escrevi.—*Simões.--Cantinho.— Raymundo Pinto Homem.*

## TESTEMUNHA 4.ª

Paulo Joaquim Gomes, alferes reformado de milicias, casado, natural da praça de Almeida e morador nesta cidade, onde vive de seu negocio, de idade que disse ter 65 annos, testemunha jurada aos Santos Evangelhos, para debaixo delle dizer a verdade do que souber e lhe for perguntado; e aos costumes disse nada. E sendo perguntado pelo conteúdo no auto retro, que todo lhe foi lido e declarado, disse elle testemunha que o réo, em virtude de uma portaria do ex-Governo Provisorio desta provincia, foi destinado para acompanhar ao Exmo. Martim Francisco Ribeiro de Andrade quando o dito ex-Governo o obrigou a sahir desta cidade, o que de facto o acompanhou até o Rio de Janeiro, o que elle testemunha sabe porque se despediu delle e lhe mostrou a portaria. Disse mais que elle testemunha que o réo, chegando ao Rio de Janeiro, foi jantar com o dito Exmo. Martim e lhe perguntou se queria alguma cousa do seu serviço, ao que o mesmo respondeu que nada queria, e depois, tratou de arranjar a sua vida e voltou para esta cidade; o que elle testemunha sobe por ouvir ao mesmo réo, e nada mais disse e se assigna com os officiaes interrogantes, sendo-lhe primeiro lido o seu depoimento e o achar conforme ao que havia deposto, e eu, José Correa Pacheco e Silva, Auditor, que o escrevi.—*Simões.*—*Cantinho.*—*Paulo Joaquim Gomes.*

___

E mandou o presidente do Conselho que se fechasse a presente sessão para se continuar no dia seguinte pelas mesmas horas, de que fiz este termo, que assignam o presidente e eu, José Correa Pacheco e Silva, Auditor, que o escrevi.—*Joaquim José de Moraes Abreu,* presidente.—O Auditor *José Correa Pacheco e Silva.*

___

## 2.ª SESSAO

Aos 2 dias do mez de Outubro de 1822, segunda sessão deste Conselho de Guerra, ahi perante elle foram perguntadas as testemunhas seguintes pelos officiaes interrogantes, o major João Pereira Simões e o capitão Matheus Fernandes Cantinho, sobre o crime que se imputa ao réo, de que fiz este termo eu, José Correia Pacheco e Silva, Auditor, que o escrevi.

### TESTEMUNHA 5.ª

João Joaquim de Carvalho, presbitero secular, natural de Mogy das Cruzes e morador nesta cidade, onde vive do seu officio de escrivão do contencioso, de idade que disse ter 38 annos, testemunha jurada aos Santos Evangelhos para debaixo delles dizer a verdade do que souber e lhe for perguntado, e aos costumes disse nada. E sendo perguntado pelo conteúdo no auto retro, que todo lhe foi lido e declarado, disse elle testemunha que o réo foi mandado pelo ex-Governo Provisorio desta provincia acompanhar ao Exmo. Martim Francisco Ribeiro de Andrada quando, por ordem do mesmo ex-Governo, partiu rapidamente desta cidade para a do Rio de Janeiro, até o Pirahy; o que sabe elle testemunha por ouvir dizer geralmente nesta cidade. Disse mais elle testemunha que o dito Exm°. Martim Francisco, encontrando-se em caminho com o corpo de milicias desta cidade, que regressava do Rio, pedira ao chefe dos mesmos que lhe desse um official para o acompanhar até ao Rio de Janeiro e, dando-se-lhe o official, mandou por este intimar ao réo que continuasse a acompanhal-o até ao Rio e que de facto fez esta intimação, e o acompanhou até áquella Corte, o que elle testemunha sabe por ter ouvido dizer-se geralmente nesta cidade e pelas villas do Norte. Disse mais que, chegando o réo ao Rio, foi ahi retido por ordem de Sua Alteza Real, como foi publico nesta cidade, e que ao depois viera fugido, o que elle testemunha sabe por lhe contar o capitão Joaquim José de Almeida. Declarou elle testemunha que a intimação feita pelo official ao réo foi que acompanhasse á ordem de Sua Alteza Real; e nada mais disse e se assigna com os officiaes interrogantes, sendo-lhe primeiro lido o seu depoimento e o achar conforme ao que havia deposto, e eu José Correia Pacheco e Silva, Auditor, que o escrivi.—*Simões—Cantinho—O padre João Joaquim de Carvalho,*

## TESTEMUNHA 6.ª

Antonio Pires de Albuquerque, soldado do 1.º regimento miliciano de infanteria, solteiro, natural de Santo Amaro e ahi morador, onde vive da sua lavoura, de edade que disse ter 20 annos, testemunha jurada aos Santos Evangelhos para dizer a verdade do que souber e lhe for perguntado, e aos costumes disse nada. E perguntado pelo conteúdo no auto retro, que todo lhe foi lido e declarado, disse elle testemunha que, voltando do Rio no corpo dos milicianos, encontrou-se com o réo para cá das Arêas, no logar chamado *Itagassava*, e que daqui voltou outra vez para o Rio na escolta que acompanhou ao Cxm°. Martim Francisco Ribeiro de Andrada e que o réo o acompanhou tambem até ao Rio de Janeiro, e nada mais disse e se assigna com os officiaes interrogantes, sendo-lhe primeiro lido o seu depoimento e o achar conforme ao que havia deposto, e eu José Correia Pacheco e Silva, Audidor, que o escrevi. —*Simões—Cantinho—Antonio Pires de Albuquerque.*

E logo no mesmo dia, mez e anno no termo retro declarados e segunda sessão deste Conselho de Guerra mandou o presidente delle vir o réo, em saa plena liberdade, á presença deste Conselho para responder as perguntas que lhe forem feitas pelos officiaes interrogantes, o major João Pereira Simões e o capitão Matheus Fernandes Cantinho, as quaes são pela maneira seguinte, de que fiz este termo eu, José Correia Pacheco e Silva, Auditor, que o escrevi:

## INTERROGATORIO DO RÉO

Foi o réo interrogado; como se chamava, de onde era natural, de quem era filho e que estado tinha e edade?

Respondeu que se chamava José Fernandes da Silva, que era natural do Porto, filho de Manoel José Fernandes da Silva, que tinha 50 annos de edade e que era casado e negociante.

Foi mais interrogado se sabe ou suspeita qual era a causa da sua prisão?—Respondeu que não sabia, nem suspeitava.

Foi mais interrogado por ordem de quem foi elle réo acompanhar ao Exmo. Martim Francisco Ribeiro de Andrada, quando foi mandado para o Rio de Janeiro? —Respondeu que foi por portaria do ex-Governo Provisorio desta provincia.

Foi mais interrogado se elle réo teve alguma ordem do dito Exmo. Martim Francisco para o acompanhar até ao Rio de Janeiro?—Respondeu que no Bananal teve do mesmo para o acompanhar até ao Rio e que essa ordem lhe foi annunciada pelo capitão Joaquim José de Almeida.

Foi mais interrogado se essa ordem lhe foi dada á ordem de Sua Alteza Real ou não.—Respondeu que a ordem lhe foi dada sem nomear-se o nome de Sua Alteza Real.

Foi mais interrogado se, no Rio elle réo teve alguma ordem para ficar ou para retirar-se? —Respondeu que não teve ordem alguma para ficar, nem para se retirar, e que jantando em casa do Exmo. Martim Francisco, lhe perguntou depois de acabado o jantar se queria mais alguma cousa e que lhe respondêra que nada mais queria

Foi mais interrogado com que licença elle réo voltou para esta cidade?—Respondeu que voltou com a mesma portaria com que tinha ido.

Foi mais interrogado se no Rio de Janeiro o capitão Joaquim José de Almeida não lhe intimou, a elle réo, a ordem do Exmo. Ministro da Guerra para que se não retirasse sem expressa ordem de Sua Alteza Real? Respondeu que não se lhe intimou ordem alguma.

Foi o réo insistido para que falasse a verdade, porquanto a parte accusatoria diz que o capitão Joaquim José de Almeida no Bananal lhe intimou que, á ordem de Sua Alteza Real, acompanhasse o Exmo. Martim Francisco até ao Rio e que ahi lhe intimou por mandato do Exmo· Ministro da Guerra que se não retirasse para esta cidade sem expressa ordem de Sua Alteza Real, como depoz em seu juramento, e assim que elle réo responda a verdade —Respondeu que era falsa a intimação da ordem, de que se faz menção, de Sua Alteza Real, tanto no caminho como no Rio de Janeiro.

Foi mais interrogado se tinha alguma defesa que allegar e provar?—Respondeu que, como não sabia, queria que este

Conselho lhe concedesse tres dias para apresentar por escripto a sua defesa.

E por esta forma e maneira houve o presidente do Conselho estes interrogatorios por findos, os quaes sendo por mim lidos ao réo os achou conformes ao que respondera, e que nada mais tinha que accrescentar, mudar e diminuir, em fé do que se assigna com os officiaes interrogantes, e eu José Correia Pacheco e Silva, Auditor, que o escrevi· —*Simões*—*Cantinho*— *José Fernandes da Silva.*

_____

## DESPACHO

E sendo ouvido por este Conselho o requerimento que fez o réo de se lhe conceder tres dias para apresentar a sua defesa por escripto, foi deliberado que se lhe concedesse, de que fiz este termo que todos assignam, e eu José Correia Pacheco e Silva, Auditor, que o escrevi.— *Joaquim José de Moraes Abreu,* presidente.—O auditor *José Correia Pacheco e Silva.*—*João Pereira Simões,* interrogante.—*Matheus Fernandes Cantinho,* interrogante. — *António José Bordini,* sargento-mór. — *Francisco da Silva Prado.*—*Segismundo Norio de Lima.*—*João Rodrigues de Camargo Pires.*—*Joaquim José da Silva.*—*Salvador Pires da Silva.*

_____

## 3.ª SESSÃO

Aos 5 dias do mez de Outubro de 1822, terceira sessão deste Conselho, tendo sido na antecedente concedido ao réo o prazo de tres dias, como havia requerido, para apresentar por escripto a sua defesa, mandou o presidente do Conselho vir o réo, afim de que apresentasse a dita sua defesa, o que elle assim cumpriu e disse que nada mais tinha a requerer; cuja defesa, acompanhada de tres documentos, é a que adeante se segue, de que fiz este termo eu, José Correia Pacheco e Silva, Auditor, que o escrevi.

_____

Artigos que em sua defesa apresenta o réo José Fernandes da Silva, capitão da 2.ª companhia do 2.º regimento de cavallaria da 2.ª linha desta cidade.

### 1.º

A culpa que se accumula ao Réo é, no dizer da testemunha capitão Joaquim José de Almeida, que intimára ordem do Prin-

cipe ao réo para acompanhar o Ill.ᵐᵒ Coronel Martim Francisco
Ribeiro de Andrada para o Rio de Janeiro, o que é falso, que
tal não houve, porquanto pelo documento n. 3 se mostra provado
que na mesma portaria já estava a dita ordem, dada pelo ex-
Governo Provisorio desta Provincia para o dito acompanhamento
até aonde o dito Ill.ᵐᵒ Coronel o despedisse.

## 2.º

Com o mesmo documento n. 3 prova o Réo que ia debaixo
das ordens daquelle Ill.ᵐᵒ Coronel já dito, para acompanhal-o e
obedecer-lhe em tudo quanto elle mandasse e ir até aonde o
mesmo o quizesse levar, até elle o despedir, o que o Réo tudo
cumpriu com humildade, respeito e obediencia, tanto para cumprir com as ordens do ex-Governo, como tambem pelo respeito
que era do seu dever ter ao mesmo Coronel.

## 3.º

Logo por este mesmo se mostra não haver necessidade, nem
precisão de se lhe intimar ordem segunda, superior, quando elle
debaixo da mesma em que ia sempre foi prompto para tudo
quanto se lhe ordenava.

## 4.º

E como por esta se mostra ser esta testemunha falsa, pelo
mesmo modo se deve julgar em tudo o mais do seu depoimento,
ficando este de nenhum effeito, visto o defeito de faltar nella á
verdade, por cujo motivo deve ser julgado, espera, por nullo
todo o seu depoimento.

## 5.º

Outrosim, que depois que cheguei ao logar destinado com
o dito Illᵐᵒ Coronel deveria usar de outra qualquer politica ou
obrigação que me competisse praticar e não pratiquei, foi por
ignorancia e falta de conhecimento, motivo este por que devo
ser desculpado no caso de que alguma houvesse.

## 6.º

Porque as tropas de milicias são compostas, em sua
maior parte, de homens do commercio e muitos com falta de
conhecimentos, que a sua maior occupação é tratar do seu negocio e é do que vivem e ganham para sustentaiem a si e suas

familias e ss fardarem e tudo o mais que é necessario, motivos estes que são bastantes para pouco conhecimento terem do regulamente e mais outros que necessarios sejam.

7.º

Pelo documento n.º 1 prova o Réo ser homem surdo, que ouve muito mal, bastante motivo este para que não fosse encarregado de tal diligencia.

8.º

Pelo documento n.º 2 prova o Réo estar occupado no emprego de juiz almotacel nesta cidade, quando foi chamado pelo ex-Governo Provisorio desta provincia para sahir em diligencia, como foi e declara o documento n.º 3.

9.º

Pelo documento n.º 3 prova o Réo que recebeu a dita portaria e seguiu, cumprindo o que nella determina, ás ordens do Ill.mo Coronel e o acompanhou até á corte do Rio de Janeiro, e porque o mesmo lhe dissera que não precisava mais delle Réo, regressou logo dahi; apromptou-se e regressou para esta com a mesma portaria, procurando dar parte da sua commissão cumprida ao ex-Governo, como fez, e apresentou-se no corpo do seu regimento, a saber, continuando com a commissão que lhe tinham encarregado de juiz almotacel até o fim do tempo destinado, como prova com o documento n.º 2, já dito, e em cuja deligencia não venceu soldo.

10.º

Pois o Réo é obediente e humilde e os seus desejos sempre foram e são cumprir com as ordens dos seus superiores e, se preciso for, derramar o ultimo pingo do seu sangue em defesa de Sua Alteza Real, e se lhe falta alguma cousa é por innocencia e iguorancia.

11.º

E por isso espera neste illustre e illuminado Conselho que, vendo as razões allegadas pelo Réo em sua defesa e os documentos n.ºs 1, 2 e 3, que junto a este offerece, e a muita ignorancia que nas tropas da 2.ª linha pela maior parte gira, mereça o Réo toda a desculpa de alguma falta que teve e seja solto e livre. O que espera ser tambem confirmado, pelas mesmas razões, no illustre e nobre tribunal do Conselho Supremo Militar. E. F. P

P. Receb. compr. de Just. 5 de Outubro de 1822.

*José Fernandes da Silva.*

## DOCUMENTO N.º 1

Ill.ᵐᵒ e Ex.ᵐᵒ Snr':—Diz o capitão José Fernandes da Silva que, para bem de sua justiça, se lhe faz preciso que o tenente coronel Joaquim José de Moraes Abreu, commandante que foi do esquadrão de cavallaria da 2.ª linha, dos Leaes Paulistanos que marcharão para a corte ao Rio de Janeiro, lhe atteste se o Supplicante foi reservado da dita marcha por andar surdo e ouvir pouco, e porque o não pode fazer sem licença, portanto,

P. a V. Ex.ª seja servido mandar que, á vista deste, o dito tenente coronel lhe atteste o que verdade for.

E. R. M.

N.º 36.

Pg. 40 reis de sello, S. Paulo, 23 de Outubro de 1822.

*Marques.*

DESPACHO:

Atteste, querendo. Quartel-General de S. Paulo, 19 de Setembro de 1822.

*Souza.*

## ATTESTADO

Joaquim José de Moraes Abreu, cavalheiro da Ordem de Christo, Tenente Coronel do 1.º Regimento da 2.ª Linha desta cidade e Commandante do mesmo Regimento etc.

Attesto que o supplicante José Fernandes da Silva, capitão da 2.ª companhia do 2.º regimento de cavallaria da 2.ª linha, me foi informado pelo seu chefe, o brigadeiro Joaquim José Pinto de Moraes Leme, em officio datado de 25 de Janeiro proximo passado, que não podia marchar com o esquadrão de cavallaria da 2.ª linha dos Leaes Paulistanos para a corte do Rio de Janeiro, que eu commandei, em razão de ser surdo. E' o que posso informar e attestar em observancia do despacho retro. Quartel de S. Paulo, em 20 de Setembro de 1822.—*Joaquim José de Moraes Abreu.*

---

## DOCUMENTO N. 2

Illmos. Snrs. do Nobre Senado:—Diz o capitão José Fernandes da Silva que elle supplicante, para bem de sua justiça, necessita que o escrivão desse Senado lhe passe por certidão o dia, mez e anno em que foi feito juiz almotacel e o dia em que tomou posse da vara no presente anno, e porque o não pode fazer sem despacho, portanto,

P. a V. S.ª se dignem mandar passar a dita certidão, em termos de fé e se é verdade que até ao presente se acha com a dita vara,

E. R. M.

N. 35

Pg. 40 réis de sello. S. Paulo, 3 de Outubro de 1822.—*Marques.*

#### DESPACHO

Accordam em vereação que passe em termos. S. Paulo, 11 Setembro de 1822.—*Penteado—Safino—Bueno.*

---

### CERTIDÃO

João Nepomuceno de Almeida, escrivão da Camara desta cidade e seu termo etc.—Certifico que a fls. 84 do livro actual de vereações se acha o termo de vereança no qual se acha a nomeação que a Camara fez ao supplicante, no dia 18 de Maio deste corrente anno, para servir o cargo de juiz almotacel nesta cidade, no triennio que seguia dalli em deante, e para seu companheiro o capitão Francisco da Silva Prado; e no dia 22 do dito mez tomaram ambos posse, como consta do livro competente, a fls. 8 verso, e tem o supplicants servido o dito emprego até hoje, 11 do corrente mez de Setembro, dia em que tomou posse o novo eleito, que o rendeu. O referido é verdade e aos ditos livros me reporto, e passo a presente em comprimento do despacho retro do Senado da Camara, que assigno. S. Paulo, 11 de Setembro de 1822.—*João Nepomuceno de Almeida.*

## DOCUMENTO N. 3

### PORTARIA DO GOVERNO PROVISORIO

O Governo Provisorio de S. Paulo manda declarar ao senhor capitão José Fernandes da Silva que, com o cabo de esquadra Felisberto Dias de Camargo e os soldados Antonio Joaquim da Silva e Francisco Pereira Bueno, deve acompanhar ao senhor coronel Martim Francisco Ribeiro de Andrada até á extrema desta provincia e dahi para deante até ao logar de onde o despedir o dito senhor coronel, ás ordens de quem marcham ; e aos senhores capitães-móres e commandantes das villas do Norte ordena o mesmo Governo que prestem ao dito senhor capitão José Fernandes da Silva os auxilios de que precisar a bem da sua commissão, principalmente cavalgaduras para si e para as praças que o acompanham, as quaes serão por elle pagas á razão de 100 réis a legua.

Palacio do Governo de S. Paulo, 30 de Maio de 1822.— *Oyenhausen—Pinto—Müller*

N. 612

Pg. 40 réis de sello. S. Paulo, 14 de Setembro de 1822.—*Azevedo Marques.*

E logo nesta mesma terceira sessão foi deliberado uniformemente que se procedesse á acareação do réo com a primeira testemunha capitão Joaquim José de Almeida, para melhor investigar-se a culpa imputada ao mesmo réo ; em consequencia do que o presidente do Conselho o mandou vir em sua plena liberdade e a testemunha capitão Joaquim José de Almeida, a quem deferiu o juramento dos Santos Evangelhos para debaixo delles dizer a verdade do que souber e lhe fôr perguntado pelos officiaes interrogantes, o major João Pereira Simões e o capitão Matheus Fernandes Cantinho, de que fiz este termo eu, José Correia Pacheco e Silva, que o escrevi.

## ACAREAÇÃO DO REO

Foi o réo interrogado separadamente se estava certo nas respostas que deu ás perguntas que se lhe fizeram e que lhe foram lidas e se as confirmava.—Respondeu que estava certo e as confirmava.

Foi perguntada separadamente a dita primeira testemunha se estava certo em seu depoimento, que deu neste Conselho, e se acaso o ratificava, sendo-lhe primeiro lido.—Respondeu que estava certo e que o ratificava, tanto assim que fez a primeira intimação ao réo na freguezia do Bananal, em casa do tenente Barbosa, onde pernoitaram, e a segunda fez no Rio de Janeiro, em casa do Exmo. José Bonifacio de Andrada e Silva, no mesmo dia em que elle testemunha e o réo chegaram áquella cidade, logo depois que elle testemunha se apresentou ao Exmo. Ministro da Guerra e ao Exmo Governador das Armas, em cujo acto o primeiro lhe deu a ordem, e fez as ditas intimações, sem que estivessem presentes outras pessoas.

Foi mais interrogado o réo, em presença da testemunha, como negava que a mesma lhe fez a primeira e segunda intimação da ordem para se não retirar da córte sem expressa licença de Sua Alteza Real, quando a mesma testemunha affirma que as fez?— Respondeu que a testemunha no Bananal lhe intimou que acompanhasse ao Exmo. Martim Francisco até o Rio, á ordem do mesmo e não de Sua Alteza Real, e que no Rio não lhe fez intimação alguma para que se não retirasse sem licença de Sua Alteza Real.

Ao que acudiu a testemunha dizendo que era verdade que no Bananal fez a intimação que acompanhasse ao Exmo. Martim Francisco até o Rio, á ordem de Sua Alteza Real, e que no Rio a fez para que se não retirasse sem expressa licença de Sua Alteza Real.—Ao que acudiu o réo dizendo que se reportava ao que já tinha dito e respondido e que nada mais tinha a dizer, porque era a verdade.—Ao que acudiu a testemunha que era verdade que intimara a ordem ao réo, pois tambem teve a mesma ordem.

E por esta forma houve o presidente do Conselho esta acareação por finda e acabada, de que fiz este termo, que assignam os officiaes interrogantes, e rèo, a testemunha e eu, José Correia Pacheco e Silva. Auditor, que o escrevi.—*Simões—Cantinho— José Fernandes da Silva—Joaquim José de Almeida.*

E logo nesta mesma terceira sessão deste Conselho foi pelo mesmo deliberado, depois de ser por mim Auditor relatado, que se lavrasse a sentença, de que fiz este termo eu José Correa Pacheco e Silva, Auditor, que o escrevi.

---

## SENTENÇA

Vendo-se nesta cidade e quartel das tropas da guarnição da mesma o processo verbal do réo capitão José Fernandes da Silva, parte accusatoria, testemunhas sobre ella perguntadas, interrogatorios feitos ao mesmo réo e sua acareação com a primeira testemunha capitão Joaquim José de Almeida, decidiu-se uniformemente que se não acha provada a culpa de desobediencia que é imputada ao réo, por isso que sómente a primeira testemunha depoz que lhe intimára as ordens primeira e segunda vez, cujas intimações constantemente tem negado o réo. vindo por esta razão a não haver prova bastante para a condemnação; portanto o absolvem.

Quartel das tropas da cidade de S. Paulo aos 5 de Outubro de 1822.—O auditor *José Corrêa Pacheco e Silva.—Joaquim José de Moraes Abreu*, presidente.—*João Pereira Simões*, interrogante.—*Antonio José Bordini*, vogal.—*Matheus Fernandes Coutinho*, interrogante.—*Francisco da Silva Prado*, vogal.— *Segismundo Norio de Lima*, vogal.—*João Rodrigues de Camargo Pires*, vogal.—*Joaquim José da Silva*, vogal.—*Salvador Pires da Silva*, alferes.

Confirmam a sentença.—Rio, 14 de Novembro de 1822.—*Barão de Bagé.— Pinto Guedes. — Oliveira. — Portelli.— Souza.—Veiga.*

A. Piza.

---

# Documentos sobre a Independencia

## 1821—1823

---

Officio da Camara de S. Paulo ao marechal Arouche, communicando-lhe a sua escolha para ir ao Rio de Janeiro levar a representação que a Camara e o povo desta cidade fizeram ao Principe Regente.

Illmo. e Exmo. Snr.—Sendo de absoluta necessidade que vá á côrte do Rio de Janeiro um deputado pela Camara desta cidade a representar a Sua Alteza Real a dignidade e interesses desta provincia, que se identificam com os de todo o Brasil, e sendo incontestavel que em V. Exa., além dos sentimentos de patriota benemerito, se acham como epilogadas todas as qualidades e virtudes que constituem o homem honrado, em sessão de hoje o nomeiam e de bom grado o elegem para tão alta e ponderosa commissão, como verá do accordam constante da copia inclusa, louvando-se, além disto, nos illustrissimos senhores deputados do governo provisorio, o coronel Martim Francisco Ribeiro de Andrada Machado e Silva e o coronel Antonio Leite Pereira da Gama Lobo, a mesma Camara se lisonjeará assaz de que V. E.ª se queira della encarregar, assim como lhe assegura sua sincera e cordial gratidão. A pessoa de V. E.ª guarde Deus muitos annos. S. Paulo, em vereação de 22 de Dezembro de 1821. Illmo. e Exmo. Snr. Marechal José Arouche de Toledo Rendon.—*José de Almeida Ramos.—Antonio de Siqueira Moraes.—Antonio da Silva Prado.—Antonio Cardoso Nogueira.—Amaro José de Moraes* (1).

---

(1) Este officio foi substituido pelo seguinte:
«Illmo. e Exmo. Snr.—Sendo de absoluta necessidade que vá á côrte do Rio de Janeiro uma deputação pela Camara desta cidade a representar a Sua Alteza Real a dignidade e os interesses desta provincia, que se identificam com os de todo o Brazil, e sendo incontestavel que em V. E.ª, além dos sentimentos de patriota benemerito, se acham como epilogadas todas as qualidades e virtudes que constituem o homem honrado, em sessão de hoje o nomeiam e de bom grado o elegem para tão alta e ponderosa commissão, como verá do accordam constante da copia inclusa; louvando-se além disto, ao excellentissimo senhor conselheiro José Bonifacio de Andrada e Silva e senhor coronel Antonio Leite Pereira da Gama Lobo, deputados do governo provisorio, a mesma Camara se lisonjeará assas de que V. E.ª se queira della encarregar, assim como lhe assegura sua sincera e cordial gratidão. S. Paulo, em Camara de 22 de Dezembro de 1821. A pessoa de V. E.ª guarde Deus muitos annos.—*José de Almeida Ra-*

Officio da Camara de S. Paulo ao conselheiro José Bonifacio de Andrada e Silva

Ill.<sup>mo</sup> e Ex.<sup>mo</sup> Snr.: — A Camara desta capital, havendo tomado em consideração o melindroso objecto de nossas circumstancias politicas e tendo visto com prazer a resolução tomada pelo nosso E.<sup>mo</sup> Governo de enviar a Sua Alteza Real uma deputação, cujo objecto é rogar-lhe que não desampare este reino do Brazil, e querendo tambem de sua parte cooperar em todas as medidas tendentes a desviar deste paiz os terriveis males que o ameaçam, resolveu, por accordam lavrado em sessão de 22 de Dezembro, enviar tambem, em nome de todos os habitantes desta cidade, uma deputação a Sua Alteza Real, composta de tres cidadãos.

A Camara, intimamente convencida de que em nenhum outro cidadão se acham reunidas, como em V. Ex.ª, as circumstancias e qualidades necessarias para o pleno desempenho de tão importante commissão, resolveu encarregal-a em primeiro logar a V. Ex.ª, em segundo ao coronel Antonio Leite Pereira da Gama Lobo e em terceiro ao marechal Arouche.

Confiada, pois, no exaltado patriotismo que tanto caracteriza a V. Ex.ª e de que tem dado tanto exuberantes provas, a Camara espera que V. Ex.ª não se negará a fazer mais este serviço a sua patria e que, chegando á augusta presença de Sua Alteza Real, lhe expressará com toda a energia, propria do caracter do um paulista honrado, nossos puros e ardentes votos e a firme resolução em que nos achamos de sustentarmos a todo o custo o seu real decoro e a dignidade e independencia do Brazil. Deus Guarde a V. Ex.ª por muitos annos. S. Paulo, em Camara de 2 de Janeiro de 1822. Ill.<sup>mo</sup> e Ex.<sup>mo</sup> Sr. Conselheiro José Bonifacio de Andrada e Silva.—*José de Almeida Ramos.— Antonio de Siqueira Moraes.—Antonio da Silva Prado.—Antonio Cardoso Nogueira.—Amaro José de Moraes.*

---

*mos.—Antonio de Siqueira Moraes.—Antonio Cardoso Nogueira.—Antonio da Silva Prado.—Amaro Jose de Moraes.* (*)

---

(*) Ha quem affirme que a substituição de Martim Francisco por José Bonifacio nesta delegação mandada pelo governo de S. Paulo ao Principe Regente, foi resolvida á ultima hora e nas vesperas da partida da delegação para o Rio, entretanto, por este documento se verifica que a troca de Martim por seu irmão foi decidida com grande antecedencia e feita no dia 22, muito cedo, tanto que deu tempo á Camara para se reunir nesse mesmo dia e expediu novo diploma ao marechal Arouche, em que já apparece o nome de Martim Francisco substituido pelo de José Bonifacio. Vide *Revista do Instituto Historico de S. Paulo*, vol. V, pags.

Copia da Portaria citada

Manda Sua Alteza Real o Principe Regente, pela Secretaria de Estado dos Negocios do Reino, participar ao Governo Provisorio da provincia de S. Paulo que lhe foi presente o seu officio de 24 de Dezembro proximo passado, e como succedesse estar a partir para Lisboa o correio *Infante Dom Sebastião* por elle o mesmo Senhor o remetteu a Sua Magestade para ser presente ás Côrtes Nacionaes, de cuja sabedoria espera Sua Alteza Real as promptas e acertadas providencias que exigem as necessidades do Brazil e que este requer como indispensaveis para o progresso de sua prosperidade e união dos dois reinos, que tão ardentemente deseja Sua Alteza promover e consolidar para ventura geral da monarchia. Palacio do Rio de Janeiro, em 4 de Janeiro de 1822.—*Francisco José Vieira.* (1)

Officio do Governo Provisorio á Camara da cidade de S. Paulo, sobre o Principe Regente ficar no Brazil

Havendo o Governo Provisorio desta provincia representado a Sua Alteza Real, o serenissimo senhor Principe Regente deste reino, em officio de 24 de Dezembro proximo passado, o quanto convinha não só ao Brasil, mas tambem á monarchia em geral, que o mesmo Augusto Senhor não se retire para Portugal e muito menos ainda para ir indecorosamente viajar por Hespanha, França e Inglaterra, como haviam determinado as Côrtes Geraes e Extraordinarias da nação, ou que ao menos Sua Alteza não partisse sem que chegassem ao Rio de Janeiro os deputados deste Governo e dessa Camara, que em nome do Governo e do povo da provincia lhe iam requerer; Sua Alteza respondeu a este governo pela portaria de 4 do corrente, expedida pela Secretaria de Estado dos Negocios do Reino, da copia inclusa, certificando que já ia remetter aquelle officio do Governo a Sua Magestade, nosso amado soberano e seu augusto pae, para ser presente ás Côrtes e se darem as providencias que exigem as necessidades do Brasil e que este requer.

O Governo se apressa em communicar esta noticia a Vossas-Mercês para sua intelligencia e para que lhe dêm a maior notoriedade possivel, por isso que essa Camara e todo o povo paulistano muito apreciam a permanencia de Sua Alteza Real

---

(1) No dia 19 de Janeiro a Camara mandou apregoar pelas ruas de S. Paulo o conteúdo desta portaria e affixal-a nos logares mais publicos da cidade, para conhecimento dos povos.

neste reino, como base fundamental da prosperidade do mesmo e
da união dos tres reinos.
Deus guarde a Vossas-Mercês. Palacio do Governo de S.
Paulo, 16 de Janeiro de 1822.—*João Carlos Augusto de Oyenhausen*, presidente.—*Martim Francisco Ribeiro de Andrade,* secretario.—*Lazaro José Gonçalves*, secretario.—Senhores Juiz de
de Fora pela Lei Presidencial e Officiaes da Camara de S.
Paulo.

OFFICIO DA CAMARA DE S. PAULO A JOSÉ BONIFACIO, FELICITANDO-O
PELA SUA ELEVAÇÃO AO CARGO DE MINISTRO DE ESTADO

Illmo. e Exmo. e Snr.:—Sendo incontestavelmente obra dos
cuidados e luzes de V. Ex.ᵃ a felicidade de que gosa esta provincia, saudosa até agora pela auzencia de seu digno filho e
vigilante pae, teria demais a lamentar hoje com justiça sua or-
phandade se, por um lado, não attendesse á gloria de que se
vê coberta pelo honoroso decreto com que o grande e incomparavel Regente do Brasil se dignou coroar o merito reconhecido
de V. Ex.ᵃ e por outro não soubesse, generosa, sacrificar seu
interesse ao bem geral de todo o Brasil e da nação inteira.
Sendo estes, Exmo. Senhor, os sentimentos puros de que
está possuida a Camara desta cidade, ella cheia de prazer, vae
por motivo tão plausivel dar a V. Ex.ᵃ os devidos parabens ou
antes os dá a si mesma, congratulando-se sobremaneira com sua
nova honra. Digne-se V. Ex.ᵃ acolher benigno aquelles em seu
vasto coração, assim como reconhecer sinceros seus ardentes votos pela saude e vida de V. Ex.ᵃ, que Deus guarde como nos
é mister. S. Paulo, em vereação de 30 de Janeiro de 1822.
Illmo. e Exmo. Snr. José Bonifacio de Andrada e Silva.—*Bento José Leite Penteado.—José Mariano Bueno.—José Pedro da
Cunha.—Luiz Manoel da Cunha Bastos.*

OFFICIO DO GOVERNO PROVISORIO Á CAMARA DA CIDADE DE S.
PAULO, COMMUNICANDO A CHEGADA DA DEPUTAÇÃO PAULISTA
AO RIO DE JANEIRO.

O Governo Provisorio, havendo recebido de seus deputados na côrte do Rio de Janeiro, o excellentissimo senhor conselheiro José Bonifacio de Andrada e Silva, ministro e secretario de Estado dos Negocios deste Reino e Extrangeiros, e o
senhor coronel Antonio Leite Pereira da Gama Lobo, um officio datado a 21 de Janeiro proximo passado, escripto e assi-

gnado tambem pelo deputado dessa Camara, o senhor marechal José Arouche de Toledo Rendon, em que participam sua chegada a aquella côrte e o muito bem que foram recebidos por Suas Altezas Reaes; o serenissimo senhor Principe Regente e sua Augusta Consorte, pedindo que esta participação seja communicada a essa Camara, o Governo remette a Vossas Mercês um extracto do dito officio para sua intelligencia e lhes dá o parabem do alto conceito em que Sua Alteza Real tem os honrados e fieis paulistas e da consideração que lhe mereceram os seus deputados,

O Governo manda agora publicar por bando que Sua Alteza Real, o serenissimo senhor Principe Regente, por portaria de 17 do mez de Janeiro, expedida pela Secretaria do Estado dos Negocios deste Reino, lhe mandou participar que resolveu no dia 9 do precitado mez suspender a sua sahida para Portugal, por entender, á vista das differentes representações que se dirigiram á sua real presença, que assim convém ao bem geral dos povos e ao importante fim da união dos dois reinos, o que igualmente o Governo manda participar a Vossas Mercês; remettendo-lhes, por cópia, a citada portaria. Deus guarde a Vossas Mercês.

Palacio do Governo de S. Paulo, 4 de Fevereiro de 1822. *João Carlos Augusto de Oyenhausen*, presidente.—*Martim Francisco Ribeiro de Andrada*, secretario.—*Miguel José de Oliveira*, secretario.—Senhores Juiz de Fóra pela Lei Presidente e Officiaes da Camara desta cidade.

———

Copia do extracto da carta dos senhores deputados deste Governo e da Camara, de 21 de Janeiro, em que participam sua chegada á côrte do Rio de Janeiro e acolhimento que lhes fizeram Suas Altezas.

. . . . . . . . . . . . . . . . . . . . . . . . .
. . . . . Chegaram felizmente a Sepetiba, levando em sua companhia o desembargador João Evangelista, que na villa de S. Sebastião desamparou a barca de vapor, em que ia, para separar-se de alguns mal intencionados que nella viajavam.

Na côrte se desejava a chegada dos senhores deputados como um bem geral. A Princeza Real estava em Santa Cruz, com seus filhos (1), em consequencia dos acontecimentos dos dias 11 e 12 e com bastante cuidado do seu esposo (2). Ella tinha

———

(1) D. Maria e D. Paula; D. Pedro só nasceu dahi a quatro annos.
(2) Revolta das tropas portuguezas no Rio, sob o commando do general Aviles.

mandado pôr em Sepetiba tres cavallos seus para serviços dos senhores deputados, com um piquete de dous soldados e um cabo para os acompanharem ao Rio de Janeiro, com ordem de se lhe dar aviso logo que os senhores deputados chegassem, e não obstante isso já tinha ido de passeio a Sepetiba no dia 16.

Chegou a Sepetiba a deputação em o dia 17 e, como achasse ahi um carro de posta em que tinha ido um particular, nelle partiu para Santa Cruz a deputação do governo logo chegou, mas em meio do caminho toparam Sua Alteza Real, a Princeza, que a ella se dirigia. Conversou com os senhores deputados com summo contentamento e ainda depois de retirar-se para Santa Cruz tornou a voltar a trote e a galope e conversou muito em francez com o exmo. sr. José Bonifacio, sendo, porêm, mui notaveis expressões: «que estimaria muito que os senho- « res deputados vissem os seus brasileirinhos (eram seus au- « gusto filhos e nossos adoraveis patricios), além dos quaes ti- « nha um terceiro no ventre (1), e que os entregaria ao cuidado « dos honrados paulistas».

Esta estimavel Princeza mandou ordem a Sepetiba para que toda a despesa que alli fizessem os senhores deputados fosse á custa da mesma Senhora, favor que não foi acceito.

Tendo já chegado a Sepetiba, pelas 10 horas da noite, o terceiro deputado da Camara, o senhor marechal Arouche, á 1 hora da manhan do dia 18 partiram para a cidade e pelas 9 horas da noite, com os mesmos vestidos de viagem e por uma porta particular, foram falar em S. Christovam a Sua Alteza Real, o Serenissimo Senhor Principe Regente, por expressa ordem sua.

Sabendo então o exmo. sr. José Bonifacio de Andrada da sua nomeação para secretario de Estado dos Negocios do Interior e Extrangeiros, resistiu quanto poude ao amavel Principe, que assim o distinguia, e só acceitou na firme certeza de poder promover a felicidade deste reino.

No mesmo dia 17 chegou ao Rio de Janeiro o desembargador Josè Teixeira da Fonseca e Vasconcellos, vice-presidente do Governo Provisorio de Minas e deputado pela mesma provincia, e está de accôrdo com os sentimentos desta provincia, que são os mesmos de Sua Alteza Real, isto é, de salvar a existencia do Reino Unido, que alguns pretendem destruir com capa de zelo e de constituição.

Estava a entrar uma fragata, que se dizia ser da Bahia e trazer deputados daquella provincia a Sua Alteza Real.

A provincia do Rio de Janeiro está no maior enthusiasmo

(1 Mais uma princeza, nascida a 11 de Março de 1822.

pela boa causa. Nos acontecimentos do dia 11 pegaram o melhor de seis mil pessoas de todas as classes.

Quanto a noticias da Europa, dizem que está a chegar a tropa destinada para o Rio de Janeiro e que só poderia estar no Rio a 15 do mez de Fevereiro e que o ténente general Palmeirim a vem commandando como futuro general das armas da provincia do Rio de Janeiro». (1)

Resposta da Camara de S. Paulo ao officio do Governo Provisorio

Illmos. e Exmos. Snrs.:—Recebemos o officio de V. Ex.ᵃˢ de 4 do corrente mez de Fevereiro, em que nos participa terem recebido de seus deputados e dos desta Camara um officio assignado por todos, em que participam a V. Ex.ᵃ sua chegada áquella côrte do Rio de Janeiro e o muito bem que foram recebidos por Suas Altezas Reaes, o Serenissimo Senhor Principe Regente e Sua Augusta Consorte, pedindo que aquella participação fosse communicada a esta Camara, remettendo-nos V. Ex.ᵃˢ o extracto do dito officio para nossa intelligencia e dando-nos o parabem do alto conceito em que Sua Alteza Real tem os honrados e fieis paulistas e da consideração que lhe mereceram seus deputados.

Igualmente recebemos, por cópia, a portaria de 17 do mez de Janeiro, pela qual Sua Alteza Real manda participar a V. Ex.ᵃˢ que resolveu no dia 9 de Janeiro proximo passado suspender a sua sahida para Portugal, cuja participação, sendo para nós a mais agradavel, não desconhecemos dever em grande parte ás sabias reflexões de V. Ex.ᵃˢ em promover a união e felicidade do Reino Unido. Deus guarde a V. Ex.ᵃˢ S. Paulo em vereação de 9 de Fevereiro de 1822.—Illmos. e Exmos. Snrs. do Governo Provisorio —*Bento José Leite Penteado.— José Pedro da Cunha.—Antonio Safino da Fonseca.—Antonio da Silva Prado.—Luiz Manoel da Cunha Bastos.*

Edital da Camara de S. Paulo, mandando illuminar a cidade em regosijo do Principe Regente ter declarado que ficava no Brazil.

O Juiz de Fóra, pela lei presidente, Vereadores e Procurador do Senado da Camara, que servimos no corrente anno por eleição e approvação de Sua Alteza Real, que Deus guarde, etc-, etc.

(1) Está o extracto assignado pelo secretario do Governo Provisorio de S. Paulo, Manoel da Cunha Azevedo Coutinho Souza Chichorro.

Fazemos saber a todos os moradores desta cidade que o Ex.<sup>mo</sup> Governo Provisorio, de accordo com o Ex.<sup>m</sup> Bispo Diocesano, tem determinado render graças ao Omnipotente pela resolução que Sua Alteza Real tomou de suspender sua partida para Portugal, deliberando que na Cathedral desta cidade se faça um Triduo dos dias 21, 22 e 23 do corrente mez de Fevereiro. E porque é um dever dos honrados paulistas applaudir tão justo festejo, dando uma evidente prova de amor para com o seu Principe e do muito que lhe deve pelo grande conceito com que o mesmo Senhor tem distinguido e considerado esta provincia, ordenamos que nas referidas noites, acima declaradas, illuminem todas as frentes de suas casas, preenchendo assim os deveres de fieis subditos, honrados e agradecidos cidadãos. E, para que chegue á noticia de todos, mandámos lavrar o presente, que será publicado e affixado no logar do costume. Dado nesta cidade de S. Paulo, sob nosso signal e real sello, em vereança do 20 dia de Fevereiro de 1822. Eu, João Nepomuceno de Almeida, escrivão, o escrevi.—Logar do real sello.—*Bento Josè Leite Penteado*—*Antonio Safino da Fonseca*—*Antonio de Siqueira Moraes*—*Luiz Manoel da Cunha Bastos.*

---

REPRESENTAÇÃO QUE O POVO E TROPA DA CIDADE DE S. PAULO LEVARAM A SUA ALTEZA REAL, NA CORTE DO RIO DE JANEIRO, POR MEIO DA QUAL SE DÁ A CONTA E OS MOTIVOS POR QUE DEPUZERAM AOS DOUS MEMBROS DO GOVERNO PROVISORIO.

*Senhor.*—O povo e tropa da cidade de S. Paulo, não podendo soffrer por mais tempo o orgulho, despotismos e arbitrariedades do coronel Martim Francisco Ribeiro de Andrada, no dia 23 de Maio tomou a nobre resolução de sacudir o jugo desse máo paulista, depondo-o do logar de secretario e membro do Governo Provisorio desta Provincia, e juntamente ao brigadeiro Manoel Rodrigues Jordão, seu socio nos crimes.

O povo de S. Paulo soffria destes dous homens, que desgraçadamente haviam alliciado maioridade de votos (1) no governo para que todas as cousas fossem ditadas e feitas ao prazer dos seu

---

(1) O governo provisorio era no começo composto de 15 membros ; tendo José Bonifacio ido ao Rio de Janeiro e aceitado o cargo de ministro de D. Pedro, ficou o governo com 14 membros. Destes eram andradistas Martim Francisco, brigadeiro Jordão, coroneis Lazaro Gonçalves e Gama Lobo, Vergueiro, padres Ferreira Bueno e Felisberto Jardim e o professor André Gomes — 8 dos quaes 3 eram portugueses — Lazaro, Gama Lobo e André Gomes. O padre Paula Oliveira era neutro ; contrario aos Andradas eram 5 sómente — João Carlos, Muller, Oliveira Pinto, Quartim e Francisco Ignacio, dos quaes só o ultimo era brazileiro, mas educado em Portugal e militar do exercito portuguez.

caprichos para esmagarem os que lhes não eram affeiçoados, ou por honrados não os coadjuvavam nos seus intuitos. Via as auctoridades de todas as classes insultadas em suas pessoas com perigosissimos exemplos, invadidas as suas jurisdicções com evidente estorvo da recta administração da justiça e menoscabo das leis. No governo, por voto do sobredito secretario e seus illudidos parciaes, se julgaram causas civeis já prevenidas no fôro contencioso; mandaram-se suspender execuçães de sentenças, soltar presos com culpa formada, prender outros arbitrariamente, dar baixa na culpa de clerigos criminosos, cujo livramento pendia ordinaria e regularmente. só porque, amontoando crimes sobre crimes, estes iam denunciar cidadãos pacificos e de probidade, que não eram panegyristas das absolutas do mencionado secretario.

Quando, Real Senhor, alguns dos membros do governo se queria oppôr a tão arbitrarias resoluções ahi chegavam a ferver na bocca daquelle soberbo as ameaças e deixava, como muitas vezes deixou, para outras occasiões serem decididos, quando estivessem mais alguns membros do seu partido ou faltasse algum mais prudente e justo, negocios que a pluralidade de votos havia já decidido (1).

Os povos desta provincia, naturalmente pacificos e amadores da ordem, pretenderam livrar-se deste ·eu ingrato compatriota, fazendo util a si e á sua patria, reprimido pela presença e vigilancia de Vossa Alteza Real, sendo nomeado procurador desta provincia, mas este fructo da vontade e pensar geral apenas foi sonhado (2), para logo o mais vergonhoso suborno foi posto em pratica, com temor de largar o sceptro de ferro com que esmagava seus patricios, que tanto o haviam mimado.

Que vileza! Que ingratidão!

Para melhor exercitar as suas tyramnias, sendo reprimido algumas vezes na carreira dellas pelo commandante da força armada, o coronel Francisco Antonio de Souza Queisoz (3) tentou depôl-o e elevar a este logar um que, por ligações com seu con·socio Jordão e por outros motivos particulares, que por injuriosos se calam, lhe promettia coadjuvação em seus manejos terriveis.

Sendo fertil em recursos oppressores, mas não tendo possibilidade para os poder manter com forças pecuniarias quando as circumstancias o exigissem, ligou-se com o brigadeiro Manoel

Rodrigues Jordão, que indevidamente occupa os logares mais importantes e responsaveis da Junta e Thesouro desta provincia (1), e nelles opprime desapiedadamente seu concidadãos, exercitando sua pessima indole, bem conhecida por todos, e assim amparados um pelo outro tentaram e por muito tempo conseguiram seus pessimos designios.

Ultimamente, como o conselheiro João Carlos Augusto de Oeynhausen, actual presidente deste governo, fosse a mais forte barreira a seus attentados, procurou o ex-secretario cavilosamente e alcançou (bem claros os motivos e via (2), uma portaria que mandava immediatamente recolher a essa Corte o dito conselheiro. Esta noticia foi espalhada pela 1 hora da tarde do dia 23 do corrente e com a brevidade do relampago conheceram todos os paulistas a illusão em que estava Vossa Alteza Real (3), qual o auctor desta portaria e o risco que todos corriam sem o escudo de suas innocencias, e viram no mesmo momento exultar meia duzia de pessimos homens e aberto o abysmo debaixo dos pés dos habitantes honrados desta cidade e da provincia (4).

Representar era o meio proprio dos portuguezes, porem a mais pequena reflexão foi sufficientissima pera todos verem que baldado seria este meio porque acharia invenciveis estorvos preparados pela intriga, em optimas circumstancias de se aproveitar, e que nunca chegariam as nossas queixas e suspiros á presença de Vossa Alteza Real (5).

O mesmo pensamento, a mesma resolução, s? apoderou ao mesmo tempo de todos os bons paulistas, que ás 4 horas da mesma tarde se apresentaram na praça de S. Gonçalo (6), como cidadãos livres, e convocadas as auctoridades requereram a conservação do conselheiro João Carlos Augusto de Oeynhausen e a deposição immediata dos dous auctores de seus males.

O maior socego e a melhor ordem presidiram a este acto, o maior socego, a melhor ordem e geral contentamento têm sido a

---

1 O brigadeiro Jordão não occupava todos os cargos mais importantes. como aqui se diz, mas era unicamente thesoureiro da Junta da Fazenda, era rico e offerecia garantias para esse cargo.

2 A portaria é de 10 de Maio de 18.2, foi obtida por via de José Bonifacio, ministro, e motivada pelas tentativas recolonizadoras dos portuguezes.

3 *Paulistas* aqui quer dizer os signatarios dest. representação, poucos em numero e na maior parte militares. os melhores elementos da cidade se abstiveeram de tomar parte na *Bernarda* e o todo o interior se revoltou contra os bernardistas, collocaddo-se ao lado dos Andradas.

4 *Honrados* eram sómente os auctores da *Bernarda*, os que nella não tomaram parte e os povos do interior que reagiram contra ella á mão armada eram naturalmente os *deshonrados*.

5 Quer dizer que D. Pedro estava de tal modo assediado por José Bonifacio, seu ministro, que não receberia sinão as noticias e queixas que José Bonifacio se dignasse consentir que chegassem a sua presença !

6 Depois Praça Municipal e hoje Largo do Dr. João Mendes.

digna partilha do povo desta cidade desde aquelle memoravel dia. O crime, que é o maior inimigo de si mesmo, cada vez mais tem justificado nossos procedimentos porque, sendo enviado da parte da Camara, a pedido do povo e tropa (1), o procurador da mesma ao governo para representar a vontade do povo e tropa, o coronel Martim, sem previa e necessaria auctorisação do governo, com injuriosas palavras maltratou aquelle procurador e na pessoa delle todo o povo e tropa, cujo representante era (2), manifestando assim a feridade e a imprudencia da sua alma, desattento um povo que em governo constitucional gosa de supremos direitos; mas elle já se havia preparado para este insulto maltratando o official da guarda e ameaçando-o por cumprir seu dever pondo-se em armas quando ouviu o toque de rebate (3).

Tentou, este mesmo homem, mandando emissarios a diversas villas desta provincia, sublevar o povo dellas, para lhe tornarem a entregar a mal obtida auctoridade de que tanto abusára (4), tendo em nénhuma monta o sangue de seus concidadãos (5), as desgraças e horrores que seriam consequencia deste attentado, se não fosse uma só a opinião de todos os paulistas contra os seus verdugos (6).

O povo e a tropa de S. Paulo, que tem sempre dado sobejas e decisivas próvas de amor, lealdade, submissão e respeito aos seu Augustissimos Monarchas, que ouviu com prazer e enthusiasmo o grito de liberdade, conheceudo as verdadeiramente reaes virtudes de Vossa Alteza Real, recolhido em seu coração, o reconheceu desde o primeiro momento por seu legitimo Regente, que obedecendo a um simples aceno de Vossa Alteza Real, se prestou generoso com indiziveis incommodos em auxilio da justissima causa de Vossa Alteza Real (7), este mesmo povo e tropa, Real Senhor, é quem hoje implora submisso inteira aprovação

---

(1) Pouco povo e bastante tropa. como se verá das assignaturas.

(2) Chamava-se esse procurador Luiz Manoel da Cunha Bastos.

(3) Ouvindo o toque de rebate a guarda do palacio se armou por prudencia e cautela e Martim, censurando-a por isso, ordenou que se desarmasse, que esperasse os sediciosos sem armas e se retirasse a uma banda.

(4) O interior sublevou-se todo contra os *bernardistas* de S. Paulo. Um illustre ytúano, Antonio Pacheco da Fonseca, que assistiu ás peripecias da Bernarda e viu Pedro Taques, Oliveira Netto, Caetano Pinto e outros sediciosos na rua, com trabuco em punho, ameaçando e convocando as auctoridades municipaes e gente para a funcção, foi quem começou a rebellião em Ytú contra os bernardistas, propagando-se ella de Ytú para os outros logares.

(5) Martim Francisco nunca derramou o sangue de ninguem: se a referencia é feita ao supplicio de Chaguinhas, Cotindiba e outros sediciosos, enforcados em Santos, cabe a censura mais a João Carlos do que a qualquer outro dos 14 membros dos Governo Provisorio, porque era o seu presidente.

(6) A opinião da maioria dos paulistas era contra os signatarios desta representação, como bem mostra a confederação dos municipios contra a capital.

(7) A referencia para ser feita a remessa dos *Leaes Paulistanos* para o Rio, em principio de 1822, em defesa de D. Pedro contra os portuguezes do general Avilles.

de tudo quanto praticára com toda a justiça no dia 23 do corrente maio; esperançados e já certos nesta graça protestam a Vossa Alteza Real a maior adhesão, o mais cordial affecto e obediencia, affirmando ao mesmo tempo e jurando por tudo quanto ha de mais sagrado nos céus e na terra que desgraçada vae ser esta provincia, vae ser victima talvez da anarchia e dos horrores da guerra civil si Vosa Alteza Real, prudente e justo, não annuir á nossa representação e ás nossas supplicas, cujos fundamentos se offerecem a provar pelos meios legaes que Vossa Alteza Real julgar mais adequados. S. Paulo, 30 de Maio de 1822. —*Matheus*, bispo—*Manoel Joaquim Gonçalves de Andrade*, arcediago—*Antonio Marques Henriques*, conego cura da Sé — *Joaquim José dos Santos*, coronel—*Mariano Pinto Tavares*, vigario — O padre *Joaquim Manoel de Oliveira*—*Gaspar Ribeiro da Rosa Ramos*, sargento-mór reformado — *José Vaz de Carvalho*, brigadeiro—O sargento-mór *Salvador de Albuquerque Bueno*— *Antonio Joaquim da Silva*, vigario—*Antonio José Vaz*, coronel reformado—*Francisco Alves Ferreira do Amaral*, coronel do 2.° regimento de infanteria de milicias (1) *Jeronymo Pereira Chrispim*, tenente-coronel — *Antonio de Padua Gusmão*, tenente-coronel—*José Rodrigues Pereira de Oliveira Netto*, sargenso-mór do 1.° regimento de infanteria da 2.ª linha (2)—*Joaquim Moreira Cesar*, capitão—*Miguel Angelo da Silveira*, tenente-coronel reformado — *Bento Alberto da Gama e Sá*, tenente-coronel de cavallaria—*João Pereira Simões*, tenente-coronel—*José Joaqnim dos Santos Prado*, sargento-mór de milicias — *Bento José de Moraes*, capitão—*Gabriel Fernandes Cantinho*, capitão — *José Pereira Jorge*, quartel-mestre—*Antonio de Siqueira Moraes*, capitão—*Rafael José Machado*, capitão, *Luiz Manoel da Cunha Bastos*, capitão—*José Floriano Lara de Moraes*, sargento-mór—*Antonio Octavio Ferrão*, coronel de milicias —*Januario Antonio de Lima*, coronel reformado—*Joaquim José dos Santos*, capitão—*Pedro Taques de Almeida Alvim*, capitão (3)—*Francisco de Paula Macedo*, major—*Francisco Gonçalves dos Santos Cruz*, capitão—*Martinho José Marques*,capitão—*Manoel José da Costa Ribeiro*, sargento-mór —*Matheus Fernandes Cantinho*, capitão—*Antonio Cardoso Nogueira*, capitão—*Joaquim Alves Moreira*, capitão—*Caetano Pinto Ho-*

---

(1) Era militar activo, rico e com bom sequito, e foi um dos chefes mais energicos da *Bernarda*.

(2) Militar violento, não se limitou a tomar parte na *Bernarda*, mas sahiu á rua de trabuco na mão a reunir gente e intimidar o povo ordeiro.

(3) Foi dos mais violentos. No dia 23 de Maio, sahiu tambem á rua armado, fazendo proezas; enlouqueceu pouco tempo depois e falleceu em 1839, sem recaperar o juizo.

*mem*, capitão (1)—*Manoel José da Silva Castro*, capitão—*Joaquim Ignacio Ribeiro*, capitão—*Francisco de Paula Leite Prestes*, capitão—*Gregorio Ignacio Ferreira Nobre*, capitão e ajudante de ordens do governo (2)—O padre *Bernardo Conrado da Cunha*, capellão da Sé--*Manoel dos Santos Lima*, ajudante—*Ignacio José de Macedo*, tenente de cavallaria—*Francisco de Paula e Oliveira*, tenente--*José dos Santos Reis*, tenente—*Rafael de Oliveira Leme*, alferes—*Francisco Antonio de Oliveira Simões*, alferes—*Manoel Felippe de Araujo*, capitão—*Luiz Antonio de Assumpção*, capitão—*Francisco José de Azevedo*, capitão—*Manoel Joaquim Coelho*, capitão—*João Baptista Tavares*, alferes—*Manoel Felizardo de Carvalho Almeida*, capitão—*Francisco de Assis do Monte Camargo*, ajudante—*Joaquim Gonçalves Gomes*, cirurgião-mór da guarnição—*Ignacio José Antunes*, tenente—*João Rodrigues de Camargo Pires*, tenente—*Vicente Ferreira da Silva*, tenente—*Joaquim Antonio da Cunha*, alferes—*Antonio Fernandes da Motta*, alferes—*Manoel Joaquim da Cruz*, cadete—*Luiz Antonio do Valle Quaresma*, capitão—*Domingos Monteiro de Carvalho*, tenente—*Antonio Joaquim de Sampaio*, ajudante—*Antonio José Pereira dos Santos*, alferes—*Francisco Xavier Ferreira da Cunha*, cadete—*Joaquim Timotheo de Araujo*—*Paulo José Rodrigues*—*José Manoel da Costa Ribeiro*, capitão—*José Gonçalves de Oliveira*, alferes reformado—*Antonio Francisco Machado*, negociante—*Francisco Candido Sagalerva*, capitão—*Luiz Antonio Pinto do Rego*, ajudante—*Antonio Joaquim de Oliveira*, alferes —*Francisco Garcia Ferreira*, tenente—*Manoel José Gonçalves Sevilha*—*José da Fonseca Carvão e Camara*, capitão—*Antonio Gonçalves*, tenente—*Francisco José de Carvalho Faro*, alferes—*Francisco Severiano dos Santos Cardim*, tenente—*Francisco de Assis*, tenente—*Manoel José Chaves*—*José Antonio de Assumpção*, tenente—O padre *Francisco de Assis Ribeiro*—O padre *Ignacio Eduardo da Silva*—O padre *Antonio Joaquim de Araujo Leite*—O padre *Manoel Thomaz dos Santos*—O padre *Francisco Figueira de Assumpção*—O padre *Antonio Romualdo Freire de Vasconcellos*—*Antonio Mariano da Silva*, sachristão da Sé—O padre *Joaquim Antonio Rodrigues de Vasconcellos*, capellão da Sé—O padre *Joaquim José de Oliveira*, capellão da Sé—O padre *João Joaquim de Carvalho Pinto*—O padre *Hygino Francisco Teixeira de Negreiros*—*Joaquim Manoel de Moraes*, alferes—*José*

---

(1) Era commensal do coronel Francisco Alves Ferreira do Amaral e, como tal *bernardista enragé*.
(2) Ajudante de ordens do governo e mettido a chefiar a sedição na praça publica! Era marinheiro portuguez e fugiu para o Brasil, seguindo o exemplo da familia real.

*Ferreira Leite*, alferes—*Antonio José Pessoa*, sargento—*Manoel José Villaça*, alferes—*Jaime da Silva Telles*, tenente—*Eleuterio José Pinto*, tenente de cavallaria—*Constantino José dos Santos*, alferes—*Hermenegildo José dos Santos—Tristão Elime de Udeval—Domingos José de Oliveira Guimarães—Rodrigo José Barbosa—Antonio José de Sampaio Guimarães—Francisco Antonio Pinto Bastos*, tenente—*Joaquim José Florindo*, negociante—*Manoel Ribeiro de Araujo*, thesoureiro dos ausentes—*Antonio José Pereira de Castro—Gabriel José Soares—João Antonio Rosa—José Pinto Teixeira—Joaquim José Marques—Joaquim José Corrêa*, negociante—*Antonio Floriano Alves Alvim*, negociante—*José Joaquim de Carvalho—Ezequiel de Moraes Santos*, sargento—*Bernardo José de Senna*, furriel—*João Dias de Oliveira*, sargento—*Joaquim Franco*, sargento—*Francisco Xavier de Brito*, sargento—*Antonio Francisco de Arruda*, sargento —*Francisco Manoel de Borja*, sargento—*Francisco Alves Ribeiro*, sargento—*Ponciano Joaquim de Góes*, sargento— *João Teixeira de Sousa*, furriel—*José Franco Penteado*, furriel—*Antonio Rodrigues dos Paços*, cabo—*João de Santiago Xavier*, cabo—*João Soares de Siqueira*, cabo—*Joaquim Dias Duarte*, cabo—*José Antonio Corrêa*, cabo—*Joaquim de Sousa*, cabo—*Salvador Roque Gonçalves*, cabo—*João José da Paixão*, cabo—*José Manoel de Macedo*, cabo—*Manoel Joaquim Espiridião*, cabo—*José Ferreira de Brito—Francisco Gomes de Moraes*, negociante—*Manoel Rodrigues Pinto—Joaquim Antonio*, cabo—*Anacleto Elias*, cabo —*José Ventura Teixeira Pinto—Constantino José de Freitas Alvim—Manoel José Pestana—Thomaz Ribeiro das Dores Vaz—Francisco Alves—Bartholomeu Alves da Silva—Vicente Ferreira de Abreu—Francisco de Lima Pinto—Gregorio José de Almeida—Antonio Lourenço Fernandes—Amaro José Vieira Joaquim Pinto de Castro—José Gonçalves Corrêa—Benedicto dos Santos — Antonio Ribeiro de Escobar*, sargento — *Francisco Antonio Borba—Joaquim José da Jesus—Joaquim Ferreira de Magalhães—José de Sousa—Joaquim de Azevedo—Francisco da Silva Lisboa—Bento José de Almeida — José Francisco de Oliveira—Rafael Simões—Thomaz de Aquino—Francisco de Paula Salgado—Martinho José—Miguel Corrêa de Mesquita—José Leonardo—Luiz Pedroso—José Joaquim de Jesus—Joaquim Miguel —Antonio José da Cruz—Leonardo Severo do Espirito Santo— Theodoro Alves Pereira—Fernando Lebsck—Antonio Dias—Manoel Egydio—José Antonio Villares—José Marcellino—Francisco de Assis — Gabriel Alves Pereira — Antonio Manoel—João Ferreira — Manoel João Pio — José Francisco Justiniano Rangel Junior—Joaquim Xavier Pinheiro—Francisco de Paula Lustosa*

—*Manoel de Jesus*, furriel—*José Corrêa de Andrade*—*Antonio de Padua Costa*— *Joaquim José Lobo* — *Benedicto Antonio de Assumpção*—*Feliciano de Jesus*—*Silveirão da Paixão*—*Joaquim Luiz de Brito* — *Manoel Baptista* — *Ricardo Benedicto*, cabo — *Francisco Rodrigues Leite* — *Ignacio José Vianna* — *Manoel Felix Leite*—*José Fernandes*—*Antonio da Silva*—*Francisco Leite Maximiano*— *José Joaquim de Camargo* — *Francisco de Borges Penteado*—*Luiz Antonio Pereira da Paixão Monati*, negociante — *Manoel Joaquim da Paixão Teco*, negociante—*José Antonio Matheus*, negociante — *Antonio José dos Santos* — *Antonio de Paiva Azevedo*— *José Antonio*— *Joaquim Francisco Gonçalves*, cabo—*Joaquim Moreira de Almeida*—*Manoel Gomes de Gouvêa* — *Manoel Teixeira Ribeiro* — *Theophilo de Sousa Dromundo* — *Manoel Joaquim de Vasconcellos*, alferes—*João Homem Guedes Portilho*, alferes—*José Joaquim de Proença*—*Manoel das Neves de Jesus*, alferes—*José Arouche de Toledo*, furriel—*Jayme Antonio Rodrigues*, sargento — *Joaquim José de Almeida*, cadete— *José Maria de Oliveira*, cabo—*José Velloso de Oliveira*, porta-bandeira—*José Branco de Barros*, sargento—*Antonio Safino da Fonseca*, sargento-mór reformado — *Francisco Corrêa Bueno* — *João Theodoro Xavier*, tenente — *Manoel Euphrasio de Azevedo Marques*, escrivão da pagadoria — *Antonio Mariano de Azevedo Marques*, professor dos moços do côro da Sé—*José Teixeira de Carvalho e Silva*—O padre *Antonio da Costa Guimarães*—*Bento Barbosa Ortiz*, alferes—*Manoel Joaquim de Oliveira*—*José de Oliveira Prado* — *Francisco de Borja* — *José Mendes da Silva*, alferes—*Pedro Fernandes de Andrade*, tenente—*Justino Pereira dos Santos* — *Fernando José do Costa* — *Antonio Justiniano de Sousa*, negociante—*Manoel José de Rezende*—*João Frederico*—*Manoel Guilherme da Silva Cruz*, sargento—*Felicio Antonio*—*Manoel José Rodrigues da Silva*—*Joaquim Elias da Silva*, porta-bandeira—*Pedro Antonio da Encarnaçãe*—*Joaquim José de Andrade Aquino*, escrivão do hospital militar—*Manoel Antonio Soares de Campos*—*Manoel Domingues Martins da Sousa*—*Bernardo Franco de Azevedo* — *João Vicente de Brito*, sargento — *Severino Pinto da Silva*, capitão — *José de Freitas Saldanha*, capitão de dragões milicianos—*Joaquim José da Silva*, alferes—*Manoel Ferreira Duarte*, negociante *Joaquim da Silva Abreu Vianna*, alferes—*José Antonio Pereira*, alferes—*Antonio Jacintho de Medeiros*—*Antonio José Fernandes*, negociante—*José Manoel Lessa*, sargento — *Antonio José Vieira Barbosa*, capitão — *Manoel José de Castro*, almoxarife do hospital militar—*Antonio José Gomes*, negociante—*José Maria Martins*—O padre *Manoel Gomes de Gouvêa* — *José Clemente de Mesquita*—*Francisco Ma-*

*noel de Abreu*—O padre *Joaqnim de Mello*—O padre *João Constantino de Camargo* — *Estolano José Barbosa*—L. *Antonio da Silva Bastos*, negociante—*Bento Miguel de Moraes*, negciante— *Joaquim Maria da Costa Terra*, capitão—*Francisco das Chagas de Jesus*, tenente—*Salvador Paes da Costa*, furriel—*Theodorico Penteado*, furriel — *José Candido de Barros* — *Messias José da Rosa*, tenente — *José Elias da Silva*, quartel-mestre—*José da Silva Marciano* — *Francisco de Paula Oliveira Montes*— *Antonio Pereira Alves da Cunha Forje*, negociante—*Franciseo Gomes da Silva*, alferes—*Francisco Antonio de Andrade*—*Luiz Gonzaga da Silva*, sargento — *Joaquim Marques* — *Manoel Jacintho de Proença*, negociante — *Manoel Corrêa Braga* — *José Elias de Carvalho* — *Manoel Ramos* — *Francisco de Assis Ludgero*, alferes.—*Marcellino Baptista*, sargento.—*José Ignacio da Fonseca*, cabo.—*Antonio João Carlos Barbosa*, tenente.— *Joaquim Cesar de Cerqueira Leme*, coronel—*José Manoel da Costa Ribeiro*, capitão—*Antonio Joaquim da Costa Ribeiro*, capitão— *José Elias da Silva*, tenente—*Manoel dos Santos Lima*, ajudante —*Joaquim Innocencio Rodrigues Cardim*, tenente—*Vasco Antonio de Toledo*, ajudante—*Antonio José Bordini*, major—*Francisco de Assis do Monte Camargo*, ajudante—*Antonio Rodrigues Moreira*—*Luiz Pedroso da Silva*—*José Gonçalves Gomide*, cirurgião-mór—*Antonio João Carlos Barbosa*, tenente—*Manoel Gonçalves da Luz Paralhão*, tenente—*Francisco Pereira Mendes*, alferes—*Maximiano Bueno da Cunha*—*Joaquim Floriano de Siqueira*, alferes—*Raymundo Pinto Homem*, alferes—*Luiz José de Oliveira*, alferes—*Antonio Joaquim de Almeida*, alferes—*Joaquim José Rozeiro*, alferes—*Pedro Antonio Ferreira*, alferes—*Francisco das Chagas Silva*, alferes—*José Joaquim de Vasconcellos Alambary*, major—*Eleuterio da Silva Prado*, capitão-mór—*Manoel Lopes Guimarães*, sargento-mór—*Antonio José Vieira Barbosa*, capitão—*Francisco José de Azevedo*, capitão—*José Rodrigues Pereira*, capitão—*Joaquim Alves Moreira*, capitão—*João Baptista Tavares*, alferes—*Antonio José Pereira dos Santos*, alferes— *Eleuterio da Silva Prado*, alferes—*Manoel Joaquim Coelho*, capitão—Guarda-mór *Manoel Alves Alvim*—O vigario *Francisco de Paula Teixeira*—*Francisco José da Silva*, major—*Manoel de Campos Penteado*, major—*Francisco Antonio de Paula Nogueira da Gama*, coronel—*Joaquim Maria da Costa Ferreira*, capitão— *José Gomes Segurado*, secretario da Caixa de Desconto—*Virgilio Gomes de Lemos*—*Francisco Manoel de Andrade Figueiredo e Albuquerque*, alferes—*José Joaquim dos Santos Prado*, major— *Luiz Antonio de Assumpção*, capitão—*Gaspar Ribeiro da Rosa Ramos*, major—*Antonio Manoel Pereira*—*João Vicente Rodrigues de Vasconcellos*, cadete—*Antonio José Osorio*, cadete—*Manoel José Rodrigues da Silva*—*Manoel Corrêa de Bittencourt*, cadete—*Amaro José Vieira*—*Gabriel Henriques Pessoa*—*Luiz Antonio Pinto do Rego*, ajudante—*Joaquim Pedroso de Oliveira Franco*—*Francisco de Assis Pinheiro*—*Francisco Gonçalves dos Santos Cruz*, capitão—*Custodio José Gomes de Lima*, sargento—*Francisco Ferreira Alves*, sargento—*Marcellino Baptista*, sargento—*Francisco Manoel de Borja*, sargento—*Francisco Alves de Siqueira*, sargento—*Francisco Xavier de Brito*, sargento—*Ponciano Joaquim de Goes*, sargento—*Antonio Jose Ferreira*, sargento—*Francisco Bernardes Correa*, sargento—*Lourenço Justiniano*, furriel—O major *João da Silva Machado*—*Anastacio de Freitas Trancoso*, coronel—*Antonio Correa de Moraes*, furriel—*José Geraldo*, furriel—*Joaquim José da Costa*, cabo—*José Joaquim Senna*, cabo—*José Vieira da Costa*, cabo—*Vicente Antonio de Camargo*, cabo *José Innocencio da Silva*, cabo—*Francisco Antonio de Paula*, cabo—*Salvador Pires de Oliveira*—*Antonio Pereira*, cabo—*Antonio Joaquim de Araujo*, cabo—*José de Jesus*, cabo—*Ignacio José de Vasconcellos*, cabo—*José Francisco de Paula*, cabo—*Joaquim de Toledo Rendon*, cabo—*Vicente Ferreira Machado*, cabo—*José Antonio de Brito*, cabo—*Benedicto Baptista*, cabo—*José Cypriano de Freitas*, cabo—*João Paes*, cabo—*José Joaquim*, cabo, *José J. Octavio de Carvalho*, cabo—*João Evangelista*, furriel—*José M. de Almeida*, cabo—*Antonio da Silva Dutra*, cabo—*João Vicente de Brito*, sargento—*João A. de Oliveira*—*Felix da Fonseca*, cabo —*Bento José Leite Penteado*, capitão—*Joaquim Cardoso*—*Joaquim José Machado*—*Thomaz de Aquino e Castro*, alferes—*Francisco Mariano de Abreu*—*Francisco S. dos Santos Cardim*, tenente—*Francisco J. Barbosa*—O padre *Antonio Romualdo Freire* —*Joaquim Pinto de Castro*--*Joaquim J. da Silva Baptista*— *Manoel das Neves de Jesus*, alferes—*José Maria*, cabo—*Benedicto J. de Carvalho*, cabo—*Agostinho dos Santos Portella Lage*—*José Vaz Aires de Carvalho*—*Joaquim J. de Oliveira*—*Benedicto Antonio de Assumpção*—*José Felippe Santiago*, alferes—*José J. Rodrigues*—*Francisco de Mesquita Vianna*, tenente—*Antonio Xavier Ferreira*, capitão—O padre *José J. de Oliveira Brazeiros* —O capitão *Bento José de Moraes*—*Manoel F. de Carvalho* e *Almeida*, ajudante—*Luiz M. da Cunha Bastos*, capitão—*José J. dos Santos*, major—*Justiniano de Mello Franco*, physico-mór—*Guilherme Tud Magessi*, capitão—*José P. Galvão de Moura Lacerda*, brigadeiro—*Joaquim M. Galvão de Moura Lacerda*, coronel—*Antonio José Vaz*, coronel—*Manoel Francisco Correa*, major —*José M. de Mello*, major—*Joaquim José de Lima*—*José da Silva Monteiro*—*João da Costa Ferreira*, brigadeiro — *Antonio*

*Pereira Mendes—Severino Pinto de Almeida*, capitão—O padre *Bento Manoel dos Passos—Manoel Leme du Guerra—Floriano da Costa e Silua*—O padre *Manoel de Faria Doria—Bento J. da Silva Rego—Bento Correa Leme*, capitão—*José Vaz de Carvalho*, brigadeiro—*Manoel Rodrigues de Mello—João de Castro Canto e Mello*, tenente-coronel—*Joaquim José de Andrade e Aquino—Joaquim Antonio Rodrigues*, sargento—*José Pires*, cabo. *Luiz Antonio Machado*, capitão—*Francisco de Salles Borralho*, ajudante.—*Francisco Pereira de Araujo.*—*Agostinho Pereira dos Santos Portella Lage.*—*Bernardo Guedes Cardoso de Vasconcellos,* tenente.—*João Domingues de Oliveira*, alferes.—*Luiz Antonio Gonçalves*, capitão.—*Joaquim Floriano de Toledo*, tenente.— *Manoel de Jesus Setubal*, furriel.—*Luiz Gonzaga de Araujo*, tenente.—*José Manoel de Abreu.*—*Francisco José de Mattos*, tenente. (1)

VEREANÇA EXTRAORDINARIA DE 23 DE MAIO DE 1822, FEITA A REQUERIMENTO DO POVO E TROPAS DA CIDADE DE S. PAULO (2)

Aos 23 dias do mez de Maio de 1822, nesta cidade de S. Paulo e Casas da Camara, Passos do Conselho della, onde foram vindos o juiz de fóra pela lei presidente, o capitão Bento José Leite Penteado, os vereadores transactos, os capitães Antonio de Siqueira Moraes e Caetano Pinto Homem e o actual procurador, abaixo assignados, assistindo o povo e as tropas, pelos quaes foram convocados os ditos extraordinariamente, e depois de ahi se acharem pelo mesmo povo e tropas foi representado a esta Camara o quanto era util a conservação do Ex.ᵐᵒ Sr. João Carlos Augusto de Oyenhausen, presidente do Governo Provisorio desta provincia, por chegar á noticia de todos que o mesmo se ausentava desta provincia por mandado de Sua Alteza Real o Principe Real do Reino Uunido e Regente deste Reino do Brasil, e que igualmente éra conveniente para o socego desta provincia a deposição de dois membros do dito Governo, o Secretario do Interior coronel Martim Francisco Ribeiro de Andrada e o brigadeiro Manoel Rodrigues Jordão. Ao que accordaram dirigir ao mesmo Ex.ᵐᵒ Governo o officio seguinte:

(1) Contem esta representação 321 assignaturas, sendo 160 de militares e seus dependentes, 140 de cidadãos civis, dos quaes apenas 5 são homens conhecidos, 5 de empregados publicos e 22 de clerigos. Os militares são classificados pelos sous postos, desde brigadeiro até sargentos, furrieis e cabos. Dos civis uma boa parte assigna sómente dois nomes e um houve que só assignou o nome de baptismo—*Maximiano*
(2) Este termo foi redigido por Costa Carvalho e escripto por seu apaniguado Amaro José de Moraes.

« Ill.ᵐᵒˢ e Ex.ᵐᵒˢ Snrs ».—Achando-nos reunidos nesta Ca-
« mara á instancia do povo e tropas, postados nesta praça. nos
« foi unanimemente representado que *sizudamente* requeriam a
« conservação do Ex.ᵐᵒ Snr. João Carlos Augusto de Oeynhau-
« sen, presidente deste Governo, bem como a disposição do Se-
« cretario dos Negocios do Interior, o sr. coronel Martim Francisco
« Ribeiro de Andrada, e igualmente do membro do mesmo
« Governo, brigadeiro Manoel Rodrigues Jordão, por serem ambos
« perniciosos a esta provincia. A vista do referido se servirão
« V.ˢ Ex.ᵃˢ dar as providencias que julgarem mais assentadas,
« fazendo-nos V. Ex.ᵃˢ a honra de participar-nos por nos achar
« em sessão. Deus guarde a V. Ex.ᵃˢ São Paulo, em Camara
« extraordinaria de 23 de Maio de 1822. Ill.ᵐᵒˢ e Ex:ᵐᵒˢ Snrs.»
« do Governo Provisorio desta Provincia.—*Bento José Leite*
« *Penteado—Antonio de Siqueira Moraes—Caetano Pinto Ho-*
« *mem—Luiz Manoel da C. Bastos.*»

Este officio, que a Camara fez apresentar na fórma acima
ao mesmo Ex.ᵐᵒ Governo por mim, foi respondido pela portaria seguinte:

« O Governo Provisorio, em resposta ao officio de V. S.ᵃ,
« desta mesma data, declara que é um verdadeiro acto de des-
« obediencia o deixar de cumprir as ordens de Sua Alteza, assim
« como não é da sua competencia demittir os dois membros
« eleitos pelo povo e sanccionados pelo mesmos Augusto Senhor.
« Mas os referidos membros, sabendo da vontade *denominada* do
« povo e tropas e desejando em tudo concorrer para o socego
« da provincia e para que nenhuma vergonha ou macula sobre ella
« recaia, deram immediata e voluntariamente a sua demissão;
« e para obter-se o mesmo fim o Ex.ᵐᵒ Snr. Presidente se obri-
« ga a ficar, o que tudo se participa a V. S.ᵃˢ para sua intel-
« ligencia. Deus guarde a V. S.ᵃˢ Palacio do Governo de S.
« Paulo a 23 de Maio de 1822.—*João Carlos Augusto de Oye-*
« *nhausen*, presidente,—*Miguel José de Oliveira Pinto*, secreta-
« rio—*Daniel Pedro Müller—Antonio Maria Quartim—Francisco*
« *de Paula e Oliveira—André da Silva Gomes—João Ferreira*
« *de Oliveira Bueno.*—Srs. Juiz Fóra pela lei presidente e mais
« officiaes da Camara desta Cidade.»

Sendo esta portaria apresentada e lida nesta sessão por mim
escrivão, foi deliberado que se a fizesse publica ao povo e tropas
que se acham postados, o que foi mim escrivão cumprido, e
immediatamente pelo povo e tropa foi requerido se lavrasse de
tudo o competente termo, bem como por parte da tropa foi protestado perante este Senado contra a palavra «insubordiuação»

indicada na portaria aqui transcripta (1); porquanto protestava
igualmenre fazer ver qual a sua conducta, que só tende a pôr
em socego esta provincia, e mostrar quem são os perturbadores
della. E que outrosim protestava a mesma tropa pelo insulto
que soffreu o procurador desta Camara quando, da parte da mesma
ma Camara, do povo e das tropas, em companhia de mim escrivão, foi participar o Ex.mo Governo para concorrer ás casas desta
Camara e lhe foi respondido que o Governo éra superior a tudo
e que não vinha a esta Camara, mas antes que as auctoridades
todas lhe eram subordinadas e que portanto, deviam concorrer
ao palacio do Governo e que pessoa nenhuma de anctoridade
tivesse mais o desaforo de subir aquellas escadas ; cujas palavras
foram proferidas pelo secretario do mesmo Governo, o coronel
Martim Francisco Ribeiro de Andrada, onde todos os mais membros do Governo se achavam reunidos.

A' vista de todo o expendido a Camara, o povo e tropas
acceitaram a demissão dos dous membros e mui positivamente a
desejada conservação do Exmo. Sr. Presidente do Governo. E
para constar todo o referido mandaram lavrar este termo de vereança, em que esta Camara, auctoridades, povo e tropas presentes se assignaram, e eu, João Nepomuceno de Almeida, escrivão da Camara, que o escrivi.—*Bento José Leite Penteado—
Antonio de Siqueira Moraes—Caetano Pinto Homem—Luiz Manoel da Cunha Bastos—José da Costa Carvalho—Francisco Alvares
Ferreira do Amaral,* coronel—*Jeronimo Pereira Chrispim de
Vasconcellos,* tenente-coronel—*José Pereira Simões,* tenente-coronel
—*José Rodrigues Pereira de Oliveira Netto,* sargento-mór—*Francisco de Paula Macedo,* sargento-mór—*Januario Antonio de Lima,*
coronel—*Manoel José da Costa Ribeiro,* sargento-mór aggregado
—*José Fernandes da Silva,* capitão—*Joaquim Ignacio Ribeiro,*
capitão—*Francisco Gonçalves dos Santos Cruz,* capitão—*Antonio
Cardoso Nogueira,* capitão—*Pedro Taques de Almeida Alvim,*
capitão—*José Manoel da Costa Ribeiro,* capitão—*Francisco Can-
dido Sagalerva,* capitão—*Luiz Antonio do Valle Quaresma,* capitão
—*Francisco de Assis do Monte Camargo,* ajudante—*José Pereira
Jorge,* tenente quartel-mestre—*Luiz Gonzaga de Araujo,* tenente
—*Sigismundo de Lima,* tenente—*Antonio Gonçalves Mamede,*
tenente—*Francisco Antonio Pinto Bastos,* tenente—*Manoel dos
Santos Lima,* ajudante—*José Gonçalves Gomide—José Elias da
Silva,* quartel-mestre—*Eleuterio José Pinto,* tenente—*Francisco

(1) Na portaria acima transcripta não se fala em « insubordinação » apenas se diz
que sería « um acto de desobediencia não cumprir as ordens do Princpe Regente » Era
a tropa que estava *comprando banha,* para ter um pretexto para mais rebelliões.

*Severiano dos Santos Cardim*, tenente—*Pedro Fernandes de Andrade*, tenente-coronel—*José Mariano de Assumpção Paião*, tenente—*Jayme da Silva Telles*, tenente—*Francisco de Paula Oliveira*... (1) ...—*Manoel das Neves de Jesus*, alferes—*Manoel Francisco de Vasconcellos*, tenente—*Manoel Felizardo de Carvalho e Almeida*, ajudante—*José Antonio de Assumpção*, tenente—*Antonio, José de Oliveira Barbosa*, capitão—*Severino Pinto da Silva*, capitão—*Francisco José de Azevedo*, capitão—*Manoel José da Silva Abreu Vianna*, alferes—*Joaquim Alves Moreira*, capitão—*Joaquim José Correa*—*João Baptista Tavares*, alferes—*Francisco Gomes da Silva*—*Antonio José Pereira dos Santos*, alferes—*Joaquim José Rodrigues* — *Manoel José Gonçalves Sevilha* — *Manoel Antonio Soares de Campos.*—*Antonio Floriano Alves Alvim.*—*Francisco Antonio de Borba.*—*Candido Ignacio da Silva.*—*Joaquim Pinto de Castro.*—*João Ribeiro da Lapa e Silva.*—*José Pinto da Silva. Domingos Affonso de Santa Anna* —*Agostinho dos Santos Portella Lage.*—*Antonio Jacintho.*—*Antonio de Padua de Gusmão*, tenente-coronel.—*Francisco de Assis*, tenente.—*Raphael de Oliveira*, alferes.—*Domingos de Araujo Roso*, tenente.—*Francisco de Assis Ludgero*, alferes.—*Joaquim José de Almeida*, cadete. —*Joaquim José do...* (2), alferes.—*Joaquim Antonio da Cunha*, alferes.—*Manoel Domingues Martins e Souza.*—*Francisco Antonio de Oliveira Simões*, alferes.—*José Gonçalves Corrêa*, sargento.—*José de Sontiago Xavier*, cabo.—*José Joaquim de Camargo*, tambor-mór.—*Francisco de Paula*, mestre da musica—*Francisco Alves Ribeiro*, sargento.·—*Joaquim Soares dos Santos*, musico.—*José Antonio Corrêa.*—*Feliciano de Jesus*, musico.—*José Manoel de Macedo*, soldado.—*Benedicto Antonio*, musico.— *João Baptista do Nascimento*, musico.—*Lucas José da Silveira*, soldado —*João Antonio de Araujo* (3).—*Joaquim Francisco Do...* (4), sargento.—*Joaquim Antonio do Carmo*, soldado.— *João Texeira de Souza*, furriel.—*Francisco Rodrigues Leite*, soldado —*João de Arruda Moraes*, furriel.—*Francisco Mendes de Paula*, soldado.—*Joaquim Luiz de Brito*, soldado.—*José Felippe de Macedo*, sargento do 2.º regimento.—*Francisco Luiz Pereira*, carcereiro.—*Manoel Joaquim Espiridião*, cabo.- *João Antonio de Oliveira*, cabo.—*José Geraldo*, furriel.—*P. João Martins de Sei-*

---

(1) A assignatura é de pessima lettra e o ultimo nome está illegivel; dahi talvez fosse que viesse a idéa de ter o padre Francisco de Paula Oliveira tomado parte na *Bernarda*. Foi outro individuo do mesmo nome e não elle, como se verificou depois por documentos no Archivo do Estado.

(2) Está illegivel o sobrenome, sendo pessima a lettra da assignatura.

(3) As assignaturas até aqui são dos que compareceram na Camara no dia 23 de Maio e fizeram a *Bernarda*; as assignaturas que seguem são de pessoas que compareceram no dia seguinte a sanccionar o feito do dia anterior.

(4) Está illegivel o resto do nome.

xas.—*José Pinto Teixeira.—Luiz Antonio de Assumpção*, capitão. *Manoel José do Patrocinio*, porta-estandarte.—*Constantino José de Freitas Alvim.—Manoel Ferreira Duarte.—Benedicto Francisco de Azevedo.—Antonio José de Oliveira Santos.—José Paulino Braga*, sargento de ordenanças.—*José Ignacio de França*, cabo. · -*Pe Francisco Manoel Junqueira.—José Joaquim de Proença*, cabo.—*Ignacio José Antunes*, tenente.—*José Antonio Pereira*, alferes.—*Floriano Antonio Rodrigues. —Manoel José de Jesus. Francisco de Lemos Pinto.—Antonio José Fernandes*, sargento. —*Manoel Lourenço*, cabo.—*João Rodrigues da Silva.—Joaquim José Xavier de Almeida.—Luiz Antonio Gonçalves.—Modesto Antonio·—Rodrigo José Barbosa.—Leandro Mendes do Amaral. —Francisco Pires da Rocha.—Manoel Domingues dos Santos.— Miguel Angelo da Silveira*, tenente-coronel reformado.—*José Joaquim dos Santos Prado*, sargento-mór de milicias.—*Francisco Cardoso de Oliveira.—Miguel Ribeiro Cardoso.—Antonio Fernandes da Motta*, alferes.—*Francisco Alves.—José S. Pinheiro.— Antonio Alves Pereira da Cunha Fórgo.—Pedro José.—Antonio Manoel Soares de Campos.—João Vicente de Brito*, sargento.— *Joaquim José de Camargo*, sargento.—*Martinho José Marques*, capitão.--*Joaquim de Souza.—Joaquim José Pedro Maia —Francisco Antonio de Araujo.—Antonio Rodrigues Leme.—Joaquim Francisco Gonçalves*, cabo.—*João Antonio Rosa.— Antonio Manoel Teixeira.—Manoel Felippe de Araujo*, capitão.—*José Manoel de Abreu Luz.—Antonio José de Sampaio Guimarães.—Balthasar de Godoy Cardoso*, capitão.—*Bento Ribeiro da Silva.—Domieiano José.—José Antonio de Oliveira.—Manoel Teixeira Ribeiro.— Aleixo Corrêa Vieira.- Joaquim José golasso.—Rogerio T. dos Reis.—Joaquim José de Lima*, sargento.—*Domingos José de Oliveira Guimarães.—Francisco de Mesquita Vianna*, tenente do 2.º regimento de cavallaria.—*Manoel Joaquim de Oliveira*, sargento.—*Antonio Joaquim Furquim Justino.—Amaro José Vieira* (1).—*Constantino José dos Santos.—João Lopes França*, capitão. —*Vicente Ferreira dos Santos Cavalheiro.—Seraphim da Silva Franco.—Francisco de Paula Leite Prestes*, capitão.— *Alexandre da Silva Collares.— José Carvão da Fonseca e Camara*, capitão.— *Antonio Joaquim de Oliveira*, alferes.— *Paulo José Rodrigues.— Manoel Thomaz dos Santos.—Feliciano Telles Gonçalves da Trindade.—Luiz Antonio Pereira Paião.—Silveiro Monati.—Antonio de Paiva Azevedo*, sargento-*Joaquim José dos Santos*, capitão — *Francisco Antonio de Miranda*, capitão—*P.e João Joaquim de Carvalho*— *Ponciano Joa-*

quim de Góes, sargento — *Martinho da Silva Santos*, meirinho geral — *Bento José Lopes*, argento — *Francisco José de Carvalho Faro*, alferes (1) — *P.º Hygino Podrigues Moreira* — *Ignacio José Cesar* — *Manoel Guilherme da Silva Cruz*, sargento — *José de Freitus Saldanha*, capitão — *Luiz Antonio Pinto do Rego*, ajudante — *Manoel Jasé Chaves* — *Manoel Lopes de Guimarães*, sargento-mór — *Jose Vaz de Carvalho*, brigadeiro.

VEREANÇA EXTRAORDINARIA DA CAMARA DE S. PAULO, EM 24 DE MAIO DE 1822

Aos 24 de Maio de 1822, nesta cidade de S. Paulo e casas da Camara, paços do Conselho della, onde foram vindos o juiz de foro pela lei presidente o capitão Bento Josè Leite Penteado, os vereadores transactos, os capitães Caetano Pinto Homem e Antonio Cardoso Nogueira, por auzencia dos actuaes, e o actual procurador, abaixo assignados, para effeito de sessão extraordinaria, a requerimento do povo (2) e tropas desta cidade, e 'em acto da mesma foi dito pela tropa e povo, de commum accordo, que elles se sbrigavam pela sua conducta e a conservar o socego publico desta provincia (3) e que o praticado por elles não foi por insubordinados, nem revoltosos, como de alguma forma dá a entender o officio dos Exmos Srs. do Governo, mas sim para que o povo e tropas possam levar á presença de Sua Alteza Real, sem receio de violencia ou despotismo, tudo quanto for a bem desta provincia, em beneficio dos cidadãos, até aqui opprimida quasi por espaço de um anno (4) e até fa-

(1) Aß assignaturas posteriores a estas já são do dia 25 de Maio, de gente recrutada para isso. São 192 ao todo, das quaes 107 são de militares, de um brigadeiro até muitos cabos e soldados, musicos, meirinho e carcereiro; sómente tres obscuros membros do clero estiverem presentes e nenhum cidadão civil de merito ou nome conhecido appareceu para sanccionar com a sua presença ou com a sua assignatura a *Bernarda* de 23 do Maio. Assignaram os vereadores transactos em ausencia dos actuaes, obrigados a se esconderem pelo trabuco de Pedro Taques, Oliveira Netto e Caetano Pinto; porém Costa Carvalho, que primou pela sua ausencia e seu silencio no dia 23 de Junho de 1821, foi quem iniciou a lista assignando-a em primeiro logar.
Comparem-se estas assignaturas com as dos que tomaram parte nos factos de 23 de Junho e ver-se-á que os 107 militares que aqui figuram e os 85 obscuros restantes individuos não representavam de modo algum o povo da cidade de S. Paulo. E' de notar que o brigadeiro Moraes Leme e o coronel Francisco Ignacio, braços fortes de Costa Carvalho na jornada de 23 do Maio, não quizeram comparecer na Camara naquelle dia, nem comprometter as suas assignaturas neste documento.
(2) Pelas assignaturas que seguem ver-se-á que o povo da capital não estava representado nessa reunião e que mesmo os militares não eram muitos
(3) A confederação dos municipios do interior, em lucta aberta com os desordeiros da capital, bem mostrou que estes anarchizaram a provincia e não garantiram a paz e e tranquillidade publica.
(4) Aqui se diz o que estavam fazendo os extrangeiros, membros do governo, que não impediam Martim Francisco e Jordão de opprimir a provincia e fazer leis arbitrarias, nem porque nunca fizeram um protesto contra isso!

zendo leis arbitrarias, o que tudo protestam levar á presença de Sua Alteza Real, como Regente deste reino do Brazil, e a quem juraram obediencia; e no mesmo acto tambem representaram que se rogasse ao Exmo Governo Provisorio declarasse aos dous mem· bros depostos que ficavam responsaveis por todo e qualquer movimento de inquietação e de desasocego que possa haver nesta cidade e provincia, motivados por elles ou por seus sequazes, cujos motivos todos serão legalizados e postos na presença de Sua Alteza Real. E por não haver mais que provir mandaram lavrar este termo em que assigna a Camara, e eu João Nepomuceno e Almeida, escrivão, a escrevi.—*Penteado— Nogueira—Pinto—Bastos*.

_____

EDITAL DA CAMARA DE S. PAULO, CONCITANDO O POVO E A TROPA
A SE MANTEREM TRANQUILLOS

O juiz de fora pela lei presidente, vereadores e procurador do Senado da Camara, que servimos no corrente anno por eleição e appiovação de Sua Alteza Real, que Deus guarde.

Fazemos saber ao povo e tropa que constitue a força armada desta cidade que havendo levado á presença do Exm. Governo Provisorio da provincia as copias dos termos de vereações extraordinarias dos dias 23 e 24 do proximo passado mez de Maio, a que deram occasião as commoções da mesma força armada e povo pelos motivos nelles expendidos, foi resultado o seguinte *reversal* officio:

« O Governo Provisorio acaba de receber o officio de V. S.ᵃˢ
« datado de hoje e com elle as cópias dos termos de sessões
« exraordinarias que essa Camara teve em os dias 23 e 24 do
« corrente, de cujos conteudos ficou sciente, e passando a
« remetter aos dous membros deste Governo depostos pelo povo
« e tropa, os senhores coronel Martim Francisco Ribeiro de
Andrada e brigadeiro Manoel Rodrigues Jordão, a copia do ultimo termo para sua intelligencia e execução, espera tambem que essa camara, desempenhando a sua promessa quanto da sua parte estiver, promova o socego publico e obediencia á Sua Alteza Real, a este Governo e ás mais auctoridades con-
ĕ stituidas na forma em que a isso se obrigam V. S.ᵃˢ e todas
« as mais pessoas a cujo pedimento se lavrou o termo de 24, ás
« quaes essa Camara fará constar isto mesmo em resposta ao
« que V. S.ᵃˢ da parte dellas nos asseguram. Palacio do Go-
« verno de S. Paulo, 25 de Maio de 1822.—*João Carlos Au-*
« *gusto de Oeynhausen*, presidente—*Miguel José de Oliveira*
« *Pinto*, secretario—*Daniel Pedro Müller*, secretario ».

A' vista do que, em seu consequente desempenho, instantissimamente pedimos e exhortamos ao mesmo povo e tropa coadjuvante que, achando-se já removidas as duas pedras do seu maior escandalo e descontentemente e por outra parte o desejado senhor presidente conservado, pela opinião a seu favor desenvolvida de uma maneira a mais energica e triumphante dos poucos facciosos em contrario (1), que de uma vez cessaram para sempre e se dissiparam similhantes accessos febris, vertiginosos e ameaçadores de mortaes ruinas, e que hajam de conter-se dentro do circulo da sua antiga moderação e socego, sem a minima discrepancia da obediencia devida ao nosso amabilissimo Principe excellente e ás mais auctoridades constituidas, sem que jámais desviem da lembrança que a civil discordia é um monstro sanguinario que traz as mãos tingidas no sangue dos seus proprios partidistas e sequazes, e castiga esses mesmos delictos que lhe inspira, do que por orações dos justos é esta a segunda vez que nos tem preservado a misericordia de Deus (2).

Paulistas! Este Senado, a quem constituistes vossos representantes, assim o espera confiado no vosso catholicismo e probidade, no emtanto que vai tomar as medidas mais proprias que estiverem ao seu alcance para pôr ao abrigo de quaesque convulsões a segurança publica estremecida, sendo o principal o requerer-se á pressa o retardado cumprimento da lei constitucional para uma nova junta de governo provincial, em cuja eleição não intervenha a malandrina influencia de novos Demetrios Ourives inculcadores de nexos da falsa Diana e por esta causa inimigos natos do grande Apostolo das Gentes e dos seus mais probos filhos, orgãos da verdade (3).

E para que chegue á noticia de todos e não se allegue ignorancia, mandámos lavrar o presente edital, que depois de ser por nós assignado, conferido e registado, será publicado pelas ruas e praças desta cidade e finalmente fixado em o logar costumado.—S. Paulo, em vereação de 1.° de Junho de 1822.—Eu, João Nepomuceno de Almeida, escrivão da Camara, o escrevi.— Logar do sello real.—*Manoel Lopes Guimarães*—*Antonio de Siqueira Moraes*—*Caetano Pinto Homem*—*Luiz Manoel da Cunha Bastos.*

---

(1) Dos signatarios deste edital dois tomaram parte activa na *Bernarda*, Siqueira Moraes e Caetano Pinto, e este ultimo andou pela rua de trabuco na mão com outros companheiros, Pedro Taques e Oliveira Netto.

(2) Não tem senso este final, que aliás vai bem copiado do original existente no archivo da Camara de S. Paulo.

(3) Está tirada da historia antiga, misturada com um pouco de mythologia, está sem sentido claro, mas como phrase bombastica podia produzir effeito no espirito dos sediciosos de 23 de Maio.

OFFICIO DA CAMARA DE S. PAULO A D. PEDRO, ACOMPANHANDO A
REPRESENTAÇÃO DOS SEDICIOSOS

Senhor: — A Camara da cidade de S. Paulo tem a honra
de levar á presença de Vossa Alteza Real os termos de vereações
extraordinarias dos dias 23 e 24 de Maio proximo passado e a
representação do povo e tropa desta cidade e unir a elles seus
votos.

Os successos do dia 23 de Maio e os motivos delle vão
agora ser patentes a Vossa Alteza Real para que, instruido da
verdade, melhor sinta a justiça com que procederam os habitantes desta cidade e a razão porque a Camara della annuiu aos
seus dezejos, posto que não legalmente, isto é, posto que ex-
primindo por outra via que era o da representação, mas a unica
que o momento permittia e que a felicidade da patria fazia indispensavel. (1)

O coronel Martim Francisco Ribeiro de Andrada tinha formado e em grande parte já posto em pratica o terrivel plano
de ser absoluto nesta cidade e provincia, servindo-lhe de gráu
á sua elevação todos os homens de bem, que, seguindo a honra,
fieis ao juramento que deram, detestavam o despotismo e cordialmente amavam a Constituição e o Principe que a jurára;
tentou reduzir, e quasi que o conseguiu, o governo ao seu unico
voto (2); as suas paixões, os seus amigos, que engraçadamente
eram o refugo da sociedade (3), os seus parentes que sempre
foram em todos os tempos máos cidadãos e pessimos subditos
(4), como é patente a todos; eram só estes os contentes porque
todos os mais lhes eram sacrificados para que o máo partido
engrossasse, a tyrannia crescesse e quando fosse occasião talvez
nem Vossa Alteza fosse poupado á sua ambição (5).

A justissima queixa de todas as auctoridades, desattendidas
a cada momento por este homem, ajudado pelo brigadeiro Manoel Rodrigues Jordão e alguns outros illudidos, mas não máos

---

1) A pretexto de que uma representação não chegaria á presença do principe, por
estar este assediado por José Bonifacio, ministro, fez-se a sedição de 23 de Maio, ex-
pulsaram-se Martim e João e fez-se representação a D. Pedro ainda assediado pelo ministro !

2) Que papel faziam no Governo Provisorio o presidente João Carlos e seus companheiros Francisco Ignacio, Müller. Oliveira Pinto e Quartim ? Das *Actas das Sessões*
não constam reclamações e protesos!

3) Paula Souza e todo o interior estavam ao lado de Martim Francisco, bem como
os marechaes Candido Xavier e Arouche o' muita gente grada da capital; mas para os
sediciosos estes eram os refugos da sociedade paulista ?

4) Deviam citar factos justificativos desta grave asserção, que é pura phantasia.

5) Aqui se procura fazer intriga, dando a entender que Martim queria derribar o
principe ou para fazer a republica, em que elle nunca pensou, ou para se fazer rei em
seu logar ; mas a intriga era muita baixa para medrar e não medrou.

e emfim o clamor geral (1) deram motivo a que no dia 23 de Maio, tendo-se divulgado a noticia de que atraiçoada e cavilosamente o coronel Martim tinha alcançado que fosse chamado á Côrte o conselheiro João Carlos Augusto de Oeynhausen, forte antemural aos seus despotismos e conservador da tranquilidade desta provincia, por sua prudencia e por seus conhecimentos na arte de governar povos brazileiros (2), o povo e tropa de S. Paulo, reunindo-se na praça de S. Gonçalo, convocaram esta Camara e lhe requereram que representasse ao governo e exigisse delle a persistencia do conselheiro nesta cidade e a deposição immediata dos dous membros—o coronel Martim e o brigadeiro Jordão.

A Camara, vendo o numero de cidadãos reunidos, a qualidade delles (3) e a boa ordem e unanimidade com que representavam, tomou em consideração sua representação e achando verdadeiros os motivos della, por serem muitos dos factos presenciados por seus proprios membros, (4) outros acontecidos com elles proprios e o resto publico e notorio com geral indignação, (5) notando mais que se não attentava contra o governo estabelecido e approvado por Vossa Alteza Real, isto é, que se não destruia a pessoa moral em quem residia uma porção do Poder Executivo (6) mas que unicamente se tirava desse todo uma parte infeccionada que não constituia a sua essencia, pois que não se acha determinado o numero de homens que devem compor esta parte executiva e tirados elles ainda restava neste governo maior numero de votos do que prudente e sabiamente tem determinado o soberano Congresso para os governos provinciaes, (7) nenhuma

---

1) No empenho de deprimir os Andradas a Camara de *bernardistas* e os sediciosos de 23 de Maio esqueceram-se de que José Bonifacio foi lente de Coimbra muitos annos, prestando bons serviços ao governo; que elle viajou por toda a Europa por conta do governo, que se alistou e commandou um batalhão de estudantes contra as forças invasoras de Junot e que foi chefe de policia do Porto durante a invasão franceza. Não podia ser máo cidadão e mao subdito quem assim procedia, tanto mais que foi elle quem mais influiu para que D. Pedro ficasse no Brasil.

2) João Carlos governou antes Ceará e Matto Grosso; mas em S. Paulo não soube manter a ordem, pois não impediu a rebellião militar de 3 de Junho de 1821, nem a revolução popular que o depoz do poder, a 23 desse mesmo mez, nem a sedição militar de Santos a 29 do mesmo mez, nem a *bernarda* de 23 de Maio de 182.'.

3) A qualidade, como se viu pelas assignaturas, não era da melhor—metade era de militares, boa parte da ralé da capital, intimada pelos trabucos de Pedro Taques, Oliveira Netto, Caetano Finto e outros desordeiros que corriam as ruas, 21 de clerigos e poucas de civis de posição social.

4 Não foram somente presenciados, mas praticados por membros da Camara; Siqueira Moraes, Cunha Bastos e Caetano Pinto foram partes activas na desordem de 23 de Maio, principalmente o ultimo, que sahiu á rua armado de trabuco.

5 Essa indignação não alcançou João Carlos, Fracisco Ignacio, Muller. Oliveira Pinto e Quartim, membros do governo, porque das *Actas das sessões* do governo nada consta, e no interior a indignação foi toda em sentido contrario.

6 Não destruia a pessoa moral do governo, mas desmoralisou-o ao ponto de se rebellar todo o interior contra o resto do esphacelado governo.

7 O governo devia, pela nova lei do congresso de Lisboa, ter sete membros, como depois teve.

duvida teve em representar ao governo, o qual, apezar do furor e crimes até aquella occasião commettidos pelo coronel Martim, (1) annuiu á supplica que pelo seu povo representado fazia esta Camara, e logo foi declarado pelo dito governo a persistencia do conselheiro João Carlos e a deposição do coronel Martim e do brigadeiro Jordão.

A ordem, o socego e a subordinação que reinaram no povo e tropa durante todo e-te tempo, (2) as geraes, publicas e muito mais que ordinarias demonstrações de contentamento, (3) fizeram ver esta Camara a ultima evidencia da justica dos passos que havia dado e conceber desde logo bem fundadas esperanças de que Vossa Alteza Real, instruido da verdade deste successo, annuiria aos rogos do benemerito e sempre leal povo e tropa desta cidade, aos quaes se une inseparavelmente esta Camara, rogando a Vossa Alteza Real humildemente inteira approvação a quanto se praticou (4).

Apezar de que estão pacificos os animos, apezar da docilidade deste povo, a Camara julga do seu dever representar a Vossa Alteza Real que para dar estabilidade á sua ventura, para remover desconfianças, para cercear partidos e para havermos uma marcha constitucional e de união com Portugal, visto estarem removidos os inconvenientes do decreto de 29 de Setembro de 1821, que mandara installar os governos no Brazil e contra o qual esta Camara representou, como devia, haja por bem mandar installar o governo provincial do modo prescripto ultimamente pelas Côrtes (5).

Si a Camara juigasse necessario para mover Vossa Alteza Real a um acto de justiça, se julgasse preciso para penhorar o magnanimo, prudente e virtuoso coração de Vossa Alteza Real, empenhar todos os importantes serviços que ella tem feito á nação, aos seus Augustos Soberanos, dignos progenitores de Vossa Alteza Real, ella, Real Senhor, o faria, protestando como sempre lealdade e respeito á Augusta Casa de Bragança, obediencia ao soberano Congresso e ardentissimos desejos de con—

---

1 Estes crimes não constam das *Actas das Sessões* do governo, ou elles são phantasticos ou os outros membros do governo foram com elles solidarios e por isso não os mencionaram naquellas actas. A primeira hypothese é a verdadeira.

2 A tropa armada, reunida na praça publica e depondo dois membr s do governo, estava em duvidosa subordinação e a ordem publica inteiramente abalada.

3 Esta alegria foi muito ephemera e só sentida pelos sediciosos; todo o resto da provincia encheu-se de dôr e de indignação, personalizadas na confederação de Ytú sob a chefia de Paula Souza e outros paulistas dos mais distinctos.

4 Foram enganados nessa esperança, pois D. Podro nada approvou e agiu com certa energia contra os sediciosos.

5 Foi installado em Janeiro do 1823, com sete membros, mas antes disto já o governo da *Bernarda* tinha sido eliminado e substituido por um triumvirato organisado por D. Pedro.

fraternidade e união com seus irmãos de Portugal (1); mas está certissima de que mais não é necessario do que a justiça com que roga a um Principe como Vossa Alteza Real, a quem Deus guarde e felicite por dilatados annos, como nos é mister. São Paulo, em Camara de 4 de Junho de 1822. — *Manoel Lopes de Guimarães*, presidente—*Antonia de Siqueira Moraes*— *Caetano Pinto Homem*— *Antonio Cardoso Nogueira*— *Luiz Manoel da Cunha Bastos.*

VEREANÇA DE 31 JULHO DE 1822

Aos 31 dias de Julho de 1822, nesta cidade de S. Paulo e salas da Camara, paços do Conselho della, onde se ajuntaram o juiz de fora pela lei presidente, sargento-mór Manoel Lopes de Guimarães, o vereador actual capitão José Mariano Bueno e os transactos, capitães Antonio de Siqueira Moraes e Caetano Pinto Homem, e actual procurador, abaixo assignados, para effeito de sessão, em acto da mesma compareceram os cidadãos de todas as classes desta cidade, abaixo assignados, e representaram a esta Camara que elles, assim reunidos, *exigiam* se mandas-e á Côrte do Rio de Janeiro uma deputação composta de seis homens, dous que reprentassem o corpo ecclesiastico, dous por parte da tropa e dous por parte do commercio, para que não sem perda de tempo representar a Sua Alteza Real e Defensor Perpetuo do Brazil que esta provincia está em pacifica paz e não submergida em anarchia (2) como talvez mal informado o mesmo Augusto Senhor por pessoas mal affeitas a esta provincia (³) e inimigos da boa ordem; e ao mesmo tempo rogassem ao mesmo Augusto Senhor se digne lançar suas benignas vistas e infallivel proteção sobre esta provincia e cidade (4), rogando-lhe ao mesmo tempo para que suspenda quaesquer medidas hostis tomadas, sobre esta provincia (5), e ultimaente supplicar-lhe com toda a *energia* para que pessoalmente venha

---

1 Com a condição de ser mantido em S. Paulo o dominio dos portuguezes; era o que pretenderam João Carlos e seus companheiros na jornada de 23 de Maio de 1822.
2 Os municipios do interior todos rebellados contra a capital e formando uma confederação com séde em Ytù, transformado em praça de guerra e guarnecida por força armada, indicavam, ao contrario disto, que a provincia não estava em pacifica paz.
3 Quem nformava o Principe Regente sobre a anarchia que reinava na provincia eram os paulistas da confederação Ytuana, que tinham mais amor a S. Paulo, seu torrão natal, do que os extrangeiros senhores do goveruo na capital.
4 Si estava a provincia em pacifica paz era desnecessarias essa proteção.
5 As medidas hostis eram a nomeação do general Arouche para commandante das armas e a marcha de general Candido de Santos sobre S. Paulo, à frente de uma boa força para occupar militarmente a cidade.

conhecer dos corações fieis dos bons paulistas, que anciosos esperam pela sua real presença. O que tudo attendido pela mesma Camara, determinaram que se precedesse a votos, ficando-assim deferida a representação supra. Em consequencia passou a mesma Camara a tomar os votos de cada um dos cidadãos e concluido, passou a apural-os, e sahiram eleitos, á maioria de votos, para deputados, por parte do clero o revdo. arcediago e vigario geral do bispado, dr. Manoel Joaquim Gonçalves de Andrade e o revdo. vigario José Lopes de Guimarães; por parte da tropa o coronel Francisco Alves Ferreira do Amaral e o tenente coronel José Antonio da Silva Valente e pelo commercio o coronel Antonio José Vaz e o capitão Francisco Gonçalves dos Santos Cruz.

Outrosim, foi por todos uniformemente requerido que este procedimento immediatamente se fizesse participação ao Exmo. Governo Provisorio para sua intelligencia e para prestar todo e qualquer auxilio que for preciso.

Assim mais: constando a todos que o coronel Francisco Ignacio de Souza Queiroz, era encarregado do commando da força armada desta provincia (1) pretende ausentar-se della, o que é muito prejudicial ao socego de que estão gosando presentemente todos os cidadãos (2) e em quem todos confiam a sua segurança, em razão da muita subordinação que a tropa e povo lhe prestam, requeriam a esta Camara que immediatamente officiasse ao Exmo. Governo Proviso io desta provincia, para que o mesmo Exmo. Governo, a quem estes factos não lhe são occultos, haja de suspender a viagem determinada pelo dito coronel, continuando elle no mesmo commando, até Sua Alteza Real, bem informado do estado desta provincia e dos relevantes serviços que o dito coronel a ella tem prestado, determinar o que for do seu real agrado (3); o que tudo sendo attendido determinou o Senado a expedição de officios e mais participações requeridas e igualmente aos senhores deputados eleitos para fazerem a sua jornada com aquella brevidade que

---

1 Era commandante da força rebellada da capital sómente : o marechal Arouche era o commandante das armas legaes o general Candido Xavier commandava as forças legaes de Santos e Pedro de Brito Caminha cheflava as forças da confederação de Yrú. Não era, portanto, verdade o que aqui se diz.

2 Os municipios do interior continuavam rebellados contra a capital e ninguem, mesmo os rebeldes aqui reunidos na Camara, gosava de socego. Era outra inverdade avançada pelos bernardistas de S. Paulo.

3 Do agrado do principe foi expedir o decreto de 25 de Junho de 1822, cassando os poderes do governo extrangeiro, e uma carta tão severa pelo espirito como aspera pela linguagem, desapprovando os seus actos.

as actuacs circumstancias pedem (1). E para constar mandaram lavrar este termo em que todos assignam com a Camara; e eu, João Nepomuceno de Almeida, escrivão, o escrevi.—*Manoel Lopes Guimarães.*—*Antonio de Siqueira Moraes.*—*Caetano Pinto Homem.*—*Luiz Manoel da Cunha Bastos.*—O arcediago da Sé *Manoel Joaquim Gonçalves de Andrade.*—*Antonio Joaquim de Abreu Pereira*, chantre.—O conego penitenciario *Antonio Paes de Camargo.*—*Frei Manoel da Natividade Marques*, presidente do mosteiro de S. Bento.—*Frei João do Espirito Santo*, guardião de S. Francisco.—*Frei José da Purificação*, presidente do Carmo.—*F.ᵉ Bernardo Conrado da Cunha Faria*—*Eleuterio da Silva Prado*, capitão-mór.—*Francisco de Paula Macedo*, major. *José Rodrigues Pereira de Oliveira Netto*, sargento-mór.—*Antonio da Silva Prado*, capitão—*Gabriel Fernandes Cantinho*, capitão.—Jeronimo *Pereira Chrispim de Vasconcellos*, tenente-coronel.—*Luiz Rodrigues da Cunha*, capitão.—*Antonio José Vieira Barbosa*, capitão.—*Manoel Joaquim Coelho*, capitão.— *Martinho José Marques*, capitão.—*Manoel Felizardo de Carvalho Almeida*, ajudante.—*Francisco José de Azevedo*, capitão.— *Manoel José da Costa Ribeiro*, sargento-mór.—*José Joaquim Rodrigues*, tenente.—*Joaquim Floriano de Siqueira*, alferes -- *Matheus Fernandes Cantinho*, capitão.—*Antonio Joaquim da Costa Ribeiro*, capitão.—*André Alves Ferreira do Amaral*, tenente.—*Francisco Candido Sagalerva*, capitão.—*Luiz Gonzaga de Araujo*, tenente.—*Luiz Antonio do Valle Quaresma*, capitão. —*Francisco Gonçalves dos Santos Cruz*, capitão.—*José Antonio de Assumpção*, tenente.—*Antonio Justino de Souza.*—*João Lopes França*, capitão.—*Antonio Cardoso Nogueira*, capitão.— *Francisco José de Carvalho Faro*, alferes.—*Joaquim Alves Moreira*, capitão.—*Joaquim da Silva Abreu Vianna*, alferes.—*João Lopes da Silva*, negociante.—*Francisco de Assis*, tenente.— *Ignacio José Antunes*, tenente.—*Eleuterio José Pinto*, tenente. *Joaquim José de Oliveira.*—*Pedro Fernandes de Andrade*, tenente. —*Francisco Gomes da Silva*, alferes.—*Severino Pinto da Silva*, capitão.—*Luiz Antonio Pinto do Rego*, ajudante.—*Antonio José Pereira dos Santos*, alferes.—*Francisco Mariano da Cunha*, capitão.—*Antonio Floriano Alves Alvim.*—*José Manoel da Silva*, capitão.—*Pedro Taques de Almeida Alvim*, capitão.— *José Gonçalves Gomide*, cirurgião-mór.—*Amaro José Vieira.*— *João Vicente de Brito.*—*Antonio de Paiva Azevedo.*—*Manoel Domingues Martins de Souza*, capitão.—*José Rodrigues Velloso*

---

1 As circumstancias eram boas, segundo os rebeldes diziam, a provincia estava em pacifica paz e nada precisava do Priucipe Regente.

*de Oliveira.—José de Oliveira Prado.—Januario Antonio de Lima,* coronel.—*José Pinto Teixeira.—Antonio de Padua Gusmão,* tenente-coronel.—*Manoel Delfino da Fonseca.—Manoel Innocencio de Vasconcellos,* sargento-mór.—*Francisco Manoel de Araujo.—Francisco de Mesquita Vianna,* tenente do 2.º regimento de cavallaria.—*José Manoel de Abreu.—José Joaquim dos Santos Silva,* alferes.—*Autonio Pereira Mendes.—Paulo José Rodrigues.—Joaquim Timotheo de Araujo.—João Theodoro Xavier.—Joaquim José Correa* (1),

VEREANÇA EXTRAORDINARIA DE 24 DE AGOSTO DE 1822

Aos 24 de Agosto de 1822, nesta cidade de S. Paulo e casas da Camara, paços do Conselho della, onde foram vindos o juiz de fora pela lei presidente, sargento-mór Manoel Lopes Guimarães, os vereadores actuaes capitães Bento José Leite Penteado e José Mariano Bueno e o vereador transacto capitão José de Almeida Ramos *(2)* e o actual procurador Luiz Manoel da Cunha Bastos, abaixo assignados, para effeito de se abrir um aviso regio de Sua Alteza Real, vindo do paço da Penha de França (3), e lendo-se o conteúdo determinava o mesmo Augusto Senhor que esta Camara fosse amanhan ás portas da cidade recebel-o e que *fossem aquelles vereadores que legalmente estavam servindo antes do acontecimento nesta cidade do dia 23 de Maio* (4), e na falta delles os transactos ds anno proximo passado, e que estes mesmos deveriam já assignar a resposta da mesma portaria, ao que logo pondo esta Camara o seu «cumpra se; accordou que o vereador mais velho e que serve de presidente, Manoel Lopes Guimarães, não deverá comparecer por tomar posse e entrar a servir de 30 de Maio em deante por excusa do capitão José Pedro da Cunha, que estava servindo

---

1 Contém este documento 76 assignaturas, das quaes mais de metade são de militares, o resto, 21, são de gente graduada da cidade, mas em pequeno numero para representar o clero e o povo.
2 Servia em ausencia de Antonio de Siqueira Queiroz, um dos mais comprometidos na *Bernarda* de 23 de Maio
3 D. Pedro, vindo do Rio de Janeiro, chegou ao arrabalde da Penha, onde pernoitou afim de chegar a S. Paulo na manhan de 25 de Agosto e dar tempo de completarem-se os festejos com que ia ser recebido. De lá mandou elle o aviso á Camara para recebel-o formalmente no dia seguinte
4 Por esta disposição se vê que D. Pedro pretendia excluir das festas officiaes os delinquentes da *Bernarda*, não permittindo que elles apparecessem nellas nem na sua qualidade de funccionarios publicos. Assim recusou elle tambem as finezas do coronel Francisco Ignacio, um dos principaes chefes da *Bernarda*.

legalmente, e deveriam comparecer em corpo de Camara o capitão Bento José Leite Penteado, como presidente, o capitão José Mariano Bueno e o capitão José de Almeida Ramos, vereador transacto do anno passado, em lugar do dito capitão José Pedro, que se acha em seu sitio doente, e o dr. Manoel Joaquim de Ornellas, vereador mais transacto, por ter sufficiencia para falar e representar por parte desta Camara o que for preciso. E passando-se a responder á mesma portaria assignaram os mesmos que aqui abaixo assignam e determinaram que eu, escrivão, levasse immediatamente ao paço da Penha. Outrosim me ordenaram que convidasse outros vereadores transactos para pegarem no pallio e no estandarte em adjutorio a esta Camara. E para constar mandaram lavrar este termo em que assignaram, e eu João Nepomuceno de Almeida, escrivão, o escrevi.—*Penteado* — *Bueno* — *Ramos* — *Bastos*.

---

VEREAÇÃO EXTRAORDINARIA PARA TRATAR DA CONVENIENCIA DE POCLAMAR D. PEDRO IMPERADOR (1)

Aos 28 de Setembro de 1822, nesta cidade de S. Paulo e casas da Camara, paços do Conselho della, achando-se presentes em acto de vereação o juiz presidente pela lei, capitão Bento José Leite Penteado e os vereadores transactos dr. Manoel Joaquim de Ornellas, sargento-mór Antonio Safino da Fonseca e capitão José de Almeida Ramos e o procurador transacto capitão Antonio José Vieira Barbosa, abaixo assignados, concorrendo ao referido acto de vereação o clero, nobreza e povo desta cidade, por convite da mesma Camara, afim de lhes ser lida a carta que lhe dirigiu a Camara da Côrte e cidade do Rio de Janeiro e darem os seus votos sobre a necessidade em que está este reino do Brasil de investir a Sua Alteza Real, em Augusto Regente e Defensor Perpetuo, de todas as attribuições do Poder Executivo, sem restricção alguma, como chefe constitucional do mesmo poder em todo este reino ; e sendo-lhes com effeito lida a mencionada carta em voz alta por mim, escrivão, por todos foi unanimemente accordado que concordavam com a sobredita Camara da Côrte e cidade do Rio de Janeiro em que Sua Alteza Real

---

1 Este documento não é mais dos *Tempos Coloniaes,* porem vae aqui transcripto sómente pelas assignaturas que contém Estas são em numero de 170 e grande parte é de gente da melhor sociedade desta capital. Quando comparadas estas assignaturas com as da acta de vereança de 23 de Maio, atraz transcripta, se verificará que nesta estão incluidos os nomes da gente civil e boa de S. Paulo e naquella os dos militares e de alguns plebeus sem responsabilidade moral.

entrasse desde já no exercicio illimitado de todas as attribuições do Poder Executivo que pela Constituição lhe devem competir na qualidade de chefe do mesmo poder, visto ser este o unico meio seguro e adequado para poder salvar este reino das indiscretas tentativas dos seus inimigos e conservar illesa a sua dignidade e independencia já proclamada pelo mesmo Augusto Senhor. E para assim constar mandou esta Camara lavrar este termo de vereação em que assignou com todos os concorrentes. Declaro mais que foi accordado na mesma vereação que se escrevesse a Sua Alteza Real e á mesma Camara da Corte do Rio de Janeiro, remettendo-se por copia o presente termo. E eu João Nepomuceno de Alme da, escrivão, o escrevi. - *Bento José Leite Penteado*—*Manoel Joaquim de Ornellas* —*Antonio Safino da Fonseca*. — *José de Almeida Ramos*.—*Antonio José Vieira Barbosa*.—*João Nepomuceno de Almeida*.—O chantre *Antonio Joaquim de Abreu Pereira* —O conego *Manoel Caetano de Oliveira*. —O conego *Francisco Joaquim de Toledo Arouche* —O conego *Lourenço Justiniano Ferreira*.—O conego *Joaquim José Carlos de Carvalho*.—O conego *Antonio Paes de Camargo* — O conego *Melchior Fernandes Nunes* —O conego *José Gomes de Almeida*. —O conego cura *Antonio Marques Henriques* —O guardião de S. Francisco *Fr. João do Espirito Santo*.—*Fr. Manoel da Natividade Marques*, presidente de S. Bento.—O vigario *Antonio Joaquim da Silva*.—*Fr José da Purificação*, presidente do Car mo.—O padre *Joaquim Antonio Fernandes de Saldanha*. lente. de Theologia.—O vigario collado *Francisco de Paula Teixeira*-—O vigario collado *José Basilio Rodrigues Cardim* —O vigario collado *José Domiciano de Meira*.— O professor publico *Manoel Joaquim do Amaral Gurgel*.—O professor publico *Antonio Mariano de Azevedo Marques* —O padre *Manoel Emygdio Bernardes*, sub chantre da Sé.—*José de Freitas Saldanha*, mestre de cerimonias —O professor *Leão José de Senna*.—O padre *José Joaquim de Toledo*.—O padre *Manoel Joaquim de Oliveira*.— O padre *José Joaquim de Oliveira*.—O padre *José Manoel de Souza*.—*Joaquim Antonio Rodrigues de Vasconcellos* —*Joaquim Manoel de Azevedo Marques*.—*José Antonio dos Reis* (1)—*Vicente Pires da Motta* (2)—*Manoel Francisco de Andrade*, capellão da cavallaria de linha.—O padre *João Joaquim de Carvalho Pinto*. — O padre *José Joaquim de Oliveira*............ (3) ...

1 Era padre e foi bispo de Cuyabá; fez figura na politica, foi deputado geral duas vezes.
2 Tambem era padre e figurou em S. Paulo, foi lente da Academia e seu director e presidente da provincia por mais de uma vez.
3 O ultimo sobrenome está illegivel.

O padre *Francisco Emygdio de Toledo—Francisco Antonio de Paula Nogueira da Gama—João Vicente da Fonseca*—O commendador *Manoel da Cunha de Azevedo Coutinho Souza Chichorro — José Joaquim Cesar de Cerqueira Leme —Joaquim José de Moraes*, tenente-coronel—*João Pereira Simões*, tenente-coronel—*Manoel de Campos Penteado*, sargento-mór—*Eleuterio da Silva Prado*, capitão-mór—*José Joaquim de Vasconcellos Alambary*, sargento mór do estado-maior do exercito e ajudante de ordens do inspector geral de milicias—*Francisco Xavier Pinheiro*, sargento mór reformado—*Antonio José Bordini*, sargento-mór da 2.ª linha—*Manoel José da Costa Ribeiro*, sargento-mór —*Thomaz Gonçalves Gomide*, sargento mór—*Bento José de Moraes*, capitão do estado maior do exercito—*Joaquim Floriano de Toledo*, 2.º official da Secretaria—*Francisco Pinto Ferraz*, capitão—*Antonio de Almeida e Silva Freire*, juiz de fóra de Taubaté e nesta cidade em diligencia—*Antonio Joaquim da Costa Ribeiro*, capitão—*Matheus Fernandes Coutinho*, capitão—*Joaquim Firmino Gonçalves—Manoel dos Santos Lima*, ajudante—*Jeronymo José de Andrade*, ajudante—*Fructuoso José de Campos*, tenente—*Luiz Antonio de Sá Brazeiro—José Manoel da Costa Ribeiro*, capitão—*José Olintho de Carvalho e Silva*, ajudante —*Luiz Gonzaga de Araujo*, tenente—*Joaquim Antonio Alves Alvim*, alferes—*José Elias da Silva*, tenente—*Francisco de Salles Borralho*, ajudante—*Francisco Bernardes Corrêa*, tenente—*Manoel José da Silva Castro—Francisco Severiano dos Santos Cardim*, tenente—*Joaquim José Machado de Oliveira*, guarda civica—*João Homem Guedes Portilho*, alferes—*Martinho José Marques*, capitão—*Januario Antonio de Araujo*, guarda civica—*José Gonçalves Gomide*, guarda civica—*Dr. Justiniano de Mello Franco*, guarda civica—*Manoel José Rodrigues da Silva*, guarda civica—*Bernardo Guedes Cardoso de Vasconcellos*, tenente—*Manoel Joaquim Coelho*, capitão—*Manoel Felizardo de Carvalho e Almeida*, ajudante—*João Olintho de Carvalho e Silva*, guarda civica—*Manoel José Chaves*, guarda civica—*Joaquim Maria da Costa Ferreira*, capitão—*João Rodrigues de Camargo Pires*, tenente—*Manoel Gonçalves da Luz Paralhão*, tenente—*Francisco de Paula Xavier de Toledo*, juiz almotacel—*Candido Gonçalves Gomide*, guarda civica—*Joaquim Cardoso*, cirurgião-mór do hospital—*José da Silva Mirceana—Luiz Manoel da Cunha Bastos*, capitão—*Manoel Innocencio de Vasconcellos*, sargento-mór—*José Maria de Mello e Souza*, sargento-mór—*Antonio Xavier Ferreira*, guarda civica—*Joaquim Theobaldo Machado*, guarda civica—*Manoel Delfino da Fonseca*, guarda-civica—*Severino Pinto da Silva*, capitão—*João Lopes França*, capitão—

*Manoel Eufrasio de Azevedo Marques*, guarda civica e escrivão da pagadoria—*José Clemente de Mesquita*, guarda civica—*Manoel Gomes de Gouvêa*, guarda civica—*José Xavier de Azevedo Marques*, guarda civica e praticante da contadoria—*Fortunato Corrêa de Mello*—*André Alves Ferreira do Amaral*, tenente — *Francisco de Assis Cruz*, tenente—*Luiz Antonio Pinto do Rego*, ajudante—*José Mathias Ferreira de Abreu*, secretario interino do expediente do governo—*Antonio da Silva Prado*, capitão e guarda civica—*Luiz Antonio da Silva Freire*, escripturario da contadoria—*Francisco da Silva Prado*, capitão—*Joaquim Theodoro de Araujo*, praticante da contadoria—*Joaquim Alves Moreira*, capitão—*João Baptista Tavares*, alferes—*José Rodrigues da Silva*, ajudante—*Antonio J Fernandes Gabizo*, tenente—*João José Moreira*, official da contadoria—*Manoel José de Castro*, almoxarife do hospital—*João Baptista Vaz*, escripturario da contadoria—*José Antonio de Abranches*, alferes—*José Francisco Serpa*—*Francisco de Paula e Oliveira*, tenente—*Antonio José Pereira dos Santos*, alferes—*José Pereira Jorge*, capitão—*João Ferreira da Silva*, escriptnrario da contadoria—*Joaquim José do Rosario*, alferes—*Joaquim Antonio da Cunha*, alferes—*Francisco de Assis Ludgero*, alferes—*Gaspar Ribeiro da Rosa*, sargento-mór reformado e guarda civica—O brigadeiro *João Jacomo de Baumann*—*Joaquim José da Silveira Baptista*—*Antonio Joaquim Furquim Justino*—*Francisco Jorge de Paula Ribeiro*. guarda civica—O padre *Hygino Francisco Teixeira*—*Bento Corrêa Leme*, capitão—*Joaquim Rodrigues Goulart*—*José da Fonseca Carvão e Camara*, capitão—*Joaquim José de Almeida*, capitão—*Bento Alberto da Gama e Sá*, tenente coronel de cavallaria—*Ignacio Antonio de Toledo*—*Ignacio José Cesar*, guarda civica—O padre *Manoel Joaquim Leite Penteado*—O padre *Joaquim de Sant'Anna Motta*—*Floriano da Costa e Silvo*, guarda civica—*Manoel José da Costa Cintra*, capitão—*João Ribeiro da Lapa e Silva*, guarda civica—O padre *Fernando Lopes de Camargo*—*Domingos de Araujo Roso*, tenente—*Antonio de Araujo Roso*—*Francisco Pinto Ferraz*, coronel—*Roberto Walkins* —O vigario—*José Joaquim Leite Penteado* -*Jose Teixeira dos Santos*—*Miguel Angelo da Silveira*, guarda civica e tenente-coronel reformado—*Felisberto Jose Machado*, capitão de ordenanças— *Segismundo de Lima*, tenente—*Francisco Jose' Barbosa*—*Luiz Manoel Feliciano Kellis*, tabellião—*José Rodrigues de Mendonça* —*José Rodrigues Velloso de Oliveira*—*Manoel Coelho Netto*— O sargento-mór *Diogo José Machado de Castro e Souza*—O sargento-mór *Antonio Xavier de Miranda Henriques*—O coronel *Bernardo José Pinto Gavião*.

ACTA DA ACCLAMAÇÃO DE D. PEDRO I, AOS 12 DE OUTUBRO DE
1822, DA CIDADE DE S. PAULO

Aos 12 de Outubro de 1822, nesta cidade de S. Paulo, em
casas da Camara e paços do Conselho, estando presentes o Ex.<sup>mo</sup>
governo actual da provincia (1), o juiz presidente do Senado,
capitão Bento José Leite Penteado, os vereadores capitão José
Mariano Bueno, doutor Manoel Joaquim de Ornellas e capitão
José Almeida Ramos, aquelle actual e estes transactos, o procurador, tambem transacto, capitão Antonio José Vieira Barbosa,
o povo e tropa, foi por todos unanimente accordado que declararam a sua independencia dos reinos de Portugal e Algarves e
por ella protestam dar a sua propria vida, e que certificados
officialmente pelo Senado da Camara da côrte e cidade do Rio
de Janeiro de que Sua Alteza Real o Principe Regente do
Brazil e seu Defensor Perpetuo, o Senhor Dom Pedro de Alcantara, é hoje, dia anniversario do seu natalicio, acclamado alli
e em algumas provincias colligadas (2), Primeiro Imperador
Constitucional do Brazil a bem deste igualmente o acclamam
como herdeiro immediato do throno portuguez (3), e lhe juram
obediencia e fidelidade debaixo da condição de que o mesmo
Senhor prestará previamente o solemne juramento de guardar,
manter e defender a constituição politica que fizer a Assembléa
Geral Constituinte e Legislativa Brazileira, fundada em solidas
bases e interessante a todo o imperio do Brazil, cuja séde se
deve forçosamente fixar dentro delle, attenta a sua vastidão e
riqueza, tendo esta felicissima acclamação por firmissimo e inabalavel fundamento, 1.º o constar com toda a certeza que as
Côrtes de Portugal, arrogando a si todos os direitos da soberania, contra as bases da promettida constituição que juraram, têm
posto em execução tudo quanto lhes agrada contra os direitos e
interesses do Brazil, afim de o recolonizarem, ameaçando proximamente com a emissão de novas tropas européas para o obri-
garem a annuir ás suas mal fundadas pretenções; 2.º, o achar-se
El-Rei Constitucional, o Senhor Dom João Septimo, Augusto Pae
de Sua Magestade Imperial, em um estado de prisioneiro em
Lisboa e sem a menor acção para o livre exercicio do Poder
Executivo, sendo um mero instrumento de que as mesmas Côrtes
abusiva e perfidamente se hão servido para vexarem e opprimi-

---

(1) O governo provincial se compunha então de tres membros, que eram o bispo
D. Matheus, o marechal Candido Xavier e o dr. Pacheco e Silva.
(2) As provincias do norte estavam desligadas das do sul e sujeitas ao governo
directo de Lisboa.
(3) Esta phrase está obscura e dá a entender que D. Pedro era acclamado imperador do Brasil por ser o herdeiro immediato da corôa portugueza e que não seria
acclamado si tal não fosse.

rem o Brazil, não podendo por isso prestarem aos habitantes deste novo impeiio aquella protecção que todo o monarcha constitucional deve dar aos seus subditos, nem tão pouco desempenhar para com elles as imprescriptiveis obrigações inherentes á sua alta dignidade, devendo o Brazil em tão criticas circumstancias prevenir quanto antes, por um tão legitimo e adequado meio, os grandes males da anarchia e da guerra civil, que podem resultar de um tal estado de oppressão e abandono e de medidas tão indiscretas, injustas e hostis, tomadas pelas referidas Côrtes, pois o povo do Brazil, sendo tão livre e soberano como é o de Portugal e Algarves, tem o inauferivel direito de lançar mão de todos os meios necessarios para a sua salvação e bem-ser na perigosa situação em que se acha, sendo um destes meios o eleger quem o reja debaixo de uma constituição liberal e judiciosa, que se propõe fazer por meio dos seus representantes (1), e possa desempenhar para com elle as importantissimas obrigações a que está ligado todo o imperante para com os seus subditos em qualquer sociedade civil (2), o que tudo concorre na pessôa de Sua Alteza Real.

Accordaram, finalmente, por unanime consentimento que, sem perda de tempo, se envie uma deputação ao novo Imperador, com carta de congratulação e uma copia da presente acta, para o felicitar pela sua exaltação aó throno, e para a mencionada deputação nomeiam aos dous procuradores geraes da provincia, os Illmos e Exmos Tenentes Geraes Manoel Martins de Castro Reis e Desembargador do Paço Antonio Rodrigues Velloso de Oliveira existentes na corte e cidade do Rio de Janeiro. E para a todo o tempo constar o referido se lavrou esta acta em que todos assignaram, e eu João Nepomuceno de Almeida, escrivão da Camara, a escrevi e assignei.—*Martins, Bispo*—*Candido Xavier de Almeida e Souza*—*José Correia Pacheco e Silva* (3)—*Bento Jose Leite Penteado*—*Manoel Joaquim de Ornellas* - *José de Almeida Ramos*—*José Mariano Bueno*—*Antonio José Vieira Barbosa*—*João Nepomuceno de Almeida*, guarda civica-- *Eleuterio da Silva Prado*—*Francisco de Paula Xavier de Toledo*, almotacel—*João Rodrigues de Camargo Pires*, almotacel—*Antonio Joaquim de Abreu Pereira*, chantre—O conego *Manoel Caetano de Oliveira* --O conego *Francisco Joaquim de Toledo Arouche*—O conego *Lourenço Justiniano Ferreira*—O conego *Joaquim José Carlos*

---

1 As ordens para eleição da Assembléa Constituinte Brasileira já estavam dadas a este tempo e as esperanças dos patriotas eram fundadas.
2 Até pouco tempo antes os subditos só tinham deveres e não direitos.
4 Estes tres primeiros signatarios eram os membros do governo de S. Paulo instalado por D. Pedro em 10 de Setembro de 1822.

*de Carvalho*—O conego *Antonio Pires de Camargo*—O conego *Melchior Fernandes Nunes*—O conego *Francisco José Lobo*—O conego *José Gomes de Almeida*—O conego cura *José Marques* —O vigario *Antonio Joaquim da Silva*—O guardião de S. Francisco—*Fr. João do Espirito Santo*—O padre *Joaquim Antonio Fernandes de Saldanha*, lente de Theologia—*Francisco de Assis Lorena*, tenente coronel—*Manoel Joaquim do Amaral Gurgel*, lente de Historia Ecclesiastica (1)—O brigadeiro *Francisco Antonio de Paula Nogueira da Gama*—O brigadeiro *João Jacomo de Baumann*—O commendador *Manoel da Cunha Azevedo Coutinho Souza Chicorro*—*Joaquim Maria da Costa Ferreira*, Capitão—*João Vicente da Fonseca*, coronel—*Anastacio de Freitas Trancoso*, coronel da guarda civica (2) - *Joaquim Theobaldo Machado*, cirurgião mór da guarda civica (3)—*Ignacio Alves de Toledo* coronel—*Diogo José Machado de Castro e Souza*—O mestre de cerimonias—*José de Freitas Saldanha* - *Manoel de Jesus Costa Cintra*—*Joaquim José dos Santos*, coronel—*Joaqdim Olintho de Carvalho*—O padre *Roque Soares de Campos*—O padre *Ildefonso Xavier Ferreira*, guarda civico—O padre *Antonio Romualdo Freire*—O padre *João Joaquim de Carvalho Pinto*—*Antonio Mariano de Azevedo Marques*—O major *José Mathias Ferreira de Abreu*—O major *José Innocencio de Vasconcellos*—*José Joaquim de Vasconcellos Alambary*, sargento-mór e ajudantes de ordens— *Francisco Jorge de Paula Ribeiro*, guarda civica—O padre *João* ..... (4) .....— *José Antonio Teixeira Cabral*—*Thomaz de Aquino e Castro*—*Bernardo José Pinto Gavião*, coronel—*José da Silva Carvalho*, major—*Fr. Manoel da Natividade Marques*, presidente de S. Bento—O padre *Joaquim Ribeiro de*...(5).a.. —O padre *Fernando Lopes de Camargo*—*Bento Alberto da Gama e Sá*—*Mariano de Almeida Leme*—*Miguel Angelo da Silveira*— *José Gonçalves Gomide*, guarda civica—*José Joaquim Cesar de Cerqueira Leme*, coronel—*João Gonçalves Bastos*, tenente coronel —*Joaquim Cardoso*, guarda civica—*Joaquim José de Moraes Abreu*, tenente coronel—*João Pereira Simões*, tenente coronel— *Francisco Pinto Ferraz*, capitão commandante do 2·. regimento —*Antonio José Bordint*, sargento-mór—*Bento José de Moraes*, capitão do estado maior—*Jeronimo José de Andrade*, ajudante— *Floriano da Costa e Silva*, guarda civica—*Luiz Antonio de Sá Brazeiro*, capitão—*Matheus Fernandes Cantinho*—*Luiz Pedroso*

---

1 Era padre e um dos mais illustres do clero paulistano.
2 Em Janeiro de 1823 entrou a faser parte do governo de S. Paulo.
3 Era o pae do grande medico e notavel politico Francisco Alves Machado.
4 O sobre nome está escripto com lettra illegivel. parecendo ser Nasianzeno.
5 Está o sobrenome em breve, mal escripto e indecifravel.

*da Silva,* ajudante—*Rafael Antonio Leite,* tenente—*Joaqaim Floriano de Toledo,* tenente—*Antonio Joaquim da Costa Ribeiro,* capitão—*Joaquim José de Almeida,* capitão—*Francisco de Assis Cruz,* tenente—*André Alves Ferreira do Amaral,* tenente - *José Manoel da Costa Ribeiro,* capitão—*Raymundo Pinto Homem,* alferes—*Bento Corrêa Leme,* capitão guarda civica—*Joaqnim José da Silva,* alferes—*Francisco da Silva Prado,* capitão—*Manoel Gonçalves da Luz Paralhão,* tenente—*Francisco Severiano dos Santos Cardim,* tenente—*Joaquim José dos Santos Silva,* alferes —*João Baptista de Oliveira,* tenente—*Sigismundo N. de Lima,* tenente *Manoel dos Santos Lima,* ajudante—*Joaquim Innocencio Rodrigues Cardim,* tenente—*José Antonio de Abranches,* alferes *José Maaiano Lara,* major—*Francisco Antonio Romano,* alferes —*Luiz Antonio do Valle Quaresma,* capitão—*Joaquim Podrigues Paes,* alferes—*Luiz Antonio Gonçalves,* capitão—*Joaquim Floriano de Godoy,* capitão—*José da Cunha e Abreu,* tenente-coronel—*Francisco Manoel de Andrada Figueiredo e Albuquerque,* alferes—*Manoel de Campos Penteado,* cadete—*Francisco Candido Sagalerva,* capitão—*Francisco de Paula e Oliveira,* tenente— *Joaquim José de Oliveira,* tenente—*José Antonio da Cunha,* tenente—*Francisco de Paula Leite Prestes.* capitão—*Maximiano Bueno da Cunha—Manoel de Campos Penieado,* sargento mór— *Pedro Fernaades de Andrade,* tenente—*José G. de Jesus,* alferes *Francisco Bernardes Corrêa,* tenente—*Joaquim Antomio da Cunha,* alferes—*Domingos Manoel Barbosa,* alferes—*Joaquim Floriano de Siqueira,* alferes—*Messias José da Rosa,* tenente—*Joaquim José Ferreira—José Leite de Souza,* alferes—*Joaquim José do Rosario,* alferes—*Antonio José Pereira dos Santos,* alferes—*Joaquim Januario Pinto Ferraz,* cadete—O prior do Carmo, *Frei Antonio de Santa Gertrudes*—O padre *Leão de Senna,* professor de Grammatica Latina—*Frei José de Santa Delfina,* visitador delegado— *Frei João de Santo Aleixo,* padre e secretario—*Jose Joaquim de Toledo—Francisco de Paula Tavares—*O padre *Antonio Teixeira Camillo*—O padre *José Domiciano de Meira—João Baptista Vaz,* alferes—*Manoel Joaquim de Vasconcellos*— *Antonio de Almeida e Silva Freire,* juiz de fóra de Santos - Dr. *Justiniano de Mello Franco,* physico-mór interino e guarda civica—*Januario Antonio de Araujo,* guarda civica—*Luiz Gonzaga de Araujo,* tenente—*João Homem Guedes Portilho,* alferes—*Joaquim José Machado,* guarda civica—*Antonio Xavier Ferreira,* guarda civica—*José Francisco Xavier dos Santos,* guarda civica - *José Gomes Segurado,* guarda civica—*Manoel José Chaves,* guarda civica - *Joaquim José Freire da Silva,* guarda civica - *Roberto Watkins,* guarda civica—*João Manoel de Almeida,* guarda civica—*Antonio Joaquim de Araujo*

*Leite,* guarda civica—*João Olintho de Carvalho,* guarda civica—
O padre *Fidelis Alves Sigmaringa de Moraes*--*Francisco Xavier
de Assis,* guarda civica e praticante da contadoria—O padre
*João Nepomuceno Fernandes Souto,* guarda civica—*Innocencio
José Rodrigues de Vasconcellos,* guarda civica—*Manoel José Rodrigues da Silva,* guarda civica--*José Elias de Carvalho,* guarda
civica—*Domingos Francisco de Andrade*—*Manoel Joaquim Coelho,*
capitão—*Manoel José da Costa,* sargento-mór—*João Lopes França,*
capitão—*José da Silva Lisboa,* coronel—*Lniz Antonio Piuto do
Rego,* ajudante—*Bernardo Guedes Cardoso de Vasconcellos,* te-
nente—*Francisco José de Azevedo,* capitão--*José Antonio de
Assumpção*—O padre *Manoel Joaquim de Oliveira,* guarda civica
*Francisco de Paula Lustosa*—*Luiz de Vasconcellos Parada e
Souza,* sargento-mór—*Severino Pinto da Silva,* capitão—*Manoel
José da Costa Ribeiro,* sargento-mór—*Manoel José da Silva Castro,*
guarda civica—*Joaquim da Silva Pontes*-*Joaquim Gonçalves
Gomide,* guarda civica –O padre *Marcelino Ferreira,* guarda civica—*José Antonio Fernandes*—*José Antonio Pimenta,* guarda
civica-*José Manoel da Silva,* capitão—*Francisco José de Car-
valho Faro*—*Luiz Antonio da Silva Freire,* escripturario da
contadoria – O padre *Jeronimo Maximo Rodrigues Cardim,*
guardacivica—*Manoel José da Silva,* alferes–O padre *Manoel
Emygdio Bernardes.* sub-chantre—*Francisco Gomes da Silva
— José Vicente Lisboa* — O padre *Manoel de Faria Doria,*
guarda civica — *Candido Gonçalves Gomide,* guarda civica —
O padre *Joaquim Manoel de Azevedo Marques,* guarda civica
—*Francisco de Assis Pinheiro Prado,* guarda civica—*Joaquim
Alves Moreira,* capitão—*Joaquim Antonio Rodrigues de Vasconcellos,* capitão — *João Baptista Tavares,* alferes — *Jeronymo de
Abreu Rangel*-*Joaquim Rodrigues Goulart,* guarda civica—*Joa-
quim Antonio Alves Alvim,* alferes—*Antonio Ribeiro de Escobar
—Thomaz Innocencio Lustosa*—*José Gonçalves Gomide,* guarda
civica—*José Felippe de Santiago*—O padre *Manoal Joaquim
Leite Penteado,* guarda civica—*José Teixeira dos Santos,* guarda
civica—*Gregorio Ignacio Ferreira Nobre,* capitão ajudante de
ordens da governo—*Francisco Gonçalves de Almeida*—O sargento
mór *Antonio Xavier de Miranda Henriques*—*José Rodrigues
Velloso de Oliveira,* guarda civica—O vigario *José Joaquim
Leite Penteado* — *Jeronymo Pinelli* — O padre *José Joaquim da
Silva Lisboa*—*Manoel José de Castro,* almoxarife do hospital—
O padre *José Joaquim de Oliveira Brazeiros,* guarda civica—
*José Joaquim de Andrade e Aquino,* escrivão do hospital—*Gaspar Pinheiro da Rosa Ramos,* sargento-mór reformado e guarda
civica—*Ignacio Teixeira de Cerqueira Cesar*—*Januario Antonio*

*de Lima*, coronel reformado — *Bernardo Justino da Silva* —*Joaquim Borges de Sampaio*, guarda civica— *Antonio da Silva Prado*, capitão e guarda civica — *João Antonio Rosa* — O padre *Vicente Pires da Motta* — *Luiz Antonio de Assumpção*, capitão— *José Antonio de Carvalho* — *João Ribeiro da Lapa e Silva*, guarda civica —*José da Silva Monteiro* — *Dyonizio E da Motta* — *Manoel Lopes Guimarães* — *Erancisco Antonio B* . (1)— *Antonio José de Faria* — *Antonio Joaquim Purquim Justino*, guarda civica— *Luiz Manoel da Cunha Bastos*, capitão— *Ignacio Lopes Cezar*, guarda civica— *Miguel Antonio de Godoy*, guarda civica— *José Rodrigues Coelho* — *José Vaz de Carvalho*, brigadeiro — *Joaquim José dos Santos*, capitão— *Constantino José dos Santos* — *Thomaz Gonçalves Gomide*, guarda civica — *João Gonçalves Gomide*, guarda civica— *Thomaz Gonçalves Gomide*, guarda civica (2) — *Erancisco de Assis Gonçalves Gomide*, guarda civica —*Martinho Gonçalves Gomide*, guarda civica — O padre *Joaquim de Sant'Anna Motta*, guarda civica — *Manoel de Rezende* — O padre *José Manoel de Souza*, guarda civica — *Erancisco Pinto do Rego Trancoso* — *Francisco J. P. de Mattos* — *Elorianno Antonio Rodrigues* — *Eleuterio José Pinto*, tenente — *Joaquim José de Camargo*, — sargento *Francisco José Paes de Camargo*, — *José Eelippe de*..... (3), sargento — O padre *Joaquim Francisco de Abreu*, capellão do hospital — *Luiz Manoel*, *Feliciano Kellis* — O padre *José Erancisco de Mendonça*, vigario de Xiririca — *Manoel Leite de Oliveira* — *Antonio Manoel Pereira* — *Joaqnim da Silva Abreu Vianna*, alleres—*Manoel Ribeiro de Araujo*, guarda civica— O padre *Antonio Felix de Oliveira*—*José Maria de Oliveira*—*José de Oliveira Prado* — *Francisco Mariano de Abreu*— *Francisco Xavier de Brito*, sargento—O padre *Elorentino José Maria* — O padre *Pedro Nolasco Cezar*—*José Joaquim de Castro* —*Francisco Xavier Pinheiro*, sargento-mór raformado e guarda civica— O vigario collado, *José Bazilio Rodrigues Cardim*, guarda civica—*Lourenço Josephino Cardim*—*Manoel Eerreira Duarte*— *José da Silva Marceana*, guarda-mór e advogado—*José Ant nio Pereira*, alferes—*Manoel Euphrazio de Azevedo Marques*, escrivão da pagadoria e guarda civica—*João José Moreira*, guarda civica —*Erancisco Antonio de Miranda*, capitão—*Erancisco José Barbosa* - *Domingos Affonso de Sant'Anna*, porteiro—*Manoel Custodio do Nascimento Cunha*, escrivão da vara do alcaide—*José Pereira Jorge*, capitão—*Erancisco Pereira de Araujo*, capitão—

---

(1) O sobrenome está escripto em bréve e é illegivel.
(2) São dous indeviduos com o mesmo nome e lettra muito diversa.
(3) O sebrenome está illegivel.

*Bento José da Silva Rego*, guarda civica—*Miguel Antunes Gar
cia—Antonio Bernardo Bueno da Veiga*, capitão e guarda civica
—*Francisco Pinto Eerraz*—O padre *João Ferreira de Oliveira
Bueno*, thesoureiro-mór da Sé—*Manoel Delfino da Fonseca*, offi-
cia da contadoria e guarda civica—O padre *Francisco de Paula
e Oliveira*, professor publico de philosophia e guarda civica--
*André da Silva Gomes*, professor publico de Grammatica Latina
—*Signal + de Antonio Jacintho Strit — Caetano + José dos
Santos—Signal + de Francisco Gomes Netto*.

REPRESENTAÇÃO DO POVO DA CIDADE DE S. PAULO, REMETTIDA A
D. PEDRO I, POR INTERMEDIO DA CAMARA MUNICIPAL, EM
QUE SE PEDE QUE JOSÉ BONIFACIO E MARTIM FRANCISCO SE-
JAM CONSERVADOS NAS SUAS PASTAS DE MINISTROS DE ESTA O.

No meio dos publicos festejos, signaes não equivocos do
regosijo que trausporta vossos corações, pela gloriosa acclamação
do senhor D. Pedro de Alcantara, imperador sem par, idolo dos
brasileiros, ouvimos e lemos com espauto que um partido de vis
carbonarios, de monstros da especie humana, solapavam a estabilidade do throno brasileiro e, servindo se de tramas e cabalas,
pretenderam murchar em flor nossas esperanças, offuscar a gloria do immortal Pedro, privando-o de um ministerio sabio, justo e forte.

Oh! Só meros automatos não se sentiri·m arrebatados de
rancor e de desesperação pela avidez de morder esses corações
perfidos que manejavam a intriga e a desordem, que pretendiam
levar de rojo o recem-nascido e florescente imperio, estabelecendo a anarchia, a destruição e a guerra civil!!!!

Como veriamos sem horror mallogrados nossos trabalhos,
menoscabado nosso nome e nossos inimigos exultando de alegria,
vendo o Basil descer do seu throno magestoso e abafando nos
labios o grito da Independencia que levantou com denodo e jurou com coragem? Como não seria insultado de novo nesse denominado «Soberano Congresso Lisbonense» o nosso anjo tutelar,
o magnanimo Pedro? Como não zombariam de suas acertadss e
maduras resoluções e de seus justos decretos, attribuindo-os ás
vacillações de um menino que, na sua opinião, devia ainda apprender os primeiros elementos de litteratura nas cortes extrangeiras?

Que serie de males, que abysmo de horrores! .. Mas, oh
ventura! os bons brasileiros, habitantes do Rio de Janeiro, idolatras da patria, do imperador e das virtudes, souberam apagar

o incendio, que começava a atear-se, e anniquilar o partido que ousadamente queria d minar. Elles viram bambalear o magestoso edificio da nossa bem entendida liberdade e ir a cahir por terra os mais firmes esteios do throno e, calculando as consequencias, dando desafogo ás suas virtudes innatas, deram o passo que só podia salvar-nos de novo: representaram ao imperador que a patria exigia que elle fizesse o sacrificio mais grato a seu coração, restituindo ao ministerio os benemeritos brasileiros, os nossos dignos patricios (com que gloria o dizemos!), os grandes, os sabios, os justos Andradas.

Os infra e criptos, pois, querendo dar um publico testemunho de seus sentimentos patrioticos, completamente identicos aos do bom povo do Rio de Janeiro, exigem que, com toda a brevidade, a Camara desta cidade, como orgam do povo, agradeça a Sua Magestade Imperial o restabelecimento dos seus bons ministros e roguem a sua conservação, pois nelles confiam a segurança da patria, a conservação e o progresso do imperio brasileiro, porqua to é incontestavel que o ministerio é a mola real dos imperios e, desde que esta se entorpece, retarda-se e até destroe-se o movimento regular destas grandes machinas.

Não é necessario procurar demonstrações desta verdade; ella é de evidencia politica e os ministerios do senhor rei D. João VI e mesmo de Sua Magestade Imperial, até os começos deste anno, são bem eloquentes testemunhos; e se renovam os protestos da mais firme adhesão á sua sagrada pessoa e á santa causa do Brasil, que os paulistas juram defender até ao ultimo alento, e rogue outrosim a Sua Magestade Imperial o mais exemplar castigo desses infames que procuraram denegrir nossa gloria.

Agradeça-se á Camara e ao honrado povo do Rio de Janeiro o passo heroico que deram, pedindo a Sua Magestade a conservação dos sabios ministros que nada têm a invejar aos Colberts, aos Sullys e aos Pitts e que rivalizam a gloria dos Franklins; assegurando lhes que os valentes e briosos paulistas, desejando imitar suas virtudes patrioticas, hão de sempre collaborar com denodo na conservação do imperio do Brasil e de seu immortal imperador e nos progressos de sua felicidade, quaesquer que sejam os sacrificios que devam fazer e quaesquer que sejam os perigos que devam affr ntar. S. Paulo, 11 de Novembro de 1822.—*Anastacio de Freitas Trancoso*, coronel reformado e commandante interino da guarda civica.—*Miguel Angelo da Silveira*, tenente coronel reformado e 2.° commandante interino da guarda civica.—*Antonio Joaquim de Abreu Pereira*, chantre.—*Francisco Nunes Ramalho*, capitão reformado e major da guarda civica.— O conego *Joaquim José Carlos de Carvalho*, guarda civica.—O conego *Francisco José Lobo.*—O conego *José Gomes de Almeida.*—O padre *Fernando Lopes de Camargo.*—O commendador *Manoel da Cunha de Azeredo Coutinho Souza Chichorro.*—*Antonio da Silva Prado,* guarda civica —O padre *Manoel Joaquim do Amaral Gurgel,* guarda civica.—O padre *Ildefonso Xavier Ferreira,* guarda civica.—*Francisco de Assis Lorena.*—O conego *Lourenço Justiniano Ferreira.*—O conego *Antonio P. de Camargo.*—*Francisco de Paula Tavares,* guarda civica.—*Manoel José Chaves,* guarda civica —*José Rodrigues Velloxo,* guarda civica.——*Ignacio José Cesar,* guarda civica.—*João Manoel de Almeida Bueno,* guarda civica.—*Francisco Jorge de Paula Ribeiro,* guarda civica.—*Francisco Pinto do Rego,* guarda civica. —*Joaquim Rodrigues Goulart,* guarda civica. — *José Maria Rodrigues Goulart,* guarda civica. — *João Nepomuceno Freire Souto,* guarda civica.—*José Porfirio,* guarda civica.—*Joaquim José da Silveira Baptista,* guarda civica. — *Thomaz Gonçalves Gomide,* guarda civica.—*Joaquim Gonçalves Gomide,* guarda civica — *José Gonçalves Gomide,* guarda civica. — *Thomaz M das Dores Ribeiro,* guarda civica. -- *Thomas de Aquino e Castro,* tenente de caçadores.—*José de Freitas Saldanha,* mestre das cerimonias.—*Antonio Mariano de Azevedo Marques,* guarda civica.—*Manoel Emygdio Fernandes,* sub-chantre da Sé —O padre *Leão Jose' de Senna.*—*Joaquim Manoel de Azevedo Marques,* guarda civica.— *João Olintho de Carvalho e Silva,* guarda civica. — *João Rodrigues de Camargo Pires,* tenente. —*Manoel Francisco da Motta.*—*Manoel Joaquim de Ornellas* —*Fr. João do Espirito Santo,* guardião de S. Francisco.—*Januario Antonio de Araujo,* guarda civica.—*Joaquim M. da Costa Ferreira,* capitão, ás ordens do governo. *João Jose' Moreira,* guarda civica. —*Joaquim Antonio Alves Alvim,* alferes.—*Jose' Gomes Segurado,* guarda civica.— *Jose' Maria da Silveira,* guarda civica. —*Joaquim Cardoso,* 1.º cirurgião mór do hospital e guarda civica —*Innocencio Jose' Rodrigues de Vasconcellos,* guarda civica. —*Thomaz Gonçalves Gomide,* official da Contadoria e guarda civica.—*Manoel Gomes de Gouvea,* guarda civica.—*Antonio Xavier Ferreira,* guarda civica.—*Joaquim Antonio Rodrigues de Vasconcellos,* guarda civica.— *Jose' Clemente de Mesquita,* guarda civica.—*Miguel Antonio de Godoy,* guarda civica.—*Jose' Antonio de Camargo,* guarda civica.—*Caetano Felix Theodoro Xavier,* guarda civica. —*João Nepomuceno de Almeida,* guarda civica — *José Francisco Xavier dos Santos,* guarda civica.—*Antonio José Pessoa,* guarda civica. — *Joaquim Borges de Sampaio,* guarda civica.—*Candido Gonçalves Gomide,* guarda civica. — *Martin Gonçalves Gomide,* guarda civica. — *João Gonçalves Gomide,* guarda civica.—*Jeronimo Maximo Rodrigues Cardim*, guarda civica.—*Francisco Martins Bonilha*, guarda civica. — *Manoel Francisco da Costa Silveira*. — *Joaquim Theodoro de Araujo*, guarda civica.—*Fr. Antonio de Santa Gertrudes*, prior do Carmo.—O major *José Mathios Ferreira de Abreu*, major da guarda civica.—*José Xavier de Azevedo Marques*, guarda civica.—*Francisco Antonio Pinto Bastos*.—*Candido Ignacio da Silva*, guarda civica.—*Joaquim Jose' Machado de Oliveira*, guarda civica.—*Antonio Marques Henriques*. conego cura da Sé. — *Antonio Manoel de Abreu*, coadjutor da Sé. — *Antonio Mariano da Silva*, sachristão da Sé. — *Antonio de Padua Gusmão*, tenente coronel. — *Francisco Antonio Romano*, alferes. — *Jose' Joaquim de Carvalho*. — O padre *Francisco de Paula Oliveira*, guarda civica.—*Jose' Joaquim Cesar de Cerqueira Leme*, coronel, *Joaquim José de Moraes Abreu*, tenente-coronel.—*Dr. Justiniano de Mello Franco*, physico-mór interino e guarda civica.—*Manoel Innocencio de Vasconcellos*, sargento-mór e guarda civica.—*Jose' Joaquim de Vasconcellos Alambary*, sargento-mór e ajudante de ordens.—*Manoel de Campos Penteado*, sargento-mór.—*Francisco Pinto Ferraz*, capitão de cavallaria.—*Francisco da Silva Prado*, capitão.—*Joaquim Jose' dos Santos Silva*, alferes.—*Antonio de Almeida e Silva Freire*, juiz de fóra de Taubaté e soldado da guarda civica.—*Manoel Joaquim Leite Penteado*, guarda civica.—*Manoel de Faria Doria*, guarda civica.—O vigario *Antonio Joaquim da Silva*.—*Pedro Antonio Ferreira*, alferes.—*Antonio Nunes Ramalho*, guarda civica.—O padre *Jose Joaquim de Oliveira Brazeiro*, guarda civica. *Joaquim Jose' de Almeida*, capitão.—O padre *Antonio Joaquim de Araujo Leite*, guarda civica.—*Joaquim Jose Freire da Silva*, guarda civica.—*Joaquim Jose' Freire Filho*, guarda civica.—*Manoel J. da Silva Castro*, guarda civica.—*Joaquim Floriano de Toledo*, tenente.—*Jose' Rodrigues da Silva*, ajudante.—*Ignacio Antonio de Toledo*, guarda civica.—*Manoel Joaquim de Toledo*, guarda civica.—*Jose' Teixeira dos Santos*, guarda civica—*Francisco de Assis Cruz*, tenente.—*Jose Francisco Serpa*.—*Bento Franco de Moraes*.—O padre *Jose' Manoel de Souza*, guarda civica.—*Manoel Delfino da Fonseca*, official da Contadoria e guarda civica. —*Francisco de Paula Xavier de Toledo*.—*Jose' Antonio Fernandes*, alferes.—*Bento Dias Vieira*.—*Thomaz Antonio Duarte*, guarda civica.—O padre *João Ferreira de Oliveira Bueno*, thesoureiro-mór da Sé e guarda civica.—O padre *Marcellino Ferreira Bueno*, guarda civica.—O padre *Vicente Pires da Motta*, guarda civica.—*Bento Correa Leme*, capitão de cavallaria.—*Manoel Jose' Rodrigues da Silva*, guarda civica.—*Manoel Nu-*

*nes Ramalho,* guarda civica.—*Roberto Watkins,* guarda civica.
—*Francisco de Assis Pinheiro Prado,* guarda civica.—*Jose' Cor-
rea Pacheco e Silva,* ouvidor da comarca.—*Segismundo Honorio
de Lima,* tenente.—*Antonio Joaquim da Costa Ribeiro,* capitão.
—*Luiz Antonio de Sá Brageiros,* capitão.—*Manoel Francisco
da Cruz Almeida,* capitão.—*João Baptista de Oliveira,* tenente.
*Francisco Bernardes Correa,* tenente.—*Manoel Gonçalves da Luz
Caralhão,* tenente.—*Manoel Ribeiro de Araujo,* guarda civica.—
*Jose' Ferreira Leite,* guarda civica.—*Jose' F. Leite Filho,* guarda civica.—*Jose' da Silva Carvalho,* sargento-mór.—O padre
*Joaquim A. Fernandes de Saldanha,* lente regio de Theologia
e guarda civica —*Manoel dos Santos Lima.*—*Luiz Jose' Carneiro,* sargento-mór de ordenanças.—*Jose' Manoel da Silva,* capitão.—*Marcellino J. de Vasconcellos Nardy,* capitão e guarda civica—*Antonio Rodrigues Moreira*—*Luiz Pedroso da Silva*—*Julião
de Moura Negrão,* coronel de milicias.—*Antonio Jose' Bordini,*
sargento-mór.—*Jose' Manoel da Luz,* sargento-mór.—*João Pereira Simões,* tenente coronel.—*Floriano da Costa e Silva,* guarda civica.—*Ignacio Jose' de Macedo,* tenente.—*Severino Pinto
da Silva,* capitão.—*Manoel B. de Toledo,* guarda civica.—*Francisco Pereira de Araujo.*—*Joaquim Jose' do Rosario,* alferes.—
*Antonio Jose' de Faria.*—*Diogo Correa Marzagão.*—*Joaquim B.
de Castro,* guarda civica,—*Jose' da Silva Marceana,* advogado e
guarda-mór da Junta de Justiça.—O padre *Sebastião A. de Oliveira Cruz.*—*Jose' Joaquim Monteiro.*—*Aleixo Correa Vieira:*—
*Salvador Pedroso de Barros,* guarda civica.—*João Homem Guedes Portilho,* alferes.—*Antonio R. Freire de Vasconcellos.*—
*João C. Marzagão.*—O padre *Manoel Dias de Abreu.*—*Andre'
da Silva Gomes,* guarda civica.—*Antonio Pedro G. da Silva
Gomes.*—*Bento Jose' de Moraes,* capitão.—*Bento Jose' da Silva
Rego,* guarda civica.—O padre *Andre' Joaquim da Silva Maca-
re'.*—*Jose' Ignacio da Silva.*—O vigario, *Jose' Bazilio Rodrigues
Cardim,* guarda civica.—*Francisco S. dos Santos Cardim,* tenente.—*Antonio B. Bueno da Veiga,* capitão de milicias e
guarda civica.—*Gregorio Ignacio F. Nobre,* capitão.—*João Lopes França,* capitão.—*Jose' Antonio Pimenta,* guarda civica.—
*Manoel Ferreira Duarte.*—*Diogo Jose' Machado de Castro,* sargento-mór.—*Francisco Jose' Barbosa.*—*Jose' Joaquim de Jesus
e Silva.*—*Jose' Rodrigues de Almeida.*—*João M. de Almeida
Bueno,* guarda civica.—*Joaquim Firmino Gonçalves,* guarda
civica.—*Luiz Manoel Feliciano Kell,.*—*Francisco de Assis Ludgero,* alferes.—*Jose' Feliciano Lara de Moraes.*—*Manoel das Neves de Jesus.*—*Luiz Antonio do Valle Quaresma.*—O padre *Florentino Jose' Maria,* guarda civica.—*Jose' Mendes da Silva,* alferes.

OFFICIO DA CAMARA DE S. PAULO A JOSÉ BONIFACIO, FELICITANDO-O
PELA SUA CONSERVAÇÃO NO MINISTERIO E PEDINDO-LHE PARA
SER O PORTADOR DE DUAS REPRESENTAÇÕES DO POVO PAULISTA.
A D. PEDRO I.

Ill.ᵐᵒ e Ex.ᵐᵒ Sr. : — A consoladora noticia de terem sido
novamente entregues as Secretarias de Estado dos Negocios deste
Imperio e Extrangeiros e dos da Fazenda Nacional ao extremoso
e vigilante cuidado dos dous benemeritos cidadãos que as regiam e
que nas actuaes circumstancias são os unicos capazes de as rege-
rem com dignidade, encheu de grande prazer os corações deste
povo, que ama devéras a sagrada causa do Brasil e a quem tanto
havia consternado a outra anterior noticia dos acontecimentos qne
ha bem pouco tempo se haviam patenteado nesta Côrte.

Esta Camara, pois, em nome do povo que representa, tem a
gostosa satisfação de levar á augusta presença de Sua Magestado.
Imperial, por intermedio de V. Ex.ᵃ, a evidentissima demonstração
de patriotismo, de gratidão e de reconhecimento do mesmo povo,.
patenteados na congratulação inclusa, pela heroica resolução do
povo dessa capital, na representação que dirigiu ao mesmo augusto Senhor para a restituição daquelles dous zelosos e honrados.
cidadãos, e juntamente pelo bem merecido acolhimento que teve
de Sua Magestade Imperial, pois que, sendo indispensavel que
grandes fins se não pódem conseguir sem grandes meios e que a
conservação de qualquer obra não é de menos importancia do
que a sua criação, era infallivel a decadencia do imperio do Brazil
na mesma feliz época da sua elevação, faltando-lhe os firmissimos.
pedestaes que o sustentavam e novamente o sustentam, quaes os.
dous grandes ministros acima designados, por isso mesmo que,
pelas suas grandes luzes, decidido patriotismo e inabalavel coragem, têm sido os dignos cooperadores para a grande obra da sua.
nova categoria e venturosa independencia.

As mesmas imperiosas circumstancias em que se vê o Brazil,.
cercado de inimigos, dentre do seu seio e fóra delle, exigem que
os governos provinciaes sejam compostos de homens dotados de
um reconhecido patriotismo, de uma inabalavel inteireza e de uma
decidida adhesão á importantissima causa do Brasil; e é por isso.
que esta Camara, movida pelos ponderosos motivos constantes da
representação junta e guiada pelo interesse do bem publico,
deseja que no novo governo da provincia, que se vae installar (1),

1) O governo de S. Paulo, então eleito pelo voto popular, se compunha do seguinte pessoal: Marechal Candido Xavier, presidente. dr. José Corrêa Pacheco e Silva,
secretario dr. Manoel Joaquim de Ornellas padre João Gonçalves de Lima e coroneis
Anastacio de Freitas Trancoso, João Baptista da Silva Passos e Francisco Corrêa de-

lhajam homens de semelhantes sentimentos, rogando por conseguinte a V. Ex.ª que para este importantissimo fim se digne
levar á alta consideração de sua Magestade Imperial a mesma
representação (1) e fazer ver ao mesmo augusto Senhor, da parte
desta Camara, o quanto convem á felicidade desta provincia que
entre no mesmo novo governo o bacharel Manoel Joaquim de
'Ornellas, attenta á pluralidade de votos que para isso tem, caso
venha a acontecer que, por effeito da mesma pluralidade de
votos, deva ir supprir a falta de algum dos deputados da Assembléa Geral Constituinte e Legislativa do Brazil, que sahiram
eleitos por parte desta provincia, visto ser elle o unico homem
formado que aqui ha e um dos que tanto tem auxiliado esta
Camara em todos os actos que ella tem figurado a bem da mesma
causa e que a mesma Camara considera muito capaz e digno de
a sustentar pela sua rectidão, actividade e energia, e é por estes
ponderosissimos fundamentos que espera merecer de Sua Magestade Imperial esta especial mercê. Deus guarde a V. Ex.ª por
muitos annos, como havemos mister. S. Paulo, em Camara de
12 de Novembro de 1822. Ill.mo e Ex.mo Sr. José Bonifacio de
Andrada e Silva, Ministro e Secretario de Estado dos Negocios
do Imperio do Brasil.—*Bento José Leite Penteado.—José Mariano
Bueno.—Antonio Safino da Fonseca —Antonio da Silva Prado.
—Antonio José Vieira Barbosa.*

---

REPRESENTAÇÃO DO POVO DE S. PAULO A D. PEDRO I, PEDINDO-LHE
QUE FAÇA O DR. MANOEL JOAQUIM DE ORNELLAS FICAR NO GO-
VERNO DESTA PROVINCIA.

Senhor·—A Camara desta cidade de S. Paulo, em nome
do povo della, tem a honra de chegar á augusta presença de
Vossa Magestade Imperial e, depois de ter ouvido o voto dos
homens bons, que se juntaram no acto de vereança de 13 de No-

---

Moraes. Este ultimo não tomou posse, por velho e doente. O dr. Ornellas, o unico
formado dos membros do governo, foi tambem eleito supplente de deputado a Assembléa Constituinte e tomou posse da vaga deixada por Fernandes Pinheiro, que optara
pelo Rio Grande do Sul. Esta vaga devia ser preenchida por Martim Francisco; porém
este fora eleito supplente de deputado pelo Rio de Janeiro e tomou assento por lá, em
uma vaga que deu-se na sua representação.

O A Camara de S. Paulo remetteu a José Bonifacio duas representações, sendo
uma do povo paulista a D. Pedro para que os Andradas fossem conservados no ministerio
e a outra para que D. Pedro ordenasse que o dr. Ornellas ficasse no governo de S.
Paulo. de que fora eleito membro, e não tomasse assento na Assembléa Constituinte em
alguma vaga na representação paulista, por necessaria a sua permanencia em S. Paulo,
onde os seus conselhos eram ouv'dos com respeito e acatamento. Ornellas, entretanto,
tomou posse de uma cadeira da Constituinte, como supplente de Fernandes Pinheiro.

Ambas as representações vão aqui transcriptas, por serem documentos de valor
sobre o caracter dos homens a que se referem.

vembro de 1822, roga a imperial aprovação para que o bacharel Manoel Joaquim de Ornellas, eleito pelo povo com 106 votos para membro do governo provincial que Vossa Magestade Imperial mandou eleger nesta provincia, e com 114 votos para deputado á Assembléa Geral Constituinte do Brasil, seja conservado no logar de membro, do governo no caso que seja preciso nomear deputados immediatos em votos para supprir a falta dos deputados ausentes, como Vossa Magestade determina do seu imperial decreto.

A Camara se lisonjêa que Vossa Magestade Imperial tomará em consideração a razão que allega, pois, dependendo nas actuaes circumstancias o socego e a tranquillidade interna da provincia de um governo justo e forte, que tome as mais energicas medidas para anniquillar qualquer facção que intente perturbal-a, é necessario que o governo não só tenha homens probos, mas que tambem reuna ao menos em um ou outro membro as luzes necessarias para ser o patriotismo bem dirigido, e igualmente administrar justiça imparcial.

Unindo-se, pois, na pessoa do referido bacharel Manoel Joaquim de Ornellas os conhecidos talentos, constante e muitas vezes provados amor e adhesão á causa do Brasil e á sagrada pessoa de Vossa Magestade Imperial, parece indispensavel que elle exerça o emprego de membro do governo para que foi nomeado com pluralidade de votos, apezar de tudo confiarmos na probidade e patriotismo dos outros membros eleitos para o governo, e que seu immediato em votos suppra o logar de deputado, no caso que temporariamente seja necessario entrar para o Congresso algum immediato pela falta dos deputados ausentes, visto que depois dos deputados que alcançaram pluralidade de votos é o dito bacharel um dos immediatos.

A Camara, em nome do povo de S. Paulo, beija respeitosamente as mãos de Vossa Majestade Imperial, a quem Deus guarde, como nos é mister. S. Paulo, em Camara de 13 de Novembro de 1822.—*Bento José Leite Penteado—Antonio Sufino da Fonseca—Antonio da Silva Prado—José Mariano Bueno—Antonio José Vieira Barbosa.*

———

OFFICIO DA CAMARA DE S. PAULO CAMARA A' DO RIO DE JANEIRO SOBRE A CONSERVAÇÃO DOS ANDRADAS COMO MINISTROS DE ESTADO.

Illms. Srs:—A Camara da cidade de S. Paulo tem o inexplicavel contentamento de remetter a Vossas Senhorias a acta da vereanção extraordinaria de 12 de Novembro do corrente anno, a que deu occasião a representação do povo, cuja copia egualmente remette, em que se exigia com urgencia que esta Camara agradecesse á Camara e ao bom povo fluminense o heroico passo que deram, rogando a Sua Magestade Imperial a reintegração dos benemeritos ministros, nossos honrados patricios, os excellentissimos srs. José Bonifacio de Andrada e Silva e Martim Francisco Ribeiro de Andrada, a despeito da infame facção carbonaria, que procurava com avidez uma brecha para destruir o grande e magestoso edificio do imperio brasiliense, para cevar seus sordidos intentos e medrar a custa do vosso bem estar, como certas plantas parasitas.

A Camara, pois, não menos avida da gloria que cobre esse benemerito Senado e ao honrado povo fluminense, se apressa a dirigir-lhe as mais sinceras felicitações, a unir suas vozes para rogar a Sua Magestade Imperial o mais severo castigo desses perfidos, desses traidores, desses monstros indignos da sociedade dos homens e que só existem para vergonha da humanidade, e assegurar que a Camara e o povo de S. Paulo jamais se arredará uma só linha da estrada da honra e da gloria e que nada a lisonjêa tanto como ter occasião de imitar os sabios e patrioticos passos de Vossas Senhorias. S. Paulo, em vereação de 13 de Novembro de 1822. Illms. Srs. Juiz Presidente e officiaes do Senado da Camara do Rio de Janeiro.—*Bento José Leite Penteado—José Mariano Bueno— Antonio Safino da Fonsca—Antonio da Silva Prado—Antonio José Vieira Barbosa.*

---

### VEREANÇA EXTRAORDINARIA DA CAMARA DE YTÚ

Aos 23 dias do mez de Julho de 1822, nesta villa de Ytú e Casas da Camara, Paços do Conselho, onde compareceram o Desembargador Ouvidor geral e Corregedor desta Comarca João de Medeiros Gomes, juiz ordinario e mais officiaes da Camara abaixo assignados, para tratar-se de assentar-se de commum accôrdo com as autoridades militares desta villa, que tambem foram presentes, sobre a segurança publica desta comarca e da CABEÇA DA PROVINCIA, que pelas noticias que tem chegado a esta villa se acha em convulsão, com pretextos sinistros a desobedecerem as Reaes determinações do Principe Regente, nosso Perpetuo Defensor, e as ordens do Governo Provisorio desta provincia, e sendo todos reunidos a este acto assentaram e ponderaram pela maneira seguinte:

1.º—Que se officiasse ao commandante militar que, com a maior brevidade promptifique a tropa que puder para o primeiro aviso que vier da Capital (S. Paulo).

2.º—Que debaixo da responsabilidade de Sua Alteza Real não deve sahir tropa alguma para o destacamento (da capital) sem ordem do commandante militar da provincia ( Cesar ou Arouche)

3.º – Que se officie ás Camaras da Comarca para estarem promptas as tropas do seus respectivos districtos para operarem em commum, rogando ellas para isso ao commandante militar do districto.

E porque assim todos concordaram com unanimidade de sentimentos, se lavrou o presente termo em que assigna o ministro presidente com o corpo da Camara e o commandante militar, e eu João Luiz Leitão Freire, escrivão da camara, que o escrevi.—*Medeiros—Botelho—Fonseca—Almeida Mello*—Caminha —Carvalho—Romano.

Depois de feito o encerramento da sessão supra compareceu o capitão-mór desta villa, Vicente da Costa Taques Goes e Aranha, ao qual sendo lida a mesma sessão, com os artigos conteúdos foi pelo mesmo declarado estar por tudo quanto se havia accôrdado, e disse mais que elle commandante militar desta villa e todo o corpo das ordenanças do seu commando se declaravam publicos inimigos de toda e qualquer auctoridade civil ou militar e de todo e qualquer homem, sem excepção alguma, que não prestar a mais prompta, fiel e cega obediencia ás sagradas ordens do Serenissimo Senhor Dom Pedro de Alcantara, nosso muito amado e respeitado Principe Regente e Perpetuo Defensor deste reino do Brazil, e que estavam promptos a derramar a ultima pinga de sangue pelo mesmo Augusto Senhor, a quem tributava o mais puro e intenso amor, incontrastavel lealdade e cordial veneração.

E para constar fiz este accresentamento, que assigno, e eu João Luiz Leitão Freire, escrivão da Camara, que o escrevi.— *Vicente da Costa Taques Gomes e Aranha. — Joaquim Jose de Andrade.*

# Prodromos da independencia na villa de Ytú [1]

## DOCUMENTOS INSTRUCTIVOS

### 1.º

#### OFFICIO DA CAMARA DE SOROCABA A' DE YTÚ

Recebemos o officio de vossas senhorias de 7 do corrente depois de termos participado ao governo de S. Paulo a deliberação de não mandar o destacamento accordado em vereação extraordinaria de 4 do corrente (2), que já participámos a vossas senhorias, consultando-se em nova vereação o objecto consultado por vossas senhorias, julgou-se necessario esperar-se resposta do governo, que hoje recebemos, cuja cópia não perdemos tempo em remetter ao conhecimento de vossas senhorias (3), que prudentemente saberão desculpar-nos de não tomarmos já as medidas que por nós outr'ora foram lembradas, emquanto não houver eguaes urgencias, o que Deus não permitta, que então nos auctorizaram. Deus guarde a vossas senhorias. Villa de Sorocaba, em vereação de 12 de Agosto de 1822.—*Joaquim de Madureira Campos.—Manoel Joaquim de Almeida Mello.—Ignacio Dias Baptista.—Antonio José de Madureira e Souza —João Luiz do Couto.*—Ill.ᵐᵒˢ Srs. Juiz Presidente e officiaes da Camara de Ytú.

#### OFFICIO DO GOVERNO DE S. PAULO A' CAMARA DE SOROCABA

O Governo Provisorio desta provincia accusa a recepção do officio de vossas mercês de 6 do corrente, acompanhado da cópia da Acta de vereança extraordinaria do dia 4, na qual em consequencia de noticias exaggeradas que se publicaram nessa villa, relativas ao estado desta cidade, que tanto tem desgraçadamente enfraquecido a força moral deste governo (4), que, sempre firme na adhesão ao nosso Augusto Principe Regente (5) se patentea

---

(1) V. Revista do Instituto H. de S. Paulo vl. VII, pags. 148 a 212, em que vem a narrativa dos factos occorridos na comarca de Ytú nas vesperas da proclamação da independencia.
(2) Vol. VII cit., pags. 185 a 197, *Annexo* T.
(3) A resposta do governo de S. Paulo vae em seguida.
(4) A acta da vereança mencionada vem no *Annexo* T do vol. VII, pags. 185 a 197. A força moral do governo estava perdida desde 25 de Junho, data do decreto cassando os seus poderes e insultando as pessoas dos membros do mesmo governo. Vide vol. VII, cit. pags. 137 a 158.
(5) *Adhesão* ao principe acompanhada da recusa de obedecer ás suas ordens, como as da remessa de João Carlos e Costa Carvalho para o Rio e resistencia aos generaes Candido Xavier e Arouche, delegados do principe!

naturalmente resentido de ser calumniado, resultando daqui o ter alterado da maneira que se expõe a opinião desse povo, vossas mercês pedem a suspensão da marcha do destacamento de milicias (1).

O Governo, deliberando com aquella prudencia que tem sempre sido a mira em suas resoluções e conhecendo quanto convem mais aplacar do que irritar os animos, até que novamente se consolidem e firmem as relações politicas entre as auctoridades constituidas e os cidadãos, participa a vossas mercês que na data desta determinou ao tenente coronel que não marche até segunda ordem o destacamento que por escala tocava dar o regimento dessa villa para a guarnição desta cidade (2). O Governo, portanto, espera que vossas mercês continuem sempre a procurar o socego desses habitantes, que elle tanto preza, procurando dissuadil-os da opinião indiscreta que se originou dos pricipios falsos com os quaes os quizeram illudir, esperando sempre que a posteridade imparcial, julgadora das acções dos homens, haja de o justificar, para o que á Augusta Presença de Sua Alteza Real, a quem se tem dado successivamente parte de todos os acontecimentos, se envia igualmente o seu officio (3). Deus guarde a vossas mercês. Palacio do governo de S. Paulo, 9 de Agosto de 1822.—*Miguel José de Oliveira Pinto*. presidente interino.—*Daniel Pedro Müller*, secretario.—*Antonio Maria Quartim.* (4)

---

### REPRESENTAÇÃO DO POVO YTUANO PEDINDO A' CAMARA A INSTALLAÇÃO DE UMA JUNTA CENTRAL

Os abaixo assignados, fieis aos protestos constantes nas actas desta camara do dia 7 e seguintes (5), representam a este senado que sendo de summa importancia a installação de uma Junta Central interina, de onde manem as providencias necessarias,

---

(1) Os municipios do interior forneciam forças para a guarnição da capital desde longa data; mas desta vez Ytú e os municipios confederados desobedeceram e não mandaram as forças requisitadas pelo governo extrngeiro de S. Paulo.

(2) Tenente coronel João Floriano da Costa, commandante do regimento de milicias de Sorocaba, que igualmente desobedeceram á ordem para remetter forças a S. Paulo.

(3) O principe regente não julgou justificados os actos do governo de S. Paulo e manteve o seu decreto cassando os seus poderes. Tambem a posteridade fez-lhe justiça de appellidar de *Bernarda* ao movimento sedicioso de 23 de Maio, que causou a desunião entre a capital e o interior da provincia

(4) Aqui estão tres militares extrangeiros, senhores do governo da provincia por um golpe de Estado, em lucta com os paulistas do interior e appellando para a posteridade. como julgadora dos actos humana, que decida se elles ou os paulistas é que defendiam melhor os interesses brasileiros!

(5) A acta da sessão de 7 de Agosto vae adeante transcripta e a da sessão do dia 9 vem no cit. vol. VII, pag. 187, *Annexo U*; são documentos importantes para a historia paulista do tempo.

não só para o progresso da justa causa que temos adoptado como
para nos assegurar contra as especulações offensivas da facção
da capital, que diariamente crescem sem que vejamos garantidos
os nossos direitos e muito menos nossa segurança, o que se con-
segue havendo um centro activo de operações; portanto, reque-
remos a este senado se digne promover a sua installação a bem
dos povos, sem o qual nada seguirá regular e ordenado assaz
necessario nas commoções politicas.

Os abaixo assignados, antevendo os males horriveis que
podem sobreviver na demora destas providencias, attendendo ao
exaltamento do espirito publico, aos solemnes protestos feitos em
publicas sessões e sobre tudo ao bem geral da comarca, reforçam
a sua representação para se cumprir o que já foi accôrdado em
vereações geraes. Os abaixo assignados, depois de responsabili
zarem a vossas senhorias para com Sua Alteza Real por qualquer
mal que resulte da omissão neste objecto, consideram fracas e
palliativas todas as medidas que não sejam para a reque-
rida installação, pois estamos convencidos que sem o Centro
cahiremos na desordem e seremos victimas de partidos fomenta-
dos pelos apaniguados da facção e da anarchia, que se desen-
volverão não se adoptando o que já tem sido accôrdado.—*José
de Pinna e Vasconcellos*, vigario encommendado.—Padre *Francisco
Leite Ribeiro.*—Padre *Francisco Novaes de Magalhães.*—Padre
*José Galvão de Barros França*—Padre *Antonio Joaquim de
Mello* (1)—Capitão *Francisco Galvão de França*—*Antonio Galvão
de França*—Alferes *Estanisláo de Campos Arruda*—Tenente *An-
tonio Correa Pacheco e Silva*—Padre *Joaquim José de Araujo*—
*Joaquim de Almeida Barros*—Padre *Luiz Mendes Ferraz da Silva*
—*José Mendes Ferraz Junior*—Tenente *Joaquim Francisco da
Cruz*—Alferes *Fernando Dias Paes Leme*—Capitão *Bento Dias
Pacheco*—Tenente *Manoel de Campos Almeida*—Tenente *Fran-
cisco de Paula Espirito Santo*—Capitão *Francisco José de Castro
— Salvador Pereira de Almeida*—*Manoel José Gonçalves da Costa
Ferrugem*—Alferes *João Manoel de Souza*—Quartel-mestre *Tho-
maz José Ferreira de Carvalho*—Padre *Antonio Luiz Pennalva
—Capitão Francisco Xavier de Barros* (2)—Alferes *Joaquim Flo-
riano de Barros*—Padre *José Joaquim de Quadros Leite*—Te-
nente *Reginaldo de Quadros Leite*—*Melchior Pereira de Almeida*
—Capitão *Ignacio Fernandes Aranha* – Capitão *Caetano José
Gomes Carneiro*—Capitão *Joaquim Dias Ferraz*—Padre Jeronimo

---

(1) Um dos sacerdotes mais notaveis que S. Paulo tem produzido nomeado bispo
desta diocese em 1851, fundou o Seminario Episcopal e falleceu em 1861.
(2) Era irmão de Bento de Barros e Antonio Paes de Barros, barões de Ytú e de
Piracicaba, e foi mais tarde perseguido pelos reaccionarios. Vide cit vol. VII, pag. 142.

*Pinto Rodrigues*—Capitão *José Cirino de Godoy*—*Joaquim Pinto de Arruda*—Padre *Braz Luiz de Pinna*—Capitão *Luiz Antonio do Amaral Gurgel*—Padre *Joaquim de Almeida Leite*—*José de Almeida Pacheco*—Ajudante *José Ferraz Leite de Sampaio*— Capitão *José Leite de Cerqueira*—*Eufrasio de Arruda Sá*—Padre *Thomaz de Mello e Silva*—Alferes *Ildefonso de Campos e Almeida*—Cirurgião *Antonio José de Babo Broxado*—*Joaquim Bento Raymundo de Souza*—*Luiz Manoel da Luz Pargino*—Tenente *Joaquim Marcelino de Oliveira Netto*—Alferes *Francisco Antonio Romano* (1) *José Carlos Duarte*—*Felix dos Santos Lisboa*—*Manoel Vidal Gonçalves*—*Carlos José Nardy de Vasconcellos*—*Vicente Dias Ferraz*—*Felippe Correa Pacheco*—Padre *Manoei Ferraz de Camargo*—Sargente Mór *João de Almeida Prado*—*Balduino de Mello Castanho*—Alferes *Luciano Francisco Pacheco*—Tenente *Francisco de Almeida Prado*—Tenente *Joaquim Galvão de Almeida*—*Francisco Mariano da Costa*—*Antonio José de Assumpção* —*José de Barros Dias*—*Francisco de Paula*—Padre *Melchior de Pontes Amaral*—Capitão *Bento Paes de Barros* (2)—*José Rodrigues do Amaral Mello*—*Francisco Xavier Pacheco.*

Reconheço verdadeiras as firmas constantes deste assignado por todas serem muito do meu meu conhecimento e de pessoas que bem distinguo, em fé do que me assigno em publico e razo. —Ytú, 18 de Agosto de 1822. Em testemunho da verdade (Lugar do signal publico).—*José Mendes Ferraz.*

---

VEREANÇA EXTRAORDINARIA DA CAMARA DE YTÚ, EM 7 DE AGOSTO DE 1822, ATRAZ MENCIONADA

Aos 7 dias do mez de Agosto de 1822 annos, nesta villa de Ytú, cabeça da comarca e paço do Conselho, onde vieram o Juiz Presidente e Officiaes da Camara, abaixo assignados, e sendo ahi em acto de vereação concorreram a Nobreza, Povo e Auctoridades e na presença de todos pelo procurador eleito Francisco de Paula Souza e Mello foram propostos varios objectos a bem do serviço nacional e utilidade da patria, e entrando em consulta geral por todos unanimemente foi accordado o seguinte: «1.°, que, como a urgencia dos ne-

---

(1) Foi outro perseguido pelos reaccionarios depois da dissolução da Assembléa Constituinte e deportação dos Andradas. Vide vol. VII, pag. 142.
(2) Foi depois barão de Ytú; era cunhado de Paula Sousa, chefe da confederação ytuana, e tambem cunhado de Costa Carvalho, a alma, o espirito director da *Bernarda de Francisco Ignacio* em S. Paulo; mas, paulista genuino, esteve ao lado dos seus patricios na lucta travada entre os municipios do interior e os extrangeiros detentores do governo da capital. Soffreu perseguições por isso; vide cit. vol VII, pag. 142.

gocios insta já e já a se darem providencias do momento, se désse ao procurador nomeado o poder necessario de ser o movel das operações da villa, ficando desde já todas as auctoridades centralizadas no mesmo, para delle e por elle haver a necessaria rapidez da marcha publica; 2.°, que logo que estivessem reunidos nesta dois procuradores se installasse a Junta, aggregando-se-lhe temporariamente o supplente de cada villa para já, até que estejam reunidos tres proprietarios (1); 3.°, que a Junta immediatamente organize e apresente o plano de suas attribuições e de sua marcha e que este seja observado já, interinamente até a necessaria approvação do povo, depois da qual se prestarão os necessarios juramentos; 4.°, que o povo confira poderes á Junta para escolher e ter um secretario, com voto, qual melhor lhe parecer; 5.°, que se vejam cidadãos ricos que emprestem dinheiro, ou a juros ou por compra de assucares, até que se organize o plano dos dinheiros publicos, a que se obrigou o cidadão Salvador Pereira de Almeida (2), a quem se deram logo muitos louvores e vivas pelo seu zelo e patriotismo e ficou elle mesmo thesoureiro; 6.°, que esta acta se remetta ás Camaras das villas colligadas para sua intelligencia. E para todo tempo constar mandaram lavrar o presente termo em que todos se assignaram, e eu José Mendes Ferraz, escrivão da Camara, que o escrevi.—*Fonseca*—*Azevedo* — *Vasconcellos*—*Prado* — *Mello*—*Vicente da Costa Taques Góes e Aranha*, capitão-mór commandante (3),—*Pedro José de Brito Caminha*, tenente coronel (4)—O vigario encommendado *José de Pinna e Vasconcellos*—Padre *Melchior de Pontes Amaral*—Padre *Luiz Mendes da Silva*—*João Manoel de Souza*—*Joaquim Manoel Pacheco da Fonseca*—*Manoel de Campos Almeida*—*Vicente Francisco da Costa*—*Joaquim José de Castro*—*Manoel José Gonçalves da Costa Ferrugem*—*Francisco José de Castro*—*Antonio José de Babo Broxado*—Capitão *Francisco Xavier de Barros*—*Bento Paes de Barros*—*Joaquim Floricno de Barros*—*Salvador Pereira de Almeida*—Padre *Miguel Archanjo do Amor Divino* (5)—*José Manoel de Mesquita*—Padre

---

(1) O supplente de Ytú era Candido José da Motta e dois dias depois dessa sessão chegaram a Ytú o sargento-mór José Custodio de Oliveira, representante de Porto Feliz, e o capitão Julio Cesar de Cerqueira Leite e o padre José Francisco de Aranha Camargo, representantes de Campinas. Vide vol. VII, pag. 164.

(2) Prestou gratuitamente a receber o dinheiro dos emprestimos e a guardai-o.

(3) Era capitão-mór de Ytú desde 1779 e muito bom; era homem instruido, latinista e poeta.

(4) Era o commandante militar da força armada de Ytú e representou bem o seu papel na confederação dos municipios. Vide cit. vol. VII. pags. 161 e 162.

(5) Foi durante muitos annos abalisado professor de latim e serviu como representante supplente da camara de Campinas na confederação de Ytú, sendo proprietario o seu collega padre José Teixeira Villela.

*Braz Luiz de Pinna*—Padre *Francisco Leite Ribeiro*—Padre *Antonio Joaquim de Mello*—Padre *José Galvão de Barros França* —Padre *Jeronimo Pinto Rodrigues.*

OFFICIO DA CAMARA DE PIRACICABA Á DE YTÚ, PARTICIPANDO A SUA SOLIDARIEDADE

Recebemos tres officios de vossas senhorias, que nos dirigiram neste mez, um com data de 6 e dois de 7, acompanhados com as copias das vereanças extraordinarias de 4 e 7 do mesmo, em os quaes nos scientifica as suas determinações; ao que respondemos que muito louvamos a vossas senhorias as justas medidas e deliberações que, a bem da nação, têm tomado.

Nós cordialmente nos congratulamos com vossas senhorias e protestamos seguir os seus bem ordenados passos na intelligencia do seu accordo de pessoas prudentes e de patriotismo. Tambem participamos a vossas senhorias que esta Camara já fez a eleição do procurador que exige em um dos officios, cuja eleição foi feita na pessoa do senhor capitão Domingues Soares de Barros. o qual se hade apresentar nessa no dia 19 do corrente, que lhe aprazámos, e nessa mesma occasião leva as pessoas que pudermos apromptar para precaução de algum accommettimento que tentem os de São Paulo, que isto mesmo nos communicarão (1). Deus guarde a vossas senhorias. Villa da Constituição, em Camara de 14 do Agosto de 1822.—*João José da Silva*—*Xisto de Quadros Aranha*—*Miguel Antonio Gonçalves*—*Garcia Rodrigues Bueno*—*Pedro Leme de Oliveira.*

OFFICIO DA CAMARA DE YTÚ AO PRINCIPE REGENTE

SENHOR:—Penetrados do mais profundo respeito temos a honra de fazer subir muito reverentemente á presença de Vossa Alteza Real a acta de vereação extraordinaria do dia 4 do corrente (2). Não querendo perder um momento não remettemos já as mais actas que tem tido lugar nesta Camara, depois do ultima que foi remmettida á Secretaria de Estado dos Negocios do Reino pelo ouvidor desta Camara.

Diremos só, Senhor, que o povo desta villa e comarca se viu na indispensavel necessidade de dar aquelle ultimo passo por se

---

(1) Chegou a Ytú e apresentou-se no dia á Junta Central, acompanhado da força armada que consigo trouxera de Piracicaba.

(2) Vide vol. VII cit., pags. 178 e 179, *Annexo* B.

subtrahir a ser victima ou instrumento do Rebelde Governo; que o povo está em massa não só para se defender na lucta, para sustentar a causa de Vossa Alteza Real, como para voar a cumprir as Augustas Ordens de Vossa Alteza Real no momento que lhe forem dirigidas e que elle respeita com idolatria, e que finalmente elle está inabalavel nos reiterados juramentos de sua obediencia e fidelidade a Vossa Alteza Real, immortal salvador do Brazil, a quem deveras reverenciamos e amamos muito mais do que ao melhor pae. Deus guarde a Vossa Alteza Real como nos é mister. Villa de Ytú, em Camara de 6 de Agosto de 1822.—De Vossa Alteza Real os mais obedientes e fieis subditos, *Bento Dias Pacheco—Antonio Pacheco da Fonseca—Antonio Victoriano de Azevedo—Lourenço de Almeida Prado—Joaquim José de Mello.*

---

### OFFICIO DA JUNTA DE YTÚ AO PRINCIPE REGENTE

Senhor: Os procuradores nomeados das villas de Ytú, Porto Feliz, São Carlos e Constituição, por ellas auctorizados, como tambem auctorizados pela villa de Itapetininga, e ja nesta reunidos para se occuparem da salvação publica da comarca, como já terá sido patente a Vossa Alteza Real pelas representações das Camaras desta e outras villas, promptos se achavam para installar-se uma Junta interina que servisse de centro á comarca contra as perfidas tentativas da existente facção da Capital, tanto mais suspeita e perigosa quanto apparente e affectadamente tranquilla, de proposito entretanto demoravam aquella installação na esperança tantas vezes annunciada da vinda de Vossa Alteza Real a esta provincia ou de suas regias providencias, decisivas e terminantes. Constando, porém, neste momento por algumas cartas que Vossa Alteza Real quanto antes tem de chegar a esta provincia e que talvez já esteja em sua capital, intimamente convencidos os ditos procuradores que só deste rasgo de sabedoria e bondade de Vossa Alteza Real é que nos póde vir o efficaz remedio de todos os males que nos tem opprimido e que ainda tanto nos ameaçam, elles, nos transportes de seus jubilos, resolveram mandar immediatamente o capitão Francisco Xavier de Barros, commandante dos voluntarios, para certificar-se da veracidade daquella noticia e, sendo certa, desde já os ditos procuradores, prostrados perante o Augusto Throno de Vossa Alteza Real e penetrados do maior acatamento e respeito, tributam seus votos da mais decidida fidelidade, obediencia, amor e gratidão a Vossa Alteza Real e protestam o seu invariavel aferro á grande causa de que Vossa Alteza Real é o defensor.

Elles imploram ao mesmo tempo muito respeitosamente a Vossa Alteza Real que se digne prescrever-lhes os seus deveres, assim como a incomparavel graça de, reunidos, irem beijar a Augusta Mão de Vossa Alteza Real e nessa mesma occasião, em nome dos seus concidadãos e por elles auctorizados, darem os motivos dos seus procedimentos e tambem manifestarem, senhor, os desejos destes povos, que tanto têm feito por Vossa Alteza e tanto ainda aspiram fazer.

Toda a tropa, todos os voluntarios e todo o povo em massa destas villas, senhor, arrebatados do mais ardente patriotismo, armados e promptos, só esperam as Augustas Ordens de Vossa Alteza Real para marcharem, impavidos, para qualquer ponto a cumpril-as. Digne-se, pois, Vossa Alteza Real fazer-nos a não merecida honra de que se nos participem as regias determinações de Vossa Alteza e permitta-nos dizer, senhor, que ninguem nos excede no amor e respeito a Vossa Alteza Real, o qual já talvez pareça idolatria. A Augusta Pessoa de Vossa Alteza Real guarde Deus por muitos, como nos é mistér. Ytú, nos Paços do Conselho aos 22 de Agosto de 1822. — Senhor, de Vossa Alteza Real subditos os mais amantes, fieis e obedientes, o padre *José Teixeira Villela—José Custodio de Oliveira—Domingos Soares de Barros—Francisco de Paula Sousa e Mello.*

---

OFFICIO DA CAMARA DE YTÚ A' DE SOROCABA

Tendo-se desenvolvido o espirito publico desta da maneira a mais energica e decisiva sobre a necessidade da installação de um centro geral da comarca, como vossas senhorias verão da representação inclusa, sendo tal, não menos, o espirito publico da villa de Porto Feliz, cujo procurador aqui está residindo desde o dia 8 do corrente; da de S. Carlos, cujo tambem hoje aqui chegou; da villa nova da Constituição, cujo igualmente hoje deve chegar (1); da de Mogy e Franca, que temos toda a certeza de serem do mesmo pensar e não tardarem a enviar os seus respectivos procuradores, vemos-nos na rigorosa obrigação de communicar isto a vossas senhorias, rogando-lhes que não permittam que a comarca, tão unanime no fim dos seus exforços, pareça dividida só porque haja discrepancia de opinião sobre o meio de obter o fim. Tanto mais nos vemos nesta obrigação,

---

(1) Chegou dahi a dois dias, por ter estado doente, conforme elle explicou um officio de 18 de Agosto, dirigido á camara de Ytú. A camara de Itapetininga tambem officiou em 16 de agosto, adherindo ao centro de Ytú e declarando que não mandava o seu procurador, por não ter na occasião um homem capaz de desempenhar esse cargo.

porque, tendo a villa de Porto Feliz por quartel de suas forças militares essa villa de Sorocaba, é da maior urgencia e necessidade que seja unico o centro de operações, não só para a rapidez e vantagens dellas como para que não se dê lugar a surgir uma semente de intriga que desdoire a heroica e magestosa marcha desta comarca.

Repetindo, portanto, tudo quanto dissemos já no nosso officio da data de 7 do corrente, concluimos rogando, por tudo quanto ha de mais sagrado pela causa e Augusta Pessoa de Sua Alteza Real, queiram vossas senhorias mandar o seu respectivo membro á necessaria Junta, certos de que ella terá por fim a salvação da comarca e provincia e por orbita as attribuições para isso necessarias, e que por isso mesmo a facção vae reconhecendo a sua fraqueza, trabalha e trabalhará cada vez mais para manejar a intriga e obter a desunião. (1) Deos guarde a vossas senhorias. Ytú em Camara de 18 de Agosto de 1822.— *Bento Dias Pacheco.—Antonio Pacheco da Fonseca.—Antonio Victoriano de Azevedo.—Lourenço de Almeida Prado.—Joaquim José' de Mello.*

---

RESPOSTA DA CAMARA DE SOROCABA Á DE YTÚ

Acabamos de receber o officio de vossas senhorias de 18 do corrente, com os exemplares annexos, a que respondemos:

Desejavamos, senhores, nesta occasião ser dotados da maior eloquencia para que, pela efficacia de nossas expressões, pudessemos persuadir a identidade de nossos sentimentos, que parece vacillarem no conceito de vossas senhorias; mas suppra a séria contemplação desse nobre Senado, a cuja presença tem sido levadas todas as nossas deliberações. (2)

E' digno de notar que vossas senhorias instem por aquillo mesmo que nós não duvidamos, mas que temos exigido unicamente a resolução de Sua Alteza Real, o nosso Augusto Principe Regente e Defensor, a quem temos representado, desejando evitar confusão de operações que pareçam acceleradas, ou talvez incompativeis, em tempo que não devemos exceder a marcha segura que adoptámos.

---

(1) A tentativa de desunião foi feita pelo governo de S. Paulo, mandando Paula Macedo a Ytú e outro emissario a Sorocaba, mas nada conseguiu. Vide vl. VII cit., pags. 161 e 162.

(2) A camara de Sorocaba adheriu lealmente ao movimento dos municipios do interior contra o governo *bernardista* de S. Paulo; mas ou porque receasse mandar suas forças a Ytú e desguarnecer a villa ou por espirito de rivalidade, que sempre existiu entre as duas povoações, tratou de agir por conta propria, com sentimentos identicos aos dos ytuanos como se vê por este officio.

Se este escrupulo dominante neste povo parece a vossas
senhorias menos digno de attenção pela nossa faculdade de ra-
ciocinar, não devem por isso duvidar da firmeza de conducta
que temos protestado pela justa causa da patria. Entretanto
exigindo vossas senhorias com o maior encarecimento a nomeação do procurador desta Camara, neste mesmo dia em que temos noticia affirmativa de Sua Alteza Real chegar por toda esta
semana a S. Paulo, contemplando como desunião essa falta de
cooperação, nós, protestando a mais firme união, com igual encarecimento exigimos de vossas senhorias, pelo que ha de mais
sagrado no céo ou na terra, que dêm tempo, que por momentos está a conhecer-se a veracidade desta noticia ; o
que unicamente nos póde servir de regra porque, verifi-
cando-se a real chegada de Sua Alteza Real a S. Paulo,
a elle cumpre o mandar e a nós o obedecer.

Esperamos que vossas senhorias, annuindo a este motivo,
que é ponderoso nesta hypothese, hajam de suster o mais, dando as medidas para reunirmo-nos, todas as Camaras, com o nosso illustre presidente, o meritissimo corregedor da comarca, afim
de irmos cumprimentar a Sua Alteza Real e renovar lhe os protestos de obediencia, amor e respeito que lhe tributamos.

Estes são, pois, os sentimentos que nos animam e que esperamos sejam egualmente os desse nobre Senado. Deus guarde
a vossas senhorias. Sorocaba, em Camara de 21 de Agosto de
1822.—*Joaquim de Madureira Campos.—Ignacio Dias Baptista
—Antonio Jose de Madureira e Souza.—João Leite do Canto.*

---

OFFICIO DA CAMARA DE YTU' AO PRINCIPE REGENTE

*Senhor:*—A Camara da villa de Ytú, provincia de São Paulo, tendo levado á Augusta Presença de Vossa Alteza Real os
successivos factos que têm occorrido nesta villa desde o fatal
acontecimento de 23 de Maio, o mesmo faz nesta occasião
enviando a Vossa Alteza Real a cópia da ultima acta sobre os
movimentos do tempo, bem como da carta dirigida á Camara de
São Paul o e sua resposta.

Esta Camara não duvida affirmar a Vossa Alteza Real a
summa urgencia da medida adoptada pelos procuradores como a
unica capaz de conter na ordem os povos, atterrar os inimigos
facciosos e num momento poder reunir uma força consideravel
para operar com rapidez as Augustas Ordens de Vossa Alteza
Real, que a todo momento esperamos na provincia e das quaes
esperamos os remedios dos horriveis males que a dilaceram.

Temos a satisfação de significar a Vossa Alteza Real que,
apezar do elevado gaz e excessivo enthusiasmo destes povos,
ainda não houve, Senhor, a menor infracção da lei ou transtor-
no da ordem publica, pois só se occupam todos na lisonjeira
esperança de servirem a Vossa Alteza e por Vossa Alteza mor-
rerem. Assim Deus permitta que seja verdadeira a vinda de
Vossa Alteza para que, fazendo brilhar os raios da Justiça,
confunda os impios e restitua a paz e a tranquillidade á provincia opprimida.

A Augusta Pessoa de Vossa Alteza Real Deus guarde por
muitos annos, como nos é mister. Ytú, em Camara de 22 de
de Agosto de 1822.—Senhor, de Vossa Alteza Real os mais re-
verentes e humildes subditos, *Bento Dias Pacheco—Antonio Pacheco da Fonseca — Antonio Victoriano de Azevedo— Lourenço
de Almeida Prado—Joaquim José de Mello.*

---

PORTARIA DO PRINCIPE REGENTE ÁS CAMARAS DE YTÚ E SOROCABA

Manda Sua Alteza Real o Principe Regente, pela Secretaria
de Estado interina, participar á Camara da villa de Ytú, cabeça
da comarca, que lhe foi presente o termo de vereança extraordinaria de 4 do corrente (1), no qual accusa a recepção do decreto de 25 de Junho do presente anno (2), e as medidas que
tomou a bem da união brasilica ; as quaes Sua Alteza Real presume terem sido tomadas por não haver então nesta provincia
um centro firme de união, e como agora dentro della existe o
chefe do Poder Executivo do reino do Brasll e seu Defensor
Perpetuo, ha por bem Sua Alteza Real anullar o sobredito termo de vereança extraordinaria visto cessarem os motivos que de
certo lhe deram causa, e ordenar que a dita Camara se dirija a
sua real pessoa directamente em tudo que houver mister a bem
do serviço nacional emquanto o novo governo de toda a provincia não estiver formado, quer Sua Alteza Real exista ou não
nesta, do modo que o mesmo senhor houver por bem mandar,
com o qual logo que organisado esteja se deve entender, como
é de sua rigorosa obrigação e conforme á ordem estabelecida.

Outrosim, há por bem Sua Alteza Real louvar á Camara,
povo e tropa dessa villa a intrepidez que tem desenvolvido pela

---

(1) Vide cit. vol. VII, pags. 178 e 179.
(2) Decreto que cassou os poderes do governo bernardista de S. Paulo. Vide cit.
vol. VII, pag. 157.

sagrada causa do Brazil e remetter-lhes incluso o seu *Manifesto* ás nações amigas. Paço de Lorena, 19 de Agosto de 1822.— *Luiz de Saldanha da Gama* (1).

---

### PORTARIA DO PRINCIPE REGENTE Á CAMARA DE YTÚ

Manda Sua Alteza Real, pela Secretaria de Estado interina, participar á Camara de Ytú, cabeça da comarca, que lhe foi presente a segunda via de participação dos termos de vereança de 23 de Julho proximo passada e de 7 e 9 do corrente.

Sua Alteza Real ha por bem fazer-lhe constar que já deu as suas reaes ordens na portaria de 19 do actual e qu°, outro-sim, eu repita em seu real nome os louvores que a Camara mui bem merece pelos seus energicos e patrioticos sentimentos. Paço de Taubaté, 21 de Agosto de 1822.—*Luiz de Saldanha da Gama.*

---

### OFFICIO DO GENERAL AROUCHE A' CAMARA DE YTÚ

Illustrissimos Senhores : — Não podendo eu responder ao officio que vossas senhorias me dirigiram de São Paulo na data de 23 do mez passado pela razão de estar a partir para esta côrte (2), como a vossas senhorias diria o portador da carta, que era um paulista honrado.

Vou nesta occasião satisfazer o meu dever, principiando por dar-lhes o parabem da sua muito honrada conducta em materia de tanta importancia. O officio de vossas senhorias fica na mão do Ministro de Estado dos Negocios do Reino, se Sua Alteza, que já se achará hoje em São Paulo, tem a melhor occasião de conhecer a conducta fiel dos seus paulistas e com particularidade dos firmes e corajosos ytúanos, que tanto se distinguiram nesta occasião, tendo á testa disto tão bons representantes do povo como o são vossas senhorias.

Eu me encho da maior satisfação quando vejo que, preten-dendo os malvados inimigos do Estado e do Principe baiulhar a provincia em funesta anarchia, acharam a barreira ytúana, que os conteve muito e impediu o seu progresso. Torno a repetir: dou a vossas senhorias o parabem porque, emquanto houver ho-

---

(1) Não pertencia á familia Andrada e nem escrevia sob a inspiração de José Bonifacio; portanto os elogios aqui feitos aos ytuanos são insuspiitos de *andradismo.*

(2) O officio que a camara de Ytú dirigia ao general não podia ser datado de São Paulo, em 23 de Julho, porque a capital estava em plena desordem nesse dia e a ca-mara de Ytú se achava de relações cortadas com o governo da *Bernarda.* A phrase deve ser «dirigiram a São Paulo», visto que Arouche lá estava.

mens, durará a memoria infame dos malvados e sobre ella a conducta firme chamada «dos ytúanos».

Taes exemplos são as melhores heranças que vossas senhorias deixarão á sua descendencia. Deus os conserve e guarde para defendermos os nossos direitos e a vossa houra debaixo do principe immortal o senhor Dom Pedro de Alcantara. Rio de Janeiro, 22 de Agosto de 1822.—*José Arouche de Toledo Rendon*, marechal de campo e governador das Armas.

---

OFFICIO DA CAMARA DE MOGYMIRIM Á CAMARA DE YTÚ

Tivemos distincta honra com a recepção do officio de vossas senhorias de 9 do presente, com demora de alguns dias, seguindo-se a de outros, para a nossa solução, por motivo de não haver promptos officiaes desta Camara, por terem sahido os actuaes para as freguezias do termo a funccionar reuniões do povo para darem os eleitores, e os do anno passado não se acharem promptos, e só agora é que pudemos satisfazer á convocação por vossas senhorias.

Sim, illustrissimos senhores, nos conformamos, como irmãos seus e egnaes comarcões, com as medidas que nos fizeram vêr as actas das sessões que nos enviaram. Vimos a real determinação do nosso Augusto Principe Regente quanto á extincção do Governo Provisorio desta Provincia pelas causas que aponta no decreto de 25 de Junho, a divisão de sujeitos da mesma, que conduz á horrifica anarchia contra esta nossa comarca, a investir a saude desta; o que tudo nos move unidos e em fervor para uma prompta defesa daquelle nosso jovem Principe Regente, salvador das provincias deste Brazil, por isso que nos promptificamos para a liga em que já entramos

Concordamos, pois, com as ditas medidas suas e fizemos concilio dos cidadãos e reunidos estes elegeram para nosso procurador ao capitão Manoel Dias de Barros, sujeito amante á paz benemerito amigo, visinho, contemporaneo de annos, fiel vassallo de Sua Magestade El-Rei constitucional e leal subdito do mesmo Augusto Senhor Principe Regente; é apto e exacto para questionar a presente causa até á feliz vinda daquelle forte redemptor que, com a sua feliz chegada, dissipará as nuvens perniciosas, obrando semilhantemente effeitos dos que ha poucos mezes se viu na visita que fez a Minas Geraes, que com a maior prudencia e previdencia deixou illesa e em boa paz, organisada liberdade e na traquillidade em que ora se acha.

Esperamos da honra do nosso deputado que desempenhe

nessa Junta interina os seus deveres officiaes com a reconhecida fidelidade e adhesão a Sua Alteza Real e da de vossas senhorias que o recebam e o agazalhem com protecção. Da mesma feliz vinda, e de tão poderoso redemptor a approvação recebendo, damos a vossas senhorias mil parabens e pela incomparavel ventura com que Deus nos soccorre. Este Omnipotente Senhor guarde e felicite muitos annos a vossas senhorias-
Villa de S. José de Mogymirim, em Camara de 25 de Agosto de 1822.—*Francisco da Silveira Franco.*—*João Gonçalves Teixeira* — *Joaquim Ferreira do Prado* —*Joaquim Bueno Barbosa*—*Joaquim José Pires*

___

TERMO DE VEREANÇA EXTRAORDINARIA DA COMARCA EE MOGY-MIRIM QUE ACOMPANHOU O OFFICIO SUPRA

Aos 25 dias do mez da Agosto de 1822 annos, nesta villa de S. José de Mogymim, comarca da villa de Ytú, da provincia de S. Paulo, no paço do Conselho da Camara, onde concorreram o juiz Presidente e Officiaes abaixo assignados, para effeito da presente vereança extraordinaria, sendo ahi, por terem no antecdente recebido do Senado da Camara da villa de Ytú, cabeça deste districto. o respeitavel officio de 9 do presente mez acompanhado do real decreto de 25 Junho do anno que corre, no qual Sua Alteza Real se dignou de cassar o Governo Provisorio desta provincia e ordenar que, pelos mesmos eleitores parochiaes convocados na cabeça de districtos, segundo seu real decreto de 3 do mesmo de Junho e relativas instrucções, ao depois de procederem á nomeação de deputados para a Assembléa Geral Constituinte e Legislativa deste reino do Brasil, passem immediatamente a nomear um novo governo provisorio para a capital desta provincia, dirigindo a esta Camara com adjuncto de duas actas de assento da mesma Camara e povos da villa de Ytú, funccionadas aos 4 e 7 do presente mez de Agosto, em que accordaram e concordaram unanimemente a prompta observancia daquelle real decreto, porquanto reconheciam e declaravam por nullo e cassado o referido Governo Provisorio e, em consequencia, isentos os povos da sua obediencia; e que para evitar os terriveis males de divisões e anarchias e conservar perfeita paz e tranquillidade publica, haviam assentado de nomear um procurador que se junte com os das demais villas colligadas e que se quizessem ligar e colligar, aos quaes se dessem os poderes necessarios para effectuarem as ditas medidas e fazerem o plano de suas attribuições, ficando desde logo

com poderes para isso; ao que procedendo sahiu a mais votos
um e o outro para na falta daquelle servir este em seu lugar,
os quaes logo houveram por empossados, e ultimamente que se
convocassem as villas colligadas.

O que tudo sendo observado accordaram em Camara unanimemente que se chamassem as pessoas da nobreza e povo
desta villa e termo a reunirem-se para a presente vereação geral e consulta sobre objecto tão importante, o que se fez por
edital que se publicou, e compareceram na presente sessão os
reunidos abaixo assignados, e pelo dito Juiz Presidente foi lido
aquelle real decreto de 15 de Junho, officio da Camara convo-
cante e suas duas actas. O que feito, todos a uma voz declararam convir nas mesmas e similhantes medidas, exaradas pela
presente Camara e Congresso da cabeça deste districto. E passando-se logo á nomeação, pelo Juiz Presidente foi proclamado
geralmente procurador-agente o capitão Manoel Dias de Barros,
para deputado á Junta interina' da cabeça deste districto, e que
na falta deste sirva em seu lugar o outro nomeado ou o mesmo
Juiz Presidente ou o Juiz de Orphãos, capitão Venancio Maria
Torriane, que tambem foi acceito por todos presentes, aos quaes
já os ha por empossados deste cargo esta Camara, que mandou-
lhes dar seus diplomas, por copia, para com elles se irem apresentar na Junta sobredita a funccionar seus deveres officiaes; o
que tudo desde já lhes ha por recommendado pela confiança que
faz das suas fidelidades, e que se remetta copia do diploma
áquella Camara.

E para todo o referido constar se lavrou o presente termo,
em que assignaram adjuntos a nobreza e povo que se achavam
presentes, e eu, Pedro Lourenço de Lima, escrivão da Camara,
pue o escrevi.—*Francisco da Silveira Franco*—*José Gonçalves
Teixeira*—*Joaquim Ferreira do Prado*—*Joaquim Bueno Barbosa*
—*Joaquim José Pires*—Capitão *Antonio da Cunha Lobo*—Sargento-mór *Martinho Dias Pacheco*—Almotacel *Francisco Luiz
de Almeida*—Jniz de Orphãos *Venancio Maria Torriane*—Capitão *José Gomes de Oliveira Franco*- Capitão *José de Moraes
Preto*—Alferes *Pedro José Frreira*—Capitão *Antonio Gonçalves
de Oliveira*—Capitão *João de Souza Nogueira*—Alferes *Urias
Emigdio Nogueira de Barros*—Alferes *Antonio Gomes Moreira*
—Alferes *Antonio José Monteiro*—*Joaquim Dias Barbosa*—*Manoel Ferreira Machado*—*Pedro José de Campos*—*José Manoel
de Souza*--*Francisco José de Souza*—*Francisco José de Barros*
—*José Fernandes da Silva*—*José Lucas de Barros*—*Domingos
Dias de Barros*—Alferes *Thomaz Carlos de Souza*.

OFFICIO DA CAMARA DE YTÚ AO PRINCIPE REGENTE

SENHOR: — A Camara de Ytú, no transporte de seu jubilo pela vinda de Vossa Alteza Real a esta provincia, accusa a recepçã-j das regias portarias das datas de 19 e 21 do corrente, na qual se digna Vossa Alteza honrar tanto a ella, ao povo e á tropa

Nós, Augusto Senhor, ingenuamente confessamos que não temos expressões que signifiquem nossa gratidão pela honra com que Vossa Alteza nos distinguiu. Nós somos fieis, Augusto Senhor, e nossos votos de fidelidade são inabalaveis, e nos apressamos apenas em reiteral-os e beijarmos as regias mãos de Vossa Alteza, que tauto desejavamos nesta malfadada provincia.

Temos a honra de participar a Vossa Alteza que, em consequencia da leitura do *Manifesto* de Vossa Alteza ao Brazil e Portaria, lidos em publica sessão aos habitantes desta reunidos nesta Camara, foi a electricidade de todos que, rompendo os diques de seu enthusiasmo em repetidos *vivas* a Vossa Alteza, representavam vivamente os gratos sentimentos de que se viam possuidos.

Quanto ás medidas que adoptamos e que foram levadas á Augusta Presença de Vossa Alteza nas differentes actas *eram filhas do aperto em que nos viamos pelo terrorismo e arbitrariedades da facção da Capital*, as quaes deveriam necessariamente cessar logo que chegassem as beneficas providencias de Vossa Alteza a esta provincia. Nós nos regosijavamos porque merecem a approvação de Vossa Alteza, alvo sempre das nossas intuições. Digne-se Vossa Alteza acceitar os fervorosos protestos de nossa inabalavel fidelidade e extremosa gratidão. Deus guarde a Vossa Alteza Real como nós é mister. Villa de Ytú, em Camara de 26 de Agosto de 1822.—*Bento Dias Pacheco — Antonio Pacheco da Fonseca.—Antonio Victoriano de Azevedo.—Lourenço de Almeida Prado.—Joaquim José de Mello*.

# Devassa sobre a Bernarda de 23 de Maio de 1822

EXPLÍCAÇÃO NECESSARIA

A *Bernarda Francisco Ignacio*, não obstante ter sido um acontecimento de caracter apparentemente local, foi um facto grave, que abalou profundamente a provincia de S. Paulo e influiu perniciosamente na politica brazileira. Abafada a sedição no fim de tres mezes, procedeu o governo de D Pedro a uma devassa para chegar ao conhecimento da verdade sobre as causas e fins daquella rebellião e sobre os personagens que nella mais se salientaram.

Essa devassa, realizada nos mezes de Setembro e Outubro de 1822, não trouxe consequencia alguma criminal e politica, porque um decreto de amnistia fez opportunamente cessar todo o procedimento legal contra os delinquentes. Entretanto, a verdade historica que devia resultar dessa devassa ficou prejudicada porque, com a amnistia, os respectivos autos desappareceram do cartorio e os factos ficaram na obscuridade ou mesmo foram alterados pela conveniencia daquelles que tinham sido seus auctores.

Azevedo Marques, nos seus *Apontamentos Historicos*, artigo BERNARDA, diz que teve em mãos esses e até delles transcreveu, com pouca fidelidade, o depoimento de uma das testemunhas, o capitão Bento José Leite Penteado, pessôa proeminente na sociedade paulista do tempo e presidente da Camara Municipal, que pouco adeantou sobre as causas e fins da sedição, de que aliás foi uma das victimas.

Passaram-se mais de trinta annos, sem que se soubesse o paradeiro dos autos e agora se descobre que elles se achavam em poder do dr. Paula de Sousa Queiroz, que gentilmente m'os cedeu para serem publicados.

Examinando o seu conteúdo, verifiquei que delles restam sómente 152 paginas do fim, contendo os depoimentos completos de vinte e tres testemunhas, unicas inquiridas, que deitam muita luz sobre aquella sedição. Era exactamente aquillo de que precisava a historia; copiei todos os depoimentos com o devido cuidado e accrescentei-lhes, por minha conta, muitas notas ao rodapé, já para dar algumas informações sobre varios personagens, já para esclarecer algumas referencias obscuras, já, finalmente, para indicar as contradicções no procedimento illogico de varios sediciosos.

Com estes esclarecimentos, entrego a devassa á apreciação dos amantes da historia patria.

S. Paulo, Março de 1905.

A. DE TOLEDO PIZA.

# ASSENTADA

Aos 16 dias do mez de Setembro de 1822, nesta cidade de São Paulo, em casas de residencia do doutor Antonio de Almeida Silva Freire da Fonseca, juiz da presente devassa (1), pelo dito ministro foram inquiridas e perguntadas as testemunhas cujos nomes, cognomes, naturalidades, moradas, idades, officios, ditos e costumes são os que adeante se seguem; do que, para assim constar, lavrei o presente teremo de assentada. Eu, o bacharel formado Manoel Joaquim de Ornellas (2), escrivão desta devassa o escrevi.

## TESTEMUNHA 1.ª

O Capitão Bento José Leite Penteado (3), casado, natural da villa de Parnahyba, desta provincia, e morador desta cidade, onde vive de seus bens e exercita o cargo de juiz de fora pela lei, de idade de 64 annos; testemuuha jurada aos Santos Evangelhos em um livro delles, em que poz sua mão direita e debaixo do juramento que prestou lhe foi encarregado pelo ministro devassante declarasse a verdade do que soubesse e lhe fosse perguntado, e assim o prometteu cumprir. E sendo perguntado pelos interrogatorios desta devassa, disse ao primeiro que sabe por ouvir vulgarmente que o sargento-mór José Rodrigues Pereira de Oliveira Netto fora quem mandou tocar a rebate na tarde do dia 23 de Maio do corrente anno, obrigando para isso, com uma pistola aos peitos, ao tenente José Ignacio de Macedo, que se achava de estado maior nos quarteis desta cidade, e que para o mesmo effeito de se tocar a rebate constrangêra os respectivos tambores, levando-os aos cachações, e querendo elle, testemuha, certificar-se do referido, perguntára ao dito tenente

---

(1) Era juiz de fóra de Taubaté e veio presidir ao feito em falta do ouvidor. Costa Carvalho, que era o ouvidor, foi um dos chefes dos sediciosos e estava no Rio a chamado de D. Pedro; era membro do governo o dr. José Corrêa Pacheco e Silva, que foi juiz nesta capital, e o de Taubaté foi chamado para a devassa.
(2) Foi membro do governo de S. Paulo, de Janeiro de 1823 a Abril de 1824 e fez boa figura na politica da provincia, sendo deputado geral varias vezes.
(3) Era o presidente da Camara de S. Paulo e, como tal, supplente do juiz de fora; soffreu violencias da parte do capitão Pedro Taques de Almeida Alvim para tomar parte na sedição. O seu depoimento foi publicado por Azevedo Marques nos *Apontamentos Historicos*, mas truncado, de modo a prejudical-o.

e este lhe assegurou que assim acontecêra, e que o mesmo lhe affirmára o capitão Francisco Candido de Sagalerva, e mais não disse.—Ao segundo, disse que nada sabia, apezar de ter entrado na indagação do que se expende no mencionado interrogatorio, se bem que ouvira vulgarmente que os agentes do motim, acontecido naquella tarde do dia 23 de Maio, foram João Carlos Augusto de Oeynhasen, presidente do extincto governo provisorio desta provincia, o ouvidor José da Costa Carvalho e o coronel Francisco Ignacio de Souza Queiroz e bem assim o coronel Francisco Alvares Ferreira do Amaral.—Ao terceiro, disse que sabe, por haver presenciado no largo de São Gonçalo, que o *coronel Francisco Alvares Ferreira do Amaral* fora o que fez sahir a tropa do quartel e postar no dito largo, comparecendo na frente della o brigadeiro Joaquim José Pinto de Moraes Leme e o coronel Francisco Ignacio de Souza Queiroz, além de outros officiaes como foram o capitão Francisco Gonçalves dos Santos Cruz, o sargento-mór Francisco de Paula Macedo, o tenente Jayme da Silva Telles, o capitão Pedro Taques de Almeida Alvim, o sargento-mór José Rodrigues Pereira de Oliveira Netto, o capitão Caetano Pinto Homem, o capitão Antonio Cardoso Nogueira e outros mais, de cujos nomes não se recorda. —Ao quarto, disse que quem commandára a tropa para sahir do quartel e ir postar-se no largo de São Gonçalo, na occasião do motim, fora o coronel Francisco Alvares Ferreira do Amaral, pondo-a alli em linha de batalha, e estando á frente della vira logo depois apparecer alli o coronel Francisco Ignacio de Souza Queiroz, entre os quaes, sabe por ouvir geralmente, houvera disputa sobre o commando da referida tropa, o que elle, testemunha, julga ser verdade por haver presenciado que o sobredito coronel Francisco Alvares Ferreira do Amaral pediu uma satisfacção ao governo a dito respeito, e mais não disse deste. — Ao quinto, disse que sendo elle, testemunha, o presidente da camara desta cidade na occasião do motim, concorrêra á vereação extraordinaria do indicado dia 23 de Maio por força e violencia que para isso lhe fez o capitão Pedro Taques de Almeida Alvim, que por duas vezes na mesma tarde fôra á rua a cavallo e armado para o conduzir, como conduziu, á casa da camara, apesar delle, testemunha, lhe perguntar o fim para que o queriam na camara, respondendo-lhe que lá o saberia (1).—Ao sexto, disse que sabe por experiencia propria que muitas das

---

(1) Na primeira intimação para ir á Camara não foi, porem na segunda Pedro Taques o ameaçou de leval-o com as mãos amarradas e atado á cincha ou á canda de seu cavallo se não fosse; seguiu então a pé para a casa da Camara, acompanhado por Pedro Taques, a cavallo, armado e com capangas!

pessoas que assignaram aquelle auto de vereação extraordinaria
o fizeram constrangidamente, como elle, testemunha, por ameaças do sargento-mór Francisco de Paula Macedo, Jayme da
Silva Telles, o capitão Pedro Taques de Almeida Alvim e outros,
de cujos nomes se não lembra, os quaes, ouviu vulgarmente,
andaram pelas casas dos que em parte se acham assignados naquelle auto de vereação extraordinaria, onvindo isto mesmo ao
tenente Ignacio, morador na rua da Quitanda desta cidade, por
sobrenome o Assumpção, a respeito das assignaturas feitas nos
dias posteriores, para cujo effeito estivera a casa da camara
aberta por alguns dias, por determinação da força armada e do
vereador transacto, o capitão Caetano Pinto Homem.—Ao setimo,
disse que sabe, por ouvir vulgarmente, que João Carlos Augusto
de Oeynhausen e o coronel Francisco Ignacio de Sousa Queiroz,
empregado no extincto governo provisorio desta provincia, influiram para o motim acontecido por intrigas particulares trava-
das entre os ditos dois empregados, o ouvidor José da Costa
Carvalho e os dois membros depostos por effeito daquelle motim,
o coronel Martim Francisco Ribeiro de Andrada e o brigadeiro
Manoel Rodrigues Jordão.—Ao oitavo, disse que não lhe consta
que o extincto governo provisorio désse providencia alguma
sobre o motim acontecido (1), e sobre o mais do interrogatorio
nada disse.—Ao nono, disse que unicamente sabe, por ouvir ao
capitão Joaquim José de Almeida (2), que já no Rio de Janeiro
se falava que estava para acontecer o referido motim, mez e
meio antes de haver acontecido.—Ao decimo, disse nada, nem
do costume, e lido o seu juramento, pelo achar conforme ao que
havia deposto, assignou com o ministro devassante. E eu, o
bacharel formado, escrivão, que o escrevi.—*Freire.*—*Bento José
Leite Penteado*.

## ASSENTADA

Aos 16 dias do mez de Setembro de 1822, nesta cidade de
São Paulo, em casas de residencia do doutor Antonio de Al-

(1) Não podia providenciar, porque, depois do motim, o governo ficou entregue a
João Carlos, Müller, Oliveira Pinto, Quartim e Francisco Ignacio, auctores do mesmo motim, e o ouvidor Costa Carvalho, que devia tomar alguma providencia, como o primeiro
magistrado da comarca, era não sómente cumplice nas desordens, mas uma das cabeças
pensantes e directoras daquelles acontecimentos.
(2) Fez este offial parte das tropas enviadas de S. Paulo ao Rio para acudir o
Principe Regente contra o general portuguez Avillez : quando voltava do Rio, com um
corpo de tropas, encontrou-se em Bananal com Martim Francisco. que seguia para o Rio,
deportado pelo governo militar e extrangeiro de S. Paulo e acompanhado pelo capitão
José Fernandes da Silva ; voltou para o Rio em companhia de Martim e do capitão Fernandes da Silva e quando regressou a S. Paulo denunciou a este, por ter sahido do Rio
contra ordem expressa do ministro da Guerra. Vide a *Deposição de Martim Francisco
e sua deportação para o Rio de Janeiro*, neste mesmo volume.

meida Silva Freire da Fonseca, juiz da presente devassa, e sendo
ahi pelo dito ministro foram inquiridas e perguntadas as testemunhas cujos nomes, cognomes, naturalidades, moradas, idades,
officios, ditos e costumes é tudo o que adeante se segue, de que
fiz este termo de assentada. E eu, o bacharel formado Manuel
Joaquim de Ornellas, escrivão nomeado, o escrevi.

## TESTEMUNHA 2.ª

O Capitão Antonio da Silva Prado (1), solteiro, natural e
morador desta cidade, de idade de 34 para 35 annos, que vive
de seus negocios ; testemunha jurada aos Santos Evangelhos em
um livro delles, em que poz sua mão direita e, debaixo do juramento que prestou, prometteu dizer a verdade do que sobesse
e perguntado lhe fosse. E sendo perguntado pelos interrogatorios desta devassa disse, ao primeiro, que sabe por ouvir em sua
casa a José Dias de Quadros Aranha, por este ter ouvido dizer,
em casa do major José Manoel da Luz, á mulher do sargento-
mór José Rodrigues Pereira de Oliveira Netto que seu marido,
estando abandonado do seu coronel Francisco Ignacio de Souza
Queiroz e até fóra do serviço, o encontrára a agradar e acari-
ciar o dito seu coronel, ainda mesmo com dinheiro para que
elle promovesse o motim acontecido no dia 23 de Maio nesta
cidade, sendo chamado para este effeito á casa do coronel Francisco Alvares Ferreira do Amaral, onde se achava João Carlos
Augusto de Oeynhausen, pelas 2 horas da madrugada daquelle
dia, e que sobre este mesmo objecto sabe por um escripto que
recebeu de seu tio, o capitão-mór desta cidade, Eleuterio da
Silva Prado, ás horas do meio dia do mesmo dia 23 de Maio e
que apresentou neste acto do seu juramento, que um alferes de
ordenanças lhe fôra participar de que tinha sido avisado por
certo official do regimento do coronel Francisco Ignacio de Souza Queiroz para ás 4 horas da tarde do mencionado dia se achar
fardado no quartel da tropa miliciana, afim de acudir a um rebate que se havia de tocar para se substar a ida do presidente
do extincto governo provisorio João Carlos Augusto de Oeynhausen para a cidade do Rio de Janeiro, por ordem de Sua
Alteza Real, e ficar general das Armas desta provincia, e ao
meio dia lhe foi dizer Gabriel Henriques Pessoa que o dito pre-

---

(1) Pertencia a uma das mais illustres familias paulistas; filho do capitão-mór
Antonio Prado. fez sua figura na politica provincial teve o titulo de Barão de Iguape e
foi avô do conselheiro Antonio Prado e do mallogrado e distincto escriptor Eduardo Prado.
O seu testemunho seria dos mais importantes, si não tivesse o seu valor diminuido pelo
facto de ser sobrinho do brigadeiro Manoel Rodrigues Jordão, o que declarou em nota
ao seu depoimento.

sidente era chamado ao Rio de Janeiro, e respondendo elle, testemunha, que de nada sabia replicou o mesmo Pessoa que desde ás 8 horas da noite do dia antecedente já se sabia da ordem por onde o mesmo presidente era chamado e que para a fazer substar se projectava tocar ao dito rebate, e nada mais disse deste.—Ao segundo, disse que os agentes do motim e cooperadores para o mesmo, da parte da tropa, foram o tenente Jayme da Silva Telles e da parte do povo o sargento–mór Franc̦isco de Paula Macedo, SEM QUE A TROPA NEM O POVO ESTIVES⁺EM DISPOSTOS PRRA SEMELHANTE ACONTECIMENTO, o que sabe por ouvir ao juiz de fóra pela lei, capitão Bento José Leite Penteado e outras muitas pessoas, que assistiram ao mesmo acontecimento; mas que é voz publica nesta cidade e em toda a provincia que um e outro eram agentes do presidente do governo, do ouvidor José da Costa Carvalho e do deputado do mesmo governo, coronel Francisco Ignacio de Souza Queiroz, que chegou mesmo ao deeaccôrdc de proferir, perante elle, testemunha, na loja do capitão Pedro Taques de Almeida Alvim, em dias do mez de Julho proximo passado, estando lendo uma folha, que tratava delle coronel como auctor das bernardas desta capital, que se Sua Alteza Real conservasse o seu primeiro ministro, o conselheiro José Bonifacio de Andrada e Silva, *ainda havia de levar com um chicote no Rio de Janeiro, o que proferiu com um semblante irado* (1), e achando-se presentes o capitão Antonio Cardoso Nogueira, o sargento–mór Francisco de Paula Macedo e José Manoel da Luz Tralhão, disse o dito capitão Nogueira ao referido coronel Francisco Ignacio de Souza Queiroz que elle era o culpado de estar o mesmo conselheiro com aquelle emprego de primeiro ministro de Estado, pois que se tivesse praticado ha seis mezos atraz o que se praticára no dia 23 de Maio, não teria obtido semelhante emprego; ao que respondeu que bem se arrependia de o não ter feito.—Ao terceiro, disse que é voz publica nesta cidade que a tropa existente nos quarteis não marchára de seu motu proprio para o largo de São Gonçalo, mas sim movida e commandada pelo coronel Francisco Alves Ferreira do Amaral e o brigadeiro Joaquim José Pinto de Moraes Leme, criaturas e intimos amigos do indicado presidente João Carlos Augusto de Oeynhausen, e naquelle largo se postára a mesma tropa em linha de batalha á ordem dos sobreditos commandantes.—Ao quarto, disse nada por ter deposto o que sabia ao artigo antecedente.

---

(1) O grypho aqui é do original. O Coronel Francisco Ignacio, que de longe ameaçava 1². Pedro com o seu chicote, era o mesmo que dahi a um mez se mettia em grandes despesas para montar um luzido corpo de tropa, com o fim de abrilhantar a chegada do Principe Regente a S. Paulo, obsequio este que elle teve o dissabor de ver regeitado por D. Pedro !

—Ao quinto, disse que sabe, por ter ouvido ao proprio capitão Bento Josè Leite Penteado, que fora levado da sua casa para a da Camara, com ameaças feitas pelo capitão Pedro Taques de Almeida Alvim, que o conduzira deante de si a pé, indo elle capitão Alvim a cavallo, e que isto mesmo ouvira a João José Moreira, o qual, estando no pateo da Sé, vira passar o mesmo juiz, capitão Benedicto Penteado, acompanhado pelo mesmo capitão Alvim pela maneira acima declarada.—Ao sexto, disse que sabe por ter ouvido o capitão Joaquim Alvares, que assistiu o acto de vereação extraordinaria do dia 23 de Maio e o assignou, que fora convidado por Antonio Gonçalves Mamede, Jayme da Silva Telles e José Manoel da Luz Tralhão e outros em casa do coronel Francisco Ignacio de Souza Queiroz, onde se acostumavam a se juntar frequentemente, afim de substar a ida do presidente do governo João Carlos Augusto de Oeynhausen para o Rio de Janeiro de ordem de Sua Alteza Real; e tendo assistido e se recusando a assignar o dito auto de vereação extraordinaria, lhe disseram de entre os circumstantes que ficava perdido se o não assignasse. Ouviu igualmente elle, testemunha, a José Clemente de Mesquita que passando este pela porta do coronel Francisco Ignacio de Souza Queiroz, fora chamado e recolhido ao escriptorio, onde se achavam o mesmo coronel, o ouvidor José da Costa Carvalho e outras muitas pessoas, que alli se acostumavam ajuntar, e alli lhe deram um papel, cujo conteúdo disse a elle, testemunha, ignorava pelo terror com que ficou quando o ouviu ler, por se achar rodeado de tantas pessoas, e que apezar disso assignára por se ver instado para isso e recear que lhe fizessem alguma desfeita se o não assignasse.—Ao setimo, disse que sabe por ter ouvido o doutor José Corrêa Pacheco e Silva (1), que este vira uma carta do proprio punho do presidente do extincto governo provisorio, João Carlos Augusto de Oeynhausen, escripta ao governador interino de Santos, o tenente coronel José Antonio da Silva Valente (2), onde mostrava grande satisfacção pelos acontecimentos de 23 de Maio passado, sobre que recebeu parabens e houvera tres dias de luminarias; andando atraz da musica de capote, no primeiro dia, o coronel Francisco Ignacio de Souza Queiroz, o ouvidor José da Costa Carvalho, o coronel Francisco

---

(1) Paulista distincto, de uma illustre familia Ytuana; foi juiz em Santos e ouvidor em S. Paulo ao tempo desta devassa era membro do governo de S. Paulo, cargo que exerceu de 10 de Setembro de 1822 a 25 de Abril de 1824, e fez boa figura na politica da provincia.

(2) Adherido ao partido retrogado se poz ao seu serviço e encravou a artilharia das fortalezas de Santos. para que não pudesse repellir a força portugueza que os sediciosos esperavam de Lisboa. Essa artilharia foi pouco depois desencravada e reparada pelo marechal Candido Xavier, nomeado por D. Pedro commandante militar de Santos.

Alvares Ferreira do Amaral, o capitão Antonio Cardoso Nogueira, o sargento-mór Francisco de Paula Macedo, Antonio Gonçalves Mumede, José Manuel da Luz Tarlbão e Joaquim Pedro Motta, espreitando os que não punham luminarias para mandar que as puzessem, CHEGANDO MESMO AO EXCESSO DE MAN-DAREM AMEAÇAR AO CORONEL MARTIM FRANCISCO RIBEIRO DE ANDRADE E AO PADRE-MESTRE FRANCISCO DE PAULA OLIVEIRA POR NÃO AS TEREM POSTO (1). — Ao oitavo, disse que sabe, por ter presenciado, que o extincto governo provisorio nenhuma providencia dera sobre aquelles acontecimentos do dia 23 de Maio preterito; antes pelo contrario os applaudiam e promoviam o desasocego da provincia, mandando emissarios para as differentes villas della (2), como foi o capitão Pedro Taques de Almeida Alvim, que foi ás villas do norte com o destino de seduzir a tropa que vinha do Rio de Janeiro e subornal-a para que deixasse de obedecer ao marechal Arouche e se unis-e ás determinações do mesmo governo (3), em que figuravam voluntariamente o presidente João Carlos Augusto de Oeynhausen com todos os outros, á excepção dos tres, do thesoureiro-mór João Ferreira de Oliveira Bueno, do padre Paula e Oliveira e do tenente coronel André da Silva Gomes, que nada concorriam para cousas de semelhante natureza, antes eram olhados com indignação pelos mais que delles occultavam muitos negocios quando viam que não coincidia com o seu parecer, tomando por seu assessor em muitas de suas deliberações ao ouvidor José da Costa Carvalho, que concorria com elles nas suas sessões, depois de despedidos dellas os dois membros padre Francisco de Paula e Oliveira e o tenente coronel André da Silva Gomes, visto que o thesoureiro-mór depois do dia 23 de Maio não comparceu no governo senão uma vez, quando se tratou de cumprir as ordens de Sua Alteza Real, em cuja occasião, sendo mal recebido, não voltou lá mais (4), como declarou a elle, testemunha o mesmo thesoureiro-mór; e quanto ao facto de Pedro Taques, acima indicado,

_(1)_ Depunham Martim do poder e ainda queriam que elle e seu amigo e ex-collega do governo, padre Paula Oliveira, puzessem luminarias!
_(2)_ Um desses emissarios foi o sargento-mór Paula Macedo, que seguiu para Ytú a subornar a força da confederação dos municipios, estacionada naquella povoação; foi agarrado e expulso violentamente da villa. Vide _Revista_ deste Instituto, vol. VII, pags. 161—162.
_(3)_ Nada conseguiu dessa missão, porque o norte, sob a influencia do marechal Arouche, ficou fiel aos interesses brazileiros e solidario com a confederação dos municipios, cuja séde era Ytú.
_(4)_ Estes factos são importantes e exigem alguns esclarecimentos: As sessões a que o depoente se refere são sessões do governo. Na acta da sessão extraordinaria da tarde de 23 de Maio, em que Martim e Jordão se deram por demittidos, assignaram os sediciosos João Carlos, Oliveira Finto, Müller, Quartim e Francisco Ignacio e mais os legalistas padres João Ferreira e Paulo Oliveira e o tenente coronel André Gomes; na acta do dia seguinte assignaram os mesmos sediciosos e mais o padre Paula e Oliveira.

veiu a saber por ter ouvido ao desembaigador João de Medeiros Gomes (1), a quem o contou o mesmo Pedro Taques de Almeida Alvim, e mais não disse deste —Ao nono, disse que sabe, por ouvir ao mesmo desembargador João Medeiros Gomes, que João Theodoro Xavier, desta cidade, lhe fora communicar no dia 3 de Maio passado que no dia seguinte havia de haver um motim, com o projecto de expulsarem do governo aos dous membros delle coronel Martim Francisco Ribeiro de Andrada e brigadeiro Manoel Rodrigues Jordão, o que lhe participava para que se não assustasse, e disto sabia o dito João Theodoro Xavier por assitir aos conventiculos que sobre este objecto faziam em casa do coronel Francisco Ignacio de Souza, no quarto do seu socio Antonio Gonçalves Mamede (2). Disse mais por ter sido avisado pelo tenente Bernardo Guedes, no dia 14 de Maio, que por se não ter verificado a deposição dos referidos dous membros do governo no dia antecedente, como se projectava, ficava reservada para se effectuar no dia de Corpo de Deus, no seguinte mez de Junho.—Ao decimo nada disse. E lido o seu juramento, pelo achar conforme ao que depoz, se assignou com o ministro devassante, e eu, bacharel formado Manel Joaquim de Ornellas, escrivão desta devassa, o escrevi. —Freire.—Antonio da Silva Prado.

## ASSENTADA

Aos 17 dias do mez de Setembro de 1822, nesta cidade de S. Paulo, em casas de residencia do juiz desta devassa, o doutor Antonio de Almeida Silva Freire da Fonseca, foram por elle inquiridas as testemunhas, cujos nomes cognomes, naturalidades moradas, idades, officios e costumes é tudo o que adeante se segue, do que, para assim constar, fiz este termo de assentada. E eu, o bacharel formado Manoel Joaquim de Ornellas, escrivão nomeado o escrevi.

Na acta da sessão de 29 de Maio, em que se revolveu a deportação immediata de Martim para o Rio, só assignaram João Carlos, Oliveira Pinto e Müller. Costa Carvalho podia ter assessorado o governo até 21 de Julho, quando seguiu para o Rio, com João Carlos, e o governo ficou entregue aos sediciosos Oliveira Pinto, Müller, Quartim e Francisco Ignacio, até ao dia em que D. Pedro aqui chegou e os despediu do poder. Vergueiro nada presenciou e Lazaro Gonçalves e Gama Lobo estavam no Rio de Janeiro.

(1) Foi por algum tempo ouvidor da comarca de Ytú, com jurisdicção que se extendia desde Mogy-mirim até Faxina e Apiahy, e se mostrou firme adepto da confederação ytuana contra o governo extrangeiro e sedicioso de S. Paulo.

(2) A sedição devia apparecer na primeira opportunidade; foi planejada para 3 de Maio, adiada para 18 e realisada a 23; a portaria de 10 de Maio, chamando para o Rio João Carlos e Costa Carvalho, nada influiu para ella e só appareceu no dia 23, como um pretexto da ultima hora e em falta de outro melhor.

# TESTEMUNHA 3.ª

João Nepomuceno de Almeida (1) casado, natural da villa de Paranaguá, desta provincia, e morador desta cidade, onde vive do seu emprego de escrivão da Camara, de edade de 37 annos; tesmunha jurada aos Santos Evangelhos, em um livro delles em que poz a sua mão direita e, debaixo do juramento que prestou, prometteu dizer a verdade do que soubesse e lhe fosse perguntado. E sendo inquirido pelos interrogatorios da presente devassa disse, ao primeiro, que sabe, por ser voz publica e por ter ouvido particularmente ao soldado miliciano José Joaquim da Luz, seu vizinho, que quem mandára tocar o rebate fôra o sargento-mór José Rodrigues Pereira de Oliveira Netto, forçando para isso com pistolas ao tenente José Ignacio de Macedo que era o official que se achava de estado-maior no quartel e que por effeito desta violencia se vira obrigado a mandar tocar o dito rebate.—Ao segundo, nada disse.—Ao terceiro, que sabe, por ouvir ao tenente Francisco Severiano dos Santos Cardim, que estando a tropa formada nos quarteis depois do rebate, debaixo do commando do tenente coronel Antonio de Padua de Gusmão, commandante do destacamento, chegára alli o coronel Francisco Alvares Ferreira do Amaral e desembainhando a espada, se puzéra á frente della para commandar, o que lhe foi muito extranhado pelo dito tenente-coronel Padua e não obstante a sua opposição, sempre a referida tropa sahira do quartel commandada pelo mencionado coronel Francisco Alvares Ferreira do Amaral, a pedido de certas pessoas do povo que alli se achavam, e se fôra postar no largo de S. Gonçalo, em linha de batalha, com os respectivos officiaes subalternos, o que elle, testemunha, presenciou.—Ao quarto, disse que na frente daquella tropa vira por commandantes os coroneis Francisco Alvares Ferreira do Amaral e Francisco Ignacio de Sousa Queiroz, que chegando posteriormente tomou uma satisfacção ao sobredito coronel Francisco Alvares Ferreira do Amaral por haver tomado o commando da tropa sem sua auctoridade, visto ser o chefe da força armada, sobre o que mostrando-se escandalizado o mesmo coronel Francisco Alvares Ferreira do Amaral, pedira no dia seguinte a sua reforma ao extincto governo provisorio na occasião em que toda a officialidade foi dar parabens ao seu presidente João Carlos Augusto de Oeynhausen por ter ficado nesta cidade apezar de ter sido chamado para a côrte do Rio de Janeiro por ordem de Sua Alteza Real. Disse mais que vira na frente da tropa o

---

(2) Residia na casa n. 1 da rua das Freiras, hoje Senador Feijó, com sua senhora, sogra, uma cunhada, seis filhos e seis escravos.

brigadeiro Joaquim José Pinto de Moraes Leme e que este alli se conservára emquanto ella esteve formada, mas que não estava com a espada desembainhada em ares de commandante, o que assim presenciára por ter ido lêr, á frente da mesma tropa por mandado do doutor ouvidor José da Costa Carvalho, uma carta que a camara dirigia ao extincto governo provisorio á instancias do tenente Jayme da Silva Telles (1), QUE ASSIM O REQUEREU COM O FIGURADO TITULO DE POVO E TROPA, sendo elle mesmo quem a notou (2). — Ao quinto, disse que sabe, por vêr, que o presidente da camara, que então era o capitão Bento José Leite Penteado, concorrêra á casa da camara levado á força pelo capitão Pedro Taques de Almeida Alvim, que o conduzia a pé adeante de si, indo a cavallo com uma espada núa na mão, concorrendo elle mesmo, testemunha, á casa da camara como escrivão della a instancias do mesmo capitão Pedro Taques de Almeida Alvim, e do procurador da camara, o capitão Luiz Manoel da Cunha Bastos, que o vieram chamar por já lá se achar o juiz presidente. — Ao sexto, disse que nada sabia sobre o conteúdo deste interrogatorio.—Ao setimo, disse que sabe, por ter ouvido geralmente nesta cidade e particularmente ao capitão Joaquim José de Almeida, que o presidente do extincto governo provisorio, João Carlos Augusto de Oeynhausen, cooperára para o motim acontecido nesta cidade em o dia 23 de Maio passado, afim de ser conservado no governo.—Ao oitavo, disse que unicamente sabe que o extincto governo provisorio recommendára á camara desta cidade fizesse conter o povo na sua antiga moderação, em consequencia do que fizéra a camara publicar um edital, lavrado por elle, testemunha.—Ao nono, disse que sabe, por ouvir a João Theodoro Xavier, que antes do dia 23 de Maio do corrente anno já se projectava pôr em execução, no dia 13, o que se effectuou naquelle dia.—Ao decimo, disse que sabe, por lhe contarem o tenente Francisco Severiano dos Santos Cardim e o capitão Joaquim José de Almeida, EM MUITO SEGREDO, QUE JOÃO CARLOS AUGUSTO DE OEYNHAUSEN PRESIDENTE DO EXTINCTO GOVERNO PROVISORIO, E O CORONEL DANIEL PEDRO MULLER TINHAM COMMUNICAÇÃO OCCULTA COM AS CORTES DE PORTUGAL CONTRA A CAUSA DO BRAZIL e que por effeito desta communicação SE ESPERAVA NO PORTO DE SANTOS, desta provincia, UMA ESQUADRA COM TROPA EUROPÉA PARA PARTE DELLA SE APODERAR DESTA MESMA PROVINCIA e OUTRA PARTE MARCHAR PARA O

---

(1) O officio da Camara ao governo foi mandado lêr-se ás tropas por ordem do ouvidor Costa Carvalho e quem o leu foi o secretario da Camara que está depondo

(2) A Camara esteve sempre debaixo de temerosa oppressão e os sediciosos Costa Carvalho e Silva Telles se faziam redactores das suas cartas e representações!

Rio de Janeiro por terra (1). E nada mais disse, nem do costume. E lido o seu juramento, pelo achar conforme ao que havia deposto, se assignou com o ministro devassante. E eu, o bacharel formado Manoel Joaquim de Ornellas, escrivão da presente devassa, o escrevi. — *Freire* — *João Nepomuceno de Almeida.*

---

## ASSENTADA

Aos 17 dias do mez de Setembro de 1822, nesta cidade de São Paulo, em casas de residencia do juiz desta devassa, o doutor Antonio de Almeida Silva Freire da Fonseca, foram por elle inquiridas as testemunhas cujos nomes, cognomes, naturalidades, idades, officios e costumes é tudo o que adeante se segue, do que para constar fiz este termo de assentada. E eu o bacharel formado Manoel Joaquim de Ornellas, escrivão nomeado, o escrevi.

## TESTEMUNHA 4.ª

O capitão Antonio Bernardo Bueno da Veiga (2), solteiro, natural e morador desta cidade, onde vive de seus bens, de idade de 50 annos mais ou menos; testemunha jurada aos Santos Evangelhos, em um livro delles em que poz sua mão direita e, debaixo do juramento que lhe foi deferido, prometteu dizer a verdade do que soubesse e perguntado lhe fosse. E sendo inquirido pelos interrogatorios desta devassa disse, ao primeiro, que sabe por ouvir ao tenente Ignacio José de Macedo, que estava de estado maior no quartel desta cidade no dia 23 de Maio proximo passado, perante o advogado capitão Manoel José de Castro e em casa deste, que naquelle dia, das 3 para as 4 horas da tarde, appareceram armados de espada e pistolas no

---

(1) Esta accusação, grave como é, tem seus fundamentos: Em primeiro logar, vemos o governo dos extrangeiros, em S. Paulo, em lucta aberta com todo o resto da provincia, que se achava sob o dominio de paulistas genuinos, como Paula Souza em Ytú, Arouche no valle do Parahyba e Candido Xavier em Santos: em segundo logar, vemos a ousadia com que estes extrangeiros desobedeciam ás ordens de D. Pedro e, fortificando a cidade com tropa armada e barricadas, offereciam resistencia ás forças vindas de Santos, sob o commando de Candido Xavier, que não se animou a tomar a cidade de assalto, tratando com os sediciosos de egual para egual; em terceiro logar vemos as fortalezas de Santos inutilizadas e a sua artilheria encravada pelo commandante Silva Valente, adepto da sedição, e, finalmente, o desembaraço com que Francisco Ignacio ameaçava de passar o chicote em D. Pedro. Todo o norte do Brazil já estava desmembrado do Rio e ligado directamente a Lisbôa e convinha aos extrangeiros do governo desta capital fazer o mesmo com S. Paulo.

(2) Era capitão de ordenanças, solteiro, morador na rua Direita n. 12, e tinha uma pequena propriedade agricola nos arredores da capital; pertencia á familia illustre dos *Bueno da Veiga*, tendo Amador Bueno da Veiga sido um dos chefes da *Guerra dos Emboabas*.

referido quartel os snagentos-móres Francisco de Paula Macedo e José Rodrigues Pereira do Oliveira Netto e bem assim os tenentes coroneis João Pereira Simões e Jeronymo Pereira Chrispim, o coronel Francisco Alvares Ferreira do Amaral e outros a mandar tocar rebate, ao que se oppuzéra elle dito tenente, como commandante do estado maior, exigindo ordem superior e não a apresentando, antes rodeando-o com espadas e pistolas, que lhe poz aos peitos o dito major Netto, e fazendo-o succumbir por meio desta força, ENTRAREM PARA DENTRO DO QUARTEL E, A ESPADEIRADAS E CHIBATADAS, OBRIGARAM OS TAMBORES A TOCAR REBATES PELAS RUAS DESTA CIDADE (1), e mais não disse deste. —Ao segundo, disse que sabe, por ouvir ao capitão Francisco Pinto Ferraz (2) que O CORONEL FRANCISCO IGNACIO, ENCARREGADO DA FORÇA ARMADA, DÉRA UM JANTAR NO INDICADO DIA 23 DE MAIO AOS ACIMA DECLARADOS, QUE DALLI SAHIRAM UM POUCO EMBRIAGADOS PARA O QUARTEL (3), TENDO SIDO JÁ PREVENIDOS DE MANHÃ PARA O REFERIDO JANTAR, e foram ordenar aquelle rebate. Disse mais que ouvira ao mesmo capitão Francisco Pinto Ferraz e ao tenente Ignacio José de Macedo que do quartel naquella occasião fôra despachado o alferes por antonomazia *O Fadiga*, com uma grande escolta, a apoderar-se da casa da polvora, a qual passou a arrombar com os soldados da escolta por não apparecer chave com que a abrissem, fazendo o arrombamento com um machado pedido a uma vizinha e ficando a casa aberta na noite do sobredito dia e no dia seguinte, do que resultou haver um grande roubo de polvora, sem embargo do tenente reformado de nome Felicio gritar toda a noite que não furtassem a polvora, chegando este roubo acima de deseseis arrobas, como elle testemunha ouvira dizer ao padre-mestre Francisco de Paula e Oliveira, membro do extincto governo provisorio, tanto assim que o *capitão* Antonio Maria Quartim (4), membro do mesmo governo, protestára em sessão, como almoxarife, não responder pela falta que havia na referida casa da polvora. Disse mais

---

(1) Deveria ser edificante o espectaculo dado pelos tambores correndo as ruas debaixo de grossa pancadaria, destinada a fornecer á sedição o caracter popular e geral que ella não tinha e de que muito necessitava!

(2) Pertencia a uma familia proeminente, que fez figura em S. Paulo, Campinas e Araraquara, de que é membro o dr. Antonio Januario Pinto Ferraz, lente de Direito da Academia e senador estadual de S. Paulo

(3) Militares, propositalmente embriagados, para dirigirem o lado marcial da sedição, faziam um bom *pendant* aos tambores surrados nas ruas da cidade para rufarem os seus instrumentos! Uma tal sedição devia ser sinão *popular*, ao menos muito admirada pela população.

(4) A' margem está escripto com a mesma lettra: «Aliás o tenente coronel A. era hespanhol, natural de Gibraltar, a serviço do governo portuguez em S. Paulo O seu protesto e muitos outros factos occorridos no seio do governo não foram registados nas actas das sessões, por não convir aos facciosos que ficassem provas de muitos dos seus actos.

que lhe disséra o mencionado capitão Francisco Pinto Ferraz
que o coronel Francisco Ignacio de Souza Queiroz, como encarregado das armas, *disséra na occasião do rebate á gentalha espe-
ctadora, assim como a pretos e mulatos forros e captivos*, que
todos os que fossem do partido de João Carlos fossem tomar
armas nos quarteis e trem, que para isso se mandou abrir, donde
resultou a grande falta que ha nas armas e pistolas, o que assim
praticaram, bem como, por exemplo, dous mulatos captivos do
coronel Francisco Pinto Ferraz (1). Disse igualmente, por ouvir ao
coronel Castro, que tanto estava premeditado o motim acontecido no dia 23 de Maio passado, que já seu genro, o capitão
Oliva, tinha sido avisado de manhã com outros muitos, que elle
coronel Castro sabia, para concorrerem ao quartel ao toque de
rebate.—Ao terceiro, disse que sabe, por ouvir geralmenre, com
especialidade ao tenente Ignacio José de Macedo e ao capitão
Francisco Pinto Ferraz, que o coronel Francisco Alvares Ferreira do Amaral tomára o commando da tropa e a conduzira ao
largo de São Gonçalo, com os officiaes alli existentes que tinham
disposto o rebate, e os que concorreram acudiram o mesmo
rebate, concorrendo áquelle largo tambem o coronel Francisco Ignacio, por assim lh'o dizer aquelle capitão Francisco
Pinto Ferraz, que lhe asseverou ter ido de ordem do governo a
pacificar o referido motim e ficára commandando a tropa. — Ao
quarto, nada disse por ter deposto ao terceiro o que sabia sobre
o seu objecto.—Ao quinto, disse que sabe, por ouvir ao capitão
Manoel José de Castro em sua casa, que o presidente da Camara, capitão Bento José Leite Penteado, se lhe queixára de que
o capitão Pedro Taques de Almeida Alvim o fizéra ir a força
para a casa da Camara na occasião do motim.- Ao sexto, disse
que é voz publica nesta cidade que taes assignaturas foram ma-
nejadas pelos facciosos e amotinados, quaes considera serem os
que mandaram tocar o rebate (2).—Ao setimo, disse que presume haverem cooperado para o acontecido motim o presidente do
extincto governo, João Carlos Augusto de Oeynhausen, e o
membro do mesmo governo coronel Francisco Ignacio de Souza
Queiroz por terem figurado nelle os seus amigos e apaniguados,
conservarem com estes a mesma anterior amizade e reprehen-
deram as camaras que detestavam semelhantes acontecimentos
(3).—Ao oitavo, disse nada por ter dito o que sabia ao interro-

(1) Com um pessoal deste quilate a sedição passou além de *popular*, para se
tornar *plebéa!*
(2) Assignaturas da acta de vereação de 23 de Maio, tomadas á força na sua
maior parte e ainda assim contendo menos de 500 nomes de militares e plebeus.
(3) Todas as camaras da provincia foram contrarias á sedição, mesmo a da Capital, que só adheriu a ella pela violencia.

gatorio antecedente.—Ao nono, disse que sabe, por ter ouvido ao capitão Francisco Pinto Ferraz, que no dia 3 de Maio estava destinada a expulsão do coronel Martim Francisco Ribeiro de Andrada e do brigadeiro Manoel Rodrigues Jordão de membros do governo, aquelle por seu grande patriotismo, amor e adhesão aos direitos e fôros do Brazil, por ser muito amante da justiça e zeloso do bem publico, tanto assim que, estando a carne no açougue a tres patacas, veiu a ficar até hoje a 880 réis pretendendo leval-a a quatro patacas o capitão Nogueira e seus socios, que para esse fim se propunham a arrematar o açougue e o não conseguiram pelas boas providencias dadas a este respeito pelo dito coronel Martim, por se oppor á pretenção do referido Nogueira (1), que tinha disposto os animos dos membros do governo, coronel Francisco Ignacio, o Intendente (2), tenente coronel Quartim e o presidente João Carlos Augusto, para o proporem para pagador da tropa com a graduação de major e habito de Christo, e por nada ter conseguido das suas pretenções se distinguiu muito no motim do dia 23 de Maio contra o mesmo coronel Martim e a favor de João Carlos Augusto; indispondo-se contra elle pela mesma razão o capitão Pedro Taques de Almeida Alvim, que pretendia a graduação de major e o habito de Christo e o não conseguira por lhe obstar o mencionado coronel Martim, com o fundamento de ser elle um official moderno e havendo outros mais benemeritos, e alguns dos empregados do extincto governo por ter-se publicado um bando, a instancias suas (3), *afim de se descobrir os que tinham deixado de ir na expedição para o Rio de Janeiro* (4) POR TEREM DADO DINHEIRO A ALG·NS COMMANDANTES E SUAS MADAMAS, como era publico, e tornar a ser-lhes restituido caso o declarassem, dando-se-lhe ao mesmo tempo a sua baixa em recompensa de o haverem declarado, e finalmente sabe, por ouvir ao indicado capitão Ferraz e ao padre-mestre Francisco de Paula e Oliveira, que tambem fora causa da indisposição contra elle coronel Martim Francisco O HAVER ESTE DESCOBERTO NAS CONTAS ANTIGAS DA REAL FAZENDA O ENGANO DE OITO CONTOS E TANTOS A FAVOR

---

(1) Capitão Antonio Cardoso Nogueira, ex-vereador da Camara desta capital e um dcs heróes da sedição de 23 de Maio de 1822.

(2) Miguel José de Oliveira Pinto, portuguez, intendente de Marinha em Santos e membro sedicioso do governo de S. Paulo.

(3) A instancias de Martim Francisco, que fazia empenho na publicação desse bando para o descobrimento das patifarias de uma parte do militarismo paulista daquelle tempo.

(4) Expedição que seguiu para o Rio em Janeiro de 1822, sob o commando de Lazaro Gonçalves, auxiliado por Gama Lobo; compunha-se de mil homens, denominados LEAES PAULISTANOS, e foi acudir D. Pedro contra a aggressão do general portuguez Aviles.

DO CORONEL FRANCISCO ALVARES FERREIRA DO AMARAL, CONTRA A MESMA REAL FAZENDA A FAVOR DO DITO CORONEL, O QUAL POR ESTA CAUSA SE DISTINGUIU MUITO NO MOTIM, e o brigadeiro Jordão por ser seu amigo (1).—Ao decimo, disse que sabe, por ter ouvido ao capitão Manoel José de Castro, em sua casa, haverá um mez mais ou menos, que lhe haviam dito algumas pessoas desta cidade que ESPERAVAM EM SANTOS MUITO BREVE TROPAS DE PORTUGAL E QUE ENTÃO SE VINGARIAM DOS PARTIDISTAS CONTRA AS CÔRTES DE PORTUGAL, accrescentando que depois da retirada de Sua Alteza Real para o Rio de Janeiro (2) havia de haver muito sangue e muita pancada nesta cidade e que o actual procurador da Camara, capitão Luiz Manoel da Cunha Bastos (3), mandára para o Porto certidões e papeis de todo o acontecido nesta cidade nos dias 23 de Maio passado e seguintes. Disse mais, por ouvir ao sargento-mór José Manoel da Luz, em o sitio delle testemunha, na freguezia da Penha, haverá dous mezes mais ou menos QUE OS ACONTECIMENTOS HAVIDOS NESTA CIDADE ERAM INSINUAÇÕES DAS CÔRTES DE PORTUGAL, A RESPEITO DAS QUAES SABIA QUE, segundo o que se havia observado nesta cidade, em Santos e pela Marinha (4), donde ha pouco tinha vindo, ESTAVAM LETRAS ABERTAS DE GRANDES SOMMAS DE CONTOS PELA COMPANHIA DOS VINHOS E COMMERCIO DO PORTO, PARA SE GASTAREM COM A TROPA E PREMIAR TODOS OS QUE SE DISTINGUISSEM.—Referindo-se esta testemunha ao que depoz ao setimo interrogatorio, accrescentou que, por ouvir ao capitão Manoel José de Castro que a este dissera o capitão Francisco Candido Sagalerva que, se tinha entrado no motim, fora para condescender com o seu coronel Francisco Ignacio de Souza Queiroz (5), e nada mais disse. E lido o seu depoimento, pelo achar conforme ao que depoz, o assignou com o ministro devassante. E eu, o bacharel formado Manoel Joaquim de Ornellas, escrivão nomeado, o escrevi.—*Freire.*—*Antonio Bernardo Bueno da Veiga.*

(1) Si havia desfalque na fazenda real, não seria difficil descobril-o, porque o brigadeiro Jordão, homem rico e amigo de Martim Francisco, entrou a occupar o cargo de thesoureiro.

(2) D. Pedro veiu a S. Paulo a 25 de Agosto e se retirou daqui a 10 de Setembro de 1822, depois de ter supprimido os residuos do governo extrangeiro e sedicioso desta capital e proclamado a independencia nos campos do Ypiranga.

(3) Foi o portador de uma das intimações a Martim Francisco, que o recebeu mal, pelo que se tornou um dos seus maiores inimigos; era portuguez, de 35 annos de edade; solteiro, negociante e capitão da 8.ª companhia de ordenanças.

(4) A's povoações paulista da costa do mar se dá o nome de Marinha; contam-se de Santos, ficando Itanhaen, Iguape e Cananéa na Marinha, ao sul, e S. Sebastião, Villa Bella, Caraguatatuba e Ubatuba na Marinha, ao norte.

(5) Sagalerva era portuguez, de 35 annos de edade, casado e com filhos: tinha loja de fazendas na rua do Commercio n. 29 e sete escravos e era capitão de milicias e, como tal, subordinado ao coronel Francisco Ignacio, que o arrastou a tomar parte na *Bernarda*; foi forçado a isso, apesar de ser natural do Porto e ter interesse na continuação do dominio portuguez no Brasil.

## ASSENTADA

Aos 18 dias do mez de Setembro de 1822, nesta cidade de S. Paulo, em casas de residencia do juiz devassante, o doutor Antonio de Almeida Silva Freire da Fonseca, por elle ministro foram inquiridas as testemunhas cujos nomes, cognomes, naturalidades, moradas, idades, officios, ditos e costumes é tudo o que adeante se segue, do que para constar lavrei este termo de assentada. E eu, o bacharel formado, Manoel Joaquim de Ornellas, escrivão desta devassa, o escrevi.

## TESTEMUNHA 5.ᵃ

O Muito Reverendo Conego José Gomes de Almeida (1) natural e morador desta cidade, onde vive do seu canonicato, de idade de 38 annos; testemunha jurada aos Santos Evangelhos, em um livro delles em que poz sua mão direita e, debaixo do juramento que lhe foi deferido, prometteu dizer a verdade do que soubesse e perguntado lhe fosse. E sendo inquirido pelos interrogatorios da presente devassa disse, ao primeiro, que sabe por ser voz publica nesta cidade que quem mandára tocar o rebate na tarde do dia 23 de Maio do corrente anno fora o sargento-mór José Rodrigues Pereira de Oliveira Netto, o qual indo aos quarteis obrigára com uma pistola aos peitos ao tenente Ignacio José de Macedo (2), que era o official que se achava de estado maior, para este mandasse tocar ao dito rebate, visto que repugnava em razão de não ter ordem superior para isso, e mais não disse.—Ao segundo, disse que sabe, tambem por ser voz publica, que os agentes e cooperadores para que a tropa e certa porção do povo se ajuntassem no largo de São Gonçalo, em consequencia daquelle rebate, foram o mencionado major Netto, o major Francisco de Paula Macedo, o capitão Pedro Taques de Almeida Alvim, o tenente Jaime da Silva Telles e outros, de quem não se lembra—o terceiro, disse que sabe, por ser voz publica, *que a tropa não marchára de seu motu proprio para o largo de São Gonçalo, mas sim por ter sido puxada pelo coronel Francisco Alvares Ferreira do Amaral.*—Ao quarto, disse que é egualmente voz publica terem sido os commandantes da tropa no

---

(1) Era arcediago da Sé e aparentado com o coronel Francisco de Almeida e dr. Honorato de Moura, sendo, portanto, pessôa de certa importancia nesta capital, pela familia e pelo sacerdócio.

(2) Ignacio José de Macedo, tenente de milicias, era natural desta cidade de S. Paulo, tinha 44 annos de edade, era viuvo, com um filho e tres escravos, e negociante de fazendas na rua do Commercio, em commodos pertencentes á egreja da Misericordia.

largo de São Gonçalo, em a occasião de motim, o referido coronel Francisco Alvares Ferreira do Amaral, o coronel Francisco Ignacio de Souza Queiroz e o brigadeiro Joaquim José
Pinto de Moraes Leme, a quem vira na rua do Rosario marchar á desfilada ao toque do rebate, e que o mesmo brigadeiro,
naquelle largo onde se achava postada a tropa, recitava varias
leis e cartas regias para apoiar a opinião de que esta provincia se podia oppor a qualquer determinação regia que não fosse
em seu beneficio, o que sabe por ouvir ao tabellião Joaquim
Rodrigues Goulart (1).—Ao quinto, disse que sabe, por ouvir
a José Manoel Lessa, que este vira da sua janella entrar o capitão Pedro Taques de Almeida Alvim em casa do juiz de fóra
pela lei e presidente da Camara e leval-o á força para a casa
da Camara, indo o referido juiz a pé adeante delle, que ia a
cavallo.—Ao sexto, disse nada.—Ao setimo, disse que presume
haverem cooperado para o acontecido motim João Carlos Augusto de Oeynhausen, presidente do extincto governo provisorio, o ouvidor José da Costa Carvalho e o coronel Francisco
Ignacio de Souza Queiroz, em razão de ver frequentemente em
casa deste ultimo aos principaes dos facciosos e amotinadores,
entre estes ao referido ouvidor que com elles conservava uma
estima e estreita amizade, bem como a conserva o sobredito
presidente (2).—Ao oitavo, disse que sabe por sua propria ob-
servação que, á excepção do thesoureiro-mór João Ferreira de
Oliveira Bueno. padre mestre Francisco de Paula e Oliveira e
tenente André da Silva Gomes, todos os mais concordavam com
a opinião dos facciosos e amotinadores e os apoiavam, condes-
cendendo com quanto elles queriam (3).—Ao nono, disse que
sabe, por ouvir ao sargento-mór Francisco de Paula Macedo,
que o acontecimento do dia 23 de Maio passado, sobre a expulsão dos dous membros do governo, o coronel Martim Francisco de Andrade e o brigadeiro Manoel Rodrigues Jordão já
estava premeditado para dias antes, o que se não verificára até
então porque *o coronel Francisco Ignacio de Souza Queiroz fora*

---

(1) Para os sediciosos não era em benefício á provincia a chamada de João Carlos
e Costa Carvalho para o Rio, e dahi esta arenga do brigadeiro, procurando nas leis uma
desculpa para a sedição longamente meditada e a que faltava um pretexto.

(2) As relações do ouvidor Costa Carvalho e coronel Francisco Ignacio eram facilmente explicaveis por outros motivos, diversos da sedição projectada. O coronel era
homem de 38 annos, genro do brigadeiro Luiz Antonio. rico, muito relacionado e commandante de um regimento de milicias ; Costa Carvalho, tinha 26 annos e era candidato
á mão da sogra do coronel, viuva do brigadeiro Luiz Antonio, com quem, com effeito,
se casou dahi a menos de dois meses.

(3) Tambem não eram partidarios da sedição Vergueiro e Felisberto Jardim, que
nella não tomou parte ; tambem Lazaro Gonçalves e Gama Lobo estavam no Rio e foram
extranhos á sedição. a julgar pelos serviços que estavam prestando naquella capital
contra os portuguezes do general Avilles e seus sequazes.

á casa do dito coronel *Martim Francisco Ribeiro de Andrada a participar-lhe*, em ar de amizade, o *projectado acontecimento* e *João Carlos Augusto fora pedir* ao mesmo coronel *Francisco Ignacio para que accommodasse* os *emprehendedores do motim* (1); porém, depois de vir a ordem para ser elle, João Carlos Augusto, recolhido ao Rio de Janeiro mudou de opinião, tanto assim que, sendo instado pelo mesmo coronel Martim, no acto da sessão extraordinaria do dia 23 de Maio, para que fosse socegar a tropa, que se achava amotinada por seu respeito, respondeu que se não mettia nisso (2), e mais não disse deste, nem do decimo. E lido o seu juramento, pelo achar conforme ao que havia deposto, depois de nada dizer ao costume, o assignou com o ministro devassante. E eu, o bacharel formado Manoel Joaquim de Ornellas, escrivão da presente devassa, o escrevi.— *Freire.—José Gomes de Almeida.*

---

## ASSENTADA

Aos dezoito dias do mez de Setembro de 1822, nesta cidade de S. Paulo, em casa de residencia do juiz devassante, o doutor Antonio de Almeida Silva Freire da Fonseca, foram por elle inquiridas as testemunhas cujos nomes, cognomes, naturalidades, moradas, idades, officios, ditos e costumes é tudo o que adeante se segue, do que para constar fiz este termo de assentada. E eu, o bacharel formado Manoel Joaquim de Ornellas, escrivão desta devassa, o escrevi.

---

(1) João Carlos foi um dos planejadores e Francisco Ignacio o principal executor do motim, que devia se realisar no dia 3 de Maio, que foi addido para 13 e estourou no dia 23. Martim Francisco, que já devia estar ao corrente da conspiração e devia tel-a communicado a José Bonifacio, ministro de D. Pedro, obteve a portaria de 10 de Maio, em que o Principe Regente chamava para o Rio João Carlos e Costa Carvalho, cabeças pensantes da projectada sedição, que rebentou finalmente com o protesto daquella portaria. Estava a sedição decidida, resolvida e combinada de longa data e os chefes se communicavam com Martim Francisco para lhe darem a entender que della não participavam e para não se comprometterem ! Era o crime planejado com dissimulação e hypocresia !

(2) A conspiração estava á espera de um pretexto e de auxilios de Portugal; os auxilios não vieram, mas podiam vir, e o pretexto appareceu na portaria de 10 de Maio, sendo aproveitado immediatamente. Que interesse especial poderiam ter os paulistas na conservação de João Carlos e Costa Carvalho em S. Paulo, quando o regimen era transitorio e elles não poderiam permanecer nos cargos por muito tempo ? Nenhum ; o interesse estava todo do lado de Francisco Ignacio e sua gente, que se communicavam com Portugal e queriam a permanencia do regimen colonial, personificado em João Carlos de Oyenhausen.

## TESTEMUNHA 6.ª

O MUITO REVERENDO CONEGO MERCHIOR FERNANDES NUNES (1), natural e morador desta cidade, onde vive de seu canonicato, de idade de 57 annos ; testemunha jurada aos Santos Evangelhos, em um livro delles em que poz sua mão direita e, debaixo do juramento que lhe foi deferido, prometteu dizer a verdade do que soubesse e lhe fosse perguntado. E sendo inquirido pelos interrogatorios desta devassa disse, ao primeiro, que sabe, por ser voz publica e ter ouvido a varias pessoas, entre as quaes fôra o conego José Gomes de Almeida, que os primeiros que compareceram no quartel a fazer tocar rebate, na tarde do dia 23 de Maio do corrente anno, foram Joaquim Pedro Maia, creatura do commandante da força armada, o coronel Francisco Ignacio de Sousa Queiroz, os majores Francisco de Paula Macedo e José Rodrigues Pereira de Oliveira Netto, capitão Antonio Cardoso Nogueira (2), o tenente-coronel João Pereira Simões, o tenente Jayme da Silva Telles, igualmente creatura do dito coronel Francisco Ignacio de Sousa Queiroz, e outros mais, como melhor dirá o tenente Ignacio José Macedo, que nessa hora estava de estado-maior e foi constrangido com espadas, bacamartes e pistolas, que lhe foram postos ao peito pelo dito major Netto, para mandar tocar a rebate, como mandou por effeito desta violencia, sahindo os tambores a pancadas pelas ruas a tocal-o, uns de chinellos e outros descalços; e quanto a ordem para tocar ao rebate presume que fôra dada ou consentida pelo referido chefe da força armada.—Ao segundo, disse que presume serem os agentes e cooperadores do ajuntamento da tropa e certa porção do povo os mesmos que mandaram tocar a rebate. — Ao terceiro, disse que sabe, por ser publico nesta cidade, que a tropa se não formára e sahira dos quarteis por seu motu proprio, mas sim por ordem de quem a fez marchar para o largo de S. Gonçalo, mas que ignora quem para alli a fez conduzir.—Ao quarto, disse que sabe por ser voz publica que na frente da tropa se acharam o brigadeiro Joaquim José Pinto de Moraes Leme, o coronel Francisco Ignacio de Souza Queiroz, o coronel Francisco Alvares Ferreira do Amaral e o

---

(1) Conego da Sé, de 1812 a 1828, de 56 annos: residia na rua do Principe n. 28, com suas irmãs e sete escravos. Mudou-se depois para Campinas, onde fez certa figura e falleceu em 1846, estando sepultado na capella de S. Benedicto Era abastado e de boa familia.

(2) Portuguez, de 33 annos, ex-vereador, casado, sem filhos: tinha loja de fazendas na rua Direita n. 34, com um caixeiro, dois aggregados e seis escravos, e fez-se inimigo de Martim e Jordão porque derrotaram o plano de um monopolio de carnes verdes.

tenente-coronel Jeronymo Pereira Chrispim (1), além de varios officiaes subalternos, como foram o capitão Pedro Taques de Almeida Alvim e o tenente Jayme da Silva Telles, o tenente Antonio Gonçalves Mamede (2) e outros.—Ao quinto, disse que sabe, por ser publico nesta cidade que o capitão Pedro Taques de Almeida Alvim fizera ir á força o presidente da camara, capitão Bento José Leite Penteado, de sua casa, oude o veio buscar, para a da mesma camara.—Ao setimo, disse que presume haverem cooperado para o motim acontecido o presidente do extincto governo João Carlos Augusto de Oeynhausen, o coronel Francisco de Sousa Queiroz, commandante da força armada, e o ouvidor José da Gosta Carvalho, aquelles por elle reverendo testemunha saber, na manhã do dia do motim e na occasião em que o governo estava em sessão, tinha vindo ordem para o referido presidente se retirar para o Rio de Janeiro, como lhe foi dito na loja do capitão Francisco Gonçalves dos Santos Cruz (3), por um negociante chamado Garcia (4), visinho do mesmo Cruz, e este dito ouvidor por lhe haverem dito Dona Anna e Maria Eufrasia, filhas do desembargador Antonio Rodrigues Velloso de Oliveira (5), *que ouviram da propria bocca do mesmo ouvidor haver-se jactado de ter disposto o motim, fazendo figurar nelle o major Macedo e o capitão Nogueira, e de ser o autor de todos os papeis feitos a semelhante respeito, os quaes eram escriptos pelo tenente Jayme da Silva Telles* (6). Disse mais que o resultado deste motim fôra a conservação de João Carlos Augusto de Oeynhausen na presidencia do extincto governo e a deposição de dois membros delle, o coronel Martim Francisco Ribeiro de Andrada e o brigadeiro Manoel Rodrigues Jordão, tudo por indisposição contra estes concebida pelo sobredito presidente e

---

(1) Era paulista, de 53 annos de idade, tenente coronel de milicias, casado, com filhos e quatro escravos; morava na rua do Piques n. 39, não se encontrando informação sobre os sens meios de vida.

(2) Foi por algum tempo criado e ordenança do coronel Francisco Ignacio, em cuja casa morava por favor; era solteiro, tinha 25 annos de idade e pela influencia do seu patrão foi nomeado tenente. Era um *agradecido*, que pagava favores recebidos, ou um suggestionado.

(3) Paulista, capitão de cavallaria, de 40 annos de idade, casado sem filhos, com loja de fazenda na rua do Commercio n. 32, com um caixeiro portuguez e sete escravos de serviço.

(4) Francisco Garcia, natural de Cuyabá, de 35 annos, solteiro, negociante de fazenda na rua do Commercio n. 33, com um caixeiro cuyabano e dois escravos. Pela numeração das casas então usada, Garcia e Santos Cruz eram visinhos de parede e meia.

(5) Um dos homens mais notaveis de S. Paulo e fez muita figura no seu tempo como deputado, procurador geral e homem de lei

(6) Costa Carvalho foi realmente o chefe da *Bernarda*, interessado como era em remover os Andradas do seu caminho politico, e se fazia o conselheiro e redactor de tudo: assessorava os extrangeiros que se apossaram do governo e só fazia inserir nas actas o que que ia; assessorava a camara e até fazia o seu escrivão Amaro José Vieira escrever papeis e officios da Camara, que aliás tinha seu secretario—João Nepomuceno de Almeida.

o coronel Francisco Ignacio de Sousa Queiroz, *visto que não concordavam com elles aquelles dois membros em cousas desairosas ao governo e á provincia*, como aconteceu a respeito de um bando organisado pelos dois membros expulsos, em que se mandava que todos os militares que tivessem dado dinheiro para não irem na expedição que desta provincia marchou para o Rio de Janeiro nos principios do corrente anno (1), comparecessem para lhes ser restituido o dinheiro que haviam dado e dar-se-lhes baixa em recompensa, *por constar que alguns commandantes e suas amasias tinham recebido esse dinheiro, cujo bando foi assignado com bastante repugnancia e depois de muitas contestações pelos mencionados João Carlos Augusto de Oeynhausen e coronel Francisco Ignacio de Sousa Queiroz (2), o que até deu causa ao coronel Martim, como secretario do governo (3), mandar entregar a pasta, protestando não ir mais ás sessões do mesmo governo emquanto aquelle bando não fosse assignado motivo este por que o* assignaram e foi publicado ; concorrendo para a deposição do mesmo coronel Martim a desavença que anteriormente houvera entre elle, em sua propria casa, e o ouvidor José Costa Carvalho (4) . — Ao oitavo, disse que sabe que, a excepção dos tres membros thesoureiro-mór João Ferreira de Oliveira Bueno, padre Francisco de Poula e Oliveira e tenente-coronel André da Silva Gomes, todos os mais não deixaram de apoiar o resultado daquelle motim, especialmente o presidente, que teve tanta satisfacção a este respeito que, em uma carta escripta ao tenente coronel José Antonio Valente, governador da villa e praça de Santos, lhe recommendava que mantivesse aquella povoação em socego porque nesta cidade tudo estava em paz e tranquillidade depois da deposição daquelles dois membros do governo, por

---

(1) Expedição dos *Leaes Paulistanos*, que seguiu para o Rio em Janeiro de 1822, sob as ordens do coronel Lazaro Gonçalves, a acudir D. Pedro ameaçado pelas tropas portuguezas 'o general Avilles.

2 Constava que muitos officiaes inferiores e soldados, que eram milicianos ou da 1.ª reserva e tinham seus negocios ou officios, não quizeram ir para o Rio com os *Leaes Paulistanos* e subornaram os seus commandantes para dispensal-os : era preciso um inquerito, mas o bando proposto por Martim e Jordão produzia o mesmo resultado, descobrindo a traficancia, que naquellas circumstancias era um crime : entretanto João Carlos e Francisco Ignacio se oppunham ao bando, fasendo-se capas dos soldados velhacos e dos commandantes venaes ! Naturalmente tinham nisso algum interesse

3 Martim Francisco não era secretario do governo, cargo este occupado por Manuel da Cunha Azeredo Coutinho Souza Chichorro ; mas era secretario da Fazenda no governo provisorio.

(4) Costa Carvalho era juiz de fora em S. Paulo e D Nuno Eugenio de Lossio Seilbs era o ouvidor quando se acclamou o governo provisorio Eliminado D. Nuno como elemento retrogrado, foi Costa Carvalho promovido a ouvidor com consentimento dos Andradas, membros do governo de S. Paulo, e mantido nesse logar por José Bonifacio, ministro de D. Pedro : entretanto fez-se o chefe intellectual da sedição e foi á casa de Martim Francisco procurar duvidas para ter um pretexto que o desculpasse aos olhos do publico !

isso mesmo que o povo os podia depor assim como os havia constituido membros do governo (1)·— Ao nono, disse que sabe, por ouvir ao vigario do Villa Bella, Luiz Antonio Lobo de Saldanha, que já no dia 4 de Maio estava para se realizarem os acontecimentos do dia 23 e, por ouvir ao conego José Gomes de Almeida, sabe que o coronel Francisco Ignacio de Souza Queiroz fôra perticipar ao coronel Martim aquelle projecto e que o presidente João Carlos Augusto de Oeynhausen pedira ao mesmo coronel Francisco Ignacio de Souza Queiroz fosse substar o tal projecto (2); e nada mais disse deste. — Ao decimo, disse que sabe, por ouvir ao vigario de S. Carlos, Joaquim José Gomes, que o CAPITÃO LUIZ MANUEL DA CUNHA BASTOS ESTAVA PROMPTO A SUSTENTAR A SUA CUSTA DUZENTOS HOMENS POR ESPAÇO DE UM ANNO DA TROPA QUE VIESSE DE PORTUGAL PARA ESTA PROVINCIA. Disse mais que lhe contára o padre Leão José de Senna (3) que o CORONEL FRANCISCO IGNACIO DE SOUZA QUEIROZ DISSERA NO QUARTEL QUE TINHA MUITA POLVORA E BALA PARA O PRINCIPE REGENTE (4), e que lhe dissera tambem a elle testemunha que o capitão-mór Manoel José de Mello, da villa de Guaratinguetá, que na mesma villa tinha dito o capitão Pedro Taques de Almeida Alvim que era tal a ascendencia que o coronel Francisco Ignacio de Souza Queiroz tinha sobre o povo e tropa desta cidade que não duvidariam dar-lhe a cabeça de Sua Alteza Real, se lh'a pedisse (5), e nada mais disse deste, e do costume· disse parente em quarto gráu de consanguinidade com o brigadeiro Manuel Rodrigues Jordão. E lido o seu juramento, pelo achar conforme ao que havia deposto, o assignou com o ministro devassante. E eu, o bacharel formado Manuel Joaquim de Ornellas, escrivão desta devassa, o escrevi.— *Antonio de Almeida Silva Freire.—Melchior Fernandes Nunes.*

---

(1) Estava João Carlos, ainda ha pouco representante do direito divino dos reis e do mais ferrenho despotismo colonial, transformado em anarchista e apregoando a doutrina do «povo que o criou o pode destruir», e isto ainda acompanhado de uma grossa falsidade sobre a paz e o socego publico da cidade, que ficou tres mezes sob o regimen do terror, até á chegada do Principe Regente.

(2) Estavam ambos açulando a sedição e não tinham interesse em fasel-a mallograr ; mas convinha fazer constar que Martim e Jordão não eram expulsos porque Francisco Ignacio o impedia, a pedido do cumplice João Carlos.

(3) Era paulista, de 38 annos de idade, morador na casa n. 20 da rua da Polvora, hoje rua da Liberdade, onde tinha dois escravos de serviço domestico

(4) Tinha chicote, polvora e bala para D. Pedro emquanto este estava no Rio mas quando teve de vir a S. Paulo, tres mezes depois, o mesmo coronel Francisco Ignacio, que lhe promettia sóva e morte, se apressou a montar á propria custa um lusido corpo de tropa para receber e abrilhantar as festas feitas pela chegada do Principe Regente !

(5) Era tanta a sua influencia que precisou da chibata para fazer os tambores tocarem rebate no quartel e nas ruas e precisou dos trabucos de Pedro Taques, Oliveira Netto, Paula Macedo e Silva Telles para que alguns vereadores e a plebe desta capital se reunissem no paço da Camara na tarde de 23 de Maio !

## ASSENTADA

Aos 19 dias do mez de Setembro de 1822, nesta cidade de São Paulo, em casas de residencia do ministro devassante, doutor Antonio de Almeida Silva Freire da Fonseca, foram por elle inquiridas as testemunhas cujos nomes, cognomes, naturalidades, moradas, idades, officios, ditos costumes é tudo que adeante se segue, do que para constar fiz este termo de assentada. E eu o bacharel formado Manuel Joaquim de Ornellas, escrivão desta devassa, o escrevi.

## TESTEMUNHA 7.ª

O MUITO REVERENDO CONEGO FRANCISCO JOAQUIM DE TOLEDO AROUCHE (1), natural e morador desta cidade, onde vive de seu canonicato, de idade de 65 annos incompletos; testemunha jurada aos Santos Evangelhos em um livro delles, em que poz sua mão direita e, debaixo do juramento que prestou, prometteu dizer a verdade do que soubesse e perguntado lhe fosse. E sendo inquirido pelos interrogatorios desta devassa disse, ao primeiro, que sabe por ser voz publica que o sargento-mór José Rodrigues Pereira de Oliveira Netto fôra quem mandou tocar a rebate na tarde do dia 23 de Maio passado, obrigando para isso com uma pistola aos peitos ao tenente Ignacio José de Macedo, que era o official que então se achava de estado-maior nos quarteis e se havia opposto á pretenção do referido major Netto; e mais não disse deste.—Ao segundo disse que ouviu falar vulgarmente nesta cidade ter sido o coronel Francisco Alvares Ferreira do Amaral um dos agentes da marcha da tropa para o largo de São Gonçalo, tomando o commando della nos quarteis do tenente coronel Antonio de Padua de Gusmão (2), que estava entregue do dito commando, e que o capitão Pedro Taques de Almeida Alvim fôra tambem um desses agentes.— Ao terceiro, disse nada.—Ao quarto, disse que sabe por ser voz publica que na frente da tropa, em o largo de São Gonçalo, estiveram o brigadeiro Joaquim José Pinto de Moraes Leme, o coronel Francisco Alvares Ferreira do Amaral, o coronel Francisco Ignacio de Souza Queiroz, o major Francisco de Paula Macedo, o

---

(1) Pertencia a uma das mais illustres familias de S. Paulo e era irmão mais moço dos drs Francisco Leandro de Toledo Rendon e Diogo de Toledo Lara e Ordonhes e do marechal José Arouche de Toledo Rendon, que figuram muito na historia da capitania e provincia de S. Paulo

(2 Era official do regimento dos Uteis, de 45 annos de idade, vivendo do seu soldo na rua de S. Bento, n. 96, com a mãe, a esposa, duas filhas, uma neta e uma escrava. Nos recenseamentos do tempo elle não dava a sua naturalidade, mas era nascido nesta capital e entrou a contra-gosto na sedição.

eapitão Pedro Taques de Almeida Alvim e outros officiaes.— Ao
quinto, disse nada.—Ao sexto, disse egualmente que nada sabia.—Ao setimo, disse que ouvira falar geralmente *haver sido o
coronel Francisco Ignacio de Souza Queiroz que não descançava
sem que lançasse fora do governo dous de seus membros* (1).—
Ao oitavo, disse que lhe não consta que o extincto governo
désse providencia alguma sobre taes acontecimentos, antes fizera
sahir desta cidade para fóra da provincia em espaço breve ao
expulso membro do governo, o coronel Martim Francisco Ribei-
de Andrada, acompanhado de um official e alguns soldados (2).
—Ao nono, disse que tem ouvido vulgarmente que já antes do
dia 23 de Maio se projectavam os successos então realizados.—Ao
decimo, disse que tem ouvido falar geralmente que *havia communicação entre as Côrtes de Portugal e o presidente do
extincto governo João Carlos Augusto de Okynhausen, o
coronel Francisco Ignacio de Souza Queiroz, membro do referido governo, e o ouvidor José da Costa Carvalho*, e que
de Agosto até o presente mez de Setembro esperavam tropas de
Portugal na villa e praça de Santos, sendo conservado como governador o tenente coronel José Antonio Valente, afim de dar
livre entrada á mesma tropa européa (3), e mais não disse; e
do costume disse ser parente remoto do brigadeiro Pinto e do
eapitão Pedro Taques de Almeida Alvim (4).   E sendo-lhe lido
o seu juramento, pelo achar conforme ao que depoz, o assignou
eom o ministro devassante.   E eu o bacharel formado Manuel
Joaquim de Ornellas, escrivão da presente devassa, o escrevi.—
*Freire.—Francisco Joaquim de Toledo Arouche.*

## ASSENTADA

Aos 19 dias do mez de Setembro de 1822, nesta cidade de
São Paulo, em casa de residencia do ministro devassante, o doutor Antonio de Almeida Silva Freire da Fonseca, foram por elle
inquiridas as testemunhas cujos nomes, cognomes, naturalidades,

---

1 Tinha elle plano formado a respeito. mas ia avisar Martim Francisco de que
se pretendia fazer-lhe violencia, ao que elle. Francisco Ignacio, se oppunha!
2 Escoltado pelo official portuguez capitão José Fernandes da Silva, com um
cabo e dois soldados, até á fronteira da provincia, donde Martim o conduziu até ao Rio
de Janeiro, preso pelo capitão Joaquim José de Almeida a pedido do mesmo Martim.
3 Não foi conservado naquelle posto, tomando o marechal Candido Xavier o commando da praça e achando a sua artilharia encravada e incapaz de laborar. Se a esquadra portugueza alli viesse acharia realmente a entrada franca.
4 Eram todos de familia iminentemente historicas de São Paulo: Pedro Taques era
neto do auctor da *Nobiliarchia Paulistana* e descendente do illustre Lourenço Castanho
Taques, de quem tambem descendia o depoente. O brigadeiro Joaquim José Pinto de
Moraes Leme descendencia dos Pinto do Rego e Brito Peixoto. multo relacionados por
casamentos com as grandes familias paulistas, como se poderá ver no *Annexo* W, do
vol. I do *Archivo do Estado de São Paulo.*

moradas, idades, officios, ditos e costumes é tudo o adeante se
segue, do que para constar lavrei este termo de assentada, e eu,
o bacharel formado Manuel Joaquim de Ornellas, escrivão desta
devassa, o escrevi.

## TESTEMUNHA 8.ª

O PADRE ILDEFONSO XAVIER FERREIRA (1), presbytero secular, natural da villa de Curityba, desta provincia, morador desta
cidade, onde vive do seu emprego de substituto da cadeira de
Philosophia, de idade de 27 annos; testemunha jurada aos Santos Evangelhos, em um livro delles em que poz sua mão direita e, debaixo do juramento que prestou, prometteu dizer a
verdade do que soubesse e perguntado lhe fosse. E sendo inquirido pelos interrogatorios da presente devassa disse, ao primeiro, que sabe por ser voz publica nesta cidade que quem
mandára tocar a rebate na tarde do dia 23 de Maio passado foram os majores Francisco de Paula Macedo e José Rodrigues
Pereira de Oliveira Netto, por ordem do commandante da força
armada, o coronel Francisco Ignacio de Souza Queiroz, forçando
ambos elles, com pistolas aos peitos, ao tenente Ignacio José de
Macedo, que nessa occasião se achava de estado maior e não
convinha no determinado rebate. Disse mais que tambem ouvira vulgarmente que foram obrigados os tambores a chibatadas
para sahirem do quartel a tocar o dito rebate.—Ao segundo,
disse que sabe por ouvir geralmente nesta cidade que os referidos dous majores e o coronel Francisco Alvares Ferreira do
Amaral foram os principaes agentes da marcha da tropa e alguma porção do povo para o largo de São Gonçalo, onde se congregaram, influindo e coadjuvando para isto o capitão Pedro
Taques de Almeida Alvim, o capitão Antonio Cardoso Nogueira,
o tenente Antonio Gonçalves Mamede, o tenente Jayme da Silva
Telles, João Theodoro Xavier, José Manuel da Luz Tralhão e
Joaquim Pedro Maia (2), que, como commensaes e apaniguados

---

1 Foi sacerdote dos mais notaveis de S. Paulo, conego da Sé, chantre e lente de
theologia; era tambem formado em direito e foi um dos mais enthusiastas da independencia. O coronel Francisco Ignacio nunca lhe perdoou este depoimento, como se vê da
correspondencia publicada do mesmo coronel.
2 Pedro Taques tinha já alguma cousa de doido e, realmente, enlouqueceu pouco
tempo depois e viveu inconsciente mais de trinta annos. Já foi dito que Cardoso Nogueira era portuguez, negociante e candidato ao monopolio das carnes verdes e que
Gonçalves Mamede foi criado da casa do coronel Francisco Ignacio, com quem morava
e que o fez tenente; Jayme da Silva Telles era um velho de 70 annos, com pequeno
sitio no bairro do Emboaçaba, onde trabalhava com a mulher, tres filhos, dois escravos
e sete aggregados, e era nas ordenanças subordinado do capitão Luiz Manoel da Cunha
Bastos, commandante da 8.ª companhia. João Theodoro Xavier morava na rua T aba-
tinguera, n. 49, e vivia do soldo do seu emprego de almoxarife, em companhia da mãe,
que era solteira e de dois escravos; tinha 30 annos, era solteiro e morava parede e meia
com o coronel Daniel Pedro Müller, um dos extrangeiros sediciosos do governo. José

do coronel Francisco Ignacio de Souza Queiroz, trabalharam em fazer apparecer o que já de antes estava projectado e o mesmo coronel Francisco Ignacio dé Souza Queiroz, *procurou occultar maliciosamente naquella occasião aos seus collegas do governo* (1), bem como coadjuvaram este motim o capitão Caetano Pinto Homem (2) e o tenente Francisco Antonio, por alcunha o *Patarata,* como socios do coronel Alvares, ccoperando igualmente para o mesmo motim o capitão Antonio de Siqueira Moraes (3), que publicamente convidava a muitos que fossem para o largo de São Gonçalo, o capitão de ordenanças Francisco José de Azevedo, o capitão Manoel Joaquim Coelho, o capitão Joaquim Alvares Moreira, o tenente Manoel Felizardo de Carvalho e Antonio Floriano Alvares Alvim (4), dos quaes viu elle testemunha uns na frente da tropa e outros na sala da Camara, persuadindo-se elle testemunha que todos estes agentes e cooperadores entraram no recontado motim por condescenderem com João Carlos Augusto de Oyenhausen, presidente do extincto governo, a quem desejavam agradar, e com o coronel Francisco Ignacio de Souza Queiroz.—Ao terceiro, disse que sabe, por ser voz publica nesta cidade, que a tropa se fôra congregar no largo de S. Gonçalo alliciada pelos indicados agentes e cooperadores para o acontecido motim, e sabe por ouvir a alguns soldados que a tropa fôra congregada naquelle largo a titulo de pedir pela conservação do memorado presidente com o fundamento de ter governado bem esta provincia, sendo um dos principaes que trabalharam a este respeito o brigadeiro Joaquim José Pinto de Moraes Leme, que appareceu na frente da tropa e a animava, citando leis e cartas regias a bem do suscitado motim que intitulava «causa publica».—Ao quarto, disse que sabe por ver que o coronel Francisco Alvares Ferreira do Amaral fôra quem tomára o commando daquella tropa na occasião do motim, conduzindo-a do quartel para o largo de São Gonçalo e pon-

---

Manoel da Lus Tralhão era paulista, de 46 annos, major reformado, casado, com seis filhos e treze escravos; era *lettrado* e morava na rua do Ouvidor n. 37. De Joaquim Pedro Maia não ha noticia e aqui se diz que todos eram commensaes de Francisco Ignacio.

1 Occultava aos collegas, recebia pedido de João Carlos para suffocar uma conspiração de que elle mesmo era o chefe e ia avisar Martim da existencia da trama!

2 Caetano Pinto era portuguez de Lamego, de 40 annos, casado e com muitos filhos: morava na casa do coronel Francisco Alvares Ferreira do Amaral, de quem era subalterno na milicia; o *Patarata* era portuguez de Lisbóa e morava com elle na mesma casa.

3 Era natural de Jundiahy, neste Estado solteiro, de 40 annos, capitão de milicias e como tal, subordinado aos coroneis Ferreira do Amaral e Francisco Ignacio. Tinha loja de fazendas na rua Direita, n. 1, com um caixeiro e cinco escravos ; foi tambem presidente da Camara, a principio muito apegado aos Andradas, a quem chamava «beneme- ritos patriotas», mas na sedição de 23 de Maio appareceu ao lado dos facciosos.

4 Não era da familia legitima dos Taques Alvim e era pardo de côr segundo um, resenseamento de tempo, solteiro, de 38 annos, negociante na rua do Commercio, n. 4, e miliciano.

do-a em linha de batalha, o que effectuado deu repetidos vivas,
e chegando logo depois o coronel Francisco Ignacio de Souza
Queiroz, mandado pelo governo, porque fizesse retirar a tropa
para o quartel visto ter affectado em governo que de nada
sabia (1), perguntou ao coronel Francisco Alvares Ferreira do
Amaral, com um ar agastado para impor ao publico, com que
ordem tinha elle ajuntado ahi aquelles soldados? Ao que lhe foi
respondido pelo dito coronel Alvares que o tinha feito em beneficio
publico, visto que as representações feitas a Sua Alteza Real
pelos habitantes desta provincia eram suffocadas pelo ministro
de Estado dos Negocios do Brasil e Extrangeiros, combinado
com seu irmão o coronel Martim Francisco Ribeiro de Andrada
nesta capital, para desta sorte chegarem suas vozes ao pé do
throno (2), *terminando-se com uma apparente e affeetada briga,
que por tal se conheceu, tanto assim que logo passaram juntos
na frente da tropa até ao fim do motim,* sem que o dito coronel
Queiroz voltasse mais ao governo a dar parte da sua commissão.—Ao quinto, disse que sabia por ser voz publica que o presidente da Camara desta cidade, o capitão José Bento Leite
Penteado, fôra violentado e constrangido pela força armada para
concorrer na casa da mesma Camara, sendo o capitão Pedro Taques de Almeida Alvim quem o conduziu (3).—Ao sexto, disse
que sabe que tudo quanto se escreveu na casa da Camara, por
parte do povo e tropa, fôra manejado pelo ouvidor José da Costa
Carvalho e ditado pelo seo escrivão Amaro José Vieira, que alli
concorreu com elle (4), presenciando elle, reverendo testemunha,
parte do que fica expendido e constando-lhe parte por ouvir, e
nada mais disse deste.—Ao setimo, disse que sabe, por ser voz
publica na cidade, que o presidente do extincto governo, João
Carlos Augusto de Oeynhausen, concorrera para o acontecido

1 Estando francamente associado com João Carlos e tendo o apoio seguro de Oliveira Pinto, Müller e Quartim, fingia nada saber da conspiração para enganar os collegas brasileiros do governo!
2 Esta scena dramatica devia ter sido bem ensaiada para produzir o effeito desejado, mas um dos actores se esqueceu do *papel contencionado* para só se lembrar da
realidade da situação e não voltar mais ao palacio communicar a João Carlos o desempenho do papel que lhe fora confiado. Dahi resultou tornar-se conhecida a combinação,
que deixou de ser tragica para ser comica. Nunca representação alguma fora suffocada
e isto facilmente se prova pelas proprias actas das sessões do governo, nas quaes não
consta cousa alguma a respeito, quando as representações deviam seguir por intermedio
do governo e ser por elle informado. E' uma falsidade para justificar o crime.
3 Já se viu como o capitão Penteado foi conduzido á casa da Camara, a pé e
acompanhado por Pedro Taques, que ia montado e armado de espada e trabuco, ameaçando-o de leval-o com as mãos amarradas, atado á cauda do seu cavallo!
4 Refere-se á representação que nesse dia se fez na Camara, planejada por Costa
Carvalho e redigida pelo seu escrivão Amaro Vieira, quando a Camara tinha o seu escrivão, que era João Nepomuceno de Almeida, sendo o mesmo Costa Carvalho o primeiro
signatario sedicioso e vindo depois os seus cumplices na sedição e a plébe recrutada por
Pedro Taques, Macedo, Oliveira Netto, Caetano Pinto e Silva Telles.

motim parte interessada, tanto assim que, sendo costume mandar elle presidente entregar ao secretario os officios da côrte apenas os recebia, não aconteceu assim a respeito daquelle por onde foi chamado á côrte, pois que, *tendo-o recebido ás 4 horas da tarde do dia 22 de Maio, só o apresentou no dia seguinte ás 10 horas, no acto da sessão, para desta sorte ter tempo de urdir o motim acontecido, andando para isso por differentes casas, como foram a do coronel Francisco Alvares Ferreira do Amaral, a do coronel Francisco Ignacio de Souza Queiroz, ONDE SE ACHAVA O OUVIDOR JOSÉ DA COSTA CARVALHO, e a do brigadeiro Pinto, a mostrar o referido officio para fazel-os interessar na sua conservação e manobrarem a disposição do coronel Martim Francisco e do brigadeiro Jordão,* para o que tudo concorreram os referidos, coronel Francisco Ignacio de Souza Queiroz e o ouvidor José da Costa Carvalho, *que era especialmente interessado na disposição do coronel Martim como seu mortal inimigo, a quem eram igualmente adversos o presidente João Carlos Augusto de Oeynhausen e o coronel Francisco Ignacio de Souza Queiroz por se opporem elle coronel Martim e o brigadeiro Jordão aos seus desaforos e injustiças* e haverem propugnado para que sahisse um bando afim de se fazer restituir o dinheiro que alguns soldados tinham dado para deixarem de ir na expedição que marchou para o Rio de Janeiro, visto constar que alguns commandantes e suas amadas o tinham recebido.—Ao oitavo, disse que sabe por ter presenciado que o extincto governo, em vez de castigar os revolucionarios, antes os approvava, tanto assim que arrombando-se e roubando-se a casa da polvora e havendo uma grande revolução nos quarteis, nenhumas providencias se deram para se cohibirem semelhantes desatinos o serem castigados os revolucionarios; antes por elles eram extranhados os que obravam de diverso modo, obedecendo a Sua Alteza Real.—Ao nono, disse que sabe, por ouvir ao padre Joaquim Manoel de Oliveira e Castro que, em casa delle reverendo testemunha, muitas vezes disse que brevemente se haviam de realizar grandes cousas, alludindo por isto aos acontecimentos do dia 23 de Maio passado, em que muito influiu, falando e aconselhando, como elle reverendo testemunha observou, e mais não disse deste.—Ao decimo, disse que sabe, por noticia, de uma carta anonyma (1), escripta ao capitão Antonio Bernardo

---

(1) As cartas anonymas e pasquins pregados nas esquinas foram muito communs em S. Paulo, desde os tempos de Rodrigo Cesar até a Independencia, periodo de 100 annos em que a dilação era um meio regular de governo e os dilatores recompensados; algumas vezes os proprios capitães generaes foram victimas de pasquins, que exprimiam verdades crueis que os povos opprimidos não tinham a coragem de falar abertamente.

da Veiga, que o presidente do governo João Carlos Augusto
de Oeynhausen, por intervenção do ouvidor José da Costa Carvalho, se communicava directamente ás Côrtes de Portugal contra a causa do Brasil, pedindo tropas para esta provincia, pelo
porto de Santos, para marcharem com a gente que aqui se
reunisse em direitura para o Rio de Janeiro afim de forçar Sua
Alteza Real a cumprir os decretos das mencionadas Côrtes, e
asseverando que nesta capital e em Santos havia dinheiro das
mesmas Côrtes, por via da companhia dos vinhos, para a compra da tropa aqui existente e arranjo da que viesse, e nada
mais disse deste, nem do costume. E lido o seu juramento, pelo
achar conforme ao que depoz, assignou com o ministro devassante. E eu, o bacharel formado Manuel Joaquim de Ornellas,
escrivão da presente devassa, o escrevi.—*Freire.—Ildefonso Xavier Ferreira* (1).

## ASSENTADA

Aos 23 dias do mez de Setembro de 1822, nesta cidade de
S. Paulo, em casas de residencia do doutor Antonio de Almeida
Silva Freire da Fonseca, juiz da presente devassa, onde eu
escrivão da mesma me achava, e sendo ahi foram por elle ministro inquiridos as testemunhas cujos nomes, cognomes, naturalidades, moradas, edades, officios, ditos e costumes é tudo o
que adeante se segue, do que para constar fiz este termo de
assentada. E eu, o bacharel formado Manoel Joaquim de Ornellas, escrivão desta devassa, o escrivi.

## TESTEMUNHA 9.ª

O capitão Bento Correia Leme (2) viuvo, natural e morador desta cidade, onde vive de negocio de tropas, de edade de

(1) Vem em nota assignada pelo juiz e depoente uma rectificação ao depocto no
oitavo item, em que diz a testemunha que o conego João Ferreira, e padre mestre Paula
Oliveira e o professor André Gomes—membros do governo—não tomaram parte alguma
nos factos sediciosos de 23 de Maio. Deviam tambem participar desta rectificação Vergueiro e Felisberto, que não tomaram parte na conspiração, estando ausentes de S.
Paulo no dia em que ella sahiu á rua, e bem assim Lazaro Gonçalves e Gama Lobo que
se achavam no Rio de Janeiro desde o começo do anno, prestando bons serviços ao
Brasil á frente do regimento dos *Leaes Paulistanos*. Parece que esta declaração do
depoente foi motivada pelo facto dos padres João Ferreira e Paula Oliveira e professor
André Gomes estarem presente á sessão do governo do dia 23 de Maio e não terem
protestado contra a sedição apatrocinada pelos outros membros presentes—João Carlos,
Oliveira Pinto, Müller, Quartim e Francisco Ignacio; porém ha desculpa para essa tacita
covardia, porque João Ferreira e André Gomes eram velhos de mais de 70 annos e
Paula Oliveira era clerigo pacifico e a cidade ficou sob o regimem do terror, com a
presença nas ruas de Oliveira Netto, Pedro Taques, Paula Macedo, Silva Telles, Caetano
Pinto, Gonçalves Mamede e outros, armados de trabuco e violentando aos que não concordavam com a sedição.
(2) Pertencia á familia Leme, que era uma das mais antigas e numerosas de S.

60 annos ; testemunha jurada aos Santos Evangelhos em um livro delles em que poz sua mão direita e, debaixo do juramento que prestou, lhe foi encarregado dissesse a verdade do que soubesse e perguntado lhe fosse. E sendo inquirido pelos interrogatorios da presente devassa disse, ao primeiro, que nada sabia, bem como ao segundo.—Ao terceiro, disse que sabe por ouvir dizer ao tenente Ignacio José de Macedo, que a tropa sahira do quartel e se fora postar no largo de S. Gonçalo por effeito de ter ido um official, cujo nome ignora, forçar com armas ao referido tenente, que se achava de estado maior, para que a mesma tropa se fosse congregar naquelle largo. — Ao quarto, disse que sabe por ver que os commandantes, que se achavam na frente da tropa congregada no referido largo, foram o brigadeiro Joaqnim José Pinto de Moraes Leme, o coronel Francisco Ignacio de Souza Queiroz e o coronel Francisco Alvares Fereira do Amaral, com os officiaes subalternos o sargento mór Francisco de Paula Macedo, o sargento-mór José Rodrigues Pereira de Oliveira Netto, o capitão Pedro Taques de Almeida Alvim, além de outros, e concorrendo elle testemunha ao logar onde se achava postada a tropa por effeito do rebate acontecido e perguntando ao referido brigadeiro Pinto qual era a causa de semelhante alvoroço, respondeu que era para socego e paz da patria, e replicando elle testemunha quaes eram os inimigos que nos dessocegavam, lhe respondeu o mesmo brigadeiro que ao depois o saberia ; e como por estas respostas viesse no conhecimento de que não havia inimigos na terra e QUE UM TAL AJUNTAMENTO LHE PARECIA ANTES UM EFFEITO DE BEBEDEIRA se retirou á sua casa e no outro dia sahiu para a sua invernada (1)—Ao quinto, disse que sabe por ser nos publica que o prisidente da Camaia, que então era o capitão Bento José Leite Penteado, fora obrigado á força de armas a concorrer á casa da mesma camara na occasião do rebate e que quem para iste o forçara fora um dos tres officiaes o capitão Pedro Taques de Almeida Alvim, o major José Rodrigues Pereira de Oliveir Netto e tenente Jayme da Silva Telles, por serem os que mais se distinguiram como perturbadores na occasião do motim —Ao sexto, disse que presume terem sido forçadas quasi todas as assigntu-

---

Paulo ; devia ter 64 annos porque em 1818 já elle apparece com 60 annos e com negocio na rua da Tabatinguera, n. 35 ; só mais tarde seria que deixou a sua profissão para se fazer negeciante de tropas.

(1) E tinha razão para assim pensar, porque outros depoimentos falam em almoços regados com abundante espirito na casa do coronel Francisco Ignacio, e André Gomes nos conta que o proprio paço municipal se transformára naquelle dia em botequim e taberna em que se prodigalizavam gratuitamente vinho e genebra aos que lá appareciam a proclamar o bem publico !

ras constando do auto de vereança extradinaria do dia 23
de Maio por ido, porquanto elle testemunha. estando no
largo de São Gonçalo, ouviu uma voz de que todos subissem á
sala da Camara debaixo de subordinação para assignarem o referido auto (1), e que tambem ouvira vulgarmente que se andara
fazendo um assignado nesta cidade para fazer expulsar della e
toda a provincia o coronel Martim Francisco Ribeiro de Andrada,
quando não havia motivo algum para semelhante procedimento
(2).—Ao setimo, disse nada —Ao oitavo, que lhe não consta que
pelo governo então existente se dessem providencias algumas
tanto sobre es acontecimentas dia 23 de Maio como sobre o ajuntamento nos quarteis na occasião em que a tropa de Santos
marchava para esta cidade, pois que então se achava fora desta
cidade.—Ao nono e decimo, nada disse, bem como do costume.
E lido o seu juramento, pelo achar conforme ao que havia deposto, e assignou com o ministro inquiridor. E eu, o bacharel
formado Manoel João de Ornellas, escrivão desta devassa, o escrevi.—*FreireBento Correa Leme.*

---

## TESTEMUNHA 10.ª

Francisco Manoel de Borja (3), solteiro, sargento do terceiro regimento de milicias, desta cidade, natural da villa de
Santos e morador desta cidade, onde vive do seu officio de al-
faiate, de idade 35 annos; testemunha jurada aos Santos Evangelhos em um livro delles em que poz a sua mão direita e debaixo
do juramento que lhe foi deferido prometteu dizer a verdade do
que soubesse e perguntado lhe fosse. E sendo inquerido pelos
interrogatorios da presente devassa, ao primeiro, disse que sabe

---

(1) Esta gente *subordinada* estava reunida no pateo, em baixo, pelos esforços dos
sedeciosos Pedro Taques, Paula Macedo Oliveira Netto e outros. que armados de espada
e trabuco e andavam recrutando pelas ruas, e a grande maioria sahiu e assignou o
auto sem saber o que nelle continha.
(2) Motivo de serviço publico não havia impotrantes inneresses particulares a at-
tender o que não podiam ser realizadas ccm a presença de Martim e Jordão no governo.
De outros depoimentos vê-se que havia a questão das carnes verdes, a inimizade de
Costa Carvalho a Martim, venalidade dos officiaes que receberam dinheiro para dispen-
sarem soldados de seguirem para o Rio. descoberto e divulgado para Martim e Jordão.
e finalmente os interesses retrogrados em lucta com os interresses brazileiros, aquelles
personificados nos estrangeiros membros do governo e no seus allidaos Francico Ignacio e Costa Carvalho e estes representados por Martim e Jordão.
() Em 1822, ao tempo desta devassa havia um Francisco de Borja. portuguez de
cerca de 40 annos. sargento, com negocio de molhados da rua do Commercio, n. 4, que
não deve ser confundido com este.
O seu depoimento tem valor por ser testemunha de vista e miliciano, subordinado
aos coroneis Ferreira do Amaral e Francisco Ignacio. Este depoimento não traz assentada, servindo para elle a mesma assentada anterior.

por ver, em razão de ser o commandante da guarda do quartel no dia 23 de Maio do corrente anno, que o major José Rodrigues Pereira de Oliveira Netto, entrando no quartel com outros officiaes, na tarde daquelle, como foram o tenente Jayme da Silva Telles e o capitão Sagalerva, se dirigiu a um dos tambores alli existentes e, perguntando-lhe pelos demais tambores, gritou que se tocasse a rebate e bem da patria e logo se encaminhou ao official do estado maior, o tenente Ignacio José de Macedo, e o obrigou com uma pistola aos peitos, gritando com elle por tres vezes que se havia de tocar a rebate e empurrando os tambores aos pescoços para que o fossem tocar, o que vendo elle testemunha se poz logo em armas e segundo as ordens que havia e que eram de se tocar a rebate sem positiva ordem do governo para se dever ou não tocar, mandou immediatamente um cabo a participar aquelle rebate á guarda principar, e lhe veiu em resposta que o official daquella guarda dava parte na sala do governo, donde lhe não veiu decisão alguma e por isso se continuou a tocar a rebate. Disse mais que chegando ao quartel o tenente coronel Antonio de Padua de Gusmão, commandante do destacamento, logo que ouviu tocar a rebate, perguntou quem o tinha mandado tocar, ao que respondeu o major José Rodrigues Pereira de Oliveira Netto que foram elle e a corporação de officiaes e povo que alli se achavam para bem commum e socego da patria. Ao segundo e terceiro, disse nada.—Ao quarto disse que sabe por ouvir vulgarmente que quem conmmanda a tropa no largo de São Gonçalo, quando alli se postou, fôra o coronel Francisco Alvares Ferreira do Amaral e que depois chegára o coronel Francisco Ignacio de Souza Queiroz e tomára o commando della.—Ao quinto, disse, que nada sabia.—Ao sexto, disse que sabe de facto proprio e por presenciar que tanto as assignaturas do auto de vereação extraordinaria do dia 23, como as que se seguiram ao depois (1) e que deram causa á expulsão dos dous membros do governo, o coronel Martim e o brigadeiro Jordão, e á sahida daquelle para fóra desta cidade e provincia, *foram determinados pelo commandante do destacamento quanto aos soldados e officiaes inferiores, que sabiam ler, sendo elle testemunha um delles, que, supposto soubesse a que se dirigiam essas assignaturas feitas na Camara e* NÃO TIVESSE MOTIVO ALGUM PARA CONVIR NO QUE FOI REQUERIDO,

---

(1) Na acta do vereação do dia 23 de Maio assignou muita gente que no dia lá. não foi. tendo o livro ficado á disposição de quem quizesse ver e assignar aquella acta e nos dias 24 e 25 de Maio foi muita gente forçada a ir á Camara prestar a sua assignatura O mesmo facto se deu com a acta do dia 29. que ficou aberta para receber mais assignaturas. Tudo isto consta das proprias actas e por isso se diz aqui « assignaturas do dia 23 e as que se seguiram ».

PELO INTITULADO' POVO E TROPA, COMTUDO PRESTOU A SUA OBRI-
GAÇÃO, de que está bem arrependido, e *a que fez no quartel foi
sem saber o fim a que se dirigia.*—Ao setimo, disse nada.—Ao
oitavo, disse que lhe não consta que o extincto governo désse
providencia alguma sobre os acontecimentos do dia 23 de Maio,
*bem como do ajuntamento de militares, paizanos e escravos, que
se conservaram no quartel por espaço de tres dias e tres noites,*
quando a tropa da villa de Santos se encaminhava para esta
cidade (1), existindo alli todos armados, até os mesmos escravos,
com armas do quartel subministradas pelo major Netto, e comprehendendo-se entre os mesmos o padre Bernardo Conrado e o
frade franciscano Frei Antonio do Menino Jesus, este com um
escravo atraz de si armado de trabuco e aquelle de espada e
pistolas, o que elle testemunha sabe por ter visto, sendo todos
sustentados a carne, farinha, arroz e vinho a custa do coronel
Francisco Ignacio de Souza Queiroz, commandante da força armada, segundo elle testemunha ouviu vulgarmente dizer ser feita
essa despesa a custa do referido commandante da força armada,
a quem davam muitos vivas, da mesma sorte que ao presidente
do extincto governo João Carlos Augusto de Oeynhausen, havendo mesa redonda para toda a officialidade, padres e paizanos de
alguma representação, sendo notados de inimigos da patria todos os
que não concorreram áquelle ajuntamento, reanimando por este modo
a todos os que alli se achavam para obstarem a entrada do
marechal Candido Xavier de Almeida e Souza e a sua tropa,
com o pretexto muitas vezes repetido no quartel de que vinham
matar e saquear (2). Disse mais que sabe, por ouvir fallar
geralmente no mesmo quartel, que querendo o governo que a
tropa entrasse desarmada e com os fusis abertos, não quizeram

---

(1) Este ajuntamento de militares. de dois clerigos desconhecidos, de alguns paisanos e escravos, teve logar em meado de Julho de 1822, quando havia já quasi dois
mezes que Martim e Jordão tinham sido depostos e estava já Martim occupando o cargo
de ministro da Fazenda do Princepe Regente. O governador militar de Santos, Silva Valente, tinha sido substituido por Candido Xavier, que teve ordem do Rio para marchar
sobre S. Paulo e restabelecer a paz na cidade; porém os sediciosos de 23 de Maio resistiram e a esta resistencia é que aqui se faz referencia. Candido Xavier voltou a
Santos e os sediciosos só cederam com a chegada de D. Pedro, em Agosto, quando se
propuzeram a fazer festas, que foram recusadas.
2 Algumas das testemunhas já disseram que na manhã do dia da *Bernarda* o coronel Francisco Ignacio déra almoço *regado a espirito* aos homens com que pretendia fazer
a sedição. e o papel que alguns delles — Pedro Taques, Paula Macedo, Oliveira Netto,
Silva Telles, Caetano Pinto, Gonçalves Mamede e outros — fizeram nas ruas parece indicar que estavam influenciados pelo lauto almoço; depois, André Gomes, velho portuguez e membro do governo; nos vem dizer que naquelle dia o *paço municipal se transformára em botequim e taberna de vinho e genebra. lautamente distribuidos aos festivos
do dia.* e agora nos conta o sargento Borja que ainda dois mezes depois da *Bernarda* a
coragem e o animo dos militares, clerigos, paizanos e escravos, reunidos no quartel,
eram mantidos a custa de carne, farinha, arroz e *vinho,* fornecidos ainda pelo coronel
Francisco Ignacio !

os aquartellados estar por isso.—Ao nono e decimo nada disse, nem do costume. E lido o seu juramento, pelo achar conforme ao que depoz, se assignou com o ministro inquiridor. E eu, o bacharel formado Manoel Joaquim de Ornellas, escrivão desta devassa ; o escrivi.—*Freire.*—*Francisco Manoel de Borja.*

## ASSENTADA

Aos 23 dias do mez de Setembro de 1822, nesta cidade de São Paulo, em casas de residencia do doutor Antonio de Almeida Silva Freire da Fonseca, onde eu escrivão desta devassa fui vindo, e sendo ahi por elle ministro foram inquiridas as testemunhas cujos nomes, cognomes, naturalidades, moradas, idades, officios, ditos e costumes é tudo o que adeante se segue, do que para constar fiz este termo de assentada. E eu, o bacharel formado Manoel Joaquim de Ornellas, escrivão da mesma devassa, o escrevi.

### TESTEMUNHA 11.ª

JACINTHO JOSÉ (1), casado, natural da villa de Santos e morador desta cidade onde vive do seu soldo de tambor-mór do 3.º regimento da infantaria miliciana, de idade de 36 annos; testemunha jurada aos Santos Evangelhos, em um livro delles em que poz a sua mão direita e debaixo do juramento que lhe foi deferido prometteu dizer a verdade do que soubesse e perguntado lhe fosse. E sendo inquirido pelos interrogatorios da presente devassa disse, ao primeiro, que estando elle testemunha dormindo sobre a tarimba do corpo da guarda do quartel na tarde do dia 23 de Maio do corrente anno accordára com o barulho dos tambores no acto de pegarem nas caixas e vira o major José Rodrigues Pereira de Oliveira Netto, acompanhado do major Francisco de Paula Macedo e do tenente Jayme da Silva Telles, a dar socos nos tambores para irem tocar rebate, e mandando elle testemunha chegar os tambores á forma lhes determinou tocassem a rebate na fóma ordenada pelos sobreditos officiaes, e querendo elle rodear o quartel na fórma praticada nas occasiões de fogo por julgar que o rebate se dirigia a este fim, se oppuzeram a isso aquelles officiaes, mandando que fossem

---

1 Em 1818 havia em S. Paulo um Jacintho José, paulista, de 33 annos, casado, branco, escripturario da Contadoria e morador na rua da Liberdade n. 31, com a mulher, um filho e tres escravos; era miliciano e por estes dados parece ser o mesmo que aqui figura como despoente e testemunha mais do que de vista, pois era o chefe dos tambores que foram espancados pela officialidade turbulenta e sediciosa.

tocar pelas ruas publicas, e indo-se já a recolher ao quartel por
detraz da cadéa, sahindo-lhe ao encontro o major Netto e man⁻
dou parar o rebate e que elle testemunna se recolhesse para o
batalhão, que já então se achava postado no largo de S. Gon-
çrlo; ignorando qual fosse a ordem que tivessem os referidos
officiaes para o determinado rebate e o fim deste, constando-lhe,
sómente por ser voz publica, que o mesmo major Netto puzera
suas pistolas ao peito do official do estado-maior, o tenente
Ignacio José de Macedo, para que mandasse tocar o exigido
rebate. — Ao segundo, disse nada.—Ao terceiro, disse que sabe,
por ouvir de alguns camaradas, que a tropa se fôra postar no
largo de S. Gonçalo conduzida pelo brigadeiro Joaquim José
Pinto de Moraes Leme e o coronel Francisco Alvares Ferreira
do Amaral.—Ao quarto, disse que quem commandou a tropa na
occasião do motim foram os ditos brigadeiro Pinto. coronel
Francisco Alvares Ferreira do Amaral e o coronel Francisco
Ignacio de Sousa Queiroz, chefe da força armada, pois que se
viu a todos elles á frente da tropa e povo. — As quinto, disse
nada.—Ao sexto, disse que sómente sabe por ACONTECER COM
ELLE E SEU FILHO E OUTROS CAMARADAS, QUE FORAM ASSIGNAR O
AUTO DE VEREAÇÃO EXTRAORDINARIA E OUTRO PAPEL POR SEREM
MANDADOS PELO SEU SUPERIOR O TENENTE-CORONEL ANTONIO DE
PADUA DE GUSMÃO, SEM SABEREM O QUE ASSIGNARAM, NEM PARA
QUE FIM, ouvindo posteriormente que fôra para a conservação do
presidente do extincto governo, João Carlos Augusto de Oeynhausen e expulsão dos dous membros. coronel Martim e o brigadeiro Jordão, *de cuja assignatura está bem arrependido por
não ter motivo algum de queixa contra os referidos dous membros* (1).
—Ao setimo, nada disse. — Ao oitavo, disse que lhe não consta
que o extincto governo désse providencias algumas sobre os
acontecimentos daquelle dia 23 de Maio passado, nem tão pouco
sobre o ajuntamento dos militares, paizanos e escravos que concorreram ao quartel, e todos se achavam alli armados com as
armas reiunas por occasião da vinda da tropa da villa de Santos,
comprehendendo se entre elles um frade franciscano de nome
Frei Antonio do Menino Jesus, armado de duas pistolas e atrás
de si um pagem mulato armado de um trabuco, e o padre Bernardo Conrado de espada e pistolas, sendo todos sustentados á
carne, farinha, arroz e vinho e dando-se rcpetidos vivas ao chefe

---

1 O depoente disse que tinha 36 annos ; não podia, portanto, ter filho emancipado
para assignar a acta de vereação de 23 de Maio. Até meninos, meirinhos, carcereiros
e musicos foram chamados durante os dias 23, 24 e 25 de Maio a assignarem aquella
acta e ainda assim ella cantém menos de 200 assignaturas ! E era o povo de S. Paulo
que alli vinha, por aquelle meio, protestar contra a tyramnia de Martim Francisco

da força armada, o coronel Francisco Ignacio de Sousa Queiroz, que ahi se conservou sempre em todo o tempo que durou este ajuntamento, ao presidente João Carlos de Oeynhausen e ao capitão Pedro Taques de Almeida Alvim, o que tudo viu elle testemunha por ser um dos que alli estiveram no mencionado ajuntamento, e doclarou que a estada de todos os acima referidos no respectivo quartel fôra para impedir a entrada da sobredita tropa vinda da villa de Santos, para cujo effeito estavam todos municiados de polvora e bala, até os mesmos escravos, e fornecidos de armas subministradas pelo major Netto e capitão Pedro Taques de Almeida Alvim.—Ao nono e decimo, disse que nada sabia, nem do costume. E lido o seu juramento, pelo achar conforme ao que havia deposto, o assignou com o ministro inquiridor. E eu, o bacharel formado Manoel Joaquim de Ornellas. escrivão da presente devassa, o escrevi.—*Ereire.*—*Jacintho José.*

## TESTEMUNHA 12.ª

IGNACIO JOSÉ' VIEIRA (1), casado, natural da freguezia da Penha e nella morador, onde vive das suas lavouras, da tdade de 4o annos mais ou menos; testemunha jurada aos Santos Evangelhos, em um livro delles em que pôz sua mão direita e, debaixo do juramento que prestou, promotteu dizer a verdade do que soubesse e perguntado lhe fosse. E perguntado pelos interrogatorios desta devassa disse. ao primeiro, que sabe por ver que quem mandou tocar a rebate na tarde do dia 23 de Maio passado foram o major José Rodrigues Pereira de Oliveira Netto e o tenente Jayme da Silva Telles, e chegando aquelle a elle testemunha, que estava limpando as armas como quarteiro e soldado miliciano do regimento dos Uteis, lhe perguntou pelo tenente Padua (2), ao que lhe respondeu que ainda não tinha vindo, de que resultou dirigir-se o dito major ao official de estado-maior, que era o tenente Ignacio José de Macedo, para que mandasse tocar a rebate, e repugnando a este fanel-o sem legitima ordem o constrangeu a isso, pondo-lhe duas pistolas ao peito, e empurrou logo os tambores a pescoções pela porta fóra do quartel para irem tocar ao dito rebate pelos ruas desta cidade. Disse mais que o tenente Jayme da Silva Telles, tanto que alli chegou na companhia do major Netto, lhe pediu a chave

---

1 Não disse muito, mas o seu testemunho é de valor por ser de vista e porque o depoente era militar em serviço na occasião. Este depoimento não traz termo de assentadas por ser em continuação do anterior.

2 Antonio de Padua de Guzmão, de quem se tem feito muita menção nos depoimentos anteriores e foi violentado a tomar parte na sedição.

do armazem das armas com um ar indignado e repugnando a elle testemunha dar-lh'a sem ordem do tenente coronel do destacamento, lh'a tomou da mão e foi dando armamento aos que concorriam ao toque do rebate, para o qual lhe não consta que precedesse legitima ordem. Ao segundo, disse por ver que os agentes e cooperadores do ajuntamento da tropa e povo no largo de São Gonçalo foram os ditos major Netto e tenente Jaime, que apenas reuniram um batalhão o fizeram marchar para aquelle largo (1), sendo o major Netto quem o puxou, concorrendo tambem ao quartel o coronel Francisco Alvares Ferreira do Amaral, o capitão Pedro Taques de Almeida Alvim, o tenente Antonio Gonçaives Mamede e outros, de cujos nomes se não recorda.—Ao terceiro, disse que sabe por ver que a *tropa se não foi postar no largo de São Gonçalo espontaneamente, mas sim por obedecer ás ordens que davam os seus officiaes, tanto assim que elle testemunha e quasi todos os soldados ignoravam o fim do rebate e do ajuntamento da mesma tropa naquelle logar.*—Ao quarto, disse que sabe por ter presenciado que quem se puzera á frente da tropa foram o coronel Francisco Alvares Ferreira do Amaral, o coronel Francisco Ignacio de Souza Queiroz, o capitão Pedro Taques de Almeida Alvim, o major Netto, os tenentes Jaime e Mamede, o tenente coronel Padua e outros de que não conserva lembrança.—Ao quinto, disse nada.—Ao sexto, disse que sabe, por ver e ter acontecido com elle testemunha, que todos os soldados que assignaram o auto de vereação extraordinaria e um papel no quartel, o fizeram por ordem dos seus superiores, ignorando o fim para que eram (2).—Ao setimo, disse nada.—Ao oitavo, disse que lhe não consta que o extincto governo desapprovasse o procedimento do dia 23 de Maio, nem tão pouco desse providencias a semelhante respeito, nem tão pouco cohibisse o ajuntamento que houve no quartel, de militares, paizanos, negros e mulatos, quando a tropa da villa de Santos se approximava a esta cidade, comprehendendo-se naquelle ajuntamento tambem o frade franciscano Frei Antonio do Menino Jesus, e o padre Bernardo Conrado armado de pistolas, e alli se achavam todos sustentados a carne, farinha, arroz, cangica e vinho e dando repetidos vivas ao presidente João Carlos Augusto de Oeynhau-

---

1 Não podia ser mais do que estes poucos militares, porque todos elles foram forçados a assignarem a acta de vereação e esta contém menos de 200 assignaturas, incluindo as da plebe e dos meninos que puderam ser apanhadas nas ruas da cidade durante tres dias consecutivos — 23, 24 e 25 de Maio, como se vê do livro das actas.
2 O que aconteceu a este depoente foi quasi geral, e raros foram os que assignaram livre e conscientemente aquella acta.

sen, ao coronel Francisco Ignacio de Souza Queiroz, ao capitão Pedro Taques de Almeida Alvim, sendo a causa daquelle ajuntamento, segundo ouviu a alguns officiaes, o impedir que a referida tropa entrasse nesta cidade (1).—Ao nono e decimo, disse nada, bem como ao costume. E lido o seu juramento, pelo achar conforme ao que havia deposto, o assignou com o ministro devassante. E eu, o bacharel formado Joaquim de Ornellas (2), escrivão da presente devassa, o escrevi.—*Freire.—Ignacio José Vieira*».

## ASSENTADA

Aos 25 dias do mez de Setembro de 1822, nesta cidade de S. Paulo, em casas de residencia do doutor Antonio de Almeida Silva Freire da Fonseca, ministro da presente devassa, onde eu escrivão della fui vindo, e sendo ahi foram por elle ministro inquiridas as testemunhas cujos nomes, cognomes, naturalidades, moradas, idades, officios, ditos e costumes é tudo o que adeante se segue, do que para constar fiz o presente termo de assentada. E eu, o bacharel formado Manoel Joaquim de Ornellas, o escrevi·

### TESTEMUNHA 13.ª

O capitão Francisco Mariano Galvão Bueno (3), casado, natural desta cidade e morador da freguezia de S. Bernardo, termo da mesma, de idade de de 26 annos, que vive de seus negocios; testemunha jurada aos Santos Evangelhos, em um livro delles em que poz sua mão direita e debaixo do juramento que lhe foi deferido prometteu dizer a verdade do que soubesse e perguntado lhe fosse. E sendo inquirido pelos interrogatorios

---

1 Nas desordens do dia 23 de Maio Costa Carvalho apparece sempre de modo a se tornar conspicuo entre os sediciosos e foi o primeiro a assignar a acta da vereação daquelle dia; mas depois disso tratou de eclipsar-se e em todas as desordens que se seguiram até :O de Julho apparecem sómente os nomes dos seus cumplices João Carlos, Francisco Ignacio e Ferreira do Amaral, chefes do movimento sedicioso. Na reunião dos quarteis, em meado de Julho, até frades e padres appareceram armados de espadas e de trabuco, acompanhados por escravos alheios á sedição e dando vivas aos chefes; mas a pessoa e o nome de Costa Carvalho primaram pela ausencia, estando elle na cidade e sendo um dos cabeças da sedição! Tropas portuguezas não vieram do Santos, a artilharia encravada por Silva Valente fora restaurada por Candido Xavier, cujas tropas marchavam sobre S. Paulo, havia perigo real e Costa Carvalho não dava mais signal de si, marchando pacificamente para o Rio alguns dias depois em obediencia aos asperos officio e portaria de 25 de Junho!

2 O nome «Manuel» foi supprimido aqui no original.

3 Pertencia a uma importante familia, ainda hoje muito conhecida nesta Capital; foi pae do dr. Carlos Mariano e Americo Galvão Bueno, avô do dr Luiz Garcia Ferreira e aparentados com outros personagens ainda vivos. Ha até uma rua «Galvão Bueno» perpetuando o nome desta familia O seu depoimento é dos mais importantes e traz muita luz sobre as causas da *Bernarda*.

da presente devassa disse. ao primeiro, que sabe por ter ouvido vulgarmente que o major José Rodrigues Pereira de Oliveira Netto e o tenente Jaime da Silva Telles foram os que mandaram tocar a rebate na tarde do dia 23 de Maio passado, forçando o dito major com uma pistola aos peitos ao official do estado maior, o tenente Ignacio José de Macedo, para que fizesse tocar o referido rebate, com ameaças de morte se assim o não praticasse, concorrendo para tocar o mesmo rebate o major Francisco de Paula Macedo, o capitão Antonio Cardoso Nogueira e o capitão Pedro Taques de Almeida Alvim e fazendo todos elles sahirem os tambores a pontapés para fóra do quartel afim de tocarem o determinado rebate, tocando ao mesmo tempo do rebate o sino da cadeia Joaquim Pedro Maia (1), tendo tudo isto por fim o não se cumprir a a ordem em virtude da qual fora chamado á côrte do Rio de Janeiro o presidente do extincto governo, João Carlos Augusto de Oeynhausen, em nome de Sua Alteza Real, e serem igualmente depostos de membros do mesmo governo o coronel Martim Francisco Ribeiro de Andrada e o brigadeiro Manoel Rodrigues Jordão *por quererem que se cumprisse a mencionada ordem de Sua . Alteza Real, como a elle testemunha disse o referido capitão Nogueira*, e mais não disse —Ao segundo, disse que sómente sabe por ouvir vulgarmente que o capitão Pedro Taques de Almeida Alvim, indo para o largo de São Gonçalo, convidava a todas as pessoas que via para que se fossem reunir na casa da Camara —Ao terceiro, disse nada.—Ao quarto, disse que. pela mesma razão de ter ouvido vulgarmente, sabe que quem commandára a tropa quando marchou para o largo de São Gonçalo, na occasião do motim, fora o coronel Francisco Alvares Perreira do Amaral e que, concorrendo áquelle logar o commandante da força armada, coronel Francisco Ignacio de Souza Queiroz, perguntára ao dito coronel Alvares com que auctoridade tomára o commando daquella tropa, de que elle era o chefe, e lhe fora respondido que, acudindo ao rebate como era da sua obrigação, *fora encarregado pelo povo e tropa de a commandar*. Disse mais que, pela indicada razão, sabe que o brigadeiro Pinto se achara tambem na frente da tropa em o largo de São Gonçalo, perante. a qual e povo alli congregado recitara um alvará ou decreto que auctorizava ao povo a fazer ou desfazer o governo, conforme lhe conviesse, não sendo por conseguinte crime o que se pretendia fazer, e que vindo o

---

1 O quartel estava como ainda está, na rua do Quartel e a cadêa e a casa da Camara, que eram um só edificio, hoje do Congresso Estadual, estavam no largo de S. Gonçalo, hoje largo do Dr. João Mendes : a distancia entre os dois predios é de cerca de cem metros, sendo facil a passagem da força do quartel para o largo mencionado

mesmo brigadeiro a reunir-se á tropa por effeito do rebate e passando pela guarda do hospital, a reprehendera por não estar em armas e não tocar a rebate, como se estava tocando na cidade (1).—Ao quinto, disse que sabe, por ter ouvido ao capitão Pedro Taques de Almeida Alvim, que fora elle mesmo quem constrangera ao presidente da Camara, o capitão Bento José Leite Penteado, para ir á casa da mesma Camara, na occasião do acontecido motim, e o levara adeante de si.—Ao sexto, disse que sabe por ser voz publica que o capitão Pedro Taques de Almeida Alvim, o major Macedo, o major Netto, o tenente Jaime e Joaquim Pedro Maia andaram convocando e rogando aos que se achavam no largo de São Gonçalo, onde estava postada a tropa, para que fossem assignar o auto de vereação extraordinarinaria celebrado naquella occasião, e sabe pela mesma razão que os ditos tenente Jaime e Joaquim Pedro Maia, adjunctos com o mesmo capitão Alvim, José Manoel de Abreu, por alcunha o Tralhão, o capitão Francisco Joé de Azevedo e o tenente Bernardo Guedes andaram de casa em casa a fazer assignar um papel para que o coronel Martim fosse expulso desta cidade dentro em vinte horas e da provincia em oito dias pelo considerarem pernicioso ao bem da mesma provincia, QUANDO ELLE TESTEMUNHA SE PERSUADE DO CONTRARIO PELO CONCEITUAR MUITO DA SUA PATRIA E ZELOSO DOS INTERESSES DA MESMA AO PONTO MESMO DE SE OPPOR A MUITAS DAS PRETENÇÕES QUE ALGUNS DOS MESMOS DO GOVERNO QUERIAM POR EM EXECUÇÃO, SENDO ALIÁS CONTRARIAS AO BEM PUBLICO, como eram : querer o capitão Nogueira e seus socios arrematar o córte desta cidade pelo preço de mil e duzentos a arroba quando aliás estava franco por preço muito mais favoravel ; o intentar o mesmo capitão—Nogueira ser reformado em major, tendo sido promovido a capitão havia bem pouco (2); o impedir-se a publicação de um bando que o coronel Martim e o brigadeiro Jordão se esforçavam a que se publicasse afim de se vir no conhecimento DOS SOLDADOS E OFFICIAES QTE TINHAM DADO DINHEIRO AOS SEUS CHEFES E SUAS AMADAS PARA NÃO IREM NA EXPEDIÇÃO QUE

1  O brigadeiro Joaquim José Pinto de Moraes Leme tinha então 68 annos e morava perto da egreja de Santa Ephigenia, com sua senhora, algumas parentas e 29 escravos. O Hospital militar era um predio visinho da sua residencia e que depois serviu para o Seminario das Educandas e hoje está alugado a particulares. O seu caminho para vir á cidade era pela pente do Acú e ladeira de S. João, passando portanto pela frente do hospital, cuja guarda não estava ainda violentada para participar da sedição que tomára posse da cidade

2  Em 1818 este Nogueira era tenente e negociante de fazendas e tinha 29 annos de idade : em 1822 continuava como negociante, prestando pouco serviço na milicia, já era capitão aos 33 annos e ainda queria reforma em major e o monopolio das carnes verdes na cidade ! Era portuguez, estava sob boas protecções e dahi as descabidas exigencias que fazia !

MARCHOU PARA A CORTE DO RIO DE JANEIRO promettendo-se, nelle a restituição do dinheiro e a baixa aos soldados em recompensa (1); a indisposição do ouvidor José Costa Carvalho contra o mesmo coronel Martim por este não consentir nas suas arbitrariedades (2) e a pretenção do capitão Venancio Antonio da Rosa relativa á rescisão da arrematação da obra do caminho do Cubatão para Santos, a que obstou o predito coronel Martim sustentando que se devia cumprir a mesma arrematação, cujos factos, que ficam relatados, foram a causal da deposição dos dous mencionados membros do extincto governo, como a elle testemunha disse o proprio capitão Nogueira em casa do alferes Francisco Martins Bonilha (3), na occasião de ter ido o mesmo Nogueira presidir a eleição parochial da freguezia de São Bernardo e em outras occasiões —Ao setimo, disse que a respeito deste artigo somente lhe consta, por ser voz publica, que o ouvidor José da Costa Carvalho fora quem dera o plano para os acontecimentos do dia 23 de Maio e seguintes e notava todos os papeis e assignados tendentes á deposição dos dois membros do extincto governo, coronel Martim e brigadeiro Jordão, á entrada do marechal Arouche e á posse do mesmo Arouche, aquem, por ouvir geralmente sabe elle testemunha, *se offerecera o Major Netto para trazer atado á cauda do seu cavallo* (4).—Ao oitavo, disse que sabe por ter presenciado que o extincto governo não dera providencia alguma sobre o ajuntamento dos que tumultuosamente concorreram para o quartel, tanto como paisanos e até negros e mulatos e mesmo alguns captivos, segundo ouviu dizer, afim de impedirem a entrada do marechal Candido Xavier de Almeida e Souza nesta cidade, com a sua tropa, de ordem de Sua Alteza Real; achando-se naquelle ajuntamento o frade franciscano Frei Antonio do Menino Jesus, armado de pistolas e o padre Berrardo Conrado tambem armado de espada e pistolas, bem como

---

! E esta famosa immoralidade encontrava protecção em Francisco Ignacio e nos seus collegas extrangeiros do governo, que ainda pretenderam passar á posteridade como exemplos de civismo !

2 Referencia já foi feita por testemunhas ao facto de Costa Carvalho ter ido á casa de Martim, onde se deu o rompimento, indicando este facto que o ouvidor lá fora com o intuito de *ageitar* o mesmo Martim e remover a sua opposição aos actos que praticava e pretendia praticar, mas que, não o conseguindo, rompeu com elle e foi se fazer o chefe dos sediciosos. Os Andradas eram um obstaculo ao seu caminho e precisavam ser removidos, mesmo á custa da *Bernarda*, da dissolução da Assembléa Constituinte e deportação e fusilamento de muitos patriotas, sendo João Carlos e Francisco Ignacio bons auxiliares para a *Bernarda* e a cortezã Domitilla para o resto.

3 Depoz tambem nesta devassa, como se verá adeante.

4 Estava na moda esta forma de ameaça e já Pedro Taques tinha obrigado o capitão Leite Penteado a ir presidir á Camara sob a ameaça de leval-o amarrado á cauda do seu cavallo. Arouche estava no valle do Parahyba, onde era inspector geral de milicias, e a execução da ameaça do major Netto era quasi tão difficil de se realizar como a sóva de chicote que Francisco Ignacio promettia a D. Pedro no Rio !

todos os paizanos, negros e mulatos, a quem foram subministradas armas reiunas pelo capitão Alvim e tenente Jaime, a quem
ouvi dizer a um negro fosse tomar armas, e quanto aos mais
sabe por ouvir dizer geralmente, lhes foram fornecidas as armas pelos ditos capitão Alvim e tenente Jaime. Disse mais
que, entrando curiosamente no quartel no dia 20 de Julho
passado, quando já lá se achava aquelle ajuntamento, lhe fora
extranhado pelo capitão Luiz Manuel da Cunha Bastos o não
ter vindo fardado e armado e ouviu dizer ao major Netto,
na frente do ajuntamento armado, que o marechal Candido
promettera a sua tropa, no alto da serra, dar lhe duas horas
de saque, asseverando-lhe com um ar indignado e com gritos
que era uma tropa de ladrões (1), e perguntando a todos se
entraria ou não a tropa lhe foi respondido que não havia de
entrar. Disse mais que entrando o coronel Müller no quartel
quando vinha de se haver encontrado com o marechal Candido
por ordem do governo, que na noite do dia antecedente tinha
ali estado em sessão (2), bem como se conservára lá o coronel
Francisco Ignacio de Souza Queiroz, commandante da força armada em todo o tempo que durou aquelle ajuntamento, disse
perante todos que o governo determinava entrasse o marechal
Candido com sua tropa visto ter marchado para dar cumprimento ás ordens de Sua Alteza Real, e chegando-se a elle o capitão Pedro Taques de Almeida Alvim lhe respondeu, em altas
vozes e na presença do proprio commandante da força armada,
que a tropa não devia entrar e, voltando-se logo para o ajuntamento armado, lhe perguntou : «não é assim, meus camaradas?»
(3) Ao que foi unanimcmente respondido que não entraria, e
voltando-se o coronel Müller ao mesmo tempo para um paizano
vestido de fardamento de soldado e batendo-lhe no hombro, lhe

---

1 Para a sedição de 23 de Maio se recorreu á cachaça, ao vinho, á genebra e á
intimidação dos pacificos por mim de espada e trabuco, e agora para a resistencia contra o marechal Candido Xavier, portador de ordens de D. Pedro, lança-se mão do recurso da calumnia e da difamação contra este marechal e suas tropas! Para os retro-
grodos e facciosos todos os meios eram bons para o alcance do fim que tinham em
vista!

2 Das actas das sessões do governo pouco consta sobre os pormenores destas scenas
do quartel; não convinha que isso ficasse registrado Müller era dos menos violentos,
porem dos mais capazes dos sediciosos; era natural de Lisboa, de 40 annos de ida'e,
habil e bom cartographo. Casára-se aqui com uma senhora paulista e tinha cinco filhas
que se casaram bem, e um filho que falleceu solteiro, com 30 annos. Estava no Brasil
a serviço, era retrogrado por nascimento e profissão, mas depois adheriu á independencia e se tornou cidadão dos mais uteis. Não era rico, vivia do seu soldo de coronel,
possuia dois escravos e residia na rua *De Tras da Boa Morte* n. 50.

3 Esta scena entre o coronel Francisco Ignacio e o capitão Pedro Taques indica
claramente que o coronel não tinha força moral para se fazer obedecer pelo capitão ou
que elle estava de antemão combinado, como a que se passou entre Francisco Ignacio
e Ferreira do Amaral no largo de S. Gonçalo na tarde de 23 de Maio, relativa ao commando do batalhão.

disse em ar rizonho que só elle era capaz de tomar uma peça de artilbaria ao inimigo, concluindo finalmente que, á vista daquella resolução do referido ajuntamento tumultuoso ia dar parte ao governo, o qual resolveu fosse o mesmo Müller segunda vez ao marechal Candido a dizer-lhe da parte do mesmo governo que a tropa fizesse alto e elle viesse conferenciar com o referido governo por se opporem o povo e tropa á sua entrada, participando esta mesma resolução ao quartel antes de ir ao marechal Candido, mas que, regressando Müller da segunda embaixada e tendo convencionado com elle o marechal Candido que, sim, viria só sem a sua tropa, não para se entender com o governo, mas sim com o marechal Arouche, general das armas, segundo as ordens que tinha de Sua Alteza Re l, fôra participal o ao governo e este lhe ordenára o fosse communicar no qual, onde se achava o tal ajuntamento, o que assim praticou, dizendo na sua sahida: *agua benta e caldo de gallinha nunca fizeram mal a doente».* Disse mais que, estando elle testemunha na noite do dia 19 do mesmo mez de Jnlho em casa do capitão Francisco Gonçalves dos Santos Cruz, ouviu da sala onde se achava dar-se-lhe um recado na escada, pelo que se lhe participava que o marechal Candido estava a entrar na cidade com a sua tropa, por cuja causa já o commandante da força armada tinha ido para o quartel, e por effeito deste recado se fardou e armou, seguindo logo para o quartel, onde havia mesa redonda para todos os officiaes e *algumas pessoas de maior consideração* (1). e os soldados e mais gente armada eram sustentados a carne, farinha, arroz e MUITO VINHO, que tudo era subministrado pelo commandante da força armada, como elle testemunha ouviu dizer geralmente e se persuade ser assim porque, estando elle mesmo, testemunha, no quartel, perto do referido commandante da força armada, o coronel Francisco Ignacio de Souza Queiroz, se chegára a elle o miliciano José Velloso e lhe dissera que tinham dado doze frascos de vinho e duas bandejas de lombo frito aos soldados artilheiros que aqui se achavam da villa de Santos pelo ter vistos descontentes, ao que lhe respondêra que estava bom. Disse mais por ter ouvido geralmente que no dia 20 de Julho de manhã fora o tenente Fadiga, com uma escolta, á casa da polvora e a arrombára (2). Disse finalmente, por ter ouvido ao coronel

---

1 Esta phrase «algumas pessoas de maior consideração» bem indica que eram poucas e que o quartel estava guardado pela tropa miliciana, auxiliada pela plebe, mulatos, negros e até alguns captivos, como affirmaram outras testemunhas.

2 A casa da polvora estava na rua da Liberdade, acima do largo deste nome, cerca de 200 metros acima do largo de S. Gonçalo e da casa da Camara e cerca de 500 metros acima do quartel. A communicação entre os tres predios era facilima.

Francisco Ignacio de Souza Queiroz, que duas horas antes de se ter tocado a rebate, na tarde do dia 23 de Maio, lhe mandára perguntar o presidente do governo, João Carlos Augusto de Oeynhausen, pelo ajudante de ordens o capitão Gregorio, se sabia de algum motim que estivesse para acontecer naquelle dia e lhe mandára em resposta que de nada sabia, e que voltára o mesmo ajudante de ordens a affirmar-lhe da parte do referido presidente que naquella tarde havia de haver uma bernarda (1), o que tendo ouvido se retirára para a sua chacara, dizendo que não queria saber de nada, e que indo em caminho ouvira tocar o rebate por assim lh'o advertir o desembargador João de Medeiros Gomes (2), com quem se encontrou, admirando-se de que elle sahisse da cidade em tempo em que nella se estava tocando a rebate, ao que lhe replicára não havia percebido que era rebate, e foi seguindo para o seu destino, o que tudo a elle testemunha foi dito pelo referido coronel Francisco Ignacio na sua casa da villa de Santos, em a noite do dia 17 do corrente perante o irmão delle testemunha, o alferes Antonio Joaquim de Oliveira, o tenente João Theodoro Xavier e o tenente Domingos Monteiro, este seu caixeiro e o dito tenente João Theodoro Xavier cobrador da casa Souza Viuva & Filhos, de quem o mesmo coronel Francisco Ignacio de Souza Queiroz é administrador.—Ao nono, disse que sabe por ouvir geralmente que no dia 13 de Maio se projectava pôr em execução o que se realizou no dia 23 pelo que respeita somente o brigadeiro Jordão por ser amigo do coronel Martim e dar-lhe maus conselhos.—Ao decimo, disse que sabe, por ouvir geralmente nesta cidade e na villa de Santos, QUE HAVIA COMMUNICAÇÃO ENTRE O PRESIDENTE DO EXTINCTO GOVERNO JOÃO CARLOS AUGUSTO DE OEYNHAUSEN, O MARECHAL JOAQUIM DE OLIVEIRA ALVARES E O TENENTE CORONEL JOSÉ ANTONIO DA SILVA VALENTE, NO TEMPO DO SEU GOVERNO NA VILLA DE SANTOS, COM AS CÔRTES DE PORTUGAL CONTRA A CAUSA DO BRAZIL, TANTO ASSIM QUE ALGUMA DAS PEÇAS DE ARTILHARIA DA BARRA DE SANTOS SE ACHARAM ENCRAVADAS QUANDO SAHIU DO GOVERNO O DITO TENENTE CORONEL VALENTE, O QUE TAMBEM LHE FORA DITO PELO MARECHAL CANDIDO XAVIER DE ALMEIDA E SOUZA, que lhe succedeu no governo, pois que teve de as mandar desencravar, como asseverou a elle testemunha (3).

---

1 Esta troca de perguntas e respostas entre João Carlos e Francisco Ignacio, quando ambos estavam combinados para a *Bernarda*, parece ter bom fim sómente salvar as apparencias, enganando aos incautos sobre a cumplicidade do governo na conspiração.

2 Era ouvidor de Ytú e tomou parte activa na confederação dos municipios do interior contra os extrangeiros sediciosos da capital.

3 O marechal Joaquim de Oliveira Alvares era ministro do Principe Regente; servindo neste posto, era collega de José Bonifacio e fez guerra aos extrangeiros sedicio-

Disse mais mais que ouvira geralmente nesta cidade e na villa de Santos que havia a mesma communicação entre o presidente do governo, o marechal Oliveira e o coronel Müller, e que assim se presumia a respeito deste pela pessima reedificação que se fez nos fortes daquella villa e montaria das peças, segundo o plano por elle feito, no que se despenderam avultadas sommas inultimente, e mais não disse. E lido o seu juramento, pelo achar conforme ao que havia deposto, se assignou com o referido ministro devassante. E eu, o bacharel formado Manuel Joaquim de Ornellas, escrivão desta devassa o escrevi.—*Freire.* —*Francisco Mariano Galvão Bueno.*

---

## ASSENTADA

Aos 26 dias do mez de Setembro de 1822, nesta cidade de São Paulo, em casas de residencia do doutor Antonio de Almeida Silva Freire da Fonseca, juiz da presente devassa. onde eu escrivão da mesma fui vindo, e seudo ahi por elle ministro foram inqueridas as testemunhas cujos nomes, cognomes, naturalides, moradas, idades, officios, ditos e costumes é tudo o que adeante se segue, do que para constar fiz este termo de assentada. E eu, o bacharel formado, Manuel Joaquim de Ornellas, o escrevi.

### TESTEMUNAA 14.ª

O ALFERES FRANCISCO MARTINS BONILHA (1), solteiro, natural da villa de Porto Feliz e morador da freguezia de São Bernardo, termo desta cidade, que vive de suas lavouras e negocios, de idade de 39 annos; testemunha jurada aos Santos Evangelhos e debaixo do juramento que lhe foi deferido prometteu dizer a verdade do que soubesse e perguntado lhe fosse. E sendo inquerido pelos interrogatorios da presente devassa disse, ao primeiro, que sabe por ser voz publica quem mandára tocar a rebate na tarde do dia 23 de Maio passado e tivera nisso principal influencia fôra o major José Rodrigues Pereira de Oliveira Netto, o qual, repugnando o official de estado maior, que era o tenente Ignacio José de Macedo, lhe puzera uma pistola aos

---

sos de S. Paulo, não podendo, portanto, estar ligado com estes para prejudicar a causa do Brasil, salvo se tinha algum plano seu a executar contra os interesses brazileiros.

1 Pertencia á familia *Toledo Piza* e era primo e sogro do conselheiro Manuel Dias de Toledo; falleceu em '871, deixando grande descendencia, que abrange as familias do conselheiro Olegario Herculano de Aquino e Castro e dr. Antonio Moreira de Barros e bom numero dos actuaes Toledo Piza, o ministro do Tribunal Federal, o ministro brazileiro em Paris e outros, inclusive o auctor destas *Notas.*

peitos e que assim mesmo não consentindo o dito tenente na sua pretenção, ella major mandara tocar ao referido rebate, e que ao mesmo tempo que se tocou a rebate pelas ruas da cidade Joaquim Pedro Maia fora tocar o sino da cadéa para se ajuntarem a Camara e povo, tendo o mesmo rebate por fim a conservação do presidente do extincto governo, João Carlos Augusto de Oeyenhausen, e a deposição dos dous membros delle o coronel Maxtim e o brigadeiro Jordão, DEBAIXO DO FALSO PRETEXTO DE TEREM FEITO OS DITOS DOUS MEMBROS DO GOVERNO VARIAS VIOLENCIAS E INJUSTIÇAS, QUANDO ASSIM NÃO É PORQUE A ELLE TESTEMUNHA SEMPRE CONSTOU SEREM ELLES BENEMERITOS CIDADÃOS E AMANTES DA BÓA ORDEM á vista do que praticaram no tempo em que estiveram no governo, e mais não disse deste.— Ao segundo, disse que sabe, por ter ouvido vulgarmente, que o tenente Jaime da Silva Telles andara convidando e angariando varias pessoas do povo para o motim do dia 23 de Maio passado.— Ao terceiro, disse que sabe pela mesma razão acima dita.que quem puxou a tropa para o largo de S. Gonçalo fora o coronel Francisco Alvares Ferreira do Amaral, a pedido de ceita porção do povo que se achava no quartel, onde elle foi.— Ao quarto disse que quem commandara a tropa no largo de S. Gonçalo, antes de alli chegar o coronel Francisco Ignacio de Souza Queiroz, fora o referido coronel Alvares, com quem o mesmo coronel Francisco Ignacio de Souza Queiroz tivera sua disputa sobre o commando daquella tropa, arguindo-o de o haver tomado sem faculdade sua como chefe da força armada, ao que replicara aquelle coronel Alvares disendo que se encarregara de commandar a tropa por assim lh'o ter requerido o povo, ficado elle coronel Francisco Ignacio desde então com o commando principal da mesma tropa, á frente da qual figurara tambem o brigadeiro Joaqnim José Pinto de Moraes Leme asseverando que o povo, na conformidade de certo alvará, tinha todo o direito para fazer e desfazer qualquer governo, e nada mais disse deste—Ao quinto, disse que é voz publica que o capitão Bento José Leite Penteado, presidente da Camara, na occasião do acontecido motim fora conduzido á força á casa da mesma Camara pelo capitão Pedro Taques de Almeida Alvim.— Ao sexto, disse que sabe por ouvir geralmente que muitas das passoas que assignaram o auto de vereacção extraordinaria do dia 23 de Maio, o fizeram por serem instadas e convidadas pelo tenente Jaime da Silva Telles, persuadindo as de que era vontade unanime do povo o que se havia accordado naquelle auto de vereação. Disse mais que sabe pela mesma razão que no assignado que apparecera para ser lançado fora desta cidade o coronel Mortim dentro em vinte e quatro horas e da provincia dentro de oito dias, figuram

varias pessoas e illudidas e enganadas, ignorando o que assigna-
vam e que o fim de semelhante assignado fora o falso pretexto
de ser elle pernicioso nesta provincia, quando elle testemunha
o considera muito preciso, pois q .e sabe que por alguns factos
por elle praticados, como foram o da publicação de nm bando
para que todo o soldado que tivesse dado dinheiro afim de
não ir na expedição que marchou para o Rio de Janeiro, o de,
nunciasse para lhe ser restitudo e réceber a sua baixa em recompensa, CUJO BANDO A INSTANCIAS SUAS É QUE SE VEIU A PUBLICAR POR
HAVER ENTRE OS DO GOVERNO ALGUNS DE OPINIÃO CONTRARIA COMO ERA
*o presidente*, mostrou bem o seu extraordinario zelo pelo bem
publico, dando a este respeito muitas outras demonstrações, quaes
foram a de se ter opposto a que o capitão Antonio Cardoso N-
gueira, PATROCINADO PELO MESMO PRESIDENTE. arrematasse o córte
do açougue pelo preço que queria, quando havia qnem cortasse
a carne por menor preço, ficando o açouque franco como ficou,
e juntamente a algumas arbitrariedades do ouvidor José da Costa
Carvalho —Ao setimo, disse que sómente sabe por ouvir a algumas pessoas; de cujos nomes se não recorda, que o referido
ouvtdor cooperara para o acontecimento do dia 23 de Maio e
seguintes, aconselhando e fazendo varios papeis tendentes aos
factos então acontecidos.—Ao oitavo disse que não consta a elle
testemunha que o extincto governo desse providencia sobre os
mencionados acontecimentos, nem punisse aos seus auctores e
cooperadores; antes deixára andar na sua liberdade ao capitão
José Fernandes da Silva e ao alferes Fadiga que vieram fogidos
do Rio de Janeiro e sem passaporte (1), e facultára ao mesmo
Fadiga o seu embarque para Portugal, não providenciando tambem o sobre tumulto do quartel, aonde concorreram militares, paizanos, negros, mulatos, forros e captivos ea té um frade franciscano de
nome Frei Antonio do Menino Jesus, armado de pistolas, e o
padre Bernardo Conrado, armado de espada e pistolas (2) por
occasião de constar pue o marechal Condido Xaxier de Almeida
marchava para esta cidade com a sua tropa, da villa de Santos,
afim de fazer cumprir as ordens de Sua Alteza Real, por sua
determinação; bem como se não providenciou o arrombamento da

---

1 Este capitão foi quem commandou a escolta que levou Martim Francisco para o
Rio de Janeiro; era portuguez e muito protegido pelos extrangeiros do governo e seu
alliado Francisco Ignacio, mas depois foi preso e mettido no calabouço da fortaleza de
Santos, processado e absolvido.
2 Este frade parece que não pertencia ao convento de S. Francisco desta capital,
porque o seu nome não é encontrado nas listas de taes frades dos annos de 1818-!822-!826.
Assim tambem o nome do padre Bernardo Conrado não apparece nos recenseamentos
da população desta capital naquelles annos E' de crer que elles tivessem vindo em
commissão politica para açular o povo e dar caracter popular á sedição, que era toda
de retrogrados e de portuguezes.

casa da polvora desta cidade, praticado por uma escolta commandada pelo alferes Fadiga, concorrendo para a conservação deste
tumulto e sua animosidade uma proclamação recitada pelo tenente
Jaime da Silva Telles no mesmo quartel, onde sempre se conservou o coronel Francisco Ignacio de Souza Queiroz, chefe da
força armada, e havia muita comida e bebida. Declarou, porem,
elle testemunha que na falta das referidas qrovidencias não foram comprehendidas os membros do governo thesoureiro-mór
João Ferreira de Oliveira Bueno, o padre-mestre Francisco de
Paula e Oliveira e o tenente coronel André da Silva Gomes,
porque estes, segundo é voz publica, eram de sentimentos contrarios.—Ao nono, disse que é voz publica que já antes do dia
23 de Maio passado se projectava a deposição dos dous membros
do governo, o coronel Martim e o brigadeiro Jordão, celebrando-
se conventiculos a este respeito em um quarto das casas do coronel Francisco Ignacio de Souza Queiroz, na rua Direita (1),
onde se ajuntavam os majores Macedo e Netto, o tenente Jaime
o capitão Pedro Taques de Almeida Alvim e o capitão Antonio
Cardoso Nogueira, sendo apoiados pelo presidente do extincto
governo João Carlos Augusto de Oeynhausen, o ouvidor José
da Costa Carvalho e o coronel Francisco Ignacio de Souza Queiroz,
entre os quaes e os dous membros expulsos é bem publica e
notoria a grande opposição que havia, visto não concordarem
com aquelles em muitas das suas pretenções contrarias ao bem
publico, como acima fica declarado, e mais não disse.—Ao decimo, disse que sabe, por ter ouvido ao tabellião Joaquim Rodrigues Goulart, que *entre o presidente João Carlos Augusto
de Oeyenhausen, o coronel Muller e o marechal Joaquim de Oliveira Alvares havia communicação com as Côrtes de Portugal
contra a causa do Brasil*, dizendo-lhe mais que sabia de muitos factos relativos ao objecto desta devassa (1), e mais não
disse, nem do costume. E lido o seu depoimento, pelo achar
conforme ao que depoz, o assignou com o ministro devassante.

_____

1 Rua Direita n. 3 onde o corenel tinha loja de fazendas: tinha elle então 38 annos, era casado e por algum tempo teve como aggregados o já conhecido tenente Antonio Gonçalves Mamede e Antonio Moreira. Na mesma casa residiam nove escravos de
serviço domestico do mesmo coronel. Em 1826 Mamede já era capitão, com 29 annos,
solteiro, e tinha loja de fazendas na mesma rua Direita, com tres caixeiros, dois aggregados e dois escravos.

1 E' insistente esta referencia a ligações e combinações de João Carlos e a sua
gente com as Côrtes de Lisbôa, que continuava na sua faina de recolonisar o Brasil,
servindo-se dos *bons elementos* de que dispunha nesta parte da colonia. O tabellião Goulart, se fosse chamado a depôr, talvez dissesse cousas curiosas a respeito: porém veio
logo a amnistia, que poz termo a esta importante devassa e assim ficamos privados de
saber toda a extensão da perfidia com que os membros extrangeiros do governo de S.
Paulo e seus alliados tratavam os interesses brazileiros, confiados pelos paulistas á sua
guarda na memoravel revolução de 23 de Maio de 1821.

E eu, o bacharel formado Manoel Joaquim de Ornellas, escrivão
desta devassa, o escrevi. —*Freire.*—*Francisco Martins Bonilha.*

## ASSENTADA

Aos 26 dias do mez de Setembro de 1822, nesta cidade
de S. Paulo, em casas de residencia do doutor Antonio de Almeida Silva Freire da Fonseca, ministro da presente devassa,
onde eu escrivão da mesma fui vindo, e sendo ahi por elle ministro foram inquiridas as testemunhas cujos nomes, cognomes,
naturalidades, moradas, idades, officios, ditos e costumes é tudo
o que adeante se segue, do que para constar fiz este termo de
assentada. E eu, o bacharel formado Manoel Joaquim de Ornellas, o escrevi.

## TESTEMUNHA 15.ª

Tomaz Rodrigues Tocha (1), natural da cidade do Porto,
do reino de Portugal, morador nesta cidade de S. Paulo, onde
vive de ser mestre da fabrica de algodões, de idade de mais de
40 annos; testemunha jurada aos Santos Evangelhos, em um
livro delles em que poz sua mão direita e, debaixo do juramento que prestou, prometteu dizer a verdade do que soubesse
e perguntado lhe fosse. E sendo inquirido pelos interrogatorios
desta devassa disse, ao primeiro, que sabe por ser publico nesta
cidade que quem mandára tocar a rebate na tarde do dia 23 de
Maio passado fora o major José Rodrigues Pereira de Oliveira
Netto e que, oppondo-se a isso o official que estava de estado
maior no quartel, lhe puzera duas pistolas aos peitos, ameaçando com a morte se não mandasse tocar, e por este motivo se
tocou o rebate pelas ruas da cidade e se ajuntaram o povo e
tropa no referido quartel.—Ao segundo, disse que sabe, por
ouvir geralmente, que quem organizára a tropa para marchar
para o largo de São Gonçalo fôra o coronel Francisco Alvares
Ferreira do Amaral, que fôra um dos primeiros que se apresentaram no quartel ao toque do rebate, aonde tambem concorreram muitos outros officiaes e juntamente o brigadeiro Pinto, que
dahi marcharam todos, com o povo e tropa, para o referido
largo.—Ao terceiro, disse que sabe, pela mesma razão de noto·
riedade publica, que a *tropa se não dispoz a marchar para*

---

1 Não obstante ser portuguez e homem obscuro o seu depoimento é de valor e
muito deprimente para os sediciosos.

*aquelle largo de sua propria vontade, mas sim por ser movida a isso pelos seus chefes e officiaes.*—Ao quarto, disse que sabe, tambem por ser publico nesta cidade, que o commandante da tropa no largo de São Gonçalo fôra o mesmo coronel Francisco Alvares Ferreira do Amaral antes de chegar alli o chefe da força armada, o coronel Francisco Ignacio de Souza Queiroz, o qual, logo que alli chegou, arguira ao coronel Alvares de ter tomado o commando da tropa sem sua auctoridade, ao que lhe respondeu o mesmo coronel Alvares que o tomára por ser o primeiro official que se apresentára no quartel e por assim lh'o terem pedido o povo e tropa que se ajuntaram no mesmo quartel, e concluida esta palliativa disputa tomou o commando da tropa o referido chefe da força armada, o coronel Francisco Ignacio de Souza Queiroz, conservando-se na frente o sobredito coronel Francisco Alvares Ferreira do Amaral, o brigadeiro Pinto e varios officiaes subalternos, como os majores Macedo e Netto, o capitão Pedro Taques de Almeida Alvim, o capião Antonio Cardoso Nogueira e o tenente Jaime da Silva Telles, o qual com o capitão Pedro Taques e o major Netto, principalmente se distinguiu no acontecido motim, que teve por objecto a conservação do presidente do extincto governo João Carlos Augusto de Oeynbausen, contra as ordens de Sua Alteza Real, e a deposição dos membros do mesmo governo o coronel Martim e o brigadeiro Jordão, *propugnando por uma e outra cousa com o maior exforço, grandes vozes e alaridos e com o figurado nome do povo* o mencionado tenente Jaime da Silva Telles.— Ao quinto, disse que ouviu falar geralmente que o presidente da Camara, que então era o capitão Bento José Leite Penteado, fôra levado á força para a casa da mesma Camara.—Ao sexto, disse que sabe pela mesma razão de ter ouvido falar e TAMBEM POR PRESENCIAR QUE MUITAS DAS PESSOAS QUE ASSIGNARAM O AUTO DE VEREAÇÃO EXTRAORDINARIA, BEM COMO O ASSIGNADO EM VIRTUDE DO QUAL SE FIZERA SAHIR O CORONEL MARTIM DESTA CIDADE DENTRO EM VINTE HORAS E DA PROVINCIA DENTRO EM OITO DIAS, O FIZERAM INSTADAS, ILLUDIDAS E ATEMORIZADAS COM RECEIO DE ALGUMA VIOLENCIA E ATÉ MESMO IGNORANDO ALGUNS O FIM A QUE SE DIRIGIA SEMELHANTE ASSIGNADO.—Ao setimo, disse que presume ter o coronel Francisco Ignacio de Souza Queiroz cooperado para o acontecimento do dia 23 de Maio em razão de lhe ter asseverado em sua casa Fortunato Correa de Mello por muitas vezes e muitos dias antes daquelle acontecimento, *que o referido coronel Francisco Ignacio de Souza Queiroz é quem havia de esmagar o coronel Martim dentro de bem pouco tempo, dizendo que assim se tinha tra-*

*tado com elle Mello.* Disse mais que indo á casa delle tes temunha o sobredito Mello depois do mesmo motim lhe perguntára em ar de chufa se não tinha sido esmagado Martim Francisco, como lh'o havia communicado, ao que replicando elle testemunha que oxalá lhe não custasse bem caro semelhante procedimento, lhe respondeu que tuto se tinha feito com muita segurança e legalidade.—Ao oitavo disse que lhe não consta que o extincto governo, em que nada influiam os tres membros thesoureiro-mór João Ferreira de Oliveira Bueno, o padre-mestre Francisco de Paula e Oliveira e o tenente-coronel André da Silva Gomes, nenhumas providencias dera sobre aquelle motim e suas consequencias, nem tão pouco castigasse os seus auctores; antes parecia approval-os, olhando mal e até punindo os que eram de opinião contraria, *como acontec*u *com a alferes Joaquim Alvim, que, por ter increpado a seu irmão o capitão Pedro Taques de Almeida Alvim por ter sido um dos cabeças do acontecido motim* (1), *foi degredado para a villa de S. Carlos.* Disse mais que tambem lhe não consta que o mencionado governo, composto do intendente Miguel José de Oliveira Pinto, do coronel Francisco Ignacio de Souza Queiroz, do coronel Müller e do tenente-coronel Antonio Maria Quartim (2), se se tratasse de obstar o ajuntamento da tropa, paizanos, negros, mulatos, forros e captivos, no quartel, onde todos foram municiados de polvora e bala e armados de patronas e armas reiunas, *Para alli convidados pelo capitão Pedro Taques, majores Macedo e Netto e tenentes Jaime e Mamede, todos apaniguados do coronel Fraucisco Ignacio,* e outros levados á força para o mesmo quartel, onde estiveram por alguns dias, tendo por seus capellães ao frade franciscano Frei Antonio do Menino Jesus e o padre Bernardo Conrado, ambos armados de pistolas, e sendo sustentados com comidas e muito vinho e aguardente, que tudo era subministrado pelo capitão Pedro Taques e tenentes Jaime e Mamede á custa do coronel Francisco Ignacio (3), menos duzentas garrafas de vinho mandadas pelo capitão Francisco Gonçalves dos Santos Cruz, o que sabe por ter ouvido geralmente, bem como

---

1 Foi simplesmente braço forte e dos mais turbulentos da sedição, mas não tinha cabeça para ser chefe; perdeu o juizo algum tempo depois e viveu muitos annos nesse triste estado Os seus irmãos Joaquim Alvim e José Innocencio Alvim eram espiritas liberaes e foram os auctores da deposição de João Carlos em 23 de Junho de 1821.

2 Isto depois de 21 de Julho de 1822, quando João Carlos já tinha seguido para o Rio. em companhia do seu amigo e cumplice Costa Carvalho. Sentia-se bem o coronel paulistá Francisco Ignacio na companhia destes tres extrangeiros sediciosos e senhores de governo de S. Paulo por um atrevido golpe de Estado.

3 Esta affirmação traz alguma luz sobre os factos, pois Mamede residia na propria casa do coronel Francisco Ignacio, era seu commensal, sua creatura, e só algum tempo depois foi que montou loja de fazendas, provavelmente abonado, auxiliado, por aquelle coronel em paga dos serviços que lhe prestára.

que o fim daquelle ajuntamento no quartel fora o impedir a entrada do marechal Candido Xavier de Almeida e Souza, que
marchava da villa de Santos com a sua tropa para esta cidade
para fazer cumprir as ordens de Sua Alteza Real, constando mais
a elle testemunha que na occasião do primeiro motim fora arrombada a casa da polvora por uma escolta commandada pelo
alferes Fadiga.—Ao nono, disse que se refere ao que depoz ao
setimo interrogatorio, DECLARANDO QUE A VERDADEIRA CAUSA DA
DEPOSIÇÃO DO CORONEL MARTIM FORA A INDISPOSIÇÃO QUE HOUVE
CONTRA ELLE POR SE HAVER OPPOSTO Á ARREMATAÇÃO DO AÇOUGUE
DESTA CIDADE, PRETENDIDA PELO CAPITÃO NOGUEIRA E SEUS SOCIOS
por muito maior preço do que veiu a ficar estando o córte
franco, por influencia e instancias do mesmo coronel Martim, e
ter feito publicar um bando, a grande pezar de alguns dos seus
collegas do governo, para que todo o soldado que tivesse dado
dinheiro para não ir na expedição que marchou desta cidade
para o Rio de Janeiro, o declarasse para lhe ser restituido e
teria em recompensa a sua baixa.—Ao decimo, disse que sabe
por ter ouvido muitas vezes em sua casa a Fortunato Correa de
Mello (1) que nunca haveria cortes no Brasil emquanto elle e
outros quizessem e elle Mello tivesse mão e pena, assim como
tambem que o marechal Oliveira é quem havia de enforcar o
conselheiro José Bonifacio de Andrada e Silva. E perguntando-lhe elle testemunha, por simplicidade, que razão tinha para
tal asseverar, lhe respondeu que o sabia porque via, por cartas
em casa do coronel Müller, a correspondencia que havia entre
este e o referido marechal Oliveira, donde conclue haver communicação entre elles e as Côrtes de Portugal contra a causa
do Brasil, dizendo-lhe mais que cá se não fazia caso algum dos
avisos de Sua Alteza Real, nem delle mesmo, ainda que cá
viesse (2), e que porisso podia mandar quantos quizesse; e nada
mais disse, nem do costume. E lido o seu depoimento, pelo
achar conforme ao que havia deposto, o assignou com o ministro
inquisidor. E eu, o bacharel formado Manoel Joaquim de Ornellas, escrivão desta devassa, o escrevi.—*Freire.*—*Thomaz Rodrigues Tocha.*

1 Era militar portuguez, imigrado para Sl Paulo por turbulento e rixoso; foi pae
de dois filhos notaveis: Joaquim Corrêa de Mello naturalista de merito, e do capitão Tito
Correa de Mello homem intelligente e chefe politico a quem se attribue muitos males que
tem affligido a certa zona do interior de S. Paulo.
2 De longe não faziam caso das ordens, nem da pessoa de D. Pedro, e até diziam
que podiam ir ao Rio passar-lhe o chicote; mas quando o Principe veiu a S. Paulo se
apresaram em render-lhe cumprimentos, que foram recusados!

## ASSENTADA

Aos 30 dias do mez de Setembro de 1822, nesta cidade de
São Paulo, em casas de residencia d* doutor Antonio de Almeida Silva Freire da Fonseca, ministro da presente devassa, onde
eu escrivão da mesma fui vindo, e sendo ahi foram por elle inquiridas as testemunhas cujos nomes, cognomes, naturalidades,
moradas, idades, officios e costumes é tudo o que adeante se
segue, do que para constar fiz este termo de assentada.—·E eu,
o bacharel formado Manoel Joaquim de Ornellas, o escrevi.

## TESTEMUNHA 16

O SARGENTO MÓR JOSÉ MARIA DE MELLO (1), solteiro, natural da provincia de Traz dos Montes, do reino de Portugal,
morador nesta cidade, onde vive do seu soldo, de idade de 33
annos ; testemunha jurada aos Santos Evangelhos e debaixo do
juramento que lhe foi deferido promotteu dizer a verdade e
perguntado lhe fosse. E sendo inquirido pelos interrogatorios
da presente devassa disse, ao primeiro, que sabe por ter ouvido
geralmente nesta cidade que quem mandára tocar a rebate, na
tarde do dia 23 de Maio do corrente anno, fora o major José
Rodrigues Pereira de Oliveira Netto, forçando para isso, com
uma pistola aos peitos, ao official do estado maior, que então
era o tenente Ignacio José de Macedo, e que o fim deste rebate tinha sido o congregarem-se o povo e tropa para obstar a sahida do
presidente do extincto governo João Carlos Augusto de Oyenhausen,
que era chamado a côrte do Rio de Janeiro por ordem de Sua Alteza
Real, fazel-o conservar na presidencia do mesmo governo e ex-
púlsar delle aos dous membros, o coronel Martim Francisco
Ribeiro de Andrada e o brigadeiro Manoel Rodrigues Jordão,
*com o figurado pretexto* de ser o dito presidente muito interessante a esta provincia e, pelo contrario. damnosos os dous mem-
bros expulsos, QUANDO ASSIM NÃO ERA PORQUE NA OPINIÃO PUBLICA
AQUELLE PRESIDENTE ERA OPPOSTO AOS VERDADEIROS INTERESSES
DA PROVINCIA E Á CAUSA DE TODO O BRASIL E OS REFERIDOS DOUS
MEMBROS TRABALHARAM QUANTO LHES FOI POSSIVEL PELO BEM GE-
RAL DA MESMA PROVINCIA, PRINCIPALMENTE NO ARTIGO DAS FIANÇAS,
COMO É PUBLICO E NOTORIO (2), assim como tambem é voz geral

---

1 Moço ainda. era já major, o que denota que não pertencia á plebe [portugueza
o seu depoimento é dos mais importantes pela gravidade dos factos que narra e pela
segurança com que affirma suas opiniões.
2 Estas affirmações e as que immediatamente se seguem, sendo feitas por um portuguez e militar, têm dobrado valor e são esmagadoras para os sediciosos do 26 de
Maio de 1823.

que o coronel Martim viera a adquirir varios inimigos por se ter opposto á arrematação do corte do açougue por maior preço do que podia ficar, como ficou, estando franco, e juntamente por ter sido a causa efficiente, ·com o brigadeiro Jordão, de se haver publicado um bando para que todo o miliciano que tivesse dado dinheiro para rão ir na expedição que marchou para a côrte do Rio de Janeiro o declarasse para lhe ser restituido e reeeber a sua baixa em recompensa, *bem como por se oppor elle*, coronel Martim, a *varias arbitr..riedades do ouvidor José da Costa Carvalho*, COMO ELLE TESTEMUNHA PRESENCIOU a respeito da galera *Conceição Esperança*, e mais não disse.—Ao segundo, disse que sabe por ter ouvido geralmente que o coronel Francisco Ignacio de Souza Queiroz, commandante da força armada na occasião do rebate, fora quem o mandou tocar e que por effeito de haver Joaquim Pedro Maia tocado o sino da cadêa ao tempo do toque do rebate se congregaram certa porção de povo no largo de São Gonçalo (1), ONDE ELLE TESTEMUNHA ACHANDO-SE POR ALGUM TEMPO OUVIU AO TENENEE JAIME DA SILVA TELLES PROFERIR Á FRENTE DA TROPA QUE SUA ALTEZA REAL ERA UM DESPOTA E QUE EM TUDO SE DEVIA ESTAR PELAS DECISÕES DAS CORTES DE PORTUGAL, não podendo Sua Alteza Real tirar o presidente do governo por isso mesmo que tinha sido feito pelo povo (2). Disse mais, por haver acontecido com elle testemunha, *que o Netto o quizera matar naquelle largo*, armado de espada e pistola, *por ser ajudante de ordens do inspector geral de milicias*, o marechal Arouche (3), e por não ter acodido ao rebate, *mas não se realizou a sua pretenção por se ouvir uma voz que o major impediu de a realizar.*—Ao terceiro, disse que sabe, por ser voz publica, que o major Netto e o capitão Pedro Taques de Almeida Alvim angariaram e reduziram a tropa do quartel para se reunir e marchar para o largo de São Gonçalo. — Ao quarto, disse que sabe, por ver á frente da tropa, que o coronel Francisco Alvares Ferreira do Amaral fora quem a commandára no referido largo, estando á frente da mesma tropa o tenente coronel Jeronimo Pereira Chrispim, os majores Netto

---

1 Foi realmente uma certa porção do povo, a arraia miuda, como disseram Machado de Oliveira e André Gomes. Essa mesma gente foi em seguida levada para a sala da Camara a assignar a acta de vereação forçada, redigida por Costa Carvalho e seu escrivente Amaro Vieira.

2 O discurso de Jaime da Silva Telles não tinha valor pelo orador, que era um velho roceiro menos que remediado do bairro da *Emboaçaba*, mas valia como expressão do pensamento de João Carlos, Francisco Ignacio, Oliveira Pinto, Muller. Quartim, Costa Carvalho e outros representantes da tyrannia colonial.

3 Arouche não estava em S. Paulo, mas no valle do Parahyba, e o depoente esteve a pagar com a vida o crime de ter sido seu ajudante de ordens e de não ter adherido á *Bernarda*.

e Macedo, os capitães Gaspar Antonio de Souza, Joaquim Ignacio Ribeiro e Caetano Pinto Homem, os tenentes Jaime, Mamede e Francisco Antonio Pinto Bastos, por alcunha *O Patarata* (1) e outros, de cujos nomes se não lembra; constando-lhe por voz publica que tambem estivera á frente da tropa o brigadeiro Joaquim José Pinto de Moraes Leme e citára um alvará em apoio daquelle motim.—Ao quinto, disse que sabe, por ter ouvido ao proprio juiz presidente (2) e a muitas outras pessoas, que elle fôra constrangido pelo capitão Pedro Taques de Almeida Alvim para ir sem demora para a casa da Camara, *ameaçando-o de que, não querendo ir por bem, iria por mal.*—Ao sexto, disse nada.—Ao setimo, disse que sabe, por ouvir geralmente e em particular ao tenente coronel João Pereira Simões, que João Caalos Augusto de Oeynhausen, presidente do extincto governo, concorrera para o referido motim, visto que algumas horas antes do seu acontecimento estiveram com elle presidente alguns dos quaes figuraram no mesmo motim. como foram o capitão Nogueira, os majores Macedo e Modesto e o capitão Pedro Taques de Almeida Alvim. Disse mais, por ter ouvido geralmente, que o coronel Francisco Ignacio de Souza Queiroz cooperára para o referido motim, endo o ouvidor José da Costa Carvalho quem déra o plano para varios papeis relativos a tal objecto.—Ao oitavo disse que sabe, porque presenciou e ouviu que fôra pessimo o comportamento do extincto governo desde o dia 23 de Maio passado em diante, exceptuando os tres membros thesoureiro mór João Ferreira de Oliveira Bueno, padre-mestre Francisco de Paula e Oliveira e tenente coronel André da Silva Gomes, por serem de sentimentos contrarios aos dos outros empregados no dito governo, visto que nenhumas providencias déra sobre o acautelar-se aquelle motim, nem punira de fórma alguma os seus fautores, antes parecia apoiar os seus procedimentos, vindo por essa causa a ficarem mais animosos e desenfreados para continuarem nas suas desenvolturas, como mostraram no successo do quartel, onde o intendente Miguel José de Oliveira Pinto animou publicamente o povo e tropa alli existentes para se não cumprirem as ordens de Sua Alteza Real que o marechal Candido Xavier de Almeida e Souza vinha fazer cumprir, *persuadindo-lhes que elle marechal vinha saquear a cidade com a sua tropa e beber o sangue de seus irmãos* (3), achan-

---

1 Era, com Caetano Pinto, commensal da casa do coronel Francisco Alvares, onde morava de favor com o nome de «aggregado».
2 Capitão Bento José Leite Penteado, juiz de fora pela lei e presidente da Camara Municipal.
3 Logo adiante se fala em *populaça embriagada com cachaça*, que representava o papel do povo ausente nos successos da *Bernarda*; a tal gente era facil illudir com estas phrases calumniosas.

do-se alli armados militares, paizanos, negros, mulatos forros e até um frade franciscano de nome Frei Antonio do Menino Jesus e o padre Bernardo Conrado, comendo e bebendo por varios dias a custa do commandante da força armada, o coronel Francisco Ignacio de Souza Queiroz, segundo elle testemunha ouviu dizer geralmente, o qual se achou alli effectivamente de dia e de noite a titulo de conter o ajuntamento aquartelado. Disse mais que tambem nenhumas medidas tomára sobre o arrombamento da casa da Polvora praticado por uma escolta commandada pelo alferes Fadiga, NEM TÃO POUCO SOBRE O FRANQUEAMENTO DAS ARMAS TIRADAS DO TREM E DADAS Á POPULAÇÃO EMBRIAGADA PELA CACHAÇA PELOS CAIXEIROS DE GABRIEL HENRIQUES PESSOA (1) comprehendendo-se nella até escravos, como foram dous mulatos do coronel Francisco Pinto Ferraz, NÃO SE TENDO MANDADO DEVASSAR SOBRE AS VOCIFERAÇÕES CONTTA SUA ALTEZA REAL E SEU GOVERNO e varias proclamações que appareceram em *abandono* do mesmo Senhor (2), quando praticára o contrario a respeito de outros papeis que atacavam alguns do governo e até consentindo que andassem soltos dous desertores, o capitão José Fernandes da Silva e o alferes Fadiga, que tinham regressado da côrte do Rio de Janeiro sem ordem. — Ao nono, disse que sabe por. ouvir geralmente, que em casa do coronel Francisco Ignacio de Souza Queiroz se fizeram dous ajuntamentos secretos para o projectado acontecimento do dia 23 de Maio passado, figurando nelles o presidente João Carlos Augusto de Oeynhausen, o ouvidor José da Costa Carvalho. o major .. (3)..., o capitão Nogueira, os tenentes Jayme e Mamede, Gabriel Henrique Pessoa e José Manuel de Abreu. —Ao decimo, disse que presume *ter havido communicação occulta entre as Côrtes de Portugal e alguns dos empregados do extincto governo contra a causa do Brasil e seu Defensor Perpetuo, tanto pelas proclamações indicadas no interrogatorio oitavo como pela qualidade de meios de que se serviram para indispor e incendiar todas as classes de pessoas e trazel-as aos seus fins,* QUE PARECE NÃO SE INCAMINHAVAM SÓMENTE Á EXPULSÃO DOS DOUS MEMBROS DO MESMO GOVERNO, O CORONEL MARTIM E O BRIGADEIRO JORDÃO. Disse finalmente que sobre este objecto sabe que um mez antes de ser deposto

---

1 Era portuguez, natural de Lisboa, solteiro, de 30 annos e negociante de fazenda e ferragens na rua Direita, n. 45, com um caixeiro e cinco escravos, secundo o recenseamento de 1822. Naturalmente empregou mais caixeiros ou alguns escravos na venda da cachaça para acudir a boa freguezia que a *Bernarda* lhe forneceu.

2 Aqui deve-se ler: «em desabono do mesmo Senhor»: a palavra está emendada no original, mas muito legivel.

3 O nome está illegivel por estar o papel roto neste logar, mas deve ser «major Machado» ou «major Netto», os dois majores mais interessados na *Bernarda* de 23 de Maio e nas suas consequencias.

ministro da Guerra, o marechal Oliveira, havia communicação
entre elle e alguns membros do governo extincto, a qual tinha
por objecto fazer suscitar na côrte do Rio de Janeiro, por via
do coronel de caçadores Lazaro José Gonsalves, um motim igual
ao acontecido nesta cidade em o dia 23 de Maio passado, afim
de facilitar e promover o plano das Côrtes, assim como se havia
de obrigar Sua Alteza Real a obedecer a seu pae, logo que chegasse a esta cidade de São Paulo, o que tudo ouviu o doutor
Justiniano de Mello Franco (1), e mais não disse, nem do costume. E lido o seu juramento, pelo achar conforme ao que
havia deposto, o assignon com o ministro devassante. E eu,
o bacharel formado Manoel Joaquim de Ornellas, escrivão desta
devassa, o escrevi. — *Freire.* — *José Maria de Mello.*

## ASSENTADA

Aos 30 dias do mez de Setembro de 1822, nesta cidade de
São Paulo, em casa de residencia do doutor Antonio de Almeida
Silva Freire da Fonseca, ministro desta devassa, onde eu escrivão della me achava, e sendo ahi foram por elle inquiridas as
testemunhas, cujos nomes, cognomes, naturalidades, moradas, idades, officios, ditos e costumes e tudo o que adeante se segue, do
que para constar fiz este termo de assentada. E eu o bacharel, formado Manuel Joaquim de Ornellas, o escrevi.

## TESTEMUNHA 17.ª

Francisco de Paula Xavier de Toledo (2), natural e morador desta cidade, onde vive de sua arte de cirurgia, de idade
de 59 annos; testemunha jurada aos Santos Evangelhos, em um

---

1 A parte deste depoimento relativa á communicação que os sediciosos de S. Paulo
tinham com o governo de Lisboa está de accordo com outros depoimentos anteriores e
bem justificada pela natureza dos acontecimentos narrados. pelas condições politicas e
sociaes de provincias em 1822 e pelo caracter dos chefes sediciosos: porem a referencia
feita a Lazaro Gonçalves precisa de mais apoio. porquanto, se fosse verdade que este
coronel dos caçadores pretendia fazer no Rio um motim igual ao que houve em S. Paulo
não havia necessidade de abrir elle lucta com os portuguezes do general Avillez, visto
que aquillo que desejava o general portuguez era isto mesmo quo se attribue a Lazaro
Gonçalves, isto é, obrigar D. Pedro a obedecer a seu pae e restabelecer o dominio aba-
lado dos portuguezes nas provincias brasileiras, do Rio ao Sul. O marechal Oliveira Alvares, como ministro da guerra, tambem se mostrou energico contra os facciosos de S.
Paulo. como se collige dos documentos officiaes daquelle tempo, e será necessario provas
*materiaes* para se crer que elle procedia abertamente de uma forma e occultamente de
forma contraria. Entretanto outras testemunhas, adeante ainda repetem esta referencia
de modo a tornar mysteriosamente contradictorio o procedimento de Oliveira Alvares.
2 Em um recenseamento da 5.ª companhia de ordenança da cidade de S. Paulo,
feito em 1818, lê que Francisco de Paula Xavier de Toledo era natural desta cidade, de
52 annos de idade, viuvo, branco, cirurgião e morador na casa n. 4 da Travessa do Col-

livro delles em que poz sua mão direita e, debaixo do juramento que prestou, prometteu dizer a verdade do que soubesse e perguntado lhe fosse. E sendo inquirido pelos interrogatorios da presente devassa disse, ao primeiro, que sabe por ser publico nesta cidade e lhe ter contado o tenente Ignacio José de Macedo, que estava de estado maior na occasião do rebate, que fora o major Netto quem o mandára tocar, forçando para isso ao dito tenente com uma pistola que lhe poz aos peitos, e deste mais não disse.—Ao segundo, disse que sabe por ser voz publica, que o coronel Francisco Aivares Ferreira do Amaral, os majores Macedo e Netto, os capitães Pedro Taques de Almeida Alvim e Antonio Cardoso Nogueira, os tenentes Jaime e Mamede, o tenente coronel Jeronimo Pereira Chrispim, o tenente Francisco Antonio Pinto Bastos, vulgarmente chamado o *Patarata*, e o alferes Fadiga foram os que dispuzeram a tropa para se congregar no largo de São Gonçalo na occasião do motim.— Ao terceiro, disse que se refere ao que expoz no segundo.—Ao quarto, disse que, por ser publico e ter ouvido ao tenente Ignacio José de Macedo, sabe que o commandante da tropa para o largo de São Gonçalo fora o referido coronel Alvares, tomando o commando do tenente coronel Antonio de Padua de Gusmão, que era o commandante do destacamento, e pondo-se alli á frente da mesma tropa com outros officiaes, como foram o brigadeiro Pinto e os demais officiaes indicados no seu depoimento ao segundo interrogatorio, bem como tambem o commandante da fcrça armada, coronel Francisco Ignacio de Souza Queiroz —Ao quinto, disse que por ser voz publica sabe que o capitão Pedro Taques de Almeida Alvim levára a força para a casa da Camara ao presidente da mesma Camara, capitão Bento José Leite Penteado.—Ao sexto, disse que lhe consta serem *convidados* para assignarem o auto de vereação extraordinaria do dia 23 muitas das pessoas que alli se acham assignadas (2), ASSIGNANDO VOLUNTARIAMENTE OS CAPITÃES ANTONIO DE SIQUEIRA MORAES E CAETANO PINTO HOMEM, QUE DE SEU MOTU PROPRIO FIGURARAM DE VERIADORES NAQUELLE AUTO, NÃO O SENDO, bem como o procu-

---

legio ; que tinha um filho, Joaquim Floriano de Toledo, de 22 annos, solteiro, alferes de milicias e morador na mesma casa, onde tambem residia a aggregada Thereza Maria de Toledo, de 55 annos, solteira e branca  O cirurgião tinha dois escravos africanos. Seu filho Joaquim Floriano fez figura na politica e foi sogro do visconde de Ouro Preto, do desembargador Tito de Mattos e do advogado Oliveira Braga.

1 *Convidadas* é um modo suave de dizer a cousa. porque os convites eram feitos á bocca de uma pistola ou á ponta da espada, como o que se fez ao proprio presidente da Camara para ir abrir a sessão e assignar aquella mesma acta, redigida por Amaro Vieira sob as ordens e inspirações de Costa Carvalho, um dos chefes sediciosos.

rador effectivo Luiz Manuel da Cunha Bastos (1), e que igualmente lhe consta que os majores Macedo e Netto, o capitão Nogueira e o tenente Bastos, por alcunha *O Patarata*, andaram de casa em casa a solicitar a assignatura de um dos papeis que enviaram para o Rio de Janeiro (2), CHEGANDO MESMO A AMEAÇAR A ALGUNS DOS QUE O NÃO O QUIZERAM ASSIGNAR —Ao setimo, disse que sabe, por ser tambem voz publica, que o coronel Francisco Ignacio de Souza Queiroz cooperára para o acontecido motim e seus apaniguados acima indicados, para o effeito de ser conservado o presidente do extincto governo João Carlos Augusto de Oeynhausen contra as ordens de Sua Alteza Real (3), que o mandava ir para a côrte do Rio de Janeiro, e de serem lançados fora do governo o coronel Martim Francisco Ribeiro de Andrada e o brigadeiro Manoel Rodrigues Jordão por intrigas que havia entre o coronel Francisco Ignacio de Souza Queiroz e os dous membros depostos, ignorando elle testemunha a causa dessas intrigas (4) e constando-lhe SÓMENTE QUE AQUELLES DOUS MEMBROS DEPOSTOS SEMPRE SE COMPORTARAM BEM NO EXERCICIO DOS SEUS SEUS EMPREGOS E TINHAM A SEU FAVOR A OPINIÃO PUBLICA.—Ao oitavo, disse que sabe por ter presenciado que os empregados no extincto governo, á excepção do thesoureiro-mór João Ferreira de Oliveira Bueno do padre mestre Francisco de Paula e Oliveira e do tenente, coronel André da Silva Gomes, que eram de sentimentos aos dos outros seus collegas e nada influiam nas decisões do governo (5), nenhumas providencias

1 Alguns vereadores, aterrados com as desordens do dia 23 de Maio, se esconderam para escaparem das violencias dos facciosos; então Siqueira Moraes e Caetano Pinto, sediciosos e vereadores transactos, isto é, da Camara anterior, se offereceram para irem occupar os logares vagos e campar de vereadores! Como taes elles estão assignados naquella acta falsa!

(2) Este papel que os sediciosos enviaram ao Rio não deixou copia. Se foi dirigido a D Pedro representa um desmentido a affirmação oos facciosos de que José Bonifacio não consentia que papel algum chegasse ás mãos do Principe Fegente; e se não foi dirigido ao Principe, tanto peor para elles, pois só poderia ser dirigido aos cumplices do Rio.

(3) Estas ordens de D. Pedro são as que constam da portaria de 10 de Maio de 1822; não serviram então para mais do que futil pretexto, visto que a sedição esteve preparada para 3 de Maio e fora adiada para 13 e, finalmente, realisada a 23. Ora, a 3 e a 13 de Maio não se tratava de conservar os *muitos necessarios* João Carlos e Costa Carvalho e a sedição não tinha um pretexto que parecesse viavel e que surgiu naquella portaria.

(4) O depoente não quis se referir ás causas das intrigas, que aliás já foram expostas pelos depoimentos anteriores e foram o monopollio gorado das carnes verdes, e o bando para restituição aos soldados de dinheiros recebidos por officiaes venaes e suas amasias para livral-os da expedição ao Rio, as arbitrariedades citadas de Costa Carvalho, já de casamento tratado com a sogra de Francisco Ignacio, e a necessidade que o ouvidor de S. Paulo sentia de remover os Andradas do seu caminho politico.

(5) Não influiam nas decisões do governo porque João Ferreira e André Gomez eram velhos de 70 annos, porque João Ferreira e Paula Oliveira eram clerigos e não militares, porque todos tres eram homens pacificos e incapazes de lucta activa e perigosa e, finalmente, porque eram sómente 3 contra 5—João Carlos, Oliveira Pinto, Müller,

deram para se cohibir o motim do dia 23 de Maio passado e as desordens acontecidas, como foram a dos quarteis e o arrombamento da casa da Polvora, nem tão pouco obstaram a reunião de alguns escravos no quartel, onde foram municiados e armados nem fizeram punir os auctores de taes desordens, consentindo de mais a mais que se conservassem tambem no quartel, armados, frade franciscano Frei Antonio do Menino Jesus e o padre Bernardo Conrado : cujo ajuntamento no quartel tivera por obejecto o obstar a entrada do masechal Candido nesta cidade para fazer cumprir as ordens de Sua Alteza Real. Disse mais que o arrombamento da casa da Polvora fora feito pelo alferes Fadiga, com uma escolta que levou comsigo, para a municiar e a mais gente armada, o coronel Francisco Ignacio de Souza Queiroz, como certificou a elle testemunha o mesmo Fadiga, que de mais mais se lhe gabou de ter elle mesmo feito aquelle arrombamento com a sua escolta, do que resultou vir a faltar muita polvora. — Ao nono, disse que sabe, por lhe dizer o capitão Antonio de Siqueira Moraes em sua casa, que já antes do dia 33 .de Maio passado se projectava aquelle acontecimento, NA ESPERANÇA DE QUE TAMBEM O CONSELHEIRO JOSÉ BONIFACIO DE ANDRADE E SILVA ESTAVA PARA SER EXPULSO DO MINISTERIO, o que tendo elle testemunha ouvido o reprehendeu e nunca mais lá voltou á sua casa (1). Disse, finalmente, por ter ouvido ao tabellião Joaquim Rodrigues Goulart, que na rua de São Bento se faziam conventiculos em certa casa, onde se ajuntavam o padre Frei José Tondella (2) e outros, e que tambem se faziam os mesmos conventiculos em casa do coronel Müller (3), e nada mais disse deste, nem do costume, E lido o seu juramento, pelo achar conforme ao que havia deposto, e assignou com o ministro inquiridor. E eu, o bacharel formado Manoel Joaquim de Ornellas, escrivão desta devassa, o escrevi. — *Freire.* — *Francisco de Paula Xavier de Toledo.*

---

Quartim e Francisco Ignacio—e nas assembléas o numero vence sempre. Vergueiro e Pelisberto Jardim não compareciam ás sessões, Lazaro e Gama Lobo estavam no Rio. Martim e Jordão depostos, e os sediciosos se fizeram senhores do governo como da sua propria casa.

(1) Esta ligação entre os sediciosos de S Paulo e do Rio devia realmente existir para ser mencionada por Siqueira Moraes, um dos facciosos desta capital, homem de certa posição social e ex-vereador da Camara. Este disse ao deponte que José Bonifacio devia ser expulso, mas o militar portuguez Fortunato Correa de Mello dissera ao outro deponte José Maria de Mello que o futuro PATRIARCHA DA INDEPENDENCIA seria enforcado pelo seu proprio collega Oliveira Alvares, ministro da Guerra do Principe Regente.

(2) O nome deste frade, assim como o do turbulento Frei Antonio do Menino Jesus, o héroe dos quarteis de S. Paulo, não está nas listas dos frades existentes nos conventos desta capital. Devia ser *missionario* politico vindo de fora.

(3) Müller devia ter 40 annos e morava na rua Detraz da Boa Morte, n. 50, com sua senhora, um filho e quatro filhas, todos menores, e dois escravos. Vivia do seu soldo e era visinho de parede e meia com o seu cumplice João Theodoro Xavier.

## ASSENTADA

Aos 2 dias do mez de Outubro de 1822, nesta cidade de
São Paulo, em casas de residencia do doutor Antonio de Almeida
Silva Freire da Fonseca, ministro da presente devassa, onde eu
escrivão della me achava, e sendo ahi foram pelo sobredito ministro inqueridas as testemunhas cujos nomes, cognomes, naturalidades, moradas, idades, officios, ditos e costumes é tudo o
que adeante se segue, do que para constar lavrei o presente
termo de assentada. E eu, o bacharel formado Manuel Joaquim
de Ornellas, o escrevi.

### TESTEMUNHA 18.ª

O BRIGADEIRO FRANCISCO ANTONIO DE PAULA NOGUEIRA DA
GAMA (1), natural da villa de São João de El-Rei, comarca do
Rio das Mortes da Provincia de Minas Geraes. e morador desta
cidade, onde vive dos seus soldos, de 48 annos; testemunha
jurada aos Santos Evangelhos, em um livro delles em que poz
sua mão direita e. debaixo do juramento que prestou, prometteu
dizer a verdade do que soubesse e perguntado lhe fosse. E sendo
inquerido pelos interrogatorios desta devassa disse, ao primeiro, que
sabe por ser publico e ter ouvido ao capitão Pedro Taques de Almeida
Alvim, nesta cidade, que quem mandára tocar a rebate na tarde
do dia 23 de Maio passado fora o major José Rodrigues Pereira
de Oliveira Netto, acompanhado de grande numero de officiaes,
como foram o coronel Francisco Alvares Ferreira do Amaral, o
tenente Jaime da Silva Telles, o major Francisco de Paula Macedo, o capitão Antonio Cardoso Nogueira e o tenente-coronel
Jeronimo Pereira Chrispim, forçando o referido major Netto para
esse effeito ao official do estado-maior, tenente Ignacio José de
Macedo, por meio de uma pistola que lhe poz aos peitos, visto
a sua opposição para o mencionado rebate, e espancando ao mesmo
tempo aos tambores para que se apressassem a tocal-o, e sabe
pela mesma razão que aquelle major Netto e seus consocios se

---

(1) A familia *Nogueira da Gama* foi sempre importante e têm tido membros que se
salientaram na sociedade fluminense. Este official assentou praça como voluntario, em
1791, em Minas, e veiu para S. Paulo em 1809, já com o posto de major de cavallaria;
voltou para Minas em 1810, com o posto de tenente coronel e lá ficou até 1814, quando
foi nomeado ajudante de ordens do governo de S. Paulo, com a patente de coronel
graduado de cavallaria, passando a coronel effectivo em 1818 e a brigadeiro em 13 de
Maio de 1822. Foi governador militar das villas de Campinas e Mogy mirim. em cujo
posto prestou bons serviços no periodo revolucionario de 1821—22 Nesta capital residia
na rua de Santa Ephigenia, n. 12, e tinha dois filhos, de 19 e 20 annos, e tres escravos
de serviço domestico. O seu depoimento é longo, minucioso, e dos mais interessantes
pelos pormenores que relata.

dispuzeram a mandar tocar este rebate por terem sido convocados, no dia antecedente, á casa do coronel Francisco Ignacio de
Souza Queiroz, commandante da força armada, onde se acharam
o presidente do extincto governo João Carlos Augusto Oyenhausen, o ouvidor José da Costa Carvalho pelo motivo de ter
vindo ordem do ministerio para o mesmo presidente se retirar
para a corte do Rio Janeiro e deliberarem sobre o modo de
obstar a sua execução.—Ao segundo, disse que sabe por ser publico e por ter ouvido ao capitão Pedro Taques de Almeida
Alvim que os agentes e cooperadores para o ajuntamento do povo
e tropa no largo de São Gonçalo, em consequencia do rebate
tocado na tarde do dia 23 de Maio passado, foram o mesmo capitão Pedro Taques, o tenente Jaime, o major Modesto e o major Macedo, que andaram avisando pelas casas e ruas, ainda
mesmo antes do toque de rebate, para que concorressem ao
quartel e dalli marchassem para aquelle largo (1).— Ao terceiro,
disse que sabe pela mesma razão que a tropa se fora postar no
referido largo movida e disposta pelos mesmos agentes e cooperadores acima indicados e outros.—Ao quarto, disse que, além de
ser vóz publica,·sabe por ouvir ao capitão Pedro Taques e ao
capitão Nogueira que o coronel Francisco Alvares Ferreira do
Amaral fora o commandante da tropa para o largo de São Gonçalo, onde se ajuntára certa porção de povo, armado por effeito
do rebate e do toque do sino da cadêa tangido por Joaquim Pedro Maia, apaniguado e protegido do coronel Francisco Ignacio
de Souza Queiroz, concorrendo aquelle ajuntamento o cirurgião Joaquim José Rodrigues, por alcunha *O Quinquim* (2), com
um bacamarte que parecia mais ser uma peça de artilharia pelo
seu desforme tamanho, e figurando á frente da tropa tambem
o brigadeiro Joaquim José Pinto de Moraes Leme, que recita-
vam certas leis que auctorizavam o povo a obstar a execução
daquellas ordens de Sua Alteza que considerasse damnosa á provincia, vindo por este modo a auctorizar aquelle procedimento
por ser especial amigo do presidente João Carlos Augusto de
Oyenhausen, de cujo valimento se servia abusivamente com grande prejuizo e escandalos de terceiros (3)  Disse mais que sabe
pela mesma razão que, estando o coronel Francisco Alvares

(1)  Do quartel ao largo de s  Gonçalo a distancia é de cerca de cem metros, por
trechos de duas toas ruas—do Quartel e do Theatro.
(2)  O cirurgião Joaquim José Rodrigues era paulista, de 44 annos, solteiro e residente na rua Direita, n. 32, com quatro escravos de 19 a 35 annos e dois aggregados—
Mariana, solteira, parda de 28 annos, e José, preto, de 16 annos.
(3)  Durante a administração de João Carlos o brigadeiro Joaquim José Pinto teve
diversas questões com seus visinhos sobre propriedades territoriaes na freguesia de
Santa Ephigenia, como consta de papeis officiaes do tempo. Dahi «o prejuizo e escandalos de terceiros» a que o depoente se refere.

Ferreira do Amaral com o commando da tropa no largo
de São Gonçalo, chegára alli o coronel Francisco Ignacio de Souza Queiroz e lhe perguntára com que auctoridade havia tomado aquelle commando, uma vez que elle como
commandante da força não havia auctorisado para isso, ao que
respondeu o referido coronel Alvares que a tropa fora quem
lhe pedira para a commandar ; mas presume elle testemunha
que a disputa era apparente e uma mera impostura de parte a
parte pelo ar com que nella se figurou.—Ao quinto, disse eue
sabe por ter ouvido ao capitão Pedro Taques que elle fora o
proprio que fez conduzir à força para a casa da Camara ao juiz
presidente, o capitão Bento José Leite Penteado, *asseverando-lhe
quado o mesmo repugnou ir*, QUE SE NÃO QUIZESSE IR COMO HOMEM
DE BEM IRÍA ATADD Á CAUDA DO SEU CAVALLO (1)—Ao sexto,
disse sabe por ser voz publica que não só as assignaturas do
auto de vereação extraordinario do dia 23 de Maio passado, mas
tambem de outros papeis que se andaram assignando de casa
em casa, *foram pela maior parte solicitadas e conseguidas por
persuasões* e ATÉ MESMO POR AMEAÇAS do tenente Jayme, capitão
Pedro Taques, major Netto e major Macedo, apaniguados e
protegidos do commandante da força armada, coronel Francisco
Ignacio de Souza Queiroz, COM CUJO NOME ATERRAVAM A MUITO DOS
QUE ASSIGNARAM *e ainda mesmo intimando-lhes ordens delle* PARA
TAES ASSIGNATURAS.—Ao setimo, disse que se persuade haverem
cooperado para o acontecimento o presidente João Carlos Au-
gusto de Oeynhaussen e o coronel Francisco Ignacio de Souza
Queiroz como principaes motores, A QUEM SERVIA DE CONSE-
SELHEIRO PARA AQUELLE E OUTROS FINS SINISTROS O OUVIDOR
JOSÉ DA COSTA CARVALHO e por condescencia com os mesmos o
intendente Miguel José de Oliveira Pinto, o coronel Daniel
Pedro Müller e o tenente coronel Antonio Maria Quartim (2),
sendo o fundamento desta sua presumpção a grande aversão que
todos elles tinham concebido contra o coronel Martim Francisco
Ribeiro de Andrada e seu irmão o conselheiro José Bonifacio de
de Andrada e Silva, contra os quaes declamavam por este se
achar no ministerio e cquelle no governo da provincia, bem como
por o coronel Martim e o brigadeiro Jordão se haverem opposto
ás pretenções de Pedro Taques e Nogueira a respeito de serem

---

1 Pedro Taques tinha noção muito *sua* do que fosse um homem de bem; tinha já
naquelle tempe pouco juizo, que logo perdeu de todo, fallecendo doido varrido em 1869,
depois de muitos annos de demencia, que degenerou em incuravel *Kleptomania*
2 Eram estes tão interessados na sedição como João Carlos, Costa Carvalho e Francisco Ignacio, por serem militares extrangeiros em rendosas commissões do governo
portuguez em S. Paulo. O declinio da influeucia portugueza só os podia prejudicar, e
pelo resto deste depoimento se vê que elles não foram *condescendentes*, mas tinham motivos para se fazerem sediciosos.

majores, ambos protegidos por João Carlos Augusto de Oeynhausen e coronel Francisco Ignacio, os quaes apoiavam a taes
prctenções; sendo igualmente uma das razões da mesma aversão
o haverem-se opposto, principalmente o coronel Martim, a arrematação do açougue pretendida por Nogueira e seus socios,
com damnos do publico, e juntamente a algumas arbitrariedades
do ouvidor José da Costa Carvalho, apoiado pelos taes do governo de opinião contraria, concorrendo tambem para esta indisposição dos mesmos o haver-se publicado um bando, a instancia do coronel Martim e brigadeiro Jordão, para que todo o miliciano que tivesse dado dinheiro para não ir para expedição que
marchou para o Rio de Janeiro, o declarasse para lhe ser
restituido e dar-se-lhe baixa em recompensa (1) visto constar
que *muitos officiaes*, COMO FOI O MAJOR MACEDO, *receberam dinheiro e varias especies para o mesmo effeito, a saber: — de um
soldado de São Carlos mais de doze dobras* (2), *de outro cem
arrobas de assucar, de outro uma ou duas bestas*, COMO A ELLE
TESTEMUNHA CERTIFICOU O REVERENDO VIGARIO DE SÃO CARLOS
JOAQUIM JOSÉ GOMES, DE QUEM SE VALEU O MESMO MAJOR MA-
CEDO PARA QUE OS TAES SOLDADOS NÃO VIESSEM DENUNCIAL-O,
ESCREVENDO-LHE PARA ISSO UMA CARTA (3). Disse mais que o
resultado do referido motim fora a conservação do presidente
João Carlos Augusto de Oeynhausen e a deposição dos dous
membros do governo, o coronel Martim e o brigadeiro Jordão.
— Ao oitavo, disse que sabe, por ter presenciado, que o presidente e os mais empregados no governo, acima designados, nenhumas providencias deram sobre o acontecido motim e que
longe de punirem os seus agentes e fautores antes positivamente
os apoiavam e conviviam com elles, concorrendo á loja do capitão Pedro Taques (4) e á do coronel Francisco Ignacio de
Souza Queiroz (5), onde quasi effectivamente se achavam o ouvidor José da Costa Carvalho, os tenentes Jaime e Mamede, os

---

1 Além dos corpos militares organizados dos *Caçadores, Dragões, Uteis, Voluntarios
Reaes, Auxiliares, Houssards, Fuzileiros* e *Sertanejos*, e tropas regulares de linha, o povo
estava dividido em corpos milicianos, ou primeira reserva, e de ordenanças ou segunda
reserva. Os milicianos estavam sempre em serviço mais ou menos activo, o coronel
Francisco Ignacio era o seu commandante e delles se servia até nas suas sedições. As
ordenanças estavam sob as ordens do capitão-mór, e o capitão-mór de S. Paulo em 1822
era Eleuterio da Silva Prado, paulista de sangue e de sentimentos.
2 A dobra valia 12$800 e, portanto, doze dobras valiam 153$600, preço então carissimo para a dispensa de um soldado de uma expedição que pouco tempo duraria e que
não lhe daria direito á baixa do serviço.
3 Hoje cidade de Campinas: a mais importante do interior, situada a 106 kilometros
a noroeste da capital.
4 Na rua Direta, n. 6; ahi residia com a sua familia.
5 Na rua Direita n 3, apenas duas portas distante de Pedro Taques: era facil
portanto, aos conspiradores passarem de uma loja á outra, sem perda de tempo e sem
darem muito na vista dos curiosos.

majores Macedo e Netto, José Manuel de Abreu, por alcunha *O
Tralhão*, o cirurgião Quinquim, o tenente João Theodoro Xavier, os capitães Nogueira e Gaspar e algumas vezes o capitão
Antonio de Siqueira Moraes, levando a mal a conducta das
villas de São Carlos e Ytú e até reprehendendo os presidentes
das camaras e capitães-móres das mesmas villas por haverem
officiado ao governo (1) e a Sua Alteza Real testemunhando-
lhes o quanto viviam penalizados a similhante respeito, o que
elle testemunho sabe haver acontecido a respeito daquellas villas
por as estar commandando militarmente e lhes haver inspirado
sentimentos contrarios aos do acontecimento dia 23, nesta cidade
(2), do que resultou ser removido do commando das mesmas villas
pelo referido governo (3), que tambem não lhe consta désse providencia alguma sobre o arrombamento da casa da polvora, praticado naquelle dia por uma escolta commandada pelo alfares
Fadiga, não mandando devassar sobre similhante facto, nem tão
pouco da reunião de povo e escravos armados no largo de São
Gonçalo no sobredito dia 23 de Maio passado e menos trataram
de averiguar e punir a deserção dos dous officiaes vindos do
Rio, o capitão José Fernandes da Silva e o alferes Fadiga, que
vindos fugidos do Rio de Janeiro e apresentando-se ao governo,
composto dos sobreditos empregados (4), este não só lhes deu liberdade para se recolherem a suas casas, mas até a um delles, que foi
o Fadiga, se facilitou a sahida para Portugal, vendendo elle os
bens que aqui tinha e dando-se-lhe de mais a mais dous contos
de réis para as suas despesas, por parte do coronel Francisco
Ignacio de Souza Queiroz, segundo dizem, levando cartas para
as Côrtes de Lisboa manifestando-lhes o estado desta provincia.
E por serem horas improprias para a continuação do depoimento
desta testemunha, se parou com elle e assignou o que havia
deposto com o ministro devassante. E eu, o bacharel formado
Manuel Joaquim de Ornellas, o escrevi.—*Freire—Francisco Antonio de Paula Nogueira da Gama.*

---

1 Não sómente Campinas e Itú, foram as villas alvejadas pelo odio dos sediciosos
da Capital, mas tambem Mogy-mirim, Piracicaba· Porto Feliz, Sorocaba e todas as outras
até Curytiba. Todas ellas formaram uma confedoração, com centro em Itú, para a defesa dos interesses brasileiros atacados pelos extrangeiros e sediciosos de S. Paulo, com
quem cortaram relações, pondo-se sob ás ordens directas do governo do Rio e do Principe Regente. Vide vol. VII. pags. 140 e seguintes.
2 Inspirou Campinas e Mogy-mirim ao mesmo tempo que Paula Sousa inspirava
Ytú, Porto Feliz e Piracicaba. Vide vol. VII, cit. pags. citadas.
3 Foi removido pelo governo sedicioso de S. Paulo do commando militar: devia
ter desobedecido, como desobedeceu Pedro de Brito em Ytú, pondo-se ás ordens directas
de D. Pedro no Rio.
4 Aos membros do governo os depoentes dão ás vezes o nome de «empregados no
governo»; eram João Carlos, Oliveira Pinto, Müller e Quartim, todos extrangeiros e
alliados de Francisco Ignacio de Souza Queiroz.

## ASSENTADA

No mesmo dia, mez e anno da assentada retro, em a residencia do ministro devassante, onde eu escrivão desta devassa me achava, compareceu a testemunha brigadeiro Francisco Antonio de Paula Nogueira da Gama para continuar o seu depoimento, do que para assim constar lavrei este termo de assentada. E eu, o bacharel formado Manuel Joaquim de Ornellas, o escrevi. Continuando esta testemunha a depor sobre o interrogatorio oitavo, disse que sabe, por lhe haver dito o proprio capitão Pedro Taques de Almeida Alvim, nesta cidade, em casa do conego José Gomes de Almeida (1), que os do governo acima indicados o enviaram á villa de Guaratinguetá com o fim de fazer persuadir a tropa que vinha do Rio de Janeiro para que não seguisse as ordens do marechal Arouche (2), officiando ao coronel Cesar (3) para que se adeantasse com a referida tropa para esta cidade, deixando atraz ao referida marechal Arouche, o qual, querendo acautelar que o dito capitão Pedro Taques seduzisse aos soldados, o privou de se communicar com elles, o que não obstante já elle havia mandado adeante tres emissarios para o mesmo fim, como contou a elle testemunha, indo-o visitar, conseguiu debaixo do pretexto dado pelos mesmos do governo, de que a tropa devia adeantar-se do marechal Arouche para socegar o povo desta cidade, que se tinha alvoroçado com a sua vinda e se oppunha á sua entrada e posse de general das Armas desta provincia, para onde tinha sido despachado por Sua Alteza Real (4). Disse mais que sabe por ser publico que, chegando o marechal Arouche a Jacarehy em companhia da tropa, recebeu alli novas ordens do governo, pelo brigadeiro João Jacome de Baumann, para que não passasse dalli e seguisse a tropa para esta cidade, o que assim se cumpriu, vindo a tropa para esta dita cidade. onde foi bem recebida pelo mesmo governo e banqueteada a officialidade no quartel de São Francisco e os soldados no quartel da legião, onde além da comida, tiveram *muito vinho, tudo fornecido a custa e por convite do coronel Francisco Ignacio de Souza Queiroz* (5),

---

1 E' a testemunha 5.ª desta devassa.

2 Esta tropa pertencia aos *Leaes Paulistanos*, que voltavam do Rio em corpos destacados um dos outros e em territorio paulista entravam na subordinação ao marechal Arouche, inspector geral de milicias, em serviço no valle do Parahyba.

3 Devo-se referir ao coronel José Joaquim Cesar, que então era commandante das Armas da provincia, paulista, de 39 annos, casado, com dois filhos pequenos e seis escravos, e morador na rua Direita n. 40: um tanto ligado aos sediciosos, foi demittido por D. Pedro e substituido pelo general Arouche no commando das Armas.

4 O commandante das Armas, aqui mencionado, era já o marechal Arouche, ultimamente nomeado, cuja posse foi impedida pelos sediciosos, senhores da cidade de S. Paulo até á chegada do Principe Regente.

5 F' sempre o coronel Francisco Ignacio quem apparece fornecendo cachaça, genebra e vinho aos soldados e pagando as despesas das festas sediciosas dos mezes de Maio a Julho de 1822 !

e que perto da noite de 19 de Julho do corrente anno, espalbando-se a noticia de que o marechal Candido Xavier de Almeida e Souza marchava com a tropa da villa de Santos para esta cidade, encarregou logo o capitão Pedro Taques, o tenente Jaime, o major Netto, o tenente Mamede, Joaquim Pedro Maia, o cirurgião Quimquim e José Manoel de Abreu a convocar o povo e tropa para o quartel, indo já muitos armados de suas casas, *e isto com o falso pretexto de que aquella tropa vinha para atacar e saquear esta cidade,* quando assim não era, pois que vinha para fazer cumprir as ordens de Sua Alteza, como depois se verificou. Daqui resultou o grande ajuntamento que houve no referido quartel, a onde concorreram negros, mulatos, e até um frade franciscano, Frei Antonio do Menino Jesus, e o padre Bernardo Conrado, ambos armados; bem como se achavam todos os mais concorrentes, com o fim de impedir a entrada da tropa, comendo e bebendo alli e vociferando contra muitas pessoas de auctoridade. Disse igualmente que, concorrendo ao quartel os membros do governo Miguel José de Oliveira Pinto, coronel Francisco Ignacio de Souza Queiroz, coronel Daniel Pedro Müller e tenente coronel Antonio Maria Quartim, a titulo de conter aquelle tumulto, alli fizera Miguel José de Oliveira Pinto uma proclamação para animar os soldados e mais gente armada, appellidando-os «honrados paulistas», conservando-se em armas todos os aquartellados, protestando não as depor emquanto o marechal Candido Xavier de Almeida e Souza se não retirasse com a sua tropa para a villa de Santos e o marechal Arouche não se demittisse do emprego de governador das Armas desta provincia, *com a declaração de não exercer mais nella emprego algum* (1); tendo-se seguido de mais a mais de semelhante tumulto o *retirarem-se muitas familias para fóra desta cidade,* POR CAUSA DO TERROR PANICO QUE ELLE HAVIA CAUSADO. Disse, finalmente, ao sobredito interrogatorio que ouvindo ao intendente Miguel José de Oliveira Pinto que o governo tinha dado ordem para o marechal Arouche tomar posse do governo das Armas e increpando-o de o não ter vindo tomar, lhe respondeu elle testemunha que se admirava daquelle seu dizer, pois que o ajudante de ordens Joaquim Maria da Costa Ferreira lhe tinha assegurado que não lhe entregára a referida ordem *por esqueci-*

---

Raumann era militar antigo e veiu ao Brasil em 1808, esteve em Pernambuco em 1810 e veiu para S. Paulo em 1815, como ajudante de ordens do governo.

1 De modo que não poderia mais occupar cargos publicos um homem da qualidade do marechal Arouche, paulista dos mais distinctos e de uma das mais illustres familias da capitania, emquanto o governo ficava entregue a extrangeiros sediciosos a quem Francisco Ignacio se havia ligado para anarchizar a provincia e trazer odios entre os paulistas, difficultando o desenvolvimento das liberdades publicas.

*mento*, e voltando-se ao mesmo tempo o dito Joaquim Maria da Costa Ferreira para o coronel Müller percebeu elle testemunha dizer-lhe em particular que a não havia entregue por elle coronel Müller lhe ter advertido que bastava entregal-a á tardinha do dia seguinte (1).—Ao nono, disse que lhe constou, por ser voz publica, que em casa do coronel Francisco Ignacio de Souza Queiroz se faziam conventiculos para o mesmo fim de serem depostos os dous membros, coronel Martim e brigadeiro Jordão, e ainda mais alguns outros, como eram o thesoureiro-mór João Ferreira de Oliveira Bueno, o padre-mestre Francisco de Paula e Oliveira e o tenente-coronel André da Silva Gomes (2).—Ao decimo, disse que sabe, por ter ouvido ao mestre da fabrica do Piques, de nome Thomaz (3), que havia communicação do presidente do governo João Carlos Augusto de Oeynhausen, do coronel Müller e marechal Oliveira, juntamente, com as Cortes de Portugal contra causa do Brasil, como elle testemunha suppõe, affirmando-lhe o mesmo Thomaz que ouvira a Fortunato Correia de Mello, que via a correspondencia de Oliveira com Müller em casa deste, e o mesmo Mello declamava em casa do sobredito Thomaz contra o Regente do Brasil e alguns dos seus ministros de Estado (4). E mais não disse deste nem do costeme. E lido o seu juramento, pelo achar conforme ao que havia deposto, o assignou com o ministro inqueridor. E eu, o bacharel formado Manoel Joaquim de Ornellas, o escrevi.—*Freire*. — *Francisco Antonio de Paula Nogueira da Gama*.

***

## ASSENTADA

Aos 3 dias do mez de Outubro de 1822, nesta cidade de S. Paulo. em casas do doutor Antonio de Almeida Silva Freire da Fonseca, juiz da presente devassa, onde eu escrivão della fui vindo, e sendo ahi por elle ministro foram inquiridas ao

---

1 Ainda aqui apparecem a falsidade e a hypocrisia a serviço dos sediciosos contra o elemento nacional !

2 André Gomes se refere a isto na exposição que fez e que foi publicado nos *Apontamentos Historicos*, de Azevedo Marques, artigo BERNARDA.

3 Thomaz Rodrigues Tocha, testemunha 15.ª deste inquerito, que fez graves referencias a respeito das ligações dos sediciosos de S. Paulo com o governo do Lisboa.

4 Thomaz Tocha era muito relacionado com Fortunato Correa de Mello e relata, no seu depoimento, as expansões sediciosas e retrogradas deste militar portuguez. João Carlos. Oliveira Pinto. Müller e Quartim, não obstante terem aceitado fazer parte de um governo popular, de origem revolucionaria, se julgavam ainda delegados do governo portuguez e procediam nessa conformidade, comquanto trahindo os paulistas liberaes que nelles confiaram. O que nao se desculpa é a cumplicidade de Francisco Ignacio, semi-paulista, e de Costa Carvalho, bahiano, com taes extrangeiros para a exploração da colonia em proveito da metropole.... e de si proprios.

testemunhas cujos nomes, cognomes, naturalidades, moradas,
édades, officios, ditos e costumes é tudo o que adeante se segue
do que para assim constar fiz este termo de assentada. E eu, o
bacharel formado Manoel Joaquim de Ornellas, o escrivi.

## TESTAMUNHA 19.ª

O CIRURGIÃO MOR JOSÉ GONÇALVES GOMIDE (1), casado, natural da freguezia de Guarapiranga, da provincia de Minas
Geraes, morador desta cidade, de edade de 40 annos, que vive
do seu emprego; testemunha jurada aos Santos Evangelhos, em
um livro delles em que por sua mão direita e, debaixo do juramento que prestou, prometteu dizer a verdade do que soubesse
e perguntado lhe fosse. E sendo inquirido pelos interrogatorios
desta devassa disse, ao primeiro, que sabe por ser voz publica
e por lhe haver contado, em ar de jactancia, o major José Rodrigues Pereira de Oliveira Netto, que fora elle mesmo quem
mandàra tocar o rebate na tarde do dia 23 de Maio passado forçando
para isso, com uma pistola aos peitos, ao official do estado maior,
o tenente Ignacio José de Macedo, que repugnava tocar-se o dito
rebate, e que a pontapés fizera subirem os tambores do quartel
pelas ruas da cidade para o tocarem.—Ao segundo, disse nada.
—Ao terceiro, disse que sabe por ouvir publicamente e ao proprio
major Netto, no largo de São Gonçalo, que elle por bem de sua
patria tomára o commando da tropa no quartel antes de alli
chegar o coronel Francisco Alvares Ferreira do Amaral, a quem
o entregou por ser official de patente superior e haver vozes, á
sua chegada, que diziam: « *Viva o nosso commandante*», donde
conclue elle testemunha que fora o mesmo major quem organi-
zara a tropa e a dispuzera para marchar para o largo de São
Gonçalo, onde se foi postar; *bem como alli concorreram certa
porção de povo e escravos armados* ao toque do sino da cadêa,
tendo este tumulto por fim a conservação do presidente do extincto
governo João Carlos Augusto de Oeynhausen e a deposição dos
dous membros do mesmo governo, o coronel Martim Francisco
Ribeiro de Andrade e o brigadeiro Manoel Rodrigues Jordão,
tudo contra as ordens de Sua Alteza Real, o que elle testemunha
sabe por se ter achado presente no corpo da tropa como cirurgião-

---

Tinha então 42 annos, era casado, com dois filhos, dois aggregados e tres escravos
e morava na rua de S. José, hoje Libero Badaró, n. 47; pertencia a uma familia de
cirurgiões, immigrada de Minas para S. Paulo alguns annos antes da *Bernarda*. Thomaz Gonçalves Gomide era tambem cirurgião, de 38 annos, e morava com sua mãe,
mulher e filhos e tres escravos, na rua do Ouvidor, hoje José Bonifacio, n. 2; era
*bernardista* e inimigo dos Andradas, de quem só falava mal. Candido Gonçalves Gomide
era igualmente cirurgião, de 33 annos, casado, com tres filhos e quatro escravos, e morava na rua do Ouvidor, n 5. Todos elles viviam da arte de cirurgião e a familia
fez figura durante o imperio.

mór della, allegando os auctores deste tumulto, como foram o tenente Jayme da Silva Telles, o major Netto, o capitão Pedro Taques de Almeida Alvim, o tenente Mamede e o major Francisco de Paula Macedo, que foi o primeiro que gritou: *«Fóra Martim Francisco»* e que a conservação daquelle presidente era necessaria a bem da provincia (1), pela qual propugnou muito o coronel Francisco Alvares Ferreira do Amaral, dizendo que para esse effeito é que elle se tinha reunido á tropa e que era igualmente necessaria a deposição dos dous indicados membros do governo por serem perniciosos á mesma provincia, *quando pelo contrario era muito proveitosa a sua conservação no governo, visto que deram muitas providencias tendentes ao bem da provincia, oppondo-se muitas vezes á opinião dos seus collegas*, QUE QUERIAM O CONTRARIO. Disse mais elle testemunha que, extranhando ao capitão Antonio Cardoso Nogueira, que era um dos agentes da deposição do coronel Martim, o comprehender semelhante pretenção quando elle, havia bem pouco tempo, tinha clamado pela sua estada no governo e não ir para o Rio de Janeiro em qualidade de procurador geral desta provincia (2), sendo ao mesmo tempo um ataque a seu irmão, o ministro de Estado José Bonifacio de Andrada e Silva, LHE RESPONDEU QUE PODIA SER QUE NAQUELLE MESMO DIA ELLE LÁ FOSSE DEPOSTO.—Ao quarto, disse que sabe por ouvir ao coronel Francisco Alvares Ferreira do Amaral, no largo de São Gonçalo, na occasião em que o coronel Francisco Ignacio de Souza Queiroz o arguia de haver tomado o commando da tropa sem sua auctoridade como commandante da força armada que elle commandara a tropa naquelle logar pelos motivos declarados ao interrogatorio antecedente. Disse mais que á frente da mesma tropa se achava o brigadeiro Joaquim José Pinto de Moraes Leme propugnando pela consevação do presidente João Carlos Augusto de Oeynhausen, contra as ordens de Sua Alteza Real, e citando leis a favor da mesma (3). — Ao quinto, disse

---

1 Mais a bem do proprio Macedo, que era muito amparado por João Carlos e Francisco Ignacio e a quem Martim e Jordão queriam obrigar a restituir os dinheiros que recebêra dos soldados dara dispensal-os de marcharem para o Rio de Janeiro.

2 A expesição aqui esta um tanto obscura e necessita de um accrescimo: Em fim de Dezembro de 1821 Martim devia seguir para o Rio, com Gama Lobo, como representantes da provincia para pedir a D. Pedro que ficasse no Brazil, sendo substituido por José Bonifacio nessa missão   Provavelmente é a isto que aqui se fas referencia, entendendo Cardoso Nogueira que Martim não devia ir ao Rio por ser necessaria a sua presença em S. Paulo. Em 1822 a provincia tinha dois procuradores geraes em commissão no Rio, mas estes eram o general Manoel Martins do Couto Reis e o desembargador Antonio Rodrigues Velloso de Oliveira, que foram eleitos em Fevereiro, alguns mezes antes da *Bernarda*

3 As Côrtes de Lisboa haviam chamado para Portugal o principe D. Pedro, que que ellas já não consideravam como regente do Brasil, sendo por isso irritos e nullos os actos que aqui praticasse. Os sediciosos de S. Paulo, estando de accordo com aquellas Côrtes, julgavam-se com o direito de proceder da mesma fórma, considerando nullos os actos de D. Pedro.

que sabe, por ser publico e pelo ter ouvido ao proprio juiz presidente (1), que fora conduzido á força para a casa da camara pelo capitão Pedro Taques. —Ao sexto, disse QUE SABE POR VER QUE OS SUBALTERNOS E INFERIORES FORAM ASSIGNAR O AUTO DE VEREAÇÃO DO DIA 23 DE MAIO PRETERITO E MAIS PAPEIS POR ORDEM QUE LHES INTIMOU O MAJOR NETTO, achando-se na casa anterior á sala da camara varios europeus (2), como eram o ajudante Manoel Felizardo de Carvalho, Joaquim Pedro Maia e o procurador do conselho, capitão Luiz Manoel da Cunha Bastos, que, ao passo que concorriam a assignar aquelle auto varias pessoas, convidavam aos que eram da sua facção para beberem vinho em applauso daquelle dia, e *conservando-se uma porção de paizanos armados na sala da camara*, AO PÉ DO OUVIDOR, QUE ALLI ESTEVE DESDE O PRINCIPIO DO TUMULTO ATÉ AO FIM E DEU VIVAS DA JANELLA DA CAMARA PARA O POVO EM APPLAUSO DAQUELLE ACTO (3), que até foi festejado cóm musica e cantoria do povo (4). —Ao setimo, disse que encontrando se elle testemunha com o alferes Thomaz de Aquino na emboccadura da rua dos Quarteis para o largo de S Gonçalo, viu elle despedir-se de varias pessoas, assim como tambem se despediu delle testemunha, dizendo a todos que na madrugada do dia seguinte ia para o Rio de Janeiro com o presidente João Carlos Augusto de Oeynhausen, e acontecendo tudo isto na tarde do dia 23 de Maio, pouco antes de se tocar a rebate, passados alguns dias perguntou elle testemunha, em conversa com o ajudante de ordens capitão Gregorio Ignacio Ferreira Nobre (5), porque motivo se andava despedindo aquelle alferes para sahir para o Rio de Janeiro, como elle testemunha observára na rua dos Quarteis e ainda aqui se conservava, lhe respondeu o dito ajudante de ordens que o mesmo alferes fora mandado por ordem daquelle presidente a

---

1 Capitão Bento José Leite Penteado, presidente da Camara e juis de fora pela lei.

2 «Europeus» aqui quer dizer «portuguezes», então geralmente cons derados como inimigos do Brasil e adversarios da nossa independencia e anarchisadores da nossa politica, até á epocha da *matança dos boaras* em Cuyabá.

3 O primeiro magistrado da cidade, o representante vivo da lei, estava trancformado em chefe da população revolta e, rodeado de capangas, estava senhor do paço municipal, onde fazia o seu escrivão Amaro Vieira redigir actas de sessões da Camara violentada pelos seus sequazes, e da janella açulava a plebe cá em baixo !

4 Este povo, já nol-o disseram varias testemunhas e o proprio André Gomes, era a arraia miuda de S. Paulo, reunida por Netto, Macedo. Mamede, Pedro Taques, Jaime e outros, excitada pela cachaça e genebra profusamente distribuidas no paço municipal, que se achava transformado em Taberna, e enthusiasmada pelas saudaçõ s que lhe dirigia o ouvidor Costa Carvalho.

5 Era um marinheiro portuguez que desertou ao tempo da invasão franceza e veio o Brasil, seguindo o exemplo de familia real. Não tem fé de officio porque não teve tempo de tiral-a antes da deserção. Veio para S Paulo em 1811 como tenente de cavallaria, passou a capitão de cavallaria addido ao estado maior em 1818 e a ajudante de ordens do governo em 1819 a major graduado em 1825 e a effectivo em 1829. Devia ter de 40 a 50 annos de idade porque entrou no serviço da marinha portugueza em 1796 e já tinha vinte e seis annos de serviços militares ao tempo da *Bernarda*.

observar se já havia algum ajuntamento de gente tanto no quartel como no largo de S. Gonçalo, donde infere elle testemunha que o mesmo presidente havia entrado no acontecido motim, e por voz publica sabe que os mais do governo, á excepção do thesoureiro-mór, do padre-mestre Francisco de Paula e Oliveira e do tenente-coronel André da Silva Gomes, eram sabedores do projectado motim, assim como o ouvidor José da Costa Carvalho, porque apenas se tocou a rebate logo se dirigiu á casa da Camara, vindo dahi a pouco em sua procura o capitão Pedro Taques. Ao oitavo, disse que, pelo que tem observado, lhe não consta que o governo désse providencia alguma sobre o motim do dia 23 de Maio, sobre o arrombamento da casa da Polvora, feito no mesmo dia por uma escolta commandada pelo alferes Fadiga, donde resultou roubar-se muita polvora, sobre a reunião dos escravos armados no Largo de São Gonçalo e sobre o ajuntamento da tropa, paizanos brancos, negros e mulatos no quartel, aonde concorreram o frade franciscano Frei Antonio do Menino Jesus e o padre Bernardo Conrado, todos armados de espadas e pistolas com o fim de obstar a entrada do marechal Candido nesta cidade, para onde marchava com sua tropa da villa de Santos para fazer cumprir as ordens de Sua Alteza Real, sendo uma destas o fazer empossar o marechal Arouche do governo das Armas da provincia que o mesmo Senhor lhe tinha conferido, de cujos factos se não devassou, nem tão pouco foram extranhados os seus auctores e antes mereciam a estima dos membros do governo, já indicados, e eram mal olhados os que nenhuma parte tiveram nos mencionados factos.—Ao nono e decimo, nada disse, nem do costume. E lido seu juramento, pelo achar conforme ao que havia deposto, o assignou com o ministro inquiridor. E eu, o bacharel formado Manoel Joaquim de Ornellas, escrivão desta devassa, o escrevi. —*Freire.—Joeé Gonçalves Gomide.*

## ASSENTADA

Aos 5 dias do mez de Outubro de 1822, nesta cidade de São Paulo, em casas de residencia do Doutor Antonio de Almeida Silva Freire da Fonseca, ministro da presente devassa, onde eu escrivão della fui vindo, e sendo ahi foram por elle ministro inquiridas as testemunhas cujos nomes, cognomes naturalidades, moradas, idades, officios, ditos e costumes é tudo o que adeante se segue, do que para constar fiz este termo de assentada. E eu, o bacharel formado Manoel Joaquim de Ornellas, o escrevi.

## TESTEMUNHA 20.ᵃ

O CAP.TÃO ANTONIO JOSÉ DE OLIVEIRA LIMA, casado, natural desta cidade e morador na villa de Sorocaba, desta provincia, onde vive de seu negocio de tropas, de idade de 58 annos; testemunha jurada aos Santos Evangelhos, em um livro delles em que poz sua mão direita e, debaixo do juramento que prestou, prometteu dizer a verdade do que soubesse e perguntado lhe fosse. E sendo inquirido pelos interrogatorios desta devassa disse, ao primeiro, que sabe por ser voz publica nesta cidade e ouvir a varios soldados do quartel, que quem mandou tocar a rebate na tarde do dia 23 de Maio passado fora o major José Rodrigues Pereira de Oliveira Netto, acompanhado do capitão Pedro Taques de Almeida Alvim e do tenente Jayme da Silva Telles, forçando com duas pistolas aos peitos ao official de estado-maior, tenente Ignacio José de Macedo, para que o mandasse tocar, visto que repugnava fazel-o, e o referido major fez sahir os tambores do quartel aos bofetões e alguns até descalços mandando-os tocar ao dito rebate pelas ruas desta cidade o que elle teste-tesmunha sabe por ter ouvido a Joaquim José Freire. empresario da casa da Opera, do qual ouviu egualmente, bem como de outras pessoas, que ao mesmo tempo do rebate tocára o sino da cadeia. Disse mais que sabe por ter ouvido a alguns soldados do quartel, cujos nomes ignora, e ao sobredito Freire que o mencionado major Netto tivera ordem do seu coronel, o commandante da força armada Francisco Ignacio de Souza Queiroz para mandar tocar o predito rebate, o que tambem ouviu a Joaquim de Almeida Salles, da villa de Ytù (1), e que sabe pelo motivo de ser publico e de ter ouvido aos mesmos Joaquim José Freire e Joaquim de Almeida Salles, que o fim daquelle rebate fora a conservação do presidente do governo João Carlos Augusto de Oeynhausen pelo considerarem proveitoso á provincia, apezar de ter sido chamado á corte do Rio de Janeiro por ordem de Sua Alteza Real, e egualmente a deposição dos dous membros do mesmo governo, o coronel Martim Francisco Ribeiro de Andrada e o brigadeiro Manoel Rodrigues Jordão, *debaixo do falso e apparente pretexto de serem prejudiciaes á mesma provincia*, QUANDO PELO CONTRARIO ERAM UTILISSIMOS, como o mostraram pelas providencias que deram sendo uma destas a de ficar o córte do açougue franco a beneficio publico, visto que o capitão Nogueira e seu socio, o coronel Francisco Ignacio, se propunham a arrematal-o por mil cento e vinte (1$120) cada

(1) Era personagem de certa proeminencia naquelle tempo e está biographado no vol. II desta *Revista*, pags. 267 e seguintes; era paulista intelligente e avesso ao despotismo politico e religioso.

arroba de carne, ao mesmo tempo que veiu a ficar a oitocentos
e oitenta (880 réis) conservando-se franco como ainda se conserva; o que elle testemunha sabe pelo haver presenciado e ter
sido o proprio que a pedido do coronel Martim deixou ficar pa a
fornecer ao córte desta cidade seiscentas rezes que levava parra
a côrte do Rio de Janeiro, em occasião que aqui havia grande
falta de carne por querer o mesmo capitão Nogueira reputar por
avultadissimo preço o grande numero de rezes que tinha (1)
bem como a de mandar o coronel Martim tirar da casa do capitão Francisco Antonio de Miranda (2) parente do coronel Francisco Ignacio de Souza Queiroz, no bairro da Luz, para cima
de trezentos alqueires de farinha e feijão, que elle havia atra-
vessado a tempo em que havia uma grande falta de mantimentos nas Casinhas (3), e mandar que aquelle mantimento viesse
para a cidade para ser vendido ao publico, e finalmente de terem
o coronel Martim e o brigadeiro Jordão feito publicar um bando
para que todo o miliciano que tivesse dado dinheiro para não
ir na expedição que marchou para o Rio ãe Janeiro, o denunciasse para lhe ser restituido o que tivesse dado e
receber em recompensa a sua baixa, visto constar que alguns dos seus commandantes receberam dinheiros e presentes para
esse fim como foram o brigadeiro Joaquim José Pinto de Moraes
Leme, QUE RECEBEU DUZENTOS MIL RÉIS DE UM SEU ALFERES DA
VILLA DE BRAGANÇA PARA NÃO IR NAQUELLA EXPEDIÇÃO, como não
foi da mesma sorte que nenhum dos soldados da companhia do
mesmo alferes; o tenente coronel Jeronimo Pereira Chrispim,
QUE RECEBEU DO CABO MARCELINO DE GODOY BUENO (4) E SESSENTA
AVES, E TRINTA E DOUS MIL RÉIS DE UM SOLDADO DA ESQUADRA
DO DITO CABO, PRATICANDO ISTO MESMO O SEU CORONEL FRANCISCO
ALVES FERREIRA DO AMARAL POR INTERMEDIO DE UMA SUA CONCU-
BINA, o que elle testemunha sabe por ser publico nas villas de

---

(1 O capitão Nogueira é socio do coronel Francisco; monopolisa as rezes entradas
em S. Paulo e o seu socio, membro do governo, trata de dar-lhe o privilegio das carnes
verdes nesta capital! E é este mesmo coronel Francisco Ignacio um dos principaes accu-
sadores dos Andradas!

2) Era capitão da companhia de ordenanças dos bairros do O' e Santa Anna, desta
capital; portugues natural da ilha do Pico, do bispado de Angra, de 40 annos, casado,
com dois filhos, tres aggregados e sete escravos, tinha negocio de seccos e molhados e
uma ferraria. Residindo ao longo da estrada para Atibaia e Bragança, por onde transitava grande parte dos mantimentos que suppriam a população da cidade, cercava os
caipiras mercadores e atravessava aquelles mantimentos, fiado na sua posição de commandante de um batalhão de ordenanças e de protegido do seu parente e amigo Francisco Ignacio de Souza Queiroz, coronel de milicias e membro do governo!

(3) Era o mercado de S. Paulo, na rua Quinze de Novembro, na esquina onde hoje
está o paço municipal, outrora Thesouro do Estado.

(4) Aqui devia estar a quantia de dinheiro que Chrispim recebeu, mas o papel do
manuscripto está estragado neste logar e a quantia illegivel. A gravidade está no acto
de receber o dinheiro e não na quantia.

Nova Bragança e Atibaia e tel-o ouvido ao referido cabo Marcellino de Godoy Bueno (1); e o MAJOR FRANCISCO DE PAULA MACEDO, QUE RECEBEU PARA CIMA DE UM CONTO DE RÉIS DE VARIOS SOLDADOS DO SEU REGIMENTO, segundo é publico na villa de Ytú e nesta cidade, onde se gabava a similhante respeito (2); resultando de todas estas providencias, por estar oppostas aos interesses dos sobreditos, a aversão que contra elles conceberam, motivo porque mais se distinguiram naquelle motim e forcejaram pela sua deposição (3).—Ao segundo disse que sabe, por ser voz publica, pue o major Netto, o tenente Jayme da Silva Telles e o major Macedo foram os que no quartel dispuzeram e organisaram a tropa para dali marchar para o largo de São Gonçalo, e fora della andaram o tenente Francisco Antonio Pinto Bastos, por alcunha o O *Patarata*, e Antonio Floriano Alvim, antes de tocar a rebate, solicitando gente de casa em casa para se reunir no referido largo, onde correu por essa causa gente de toda a classe e até escravos armados.—Ao terceiro, disse que se refere ao que disse ao segundo.—Ao quarto, disse que sabe, por ser publico nesta cidade e tel-o ouvido a Joaquim José Freire e Joaquim de Almeida Salles, que quem commandára a tropa para o largo de São Gonçalo fôra o coronel Francisco Alvares Ferreira do Amaral, por assim lh'o haver pedido a mesma tropa, conservando o commando até que chegasse o coronel Francisco Ignacio de Souza Queiroz, que com elle teve uma apparente disputa a semelhante respeito, arguindo-o de haver tomado o dito commando sem sua auctoridade, como chefe da força armada; apparecendo á frente da mesma tropa tambem o brigadeiro Pinto, o qual, entrando na indagação da causa da sua reunião naquelle largo e sabendo que éra para a conservação do presidente do governo João Carlos Augusto de Oeynhausen contra as ordens de Sua Alteza, passou a persuadir a todos que éra muito justo por ter sido um bom general e servindo de pae a esta provincia (4), ao que logo acudiram o major

---

(1) Por uma só despensa seriam demasiado os preços pagos pelos subornos; porém como era para o official e os soldados da sua companhia pode-se classificar de «modesta» a venalidade dos officiaes *bernardistas!*

(2) Aqui e fala em Ytú e S. Paulo sómente, mas o brigadeiro Nogueira da Gama affirmou, no seu depoimento, que a venalidade do major Macedo se fez sentir tambem em Campinas e Mogy mirim. De que gente se serviram João Carlos e Costa Carvalho para removerem Martim Francisco do seu caminho politico!

(3) Era a *lucta pela vida* que esta gente travou contra Martim e Jordão, e foi ella tão feliz que encontrou protecção no presidente do governo, João Carlos, e no ouvidor da comarca, Costa Carvalho!

(4) Isto dito, a respeito de seu protector, por um official accusado de venalidade e ameaçado de vergonhoso processo, não tem valor algum intrinseco, tanto mais que quando se tratou de depor este mesmo João Carlos de Oeynhausen do seu cargo de capitão general de S. Paulo, no dia 23 de Junho de 1821, foram este mesmo brigadeiro Pinto e o coronel Francisco Ignacio que commandaram as tropas rebelladas e fizeram João Carlos passar pelas *forcas caudinas!*

Macedo, o capitão Nogueira e o tenente Jaime propugnando pela conservação do mesmo presidente e clamando que sahissem do governo o coronel Martim e o brigadeiro Jordão, e dizendo o mesmo capitão Nogueira por fim do acto que viesse a nossa liberdade, respondeu-lhe um dos circumstantes que elle perdera uma boa occasião de vender a carne a quatro patacas para vexar o povo, como pretendia a bem dos seus interesses, e que tambem lhe contara Francisco Pinto, filho do coronel Anastacio de Freitas Trancoso (1).—Ao quinto, disse que sabe por ser publico e lhe ter contado o proprio presidente da Camara, capitão Bento José Leite Penteado, que fora levado á força para a casa da Camara pelo capitão Pedro Taques de Almeida Alvim, o qual lhe asseverava que, se não quizesse ir por bem, iria atado á cauda do seu cavallo.—Ao sexto, disse que sabe sómente por ter presenciado que o tenente Bernardo Guedes andara de casa em casa, solicitando as assignaturas da representação feita para o coronel Martim sahir fóra desta cidade dentro em vinte e quatro horas e da provincia dentro em oito dias, observando isto em casa do capitão Francisco Gonçalves dos Santos Cruz, a quem foi falar para assignar (2).—Ao setimo, disse que sabe, por ser voz publica, que o presidente do governo João Carlos Augusto de Oeynhausen e o coronel Francisco Ignacio de Souza Queiroz, membro do mesmo governo, foram os auctores do acontecido motim, por se terem declarado inimigos do coronel Martim e do brigadeiro Jordão, e que para o mesmo cooperára o ouvidor José da Costa Carvalho pela mesma razão, aconselhando e dirigindo os facciosos. —Ao oitavo, disse que sabe que o extincto governo nenhuma providencia déra sobre o tumulto do dia 23 de Maio, arrombamento da casa da Polvora, feito naquelle mesmo dia por uma escolta commandada pelo alferes Fadiga, e reunião de tropa, paizanos e até negros e mulatos no quartel, um frade franciscano de nome Frei Antonio do Menino Jesus, e padre Bernardo Conrado, todos armados e municiados para se opporem á entrada

---

(1) Anastacio Trancoso pertencia a uma illustre familia paulista; rico e de gosto militar, montou uma companhia á sua custa e seguiu para o Sul no tempo de Martim Lopes, prestando bons serviços ao seu paiz. Era natural de Paranaguá e foi membro do governo de S. Paulo em 1823-24 ; tinha então 70 annos de idade, era viuvo e risidia na rua de S. Bento n. 11, com seu filho Francisco Pinto, moço de 32 annos e solteiro tres filhas e seis escravos. Sua fallecida esposa era irmã do brigadeiro Joaquim José Pinto de Moraes Leme, um dos sediciosos da *Bernarda*, mas o coronel Anastacio se manteve leal aos paulistas e fiel servidor dos interesses brazileiros em lucta com os extrangeiros senhores do governo faccioso de S. Paulo; falleceu em 1839 na idade de 87 annos.

(2) As testemunhas anteriores, referindo-se ás *solicitações* de assignaturas por parte dos sediciosos contra Martim e Jordão, não fazem menção deste Bernardo Guedes, que foi visto por este deponente empenhado no mesmo mister de *angariar* assignaturas. E' mais um official militar que apparece filiado á escola do coronel Francisco Ignacio

do marechal Candido nesta cidade, com a sua tropa da villa de Santos, para fazer cumprir as ordens de Sua Alteza Real; nem tão pouco castigou os amotinadores, nem mandou devassar sobre taes procedimentos, antes pareciam ser louvados pelo referido governo, que então era composto do presidente João Carlos Augusto Oeynhausen, do intendente Miguel José de Oliveira Pinto, do coronel Francisco Ignacio de Souza Queiroz, do coronel Daniel Pedro Müller e do tenente coronel Antonio Maria Quartim (1), e eram por elle governo mal olhados os que eram de sentimentos contrarios. — Ao nono, disse que sabe, por ser publico e lhe ter contado o tenente Francisco Severino dos Santos Cardim, que em casa do coronel Francisco Ignacio de Souza Queiroz se faziam conventiculos sobre o projectado tumulto do dia 23 de Maio passado, que já estava premeditado para os dias 4 e 13 do dito mez (2), e alli se davam e traçavam os planos para serem postos em execução, como foi no sobredito dia 23 de Maio.—Ao decimo, disse que sabe sómente sobre o seu conteúdo, *por ter ouvido ao marechal Candido*, além de algumas vozes vagas, QUE O TENENTE CORONEL JOSÉ ANTONIO DA SILVA VALENTE, SENDO GOVERNADOR DA VILLA E PRAÇA DE SANTOS, FIZERA ENCRAVAR AS PEÇAS DE ARTILHERIA DA FORTALEZA DA BARRA DE ORDEM DO SOBREDITO PRESIDENTE DO GOVERNO (3), e por lhe contar o thesoureiro-mór João Ferreira de Oliveira Bueno, sabe tambem que, havendo desertado seis soldados artilheiros da tropa européa do brigadeiro Madeira (4), governador das Armas da Bahia, para a mesma villa e praça de Santos, do que dando parte ao governo o mesmo governador Valente e pedindo para alli ficarem afim de ensinarem aos soldados daquella praça, assim o determinára o presidente João Carlos de Oeynhausen apesar da opposição do referido thesoureiro-mór, do padre-mestre Francisco de Paula e Oliveira e do tenente-coronel

---

(1) De quinze membros de que se compunha o primitivo governo restavam sómente estes cinco-quatro extrangeiros e um seu alliado, ficando expulsos ou retirados todos quantos *cheiravam* a brazileirismo, incluindo mesmo Vergueiro e André Gomes, portuguezes amigos do Brazil.

2 Então não se tratava da permanencia de João Carlos e Costa Carvalho em S. Paulo; este pretexto só appareceu depois, em falta de melhor.

3 Silva Valente era official da infanteria da marinha portugueza; emigrado para o Brasil, foi feito tenente coronel de cavallaria, addido ao estado maior, em 1818, com exercicio do cargo de ajudante de ordens do capitão general de S. Paulo, sendo depois nomeado governador militar de Santos em logar de Bento Alberto da Gama Sá, removido por causa do levante do 1.º batalhão de caçadores e consequente saque daquella villa, em Junho de 1821. Estava no seu papel encravando aquellas peças e defendendo os interesses portuguezes.

4 Era official portuguez a serviço do seu governo na Bahia; onde se oppoz á independencio do Brasil. A sua expulsão foi um dos bons serviços de José Bonifacio, ministro, e é o motivo das festas annuaes de 2 de Julho na Bahia.

André da Silva (1), que suppunham ser aquelles seis soldados antes espias do Madeira do que desertores, donde elle testemunha presume que havia communicação entre o extincto governo e as Côrtes de Portugal contra a causa do Brasil. E mais não disse, nem do costume. E lido o seu juramento, pelo achar conforme ao que havia deposto, o assignou com o ministro devassante. E eu, o bacharel formado, Manuel Joaquim de Ornellas, escrivão desta devassa, o escrevi.—*Freire.*—*Antonio José de Oliveira Lima.*

## ASSENTADA

Aos 5 dias do mez de Outubro de 1822, nesta cidade de São Paulo, em casas de residencia do doutor Antonio de Almeida Silva Freire da Fonseca, juiz da presente devassa, onde eu escrivão della me achava, e sendo ahi foram por elle ministro inquir-das as testemunhas cujos nomes, cognomes, naturalidades, moradas, idades, officios, ditos e costumes é tudo o que adeante se segue, do que para constar fiz este termo de assentada. E eu, o bacharel formado Manuel Joaquim de Ornellas, escrivão da mesma devassa, o escrevi.

## TESTEMUNHA 21

O TENENTE ANTONIO DE PADUA DE GUSMÃO (2), casado, natural e morador desta cidade, onde vive do seu soldo, de 7 annos de idade (3); testemunha jurada aos Santos Eva m um livro delles em que poz sua mão direita e de' jura- mento que prestou, prometteu dizer a verdade c nbesse e perguntado lhe tosse. E sendo inquirido pelos ratorios desta devassa di-se, ao primeiro, que sabe por lhe ter dito o official do estado maior, tenente Ignacio José de Macedo, quando do elle testemunha acudiu ao quartel ao toque do rebate como commandante do destacamento (4), que quem mandou tocar a

---

1 Eram membros do governo, mas muito fracos para a lucta contra os extrangeiros e seu alliado Francisco Ignacio, membro tambem do governo: deixaram os seus logares e os cinco sediciosos ficaram senhores do poder como da propria casa, em sessão permanente por semanas inteiras até á sua agonia em Agosto de 1822.

2 Em nota ao depoimento do conego Toledo Arouche, testemunha 7.ª, foram dadas algumas informações sobre este militar

3 Nos recenceamentos do tempo a idade que se lhe dava não combina com esta com esta; no de 1822 elle apparece com 45 annos. O seu depoimento é importante porque tomou parte nos motins de 23 de Maio, embora constrangido.

4 No quartel da cidade havia sempre força prompta, ora da milicia da cidade, ora da milicia do interior, que vinha fazer o serviço de guarnição por um ou dois mezes. Essa força, variavel em parte do seu pessoal e na sua procedencia, mas permanente no quartel, é que se chamava «destacamento» e era commandada pelo depoente, como capitão de carreira. O coronel Francisco Ignacio era o commandante da milicia toda da capital, quer aquartelada, quer fora dos quarteis.

rebate na tarde do dia 23 de Maio passado fôra o major José Rodrigues Pereira de Oliveira Netto, obrigando para isco o mesmo official com uma pistola aos peitos, por elle não querer mandal-o tocar, e fizera sahir os tambores do quartel a bofetões a tocar a rebate pelas ruas da cidade. Disse mais que, chegando ao quartel e perguntando ao mesmo official do estado-maior como se havia tocado a rebate sem sua ordem, logo lhe sahiu ao encontro o referido major Netto, com o major Macedo, o capitão Nogueira e o tenente Jayme, dizendo que a tropa e povo foram quem mandára tocar a rebate (1), e dahi a pouco, chegando o coronel Francisco Alvares Ferreira do Amaral, tomou conta do batalhão pelos gritos da multidão, que dizia para elle : «Viva o nosso commandante», e que fazendo o mesmo ao brigadeiro Pinto, não poude este tomar o commando por já estar dado ao dito coronel Alvares (2), e vindo elle testemunha ao quartel en.... ().... O ajuntamento de tropa e povo alli existente, que o fim deste tumulto era a conservação de João Carlos Augusto, presidente do extincto governo, visto ter sido chamado ao Rio de Janeiro por ordem de Sua Alteza Real, e que ao depois no largo de São Gonçalo, estando alli já postada a tropa, ouvira gritar o tenente Jayme, os majores José Rodrigues Pereira de Oliveira Netto e Macedo, o capitão Pedro Taques, Joaquim Pedro Maia, o tenente Mamede, o alferes Fadiga e o tenente Francisco Antonio Pinto Bastos, por alcunha O Patarata, que se depuzessem aos membros do governo coronel Martim e brigadeiro Jordão pelos considerarem prejudiciaes á provincia, QUANDO A ELLE TESTEMUNHA NUNCA CONSTOU QUE DESMERECESSEM NA OPINIÃO PUBLICA (3).— Ao segundo, disse que sabe, por ver, que quem dispoz a tropa no quartel e a arranjou para marchar para o largo de São Gonçalo foram o tenente Jayme, os majores Netto e Macedo, o tenente Patarata, que em ar de ajudante se poz a dividir o batalhão, o tenente Mamede, o capitão Pedro Taques e o capitão Nogueira, sendo o tenente Jayme o que mais se distinguiu, pois até sem ordem delle testemunha obrigou ao quarteleiro do armazem do armamento.... (2) .. a armar o povo e tropa á proporção que iam chegando,

---

1  O rebate foi uma surpresa para o publico e para as mesmas tropas, sendo necessario o emprego de violencias para ser tocado ; entretanto estes officiaes sediciosos vem dizer que o rebate fora tocado a pedido do povo e tropa !

2  O manuscripto está roto neste logar e o resto da palavra desappareceu

3  Esta declaração é importante por partir de um official que tomou parte na Bernarda ; desmentindo assim as affirmações dos seus companheiros de sedição, elle bem mostra que fora violentado, para tomar parte nella, como o foram os tambôres, o tenente Ignacio Macedo, o presidente da Camara, capitão Leite Penteado, e tantas outras victimas da sanha reaccionaria da officialidade venal daquelles tempos.

4  Falta aqui uma palavra estragada no manuscripto, que aliás não obscurece o sentido da phrase.

não se distinguindo menos o alferes Fadiga, que, sendo nomeado para commandante da guarda da polvora pelo coronel Francisco Alvares á instancia do major Netto e tenente Jayme e chegando lá, arrombou a porta e tirou o cartuchame que bem lhe pareceu, conservando arrombada até ao outro dia, sem que para tal arrombamento tivesse ordem alguma superior, o que elle testemunha ouviu do mesmo alferes Fadiga.— Ao terceiro, disse que sabe, por ver, que a tropa e algum povo que existiam no quartel, por effeito do rebate, foram angariados pelos mesmos agentes e cooperadores do motim, acima referidos.— Ao quarto, disse que quem commandou a tropa para o largo de São Gonçalo fora o coronel Francisco Alvares como official superior, e além dos diversos outros officiaes acima indicado, que commandavam diversos pelotões, commandou um destes o capitão Gaspar, do regimento dos Caçadores (1), conservando-se a frente da tropa o brigadeiro Pinto, que citava leis em apoio do que elle testemunha ignorava (2); mas logo que chegou o coronel Francisco Ignacio, commandante da força armada o que terminou uma apparente disputa que teve com o coronel Francisco Alvares, por haver este tomado o commando da tropa sem sua auctoridade, tomou o commando da mesma e alli se conservou até que se recolheu para o quartel.— Ao quinto, disse nada.— Ao sexto, disse que sabe, por ter ouvido uma voz espalhada entre a tropa que os soldados e officiaes fossem assignar o auto de vereação, e assim o praticaram por essa causa, bem como outros assignados que ao depois se seguiram e foram apresentados no quartel pelo major Netto.— Ao setimo, disse nada.— Ao oitavo, disse que lhe não consta que o governo, composto do presidente João Carlos Augusto de Oeynhausen, do intendente Miguel José de Oliveira Pinto, do coronel Francisco Ignacio de Souza Queiroz, do coronel Müller e do tenente coronel Antonio Maria Quartim, désse providencia alguma sobre os factos que ficam relatados, bem como sobre o ajuntamento no quartel, aonde concorreram militares, paizanos, negros e mulatos e até o frade franciscano Frei Antonio do Menino Jesus e o padre Bernardo Conrado, cada um dos quaes era capellão do

---

1 Havia dois batalhões de caçadores, estando o 1.º de guarnição em Santos e o 2.º aquartelado nesta capital. Este se rebellou contra João Carlos a 3 de Junho de 1821, por falta de pagamento de seus soldos, e aquelle se rebellou em Santos pelo mesmo motivo na noite de 28 do mesmo mez de Junho. A primeira rebellião foi apaziguada pelo coronel Joaquim José dos Santos sem derramamento de sangue; porém a segunda trouxe o saque da villa de Santos e alguns assassinatos, acabando a vida na força alguns dos rebeldes e nas galés, com ferros, muitos outros. Vide a respeito vol. V desta *Revista*, pags. 38 e seguintes.

2 Se o depoente, que era militar de carreira e capitão, ignorava a natureza das citações feitas pelo brigadeiro Pinto, que se poderá dizer da soldadesca e da plébe reunidos pelos sediciosos no largo de S. Gonçalo?

seu batalhão, todos armados e municiados para impedirem a entrada do marechal Candido nesta cidade, com a sua tropa vinda de Santos com o fim de fazer cumprir as ordens de Sua Alteza Real, uma das quaes era empossar o marechal Arouche do governo das Armas desta provincia, proclamando no mesmo quartel o capitão Pedro Taques, o major Netto e o tenente Jayme *que aquella tropa, que vinha marchando, era uma caterva de ladrões que vinha atacar e saquear a cidade, para desta sorte animar a gente amotinada que alli se achava* (1), e proferindo tudo isto sem respeito algum ao commandante da força armada, que nenhum caso fazia disso, achando alli e observando todos estes movimentos (2); e chegou a tal ponto a falta de disciplina que o tenente coronel Jeronimo Pereira Crispim, que succedera a elle testemunha no commando do destacamento pelo deitarem para fóra depois do acontecido rebate, *andou convidando os officiaes para servirem a mesa aos soldados e á mais gente amotinada no quartel, onde havia muita comida e muito vinho* (3), e vivas ao coronel Francisco Ignacio e ao capitão Pedro Taques, a quem trouxeram em braços em ar de triumpho.—Ao nono, disse que muitos dias antes do motim acontecido na tarde do dia 23 de Maio, fôra rogado pelo capitão Nogueira, que o mandou chamar á sua casa, para uma reunião em casa do coronel Francisco Ignacio de Souza Queiroz, na rua Direita, na noite daquelle dia, em que o mandou chamar por um bilhete, pois lá se encontraria com muitas pessôas de bem para se tratar de um rebate afim de se expulsarem do governo ao coronel Martim e ao brigadeiro Jordão (4): e comparecendo elle testemunha alli na referida noite e achando lá o coronel Francisco Ignacio, o coronel Francisco Alvares, o ouvidor José da Costa Carvalho, o major Macedo, o capitão Nogueira e o tenente Jayme, concordaram entre si e instaram com elle testemunha para que houvesse o premeditado rebate, ao que não quiz elle testemunha annuir por ser um grande crime em que incorria, o que ouvindo o coronel Francisco Ignacio, que até alli estivera calado, disse

---

1 Não bastavam a cachaça, a genebra e o vinho para animar a gente amotinada; era necessario ainda inventar estas calumnias contra Candido Xavier e a sua tropa, que representavam a ordem e os sentimentos brasileiros em lucta contra os retrogrados e contra a officialidade venal que figurava na sedição!

2 Não podia fazer caso disso porque era obra sua, consciente e proposital, resultado immediato do emprego da cachaça, da genebra e do vinho como meio de levar aos fins desejados a soldadesca e a plébe paulistana; era elle quem pagava as despesas da festa revolucionaria.

3 Foi o elemento predominante nas desordens que affligiram esta capital desde 23 de Maio até 20 de Agosto de 1822; até o paço municipal foi transformado em botequim e taberna para regalo de soldados boçaes e da plébe inconsciente !

4 Não era só gente de bem, pois lá estavam officiaes que se deixavam subornar por soldados desejosos de escapar ao serviço militar activo.

que fizessem o que quizessem com tanto que o não compromettessem (1). A' vista da resolução que elle testemunha tomou sahiu o tenente Jayme muito inflammado dizendo-lhe que désse parte de doente e lhe apresentou papél e tinta; e não querendo elle testemunha fazer, por temer alguma desfeita, se retirou para sua casa, apezar de o continuarem a instar sobre o seu intentado projecto, e no outro dia deu parte de doente.—Ao decimo, disse nada e ao costume disse ser parente do coronel Daniel Pedro Müller em segundo gráu de affinidade, mixto ao primeiro. E lido o seu juramento, pelo achar conforme ao que havia deposto, o assignou com o miuistro inquiridor. E eu, o bacharel formado Manuel Joaquim de Ornellas, o escrevi.—*Freire.*—*Antonio de Padua de Gusmão.*

## ASSENTADA

Aos sete dias do mez de Outubro de 1822, nesta cidade de S. Paulo, em casas de residencia do doutor Antonio de Almeida Silva Freire da Fonseca, ministro da presente devassa, onde eu escrivão della fui vindo, e sendo ahi foram, por elle, ministro, interrogadas as testemunhas cujos nomes, cognomes, naturalidades, moradas, edades, officios, ditos e costumes é tudo o que adeante se segue, do que para constar fiz este termo de assentada. E eu, o bacharel formado Manoel Joaquim de Ornellas, u escrevi.

## TESTEMUNHA 22.ª

O CAPITÃO ANTONIO XAVIER FERREIRA (2), casado, natural da villa de Curityba e morador desta cidade, onde vive do seu ordenado de primeiro official da Caixa de Descontos da mesma, de edade de 55 annos; testemunha jurada aos Santos Evangelhos, em uns livros delles em que poz sua mão direita e, debaixo do juramento que prestou, prometteu dizer a verdade do que soubesse e perguntado lhe fosse. E sendo inquirido pelos interrogatorios da presente devassa disse, ao primeiro, que sabe, por lhe ter dito José Velloso de Oliveira, morador desta cidade, caixeiro ou socio de D. Thomaz de Molina, que quem mandára tocar a rebate, na tarde do dia 23 de Maio passado, fôra o major José Rodrigues Pereira de Oliveira Netto e que repugnando o official do estado-maior, tenente Ignacio José de

---

1 Era um dos chefes e o braço forte da sedição; mas antes de realizar o motim fazia-se de Pilatos e pedia que o não compromettessem!

2 Pelo nome, naturalidade e idade deve ser o pae do conego Ildefonso Xavier Ferreira, cujo depoimento já foi transcripto, testemunha 5.ª

Macedo, o forçára a mandal-o tocar pondo-lhe uma pistola aos peitos.—·Ao segundo, disse que nada sabia, bem como ao terceiro. —Ao quarto, disse que sómente sabe, por ver, que na frente da tropa, depois de estar postada no largo de S. Gonçalo, estiveram varios officiaes, como foram o brigadeiro Joaquim José Pinto de Moraes Leme, o coronel Francisco Alvares Ferreira do Amaral, os majores Francisco de Paula Macedo e José Rodrigues Pereira de Oliveira Netto, o capitão Antonio Cardoso Nogueira e o sargento-mór Antonio José de Jesus Andrade, e consta-lhe, por ser voz publica, que este motim tivera por objecto a conservação do presidente do extincto governo João Carlos Augusto de Oeynhausen e a deposição dos dois membros delle o coronel Martim Francisco Ribeiro de Andrade e o brigadeiro Manoel Rodrigues Jordão, sendo tudo contrario ás ordens de Sua Alteza Real, ouvindo elle testemunha publicamente na sala da camara ao capitão Pedro Taques de Almeida Alvim, em o 1.º de Julho do corrente anno *que não se tinha deposto a dois illustres membros do governo*, como se lia na carta de participação do mesmo governo a Sua Alteza Real, *mas sim a dois ladrões e a dois desavergonhados* (1), quando sempre constou a elle testemunha que aquelles dois membros do governo nunca tiveram semelhante nota e antes foram em todo o tempo bem conceituados na opinião publica (2).—Ao quinto, disse que sabe por ser publico e ter ouvido ao proprio juiz presidente que fôra para a casa da camara levado á força pelo capitão Pedro Taques de Almeida Alvim. — Ao sexto, disse que sabe por ser publico que muitos soldados e officiaes assignaram o auto de vereação extraordinaria do dia 23 de Maio preterito e algus outros papeis relativos aos acontecimentos daquelle dia obrigados e atemorizados pelos seus superiores e que os principaes agentes de tudo quanto se obrou em camara naquella occasião foram o ouvidor José da Costa Carvalho, o seu escrivão Amaro José Vieira, Joaquim Pedro Maia e o tenente Jayme da Silva Telles, o qual disse alli publicamente que o seu coronel Francisco Ignacio de Sousa Queiroz mandava saber por elle quaes eram os de opinião contraria ao que se projectava então fazer, porque então tinha alli aquella tropa para os fazer assentir ao seu projecto. Disse mais que lhe dissera o coronel Antonio José Vaz (3) que, tendo sido chamado na occasião do motim,

---

1 Pedro Taques era mero porta-voz dos seus companheiros de sedição; pessoalmente era já quasi irresponsavel pelo seu desequilibrio mental.

2 Estava o depoente no caso de saber por ser funccionario do Thesouro, assim como o brigadeiro Jordão, que era o thesoureiro da Junta da Fazenda.

3 Em um documento official de 1797 se lê que Antonio José Vaz já era capitão e que assentára praça em 1766, «sendo limpo de mãos, obediente, fiel e versado nos estudos» : nos serviços militares era exacto e prompto em as occasiões, «sendo a companhia de que elle era o capitão o modelo do 3.º regimento». Era paulista e tem muitos

fora ao palacio do governo, dalli ao quartel e depois á sala da Camara, onde se lhe fizera ver que a mesma Camara o tinha mandado procurar para que lhe notasse a acta de vereação e as participações que se fizeram por occasião della, ao que elle não quiz assentir por ver que tudo já estava arranjado e quasi concluido pelo referido ouvidor e seu escrivão Amaro José Vieira, que alli se acharam effectivamente até ao fim do acto, .... (1) .... déra sómente a norma .... (2) .... em que se fazia ver ao publico que ficasse tranquillo porque era conservado João Carlos Augusto de Oeynhausen na presidencia do governo e tinham sido depostos os dous membros que eram as duas maiores pedras de escandalo.—Ao decimo, disse nada.—Ao oitavo, disse que não lhe consta que o extincto governo, que então era composto do presidente João Carlos Augusto de Oeynhausen, do intendente Miguel José de Oliveira Pinto, do coronel Francisco Ignacio de Souza Queiroz, do coronel Daniel Pedro Müller e do tenente coronel Antonio Maria Quartim, désse providencia alguma sobre os acontecimentos do dia 23 de Maio passado, como a respeito dos mais que se seguiram, nem tão pouco tratou de punir os amotinadores, antes parecia approvar os seus desatinos, visto que o alferes Fadiga, que acompanhado de uma escolta havia arrombado a casa da Polvora no mencionado dia 23, fora um dos emissarios de que o governo se servira para levar o officio do mesmo governo ao Rio de Janeiro e que depois, regressando a esta cidade com o capitão José Fernandes da Silva sem despacho (3), como elle testemunha ouviu ao mesmo capitão José Fernandes da Silva, nem ao menos fora extranhado semelhante procedimento.—Ao nono e decimo, nada

descendentes nesta capital : rico e dado á poesia e á politica, foi eleitor e teve votos para alguns altos cargos da provincia no tempo da dependencia. Diz Azevedo Marquez que elle falleceu em 1843, sem dar-lhe a idade.

1 Faltam aqui duas ou tres palavras estragadas no original.

2 Está roto o original e devem faltar duas ou tres palavras.

3 O capitão José Fernandes da Silva, portuguez, foi o commandante da guarda encarregada de escoltar Martim Francisco até as divisas do Rio de Janeiro, com ordem de pôr-se desse ponto em deante á disposição do mesmo Martim, que dalli o levou preso até a cidade do Rio. De lá voltou, em companhia do alferes Fadiga, sem despacho algum e sem passaporte, allegando que a portaria, com que foi encarregado de levar Martim, para fóra da provincia, devia servir para fazel-o voltar a S. Paulo. Emquanto os sediciosos estiveram senhores desta Capital ficou elle impune ; porém depois foi preso e mettido na fortaleza, fazendo-se um processo regular sobre o facto e sahindo elle absolvido.

Elle e Fadiga eram dois agentes do governo sedicioso de S. Paulo, que estava cassado pelo decreto de 25 de Junho de 1822. Se José Bonifacio fosse aquelle ministro arbitrario e violento pintado pelos seus adversarios, tel-os-ia prendido no Rio como cumplices dos facciosos de S. Paulo : entretanto, podendo tel-o feito com razão e justos motivos, não o fez e elles voltaram a S. Paulo sem embaraços e daqui Fadiga fugiu para Portugal com o auxilio dos seus patrões.

disse, bem como ao costume. E sendo-lhe lido o seu juramento, pelo achar conforme ao que havia deposto, o assignou com o ministro devassante. E eu, o bacharel formado Manoel Joaquim de Ornellas, o escrevi.—*Freire.*—*Antonio Xavier Ferreira.*

---

## ASSENTADA

Aos 7 dias do mez de Outubro de 1822, nesta cidade de São Paulo, em casas de residencia do doutor Antonio de Almeida Silva Freire da Fonseca, ministro da presente devassa, onde eu escrivão da mesma me achava, e sendo ahi foram por elle inquiridas as testemunhas cujos nomes, cognomes, naturalidades, moradas, idades, officios, ditos e costumes é tudo o que adeante se segue, do que para constar fiz este termo de assentada. E eu, o bacharel formado Manoel Joaquim de Ornellas, o escrevi.

### TESTEMUNHA 23.ª

O SARGENTO-MÓR GASPAR RIBEIRO, viuvo, natural e morador desta cidade, onde vive do seu soldo, de idade de 54 para 55 annos; testemunha jurada aos Santos Evangelhos, em um livro delles em que poz sua mão direita e, debaixo do juramento que prestou, prometteu dizer a verdade do que soubesse e perguntado lhe fosse. E sendo inquirido pelos interrogatorios desta devassa disse, ao primeiro, que sabe, por ser publico nesta cidade e ter ouvido ao tenente Ignacio José de Macedo, que era o official do Estado maior na occasião do rebate, que fôra o major José Rodrigues Pereira de Oliveira Netto quem o mandou tocar, e ouviu aos tambores, que o andavam tocando pelas ruas, que o fim deste rebate éra para ser conservado na presidencia do governo o conselheiro João Carlos Augusto de Oeynhausen, que tinha sido chamado ao Rio de Janeiro por ordem de Sua Alteza Real; e depois de reunida a tropa no largo de São Gonçalo ouviu elle testemunha varios gritos que diziam: «*Fóra Martim Francisco, fóra Jordão!*», sem conhecer quem eram os que deram aquelles gritos, mas ouviu dizer geralmente que foram os majores Macedo e Netto, o capitão Pedro Taques de Almeida Alvim e os tenentes Mamede e Jayme, dizendo a elle testemunha o dito tenente Mamede que tinham sido depostos aquelles dous membros por serem prejudiciaes á patria.—Ao segundo, disse nada, bem como ao terceiro.—Ao quarto, disse que sabe, por ver, que quem puxou a tropa para o largo de São Gonçalo fóra o coronel Francisco Alves Ferreira do Amaral indo á frente della o brigadeiro Pinto, o tenente coronel Jeronimo Pereira Chrispim, o major Netto, e outros offciaes, de quem não tem lembrança, e que o referido major Netto ameaçou a elle testemunha com um conselho de guerra por não ter acudido ao rebate, sendo militar ao que elle mesmo testemunha respondeu que não estava para acudir á suas asneiras.—Ao quinto, disse que sabe, por ver, que o presidente da Camara, capitão Bento José Leite Penteado, fôra levado á força para a casa da Camara pelo capitão Pedro Taques de Almeida Alvim, indo este a cavallo e adeante delle o referido presidente a pé.—Ao sexto, disse que sabe, por ser publico, que varias pessoas assignaram o auto de vereação extraordinaria do dia 23 de Maio e outros papeis relativos aos acontecimentos daquelle dia por *serem illudidas e aterradas por alguns dos agentes do motim*, como eram Joaquim Pedro Maia, o major Netto e o tenente Patarata, QUE ILLUDIO E ATERROU A ELLE TESTEMUNHA AO PONTO DE O FAZER ASSIGNAR UM DOS REFERIDOS PAPEIS SEM O LER, NEM SABER O QUE ASSIGNAVA. —Ao setimo, disse nada.—Ao oitavo, disse que não lhe consta que pelo governo, em que só então tinham influencia o presidente João Carlos Augusto de Oeynhausen, o intendente Miguel José de Oliveira Pinto, o coronel Francisco Ignacio de Souza Queiroz, o coronel Daniel Pedro Müller e o tenente coronel Antonio Maria Quartim, se désse providencia alguma sobre os acontecimentos do dia 23 de Maio passado e os que posteriormente se seguiram, como foi o ajuntamento de militares, paizanos, negros e mulatos no quartel, aonde tambem concorreram um frade franciscano por nome Frei Antonio do Menino Jesus e o padre Bernardo Conrado, todos armados e municiados para impedirem a entrada do marechal Candido nesta cidade, com sua tropa vinda da villa de Santos, nem tão pouco se mandasse devassar de semelhantes factos, nem fossem punidos os seus perpetradores e fautores.—Ao nono e decimo, disse nada, nem do costume. E lido o seu depoimento, pelo achar conforme ao que havia deposto, o assignou. E eu, o bacharel formado Manuel Joaquim de Ornellas, o escrevi.—*Freire.—Gaspar Ribeiro da Rosa Ramos.*

# Campanha de 1827

DISCURSO PRONUNCIADO A 20 DE MAIO DE 1905

PELO

SR. CORONEL HENRIQUE DE MACEDO

*Exmo. sr. presidente. Dignissimos srs. consocios do Instituto:*

« Em nós palpita o amor da historia, alicerce do sentimento patriotico e condição do espirito de nacionalidade ».

Em cumprimento da nossa promessa feita na sessão de 4 do corrente, vimos dar-vos hoje as razões pelas quaes mais convencidos nos achamos do diagnostico que formulamos a respeito do general argentino Carlos M. de Alvear, no estudo que tivemos a honra de apresentar-vos, anteriormente, sobre a memoravel batalha do Passo do Rosario ou Ituzaingo, em 20 de Fevereiro de 1827 ganha com incrivel bravura por nossos soldados e chefes ao mando do preclaro general marquez de Barbacena.

Dissemos, então, que, pela leitura minuciosa feita por nós sobre a individualidade de Alvear, estudo todo elle feito por nós em livros argentinos, pois que não os ha de outra nacionalidade que tratem desse assumpto, verificamos ser o mesmo general um bem acabado typo morbido, um nevrotico, um desequilibrado em fim, condemnado *a priori* a ser batido como foi, desde que enfrentasse com um exercito regular e um general methodico.

Agora, lendo um interessante livro *As nevroses dos homens celebres da historia argentina*, por J. M. Ramos Mejia, presidente do *Circolo-medico* de Bueno Aires, tivemos occasião de verificar que se achava perfeitamente corroborada essa nossa asserção por esse notavel clinico, pois, a pagina 28 na citada obra: vem declinado o nome de Alvear, como alistado nas sombrias phalanges de que fazem parte em gráu excessivo os nevroticos Francia, Belgrano, Aldáo, Ramires e tantos outros que por seus proprios desatinos sobrenadaram aos successos daquelles tempos.

Devemos á obsequiosidade do nosso distincto consocio o mui illustre sr. dr. Domingos Jaguaribe a leitura dessa obra prima que generosamente nol-a confiou emprestada (baldos que nos vemos, ha longos annos, de todos os recursos, especialmente de bons livros, nossa innocente paixão!) Nossos agradecimentos.

Estudando o campo de batalha de Ituzaingo, as peripecias que a precederam, o epilogo daquelle sanguinolento drama internacional, ficamos admirados dos erros commettidos pelo general invasor Alvear, victima, sem duvida, de um estado morbido que o incapacitava de desempenhar com acerto as graves e elevadas funcções de commandante em chefe de um exercito em campanha.

Em sua vida anterior, nas differentes commissões que desempenhava, era sempre infeliz, ao ponto de ser expulso de sua patria e alli ter o nome de Catilina II. Rodeado sempre dos peiores elementos como os Lopes. os Carreras, e outros que se assignalavam pelo roubo, pelo saque, por todos os crimes, que arrhas daria de si nessa campanha?

De principio a fim, Alvear infringia os principios da bôa politica; hostilizava os orientaes, seus alliados, e maltratava os habitantes pacificos por onde transitava com suas hordas devastadoras.

Conculcava as regras da estrategia, escolhendo os mais longos e peiores caminhos para alcançar nossa aberta fronteira; assignalava sua marcha com o incendio, a destruição, a deshonra, a morte!

No Camacuan Chico e em S. Gabriel, enchia se de terrores vãos ao ouvir a trovoada, ou o ribombo do canhão, e, alli, as suas vacillações deram ganho definitivo de causa ao exercito bra-ileiro, que operou a sua juncção com a ala esquerda remota, sem o minimo obstaculo, quando devêra ser esmagado em detalhe. Os panicos subitos que o assaltaram bem indicavam ser o general Alvear incompativel com serviço das armas que demanda *mens sana in corpore sano.*

Tendo ás suas ordens forças duplas ás nossas; tendo previamente escolhido terreno para o combate, além de outras vantagens, Alvear foi batido pelas disposições pessimas que tomou, filhas de um cerebro enfermo.

Não podemos attribuir á ignorancia os erros palmares de tactica, manobras impossiveis e condemnadas pela sciencia, pela prudencia, pela experiencia.

No dia da acção, os seus melhores cabos de guerra Brandzem, José Maria Paz, Lavalle e outros foram pelo general Alvear insultados, levados ao desespero, á desobediencia ou ao suicidio!

Infelizmente para Alvear, até a natureza nesse dia era contra elle, pois, além de sol abrazador, ventava o ardente norte, impregnado das emanações mephiticas dos banhados existentes ás margens do Santa Maria e do Inhatium; ora, o mesmo dr. Mejia affirma que Francia, tyranno do Paraguay, quando ventava o calido norte nas ruas arenosas de Assumpção, tornava se feroz, cruel, impossivel, devido á nevrose, cujas crises se aggravavam com aquelle phenomeno da natureza.

Por tudo que lemos, repetimos que os erros do general Alvear, sem que queiramos invadir os terrenos pertencentes aos filhos de Hippocrates, não podiam ter outro diagnostico qual o que fizemos, principalmente quando soubemos pelos historiadores argentinos que Alvear pretendia fazer passear triumphantes pelas ruas do Rio de Janeiro as bandeiras argentinas!

Dissemos, então, que essas velleidades já não são simples hespanholadas mas accusavam um producto morbido, senhor de um individuo nevrotico e prognosticamos que esse general Alvear levaria inconscientemente suas massas, sua multidão, á derrota, á perdição: e foi o que se deu em Ituzaingo.

Orgulhamo-nos de ter achado a confirmação desse nosso diagnostico, nas primorosas paginas escriptas por tão insigne especialista clinico argentino, que, sem o querer, veiu ajudar-nos no empenho em que estamos de restabelecer a verdade historica e a reivindicação de nossos sagrados direitos, quanto aos louros da victoria que ornou a fronte de nossos bravos, a 20 de Fevereiro de 1827, em Ituzaingo, na memoravel batalha do Passo do Rozario.»

Ao terminar a leitura, o orador foi muito applaudido.

# Parecer sobre um Projecto de Estrada de Ferro de tracção electrica para Matto Grosso do Sr. Augusto Cambraia

*Non quis, sed quid*

A invasão de Matto Grosso em 1865, com todas suas dolorosas consequencias, pois os Paraguayos em vastissima zona tudo levaram a ferro e a fogo, obrigou o nosso descuidoso governo a invocar o nunca desmentido valor e patriotismo dos Paulistas que, presurosos, acudiram ao reclamo, tendo porém de marchar para debellar o audaz inimigo por mais de tresentas legoas de invios desertos, soffrendo a fome, mil miserias, e... *calcante pede*.

Entretanto encho-me de orgulho quando olho para esse passado no qual figurei.

Terminada a custosa campanha com honra e gloria para os nossos fóros, os restos do Exercito Brazileiro regressaram á Patria que bem depressa delles se esqueceu e nem cuidou de tirar proveito da licção. Continnamos a seguir o adagio: «Quartel General de Abrantes, tudo como dantes». Nossos vizinhos prosperaram, se prepararam para novas surprezas; mas declarando sempre *mui buenas intenciones*, muita confraternização e solidariedade americanas! E se prepararam!

Do lethargo em que jazia o Brazil e da sinceridade dos protestos diplomaticos dos vizinhos estamos colhendo fructos bem. amargos, addicionados aos terriveis males internos que nos assoberbam!

Si Palinuros adestrados talvez conseguem livrar hoje a náu com os destinos patrios de se despedaçar em forjados parceis; quiçá amanhã a temerosa borrasca que sente surgir nol-a arrebate; e,... então, a imprevidencia, a ignorancia o *laisser faire* nos deparará dias amargos! Si não nós, quem sabe nossos filhos irão cultivar as frias pampas da Patagonia, sob a ameaça do cuchillo degolador!

Não é devaneio; fomos dos que libertamos milhares de brazileiros levados captivos do Rio Grande do Sul e Matto Grosso para trabalhar nos hervaes febricitantes do Igatimi!

Não é devaneio; agora mesmo soubemos que nossos patricios, quando não fuzilados, são marcados a ferro em braza, qual
rebanho de gado vil!

Não é devaneio; a America do Sul, a do Norte, a Europa,
o mundo inteiro, zomba de nós, de nossa fraqueza, da instabili-
dade de nossos governos, da tibieza revelada nas relações diplomaticas, da venalidade dos tribunaes, da corrupção geral!

Não é devaneio; os échos do jornalismo de Buenos-Ayres,
Assumpcion e La Paz só nos trazem insultos e ameaças que
quebrantam os brios e abatem o amor proprio! E tudo impune-
mente! Tal o abatimento e fraqueza do Brazil.

Visões por toda a parte! Mil escriptores assalariados do Velho e Novo Mundo espalham mil balelas, mil embustes contra
nós: ora é o Pan-germanismo alongando vistas cubiçosas para
as nossas colonias de Santa Catharina e do Rio Grande; ora,
o inventado imperialismo norte-americano; ora, uma procuradis-
sima alliança de certas Republicas Sul Americanas contra as
pretenções expansivas da Europa, mas, na realidade para em-
maranhar o Brazil em teias platinas; ora, conselhos ao Paraguay
quanto ao perdão da divida de guerra; mas cujo fim, é preparar um futuro alliado, bem como a Bolivia, o Perú e o Estado
Oriental; verdadeira leva de broqueis desses paizes todos contra
nós nas relações diplomaticas, na imprensa, nos livros, até nas
intrigas com os proprios Brazileiros Nacionaes!

Bem se vê que tudo isso é movido por uma só mão occulta de inimigo invejoso, rancoroso, secular! *Carthago* a exigir
uma *delenda!*

Seculares são as pendencias que alimentam contra o magnanimo Brazil, liliputianos vizinhos incommodos! Enriqueci-
dos com a farta bolsa do Brasil durante a guerra, medraram á
nossa sombra; engrandeceram-se em territorios; criaram apara-
tosa esquadra; e, ... escalonaram uma cintura de bayonetas ca-
ladas, ameaçando nossos flancos! E a esquadra branca não viu
isso!...

Agora, riem-se de nós e com razão!... Com os seus celebres boletins, com os seus historiadores *sui generis;* com os
seus *cuentos* adormecem a fibra patriotica dos nossos Patricios!
Os brasileiros perseguindo os justos, opprimindo a virtude exal-
tando a ignorancia, offuscando a verdade, abatendo o caracter
nacional muito se debilitaram!

Esquecida a nação Brasileira das verdades eternas, entre
outras, das maximas militares: *Si vis pacem, para bellum,* e
dest'outra.: *La paix est le rêve des sages, mais la guerre est
d'histoire des hommes,* imprudentemente desorganisou as finanças,

desmantellou a marinha, aliás tão gloriosa; debilitou o exercito soffredor, egyde da Nação e subverteu as instituições bellicas, esteios da classe militar, penhor de nossas glorias!

Si amanhan se declarar a guerra, o que é muito possivel, e, *quod Deus avertat*, como abriremos a campanha? Podindo ao inimigo preparado e rapido *sicut fulmen*, que nos espere? Não! Teremos de soffrer descalabros, devido a incuria criminosa em que jazemos!

E, no emtanto, ha um meio bem facil de conjurar muitas desgraças, muitos perigos, e ainda ficaremos, nós, Paulistas especialmente, ricos e fortes eternamente! Parece incrivel!? Mas é a verdade:

Basta prolongarmos de qualquer ponto terminal uma de nossas linhas de estrada de ferro do oeste demandando o Paraná, o Paraguay, os Andes, o Pacifico emfim. Esta foi a rota batida por nossos maiores, com menos recursos, os legendarios Bandeirantes Paulistas!

Não vacillemos em amparar siquer com o nosso influxo moral qualquer idéa como o projecto da estrada de que cogitamos, nypothese mais que realisavel do cidadão Augusto Cambraia, pois que é inadiavel a resolução desse problema grandioso, que nos trará uma communicação sempre segura. rapida directa com o riquissimo inexplorado Estado de Matto Grosso, sem dependencia da hostil, da duvidosa linha fluvial, por entre odientos paizes estrangeiros!

Quer o prolongamento parta do ponto terminal da Paulista no Bebedouro, marginando o piscoso Mogy-Guassú até cabir no imponente Rio Grande, e dahi seguindo pelas verdes campinas de Barretos, fartas de gado, para o magestoso Paraná, podendo aproveitar a famosa cachoeira do Marimbondo como poderosa força motora; quer seguindo de Ribeirãozinho pelo traçado antigo e já estudado do nosso malogrado patricio e distincto engenheiro Dr. Pimenta Bueno procurando o conhecido porto do Taboado, acima de Itapura, ou mesmo avançando pela margem esquerda e sul do nosso querido Tieté nas alturas de Agudos abeirando e talvez aproveitando como *carvão branco* seus imponentes saltos até enfrentar, além do Paraná, com os magnificos e historicos campos da Vaccaria; emfim, parta donde partir, e de qualquer daquellas linhas, ou mesmo das intermediarias como de Jahú e de Dourados; o que se deve fazer é prolongar a estrada, e com urgencia, por ser o unico traçado intuitivo, scientifico, commercial, estrategico; (veja-se qualquer mappa daquellas regiões).

A esse prolongamento, seja qual fôr o traçado que se adoptar, dar-se-á o nome—*velis, nolis*,—de linha geral estrategica,

unica que servirá para todo o Brazil; será uma especie de—
*divortium viarum*—por isso que unica e invulneravel cobrirá todo
o sul do Brazil e defenderá todo Oeste pela rapidez de suas
communicações. Ainda mais: si abrisse uma communicação, um
canal, nas cabeceiras do rio Paraguay com as vertentes do Amazonas, entre o Aguapehy e o Alegre, (distão apenas um do outro
oitocentos metros!) poderá servir para toda a zona do Norte.

Nós Paulistas, mui particularmente os engenheiros e militares estrategicos devemos empregar todos os esforços para desviar
o governo de commetter dois grandes erros: 1.º levar a linha
estrategica, ainda que parta de S. Paulo, para os sertões inter-
minos de Goyaz: 2.° vender qualquer fracção de via ferrea a
companhias extrangeiras. Os perigos são palpaveis. Já os Ro-
manos o dizião: *hospes, hostis*. As companhias extrangeiras
visam apenas bons dividendos, attentando ao nosso futuro; ellas
virão sugar a pouca seiva de nossa comballida lavoura; intervirão
fatalmente na nossa politica interna, avassalando caracteres; fi-
carão, afinal, com as chaves de nossas communicações internas.

Seria nos livrar de Scylla para cahir em Charibides; isto
é, evitarmos o perigo da navegação fluvial burlada, onerada,
atravancada com os Martim Garcia do Prata, e crearmos outro
maior, interno, terrestre, no seio de nosso bello e livre Estado,
aliás já tão sobrecarregado de difficuldades.

Desviemos o governo das syrtes enganadoras; e tratemos,
quanto antes de avançar para a conquista do desconhecido Oeste.

Este é o succinto parecer que damos sobre o requerimento
do cidadão A. Cambraia, em que pede ao Instituto o apoio para
construir uma estrada de ferro, por tracção electrica que sahindo
dos nossos portos do Atlantico, procure nos ligar com Matto-
Grosso.

Não tendo o Instituto outros meios, entendo que deve dar
todo o apoio moral a commettimentos tão grandiosos, não se im-
pressionando com o —quis—porém sim com o—quid.

S. Paulo, 5 de Maio de 1903.

HENRIQUE AFFONSO DE ARAUJO MACEDO.

# Os primitivcs aldeiamentos Indigenas e indios mansos de Itanhaen

No tomo II — n. 1 da «Revista da Sociedade de Ethnographia e Civilização dos Indios», vem uma importante *Memoria sobre as aldeias de Indios da Provincia*, pelo general José Arouche de Toledo Rendon, bem como *Uma noticia raciocinada sobre as aldeias dos Indios da mesma provincia, desde o seu começo até a actualidade* (1845) pelo brigadeiro José Joaquim Machado de Oliveira; e ainda uma *Memoria sobre a catechese e civilização dos indigenas da provincia de S. Paulo*, pelo dr. Joaquim Antonio Pinto Junior.

O general Arouche trata de todas as aldeias e occupa-se em descrever as atrocidades praticadas contra esses infelizes indios aldeados, e da expoliação de que foram victimas nas terras em que constituiram as suas aldeias.

Diz o general Arouche que parte dessas aldeias, depois da expulsão dos jesuitas, e algumas, mesmo desde a sua fundação, foram dadas em apanagio aos frades Carmelitas, Benedictinos e Capuchos. Neste numero, não sei com que fundamento, elle dá á aldeia de Itanhaem e Peruhibe como regida, desde seus principios por estes ultimos, os Capuchos.

Na descripção que o auctor faz das demais aldeias, comprovando as suas asserções com alguns documentos, e determinando a extensão dos terrenos que cada uma dessas aldeias possuia; vê-se, entretanto, que elle estava mal informado quanto aos aldeamentos de Itanhaem, pois, apenas, toca por alto quando se refere a ellas, ou francamente confessa-se mal seguro da materia, quando diz: «Ignoro as terras que possue a aldeia de S. João de Peruhibe; mas pelo menos deve ter uma legua, que no caso de não ter outras lhe devia ser dada; em observancia ao alvará de 23 de Novembro de 1700, pelo qual Sua Magestade mandou que se désse a cada aldeia, tendo 100 casaes, uma legua de terra em quadra, etc.»

Diremos adiante quaes foram os administradores dessas aldeias; quaes as terras que possuiam as mesmas desde os seus principios e as que possuem ainda actualmente.

O brigadeiro Machado de Oliveira é mais extenso na sua *Noticia Raciocinada*, onde dá uma noticia especial sobre a fundação da aldeia de Itanhaem, embora não concordemos com as accusações, que faz aos capuchos e jesuitas, acceitando o auctor, neste ponto as informações do general Arouche.

Na pequena monographia a *Villa de Itanhaem*, que publicamos em folheto, já nos occupamos em uma ligeira noticia sobre a fundação da aldeia de Itanhaem e da sua egreja. Ao fazermos essas referencias não podemos deixar sem alguns reparos e mesmo de censurar o facto de não ter o brigadeiro Machado de Oliveira se occupado sériamente no seu importante livro *Quadro Historico da Provincia de S. Paulo*, dos fundamentos e annaes dessa aldeia, unica no littoral do nosso Estado, e uma das primitivas da antiga capitania de Martim Affonso, mórmente sendo s. s., além de erudito escriptor — o director geral das aldeias da provincia.

Lamentamos que não tivesse dito o auctor consultado os annaes e archivos de Itanhaem, quando em 1855 foi s. s. commissionado pelo Instituto Historico e Geographico do Brazil para vir a S. Vicente consultar os archivos dessa Camara e de outras povoações primitivas, antes de escrever o seu citado livro. Nessa época teria ainda encontrado nos archivos de Itanhaem os documentos que ahi pereciam de velhice e em abandono completo, sem jámais serem consultados pelos chronistas... Como esse nosso folheto é pouco conhecido, convém que registemos aqui algumas das considerações e noticias que nelle formulamos, rectificando ainda outros enganos e faltas que se encontram na parte em que o auctor da *Noticia Racionada* se refere ao aldeamento de Itanhaem.

«Pelo que se infere, diz o dito brigadeiro Machado, das poucas noticias historicas que ha sobre os tempos primitivos de S. Paulo, parece provavel que a fundação da aldeia da Conceição de Itanhaem fosse um pouco posterior á da villa de S. Vicente, e coetanea com a de S. Paulo. Na categoria de villa tem S. Paulo a prioridade de um anno, porque, tendo a povoação de Piratininga o predicamento de villa em 1560, a aldeia de Itanhaem só a teve em 1561». De facto, a elevação de Itanhaem ao predicamento de villa teve logar em 1561, porêm, a fundação desse povoado fundado por Martim Affonso no certo periodo de dous annos que elle demorou em sua capitania é contemporanea ao de S. Vicente. Foram essas as duas unicas povoações fundadas pelo donatario.

Além de outros chronistas, é o proprio Machado de Oliveira quem o affirma no seu excellente livro *Quadro Historico da Provincia de S. Paulo*, que foi escripto e publicado muito tempo depois delle ter escripto a sua *Noticia Raciocinada*, à qual nos referimos.

Possuindo então melhores dados e informações e obedecendo a estudos acurados sobre este assumpto, diz elle no seu *Quadro Historico*:

«Pareceu a Martim Affonso que o povoamento do primeiro quinhão de suas terras devia começar da ilha de S. Vicente para o sul, visto que, em sentido contrario, ia confundir-se com a doação de seu irmão, que fôra designada de S. Vicente para o norte».

«Neste intento dirigiu-se, antes de partir para Portugal, ás terras occupadas no littoral pela tribu dos Itanhaens e, na barra do rio do mesmo nome, distante de S. Vicente oito leguas, designou o local onde devia ter assento a povoação, que desde seu fundamento teve o nome de villa da Conceição de Itanhaem, e já com o pensamento que seria alli a séde de sua colonia, por apresentar melhores condições de segurança e vantagens agricolas .. »

No citado folheto *A Villa de Itanhaem*, nos occupamos longamente deste assumpto, provando que a povoação de Itanhaem foi a segunda fundada pelo donatario; e só este periodo que vimos de citar destroe as asserções contrarias que o escriptor faz na sua anterior *Noticia*, sobre a época da fundação da aldêa e povoação de Itanhaem, na qual refere ainda que: «A elevação de S. Vicente, Santos, Santo André e Piratininga, á categoria de villas, foi que excitou em seu primeiro capitão-mór Francisco de Moraes, a fatuidade de dar identico predicamento á sua pequena, colonia de Itanhaem».

Quando, na nossa citada monographia, dissemos,—ser a villa de Itanhaem a segunda povoação fundada por Martim Affonso, —foi baseado, não só nesta affirmação que vimos de citar, do Brigadeiro Machado de Oliveira, como na opinião de outros chronistas.

Só mais tarde, após a publicação deste nosso folheto, é que tivemos conhecimento do «Diario de Pedro Lopes de Souza» e da «Carta do Padre Manoel da Nobrega»; documento esse que consta da preciosa collecção de manuscriptos, da cidade de Evora, mandados copiar para a bibliotheca do Instituto Historico do Brazil.

Uma dessas cartas, datadas de S. Vicente, 1556, e dirigidas a Santo Ignacio de Loyola, vem o primeiro apostolo do

Brazil esclarecendo definitivamente esse ponto dizer-nos, que «a povoação de Piratininga é anterior a de Santo André, e foi fundada pelo primeiro donatario», dando assim razão ao que diz o «Diario de Pedro Lopes» tão contestado. O sr. dr. Candido Mendes de Almeida, nas suas «Notas para a Historia Patria», tambem affirmava, como nós, que a 2.ª povoação era Itanhaem. Em vista porêm destes ultimos documentos o illustre escriptor rectificou depois o seu engano; como nós o fazemos de bom grado.

As povoações fundadas por Martim Affonso, são portanto S. Vicente, Piratininga e Itanhaem.

Ao referir-se á aldeia de Peruhibe diz o mesmo auctor que : « nem siquer sabe-se com evidencia qual fosse a sua origem. Presume-se que o seu local serviu de refugio aos grupos de indigenas que evitaram o encontro da expedição de Moraes, quando este se lançou sobre as tribus dos Itanhaens, que habitavam as margens do rio Conceição ; e amalgamando-se elles com uma fracção de Carijós, seus inimigos, que então dominavam e fruiam pacificamente todo o littoral, que vae do rio Conceição ao dos Patos. O commum perigo os obrigou a darem-se as mãos.

Este sitio ficando quatro leguas distante de Itanhaem, encerra os mesmos inconvenientes daquelle ».

Não sabemos donde hauri o escriptor estas noticias sobre a posição pessima das terras de Itahanhaen e Peruhibe e principalmente quando se refere a essa expedição organizada por Francisco de Moraes antes de ser Itanhaem elevada á Villa, na qual expedição o mesmo Moraes « levou a ferro e a fogo os indigenas que alli deparou, subjugando os que não puderam fugir e com estes, sob a condição de escravos, erigiu a aldeia que foi conhecida com o nome de Itanhaem, derivado da tribu que anteriormente tivera por solar esse territorio ».

Alguns annos após, quando o brigadeiro Machado de Oliveira, melhor orientado sem duvida em todos estes assumptos, dá alguns dados historicos sobre Itanhaem, no seu citado livro Quadro Historico da Provincia de S. Paulo, não faz a menor referencia a estes factos e a estas correrias de Francisco de Moraes contra os miseros indios de Itanhaem.

Isto nos leva a suppôr que, tendo então, seguramente, conhecimentos mais positivos sobre o facto, não quiz servir-se desses, porque os julgava, talvez, pouco provaveis.

Os indios da tribu dos Itanhaens, fugindo ás perseguições de Moraes, não podiam ir unir-se aos Carijós e refugiar-se em Peruhybe, tão perto de Itanhaem e ahi formar essa outra aldeia

Não, os indigenas que compunham esse aldeamento já viviam ahi em commum desde épocas prehistoricas.

Essa aldêa estava, ha muito desfalcada, e quasi extincta, quando Francisco de Moraes ahi chegou.

Não dizemos isto para pretender isentar a memoria desse primeiro capitão-mór de Itanhaem, da atroz perseguição que, por ventura, moveu aos pobres indios dessa tribu, porque sabemos bem que nesse tempo de barbarismo, esses audazes aventureiros, a começar pelo primeiro donatario Martim Affonso, que *tão bôa fama* deixou na India, todos quasi sem excepção, viviam animados da mesma disposição, hostis contra os desventurados aborigenes.

Sabe se hoje que, todo esse territorio da marinha que vae do rio Itanhaen ao dos Patos, isto è, entre Santa Catharina e Conceição de Itanhaem, foi outr'ora theatro das horrorosas façanhas do celebre bacharel, o *mestre Cosme*, Pedro Corrêa, Ruy Mochéra e outros audazes e temiveis aventureiros que viviam do barbaro e exclusivo commercio de escravizar e vender indios.

Peruhybe não podia, portanto, servir de refugio ás victimas de Moraes, porque nesse tempo, já estava ahi o celebre Pedro Corrêa com suas naus atracadas na ilha grande do Guarahú ; e suas hostes terriveis batiam toda essa zona dos Itatins (Itatinga) até as fraldas do Paranápiacaba.

E' bastante conhecida hoje, aos que se dedicam aos estudos da nossa historia primitiva, essa segunda carta de data que Pedro Corrêa pediu a 25 de Maio de 1542 ao loco-tenente de Martim Affonso, das terras de Peruhybe e Guarahú, por ter perdido a primeira carta em um naufragio.

Esses terrenos, antes de serem doados a Pedro Corrêa já tinham pertencido ao tal bacharel de Cananéa o *mestre Cosme* que habitava já este litoral quando Martim Affonso nelle aportou. Essas terras estavam, portanto, devolutas quando Martim Affonso as deu a Pedro Corrêa. Por ahi se vê que antes mesmo de Martim Affonso chegar a S. Vicente, já esses aventureiros devastavam os sertões do littoral e destruiam as aldêas, escravizando e vendendo os seus habitantes.

Trasladamos para aqui uma parte desse importante documento, não obstante ser bem conhecido e fazer parte da nossa citada monographia : «...a 2.ª parte (de terras) que dizem Peruhibe, dada ao dito Pedro Corrêa, pelo dito Gonçalo Monteiro, (Loco-tenente), e nomeadamente para elle Pedro Corrêa, e para um seu irmão que esperava vir a esta terra, e que não vindo fica-se toda a elle Pedro Corrêa ; e parte (divide) nesta maneira, trasladada letra por letra do dito registro de terras seguinte : em Peruhibe, convem a saber : *onde foi aldeia dos indios*, indo desta villa de S. Vicente para a dita aldeia dos indios.

Peruhibe começa a partir de um regato que está aquem da dita aldeia, que chamam em lingua dos indios Tapirama (hoje Tapirêma) que está da banda do levante, e da outra banda do poente passando o rio grande que se chama Guarahype (Guarahú) e em nosso nome lhe puzemos Santa Catharina, partindo pelo mar, assim como vai a costa de maneira que tanto haja na bocca, pelo mar e costa, como na entrada pela dita terra, as quaes terras dou ao dito Pedro Corrêa novamente, e mais lhe dou a dita ilha que já atrás digo... etc., etc... »

Essa ilha, da qual trata a primeira parte deste documento, é a que fica em frente á fôz do rio Guarahú. E' uma ilha tristemente celebre, pois além de servir de porto e amparo ás náus empregadas nesse barbaro trafico primitivo, serviu ainda em nossos dias como *excellente refugio e abrigo* aos navios de *negros novos*, depois que os nossos portos foram trancados a esse infame commercio africano, quando os navios britanicos começaram a dar-lhes caça nos mares do nosso extenso littoral.

A primeira parte do documento que se refere a tal ilha, diz assim: « Faço saber aos que esta minha carta de confirmação virem, como por Pedro Corrêa, morador nesta villa de S. Vicente, me foi feita uma petição em que diz, que por Gonçalo Monteiro, que aqui foi capitão, lhe foram dadas umas terras, da outra banda desta ilha (S. Vicente) que é porto das náus, terra que era dada a um *mestre Cosme bacharel*, e outra d'onde chamam Peruhibe, e é dez ou doze legu s desta villa, das quaes terras elle Pedro Corrêa tinha carta e lhe cahira ao mar, etc... e me pedindo pelas ditas confrontações que no dito livro do tombo estavam, lhe mandasse passar nova carta das ditas terras que me pedia, e mais umn ilha, de tres que estão defronte da dita terra de Peruhibe, para seu *aposentamento de carga e descarga das suas náus*; (1) convem a saber: das ditas tres ilhas a maior... etc... »

Todas essas terras, como já referimos, não só as que ficavam « defronte da ilha de S. Vicente », no porto das náus, bem como essa vasta extensão que vai desde o ribeiro de Itapirêma até o rio do Guarahú, no municipio de Itanhaem, já tinham pertencido ao celebre bacharel de Cananéa, e se achavam devolutas quando Pedro Corrêa pela primeira vez pediu ao substituto de Martim Affonso que lh'as concedesse por carta de data, como provam estes documentos.

_____

(1) O grypho é nosso.

E' bastante conhecida tambem a vida de Pedro Corrêa, para que nos detenhamos longamente com a figura importante desse temivel aventureiro, desse heróe e martyr! E' entretanto necessario registar aqui alguns factos que se relacionam com o objecto de que tratamos, pois a vida desse heróe está extremamente ligada aos factos mais importantes do desaparecimento da aldeia de Peruhibe e da fundação da de Itanhaem.

A aldeia de Peruhibe, assente a margem esquerda do rio do mesmo nome, já estava, como se vê, despovoada nesse tempo.

Dos seus habitantes, parte refugiou-se nos sertões e parte foi presa e vendida como escravos. Um numero de indigenas pertencentes a tribu dos Itanhaens reduzidos a condições de es-cravos, ou de colonos, viviam então aggregados á pequena colonia fundada pelo donatario. Essa colonia cuja fundação data, sem duvida, de 1532, foi estabelecida, não á margem esquerda do rio Itanhaem, como diz o *Quadro Historico*, mas no meio da praia de Peruhibe, entre o ribeirão de Itapirêma e o pequeno rio Paranámirim. (Ponta da aldeia).

Em 1549 o castelhano João Rodrigues e o portuguez Christovam Gonçalves, foram estabelecer-se no mesmo littoral, escolhendo para isso um local, á margem esquerda da fóz do rio Itanhaem, duas leguas aquem da referida colonia ou aldeia. Estes dois individuos, não quizeram juntar-se á povoação fundada por Martim Affonso, porque julgaram aquelle sitio mais vantajoso.

Em fins desse anno de 1549 chegara tambem a S. Vicente o padre Leonardo Nunes e o *irmão* Diogo Jacome, com o fim de doutrinarem os gentios. Estes dois missionarios jesuitas, os primeiros que aportaram a nossas plagas, vinham da Bahia, mandados pelo padre Nobrega que ali, naquelle mesmo anno, aportára em companhia de Thomé de Souza.

Leonardo Nunes *o obarè bebé* visitou logo os indigenas de Itanhaem: viu a devastação cruel que por ali reinava: conheceu o estado de aviltamento a que estavam sujeitos os pobres indios de Itanhaem e de todo esse littoral, onde dominava a vontade potente de Corrêa e dos seus barbaros sequazes. Cedo, como se vê, começou a lucta entre os ambiciosos aventureiros e missionarios que tenazmente se oppuzeram contra a escravidão e flagicios impostos aos pobres indios...

Os jesuitas, que missionavam o littoral, fizeram sua parada habitual, no meio dessa tribu de Itanhaens. Ahi começaram elles por edificar uma ermida, que mais tarde foi transformada em egreja parochial, cujas ruinas ainda alli vemos e admiramos.

Os colonos portuguezes que ahi habitavam, não podendo mais exercer sobre os indios aldeados a mesma prepotencia de antes, porque então a vóz e o braço do missionario já se erguiam em defesa dos miseros captivos, e sobre tudo oppunham-se ao barbaro *commercio* que Correia e seus prepostos alli exerciam, resolveram portanto, os ditos colonos, deixar a aldeia e reuniram-se aos dois aventureiros que tinham vindo situar-se á margem esquerda da barra do rio Itanhaem.

Quando em 1556, as hordas bellicosas dos Tamoyos investiram sobre S. Vicente e desvastaram a povoação, parte dos seus habitantes se refugiram no littoral do sul e vieram abrigar-se no pov' ado que começava a surgir em torno das habitações dos dois individuos já citados.

Dahi em deante essa povoação foi sempre em augmento, pois que, em 1561 era elevada á categoria de villa, sob a denominação de Villa da Conceição de Itanhaem, sendo seu primeiro capitão-mór o dito Francisco de Moraes, do qual já nos occupamos.

A aldeia de Itanhaem, no meio da qual se estabeleceram os primeiros jesuitas, e na qual edificaram sua egreja, nada tinha de commum com a povoação, que teve o predicamento de villa nesse anno de 1561.

Essa aldeia, a quem o donatario Martim Affonso deu o nome e invocação de N. S. da Conceição, conservou ainda por muitos annos esse titulo. Era, entretanto, uma verdadeira anomalia, para não dizer um absurdo, a existencia dessas duas povoações, tão proximas, tendo ambas a mesma denominação.

A aldeia cedeu, entretanto, o titulo á villa; porém, os indios jámais consentiram que a veneranda imagem de N. S. da Conceição que existia na sua egreja, fosse transladada para a villa.

Dahi em deante a aldeia de Itanhaem passou á invocação de S. João Baptista.

Estes factos, já relatamos longamente na nossa referida obra «A Villa de Itanhaem».

Terminadas estas explicações, reatemos o fio da nossa narração.

Em 1553 voltou o padre Leonardo Nunes á Bahia, para solicitar do superior Manoel da Nobrega. mais alguns companheiros para o coadjuvar na catechese dos indios da capitania S. Vicente. Nobrega veiu então a esta capitania, afim de tomar conhecimento pessôal das necessidades que havia e da maneira porque se estava fazendo a catechese e principalmente do modo barbaro porque eram tratados os indios do littoral.

Os resultados dessa visita e as providencias e bens que de la resultaram para a nascente povoação de Itanhaem e para a capitania em geral, são bem conhecidos.

Teve, então, começo nessa epocha um dos acontecimentos mais estupendos na vida desta humilde povoação e nos factos miraculosos desses companheiros de Anchieta: — Pedro Correia, o temivel e feroz caçador e escravizador de indios, ahi mesmo nesse littoral, sendo fortemente admoestado dos seus crimes pelo padre Leonardo Nunes, submette-se, humilha-se ante a voz e o exemplo do humilde Filho de S. Ignacio; arrependeu-se de seus crimes; converteu-se e . fez-se tambem missionario! Tal foi, pois, a influencia, o poder da abnegação e caridade que em seu espirito se operou, em vista das acções praticadas por esses santos missionarios, que elle abandonando tudo quanto lhe prendia á vida material, vota-se de corpo e alma ás praticas da caridade christã e ao bem commum dos indios, morrendo afinal, martyr e resignado como um santo, em companhia de outros missionarios, nos sertões da Cananéa, victima da sua abnegação, nas mãos desses mesmos indios a quem elle então tanto amava e protegia.

Como homem versado na lingua dos aborigenes, e conhecedor dos seus habitos e costumes, muito util foi o seu novo ministerio, a causa santa dos primeiros missionarios a quem elle tanto auxiliou, principalmente nesta parte do liltoral, entre Itanhaem e Cananéa.

Pedro Correia fez doação de todos os seus bens á *Companhia de Jesus*, e as terras que comprehendiam parte do seu dominio, que lhe foram dadas pelo donatario, desde Tapirêma até o Guarahú ficaram como patrimonio da egreja da aldeia de Itanhaen. Essas terras, como tudo quanto pertenceu aos jesuitas, foram confiscadas e revertidas aos bens da corôa por occasião da expulsão e extincção da companhia, no tempo de Pombal.

Em 1813, o governador de S. Paulo, capitão general marquez de Alegrete, concedeu, por carta de Sesmaria, ao licenciado João José Leite da Fonseca, parte dessas terras do Guarahú. Essa sesmaria contém cinco mil e oitocentas braças de frente, na costa, e divide pelo lado do sul com o morro Paranápôamguassú e pelo lado do norte com as vertentes do morro de Perubibe, fazendo fundo na extensão de muitas leguas com a serra Paranápiacaba, ou serra do mar, que serve de limite ao municipio de Itanhaen com os da serra acima.

O resto das terras de Pedro Correia ficaram ainda, parte devolutas e parte pertencendo a alguns habitantes de Peruhibe, que alli fizeram seus cultivados, e registraram-nas por occasião da lei de 1851, constituindo-se dahi em deante seus legitimos possuidores. Nessa mesma epoca, estando já em abandono a egreja da aldeia de S. João Baptista, que era apenas habitada por mestiços, o fabriqueiro da matriz de Itanhaen, João Pedro de Jesus, registou, a 14 de Junho de 1857, uma parte dessas terras de Peruhibe, no logar conhecido por *Fazenda*, afim de ficarem como patrimonio da matriz, visto achar-se nessa egreja não só o orago com todas as imagens que pertenceram á antiga egreja da aldeia. O uso-fructo dessas terras foi concedido aos habitantes de Peruhibe.

A denominação de *Fazenda*, demonstra o estabelecimento agricola que os «padres» tinham nesse logar, onde houve uma pequena capella, para seu uso exclusivo, conforme havia em todos estabelecimentos deste genero que elles possuiam.

Essas terras partem pelo lado do mar com os terrenos do *Vilão* e pelos lados da terra com a cachoeira do *Quatinga;* para o lado do nascente com o rio Peruhibe e para o poente com as terras de Sesmaria do Guarahú. Além dessas terras, o mesmo fabriqueiro João Pedro de Jesus havia registrado mais, a 12 de Maio de 1856, uma outra *sorte* de terrenos, na aldeia de S. João Baptista, na referida praia ' de Peruhibe, em torno da antiga egreja. Essas terras têm de frente, mais ou menos, uma legua, e, dividem pelo lado do oriente, com as terras de Francisco Patricio Gomes, pelo occidente com as terras de João do Prado e pelos fundos com o rio do Crasto. Os mestiços que ahi habitam gosam tambem, até hoje, do usofructo desssas terras, que fazem parte do patrimonio da matriz de Itanhaem, conhecidas como—Terras de S. João.

———

Não consta absolutamente, nem da tradição ainda tão viva na memoria dos habitantes de Itanhaem, nem de documentos escriptos, que a aldeia de S. João Baptista de Itanhaem estivesse algum tempo sob o dominio dos Capuchos, ou de outros frades, depois que sahiu da administração dos jesuitas, como pretende o general Arouche. Nem è crivel que havendo na villa de Itanhaem um excellente convento de franciscanos, tão bem provido de frades, desde os seus principios, fosse a administração espiritual dessa aldeia, após a retirada dos jesuitas, dada a outros ecclesiasticos que não fossem os frades desse convento, que dista apenas duas leguas dessa aldeia.

Em 1761, quando se concluiu e benzeu a actual matriz de Itanhaem, sob a invocação de Santa Anna, já essa aldeia estava muito decadente, e a sua egreja em estado ruinoso. Nessa época foi determinado que se lhes tirassem as telhas, e que as suas imagens e demais alfaias fossem trasladadas para a matriz de Itanhaem.

Os pobres indios e mestiços vieram em procisão acompanhar as imagens venerandas de seus santos, até a margem do rio Itanhaem, de onde voltaram tristes e chorosos para a sua aldeia. Ahi, sem pastor espiritual, agrupados em torno de sua egreja arruinada, têm, os descendentes desses indios, vivido até os nossos dias nesse estado de abatimento e desanimo, em que os vemos cultivando as suas terras, que não são hoje mais do que uma pequena parte de seu extenso patrimonio de outr'ora. Essas terras, ainda que exgottadas e empobrecidas pelo contínuo cultivo, não são e nem foram jámais tão estereis como affirmam os srs. generaes Arouche e o brigadeiro Machado de Oliveira. ·

Ellas produzem o necessario para a subsistencia dos seus habitantes, principalmente os terrenos de Peruhibe que são considerados excellentes para toda e qualquer cultura e criação.

Não consta tambem da tradição desse povo, as taes atrocidades e espoliações que eram infringidas aos habitantes dessa aldeia e das demais, pelos seus administradores espirituaes, segundo referem os dois citados escriptores.

Ao contrario, essa região, toda occupada pelos aldeados de Itanhaem, foi outr'ora bem prospera e feliz.

Quem couviveu sempre com os descendentes dos indios aldeados e sonda ainda a tradição, latente na memoria desses incolas, hade notar quo elles ainda têm reminiscencias saudosas dos tempos primitivos e dos seus chefes espirituaes.

Hoje infelizmente esse povoado tem, de facto, decahido muito, porém, ha trinta ou quarenta annos era ainda uma população laboriosa e morigerada nos seus costumes, viviam em abastança relativa, sempre em paz, respeitando com muito acatamento os seus anciãos e seguindo sem discrepancia as praticas religiosas dos antepassados.

Tres ou quatro familias de extrangeiros portuguezes, ou descendentes destes, constituiam o unico elemento extranho no meio dessa população aborigene, que se extende de um a outro extremo da praia de Peruhibe.

Alguns desses *brancos* (emboavas) possuiam escravos, na mór parte mulatos e caboclos, porém onde o elemento africano foi sempre escasso. Esses senhores e captivos, foram pouco a pouco assimilando-se á população e extinguindo-se afinal; ou por outra, misturando-se com a raça indigena, formou essa mescla de mestiços que hoje vemos, mas onde predomina ainda o typo indigena.

Um dos caracteristicos dessa raça de mestiços é a sua má disposição ou *birra* contra os indios mansos, *os Guainas*, a quem repellem.

Estes mestiços chegam mesmo a insultar se quando se lhes diz que descendem dos indios, dos *bugres ou gente do matto*, como lhes chamma.

A aldeia de Peruhibe que só existiu em periodo remoto é foi depois, *fazenda* dos jesuitas, é hoje um bairro bastante populoso.

A amenidade de seu clima e fertilidade de suas terras, attrahiram sempre para ahi maior numero de extrangeiros, na mór parte portuguezes, que ali têm constituido familia.

Devido a isso o estado da raça é ahi muito mais desenvolvido; o typo mais robusto, bem proporcionado e a tez menos bronzeada.

Ali nunca houve capella curada. A pequena capella que existiu, foi no sitio da *fazenda* dos padres, á margem direita do rio Peruhibe, para uso exclusivo e particular destes, como já demonstramos.

A igreja da aldeia de S. João Baptista na Ponta da Praia, ou Ponto da Aldeia era, entretanto, relativamente vasta, conforme demonstram as suas ruinas. Tinha pia baptismal, capellamór, arco-cruzeiro, e dois altares collateraes, além de outras edificações annexas para escola e residencia dos padres.

No livro «*A vida do veneravel José de Anchieta*», de Charles de Saint'Foy, onde se relatam os factos miraculosos deste santo thaumaturgo, vem frequentes referencias de factos occorridos na egreja desta aldeia e outros na egreja de Itanhaem, que já era villa no tempo de Anchieta.

Na pagina 143 da dita obra, diz o auctor: «Estava o servo de Deus pregando em uma egreja na aldeia de Itanhaem, dedicada a Maria Santissima etc...» e relata longamente o milagre.

Mais adeante, pagina 261, diz entretanto: «na egreja da Immaculada Conceição, em Itanhaem, (na povoação) arrebatado em extasis, elle foi envolto em luz tão viva...» O milagre aqui se opera na villa e não na aldeia.

O auctor faz ainda muitas referencias aos milagres que se operaram não só nessa egreja, como em toda essa região do littoral a qual «o santo missionario chamava o *seu Perú* e onde elle cultivava com particular disvello e amava com preferencia, por lhe proporcionar maior occasião de soffrer, e por isso mesmo de acrysolar mais merecimentos».

Comquanto, diz ainda o escriptor, «o ardente zelo do padre Anchieta se extendeu por todo o Brazil, havia comtudo esse recanto (praia de Peruhybe) que era por elle preferido...etc...»

Nas cartas de Nobrega lê-se tambem que: «quando se effectuou a paz com os tamoyos, houve festas em Itanhaem e na aldeia com os tupys dos padres...»

Identicas referencias vêm nos «Apontamentos para a historia dos jesuitas no Brazil»pelo dr. A. Henrique Leal, Revista do Instituto Historico do Brazil, tomo XXXIV.

Os terrenos onde actualmente se acham aldeiados os indios mansos estão afastados das terras de S. João Baptista pelo rio Castro. Esse aldeiamento é nas cabeceiras do rio Preto, no logar denominado Bananal e Tariruhú.

O outro aldeamento de indios mansos, é no rio Itariry affluente da Ribeira de Iguape, no municipio de Itanhaem, conforme explicaremos no capitulo immediato: «Os indios mansos de Itanhaem».

Taes são pois as rectificações e apontamentos que offerecemos, com relação ás noticias publicadas no 1.º volume da «Revista da Sociedade de Ethnographia e Civilização dos Indios» pelos eruditos chronistas general Arouche, Brigadeiro Machado de Oliveira e dr. Pinto Junior, na parte que se referem aos aldeiamentos de Itanhaem.

## II

A tribu indigena que habita o municipio de Itanhaem está dividida hoje em dois pequenos aldeiamentos: um no rio Itariry, nos sertões de Peruhybe, ha dois dias de viagem desta povoação, e o outro no Bananal, dois dias de viagem da villa de Itanhaem.

O aldeiamento de Itariry compõe-se de cinco familias, a saber: Ignacio Pequeno, que é o chefe *Ureubichá*, casado, com sete filhos.—Pedrinho, casado, com seis filhos.—Salvador Candido, casado, com tres filhos.—Reducinio, casado, sem filhos.—Antonio Ribeiro, casado, com dois filhos.

Além destas familias, que são indios genuinos, falando entre si o idioma tupy, existem ainda de mistura, grande numero de mestiços cohabitando a mesma aldeia, porém, que não falam o idioma indigena.

O aldeiamento do Bananal compõe-se de oito familias, que são: Bento Pires, *Ureuhichá*, casado, com oito filhos.—Joaquim Bento, casado, com seis filhos.—Pedrinho, casado, com quatro filhos.—Americo, casado, com quatro filhos.—Joaquim Branco, casado, com tres filhos.—Joaquim Pinto, casado, com cinco filhos.—Joaquim Ignacio, casado, sem filhos.—Maria Lucia, viuva, com cinco filhos.

Neste aldeiamento não existe absolutamente mestiço algum; os indios ahi vivem isolados completamente do povoado, conservando entre si não só seu idioma puro, como todos os habitos e costumes peculiares á raça. Amando sobre modo a sua liberdade, e muito ciosos nesse ponto, elles preferem as solidões remotas das florestas, onde possam viver livres, sem peias e vexames; é por isso que se retraem, repellindo mesmo o convivio com os mestiços, dos quaes conservam sempre, por tradição e por indole uma especie de receio ou desconfiança. E' sem duvida ainda - a vaga reminiscencia dos terriveis *mamelucos*.

Estes indios estão em communicação constante com os outros que habitam o aldeiamento de S. João Baptista do Rio Verde.

São ambos da mesma tribu e dizem; «somos a mesma gente».

De facto: todos esses indios mansos, descendem de uma numerosa tribu de Caiuá, ou *Guainá* descendentes da grande nação Guainaz ou talvez um ramo da Nação Tupy, que habitava o planalto no tempo da descoberta e que, desde o começo do seculo passado, 1819, segundo referem alguns chronistas, vagava errante pelos sertões meridionaes da Provincia de S. Paulo, acossados já por outras tribus ferozes, que os odeiam e repellem até hoje, em consequencia do constante commercio e trato que esta nação manteve sempre com os paulistas. A sua peculiar mansidão, tornou sempre esta nação accessivel; foi ella que maior contingente de indios forneceu ás antigas aldeias e *melhor* se submetteu ao aviltante captiveiro.

Em 1843, uma grande parte dessa tribu foi habitar no municipio de Itapéva da Faxina e ahi deu origem á povoação de S. João Baptista do Rio Verde, que foi creada freguezia por lei provincial de 5 de Março de 1855.

A outra fracção dessa tribu errante havia anteriormente emigrado para o littoral, vindo formar o aldeiamento do Itariry, perto do rio Juquiá, no municipio de Itanhaem.

O governo Imperial concedeu, por essa occasião, uma sórte de terras a esse aldeiamento do Itarery, que ainda hoje constitue o patrimonio desses indios. Essas terras dividem, para o lado de baixo do Itarery, com o sitio *Caracól* e para cima com o ribeirão do *Attiage*. Têm de frente meia legua e de fundo todo o percurso do *Rio do Peixe*, até as vertentes da serra dos Itatins ou Itatinga.

Essas duas pequenas aldeias, Itariry e Bananal, das quaes nos occupamos, e ainda algumas familias dispersas pelo littoral, é apenas o que resta desse primeiro nucleo, hoje tão desfalcado e tendente a desapparecer.

Todo esse sertão, quasi inculto e deshabitado, que se extende desde o immenso valle da Ribeira de Iguape e grande parte do municipio de Itanhaem, até as margens do Rio Verde e Itararé, abrangendo os municipios de Faxina, Apiahy, Piedade, Una, Itapecirica, etc., é ainda hoje constantemente percorrido por essa tribu de *Guainá* nas suas idas e vindas para o littoral. Esta zona pouco povoada do nosso prospero Estado, incontestavelmente uma das mais incultas, foi sempre a mais pre ferida pelos indios. Ahi se encontram ainda verdadeiros sertões, nos quaes o elemento civilizador é por emquanto muito escasso.

No littoral, a parte justamente a mais agreste e inculta, entre a Ribeira de Iguape e a bacia fluvial do rio Conceição, foi a zona por elles preferida. Ahi estão elles verdadeiramente «em sua casa»; toda essa região é inteiramente despovoada, ninguem os encommoda, a não ser algum caçador que uma ou outra vez penetra nessas florestas.

Dahi tambem lhes são faceis as suas viagens para os centros povoados, pois estão apenas a tres e quatro dias de Santos e S. Paulo, e a dia e meio de Itanhaem, aonde vêm vender o producto de suas industrias e fazer seus pequenos provimentos.

Os antigos habitantes da aldeia Irariry, faziam as suas sortidas para o interior, subindo o curso do rio Guanhanhá, que desagua no rio Itariry; dahi seguiam até S. Lourenço; subiam a serra e tomando o rumo de oeste, transpunham os sertões que medeiam os municipios de Piedade, Pilar, Lavrinhas e Apiahy, atravessando nesse ponto o valle do Taquary que confina com o Rio Verde, onde existe o principal nucleo de aldeiamento, como já referimos.

Hoje, esse trajecto está quasi abandonado e suas viagens para o Rio Verde, são feitas por outro itenerario: ou seguem pelo rio Branco de Itanhaem, subindo a serra até Santa Cruz dos Parelheiros e dahi a Santo Amaro, onde tomam a estrada geral até Sorocaba e Faxina; ou descendo pela rio Juquiá, seguem até Xiririca e dalli a Itapeva da Faxina, que dista apenas doze leguas de S. João Baptista e do Rio Verde.

São estes, pois, os pontos por elles preferidos para os seus trajectos, entre esses dois nucleos, um no littoral, e outro no interior, ambos isolados dos centros populosos.

E' necessario que nos esforcemos por conserval-os nessa posição, tão vantajosa para elles, protegendo-os e procurando de alguma fórma pol-os a coberto da ganancia e do odio dos mestiços e demais invejosos que os aborrecem por indole e que os vão a pouco e pouco expulsando do aldeiamento do Itariry e do Rio Verde.

Lembramos que seria de grande vantagem mandar dois missionarios intelligentes e abnegados para cuidar dessa pobre gente, proporcionando-lhes instrucção religiosa e civil de que tanto carecem, e ao mesmo tempo protegel-os contra a ganancia dos invasores.

Esses missionarios, aproveitando-se da convivencia intima com os indios, poderão apprender o seu idioma, que se vae perdendo pouco a pouco e se perderá completamente, si nós não tratarmos quanto antes de amparal-os.

Para a collocação desses missionarios e estabelecimento provisorio de suas escolas, nos aldeiamentos de Itanhaem, que a nosso ver são os primeiros de que nos compete cuidar, por serem os mais proximos e os que estão tendentes a desapparecer, lembramos o convento de Nossa Senhora da Conceição de Itanhaem, que se presta admiravelmente para o fim.

Ahi lhes ficará facil, aos missionarios, as suas visitas aos respectivos aldeiamentos.

Uma vez que possamos captar a sympathia e a confiança desses indios, prestando-lhes reaes serviços, elles mesmo, pelo contacto e commercio constante com os aldeiamentos de S. João do Rio Verde e com o resto da tribu que vaga errante por toda essa zona, se encarregarão de fazer propaganda dos beneficios que lhes forem prestados, chamando desta fórma para alli, todos ou parte dos indios que existem dispersos, formando assim um bom nucleo, nessa vasta região do nosso littoral, tão preferida por elles e tão abandonada, tão esquecida dos poderes publicos e ecclesiasticos.

O indio, desde os tempos primitivos, na sua vida livre, teve sempre por habito, em determinada época do anno, fazer suas excursões ás praias do mar, e entreter relações e commercio com as tribus ichtyophagas do littoral.

Das regiões mais centraes vinham as tribus contemplar — o grande mar — das cuspides abruptas da serra Paranapiacaba; e dalli, desciam nos mezes de Maio, Junho e Julho, no tempo *do curumã* (as tainhas) para visitar as praias e fazer provisão de peixes e de aves que, como as tainhas, emigram das regiões meridionaes, em busca da zona tropical: e tambem das aves das florestas do interior que, como os Jacutingas descem do planalto de Paranapiacaba e, como elles, os selvagens, vêm na zona do littoral, fugindo dos frios rigorosos do planalto, procurar o ar mais calido, e prover-se do necessario que a Providencia Divina tão caridosa e tão sabiamente lhes propoiciona.

O indio manso, o *guainá*, procurando ainda hoje manter, com tanto custo, as relações com o littoral, obedece, talvez inconscientemente, ao instincto dos seus antepassados.

Elles, como todos nós, que nascemos sob este céu tropical, têm por instincto a predilecção, o amôr por tudo quanto é vasto e grandioso!

Elles, como nós, têm a nostalgia do mar!

Sentindo ques o terreno lhes escasseia, que a vastidão das florestas vae-lhe cada dia fugindo nos horizontes, elles querem ainda um momento, das alturas de Paranapiacaba e dos pincaros altaneiros do Itatinga e Cahepupú, divagar o olhar melancolico por essa vastidão de verdejantes e incultas florestas de beira mar e por essa outra vastidão ainda mrior, cujos horisontes são ainda livres — o oceano!...

Deixemos pois que elles saciem esse desejo e que continuem todos os annos a percorrer esse itinerario predilecto até as praias do mar, ao menos emquanto ellas são solitarias e livres....

Acossados, espoliados, de um lado pela população sempre crescente, que se desdobra, se estende para o oeste do nosso vasto Estado, e do outro lado, nos sertões do Paranapanema; pelas hordas ferozes e indomitas dos Chavantes e Coroados que os odeiam de morte, esses pobres indios mansos, espurios remanescentes da grande nação Tupy, victimas perennes, filhos dos nossos captivos de outr'ora, vão cada dia recuando; sempre tristes e resignados com a sua sorte, levando ainda na alma o fel e o estigma latente; a procurar no limite meridional do Estado, nas já escassas florestas, um abrigo, um refugio, afim de repousar os ultimos instantes da vida, nessa terra que para elles já foi um dia tão vasta, tão fertil e tão livre !

Esforcemo-nos, portanto, em garantir a esses pobres incolas, a esses indios mansos, um cantinho no nosso Estado, onde elles possam estar socegados, e tratemos de suavizar um pouco a sua triste sorte.

Os terrenos do municipio de Itanhaem, em que esses indios estão situados, prestam-se perfeitamente para qualquer cultura. Tratemos de instruil-os e de animal-os neste nucleo do littoral.

Os indios mansos, apesar da sua proverbial indolencia, devido ao estado de abandono em que os temos deixado viver, e da sua tendencia para a vida nomada, são entretanto robustos e sadios, podendo vir a ser bons trabalhadores e uteis a si mesmo.

Alguns desses incolas possuem nos aldeiamentos de Itanhaem habitações relativamente confortaveis   Têm plantações de mandioca, milho. feijão e algum café e arvores fructiferas em torno de suas palhoças.   São bastante industriosos, fabricam, para seu uso, todos os utensilios de carpintaria de que precisam, como rodas de ral r mandioca, prensas, monjolos, etc.

Trabalham perfeitamente em obras de barro, modelando perfeitamente e com certa arte os seus utensilios domesticos, como panellas, pratos, canecas, moringas e toda a sorte de vasos, que vêm vender em Peruhibe e Itanhaem.

Construóem aś suas canôas para os trajectos fluviaes e pescarias, no que são muito dextros.

Trabalham admiravelmente em tecidos de palha, junco e taquara, fabricando vassouras, balaios, cestas, peneiras, tipitys, cóvos, etc., etc. De fòrma que, vivendo elles inteiramente isolados em suas aldeias, dispensam o concurso e convivio com os mestiços, com quem não fazem liga e dos quaes, de facto, nada dependem, porque o seu limitado commercio, a sua industria e modo de vida, é inteiramente á parte.

Por natureza e por habito desconfiados, (não sem motivo), jámais elle procuram intrometter-se na vida, nos trabalhos e folguedos dos mestiços.

Só vêm ao povoado, quando necessitam negociar os seus productos, solicitar um beneficio das auctoridades, ou articular uma queixa, quando, não raras vezes, se lhes quer expoliar os terrenos de sua pequena cultura, ou vexal-os em sua vida solitaria e misanthropa.

Taes são pois, as condições em que se acham estes infelizes *guaianás* um ramo, talvez, da antiga e importante nação *Tupy*, primeiros habitantes e donos desta vasta região, e que tão importantes serviços prestaram ao estabelecimento da primeira capitania.

A Sociedade de Ethnographia e Civilização dos Indios, da qual fazemos parte, que tem por fim exclusivo proteger e civilizar os indigenas deste Estado, deve primeiro que tudo, antes de encetar commettimentos mais audazes, como sejam os da cathechese dos indios selvagens do Paranapanema, tratar de proteger e salvar estes.

Si esta Sociedade, ou o governo do Estado não tomarem providencias, quanto antes, talvez que ao depois já seja tarde, pois que, estes indios, mesclando-se e viciando-se no meio da população, tendem cada dia a degenerar, a dissolver-se perdendo quasi que completamente os seus habitos e idioma. E' isto o que temos observado nas familias que abandonam os aldeiamentos e vêm viver nos povoados, onde adquirem toda a sorte de vicios, sobre tudo o da embriaguez.

Para terminar esta breve noticia, diremos ainda que, embora exista como se pretende, um odio de morte entre a tribu dos indios mansos e as tribus ferozes do sertão, acreditamos entretanto que será só com o auxilio daquelles, que se poderá com vantagem e segurança tentar a salvação destes.

S. Vicente, Julho de 1902.

BENEDICTO CALIXTO.

# O meu papel no advento da Republica em São Paulo

## O DIA 15 DE NOVEMBRO

A 15 de Novemhro de 1889, pouco depois do meio-dia, achava-me no Quartel do largo do Carmo, occupado pelo Corpo de Permanentes do qual eu era então o Coronel-Commandante, quando fui chamado, com urgencia, pelo Presidente da Provincia, General Couto de Magalhães.

Dei algumas ordens a meus officiaes, no sentido de ninguem sahir do Quartel até a minha vinda, e immediatamente puz me a caminho.

Ao chegar ás escadas de Palacio topei com o Chefe de Policia, Dr. Leão Velloso, o qual visivelmente nervoso e extremamente pallido, deu-me o braço, dizendo:—Commandante! sabe o que ha? Rebentou no Rio uma revolta muito séria e já assassinaram o Maracajú, Ministro da Guerra! (Verificou se, no outro dia, que o facto sanguinolento se déra com o Barão do Ladario).

Essa noticia, dada assim á queima roupa, bastante me impressionou, não só pela gravidade do facto em si, como porque o Visconde de Maracajú é um militar verdadeiro ornamento da classe, pelo seu saber e serviços, e pessôa com quem eu sempre entretive relações de amizade, desde a gloriosa campanha do Paraguay.

Disse-me mais o Dr. Chefe de Policia:—Não ha pormenores, mas os promotores da revolta são os republicanos de mãos dadas com os militares que começam mal a revolução, servindo de instrumento e derramando sangue até de seus companheiros e superiores!

Nisto chegámos á sala onde estava o General, o qual, logo que me viu, disse-me, com voz muito alterada pela emoção:—Commandante! estamos em plena revolução; o telegrapho está interrompido; não sei o que fazer; o sr. o que pensa?

Esta phrase «o telegrapho está interrompido» a meu vêr explica perfeitamente a causa, o motivo por que, tendo tão bons elementos de resistencia em S. Paulo, o Governo e os monarchistas daqui deixaram perecer as instituições! O General, bem como a maior parte dos Administradores Provinciaes, apenas moviam-se pelas ordens emanadas do Rio, e desde que estas dali não vinham, por uma força maior, elles estacavam indecisos, não sabendo ou não querendo deliberar por si, receiando talvez o comprometter-se. Retrahindo-se, como elle o fez, a causa resentiu-se; os politicos ficaram sem o calor do Palacio, que lhes dá vida. Nem uns nem outros tinham o *self government*; a demasiada centralização; a má comprehensão de deveres civicos para com a Patria perdeu a monarchia—*Voila tout*.

Tanto foi assim, que o General confessou várias vezes: «Não sei o que fazer», quando aliás era tão clara a rota a seguir: bater-se pelas instituições e salvar o Paiz. Mais tarde quiz fazel-o, mas a occasião é calva. Já elle não tinha os poderosos elementos que esterilizou a 15 e 16 de Novembro; então chorava, como Boabdil, nas portas de Granada, como débil mulher, o poder que não quiz e não soube defender como homem, em tempo, compromettendo inutilmente tanto esforço, tanta lealdade, e pedindo ao inimigo que «mantivesse a ordem na Capital», como só naquelles dias supremos se tratasse disso! Inaudito, incrivel!...

Depois de pequena pausa respondi:—Sr. General, não se commova tanto; isto era de esperar mais dia menos dia; o que devemos fazer é aguardar noticias e procurar dominar os acontecimentos.

O General, depois de prolongado silencio, perguntou-me:—Entre os militares que se faz quando ha um facto destes? Que farei?

Respondi:—As tropas ficam logo de promptidão, medida que já tomei: as auctoridades preparam-se para o que dér e viér; e o Governo age movendo toda a engrenagem, para dominar os acontecimentos.

Passados alguns instantes o General abraçou-me muito commovido e disse-me:—Vá, amigo e Commandante! Não lhe dou instrucções; faça tudo o que achar bem, pois confio muito na sua honra e capacidade etc. etc.

Ao retirar-me desta curta, mas pathetica entrevista, um dos homens eminentes que alli se achavam, apontando-me disse:—Quem diria! Alli vae o nosso...! Voltei a cabeça e agradeci aquella doce palavra de labios amigos.

Que pensamentos agitaram então minh'alma ao receber tão tristes noticias! Como logo se desenhou a meus olhos não só o descalabro da Patria, mas tambem as scenas que eu presenciaria e soffreria sem poder remediar!

Immerso em profunda dôr, mas dominando-me, porque tinha deveres a cumprir, segui para o meu Quartel rapidamente, onde ia providenciar para resistir em S. Paulo á onda revolucionaria que se abatia ameaçadora, sanguinosa, sobre o meu caro Brazil, ao qual, como filho e ardente patriota, servia com abnegado amor desde os mais verdes annos!

A tarefa não era facil nem isenta de perigos! (1)

Reconheci o pesado fardo que se atirava aos meus débeis hombros, a immensa responsabilidade que sobre mim recahiria! Nada mais, nada menos do que sahir com honra de uma situação difficil para todos, e isto, quando as paixões alçavam o collo!

Mas não vacillei um só instante, comquanto logo reconhecesse que me achava só e abandonado, (2) e acceitei com orgulho e sem temer a situação, confiado na Providencia.

Invoquei ao Divino Espirito Santo para que com suas luzes me guiasse naquelle transe, naquelle dia de perturbação geral e me indicasse qual o caminho que devia trilhar, apontando-me o dever!

Porque, nas commoções e revoluções sociaes, justamente o mais difficil, para os militares, é acertar onde está o direito e o dever!

E não foi em vão a minha supplica! Fui attendido muito alem de minha espectativa porque, tenho certeza de ter cumprido cabalmente com os meus deveres. Como christão, não perjurei. Lealmente sustentei e defendi as instituições, o governo, e os amigos, além da ultima hora, (dia 16, depois do meio dia). Como militar, não atraiçoei os meus superiores: defendi-os, e mesmo guiei-os. (3) Fui fiel á minha bandeira, a mesma que sempre falava á minha imaginação juvenil e saudosa, quando gloriosa fluctuava nas ameias dos fortes ou nos campos de batalha do longinquo e bellicoso Paraguay!

Como patriota, tendo verdadeiras apprehensões sobre os destinos da Patria que eu servia, procurando acertar, não obstei vio-

(1) Calarei o que miseraveis intentaram contra mim; devendo eu, talvez, a vida, ao benemerito Dr. Antonio Bento, meu companheiro de abolicionismo.

(2) O general presidente e chefe de policia nullificaram-se, apagaram-se; o povo bem o comprehendeu, tanto que o palacio e largo do palacio estavam ermos, sem vida, desertos! O largo do Carmo, pelo contrario, enchia-se de multidão de patriotas de calor vital!

(3) Aos meus subordinados só dei bôas normas a seguir; e o corpo de Permanentes sob meu commando, chegou ao auge da moralidade; conquistou fama e gloria!

lentamente a implantação do novo regimem; pelo contrario, mantive a ordem, observando as regras da mais estricta disciplina numa corporação hecterogenea e numerosa, em dia de effervescencia popular; aplainei, e como que semeei de flores o caminho a percorrer; apontando todos os perigos com sombranceria e calma. Como amigo, não abandonei os meus, visando lucros e proventos futuros, embora nenhum delles (1) me apparecesse, nesses momentos criticos, para me levar conselhos e conforto: finalmente, como chefe de tão forte e numerosa corporação, consegui que ninguem discrepasse; pela disciplina implantada, pela energica e correcta attitude que assumi, impuz aos discolos; desprezei ameaças; e só, póde-se dizer, que absolutamente só, resisti até o ultimo momento á revolução triumphante! E resistindo, a servi melhor!

Por ser dia 15 do mez, destinado pelo regulamento do corpo ao pagamento dos fornecedores, á abertura do cofre e lançamento dos termos do conselho nos respectivos livros, e porque, assim eu ordenára, se achavam todos os officiaes reunidos na sala do Estado-Maior, onde eu, chegando de Palacio, depois de feitos e encerrados esses trabalhos, expliquei-lhes o que havia; a melindrosa situação da Patria; e em patrioticas phrases concitei-os a serem leaes e obedientes, porque eu lhes asseverava que ao disciplinado Corpo de Permanentes estava reservado um bellissimo papel, succedesse o que succedesse; o que prometteram e cumpriram fielmente.

Mas uma vez daqui lhes agradeço não em meu nome, proscripto e gloriosamente *suspeito*, (2) mas em nome da Patra.

Dalli, me dirigi ao alojamento das praças, ás quaes fiz identico appello, com egual resultado. E como não? Acaso quem lhes falava era um commandante nominal? Não. Era um patricio, cheio de notaveis serviços; era um irmão; um amigo que diariamente elevava o seu nivel moral falando-lhes á mente, ao coração, e praticando acções grandes e inauditas. (3) Basta dizer que durante o meu commando não houve deserções, crimes ou sique faltas simples, mandando eu fechar, por não haver mais soldados presos, as portas do xadrez, significando com isso que os meus soldados viviam satisfeitos, em paz com suas consciencias, com a severa disciplina, com as leis; assim era o templo de

---

1 Me refiro aos politicos. porquanto os meus collegas de estudos e camaradas da vida militar e meretissimos conhecidos civis, estiveram sempre me coadjuvando; me refiro aos amigos politicos de ambos os credos, os quaes, desde aquelle momento até hoje só procuraram amesquinhar-me: parece que uma condição foi-lhes imposta ao adherirem: hostilisar-me!

2 Pela impatriotica, anti-paulista politica vesga dos divinos.

3 Vide o documento n. 1 ordem do dia.

Jano na antiga Roma, cujas portas se fechavam em tempo de paz. (1).

Passei a tomar as providencias militares que por serem variadissimas, innumeras e sem interesse para o auditorio, deixarei de mencionar. Entretanto ellas foram importantes; e dariam ganho de causa ás Instituições, si não fosse... o governo fraquear e... o destino intervir! ...

O corpo ficou de rigorosa promptidão, como já disse : ninguem mais sahiu do quartel até o dia 16 depois do meio dia, isto é, depois que o general presidente, contra toda a espectativa se retirou, voluntariamente, de Palacio.

E' portanto falso, falsissimo mesmo, que os meus officiaes no dia 15 alli, em Palacio, tivessem ido fazer offerecimentos extemporaneos e descabidos ; não, aquella officialidade modesta, briosa, digna, disciplinada a capricho por mim, não deu similhante cincada.

Pessôas pouco, observadoras e incompetentes occuparam-se nesse dia, e sempre, em espalhar ballelas e calumnias que muito mal fizeram então e o tem produzido ainda até hoje! E' que as sementes damninhas medram em qualquer terreno e estação. Os officiaes que essas pessôas viram, no dia 15, fazer offerecimentos de devotação e fidelidade ao governo, foram os do 10.º Regimento de Linha, que ha muitos dias já estavam de combinação com os republicanos, de quem recebiam o santo e a senha!!

Mas, voltemos ao assumpto (2)

Pelas 5 horas da tarde, desse dia 15, vieram me dar parte, dentro do quartel onde eu me achava, de que um alferes, com duas ordenanças do 10.º Regimento de Cavallaria de Linha, intitulando-se Ajudante de Campo (!) do General Presidente, queria entrar no quartel e saber quantas praças estavam lá dentro.

Reconhecendo eu que isso era um ardil, visando qualquer fim, dei ordem para não ser consentida a sua entrada no Quartel, mandando-lhe dizer que tinha 1.2000 homens em armas ; retirando-se elle, confundido e desabusado, em vista dessa resposta dada em tom secco e desabrido, por minha ordem.

Passou-se o resto do dia calmamente: — resultante da ordem e diciplina rigorosa que reinava no Quartel que regorgitava de soldados e officiaes, os quaes, conforme eu determinára, a cada momento, chegavam de differentes destacamentos e destinos, au-

---

(1) Sendo secretario da Justiça o cidadão Mello Peixoto desertaram em um só anno mais de 700 soldados !!! Um terço do pessoal! cansando só em fardamento um prejuizo de noventa e tantos contos de réis. E ninguem foi responsabilizado! O armamento extrahido era innumeravel e carissimo !

(2) Vide o documento n. 4.

gmentando consideravelmente o effectivo do corpo. Além desse pessôal, eu ainda convidára os reformadcs e os Voluntarios da Patria, que então, numerosos e auxiliados por amigos paizanos, muito me ajudaram ; e, com enthusiasmo davam-me parte de tudo que se passava na cidade, no Club Republicano, no Quartel de linha etc. etc.

A's 6 horas da tarde recebi um officio do cidadão dr. Campos Salles na qualidade de Secretario, dando-me sciencia de que o Governo Provisorio se achava installado no Paço da Camara Municipal, e, dizendo mais, que contava com os meus bons serviços para continuar a garantir a ordem (1); momentos depois recebi um telegrama directo do cidadão Quintino Bocayuva, dizendo que, no Rio, o Exercito e a Armada, em nome da Nação, ião installar o Governo Provisorio; que consultaria o Povo; etc.

Dei esses documentos aos officiaes, para que delles se inteirassem. (Ahi estão ns. 2 e 3).

Pelo telephone, dei disso sciencia ao General Presidente a quem, antes, eu tinha pedido que não se afastasse mais de Palacio para evitar qualquer surpreza (2); promettendo-me elle dormir alli; e isto fiz, por ter sido informado que o mesmo General fôra desrespeitado no Quartel de linha pelos officiaes! Sem commentarios!

Durante o dia o sól tinha sido abrazador; mas branda viração corria ao crepusculo. A bella estrella Sirius elevava-se vagarosa, adamantina, do lado do aurifero Jaraguá; em quanto, Marte rubro e agourento perpassava sobre os Campos de Piratininga. Findára-se o derradeiro dia do que fôra grande Imperio Brazileiro!

Pelas dez ou onze horas da noite, que tornara-se trevosa, brilhando poucas estrellas no céu escurissimo, o official de serviço participou-me que dois paizanos, dizendo-se meus amigos, pediam com insistencia, ás sentinellas exteriores que eu collocára no Largo do Carmo, licença para passar e vir falar commigo.

Extranhando o facto, por ser aquella hora tardia, mandei franquear-lhes o passo e verificar quem eram. Soube logo que eram

---

(1) Esse officio, veja-se bem, e os factos anteriores e posteriores, demonstram que eu era a garantia da ordem em São Paulo; ficando, destruida a asserção de que o General Couto de Magalhães tivesse pedido aos republicanos que se responsabilizassem e mantivessem a ordem e tranquilidade na cidade. Seria uma inepcia de sua parte: maximé quando elle sabia dos manejos quo havia... Justamente para garantia da ordem é que o Presidente tinha me dado carta branca... e, para mantel a - Campos Salles podia o meu concurso. Ainda muito tempo depois de proclamada a Republica eu continuei a commandar o corpo, mantendo a ordem!

(2) Uma deposição por exemplo, allegando-se estar o Palacio desoccupado, o aproveitando-se dessa circumstancia; segundo informações quo colhemos.

os cidadãos Lopes de Oliveira e dr. Campos Salles. Não tendo segredos nem reservas em serviço publico pareceu-me conveniente convidar os meus officiaes a assistirem a conferencia, para que de tudo soubessem e deliberassem livremente; e mesmo para afastar de mim qualquer suspeita, em dias e momentos tão agitados. Chegando ao ponto em que se achavam aquelles dois cavalheiros, apresentei-lhes, si bem que no escuro, os meus companheiros militares, meus subordinados, os quaes, logo, expontaneamente, se collocaram a pequena distancia, podendo, entretanto, ouvir tudo.

O Sr. Lopes de Oliveira disse-me que tendo ambos ido a minha casa, alli souberam por bocca de minha Senhora e filhas que dezenas de pessôas tinham ido procurar-me e muitos republicanos; entre outros o dr. Carlos Garcia etc.; disseram-lhes mais, que, desde pela manhã eu me achava occupado no Quartel; que nem tinha ido jantar com a familia.

Então elles, «urgidos pelas circumstancias, vinham falar commigo, apezar do apparato bellico, pois parecia-lhes que estavam numa praça de guerra»! Respondi-lhes que effectivamente assim era; mas esse apparato não era para os amigos pacificos; que cada um cumpria o seu dever, conforme o seu criterio; que o meu ordenava aquellas disposições; disse mais, que, si tivessem vindo, de dia, ao Quartel onde me achava, em vista da angustiosa situação politica desde pela manhã, até aquella hora, não extranhariam essas elementares visiveis precauções militares e outras de quem sabe o officio; mas que tendo elles apparecido tão tarde, nem me era licito convidal-os para entrar no Quartel. Responderam-me dizendo que não censuravam, mas antes gabavam-me por verem que realmente eu era um Commandante *comme il faut!*

Depois de mais algumas phrases banaes fui convidado para ir ao Club Republicano, a rua de São Bento, para proclamar a Republica, ou pelo menos, para eu consentir que a officialidade, com a respectiva banda de musica lá se achasse; ao que, em phrases cortezes, formalmente me neguei, como me cumpria, dizendo-lhes que elles julgaram prescindir do concurso dos genuinos militares Paulistas, dos meus commandados e do meu debil esforço, até aquella hora calada, indo procurar algures a força de que precisavam e que assim, por tanto, deviam continuar a proceder.

A conferencia prolongou-se muito, falando com a reconhecida eloquencia o cidadão dr. Campos Salles; e eu, ouvindo-o, sempre com religiosa atenção, embóra discordando em alguns pontos.

Perguntei, nesse intervallo, ao cidadão Lopes de Oliveira, se a revolução era pela separação de S. Paulo, como elle e os patriotas trabalhavam, diziam e escreviam.

—Respondeu que—não, porque isso, então, não convinha,—
Essa resposta bastante me impressionou e por isso a consigno aqui.

No correr da conversação affirmei que a attitude do Corpo de Permanentes era a unica possivel e digna naquellas actuaes circumstancias, porquanto nem era licito estabelecer o precedente de militares, e principalmente de um corpo provincial da inteira confiança do Governo que o creára e nelle se estribava andar pela rua fazendo patriotadas interesseiras, promovendo desordens, assassinando cidadãos como a 24 de Novembro de 1888, na Bernarda do 17.° batalhão (1), porque isso provaria indisciplina dos soldados, inépcia dos officiaes, do commandante e falta de previsão politica dos chefes ; muito menos, era permittido arvorar-se em classe dirigente para, á sombra de bayonetas e espadas, destruir o governo legal e subverter a ordem publica, influenciados, por telegramas, apenas !

Ao fazer estas e outras considerações que os meus brios e poucas luzes dictavam fui muito aparteado ; mas, em resumo, é de crêr que, na occasião, minhas theorias e meu proceder leal e sincero não conviessem ; hoje, porêm, desvaneço-me de ter, com minha conducta, evitado derramamento de sangue, como desde as vesperas, vinham fazendo, preparando e iniciando o advento da Republica em S. Paulo (2) os soldados de linha ; gabo-me de ter sustentado o governo legal e amigo ; e, resistindo, *suaviter in modo fortiter in re*, isto é, em termos, cedi em quanto pude ás exigencias do momento histórico sem, quebra da lealdade e honra de funccionario publico e militar, sem menoscabo da dignidade pessoal, e da disciplina da corporação da qual eu era chefe.

Não podendo chegar a um accôrdo, porque eu não podia alterar a linha de conducta que me tinha traçado, retiraram-se os emissarios da revolução, naturalmente meus inimigos ; mas, com a retirada delles, redobrou o devotamento e enthusiasmo da corporação, para commigo, por terem presenciado a repulsa nobre e altiva que fiz então.

A solução da crise, verdadeira batalha politica, ficou para se decidir no dia seguinte, 16 de Novembro.

Era preciso dar-se tempo ao tempo... *et, la nuit porte conseil...*

_____

(1) Escrevendo hoje estas linhas, lembro ao auditorio as sanguinolentas scenas que precederam á desposição e fuga do dr. Americo Brasiliense e outros.

(2) Os officiaes do 10.° Regimento, com o seu respectivo commandante, gabam-se de ter feito a Republica em S. Paulo! E de facto, assim foi, porque elles têm sido bem recompensados pelo Estado e pela União. Para nos livrarmos desse borrão é que eu me batia ; isto é, intervenção da força armada na eleição do governo.

Seria facil verificar-se então que a população em geral na calma do silencio, era insciente do phenomeno social, da transformação radical e politica que se operava sem o concurso della; seria facil verificar-se que esse povo durante o dia estivéra apprehensivo, como que receoso do futuro; os monarchistas sem acção, sem iniciativa, inertes; os republicanos, si bem que em pequeno numero, agitavam-se de um lado e outro pelas ruas e redacções dos jornaes, mas, inermes. E' que não tinham elles o principal para dirigir qualquer movimento, o caudilho, o homem carbono, a alma que move as massas, e, por isso, nada elles e ellas produziam; entretanto, alguns se puzeram em evidencia, cautelosamente arregimentando forças, preparando elementos para o desenlace da lucta, talvez em outro terreno; os desordeiros (e os ha sempre, mórmente nessas occasiões), suspiravam pelo alvorecer, para se desforrarem da inacção que minha prudencia, minhas medidas militares lhes tinha imposto.

O quartel de linha, anarchizado, recebia armamento de casas commerciaes e armava centenares de paizanos, caixeiros do commercio e até extrangeiros; ali, conspiravam insofridos, mas divididos, impotentes.

O presidente, fraco, doente, pusillánime, mas respeitado no fundo do palacio, nada fazia (1), de nada se lembrava para debellar a tormenta que ganhava corpo no tempo e no espaço; os elementos conservadores retrahiam-se commodamente no *dolce far niente* do *laissez aller, laissez faire, laissez passer;* muitos, doloroso é confessal-o, sopesavam já nas conchas da balança os ouropeis da monarchia e as lantejoilas da republica!

Que terriveis combates se travaram naquelles momentos em minha alma?

E, eram bem acabrunhadores, bem fortes, pois, melancholicamente, passeava de um lado para outro, no espaçoso Largo do Carmo, com a fronte banhada em abundante suor; a cada momento, como que tentando devassar arcanos, alçava os olhos para os céos fitando o Alpha da Cruz do Sul, que desde as longas noites da Campanha do Paraguay eu elegêra para minha *stella confidente*, procurando buscar inspirações: ora aprehensivo, baixava a vista á terra esquadrinhando o lar, bem proximo, onde estava tudo que me era caro—a extremosa familia;—ora, contemplava a bandeira, sagrado emblema da Patria, os instrumentos marciaes que a ladeavam e aquelles bravos que commandava; cidadão,

---

(3) Quem ignora que o general Conto de Magalhães, apesar das bellas qualidades que o ornavam, não era, entretanto, o homem o proprio para, naquelles dias, presidir S. Paulo? Não tendo seguido meu conselho, convocando, em tempo, em Palacio, os homens eminentes de todas as classes, o alto clero, o corpo docente da Academia. Viu-se isolado, e não poude arcar.

pae de familia e chefe militar com pleno conhecimento de causa e cura d'almas, só, isolado, incomprehendido, estremecia pela incognoscivel do dia seguinte, pelo porvir !

Seriamos mais felizes ?

Eu ficára no Paraguay de guarnição na Capital, em Assumpção, cinco annos após a guerra, e presenciára uma dezena de revoluções bem cruentas ; em todas o povo só é quem perdia. (1) Isso se dava com um povo anemico, pobre e enfraquecido pella guerra. Eu perguntava-me : o que não seria com o Brazil, com São Paulo, rico, exhuberante de seiva e vigor ?

Eu tinha pois razões bem plausiveis de querer afastar aquella desgraça — a revolução, — da nossa sociedade, da nossa terra, maximé, tendo ella um exordio condemnavel !

Finalmente, eu receiava, e ainda hoje mais se robustece esse terror, infelizmente, de que o Brazil, grande e poderoso, se debilitaria ; e, retalhado, passaria a muitos donos ; perdendo nós a independencia, a nacionalidade, a lingua a religião, a Patria emfim !

No quartel de Permanentes, porém quem o diria ?... constituido por uma lei de Deus, em ultimo baluarte do imperio que se desmoronava, centenares de homens dormiam tranquillamente ao lado de armas ensarilhadas emquanto a bandeira docemente reclinada sobre as baionetas, emquanto, por todos, velava, um obscuro campeão, qual moderno Stilicon que procurava suster nas bordas do abysmo a Patria que se derruia ! Cheio de fé, destemido, tentava salvar ainda as instituições que jurára defender !

Baldado intento !

A' meia noite o céu cobrio-se de fulgentes estrellas ; a via lactea, com os seus milhões de sóes, olhos luminosos, deslumbrantes, lançava vivo clarão sobre a silenciosa Cidade ; a formosa constellação do Cruzeiro, com o que procurando pouso, reclinava-se explendorosa no seio das nuvens, lá para as bandas do historico Ypiranga . . .

E, assim, findou-se a ultima noite do que fôra poderoso Imperio Sul-Americano !                                        Dixi.

São Paulo, Alto da Moóca, 196. 15 de Novembro de 1905.

HENRIQUE AFFONSO DE ARAUJO MACEDO.

---

(1) E' bem conhecida a sentença latina:
In commutando civium, nihil mutans homines, præter nomem domini.

## DOCUMENTO N. 1

Cópia.—Quartel do Commando do Corpo Policial Permanente em São Paulo, 13 de Dezembro de 1889.

ORDEM DO DIA N. 23 (ADDICIONAL)

O Major Commandante interino publica ao Corpo para seu conhecimento e fins convenientes o seguinte:

Que seguindo amanhan para a Côrte o Cidadão Coronel Commandante Henrique Affonso de Araujo Macedo, a chamado do Ministerio da Guerra e por ordem do Governo Provisorio deste Estado, assumi nesta data o Commando interino do Corpo, que me foi passado pelo referido Cidadão Coronel que pelos seus esforços conseguiu por em dia a escripturação do mesmo e empregou os mais herculeos, denodados e ingentes trabalhos afim de elevar o prestigio e o nivel moral desta Corporação, o que com brilhantismo conseguiu; e, por esta occasião, me é agradavel reconhecer, neste publico documento; e, faço votos para que tão distincto e nobre irmão de armas em breves dias se ache ao nosso lado para com suas luzes e o elevado patriotismo que todos lhe reconhecemos nos coadjuvar na grande obra da regeneração deste collosal Estado nosso tão querido.

*Guilherme J. do Nascimento*, Major Commandante interino.

Reconheço a firma supra. São Paulo, em 17 de Fevereiro de 1890.—Em test.° ELB de verd.°—*Estevam Leão Bourroul* — São Paulo, era ut supra (1)—*E. L. Bourroul.*

## DOCUMENTO N. 2

Cópia.—Governo Provisorio de S. Paulo, Paço da Camara Municipal, 15 de Novembro de 1889.

Ill.ᵐᵒ Snr.

Tendo o Governo Provisorio, acclamado pelo povo, tomado perante a Camara Municipal posse da administração e governo da Provincia, communico esse facto a V. S.ᵃ para que se sirva levar ao conhecimento do seu batalhão para os devidos effeitos.

---

(1) As duas ultimas linhas estão inutilisando uma estampilha de 200 réis.

O Governo Provisorio conta com os bons serviços de V. S.ª e de seus dignos commandados para garantia da ordem no regimen da mais plena liberdade,

Ill.mo Snr. Coronel Henrique Affonso de Araujo Macedo, Dig.mo Commandante do Corpo de Permanentes.

(Assignado) *M. Ferraz de Campos Salles*,
secretario interino.

\*\*\*

## DOCUMENTO N. 3

Cópia.—REPARTIÇÃO GERAL DOS TELEGRAPHOS

Estação—15 de Novembro de 1889.

Telegrama n.                Numero de ordem
Hora de apresentação        Remettido á
Numero de palavras   pagas  Hora de expedição
Recebido de                 Aviso

A's 5 horas, 73 minutos, p.m.    Carimbo— Estação Central
                                 dos Telegraphos.

Novembro 15 de 1889
Brazil, S. Paulo.

Assignatura do Telegraphista expedidor—O.N.

Procedente de Rio—Data 15.

Endereço—Coronel Henrique Macedo—Commandante Força Policial—Provincia de S.Paulo.

. . . . . . . . . . . . . . .

Povo, Exercito, Armada vão installar Governo Provisorio que Consultará Nação, Convocação Constituinte. Acclamações Geraes. Republica.

(Assignado)—*Q. Bocayuva.*

\*\*\*

## DOCUMENTO N. 4 (*)

Meu illustre amigo Dr. Miranda Azevedo.

Não podendo ainda comparecer ás sessões do Instituto desejava merecer um obsequio.

Tendo sido publicado na nossa *Revista* as notas que offereci sobre o — *Quinze de Novembro em S. Paulo* — queria tornar bem claro um ponto, para que de futuro não se venha dar algum equivoco.

No correr daquella narrativa, referi uma anedocta (aliás verdadeira) occorrida entre o Dr. Campos Salles e o *Coronel Commandante* da força de linha que aqui estacionava.

Finalizando a narrativa, fiz um appello ao nosso illustre consocio Coronel Araujo de Macedo que naquelles tempos era *Commandante da Força Provincial*, para que completasse e rectificasse os pontos omissos do meu trabalho, para facilitar o estudo aos futuros historiadores.

Desejo como disse, que fique bem claro, que aquella anedocta não se refere ao nosso illustre consocio Coronel Araujo Macedo.

Esta resalva seria desnecessaria para os contemporaneos, que conhecem e respeitam ao militar illustrado e leal, que naquelles momentos soube proceder com correcção, calma e prudencia com o mesmo patriotismo que sempre deixou transparecer, quer nas fileiras, quer nos campos de batalha.

Accedendo a este meu pedido muito grato ficará quem é

Am.º Consocio Obr.º

João C. de Moraes.

Setembro — 1905.

———— •❍❀❍• ————

(*) Esta carta vem restabelecer o ponto a que se refere o boato de que o official da Policia tinha ido a Palacio no dia 15 de Novembro de 1889.
Vide *Revista Inst. Hist. de S. Paulo. Proclamação da Republica em S. Paulo pelo dr. João Moraes*—Vol. 8.º, pg. 205.

N. R.

# Noticia historica sobre Cuyabá

Nasce o Coxipó-merim no planalto da *Chapada* (1), de onde precipita-se depois de um sinuoso percurso de cerca de doze kilometros, engrossando logo o seu volume as aguas de cinco contribuintes, cuja série fecha-se com o ribeirão das *Tres Barras*.

Pouco abaixo dessa corrente, na paragem em que o rio primitivamente se repartia em dous braços, formando a extincta ilhota do *Capitão-mór*, assentava-se outrora a povoação da *Forquilha*, em terreno circumjacente ao arraial hoje existente do Coxipó do Ouro.

Em sua origem, modesto acampamento de uma turma de *bandeirantes*, sem destino prefixado, occupou ella a principio apenas a nesga de lerra delimitada a léste pelo braço occidental daquella ilha, e só mais tarde desceu ao sitio antes semeado de malocas *Carijós*.

Da lucta travada entre os invasores e os incolas, lucta sem duvida desegual, mas renhida, a historia local nada menciona, chegando mesmo os raros documentos comtemporaneos a silenciarem inteiramente a respeito, silencio que tambem se reproduz nas chronicas do tempo.

O que parece certo, e a tradição confirma, é que se parte daquella tribu conseguiu furtar-se ao contacto dos brancos, emigrando para o interior, a outra parte talvez mais numerosa submetteu-se á escravidão que lhe era imposta pela lei do mais forte, tendo, entretanto, com o decorrer dos dias, apparecido casos de revolta contra esse jugo, expressos em deserções isoladas.

Naturalmente indolentes, incapazes por isso de qualquer esforço demorado, os individuos desse grupo denunciaram-se fracos auxiliares quando applicados em trabalhos de ordem sedentaria, sendo que seus serviços foram utilizados com melhor vantagem na mineração, e mais ainda como dextros caçadores e experimentados guias através das mattas.

Conhecedores da região, e já por fim sabedores da estima votada ao ouro, vemos dous de seus membros conduzirem em 1722 (2) o sorocabano Miguel Sutil ao declive da collina de N. S. do

---

1) Tem origem nas immediações da fazenda do Burity, numa altitude correspondente a 434 metros sobre a matriz de Cuyabá, ou sejam 653 metros sobre e nivel do mar (Dr. P. Vagel.—*Reisen in Matto-Grosso*—1887 e 1888).

2) João Severiano da Fonseca data esse facto como occorrido em 1720 (*Viagem ao redor do Brasil*, vol. II). Leverger indica o anno de 1722 (*Apontamentos chorographicos da provincia de Matto-Grosso*).

Rosario, onde lhe desvendam por entre o grammado virente grande cópia do precioso metal.

Era a situação da Forquilha naquella epocha sobremodo lisongeira—quatro annos de existencia relativamente tranquilla haviam alterado o seu aspecto, substituindo pouco a pouco as rudes paliçadas de uacoris, por solidos ranchos de páu a pique, e multiplicando prodigiosamente o numero de habitantes.

A noticia daquella descoberta, porêm, exerceu influencia tão preponderante no espirito dos moradores da povoação, gente ferretoada pelo anhelo de espantosas riquezas, que em menos de um anno na outr'ora prospera localidade sómente restavam cercas cahidas e esteios desaprumados para attestarem a passagem ahi de uma população civilizada.

O abandono fóra completo, e a emigração para a nova lavra, que recebeu a denominação de Cuyabá—do rio mais proximo—operou-se com açodamento só explicavel pela abundancia mineral do sitio, de cujos arredores foram extrahidas em menos de um mez, quatrocentas arrobas de ouro, sem que as excavações fossem além de uma camada correspondente a quatro braças abaixo da suberficie do solo (1).

Essa pujança arrastou com sofreguidão para ahi sertanistas e aventureiros de S. Paulo, Minas, Bahia, Piauhy e Maranhão, aos quaes se encorporaram tambem individuos de várias nacionalidades, muitos embora os perigos de uma longa travessia de mais de quinhentas legoas (2), não tendo sido reduzido o numero dos que nella succumbiram.

«Estavam esses homens, escreve o brigadeiro Machado de Oliveira, exclusivamente dominados pelo objecto que os levou a emigrarem do seu paiz, e tanto assim que lhe foi cousa secundaria o curarem da propria manutenção e segurança para viagem tão prolongada e perigosa, em que por certo depaririam com mil difficuldades e riscos. Assim desprecavidos, não tardou muito que *não* cahissem victimas, uns de fome, outros das intermittentes dos paúes do Tieté, e muitos dos Payaguás, que em numerosas canôas affrontavam as expedições n'aquellas paragens em que não podiam ser evitados».

Por impaciencia, sinão por imprevidencia, esses *flibusteiros do sertão*, no dizer de Humboldt, «padeceram grandes destroços, mortandades de gentes por falta de mantimentos, doenças, comidos das onças e outras muitas misérias.»

---

(1) Felippe José Nogueira Coelho.—*Memorias chronologicas da capitania de Matto-Grosso*.

(2) De Araraytaguaba a Cuyabá a distancia pela via fluvial é reputada em 530 1/2 leguas, segundo Lacerda e Almeida, incluindo se o trecho de dezesete leguas comprehendido na voradouro de Camapuam *(Diario de Viagem)*.

«Houve comboyo de canôas, relata Barbosa de Sá (1), em que morreram todos sem ficar um vivo, pois eram achadas as canôas e fazendas podres pelos que vinham atrás, e os corpos mortos pelos reductos e barrancos.»

A uma monção, porêm, que se espedaçava de encontro ás cachoeiras do Tieté ou do Taquary—roteiro preferido posteriormente á navegação do Anhanduhy-assú—ou era destroçada pelos selvagens ,succediam-se outras mais ousadas, ou quiçá mais adextradas, porque em São Paulo repetia-se sempre que «o ouro em Cuyabá era em tanta abundancia, que os caçadores serviam-se delle em vez de chumbo »

Assim, apezar de taes obstaculos, as novas minas já em 1726 tinham-se metamorphoseado em pittoresco arraial de cerca de tres mil habitantes, contando mais de cem casas de edificação regular e duas egrejas. (2)

De todos os acontecimentos teve a metropole exacto conhecimento, e no interesse de melhor assegurar a arrecadação da fazenda real, até então effectuada sem o rigor que convinha á corôa, ordenou que para o arraial se transportasse o governador Rodrigo Cesar de Menezes, incumbindo-o tambem da erecção de Cuyabá em villa.

E a 15 de Novembro daquelle anno, aqui aportava esse funccionario, em cumprimento á determinação régia, tendo-se feito acompanhar do dr. Antonio Alves Lanhas Peixoto, ouvidor de Paranaguá, do padre Lourenço de Toledo Taques, como visitador, e do ajudante Antonio Borba, que se fez tristemente celebre pelo seu comportamento brutal e violento

A expedição que os conduziu compunha-se de trezentas canôas tripuladas por tres mil pessôas, e esse accrescimo de população—despejada assim de chofre sobre um centro afastado de todos os recursos—trouxe como corollario a elevação do preço dos generos de consumo immediato, e foi o annuncio dos males que viéram em pouco flagellar o povo.

Dez-ssis dias depois—a 1.º de Janeiro de 1727—era Cuyabá elevada á categoria de villa lavrando-se do acto o seguinte termo:

«Ao primeiro dia de mez de Janeiro de 1727, nesta Villa Real do Senhor Bom Jesus do Cuyabá, sendo mandado por S. M., que Deus Guarde, a creal-a de novo o Exm. Sr. Rodrigo Cesar de Menezes, governador e capitão-general desta capitania, e que o acompanhasse para o necessario, o Dr. Antonio Alves Lanhas Peixoto, ouvidor geral da comarca de Paranaguá, sendo por

---

(1) José Barbosa de Sá.— *Chronicas de Cuyabá.*
(2) Bom Despacho e Senhor Bom Jesus. Nesta ultima, edificada em 1722 pelo capitão-mòr Jacintho Barbosa Lopes, repousam os restos de Paschoal Moreira Cabral, fallecido em 1724, aos setenta annos de edade.

elle eleitas as justiças, juizes ordinarios, Rodrigo Bicudo Chacim, o thesoureiro coronel João de Queiroz Magalhães, e vereadores Marcos Soares de Faria, Francisco Xavier de Mattos, João de Oliveira Garcia, e procurador do conselho Paulo Anhayá Lima, servindo de escrivão da comarca Luiz Teixeira de Almeida, almotacé o brigadeiro Antonio de Almeida Lara, e o capitão-mór Antonio José de Mello, levando o estandarte da villa Mathias Gomes de Faria, foi mandado pelo dito Snr. governador capitão· general que com o dito Dr. Ouvidor, todos juntos com a nobreza e povo, fossem á praça levantar o pelourinho desta villa, a que nome d'El Rei deu o nome de Villa Real do Bom Jesus, e declarou que sejam as armas de que usasse um escudo dentio com o campo verde e um morro ou monto no meio todo salpicado com folhetas e granitos de ouro, e por timbre, em cima do escudo, uma phenix; e nomeou para levantar o pelourinho ao capitão mór regente Fernando Dias Falcão, e todos sobreditos com o dito Dr. Ouvidor, nobreza e povo foram á praça desta villa, aonde o dito Fernando Dias Falcão levantou o pelourinho, do que para constar a todo o tempo fiz este termo, que assignou o dito Snr. General com os sobreditos.

E eu Gervasio Leite Rabello, secretario deste governo, que o escrevi, dia e era ut supra.—Rodrigo de Menezes—Antonio Alves Lanhas Peixoto—Rodrigo Bicudo Chacim—Marcos Soares de Faria—Francisco Xavier de Mattos—João de Queiroz Magalhães—João de Oliveira Garcia—Luiz Ferreira de Almeida—Antonio José de Mello—Paulo de Anhayá Lemos—Antonio de Almeida Lara—Mathias Soares de Faria—Fernando Dias Falcão —João Pereira da Cruz—Manoel Dias de Barros—Luiz de Vasconcellos Pessoa—Manoel Vicente Neves—Salvador Martins Bonella.»

Rodrigo Cesar só regressou a S. Paulo em Setembro de 1728, e a sua permanencia na villa foi assignalada por uma série de extorsões, processos e actos de requintada violencia—do que dá justa medida a perseguição movida contra os irmãos Lourenço e João Leme—forçando desse modo os seus habitantes abandonarem interesses e propriedades, e a se internarem pelos sertões uns, e outros tomarem caminho para Goyaz e São Paulo. (1)

Do grau de decadencia a que chegou Cuyabá, logo depois da partida daquelle governador, dá uma testemunha a noticia que segue

«A villa só tem oito ou nove casas de telha, entre as quaes

_____

(1) Só em 1728, mais de mil pessôas abandonaram Cuyabá em busca de Goyaz.

a melhor é a que foi do General Rodrigo Cesar; as mais são
de capim, mas como serem assim se não vendiam quando cheguei,
por mais pequenas que fossem, por menos de 200 a 500 oitavas
cada uma, e as que tinham mais algum commodo chegaram a
700, porêm dahi a dois annos as vi vender a 40 e 50 oitavas,
quando as não desamparavam os donos que vinham para o povoado: o mesmo succedeu ás roças que pedindo por algumas
quando fui, 300 a 400 oitavas, as venderam ao depois por 50 a
100, e muitas as abandonaram os donos, retirando-se para S.
Paulo ». (1)

« Erão tudo misérias, queixas e lamentos; a terra falta de
roças, que brotavão os milhos espigas sem gram algum; as doenças
actuaes, os que escapavão dellas não escapavão da fome; assim
que tudo era gemer, chorar, morrer. » (2)

A decadencia manifesta-se notoria e constante em todos os
sentidos, e esse estado de cousas vigorou até que os primeiros
actos do general Joaquim da Silva Caldeira Pimentel viéram
pela moderação reanimar a confiança publica.

O germen do mal, porêm, estava lançado e a lembrança dos
calamitosos dias que a presença de Rodrigo Cesar assignalára, per-
durava ainda na memoria de todos, actuando de modo que os poucos
moradores da villa buscavam apenas pretexto para abandonal-a.

Dessa irradiação, e mais ainda pela indole aventureira dos
primeiros povoadores do sertão matto-grossense, nasceram as
entradas para a região occidental, que tomaram vulto depois dos
descobrimentos dos irmãos Fernando e Arthur Paes de Barros,
originando-se dahi o povoamento do valle do Guaporé.

Indirectamente, pois, os desmandos de um governo mal intencionado e pessimamente orientado, foram os factores de um
conjuncto de acontecimentos que trouxeram ao Brazil maior ampli-
dão territorial, e a Portugal feliz opportunidade de indemnizar-se
dos prejuizos que a má fé da politica hespanhola lhe havia acarre-
tado com a occupação dos Felippinas, procedimento contrario ao
estabelecido no tratado de Tordesilhas de 1494 e extranhavel em
face da convenção de Saragoça de 1523.

Apezar da sua preoccupação doentia de imitador de Luiz XIV,
bem comprehendeu d. João V o alcance dos novos successos e
para melhor assegurar o dominio portuguez naquella zona, apressou-se em crear, por acto de 9 de Maio de 1748, a capitania
independente de Matto-Grosso.

Cuyabá.                                          Estevão de Mendonça

(1) Noticias praticas das minas de Cuyabá, etc.. que dá ao Rev. Padre Diogo
Soares o capitão João Antonio Cabral Camello etc. (Revista do Instituto Historico, vol. IV).
(2) Barbosa de Sá.—Chronicas do Cuyabá.

# A fundação da cidade de S. Paulo

---

Quando d. João III viu por terra anniquilados os projectos do seu ministro, quando viu os seus validos a braços com o infortunio, os heróes da India, que julgou galardoar com essas terras da America, acabando com a morte escura, ás mãos dos barbaros que elles não souberam vencer, comprehendeu então que, para domar esse povo, para conquistar o Brazil, só uma arma se lhe deparava irresistivel — o Evangelho.

E de facto, o que não pudera conseguir o favoritismo bafejado, nem a valentia tantas vezes provada nas pugnas do Oriente, nem o trafico do contractador, obteve-o, e triumphantemente, a palavra unctuosa e persuasiva do missionario.

O rei appellou então para a obra, ainda nascente, de Ignacio de Loyola, para essa Companhia de Jesus, instituição formidavel, que tinha de levar o catholicismo a todos os recantos da terra, e entregou-lhe a evangelização do Brazil.

Dentro das traças a que ia obedecer o novo regimen, o padre Nobrega, ao lado de Thomé de Sousa, não é um simples collaborador: é o pensamento, é o conselho na fundação da metropole da colonia, como foi a acção mais efficaz na defesa desta e no seu engrandecimento.

Effectivamente, quando em 1549 desembarcavam nas plagas bahianas os primeiros Jesuitas, companheiros de Nobrega, começa, para o Brazil, essa sublime epopéa do Evangelho nas selvas, que já teve de um dos nossos peregrinos cantores a condigna consagração.

Nas praias do mar, como na floresta secular, onde quer que houvesse um povo a salvar, uma tribu errante a redimir, onde da palavra de Deus podia brotar uma sociedade christã, a cruz redemptora, hasteada pela fé, mantida por sublime devotamento, regada com o sangue de martyres, precede a bandeira das quinas, a bandeira desses heróicos marinheiros para quem não ha Adamastores a empecer-lhes, para os mundos escondidos, a marcha victoriosa.

* * *

Quando José de Anchieta, com mais quatro companheiros, desembarca em S. Vicente, em 1553, pequena era ainda a população da colonia, precaria e até humilhada a sua situação.

A despeito dos esforços de Nobrega e principalmente do padre Leonardo Nunes, enfraquecido estava ainda o sentimento religioso, quasi obliterado o senso moral entre os colonos, tão profundo cavára o vicio nesse longo periodo de doze annos, desde a morte de Gonçalo Monteiro, o primeiro parocho e logar tenente do Donatario, até á vinda dos primeiros jesuitas em 1549.

Fóra das ilhas onde a agricultura apenas medrava, timidas e arriscadas eram as tentativas dos colonos e povoadores. Quasi ninguem se atrevia a estabelecer-se no continente, em pontos mais distantes, ou fóra da protecção natural dos esteiros ou braços de mar, que serviam, a um tempo, de estradas e de fossos interpostos entre christãos e gentios.

Itanhaen, na terra firme, pouco havia que recebera os seus primeiros povoadores. Santo André, no alto dos campos, mais era uma traição á idéa civilizadora do que uma villa de portuguezes. E, comtudo, eram estes dois pontos excepções em que aliás bem pouco se confiava. A prohibição expressa do Donatario de irem europeus serra acima a traficar com os indios, e aquelle movimento de concentração, annos antes, ordenado pela Camara de S. Vicente, são disso a prova irrefragavel

Uma série de desastres occorridos a curtos intervallos acabára por encurralar os europeus nas suas ilhas, onde se quedavam timidos deante do Tupi, emboscado nas mattas vizinhas, como deante da arrogancia audaciosa dos Tamoyos.

Por isso, o continente permanecia vedado á civilização, como por um véo de mysteriosos, terrores e incertezas, pois só partidas bem armadas ousavam pisar a terra firme, com tal ou qual probalidade de sucesso...

*<br>* *

Entretanto, ainda que sitiados nas suas ilhas, e sem forças para os rasgos audaciosos, viviam os portuguezes como si fossem barbaros tambem. Diz Vasconcellos que além dos desregramentos dos costumes e do nenhum respeito pela religião, viviam os colonos do rapto traiçoeiro dos indios, tendo entre si o officio de salteal-os por valentia e por elle eram os homens estimados...

Comprehendeu o padre Manoel da Nobrega que não era essa região de beira-mar a mais propria para fazer fructificar entre o gentio a tão desejada catechese. Determinou, portanto, de ir-se pelo sertão dentro á escolha de melhor sitio, onde «... fundar de novo um povo principiado em sinceridade, verdadeira religião e amor de Christo».

Apparelhada a apostolica missão de que fazia parte o joven José de Anchieta, aos vinte annos de sua edade, o padre Nobrega, já então provincial no Brasil, enviou-a a fundar um collegio entre os indios nos campos de Piratininga.

Começa então, de facto, e incontestavelmente, a obra da conquista do planalto brasileiro, a expansão do Brasil.

Aquelles treze religiosos, que compunham a missão, ao pisarem a prancha da barca que os devia conduzir á terra firme, para as santas e amarguradas pelejas, postos os olhos na alterosa serrania, coroada de nevoas que em revoada se despenham pelas quebradas daquelles montes, como occultando-lhes as indiziveis agruras, certo, occorreu-lhes a grandeza dos sacrificios do apostolado. Maior, porém, era a grandeza da sua fé, que não só galga as montanhas, mas tem tambem o poder de removel-as.

Transposta a asperrima serrania, atravessaram a matta, e, já distante della cerca de tres leguas, foram ter ao logar escolhido para o Collegio nesta lombada de campo alto, interposta ás aguas dos ribeiros Tamanduatehy e Anhangabahú, onde já estavam residindo, com as suas tribus, os dous chefes indios Tebiriçá e e Cai-Uby, aguardando a annunciada vinda dos missionarios.

A importancia e a capacidade do logar escolhido ahi estão a attestar-nos, pela benignidade do clima, pelo relevo topographico, pela abundancia das aguas, pela belleza do horizonte, o summo tacto, a discreta prudencia, a elevação de vistas dos discipulos de Santo Ignacio.

Aqui, nesse pequeno espaço de não mais de quatro alqueires de terra, a que aquelles dous ribeiros convergentes davam a figura de um triangulo, aqui se lançaram os fundamentos da cidade que, nos accidentes naturaes do terreno, encontrava a mais efficaz defesa.

Foram alojar-se os padres para uma pequena casa que os indios por si mesmos edificaram, e que, coberta de palha, com as paredes de taipa de mão, não tendo mais de quatorze passos de comprimento e dez de largo, serviu por quasi um anno de egreja e de collegio, o qual se denominou de S. Paulo, por se haver nelle celebrado a primeira missa a 25 de janeiro de 1554, quando a Egreja Catholica commemora a conversão do Apostolo das Gentes.

A posição escolhida para a egreja era, entretanto, a mais propicia. A face de terreno voltada para o Tamanduatehy, outr' ora Piratininga, onde se espraiava extensa varzea, era talhado em encosta abrupta, e exhibia nesse tempo os desbarrancados vermelhos de grês e schisto occultos pela moderna casaria. A escarpa tinha resaltos, curvas e recortes, e nella formava profunda depressão a actual rua João Alfredo. Esta elevação, que lembrava as acropoles gregas, dominava de vinte e cinco a trinta metros de alto toda a extensa varzea alagadiça até ao Tieté ou Anhemby, distante meia legoa ao norte.

Da pequena egreja, collocada á beira dessa escarpa e no angulo da mais funda das suas reentrancias, não só se dominava o horizonte donde era possivel um ataque ou surpreza, como se podia fazer a policia da povoação que lhe crescia na vizinhança.

Os indios, a principio reduzidos pelos padres, foram os Tupinaquis, Carijòs, Tupis e Guayanazes, que assentaram suas cabanas segundo os mesmos arrumamentos ainda hoje não obliterados pelas modernas construcções.

No plano então observados se descobrem perfeitamente os lineamentos dessa cauta prudencia, dessa estrategia que convinha para com os de dentro e desse calculado retrahimento ou exclusão inteira que observava para com os de fóra. O chefe Tebiriçá e os da sua sequela ficaram alli para o vertice do triangulo, na altura do actual convento de S. Bento, que era a porta norte da cidadella de catechumenos e protegendo o accesso desse lado do sinuoso Tieté. Os do sequito do do velho Cai-Uby localisaram-se alli para o extremo sul, proximo do sitio que depois se chamou *Tabatagoera* e tinham sob sua guarda o caminho que do alto do espigão descia para a varzea e tomava para S. Vicente, por Santo André.

No meio ficava o collegio dos Padres como centro donde irradiavam os caminhos ou futuras ruas da cidade.

No beiço da escarpa que dá para o Anhangabahú, sulco profundo onde crescia espesso matto e onde a lenda selvagem fazia deslisar mysteriosamente essa *agua da maldade*, rasgava-se o caminho de cintura, mais tarde transformado em rua de Martim Affonso, e hoje de S. Bento, outr'ora habitado em sua maior extensão pela gente de Tebiriçá....

*
* *

O primeiro anno da fundação do Collegio passou-se todo a conciliar os interesses do gentio com os da religião. Foi preciso ensinar-lhe a construir com mais apuro as suas cabanas, dando-lhes alinhamento e proporções. Os padres eram elles mesmos os mestres da obra e tambem os operarios, quando cumpria ensinar com o exemplo. O irmão Affonso Braz improvisou-se carpinteiro e fez prodigios.

Escassa, comtudo, era a população de S. Paulo. José de Anchieta contava tão somente cento e trinta pessoas. de todo o sexo e edade, no ensino do catecismo, e destes só trinta e seis foram baptisados no primeiro anno.

O irmão Antonio Rodrigues, que sabia bem o *tupi*, encarregou-se do ensino na escola, frequentada então por quinze baptisados e alguns catechumenos. José de Anchieta, regente do Collegio, ensinava aos outros irmãos o latim, o portuguez e o castelhano, e, por sua vez, aprendia a lingua do paiz, em que se fez mestre consummado.

Cedo, porém, a fama dos Padres, amigos do gentio e seus protectores, se espalhou pelos sertões, determinando um exodo verdadeiro dos selvagens, que, ou vinham trazer os filhos para aprenderem com os religiosos ou para se acolherem elles mesmos á sombra da Egreja de Deus.

Por muito tempo viveram os padres e os seus indios separados dos portuguezes. E assim era preciso, para que a sementeira do Evangelho se não perdesse com o degradante proceder e triste exemplo dos maus christãos. Critiquem embora os sabios e liberaes de gabinete a prudentissima deliberação dos religiosos; condemnem o seu systema, á luz da moderna sciencia: o caso é que, si quizerem, ainda hoje, catechisar indios, hão de fazel-o como elles, os religiosos, outr'ora o fizeram; sinão, não.

O abandono dos indigenas, a sua volta á vida selvagem, depois do desapparecimento dos jesuitas, é a melhor prova de quanto valiam aquelles padres, como civilizadores dos indios.

Quando, em 1886, desci explorando as aguas encachoeiradas do Paranapanema, até onde, outr'ora, se estenderam as missões de Guayrá, tocou-me a alma, naquelle deserto immenso, o bosque marginal das bravas e incultas laranjeiras. Dos seus pomos de ouro, abundantes, bellos, pendidos sobre as nossas cabeças, não resumavam, entretanto, sinão acidez e fel.

O indio, abandonado ou perseguido, ficou como essas laranjeiras, esplendidas na sua grandeza selvagem, mas cujos fructos a corrente dispersou e corrompeu

Azedume e fel, desconfiança e odio, eis o que sobra hoje na alma do indio, contra essa civilização cujo alvorecer apenas entrevira e que tão cedo lhe arrebataram....

THEODORO SAMPAIO.

## Relación de la guerra y victoria alcanzada contra los Portugueses del Brasil año 1641 en 6 de Abril

---

Pax Christi etc.

Mucho antes que el p.° D.° de Boroa, amoroso P.° de las Red.ᵉˢ, nos avisasse de la venida cierta de los Portugueses de S. Pablo con animo de destruyr a las Red.ᵉˢ puse particular cuydado que en las fronteras todas se viviesse con particular cuydado y vigilansia, ordenando se cuydasse de que jamas faltassen sentinelas y espias, y juntamente se atendiesse en todos los pueblos a bazer sentinelas, alardes y exercicios militares con que nuestros hijos notablemente se animaron y ya no vian la hora de probar las manos con los enemigos que les dava alguna molestia y enfado el que tardassen tanto que hazian el caso ya del que hazen valerosos soldados de afeminados hombres. Entre tanto deseo de probar las armas, estando con notable suspension sin saver de cierto de la llegada del enemigo a las cabesadas deste Uruguay; teniendo por casi cierto, que de su numerosa infidelidad se deslisarian alguna canoa de infieles, huyendo de los portugueses, atendiendo a las muchas ofertas que les aviamos hecho y partidos aqueles aviamos salido si nos avisassen, asegurando-nos lo harian el suceder siempre aquesto las vezes que el enemigo desta nacion guaraní les a infestado sus tierras, y dando nos seguro desto, el tener tantos parientes tan sercano suyos en la Red.ᵒⁿ de S. Maria. Pero ya que ellos por justos juisios de Dios en castigo quisas de su duresa no lo hisieron ni arrostraron a admitir las ofertas hechas continuamente de nuestra parte, entregandose a los Portugueses infamemente, nro S. P.° Piadoso destos pobrecitos hijos nros lo hizo con el aviso que el P.° D.° de Boroa nos enbió tan atiempo e con tantas ayudas de cosas para la guerra y premios para los soldados enviando al H.° P.° Sadorni, su compañero para que nos traxesse el aviso con prestesa y cuidado, el qual le mostro viniendo con brevedad y a tiempo, con que tuve lugar de embiar a llamar a los P.ᵉˢ que iban ya a la mission de la sierra y estaban ya en el ...iro que a tardar algo mas fuera cosa trabajosa el detenerlos y nos bizieron grande falta assi los P.ᵉˢ como los indios, por yr mas de mil indios con sus armas de fuego y para la mision de S.ᵃ Theresa estabau ya para salir del Uruguay otros dos P.ᵉˢ con mas de docientos indios y sus armas de fuego.

Con el avi·o pues y ayudas de costa del P.ᵉ D.ᵒ de Boroa crecio el cuydado y deligencia y viendo que el golpe nos amenasaba por el Uruguay, fuera de los espias que avian para poner mas cuydado y animar las mas, enbié al P.ᵉ D.ᵒ Suarez que asistiesse a los Indios que hazian la ordinaria sentinella lo qual hizo con cuydado quinze dias que alli estuvo, en estos nos dió otro aviso casi cierto nro Sr. y de la llegada a este rio de los Portugueses de S. Pablo enviando a tiempo extraordinario qual es el de dicienbre y Henero una cresciente deste rio Uruguay con que rodaron mas de cien canoas y con ellas muchas cosas de la pobresa de los indios de arriba y algumas canoas ya acabadas de escoplear para balsas y mucha flecheria. Con estos indicios casi evidentes, pues denotaban claro el rodar canoas buenas llenas de la hacienda de los Indios el estar apurados y huyr y las balsas indicaban ser obra de gente mas ladina y perita que los Indios infideles, dando gracias a Dios por el aviso y recuerdo con parecer de los P.ᵉˢ a los ocho de henero hize convocacion de solos dos mil indios de los pueblos, dexando lo mas de la fuerza en pié y con orden de que al primer aviso cierto se havian de juntar todos. Parti con ellos al Acaragua con animo de hazer alli rostro al enemigo y de camino acabar aquellas comidas, por que el enemigo si· viniesse no se apoderasse de ellas y cobrasse brios. Alli determiné con parecer de los P.ᵉˢ enviar gente a saver lo que passava el rio arriba, y para esta mision escogi a los Padres Xpobal de Altamirano, D.ᵒ de Salasar, Ant.ᵒ de Alarcon y al H.ᵒ P.ᵒ Sadorni con buen numero de soldados, con orden de que se informassen y tomasen lengua del enemigo y de sus intentos y si se ofreciesse alguna ocasion buena de ofender a lo enemigo no la perdiesen; fueron los P.ᵉˢ y por el camino luego encontraron algunos cuerpos muertos y algunos daban muestras aver muerto pocos dias antes, segun estaban de frescos, gran cantidad de flechas, canoas que se cruzaban, rodando, y sobre todo encontraron mas de diez o doze balsas hechas de unas cañas de la tierra, que los Indios llaman taquaras, muy bien hechas y acabadas. Con esto los P.ᵉˢ discurrieron de la cercania del enemigo y vecindad ya a nros fines, y assi llegados a un puesto serca del salto deste rio Uruguay enbiaron los P.ᵉˢ gente por tierra y agua a ver si cogian algun espia o gente que les alumbrasse de lo que avia en la tierra: los que yban por tierra tuvieron muy buena suerte, pues ya con tres horas poco mas o menos de la noche volv.eron con unas dies y sois almas que avian venido, dexadas sus canoas

por tierra huyendo de los Portugueses que ya avian visto el rio
arriba y hallado se en juntas que los del rio arriba avian hecho
contra los Portugueses y juntamente avisaron a los P.ᵉˢ de la
determinacion de ellos, que era ir unos al Para..., otros
por S. Teresa a la Concep.ⁿ y otros por el Uruguay avajo en
canoas para divertir las fuerzas de nuestras Red.ᵉˢ Con este aviso
cierto los P.ᵉˢ determinaron llegarse al salto y esperar los espias
que avian enviado, adonde los esperaron hasta casi las tres de
la tarde del dia siguiente y alli vieron grandissima cantidad de
canoas y balsas de los Portugueses que avian rodado; passó
nuestra gente dos leguas arriva del Salto donde hallaron todos
los Pueblos y puertos desiertos ya, sin gente ni canoas con que
se persuadieron los P.ᵉˢ que ya el Portugues era buelto a su
tierra o hecho lo que se sospechaba y decian los indios cogidos,
y assi los P.ᵉˢ se volvieron luego con la gente para estar apercebidos
para qualquier successo y tener las fuerzas todas juntas, y con
esto salieron del Acaraguá los dos mil indios que yo avia
ordenado se juntassen y por el reselo que avia de que el
Portugues tomasse los campos y camino que siempre avian
traydo, por mayor cuydado los P.ᵉˢ missioneros que en esta
occasion como en otras xamas an perdonado a trabajo por el
amor de Dios y de sus hijos se encargaron los P.ᵉˢ Pablo de
Benabides, P.ᵉ de Mola y Xpóbal Portel aunque en tiempo de
excesivos calores y con extraordinarias incomodidades a la sombra
de una pobre chosuela de hazer continua sentinella por aquela
parte estando por quinse dias, y ves ubo que un mez, padeciendo
lo que Dios sabe, y lo mesmo paso en el Parana, en lo qual los
P.ᵉˢ mostraron como suelen la fuerza del divino amor, y de los
Proximos que en sus coraçones reyna   En el Acaragua aunque
parece no amenasaba ya tanto peligro ordene al P.ᵉ Xpóbal
de Altamirano se encargase de que sus hijos acudiessen a
espiar y hazer continuas centinelas el rio arriba, y assi dexe al
P.ᵉ en aquel puesto aunque tenia ya la gente un dia de camino
mas abajo en el Borore, y segura; por que a su sombra y con
su presencia los Indios hiziessen aprecio de la centinela que
hazian en que gastaron mes y medio sin parar ocupacion que
el P.ᵉ y sus hijos han tenido quatro años ha con muy grande
diligencia y cuydado. Finalmente allos 25 de febrero quiso el
Señor avisar-nos de la venida cierta de los Portuguezes a nras
Red.ᵉˢ con aver cogido el dia que dize los del Acaragua que
estaban en sentinela dos muchachos huydos de los Portugueses
que trahydos ao P.ᵉ Altamirano le dizeron lo que avia, y
constantes mas que una roca afirmaron ser cierta la determinacion
y venida de los Portugueses, que estaban muy a priessa y deveras

haziendo canoas y matalotage para vajar por rio a dar sobre las Red.°°. A la hora misma despacho el P.° alguna chusma que avia ydo a su pueblo antiguo por mays en balsas a que acudio la gente con cuydado y luego se me aviso de todo, y el P.° doblo los espias y puso docientos indios en varios puestos para saber de cierto de los enemigos. Volvi recebido el aviso del Parana adonde ubo algum rumor de enemigos, y adonde para disponer de cosas avia ydo llegado a este Uruguay ordené estuviesse todo a punto, y asi mesmo encargué al dicho padre Altamirano cuydasse de aquella frontera pues de su cuydado dependia el bien de las Red.°° hizolo como se le encargo y assi nro Señor nos ayudo pues aviendo el P.° enviado ocho canoas el rio arriba, y conforme a la instruccion del P.° salido de mañana a reconocer el rio al salir del sol vieron al enemigo volvieron con prestesa las proas por que al mismo punto el enemigo tomando las canoas ligeras que para esto traya ya prevenidas con deseo de coger nuestras espias de que tenian ya noticia de los infieles del rio arriba y de los puestos en que se hazian, comenso con seys canoas y con esforzados bogadores a darles caça y seguillos como media legua larga a toda furia y con tal denuedo que casi llegaron a ygualar las proas y a dar voces y hazer otras cosas con deseo de turbar nros hijos y hazerlos desmayar para tener lugar de coger les la delantera y rendirlos, y hazerlos desmayar para tener, digo, y rendirlos, y coger nos de repente cogidas las espias, pero estando ya las dos canoas de nros hijos en este parage y ya casi como vencidas (pues lo mas probable es que con trabajo se escaparan de los enemigos) salieron a su ayuda de una media enboscada las otras seys canoas, y disparando un arcabus y dando voceria, con todo su pingolleria (?) que el P.° previniendo este lance les havia hecho llevar se detuvo el enemigo y dejo libres a nros hijos, quedando avergononzados y muy burlados, y frustrados sus intentos, y nros hijos les dieron la vaya, y desafiaron y avisaron al P.° de la cercania del enemigo, el qual por temor de alguna celada disparo toda su arcabuceria, enarbolo sus banderas, toco sus cajas y entro por una tabla que ay grande de rio por alli en forma de guerra. nros hijos por saber de sus designios se yban poniendo de punta en punta en el rio y asi le fueron trayendo hasta serca del Acaragua. eneste interim el P.° aviendo me avisado de todo pontualmente apurado destos indios con un grande aguasero, y con el agua hasta media pierna en una canoa, de las olas, vino al Borore que es adonde se mudo la Red.ⁿ a dar orden de retirar la chusma y encargando se dello el P.° P.° de Mola volvio el mesmo P.° aquella mesma hora al Açaragua adonde avia dejado ordenado a los indios lo que avian de hazer, y lo que les importaba por que el enemigo no los cogiesse desapercebidos; que les dio la vida, pues aviendo los antes confessado a todos y exortadolos a la defensa de sus tierras con un Christo en las manos animandoles a hazer siquiera alguna demonstracion; hizieron mas que el P.ᵉ pensaba como luego diere. Aquella noche el enemigo con deseo de coger la gente desapercebida, y algunas indias que el deseaba muchissimo, sercaron con todo el aguasero el pueblo por tres partes, y por el rio se esparcieron con canoas. nuestros hijos que no dormian y se avian puesto en otra parte hizieron lo mismo velando y poniendose en la parte contraria al puesto del enemigo. pero las centinelas del rio de tal suerte se mesclaron que encontraban las unas espias con las otras sin coneserse, pues perguntando las del enemigo a las nuestras quienes eran y como se llamaban se hizieron como indios nuebos respondiendo ad efesios y diziendo; mi nombre? perguntaronles mas quien os a enbiado aqui respondieron el capitan Mayor, y con esto se apartaron los nuestros a priesa por no ser conosidos. amanecio, y el enemigo acometio al pueblo y hallose burlado por no hallar alma en el; en esto nros hijos salieron en sus canoas a desafiar al enemigo, aunque tan pocos que que no pasaban de docientos y sinquenta de las Red.ᵉˢ del Acaragua y S. Xavier en solas treynta canoas, y el enemigo tenia mas de ciento, que accepto la batalla teniendo por cierta la victoria, mas ayudando Dios a los nuestros, y guiados de S. Fran.ᶜᵒ Xavier nro Patron el capitan Ignacio Abiaru con quince canoas acometio a mas de sinquenta del Portugues y durando la pelea mas de dos horas, um mosquetero nuestro disparo y guiando la bala S. Fran.ᶜᵒ Xavier dio en un muslo a Portugues y se le quebro dando con el en el agua, y otro de otra canoa dio a otro Portugues en un costado y le derribo; otro con una bala de mosquete algo de serca limpio una canoa de enemigos.

En este interim llego el P.ᵉ Altamirano animando de nuebo a los indios que alentandose de nuebo dieron sobre el enemigo y le hizieron huyr infamemente mas de ocho quadras, y saltaron en tierra no queriendo pelear mas aunque le desafiaron e incitaron muchissimo los nuestros. llegaron en esto otras tres banderas del enemigo, y viendo el P.ᵉ que el poder que traya era grande retiro los indios contra su voluntad pues aunque se vian pocos deseaban murir pro Patria, et lege. trajolos el P.ᵉ a todos al Borore sin aver avido herido alguno ni succedido de-man que harto se temio pues llovian balas como granizo, y flechas a montones sobre los nuestros pero sin daño alguno que fue de mucho provecho por que cobraran con esto mucho aliento y esfuerzo todos nrõs hijos pues la consequensia estaba en la mano que si pocos bazian huyr infamemente a tantos quanto mejor lo haria todo nuestro exercito junto y con tantas armas.

A quel mesmo dia sabado nuebe de março envio nuestro Señor un terrible aguasero y tormenta con que el enemigo se quedo en el Acaragua aquel dia, y el domingo en que se junto la gente toda del Uruguay que a no aver enbiado nro Sr el temporal tan a tiempo, cumpliera el enemigo lo que deseaba que era venirse luego tras las canoas que le hisieron rostro, y se ubiera apoderado de las comidas del Mborore con que nos dieran bien en que entender y fuera muy dificultoso el echarlo de la tierra, cobrando brio, y creciendo su soberbia y orgulho que era grande y fiado en ella se prometia ya el buen successo y la destruccion de todas nuestras Reducciones que ya traya hecha partixa dellas y de su gente, pero despues muy en brebe se desenganaron de todo viendo en el Acaragua adonde pensaban dar un terrible assalto como lo tenian determinado desde S. Pablo segun dize la gente que se a salido de ellos, se vieron sin gente alguna, las casas deciertas y ahuyentados de pocos indios con todo esto llebados de aquel deseo tan conatural de coger indios no descansaron haciendo varias correrias por las chacras y demas puestos de aquel pueblo, y volviendo Tupis (que son sus corredores mayores) sin presa alguna los azotaban y apaleaban atribuyendo a poco cuydado y a demasiada flogedad el no traer un alma tan sola, con esto se los cayo el animo y dixeron entre si y a sus basallos cansarse enbalde y que mejor fuera no aver venido pues se abrian de volver heridos dexando muchos muertos, y al fin vasios y sin presa alguna y de hecho trataron con grandes veras de volverse como lo afirman todos quantos an salido dentre ellos. Ciegos en pero de cudicia y queriendo nro Sr pagassen muchos dellos sus pecados, y humillarlos, y trabajarlos pessadamente, por el que el se sabe no fomento esta determinacion permitiendo que derepente mudassen determinacion y baxassen este Uruguay abajo.

En nro real del Mborore, mientras el enemigo quedaba perplexo en el Acaragua trataron los P.⁰ˢ de ver lo que se avia de hazer, y en primer lugar de dia y de noche se expusieron a confessar a sus hijos, estando tan continuos en esto, y no perdoando a trabajo alguno, que la ubo grande pues la junta era ya de mas de tres mill indios; animaba ver la fee de los indios, y las ansias con que deseaban aver a los P.⁰ˢ para confesssarse aun que lo estaban todos, aprehendiendo vivamente el temor de la muerte en peccado: en este exercicio gastaron los P.⁰ˢ sabado y domingo hasta el lunes como a los dos de la tarde ayunando tan

rigurosamente, que no exedia la comida de medio medio dia a
una media colacion por ser fuerza acudir a tantas cosas, y ayuda
de las almas y cuerpos de sus hijos, pues de esto dependia el
bien y augmento dellas, atendiendo con toda diligencia, a disponer
la gente y las cosas para la pelea pues del buen successo della
dependia la conservacion de todas las Red.ᶜᵃ.

En este interim que los P.ᶜˢ y sus hijos trataban tan deveras
de disponerse para la guerra: el enemigo Portugues viendo que
no hallaban rastro alguno de gente, si determinaron arestados
(como dixe) vajar el rio abajo pero con tan poca union y tan
temerosos que dos veces se volvieron al puesto del Acaragua de
mas de media legua de camino, hasta que alfin se resolvieron
a vaxar, mas con tal miedo que apenas vogaban, con reselos
grandes, de alguna selada. En nuestro exercito advirtiendo la
vecindad del enemigo se puso todo a punto conforme al orden
del P.ᵉ Pedro de Mola que tenia mis veces por estar yo
enfermo con tercianas en S. Nicolas, que esta tres leguas del
Borore, mientras venia el P.ᵉ P.ᵉ Romero, que por ordem
del P.ᵉ Provincial pasado D.ᵒ de Boroa avia de acudir de la
guerra, el qual llego el segundo dia, y se encargo della. Aprestose
la armada de Rio en que se hallaron setenta canoas con sinquenta
y siete arcabuces, senalandose por Cap.ⁿ general del rio al capitan
Don Ignacio Abiaru que cumplio con su oficio exelentemente,
con aplauso de los P.ᶜˢ e indios, hablando, industriando a sus
soldados del modo que avian de tener en pelear con el enemigo
que aguardaban con deseos; lo de tierra se dispuso tanbien muy
bien encargandose al H.ᵒ Domingo de Torres la execucion a que
acudio con notables veras, grande animo y esfuerço, que lo mostro
en las ocaciones y peleas en que andaba personalmente animando
a los indios y ayudandolos con su industria, sin reparar en trabajos,
y los padecio muy grandes, y nos ayudo muchissimo, y el H.ᵒ
P.ᵒ Sadorni por su parte nos ayudo tambien, con muy grandes
veras, en todo, cuydando tambien de curar los heridos, a que
asistio con muy grande aplicacion y caridad hasta mas de tres
o quatro horas de la noche, edificando notablemente a los P.ᶜˢ que
unos acudian a confessar heridos, otros a hazerlos traer de la
guerra y hazerles fuego por que no se resfriassen desacomodandose
todos, pues la choza donde todos vivian servio de enfermaria,
y hospital, trazendo los mesmos P.ᶜˢ el fuego, solicitando el
foguear y cauterisar a los heridos, arropandolos con sus mesmas
ropas y frezadas, haziendo tiras sus camisas para bendas y otras
cosas de que necessitan los heridos.

Amenasando ya proximo el peligro de la guerra se hablo a los
Indios para que hiciessen actos fervorosos de contricion y pidiessen

a Dios misericordia; absolviendolos a tropas por no dar ya el tiempo lugar a mas. Hizieron lo nrõs hijos con afecto y devocion que enternecian a sus Padres, pidiendo a Dios misericordia e perdon de sus peccados y defectos. Absueltos todos, Lunes once de Março como a las dos de la tarde vino como de boga arrancada una canoa nuestra avisando venia ya el enemigo; ya segundando, otra, y luego otra que las teniamos dispuestas para que no nos cogiessen de repente saltaron nuestros hijos en sus canoas y se pusieron a punto de guerra, y ya todo dispuesto, começo a descubrirse por una punta de rio la armada enemiga, que venia ostentando su poder, y arrogancia: luego que descubrieron la caseria del Borore se arrimaron a una chacra grande que estaba a la orilla del rio donde se juntaron todos, y saltando algunos en tierra la reconocieron. El cap.ᵐ general Don Ignacio salio impaciente (antes que se hiziesse mas tarde) apresentarles batalha sacando solas sinco canoa y para obligarle a salir luego, antes que descansasse el enemigo le comenso a referir los agravios que a los Indios bazian destruyendolos y acabandolos, quitandoles sus yglesias, cautibandolos y quitandoles su libertad, y la vida del cuerpo y alma, y exortando a voces a la gente que traya el Portugues, a que se saliesse y se recogiesse a los nuestros y viendo que a todo esto no se meneaba el enemigo y al parecer mostraba algun recelo en querer dar la batalla, insto en que saliesse luego y que no mostrase cobardia, diziendoles que tuviessen verguensa de que unos Indios desnudos se expusiessen a salirles al encuentro, diciendoles otras palabras de vituperio y desprecio; la demas gente de nros hijos que estaban en las canoas viendo a sucap.ⁿ en peligro e impacientes ya con la tardança salieron conorden en forma de media luna, y en la manguardia se puso un verso que yba en una balsa fuerte y bien acomodada con sus parapetos etc. y en ella una bandera con la ymagen de N. S.ᵗᵒ Pᵉ y Patron S. Fran.ᶜᵒ Xavier. Afrentados los Portugueses de ver la valentia de nros hijos y corridos con las palabras de desden y mofa que les decian, se volvieron a poner en sus canoas y comensaron a ponerse en orden. Al punto los Padres viendo que de aquella ves que daba el enemigo en pie, o por el suelo comensaron a pedir de rodillas a nro Sr. por medio del Sᵗᵒ Xavier victoria, qual ofrecia ajunaile la vigilia a pan e agua, qual ofrecia 50 misas a las animas y destos ubo muchos, y a voces instaban los P.ᵉˢ a nros hijos pidiessen misericordia a Dios, e invocassen al glorioso San Fran.ᶜᵒ Xavier, como lo hizieram con grande afecto e luego se pusseron a coros los P.ᵉˢ a decir las letanias, y al tiempo que con grande affecto invocaban el Sᵗᵒ Patron los Indios dispararon el tiro, con tan buen acierto, que con el mataron dos Portugueses y trastornaran tres canoas de los enemigos hiriendo y matando muchos Indios, cosa que los atemoriso grandemente y dio singular esfuerzo a nros hijos, y assi dando voces y poniendose en hila el euemigo se trabo la batalla, con brabo corage de una y de otra parte, comenso la arcabuceria, de entranbas partes. cargando y disparando nros hijos tan apriesa y con tal destresa que parecian soldados de Flandes. Fueron se retirando nros hijos con deseo de empeñar al enemigo (que deseaban sacarle lexos de su chusma para a su salvo arcabucearlo y dar cabo del. En este tiempo salto en tierra el cap.ⁿ Pedroso (el mayor bellaco de todos) con treynta hombres, y passando montes y un arroyo grande, de repente comensaron por las espaldas a arcubucear a nros hijos que estaban en tierra, y como lo cogieron asi de repente mataron tres e hirieron a mas de treynta. Pero volviendo sobre sí los Indios viendo les acometian por tantas partes acometieron a los Portuguese defendiendose varonilmente y matando luego a un Portugues y a quatro tupis, hizieron huyr a los demas enbiando los muy mal heridos, y arrastrandose unos a otros, de los quales murieron algunos en su palisada con los demas tambien fue herido en una musslo el traydor de su Cap.ⁿ a quien mas que a otro deseaban matar los Indios y les falto bien poco para hazerlo. Volvieron a su rancho o palizada tan escarmentados que ninguno se atrevio mas a salir por tierra a acometer a los nuestros. Al ruydo de sus escopetas tres canoas que peleaban con nuestros hijos enbistieron a nuestra palisada pensando teniamos toda nra fuerza en el rio, y que los Indios y chusmas estaba en la palisada solam.ᵗᵉ porque con industria estaban todos los Indios encubiertos y las banderas escondidas, para que se llegassen por alli donde estaba toda la mosqueteria aguardandolos, llegaron las dichas tres canoas enemigas con brabo de mucho muy serca de la palisada, y viendo ya la hya los nuestros de improviso le disparon tantos mosquetas que parecian graniso los valas que cayan sobre ellos, mostrose toda la gente lebantando y tremolando las banderas con grande voceria, espantolos y asombrolos de suerte que las canoas se pusieron surtas tendidos todos ellos por los planes de las canoas, y avista de todos alli quedo un Portugues muerto, y todos o casi todos sus vogadores, y los demas quedaron mal heridos y destrosados, y tan sin aliento que depues de un grande rato vogando con las manos se apartaron retirandose a su chusma, por no tener alli nosotros una canoa, que a tenerla todos quedaron alli captibos y muertos. Los Indios del rio menos en numero que los Portugueses (pues los que pelearon de los enemigos eran mas de ciento y treynta canoas, y casi trecientos Portugueses en ellas y mas de seyscientos tupis fuera de los bogadores y los nuestros solas setenta canoas, y trecientos Indios. anduvieron tan valerosos que aviendo traydo a los Portugueses muy gran trecho de su chusma rio abajo, retirandose con buen orden, sin reparar en los muchos arcabusasos que les disparaban se bolvieron sobre ellos con tal denuedo y esfuerso que le obligaron al enemigo a bolver mas que de paso, y los nuestros tras ellos a arcabusasos y flechasos apretaron los de suerte que unos arrojando sus escopetas al agua se arrojaron de las canoas saltando en tierra de essotra banda del rio. a esconderse por el monte, dexando sus canoas (que fueron catorce) con todo su hato vestido hachas (?) rescates y otras cosas en manos de los nuestros. Otros se bieron obligados para escaparse a dexar la escopeta y tomar la pala para bogar desta manera los llevaron grande trecho, matando los y hiriendolos. Quedaron muertos nuebe Portugueses, heridos assi de Portugueses como de sus Indios muchissimos, quitaron les una bandera, polbora y valas y una escopeta (que otras los arrojaron como dixe al agua porque no viniessen a poder de los nuestros). Finalmente los arrimaron adonde estaba su chusma con su presidio, corridos y afrentados, quedando los nuestros victoriosos, tremolando sus banderas tocando sus cajas, y pingo lleria, señores del campo asi por tierra como por el rio; y lo que mas admira, no salieron por el rio mas que seys o siete Indios heridos nuestros, y ninguno muerto; quien no ve claro aqui el favor del cielo y amparo del glorioso S.<sup>to</sup> y P.<sup>e</sup> Nuestro S. Fran.<sup>co</sup> Xavier; aun los mesmos inemigos, tan ciegos, lo conocieron y confesaron. Era ya puesto el sol y asi se desistio de seguir el alcance y victoria con que quedamos todos consoladissimos y dando infinitas gracias al S.<sup>r</sup> y a nro S.<sup>to</sup> Patron.

El dia siguiente doce de Março trataron los nuestros de dar otra vez sobre el enemigo, que ya no le temian. El Portugues aviendo visto el poder nuestro y el animo y valor de nuestros hijos, trabajo toda aquella noche haziendo una fuerte palizada por temor de algun asalto, ya la mañana la tenian casi acabada. Nuestros hijos no haziendo caso de sus heridos ni muertos salieron por la mañana a desafiar al enemigo otra vez y a decirles las mil leyes (como dizen) mas el se estuvo quedo sin querer salir a batalla, antes bien enbio una carta con dos viejos, del tenor seguiente, que traducida en español dize assi:

Mui R.<sup>os</sup> P.<sup>es</sup> Emos llegado aqui adonde veniamos a hablar a V. P.<sup>es</sup> para saber de los hombres que V. P.<sup>es</sup> cogieron los años passados, es a saber Pasqual Leyte Paes, y los demas de los quales nunca emos tenido noticia ni por mar ni por tierra si son vivos o muertos por lo que vi ante ayer veo que V. P.<sup>es</sup> estan

puestos en arma, y antes que ubiessemos bien llegado ya hallamos
este rio lleno de canoas de guerra por orden de V. P.ᶜˢ a las
quales quatro moços mal mirados sin orden mio se dispusieron
a salir al encuentro, lo qual V. P.ᶜˢ sin ninguna razon ni
christiandad lo hizieron que si yo viniera a hazer mal barloara
con todo mi exercito, pero antes mande recoger la gente toda y
asi lo hizieron como V. P.ᶜˢ bien vieron por ver que eran religiosos
y siervos de Dios y nosotros christianos : y sin avernos primero
hablado los unos a los otros ni dicho a lo que veniamos ; y luego
rio arriba queriendo hablar a las canoas de V. P.ᶜˢ echamos una
bandera blanca a la qual nos respondieron con muchos arcabusasos,
cosa que cada vez va de mal en peor. y asi requiero a V. P.ᶜˢ de
parte de Dios y de su Magestad una y muchas veses descargando
mi conciencia y la de todo este real sobre V. P.ᶜˢ de lo que
sucediere de oy en adelante de parte a parte, pues lo an causado
V. P.ᶜˢ pues es claro que no e tenido tal intencion y para esto
dejo traslado desta misma carta para que en todo tiempo conste
desta verdad pues nos otros no tenemos intencion de hazer mal
a christianos Assi que a lo que venimos no es mas que
a saber de nuestros H.ᵒˢ y parientes que los mas dellos son
casados y estan cargados de hijos e hijas que estan oy dia en
grande desamparo y clamando y pidiendo justicia a Dios contra
V. P.ᶜˢ por el desamparo y miserias en que se ven : y a mi
como a p.ᵉ del P.ᵉ Vicente Rodrigues de la Comp.ᵃ de Jesus
me pidieron las partes me llegasse aca a saber dellos ; y assi
estimare que V. P.ᶜˢ me hagan caridad y merced de que nos
veamos y principalmente para que nos digan missa, y oygan
algunas confesiones pues estamos en la S.ᵗᵃ quaresma. y assi no
ymaginen V. P.ᶜˢ que emos venido aca con cudicia de sus
Indios que muy bien saben V. P.ᶜˢ el mucho gentio que tenia
este rio en si al qual lo e enbiado por delante, y con que
V. P.ᶜˢ se vengan aca a verse con migo veran que hallaran ser
todo esto cierto y verdadero, yo quedo esperando a V. P.ᶜˢ o
respuesta ; y no sea la que se dio a Antonio Raposo Tabares en
Jh. M.ᵃ y V. P.ᶜˢ muy bien saben lo que de alli resulto, lo qual
entiendo que no haran V. P.ᶜˢ y assi queriendo V. P.ᶜˢ llegarse
aca lo pueden hazer confiadamente sin recelo ninguno, yo quedo
esperando a V. P.ᶜˢ a quien Dios guarde etc. 13 de Março de
1641 anos. De V. P.ᶜˢ servidor que sus manos vesa el cap.ⁿ
Manuel Peres.

    Hasta qui la carta que ley da por conocer ya por expe-
riencia de tantos años y tan acosta de nros Red.ᵉˢ ser traza
suya para con esto entretener el tiempo en demandas y res-
puestas, enfadar y entibiar los animos de nuestros hijos y

hazernos sospechosos a ellos lebantandonos mil testimonios y diziendo que nos otros tenemos trato con ellos y los etregamosen sus manos, por esto la respuesta que se le dio a esta carta, aviendo hablado a nros hijos y rasgado delante dellos un traslado della, fue, que animados se determinaron de sercarle por rio y tierra para acabarle y consumirle dentro en su misma palisada, y assi aunque mas sacaban bandera blanca los enemigos de Dios su pusieron en orden tres mil Indios por un monte espeso y con gran silencio llegaron a tiro de arcabus a la palisada de los Portugueses y assi comensaron a darles luego una famosa rosiada de arcabuseria y flecheria. Turbaron se luego luego, mas viendo el daño que se les seguiria del serco y vesindad e nro exercito, salieron todos arestados fuera de su palisada a pelear contra nra gente, para retirala y hazer la desistir de una palisada que al mesmo tiempo yban alli haziendo y peleando juntamente, mas los nuestros pelearon con tal valor que por tres veces hizieron huyr a los Portugueses y entrar en su palizada mas que de paso, matando quatro portugueses e hiriendo a muchos, y de sus tupis mataron gran cantidad, y aunque duro la pelea casi tres horas no desistio della hasta muy noche, que la deseaban harto, viendo a nros hijos tan balientes que llegaban a quitar palos de su mesma palisada, y si durara mas el dia quedar an del todo vencidos, porque ya los Portugueses estaban cansadissimos y medrosis.", y las Indias de su real lloraban y lamentaban su destruccion, viendose ya muchas heridas y maltratadas y los mesmos Portugueses unos con otros reñian, y se echaban maldiciones por aver venido a dar sobre nuestros Red.** viendo el estrago que nuestros hijos hazian en ellos y en su gente. Al mesmo tiempo se le acometio tambien por el rio, con seys balsas bien armadas de mosquetes con sus parapetos, de donde los cañonearon e hizieron mucho daño.

La noche despartio nros hijos de los Portugueses, y por ser el puesto malo y no aproposito para sercar el enemigo aunque a pesar suyo se avia ya acabado un muy gran lienso de palisada, se retiraron otra vez al real de noche dexando al Portugues bien castigado y mal contento de la respuesta que a su carta se le dio.

El dia seguiente se le hizo otra guerra mas fuerte y cruel, y fue que aviendo se salido dellos algunos tupis y venido se a nos otros, y entre ellos un famoso arcabucero trayendo se alguños machetes y un escupil y alguna municion, los llevaron en una balsa y se los mostraron a los Portugueses, y exortaron a sus Indios que se saliessen dentro ellos, y los dexassen para gozar de la libertad que Dios y el Rey les daban. Enfadados de aquesto los Portugueses com colera y despecho tiraron muchos arcabusasos a la balsa, y los della les pagaron la salva con otra de buenos mosquetasos; surtio buen effecto esta accion pues despues de ella se les salieron muchos y se entregaron a los nuestros: No sesaban por el rio las seys balsas de inquietar el enemigo de dia y de noche dando le cargas de mosqueteria a sus ranchos que por estar en una chacra descombrada y eminente a la mesma orilla del rio resevia muy grande daño; a un Portugues que estaba soplando el fogon de su rancho entro una bala y dandole en la boca lo dexo alli muerto. A otro miserable estando acostado en su hamaca, y una India (que despues se salio dellos) junto a el entro otra bala por entre unos palos, y taubien le dexo alli muerto. A otro estando cenando, vino otra bala y dando por sima de la mesa quebrandole el plato en que comia le dio en el ombligo y lo mato luego ; y assi temerosos con estos successos tomaron por partido dormir por los suelos y sin ensender fuegos, no contentandose con una palisada, y otra sino que cada uno de sus ranchos tenia su contrapalisada hazia el rio; daban muchas valas en los arboles que dentro de la palisada avia y desgajando gajos descalabraban a los que debajo avia, causando esto tal horror en los infieles del rio arriba que no savian que hazerse, y se lamentaban por no aver creydo nuestras amonestaciones. Advirtiendo el enemigo el grave daño que resevia con las balsas cubiertas de tablas que teniamos intento hazer otras el, mas las nuestras se lo impidieron con los mosquetes con muerte de algunos que andaban en la obra. Otra ves muy noche quisieron dar asalto a nuestras canoas y sintiendolos los nuestros les dieron tal rosiada que con desconcertada priesa salieron de las canoas y entraron a su palisada, porque el P.° Juan de Porras que cuydaba de la gente del rio no reposaba andando en continua vela y cuydado. Persuadidos ya y resueltos ellos de no pelear mas por rio aunque nuestros hijos mas los desafiaban, y se ponian a tiro de arcabus todas las canoas con reselo no se nos huyessen por el rio, como saviamos de sus tupis intentaban hazerlo. dabamos trasas de quitarles las canoas; y algunos de nros hijos echandose al agua de noche se fueron poco a poco, y llegando a las canoas no pudieron quitarles mas de dos o tres por tenerlas tan amarradas, y con muchas guardas, y para poderlo mejor hazer llegaron derepente nras balsas y dieron una rosiada con que hirieron algunos y los espantaron.

En estas continuas refriegas gastaron nuestros hijos desde el lunes once de Março hasta el sabado 16 del dicho mes, el qual dia como a las once salio de su real una canoa con una banderica blanca, y los Indios con deseo de que no se tratase de concierto alguno, cogieron el papel y lo hizieron pedasos. Al mesmo punto todos a una los portugueses despechados, viendo que no se trataba de o yrles ni admitirles medios algunos de paz, acometieron con gran furia a sus canoas, y con una furia infernal ellos y sus Indios la comensaron arrajar a toda priessa, salio nuestra armada a impedirlo, con la mosqueteria, y matando de un mosquetaso un Portugues, cesaron de razarlas, contodo razaron mas de ciento, perque trayan mas de docientas y sinquenta canoas las mas eran de los pobres Indios del rio arriba, otras avian ellos echo de mala figura aunque de buen porte. Fue causa desta su determinacion el verse de repente sercados hazia el rio arriba por donde les era fuersa passar queriendo volverse al Acaragua por tierra, de mas de mil y docientos yndios, que por orden del P.° P.° Romero, avian venido del Parana y los avia despachado a la boca del Tabay con orden de que alli biziessen su palisada y cogiessen al passo al enemigo como lo hizieron, lo qual advirtio el enemigo este dia por ver enalbolar una bandera y tocar cajas en aquel puesto.

Esta mesma noche yendo tres P.ᵉˢ a visitar la gente que estaba en el real del Tabay y consolar los de la armada comenso un Portugues a hallar y el P.° Joseph Domenech les hablo, afeandoles su mala vida, ponderandoles sus maldades y la descomunion en que avian incurrido; la deslealtad que a su Rey tenian haziendo estas entradas contra sus reales sedulas, cometiendo en ellas tantos y tan enormes peccados, con que les toco un punto de la eternidad, y ultimamente les dixo que se tenian algunos heridos mortales los enbiassen que los confessariamos. Dixo el cap.ⁿ que tenian once brancos (que assi llaman a los Portugueses) y otros Indios. Entonces un mal moço salio diziendo no eran sino solos dos los heridos de muerte, por no descubrir la flaquesa y el daño que avian resevido de nros hijos, que au peleado en esta occacion tan valiente y esforsadamente, que el H° Domingos de Torre decia que soldados de Flandes no lo harian mexor, y aun los mesmos Portugueses viendo el esfuerso tan estraño y la perseverancia, sin asombrarse con la vista de heridos y muertos, hasta oy dia se an persuadido peleaban no con Indios si no con Españoles, ayudandoles a esta persuacion el ver tanta gente, y tantos arcabuceros con escupiles en nuestro exercito. Ya mi P.ᵉ Provincial nros hijos son cides ya ayudados de Dios y dela intersesion de nro S.ᵗᵒ P.ᵉ S. Fran.ᶜᵒ Xavier son otros en valor, brio y esfuerso, y bien lo an mostrado pues an hecho rostro a mas de trecientos y sinquenta Portugueses, y mas de mil y docientos tupis, tan bien armados y prevenidos, y que avian salido con animo de acabar con todas las Reducciones, pero no lo permitio nro Sr. que ayuda a los Pobres, y ayuda las

ordinarias y extraordinarias oraciones de V. R.ª y toda la
provincia. Ellas son las que dieron animo a nros hijos, ellas las
que nos defendieron con confusion grande de nros enemigos, los
quales desearon se les diesse passo franco para volverse el
Uruguay arriba, envio nuebos papeles en un calabaso, muy bien
serrado, el qual nros hijos dexaron yr rio abajo sin tocarle con
deseo de dar a tan malos hombres el castigo que merecian, con
esto viendo ya su negocio tan mal parado, diziendo a su gente,
y unos a otros, ya no ay remedio de vencer ni sugetar a los
hijos de los P.ᵉˢ pues claramente vemos Dios los ayuda y defiende;
despechados y ll nos de una cruel yra conmensaron entre si la
guerra, tratandose muy mal, y casi viniendo a las manos, echandose
la culpa unos a otros desenvaynando espadas, levantando escopetas
y apuntandose los unos a los otros, dando desmedidas voces como
gente totalmente fuera de juizio y razon, viendo perdidos los
trabajos de tantos meses acordandose de las deudas en que se
avian empeñado por los grandes gastos que avian hecho de
municion y polvora y otras cosas de su matalotage cuya paga
avian de ser nuestros pobrecitos hijos si Dios no los defendera
y sus P.ᵉˢ con tanto cuydado no los animaran y principalmente
el P.ᵉ Diego de Boroa antecessor de V. R.ª no ubiera puesto
tan extraordinario cuydado en aumentarles las armas de fuego,
animarles de palabra y por escrito y sobre tudo no perdonando a
trabajo alguno solicitando quitassen peccados causa de semejantes
castigos. Con lo qual al fin, fin se libraron contra el poder de
tantos sertonistas del Brasil, hombres que an gastado su vida
en destruir pueblos de Indios, hombres que an arruynado la
christiandad del Guayra, sierra del Tape, Pinales y parte del
Uruguay, hombres que fiados en sus armas se prometian ya
el dicho Uruguay todo en sus manos y juntar su destruycion
con la del Parana, hombres que blasonaban aver de enbiar a sus
tierras a los P.ᵉˢ y aun de matallos o a lo menos llevarlos a sus
tierras maniatados, despues de aver les quitados sus queridos
hijos de tanto dolor, hombres que llevados de loca y siega
pacion se jactaban ya y complacian como que tuviessen en su poder
las mugeres e hijos de los pobresitos Indios de quienes se
prometian muy a su salvo gozar y no se enpachaban decirlo a
voces a sus mesmos maridos y P.ᵉˢ : hombres que trayan montones
de cadenas y grillos, esposas y colleras para que sugetandolos y
venciendolos quedassen: en ellas, puestos en miserable cautiverio:
hombres tan desalmados que algunos dellos a voces decian a los
P.ᵉˢ los avian de matar a escopetasos, otros que los avian de
ahorcar y asaetiar; estos pues que tan hinchados y sobervios
dezian a voces que avian de destruyr aun a los mesmos pueblos

de los españoles se quedaron vencidos, destruidos y ahuyentados por la mano poderosa del Sr tomando por instrumento a estos nros pobrecitos hijos.

Viendose pues ya con tantos heridos y muertos y sus fuerzas disminuydas, porque cada dia se le yba saliendo la gente en mayor numero, hizieron lo que otras vezes, que es hyr por entre montes y malessas a toda priesa quedando se muchos dellos entre los palos de su palisada escondidos en selada con deseo de engañar a nros hijos y matarlos ; pero nro Sr que los defendia y amparaba les dio reportacion y envio un grande aguasero con que a gatas por no ser vistos se metieron entre los montes y huyeron como los demas lo qual vieron las espias que teniamos puestas por lo alto de los arboles que nos avisaron, y luego se reconocio la palisada, y se comenso a seguir el alcanse con grande ánimo de nros hijos, no reparando en la espesura de los montes asperesa de las sierras, que con el aguasero antecedente estaban tales que por momentos cayan los que por ellas subian, con todo nros hijos deseosos de coger a los que nro Sr les daba en sus manos no perdonaban a trabajo alguno, assitiendoles como siempre sus P<sup>es</sup> con todo aquel aguasero en sima sin tener muchos que mudarse, ni a que recoger-se en todo el dia a hazerlo ni enjugarse hasta la noche de que a algunos se les occasiono alguna enfermedad dandola por muy bien enpleada por amor de mo Sr y de sus hijos, y mas alcansando como alcansaron al enemigo ya como a las cinco de la tarde que apriesa hazia palisada y se procuraba fortificar. Antes que lo hiziesse aunque defendido de unas terribles serranias nros hijos (valerosos soldados honra de la nacion guarani) les acometieron denodadamente, afligiendolos, y apurandolos tanto que decian perdidos somos ; y a los Indios no nos matemos en quaresma y otras palabras de grande sumicion y lastima ; mas nros hijos reconocidos a la mersed del cielo les apretaban mas y mas hasta que al fin la noche los despartio.

Muy de mañana se puso en huyda el enemigo y sintiendolo los nuestros fueron en su seguimiento dandoles braba bateria sin consensio alguno (no aviendo casi dormido la noche antecedente lloviendo a cantaros sobre ellos, haziendo grande frio, y, no haviendo aun sesado el agua pero nada desto lesinmuto ni estorbo el dar tras del enemigo que desia viendo su corage no ser hombres sino demonios, otros les llamaban tigres crueles pues no se hartaban de deramar sangre humano, pero nada les immutaba a nros hijos si no que animosos mas cada hora hizieron una temeridad grande, que fue meterse por unos especiss.<sup>os</sup> montes y por unas enpinadas serranias, arcabuceando y flechando con

que mataron seys portugueses e hirieron muchissimos, y de sus
tupis de quatr · en quatro estaban los cuerpos muertos y con ver
nra gente que en los montes no se conosian ni viau y que yban
expuestos a grandes peligros se enpeñaron de suerte que duro la
pelea desde la mañanita hasta las dos de la tarde, corriendo por
aquelles montes y tierras cayendo y levan'ando por momentos,
haziendo al enemigo grande daño y poniendole en tales trances
que ultimamente viendo a todos sus Indios tan amedrentados y
mal heridos tomaron ellos mesmos, digo los portugueses, las
rodelas y machetes y hisieron rostro a nuestros hijos mientras
pasaban las serranias los heridos y de mas chusma, que a todo
correr yba delante, y todos ellos se esforsaban quanto podian por
ver les yba la vida, y assi hirieron a mas de treynta de los
nuestros, quebrando a algunos brasos, y pasando muslos y
mataron tres; entonces nros hijos arrestados arremetieron de
suerte que se mesclaron tanto entre los mesmos Portugueses que
a palos y machatasos y valasos mataron quatro Portugueses
y de sus tupis tantos que quedaron los montes sembrados de sus
cuerpos muertos, no si grande riesgo de los nuestros, porque sin
saver unos de otros se metian entre los Portugueses, y asi estuvo
ya cojido el Capitan general Don Nicolas Neengiru pero acudiole
a defender su gente matando a los gualachos que le asieron. El
capitan Arazas estuvo ya casi rendido mas acudiole bien acaso
otro que dexo alli muerto al enemigo. Al capitan Don Ignacio
del Acaragua ya le arrastraban para llevar a los Portugueses, a
quien libro nro Sr enbiando a un rodelero de su mesmo pueblo
que hizo campo contra dos Portugueses y quatro Tupis, y
ayudandose el Capitan tanbien, se puso en pie y dio tras los
enemigos matando uno de ellos y descalabrando e hiriendo a los
otros, poniendolos en huyda; al Capitan Don Francisco Mbayroba
de S. Nicolas tanbien lo tubo ya casi rendido un Portugues, al
qual mato un Indio de la mesma Red.ⁿ y libro a su Capitan
(que como los capitanes son los mas valerosos van delante de
todos y entran primero en los peligros. Otro Indio se empeño de
suerte que se hallo entre los mesmos Portugueses, y viendose solo y
advirtiendo su peligro se hizo de su banda y sin ser conocido de
ellos les ofrecio ayudar mostrandose valeroso defensor pero en
breve vieron el engaño pues de repente viendose con alguna
seguridad volvio su arco y flechas contra ellos. Otro dio en una
celada de los mesmos Tupis y Portugueses y advirtiendo su
peligro con grande disimulo se quito el rosario que traya al cueilo
por no ser conocido y se puso en selada con ellos y dexandolos
descuydar empleo sus flechas en los Portugueses. dexandolos
burlados y heridos. Otros muchos casos ubo semejantes, que por

no cansar se dejan, pero los referidos bastan para mostrar quan animosos, y quan sobre si andaban los nuestros. En medio de toda esta confusion se le yba saliendo, y entregandose a los nuestros mucha de su gente, y los Portugueses mesmos con aquella revolucion y turbacion se hirieron unos a otros y mataron a sus tupis pensando eran hijos nuestros. Con esta confusion creciendo cada hora con el humo de la polvora y ñeblina la obscuridad de los montes, no conociendose ya los unos a los otros, los Portugueses medrosos viendo tantos de los suyos muertos y reparando en la diminucion de sus tupis, y sobre todo asombrados del valor de los nros, y de su constancia aprovechandose desta confusion se pusieron en huyda dando voces y diciendo dexadnos ya capitan Nêengiru hased suelta de nos otros, vasta que nos aveys muerto a todos los blancos, mas los nros ensendidos en justo enojo todabia los seguian hasta que al fin la fragosidad de los montes, lo aspero de las sierras, la obscuridad del humo, y el continuo trabajo de aver peleado desde las seys de la mañana hasta las dos y media o tres de la tarde cansados de trepar cuestas tras los Portugueses (que esta fue su defensa) baldonandolos porque no les hazian rostro, llenos de injurias, a que corridos no respondian, dando grande voceria y haziendo grande algasara si retiraron nros hijos a descansar, gososos y alegres, por aver les salido tan bien lo que a todos nos tenia en tanto cuydado; quedando solos dies de los nuestros muertos en todas las guerras que ubo por espacio de ocho dias continuos; contandose casi sesenta Portugueses muertos; y casi todos heridos; y de sus Tupis sin comparacion mas, dexando sembrados los montes de cuerpos muertos, y los ranchos donde paran llenos, pues en uno solo se contaron dies muertos a flechasos y arcabusasos.

Uno de los mas crueles enemigos que el Portugues tubo fue la hambre porque se le defendieron todas las chacras de suerte que no cogieron una espiga de mays fuera de lo que hallaron en la chacra donde hizieron su palisada que no era mucho y asi no comian otra cosa que palmitos y su gente se caya de.. ? estado muertos de hambre, y en todas sus rancherias o dormidas an dejado criaturas muertas y gente tan flaca que apenas se podia menear, hechos unos esqueletos: otras criaturas las an muerto con machetes, abriendoles las cabesas, otras con flechas y a los enfermos los an dexado en su mesma palisada sin remedio alguno ni comida ya muy flacos, otros no tan flacos sin dexarles una tan sola espiga de mays, ni aun fuego para poderse calentar, haziendo entonces mucho frio, y lloviendo y los pobres tiritando de frio, y apurados con camaras de sangre. En estos se empleo la caridad de los P.<sup>es</sup> ayudados de sus hijos, cargandolos, poniendolos en las canoas dandoles algun refresco y sobre todo catequisandolos, y a los que estaban muy al cabo baptisando, quedando los tales consoladissimos de verse morir entre Christianos y los Padres gososissimos de ver los acabar con los sacramentos.

Luego que el enemigo huyo se enbio al Acaragua a ver que rumbo tomaba, y por estar tan maltratado, y haverse retirado por tan extraordinarios caminos y serranias, llevado del miedo, que muchas veces les fue fuersa atarse sogas a las sinturas para descolgar-se por ellas entre las quales dexo muerta mucha de su chusma, y se le salio otra, aun de sus mismos pages y confidentes, yendo con tal miedo que por momentos se asombraban, y al ruydo pequeño de un arbol o buelo de pajaro tenian por numeroso exercito, y una noche se asombraron de suerte que pensando estaba ya sercado de nuestros hijos se puso apunto de guerra y ocupado del temor teniendo a sus mesmos Tupis por enemigos les tiraron dos arcabusasos con que los mataron hiriendo a otros, y aun los mesmos Indios que en su compañia estaban se tiraron flechas, y se ubieran acabado unos a otros sino se quietaran y advirtieran en su vano espanto; Jamas le falto al enemigo mientras fue por los montes quien le desasosegasse pues aun los mesmos tigres les desasosegaban de noche no dejandeles dormir, que sebados en los muchos cuerpos muertos, buscaban al dicho enemigo para hazer presa en el por estas y otras muchas causas se detubo el enemigo seys dias en los montes sin saverse de cierto del, ni del rumbo que tomaba. La gente que fue al Acaragua abraso ochenta hanegas de trigo, y otras cosas de sustento a que llebaba ojo el enemigo para su avio; hallaron los dichos hijos nuestros cuerpos muertos en las rancherias que avian sido de los Portugueses quando bajaron rio abajo, y entre los que hallaron fue uno el de una India ya casi deshecha y encima de los huesos della una criatura como de cinco años, adonde avia estado dies dias, y preguntandola por lo que avia comido respondio balbuciente que un poco de mays quemado le avia servido de sustento el dicho tiempo, y concervadole la vida hasta aquel dia que fue el de la espiritual de su alma, trayendola adonde fue baptizada y vive agora, Quemaron los Indios los ranchos y caserias y demas cosas que podian servir de alivio alguno al Portugues y a sus vasallos; retiraron les siete canoas que avian dexado escondidas, quando vajaron a dar sobre nras reducciones y de buelta al sexto dia despues de la batalla serca del Acaragua como media leguesita corta cintieron al enemigo a la orilla del Uruguay a quien vocearon y dispararon dos mosquetasos con que fuera de si el Portugues lleno de miedo no reparando eran solas espias se alboroto de suerte que huyo a los montes con toda su chusma,

intentando romper de nuebo los montes y salir donde su ventura
les llevasse. La espia volvio y trate luego de entrar tras ellos
como se executo, saliendo en su alcanse mas de mill y docientos
Indios para apurarlos lo possible y hallando buena occasion darles
una buena manotada para esto enbie a los P.ᵉˢ P.ᵉ de Mola,
Cristobal de Altamirano, Juan de Porras y Miguel Gomes y
D.ᵒ Suarez. Partido el exercito, el capitan Don Ignacio, con
algunos de los suyos, se ofrecio a yr delante, para como tan
practico de la tierra tomar lengua del enemigo. y de sus intentos;
el qual antes de llegar el Acaragua salio por tierra, tras el rastro
de los Portugueses y hallo un Indio muy flaco que con su muger
y hija descaminados no sabian que rumbo tomar, y sin cosa que
llegar a la boca, llevolos a su canoa dioles de comer con que
volvieron en si y se alentaron y llorando decian, o quien ubiera
creydo a los Padres siendo hijo suyo pues no me viera agora
en la miseria en que me e visto y en la que estan agora
actualmente mis desdichados parientes, esclavos de sus enemigos
los Portugueses. Tanbien hallo otro indio pasado el muslo de un
arcabusaso, y una pierna mal herida de un flechaso. que apenas
se podia menear, que a no aver ydo por alli y deparado se le
Dios muriera de hambre con el qual cargandole a sus cuestas
uso de la mesma caridad que con los primeros. Prosiguio su
camino el miercoles santo, y dexando anochecer fue y dio con la
espia del Portugues, y maniatandole, el jueves santo por la
mañana le trajo a los Padres que informo del puesto del enemigo,
y de su determinacion que era luego por la Pasqua partirse del
dicho Acaragua tomando su derota por los montes para salir a
un arroyo que esta este Uruguay arriba llamado Guarumbaca, y
alli dividirse unos hazia el Iguazu; otros passar por el salto el
Uruguay hazia Santa Theresa, para yr arresbuscar las taperas
de Jesu Maria y do alli al Caamo, Caagua ett.ᵃ y otros
determinaban yr el Uruguay arriba arrebuscar los pueblos de los
infieles. Con deseo de darle bien en que entender antes que
saliesse de nuestros terminos esperaron los P.ᵉˢ todo el Jueves
santo en parte escondida a que llegasse todo nro exercito, llego
lo mas del, y casi a puertas de sol salieron del rancho, y se
pusieron serca del Acaragua, y muy de mañana reconocidos los
puestos de los Portugueses que por seguridad y miedo se avian
puesto de escotra banda del rio Acaragua, dieron los nuestros en
sus tupis y gente que estaba como descuydada por quatro partes
de la una y otra banda del dicho rio con tan buen orden y tan
a tiempo que mataron muchos dellos y cogieron otros y los
maniataran asi a Indios como algunas Indias, y a los que huyeron
los fueron siguiendo flechandolos muy apriessa hasta dar con

ellos en el mesmo Acaragua al qual se arrojaron y les servio de
defensa para escapar las vidas aunque mal heridos pues no
se perdia golpe en ellos, todo lo qual se hizo sin ruydo de
arcabuses por no ser sentido del Portugues. Con este inopinado
successo los Portugueses que estaban occupados en lebantar
cruces hazer calbarios, enramar arcos y andar estaciones, diziendo
a los Indios que nuestros hijos no les acometerian en dias tan
santos y quietos, asombrados de tan inopinado succeso hizieron
suelta de los altares, interrumpieron sus estaciones, desampararon
sus calbarios, y se retiraron a los montes tratando luego de huyr
aquella mesma noche. Mucha de la gente del Portugues que
deseaba como el agua de Mayo la venida de nuestros hijos
a nado unos y corriendo otros comensaron a salirse de entre los
Portugueses y asi todo el viernes santo, desde las doce del dia
hasta la tarde de citano dexaron de salirse dellos viniendose
a los nuestros, aunque el Portugues reparando en ello hizo todo
el esfuerso possible para impedirselo con que no pudieron salirse
tantos, quantos deseaban hazerlo con amenasas y lebantandonos
gravissimos testimonios como suelen. El primero que nosotros les
aviamos escrito ahorcariamos a quantos de los suyos saliessen a
los nuestros. El segundo que de hecho lo aviamos executado, y
que la yglesia del Acaragua estaba llena de cabesas de los
ahorcados por orden nuestro, por averse salido de los Portugueses;
el tercero que a los huydos se los aviamos de volver luego; el
quarto que nuestros hijos los avian de matar donde quiera que
los halassen y sin avisar a los Padres con que algunos medrosos
y de corta capacidad se quedaron entre ellos, pero otros mas
advertidos riyendose de semelhantes dichos teniendoles por
calificadas mentiras y patrañas, diziendo no poder persuadirse
que Padres tan amorosos suyos como lo eran los de la Compañia
de Jesu y avian sido siempre, se mudassen asi derepente; sin
reparar en nada fiados en nro Sr y en la caridad de los Padres
con deseo de vivir como christianos y dexar aquella mala vida
que entre los Portugueses tenian sin confesion ni misa, ni obra
alguna de christianos dexando quanto tenian se nos vinieron. Otros
mas animosos y sagases se nos vinieron trayendose juntamente
todo el hato de sus amos, dexandolos a ellos sin hamacas, sin
fresadas, vestidos, ni camisas todo lo qual repartian luego con
los nuestros. En esto se paso el viernes santo hasta la tarde, y
aviendo descansado un poco nros hijos se les predico la passion
que oyeron con atencion acompañando al predicador con lagrimas y gemidos y actos fervorosos de contricion que consolaba a
los Padres el berlo. A lo qual se siguieron muchas confesiones
de manera que mas parecia congregacion devota que exercito de
soldados victoriosos.

Aquella mesma noche el capitan Don Ignacio Abiaru con dos Indios fue y reconocio los ranchos y palisadas del enemigo, y lo vio todo, y gasto toda la noche en continua vela no reparando en que si fuesse sentido seria muerto o preso pero ayudole nro Sr por las oraciones de los Padres que aquella noche se lo suplicaron afectuosamente, y en amaneciendo estando con grande cuydado del successo nos vino a dar cuenta de todo, y de la disposicion en que estaba el enemigo y que parece huya ya pues no tenia chusma consigo como fue cierto, porque nos lo certifico un Indio de los Portugueses Cap$^n$· de sus tupis que cansado de aquella vida vestial que entre los Portugueses teñia deseoso de vivir como christiano aunque estimado dellos y tratado como se fuera uno dellos por su valor y esfuerso posponiendo todos estos regalos y gustos al que deseaba tener verdadero se salio de entre ellos al tiempo que se partian y nos dixo que asombrados ya de nuestro poder y admirandose de la perseverancia de nuestros hijos, temiendo ser acabados se avian puesto ya en huyda diziendo a voces avian de matar a quien quisiesse probar las manos con nuestros hijos.

Con esta nueba nros hijos quisieron yr luego al alcance pero el mesmo tupi les advirtio no lo hiziessen, lo uno porque era la tierra fragosiss.ᵃ lo otro porque los estarian quisas aguardando en alguna selada de que ya avian tratado y seria muy factible cayessen en ella, con esto los Indios muy mal de su grado y como violentados se detuvieron todo el sabado santo y el domingo de pasqua muy temprano aviendo oydo misa y comulgado algunos y confessado otros muchos fiados en nuestro Sr fueron tras los Portugueses y reconocer su palisada y rastro y le siguieron hasta muy tarde sin poder le dar alcance por ir a toda priessa y tener algunos dias antes ya hecho los caminos mal aviertos y defendidos con muchas serrarias y malesa, pero ya que no le alcansaron, traxeron muchos de los pobrecitos Indios e Indias que de los Portugueses se yban saliendo, trayendo casi todos algo de sus amos dexandolos muy desventurados, y desacomodados arrojando por los montes las cargas de comida. Lo que consolo mucho a los Padres en esta occacion fue muchas criaturas flacas y ya para morir que les traxeron sus hijos a quienes despues de aver baptisado les procuraban la salud y regalo del cuerpo dandoles de comer de su pobresa a que sin tiento alguno se arrojaban perdidos de hambre, cuydando de la leña, de los ranchos y encomendandolos muchas voces a sus hijos y visitandolos para ver si se cumplia lo que se les encargaba, quebraba el coracon el verlos y enternecia su vista a los Padres e Indios; los quales mostraron su caridad trayendo de muy lejos a cuestas Indios e Indias flaquissimas y algunas que no esperaban mas que el agua del baptismo para salir deste miserable mundo. Estas fueron las pasquas que los Padres celebraron baptizando criaturas y cathequisando adultos. Aquella noche trataron los Padres entre si de yr siguiendo el rastro de los Portugueses no tanto a seguirles el alcance quanto a buscar enfermos flacos y criaturas y aviendo dicho misa muy temprano el lunes segundo dia de Pasqua, ofreciendo el trabajo del camino a nro Sr muy deveras, todos nuestros hijos asi capitanes como soldados no lo concintieron oponiendose eficazmente a los designios y determinacion de los Padres ofreciendose a yr ellos en persona a hazer lo que los Padres quisa no pudieron totalmente alcansar por la fragosidad y asperesa de la tierra y pantanos grandes que dificultaban el camino. Y en efecto con grande aliento se partieron y repartieron por los montes, y sendas de los Portugueses yendo hasta muy serca dellos sin atender a peligro, y como a las quatro de la tarde fueron volviendo muchos con los enfermos y flacos (dexados de los dichos enemigos) para que los Padres enpleasen sus fervorosos deseos, ayudandoles. Entre los que traxeron fue una muchacha cuyos pies estaban todos quemados vertiendo sangre, desollados hasta los enpeynes y colgandole el cuero de las plantas, quexandose lastimosamente acudiosele como se pude y preguntada, respondio que un Portugues que la tenia a cargo enfadado ya de traerla y viendo que ya no le podia seguir por su pie cogio el rescaldo todo de un fogon y con brasas y seniza se lo arrojo ensima abrasandoselos entrambos.

Hallaronse cuerpos muertos asi de criaturas como de viejos y viejas y algunos moços muertos violentamente con cuchillos y palos, porque de puros flacos no los podian seguir : quebraba el coraçon oyrlo, quanto y mas verlo; y a nuestros hijos fueron estos espectaculos unas exortaciones muy vivas de lo que les inportaba vivir con los Padres y defenderse de sus enemigos. Tuvo se noticia de algunos enfermos flaquissimos que quedaban muy junto al corral de los Portugueses y aunque avia peligro en yr alla, por amor de aquellas almas se ofrecieron los Padres a yr, pero nuestros hijos reconosidos a lo mucho que a sus Padres deben, se animaron y fueron y traxeron los enfermos que eran dos indias flaquisimas, que la una dellas murio luego aquella noche despues de bautizada y otras criaturas muy flacas que tanbien fueron bautizadas, fue tanbien con los soldados un cathequista muy industriado por si acaso ubiesse alguno para morir, y fue advertencia del cielo aquesta, porque hallo a una India que estaba ya acabando y cathequisada la bautizo y luego se murio:

con lo qual alegres volvieron de su micion no dexando enfermo ni flaco que no traxessen; en pago destas buenas obras sin duda se servio nuestro Sr de que los nuestros sin perdida alguna ni deramamiento de sangre propria ahuyentassen al enemigo de todas sus tierras. El qual queda tan destrosado que como afirman los que del an salido ban sartas enteras de heridos, con baculos en las manos, mas umildes a sus tierras (si es que a ellas llegan) de lo que vinieron, dexando nuestras reducciones no solo no destruydas como ellos orgullosamente se prometian, sino augmentadas con lo mejor de su gente que se nos a quedado, con harto dolor de sus coraçones como lo lamentaban diziendo, aver venido por lana y volver tresquilados.

Echados ya los enemigos de todos nuestros confines se volvieron los P.es y sus hijos victoriosos, y reconocidos a los favores del cielo y a la intercesion del glorioso apostolo S. Francisco Xavier, se fueron a su yglesia y alli le cantaron uina misa solemne, y un Tedeum laudamus en accion de gracias viendose ya libres de sus enemigos tan gloriosamente Lo mesmo hize yo aqui en esta reduccion de S. Nicolas donde me halle y lo mesmo han hecho los demas P.es en todas las reducciones y fuera deso en cada una de ellas se a cantado una solemne misa de requien por nuestros hijos difuntos que murieron en la pelea, quedando muy reconocidos a nuestro Sr por la multitud de mercedes que de su liberaliss.ª mano emos recebido en esta occasion, y juntam.te muy agradecidos a V. R.ª y a toda la provincia que con tantas veras nos an ayudado, y alcansado con sus oraciones de nuestro Sr esta victoria, en la qual an quedado muertos, heridos y afrentados la flor de los certonistas de S. Pablo, y del Brasil, enemigos declarados desta afligida christiandad y de sus P.es.

Agora vuelvo a enbiar al P.e Christoval de Altamirano, el rio arriba para que recoja la gente que del Portugues cada dia se sale y acuda a los enfermos y criaturas que sin duda yra quedando en todos los ranchos, y sepa el rumbo que este enemigo lleba, de lo que resultare avisare a V. R.ª en otra occasion. Pido a V. R.ª con todo el afecto de mi alma se sirva de mandar encomendar a nuestro Sr. esta mision y la de la sierra que se hará presto, y en sus santos sacrificios no me olvide, desta reduccion de S. Nicolas y Abril 6, de 1641.

CLAUDIO RUYER.

## NOTA EXPLICATIVA

A carta do padre Claudio Ruger agora impressa entrou para a Bibliotheca Nacional do Rio de Janeiro, com a collecção Angelis. Consta de nove folhas escriptas de ambos os lados, excepto a ultima, reunida posteriormente onde tres vezes se lê no dorso o titulo e mais: *archivo de Buenos Ayres, gaveta 6— legax 4.*

O catalogo de Angelis considera-a autographa; o caracter da lettra, a qualidade do papl, certos accrescimos e emendas difficeis de explicar si não se tratasse da redacção primitiva, persuadem á realidade do asserto.

Serviu agora para a impressão na *Revista* uma cópia extrahida, vae para muitos annnos, a pedido do benemerito Barão do Rio Branco, por A. do Valle Cabral, de saudosa memoria, e pelo abaixo assignado.

Por motivo hoje impossivel de apurar, deixou de ser remettida em tempo a seu destino.

A correcção das próvas foi feita pelo autographo. Pontos de interrogação indicam leituras duvidosas.

Rio—Novembro 1905.

CAPISTRANO DE ABREU.

# Observações sobre a fauna paulista; recentes explorações do naturalista E. Garbe

PELO

## DR. H. VON IHERING

Sr. presidente; meus senhores.—A exploração scientifica da natureza do Estado de S. Paulo, que é uma das principaes tarefas do Museu Paulista, tem continuado regularmente nos ultimos annos, chegando ao feliz resultado de hoje podermos conhecer mais ou menos as differentes partes do Estado.

Este resultado lisongeiro de possuirmos já conhecimentos mais aprofundados da natureza deste grandioso Estado, devemos, em parte, á actividade e aos multiplos esforços empregados pelo sr. Ernesto Garbe, naturalista-viajante do Museu, que, vencendo innumeras difficuldades, conseguiu reunir de differentes regiões deste e de outros Estados da União, as mais ricas e variadas collecções.

Encarregado pelo nosso Museu, o sr. Ernesto Garbe, ha dois annos, fez a exploração do Rio Juruá, Estado do Amazonas, donde trouxe magnificas collecções que bem caracterizam a riqueza daquella parte do territorio nacional. Esta expedição, além do bom resultado que deu ao nosso Museu, representa ainda um successo completo.

Nos ultimos dois annos este mesmo senhor tem trabalhado aqui, no interior do Estado, achando-se, actualmente, em Ubatuba, de cuja expedição eu espero ter bôa representação em nossas collecções no Museu.

Ainda ha pouco utilisei-me dos serviços do sr. E. Garbe na exploração do curso inferior do rio Tieté, cujos resultados vieram convencer-me da grandeza desta zona.

E' com a maior satisfação que communico aos meus illustres consocios que uma viagem feita a Itapura, nas mesmas condições que as anteriores, foi coroada de completo exito, estando eu muito satisfeito pelas excellentes collecções obtidas e pelas interessantes notas de viagem desta vasta região, que me foram fornecidas pelo mesmo sr. E. Garbe.

Em geral, dentre os Estados, o de S. Paulo já ha muito é considerado, scientificamente, o melhor explorado, e isto devido principalmente ao trabalho do illustre sabio e excellente collecionador João Natterer, que durante os annos de 1818 a 1822 percorreu o Estado de S. Paulo.

Acontece, entretanto, que naquella épocha, apesar dos esforços empregados e do muito que relativamente conseguiu, não pôde este illustre naturalista chegar a um resultado tão completo como o que o nosso Museu acaba de obter com as collecções adquiridas dessas expedições e que são acompanhadas de photographias e de notas importantissimas das respectivas localidades.

Fazendo um pequeno estudo comparativo, notei, por exemplo, que a litteratura existente dá para o Estado de S. Paulo quatro-centas e setenta especies de aves, quando, entretanto, até agora, já temos conseguido elevar esse numero de especies a seiscentas e setenta, ou seja quasi 50 % para mais, esperando que daqui a pouco possamos chegar provisoriamente a um resultado concludente.

Um caso analogo tive occasião de verificar com a familia dos *Marsupiaes* (*Didelphis*), gambás, raposas, guaiguicas e muitas outras especies pequenas do tamanho de camondongos e ratos que são tambem conhecidos por chupatis.

Em geral, todos estes animaes pouca gente aqui os conhece, acontecendo até que só raramente tenho conseguido bons exemplares das especies pequenas desta familia. Eu verifiquei que deste grupo existem no Brasil trinta e uma especies conhecidas e estas mesmas distribuidas de modo que no Rio Grande do Sul e em Minas Geraes se encontram onze, no Rio de Janeiro e no Pará, sete ou oito, e no Estado de S. Paulo vinte e uma.

Neste sentido, julgo que as nossas explorações têm sido bem dirigidas, ou antes, tem dado o resultado que almejamos, porquanto já conseguimos saber que as especies que devem existir no Estado de S. Paulo não pódem exceder de vinte e cinco, o que já se póde considerar um resultado quasi que definitivo.

O sr. E. Garbe, durante o anno proximo findo, percorreu a zona que margeia o Rio Grande e a de Barretos, donde seguiu para a povoação de Avanhandava, fazendo a viagem dahi por deante embarcado em canôa pelo rio Tieté abaixo até Itapura.

Ahi conservou-se por espaço de muitos mezes, regressando em Novembro, em virtude de ser o tempo das aguas e de estar, por conseguinte, muite cheío o mesmo rio, tornando difficil e mui desfavoravel a sua navegação. Desta viagem os resultados obtidos foram de muita vantagem para o nosso Museu, que viu as suas collecções enriquecidas com excellentes especimens.

Dentre os caracteres geraes do curso inferior do rio Tieté, existe para mim um de grande importancia, que passarei a examinar, em vista de serem muito contradictorias as informações que se encontram na litteratura, relativamente a esta zona.

Alguns, por exemplo, dizem que toda esta região é, occupada por matto, e outros que o rio nos dois lados é margeado de campos.

Pois bem ; o exame feito nesta expedição deu-me um resultado que é não existir de ambos os lados do rio, zonas, em que não haja matto, assim como extensos banhados que durante a épocha das chuvas transbordam. E', pois, um systema de banhados cu lagos que acompanham o rio Tieté, e que no tempo da sêcca se apresentam cobertos de uma vegetação de *gramineas* e de outras plantas arbustinhos. Não se póde por conseguinte chamar campo a um tal systema de banhados.

Effectivamente a zona é consistente de matto, porquanto, todas as collecções confeccionadas pelo sr. E. Garbe, naquella região, apenas se referem a elementos proprios á fauna de matto.

A zona do rio Tieté, entre Avanhandava e Itapura, é pouco appropriada e mui desfavoravel á navegação.

Entre os grandes saltos do Avanhandava e Itapura, ha mais de vinte pequenas cachoeiras e saltos, sendo alguns delles difficeis de serem vencidos.

Referir-me-ei primeiramente áquelles de Avanhandava dos quaes foram tiradas algumas photographias.

Do salto das Cruzes tenho aqui duas vistas que são muitissimo interessantes, sendo uma tirada com aguas baixas e outra com aguas altas. Em ambas vê-se a canôa vasia, isto é, descarregada, passando pelo canal, cuja travessia é perigosa em virtude da passagem dar logar apenas para uma embarcação estreita.

A carga da canôa é transportada pela picada, ao lado do salto, por trabalhadores, ou camaradas, até o ponto do novo embarque.

Aqui, finalmente, tenho varias photographias do salto de Itapura, que é intransitavel.

Fecharei esta demonstração de cachoeiras e saltos, citando o do rio Paraná, denominado Urubupunga, que se divide em duas partes de passagens muito poéticas e interessantes.

Continuando nas minhas considerações apresento agora, aos meus illustres consocios, diversas vistas das ultimas duas povoações existentes nesta parte do rio, que são Avanbandava e Itapura. A ultima destas povoações, outr'ora prospera e bastante important-, hoje acha se em decadencia.

Para as embarcações que quizerem transitar por estas regiões, torna-se tambem necessario o descarregamento do seu conteúdo, que é transportado pelas grandes picadas alli existentes ao lado dos saltos

Deste trabalho encarregava-se antigamente, com especialidade em Avanhandava, um grupo de trabalhadores que, com este serviço sempre faziam uma receita regular, e o transporte era feito em menos de tres horas. Hoje, entretanto, o proprio viajante é obrigado a fazer este serviço penosissimo, que, pelas difficuldades que encontra e pela má qualidade dos caminhos, não gasta menos de dois dias. E' para lastimar-se que no interior do nosso adeantado Estado, em uma zona que, pela sua riqueza natural e pela força motriz dos saltos, parece estar destinada a grande futuro, ainda se encontre tamanha falta de communicações não só para o viajante, como principalmente para o commercio.

Na povoação de Itapura, que ha quinze annos mais ou menos era de grande importancia, achava se estabelecida uma colonia militar naturalmente que tinha por mister garantir a ordem. Era, pois, uma povoação florescente, quando ha nove ou dez annos foi dissolvida a colonia militar e as praças dos batalhões se retiraram.

As poucas pessoas que não faziam parte da guarnição encetaram então a rapida destruição desta colonia, o que lhes foi muito facil pela ausencia dos guardas.

Imagine-se o que póde acontecer a uma cidade ou povoação abandonada !

Chegaram logo os visinhos e começaram a carregar as portas, as telhas e tudo que ahi existia de melhor nas casas da colonia militar.

Assim, em pouco tempo, ficou tudo em ruinas e até a propria casa que servira de moradia ao director da colonia, da qual tenho aqui uma photographia, ficou sem moveis.

E' interessante a lucta que se observa entre o trabalho do homem e a natureza !

A vegetação é alli tão rica e resistente que, successivamente, o matto invade as casas, em cima das quaes cresceram figueiras bravas que, por sua parte, contribuem para a destruição dos edificios.

Neste sentido, é notavel o contraste que se dá entre a construcção destes edificios modernos, de tijolos, e as construcções de pedra do tempo antigo como existem no municipio de Santos, e que, embora tenham signaes de destruição, resistiram por seculos á acção do tempo e da vegetação, ao passo que a daquelles, depois de nove ou dez annos, em grande parte, estão completamente em ruinas.

Acontecendo ter fallecido o antigo director da colonia os moradores estão scismados de que á noite, na casa em que o mesmo residiu, apparece a alma do fallecido, e com esta superstição tiveram medo de continuar a retirar materiaes deste edificio, que juntamente com a egreja, talvez por sentimento religioso, são os unicos edificios da antiga colonia que escaparam á destruição, e que ainda hoje se encontram regularmente conservados.

A povoação de Itapura, nestas condições é composta, actualmente, apenas de elementos desprovidos de instrucção e de recursos.

O numero de casas occupadas é unicamente de quatorze, e dentre estas familias que ahi habitam ainda existem tres, cujos chefes sabem lêr e escrever.

Ha alli uma agencia do correio que para o exterior muito pouca, ou mesmo nenhuma correspondencia póde ter, em virtude de serem os moradores verdadeiros caipiras do nosso sertão, que nenhuma relação tem com o extrangeiro.

Vem ao caso narrar aos meus illustres consocios, um facto que ha pouco deu-se commigo relativamente a diversas cartas qui dirigi ao naturalista-viajante do Museu, então em excursão naquella zona.

Tendo escripto a este funccionario do Museu varias cartas, das quaes não obtive resposta, apesar de terem algumas seguido registradas, e ficando por conseguinte sem noticias suas, quando tinha elle por costume escrever-me com regularidade, dando-me conhenhecimento das occorrencias das expedições, e como já tivesse deccorrido muito tempo sem que conseguisse informações do seu paradeiro, fiquei na supposição de que o mesmo tinha sido victima, cahindo em poder dos indigenas que ainda habitam aquella região do Estado. Assim, incommodado, dirigi-me á administração geral dos correios, pedindo informações acêrca do modo pelo qual era feito o serviço postal para aquella localidade, e tendo resposta de que o serviço era feito por um estafeta que para lá seguia tres vezes por semana e com a maior regularidade, maiores foram as minhas apprehensões. Finalmene, deccorridos muitos mezes, consegui receber com a maior satisfação uma carta sua, dando-me boas noticias de sua saúde, e pondo-me a par das occorrencias da expedição. Nessa mesma carta communicou-me ainda que se achava em Itapura, donde não saía sinão para os pontos vizinhos, e que as difficuldades na transmissão da correspondencia, em parte era motivada pelos disturbios politicos em Sant'Anna do Parnahyba e em parte pela grande distancia, visto que as malas postaes vão de S. Paulo á Uberaba, passando pelos Estados de Minas Geraes e de Matto Grosso!

Este serviço postal, apesar de ser muito demorado e quasi desnecessario, convém todavia ser conversado, porque tanto a União como o Estado de S. Paulo têm o dever de cuidar não só das localidades de povoação densa, como tambem das zonas pouco favorecidas e de população pequena, como a colonia de Itapura, que sobre ser uma parte historica do Estado de S. Paulo, é uma parcella do territorio nacional que jamais deveficar desamparada completamente.

Se em tempo os edificios da colonia tivessem sido entregues a uma ordem religiosa qualquer, com a condição de serem os mesmos conservados sempre em bom estado, hoje, talvez, não estariam nas condições lastimaveis em que se encontram acreditando eu ainda que o estabelecimento de uma ordem religiosa naquella zona teria concorrido tambem para o progresso da mesma e seria sobretudo de muita vantagem para os seus moradores, que nada conhecem da vida de fóra e cujos filhos alli crescem sem instrucção.

E' difficil fazer-se uma ideia da miseria que reina actualmente nesta parte esquecida do Estado, que podia ser aproveitada e com maiores vantagens. A pescaria, por exemplo, poderia ser uma fonte de renda magnifica para aquelles infortunados, e quando não o fosse, o resultado della só por si constituiria um elemento pàra a sua manutenção, mas, para isso é penoso confessar, faltam-lhes até os apetrechos primordiaes, como sejam a rêde, a canôa, etc. Algumas canôas que alli existiam foram roubadas pelos indios. Existe alli uma unica canôa que os indios não levaram, que é empregada no serviço do estafeta do correio. Era desta canôa que, na ausencia deste empregado do correio, o nosso viajante se utilisava nas suas excursões, aproveitando se para isto da auctorisação que o mesmo estafeta lhe havia dado.

O nosso viajante, com o auxilio de alguns camaradas daquella gente, abriu uma picada na extensão de seis leguas, tendo assim um campo para fazer caçadas, e armar arapucas, mondiés etc.

Uma vez conseguiu matar um cervo e este em condições singulares. Seguindo o rastro do animal em companhia de seu filho e de um camarada que atirou ao cervo na distancia de sessenta metros, verificou que o mesmo se precipitou nagua, apesar de ferido.

Em vista desse facto, que não esperava, teve o sr. Garbe de perseguir o aninal dentro dagua, conseguindo retiral-o para a margem opposta do banhado, que então verificou ser-lhe a mais proxima De posse do cervo, tirou-lhe a pelle e o cráneo que, depois de bem acondicionados, amarrou—os nas costas e no cabeça, e, tornando novamente ao banhado, regressou ao seu ponto de partida, com aguu até ao pescoço.

Tambem as condições sanitarias daquella região não são favoraveis. Não se póde beber a agua, senão fervida porque, em geral é de péssima qualidade e já tém occasionado alli febres de máu caracter que, com facilidade, já tem feito muitas victimas. Assim, o sr Ernesto Garde, correndo innumeros perigos, precavido como é, conseguiu passar alli, e no rio Juruá, cerca de anno e meio, sem o menor incommodo na sua saúde.

As collecções de mammiferos e de aves que trouxe para o nosso museu, desta expedição a Itapura, já estão em parte estudadas e classificadas. Naturalmente estas collecções não pódem corresponder em seu resultado de modo egual a todos os grupos, e mesmo não se póde com um tão resumido pessoal emprehender o estudo de todos os differentes grupos do reino animal, de modo que com especialidade encarreguei o naturalista viajante do nosso Museu de colligir com especialidade os animaes, que, pela nossa literatura, estivessem nas condições de serem examinados.

O resultado destas expedições é muito interessante, principalmente quanto ás aves.

Constatei nas collecções verdadeiros typos amazonicos, dos quaes recebi mais de dez especies que faltavam em nossas collecções, e que ainda não eram conhecidas no Estado de São Paulo, e sómente no rio Juruá (Amazonas), que haviam sido colligidas tambem pelo nosso viajante.

Certos mammiferos que nos foram remettidos do rio Juruá, do mesmo modo que as aves, apenas conheciamos do Estado de Matto Grosso e até ha pouco ignoravamos a sua existencia neste Estado.

Estes interessantes resultados, por outro lado, foram tambem completados com o estudo das collecções procedentes da Franca. Estas ricas collecções da Franca representam principalmente os elementos dos campos do Estado de Minas.

De sorte que não é para extranhar que daqui a pouco tempo tenhamos um conhecimento mais amplo, e menos completo, desta rica e variada fáuna do Estado de S. Paulo em comparação com a dos outros Estados.

Não é só o nosso trabalho systematico de exploração em todas as regiões do Estado de S. Paulo que contribue para tal resultado, mas tambem o facto de pertencer ao territorio paulista parte de diversas provincias fáunisticas.

A fáuna dos mattos da zona litoral é quasi identica á dos da Bahia e do Rio Grande do Sul.

Assim, temos esta em S. Paulo e em Santos, para o norte e para o sul, e em partes os mesmo typos se estendem ao oeste até Bahurú e rio Paranapanema.

O bugio ruivo, por exemplo, é commum na Serra de Santos, ao passo que na região do rio Paraná vive o bugio preto. Esta ultima especie occorre desde Itapura e Franca, Estado de S. Paulo, até as costas do Oceano Pacifico, no Equador.

Tenho procurado successivamente conhecer as divisas zoogeographicas do Estado de S. Paulo.

Em parte aqui ainda occorrem especies caracteristicas do Brazil Meridional, e por outro lado não é pequeno o numero de animaes dos Estados da Bahia e do Rio de Janeiro, que ainda são representados em o norte do nosso Estado, ou a zona do litoral.

Uma fáuna toda differente é a do Brazil Central, cuja occorrencia da região occidental do Estado de S. Paulo já mencionei.

Assim, estou satisfeito por vêr sempre progredindo o trabalho de discriminação das diversas provincias zoogeographicas que temos. Nestas condições, já possuimos a provincia do littoral; fomos depois á de Matto Grosso e á dos campos de Minas Geraes que, entrando pela Franca, váe até Jaboticabal.

A fauna do Estado de S. Paulo é, por conseguinte, composta de varios elementos differentes, sendo esta a razão especial da grande importancia que para os estudos zoogeographicos, em geral, tem a fáuna do nosso Estado.

Assim, proseguindo na exploroção de sua natureza, o nosso Estado prestará um grande serviço á sciencia, formando um ponto de partida para futuros estudos sobre a zoogeographia de todo o Brazil.

(Ao terminar o seu discurso, o Dr. H. von Ihering foi muito applaudido pelos socios presentes.)

## Discurso proferido pelo orador dr. João Coelho Gomes Ribeiro, na sessão anniversaria de 1 de Novembro de 1905

EXMO. SR. PRESIDENTE—EXMAS. SENHORAS—MEUS SENHORES.

Antes de tudo, obediente á bôa pragmatica, peço venia para apresentar-vos as minhas credenciaes.

O Instituto Historico e Geographico de S. Paulo deliberou que o mais incompetente de seus consocios commemorasse hoje a data gloriosa de sua fundação e fizesse o elogio historico dos confrades fallecidos, durante o anno findo e eu, bem a contra gosto, acceitei essa missão tão ardua, tão superior ás minhas forças, confiado apenas na benevolencia generosa de vós todos.

Ainda repercute nesta sala o éco attenuado das vozes eloquentes de um João Monteiro, de um Eduardo Prado, de um Theodoro Sampaio, meus antecessores nesta tribuna, e só isso basta para augmentar a minha commoção, ao tomar a palavra nesta sessão solemne, onde se vêm representadas as classes dirigentes da nossa sociedade, o poder publico, a illustração, o talento e a virtude.

Não desertarei porém, o meu posto porque, o mandato recebido é daquelles que se não podem solicitar nem recusar, pois constituem um dever social honrosissimo e indeclinavel, para o mandatario.

Minha missão, neste momento, é dupla : devo commemorar a fundação do Instituto e fazer o elogio historico dos socios fallecidos.

A historia não é o drama cambiante das paixões, nem um problema de mechanica psychologica como quer Taine, que faz do homem *theorema que caminha*; mas, sim, é a epopéa mysteriosa da Justiça e da Providencia, porque se baseia na lei da finalidade, e, como diz Ihering «a marcha das idéas moraes, no tempo, é mais maravilhosa ainda do que o movimento dos corpos celestes, no espaço».

Parte integrante da sociologia geral, como querem muitos, é ella uma elevada sciencia, tomada essa palavra no sentido

DR. JOÃO MONTEIRO

amplo, e neste ponto sinto divergir de um eminente mestre da Faculdade de Direito, que sustentou, ha pouco, these em contrario com proficiencia notavel.

Embora, porém, sciencia e sciencia elevada como disse, a Historia invade fodos os recantos da nossa sociedade, faz-se popular e amiga de todos, e com ella vemos, em familiar convivencia. todas as classes desde a mais illustrada até á analphabeta do nosso povo.

De facto, senhores, o que significam muitas denominações de nossas praças publicas, de nossas ruas, de nossos bairros, de nossas capitaes, em uma palavra, de nosso proprio paiz? — factos historicos que se quiz perpetuar em taes nomes.

A denominação de *bondes* dada aos ferro-carris, recorda um facto da nossa historia financeira.

Os proprios nomes de baptismo, usados entre nós, como *Tibiriçá, José Bonifacio, Washington* tantos outros, recordam vultos historicos; e até no trage, temos o nome *Cavour,* do estadista italiano, dado a uma variedade de sobretudo, e, na barba, temos o nome do prestigioso politico francez *Cavaignac.*

A historia, pois, tudo invade e até o povo ignaro muitas vezes rende-lhe culto inconscientemente.

Ella é a verdadeira *Religião da Humanidade,* muito mais racional e comprehensiva do que a outra, creação fantasista de A. Comte, que mutilou a verdade historica pelo seu criterio exclusivista.

E' justo, pois, que commemoremos hoje o undecimo anniversario da unica sociedade que, neste Estado, se devota especialmente ao culto do passado, sem ambições de gloria, sem incentivos interesseiros e sem desfallecimentos mesquinhos.

A legendaria Piratininga, a predilecta de João Ramalho e de Martim Affonso, contendo em seu seio a mais antiga povoação erigida em terras brazileiras pelo nauta portuguez, não podia deixar de possuir um gremio de estudiosos, um retiro scientifico, onde, longe das paixões irritantes da politica e da lucta pela vida, se evocasse em horas de silencio a sombra grandiosa do passado, como o fazia o gardingo Eurico, no vizo escarpado do Calpe, para fugir á obsessão da orgia final das Hespanhas!

E fundou-se e desenvolveu-se o Instituto, aggremiando em seu seio as notabilidades mais conspicuas do nosso mundo litterario, que se interessavam pelo seu objectivo social.

E são passados onze annos de gloriosa carreira, de serviços valiosos, de esforços patrioticos, prestados á nossa historia e geographia, não já só estaduaes, mas de todo o Brazil, pois que homens como E. Prado, J. Monteiro, Orville Derby, Ihering,

Miranda Azevedo, T. Sampio e tantos outros não sabem reduzir os seus horizontes intellectuaes ao ambito restricto de um Estado sómente e voam além, muito além de suas fronteiras, para abranger, com a vista, o Brazil inteiro, só estacando, deante dos Andes e do Oceano.

Essa carreira gloriosa, porêm, teve, no ultimo anno que findou, a exemplo dos anteriores (dolorosa contingencia humana!) transes angustiosos a soffrer, pela morte de muitos companheiros de luctas, que vinham jubilosos e valentes, elevando bem alto o estandarte da sciencia.

Na antiga Roma, antes della mesmo, nos primórdios da historia dos Arias, o culto dos mortos, a reverencia dos antepassados foi o fundamento da religião primitiva.

O culto dos deuses Lares ou Manes, que se confundia com o do *fogo sagrado*, era a face mais poetica e tocante do polytheismo antigo.

Nós tambem temos os nossos Manes, tambem sabemos prestar culto aos nossos mortos, aos nossos irmãos que tombaram no pó da estrada, victimados muitos delles pela febre ardente da sciencia ou pelas provações durissimas da virtude e do patriotismo.

No anno que findou, vimos abandonarem para sempre as nossas fileiras os socios fundadores: dr. J. Pereira Monteiro, dr. Augusto Cesar de Barros Cruz e dr. Hypolito de Camargo; honorarios: dr. Antonio Joaquim de Macedo Soares, dr. Martim Garcia Merou, d. João Lourenço da Costa Aguiar, bispo do Amazonas, e Anatolio Luiz Garraux; correspondente: coronel Agostinho José Moreira Rollo.

Passo a occupar-me de cada um delles, tendo em consideração a precedencia que merece a somma de trabalho, representada em publicações attinentes aos fins do Instituto e por elles feitas.

E' justo que, na partilha dos louros e recompensas, tenha aqui a preeminencia, o merito demonstrado pelos socios no empenho de exalçar e cumprir os intuitos do programma da Associação.

O dr. João P. Monteiro foi, sem duvida, especialmente um cultor do Direito, mas a tendencia fatal do seu espirito dirigia-se de continuo para a Historia; e assim é que neste recinto trabalhava elle com zelo para o engrandecimento do Instituto e, em prova disso, foi eleito seu orador official.

Por occasião do quarto centenario do descobrimento da India, em 1898, proferiu elle, na Sociedade de Geographia, em Lisboa, um notavel discurso sobre Vasco da Gama; e em todas as suas obras e, principalmente, em seus discursos, sente-se o calor de uma paixão enthusiastica pelo estudo da Historia, como provou em Paris, por occasião do Congresso de Historia comparada, em 1900.

Para elle o Direito, como disse Ihering, era um filho da Historia; *era um ideal que actua na historia*, na phrase incisiva de J. B. Vico.

E, pois, mesmo, como jurista, o dr. João Monteiro nunca deixava de ser um historiador.

Eis porque o collocamos em primeiro logar aqui.

Nascido no Rio de Janeiro e vindo para esta capital para fazer o curso de Direito, sua carreira academica foi brilhante e rapida.

Formado em 1872, pertenceu á geração illustre dos Oliveiras Bello, Brasilio Machado, Valladares e muitos outros, cujo nomes não nos occorrem agóra.

Contemporaneo delle na Faculdade, recordo-me apenas, de que, no seu tempo, só tinha, como rival na tribuna, Oliveira Bello, o orador academico, mais espontaneo e fluente que temos ouvido; João Monteiro, porém, excedia-o na illustração e no talento·

Doutorando-se em Direito em 1874, foi nomeado lente substituto em 1882, e cathedratico em 1883 e elevado a vice-director em 1893 foi a director, em 1903.

Para assim galgar com dignidade e brilhantismo, todas essas posições academicas, elle indefesamente trabalhou, na imprensa, publicando livros de valor inestimavel, na cathedra, preleccionando com profundeza e eloquencia, ne tribuna, arrebatande e auditorio com surprehendentes rasgos de eloquencia imaginosa e erudita, e na banca de advogado, com os ensinamentos e pareceres de um tino juridico notavel e de uma profusão extranha de fundamentos e de provas.

No Congreso Constituinte do Estado, occupou elle uma cadeira como senador e tambem fez parte do Congresso Juridico Americano.

Seu parecer de profissional emerito era geralmente acatado até p·lo governo, que lhe confiou a elaboração dos codigos do processo criminal e civil e commercial, de collaboração com o nosso illustrado presidente.

Em diversas campanhas, empenhou-se elle com brilho para o seu nome, como a da Universalisação do Direito, a da organi-sação de uma Ordem dos Advogados entre nós, a do adiamento da creação da Universidade, etc.

Espirito eminentemente generalisador e synthetico; imaginação ardente e rebelde ás imposições do direito positivo, quando contrarias ao seu ideal, palavra facil, vocabulario riquissimo, erudição vasta, tudo isso fazia de João Monteiro um orador, não, um tribuno de praça publica ou um parlamentar á ingleza mas sim, um conferencista, um orador academico notavel, um emulo dos professores livres da Sorbonna de Pariz.

Elle, para nós tinha, porém, uma qualidade preponderante e sympathica sobre todas; era o seu amor á Patria e, em especial, o seu culto carinhoso á Academia de S. Paulo.

Na Europa, em todos os meios cultos que frequentou, procurava sempre elevar bem alto o nome brasileiro e, sobre tudo o nome da nossa Faculdade.

E morreu curvado sobre os livros de Direito, deixando-nos como legado precioso, seu livro posthumo sobre as «Acções».

Vendo-o e ouvindo-o, impressionavam-se todos com o calor juvenil de sua palavra iflammada, em confronto com as cans prematuras que lhe cobriam a cabeça: dir-se-ia um vulcão das regiões polares coberto de neves perpetuas.

De João Monteiro o Macedo Soares a transição parece brusca mas não é.

Ambos foram emeritos cultores de Direito, que amavam com o mais acendrado dos affectos.

João Monteiro visava no Direito sobretudo, o ideal, *o jus constituendum ;* Macedo Soares—a lei, o *jus constitutum.*

João Monteiro tinha o enthusiasmo dos corações expansivos; Macedo Soares era frio, como a razão, e só visava a verdade, atravez da Justiça. Um—advogado e lente; outro—juiz e só juiz.

Ambos, porém, foram dois jurisconsultos notaveis, porque, como diz Vico, *Verum et fatum reciprocantur.*

O dr. A J. de Macedo Soares, nascido em Maricá, Estado do Rio de Janeiro, formou-se em direito pela nossa Faculdade em 1861, pertencendo à notavel turma de Antonio Prado, Francisco Belisario, Ribeiro de Almeida, A. Moreira de Barros e outros. Foi juiz municipal e advogado em Araruama, juiz de direito das comarcas de Campo Largo, no Paraná, de Cabo Frio, no Rio de Janeiro, e de Mar de Hespanha, em Minas, juiz de uma das varas commerciaes da antiga Côrte e, emfim, ministro do Supremo Tribunal Federal.

Chegou, portanto, na magistratura, do mesmo modo que João Monteiro no magisterio, ao pinaculo das posições sociaes.

Seus titulos foram notaveis: além de varias obras de Direito de merito notorio, publicadas, foi elle um juiz honestissimo, independente e zeloso dos seus deveres.

Sua altivez, perante o poder executivo, do qual, aliás, dependia, tornou-se notavel, sobretudo na reacção que oppunha aos avisos do governo, sobre questões judiciarias.

Seu conhecido opusculo sobre a Liberdade Religiosa, que

foi criticado pelo bispo do Pará, d. Antonio Macedo Costa e pelo conselheiro Zacharias, no Senado, causando-lhe a decepção da não reconducção no cargo de juiz municipal, accentuou sua energia de caracter, e tornou-o muito conhecido, vindo talvez dahi sua elevação aos cargos superiores da Maçonaria e afinal ao de grão-mestre.

Importa-nos, porém, examinar o seu espolio litterario que interessa ao Instituto.

Discipulo de Baptista Caetano de Almeida Nogueira, de quem escreveu a biographia, Macedo Soares publicou alguns trabalhos sobre a lingua tupi e tambem, na *Revista Brasileira*, parte do seu *Vocabulario luso-brasileiro*, obra importantissima, que infelizmente ficou incompleta e em manuscripto.

Nesse vocabulario, sustenta elle a necessidade do estudo do dialecto brazileiro, acompanhando assim Baptista Caetano, B. Rohan, Paranhos da Silva e outros, aliás, com o apoio de Adolpho Coelho que reconhece a existencia de tal dialecto.

Nesse vocabulario, Macedo revela profundo conhecimento das linguas indigenas e até de linguas africanas.

Gloria da magistratura e das letras brazileiras, sua morte, foi, como a de João Monteiro, nestas ultimas, uma perda irreparavel para o nosso paiz.

O dr. Martim Garcia Merou, comquanto extrangeiro, merece occupar aqui a nossa attenção, porque, além de historiador notavel foi elle auctor desse livro sincero e carinhoso para nós— *O Brasil Intellectual*, que, com o de F. Wolff, constitúe a unica contribuição allienigena para a historia da litteratura patria.

Garcia Merou, poeta, romancista, publicista, historiador e diplomata argentino, teve, segundo o diz E. Quesada, uma carreira auspiciosa e brilhante, quer nas letras, quer na diplomacia; morreu, moço ainda, ministro argentino em Berlim.

Delle disse Araripe Junior: «Garcia Merou é um escriptor de raça e, nos seus livros, encontra-se sempre a clareza das ideias, junto ao conceito da phrase, a um tempo familiar e elegante».

Egualmente, José Verissimo e o visconde Taunay lhe fizeram os mais calorosos encomios.

Para que se veja o enthusiasmo espontaneo, com que elle se exprime sobre os nossos escriptores, basta citar a seguinte phrase do seu livro:

« O Brasil póde mostrar com orgulho no passado e no presente um nucleo compacto de sabios, de escriptores e de estadistas dignos de figurar em qualquer dos centros mais adiantados do velho mundo.

Accrescenta elle, referindo-se as diversas causas desse facto : —taes causas tem concorrido para dar ao Brasil *uma cultura litteraria mais solida e original do que a das outras nações sul-americanas* »

Isto dito por um argentino, é digno de ser consignado com apreço.

Além de muitas obras litterarias e de critica, escreveu elle uma *Historia da Republica Argentina*, em 3 vols., que não sabemos si foi terminada.

O Instituto curva se reverente, ante seu tumulo, lamentando o seu prematuro e infausto passamento, não só para as letras argentinas, como para as das nações irmaus. Na diplomacia, aliás, seria mais um bom amigo do Brasil.

Anato'io L. Garraux, o fundador da conhecida livraria desta capital, deixou uma bibliographia de publicações sobre o Brasil, que lhe é titulo de honra, para es a commemoração.

Nascido em Pariz, a 3 de Abril de 1833, elle veiu para o Riô de Janeiro em 1850, e ahi, collocou-se na livraria Garnier; em 1860, creou em S. Paulo a *Livraria Academica*, que, em 1863, por sua associação com o sr. Lailhacar, tornou-se o importante estabelecimento tão conhecido hoje—a *Casa Garraux*.

Sobre o seu livro *Bibliographie Brésilienne* já publicou o nosso illustrado vice-presidente um substancioso artigo na *Revista do Instituto*, volume III, e sobre elle, pois, nada accrescentaremos, a tão competente e encomiastico juizo.

E' mais um extrangeiro que cumulou a nossa gratidão concorrendo para o edificio da nossa historia, espontaneamente, com uma obra de valor, honrando assim a qualidade de socio que, em bôa hora, lhé fôra attribuida pelo Instituto, o qual, por minha mão, desfolha uma saudade sobre o seu tumulo.

D. João Lourenço da Costa Aguiar, um principe da egreja que tambem a morte eliminou de nossas fileiras, era filho de paes humildes, da comarca de Sobral, no Ceará, nascido em 1850, pelas suas virtudes, talento e amor ao estudo, percorreu a carreira ecclesiastica até a séde episcopal, sendo preconizado primeiro bispo do Amazonas pelo Summo Pontifice Leão XIII. Foi deputado pelo Ceará, na legislatura que fez a libertação dos escravos, e por ella muito trabalhou.

Dedicava-se muito á catechese dos indigenas e assim publicou uma exposição da doutrina christã em lingua tupy, da qual enviou um exemplar ao Instituto. Sacerdote de virtudes verdadeiramente evangelicas, bispo de accendrado zelo apostolico, foi muito lamentada sua perda em sua diocese, e o Instituto não póde deixar de unir os seus sentimentos de pezar aos do povo amazonense. Muito podia e devia esperar-se dos seus esforços, em prol da civilisação dos selvicolas, em tão grande numero naquella extensa região.

O dr. Augusto C. de Barros Cruz, formado em direito pela nossa faculdade, em 1884, foi director de collegio em Avaré e advogado em Ytú. Espirito estudioso e investigador deixou publicado o interessante romance historico—*O Paulista*, no qual descreve expedições dos antigos *bandeirantes* pelos sertões de nossa terra. Esse livro, embora tenha defeitos de forma e de contexto, é por si só um titulo bastante para demonstrar que o dr. B. Cruz não era um anonymo, no mundo das lettras; tinha amor á nossa historia e procurava conhecel-a sériamento.

Paz a sua memoria.

O coronel Agostinho José Moreira Rollo não deixou trabalho publicado sobre as materias de que se occupa o Instituto. Era, porêm, um socio dedicado deste e conjunctamente com o seu amigo E. Young, não poupava occasião de demonstral-o.

Era elle o cidadão de maior prestigio hoje, na zona iguapense. Natural do Rio de Janeiro, veiu joven ainda para Iguape, ahi casou-se e ao lado do coronel Sousa Castro e tenente Peniche tomou posição saliente na politica, sendo vereador, delegado de policia, inspector litterario e presidente da camara. Prestou grandes serviços como provedor da Santa Casa de Misericordia.

Com o coronel Ludgero de Castro e Joaquim de Oliveira muito trabalhou pela abolição do elemento servil, e sua morte foi muito sentida no municipio de Iguape, ao qual tambem se associa pesaroso o Instituto.

O dr. Hyppolito de Camargo, embora não tivesse publicado trabalho algum sobre materia do programma do Instituto, deixou, entretanto, varias obras de direito, de merecimento, sobretudo pratico. Formado em 1872, com o dr. João Monteiro, dedicouse á magistratura, sendo juiz de direito em Jacarehy e nesta capital

Era intelligente e estudioso e sua morte foi geralmente sentida no fôro e no seio do Instituto, onde tinha amigos.

Eis-nos ao termo da nossa *via dolorosa*, por entre tumulos recem abertos, de vultos illustres, de amigos e de consocios queridos, que desappareceram para sempre de nossos olhos...

Deante da contigencia do facto mysterioso da morte, não nos domina, porém, o gélido torpor da descrença, para que nos deixemos succumbir ás maguas que ella produz em nossos corações.

Si as conclusões da psychologia moderna, como o demonstra Guido Villa, o illustre professor da Universidade de Roma, forçam a reconhecer-se — *em face da realidade da materia, a realidade do espirito*, isto é, a verdade do dualismo scientifico, e si, por outro lado, é verdadeira a lei da conservação da energia é claro que assim como toda a materia existente se transforma, mas não se extingue no universo, assim tambem o espirito ou principio peychico não se anniquila, não morre, antes se trannsforma tambem, como o corpo, e subsiste além delle, após a morte orgánica ; em uma palavra, é immortal !

Eis o nosso consolo animador, ao concluir esta missão difficil, consolo esse que o grande cantor da *Divina Comedia* ja exprimira nos seguinte melodiosos versos :

> « *Non v'accorgete voi che noi siam vermi,*
> *Nati a formar l'angelica farfalla?* »

Verso esse que ao nosso poeta dos *Tymbiras* inspirou talvez esta bellissima quadra tão conhecida :

> « *Sáe da larva a borboleta,*
> *Sáe da rocha o diamante ;*
> *De um cadaver mudo e frio*
> *Sáe uma alma radiante.* »

Anatolio Luiz Garraux

# ACTAS DAS SESSÕES

---

## Acta da 1.ª sessão ordinar.a, em 25 de Janeiro de 1905

PRESIDENCIA DO EXMO. SR. CONS°. MANOEL A. DUARTE DE
AZEVEDO

Aos vinte e cinco dias do mez de Janeiro de mil novecentos
e cinco, nesta Capital á rua General Carneiro n. 1-A, edificio
em que funcciona o Instituto Historico e Geographico de São
Paulo, ás sete e meia horas da noite, presentes os socios srs.
Conselheiro Duarte de Azevedo, Presidente, drs. Miranda Aze-
vedo, Vice-Presidente, Pereira Guimarães, 1.° Secretario, Carlos
Reis, Domingos Jaguaribe, Eugenio Alberto Franco, Antonio de
Toledo Piza, Torres de Oliveira, Orville Derby, Eduardo Loschi,
Coronel Araujo Macedo, drs. Silveira Cintra, Alberto Löefgren,
Assis Moura, Alfredo de Toledo, srs. Jules Martin, H. E. William,
Luiz de Vasconcellos, comigo segundo Secretario abaixo nomeado,
foi pelo sr. Presidente declarada e aberta a sessão, presentes
tambem os representantes do *Estado de S. Paulo* e *Commercio
de S. Paulo.*

O sr. Presidente ao encetar os trabalhos do anno, fal-o em
termos elevados, concitando os companheiros e consocios a pro-
seguirem com amor e dedicação á causa que ora nos reune.

Não se achando na occasião o livro de actas deixa de ser
lida a da ultima sessão e passa-se ao «Expediente» :

Consta este de diversos officios de sociedades, cartões de
cumprimentos e felicitações das nossas congeneres e de varios
socios ausentes, bem assim de varias offertas que vão ser relacionadas e que o Instituto agradece com especial affecto,

Merecendo menção especial a seguinte, que constitue documento de alta importancia historica :

« Prefeitura do "Alto Juruá".—Cruzeiro do Sul em 28 de
« Setembro de 1904.—Circular.—Illmo. e Exmo. Sr.—Cabe-me
« a honra de levar ao conhecimento de V. Exma., que pelo De-
« creto desta Prefeitura, n. 1 de 7 deste mez, installei solemne-
« mente o Departamento do Alto Juruá e tomei posse do seu
« territorio; pelo Decreto n. 2 de 12 estabeleci a séde provisoria
« da Prefeitura no logar «Invencivel» á margem direita do rio
« Juruá, onde se acha acampada a força federal em operações
« sob o meu commando; pelo Decreto n. 8 desta data lancei a
« pedra fundamental da séde permanente da mesma Prefeitura,
« a que dei o nome de «Cruzeiro do Sul», na antigo logar
« «Centro Brazileiro», situado á margem esquerda daquelle rio,
« no augulo inferior por elle formado com o Móá, seu affluente.
« Saudações: assignado— Gregorio Thaumaturgo de Azevedo ».

A presente transcripção fez-se para constar em qualquer
tempo, como documento de valor historico, e será publicado, a
requerimento do dr. Miranda Azevedo, na Revista do Instituto.

Pela ordem, pede a palavra o socio dr. Deiby e em nome
do socio Condo de Wetlstein offerece um autographo do mappa
do Estado de S. Paulo, do tempo colonial, organizado pelo Coronel João da Costa Azevedo, digo Coronel João da Costa Ferreira, portuguez, que esteve no serviço da Metropole.

O sr. dr. Carlos Reis, digno Thesoureiro, apresenta o balancete do anno findo, que posto em discussão com o respectivo
parecer da commissão de contas, é approvado por unanimidade,
sendo lançado um voto de louvor ao digno Thesoureiro, na acta
presente.

Tem a palavra o sr. dr. Miranda Azevedo que, depois de
memorar as palavras com que se manifestou no encerramento dos
nossos trabalhos do anno passado, vinha, no doloroso cumprimento do dever, pedir á casa que fizesse inserir na acta da
sessão presente, um voto de pezar pelo fallecimento do dr. João
Pereira Monteiro, nosso digno e saudoso confrade, cujo desapparecimento de entre os vivos enlutou a Patria, a quem servia como
homem de sciencia e cultor das letras. Egualmente pediu o
digno orador um voto de pezar pelo passamento do consocio sr.
Anatole Garraux, um amigo do Brazil, que jámais se esqueceu
do nosso Instituto. Taes propostas foram approvadas por unanimidade.

O mesmo dr. Miranda Azevedo, em nome do dr. Theodoro
Sampaio, ausente, membro da Commissão de Redacção da Revista,
pede que o Instituto auctorize a inserção dos mappas necessarios
ao enriquecimento da mesma, cuja impressão de seu 9.° volume
já vai adeantada.

Achando-se presente á sessão o sr. dr. Miguel Guedes Nogueira, digno representante do Estado de Alagoas, o sr. dr. Miranda Azevedo o sauda e requer que conste da acta a honrosa visita.

Pede a palavra o dr. Domingos Jaguaribe, que passa a ler um trabalho sob o titulo : *Porque não creio no perigo Allemão.* Commentando as opiniões do sr. Morviskow, o illustre consocio expande sensatas considerações, sendo muito applaudido ao terminar a leitura. Encerrou-se, em seguida, a sessão, marcando o sr. dr. presidente o dia 4 do mez proximo, para a 2.ª sessão, por ser domingo o dia 5, designado pelo nosso regimento.

Para constar, eu, Dionysio Caio da Fonseca, escrevi. — *Duarte de Azevedo.—Dionysio Caio da Fonseca.—Alfredo de Toledo.*

---

## Acta da 2.ª sessão, em de 4 de Fevereiro de 1905

PRESIDENCIA DO SR. CONSELHEIRO DUARTE DE AZEVEDO

Aos quatro dias do mez de Fevereiro de mil novecentos e cinco, ás sete e meia horas da noite, nesta Capital do Estado de São Paulo, no predio á rua General Carneiro n. 1 A, onde funcciona o Instituto Historico e Geographico de São Paulo, sendo presentes os socios srs. conselheiro Duarte de Azevedo, presidente; drs. Miranda de Azevedo, Carlos Reis, Orville Derby, Alfredo de Toledo, H. von Ihering, coronel Henrique de Araujo Macedo, conego Ezechias Galvão da Fontoura, Francisco Gaspar da Silveira Martins, comigo segundo secretario, abaixo assignado, foi declarada aberta a sessão.

Tendo o sr. dr. Pereira Guimarães, 1.º secretario. communicado que não podia comparecer á presente sessão, foi convidado pelo sr. presidente o dr. Alfredo de Toledo, na ausencia do substituto, para servir de 2.º secretario, assumindo, na fórma dos Estatutos o logar de primeiro, quem está lavrando esta.

Foi lida a acta da sessão anterior, após o que o sr. dr. Orville Derby, pediu rectificação na parte referente á importante offerta de um mappa que s. s. fizera, na sessão anterior, e que em nome do offertante, desejava ser bem expressa, offerecendo ainda os seguintes detalhes :

« Que o nosso consocio honorario dr. barão Ricardo von
« Wetlstein fazia doação de um mappa autographo de um no-
« tavel geographo e geologo allemão — Barão Guilherme von
« Eschwege, a quem o Brasil deve as primeiras contribuições ao
« estudo da sua geologia e geographia physica, as quaes são

« em alguns respeitos as mais importantes que até hoje tem
« sido feitas. Conforme declaração á margem do referido mappa
« doado, foi copiado para seu uso particular, pelo Barão von
« Eschwege de um original feito em 1811 pelo coronel João da
« Costa Ferreira. Este mappa foi reproduzido no Atlas que
« acompanha a grande obra de Spix e Martius, onde é attribuido
« ao Barão von Eschwege.

« De uma outra cópia existente no Archivo Militar foi li-
« thographado nas officinas daquelle estabelecimento, mas sem
« indicação do nome do auctor; o mappa que figura no Catalogo
« da Exposição da Historia do Brasil, sob numero 2816.

« Existem no Archivo Militar outras cópias manuscriptos
« de um mappa sem nome do auctor mas que são indubitavelmente
« da mão do Coronel João da Costa Ferreira, e essencialmente
« identicas com o que agora se offerece ao Instituto. Por sua
« vez este e outros mappas confeccionados pelo Coronel João
« da Costa Ferreira são reproducções do Mappa da Capitania de
« São Paulo, organisado em 1791 e 1792 por Antonio Rodrigues
« Montezinho, collaborando nelles o citado coronel Costa Ferreira.

« Este ultimo mappa nunca foi publicado, mas existe cópia
« no Archivo da Secretaria de Extrangeiros da qual a Commis-
« são Geographica e Geologica de São Paulo possue uma cópia.

« No mappa impresso pelo Archivo Militar vem represen-
« tadas as linhas, digo, tres linhas de fronteiras entre as Capi-
« tanias de São Paulo e Minas Geraes, figurando as diversas
« hypotheses a respeito dos limites. Nas outras cópias existentes
« no mesmo Archivo e na offerecida ao Instituto vem apenas a
« linha pretendida pelos mineiros.

« Isto se explica, provavelmente, pela circumstancia de que
« os cópistas, inclusive o proprio Barão von Eschwege, sendo mais
« interessado na Capitania de Minas do que na de São Paulo,
« copiaram do original do Coronel João da Costa Ferreira ape-
« nas a linha que correspondia melhor as suas sympathias pes-
« soaes ».

Após a inserção do presente requerimento, fielmente transcripto em additamento foi a acta approvada.

Passou-se ao expediente, que constou da apresentação de
varias offertas de jornaes, livros e revistas e que o Instituto ac
ceitando agradece, e vão relacionados no fim desta.

Foram propostos, na ordem do dia, para socios effectivos os
snrs. Drs. Alberto Penteado e Euclides Silva, e Exma Sra. D.
Ibrantina Cardona. Taes propostas são remettidas á commissão
respectiva.

Conforme promettera na sessão anterior o snr. Cons. Presidente apresenta o Relatorio da gestão do anno p. findo. A casa ouviu a leitura desse documento ficando depois de approvado sobre a meza com os appensos para serem examinados pelos srs. socios que o desejarem.

O Snr. Dr. Miranda Azevedo propõe um voto de pezar pelo fallecimento do notavel jornalista e membro da Academia Brazileira José do Patrocinio, a cuja familia se deverá officiar, transmittindo os pezames desta Instituição que, rendendo preito de justa homenagem de saudade ao illustre brazileiro aqui inscreve por unanimidade a parte que toma no lucto da nação.

Levanta-se a sessão, sendo convidados os snrs. socios para a seguinte. Eu Dionysio Caio da Fonseca, segundo secretario, escrevi.—*Duarte de Arevedo.*--*Dionysio Caio da Fonseca.*—*Alfredo de Toledo.*

---

## Acta da 3.ª sessão ordinaria, em 20 de Fevereiro de 1905,

### PRESIDENCIA DO SNR. DR. MIRANDA AZEVEDO

Aos vinte dias do mez de Fevereiro de mil novecentos e cinco, ás sete e meia horas da noite, no edificio da rua General Carneiro n. 1 A, nesta Capital, onde funcciona o Instituto Historico e Geographico de São Paulo, presentes os socios Drs. Miranda Azevedo, Pereira Guimarães, Orville Derby, H. von Ihering, Carlos Reis, Eduardo Lorschi, Torres de Oliveira, Antonio Piza, Dinamerico Rangel, commigo segundo secretario que a presente lavro, foi declarada aberta a sessão.

O Snr. Presidente declara que não pode ser lida a acta da sessão anterior por não ter sido lavrada pelo secretario, por accumulo de serviço. Passa-se ao Expediente, constando de varias offertas em livros, revistas e jornaes do costume que o Instituto acceita e agradece desvanecido.

Achando-se na ante-sala o entomologista de Hamburgo, Sr. F. Chaus, o Snr. Presidente nomea uma commissão composta dos Snrs. Orville Derby, e H. von Ihering para convidal-o a assistir a sessão presente, ao que acquiescendo lhe foi feita solemne recepção.

Foram lidos na primeira parte da ordem do dia os pareceres da commissão de syndicancia e admissão de socios opinando pela acceitação dos Snrs Drs Euclides Silva, Alberto Penteado, e Ex.ma Snr.ª D.ª Ibrantina Cardona, esta na qualidade de socia correspondente, os primeiros na de effectivo, satisfeitas as formalidades dos estatutos.

Foram propostos socios correspondentes os snrs.: dr. Pablo Barrane e Major José C. Soto, residente em Buenos-ayres, o primeiro advogado e homem de letras, o segundo,, auctor de um livro—Historia da guerra do Paraguay, A' Commissão de admissão de socios.

Tem a palavra o sr. dr. H von Ihering que passa a ler a seguinte conferencia, conforme notas tomadas sobre explorações que tem sido feitas no Estado de São Paulo donde tem resultado o seu invejavel progresso.

O illustre conferente apresenta dados comprobativos das descobertas scientificas no nosso Estado que corroboram a sua riqueza quer na fauna, quer na flora, quer na mineralogia.

Falou longamente sobre as investigações e explorações feitas nas margens do Tieté por um membro deste Instituto, e apresenta photographias interessantes do—Salto do Avanhandava—Cachoeira das Cruzes, e outras da Colonia do Itapura.

Explanando-se em considerações de alto valor historico e scientifico e no intuito de bem assignalar o subsidio das informações que tem colhido e com prazer expõe, aponta falhas sanaveis como a melhoria do serviço postal, moroso pelo itenerario que soffre no trajecto para Itapura. (*)

Ouvido com o maior interesse o conferente é muito felicitado ao terminar.

Additando, pede a palavra o sr. Orville Derby, que considerando de inestimavel importancia as revelações do illustre consocio seu antecessor na «Tribuna», diz: Que considerava extremamente importante a communicação feita pelo sr von Ihering, no seu entender nem um ponto do Centro do Brazil, com possivel excepção de Manáos, reunia como o pontal do Tieté no Paraná, tanto em condições naturaes para, uma vez chegada a épocha do desenvolvimento dos desertos, rivalisar com as cidades novas do interior dos Estados Unidos.

Estas condições se assemelhavam com as das cidades gemeas — St. Paul e Miniapolis situadas juntas ao Salto de St. Antony, no extremo da parte navegavel do Mississipe, cujo desenvolvimento rivalisava em rapidez com Chicago e St. Luiz. No pontal do Tieté a extraordinaria força hydraulica dos dois saltos de Itapura e Urubupungá, muito superior á do Salto de St. Antony, indicava o centro industrial e commercial para a população que, algum dia ha de encher os sertões do valle do Paraná actualmente quasi despovoados.

Por um accaso, remexendo na vespera, em papeis velhos encontrou um quadro contrastando a Chicago de 1832 com a de 1893

(*) Esta conferencia vae publicada á pag. 554.

O primeiro apresentava um aspecto tão desolador como o das photographias da actual povoação de Itapura apresentadas pelo Dr. von Ihering, o segundo é o collosso que todo o mundo conhece. Não se atreve em prophetisar que em igual intervallo de sessenta annos fará uma differença igual á do aspecto do Itapura, mas espera com confiança, haverá alguma cousa de comparavel. Para tanto basta que algum espirito emprehendedor incite na população, influindo tambem o tino administractivo.

O primeiro não falta entre os habitantes de S. Paulo. As photographias exhibidas mostrando o que era e o que é a povoação do Itapura, denotam a vida que pelo menos com referencia a este ponto tem havido falta de segundo, mas é de esperar que seja corrigida pela actual administração ou por seus successores. »

O orador foi muito cumprimentado ao terminar a serie de observações que ahi ficam. O sr. Presidente em seguida faculta a palavra aos socios que desejassem propor algum assumpto: e não havendo mais quem quizesse usar da palavra foi a sessão encerrada: do que lavrei eu Dyonisio Caio da Fonseca segundo secretario.—*Duarte de Azevedo*, Presidente.—*Alfredo de Toledo*— *Dyonisio Caio da Fonseca.*

_____

## Acta da 4.ª sessão ordinaria em 4 de Março de 1905

PRESIDENCIA DO SR. CONSELHEIRO DUARTE DE AZEVEDO

Aos quatro dias do mez de Março de mil novecentos e cinco, nesta Capital e séde do Instituto Historico e Geographico de S. Paulo no predio á rua General Carneiro n. 1 A, presentes os srs. Conselheiro Duarte de Azevedo, dr. Carlos Reis, Alfredo de Toledo, Assis Moura, coronel Araujo Macedo, commigo segundo secretario abaixo nomeado, tendo justificado sua falta o dr. Pereira Guimarães, 1.º secretario, foi pelo sr. presidente convidado o dr. Alfredo de Toledo para substituir o segundo passando este a occupar o de 1.º na fórma estatuida.

E' declarada aberta a sessão e, sendo lidas pelo dr. 2.º secretario as actas dos dias 4 e 20 do mez de Fevereiro p. passado, foram approvadas depois de postas em discussão e sem debates.

O expediente constou de diversos officios de sociedades congeneres e de uma carta do consocio sr. Henrique R. Leang, de New Haven, agradecendo sua admissão como socio correspondente. São apresentadas as offertas relacionadas no fim da presente, constantes de revistas, jornaes e boletins que o Instituto manda agradecer aos dignos offertantes, com especial agrado,

Na primeira parte da ordem do dia foi submettida á discussão e votação a proposta que transfere os socios effectivos srs. dr. José Alves de Cerqueira Cesar e o Exm. Sr. D. Duarte Leopoldo, bispo de Curytiba desta para a categoria de honorarios. Approvados.

A commissão de admissão de socios apresenta parecer concluindo pela admissão de socios Pablo Banancbea e major José Souto, residentes em Buenos-Ayres, na qualidade de socios correspondentes, ficando o parecer sobre a mesa para ser discutido na sessão posterior.

São apresentadas propostas para socios effectivos os srs. dr. Jacob Thomaz Itapura de Miranda e Francisco Teixeira, e para correspondente o sr. Eurico Doria de Araujo Góes.

O dr. Carlos Reis na qualidade de thesoureiro, pede auctorização para, nos recibos que extrahir no corrente anno, aos socios cuja annuidade não correcem de Janeiro, a faculdade de equiparar aos demais socios.

Posta em discussão a indicação, foi approvada.

Na segunda parte da ordem do dia o socio coronel Henrique de Araujo Macedo pede ao sr. presidente, sua inscripção para a leitura de um trabalho seu, na primeira parte da ordem do dia da proxima sessão, sobre um ponto a esclarecer da Historia Militar do Brazil de que já tratou em conferencia anterior e que ora vê corroborado pelo illustre escriptor argentino sr. Ramos Mejia, lente da escola militar de Buenos-Ayres. O sr. presidente declara o associado inscripto e termina a sessão convidando os socios do Instituto a apresentarem trabalhos que sejam lidos em nossas sessões futuras, trabalhos esses que serão apreciados como de valor pelo Instituto que tão novo ainda já se póde ufanar de gloriosas tradições. Nada mais havendo a tratar-se foi suspensa a sessão ás 8 e meia horas da noite. Eu, Dionysio Caio da Fonseca, lavrei a presente.—*Duarte de Azevedo.—M. Pereira Guimarães.—Alfredo de Toledo.*

---

## Acta da 5.ª sessão ordinaria em 20 de Março de 1905

PRESIDENCIA DO DR. MIRANDA AZEVEDO

Aos vinte dias do mez de Março de 1905, nesta capital e séde do Instituto Historico e Geographico de S. Paulo, no predio á rua General Carneiro, n. 1 A, presentes os socios senhores Dr. Miranda Azevedo, vice-presidente, Pereira Guimarães, 1.° Secretario, Carlos Reis, Thesoureiro, Antonio Piza, Mello Barreto

Domingos Jaguaribe, Alberto Löfgren, Eduardo Loschi, H von Ihering, Gomes Ribeiro, Alfredo de Toledo, coronel Henrique Affonso de Araujo Macedo; tendo participado a falta de presença o 2.° Secretario, foi convidado, ao assumir a presidencia o Dr Miranda Azevedo, para occupar o logar de 2.° secretario o Dr Alfredo de Toledo que acceitou. Aberta a sessão foi lida e approvada, sem debate, a acta da anterior.

Expediente constante da leitura de officios de interesse social e recebimento de revistas e jornaes, que o Instituto agradece com particular affecto.

São apresentados os pareceres que concluem pela admissão de socios dos senhores dr. Pablo Barrene, major José Sotto, na qualidade de socios correspondentes. Sobre a mesa para ser votado. Foi proposto o sr dr. Augusto Elisio de Castro Fonseca, advogado, residente nesta capital, para socio effectivo: á commissão respectiva.

Foram lidos ainda os pareceres da Commissão opinando pela admissão dos srs. dr. Eurico Doria de Araujo Góes, como correspondente e Jacob Itapura de Miranda, e Francisco Teixeira, na qualidade de effectivos. Os pareceres sobre os primeiros foram approvados, ficando os dos ultimos mencionados, sobre a mesa, na fôrma regimental.

O sr. Alberto Löfgren offereceu ao Instituto um documento que pertenceu a S. M. rei da Suecia; e consiste em notas de viagem ao Brazil em 1813, tal documento existe na bibliotheca particular daquelle monarcha e foi delle extrahida a cópia presente, a pedido do digno consocio, que explicando a procedencia declara ser original a sua offerta. O Presidente agradeceu a importante dadiva e pediu ao sr. Löfgren de o fazer tambem ao referido monarcha.

O dr. Piza explicando a offerta que vem fazer ao instituto apresenta a cópia de uma carta escripta, no dizer do informante, pelo sabio Martius, quando em viagem pelo nosso paiz no primeiro quartel do seculo passado.

São ainda presentes documentos sobre a fundação da villa Caçapava-Velha, e uma curiosa noticia geneologica sobre a familia Alvarenga pelo sr. dr. Francisco Eugenio de Toledo.

Memoria da fundação de Santos pelo capitão-mór Francisco Xavier Aguiar Andrade.

Na 2.ª parte da ordem do dia tem a palavra o digno socio coronel Araujo Macedo. que se achava inscripto e que passou a ler um substancioso trabalho sobre assumpto palpitante, que tal é o de justificar direitos a verdadeira historia «Sobre a batalha de Passo do Rosario ou Itusaingo, em 20 de Fevereiro de 1828».

O illustre conferente corroborando suas opiniões já expressas luminosamente em anterior trabalho, cita o recente trabalho «As nevroses dos homens celebres da historia argentina» e outros factos que, ouvidos com a maior attenção constituem o triumpho das nossas armas naquella memoravel lucta.

O dr. Piza pede para ser inscripto para a proxima sessão, depois de ter o Instituto applaudido o conferente anterior.

O sr. Presidente, antes de encerrar a sessão, propõe a inserção de um voto de pesar na acta presente pelo fallecimento do dr. Hippolyto de Camargo, illustre jurisconsulto e ex-magistrado. O Instituto vota por unanimidade pela proposta do sr. Presidente e aqui inscreve o voto de pesar como justa homenagem aos meritos do saudoso morto fundador desta associação e quem as letras patrias devem assignalados serviços.

Nada mais havendo a tratar-se o sr. Presidente convida os senhores consocios para a sessão seguinte que terá logar a cinco de Abril e encerra a presente. Eu, Dionisio Caio da Fonseca, segundo secretario, a escrevi. — *Duarte de Azevedo.* — *Pereira Guimarães.* — *Dionisio Caio da Fonseca.*

---

## Acta da 6.ª sessão em 5 de Abril de 1905

PRESIDENCIA DO SR. CONS.º DUARTE DE AZEVEDO

Aos cinco dias do mez de Abril de 1905 (mil novecentos e cinco), nesta Capital e séde do Instituto Historico e Geographico de São Paulo, ás 7 e meia horas da noite, presentes os socios srs. Conselheiro Manoel Antonio Duarte de Azevedo, drs. Domingos Jaguaribe, João N. Jaguaribe, Carlos Reis, Pereira Guimarães, Desembargador José Maria do Valle, drs. Alfredo de Toledo, Antonio Piza, Eugenio Franco, Eduardo Lorschi, Jorge Maia, representantes do «Estado de São Paulo, do Commercio de São Paulo e Correio Paulistano, alguns assistentes na qualidade de visitantes, sob a presidencia do primeiro dos acima nomeados, commigo segundo secretario, lavrando a presente, foi declarada aberta a sessão. Lida a acta da anterior foi posta em discussão e approvada sem debates, por unanimidade. Passando se ao expediente: Tem a palavra o sr. primeiro secretario Pereira Guimarães que, lendo os titulos de diversas offertas em livros, revistas e jornaes que vão mencionados no fim desta termina-o, agradecendo o Instituto com especial

affecto aos seus offertantes. Pede a palavra o dr. Antonio Piza
e offerece ao Instituto o n. 60 do «O Pharol Paulistano» publicado em 1827, sabbado 3 de Novembro e o numero 172 do
«O Novo Farol Paulistano»—terça-feira, 14 de Maio do anno
1833—: o numero 8 do «O Observador Constitucional», segunda-
feira 16 de Novembro de 1829—: o numero 202, do «O Observador Constitucional», segunda-feira, 16 de Janeiro de 1832—
impresso na Typographia Patriotica—rua da Esperança n. 9.

Taes offertas que aqui merecem especial assignalado, constituem importante dadiva para o nosso archivo e repositorio
historico.

Passa-se á seguinte

## ORDEM DO DIA

Inscripto o socio dr. Antonio Piza o sr. Presidente dá-lhe
a palavra. Antes, porém da dissertação o sr. dr. Carlos Reis,
thesoureiro, apresenta o balancete referente ao trimestre findo,
que foi lido pelo 1.º secretario e ficou sobre a mesa para ser
examinado na sessão seguinte—e discutido.

São propostos socios correspondentes os srs. drs. Ataliba
Leonel e Cicero Leonel, o primeiro advogado e o segundo poeta
e advogado.

As propostas vão á respectiva commissão de admissão de
socios para apresentar parecer.

São postos em discussão e approvados os pareceres opinando pela admissão dos srs. dr. Jacob Itapura de Miranda,
effectivo; e drs. Eurico Doria de Araujo Góes e Francisco Teixeira, na qualidade de correspondentes.

Tem a palavra o sr. dr. Antonio Piza que, por espaço de
uma hora se occupa do facto historico «Bernarda de Francisco
Ignacio»—documentando-a com opiniões de diversos os factos
que antecederam a independencia do Brazil.

O orador, promettendo continuar a leitura do interessante
trabalho, foi muito applaudido. Encerrada a sessão, foi designado o dia 5 de Maio p. futuro, para o proseguimento dos
trabalhos, por occorrer a circumstancia de ser feriado o dia 20
de Abril corrente. Eu, Dionysio Caio da Fonseca, segundo
secretario, escrevi —*Dr. Miranda Azevedo*, presidente.—*Pereira
Guimarães*, primeiro-secretario.—*Dionysio Caio da Fonseca.*

# de 1905

Aos cinco dias do mez de Maio de mil novecentos e cinco, nesta capital e séde do Instituto Historico e Geographico de S. Paulo, ás sete e meia horas da noite, presentes os srs. drs. Miranda Azevedo, Pereira Guimarães, Assis Moura, Jorge Krichbaum, coronel Araujo Macedo, Eduardo Loschi, Antonio de Toledo Pisa, Alfredo de Toledo, H. von Ihering, Gomes Ribeiro, Ernesto Goulart, Assumpção, commigo segundo secretario, abaixo assignado, foi aberta a sessão, sob a presidencia do dr. Miranda Azevedo.

Lida a acta da sessão anterior foi approvada sem debates.

O expediente constou de offertas e leitura de officios, sendo as primeiras recebidas com agrad·› especial, e mandadas agradecer.

Pede a palavra o socio von Ihering que apresentou ao Instituto o sr. Barão de von Branse, sabio e naturalista em excursão pelo nosso paiz e que de passagem por esta capital nos visita.

E' recebido com demonstração de amizade o nosso visitante, que tendo assignado o livro de visitantes, tomou assento e assistiu a sessão presente.

São lidos os pareceres da commissão de syndicancia concluindo pela acceitação de socios dos srs. drs. Augusto Elysio de Castro Fonseca, na qualidade de effectivo, e dos srs. Cicero Leonel e Ataliba Leonel na de correspondentes. Ficam sobre a mesa para discussão na seguinte.

Foram proclamados socios, por terem sido aprovados os srs. dr. Jacob Itapura de Miranda, effectivo e dr. Eugenio Doria de Araujo Góes e Francisco Teixeira, na qualidade de correspondentes.

Pela ordem : Propõe o sr. dr. Pereira Guimarães um voto de pezar pelo fallecimento do dr. Antonio de Godoy, chefe de policia do Estado. O Instituto approva e manda inserir tal voto que ahi fica como tributo de saudosa homenagem ao illustre morto.

O mesmo dr. Pereira Guimarães propõe e justifica com argumentos, que se nomeasse uma commissão que se entendesse com o sr. Bispo diocesano afim de serem acautelados os documentos pertencentes ao Convento do Carmo, e que foram arrecadados por ordem superior. A proposta foi approvada e nomeada uma commissão dos srs drs. Manoel Antonio Duarte de Azevedo, Antonio de Toledo Pisa e revm.° conego Francisco de Paula Rodrigues, a qual se entenderá com o sr. Bispo da diocese e delle solicitará o resolvido em sessão e de accôrdo com a proposta. Na segunda parte da ordem do dia tem a palavra o socio dr. Toledo Pisa que continúa a leitura do seu interessante trabalho sobre os factos occorridos neste Estado anteriores á Independencia do Brazil. Ouvido com attenção e interesse que dispertam á casa taes assumptos em referencia á nossa historia, o orador é muito applaudido ao terminar.

Pede para ser inscripto caso aja tempo, para a sessão seguinte o sr. dr. Gomes Ribeiro que lerá tambem um trabalho de sua lavra.

Levanta-se a sessão, e o sr. Presidente convida os srs. socios para a seguinte, que terá logar a vinte do corrente. Eu Dionysio Caio da Fonseca, segundo secretario, a escrevi.

Em tempo. A commissão nomeada para entender-se sobre os manu-criptos do Convento do Carmo é composta dos senhores socios dr Manoel Pereira Guimarães, dr. Antonio Toledo Pisa e arcediago dr. Francisco de Paula Rodrigues. —Dr. *Miranda Azevedo.—M. Pereira Guimarães.—J. C. Gomes Ribeiro.*

---

## Acta da 8.ª sessão ordinaria, em 20 de Maio de 1905

PRESIDENCIA DO SR. DR. MIRANDA AZEVEDO

Aos vinte dias do mez de Maio de mil novecentos e cinco, ás sete e meia horas da noite, no salão nobre deste Instituto Historico, presentes os srs. drs. Miranda Azevedo, Toledo Piza, Carlos Reis, Pereira Guimarães, Jorge Krichbaum, H. von Ihering, Eduardo Loschi, Gomes Ribeiro, Coronel Henrique Affonso de Aranjo Macedo, Dra. Maria Rennotte, commigo segundo secretario e sob a presidencia da dr. Miranda Azevedo, foi declarada aberta a sessão. Procede-se á leitura da acta da sessão anterior que, posta em discussão, foi approvada sem debates e em seguida, na fórma do regimento, assignada pela mesa.

Passando-se ao expediente, constou este da leitura de officios e apresentações de offertas em livros e em jornaes e revistas, que são acceitos pelo Instituto com particular agrado.

Ordem do dia, 1.ª parte: São lidos e approvados os pareceres da respectiva commissão, opinando pela admissão do srs.

dr: Augusto Elysio de Castro Fonseca, na qualidade de socio effectivo ; drs. Ataliba Leonel e Cicero Leonel, de correspondentes. Fica sobre a mesa o parecer que será discutido em sessão posterior sobre admissão do srs dr. Julio Brandão Sobrinho. Foram lidas as propostas dos srs. Andréა Lupeña, residente em Buenos-Ayres, e Gustavo Enge, para cocios correspondentes, este ultimo residente em Campinas; a do dr. Joaquim Rodrignes dos Santos, para socio effectivo.

Para socios correspondentes, os srs drs. Manoel Monteiro da Rocha, residente no interior, Abilio Sampaio, residente em Tambahú, e Rabello Pestana, medicos ; como effectivos, os srs. drs. Jorge Blackscorrar, Olavo Hummel, Geraldo Machado e agrimensor Cornelio Schmidt, chefe das turmas da Commissão Geographica do Estado, actualmente em estudos no interior.

Segundo a praxe, essas propostas vão á commissão respectiva

O sr. von Ihering apresenta um curioso estudo que fez sobre algumas moluscos que lhe foram enviados da Bahia, pelo nosso consocio dr. Orville Derby, denotando pacientes curiosidades.

O dr. Pereira Guimarães faz eutrega ao Instituto de uma planta de S. Paulo, com data de 1870 a 1874. O mesmo dr. se-cretario faz sciente á casa que tem recebido reclamações de alguns socios correspondentes, que solicitam diplomas. Nao sendo dos Estatutos a concessão de taes diplomas aos seus acceitos na qualidade de correspondentes e mesma dada a exiguidade de impressos actualmente, consulta á casa se é da sua competencia deliberar ou se a mesa póde por si concedel-os.

O sr. Toledo Piza acha que deve mandar imprimir outra edição de diplomas com a suppressão da palavra—socio—afim de ser preenchida conforme a cathegoria dos acceitos· Essa consul-ta é feita pelo sr. Presidente, opinando o sr. Carlos Reis que seja addiada a discussão do assumpto, como pede, para a sessão seguinte.

Passa-se a segunda parte da ordem da dia, tendo a palavra o sr. Toledo Piza. que continúa a leitura do seu trabalho sobre «Os factos occorridos em S. Paulo», antecedendo ao advento da Independencia do Brazil. A phase tersa e convicta do illus-tre consocio foi ainda uma vez ouvida com attenção pelo In-stituto que o appláude ao terminar a leitura.

Pede inscripção o sr. dr. João Gomes Ribeiro para falar na sesão seguinte, sendo levantada a presente, após o convite feito pelo dr. Presidente, que marca o dia 5 de Junho proximo. Nada mais havendo a tratar-se, foi suspensa, como acima se diz. Eu, Dionysio Caio da Fonseca, segundo secretario escrevi.—Dr. *Mi-randa Azevedo.—Pereira Guimarães.—Dionysio Caio da Fonseca.*

## Acta da 9ª sessão ordinaria em 5 de Julho de 1905

Aos cinco dias do mez de Julho de mil novecentos e cinco, nesta capital de São Paulo, na séde do Instituto Historico e Geographico de São Paulo, ás 7 e meia horas da noite, presentes os srs. drs. Manoel Pereira Guimarães, 1.º secretario, Carlos Reis, J. C. Gomes Ribeiro, Domingos Jaguaribe, José Torres de Oliveira, H. von Ihering, Antonio Piza, commigo segundo secretario abaixo assignado foi declarada aberta a sessão, cuja presidencia assumiu o dr. Pereira Guimarães, por se acharem ausentes os srs. presidente e vice-presidente.

Foi convidado para substituir o segundo secretario o sr. dr. Torres de Oliveira, que passou a ler a acta digo, que, acceitando, tomou assento.

O segundo secretario communica que por falta de tempo deixou de lavrar a acta da sessão anterior. Achando-se em sala contigua o sr. professor Antonio Alexandre Borges dos Reis, o sr. presidente nomeia uma commissão para acompanhal-o á sala dos nossos trabalhos, convidando-o a tomar assento, após ter assignado o livro de presença.

O abaixo essignado apresenta ao Instituto o nobre consocio correspondente, deputado estadual e professor do Gymnasio da Bahia, congratulando-se com s. s. e com a casa, pela honra da vista.

O sr. Borges dos Reis agradece ao Instituto a sua acceitação no numero dos que aqui trabalham pelos interesses da Patria, registrando os documentos que nos honram e promette quanto em si couber pugnar pelo bom nome da associação

O expediente consta da apresentação e leitura dos titulos das varias offertas em livros, revistas e jornaes, todas as quaes o Instituto agradece. Vota-se o parecer da Commissão admittindo na qualidade de socio effectivo o sr. dr. Julio Brandão Sobrinho, o qual é proclamado pelo sr. presidente.

Tem a palavra o socio inscripto sr. Gomes Ribeiro, que passa a ler a introducção do trabalho «A Revolução de 7 de Abril e seu alcance politico».

O Instituto ouve com o maior interesse a leitura feita pelo nobre consocio, que continúa inscripto para a proxima sessão.

O sr. presidente convida os presentes á sessão do dia 20 do corrente e encerra os trabalhos do dia. Eu, Dionysio Caio da Fonseca, escrevi.—Dr. *A. C. Miranda Azevedo.*—*M. Pereira Guimarães.*—*Dionysio Caio da Fonseca.*

Acta da 10ª sessão ordinaria em 5 de Julho
de 1905

Aos cinco dias do mez de Julho de mil novecentos e cinco,
nesta capital e séde do Instituto Historico e Geographico
de S. Paulo, á rua General Carneiro n. 1-A, presentes os srs.
drs. Miranda Azevedo, Pereira Guimarães, Eugenio Franco,
Francisco Campos Andrade, Alfredo de Toledo, João C.
Gomes Ribeiro, Carlos Reis, Eduardo Loschi, José Torres de Oliveira,
commigo, segundo secretario, abaixo nomeado, foi, sob a presidencia do dr. Miranda Azevedo, declarada aberta a sessão.
Ordenada a leitura da acta da sessão antecedente, passei a lêr
a de 5 de Junho, que foi approvada, tendo o sr. presidente declarado que por falta de numero deixou o Instituto de celebrar
a sessão do dia 20 do mez p. p. Passa-se a leitura do expediente seguinte: Offertas que vão mencionadas no fim da pre
sente e que o Instituto manda agradecer. Leitura de varias
communicações de instituições. Sciente.

Ordem do dia. Não havendo parecer da commissão de
admissão de socios, é lida a proposta para socio correspondente
do sr. Antonio Viotti, homem de letras e inspector litterario na
cidade de Limeira, onde reside: a proposta vae á commissão
respectiva. Tem a palavra o socio dr. Gomes Ribeiro que passa
a lêr, em continuação, o seu trabalho «A Revolução de 7 de
Abril e seu alcance politico».

Dissertou o illustre consocio, por espaço de quarenta e cinco
minutos, sendo ouvido com o maior interesse pela casa, sendo
applaudido ao terminar a leitura e felicitado pela mesa e consocios. Nada mais havendo a tratar-se, foi encerrada a presente
e convidados pelo sr. presidente os srs. socios para a sessão ordinaria do dia 20 do corrente. Eu, Dionysio Caio da Fonseca,
segundo secretario, o lavrei e assigno.

Em tempo. O sr. dr. Torres Oliveira communica á casa
que, em companhia do dr. Eugenio Franco, foi em desempenho
á commissão, ao Ipanema, correspondendo ao gentil convite da
sociedade. A mesa agradece. O dr. 1.º secretario apresenta um
interessante trabalho do sr. Affonso A. de Freitas sobre a geographia e historia de S. Paulo — vae á commissão respectiva,
representada pelo socio Eduardo Loschi. O dr. Miranda Azevedo propõe voto de pezar pelo fallecimento do notavel geographo Elisée Rèclus, e que se officie ao ministro em Paris,
enviando pezames. Bem assim propõe o mesmo sr. que a casa
se manifeste egualmente pezarosa pela perda do consocio Garcia

Merou, e do bispo do Amazonas D. João Lourenço da Costa Aguiar. Consultada a casa, resolve esta que se inscreva voto de pezar e que aqui fica, em homenagem de saudosa lembrança. Eu, 2.º secreterio escrevi.—*Dr. A. C. de Miranda Azevedo.* —*M. Pereira Guimarães.*—*Dionysio Caio da Fonseca.*

---

## Acta da 11.ª sessão ordinaria, em 5 de Agosto de 1905

### PRESIDENCIA DO EXM. SR. DR. MIRANDA AZEVEDO

Aos cincos dias do mez de Agosto de mil novecentos e cinco ás sete e meia horas da noite, no edificio do Instituto Historico e Geographico de São Paulo, á rua General Carneiro n. 1 A, presentes os socios srs. drs. Miranda Azevedo, vice-presidente, Domingos Jaguaribe, Pereira Guimarães, 1.º secretario, Raphael Correia e Carlos Reis—assume a presidencia, na fórma dos estatutos, o primeiro dos acima citados e declara aberta a sessão.

Achando-se ausente o segundo secretario, abaixo nomeado, o sr. presidente convida a occupar esse logar ao sr. dr. Raphael Correia Sampaio, que acceita e toma assento.

Não estando lavrada a acta da sessão anterior, digo da ultima sessão, o senhor segundo secretario interino dá conhecimento á casa e passa-se ao expediente seguinte: Officio do Instituto Geologico do Mexico, solicitando que este Instituto se faça representar na decima sessão do Congresso Geologico Internacional, em 1906.

A casa resolverá opportunamente e desde já agradece a gentileza do nosso congenere.

Segue-se a apresentação de varias e importantes offertas em livros, revistas e jornaes, boletins entre os quaes «Contribuicion de Estudio de la Cartographia de los paizes del Rio de la Plata», (Mappa inedito de Ruy Dias Gusman), por Daniel Garcia Acevedo e outras dadivas de real importancia, que o Instituto agradece com especial menção.

Por offerta da exm.ª Sr.ª d Veridiano Prado, acha-se na mesa um retrato do socio benemerito sr. dr. Orville Derby. Agradecendo o sr Presidente a delicada offerta, propõe que seja o retrato inaugurado na sala das nossas sessões, o que foi unanimemente approvado. Ordem do dia: Parecer da commissão de admissão de socios sobre a do sr. Antonio Viotti, foi, sem discussão acceita e proclamado socio correspondente, e vae se communicar. Propostas para socios correspondentes : exm.ª sr.ª Viscondessa de Cavalcanti, brazileira, auctora de varios escriptos litterarios e scientificos e de um Diccionario Biographico Brazileiro, residente em Paris; mais os srs. Daniel Garcia Acevedo, advogado natural do Uruguay, residente em Montevidéo, auctor de diversos trabalhos litterarios; dr. Fabio Ramos, braziloiro, advogado, e homem de lettras. residente em Rio Claro, São Paulo; dr. Ernesto Martiniano Pedroso, advogado, homem de letras, residente na Capital; dr. Edmundo Navarro de Andrade, agrimensor, director do Horto Florestal de Jundiahy, residente na Capital, sendo os dois ultimos propostos na qualidade de socios effectivos. A requerimento do dr. presidente a casa dispensa o intersticio, sendo taes propostas acceitas e reconhecidos e aclamados socios os srs. propostos. O dr Jaguaribe consulta a casa e propõe que o Instituto se congratule com o Congresso Latino Americano, ora reunido no Rio de Janeiro: a proposta foi acceita com demonstrações de viva sympathia. O dr Pereira Guimarães.propõe um voto de pesar na acta presente pelo passamento do Conselheiro Corrêa, vice-presidente do Instituto Historico Brazileiro, bem assim que se officie ao mesmo Instituto dando pezames, o que foi unanimemente approvado. Officie se.

O dr. Raphael Corrêa Sampaio igualmente propõe um voto de pezar pelo fallecimento do illustre paulista dr. A. Francisco de Aguiar e Castro : tal proposta é acceita e approvada, fica inscripto um voto de pezar como preito de homenagem e justa saudade por tão uteis e prestimosos concidadãos. Nada mais havendo a tratar-se foi encerrada a presente, sendo convidados os socios para a sessão ordinaria que tera logar e 20 do corrente. Eu Dionysio Caio da Fonseca, reportando-me ás notas que encontrei, por me achar ausente, lavrei esta acta, e em tempo declaro que a seguinte sessão terá logar no dia 19, por ser domingo o dia 20 marcado pelo regimento Dionysio Caio da Fonseca.—Dr. Miranda Azevedo.—Pereira Guimarães.—Dionysio Caio da Fonseca·

Acta da 12.ª sessão ordinaria, em 19 de Agosto de 1905

PRESIDENCIA DO DR. MIRANDA AZEVEDO

Aos dezenove dias do mez de Agosto de mil novecentos e cinco, nesta capital e séde do Instituto Historico e Geographico de S. Paulo, ás 7 e meia horas da noite, presentes os srs. Augusto de Siqueira Cardoso, Antonio Piza, Pereira Guimarães, coronel Henrique A. de Araujo Macedo, von Ihering, Alfredo de Toledo, Miranda Azevedo, vice presidente; foi declarada aberla a sessão.

Em seguida, foram lidas as actas de 5 de Agosto, que, postas em discussão, foram unanimemente approvadas. Passando-se ao expediente: foi lido um officio do sr. dr. Lechamann Nitsche, chefe da secção anthropologica do «Museu de La Plata», pedindo a permuta de nossas publicações. O sr. dr. primeiro secretario communica á casa que diversas associações congeneres têm feito identicos pedidos, propondo s. s. que sejam attendidas; a casa depois de ouvir as considerações feitas que vão mencionadas no fim da presente e constantes de livros, revistas, relatorios e jornaes, as quaes são recebidas com agrado especial.

Pede a palavra o sr. dr. Antonio Piza para fazer entrega ao Instituto de uma offerta feita pelo dr. Estevam Bourroul e apresenta um manuscripto do dr. Estevam de Mendonça, director do Archivo Publico do Estado de Matto Grosso, sob a epigraphe «Noticia Historica de Cuyabá». O dr. Piza pede que o Instituto se pronuncie sobre a importancia historica da offerta. Com esta offerece tambem para o nosso archivo a «Planta de Cuyabá» e antigo palacio dos capitaes—generaes em Cuyabá: duas photographias.

O sr. presidente nomeia uma commissão composta do mesmo dr. Piza, Alfredo de Toledo e coronel Araujo Macedo por se acharem ausentes da capital os membros da commissão effectiva.

A commissão nomeada acceita a incumbencia para se pronunciar opportunamente.

Ordem do dia: Propostas para socios effectivos os srs. dr. Antonio Baptista de Campos Pereira, ministro do Tribunal de Justiça do Estado; João Pedro Cardoso, chefe da Commissão Geographica e Geologica do Estado; e para correspondentes: os srs. Benedicto Calixto, artista notavel e auctor da «Historia do Itanhaen», e dr. Estevam de Mendonça, residente em Cuyabá.

As propostas vão á commissão respectiva.

Pede a palavra o sr. coronel Araujo Macedo, veterano da guerra do Paraguay; e memorando os factos da historia que se relacionam com aquella época, sente-se feliz em vir propôr ao Instituto Historico que se congratule, em mensagem com o Congresso Nacional pelo projecto apresentado pelo coronel Marcolino Moura, lembrando o cumprimento de promessas aos voluntarios da Patria. O orador fala como brasileiro e como membro deste Instituto, e, em extremo commovido relembra os feitos dos voluntarios nas campanhas do Sul. A casa adopta por unanimidade a proposta e resolve proceder de accôrdo com o pedido feito.

O sr. presidente pede que seja inserto na acta presente um voto de pezar pelo fallecimento dos ministro Macedo Soares e conego Augusto Cavalheiro e Silva. Aqui ficam taes manifestações como tributo de respeitosa homenagem aos saudosos extinctos.

Pede a palavra o dr. von Ihering e apresenta o esboço de um seu trabalho «Distribuição de mattas e campos da America do Sul» com um mappa de caracter provisorio, confeccionado s. s. e desenhado pelo joven engenheiro Fausto Leff. Entrando em diversas considerações o orador pede a collaboração dos consocios afim de que possa esclarecer quanto possivel o assumpto já tentado por alguns naturalistas a cuja frente cita o sabio Martius. O orador salienta os nomes dos srs. coronel Maia, Orville Derby e Eugenio Loefregen e Affonso Artung, bem assim a Commissão Geographica e Geologica do Estado.

O sr. presidente encarece o valor do trabalho do dr. von Ihering e bem assim louva a dedicação do sr. Fausto Leff sendo distribuido por todos os socios o mappa que acima vem citado, assignalando as zonas occupadas pelas mattas e pelos campos.

Foi levantada a sessão ás 9 e meia horas da noite e convidados os socios para a seguinte. E u, lavrei e assigno. Dyonisio Caio da Fonseca —Dr. A. C. Miranda Azevedo, —Pereira Guimarães.—Dyonisio Caio da Fonseca.

---

## Acta da 13.ª sessão ordinaria, em 5 de Setembro de 1905

PRESIDENCIA DO SR CONSELHEIRO DUARTE DE AZEVEDO.

Aos cinco dias do mez de Setembro de mil novecentos e cinco, nesta Capital, e edificio em que funcciona o Instituto Historico e Geographico de São Paulo, ás 7 e meia horas da noite, sob a presidencia do sr. conselheiro Manoel Antonio Duarte de Azevedo, presentes os socios drs Pereira Guimarães, primeiro secretario, Toledo Piza, Alfredo de Toledo. Torres de Oliveira, Domingos Jaguaribe, Silveira Cintra, Orville Derby, Gomes Ribeiro, Drª. Maria Renotte, conego Ezechias Galvão da Fontoura, conego Araujo Marcondes, commigo segundo secretario, abaixo nomeado, foi declarada aberta a sessão. Lida e

approvada, sem debates, a acta da sessão anterior, passou-se á leitura do seguinté expediente, cuja apresentação foi feita pelo sr. dr. Pereira Guimarães: Officio do sr Raphael de Aguiar agradecendo ao Instituto os pezames que lhe foram dirigidos, conforme resolução anterior.— Sciente. São apresentados lidos e approvados os pareceres da commissão de admissão, reconhecendo, de conformidade com os estatutos, os srs drs Antonio Baptista de Campos Pereira, e João Pedro Cardoso, como effectivos e Benedicto Calixto, na qualidade de correspondenfe.
—Ficam sobre a mesa.

Proposta para socio effectivo o sr. dr. Clodomiro Pereira da Silva - A' commissão respectiva para emittir parecer.

Em tempo—o Instituto recebe e agradece varias offertas em livros, jornaes e revistas, que vão enriquecer suas collecções e mencionadas no fim desta

O dr. Alfredo de Toledo propõe e o Instuto approva por unanimidade um voto de pezar lançado na acta, pelo falecimento do sr conselheiro Carlos Augusto de Carvalho, autor da Consolidação das Leis Brazileiras, e cidadão notavel por serviços á causa publica. O sr. conselheiro presidente additando palavras á proposta, submette á approvação da casa a dita proposta, e aqui se inscreve o voto como homenagem de respeitosa saudade.

Pede a palavra o sr. 1.° Secretario e offerece ao Instituto a copia de um documeuto por s. s. extrahida do Archivo Convento do Carmo, em Santos O Instituto resolve que, pela importancia historica ligada a tão precioso folio, seja o mesmo enviado á commissão de redacção da *Revista* para ser nella publicado.

O dr. Domingos Jaguaribe propõe que o Instituto officie ao nosso pre timoso consocio dr. Alfredo Ellis, digno senador federal, afim de solicitar sua intervenção tendente á dispensa do imposto de sello á correspondencia que fôr dirigida pelo mesmo aos seus congeneres.

Tal proposta é apoiada e approvada pela casa que resolve dirigir-se ao citado senador

Pede inscripção para a proxima sessão o consocio dr. Gomes Ribeiro que lerá seu trabalho « Origens da Civilisação Americana antes da conquista».

Nada mais havendo a tractar-se, o sr. Presidente convida os srs. socios para a seguinte sessão, que terá logar a 20 do corrente e levanta se a sessão.

Eu, Dionysio Caio da Fonseca, segundo secretario, escrevi —*Dr. Miranda Azevedo.*—*Pereira Guimarães*—*Dionysio Caio da Fonseca.*

# Acta da 14.ª sessão ordinaria, em 20 de Setembro de 1905

PRESIDENCIA DO SR. DR. MIRANDA AZEVEDO

Aos vinte dias do mez de Setembro de mil novecentos e cinco, nesta capital, ás 7 e meia horas da noite, no edificio em que funcciona o Instituto Historico e Geographico de São Paulo, á rua General Carneiro n. 1 H, presentes os srs. drs. Miranda Azevedo, Vice-Presidente, Pereira Guimarães, primeiro Secretario, As-is Moura, Eduardo Loschi, H. von Ihering, Eugenio Franco, Silveira Cintra, Domingos Jaguaribe, commigo segundo Secretario abaixo nomeado, presidencia do dr. Miranda Azevedo, foi por este declarada aberta a sessão.

Achando-se na sala da Bibliotheca o sr. dr. Augusto Elysio de Castro Fonseca, socio acceito, o sr. dr. Presidente, seguindo as praxes, noméa uma commissão para dar-lhe entrada no recinto da assembléa

Introduzido e recebido no salão pelos socios presentes foi s. s. convidado a assignar o livro de presença, o que, feito, passei a ler a acta da sessão anterior. Esta, posta em discussão, foi approvada, sem debates.

Não tendo comparecido o socio dr. Gomes Ribeiro, que se achava inscripto, passou-se á leitura do expediente, constante da apresentação de diversas offertas em livros, revistas e jornaes, mencionados no fim, o que o Instituto agradece.

Leitura de um officio do sr. dr. Daniel Garcia Azevedo, agradecendo a sua admissão de socio do Instituto.

Ordem do dia—primeira parte: lido e approvado o parecer da commis-ão de admissão de socios, sendo proclamados depois socios effectivos os srs. dr. Antonio Baptista de Campos Pereira ministro do Tribunal de Justiça e dr. João Pedro Cardozo, chefe da Commissão Geographica e Geologica do Estado; socios correspondentes os srs. Benedicto Calixto, e dr. Estevam de Mendonça, director do Archivo publico de Matto Grosso.

Fica sobre a mesa, na forma regimental, o parecer favoravel á admissão do sr. dr. Clodomiro Pereira da Silva.

O sr. dr. primeiro Secretario pede a palavra e propõe um voto de pezar pelo passamento do eugenheiro Alberto Kulmann, que fez parte da Constituinte do Estado, e Busche Varella notavel orador e cultor da tribuna judiciaria: o proponente enaltece com palavras sentidas os merecimentos dos falecidos cidadãos, sendo votados por unanimidade e inscriptos votos de homenagem saudosa.

Continúa inscripto para a sessão proxima o digno consocio dr. João Gomes Ribeiro, tendo tambem pedido inscripção os srs. Coronel Henrique S. de Araujo Macedo e dr. Eduardo Loschi; este lerá um trabalho seu subordinado á these «A posição geographica da capital do Estado de São Paulo».

Levanta-se a sessão, sendo convidados os srs. socios para a de 5 de Outubro proximo. Em tempo, antes de encerrada a sessão o sr. Miranda Azevedo congratula-se com o socio hoje empossado, dr. Augusto Elysio de Castro Fonseca e com o Instituto pela acquisição que acaba de fazer, na pessoa do digno consocio, de quem espera valioso concurso no emprehendimento patriotico que nos congrega. Eu Dionysio Caio da Fonseca, segundo Secretario, escrevi.—*Pereira Guimarães*, Presidente.—*Dionysio Caio da Fonseca*, 1.° Secretario.—*Eugenio A. Franco*, 2.° Secretario.

---

## Acta da 15.ª sessão ordinaria, em 5 de Outubro de 1905

PRESIDENCIA DO SR. DR. PEREIRA GUIMARÃES

Aos cinco dias do mez de Outubro de mil novecentos e cinco, ás 7 e meia horas da noite, nesta capital de S. Paulo, edificio do Instituto Historico e Geographico de S. Paulo, presentes os srs. drs. Pereira Guimarães, 1.° secretario, Silveira Cintra, Eugenio Franco, Gomes Ribeiro, Torres de Oliveira, Carlos Reis, Alfredo de Toledo, Horace Lane, Eduardo Loschi, von Ihering, commigo segundo secretario abaixo nomeado, foi declarada aberta a sessão. Achando-se na sala da Bibliotheca o consocio correspondente desembargador Thomaz Garcez Paranhos Montenegro, deputado federal pelo Estado da Bahia, o sr. sr. dr. Pereira Guimarães, presidente da Assembléa, nomeou uma commissão composta dos drs. Carlos Reis e Torres de Oliveira, para na fórma do nosso regimento, dar entrada em sessão ao digno consocio, que foi recebido, assignou a presença e tomou assento. Foi em seguida approvada a acta da sessão anterior, depois de lida e sem debate passando-se ao expediente seguinte. Recebimento de varias offertas que vão no fim relacionadas, livros, revistas e jornaes, que o Instituto agradece com especial agrado.

A casa ouve a leitura do parecer da commissão de admissão de socios, favoravel á acceitação do sr. dr. Clodomiro Pereira da

Silva, na qualidade de effectivo, conforme o proclama o sr. Presidente.

Foram propostos os srs. drs. Francisco Antonio de Souza Queiroz Netto e Edmundo Krug para socios effectivos. — A' commissão respectiva. O sr. dr. Thesoureiro apresentou o balancete da Receita e Despeza no trimestre terceiro do corrente anno e o orçamento para o anno de 1906. Ficam sobre a mesa ambos para discussão posterior. Na ordem do dia tem a palavra o sr. dr. Gomes Ribeiro que subindo á tribuna das conferencias adduz a leitura de seu trabalho «Origem da civilização sul-americana antes da conquista». O digno consocio prende a attenção do auditorio durante meia hora sendo muito applaudido ao terminar e felicitado.

O dr. Eduardo Loschi que se acha inscripto communica que não tendo podido completar seus estudos pelas condições atmosphericas dos ultimos dias, deixa de apresentar o trabalho annunciado.

O sr. 2.º secretario pede permissão para lêr um artigo do consocio dr. Luciano Esteves Junior publicado no *Jornal de Limeira* do dia 7 de Setembro, e epigraphado por essa data. A casa consente sendo muito apreciados os conceitos historicos emittidos no patriotico escripto, dedicado á mocidade brasileira.

Estando proxima a sessão magna, para encerramento dos trabalhos e commemoração do nosso anniversario, o dr. Presidente, faz ver que estando ausente o orador eleito, dr. Theodoro Sampaio, devia a casa eleger outro: tal escolha recahe por acclamação e proposta do dr. Carlos Reis, no consocio dr. Gomes Ribeiro que depois de pedir excusa termina acceitando a commissão. O sr. Presidente congratula-se com o dr. Paranhos Montenegro e com o Instituto pela acquisição feita dos dotes de mais um preclaro brasileiro tão notavel como jurisconsulto e como representante da nação. O sr. dr. Montenegro agradece a sua eleição e acceitando prometteu seu valioso auxilio e pediu a collaboração dos estudiosos e dos homens de bôa vontade, para a verdade historica que é o motivo pelo qual se criam os Institutos desta natureza.

O sr. Presidente encerra a sessão e convida os socios para a de vinte do corrente, penultima dos nossos trabalhos lectivos. Eu, Dionysio Caio da Fonseca. escrevi. — Dr. *A. C. Miranda Azevedo.* — *M. P. Guimarães.* — *Eugenio Franco.*

Acta da 16.ª sessão ordinaria, em 20 de Outubro
de 1905

Aos vinte dias do mez de Outubro de mil novecentos e
cinco, ás sete e meia horas da noite, no edificio do Instituto
Historico e Geographico de São Paulo, á rua General Carneiro
n. 1 A, presentes os socios srs. drs. Miranda Azevedo, Pereira
Guimarães, Eugenio Franco, Carlos· Reis, Silveira Cintra, Assis
Moura, Torres de Oliveira, Jules Martin, Augusto Egydio de
Castro Fonseca, foi sob a presidencia do primeiro dos acima
mencionados declarada aberta a sessão, na fórma do regimento,
occupando a cadeira de 2.º secretario o sr. dr. Eugenio Franco, por convite da sr. presidente, na ausencia de quem esta
lavra. Em seguida o sr. 2.º secretario passa a ler a acta da
sessão anterior, que, depois de posta em discussão foi approvada sem debate. Passando-se ao expediente, constou este da
leitura pelo sr. dr. 1.º secretario de um officio do digno consocio
dr. Eduardo Loschi, excusando-se da leitura do trabalho para
que se inscrevera anteriormente, por motivo de molestia. São
apresentadas diversas offertas que vão mencionadas afinal, as
quaes recebidas com especial agrado o Instituto agradece. O
socio sr. Jules Martin offerece uma collecção do « São Paulo
Antigo e Moderno». O sr. dr. Pereira Guimarães communica
á casa que o sr. dr Miranda Azevedo, nosso digno Vice-Presidente fez donativo importante ao Instituto, de um movel, se-
cretária de valor real historico, objecto de arte e de mais de
um seculo e que ora se acha na nossa sala da Bibliotheca. Pede
que a casa approve um voto de louvor ao offertante, voto que
por unanimidade, aqui fica consignado.
Passa-se á seguinte ordem do dia:
Parecer da Commissão de admissão de socios, opinando pela
acceitação dos srs. drs. Antonio de Souza Queiroz Netto e Edmundo Krug na qualidade de effectivos. Declara o dr. Pereira
Guimarães que pela praxe devia ser votado o parecer na sessão
seguinte, mas indicava que fosse a votação immediata visto occorrer a circumstancia do proximo termo dos trabalhos do anno,
o que foi acceito e resolvido pela casa, sendo acclamados os
propostos a quem se officiará.
Não tendo comparecido, por motivos allegados, os socios dr.
Eduardo Loschi e coronel Henrique A. de Araujo Macedo, inscriptos em sessão anterior, o sr. dr. Presidente faculta a palavra a algum dos presentes que queira della usar, e, não haven-

do quem requeresse, o sr. presidente propõe que a acta consigne voto de pesar pelo fallecimento dos srs. dr. Augusto Cesar de Barros Cruz e Agostinho José Moreira Rollo, cidadãos que se fizeram dignos pelos seus actos de patriotismo, da homenagem e respeito desta casa, interprete fiel dos sentimentos da geração contemporanea. São convidados os socios para a sessão do dia 25 do corrente, á mesma hora, neste mesmo local, afim de serem encerrados os trabalhos do anno, e levantou a sessão: e eu, Dionysio Caio da Fonseca, segundo secretario, escrevi.

Em tempo: foi proposto para socio correspondente o sr. capitão José Leite da Costa Sobrinho, residente em Santos, sendo dispensado do intersticio regimental e acclamado por unanimidade. Eu Dionysio Caio da Fonseca, escrevi.—Dr. *A. C Miranda Azevedo.—Pereira Guimarães*, 1.° secretario. - *Dionysio Caio da Fonseca*, 2.° secretario.

---

## Acta da 17ª sessão ordinaria, em 25 de Outubro de 1905 Encerramento dos trabalhos.

### PRESIDENCIA DO DR. MIRANDA AZEVEDO

Aos vinte e cinco dias do mez de Outubro de mil novecentos e cinco, nesta capital e predio onde funcciona o Instituto Historico e Geographico de São Paulo, á rua General Carneiro n 11, presentes ás 7 e meia horas da noite os srs. drs. Miranda Azevedo, vice-presidente, Pereira Guimarães, primeiro secretario, Eugenio Franco, Carlos Reis, Conego Ezechias Galvão da Fontoura, Coronel Affonso de Araujo Macedo, Major Luiz A. de Vasconcellos, Dr. Eduardo Loschi, H. von Ihering, João C. Gomes Ribeiro, Leoncio A. Gurgel, commigo, segundo secretario, abaixo nomeado, foi declarada aberta a sessão.

O sr. dr, Carlos Reis communica á casa que o sr. conselheiro Duarte de Azevedo deixa de comparecer por motivo de molestia e disto faz sciente. O sr. dr. Miranda Azevedo auctoriza a leitura da acta da sessão anterior que depois de posta em discussão foi approvada.

Não havendo expediente passa-se á ordem do dia, e na primeira parte desta pede a palavra o sr. Carlos Reis que apresenta á mesa uma proposta assignada por varios socios para a elevação do nosso digno vice-presidente dr, Miranda Azevedo á categoria de socio honorario.

Tal proposta fundamentada com palavras de louvor aos importantes serviços que ao Instituto tem prestado o proposto é unanimemenre approvada.

O dr. Miranda Azevedo commovido agradece ao Instituto a distincção com que é galardoado e promette continuar o seu auxilio em bem do desenvolvimento da Instituição scientifica de que faz parte O parecer da Commissão de Contas e projecto da receita e despesas, apresentados pelo digno dr. thesoureiro são approvados por unanimidade, após a faculdade da discussão. Tal projecto refere-se ao orçamento do anno vindouro Na segunda parte da ordem do dia tem a palavra o socio coronel Araujo Macedo para ler o trabalho para que se inscrevera na sessão anterior.—«A Bernarda de Francisco Ignacio».—O illustre conferente em opposição a varios topicos desse trabalho adduz alguns argumentos que foram ouvidos pelo Instituto com a attenção merecida.

Em seguida o dr. Eduardo Loschi leu um desenvolvido estudo «Memorial discriptivo da determinação do Meridiano, da latitude e da longitude do Observatorio Astronomico» na Avenida Paulista, n. 215, e da orientação geographica do mappa da capital do Estado. O interessante estudo vae á Commissão da Redacção da Revista para dar parecer e publicar.

Foi proposto pelo dr. Miranda Azevedo um voto de pesar pelo fallecimento do desembargador Bernardino Ferreira, membro aposentado do Supremo Tribunal Federal, antigo magistrado e jurisconsulto. O Instituto approva a indicação do sr. presidente e aqui inscreve o voto de pesar pelo passamento do pintor nacional sr. Pedro Americo, e que o Instituto officie á Academia de Bellas Artes do Rio de Janeiro com quem partilha os pezames pelo funebre acontecimento.

Vae a encerrar-se a sessão; o sr. Miranda Azevedo agradece aos socios o empenho denotado durante o anno concitando-os á continuação do patriotico feito, convidando para a sessão magna de anniversario o 1.° de Novembro proximo futuro para o qual serão convidados o sr. presidente do Estado e membros do governo Estão encerrados os trabalhos: Eu, Dionysio Caio da Fonseca, segundo secretario, lavrei a presente: Em tempo, são presentes as offertas abaixo, que o Instituto agradece.

1 «A Nova Cruz», Novembro de 1905.

4 Fasciculos – Boletim da Agricultura, ns. 8 e 9, em duplicata.

1 «Le Bibliophile Americain», Outubro a Dezembro 1905,

4 Relatorio de 1904 a 1905.—Policlinica de S. Paulo, pelo socio dr. Sergio Moreira.

1 Boletim «Of The New-York Public Library», Setembro de 1905.

2 Boletins ns. 15—Flora Paulista—VI familia Myrsinaceae. (Dr. João Pedro Cardoso) 1095.

1 «Santa Cruz» n. 1—Anno 6.º—Outubro 1905.

1 Boletim Postal n. 6—Maio de 1905.

*Dr. A. C. de Miranda Azevedo.—M Pereira Guimarães. —Dionysio Caio da Fonseca*, segundo secretario.

---

## Acta da Sessão Magna Commemorativa de um decimo anniversario do Instituto Historico em 1.º de Novembro de 1905.

PRESIDENCIA DO SR. CONSELHEIRO MANOEL ANTONIO DUARTE DE AZEVEDO

A primeiro de Novembro de um mil novecentos e cinco, nesta Capital do Estado de São Paulo, ás oito horas da noite, no predio n. 1-A da Rua General Carneiro, onde funcciona o Instituto Historico e Geographico de São Paulo, presentes os Srs. Conselheiro Monoel Antonio Duarte de Azevedo—Presidente Drs. Miranda Azevedo—Vice-Presidente, Manoel Pereira Guimarães, primeiro secretario. Gomes Ribeiro, orador, Eugenio A. Franco, Silveira Cintra, H. von Ihering, coronel Henrique A. de Araujo Macedo, conegos Ezechias Galvão da Fontoura, Araujo Marcoudes, Srs. Jules Martin, Dr. Americo Braziliense de Almeida Mello, Professor Arthur Goulart, Henry White, Eduardo Lorschi, Augusto Elysio de Castro Fonseca, Leoncio Gurgel, representantes do Governo do Estado, do Dr. Chefe de Policia, do Dr. Secretario do Interior, do Commando Geral da Força Publica, do Commando Superior da Guarda Nacional, do Ex.ᵐᵒ Sr. Bispo Diocesano, Ex.ᵐᵃˢ Senhoras, e representantes da imprensa da Capital e varios convidados, commigo segundo secretario abaixo nomeado foi declarada aberta a sessão.

O Sr. Conselheiro Duarte de Azevedo faz uma breve allocução passando em revista os serviços assignalados que á historia Patria e principalmente á do Estado de São Paulo presta ha onze annos este Instituto, cuja existencia dia a dia é encarecida pelo apoio que o mesmo prestam os associados, o governo e associações congeneres no paiz e fóra delle. Na fórma da letra dos nossos Estatutos diz S. Ex.ª a sessão magna é destinada a lembrar os nomes dos companheiros que na jornada do anno tombaram assignalando seu amor pela causa que nos reune. Convida S. Ex.ª o orador official a fazer o elogio dos socios fallecidos, dando a palavra ao consocio Dr. João C. Gomes Ribeiro que sóbe á tribuna entre applausos dos presentes. O digno consocio passa em rapida revista os feitos dos socios fallecidos durante o anno, tendo para cada um, uma phrase de saudade. Ao terminar a oração o orador é comprimentado pela casa. Em seguida o Sr. Presidente depois de facultar a palavra a qualquer dos consocios ou convidado, agradeceu a presença dos que nos vieram animar com suas presenças, abrilhantando a modesta festa do nosso anniversario, e encerrou a sessão. Eu Dionysio Cais da Fonseca. segundo secretario lavrei a presente—*Dionysio Cais da Fonseca.*—*Duaate de Azevedo.*—*Manoel Pereira Guimarães.*—*João Coelho Gomes Ribeiro.*

# RELATORIO

*Trabalhos e occorrencias do Instituto Historico e Geographico de S Paulo, no anno de 1905, apresentado pela Directoria, na sessão de 25 de Janeiro de 1906*

Srs. membros do Instituto Historico e Geographico de S Paulo —Em obediencia ao preceito contido no art. 16 § 5 dos Estatutos, a directoria vem apresentar-vos o relatorio das occorrencias do anno social de 1905.

### ADMINISTRAÇÃO

Continúa em exercicio a diretoria eleita em sessão de 25 de Outubro de 1903 e empossada em 25 de Janeiro de 1904, com excepção do orador, ausente desta capital.

### COMMISSÕES

As permanentes, nomeadas em sessão de 25 de Janeiro de 1904, soffreram as modificações adiante indicadas.

### SESSÕES E TRABALHOS

Durante o anno foram realizadas 18 sessões, sendo 16 ordinarias, 1 extraordinaria e 1 magna. Nas sessões foram lidos os seguintes trabalhos:

Na de 25 de Janeiro — «Porque não creio no perigo allemão» —pelo dr. Domingos Jaguaribe.

Na de 20 de Fevereiro—«Investigações e explorações feitas nas margens do Tieté»—Pelo dr. Ihering.

No de 20 de Março—«Batalha do Passo do Rosario, em 20 de Fevereiro de 1828»—pelo Cel Araujo Macedo.

Nas de 5 de Abril, 5 e 20 de Maio—»Factos occorridos em S. Paulo, antecedendo ao advento da Independencia do Brasil» —pelo dr. A. Piza.

Nas de 5 de Junho e 5 de Julho — «Revolução de 7 de Abril e seu alcance politico»—pelo dr. Gomes Ribeiro.

Na de 5 de Outubro—«Origens da civilização sul-americana antes da conquista»—pelo dr. Gomes Ribeiro.

Na de 5 de Outubro—«A bernarda de Francisco Ignacio»—
pelo Cel. A. Macedo; — «Memorial descriptivo da determinação
do Meridiano, da latitude e da longitude do Observatorio Astronomico, na Avenida Paulista e da Orientação Geographica do
mappa da Capital »—pelo dr. E. Loschi.

### BIBLIOTHECA E ARCHIVO

Como nos annos anteriores, o archivo e a bibliotheca do
Instituto foram contemplados com as importantissimas offertas
de livros, mappas, moédas, medalhas, jornaes, etc., constantes
do catalogo annexo.

A todos os generosos doadores a directoria, em nome do
Instituto, manifesta a mais profunda gratidão.

### SOCIOS

Foram acceitos durante o anno 36 novos socios, sendo 18
effectivos e 18 correspondentes.

Foram tranferidos para a cathegoria de socios honorarios
os srs. dr. J. A. Cerqueira Cesar, D. Duarte Leopoldo e dr.
A C. Miranda Azevedo.

Durante o anno de 1905, falleceram os illustres consocios
seguintes: drs. Hyppolito de Camargo, Garcia Mérou, A. J.
Macedo Soares, A. C. de Barros Cruz, D. J L. Costa Aguiar,
A. J. Moreira Rollo e. posteriormente ao encerramanto dos
trabalhos, dr. A. de Toledo Piza.

Perante os seus tumulos curva-se saudoso o Instituto.

### REVISTA

Foi distribuido o 9.º volume da Revista, devendo o 10.º
entrar em breve para o prélo.

### FINANÇAS

Continuam florescentes as finanças do Instituto. No orçamento da receita e despesa do Estado foi consignada a verba
de 3:600$000 de auxilio á nossa associação, sendo mantida a
auctorização para ser publicada a Revista na typographia do
*Diario Official*.

Continúa tambem a camara municipal a auxiliar-nos com a
verba de 2:000$000 annuaes.

A directoria aqui consigna, em nome do Instituto, os seus
fervorosos agradecimentos aos dignissimos e illustres membros

de ambas as casas do Congresso Legislativo do Estado e da camara municipal da capital

Pelo balanço annexo verificareis qual o estado das finanças do Istituto.

A receita foi de 9:960$900, e a despesa de 5:035$000, havendo, pois, um saldo de 4:925$900, que unido ao de 12:055$600 de 1904, eleva-se ao total de 16:961$507, sendo em conta corrente no Banco Commercio e Industria, 16:746$300; em mão do thesoureiro do Instituto, 215$200.

Ao vos-o exame a directoria sujeita o balanço e as contas do anno findo, aguardando a vossa deliberação a respeito.

### CONCLUSÃO

Taes, são srs. membros do Instituto Historico e Geographico de São Paulo as informações que a directoria entendeu dignas de trazer ao vosso conhecimento, estando prompta a prestar todos os esclarecimentos que exigirdes.

São Paulo, 25 de Janeiro de 1905.

MANOEL ANTONIO DUARTE DE AZEVEDO, Presidente.
MANOEL PEREIRA GUIMARÃES, 1.º Secretario.
DIONYSIO CAIO DA FONSECA, 2.º Secretario.

---

S. Paulo, 8 de Fevereiro de 1906.—Ex.ᵐᵒ Sr.—De conformidade com o § 7.º do art. 22 dos estatutos, tenho a honra de passar ás vossas mãos o balanço da receita e despesa do anno findo, acompanhado dos competentes documentos, afim de que seja transmittido á Commissão de Contas para o devido exame e respectivo parecer, ficando á disposição da mesma os livros e talões da thesouraria.

Annexo ao Balanço, junto as relações dos socios que, durante o anno, pagaram joias de admissão e annuidades. Junto tambem a relação dos socios que estão em debito de mais de 2 annos de annuidades e no caso de lhe ser applicada a disposição do art. 58 dos estatutos, afim de que o Instituto resolva a respeito.

Exᵐᵒ Sr. Presidente do Instituto Historico e Geographico de S. Paulo.

O Thesoureiro, CARLOS REIS.

# Instituto Historico e Geographico do Estado São Paulo

## BALANÇO DA RECEITA E DESPESA DO ANNO DE 1905

## (Fechado em 31 de Dezembro de 1905)

### RECEITA

| | | |
|---|---:|---:|
| Saldo do balanço de 1904 . . . . | | 12:035$600 |
| *Subvenções:* | | |
| Concedidas para o anno de 1905: | | |
| Pelo Congresso Legislativo do Estado. | 3:600$000 | |
| Pela Camara Municipal da Capital . | 2:000$000 | 5:600$000 |
| | | |
| *Joias e annuidades:* | | |
| Joias de admissão de 9 socios, sendo 6 effectivos e 3 correspondentes . | 450$000 | |
| Annuidades recebidas durante o anno. | 3:492$000 | 3:942$000 |
| | | |
| *Receita eventual:* | | |
| Venda de volumes da *Revista* . . . | 107$200 | |
| Juros da conta corrente do Instituto no Banco Commercio e Industria de S. Paulo, relativos ao 1.º e 2.º semestres deste anno . . . . | 311$700 | 418$900 |
| | | 21:996$500 |

### DESPESA

| | | |
|---|---:|---:|
| *Casa e luz:* | | |
| Aluguel e illuminação das salas durante o anno (documentos ns. 1 a 11). . . . . . . . | | 2:400$000 |
| *Empregado:* | | |
| Gratificação ao zelador, durante o anno (documen- mentos ns. 12 a 23) . . . . . . . . | | 600$000 |
| *Cobrança:* | | |
| Porcentagem sobre a cobrança de joias e annuida- des effectuada durante o anno (documentos ns. 24 a 25) . . . . . . . . . . . | | 394$200 |
| *Expediente:* | | |
| Dispendido durante o anno a saber: | | |
| Sellos, estampilhas, etc. (documentos ns. 25, 26, 27, 28 a 31, 33 e 34) | 126$640 | |
| Véos, globos, etc., para os apparelhos de gaz (docs. ns. 36 a 38) . . | 14$500 | |

Carretos da *Revista* e de uma secretaria, bandeja e copos para agua
(documentos ns. 39 a 41) . .           23$000
Contas de Espindola, Siqueira & Comp.
(documentos ns. 42 e 43). . .       63$500     227$640

*Compra de livros:*
Collecção completa da revista *La Science Sociale* e
assignatura da mesma para 1906 e despesas
de alfandega (documentos ns. 44 e 45) . .    405$160
*Impressões:*
Mappas e plantas para a *Revista* ( doc. n. 46 ) .    950$000
*Despesa eventual:*
Ornamentação da casa e aluguel de cadeiras, etc.,
para a sessão magna de anniversario ( do-
cumentos ns. 47 e 48) . . . . . . . .    58$000
*Saldo:*
Saldo nesta data que passa para 1906 . . . .    16:961$500

                                          21:996$500

## RESUMO DO BALANÇO

Saldo de 1904 . . .    12:035$600
Receita arrecadada . .    9:960$900    21:996$500

Despesa effectuada . . . . . .    5:035$000

Saldo nesta data . . . . . . . . . . . .    16:961$500
    Sendo :
Em conta corrente no Banco do Commercio e Industria de S. Paulo,
conforme a respectiva caderneta    16:746$300
Em mão do thesoureiro do Instituto.    215$200    16:961$500

S. E. O.

S. Paulo, 31 de Dezembro de 1905.—O thesoureiro, *Carlos Reis*.

---

## PARECER

A Commissão de Contas, abaixo assignada, tendo examinado cuidadosamente o balanço da receita e despesa do anno findo, e encontrando tudo na melhor ordem, é de parecer que seja acceito e approvado. — São Paulo, 22 de Janeiro de 1906. — ARTHUR VAUTIER.—EUGENIO A. W. FRANCO.

Relação dos socios acceitos que, durante o anno de 1905, satisfizeram a respectiva joia de admissão

| | | |
|---|---|---|
| Dr. Armando Prado . . . . . | Effectivo | 50$000 |
| » Augusto Ely-io de Castro Fonseca | » | 50$000 |
| » Eurico Doria de Araujo Goes | Corresp. | 50$000 |
| D. Ibrautina Cardona . . . . | » | 50$000 |
| Dr. Jacob Itapura de Miranda . . | Effectivo | 50$000 |
| » João Pamphilo de Assumpção . | » | 50$000 |
| » João Pedro Cardoso . . . . | | 50$000 |
| » Julio Brandão Sobrinho. . . | » | 50$000 |
| C.el Septimio Augusto Werner . . | Corresp | 50$000 |
| | | 450$000 |

Relação dos socios que pagaram annuidades durante anno de 1905

| | | |
|---|---|---|
| Dr. Armando Prado . . . . . | 1.ª annuidade | 24$000 |
| » Augusto Elysio de Castro Fonseca | » | 24$000 |
| » Jacob Itapura de Miranda . . | » | 24$000 |
| » João Pamphilo de Assumpção . | » | 24$000 |
| ι João Pedro Cardoso . . . . | » | 24$000 |
| » Julio Brandão Sobrinho. . . | » | 24$000 |
| » Adolpho Augusto Pinto . . | 1905 | 24$000 |
| » Affonso Arinos de Mello Franco | 1903 e 1904 | 48$000 |
| Alberto Löfgren . . . . . . | 1904 | 24$000 |
| Prof. Alfredo Bresser da Silveira . | 1905 | 24$000 |
| Dr. Alfredo Ellis . . . . . . | 1905 | 24$000 |
| » Alfredo de Toledo . . . . | 1905 | 24$000 |
| » Alvaro A. da C. Carvalho . | 1904 | 24$000 |
| » Alvaro A. de Toledo . . . | 1903 e 1904 | 48$000 |
| » Alvaro de Souza Queiroz . | 1905 | 24$000 |
| » Americo Braziliense de A. Mello— 6 mezes . . . . . . | 1905 | 12$000 |
| Dr. Antonio A. Moreira de Toledo. | 1905 | 24$000 |
| C.el Antonio Borges Sampaio . . | 1905 e 1906 | 30$000 |
| » Antonio Dino da C. Bueno. . | 1905 | 24$000 |
| » Antonio F. de Araujo Cintra . | 1904 | 24$000 |
| » Antonio F de Paula Souza . | 1905 | 24$000 |
| » Antonio J. Pinto Ferraz . . | 1905 | 24$000 |
| » Antonio M. Fontes Junior . . | 1905 | 24$000 |
| » Antonio de Padua Salles . . | 1905 | 24$000 |
| » Antonio da Silva Prado . . . | 1905 | 24$000 |

| | | | |
|---|---|---|---|
| » Antonio de Toledo Piza. . . | 1905 | 24$000 |
| » Aristides Salles . . . . . | 1905 | 24$000 |
| Prof. Arthur Goulart . . . . . | 1904 | 24$000 |
| Dr. Arthur Vautier . . . . . | 1905 | 24$000 |
| » Augusto C. da Silva Telles. . | 1905 | 24$000 |
| Augusto C. Barjona . . . . . | 1903 | 24$000 |
| Dr. Augusto C. de Barros Cruz . | 1904 | 24$000 |
| » Augusto C. de Miranda Azevedo | 1904 | 24$000 |
| » Augusto de Siqueira Cardoso . | 1905 | 24$000 |
| » Augusto de Meirelles Reis . . | 1905 | 24$000 |
| Barão de Rezende. . . . . . | 1905 | 24$000 |
| Dr. Bento Bueno . . . . . . | 1909 | 24$000 |
| » Bernardino de Campos . . . | 1905 | 24$000 |
| Des.or Bernardo A. Gavião Peixoto. | 1905 | 24$000 |
| Dr. Bernardo de Campos. . . . | 1905 | 24$000 |
| Dr. Bernardo Morelli. . . . . | 1905 | 24$000 |
| Dr. Brazilio A Machado de Oliveira | » | 24$000 |
| Mons.or dr. Camillo Passalacqua. . | » | 24$000 |
| Dr Candido N. N. da Motta . . | » | 24$000 |
| Dr. Carlos A. de F. Villalva . . | 1903 | 24$000 |
| Dr. Carlos de Campos . . . . | 1905 | 24$000 |
| Dr. Carlos Paes de Barros . . . | » | 24$000 |
| Dr. Cincinato Braga. . . . . | | 24$000 |
| Dr. Clementino de Sousa e Castro. | » | 24$000 |
| Conde de Prates . . . . . . | 1904 a 1905 | 24$000 |
| Dr. Constante A. Coelho . . . | 1905 | 24$000 |
| Eduardo Carlos Pereira . . . . | » | 24$000 |
| Eduardo Loschi . . . . . . | | 24$000 |
| Emannuel Vanorden . . . . . | » | 24$000 |
| Dr. Eugenio Alberto Franco . . | 1903 a 1904 | 48$000 |
| Eugenio Hollender . . . . . | 1905 | 24$000 |
| Cons.° Ezechias G da Fontoura . | » | 24$000 |
| C.el Felicio de Campos Cintra . . | | 24$000 |
| Mons.or dr. Fergo O'Connor de C. Dauntre . . . . . . . | 1904 a 1905 | 48$000 |
| Prof. Fernando M. Bonilha Junior | 1904 a 1905 | 24$000 |
| Dr. Firmiano de M. Pinto. . . | 1905 | 24$000 |
| Dr. Francisco de A. Peixoto Gomide | » | 24$000 |
| Dr. Francisco de Campos Andrade— 8 mezes . . . . . . . | | 16$000 |
| Dr. Francisco Ferreira Ramos . . | » | 24$000 |
| Dr. Francisco Franco da Rocha . | 1904 a 1905 | 48$000 |
| Francisco Gaspar da S. Martins . | 1905 | 24$000 |
| Francisco Nicolau Baruel . . . | » | 24$000 |

| | | |
|---|---|---|
| Dr. Francisco de P. Ramos de Aze-vedo . . . . . . . . . | 1905 | 24$000 |
| Dr. Francisco de Paula Rodrigues. | » | 24$000 |
| Dr. Francisco de Toledo Malta . . | » | 24$000 |
| Dr. Frederico de Barros Brotero . | 1904 a 1905 | 30$000 |
| C.el Gabriel Prestes . . . . . | 1905 | 24$000 |
| Dr. Galeno M. de Almeida. . . | » | 24$000 |
| Dr. H. von Ihering . . . . . | | 24$000 |
| Dr. Henrique Coelho. . . . . | | 24$000 |
| Henry White . . . . . . . | | 24$000 |
| Horace E. Williams—8 mezes . . | | 16$000 |
| Dr. Horace M Lane. . . . . | | 24$000 |
| Horacio de Carvalho . . . . . | | 24$000 |
| Dr. Ignacio de Rezende—8 mezes. | | 16$000 |
| Dr. Ignacio Ignacio W. da G. Co-chrane . . . . . . . . | | 24$000 |
| Dr. João A. Rubião Junior. . . | | 24$000 |
| Dr. João A. de Lima . . . . | | 24$000 |
| Dr. João A. Oliveira Cesar . . | | 24$000 |
| Dr. João B. de Mello Peixoto . . | | 24$000 |
| Dr. João B. de Oliveira Penteado. | | 24$000 |
| Dr. João C Gomos Ribeiro. . . | | 24$000 |
| Dr. João Eboli . . . . . . | » | 24$000 |
| Prof. João Lourenço Rodrigues. . | 1904 a 1905 | 48$000 |
| Dr. João Mendes de Almeida Junior | 1904 a 1905 | 40$000 |
| Dr. João Nogueira Jaguaribe . . | 1905 | 24$000 |
| C.el Joaquim de T. Piza e Almeida | » | 24$000 |
| Dr. Jorge Krichbaum . . . . | | 24$000 |
| Dr. Jorge Tibiriçá . . . . . | | 24$000 |
| Dr. José A. Guimarães Junior. . | | 24$000 |
| Dr. José E. de Macedo Soares. . | | 24$000 |
| José F. Soares Romeo . . . . | | 24$000 |
| Dr José Getulio Monteiro . . . | | 24$000 |
| José Hippolyto da Silva Dutra . . | » | 24$000 |
| Dr. José M. de Azevedo Marques. | » | 24$000 |
| Desembargador José Maria do Valle | 1905 | 24$000 |
| Conselheiro José Pedro de Araujo Marcondes — 8 mezes . . | 1905 | 8$000 |
| Dr. José Pinto do Carmo Cintra . | 1905 | 24$000 |
| Dr. José Torres de Oliveira . . | 1904 e 1905 | 30$000 |
| Conego dr José Valois de Castro . | 1905 | 24$000 |
| Dr. José Vicente de Azevedo . . | 1905 | 24$000 |
| Dr. José V. de Azevedo Sobrinho | 1905 | 24$000 |
| Dr. José Vieira Couto de Magalhães | 1905 | 24$000 |

| | | |
|---|---|---|
| Dr. Julio C. F. de Mesquita . . | 1905 | 24$000 |
| Leoncio do Amaral Gurgel — 8 mezes | 1905 | 16$000 |
| Dr. Luiz Arthur Varella — 6 mezes | 1905 | 12$000 |
| Coronel Luiz Gonzaga de Azevedo. | 1905 | 24$000 |
| Dr. Luiz Gonzaga da Silva Leme. | 1905 | 24$000 |
| Dr. Luiz de T. Piza e Almeida . | 1905 | 24$000 |
| Major Luiz de Vasconcellos . . | 1905 | 24$000 |
| Dr. Manoel A. Duarte de Azevedo | 1905 | 24$000 |
| Dr. Manoel Corrêa Dias. . . . | 1905 | 24$000 |
| Dr. Manoel P. Monteiro Tapajós . | 1905 | 24$000 |
| Dr. Manoel P. Guimarães . . . | 1905 | 24$000 |
| Dr. Manoel P. de Siqueira Campos | 1905 | 24$000 |
| Monsenhor Manoel Vicente da Silva | 1905 | 24$000 |
| Dra. Maria Rennotte — 8 mezes. . | 1905 | 16$000 |
| Dr. Mario Bulcão. . . . . . | 1904 | 24$000 |
| Dr. Martim Francisco R. de Andrada Sobrinho . . . . . . . | 1904 | 24$000 |
| Dr. Martinho Prado Junior . . . | 1905 | 24$000 |
| Nereu Rangel Pestana . . . . | 1905 | 24$000 |
| Dr. Octaviano Mello Barreto-3 mezes | 1905 | 6$000 |
| Dr. Oscar Thompson . . . . . | 1905 | 24$000 |
| Dr. Othoniel Campos Motta—4 mezes | 1905 | 8$000 |
| Dr. Pedro Arbues da Silva . . . | 1905 | 24$000 |
| Dr. Pedro A. C. Lessa . . . . | 1905 | 24$000 |
| Dr. Pedro Vicente de Azevedo . . | 1905 | 24$000 |
| Dr. Plinio de Mendonça Uchôa. . | 1904 e 1905 | 28$000 |
| Dr. Raymundo Furtado Filho . . | 1905 | 24$000 |
| Dr. Rodolpho Miranda . . . . | 1905 | 24$000 |
| Dr. Sergio Meira. . . . . . | 1905 | 24$000 |
| Dr. Silvio de Almeida — 8 mezes . | 1905 | 16$000 |
| Dr. Theodoro D. de Carvalho Junior | 1905 | 24$000 |
| Dr. Theodoro Sampaio . . . . | 1904 | 24$000 |
| Dr. Tullio de Campos . . . . | 1904 e 1905 | 48$000 |
| Dr. Victor da Silva Freire . . . | 1905 | 24$000 |
| Dr. Washington L. Pere.ra de Souza | 1905 | 24$000 |
| | | 3:492$000 |

# Lista das offertas

Revistas: — *Santa Cruz* —Anno V. — N. 1—Outubro de 1904. *Pharmaceutica e Odontologica.* N. 9, 11 e 12 de Setembro, Novembro e Dezembro de 1904.—*Ensino* (orgam beneficente do professorado publico de S. Paulo) Dezembro, 1904 n. 5.

Boletins: —*Postal* n 5 e 6. 1904.—Anno XVI —*Demographo Sanitaria.*—*Agricultura.* (Da) n. 8. 5.ª Série.—Agosto 1904. —*Museu Goeldi.* (Estracto do boletim do)

Volumes avulsos:—*Annaes da Bibliotheca Nacional do Rio de Janeiro,* 2 Volumes. Brochura.--1904. *Pratica Civil e Commerciaes — Contos Sertanejos,* offerta do seu auctor, Pelayo Serrano.—*Recuerdos de mi vida diplomatica,* 2 volumes. Offerecido ao Instituto pelo seu auctor, Vicente Quesada.

Revistas :—*Pharmaceutica.*—*Agricola,* Março de 1904—n. 116.

Boletins :—*Postal,* n. 7, 8, 10, e 11, Junho a Outubro de 1904.—Da *Secretaria Viação Industria e Obras Publicas do Estado da Bahia.* Volume 4, ns. 9 e 10, Setembro e Outubro de 1904.—*Da Agricultura.*—*Demographo Sanitaria*—Da la *Bibliotheca Publica de la Provincia de Buenos-Ayres.*

Avulsos:—*O Archivo Publico Mineiro* vol. IX—Fasciculo III e IV—Julho e Dezembro de 1904.—*Annuario Estatistico de S. Paulo de 1904.*— *Railwais in the State of S. Paulo.*— 1903.—*Geographia Fisica y Esferica de las Provincias del Paraguay e Missiones Guaranies.*—Relatorio elaborado pelo secretario do Interior.—Dr. Cardoso de Almeida; offerta da Secretaria do Interior.

Volumes :—Relatorio apresentado ao sr. Secretario do Interior pelo Inspector geral do Ensino, Dr. Mario Bulcão em 1904.

Os ns. 44.º e 46.º do Relatorio da Sociedade Artistica e Beneficente—1905.

Annaes da Camara Municipal de S. Paulo.—1904

« La Science Sociale » 20 Année—Deuxiéme periode—13ª fasciculo.

«Campinas Antiga» as festas de 1846—offerta do seu auctor e membro do Instituto, B. Octavio.

« Almanak Illustrado do Lavrador Paulista » offerta do seu Julio Brandão Sobrinho

Revistas:— Pharmaceutica—*Revista* Polytechnica — *Revista* A Santa Cruz—*Revista* Maritima Brasileira,—Estatistica Demographo Sanitaria

*Boletins* —« New York Public Library—Boletim da Secretaria de Agricultura—Viação Industria e Obras Publicas do Estado da Bahia.

*Ravista* Agricola—Trimensal do Instituto do Ceará—Tomo XIX — ns. 1.° e 2 ° de 1905

*Revista* Pharmaceutica—1905.

» Odontologica—19ᵒᵒ5.

1 *Boletim da Secretaria da Agricultura do Estado da Bahia*—Anno 3.°—vol. 5.°—Janeiro a Março de 1905.

1 *Summario Estatistico da Secção de Demographia*—Anno 3.° e 6.°—1904 a 1905.

8 *Boletins da Agricultura*, ns· 3, 4, 5 e 6 (em duplicata).

1 *Boletim del Cuerpo de Ingeniero de Minas del Perú*— 1905.

2 *Boletins of the New-York Public Leibrary* -Abril de 1905—Maio—2 folhetos—1905.

15 Boletins - *Hebdomadario de Estatistica demographo sanitaria*—Ns. 12 a 20; 25 a 30.

1 *La Science Sociale* 20.° année—fasciculo 15—1905.

1 *Revista do Instituto do Ceará* —Tom. 19 de—1905.

1 *Revista do Ensino Associação Beneficente*—n. 1—1905.

3 *Revista Pharmaceutica* - ns. 4, 6 e 7—1905.

1 *Revista Militar*—Junho de 1905.

1 *Revista Agricola*—n, 120—Julho de 1905.

1 *Revista da Sociedade Scientifica de S. Paulo*—Junho de 1905.

1 *Santa Cruz.*—Anno 5.°—n. 10—1905.

1 *O Nenê*—Anno 1.°—n. 2—1905.

2 *Cartophilia*—Anno 1.°—n. 3 e 6—1905.

2 *A Nova Cruz*—Junho a Julho de 1905.

1 *Verdade e Luz*—n. 360—1905.

2 *Onze de Agosto e Jornal de Limeira*—1905·

1 Alexandro Rosa—*Numismatica—Los Paizes Bajos y Francia en America (siglo XVII)—Buenos-Ayres*—1905—pelo *auctor*.

1 Catalogo dos jornaes, revistas e outras publicações do Ceará—pelo auctor João Baptista Perdigão de Oliveira—1905.

1 *Da Unidade do Espirito Humano*—Pelo auctor dr. Alonso Guayanaz da Fonseca.

3 Brochura — *Genealogia Paulistana* — pelo auctor—socio dr. Luiz Gonzaga Silva Leme—Vols. 6.°, 7.° e 8.°

1 *Boletim of The New-York Public Leibrary Astor Le-enox-and-Filden Fundations*—Julho de 1905.

3 *Boletins da Agricultura*—fasc. ns. 7—3.

4 *Boletins hebdomadario da Estatistica Demographo Sanitaria de Santos, S. Paulo e Campinas*—ns. 34, 32 e 33.

Varios jornaes da Capital e do Interior.

## CONTINUAÇÃO DAS OFFERTAS

1 *As Caixas Economicas*—Memoria apresentada pelo dr. Alfredo Rocha—ao Congresso Brazileiro—1905.

4 *Fasciculos La Science Sociale* - 20 année—ns. 13, 14, 15 e 16.

*Relatorio do ministro do. J J. Seabra, sobre a bibliotheca Nacional*—pelo dr. Manoel C. Pecegueiro Silva.

1 *Conferencia Internacional de Compenhague sobre o Tuberculose*—pelo dr. Hilario de Gouveia.

22 brochuras—opusculos, boletins e publicações da Commissão Geographica e Geologica do Estado de São Paulo—a datar de 1887 a 1901—Offertas do socio dr. João Pedro Cardoso.

1 *Historia do Estado de Sergipe*—pelo dr. Felidello Freire.

1 *Historia do Rio de Janeiro*—pelo mesmo.

1 *Noções do Direito Patria*—pelo mesmo.

1 *Historia Constitucional da Republica dos Estados Unidos do Brasil*, e 3 vols—pelo mesmo.

1 *As Constituições dos Estados*—pelo mesmo.

1 *Memorias do Museu de Goeldi*—Vol. IV.

1 *Os Mosquitos no Pará* (Goeldi)—1.05.

2 *Fasciculos Lacience Sociale*—15.° fasc. n. 16.

1 *Revista Agricola*- n. 121—Agosto de 1905.

1 *Revista A Nova Cruz*—n. 3—Agosto de 1905.

1 *Revista—Parecer da Congregação da Faculdade de Direito de S. Paulo sobre os projectos da Creação de sua universidade no Brazil*—1 broch.—1905, pelo Dr. A. C. de Miranda Azevedo.

1 *As molestias infectuosas e a hygiene em São Paulo.*—1 broch —1905.

1 *Relatorio do dr. Manoel Cicero P. do Amaral ao dr. J. J. Seabra*—1 broch.—1905.

1 *Revista—Santa Cruz*—n, II—Agosto de 1905.

1 *Boletim da Estatistica Demographia-Sanitaria*—vols. 23 a 24—Janeiro de 1905.

3 *Boletim del Ministerio Agric.*—Buenos-Ayres—de Abril e Maio—1905.

1 *Fasc.—Appellação Civel n. 4270*—Offerta do socio dr. Alfredo Toledo.

4 *Theses do dr. João Baptista da Costa Rodrigues* — Offerta do mesmo auctor.

1 *Fascicolo — Uma visita agradavel* — Francisco Gaspar — 1905.

1 *Annaes do Brazil.* — Offerta do socio dr. Felisbello Freire.

## BOLETINS

*Boletim Museu Goeldi* — ( Museu Paraense — 1904 — 2.° Vol. — *Boletim da Agricultura* — Del Ministerio de Agricultura «Buenos Ayres — 1904 — 2 exemplares — *Boletim del Cuerpos de Ingenieros de Minas del Peru* ns. 11 e 13 — 1904 — *Boletim Postal — Boletim da Secretaria da Agricult. Viação, Industria e Obras Publicas da Bahia — Boletim de Estatisca Demographo Sanitario — Boletim de la Biblioteca Publica.*

*Opusculos — Brochuras: — O Estado de Minas Geraes na Exposição de San Luiz* — Offerta do auctor dr. Nelson Coelho de Lima.

*Santa Ephigenia* — dr. Nelson de Mima.

*Comarca de Bello Horizonte* — 1 *As vespas sociaes do Brasil* — Offerta do auctor Rodolpho Von Ihering — *Le Bibliophile Americaine* — 1 *Appellação de Casa Branca* — 1 *Estatutos do Gremio Eitterario «Carlos Ferreira»* — 1 *La Scienc Sociale.*

1 *Noções e Conselhos praticos para uso dos banhos de mar e de rio* — pelo auctor capitão José Leite da Costa Sobrinho — 1 *A Cartophila da Sociedade de Cartophila Internacional* — 1 *Catalogo da Bibliotheca Americana — Almanach de Casa Branc* — 1904.

## REVISTAS

*Revista Militar* n. 4, 5 Abril e Maio de 1905 — *A Santa Cruz* — Maio, Junho de 1905 — *Revista Pharmaceutica* — de 31 de Maio 1995 — v. 5 — *Revista Polytechinica* de Abril e Maio 1905 v. 5, 6 — *Revista do «Museu Paulista»* 1904 — *Rev. Agricola* — Junho 1905 — *Rev. Ensino* — v. 6 — *Rev. de Santa Cruz* v. Junho 905.

*Bolentim — Del Cuerpo de Ingenieros de Minas* v. 23 — *Boletim Ministerio da Agricultura — Buenos-Ayres*

*Volumen — As Minas do Brasil e sua Legislação,* tom. 2.°.

*Anales do Museu Nacional de Montevideo,* tom. 2.°.

1 *Brazil at the Leovisiana Porchase Expositiva* — St. Louis 1904 — offerta da Directoria do Interior

1 *Horas vagas* — do auctor Tullio de Campos.

1 *Mensagem* apresentada ao Cong. Nacional na 3.ª sessão da 5.ª legislatura pelo Presidente da Republica dr. Rodrigues Alves 1905.

*Boletim de Estatistica Demographo Sanitaria.*
*Boletim de la Bibliotheca Publica de Buenos Ayres.*
1 *Ajuste de Contas* pelo dr. Salvador de Mendonça—offerta do sr. Carmo Cintra.
1 *Annuaire Astronomique*—para 1905—1 *Serviço Metereologico* do anno 1902 – *Dados Climatologicos*.
1 *Annuario Estatistico de São Paulo*—1903—Uma collecção de opusculos—*Estatutos da Associoção Typographica Paulistana de Socorros Mutuos*, desde 1897 até 1905—por Jesuino Antonio de Castro—*A Medicina Legal no Brazil*—offerta do auctor socio dr. Nina Rodrigues.
1 *Mappa de Chicago*— offerta do dr. Orville Derby—de 1832 a 1893.
1 Folheto broch. *Noções e Conselhos praticos para uso dos Banhos de Mar*—pelo capitão José Leite da Costa Sobrinho.
1 *Almanach Illustrado do Lavrador Paulista*—1905.
1 Brochura—*O Poder Legislativo e o Poder Executivo*— Henrique Coelho—1905.
1 Brochura—*Vias de Communicação*—Matto Grosso—1905.
1 *Documentos para a Historia de Martim Soares Moreno*— pelo Barão de Studar—1905.
*Documentos para a Historia da Conquista e Civilisação da costa leste e oeste do Brasil*—1905.
1 *Relatorio*—*A Bibliotheca Nacional* em 1903—1905.
1 Brochura-- *Metropolitana Paulistana* — José de Campos Novaes 1905.
1 Brochura—*Contribucion al estudio de la Cartographia de los paizes del Rio de la Plata.*
1 Bulletin ns. 11 a 12—*The Geological Institution—The University of Upsada*—1905.
1 *Bulletin Of The New-York Public Leibrauj*—June—1905.
1 *Geschichte*—Katalog. n. 255.
1 *Catalogo dos retratos*—coll. por Diogo Barbosa Machado,
1 *Catalogo de Discos e Apparelhos*—Casa Edson.
1 *Folheto—Frosa The Ibis*—for october— Emilio A. Goeldi —1904.
Idem de 1904.
1 *White Henns and Bell Ibises*—Pará—1904.
1 *On The Rau Rodent*—Dinomys Branichü—Pará—1904.
1 *Souderakuck ans Globus Bd*—Stocholm.
1 *Bulletim du Musée Oceanographiqno de Monaco*—12-1— 1904.
1 *Boletim del Ministerio de Agricultura*—Buenos Ayres— Ereno a Marso—1905.
*Hilario de Gouvêia* — 1905.

## REVISTAS

1 *Santa Cruz* –Anno 5.°– n. 12—Setembro de 1905.
1 *A Nova Cruz*—Anno 1.°–n. 4—Setembro de 1905.
1 *Agricolu*—n. 122—15 de Setembro de 1905.
1 *Militar*—Anno 7.°–n. 7—Julho de 1905.
1 *Pharmaceutica*– Anno 10—n. 8—Julho de 1905
1 *O Nenê*—Anno 1.°– n. 2—Julho de 1905.
1 Numero especial da *A Comarca*—Anno 6.°—n. 572— de 1905.

## BOLETINS

2 Fasciculos da—*Secretaria de Agricultura, Viação e Industria, Obras Publicas da Bahia*—Abril a Junho de 1905.
De *Demographia Sanitaria do Estado de S. Paulo*—fasciculo ns. 34, 35 e 36—1905

## JORNAES

*El Mundo Latino*—Anno 6.°—n. 109 e 110.
*O Onze de Agosto*—Anno 3.°–n. 3—Setembro de 1905.
*Verdade e Luz*—Julho de 1905.
2 *Boletins del Ministerio de Agricultura de Buenos-Ayres* n. 1—Junho—Tomo 3.°.
1 *Politica e Legislação de Estradas de Ferro*, pelo seu auctor dr. Clodomiro Pereira da Silva, em 2 volumes—Brochura.
1 Brochura—*As Minas do Brasil e sua Legislação*—vol. 3.°
—Pelo dr. João Pandia Callogus
1 *Relatorio do dr. Carlos Botelho, Secretaria da Agricultura ao dr. Jorge Tibiriçá*—Anno de 1904.
1 *Annuario da Escola Polytechnica*—5.° anno—1905.
1 *Revista Militar*—anno 7.°–n. 8—Agosto de 1905.
1 *Dados Climatologicos*—Pelo J Belforte Mattos, referentes ao anno de 1902. *Verdade e Luz*—ns. 261 e 62.
1 Mappa—*Distribuição das Mattas e dos Campos na America do Sul*—pelo dr H. von Ihering.
1 Brochura – *Nova lei do systhema do mundo*, pelo auctor dr. Alves de Magalhães, residente na cidade do Porto—1905.
1 Brochura—*Liberdade profissional*—pelo dr. Bernardo de Campos—1905
1 Encadernado em percaline—*Serviço Sanitario de S. Paulo*
—Offerta da Directoria respectiva.
1 Fasciculo—*La Science Sociale*—17.° fasciculo.
1 *Revista da Sociedade Scientifica de S. Paulo*—n. 2—Setembro de 1905.

1 *Revista Agricola de S. Paulo*—n. 123.

1 *O Archivo*—Matto Grosso—vol. IV—Agosto de 1905.

1 *Boletim del Ministerio de Agricultura*—Julio—Buenos-Ayres—1905

1 Boletim—*Of the New-york Public Library*—Agosto de 1505.

2 *Boletins Postal*—ns. 3 e 4—Março e Abril de 1905.

2 *Boletins da Agricultura*—6.ª serie—Agosto ns. 8—1905.

1 *Annuario Estatistico da Secção de Demographia*—Anno X—1903—S. Paulo 1904.

1 *Boletim trimensal* -Janeiro a Março da Estatistica Demographo Sanitaria—Anno 12—n. 1—1905.

3 *Boletins de Estatistica Demographo Sanitaria*—ns. 38 a 40.

2 *Verdade e Luz*—ns. 366 e 365

1 Brochura—*Commentario*—Revista de critica litteraria—Alfredo Rocca—1905

1 Collecção do *S. Paulo antigo e S. Paulo moderno*—em 6 fasciculos 1 a 6—pelo socio Jules Martin.

3 *Boletins de Estatistica Demographo Sanitaria*—fasciculos ns. 41, 42 e 43.

1 *Relatorio do dr. Guilherme Alvaro*, sobre a Prophylaxia e tratamento da ophtalmia do Oeste de S. Paulo—1904.

1 *Fasciculo do mesmo trabalho*, em lingua italiana—1904.

3 *Verdade e Luz*—Revista—ns. 366, 367 e 368—1905.

1 Levista—*O Nenê*—ns. 6—Setembro de 1905.

1 Brochura—*Fauna Fluvial de Goyaz*—pelo auctor Henrique Silva.

1 Revista—*A Nova Cruz*—Outubro de 1905.

1 Revista n. 9—*Pharmaceutica*—Setembro—1905.

1 *La Science Sociale*—18 fasciculo.

1 *Revista Militar*—n. 9—Setembro de 1905.

1 *Revista de ensino*—Julho de 1905—n. 2—1905.

1 *Revista do Centro de Sciencias*—Campinas—n. 8—Outubro—1905.

1 *Boletim del Cuerpo de Ingenieros de Minas del Perú*—n. 124—1905.

1 *Boletim Postal*—n. 5—Junho de 1905.

1 Relatorio de 1904 a 1905—*Polytechnica de S. Paulo*—pelo socio dr. Sergio Meira,

1 Boletim—*Of the Now-York Public Library*—Setembro de 1905.

2 Boletins—n. 15—*Flora Paulista*—IV familia Nupsinacede (dr. Joaquim Cardoso)—1905.

1 Revista—*Santa Cruz*—n. 1—Anno 6.º—Outubro de 1905.

1 *Boletim Postal*—n. 6—Maio de 1905.

# O Dr. Antonio Piza

No correr do anno que findou,—notavamos todos –com surpreza—a principio—e depois com pezar--que não era assiduo—como costumava, ás sessões do Instituto Historico--o nosso illustre consocio Dr. Antonio Piza.

No mez de Julho—confiou a um dos companheiros da commissão da *Revista*, a incumbencia—que lhe era cara—de continuar a dirigir, a publicação do presente volume—já em mais de meio; era symptoma grave – de que o luctador estava ferido seriamente.

Não era indifferente aos nossos trabalhos ainda assim—e com amor—informava-se do que occorria em nossas reuniões —e indagava—o ponto em que estava a impressão d'este volume - o material que tinhamos, e promettia que em breve retomaria o seu lugar na fileira dos activos, sentindo-se contrariado por não ter vindo assistir a sessão magna de encerramento de trabalhos—e discurso do orador—que commemorava a vida e meritos dos socios fallecidos.

— 618 —

Não mais o veremos—partilhar de nossas discussões—e concorrer com sua valioza erudição para elucidar os problemas de historia, de archeologia ou de geographia patria. Ao orador no proximo anno cabe dizer quem foi o finado—e o quanto perdeu a patria com a morte do Dr. Antonio Piza—capaz de prestar ainda os melhores serviços ás lettras nacionaes.

Por hoje—limitamo-nos a transcrever—do mais antigo jornal paulista—de que foi assiduo collaborador—a seguinte noticia necrologica. (1)

« Fomos hontem pela manhã dolorosamente surprehendidos com a noticia de ter fallecido o nosso presado collaborador Dr. Antonio de Toledo Piza, ha muitos dias prostrado por pertinaz enfermidade.

« Sentimo nos surpresos com o infausto passamento por isso que, ainda nas vesperas do desenlace, alguma esperança pelo restabelecimento do illustre enfermo voltára a animar os innumeros amigos e admiradores que possuia o extincto.

« Sabiamos estarem contados os dias da preciosa existencia do Dr. Antonio Piza, tal a gravidade do seu estado, mas porque tanto o estimavamos, parecia-nos que o nosso saudoso amigo resistiria ainda por algum tempo, á enfermidade que, emtanto, trahiçoeira, sahiu afinal victoriosa. privando-nos e á nossa sociedade de um cavalheiro distinctissimo, cheio de serviços ao seu Estado.

« O dr. Antonio Piza falleceu pelas 2 horas da madrugada em consequencia de uma syncope cardiaca.

« Dessappareceu assim, de um instante para outro, um homem que se tornou desde sua mocidade notavel pela sua intelligencia e energia  Dotado desses elementos bem facil foi ao Dr. Antonio Piza conquistar a posição em que a morte o veiu colher, prestando ao seu Estado natal o brilhante concurso do seu valor.

«Os seus conhecimentos de profissional, tendo abraçado a carreira da engenharia, os seus estudos pacientemente feitos sobre historia do seu paiz e em especial a de seu Estado o tornaram em evidencia no nosso meio intellectual e á frente da Repartição de Estatistica, cargo que exerceu com admiravel competencia e correcção, no seio do Instituto Historico e Geographico de que foi um dos fundadores, ou nas columnas dos jornaes, o dr. Antonio Piza se revelou sempre em evidente destaque.

«O serviço da Repartição de Estadistica que é hoje um modelo entre os existentes no Brazil, tão bem organizado está, prestando-se mesmo de molde a repartições eguaes de outros

(1) *Correio Paulistano*, 9 de Novembro de 1905.

Estados, foi trabalho seu, fructo da sua dedicação de infatigavel
e não é pequeno o subsidio que para a reconstrucção hitorica
do nosso passado nos legou a sua penna de estudioso para quem
não possuiam segredos os velhos documentos nem a chronica
complicada e vaga dos primeiros tempos coloniaes.

«Nesse terreno a competencia do illustre extincto tornou-se
entre nós unica, insubstituivel, tão profundos foram os seus
trabalhos de excavação sobre os primitivos estadios da então
nascente nacionalidade brasileira.

«Para comprovar o merecimento do dr. Antonio de Toledo
Piza, em materia de historia patria, bastariam os interessantes
e preciosos artigos que ainda ha pouco na nossa folha estampavamos.
Em qualquer delles, para não falar dos estudos que deixa espar-
sos, pricipalmente nas paginas da *Revista* do Instituto Historico
desta capital, se demonstra o que com a morte do distincto
paulista perderam as letras patrias.

«O morto de hontem teve tambem seu nome ligado ao
movimento republicano operado no nosso paiz, Republicano con-
victo, intransigente nos seus ideaes democraticos bateu-se pelo
actual regimen conscientemente e foi assim que se declarou com
independencia partidario dos principios triumphantes a 15 de
Novembro de 1889, sendo um dos signatarios do celebre manifesto de 3 de Dezembro de 1870 (1) e agindo activamente como
presidente do Club Republicano de Porto Feliz.

«O dr. Antonio de Toledo Piza pertencia a uma das mais
distinctas familias paulistas, era solteiro e irmão do, sr. Francisco
Piza e dos drs. Joaquim Piza e Almeida ministro do Supremo
Tribunal Federal, Gabriel Piza, ministro plenipotenciario em
Paris e tio do dr. Luiz Piza, senador estadual.

«Do trabalho *Chronologia Paulista*, do sr. José Jacintho
Ribeiro, retiramos os seguintes dados biographicos sobre o finado.

«Antonio de Toledo Piza, nascido a 2 de Abril de 1848,
em Capivary.

«Deposito de haver estudado os preparatorios com seu pae,
na fazenda, e com o professor particular Seraphim José do Horto
e Mello, a quem Julio Ribeiro dedicou a sua Grammatica Portugueza, applicou-se á lavoura de canna até á edade de 23 annos,
mudando-se para Porto Feliz, onde occupou-se em ensinar
meninos até 1874. Levado pela *febre* que impellia a mocidade

---

(1) Ha aqui erro;—o *Manifesto* de 3 de Dezembro de 1870 do Club Republicano do
Rio de Janeiro—não tem a assignatura e Dr. A Piza, pois só foi assignado pelos republicanos residentes no Rio de Janeiro. A organisação do partido em S. Paulo, foi posterior e só effectuas-se aqui depois da Convenção de Itú em 1872.

brasileira para os Estados Unidos e um pouco pelo mau estado de sua saúde, partiu para aquella grande Republica onde em 14 mezes reviu todos os preparatorios, fez os respectivos exames e matriculou-se, em 1875, no curso de Engenharia da Universidade de Cincinnati, no Estado de Ohio.

«Em quatro annos completou o seu curso, recebendo o diploma de engenheiro civil com distincção (unico obtido nesse anno por brasileiros naquelle paiz), e esteve algum tempo empregado em diversos caminhos de ferro em construcção nos Estados de Kentucky e de Tennessee.

«Em 1880 voltou ao Brasil e foi, por quatro annos, director do Engenho Central de Porto Feliz.

«Em 1885 voltou aos Estados-Unidos, como representante da casa Joaquim de Salles & Comp., para comprar os machinismos necessarios para a montagem da fabrica Antarctica Paulista, no bairro da Agua Branca, nesta Capital, trazendo, em dezembro desse anno, comsigo, esses machinismos, que montou e fez funccionar.

«Em fins de 1886 e principios de 1887, foi residir em Jaboticabal e Araraquara, onde se entregou ao trabalho de divisão de terras e construcções de edificios. A actual egreja matriz de Araraquara é obra sua, construida em poucos mezes nos annos de 1889 e 189'.

«Em Fevereiro de 1891, foi nomeado engenheiro das obras publicas do Estado, onde ficou até maio de 1893, quando nomeado para o cargo de director da Repartição de Estatistica e do Archivo do Estado.

«Enthusiasmado pelo manifesto republicano de 3 de dezembro de 1870, foi com seus irmãos Francisco e Gabriel, dos primeiros a acceitar as idéas nelle contidas e a subscrevel-o. (1)

«Foi de 1871 a 1874, director do Club Republicano de Porto Feliz, que encetou as primeiras conferencias publicas no Estado.

«Em 1873, foi delegado desse Club á Convenção de Ytú e em 1874 foi membro do Congresso Republicano que se reuniu em S. Paulo no mez de abril, como representante do Club Republicano de Capivary.

«Dado ás lides do jornalismo, na imprensa dos Estados Unidos, escreveu sobre a politica e lavoura do Brazil; foi correspondente da *Provincia*, hoje *Estado S. Paulo* e nas co-

---

(1) Vide a nota anterior. O que falta nestes dados—pelo lado politico—é a noticia de que o dr. A Pisa—foi presidente do *Club Republicano de - S. Paulo* ·· durante o anno de 1896- tendo se esforçado em vão para reanimar aquella historica associação.

lumnas desse jornal se encontram grande numero de artigos seus nos annos de 1886 a 1888.

« Em Araraquara fez parte da redacção da *Folha do Povo*, de 1889 a 1890.

« Collaborador do *Correio Paulistano*, ahi tem publicado grande numero de artigos sobre politica, historia, estatistica, instrução e jornalismo.

« E' um dos fundadores do Instituto Historico de S. Paulo, socio correspondente do Instituto Historico e Geographico do Brazil e redactor da *Revista* do Archivo do Estado de S. Paulo.

« O enterro realizou-se hontem mesmo, ás 4 e meia horas da tarde, partindo o feretro da rua de S. João, 138, para o cemiterio da Consolação, ficando depositado o caixão mortuario na capella dessa necropole afim de ser dado á sepultura hoje, ás 7 horas da manhã. »

\*\*\*

Não podiamos encerrar este volume sem deixar assignalada a lutuosa data da morte do querido e illustre consocio que deixa uma vaga muito difficil de ser preenchida.

Honra á sua memoria.

*M. A.*

Lightning Source UK Ltd.
Milton Keynes UK
UKHW02f0657210818
327557UK00011B/814/P

9 780332 214252